THE AMERICAN NEGRO

HIS HISTORY AND LITERATURE

THE
UNDERGROUND RAILROAD

William Still

ARNO PRESS and THE NEW YORK TIMES

NEW YORK 1968

General Editor
WILLIAM LOREN KATZ

THOUGH THE HEROISM OF THE UNDERGROUND RAILROAD HAS WON a place in our history and folklore, only one nearly complete record of its operations has been preserved, that kept by William Still of Philadelphia. At the risk of heavy fines and long imprisonment, Still and other members of the Philadelphia Vigilance Committee helped hundreds of runaway slaves to find safety in Canada. By merely setting down and preserving these records during the 1850's, Still risked the penalties of the Fugitive Slave Law, but record and preserve them he did, and his illustrated compilation forms a series of black profiles in courage of the men, women and children who passed through his station.

Born in New Jersey in 1821, to parents who had emancipated themselves from slavery (one through escape and the other through self-purchase), William Still labored on his parents' farm until 1844. He moved to Philadelphia and within three years had taught himself to read and write. He joined the Philadelphia Vigilance Committee, which offered aid and comfort to the slave runaways, and soon became the organization's most important link to the city's black community (largest in the country at that time). By 1851 Still was Chairman of the Pennsylvania Abolition Society.

During his fourteen years of service for the Underground Railroad, Still interviewed hundreds of Southern bondsmen as they made their way North. In one interview he made the dramatic discovery that the fugitive confronting him was his own brother, from whom he had been separated since childhood.

Intending originally to use the material to assist other escaped slaves find their relatives and loved ones, he decided to compile the detailed information he had gathered. To avoid arrest for his illegal labors, for these records were evidence of a willful effort to violate the law, he concealed his notes in the loft of Lebanon Seminary and in a graveyard. In 1873 he published his best material in book form. Always a successful businessman, he made sure that the book would have a wide circulation by hiring agents to sell it in major cities and twice reprinted it (1879 and 1883).

Until his death in 1902, William Still supported many projects for the improvement of the local Negro population. Before the Civil War he launched a campaign to end Philadelphia streetcar segregation. His ability to unite prominent whites and Negroes behind this effort, and particularly the giant interracial rally he organized on January 13, 1865, finally led to the elimination of these Jim Crow practices.

Still's record is a monumental tribute to Negro bravery and resourcefulness during this critical period. Its heroes are the daring and intrepid Negro fugitives, male and female, who risked all in a hostile white land to secure liberty. Not the least of the volume's many heroic figures is its black author.

William Loren Katz
GENERAL EDITOR

THE

UNDERGROUND RAIL ROAD

W Still

THE

UNDERGROUND RAIL ROAD.

A RECORD

OF

FACTS, AUTHENTIC NARRATIVES, LETTERS, &C.,

Narrating the Hardships Hair-breadth Escapes and Death Struggles

OF THE

Slaves in their efforts for Freedom,

AS RELATED

BY THEMSELVES AND OTHERS, OR WITNESSED BY THE AUTHOR;

TOGETHER WITH

SKETCHES OF SOME OF THE LARGEST STOCKHOLDERS, AND

MOST LIBERAL AIDERS AND ADVISERS,

OF THE ROAD.

BY

WILLIAM STILL,

For many years connected with the Anti-Slavery Office in Philadelphia, and Chairman
of the Acting Vigilant Committee of the Philadelphia Branch of
the Underground Rail Road.

Illustrated with 70 fine Engravings by Bensell, Schell and others, and
Portraits from Photographs from Life.

Thou shalt not deliver unto his master the servant that has escaped from his master unto thee.—*Deut.* xxiii. 15.

SOLD ONLY BY SUBSCRIPTION.

PHILADELPHIA:

PORTER & COATES,

822, CHESTNUT STREET.

1872.

JAS. B. RODGERS CO.
Electrotypers & Printers,
52 & 54 North 6th Street, Philad'a.

DEDICATION.

———

TO THE

FRIENDS OF FREEDOM, TO HEROIC FUGITIVES AND THEIR

POSTERITY IN THE UNITED STATES,

THESE MEMORIALS OF THEIR LOVE OF LIBERTY

ARE INSCRIBED

By the AUTHOR.

PREFACE.

Whereas, The position of William Still in the vigilance committee connected with the "Underground Rail Road," as its corresponding secretary, and chairman of its active sub-committee, gave him peculiar facilities for collecting interesting facts pertaining to this branch of the anti-slavery service; therefore

Resolved, That the Pennsylvania Anti-Slavery Society request him to compile and publish his personal reminiscences and experiences relating to the "Underground Rail Road."

In compliance with this Resolution, unanimously passed at the closing meeting of the Pennsylvania Anti-Slavery Society held last May in Philadelphia, the writer, in the following pages, willingly and he hopes satisfactorily discharges his duty.

In these Records will be found interesting narratives of the escapes of many men, women and children, from the prison-house of bondage; from cities and plantations; from rice swamps and cotton fields; from kitchens and mechanic shops; from Border States and Gulf States; from cruel masters and mild masters;—some guided by the north star alone, penniless, braving the perils of land and sea, eluding the keen scent of the blood-hound as well as the more dangerous pursuit of the savage slave-hunter; some from secluded dens and caves of the earth, where for months and years they had been hidden away waiting for the chance to escape; from mountains and swamps, where indescribable suffering from hunger and other privations had patiently been endured. Occasionally fugitives came in boxes and chests, and not infrequently some were secreted in steamers and vessels, and in some instances journeyed hundreds of miles in skiffs. Men disguised in female attire and women dressed in the garb of men have under very trying circumstances triumphed in thus making their way to freedom. And here and there when all other modes of escape seemed cut off, some, whose fair complexions have rendered them indistinguishable from their Anglo-Saxon brethren, feeling that they could endure the yoke no longer, with assumed airs of im-

1

portance, such as they had been accustomed to see their masters show when traveling, have taken the usual modes of conveyance and have even braved the most scrutinizing inspection of slave-holders, slave-catchers and car conductors, who were ever on the alert to catch those who were considered base and white enough to practice such deception. Passes have been written and used by fugitives, with their masters' and mistresses' names boldly attached thereto, and have answered admirably as a protection, when passing through ignorant country districts of slave regions, where but few, either white or colored, knew how to read or write correctly.

Not a few, upon arriving, of course, hardly had rags enough on them to cover their nakedness, even in the coldest weather.

It scarcely needs be stated that, as a general rule, the passengers of the U. G. R. R. were physically and intellectually above the average order of slaves.

They were determined to have liberty even at the cost of life.

The slave auction block indirectly proved to be in some respects a very active agent in promoting travel on the U. G. R. R., just as Jeff. Davis was an agent in helping to bring about the downfall of Slavery. The horrors of the block, as looked upon through the light of the daily heart-breaking separations it was causing to the oppressed, no pen could describe or mind imagine; hence it will be seen that many of the passengers, whose narratives will be found in this work, ascribed their first undying resolution to strike for freedom to the auction block or to the fear of soon having to take their chances thereon. But other agencies were at work in the South, which in various ways aided directly or tacitly the U. G. R. R. cause.

To refer in detail to any considerable number of these agents would be impossible, if necessary. Some there were who nobly periled their all for the freedom of the oppressed, whose sufferings and deeds of bravery must have a fitting place in this volume.

Where in history, modern or ancient, could be found a more Christlike exhibition of love and humanity, of whole-souled devotion to freedom, than was proven in the character of the hero, Seth Concklin, who lost his life while endeavoring to rescue from Alabama slavery the wife and children of Peter Still?

So also do the heroic and faithful services of Samuel D. Burris demand special reference and commemoration, for his connection with the U. G. R. R. cost him not only imprisonment and the most barbarous treatment, but likewise the loss of his freedom. He was sold on the auction block.

Here too come the overwhelming claims of S. A. Smith, who at the sad cost to himself of many of the best years of his life in the Richmond penitentiary, boxed up Henry Box Brown and others in Richmond, and committed them to Adams' Express office, to be carried in this most extraordinary manner to freedom.

We must not omit from these records the boldness and the hazard of the unparalleled undertakings of Captains Drayton, Lee, Baylis, &c.

While the Vigilance Committee of Philadelphia was in no wise responsible for the suffering incurred by many of those who helped the slave, yet in order to show how men were moved to lend an ear to those hungering and thirsting for freedom, and to what extent the relentless spirit of Slavery would go in wreaking vengeance upon them—out of the many who were called upon to suffer thus, the individual cases here brought forward must suffice. Without introducing a few of such incidents the records would necessarily be incomplete.

Those who come after us seeking for information in regard to the existence, atrocity, struggles and destruction of Slavery, will have no trouble in finding this hydra-headed monster ruling and tyrannizing over Church and State, North and South, white and black, without let or hindrance, for at least several generations. Nor will posterity have any difficulty in finding the deeds of the brave and invincible opposers of Slavery, who in the language of Wm. Lloyd Garrison, declared without concealment and without compromise : " I am in earnest, I will not equivocate—I will not excuse—I will not retreat a single inch—and I will be heard."

While this resolute spirit actuated the hearts of all true abolitionists, it was a peculiar satisfaction and gratification to them to know that the slaves themselves were struggling and hungering for deliverance. Hence such evidence from this quarter never failed to meet with hearty sympathy and aid. But here the enemy was never willingly allowed to investigate.

The slave and his particular friends could only meet in private to transact the business of the Underground Rail Road ground. All others were outsiders. The right hand was not to know what the left hand was doing.

Stockholders did not expect any dividends, nor did they require special reports to be published. Indeed prudence often dictated that even the recipients of our favor should not know the names of their helpers, and *vice versa* they did not desire to know theirs.

The risk of aiding fugitives was never lost sight of, and the safety of all concerned called for still tongues. Hence sad and thrilling stories were listened to, and made deep impressions; but as a universal rule, friend and fugitive parted with only very vivid recollection of the secret interview and with mutual sympathy; for a length of time no narratives were written. The writer, in common with others, took no notes. But after the restoration of Peter Still, his own brother (the kidnapped and the ransomed), after forty years' cruel separation from his mother, the wonderful discovery and joyful reunion, the idea forced itself upon his mind that all over this wide and extended country thousands of mothers and children, separated by Slavery, were in a similar way living without the slightest knowledge of each other's whereabouts, praying and weeping without ceasing, as did this mother and son. Under these reflections it seemed reasonable to hope that by carefully gathering the narratives of Underground Rail Road passengers, in some way or other some of the bleeding and severed hearts might be united and comforted; and by the use that might be made privately, if not publicly, of just such facts as would naturally be embraced in their brief narratives, re-unions might take place. For years it was the writer's privilege to see many travelers, to receive from their own lips the most interesting and in many cases exceedingly thrilling accounts of their struggles for liberty, and to learn who had held them in bondage, how they had been treated, what prompted them to escape, and whom that were near and dear to them they had left in chains. Their hopes, fears and sufferings were thus recorded in a book. It scarcely need be added with no expectation, however, that the day was so near when these things could be published.

It is now a source of great satisfaction to feel that not

only these numerous narratives may be published, but that in connection therewith, for the completeness of the work, many interesting private letters from fugitives in Canada, slaves in the South, Underground Rail Road conductors and stockholders, and last and least, from slaveholders, in the bargain—all having a direct bearing on the mysterious road.

In the use of these various documents, the writer begs to assure his readers that the most scrupulous care has been taken to furnish artless stories, simple facts,—to resort to no coloring to make the book seem romantic, as he is fully persuaded that any exaggerations or additions of his own could not possibly equal in surpassing interest, the original and natural tales given under circumstances, when life and death seemed about equally balanced in the scale, and fugitives in transit were making their way from Slavery to Freedom, with the horrors of the Fugitive Slave-law staring them in the face.

Thousands were either directly or indirectly interested in this enterprise, and in all probability two generations will pass away before many who are now living witnesses to the truth of these records will cease to bring vividly to mind the hour and circumstance when for the first time they were led to resort to this road to escape the " barbarism" of Slavery.

Far be it from the writer to assume, however, that these Records cover the entire Underground Rail Road operations. Many local branches existed in different parts of the country, which neither time nor limit would allow mention of in this connection. Good men labored and suffered, who deserve to be held in the highest admiration by the friends of Freedom, whose names may be looked for in vain in these pages; for which reason some may be inclined to complain. With respect to these points it may here be remarked that in gathering narratives from unwritten sources—from memory simply—no amount of pains or labor could possibly succeed in making a trustworthy history. The writer has deemed it best, therefore, to confine himself to facts coming within his personal knowledge, and to the records of his own preserving, which, by the way, are quite too voluminous to be all used in this work. Frequent abridgements and omissions must be made.

The writer is fully conscious of his literary imperfections. The time allotted him from other pressing duties is, moreover, exceedingly limited. Nevertheless he feels that he owes it to the cause of Freedom, and to the Fugitives and their posterity in particular, to bring the doings of the U. G. R. R. before the public in the most truthful manner; not for the purpose of amusing the reader, but to show what efforts were made and what success was gained for Freedom under difficulties. That some professing a love of liberty at this late date will be disposed to criticise some of the methods resorted to in aiding in the escape of fugitives as herein recounted, may be expected. While the writer holds the labors of Abolitionists generally in very grateful appreciation, he hopes not to be regarded as making any invidious discriminations in favor of the individual friends of the slave, whose names may be brought out prominently in this work, as it is not with the Anti-Slavery question proper that he is dealing, but simply the Underground Rail Road. In order, therefore, fittingly to bring the movements of this enterprise to light, the writer could not justly confine himself to the Acting Committee, but felt constrained to bring in others—Friends—who never forsook the fugitive, who visited him in prison, clothed him when naked, fed him when hungry, wept with him when he wept, and cheered him with their warmest sympathies and friendship. In addition to the names of the Acting Committee, he has felt constrained to beg the portraits of the following stockholders and advisers of the Road, whose names will be found on the next page, and in thus presenting a brief sketch of their labors, he feels that the true friends of the slave in recognizing them in this connection with many of the once Fugitives (now citizens), will regard it as a tribute to the Anti-Slavery cause rather than the individuals themselves.

WILLIAM STILL.

Philadelphia, *January,* 1872.

ILLUSTRATIONS.

7

CONTENTS.

HEAVY REWARD.

ARRIVAL FROM UNIONVILLE, 1857.

ARRIVAL FROM MARYLAND, 1857.

ARRIVAL FROM CAMBRIDGE, 1857.

BENJAMIN ROSS AND HIS WIFE HARRIET

2

THE

UNDERGROUND RAIL ROAD.

SETH CONCKLIN.

In the long list of names who have suffered and died in the cause of freedom, not one, perhaps, could be found whose efforts to redeem a poor family of slaves were more Christlike than Seth Concklin's, whose noble and daring spirit has been so long completely shrouded in mystery. Except John Brown, it is a question, whether his rival could be found with respect to boldness, disinterestedness and willingness to be sacrificed for the deliverance of the oppressed.

By chance one day he came across a copy of the Pennsylvania Freeman, containing the story of Peter Still, "the Kidnapped and the Ransomed,"—how he had been torn away from his mother, when a little boy six years old; how, for forty years and more, he had been compelled to serve under the yoke, totally destitute as to any knowledge of his parents' whereabouts; how the intense love of liberty and desire to get back to his mother had unceasingly absorbed his mind through all these years of bondage; how, amid the most appalling discouragements, prompted alone by his undying determination to be free and be reunited with those from whom he had been sold away, he contrived to buy himself; how, by extreme economy, from doing over-work, he saved up five hundred dollars, the amount of money required for his ransom, which, with his freedom, he, from necessity, placed unreservedly in the confidential keeping of a Jew, named Joseph Friedman, whom he had known for a long time and could venture to trust,—how he had further toiled to save up money to defray his expenses on an expedition in search of his mother and kindred; how, when this end was accomplished, with an earnest purpose he took his carpet-bag in his hand, and his heart throbbing for his old home and people, he turned his mind very privately towards Philadelphia, where he hoped, by having notices read in the colored churches to the effect that "forty-one or forty-two years before two little boys*

---

* Sons of Levin and Sidney—the last names of his parents he was too young to remember.

were kidnapped and carried South "—that the memory of some of the older members might recall the circumstances, and in this way he would be aided in his ardent efforts to become restored to them.

And, furthermore, Seth Concklin had read how, on arriving in Philadelphia, after traveling sixteen hundred miles, that almost the first man whom Peter Still sought advice from was his own unknown brother (whom he had never seen or heard of), who made the discovery that he was the long-lost boy, whose history and fate had been enveloped in sadness so long, and for whom his mother had shed so many tears and offered so many prayers, during the long years of their separation; and, finally, how this self-ransomed and restored captive, notwithstanding his great success, was destined to suffer the keenest pangs of sorrow for his wife and children, whom he had left in Alabama bondage.

Seth Concklin was naturally too singularly sympathetic and humane not to feel now for Peter, and especially for his wife and children left in bonds as bound with them. Hence, as Seth was a man who seemed wholly insensible to fear, and to know no other law of humanity and right, than whenever the claims of the suffering and the wronged appealed to him, to respond unreservedly, whether those thus injured were amongst his nearest kin or the greatest strangers,—it mattered not to what race or clime they might belong,—he, in the spirit of the good Samaritan, owning all such as his neighbors, volunteered his services, without pay or reward, to go and rescue the wife and three children of Peter Still.

The magnitude of this offer can hardly be appreciated. It was literally laying his life on the altar of freedom for the despised and oppressed whom he had never seen, whose kins-folk even he was not acquainted with. At this juncture even Peter was not prepared to accept this proposal. He wanted to secure the freedom of his wife and children as earnestly as he had ever desired to see his mother, yet he could not, at first, hearken to the idea of having them rescued in the way suggested by Concklin, fearing a failure.

To J. M. McKim and the writer, the bold scheme for the deliverance of Peter's family was alone confided. It was never submitted to the Vigilance Committee, for the reason, that it was not considered a matter belonging thereto. On first reflection, the very idea of such an undertaking seemed perfectly appalling. Frankly was he told of the great dangers and difficulties to be encountered through hundreds of miles of slave territory. Seth was told of those who, in attempting to aid slaves to escape, had fallen victims to the relentless Slave Power, and had either lost their lives, or been incarcerated for long years in penitentiaries, where no friendly aid could be afforded them; in short, he was plainly told, that without a very great chance, the undertaking would cost him his life. The occasion of this interview and conversation, the seriousness of Concklin and the utter failure in presenting the various obstacles to his plan, to create the slightest apparent misgiving in his mind, or to produce the slightest sense of fear or hesitancy, can never be effaced from the memory of the writer. The plan was, however, allowed to rest for a time.

In the meanwhile, Peter's mind was continually vacillating between Alabama, with his wife and children, and his new-found relatives in the North. Said a brother, " If you cannot get your family, what will you do ? Will you come North and live with your relatives?" " I would as soon go out of the world, as not to go back and do all I can for them," was the prompt reply of Peter.

The problem of buying them was seriously considered, but here obstacles quite formidable lay in the way. Alabama laws utterly denied the right of a slave to buy himself, much less his wife and children. The right of slave masters to free their slaves, either by sale or emancipation, was positively prohibited by law. With these reflections weighing upon his mind, having stayed away from his wife as long as he could content himself to do, he took his carpet-bag in his hand, and turned his face toward Alabama, to embrace his family in the prison-house of bondage.

His approach home could only be made stealthily, not daring to breathe to a living soul, save his own family, his nominal Jew master, and one other friend—a slave—where he had been, the prize he had found, or anything in relation to his travels. To his wife and children his return was unspeakably joyous. The situation of his family concerned him with tenfold more weight than ever before.

As the time drew near to make the offer to his wife's master to purchase her with his children, his heart failed him through fear of awakening the ire of slaveholders against him, as he knew that the law and public sentiment were alike deadly opposed to the spirit of freedom in the slave. Indeed, as innocent as a step in this direction might appear, in those days a man would have stood about as good a chance for his life in entering a lair of hungry hyenas, as a slave or free colored man would, in talking about freedom.

He concluded, therefore, to say nothing about buying. The plan proposed by Seth Concklin was told to Vina, his wife; also what he had heard from his brother about the Underground Rail Road,—how, that many who could not get their freedom in any other way, by being aided a little, were daily escaping to Canada. Although the wife and children had never tasted the pleasures of freedom for a single hour in their lives, they hated slavery heartily, and being about to be far separated from husband and father, they were ready to assent to any proposition that looked like deliverance.

So Peter proposed to Vina, that she should give him certain small articles, consisting of a cape, etc., which he would carry with him as memorials, and, in case Concklin or any one else should ever come for her from him, as an unmistakable sign that all was right, he would send back, by whoever was to befriend them, the cape, so that she and the children might not doubt but have faith in the man, when he gave her the sign, (cape).

Again Peter returned to Philadelphia, and was now willing to accept the offer of Concklin. Ere long, the opportunity of an interview was had, and Peter gave Seth a very full description of the country and of his family, and made known to him, that he had very carefully gone over with his wife and children the matter of their freedom. This interview interested Concklin most deeply. If his own wife and children had been in bondage, scarcely could he have manifested greater sympathy for them.

For the hazardous work before him he was at once prepared to make a start. True he had two sisters in Philadelphia for whom he had always cherished the warmest affection, but he conferred not with them on this momentous mission. For full well did he know that it was not in human nature for them to acquiesce in this perilous undertaking, though one of these sisters, Mrs. Supplee, was a most faithful abolitionist.

Having once laid his hand to the plough he was not the man to look back,—not even to bid his sisters good-bye, but he actually left them as though he expected to be home to his dinner as usual. What had become of him during those many weeks of his perilous labors in Alabama to rescue this family was to none a greater mystery than to his sisters. On leaving home he simply took two or three small articles in the way of apparel with one hundred dollars to defray his expenses for a time ; this sum he considered ample to start with. Of course he had very safely concealed about him Vina's cape and one or two other articles which he was to use for his identification in meeting her and the children on the plantation.

His first thought was, on reaching his destination, after becoming acquainted with the family, being familiar with Southern manners, to have them all prepared at a given hour for the starting of the steamboat for Cincinnati, and to join him at the wharf, when he would boldly assume the part of a slaveholder, and the family naturally that of slaves, and in this way he hoped to reach Cincinnati direct, before their owner had fairly discovered their escape.

But alas for Southern irregularity, two or three days' delay after being advertised to start, was no uncommon circumstance with steamers ; hence this plan was abandoned. What this heroic man endured from severe struggles and unyielding exertions, in traveling thousands of miles on water and on foot, hungry and fatigued, rowing his living freight for seven days and seven nights in a skiff, is hardly to be paralleled in the annals of the Underground Rail Road.

The following interesting letters penned by the hand of Concklin convey minutely his last struggles and characteristically represent the singleness of heart which impelled him to sacrifice his life for the slave—

EASTPORT, MISS., FEB. 3, 1851.

To Wm. Still :—Our friends in Cincinnati have failed finding anybody to assist me on my return. Searching the country opposite Paducah, I find that the whole country fifty miles round is inhabited only by Christian wolves. It is customary, when a strange negro is seen, for any white man to seize the negro and convey such negro through and out of the State of Illinois to Paducah, Ky., and lodge such stranger in Paducah jail, and there claim such reward as may be offered by the master.

There is no regularity by the steamboats on the Tennessee River. I was four days getting to Florence from Paducah. Sometimes they are four days starting, from the time appointed, which alone puts to rest the plan for returning by steamboat. The distance from the mouth of the river to Florence, is from between three hundred and five to three hundred and forty-five miles by the river; by land, two hundred and fifty, or more.

I arrived at the shoe shop on the plantation, one o'clock, Tuesday, 28th. William and two boys were making shoes. I immediately gave the first signal, anxiously waiting thirty minutes for an opportunity to give the second and main signal, during which time I was very sociable. It was rainy and muddy—my pants were rolled up to the knees. I was in the character of a man seeking employment in this country. End of thirty minutes gave the second signal.

William appeared unmoved; soon sent out the boys; instantly sociable; Peter and Levin at the Island; one of the young masters with them; not safe to undertake to see them till Saturday night, when they would be at home : appointed a place to see Vina, in an open field, that night; they to bring me something to eat; our interview only four minutes; I left; appeared by night; dark and cloudy; at ten o'clock appeared William; exchanged signals; led me a few rods to where stood Vina; gave her the signal sent by Peter; our interview ten minutes; she did not call me " master," nor did she say " sir," by which I knew she had confidence in me.

Our situation being dangerous, we decided that I meet Peter and Levin on the bank of the river early dawn of day, Sunday, to establish the laws. During our interview, William prostrated on his knees, and face to the ground; arms sprawling; head cocked back, watching for wolves, by which position a man can see better in the dark. No house to go to safely, traveled round till morning, eating hoe cake which William had given me for supper; next day going around to get employment. I thought of William, who is a Christian preacher, and of the Christian preachers in Pennsylvania. One watching for wolves by night, to rescue Vina and her three children from Christian licentiousness; the other standing erect in open day, seeking the praise of men.

During the four days waiting for the important Sunday morning, I thoroughly surveyed the rocks and shoals of the river from Florence seven miles up, where will be my place of departure. General notice was taken of me as being a stranger, lurking around. Fortunately there are several small grist mills within ten miles around. No taverns here, as in the North; any planter's house entertains travelers occasionally.

One night I stayed at a medical gentleman's, who is not a large planter; another night at an ex-magistrate's house in South Florence—a Virginian by birth—one of the late census takers; told me that many more persons cannot read and write than is reported; one fact, amongst many others, that many persons who do not know the letters of the alphabet, have learned to write their own names; such are generally reported readers and writers.

It being customary for a stranger not to leave the house early in the morning where he has lodged, I was under the necessity of staying out all night Saturday, to be able to meet Peter and Levin, which was accomplished in due time. When we approached, I gave my signal first; immediately they gave theirs. I talked freely. Levin's voice, at first, evidently trembled. No wonder, for my presence universally attracted attention by the lords of the land. Our interview was less than one hour ; the laws were written. I to go to Cincinnati to get a rowing boat and provisions ; a first class clipper boat to go with speed. To depart from the place where the laws were written, on Saturday night of the first of March. I to meet one of them at the same place Thursday night, previous to the fourth Saturday from the night previous to the Sunday when the laws were written. We to go down the Tennessee river to some place up the Ohio, not yet decided on, in our row boat. Peter and Levin are good oarsmen. So am I. Telegraph station at Tuscumbia, twelve miles from the plantation, also at Paducah.

Came from Florence to here Sunday night by steamboat. Eastport is in Mississippi. Waiting here for a steamboat to go down ; paying one dollar a day for board. Like other taverns here, the wretchedness is indescribable; no pen, ink, paper or newspaper to be had ; only one room for everybody, except the gambling rooms. It is difficult for me to write. Vina intends to get a pass for Catharine and herself for the first Sunday in March.

The bank of the river where I met Peter and Levin is two miles from the plantation. I have avoided saying I am from Philadelphia. Also avoided talking about negroes. I never talked so much about milling before. I consider most of the trouble over, till I arrive in a free State with my crew, the first week in March ; then will I have to be wiser than Christian serpents, and more cautious than doves. I do not consider it safe to keep this letter in my possession, yet I dare not put it in the post-office here ; there is so little business in these post-offices that notice might be taken.

I am evidently watched ; everybody knows me to be a miller. I may write again when I get to Cincinnati, if I should have time. The ex-magistrate, with whom I stayed in South Florence, held three hours' talk with me, exclusive of our morning talk. Is a man of good general information ; he was exceedingly inquisitive. "I am from Cincinnati, formerly from the *State of New York.*" I had no opportunity to get anything to eat from seven o'clock Tuesday morning till six o'clock Wednesday evening, except the hoe cake, and no sleep.

Florence is the head of navigation for small steamboats. Seven miles, all the way up to my place of departure, is swift water, and rocky. Eight hundred miles to Cincinnati. I found all things here as Peter told me, except the distance of the river. South Florence contains twenty white families, three warehouses of considerable business, a post-office, but no school. McKiernon is here waiting for a steamboat to go to New Orleans, so we are in company.

PRINCETON, GIBSON COUNTY, INDIANA, FEB. 18, 1851.

To WM. STILL:—The plan is to go to Canada, on the Wabash, opposite Detroit. There are four routes to Canada. One through Illinois, commencing above and below Alton ; one through to North Indiana, and the Cincinnati route, being the largest route in the United States.

I intended to have gone through Pennsylvania, but the risk going up the Ohio river has caused me to go to Canada. Steamboat traveling is universally condemned; though many go in boats, consequently many get lost. Going in a skiff is new, and is approved of in my case. After I arrive at the mouth of the Tennessee river, I will go up the Ohio seventy-five miles, to the mouth of the Wabash, then up the Wabash, forty-four miles to New Harmony, where I shall go ashore by night, and go thirteen miles east, to Charles Grier, a farmer, (colored man), who will entertain us, and next night convey us sixteen miles to David Stormon, near Princeton, who will take the command, and I be released.

David Stormon estimates the expenses from his house to Canada, at forty dollars, without which, no sure protection will be given. They might be instructed concerning the course, and beg their way through without money. If you wish to do what should be done, you will send me fifty dollars, in a letter, to Princeton, Gibson county, Inda., so as to arrive there by the 8th of March. Eight days should be estimated for a letter to arrive from Philadelphia.

The money to be State Bank of Ohio, or State Bank, or Northern Bank of Kentucky, or any other Eastern bank. Send no notes larger than twenty dollars.

Levi Coffin had no money for me. I paid twenty dollars for the skiff. No money to get back to Philadelphia. It was not understood that I would have to be at any expense seeking aid.

One half of my time has been used in trying to find persons to assist, when I may arrive on the Ohio river, in which I have failed, except Stormon.

Having no letter of introduction to Stormon from any source, on which I could fully rely, I traveled two hundred miles around, to find out his stability. I have found many Abolitionists, nearly all who have made propositions, which themselves would not comply with, and nobody else would. Already I have traveled over three thousand miles. Two thousand and four hundred by steamboat, two hundred by railroad, one hundred by stage, four hundred on foot, forty-eight in a skiff.

I have yet five hundred miles to go to the plantation, to commence operations. I have been two weeks on the decks of steamboats, three nights out, two of which I got perfectly wet. If I had had paper money, as McKim desired, it would have been destroyed. I have not been entertained gratis at any place except Stormon's. I had one hundred and twenty-six dollars when I left Philadelphia, one hundred from you, twenty-six mine.

Telegraphed to station at Evansville, thirty-three miles from Stormon's, and at Vinclure's, twenty-five miles from Stormon's. The Wabash route is considered the safest route. No one has ever been lost from Stormon's to Canada. Some have been lost between Stormon's and the Ohio. The wolves have never suspected Stormon. Your asking aid in money for a case properly belonging east of Ohio, is detested. If you have sent money to Cincinnati, you should recall it. I will have no opportunity to use it.

SETH CONCKLIN, Princeton, Gibson county, Ind.

P. S. First of April, will be about the time Peter's family will arrive opposite Detroit. You should inform yourself how to find them there. I may have no opportunity.

I will look promptly for your letter at Princeton, till the 10th of March, and longer if there should have been any delay by the mails.

In March, as contemplated, Concklin arrived in Indiana, at the place designated, with Peter's wife and three children, and sent a thrilling letter to the writer, portraying in the most vivid light his adventurous flight from the hour they left Alabama until their arrival in Indiana. In this report he stated, that instead of starting early in the morning, owing to some unforeseen delay on the part of the family, they did not reach the designated place till towards day, which greatly exposed them in passing a certain town which he had hoped to avoid.

But as his brave heart was bent on prosecuting his journey without further delay, he concluded to start at all hazards, notwithstanding the dangers he apprehended from passing said town by daylight. For safety he endeavored to hide his freight by having them all lie flat down on the bottom of the skiff; covered them with blankets, concealing them from the effulgent beams of the early morning sun, or rather from the " Christian Wolves" who might perchance espy him from the shore in passing the town.

The wind blew fearfully. Concklin was rowing heroically when loud voices from the shore hailed him, but he was utterly deaf to the sound. Immediately one or two guns were fired in the direction of the skiff, but he heeded not this significant call; consequently here ended this difficulty. He supposed, as the wind was blowing so hard, those on shore who hailed him must have concluded that he did not hear them and that he meant no disrespect in treating them with seeming indifference. Whilst many straits and great dangers had to be passed, this was the greatest before reaching their destination.

But suffice it to say that the glad tidings which this letter contained filled the breast of Peter with unutterable delight and his friends and relations with wonder beyond degree.* No fond wife had ever waited with more longing desire for the return of her husband than Peter had for this blessed news. All doubts had disappeared, and a well grounded hope was cherished that within a few short days Peter and his fond wife and children would be reunited in Freedom on the Canada side, and that Concklin and the friends would be rejoicing with joy unspeakable over this great triumph. But alas, before the few days had expired the subjoined brief paragraph of news was discovered in the morning Ledger.

RUNAWAY NEGROES CAUGHT.—At Vincennes, Indiana, on Saturday last, a white man and four negroes were arrested. The negroes belong to B. McKiernon of South Florence, Alabama, and the man who was running them off calls himself John H. Miller. The prisoners were taken charge of by the Marshall of Evansville.—*April 9th.*

How suddenly these sad tidings turned into mourning and gloom the hope and joy of Peter and his relatives no pen could possibly describe; at least the writer will not attempt it here, but will at once introduce a witness who met the noble Concklin and the panting fugitives in Indiana and proffered them sympathy and advice. And it may safely be said from a truer and more devoted friend of the slave they could not have received counsel.

EVANSVILLE, INDIANA, MARCH 31st, 1851.

WM. STILL: *Dear Sir,*—On last Tuesday I mailed a letter to you, written by Seth Concklin. I presume you have received that letter. It gave an account of his rescue of the family of your brother. If that is the last news you have had from them, I have very painful intelligence for you. They passed on from near Princeton, where I saw them and had a lengthy interview with them, up north, I think twenty-three miles above Vincennes, Ind., where they were seized by a party of men, and lodged in jail. Telegraphic dispatches were sent all through the South. I have since learned that the Marshall of Evansville received a dispatch from Tuscumbia, to look out for them. By some means, he and the master, so says report, went to Vincennes and claimed the fugitives, chained Mr. Concklin and hurried all off. Mr. Concklin wrote to Mr. David Stormon, Princeton, as soon as he was cast into prison, to find bail. So soon as we got the letter and could get off, two of us were about setting off to render all possible aid, when we were told they

* In some unaccountable manner this the last letter Concklin ever penned, perhaps, has been unfortunately lost.

all had passed, a few hours before, through Princeton, Mr. Concklin in chains. What kind of process was had, if any, I know not. I immediately came down to this place, and learned that they had been put on a boat at 3 P. M. I did not arrive until 6. Now all hopes of their recovery are gone. No case ever so enlisted my sympathies. I had seen Mr. Concklin in Cincinnati. I had given him aid and counsel. I happened to see them after they landed in Indiana. I heard Peter and Levin tell their tale of suffering, shed tears of sorrow for them all; but now, since they have fallen a prey to the unmerciful blood-hounds of this state, and have again been dragged back to unrelenting bondage, I am entirely unmanned. And poor Concklin! I fear for him. When he is dragged back to Alabama, I fear they will go far beyond the utmost rigor of the law, and vent their savage cruelty upon him. It is with pain I have to communicate these things. But you may not hear them from him. I could not get to see him or them, as Vincennes is about thirty miles from Princeton, where I was when I heard of the capture.

I take pleasure in stating that, according to the letter he (Concklin) wrote to Mr. D. Stewart, Mr. Concklin did not abandon them, but risked his own liberty to save them. He was not with them when they were taken; but went afterwards to take them out of jail upon a writ of Habeas Corpus, when they seized him too and lodged him in prison.

I write in much haste. If I can learn any more facts of importance, I may write you. If you desire to hear from me again, or if you should learn any thing specific from Mr. Concklin, be pleased to write me at Cincinnati, where I expect to be in a short time. If curious to know your correspondent, I may say I was formerly Editor of the "New Concord Free Press," Ohio. I only add that every case of this kind only tends to make me abhor my (no!) *this* country more and more. It is the Devil's Government, and God will destroy it.   Yours for the slave, N. R. JOHNSTON.

P. S. I broke open this letter to write you some more. The foregoing pages were written at night. I expected to mail it next morning before leaving Evansville; but the boat for which I was waiting came down about three in the morning; so I had to hurry on board, bringing the letter along. As it now is I am not sorry, for coming down, on my way to St. Louis, as far as Paducah, there I learned from a colored man at the wharf that, that same day, in the morning, the master and the family of fugitives arrived off the boat, and had then gone on their journey to Tuscumbia, but that the "white man" (Mr. Concklin) had "got away from them," about twelve miles up the river. It seems he got off the boat some way, near or at Smithland, Ky., a town at the mouth of the Cumberland River. I presume the report is true, and hope he will finally escape, though I was also told that they were in pursuit of him. Would that the others had also escaped. Peter and Levin could have done so, I think, if they had had resolution. One of them rode a horse, he not tied either, behind the coach in which the others were. He followed apparently "contented and happy." From report, they told their master, and even their pursuers, before the master came, that Concklin had decoyed them away, they coming unwillingly. I write on a very unsteady boat.   Yours, N. R. JOHNSTON.

A report found its way into the papers to the effect that "Miller," the white man arrested in connection with the capture of the family, was found drowned, with his hands and feet in chains and his skull fractured. It proved, as his friends feared, to be Seth Concklin. And in irons, upon the river bank, there is no doubt he was buried.

In this dreadful hour one sad duty still remained to be performed. Up to this moment the two sisters were totally ignorant of their brother's whereabouts. Not the first whisper of his death had reached them. But they must now be made acquainted with all the facts in the case. Accordingly an interview was arranged for a meeting, and the duty of conveying this painful intelligence to one of the sisters, Mrs. Supplee, devolved upon Mr. McKim. And most tenderly and considerately did he perform his mournful task.

Although a woman of nerve, and a true friend to the slave, an earnest worker and a liberal giver in the Female Anti-Slavery Society, for a time she was overwhelmed by the intelligence of her brother's death. As soon as possible, however, through very great effort, she controlled her emotions, and calmly expressed herself as being fully resigned to the awful event. Not a word of complaint had she to make because she had not been apprised of his movements; but said repeatedly, that, had she known ever so much of his intentions, she would have been totally powerless in opposing him if she had felt so disposed, and as an illustration of the true character of the man, from his boyhood up to the day he died for his fellowman, she related his eventful career, and recalled a number of instances of his heroic and daring deeds for others, sacrificing his time and often periling his life in the cause of those who he considered were suffering gross wrongs and oppression. Hence, she concluded, that it was only natural for him in this case to have taken the steps he did. Now and then overflowing tears would obstruct this deeply thrilling and most remarkable story she was telling of her brother, but her memory seemed quickened by the sadness of the occasion, and she was enabled to recall vividly the chief events connected with his past history. Thus his agency in this movement, which cost him his life, could readily enough be accounted for, and the individuals who listened attentively to the story were prepared to fully appreciate his character, for, prior to offering his services in this mission, he had been a stranger to them.

The following extract, taken from a letter of a subsequent date, in addition to the above letter, throws still further light upon the heart-rending affair, and shows Mr. Johnston's deep sympathy with the sufferers and the oppressed generally—

EXTRACT OF A LETTER FROM REV. N. R. JOHNSTON.

My heart bleeds when I think of those poor, hunted and heart-broken fugitives, though a most interesting family, taken back to bondage ten-fold worse than Egyptian. And then poor Concklin! How my heart expanded in love to him, as he told me his adventures, his trials, his toils, his fears and his hopes! After hearing all, and then seeing and communing with the family, now joyful in hopes of soon seeing their husband and father in the land of freedom; now in terror lest the human blood-hounds should be at their heels, I felt as though I could lay down my life in the cause of the oppressed. In that hour or two of intercourse with Peter's family, my heart warmed with love to them. I never saw more interesting young men. They would make Remonds or Douglasses, if they had the same opportunities.

While I was with them, I was elated with joy at their escape, and yet, when I heard their tale of woe, especially that of the mother, I could not suppress tears of deepest emotion.

My joy was short-lived. Soon I heard of their capture. The telegraph had been the means of their being claimed. I could have torn down all the telegraph wires in the land. It was a strange dispensation of Providence.

On Saturday the sad news of their capture came to my ears. We had resolved to go to their aid on Monday, as the trial was set for Thursday. On Sabbath, I spoke from Psalm xii. 5. "For the oppression of the poor, for the sighing of the needy, now will I arise," saith the Lord: "I will set him in safety from him that puffeth at (from them that would enslave) him." When on Monday morning I learned that the fugitives had passed through the place on Sabbath, and Concklin in chains, probably at the very time I was speaking on the subject referred to, my heart sank within me. And even yet, I cannot but exclaim, when I think of it—O, Father! how long ere Thou wilt arise to avenge the wrongs of the poor slave! Indeed, my dear brother, His ways are very mysterious. We have the consolation, however, to know that all is for the best. Our Redeemer does all things well. When He hung upon the cross, His poor broken-hearted disciples could not understand the providence; it was a dark time to them; and yet that was an event that was fraught with more joy to the world than any that has occurred or could occur. Let us stand at our post and wait God's time. Let us have on the whole armor of God, and fight for the right, knowing, that though we may fall in battle, the victory will be ours, sooner or later.

* * * * * * * * * *

May God lead you into all truth, and sustain you in your labors, and fulfill your prayers and hopes. Adieu.   N. R. JOHNSTON.

LETTERS FROM LEVI COFFIN.

The following letters on the subject were received from the untiring and devoted friend of the slave, Levi Coffin, who for many years had occupied in Cincinnati a similar position to that of Thomas Garrett in Delaware, a sentinel and watchman commissioned of God to succor the fleeing bondman—

CINCINNATI, 4TH MO., 10TH, 1851.

FRIEND WM. STILL:—We have sorrowful news from our friend Concklin, through the papers and otherwise. I received a letter a few days ago from a friend near Princeton, Ind., stating that Concklin and the four slaves are in prison in Vincennes, and that their trial would come on in a few days. He states that they rowed seven days and nights in the skiff, and got safe to Harmony, Ind., on the Wabash river, thence to Princeton, and were conveyed to Vincennes by friends, where they were taken. The papers state, that they were all given up to the Marshal of Evansville, Indiana.

We have telegraphed to different points, to try to get some information concerning them, but failed. The last information is published in the *Times* of yesterday, though quite incorrect in the particulars of the case. Inclosed is the slip containing it. I fear all is over in regard to the freedom of the slaves. If the last account be true, we have some hope that Concklin will escape from those bloody tyrants. I cannot describe my feelings on hearing this sad intelligence. I feel ashamed to own my country. Oh! what shall I say. Surely a God of justice will avenge the wrongs of the oppressed.

    Thine for the poor slave,   LEVI COFFIN.

N. B.—If thou hast any information, please write me forthwith.

CINCINNATI, 5TH MO., 11TH, 1851.

WM. STILL:—*Dear Friend*—Thy letter of 1st inst., came duly to hand, but not being able to give any further information concerning our friend, Concklin, I thought best to wait a little before I wrote, still hoping to learn something more definite concerning him.

We that became acquainted with Seth Concklin and his hazardous enterprises (here at Cincinnati); who were very few, have felt intense and inexpressible anxiety about them. And particularly about poor Seth, since we heard of his falling into the hands of the tyrants. I fear that he has fallen a victim to their inhuman thirst for blood.

I seriously doubt the rumor, that he had made his escape. I fear that he was sacrificed.

Language would fail to express my feelings; the intense and deep anxiety I felt about them for weeks before I heard of their capture in Indiana, and then it seemed too much to bear. O! my heart almost bleeds when I think of it. The hopes of the dear family all blasted by the wretched blood-hounds in human shape. And poor Seth, after all his toil, and dangerous, shrewd and wise management, and almost unheard of adventures, the many narrow and almost miraculous escapes. Then to be given up to Indianians, to these fiendish tyrants, to be sacrificed. O! Shame, Shame!!

My heart aches, my eyes fill with tears, I cannot write more. I cannot dwell longer on this painful subject now. If you get any intelligence, please inform me. Friend N. R. Johnston, who took so much interest in them, and saw them just before they were taken, has just returned to the city. He is a minister of the Covenanter order. He is truly a lovely man, and his heart is full of the milk of humanity; one of our best Anti-Slavery spirits. I spent last evening with him. He related the whole story to me as he had it from friend Concklin and the mother and children, and then the story of their capture We wept together. He found thy letter when he got here.

He said he would write the whole history to thee in a few days, as far as he could. He can tell it much better than I can.

Concklin left his carpet sack and clothes here with me, except a shirt or two he took with him. What shall I do with them? For if we do not hear from him soon, we must conclude that he is lost, and the report of his escape all a hoax. . . . .

Truly thy friend,   LEVI COFFIN.

Stunning and discouraging as this horrible ending was to all concerned, and serious as the matter looked in the eyes of Peter's friends with regard to Peter's family, he could not for a moment abandon the idea of rescuing them from the jaws of the destroyer. But most formidable difficulties stood in the way of opening correspondence with reliable persons in Alabama. Indeed it seemed impossible to find a merchant, lawyer, doctor, planter or minister, who was not too completely interlinked with slavery to be relied upon to manage a negotiation of this nature. Whilst waiting and hoping for something favorable to turn up, the subjoined letter from the owner of Peter's family was received and is here inserted precisely as it was written, spelled and punctuated—

McKIERNON'S LETTER.

SOUTH FLORENCE ALA 6 Augest 1851

Mr WILLIAM STILL *No* 31 *North Fifth street Philadelphia*

Sir a few days sinc mr Lewis Tharenton of Tuscumbia Ala shewed me a letter dated 6 June 51 from cincinnati signd samuel Lewis in behalf of a Negro man by the name of peter Gist who informed the writer of the Letter that you ware his brother and wished an answer to be directed to you as he peter would be in philadelphi. the object of the letter was to purchis from me 4 Negros that is peters wife & 3 children 2 sons & 1 Girl the Name of said Negres are the woman Viney the (mother) Eldest son peter 21 or 2 years old second son Leven 19 or 20 years 1 Girl about 13 or 14 years old. the Husband & Father of these people once Belonged to a relation of mine by the name of Gist now

Decest & some few years since he peter was sold to a man by the Name of Freedman who removed to cincinnati ohio & Tuck peter with him of course peter became free by the volentary act of the master some time last march a white man by the name of Miller apperd in the nabourhood & abducted the bove negroes was caut at vincanes Indi with said negroes & was thare convicted of steling & remanded back to Ala to Abide the penalty of the law & on his return met his Just reward by Getting drownded at the mouth of cumberland River on the ohio in attempting to make his escape I recovered & Braught Back said 4 negroes or as You would say coulard people under the Belief that peter the Husband was accessery to the offence thareby putting me to much Expense & Truble to the amt $1000 which if he gets them he or his Friends must refund these 4 negroes are worth in the market about 4000 for thea are Extraordinary fine & likely & but for the fact of Elopement I would not take 8000 Dollars for them but as the thing now stands you can say to peter & his new discovered Relations in philadelphia I will take 5000 for the 4 culerd people & if this will suite him & he can raise the money I will delever to him or his agent at paduca at mouth of Tennessee river said negroes but the money must be Deposeted in the Hands of some respectabl person at paduca before I remove the property it wold not be safe for peter to come to this countery write me a line on recpt of this & let me Know peters views on the above

I am Yours &c B. McKIERNON

N B say to peter to write & let me Know his viewes amediately as I am determined to act in a way if he dont take this offer he will never have an other oppertunity

B McKIERNON

WM. STILL'S ANSWER.

PHILADELPHIA, Aug. 16th, 1851.

To B. McKIERNON, ESQ.: *Sir*—I have received your letter from South Florence, Ala., under date of the 6th inst. To say that it took me by surprise, as well as afforded me pleasure, for which I feel to be very much indebted to you, is no more than true. In regard to your informants of myself—Mr. Thornton, of Ala., and Mr. Samuel Lewis, of Cincinnati—to them both I am a stranger. However, I am the brother of Peter, referred to, and with the fact of his having a wife and three children in your service I am also familiar. This brother, Peter, I have only had the pleasure of knowing for the brief space of one year and thirteen days, although he is now past forty and I twenty-nine years of age. Time will not allow me at present, or I should give you a detailed account of how Peter became a slave, the forty long years which intervened between the time he was kidnapped, when a boy, being only six years of age, and his arrival in this city, from Alabama, one year and fourteen days ago, when he was re-united to his mother, five brothers and three sisters.

None but a father's heart can fathom the anguish and sorrows felt by Peter during the many vicissitudes through which he has passed. He looked back to his boyhood and saw himself snatched from the tender embraces of his parents and home to be made a slave for life.

During all his prime days he was in the faithful and constant service of those who had no just claim upon him. In the meanwhile he married a wife, who bore him eleven children, the greater part of whom were emancipated from the troubles of life by death, and three only survived. To them and his wife he was devoted. Indeed I have never seen attachment between parents and children, or husband and wife, more entire than was manifested in the case of Peter.

Through these many years of servitude, Peter was sold and resold, from one State to another, from one owner to another, till he reached the forty-ninth year of his age, when, in a good Providence, through the kindness of a friend and the sweat of his brow, he regained the God-given blessings of liberty. He eagerly sought his parents and home with all possible speed and pains, when, to his heart's joy, he found his relatives.

Your present humble correspondent is the youngest of Peter's brothers, and the first one of the family he saw after arriving in this part of the country. I think you could not fail to be interested in hearing how we became known to each other, and the proof of our being brothers, etc., all of which I should be most glad to relate, but time will not permit me to do so. The news of this wonderful occurrence, of Peter finding his kindred, was published quite extensively, shortly afterwards, in various newspapers, in this quarter, which may account for the fact of "Miller's" knowledge of the whereabouts of the "fugitives." Let me say, it is my firm conviction that no one had any hand in persuading "Miller" to go down from Cincinnati, or any other place, after the family. As glad as I should be, and as much as I would do for the liberation of Peter's family (now no longer young), and his three "likely" children, in whom he prides himself—how much, if you are a father, you can imagine; yet I would not, and could not, think of persuading any friend to peril his life, as would be the case, in an errand of that kind.

As regards the price fixed upon by you for the family, I must say I do not think it possible to raise half that amount, though Peter authorized me to say he would give you twenty-five hundred for them. Probably he is not as well aware as I am, how difficult it is to raise so large a sum of money from the public. The applications for such objects are so frequent among us in the North, and have always been so liberally met, that it is no wonder if many get tired of being called upon. To be sure some of us brothers own some property, but no great amount; certainly not enough to enable us to bear so great a burden. Mother owns a small farm in New Jersey, on which she has lived for nearly forty years, from which she derives her support in her old age. This small farm contains between forty and fifty acres, and is the fruit of my father's toil. Two of my brothers own small places also, but they have young families, and consequently consume nearly as much as they make, with the exception of adding some improvements to their places.

For my own part, I am employed as a clerk for a living, but my salary is quite too limited to enable me to contribute any great amount towards so large a sum as is demanded. Thus you see how we are situated financially. We have plenty of friends, but little money. Now, sir, allow me to make an appeal to your humanity, although we are aware of your power to hold as property those poor slaves, mother, daughter and two sons,—that in no part of the United States could they escape and be secure from your claim—nevertheless, would your understanding, your heart, or your conscience reprove you, should you restore to them, without price, that dear freedom, which is theirs by right of nature, or would you not feel a satisfaction in so doing which all the wealth of the world could not equal? At all events, could you not so reduce the price as to place it in the power of Peter's relatives and friends to raise the means for their purchase? At first, I doubt not, but that you will think my appeal very unreasonable; but, sir, serious reflection will decide, whether the money demanded by you, after all, will be of as great a benefit to you, as the satisfaction you would find in bestowing so great a favor upon those whose entire happiness in this life depends mainly upon your decision in the matter. If the entire family cannot be purchased or freed, what can Vina and her daughter be purchased for? Hoping, sir, to hear from you, at your earliest convenience, I subscribe myself,　　　　　　　Your obedient servant,　　　　　　WM. STILL.

To B. McKIERNON, Esq.

No reply to this letter was ever received from McKiernon. The cause of his reticence can be as well conjectured by the reader as the writer.

Time will not admit of further details kindred to this narrative. The life, struggles, and success of Peter and his family were ably brought before

PETER STILL,
THE KIDNAPPED AND RANSOMED.

CHARITY STILL,
TWICE ESCAPED FROM SLAVERY. See p. 37.

the public in the "Kidnapped and the Ransomed," being the personal
recollections of Peter Still and his wife "Vina," after forty years of slavery,
by Mrs. Kate E. R. Pickard; with an introduction by Rev. Samuel J. May,
and an appendix by William H. Furness, D. D., in 1856. But, of course,
it was not prudent or safe, in the days of Slavery, to publish such facts as
are now brought to light; all such had to be kept concealed in the breasts
of the fugitives and their friends.

The following brief sketch, touching the separation of Peter and his
mother, will fitly illustrate this point, and at the same time explain certain
mysteries which have been hitherto kept hidden—

THE SEPARATION.

With regard to Peter's separation from his mother, when a little boy, in
few words, the facts were these: His parents, Levin and Sidney, were both
slaves on the Eastern Shore of Maryland. " I will die before I submit to
the yoke," was the declaration of his father to his young master before either
was twenty-one years of age. Consequently he was allowed to buy himself
at a very low figure, and he paid the required sum and obtained his "free
papers" when quite a young man—the young wife and mother remaining
in slavery under Saunders Griffin, as also her children, the latter having
increased to the number of four, two little boys and two little girls. But to
escape from chains, stripes, and bondage, she took her four little children and
fled to a place near Greenwich, New Jersey. Not a great while, however,
did she remain there in a state of freedom before the slave-hunters pursued
her, and one night they pounced upon the whole family, and, without judge
or jury, hurried them all back to slavery. Whether this was kidnapping or
not is for the reader to decide for himself.

Safe back in the hands of her owner, to prevent her from escaping a
second time, every night for about three months she was cautiously "kept
locked up in the garret," until, as they supposed, she was fully "cured of
the desire to do so again." But she was incurable. She had been a witness
to the fact that her own father's brains had been blown out by the discharge of a heavily loaded gun, deliberately aimed at his head by his
drunken master. She only needed half a chance to make still greater struggles than ever for freedom.

She had great faith in God, and found much solace in singing some of
the good old Methodist tunes, by day and night. Her owner, observing
this apparently tranquil state of mind, indicating that she "seemed better
contented than ever," concluded that it was safe to let the garret door
remain unlocked at night. Not many weeks were allowed to pass before
she resolved to again make a bold strike for freedom. This time she had to
leave the two little boys, Levin and Peter, behind.

On the night she started she went to the bed where they were sleeping, kissed them, and, consigning them into the hands of God, bade her mother good-bye, and with her two little girls wended her way again to Burlington County, New Jersey, but to a different neighborhood from that where she had been seized. She changed her name to Charity, and succeeded in again joining her husband, but, alas, with the heart-breaking thought that she had been compelled to leave her two little boys in slavery and one of the little girls on the road for the father to go back after. Thus she began life in freedom anew.

Levin and Peter, eight and six years of age respectively, were now left at the mercy of the enraged owner, and were soon hurried off to a Southern market and sold, while their mother, for whom they were daily weeping, was they knew not where. They were too young to know that they were slaves, or to understand the nature of the afflicting separation. Sixteen years before Peter's return, his older brother (Levin) died a slave in the State of Alabama, and was buried by his surviving brother, Peter.

No idea other than that they had been "kidnapped" from their mother ever entered their minds; nor had they any knowledge of the State from whence they supposed they had been taken, the last names of their mother and father, or where they were born. On the other hand, the mother was aware that the safety of herself and her rescued children depended on keeping the whole transaction a strict family secret. During the forty years of separation, except two or three Quaker friends, including the devoted friend of the slave, Benjamin Lundy, it is doubtful whether any other individuals were let into the secret of her slave life. And when the account given of Peter's return, etc., was published in 1850, it led some of the family to apprehend serious danger from the partial revelation of the early condition of the mother, especially as it was about the time that the Fugitive Slave law was passed.

Hence, the author of "The Kidnapped and the Ransomed" was compelled to omit these dangerous facts, and had to confine herself strictly to the "personal recollections of Peter Still" with regard to his being "kidnapped." Likewise, in the sketch of Seth Concklin's eventful life, written by Dr. W. H. Furness, for similar reasons he felt obliged to make but bare reference to his wonderful agency in relation to Peter's family, although he was fully aware of all the facts in the case.

UNDERGROUND RAIL ROAD LETTERS.

Here are introduced a few out of a very large number of interesting letters, designed for other parts of the book as occasion may require. All letters will be given precisely as they were written by their respective authors, so that there may be no apparent room for charging the writer with partial colorings in any instance. Indeed, the originals, however ungrammatically written or erroneously spelt, in their native simplicity possess such beauty and force as corrections and additions could not possibly enhance—

LETTER FROM THOMAS GARRETT (U. G. R. R. DEPOT).

WILMINGTON, 3mo. 23d, 1856.

DEAR FRIEND, WILLIAM STILL :—Since I wrote thee this morning informing thee of the safe arrival of the Eight from Norfolk, Harry Craige has informed me, that he has a man from Delaware that he proposes to take along, who arrived since noon. He will take the man, woman and two children from here with him, and the four men will get in at Marcus Hook. Thee may take Harry Craige by the hand as a brother, true to the cause; he is one of our most efficient aids on the Rail Road, and worthy of full confidence. May they all be favored to get on safe. The woman and three children are no common stock. I assure thee finer specimens of humanity are seldom met with. I hope herself and children may be enabled to find her husband, who has been absent some years, and the rest of their days be happy together. I am, as ever, thy friend, THOS. GARRETT.

LETTER FROM MISS G. A. LEWIS (U. G. R. R. DEPOT).

KIMBERTON, October 28th, 1855.

ESTEEMED FRIEND :—This evening a company of eleven friends reached here, having left their homes on the night of the 26th inst. They came into Wilmington, about ten o'clock on the morning of the 27th, and left there, in the town, their two carriages, drawn by two horses. They went to Thomas Garrett's by open day-light and from thence were sent hastily onward for fear of pursuit. They reached Longwood meeting-house in the evening, at which place a Fair Circle had convened, and stayed a while in the meeting, then, after remaining all night with one of the Kennet friends, they were brought to Downingtown early in the morning, and from thence, by daylight, to within a short distance of this place.

They come from New Chestertown, within five miles of the place from which the nine lately forwarded came, and left behind them a colored woman who knew of their intended flight and of their intention of passing through Wilmington and leaving their horses and carriages there.

I have been thus particular in my statement, because the case seems to us one of unusual danger. We have separated the company for the present, sending a mother and five children, two of them quite small, in one direction, and a husband and wife and three lads in another, until I could write to you and get advice if you have any to give, as to the best method of forwarding them, and assistance pecuniarily, in getting them to Canada. The mother and children we have sent off of the usual route. and to a place where I do not think they can remain many days.

We shall await hearing from you. H. Kimber will be in the city on third day, the 30th, and any thing left at 408 Green Street directed to his care, will meet with prompt attention.

Please give me again the direction of Hiram Wilson and the friend in Elmira, Mr. Jones, I think. If you have heard from any of the nine since their safe arrival, please let us know when you write. Very Respectfully, G. A. LEWIS.

2d day morning, 29th.—The person who took the husband and wife and three lads to E. F. Pennypecker, and Peart, has returned and reports that L. Peart sent three on to Norristown. We fear that there they will fall into the hands of an ignorant colored man Daniel Ross, and that he may not understand the necessity of caution. Will you please write to some careful person there? The woman and children detained in this neighborhood are a very helpless set. Our plan was to assist them as much as possible, and when we get things into the proper train for sending them on, to get the assistance of the husband and wife, who have no children, but are uncle and aunt to the woman with five, in taking with them one of the younger children, leaving fewer for the mother. Of the lads, or young men, there is also one whom we thought capable of accompanying one of the older girls—one to whom he is paying attention, they told us. Would it not be the best way to get those in Norristown under your own care? It seems to me their being sent on could then be better arranged. This, however, is only a suggestion,

Hastily yours, G. A. LEWIS.

LETTER FROM E. L. STEVENS, ESQ.

(The reader will interpret for himself.)

WASHINGTON, D. C., July 11th, 1858.

MY DEAR SIR :—Susan Bell left here yesterday with the child of her relative, and since leaving I have thought, perhaps, you had not the address of the gentleman in Syracuse where the child is to be taken for medical treatment, etc. His name is Dr. H. B. Wilbur. A woman living with him is a most excellent nurse and will take a deep interest in the child, which, no doubt, will under Providence be the means of its complete restoration to health. Be kind enough to inform me whether Susan is with you, and if she is give her the proper direction. *Ten packages* were sent to your address last evening, one of them belongs to Susan, and she had better remain with you till she gets it, as it may not have come to hand. Susan thought she would go to Harrisburg when she left here and stay over Sunday, if so, she would not get to Philadelphia till Monday or Tuesday. Please acknowledge the receipt of this, and inform me of her arrival, also when the packages came safe to hand, inform me especially if Susan's came safely.

Truly Yours, E. L. STEVENS.

LETTER FROM S. H. GAY, ESQ., EX-EDITOR OF THE ANTI-SLAVERY STANDARD AND NEW YORK TRIBUNE.

FRIEND STILL:—The two women, Laura and Lizzy, arrived this morning. I shall forward them to Syracuse this afternoon.

The two men came safely yesterday, but went to Gibbs'. He has friends on board the boat who are on the lookout for fugitives, and send them, when found, to his house. Those whom you wish to be particularly under my charge, must have careful directions to this office.

There is now no other sure place, but the office, or Gibbs', that I could advise you to send such persons. Those to me, therefore, must come in office hours. In a few days, however, Napoleon will have a room down town, and at odd times they can be sent there. I am not willing to put any more with the family where I have hitherto sometimes sent them.

When it is possible I wish you would advise me two days before a shipment of your intention, as Napoleon is not always on hand to look out for them at short notice. In special cases you might advise me by Telegraph, thus: " One M. (or one F.) this morning. W. S." By which I shall understand that one Male, or one Female, as the case may be, has left Phila. by the 6 *o'clock train*—one or more, also, as the case may be.

Aug. 17th, 1855. Truly Yours, S. H. GAY.

LETTER FROM JOHN H. HILL, A FUGITIVE, APPEALING IN BEHALF OF A POOR SLAVE IN PETERSBURG, VA.

HAMILTON, Sept. 15th, 1856.

DEAR FRIEND STILL :—I write to inform you that Miss Mary Wever arrived safe in this city. You may imagine the happiness manifested on the part of the two lovers, Mr. H. and Miss W. I think they will be married as soon as they can get ready. I presume Mrs. Hill will commence to make up the articles to-morrow. Kind Sir, as all of us is concerned about the welfare of our enslaved brethren at the South, particularly our friends, we appeal to your sympathy to do whatever is in your power to save poor Willis Johnson from the hands of his cruel master. It is not for me to tell you of his case, because Miss Wever has related the matter fully to you. All I wish to say is this, I wish you to write to my uncle, at Petersburg, by our friend, the Capt. Tell my uncle to go to Richmond and ask my mother whereabouts this man is. The best for him is to make his way to Petersburg; that is, if you can get the Capt. to bring him. He have not much money. But I hope the friends of humanity will not withhold their aid on the account of money. However we will raise all the money that is wanting to pay for his safe delivery. You will please communicate this to the friends as soon as possible.

Yours truly, JOHN H. HILL.

LETTER FROM J. BIGELOW, ESQ.

WASHINGTON, D. C., June 22d, 1854.

MR. WILLIAM STILL :—*Sir*—I have just received a letter from my friend, Wm. Wright, of York Sulphur Springs, Pa., in which he says, that by writing to you, I may get some information about the transportation of some *property* from this neighborhood to your city or vicinity.

A person who signs himself Wm. Penn, lately wrote to Mr. Wright, saying he would pay $300 to have this service performed. It is for the conveyance of *only one* SMALL package; but it has been discovered since, that the removal cannot be so safely effected without taking *two larger* packages with it. I understand that the *three* are to be brought to this city and stored in safety, as soon as the forwarding merchant in Philadelphia shall say he is ready to send on. The storage, etc., here, will cost a trifle, but the $300 will be promptly paid for the whole service. I think Mr. Wright's daughter, Hannah, has also seen you. I am also known to Prof. C. D. Cleveland, of your city. If you answer this promptly, you will soon hear from Wm. Penn himself.

Very truly yours, J. BIGELOW.

LETTER FROM HAM & EGGS, SLAVE (U. G. R. R. AG'T).

PETERSBURG, VA., Oct. 17th, 1860.

MR. W. STILL:—*Dear Sir*—I am happy to think, that the time has come when we no doubt can open our correspondence with one another again. Also I am in hopes, that these few lines may find you and family well and in the enjoyment of good health, as it leaves me and family the same. I want you to know, that I feel as much determined to work in this glorious cause, as ever I did in all of my life, and I have some very good hams on hand that I would like very much for you to have. I have nothing of interest to write about just now, only that the politics of the day is in a high rage, and I don't know of the result, therefore, I want you to be one of those wide-a-wakes as is mentioned from your section of country now-a-days, &c. Also, if you wish to write to me, Mr. J. Brown will inform you how to direct a letter to me.

No more at present, until I hear from you; but I want you to be a wide-a-wake.

Yours in haste,   HAM & EGGS.

LETTER FROM REV H. WILSON (U. G. R. R. AG'T).

ST. CATHARINE, C. W., July 2d, 1855.

MY DEAR FRIEND, WM. STILL :—Mr. Elias Jasper and Miss Lucy Bell having arrived here safely on Saturday last, and found their "companions in tribulation," who had arrived before them, I am induced to write and let you know the fact. They are a cheerful, happy company, and very grateful for their freedom. I have done the best I could for their comfort, but they are about to proceed across the lake to Toronto, thinking they can do better there than here, which is not unlikely. They all remember you as their friend and benefactor, and return to you their sincere thanks. My means of support are so scanty, that I am obliged to write without paying postage, or not write at all. I hope you are not moneyless, as I am. In attending to the wants of numerous strangers, I am much of the time perplexed from lack of means; but send on as many as you can and I will divide with them to the last crumb.

Yours truly,   HIRAM WILSON.

LETTER FROM SHERIDAN FORD, IN DISTRESS.

BOSTON, MASS., Feb. 15th, 1855.

No. 2, Change Avenue.

MY DEAR FRIEND:—Allow me to take the liberty of addressing you and at the same time appearing troublesomes you all friend. but subject is so very important that i can not but ask not in my name but in the name of the Lord and humanity to do something for my Poor Wife and children who lays in Norfolk Jail and have Been there for three month i Would open myself in that frank and hones manner. Which should convince you of my cencerity of Purpoest don't shut your ears to the cry's of the Widow and the orphant & i can but ask in the name of humanity and God for he knows the heart of all men. Please ask the friends humanity to do something for her and her two lettle ones i cant do any thing Place as i am for i have to lay low Please lay this before the churches of Philadelphaise beg them in name of the Lord to do something for him i love my freedom and if it would do her and her two children any good i mean to change with her but cant be done for she is Jail and you most no she suffer for the jail in the South are not like yours for any thing is good enough for negros the Slave hunters Says & may God interpose in behalf of the demonstrative Race of Africa Whom i claim desendent i am sorry to say that friendship is only a name here but i truss it is not so in Philada i would not have taken this liberty had i not considered you a friend for you treaty as such Please do all you can and Please ask the Anti Slavery friends to do all they can and God will Reward them. for it i am shure for the earth is the Lords and the fullness there of as this note leaves me not very well but hope when it comes to hand it may find you and family enjoying all the Pleasure life Please answer this and Pardon me if the necessary sum can be required i will find out from my brotherinlaw i am with respectful consideration   SHERIDAN W. FORD.

Yesterday is the fust time i have heard from home Sence i left and i have not got any thing yet i have a tear yet for my fellow man and it is in my eyes now for God knows it is tha truth i sue for your Pity and all and may God open their hearts to Pity a poor Woman and two children. The Sum is i believe 14 hundred Dollars Please write to day for me and see if the cant do something for humanity.

LETTER FROM E. F. PENNYPACKER (U. G. R. R. DEPOT).

SCHUYLKILL, 11th mo., 7th day, 1857.

WM. STILL:—*Respected Friend*—There are three colored friends at my house now, who will reach the city by the Phil. & Reading train this evening. Please meet them.

Thine, &c.,   E. F. PENNYPACKER.

We have within the past 2 mos. passed 43 through our hands, transported most of them to Norristown in our own conveyance.   E. F. P.

LETTER FROM JOS. C. BUSTILL (U. G. R. R. DEPOT).

HARRISBURG, March 24, '56.

FRIEND STILL:—I suppose ere this you have seen those five large and three small packages I sent by way of Reading, consisting of three men and women and children. They arrived here this morning at 8½ o'clock and left twenty minutes past three. You will please send me any information likely to prove interesting in relation to them.

Lately we have formed a Society here, called the Fugitive Aid Society. This is our first case, and I hope it will prove entirely successful.

When you write, please inform me what signs or symbols you make use of in your despatches, and any other information in relation to operations of the Underground Rail Road.

Our reason for sending by the Reading Road, was to gain time; it is expected the owners will be in town this afternoon, and by this Road we gained five hours' time, which is a matter of much importance, and we may have occasion to use it sometimes in future. In great haste,   Yours with great respect,   Jos. C. BUSTILL.

LETTER FROM A SLAVE SECRETED IN RICHMOND.

RICHMOND, VA., Oct. 18th, 1860.

To MR. WILLIAM STILL:—*Dear Sir*—Please do me the favor as to write to my uncle a few lines in regard to the bundle that is for John H. Hill, who lives in Hamilton, C. W. Sir, if this should reach you, be assured that it comes from the same poor individual that you have heard of before; the person who was so unlucky, and deceived also. If you write, address your letter John M. Hill, care of Box No. 250. I am speaking of a person who lives in P.va. I hope, sir, you will understand this is from a poor individual.

LETTER FROM G. S. NELSON (U. G. R. R. DEPOT).

MR. STILL:—*My Dear Sir*—I suppose you are somewhat uneasy because the goods did not come safe to hand on Monday evening, as you expected—consigned from Harrisburg to you. The train only was from Harrisburg to Reading, and as it happened, the goods had to stay all night with us, and as some excitement exists here about goods of the kind, we thought it expedient and wise to detain them until we could hear from you. There are two small boxes and two large ones; we have them all secure; what had better be done? Let us know. Also, as we can learn, there are three more boxes still in Harrisburg. Answer your communication at Harrisburg. Also, fail not to answer this by the return of mail, as things are rather critical, and you will oblige us.

G. S. NELSON.

Reading, May 27, '57.

We knew not that these goods were to come, consequently we were all taken by surprise. When you answer, use the word, goods. The reason of the excitement, is: some three weeks ago a big box was consigned to us by J. Bustill, of Harrisburg. We received it, and forwarded it on to J. Jones, Elmira, and the next day they were on the fresh hunt of said box; it got safe to Elmira, as I have had a letter from Jones, and all is safe.

Yours,   G. S. N.

LETTER FROM JOHN THOMPSON.

MR. STILL:—You will oblige me much Iff you will Direct this Letter to Vergenia for me to my Mother & iff it well sute you Beg her in my Letter to Direct hers to you & you Can send it to me iff it sute your Convenience I am one of your Chattle.

JOHN THOMPSON,
Syracuse, Jeny 6th.

Direction—Matilda Tate Care of Dudley M Pattee Worrenton Farkiear County Verginia.

LETTER FROM JOHN THOMPSON, A FUGITIVE, TO HIS MOTHER.

MY DEAR MOTHER:—I have imbrace an opportunity of writing you these few lines (hoping) that they may fine you as they Leave me quite well I will now inform you how I am geting I am now a free man Living By the sweet of my own Brow not serving a nother man & giving him all I Earn But what I make is mine and iff one Plase do not sute me I am at Liberty to Leave and go some where elce & can ashore you I think highly of Freedom and would not exchange it for nothing that is offered me for it I am waiting in a Hotel I supose you Remember when I was in Jail I told you the time would Be Better and you see that the time has come when I Leave you my heart was so full & yours But I new their was a Better Day a head, & I have Live to see it I hird when I was on the Underground R. Road that the Hounds was on my Track but it was no go I new I was too far out of their Reach where they would never smell my track when I Leave you I was carred to Richmond & sold & From their I was taken to North Carolina & sold & I Ran a way & went Back to Virginna Between Richmond & home & their I was caught & Put in Jail & their I Remain till the oner come for me then I was taken & carred Back to Richmond then I was sold to the man who I now Leave he is nothing But a But of a Feller Remember me to your Husband & all in quirin Friends & say to Miss Rosa that I am as Free as she is & more happier I no I am getting $12 per month for what Little work I am Doing I hope to here from you a gain I your Son & ever By

JOHN THOMPSON.

LETTER FROM "WM. PENN" (OF THE BAR).

WASHINGTON, D. C., Dec. 9th, 1856.

DEAR SIR:—I was unavoidably prevented yesterday, from replying to yours of 6th instant, and although I have made inquiries, I am unable *to-day*, to answer your questions satisfactorily. Although I know some of the residents of Loudon county, and have often visited there, still I have not practiced much in the Courts of that county. There are several of my acquaintances here, who have lived in that county, and *possibly*, through my assistance, your commissions might be executed. If a better way shall not suggest itself to you, and you see fit to give me the *facts* in the case, I can better judge of my ability to help you; *but I know not the man resident there, whom I would trust with an important suit.* I think it is now some four or five weeks since, that some packages left this vicinity, said to be from fifteen to twenty in number, and as I suppose, went through your hands. It was at a time of uncommon vigilance here, and to me it was a matter of extreme wonder, *how and through whom,* such a work was accomplished. Can you tell me? It is *needful* that I should know! Not for curiosity merely, but for the good of others.

An enclosed slip contains the *marks* of one of the packages, which you will read and then *immediately burn.*

If you can give me any light that will *benefit others,* I am sure you will do so.

A traveler here, *very reliable,* and who knows his business, has determined not to leave home again till spring, at least not without extraordinary temptations.

I think, however, he or others, might be tempted to travel in Virginia.

Yours,   W<small>M</small>. P.

LETTER FROM MISS THEODOCIA GILBERT.

S<small>KANEATELES</small> (G<small>LEN</small> H<small>AVEN</small>) C<small>HUY</small>., 1851.

W<small>ILLIAM</small> S<small>TILL</small>:—*Dear Friend and Brother*—A thousand thanks for your good, generous letter!

It was so kind of you to have in mind my intense interest and anxiety in the success and fate of poor Concklin! That he desired and intended to hazard an attempt of the kind, I well understood; but what particular one, or that he had actually embarked in the enterprise, I had not been able to learn.

His memory will ever be among the sacredly cherished with me. He certainly displayed more real disinterestedness, more earnest, unassuming devotedness, than those who *claim* to be the sincerest friends of the slave can often boast. What more *Saviour*-like than the *willing* sacrifice he has rendered!

Never shall I forget that night of our extremest peril (as we supposed), when he came and so heartily proffered his services at the hazard of his liberty, of life even, in behalf of William L. Chaplin.

Such generosity! at *such* a moment! The emotions it awakened no words can bespeak! They are to be sought but in the inner chambers of one's own soul! He as earnestly devised the means, as calmly counted the cost, and as unshrinkingly turned him to the task, as if it were his own freedom he would have won.

Through his homely features, and humble garb, the intrepidity of soul came out in all its lustre! Heroism, in its native majesty, *commanded* one's admiration and love!

Most truly can I enter into your sorrows, and painfully appreciate the pang of disappointment which must have followed this sad intelligence. But so inadequate are words to the consoling of such griefs, it were almost cruel to attempt to syllable one's sympathies.

I cannot bear to believe, that Concklin has been actually murdered, and yet I hardly dare hope it is otherwise.

And the poor slaves, for whom he periled so much, into what depths of hopelessness and woe are they again plunged! But the deeper and blacker for the loss of their dearly sought and new-found freedom. How long must wrongs like these go unredressed? "*How long, O God, how long?*" . . . .

Very truly yours,   T<small>HEODOCIA</small> G<small>ILBERT</small>.

WILLIAM PEEL, ALIAS WILLIAM BOX PEEL JONES.

ARRIVED PER ERRICSON LINE OF STEAMERS, WRAPPED IN STRAW AND BOXED UP,
APRIL, 1859.

William is twenty-five years of age, unmistakably colored, good-looking, rather under the medium size, and of pleasing manners. William had himself boxed up by a near relative and forwarded by the Erricson line of steamers. He gave the slip to Robert H. Carr, his owner (a grocer and commission merchant), after this wise, and for the following reasons: For some time previous his master had been selling off his slaves every now and then, the same as other groceries, and this admonished William that he was liable to be in the market any day; consequently, he preferred the box to the auction-block.

He did not complain of having been treated very badly by Carr, but felt that no man was safe while owned by another. In fact, he "hated the very name of slaveholder." The limit of the box not admitting of straightening himself out he was taken with the cramp on the road, suffered indescribable misery, and had his faith taxed to the utmost,—indeed was brought to the very verge of "screaming aloud" ere relief came. However, he controlled himself, though only for a short season, for before a great while an excessive faintness came over him. Here nature became quite exhausted. He thought he must "die;" but his time had not yet come. After a severe struggle he revived, but only to encounter a third ordeal no less painful than the one through which he had just passed. Next a very "cold chill" came over him, which seemed almost to freeze the very blood in his veins and gave him intense agony, from which he only found relief on awaking, having actually fallen asleep in that condition. Finally, however, he arrived at Philadelphia, on a steamer, Sabbath morning. A devoted friend of his, expecting him, engaged a carriage and repaired to the wharf for the box. The bill of lading and the receipt he had with him, and likewise knew where the box was located on the boat. Although he well knew freight was not usually delivered on Sunday, yet his deep solicitude for the safety of his friend determined him to do all that lay in his power to rescue him from his perilous situation. Handing his bill of lading to the proper officer of the boat, he asked if he could get the freight that it called for. The officer looked at the bill and said, "No, we do not deliver freight on Sunday;" but, noticing the anxiety of the man, he asked him if he would know it if he were to see it. Slowly—fearing that too much interest manifested might excite suspicion—he replied: "I think I should." Deliberately looking around amongst all the "freight," he discovered the box, and said, "I think that is it there." Said officer stepped to it, looked at the directions on it, then at the bill of lading, and said, "That is right, take it along." Here the interest in these two bosoms was thrilling in the highest degree. But the size of the box was too large for the carriage, and the driver refused to take it. Nearly an hour and a half was spent in looking for a furniture car. Finally one was procured, and again the box was laid hold of by the occupant's particular friend, when, to his dread alarm, the poor fellow within gave a sudden cough. At this startling circumstance he dropped the box; equally as quick, although dreadfully frightened, and, as if helped by some invisible agency, he commenced singing, "Hush, my babe, lie still and slumber," with the most apparent indifference, at the same time slowly making his way from the box. Soon his fears subsided, and it was presumed that no one was any the wiser on account of the accident, or coughing. Thus, after summoning courage, he laid hold of the box a third time, and the Rubicon was passed. The car driver, totally ignorant of the contents of the box, drove to the number to which he was directed to take it—left it and went about his business. Now is a moment of intense interest—now of inexpressible delight. The box is opened, the straw removed, and the poor fellow is loosed; and is rejoicing, I will venture to say, as mortal never did rejoice, who had not been in similar peril. This particular friend was scarcely less overjoyed, however, and their joy did not abate for several hours; nor was it confined to themselves, for two invited members of the Vigilance Committee also partook of a full share. This box man was named Wm. Jones. He was boxed up in Baltimore by the friend who received him at the wharf, who did not come in the boat with him, but came in the cars and met him at the wharf.

The trial in the box lasted just seventeen hours before victory was achieved. Jones was well cared for by the Vigilance Committee and sent on his way rejoicing, feeling that Resolution, Underground Rail Road, and Liberty were invaluable.

On his way to Canada, he stopped at Albany, and the subjoined letter gives his view of things from that stand-point—

MR. STILL :—I take this opportunity of writing a few lines to you hoping that tha may find you in good health and femaly. i am well at present and doing well at present i am now in a store and getting sixteen dollars a month at the present. i feel very much o blige to you and your family for your kindnes to me while i was with you i have got a long without any trub le a tal. i am now in albany City. give my lov to mrs and mr miller and tel them i am very much a blige to them for there kind ns. give my lov to my Brother nore Jones tel him i should like to here from him very much and he must write. tel him to give my love to all of my perticular frends and tel them i should like to see them very much. tel him that he must come to see me for i want to see him for sum thing very perticler. please ansure this letter as soon as posabul and excuse me for not writting sooner as i dont write myself. no more at the present. WILLIAM JONES.

derect to one hundred 125 lydus. stt

His good friend returned to Baltimore the same day the box man started for the North, and immediately dispatched through the post the following brief letter, worded in Underground Rail Road parables:

BALTIMO APRIL 16, 1859.

W. STILL:—Dear brother i have taken the opportunity of writing you these few lines to inform you that i am well an hoping these few lines may find you enjoying the same good blessing please to write me word at what time was it when isreal went to Jerico i am very anxious to hear for thare is a mighty host will pass over and you and i my brother will sing hally luja i shall notify you when the great catastrophe shal take place No more at the present but remain your brother N. L. J.

WESLEY HARRIS,* ALIAS ROBERT JACKSON, AND THE MATTERSON BROTHERS.

In setting out for freedom, Wesley was the leader of this party. After two nights of fatiguing travel at a distance of about sixty miles from home, the young aspirants for liberty were betrayed, and in an attempt made to capture them a most bloody conflict ensued. Both fugitives and pursuers were the recipients of severe wounds from gun shots, and other weapons used in the contest.

Wesley bravely used his fire arms until almost fatally wounded by one of the pursuers, who with a heavily loaded gun discharged the contents with deadly aim in his left arm, which raked the flesh from the bone for a space of about six inches in length. One of Wesley's companions also fought heroically and only yielded when badly wounded and quite overpowered. The two younger (brothers of C. Matterson) it seemed made no resistance.

In order to recall the adventures of this struggle, and the success of Wesley Harris, it is only necessary to copy the report as then penned from the lips of this young hero, while on the Underground Rail Road, even then in a very critical state. Most fearful indeed was his condition when he was brought to the Vigilance Committee in this City.

UNDERGROUND RAIL ROAD RECORD.

November 2d, 1853.—Arrived: Robert Jackson (shot man), *alias* Wesley Harris; age twenty-two years; dark color; medium height, and of slender stature.

Robert was born in Martinsburg, Va., and was owned by Philip Pendleton. From a boy he had always been hired out. At the first of this year he commenced services with Mrs. Carroll, proprietress of the United States Hotel at Harper's Ferry. Of Mrs. Carroll he speaks in very grateful terms, saying that she was kind to him and all the servants, and promised them their freedom at her death. She excused herself for not giving them

* Shot by slave-hunters.

their freedom on the ground that her husband died insolvent, leaving her the responsibility of settling his debts.

But while Mrs. Carroll was very kind to her servants, her manager was equally as cruel. About a month before Wesley left, the overseer, for some trifling cause, attempted to flog him, but was resisted, and himself flogged. This resistance of the slave was regarded by the overseer as an unpardonable offence; consequently he communicated the intelligence to his owner, which had the desired effect on his mind as appeared from his answer to the overseer, which was nothing less than instructions that if he should again attempt to correct Wesley and he should repel the wholesome treatment, the overseer was to put him in prison and sell him. Whether he offended again or not, the following Christmas he was to be sold without fail.

Wesley's mistress was kind enough to apprise him of the intention of his owner and the overseer, and told him that if he could help himself he had better do so. So from that time Wesley began to contemplate how he should escape the doom which had been planned for him.

" A friend," says he, " by the name of C. Matterson, told me that he was going off. Then I told him of my master's writing to Mrs. Carroll concerning selling, etc., and that I was going off too. We then concluded to go together. There were two others—brothers of Matterson—who were told of our plan to escape, and readily joined with us in the undertaking. So one Saturday night, at twelve o'clock, we set out for the North. After traveling upwards of two days and over sixty miles, we found ourselves unexpectedly in Terrytown, Md. There we were informed by a friendly colored man of the danger we were in and of the bad character of the place towards colored people, especially those who were escaping to freedom; and he advised us to hide as quickly as we could. We at once went to the woods and hid. Soon after we had secreted ourselves a man came near by and commenced splitting wood, or rails, which alarmed us. We then moved to another hiding-place in a thicket near a farmer's barn, where we were soon startled again by a dog approaching and barking at us. The attention of the owner of the dog was drawn to his barking and to where we were. The owner of the dog was a farmer. He asked us where we were going. We replied to Gettysburg—to visit some relatives, etc. He told us that we were running off. He then offered friendly advice, talked like a Quaker, and urged us to go with him to his barn for protection. After much persuasion, we consented to go with him.

"Soon after putting us in his barn, himself and daughter prepared us a nice breakfast, which cheered our spirits, as we were hungry. For this kindness we paid him one dollar. He next told us to hide on the mow till eve, when he would safely direct us on our road to Gettysburg. All, very much fatigued from traveling, fell asleep, excepting myself; I could not sleep; I felt as if all was not right.

4

"About noon men were heard talking around the barn. I woke my companions up and told them that that man had betrayed us. At first they did not believe me. In a moment afterwards the barn door was opened, and in came the men, eight in number. One of the men asked the owner of the barn if he had any long straw. 'Yes,' was the answer. So up on the mow came three of the men, when, to their great surprise, as they pretended, we were discovered. The question was then asked the owner of the barn by one of the men, if he harbored runaway negroes in his barn? He answered, 'No,' and pretended to be entirely ignorant of their being in his barn. One of the men replied that four negroes were on the mow, and he knew of it. The men then asked us where we were going. We told them to Gettysburg, that we had aunts and a mother there. Also we spoke of a Mr. Houghman, a gentleman we happened to have some knowledge of, having seen him in Virginia. We were next asked for our passes. We told them that we hadn't any, that we had not been required to carry them where we came from. They then said that we would have to go before a magistrate, and if he allowed us to go on, well and good. The men all being armed and furnished with ropes, we were ordered to be tied. I told them if they took me they would have to take me dead or crippled. At that instant one of my friends cried out—'Where is the man that betrayed us?' Spying him at the same moment, he shot him (badly wounding him). Then the conflict fairly began. The constable seized me by the collar, or rather behind my shoulder. I at once shot him with my pistol, but in consequence of his throwing up his arm, which hit mine as I fired, the effect of the load of my pistol was much turned aside; his face, however, was badly burned, besides his shoulder being wounded. I again fired on the pursuers, but do not know whether I hit anybody or not. I then drew a sword, I had brought with me, and was about cutting my way to the door, when I was shot by one of the men, receiving the entire contents of one load of a double barreled gun in my left arm, that being the arm with which I was defending myself. The load brought me to the ground, and I was unable to make further struggle for myself. I was then badly beaten with guns, &c. In the meantime, my friend Craven, who was defending himself, was shot badly in the face, and most violently beaten until he was conquered and tied. The two young brothers of Craven stood still, without making the least resistance. After we were fairly captured, we were taken to Terrytown, which was in sight of where we were betrayed. By this time I had lost so much blood from my wounds, that they concluded my situation was too dangerous to admit of being taken further; so I was made a prisoner at a tavern, kept by a man named Fisher. There my wounds were dressed, and thirty-two shot were taken from my arm. For three days I was crazy, and they thought I would die. During the first two weeks, while I was a prisoner at the tavern, I raised a great deal of blood, and was considered in a very dangerous condition—so much so that persons desiring to see me were not

DESPERATE CONFLICT IN A BARN.

permitted. Afterwards I began to get better, and was then kept very privately—was strictly watched day and night. Occasionally, however, the cook, a colored woman (Mrs. Smith), would manage to get to see me. Also James Matthews succeeded in getting to see me; consequently, as my wounds healed, and my senses came to me, I began to plan how to make another effort to escape. I asked one of the friends, alluded to above, to get me a rope. He got it. I kept it about me four days in my pocket; in the meantime I procured three nails. On Friday night, October 14th, I fastened my nails in under the window sill; tied my rope to the nails, threw my shoes out of the window, put the rope in my mouth, then took hold of it with my well hand, clambered into the window, very weak, but I managed to let myself down to the ground. I was so weak, that I could scarcely walk, but I managed to hobble off to a place three quarters of a mile from the tavern, where a friend had fixed upon for me to go, if I succeeded in making my escape. There I was found by my friend, who kept me secure till Saturday eve, when a swift horse was furnished by James Rogers, and a colored man found to conduct me to Gettysburg. Instead of going direct to Gettysburg, we took a different road, in order to shun our pursuers, as the news of my escape had created general excitement. My three other companions, who were captured, were sent to Westminster jail, where they were kept three weeks, and afterwards sent to Baltimore and sold for twelve hundred dollars a piece, as I was informed while at the tavern in Terrytown."

The Vigilance Committee procured good medical attention and afforded the fugitive time for recuperation, furnished him with clothing and a free ticket, and sent him on his way greatly improved in health, and strong in the faith that, " He who would be free, himself must strike the blow." His safe arrival in Canada, with his thanks, were duly announced. And some time after becoming naturalized, in one of his letters, he wrote that he was a brakesman on the Great Western R. R., (in Canada—promoted from the U. G. R. R.,) the result of being under the protection of the British Lion.

DEATH OF ROMULUS HALL—NEW NAME GEORGE WEEMS.

In March, 1857, Abram Harris fled from John Henry Suthern, who lived near Benedict, Charles county, Md., where he was engaged in the farming business, and was the owner of about seventy head of slaves. He kept an overseer, and usually had flogging administered daily, on males and females, old and young. Abram becoming very sick of this treatment, resolved, about the first of March, to seek out the Underground Rail Road. But for his strong attachment to his wife (who was owned by Samuel

Adams, but was "pretty well treated"), he never would have consented to "suffer" as he did.

Here no hope of comfort for the future seemed to remain. So Abram consulted with a fellow-servant, by the name of Romulus Hall, alias George Weems, and being very warm friends, concluded to start together. Both had wives to "tear themselves from," and each was equally ignorant of the distance they had to travel, and the dangers and sufferings to be endured. But they "trusted in God" and kept the North Star in view. For nine days and nights, without a guide, they traveled at a very exhausting rate, especially as they had to go fasting for three days, and to endure very cold weather. Abram's companion, being about fifty years of age, felt obliged to succumb, both from hunger and cold, and had to be left on the way. Abram was a man of medium size, tall, dark chestnut color, and could read and write a little and was quite intelligent; "was a member of the Mount Zion Church," and occasionally officiated as an "exhorter," and really appeared to be a man of genuine faith in the Almighty, and equally as much in freedom.

In substance, Abram gave the following information concerning his knowledge of affairs on the farm under his master—

"Master and mistress very frequently visited the Protestant Church, but were not members. Mistress was very bad. About three weeks before I left, the overseer, in a violent fit of bad temper, shot and badly wounded a young slave man by the name of Henry Waters, but no sooner than he got well enough he escaped, and had not been heard of up to the time Abram left. About three years before this happened, an overseer of my master was found shot dead on the road. At once some of the slaves were suspected, and were all taken to the Court House, at Serentown, St. Mary's county; but all came off clear. After this occurrence a new overseer, by the name of John Decket, was employed. Although his predecessor had been dead three years, Decket, nevertheless, concluded that it was not 'too late' to flog the secret out of some of the slaves. Accordingly, he selected a young slave man for his victim, and flogged him so cruelly that he could scarcely walk or stand, and to keep from being actually killed, the boy told an untruth, and confessed that he and his Uncle Henry killed Webster, the overseer; whereupon the poor fellow was sent to jail to be tried for his life."

But Abram did not wait to hear the verdict. He reached the Committee safely in this city, in advance of his companion, and was furnished with a free ticket and other needed assistance, and was sent on his way rejoicing. After reaching his destination, he wrote back to know how his friend and companion (George) was getting along; but in less than three weeks after he had passed, the following brief story reveals the sad fate of poor *Romulus Hall*, who had journeyed with him till exhausted from hunger and badly frost-bitten.

A few days after his younger companion had passed on North, Romulus

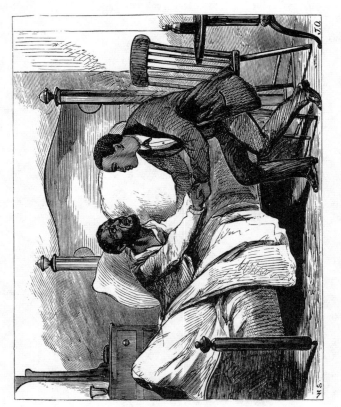

DEATH OF ROMULUS HALL.

was brought by a pitying stranger to the Vigilance Committee, in a most shocking condition. The frost had made sad havoc with his feet and legs, so much so that all sense of feeling had departed therefrom.

How he ever reached this city is a marvel. On his arrival medical attention and other necessary comforts were provided by the Committee, who hoped with himself, that he would be restored with the loss of his toes alone. For one week he seemed to be improving; at the expiration of this time, however, his symptoms changed, indicating not only the end of slavery, but also the end of all his earthly troubles.

Lockjaw and mortification set in in the most malignant form, and for nearly thirty-six hours the unfortunate victim suffered in extreme agony, though not a murmur escaped him for having brought upon himself in seeking his liberty this painful infliction and death. It was wonderful to see how resignedly he endured his fate.

Being anxious to get his testimony relative to his escape, etc., the Chairman of the Committee took his pencil and expressed to him his wishes in the matter. Amongst other questions, he was asked: "Do you regret having attempted to escape from slavery?" After a severe spasm he said, as his friend was about to turn to leave the room, hopeless of being gratified in his purpose: "Don't go; I have not answered your question. I am glad I escaped from slavery!" He then gave his name, and tried to tell the name of his master, but was so weak he could not be understood.

At his bedside, day and night, Slavery looked more heinous than it had ever done before. Only think how this poor man, in an enlightened Christian land, for the bare hope of freedom, in a strange land amongst strangers, was obliged not only to bear the sacrifice of his wife and kindred, but also of his own life.

Nothing ever appeared more sad than seeing him in a dying posture, and instead of reaching his much coveted destination in Canada, going to that "bourne whence no traveler returns." Of course it was expedient, even after his death, that only a few friends should follow him to his grave. Nevertheless, he was decently buried in the beautiful Lebanon Cemetery.

In his purse was found one single five cent piece, his whole pecuniary dependence.

This was the first instance of death on the Underground Rail Road in this region.

The Committee were indebted to the medical services of the well-known friends of the fugitive, Drs. J. L. Griscom and H. T. Childs, whose faithful services were freely given; and likewise to Mrs. H. S. Duterte and Mrs. Williams, who generously performed the offices of charity and friendship at his burial.

From his companion, who passed on Canada-ward without delay, we received a letter, from which, as an item of interest, we make the following extract :

"I am enjoying good health, and hope when this reaches you, you may be enjoying the same blessing. Give my love to Mr. —— ——, and family, and tell them I am in a land of liberty! I am a man among men!" (The above was addressed to the deceased.)

The subjoined letter, from Rev. L. D. Mansfield, expressed on behalf of Romulus' companion, his sad feelings on hearing of his friend's death. And here it may not be inappropriate to add, that clearly enough is it to be seen, that Rev. Mansfield was one of the rare order of ministers, who believed it right "to do unto others as one would be done by" in practice, not in theory merely, and who felt that they could no more be excused for "falling down," in obedience to the Fugitive Slave Law under President Fillmore, than could Daniel for worshiping the "golden image" under Nebuchadnezzar.

AUBURN, NEW YORK, MAY 4TH, 1857.

DEAR BR. STILL :—Henry Lemmon wishes me to write to you in reply to your kind letter, conveying the intelligence of the death of your fugitive guest, Geo. Weems. He was deeply affected at the intelligence, for he was most devotedly attached to him and had been for many years. Mr. Lemmon now expects his sister to come on, and wishes you to aid her in any way in your power—as he knows you will.

He wishes you to send the coat and cap of Weems by his sister when she comes. And when you write out the history of Weems' escape, and it is published, that you would send him a copy of the papers. He has not been very successful in getting work yet.

Mr. and Mrs. Harris left for Canada last week. The friends made them a purse of $15 or $20, and we hope they will do well.

Mr. Lemmon sends his respects to you and Mrs. Still. Give my kind regards to her and accept also yourself,　　　Yours very truly,　　　L. D. MANSFIELD.

JAMES MERCER, WM. H. GILLIAM, AND JOHN CLAYTON.

STOWED AWAY IN A HOT BERTH.

This arrival came by Steamer. But they neither came in State-room nor as Cabin, Steerage, or Deck passengers.

A certain space, not far from the boiler, where the heat and coal dust were almost intolerable,—the colored steward on the boat in answer to an appeal from these unhappy bondmen, could point to no other place for concealment but this. Nor was he at all certain that they could endure the intense heat of that place. It admitted of no other posture than lying flat down, wholly shut out from the light, and nearly in the same predicament in regard to the air. Here, however, was a chance of throwing off the yoke, even if it cost them their lives. They considered and resolved to try it at all hazards.

Henry Box Brown's sufferings were nothing, compared to what these men submitted to during the entire journey.

They reached the house of one of the Committee about three o'clock, A. M.

All the way from the wharf the cold rain poured down in torrents and they got completely drenched, but their hearts were swelling with joy and gladness unutterable. From the thick coating of coal dust, and the effect of the rain added thereto, all traces of natural appearance were entirely obliterated, and they looked frightful in the extreme. But they had placed their lives in mortal peril for freedom.

Every step of their critical journey was reviewed and commented on, with matchless natural eloquence,—how, when almost on the eve of suffocating in their warm berths, in order to catch a breath of air, they were compelled to crawl, one at a time, to a small aperture; but scarcely would one poor fellow pass three minutes being thus refreshed, ere the others would insist that he should "go back to his hole." Air was precious, but for the time being they valued their liberty at still greater price.

After they had talked to their hearts' content, and after they had been thoroughly cleansed and changed in apparel, their physical appearance could be easily discerned, which made it less a wonder whence such outbursts of eloquence had emanated. They bore every mark of determined manhood.

The date of this arrival was February 26, 1854, and the following description was then recorded—

Arrived, by Steamer Pennsylvania, James Mercer, William H. Gilliam and John Clayton, from Richmond.

James was owned by the widow, Mrs. T. E. White. He is thirty-two years of age, of dark complexion, well made, good-looking, reads and writes, is very fluent in speech, and remarkably intelligent. From a boy, he had been hired out. The last place he had the honor to fill before escaping, was with Messrs. Williams and Brother, wholesale commission merchants. For his services in this store the widow had been drawing one hundred and twenty-five dollars per annum, clear of all expenses.

He did not complain of bad treatment from his mistress, indeed, he spoke rather favorably of her. But he could not close his eyes to the fact, that at one time Mrs. White had been in possession of thirty head of slaves, although at the time he was counting the cost of escaping, two only remained—himself and William, (save a little boy) and on himself a mortgage for seven hundred and fifty dollars was then resting. He could, therefore, with his remarkably quick intellect, calculate about how long it would be before he reached the auction block.

He had a wife but no child. She was owned by Mr. Henry W. Quarles. So out of that Sodom he felt he would have to escape, even at the cost of leaving his wife behind. Of course he felt hopeful that the way would open by which she could escape at a future time, and so it did, as will appear by and by. His aged mother he had to leave also.

Wm. Henry Gilliam likewise belonged to the Widow White, and he had been hired to Messrs. White and Brother to drive their bread wagon. William was a baker by trade. For his services his mistress had received one hundred and thirty-five dollars per year. He thought his mistress quite as good, if not a little better than most slave-holders. But he had never felt persuaded to believe that she was good enough for him to remain a slave for her support.

Indeed, he had made several unsuccessful attempts before this time to escape from slavery and its horrors. He was fully posted from A to Z, but in his own person he had been smart enough to escape most of the more brutal outrages. He knew how to read and write, and in readiness of speech and general natural ability was far above the average of slaves.

He was twenty-five years of age, well made, of light complexion, and might be put down as a valuable piece of property.

This loss fell with crushing weight upon the kind-hearted mistress, as will be seen in a letter subjoined which she wrote to the unfaithful William, some time after he had fled.

LETTER FROM MRS. L. E. WHITE.

RICHMOND, 16th, 1854.

DEAR HENRY:—Your mother and myself received your letter; she is much distressed at your conduct; she is remaining just as you left her, she says, and she will never be reconciled to your conduct.

I think Henry, you have acted most dishonorably; had you have made a confidant of me I would have been better off; and you as you are. I am badly situated, living with Mrs. Palmer, and having to put up with everything—your mother is also dissatisfied—I am miserably poor, do not get a cent of your hire or James', besides losing you both, but if you can *reconcile* so do. By renting a cheap house, I might have lived, now it seems starvation is before me. Martha and the Doctor are living in Portsmouth, it is not in her power to do much for me. I know you will repent it. I heard six weeks before you went, that you were trying to persuade him off—but we all liked you, and I was unwilling to believe it—however, I leave it in God's hands He will know what to do. Your mother says that I must tell you servant Jones is *dead* and old *Mrs. Galt*. Kit is well, but we are very uneasy, losing your and *James' hire*, I fear poor little fellow, that he will be obliged to go, as I am compelled to live, and it will be your fault. I am quite unwell, but of course, you don't care. Yours, L. E. WHITE.

If you choose to come back you could. I would do a very good part by you, Toler and Cooke has none.

This touching epistle was given by the disobedient William to a member of the Vigilant Committee, when on a visit to Canada, in 1855, and it was thought to be of too much value to be lost. It was put away with other valuable U. G. R. R. documents for future reference. Touching the "rascality" of William and James and the unfortunate predicament in which it placed the kind-hearted widow, Mrs. Louisa White, the following editorial clipped from the wide-awake Richmond Despatch, was also highly appreciated, and preserved as conclusive testimony to the successful working of the U. G. R. R. in the Old Dominion. It reads thus—

"RASCALITY SOMEWHERE.—We called attention yesterday to the advertisement of two negroes belonging to Mrs. Louisa White, by Toler & Cook, and in the call we expressed the opinion that they were still lurking about the city, preparatory to going off. Mr. Toler, we find, is of a different opinion. He believes that they have already cleared themselves—have escaped to a Free State, and we think it extremely probable that he is in the right. They were both of them uncommonly intelligent negroes. One of them, the one hired to Mr. White, was a tip-top baker. He had been all about the country, and had been in the habit of supplying the U. S. Pennsylvania with bread; Mr. W. having the contract. In his visits for this purpose, of course, he formed acquaintances with all sorts of sea-faring characters; and there is every reason to believe that he has been assisted to get off in that way, along with the other boy, hired to the Messrs. Williams. That the two acted in concert, can admit of no doubt. The question is now to find out how they got off. They must undoubtedly have had white men in the secret. Have we then a nest of Abolition scoundrels among us? There ought to be a law to put a police officer on board every vessel as soon as she lands at the wharf. There is one, we believe for inspecting vessels before they leave. If there is not there ought to be one.

"These negroes belong to a widow lady and constitute all the property she has on earth. They have both been raised with the greatest indulgence. Had it been otherwise, they would never have had an opportunity to escape, as they have done. Their flight has left her penniless. Either of them would readily have sold for $1200; and Mr. Toler advised their owner to sell them at the commencement of the year, probably anticipating the very thing that has happened. She refused to do so, because she felt too much attachment to them. They have made a fine return, truly."

No comment is necessary on the above editorial except simply to express the hope that the editor and his friends who seemed to be utterly befogged as to how these "uncommonly intelligent negroes" made their escape, will find the problem satisfactorily solved in this book.

However, in order to do even-handed justice to all concerned, it seems but proper that William and James should be heard from, and hence a letter from each is here appended for what they are worth. True they were intended only for private use, but since the "True light" (Freedom) has come, all things may be made manifest.

LETTER FROM WILLIAM HENRY GILLIAM.

ST. CATHARINES, C. W., MAY 15th, 1854.

MY DEAR FRIEND:—I receaved yours, Dated the 10th and the papers on the 13th, I also saw the pice that was in Miss Shadd's paper About me. I think Tolar is right

About my being in A free State, I am and think A great del of it.   Also I have no compassion on the penniless widow lady, I have Served her 25 yers 2 months, I think that is long Enough for me to live A Slave.   Dear Sir, I am very sorry to hear of the Accadent that happened to our Friend Mr. Meakins, I have read the letter to all that lives in St. Catharines, that came from old Virginia, and then I Sented to Toronto to Mercer & Clayton to see, and to Farman to read fur themselves.   Sir, you must write to me soon and let me know how Meakins gets on with his tryal, and you must pray for him, I have told all here to do the same for him.   May God bless and protect him from prison, I have heard A great del of old Richmond and Norfolk.   Dear Sir, if you see Mr. or Mrs. Gilbert Give my love to them and tell them to write to me, also give my respect to your Family and A part for yourself, love from the friends to you Soloman Brown, H. Atkins, Was. Johnson, Mrs Brooks, Mr. Dykes.   Mr. Smith is better at presant.   And do not forget to write the News of Meakin's tryal.   I cannot say any more at this time; but remain yours and A true Friend ontell Death.   W. H. GILLIAM, the widow's Mite.

"Our friend Minkins," in whose behalf William asks the united prayers of his friends, was one of the "scoundrels" who assisted him and his two companions to escape on the steamer.   Being suspected of "rascality" in this direction, he was arrested and put in jail, but as no evidence could be found against him he was soon released.

JAMES MERCER'S LETTER.

TORONTO, MARCH 17th, 1854.

MY DEAR FRIEND STILL :—I take this method of informing you that I am well, and when this comes to hand it may find you and your family enjoying good health.   Sir, my particular for writing is that I wish to hear from you, and to hear all the news from down South.   I wish to know if all things are working Right for the Rest of my Brotheran whom in bondage.   I will also Say that I am very much please with Toronto, So also the friends that came over with.   It is true that we have not been Employed as yet; but we are in hopes of be'en so in a few days.   We happen here in good time jest about time the people in this country are going work.   I am in good health and good Spirits, and feeles Rejoiced in the Lord for my liberty.   I Received cople of paper from you to-day. I wish you see James Morris whom or Abram George the first and second on the Ship Penn., give my respects to them, and ask James if he will call at Henry W. Quarles on May street oppisit the Jews synagogue and call for Marena Mercer, give my love to her ask her of all the times about Richmond, tell her to Send me all the news.   Tell Mr. Morris that there will be no danger in going to that place.   You will also tell M. to make himself known to her as she may know who sent him.   And I wish to get a letter from you.   JAMES M. MERCER.

JOHN H. HILL'S LETTER.

MY FRIEND, I would like to hear from you, I have been looking for a letter from you for Several days as the last was very interesting to me, please to write Right away.
            Yours most Respectfully, JOHN H. HILL.

Instead of weeping over the sad situation of his "penniless" mistress and showing any signs of contrition for having wronged the man who held the mortgage of seven hundred and fifty dollars on him, James actually "feels rejoiced in the Lord for his liberty," and is "very much pleased with

Toronto;" but is not satisfied yet, he is even concocting a plan by which his wife might be run off from Richmond, which would be the cause of her owner (Henry W. Quarles, Esq.) losing at least one thousand dollars.

ST. CATHARINE, CANADA, JUNE 8th, 1854.

MR. STILL, DEAR FRIEND:—I received a letter from the poor old widow, Mrs. L. E. White, and she says I may come back if I choose and she will do a good part by me. Yes, yes I am choosing the western side of the South for my home. She is smart, but cannot bung my eye, so she shall have to die in the poor house at last, so she says, and Mercer and myself will be the cause of it. That is all right. I am getting even with her now for I was in the poor house for twenty-five years and have just got out. And she said she knew I was coming away six weeks before I started, so you may know my chance was slim. But Mr. John Wright said I came off like a gentleman and he did not blame me for coming for I was a great boy. Yes I here him enough he is all gas. I am in Canada, and they cannot help themselves.

About that subject I will not say anything more. You must write to me as soon as you can and let me here the news and how the Family is and yourself. Let me know how the times is with the U G. R. R. Co. Is it doing good business? Mr. Dykes sends his respects to you. Give mine to your family. Your true friend, W. H. GILLIAM.

John Clayton, the companion in tribulation of William and James, must not be lost sight of any longer. He was owned by the Widow Clayton, and was white enough to have been nearly related to her, being a mulatto. He was about thirty-five years of age, a man of fine appearance, and quite intelligent. Several years previous he had made an attempt to escape, but failed. Prior to escaping in this instance, he had been laboring in a tobacco factory at $150 a year. It is needless to say that he did not approve of the "peculiar institution." He left a wife and one child behind to mourn after him. Of his views of Canada and Freedom, the following frank and sensible letter, penned shortly after his arrival, speaks for itself—

TORONTO, March 6th, 1854.

DEAR MR. STILL:—I take this method of informing you that I am well both in health and mind You may rest assured that I fells myself a free man and do not fell as I did when I was in Virginia thanks be to God I have no master into Canada but I am my own man. I arrived safe into Canada on friday last. I must request of you to write a few lines to my wife and jest state to her that her friend arrived safe into this glorious land of liberty and I am well and she will make very short her time in Virginia. tell her that I likes here very well and hopes to like it better when I gets to work I don't meane for you to write the same words that are written above but I wish you give her a clear understanding where I am and Shall Remain here untel She comes or I hears from her.

Nothing more at present but remain yours most respectfully, JOHN CLAYTON.

You will please to direct the to Petersburg Luenena Johns or Clayton John is best.

CLARISSA DAVIS.

ARRIVED DRESSED IN MALE ATTIRE.

Clarissa fled from Portsmouth, Va., in May, 1854, with two of her brothers. Two months and a half before she succeeded in getting off, Clarissa had made a desperate effort, but failed. The brothers succeeded, but she was left. She had not given up all hope of escape, however, and therefore sought " a safe hiding-place until an opportunity might offer," by which she could follow her brothers on the U. G. R. R. Clarissa was owned by Mrs. Brown and Mrs. Burkley, of Portsmouth, under whom she had always served.

Of them she spoke favorably, saying that she "had not been used as hard as many others were." At this period, Clarissa was about twenty-two years of age, of a bright brown complexion, with handsome features, exceedingly respectful and modest, and possessed all the characteristics of a well-bred young lady. For one so little acquainted with books as she was, the correctness of her speech was perfectly astonishing.

For Clarissa and her two brothers a "reward of one thousand dollars" was kept standing in the papers for a length of time, as these (articles) were considered very rare and valuable; the best that could be produced in Virginia.

In the meanwhile the brothers had passed safely on to New Bedford, but Clarissa remained secluded, "waiting for the storm to subside." Keeping up courage day by day, for seventy-five days, with the fear of being detected and severely punished, and then sold, after all her hopes and struggles, required the faith of a martyr. Time after time, when she hoped to succeed in making her escape, ill luck seemed to disappoint her, and nothing but intense suffering appeared to be in store. Like many others, under the crushing weight of oppression, she thought she "should have to die" ere she tasted liberty. In this state of mind, one day, word was conveyed to her that the steamship, City of Richmond, had arrived from Philadelphia, and that the steward on board (with whom she was acquainted), had consented to secrete her this trip, if she could manage to reach the ship safely, which was to start the next day. This news to Clarissa was both cheering and painful. She had been "praying all the time while waiting," but now she felt "that if it would only rain right hard the next morning about three o'clock, to drive the police officers off the street, then she could safely make her way to the boat." Therefore she prayed anxiously all that day that it would rain, " but no sign of rain appeared till towards midnight." The prospect looked horribly discouraging; but she prayed on, and at the appointed hour (three o'clock—before day), the rain descended in torrents. Dressed in male attire, Clarissa left the miserable coop where she had been almost without light or air for two and a half months, and unmolested, reached the boat safely, and was secreted in a box by Wm. Bagnal, a clever young man who sincerely sympathized with the slave, having a wife in slavery himself; and by him she was safely delivered into the hands of the Vigilance Committee.

Clarissa Davis here, by advice of the Committee, dropped her old name, and was straightway christened "Mary D. Armstead." Desiring to join her brothers and sister in New Bedford, she was duly furnished with her U. G. R. R. passport and directed thitherward. Her father, who was left behind when she got off, soon after made his way on North, and joined his children. He was too old and infirm probably to be worth anything, and had been allowed to go free, or to purchase himself for a mere nominal sum. Slaveholders would, on some such occasions, show wonderful liberality in letting their old slaves go free, when they could work no more. After reaching New Bedford, Clarissa manifested her gratitude in writing to her friends in Philadelphia repeatedly, and evinced a very lively interest in the U. G. R. R. The appended letter indicates her sincere feelings of gratitude and deep interest in the cause—

NEW BEDFORD, August 26, 1855.

MR. STILL:—I avail my self to write you thes few lines hopeing they may find you and your family well as they leaves me very well and all the family well except my father he seams to be improveing with his shoulder he has been able to work a little I received the papers I was highly delighted to receive them I was very glad to hear from you in the wheler case I was very glad to hear that the persons ware safe I was very sory to hear that mr Williamson was put in prison but I know if the praying part of the people will pray for him and if he will put his trust in the lord he will bring him out more than conquer please remember my Dear old farther and sisters and brothers to your family kiss the children for me I hear that the yellow fever is very bad down south now if the underground railroad could have free course the emergrant would cross the river of gordan rapidly I hope it may continue to run and I hope the wheels of the car may be greesed with more substantial greese so they may run over swiftly I would have wrote before but circumstances would not permit me Miss Sanders and all the friends desired to be remembered to you and your family I shall be pleased to hear from the underground rail road often Yours respectfully, MARY D. ARMSTEAD.

ANTHONY BLOW, ALIAS HENRY LEVISON.

SECRETED TEN MONTHS BEFORE STARTING—EIGHT DAYS STOWED AWAY ON A STEAMER BOUND FOR PHILADELPHIA.

Arrived from Norfolk, about the 1st of November, 1854. Ten months before starting, Anthony had been closely concealed. He belonged to the estate of Mrs. Peters, a widow, who had been dead about one year before his concealment.

On the settlement of his old mistress' estate, which was to take place one year after her death, Anthony was to be transferred to Mrs. Lewis, a daughter of Mrs. Peters (the wife of James Lewis, Esq.). Anthony felt well satisfied that he was not the slave to please the "tyrannical whims" of his anticipated master, young Lewis, and of course he hated the idea of having to come under his yoke. And what made it still more unpleasant for Anthony was that Mr. Lewis would frequently remind him that it was his intention to "sell him as soon as he got possession—the first day of January." "I can get fifteen hundred dollars for you easily, and I will do it." This contemptuous threat had caused Anthony's blood to boil time and again. But Anthony had to take the matter as calmly as possible, which, however, he was not always able to do.

At any rate, Anthony concluded that his "young master had counted the chickens before they were hatched." Indeed here Anthony began to be a deep thinker. He thought, for instance, that he had already been shot three times, at the instance of slave-holders. The first time he was shot was for refusing a flogging when only eighteen years of age. The second time, he was shot in the head with squirrel shot by the sheriff, who was attempting to arrest him for having resisted three "young white ruffians," who wished to have the pleasure of beating him, but got beaten themselves. And in addition to being shot this time, Anthony was still further "broke in" by a terrible flogging from the Sheriff. The third time Anthony was shot he was about twenty-one years of age. In this instance he was punished for his old offence—he "would not be whipped."

This time his injury from being shot was light, compared with the two preceding attacks. Also in connection with these murderous conflicts, he could not forget that he had been sold on the auction block. But he had still deeper thinking to do yet. He determined that his young master should never get "fifteen hundred dollars for him on the 1st of January," unless he got them while he (Anthony) was running. For Anthony had fully made up his mind that when the last day of December ended, his bondage should end also, even if he should have to accept death as a substitute. He then began to think of the Underground Rail Road and of Canada; but who the agents were, or how to find the depot, was a serious puzzle to him. But his time was getting so short he was convinced that whatever he did would have to be done quickly. In this frame of mind he found a man who professed to know something about the Underground Rail Road, and for "thirty dollars" promised to aid him in the matter.

The thirty dollars were raised by the hardest effort and passed over to the pretended friend, with the expectation that it would avail greatly in the emergency. But Anthony found himself sold for thirty dollars, as nothing was done for him. However, the 1st day of January arrived, but Anthony was not to be found to answer to his name at roll call. He had "took out" very early in the morning. Daily he prayed in his place of concealment how to find the U. G. R. R. Ten months passed away, during which time he suffered almost death, but persuaded himself to believe that even that was better than slavery. With Anthony, as it has been with thousands of others similarly situated, just as everything was looking the most hopeless, word came to him in his place of concealment that a friend named Minkins, employed on the steamship City of Richmond, would undertake to conceal him on the boat, if he could be crowded in a certain place, which was about the only spot that would be perfectly safe. This was glorious news to Anthony ; but it was well for him that he was ignorant of the situation that awaited him on the boat, or his heart might have failed him. He was willing, however, to risk his life for freedom, and, therefore, went joyfully.

The hiding-place was small and he was large. A sitting attitude was the only way he could possibly occupy it. He was contented. This place was "near the range, directly over the boiler," and of course, was very warm. Nevertheless, Anthony felt that he would not murmur, as he knew what suffering was pretty well, and especially as he took it for granted that he would be free in about a day and a half—the usual time it took the steamer to make her trip. At the appointed hour the steamer left Norfolk for Philadelphia, with Anthony sitting flat down in his U. G. R. R. berth, thoughtful and hopeful. But before the steamer had made half her distance the storm was tossing the ship hither and thither fearfully. Head winds blew terribly, and for a number of days the elements seemed perfectly mad. In addition to the extraordinary state of the weather, when the storm subsided the fog took its place and held the mastery of the ship with equal despotism until the end of over seven days, when finally the storm, wind, and fog all disappeared, and on the eighth day of her boisterous passage the steamship City of Richmond landed at the wharf of Philadelphia, with this giant and hero on board who had suffered for ten months in his concealment on land and for eight days on the ship.

Anthony was of very powerful physical proportions, being six feet three inches in height, quite black, very intelligent, and of a temperament that would not submit to slavery. For some years his master, Col. Cunnagan, had hired him out in Washington, where he was accused of being in the schooner Pearl, with Capt. Drayton's memorable " seventy fugitives on board, bound for Canada." At this time he was stoker in a machine shop, and was at work on an anchor weighing "ten thousand pounds." In the excitement over the attempt to escape in the Pearl, many were arrested, and the officers with irons visited Anthony at the machine shop to arrest him, but he declined to let them put the hand-cuffs on him, but consented to go with them, if permitted to do so without being ironed. The officers yielded, and Anthony went willingly to the jail. Passing unnoticed other interesting conflicts in his hard life, suffice it to say, he left his wife, Ann, and three children, Benjamin, John and Alfred, all owned by Col. Cunnagan. In this bravehearted man, the Committee felt a deep interest, and accorded him their usual hospitalities.

PERRY JOHNSON, OF ELKTON, MARYLAND.
EYE KNOCKED OUT, ETC.

Perry's exit was in November, 1853. He was owned by Charles Johnson, who lived at Elkton. The infliction of a severe "flogging" from the hand of his master awakened Perry to consider the importance of the U. G. R. R. Perry had the misfortune to let a "load of fodder upset," about which his master became exasperated, and in his agitated state of mind he succeeded in affixing a number of very ugly stationary marks on Perry's back. However, this was no new thing. Indeed he had suffered at the hands of his mistress even far more keenly than from these " ugly marks." He had but one eye; the other he had been deprived of by a terrible stroke with a cowhide in the " hand of his mistress." This lady he pronounced to be a " perfect savage," and added that " she was in the habit of cowhiding any of her slaves whenever she felt like it, which was quite often." Perry was about twenty-eight years of age and a man of promise. The Committee attended to his wants and forwarded him on North.

ISAAC FORMAN, WILLIAM DAVIS, AND WILLIS REDICK.
HEARTS FULL OF JOY FOR FREEDOM—VERY ANXIOUS FOR WIVES IN SLAVERY.

These passengers all arrived together, concealed, per steamship City of Richmond, December, 1853. Isaac Forman, the youngest of the party— twenty-three years of age and a dark mulatto—would be considered by a Southerner capable of judging as "very likely." He fled from a widow by the name of Mrs. Sanders, who had been in the habit of hiring him out for " one hundred and twenty dollars a year." She belonged in Norfolk, Va.; so did Isaac. For four years Isaac had served in the capacity of steward on the steamship Augusta. He stated that he had a wife living in Richmond, and that she was confined the morning he took the U. G. R. R. Of course he could not see her. The privilege of living in Richmond with his wife " had been denied him." Thus, fearing to render her unhappy, he was obliged to conceal from her his intention to escape. " Once or twice in the year was all the privilege allowed" him to visit her. This only added "insult to injury," in Isaac's opinion ; wherefore he concluded that he would make one less to have to suffer thus, and common sense said he was wise in the matter. No particular charges are found recorded on the U. G. R. R. books against the mistress. He went to Canada.

In the subjoined letters (about his wife) is clearly revealed the sincere gratitude he felt towards those who aided him: at the same time it may be seen how the thought of his wife being in bondage grieved his heart. It would have required men with stone hearts to have turned deaf ears to such appeals. Extract from letter soon after reaching Canada—hopeful and happy—

EXTRACT OF LETTER FROM ISAAC FORMAN.

TORONTO, Feb. 20th, 1854.

MR. WILLIAM STILL :—*Sir*—Your kind letter arrived safe at hand on the 18th, and I was very happy to receive it. I now feel that I should return you some thanks for your kindness. Dear sir I do pray from the bottom of my heart, that the high heavens may bless you for your kindness ; give my love to Mr. Bagnel and Mr. Minkins, ask them if they have heard anything from my brother, tell Mr. Bagnel to give my love to my sister-in-law and mother and all the family. I am now living at Russell's Hotel ; it is the first situation I have had since I have been here and I like it very well. Sir you would oblige me by letting me know if Mr. Minkins has seen my wife ; you will please let me know as soon as possible. I wonder if Mr. Minkins has thought of any way that he can get my wife away. I should like to know in a few days. Your well wisher, ISAAC FORMAN.

Another letter from Isaac. He is very gloomy and his heart is almost breaking about his wife.

SECOND LETTER.

TORONTO, May 7, 1854.

MR. W. STILL :—*Dear Sir*—I take this opportunity of writing you these few lines and hope when they reach you they will find you well. I would have written you before, but I was waiting to hear from my friend, Mr. Brown. I judge his business has been of importance as the occasion why he has not written before. Dear sir, nothing would have prevented me from writing, in a case of this kind, except death.

My soul is vexed, my troubles are inexpressible. I often feel as if I were willing to die. I must see my wife in short, if not, I will die. What would I not give no tongue can utter. Just to gaze on her sweet lips one moment I would be willing to die the next. I am determined to see her some time or other. The thought of being a slave again is miserable. I hope heaven will smile upon me again, before I am one again. I will leave Canada again shortly, but I don't name the place that I go, it may be in the bottom of the ocean. If I had known as much before I left, as I do now, I would never have left until I could have found means to have brought her with me. You have never suffered from being absent from a wife, as I have. I consider that to be nearly superior to death, and hope you will do all you can for me, and inquire from your friends if nothing can be done for me. Please write to me immediately on receipt of this, and say something that will cheer up my drooping spirits. You will oblige me by seeing Mr. Brown and ask him if he would oblige me by going to Richmond and see my wife, and see what arrangements he could make with her, and I would be willing to pay all his expenses there and back. Please to see both Mr. Bagnel and Mr. Minkins, and ask them if they have seen my wife. I am determined to see her, if I die the next moment. I can say I was once happy, but never will be again, until I see her; because what is freedom to me, when I know that my wife is in slavery? Those persons that you shipped a few weeks ago, remained at St. Catherine, instead of coming over to Toronto. I sent you two letters last week and I hope you will please attend to them. The post-office is shut, so I enclose the money to pay the post, and please write me in haste.

I remain evermore your obedient servant, I. FORMAN.

5

WILLIS REDICK.

He was owned by S. J. Wilson, a merchant, living in Portsmouth, Va. Willis was of a very dark hue, thick set, thirty-two years of age, and possessed of a fair share of mind. The owner had been accustomed to hire Willis out for "one hundred dollars a year." Willis thought his lot "pretty hard," and his master rather increased this notion by his severity, and especially by "threatening" to sell him. He had enjoyed, as far as it was expected for a slave to do, "five months of married life," but he loved slavery no less on this account. In fact he had just begun to consider what it was to have a wife and children that he "could not own or protect," and who were claimed as another's property. Consequently he became quite restive under these reflections and his master's ill-usage, and concluded to "look out," without consulting either the master or the young wife.

This step looked exceedingly hard, but what else could the poor fellow do? Slavery existed expressly for the purpose of crushing souls and breaking tender hearts.

WILLIAM DAVIS.

William might be described as a good-looking mulatto, thirty-one years of age, and capable of thinking for himself. He made no grave complaints of ill-usage under his master, "Joseph Reynolds," who lived at Newton, Portsmouth, Va. However, his owner had occasionally "threatened to sell him." As this was too much for William's sensitive feelings, he took umbrage at it and made a hasty and hazardous move, which resulted in finding himself on the U. G. R. R. The most serious regret William had to report to the Committee was, that he was compelled to "leave" his "wife," Catharine, and his little daughter, Louisa, two years and one month, and an infant son seven months old. He evidently loved them very tenderly, but saw no way by which he could aid them, as long as he was daily liable to be put on the auction block and sold far South. This argument was regarded by the Committee as logical and unanswerable; consequently they readily endorsed his course, while they deeply sympathized with his poor wife and little ones. "Before escaping," he "dared not" even apprise his wife and child, whom he had to leave behind in the prison house.

JOSEPH HENRY CAMP.

THE AUCTION BLOCK IS DEFEATED AND A SLAVE TRADER LOSES FOURTEEN HUNDRED DOLLARS.

In November, 1853, in the twentieth year of his age, Camp was held to "service or labor" in the City of Richmond, Va., by Dr. K. Clark. Being uncommonly smart and quite good-looking at the same time, he was a saleable piece of merchandise. Without consulting his view of the matter or making the least intimation of any change, the master one day struck up a bargain with a trader for Joseph, and received *Fourteen Hundred Dollars cash* in consideration thereof. Mr. Robert Parrett, of Parson & King's Express office, happened to have a knowledge of what had transpired, and thinking pretty well of Joseph, confidentially put him in full possession of all the facts in the case. For reflection he hardly had five minutes. But he at once resolved to strike that day for freedom—not to go home that evening to be delivered into the hands of his new master. In putting into execution his bold resolve, he secreted himself, and so remained for three weeks. In the meantime his mother, who was a slave, resolved to escape also, but after one week's gloomy foreboding, she became "faint-hearted and gave the struggle over." But Joseph did not know what surrender meant. His sole thought was to procure a ticket on the U. G. R. R. for Canada, which by persistent effort he succeeded in doing. He hid himself in a steamer, and by this way reached Philadelphia, where he received every accommodation at the usual depot, was provided with a free ticket, and sent off rejoicing for Canada. The unfortunate mother was "detected and sold South."

SHERIDAN FORD.
SECRETED IN THE WOODS—ESCAPES IN A STEAMER.

About the twenty-ninth of January, 1855, Sheridan arrived from the Old Dominion and a life of bondage, and was welcomed cordially by the Vigilance Committee. Miss Elizabeth Brown of Portsmouth, Va. claimed Sheridan as her property. He spoke rather kindly of her, and felt that he "had not been used very hard" as a general thing, although, he wisely added, "the best usage was bad enough." Sheridan had nearly reached his twenty-eighth year, was tall and well made, and possessed of a considerable share of intelligence.

Not a great while before making up his mind to escape, for some trifling offence he had been "stretched up with a rope by his hands," and "whipped unmercifully." In addition to this he had "got wind of the fact," that he was to be auctioneered off; soon these things brought serious reflections to Sheridan's mind, and among other questions, he began to ponder how he could get a ticket on the U. G. R. R., and get out of this "place of torment," to where he might have the benefit of his own labor. In this state of mind, about the fourteenth day of November, he took his first and daring step. He went not, however, to learned lawyers or able ministers of the Gospel in his distress and trouble, but wended his way "directly to the woods," where he felt that he would be safer with the wild animals and reptiles, in solitude, than with the barbarous civilization that existed in Portsmouth.

The first day in the woods he passed in prayer incessantly, all alone. In this particular place of seclusion he remained "four days and nights," "two days suffered severely from hunger, cold and thirst." However, one who was a "friend" to him, and knew of his whereabouts, managed to get some food to him and consoling words; but at the end of the four days this friend got into some difficulty and thus Sheridan was left to "wade through deep waters and head winds" in an almost hopeless state. There he could not consent to stay and starve to death. Accordingly he left and found another place of seclusion—with a friend in the town—for a pecuniary consideration. A secret passage was procured for him on one of the steamers running between Philadelphia and Richmond, Va. When he left his poor wife, Julia, she was then "lying in prison to be sold," on the simple charge of having been suspected of conniving at her husband's escape. As a woman she had known something of the "barbarism of slavery," from every-day experience, which the large scars about her head indicated—according to Sheridan's testimony. She was the mother of two children, but had never been allowed to have the care of either of them. The husband, utterly powerless to offer her the least sympathy in word or deed, left this dark habitation of cruelty, as above referred to, with no hope of ever seeing wife or child again in this world.

The Committee afforded him the usual aid and comfort, and passed him on to the next station, with his face set towards Boston. He had heard the slaveholders "curse" Boston so much, that he concluded it must be a pretty safe place for the fugitive.

JOSEPH KNEELAND, ALIAS JOSEPH HULSON.

Joseph Kneeland arrived November 25, 1853. He was a prepossessing man of twenty-six, dark complexion, and intelligent. At the time of Joseph's escape, he was owned by Jacob Kneeland, who had fallen heir to him as a part of his father's estate. Joseph spoke of his old master as having treated him "pretty well," but he had an idea that his young master had a very "malignant spirit;" for even before the death of his old master, the heir wanted him, "Joe," sold, and after the old man died, matters appeared to be coming to a crisis very fast. Even as early as November, the young despot had distinctly given "Joe" to understand, that he was not to be hired out another year, intimating that he was to "go somewhere," but as to particulars, it was time enough for Joe to know them.

Of course "Joe" looked at his master "right good" and saw right through him, and at the same time, saw the U. G. R. R., "darkly." Daily slavery grew awfully mean, but on the other hand, Canada was looked upon as a very desirable country to emigrate to, and he concluded to make his way there, as speedily as the U. G. R. R. could safely convey him. Accordingly he soon carried his design into practice, and on his arrival, the Committee regarded him as a very good subject for her British Majesty's possessions in Canada.

EX-PRESIDENT TYLER'S HOUSEHOLD LOSES AN ARISTO-CRATIC "ARTICLE."

James Hambleton Christian is a remarkable specimen of the "well fed, &c." In talking with him relative to his life as a slave, he said very promptly, "I have always been treated well; if I only have half as good times in the North as I have had in the South, I shall be perfectly satisfied. Any time I desired spending money, five or ten dollars were no object." At times, James had borrowed of his master, one, two, and three hundred dollars, to loan out to some of his friends. With regard to apparel and jewelry, he had worn the best, as an every-day adornment. With regard to food also, he had fared as well as heart could wish, with abundance of leisure time at his command. His deportment was certainly very refined and gentlemanly. About fifty per cent. of Anglo-Saxon blood was visible in his features and his hair, which gave him no inconsiderable claim to sympathy and care. He had been to William and Mary's College in his younger days, to wait on young master James B. C., where, through the kindness of some of the students he had picked up a trifling amount of book learning. To be brief, this man was born the slave of old Major Christian, on the Glen Plantation, Charles City county, Va. The Christians were wealthy and owned many slaves, and belonged in reality to the F. F. V's. On the death of the old Major, James fell into the hands of his son, Judge Christian, who was executor to his father's estate. Subsequently he fell into the hands of one of the Judge's sisters, Mrs. John Tyler (wife of Ex-President Tyler), and then he became a member of the President's domestic household, was at the White House, under the President, from 1841 to 1845. Though but very young at that time, James was only fit for training in the arts, science, and mystery of waiting, in which profession, much pains were taken to qualify him completely for his calling.

After a lapse of time; his mistress died. According to her request, after this event, James and his old mother were handed over to her nephew, William H. Christian, Esq., a merchant of Richmond. From this gentleman, James had the folly to flee.

Passing hurriedly over interesting details, received from him respecting his remarkable history, two or three more incidents too good to omit must suffice.

"How did you like Mr. Tyler?" said an inquisitive member of the Vigilance Committee. "I didn't like Mr. Tyler much," was the reply. "Why?" again inquired the member of the Committee. "Because Mr. Tyler was a poor man. I never did like poor people. I didn't like his marrying into our family, who were considered very far Tyler's superiors." "On the plantation," he said, "Tyler was a very cross man, and treated the servants very cruelly; but the house servants were treated much better, owing to their having belonged to his wife, who protected them from persecution, as they had been favorite servants in her father's family." James estimated that "Tyler got about thirty-five thousand dollars and twenty-nine slaves, young and old, by his wife."

What prompted James to leave such pleasant quarters? It was this: He had become enamored of a young and respectable free girl in Richmond, with whom he could not be united in marriage solely because he was a slave, and did not own himself. The frequent sad separations of such married couples (where one or the other was a slave) could not be overlooked; consequently, the poor fellow concluded that he would stand a better chance of gaining his object in Canada than by remaining in Virginia. So he began to feel that he might himself be sold some day, and thus the resolution came home to him very forcibly to make tracks for Canada.

In speaking of the good treatment he had always met with, a member of the Committee remarked, "You must be akin to some one of your master's family?" To which he replied, "I am Christian's son." Unquestionably this passenger was one of that happy class so commonly referred to by apologists for the "Patriarchal Institution." The Committee, feeling a deep' interest in his story, and desiring great success to him in his Underground efforts to get rid of slavery, and at the same time possess himself of his affianced, made him heartily welcome, feeling assured that the struggles and hardships he had submitted to in escaping, as well as the luxuries he was leaving behind, were nothing to be compared with the blessings of liberty and a free wife in Canada.

EDWARD MORGAN, HENRY JOHNSON, JAMES AND STEPHEN BUTLER.

"Two Thousand Dollars Reward.—The above Reward will be paid for the apprehension of two blacks, who escaped on Sunday last. It is supposed they have made their way to Pennsylvania. $500 will be paid for the apprehension of either, so that we can get them again. The oldest is named Edward Morgan, about five feet six or seven inches, heavily made—is a dark black, has rather a down look when spoken to, and is about 21 years of age.

"Henry Johnson is a colored negro, about five feet seven or eight inches, heavily made, aged nineteen years, has a pleasant countenance, and has a mark on his neck below the ear.

"Stephen Butler is a dark-complexioned negro, about five feet seven inches; has a pleasant countenance, with a scar above his eye; plays on the violin; about twenty-two years old.

"Jim Butler is a dark-complexioned negro, five feet eight or nine inches; is rather sullen when spoken to; face rough; aged about twenty-one years. The clothing not recollected. They had black frock coats and slouch hats with them. Any information of them address Elizabeth Brown, Sandy Hook P. O., or of Thomas Johnson, Abingdon P. O., Harford county, Md. "ELIZABETH BROWN.

"THOMAS JOHNSON."

FROM THE UNDERGROUND RAIL ROAD RECORDS.

The following memorandum is made, which, if not too late, may afford some light to "Elizabeth Brown and Thomas Johnson," if they have not already gone the way of the " lost cause "—

June 4, 1857.—Edward is a hardy and firm-looking young man of twenty-four years of age, chestnut color, medium size, and "likely,"—would doubtless bring $1,400 in the market. He had been held as the property of the widow, "Betsy Brown," who resided near Mill Green P. O., in Harford county, Md. "She was a very bad woman; would go to church every Sunday, come home and go to fighting amongst the colored people; was never satisfied; she treated my mother very hard, (said Ed.); would beat her with a walking-stick, &c. She was an old woman and belonged to the Catholic Church. Over her slaves she kept an overseer, who was a very wicked man; very bad on colored people; his name was 'Bill Eddy;' Elizabeth Brown owned twelve head."

Henry is of a brown skin, a good-looking young man, only nineteen years of age, whose prepossessing appearance would insure a high price for him in the market—perhaps $1,700. With Edward, he testifies to the meanness of Mrs. Betsy Brown, as well as to his own longing desire for freedom. Being a fellow-servant with Edward, Henry was a party to the plan of escape. In slavery he left his mother and three sisters, owned by the "old woman" from whom he escaped.

James is about twenty-one years of age, full black, and medium size. As he had been worked hard on poor fare, he concluded to leave, in company with his brother and two cousins, leaving his parents in slavery, owned by the "Widow Pyle," who was also the owner of himself. "She was upwards of eighty, very passionate and ill-natured, although a member of the Presbyterian Church." James may be worth $1,400.

Stephen is a brother of James', and is about the same size, though a year older. His experience differed in no material respect from his brother's; was owned by the same woman, whom he "hated for her bad treatment" of him. Would bring $1,400, perhaps.

In substance, and to a considerable extent in the exact words, these facts are given as they came from the lips of the passengers, who, though having been kept in ignorance and bondage, seemed to have their eyes fully open to the wrongs that had been heaped upon them, and were singularly determined to reach free soil at all hazards. The Committee willingly attended to their financial and other wants, and cheered them on with encouraging advice.

They were indebted to "The Baltimore Sun" for the advertisement information. And here it may be further added, that the "Sun" was quite famous for this kind of U. G. R. R. literature, and on that account alone the Committee subscribed for it daily, and never failed to scan closely certain columns, illustrated with a black man running away with a bundle on his back. Many of these popular illustrations and advertisements were preserved, many others were sent away to friends at a distance, who took a special interest in the U. G. R. R. matters. Friends and stockholders in England used to take a great interest in seeing how the fine arts, in these particulars, were encouraged in the South ("the land of chivalry").

HENRY PREDO.
BROKE JAIL, JUMPED OUT OF THE WINDOW AND MADE HIS ESCAPE.

Henry fled from Buckstown, Dorchester Co., Md., March, 1857. Physically he is a giant. About 27 years of age, stout and well-made, quite black, and no fool, as will appear presently. Only a short time before he escaped, his master threatened to sell him south. To avoid that fate, therefore, he concluded to try his luck on the Underground Rail Road, and, in company with seven others—two of them females—he started for Canada. For two or three days and nights they managed to outgeneral all their adversaries, and succeeded bravely in making the best of their way to a Free State.

In the meantime, however, a reward of $3,000 was offered for their arrest. This temptation was too great to be resisted, even by the man who had been intrusted with the care of them, and who had faithfully promised to pilot them to a safe place. One night, through the treachery of their pretended conductor, they were all taken into Dover Jail, where the Sheriff and several others, who had been notified beforehand by the betrayer, were in readiness to receive them. Up stairs they were taken, the betrayer remarking as they were going up, that they were "cold, but would soon have a good warming." On a light being lit they discovered the iron bars and the fact that they had been betrayed. Their liberty-loving spirits and purposes, however, did not quail. Though resisted brutally by the sheriff with revolver in hand, they made their way down one flight of stairs, and in the moment of excitement, as good luck would have it, plunged into the sheriff's private apartment, where his wife and children were sleeping. The wife cried murder lustily. A shovel full of fire, to the great danger of burning the premises, was scattered over the room ; out of the window jumped two of the female fugitives. Our hero Henry, seizing a heavy andiron, smashed out the window entire, through which the others leaped a distance of twelve feet. The railing or wall around the jail, though at first it looked forbidding, was soon surmounted by a desperate effort.

At this stage of the proceedings, Henry found himself without the walls, and also lost sight of his comrades at the same time. The last enemy he spied was the sheriff in his stockings without his shoes. He snapped his pistol at him, but it did not go off. Six of the others, however, marvellously got off safely together; where the eighth went, or how he got off, was not known.

DANIEL HUGHES.

Daniel fled from Buckstown, Dorchester Co., also. His owner's name was Richard Meredith, a farmer. Daniel is one of the eight alluded to above. In features he is well made, dark chestnut color, and intelligent, possessing an ardent thirst for liberty. The cause of his escape was : " Worked hard in all sorts of weather—in rain and snow," so he thought he would " go where colored men are free." His master was considered the hardest man around. His mistress was " eighty-three years of age," " drank hard," was " very stormy," and a " member of the Methodist Church" (Airy's meeting-house). He left brothers and sisters, and uncles and aunts behind. In the combat at the prison he played his part manfully.

THOMAS ELLIOTT.

Thomas is also one of the brave eight who broke out of Dover Jail. He was about twenty-three years of age, well made, wide awake, and of a superb black complexion. He too had been owned by Richard Meredith. Against the betrayer, who was a black man, he had vengeance in store if the opportunity should ever offer. Thomas left only one brother living; his " father and mother were dead."

The excitement over the escape spread very rapidly next morning, and desperate efforts were made to recapture the fugitives, but a few friends there were who had sympathy and immediately rendered them the needed assistance.

The appended note from the faithful Garrett to Samuel Rhoads, may throw light upon the occurrence to some extent.

WILMINGTON, 3d mo. 13th, 1857.

DEAR COUSIN, SAMUEL RHOADS :—I have a letter this day from an agent of the Underground Rail Road, near Dover, in this state, saying I must be on the look out for six brothers and two sisters, they were decoyed and betrayed, he says by a colored man named Thomas Otwell, who pretended to be their friend, and sent a *white scamp* ahead to wait for them at Dover till they arrived ; they were arrested and put in Jail there, with Tom's assistance, and some officers.   On third day morning about four o'clock, they broke jail ; six of them are secreted in the neighborhood, and the writer has not known what became of the other two.   The six were to start last night for this place.   I hear that their owners have persons stationed at several places on the road watching.   I fear they will be taken.   If they could lay quiet for ten days or two weeks, they might then get up safe.   I shall have two men sent this evening some four or five miles below to keep them away from this town, and send them (if found to Chester County).   Thee may show this to Still and McKim, and oblige thy cousin,   THOMAS GARRETT.

Further light about this exciting contest, may be gathered from a colored conductor on the Road, in Delaware, who wrote as follows to a member of the Vigilance Committee at Philadelphia.

CAMDEN, DEL., March 23d, 1857.

DEAR SIR:—I tak my pen in hand to write to you, to inform you what we have had to go throw for the last two weaks.   Thir wir six men and two woman was betraid on the tenth of this month, thea had them in prison but thea got out was conveyed by a black man, he told them he wood bring them to my hows, as he wos told, he had ben ther Befor, he has com with Harrett, a woman that stops at my hous when she pases tow and throw yau.   You don't no me I supos, the Rev. Thomas H. Kennard dos, or Peter Lowis. He Road Camden Circuit, this man led them in dover prisin and left them with a whit man ; but tha tour out the winders and jump out, so cum back to camden.   We put them throug, we hav to carry them 19 mils and cum back the sam night wich maks 38 mils. It is tou much for our littel horses.   We must do the bes we can, ther is much Bisness dun on this Road.   We hav to go throw dover and smerny, the two wors places this sid of mary land lin.   If you have herd or sean them ples let me no.   I will Com to Phila be for long and then I will call and se you.   There is much to do her.   Ples to wright, I Remain your frend,   WILLIAM BRINKLY.
Remember me to Thom. Kennard.

The balance of these brave fugitives, although not named in this connection, succeeded in getting off safely.   But how the betrayer, sheriff and hunters got out of their dilemma, the Committee was never fully posted.

The Committee found great pleasure in assisting these passengers, for they had the true grit.   Such were always doubly welcome.

MARY EPPS, ALIAS EMMA BROWN—JOSEPH AND ROBERT ROBINSON.

A SLAVE MOTHER LOSES HER SPEECH AT THE SALE OF HER CHILD—BOB ESCAPES FROM HIS MASTER, A TRADER, WITH $1500 IN NORTH CAROLINA MONEY.

Mary fled from Petersburg and the Robinsons from Richmond.   A fugitive slave law-breaking captain by the name of B., who owned a schooner, and would bring any kind of freight that would pay the most, was the conductor in this instance.   Quite a number of passengers at different times availed themselves of his accommodations and thus succeeded in reaching Canada.

His risk was very great. On this account he claimed, as did certain others, that it was no more than fair to charge for his services—indeed he did not profess to bring persons for nothing, except in rare instances. In this matter the Committee did not feel disposed to interfere directly in any way, further than to suggest that whatever understanding was agreed upon by the parties themselves should be faithfully adhered to.

Many slaves in cities could raise, "by hook or by crook," fifty or one hundred dollars to pay for a passage, providing they could find one who was willing to risk aiding them. Thus, while the Vigilance Committee of Philadelphia especially neither charged nor accepted anything for their services, it was not to be expected that any of the Southern agents could afford to do likewise.

The husband of Mary had for a long time wanted his own freedom, but did not feel that he could go without his wife; in fact, he resolved to get her off first, then to try and escape himself, if possible. The first essential step towards success, he considered, was to save his money and make it an object to the captain to help him. So when he had managed to lay by one hundred dollars, he willingly offered this sum to Captain B., if he would engage to deliver his wife into the hands of the Vigilance Committee of Philadelphia. The captain agreed to the terms and fulfilled his engagement to the letter. About the 1st of March, 1855, Mary was presented to the Vigilance Committee. She was of agreeable manners, about forty-five years of age, dark complexion, round built, and intelligent. She had been the mother of fifteen children, four of whom had been sold away from her; one was still held in slavery in Petersburg; the others were all dead.

At the sale of one of her children she was so affected with grief that she was thrown into violent convulsions, which caused the loss of her speech for one entire month. But this little episode was not a matter to excite sympathy in the breasts of the highly refined and tender-hearted Christian mothers of Petersburg. In the mercy of Providence, however, her reason and strength returned.

She had formerly belonged to the late Littleton Reeves, whom she represented as having been "kind" to her, much more so than her mistress (Mrs. Reeves). Said Mary, "She being of a jealous disposition, caused me to be hired out with a hard family, where I was much abused, frequently flogged, and stinted for food," etc.

But the sweets of freedom in the care of the Vigilance Committee now delighted her mind, and the hope that her husband would soon follow her to Canada, inspired her with expectations that she would one day "sit under her own vine and fig tree where none dared to molest or make her afraid."

The Committee rendered her the usual assistance, and in due time, forwarded her on to Queen Victoria's free land in Canada. On her arrival she wrote back as follows—

TORONTO, March 14th, 1855.

DEAR MR. STILL:—I take this opportunity of addressing you with these few lines to inform you that I arrived here to-day, and hope that this may find yourself and Mrs. Still well, as this leaves me at the present. I will also say to you, that I had no difficulty in getting along. the two young men that was with me left me at Suspension Bridge. they went another way.

I cannot say much about the place as I have ben here but a short time but so far as I have seen I like very well. you will give my Respect to your lady, & Mr & Mrs Brown. If you have not written to Petersburg you will please to write as soon as can I have nothing More to Write at present but yours Respectfully

EMMA BROWN (old name MARY EPPS).

Now, Joseph and Robert (Mary's associate passengers from Richmond) must here be noticed. Joseph was of a dark orange color, medium size, very active and intelligent, and doubtless, well understood the art of behaving himself. He was well acquainted with the auction block—having been sold three times, and had had the misfortune to fall into the hands of a cruel master each time. Under these circumstances he had had but few privileges. Sundays and week days alike he was kept pretty severely bent down to duty. He had been beaten and knocked around shamefully. He had a wife, and spoke of her in most endearing language, although, on leaving, he did not feel at liberty to apprise her of his movements, "fearing that it would not be safe so to do." His four little children, to whom he appeared warmly attached, he left as he did his wife—in Slavery. He declared that he "stuck to them as long as he could." George E. Sadler, the keeper of an oyster house, held the deed for "Joe," and a most heartless wretch he was in Joe's estimation. The truth was, Joe could not stand the burdens and abuses which Sadler was inclined to heap upon him. So he concluded to join his brother and go off on the U. G. R. R.

Robert, his younger brother, was owned by Robert Slater, Esq., a regular negro trader. Eight years this slave's duties had been at the slave prison, and among other daily offices he had to attend to, was to lock up the prison, prepare the slaves for sale, etc. Robert was a very intelligent young man, and from long and daily experience with the customs and usages of the slave prison, he was as familiar with the business as a Pennsylvania farmer with his barn-yard stock. His account of things was too harrowing for detail here, except in the briefest manner, and that only with reference to a few particulars. In order to prepare slaves for the market, it was usual to have them greased and rubbed to make them look bright and shining. And he went on further to state, that "females as well as males were not uncommonly stripped naked, lashed flat to a bench, and then held by two men, sometimes four, while the brutal trader would strap them with a broad leather strap." The strap being preferred to the cow-hide, as it would not break the skin, and damage the sale. "One hundred lashes would only be a common flogging." The separation of families was thought nothing of. "Often I have been flogged for refusing to flog others." While not yet twenty-three years of age, Robert expressed himself as having become so daily sick of the brutality and suffering he could not help witnessing, that he felt he could not possibly stand it any longer, let the cost be what it might. In this state of mind he met with Captain B. Only one obstacle stood in his way—material aid. It occurred to Robert that he had frequent access to the money drawer, and often it contained the proceeds of fresh sales of flesh and blood; and he reasoned that if some of that would help him and his brother to freedom, there could be no harm in helping himself the first opportunity.

The captain was all ready, and provided he could get three passengers at $100 each he would set sail without much other freight. Of course he was too shrewd to get out papers for Philadelphia. That would betray him at once. Washington or Baltimore, or even Wilmington, Del., were names which stood fair in the eyes of Virginia. Consequently, being able to pack the fugitives away in a very private hole of his boat, and being only bound for a Southern port, the captain was willing to risk his share of the danger. "Very well," said Robert, "to-day I will please my master so well, that I will catch him at an unguarded moment, and will ask him for a pass to go to a ball to-night (slave-holders love to see their slaves fiddling and dancing of nights), and as I shall be leaving in a hurry, I will take a grab from the day's sale, and when Slater hears of me again, I will be in Canada." So after having attended to all his disagreeable duties, he made his "grab," and got a hand full. He did not know, however, how it would hold out. That evening, instead of participating with the gay dancers, he was just one degree lower down than the regular bottom of Captain B's. deck, with several hundred dollars in his pocket, after paying the worthy captain one hundred each for himself and his brother, besides making the captain an additional present of nearly one hundred. Wind and tide were now what they prayed for to speed on the U. G. R. R. schooner, until they might reach the depot at Philadelphia.

The Richmond *Dispatch*, an enterprising paper in the interest of slave-holders, which came daily to the Committee, was received in advance of the passengers, when lo! and behold, in turning to the interesting column containing the elegant illustrations of "runaway negroes," it was seen that the unfortunate Slater had "lost $1500 in North Carolina money, and also his dark orange-colored, intelligent, and good-looking turnkey, Bob." "Served him right, it is no stealing for one piece of property to go off with another piece," reasoned a member of the Committee.

In a couple of days after the Dispatch brought the news, the three U. G. R. R. passengers were safely landed at the usual place, and so accurate were the descriptions in the paper, that, on first seeing them, the Committee recognized them instantly, and, without any previous ceremonies, read to them the advertisement relative to the "$1500 in N. C. money, &c.," and put the question to them direct: "Are you the ones?" "We are," they owned up without hesitation. The Committee did not see a dollar of their money, but understood they had about $900, after paying the captain; while Bob considered he made a "very good grab," he did not admit that the amount advertised was correct. After a reasonable time for recruiting, having been so long in the hole of the vessel, they took their departure for Canada.

From Joseph, the elder brother, is appended a short letter, announcing their arrival and condition under the British Lion—

SAINT CATHARINE, April 16, 1855.

MR. WILLIAM STILL, DEAR SIR:—Your letter of date April 7th I have just got, it had been opened before it came to me. I have not received any other letter from you and can get no account of them in the Post Office in this place, I am well and have got a good situation in this city and intend staying here. I should be very glad to hear from you as soon as convenient and also from all of my friends near you. My Brother is also at work with me and doing well.

There is nothing here that would interest you in the way of news. There is a Masonic Lodge of our people and two churches and societys here and some other institutions for our benefit. Be kind enough to send a few lines to the Lady spoken of for that mocking bird and much oblige me. Write me soon and believe me your obedient Servt

Love & respects to Lady and daughter   JOSEPH ROBINSON.

As well as writing to a member of the Committee, Joe and Bob had the assurance to write back to the trader and oyster-house keeper. In their letter they stated that they had arrived safely in Canada, and were having good times,—in the eating line had an abundance of the best,—also had very choice wines and brandies, which they supposed that they (trader and oyster-house keeper) would give a great deal to have a "smack at." And then they gave them a very cordial invitation to make them a visit, and suggested that the quickest way they could come, would be by telegraph, which they admitted was slightly dangerous, and without first greasing themselves, and then hanging on very fast, the journey might not prove altogether advantageous to them. This was wormwood and gall to the trader and oyster-house man. A most remarkable coincidence was that, about the time this letter was received in Richmond, the captain who brought away the three passengers, made it his business for some reason or other, to call at the oyster-house kept by the owner of Joe, and while there, this letter was read and commented on in torrents of Billingsgate phrases; and the trader told the captain that he would give him "two thousand dollars if he would get them;" finally he told him he would "give every cent they would bring, which would be much over $2000," as they were "so very likely." How far the captain talked approvingly, he did not exactly tell the Committee, but they guessed he talked strong Democratic doctrine to them under the frightful circumstances. But he was good at concealing his feelings, and obviously managed to avoid suspicion.

GEORGE SOLOMON, DANIEL NEALL, BENJAMIN R. FLETCHER AND MARIA DORSEY.

The above representatives of the unrequited laborers of the South fled directly from Washington, D. C. Nothing remarkable was discovered in their stories of slave life; their narratives will therefore be brief.

George Solomon was owned by Daniel Minor, of Moss Grove, Va. George was about thirty-three years of age; mulatto, intelligent, and of prepossessing appearance. His old master valued George's services very highly, and had often declared to others, as well as to George himself, that without him he should hardly know how to manage. And frequently George was told by the old master that at his "death he was not to be a slave any longer, as he would have provision made in his will for his freedom." For a long time this old story was clung to pretty faithfully by George, but his "old master hung on too long," consequently George's patience became exhausted. And as he had heard a good deal about Canada, U. G. R. R., and the Abolitionists, he concluded that it would do no harm to hint to a reliable friend or two the names of these hard places and bad people, to see what impression would be made on their minds; in short, to see if they were ready to second a motion to get rid of bondage. In thus opening his mind to his friends, he soon found a willing accord in each of their hearts, and they put their heads together to count up the cost and to fix a time for leaving Egypt and the host of Pharaoh to do their own "hewing of wood and drawing of water." Accordingly George, Daniel, Benjamin and Maria, all of one heart and mind, one "Saturday night" resolved that the next Sunday should find them on the U. G. R. R., with their faces towards Canada.

Daniel was young, only twenty-three, good looking, and half white, with a fair share of intelligence. As regards his slave life, he acknowledged that he had not had it very rough as a general thing; nevertheless, he was fully persuaded that he had "as good a right to his freedom" as his "master had to his," and that it was his duty to contend for it.

Benjamin was twenty-seven years of age, small of stature, dark complexion, of a pleasant countenance, and quite smart. He testified, that "illtreatment from his master," Henry Martin, who would give him "no chance at all," was the cause of his leaving. He left a brother and sister, belonging to Martin, besides he left two other sisters in bondage, Louisa and Letty, but his father and mother were both dead. Therefore, the land of slave-whips and auction-blocks had no charms for him. He loved his sisters, but he knew if he could not protect himself, much less could he protect them. So he concluded to bid them adieu forever in this world.

Turning from the three male companions for the purpose of finding a brief space for Maria, it will be well to state here that females in attempting to escape from a life of bondage undertook three times the risk of failure that males were liable to, not to mention the additional trials and struggles they had to contend with. In justice, therefore, to the heroic female who was willing to endure the most extreme suffering and hardship for freedom, double honors were due.

Maria, the heroine of the party, was about forty years of age, chestnut color, medium size, and possessed of a good share of common sense. She was owned by George Parker. As was a common thing with slave-holders, Maria had found her owners hard to please, and quite often, without the slightest reason, they would threaten to "sell or make a change." These threats only made matters worse, or rather it only served to nerve Maria for the conflict. The party walked almost the entire distance from Washington to Harrisburg, Pennsylvania.

In the meantime George Parker, the so-called owner of Daniel and Maria, hurriedly rushed their good names into the "Baltimore Sun," after the following manner—

"Four Hundred Dollars Reward.—Ranaway from my house on Saturday night, August 30, my negro man 'Daniel,' twenty-five years of age, bright yellow mulatto, thick set and stout made.

Also, my negro woman, 'Maria,' forty years of age, bright mulatto. The above reward will be paid if delivered in Washington city.   George Parker."

While this advertisement was in the Baltimore papers, doubtless these noble passengers were enjoying the hospitalities of the Vigilance Committee, and finally a warm reception in Canada, by which they were greatly pleased. Of Benjamin and Daniel, the subjoined letter from Rev. H. Wilson is of importance in the way of throwing light upon their whereabouts in Canada:

St. Catharine, C. W., Sept. 15th, 1856.

Mr. William Still :—*Dear Sir*—Two young men arrived here on Friday evening last from Washington, viz : Benjamin R. Fletcher and Daniel Neall. Mr. Neall (or Neale) desires to have his box of clothing forwarded on to him. It is at Washington in the care of John Dade, a colored man, who lives at Doct. W. H. Gilman's, who keeps an Apothecary store on the corner of 4½ and Pennsylvania Avenue. Mr. Dade is a slave, but a free dealer. You will please write to John Dade, in the care of Doct. W. H. Gilman, on behalf of Daniel Neale, but make use of the name of George Harrison, instead of Neale, and Dade will understand it. Please have John Dade direct the box by express to you in Philadelphia ; he has the means of paying the charges on it in advance, as far as Philadelphia; and as soon as it comes you will please forward it on to my care at St. Catherine. Say to John Dade, that George Harrison sends his love to his sister and Uncle Allen Sims, and all inquiring friends. Mr. Fletcher and Mr. Neale both send their respects to you, and I may add mine.   Yours truly,   Hiram Wilson.

P. S.—Mr. Benjamin R. Fletcher wishes to have Mr. Dade call on his brother James, and communicate to him his affectionate regards, and make known to him that he is safe, and cheerful and happy. He desires his friends to know, through Dade, that he found Mrs. Starke here, his brother Alfred's wife's sister; that she is well, and living in St. Catharine, C. W., near Niagara Falls. H. W.

HENRY BOX BROWN.

ARRIVED BY ADAMS' EXPRESS.

Although the name of Henry Box Brown has been echoed over the land for a number of years, and the simple facts connected with his marvelous escape from slavery in a box published widely through the medium of anti-slavery papers, nevertheless it is not unreasonable to suppose that very little is generally known in relation to this case.

Briefly, the facts are these, which doubtless have never before been fully published—

Brown was a man of invention as well as a hero. In point of interest, however, his case is no more remarkable than many others. Indeed, neither before nor after escaping did he suffer one-half what many others have experienced.

He was decidedly an unhappy piece of property in the city of Richmond, Va. In the condition of a slave he felt that it would be impossible for him to remain. Full well did he know, however, that it was no holiday task to escape the vigilance of Virginia slave-hunters, or the wrath of an enraged master for committing the unpardonable sin of attempting to escape to a land of liberty. So Brown counted well the cost before venturing upon this hazardous undertaking. Ordinary modes of travel he concluded might prove disastrous to his hopes; he, therefore, hit upon a new invention altogether, which was to have himself boxed up and forwarded to Philadelphia direct by express. The size of the box and how it was to be made to fit him most comfortably, was of his own ordering. Two feet eight inches deep, two feet wide, and three feet long were the exact dimensions of the box, lined with baize. His resources with regard to food and water consisted of the following: One bladder of water and a few small biscuits. His mechanical implement to meet the death-struggle for fresh air, all told, was one large gimlet. Satisfied that it would be far better to peril his life for freedom in this way than to remain under the galling yoke of Slavery, he entered his box, which was safely nailed up and hooped with five hickory hoops, and was then addressed by his next friend, James A. Smith, a shoe dealer, to Wm. H. Johnson, Arch street, Philadelphia, marked, "This side up with care." In this condition he was sent to Adams' Express office in a dray, and thence by overland express to Philadelphia. It was twenty-six hours from the time he left Richmond until his arrival in the City of Brotherly Love. The notice, "This side up, &c.," did not avail

6

with the different expressmen, who hesitated not to handle the box in the usual rough manner common to this class of men. For a while they actually had the box upside down, and had him on his head for miles. A few days before he was expected, certain intimation was conveyed to a member of the Vigilance Committee that a box might be expected by the three o'clock morning train from the South, which might contain a man. One of the most serious walks he ever took—and they had not been a few—to meet and accompany passengers, he took at half past two o'clock that morning to the depot. Not once, but for more than a score of times, he fancied the slave would be dead. He anxiously looked while the freight was being unloaded from the cars, to see if he could recognize a box that might contain a man; one alone had that appearance, and he confessed it really seemed as if there was the scent of death about it. But on inquiry, he soon learned that it was not the one he was looking after, and he was free to say he experienced a marked sense of relief. That same afternoon, however, he received from Richmond a telegram, which read thus, "Your case of goods is shipped and will arrive to-morrow morning."

At this exciting juncture of affairs, Mr. McKim, who had been engineering this important undertaking, deemed it expedient to change the programme slightly in one particular at least to insure greater safety. Instead of having a member of the Committee go again to the depot for the box, which might excite suspicion, it was decided that it would be safest to have the express bring it direct to the Anti-Slavery Office.

But all apprehension of danger did not now disappear, for there was no room to suppose that Adams' Express office had any sympathy with the Abolitionist or the fugitive, consequently for Mr. McKim to appear personally at the express office to give directions with reference to the coming of a box from Richmond which would be directed to Arch street, and yet not intended for that street, but for the Anti-Slavery office at 107 North Fifth street, it needed of course no great discernment to foresee that a step of this kind was wholly impracticable and that a more indirect and covert method would have to be adopted. In this dreadful crisis Mr. McKim, with his usual good judgment and remarkably quick, strategical mind, especially in matters pertaining to the U. G. R. R., hit upon the following plan, namely, to go to his friend, E. M. Davis,* who was then extensively engaged in mercantile business, and relate the circumstances. Having daily intercourse with said Adams' Express office, and being well acquainted with the firm and some of the drivers, Mr. Davis could, as Mr. McKim thought, talk about "boxes, freight, etc.," from any part of the country without risk. Mr. Davis heard Mr. McKim's plan and instantly approved of it, and was heartily at his service.

---

* E. M. Davis was a member of the Executive Committee of the Pennsylvania Anti-Slavery Society and a long-tried Abolitionist, son-in-law of James and Lucretia Mott.

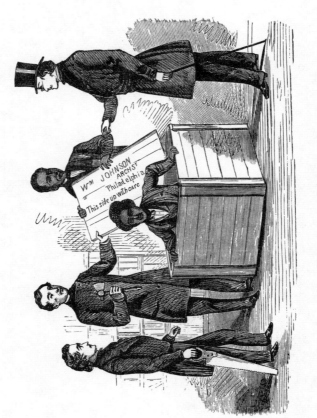

RESURRECTION OF HENRY BOX BROWN.

"Dan, an Irishman, one of Adams' Express drivers, is just the fellow to go to the depot after the box," said Davis. " He drinks a little too much whiskey sometimes, but he will do anything I ask him to do, promptly and obligingly. I'll trust Dan, for I believe he is the very man." The difficulty which Mr. McKim had been so anxious to overcome was thus pretty well settled. It was agreed that Dan should go after the box next morning before daylight and bring it to the Anti-Slavery office direct, and to make it all the more agreeable for Dan to get up out of his warm bed and go on this errand before day, it was decided that he should have a five dollar gold piece for himself. Thus these preliminaries having been satisfactorily arranged, it only remained for Mr. Davis to see Dan and give him instructions accordingly, etc.

Next morning, according to arrangement, the box was at the Anti-Slavery office in due time. The witnesses present to behold the resurrection were J. M. McKim, Professor C. D. Cleveland, Lewis Thompson, and the writer.

Mr. McKim was deeply interested; but having been long identified with the Anti-Slavery cause as one of its oldest and ablest advocates in the darkest days of slavery and mobs, and always found by the side of the fugitive to counsel and succor, he was on this occasion perfectly composed.

Professor Cleveland, however, was greatly moved. His zeal and earnestness in the cause of freedom, especially in rendering aid to passengers, knew no limit. Ordinarily he could not too often visit these travelers, shake them too warmly by the hand, or impart to them too freely of his substance to aid them on their journey. But now his emotion was overpowering.

Mr. Thompson, of the firm of Merrihew & Thompson—about the only printers in the city who for many years dared to print such incendiary documents as anti-slavery papers and pamphlets—one of the truest friends of the slave, was composed and prepared to witness the scene.

All was quiet. The door had been safely locked. The proceedings commenced. Mr. McKim rapped quietly on the lid of the box and called out, " All right!" Instantly came the answer from within, " All right, sir!"

The witnesses will never forget that moment. Saw and hatchet quickly had the five hickory hoops cut and the lid off, and the marvellous resurrection of Brown ensued. Rising up in his box, he reached out his hand, saying, "How do you do, gentlemen?" The little assemblage hardly knew what to think or do at the moment. He was about as wet as if he had come up out of the Delaware. Very soon he remarked that, before leaving Richmond he had selected for his arrival-hymn (if he lived) the Psalm beginning with these words: "*I waited patiently for the Lord, and He heard my prayer.*" And most touchingly did he sing the psalm, much to his own relief, as well as to the delight of his small audience.

He was then christened Henry Box Brown, and soon afterwards was sent to the hospitable residence of James Mott and E. M. Davis, on Ninth street, where, it is needless to say, he met a most cordial reception from Mrs. Lucretia Mott and her household. Clothing and creature comforts were furnished in abundance, and delight and joy filled all hearts in that stronghold of philanthropy.

As he had been so long doubled up in the box he needed to promenade considerably in the fresh air, so James Mott put one of his broad-brim hats on his head and tendered him the hospitalities of his yard as well as his house, and while Brown promenaded the yard flushed with victory, great was the joy of his friends.

After his visit at Mr. Mott's, he spent two days with the writer, and then took his departure for Boston, evidently feeling quite conscious of the wonderful feat he had performed, and at the same time it may be safely said that those who witnessed this strange resurrection were not only elated at his success, but were made to sympathize more deeply than ever before with the slave. Also the noble-hearted Smith who boxed him up was made to rejoice over Brown's victory, and was thereby encouraged to render similar service to two other young bondmen, who appealed to him for deliverance. But, unfortunately, in this attempt the undertaking proved a failure. Two boxes containing the young men alluded to above, after having been duly expressed and some distance on the road, were, through the agency of the telegraph, betrayed, and the heroic young fugitives were captured in their boxes and dragged back to hopeless bondage. Consequently, through this deplorable failure, Samuel A. Smith was arrested, imprisoned, and was called upon to suffer severely, as may be seen from the subjoined correspondence, taken from the New York Tribune soon after his release from the penitentiary.

THE DELIVERER OF BOX BROWN—MEETING OF THE COLORED CITIZENS OF PHILADELPHIA.

[Correspondence of the N. Y. Tribune.]

PHILADELPHIA, Saturday, July 5, 1856.

Samuel A. Smith, who boxed up Henry Box Brown in Richmond, Va., and forwarded him by overland express to Philadelphia, and who was arrested and convicted, eight years ago, for boxing up two other slaves, also directed to Philadelphia, having served out his imprisonment in the Penitentiary, was released on the 18th ultimo, and arrived in this city on the 21st.

Though he lost all his property; though he was refused witnesses on his trial (no officer could be found, who would serve a summons on a witness); though for five long months, in hot weather, he was kept heavily chained in a cell four by eight feet in dimensions; though he received five dreadful stabs, aimed at his heart, by a bribed assassin, nevertheless he still rejoices in the motives which prompted him to "undo the heavy burdens, and let the oppressed go free." Having resided nearly all his life in the South, where he had traveled and seen much of the "peculiar institution," and had witnessed the most horrid enormities inflicted upon the slave, whose cries were ever ringing in his ears, and for whom he had the warmest sympathy, Mr. Smith could not refrain from believing that the black man, as well as the white, had God-given rights. Consequently, he was not accustomed to shed tears when a poor creature escaped from his " kind master ;" nor was he willing to turn a deaf ear to his appeals and groans, when he knew he was thirsting for freedom. From 1828 up to the day he was incarcerated, many had sought his aid and counsel, nor had they sought in vain. In various places he operated with success. In Richmond, however, it seemed expedient to invent a new plan for certain emergencies, hence the Box and Express plan was devised, at the instance of a few heroic slaves, who had manifested their willingness to die in a box, on the road to liberty, rather than continue longer under the yoke. But these heroes fell into the power of their enemies. Mr. Smith had not been long in the Penitentiary before he had fully gained the esteem and confidence of the Superintendent and other officers. Finding him to be humane and generous-hearted—showing kindness toward all, especially in buying bread, &c., for the starving prisoners, and by a timely note of warning, which had saved the life of one of the keepers, for whose destruction a bold plot had been arranged—the officers felt disposed to show him such favors as the law would allow. But their good intentions were soon frustrated. The Inquisition (commonly called the Legislature), being in session in Richmond, hearing that the Superintendent had been speaking well of Smith, and circulating a petition for his pardon, indignantly demanded to know if the rumor was well founded. Two weeks were spent by the Inquisition, and many witnesses were placed upon oath, to solemnly testify in the matter. One of the keepers swore that his life had been saved by Smith. Col. Morgan, the Superintendent, frequently testified in writing and verbally to Smith's good deportment; acknowledging that he had circulated petitions, &c.; and took the position, that he sincerely believed, that it would be to the interest of the institution to pardon him; calling the attention of the Inquisition, at the same time, to the fact, that not unfrequently pardons had been granted to criminals, under sentence of death, for the most cold-blooded murder, to say nothing of other gross crimes. The effort for pardon was soon abandoned, for the following reason given by the Governor : " I can't, and I won't pardon him !"

In view of the unparalleled injustice which Mr. S. had suffered, as well as on account of the aid he had rendered to the slaves, on his arrival in this city the colored citizens of Philadelphia felt that he was entitled to sympathy and aid, and straightway invited him to remain a few days, until arrangements could be made for a mass meeting to receive him. Accordingly, on last Monday evening, a mass meeting convened in the Israel church, and the Rev. Wm. T. Catto was called to the chair, and Wm. Still was appointed secretary. The chairman briefly stated the object of the meeting. Having lived in the South, he claimed to know something of the workings of the oppressive system of slavery generally, and declared that, notwithstanding the many exposures of the evil which came under his own observation, the most vivid descriptions fell far short of the realities his own eyes had witnessed. He then introduced Mr. Smith, who arose and in a plain manner briefly told his story, assuring the audience that he had always hated slavery, and had taken great pleasure in helping many out of it, and though he had suffered much physically and pecuniarily for the cause' sake, yet he murmured not, but rejoiced in what he had done. After taking his seat, addresses were made by the Rev. S. Smith, Messrs. Kinnard, Brunner, Bradway, and others. The following preamble and resolutions were adopted—

WHEREAS, We, the colored citizens of Philadelphia, have among us Samuel A. Smith, who was incarcerated over seven years in the Richmond Penitentiary, for doing an act that was honorable to his feelings and his sense of justice and humanity, therefore,

Resolved, That we welcome him to this city as a martyr to the cause of Freedom.

Resolved, That we heartily tender him our gratitude for the good he has done to our suffering race.

Resolved, That we sympathize with him in his losses and sufferings in the cause of the poor, down-trodden slave.   W. S.

During his stay in Philadelphia, on this occasion, he stopped for about a fortnight with the writer, and it was most gratifying to learn from him that he was no new·worker on the U. G. R. R. But that he had long hated slavery thoroughly, and although surrounded with perils on every side, he had not failed to help a poor slave whenever the opportunity was presented.

Pecuniary aid, to some extent, was rendered him in this city, for which he was grateful, and after being united in marriage, by Wm. H. Furness, D.D., to a lady who had remained faithful to him through all his sore trials and sufferings, he took his departure for Western New York, with a good conscience and an unshaken faith in the belief that in aiding his fellow-man to freedom he had but simply obeyed the word of Him who taught man to do unto others as he would be done by.

TRIAL OF THE EMANCIPATORS OF COL. J. H. WHEELER'S SLAVES, JANE JOHNSON AND HER TWO LITTLE BOYS.

Among other duties devolving on the Vigilance Committee when hearing of slaves brought into the State by their owners, was immediately to inform such persons that as they were not fugitives, but were brought into the State by their masters, they were entitled to their freedom without another moment's service, and that they could have the assistance of the Committee and the advice of counsel without charge, by simply availing themselves of these proffered favors.

Many slave-holders fully understood the law in this particular, and were also equally posted with regard to the vigilance of abolitionists. Consequently they avoided bringing slaves beyond Mason and Dixon's Line in traveling North. But some slave-holders were not thus mindful of the laws, or were too arrogant to take heed, as may be seen in the case of Colonel John H. Wheeler, of North Carolina, the United States Minister to Nicaragua. In passing through Philadelphia from Washington, one very warm July day in 1855, accompanied by three of his slaves, his high official equilibrium, as well as his assumed rights under the Constitution, received a terrible shock at the hands of the Committee. Therefore, for the readers of these pages, and in order to completely illustrate the various phases of the work of the Committee in the days of Slavery, this case, selected from many others, is a fitting one. However, for more than a brief recital of some of the more prominent incidents, it will not be possible to find room in this volume. And, indeed, the necessity of so doing is precluded by the fact that Mr. Williamson in justice to himself and the cause of freedom, with great pains and singular ability, gathered the most important facts bearing on his memorable trial and imprisonment, and published them in a neat volume for historical reference.

In order to bring fully before the reader the beginning of this interesting and exciting case, it seems only necessary to publish the subjoined letter, written by one of the actors in the drama, and addressed to the New York Tribune, and an additional paragraph which may be requisite to throw light on a special point, which Judge Kane decided was concealed in the "obstinate" breast of Passmore Williamson, as said Williamson persistently refused before the said Judge's court, to own that he had a knowledge of the mystery in question. After which, a brief glance at some of the more important points of the case must suffice.

LETTER COPIED FROM THE NEW YORK TRIBUNE.

[Correspondence of The N. Y. Tribune.]

PHILADELPHIA, Monday, July 30, 1855.

As the public have not been made acquainted with the facts and particulars respecting the agency of Mr. Passmore Williamson and others, in relation to the slave case now agitating this city, and especially as the poor slave mother and her two sons have been so grossly misrepresented, I deem it my duty to lay the facts before you, for publication or otherwise, as you may think proper.

On Wednesday afternoon, week, at 4½ o'clock, the following note was placed in my hands by a colored boy whom I had never before seen, to my recollection:

"Mr. Still—*Sir:* Will you come down to Bloodgood's Hotel as soon as possible—as there are three fugitive slaves here and they want liberty. Their master is here with them, on his way to New York."

The note was without date, and the signature so indistinctly written as not to be understood by me, having evidently been penned in a moment of haste.

Without delay I ran with the note to Mr. P. Williamson's office, Seventh and Arch, found him at his desk, and gave it to him, and after reading it, he remarked that he could not go down, as he had to go to Harrisburg that night on business—but he advised me to go, and to get the names of the slave-holder and the slaves, in order to telegraph to New York to have them arrested there, as no time remained to procure a writ of habeas corpus here.

I could not have been two minutes in Mr. W.'s office before starting in haste for the wharf. To my surprise, however, when I reached the wharf, there I found Mr. W., his mind having undergone a sudden change; he was soon on the spot.

I saw three or four colored persons in the hall at Bloodgood's, none of whom I recognized except the boy who brought me the note. Before having time for making inquiry some one said they had gone on board the boat. "Get their description," said Mr. W. I instantly inquired of one of the colored persons for the desired description, and was told that she was "a tall, dark woman, with two little boys."

Mr. W. and myself ran on board of the boat, looked among the passengers on the first deck, but saw them not. "They are up on the second deck," an unknown voice uttered. In a second we were in their presence. We approached the anxious-looking slave-mother with her two boys on her left-hand; close on her right sat an ill-favored white man having a cane in his hand which I took to be a sword-cane. (As to its being a sword-cane, however, I might have been mistaken.)

The first words to the mother were: "Are you traveling?" "Yes," was the prompt answer. "With whom?" She nodded her head toward the ill-favored man, signifying with him. Fidgeting on his seat, he said something, exactly what I do not now recollect. In reply I remarked: "Do they belong to you, Sir?" "Yes, they are in my charge," was his answer. Turning from him to the mother and her sons, in substance, and word for word, as near as I can remember, the following remarks were earnestly though calmly addressed by the individuals who rejoiced to meet them on free soil, and who felt unmistakably assured that they were justified by the laws of Pennsylvania as well as the Law of God, in informing them of their rights:

" You are entitled to your freedom according to the laws of Pennsylvania, having been brought into the State by your owner. If you prefer freedom to slavery, as we suppose everybody does, you have the chance to accept it now. Act calmly—don't be frightened by your master—you are as much entitled

RESCUE OF JANE JOHNSON AND HER CHILDREN.

to your freedom as we are, or as he is—be determined and you need have no fears but that you will be protected by the law. Judges have time and again decided cases in this city and State similar to yours in favor of freedom! Of course, if you want to remain a slave with your master, we cannot force you to leave; we only want to make you sensible of your rights. *Remember, if you lose this chance you may never get such another,"* etc.

This advice to the woman was made in the hearing of a number of persons present, white and colored; and one elderly white gentleman of genteel address, who seemed to take much interest in what was going on, remarked that they would have the same chance for their freedom in New Jersey and New York as they then had—seeming to sympathize with the woman, etc.

During the few moments in which the above remarks were made, the slaveholder frequently interrupted—said she understood all about the laws making her free, and her right to leave if she wanted to; but contended that she did not want to leave—that she was on a visit to New York to see her friends—afterward *wished to return to her three children whom she left in Virginia, from whom it would be* HARD *to separate her.* Furthermore, he diligently tried to constrain her to say that she did not want to be interfered with—that she wanted to go with him—that she was on a visit to New York—had children in the South, etc.; but the woman's desire to be free was altogether too strong to allow her to make a single acknowledgment favorable to his wishes in the matter. On the contrary, she repeatedly said, distinctly and firmly, "*I am not free, but I want my freedom*—ALWAYS *wanted to be free ! ! but he holds me.*"

While the slaveholder claimed that she belonged to him, he said *that she was free!* Again he said that he was *going to give her her freedom,* etc. When his eyes would be off of hers, such eagerness as her looks expressed, indicative of her entreaty that we would not forsake her and her little ones in their weakness, it had never been my lot to witness before, under any circumstances.

The last bell tolled! The last moment for further delay passed! The arm of the woman being slightly touched, accompanied with the word, "Come!" she instantly arose. "Go along—go along!" said some, who sympathized, to the boys, at the same time taking hold of their arms. By this time the parties were fairly moving toward the stairway leading to the deck below. Instantly on their starting, the slave-holder rushed at the woman and her children, to prevent their leaving; and, if I am not mistaken, he simultaneously took hold of the woman and Mr. Williamson, which resistance on his part caused Mr. W. to take hold of him and set him aside quickly.

The passengers were looking on all around, but none interfered in behalf of the slaveholder except one man, whom I took to be another slaveholder. He said harshly, "Let them alone; they are his *property!*" The youngest boy, about 7 years of age—too young to know what these things meant—cried "Massa John! Massa John!" The elder boy, 11 years of age, took the matter more dispassionately, and the mother *quite calmly.* The mother and her sympathizers all moved down the stairs together in the presence of quite a number of spectators on the first deck and on the wharf, all of whom, as far as I was able to discern, seemed to look upon the whole affair with the greatest indifference. The woman and children were assisted, but not forced to leave. Nor were there any violence or threatenings as I saw or heard. The only words that I heard from any one of an objectionable character, were: " Knock him down ; knock him down !" but who uttered it or who was meant I knew not, nor have I since been informed. However, if it was uttered by a colored man, I regret it, as there was not the slightest cause for such language, especially as the sympathies of the spectators and citizens seemed to justify the course pursued.

While passing off of the wharf and down Delaware-avenue to Dock st., and up Dock to Front, where a carriage was procured, the slaveholder and one police officer were of the party, if no more.

The youngest boy on being put in the carriage was told that he was " a fool for crying so after ' Massa John,' who would sell him if he ever caught him." Not another whine was heard on the subject.

The carriage drove down town slowly, the horses being fatigued and the weather intensely hot ; the inmates were put out on Tenth street—not at any house—after which they soon found hospitable friends and quietude. The excitement of the moment having passed by, the mother *seemed very cheerful, and rejoiced greatly that herself and boys had been, as she thought, so " providentially delivered from the house of bondage !"* For the first time in her life she could look upon herself and children and feel free !

Having felt the iron in her heart for the best half of her days—having been sold with her children on the auction block—having had one of her children sold far away from her without hope of her seeing him again—she very naturally and wisely concluded to go to Canada, fearing if she remained in this city—as some assured her she could do with entire safety— that she might again find herself in the clutches of the tyrant from whom she had fled.

A few items of what she related concerning the character of her master may be interesting to the reader—

Within the last two years he had sold all his slaves—between thirty and forty in number—having purchased the present ones in that space of time. She said that before leaving Washington, coming on the cars, and at his father-in-law's in this city, a number of persons had told him that in bringing his slaves into Pennsylvania they would be free. When told at his father-in-law's, as she overheard it, that he " could not have done a worse thing," &c., he replied that " Jane would not leave him."

As much, however, as he affected to have such implicit confidence in Jane, he scarcely allowed her to be out of his presence a moment while in this city. To use Jane's own language, he was "on her heels every minute," fearing that some one might get to her ears the sweet music of freedom. By the way, Jane had it deep in her heart before leaving the South, and was bent on succeeding in New York, if disappointed in Philadelphia.

At Bloodgood's, after having been belated and left by the 2 o'clock train, while waiting for the 5 o'clock line, his appetite tempted her "master" to take a hasty dinner. So after placing Jane where he thought she would be pretty secure from "evil communications" from the colored waiters, and after giving her a double counselling, he made his way to the table; remained but a little while, however, before leaving to look after Jane; finding her composed, looking over a bannister near where he left her, he returned to the table again and finished his meal.

But, alas, for the slave-holder! Jane had her "top eye open," and in that brief space had appealed to the sympathies of a person whom she ventured to trust, saying, "I and my children are slaves, and we want liberty!" I am not certain, but suppose that person, in the goodness of his heart, was the cause of the note being sent to the Anti-Slavery office, and hence the result.

As to her going on to New York to see her friends, and wishing to return to her three children in the South, and his going to free her, &c., Jane declared repeatedly and very positively, that there was not a particle of truth in what her master said on these points. The truth is she had not the slightest hope of freedom through any act of his. She had only left one boy in the South, who had been sold far away, where she scarcely ever heard from him, indeed never expected to see him any more.

In appearance Jane is tall and well formed, high and large forehead, of genteel manners, chestnut color, and seems to possess, naturally, uncommon good sense, though of course she has never been allowed to read.

Thus I have given as truthful a report as I am capable of doing, of Jane and the circumstances connected with her deliverance.   W. STILL.

P. S.—Of the five colored porters who promptly appeared, with warm hearts throbbing in sympathy with the mother and her children, too much cannot be said in commendation. In the present case they acted nobly, whatever may be said of their general character, of which I know nothing. How human beings, who have ever tasted oppression, could have acted differently under the circumstances I cannot conceive.

The mystery alluded to, which the above letter did not contain, and which the court failed to make Mr. Williamson reveal, might have been truthfully explained in these words. The carriage was procured at the wharf, while Col. Wheeler and Mr. Williamson were debating the question relative to the action of the Committee, and at that instant, Jane and her two boys were invited into it and accompanied by the writer, who procured it, were driven down town, and on Tenth Street, below Lombard, the inmates were invited out of it, and the said conductor paid the driver and discharged him. For prudential reasons he took them to a temporary resting-place, where they could tarry until after dark; then they were invited to his own residence, where they were made welcome, and in due time forwarded East. Now, what disposition was made of them after they had left the wharf, while Williamson and Wheeler were discussing matters—(as was clearly sworn to by Passmore, in his answer to the writ of Habeas Corpus)—he Williamson did not know. That evening, before seeing the member of the Committee, with whom he acted in concert on the boat, and who had entire charge of Jane and her boys, he left for Harrisburg, to fulfill business engagements. The next morning his father (Thomas Williamson) brought the writ of Habeas Corpus (which had been served at Passmore's office after he left) to the Anti-Slavery Office. In his calm manner he handed it to the writer, at the same time remarking that "Passmore had gone to Harrisburg," and added, "thee had better attend to it" (the writ). Edward Hopper, Esq., was applied to with the writ, and in the absence of Mr. Williamson, appeared before the court, and stated "that the writ had not been served, as Mr. W. was out of town," etc.

After this statement, the Judge postponed further action until the next day. In the meanwhile, Mr. Williamson returned and found the writ awaiting him, and an agitated state of feeling throughout the city besides. Now it is very certain, that he did not seek to know from those in the secret, where Jane Johnson and her boys were taken after they left the wharf, or as to what disposition had been made of them, in any way; except to ask simply, "are they safe?" (and when told "yes," he smiled) consequently, he might have been examined for a week, by the most skillful lawyer, at the Philadelphia bar, but he could not have answered other than he did in making his return to the writ, before Judge Kane, namely: "*That the persons named in the writ, nor either of them, are now nor was at the time of issuing of the writ, or the original writ, or at any other time in the custody, power, or possession of the respondent, nor by him confined or restrained; wherefore he cannot have the bodies,*" etc.

Thus, while Mr. W. was subjected to the severest trial of his devotion to Freedom, his noble bearing throughout, won for him the admiration and sympathy of the friends of humanity and liberty throughout the entire land, and in proof of his fidelity, he most cheerfully submitted to imprisonment rather than desert his principles. But the truth was not wanted in this instance by the enemies of Freedom; obedience to Slavery was demanded to satisfy the South. The opportunity seemed favorable for teaching abolitionists and negroes, that they had no right to interfere with a "chivalrous southern gentleman," while passing through Philadelphia with his slaves. Thus, to make an effective blow, all the pro-slavery elements of Philadelphia were brought into action, and matters looked for a time as though Slavery in this instance would have everything its own way. Passmore was locked up in prison on the flimsy pretext of contempt of court, and true bills were found against him and half a dozen colored men, charging them with "riot," "forcible abduction," and "assault and battery," and there was no lack of hard swearing on the part of Col. Wheeler and his pro-slavery sympathizers in substantiation of these grave charges. But the pro-slaveryites had counted without their host—Passmore would not yield an inch, but stood as firmly by his principles in prison, as he did on the boat. Indeed, it was soon evident, that his resolute course was bringing floods of sympathy from the ablest and best minds throughout the North. On the other hand, the occasion was rapidly awakening thousands daily, who had hitherto manifested little or no interest at all on the subject, to the wrongs of the slave.

It was soon discovered by the "chivalry" that keeping Mr. Williamson in prison would indirectly greatly aid the cause of Freedom—that every day he remained would make numerous converts to the cause of liberty ; that Mr. Williamson was doing ten-fold more in prison for the cause of universal liberty than he could possibly do while pursuing his ordinary vocation.

With regard to the colored men under bonds, Col. Wheeler and his satellites felt very confident that there was no room for them to escape. They must have had reason so to think, judging from the hard swearing they did, before the committing magistrate. Consequently, in the order of events, while Passmore was still in prison, receiving visits from hosts of friends, and letters of sympathy from all parts of the North, William Still, William Curtis, James P. Braddock, John Ballard, James Martin and Isaiah Moore, were brought into court for trial. The first name on the list in the proceedings of the court was called up first.

Against this individual, it was pretty well understood by the friends of the slave, that no lack of pains and false swearing would be resorted to on the part of Wheeler and his witnesses, to gain a verdict.

Mr. McKim and other noted abolitionists managing the defense, were equally alive to the importance of overwhelming the enemy in this particular issue. The Hon. Charles Gibbons, was engaged to defend William Still, and William S. Pierce, Esq., and William B. Birney, Esq., the other five colored defendants.

In order to make the victory complete, the anti-slavery friends deemed it of the highest importance to have Jane Johnson in court, to face her master, and under oath to sweep away his "refuge of lies," with regard to her being "abducted," and her unwillingness to "leave her master," etc. So Mr. McKim and the friends very privately arranged to have Jane Johnson on hand at the opening of the defense.

Mrs. Lucretia Mott, Mrs. McKim, Miss Sarah Pugh and Mrs. Plumly, volunteered to accompany this poor slave mother to the court-house and to occupy seats by her side, while she should face her master, and boldly, on oath, contradict all his hard swearing. A better subject for the occasion than Jane, could not have been desired. She entered the court room veiled, and of course was not known by the crowd, as pains had been taken to keep the public in ignorance of the fact, that she was to be brought on to bear witness. So that, at the conclusion of the second witness on the part of the defense, "Jane Johnson" was called for, in a shrill voice. Deliberately, Jane arose and answered, in a lady-like manner to her name, and was then the observed of all observers. Never before had such a scene been witnessed in Philadelphia. It was indescribable. Substantially, her testimony on this occasion, was in keeping with the subjoined affidavit, which was as follows—

"*State of New York, City and County of New York.*

"Jane Johnson being sworn, makes oath and says—

"My name is Jane—Jane Johnson; I was the slave of Mr. Wheeler of Washington; he bought me and my two children, about two years ago, of Mr. Cornelius Crew, of Richmond, Va.; my youngest child is between six and seven years old, the other between ten and eleven; I have one other child only, and he is in Richmond; I have not seen him for about two years; never expect to see him again; Mr. Wheeler brought me and my two children to Philadelphia, on the way to Nicaragua, to wait on his wife; I didn't want to go without my two children, and he consented to take them; we came to Philadelphia by the cars; stopped at Mr. Sully's, Mr. Wheeler's father-in-law, a few moments; then went to the steamboat for New York at 2 o'clock, but were too late; we went into Bloodgood's Hotel; Mr. Wheeler went to dinner; Mr. Wheeler had told me in Washington to have nothing to say to colored persons, and if any of them spoke to me, to say I was a free woman traveling with a minister; we staid at Bloodgood's till 5 o'clock; Mr. Wheeler kept his eye on me all the time except when he was at dinner; he left his dinner to come and see if I was safe, and then went back again; while he was at dinner, I saw a colored woman and told her I was a slave woman, that my master had told me not to speak to colored people, and that if any of them spoke to me to say that I was free; but I am not free; but I want to be free; she said: 'poor thing, I pity you;' after that I saw a colored man and said the same thing to him, he said he would telegraph to New York, and two men would meet me at 9 o'clock and take me with them; after that we went on board the boat, Mr. Wheeler sat beside me on the deck; I saw a colored gentleman come on board, he beckoned to me; I nodded my head, and could not go; Mr. Wheeler was beside me and I was afraid; a white gentleman then came and said to Mr. Wheeler, 'I want to speak to your servant, and tell her of her rights;' Mr. Wheeler rose and said, 'If you have anything to say, say it to me—she knows her rights;' the white gentleman asked me if I wanted to be free; I said 'I do, but I

JANE JOHNSON.

PASSMORE WILLIAMSON.

belong to this gentleman and I can't have it;' he replied, 'Yes, you can, come with us, you are as free as your master, if you want your freedom come now; if you go back to Washington you may never get it;' I rose to go, Mr. Wheeler spoke, and said, 'I will give you your freedom,' but he had never promised it before, and I knew he would never give it to me; the white gentleman held out his hand and I went toward him; I was ready for the word before it was given me; I took the children by the hands, who both cried, for they were frightened, but both stopped when they got on shore; a colored man carried the little one, I led the other by the hand. We walked down the street till we got to a hack; nobody forced me away; nobody pulled me, and nobody led me; I went away of my own free will; I always wished to be free and meant to be free when I came North; I hardly expected it in Philadelphia, but I thought I should get free in New York; I have been comfortable and happy since I left Mr. Wheeler, and so are the children; I don't want to go back; I could have gone in Philadelphia if I had wanted to; I could go now; but I had rather die than go back. I wish to make this statement before a magistrate, because I understand that Mr. Williamson is in prison on my account, and I hope the truth may be of benefit to him."

her
JANE ✕ JOHNSON.
mark.

It might have been supposed that her honest and straightforward testimony would have been sufficient to cause even the most relentless slaveholder to abandon at once a pursuit so monstrous and utterly hopeless as Wheeler's was. But although he was sadly confused and put to shame, he hung on to the "lost cause" tenaciously. And his counsel, David Webster, Esq., and the United States District Attorney, Vandyke, completely imbued with the pro-slavery spirit, were equally as unyielding. And thus, with a zeal befitting the most worthy object imaginable, they labored with untiring effort to convict the colored men.

By this policy, however, the counsel for the defense was doubly aroused. Mr. Gibbons, in the most eloquent and indignant strains, perfectly annihilated the "distinguished Colonel John H. Wheeler, United States Minister Plenipotentiary near the Island of Nicaragua," taking special pains to ring the changes repeatedly on his long appellations. Mr. Gibbons appeared to be precisely in the right mood to make himself surpassingly forcible and eloquent, on whatever point of law he chose to touch bearing on the case; or in whatever direction he chose to glance at the injustice and cruelty of the South. Most vividly did he draw the contrast between the States of "Georgia" and "Pennsylvania," with regard to the atrocious laws of Georgia. Scarcely less vivid is the impression after a lapse of sixteen years, than when this eloquent speech was made. With the District Attorney, Wm. B. Mann, Esq., and his Honor, Judge Kelley, the defendants had no cause to complain.   Throughout the entire proceedings, they had reason to feel, that neither of these officials sympathized in the least with Wheeler or Slavery.   Indeed in the Judge's charge and also in the District Attorney's closing speech the ring of freedom could be distinctly heard—much more so than was agreeable to Wheeler and his Pro-Slavery sympathizers.   The case of Wm. Still ended in his acquittal ; the other five colored men were taken up in order.   And it is scarcely necessary to say that Messrs. Peirce and Birney did full justice to all concerned.   Mr. Peirce, especially, was one of the oldest, ablest and most faithful lawyers to the slave of the Philadelphia Bar.   He never was known, it may safely be said, to hesitate in the darkest days of Slavery to give his time and talents to the fugitive, even in the most hopeless cases, and when, from the unpopularity of such a course, serious sacrifices would be likely to result.   Consequently he was but at home in this case, and most nobly did he defend his clients, with the same earnestness that a man would defend his fireside against the approach of burglars. At the conclusion of the trial, the jury returned a verdict of " not guilty," as to all the persons in the first count, charging them with riot.   In the second count, charging them with " Assault and Battery " (on Col. Wheeler) Ballard and Curtis were found " guilty," the rest " not guilty."   The guilty were given about a week in jail.   Thus ended this act in the Wheeler drama.

The following extract is taken from the correspondence of the New York Tribune touching Jane Johnson's presence in the court, and will be interesting on that account :

" But it was a bold and perilous move on the part of her friends, and the deepest apprehensions were felt for a while, for the result.   The United States Marshal was there with his warrant and an extra force to execute it. The officers of the court and other State officers were there to protect the witness and vindicate the laws of the State.   Vandyke, the United States District Attorney, swore he would take her.   The State officers swore he should not, and for a while it seemed that nothing could avert a bloody scene.   It was expected that the conflict would take place at the door, when she should leave the room, so that when she and her friends went out, and for some time after, the most intense suspense pervaded the court-room. She was, however, allowed to enter the carriage that awaited her without disturbance.   She was accompanied by Mr. McKim, Secretary of the Pennsylvania Anti-Slavery Society, Lucretia Mott and George Corson, one of our most manly and intrepid police officers.   The carriage was followed by another filled with officers as a guard ; and thus escorted she was taken back in safety to the house from which she had been brought.   Her title to Freedom under the laws of the State will hardly again be brought into question.

Mr. Williamson was committed to prison by Judge Kane for contempt of

Court, on the 27th day of July, 1855, and was released on the 3d day of November the same year, having gained, in the estimation of the friends of Freedom every where, a triumph and a fame which but few men in the great moral battle for Freedom could claim.

THE ARRIVALS OF A SINGLE MONTH.

SIXTY PASSENGERS CAME IN ONE MONTH—TWENTY-EIGHT IN ONE ARRIVAL—GREAT PANIC AND INDIGNATION MEETING—INTERESTING CORRESPONDENCE FROM MASTERS AND FUGITIVES.

The great number of cases to be here noticed forbids more than a brief reference to each passenger. As they arrived in parties, their narratives will be given in due order as found on the book of records:

William Griffen, Henry Moor, James Camper, Noah Ennells and Levin Parker. This party came from Cambridge, Md.

WILLIAM is thirty-four years of age, of medium size and substantial appearance. He fled from James Waters, Esq., a lawyer, living in Cambridge. He was "wealthy, close, and stingy," and owned nine head of slaves and a farm, on which William served. He was used very hard, which was the cause of his escape, though the idea that he was entitled to his freedom had been entertained for the previous twelve years. On preparing to take the Underground, he armed himself with a big butcher-knife, and resolved, if attacked, to make his enemies stand back. His master was a member of the Methodist Church.

HENRY is tall, copper-colored, and about thirty years of age. He complained not so much of bad usage as of the utter distaste he had to working all the time for the "white people for nothing." He was also decidedly of the opinion that every man should have his liberty. Four years ago his wife was "sold away to Georgia" by her young master; since which time not a word had he heard of her. She left three children, and he, in escaping, also had to leave them in the same hands that sold their mother. He was owned by Levin Dale, a farmer near Cambridge. Henry was armed with a six-barreled revolver, a large knife, and a determined mind.

JAMES is twenty-four years of age, quite black, small size, keen look, and full of hope for the "best part of Canada." He fled from Henry Hooper, "a dashing young man and a member of the Episcopal Church." Left because he "did not enjoy privileges" as he wished to do. He was armed with two pistols and a dirk to defend himself.

NOAH is only nineteen, quite dark, well-proportioned, and possessed of a fair average of common sense. He was owned by "Black-head Bill Le-Count," who "followed drinking, chewing tobacco, catching 'runaways,' and hanging around the court-house." However, he owned six head of slaves, and had a "rough wife," who belonged to the Methodist Church. Left be-

7

cause he " expected every day to be sold "—his master being largely in " debt." Brought with him a butcher-knife.

LEVIN is twenty-two, rather short built, medium size and well colored. He fled from Lawrence G. Colson, " a very bad man, fond of drinking, great to fight and swear, and hard to please. His mistress was " real rough ; very bad, worse than he was as ' fur ' as she could be." Having been stinted with food and clothing and worked hard, was the apology offered by Levin for running off.

STEBNEY SWAN, John Stinger, Robert Emerson, Anthony Pugh and Isabella ——. This company came from Portsmouth, Va. Stebney is thirty-four years of age, medium size, mulatto, and quite wide awake. He was owned by an oysterman by the name of Jos. Carter, who lived near Portsmouth. Naturally enough his master " drank hard, gambled " extensively, and in every other respect was a very ordinary man. Nevertheless, he " owned twenty-five head," and had a wife and six children. Stebney testified that he had not been used hard, though he had been on the " auction-block three times." Left because he was "tired of being a servant." Armed with a broad-axe and hatchet, he started, joined by the above-named companions, and came in a skiff, by sea. Robert Lee was the brave Captain engaged to pilot this Slavery-sick party from the prison-house of bondage. And although every rod of rowing was attended with inconceivable peril, the desired haven was safely reached, and the overjoyed voyagers conducted to the Vigilance Committee.

JOHN is about forty years of age, and so near white that a microscope would be required to discern his colored origin. His father was white, and his mother nearly so. He also had been owned by the oysterman alluded to above ; had been captain of one of his oyster-boats, until recently. And but for his attempt some months back to make his escape, he might have been this day in the care of his kind-hearted master. But, because of this wayward step on the part of John, his master felt called upon to humble him. Accordingly, the captaincy was taken from him, and he was compelled to struggle on in a less honorable position. Occasionally John's mind would be refreshed by his master relating the hard times in the North, the great starvation among the blacks, etc. He would also tell John how much better off he was as a " slave with a kind master to provide for all his wants," etc. Notwithstanding all this counsel, John did not rest contented until he was on the Underground Rail Road.

ROBERT was only nineteen, with an intelligent face and prepossessing manners ; reads, writes and ciphers ; and is about half Anglo-Saxon. He fled from Wm. H. Wilson, Esq., Cashier of the Virginia Bank. Until within the four years previous to Robert's escape, the cashier was spoken of as a " very good man ;" but in consequence of speculations in a large Hotel in Portsmouth, and the then financial embarrassments, "he had become seri-

ESCAPING FROM NORFOLK IN CAPT. LEE'S SKIFF.

ously involved," and decidedly changed in his manners. Robert noticed this, and concluded he had "better get out of danger as soon as possible."

ANTHONY and Isabella were an engaged couple, and desired to cast their lot where husband and wife could not be separated on the auction-block.

The following are of the Cambridge party, above alluded to. All left together, but for prudential reasons separated before reaching Philadelphia. The company that left Cambridge on the 24th of October may be thus recognized: Aaron Cornish and wife, with their six children; Solomon, George Anthony, Joseph, Edward James, Perry Lake, and a nameless babe, all very likely; Kit Anthony and wife Leah, and three children, Adam, Mary, and Murray; Joseph Hill and wife Alice, and their son Henry; also Joseph's sister. Add to the above, Marshall Dutton and George Light, both single young men, and we have twenty-eight in one arrival, as hearty-looking, brave and interesting specimens of Slavery as could well be produced from Maryland. Before setting out they counted well the cost. Being aware that fifteen had left their neighborhood only a few days ahead of them, and that every slave-holder and slave-catcher throughout the community, were on the alert, and raging furiously against the inroads of the Underground Rail Road, they provided themselves with the following weapons of defense: three revolvers, three double-barreled pistols, three single-barreled pistols, three sword-canes, four butcher knives, one bowie-knife, and one paw.* Thus, fully resolved upon freedom or death, with scarcely provisions enough for a single day, while the rain and storm was piteously descending, fathers and mothers with children in their arms (Aaron Cornish had two)—the entire party started. Of course, their provisions gave out before they were fairly on the way, but not so with the storm. It continued to pour upon them for nearly three days. With nothing to appease the gnawings of hunger but parched corn and a few dry crackers, wet and cold, with several of the children sick, some of their feet bare and worn, and one of the mothers with an infant in her arms, incapable of partaking of the diet,—it is impossible to imagine the ordeal they were passing. It was enough to cause the bravest hearts to falter. But not for a moment did they allow themselves to look back. It was exceedingly agreeable to hear even the little children testify that in the most trying hour on the road, not for a moment did they want to go back. The following advertisement, taken from *The Cambridge Democrat* of November 4, shows how the Rev. Levi Traverse felt about Aaron—

 $300 REWARD.—Ran away from the subscriber, from the neighborhood of Town Point, on Saturday night, the 24th inst., my negro man, AARON CORNISH, about 35 years old. He is about five feet ten inches high, black, good-looking, rather pleasant countenance, and carries himself with a confident manner. He went off with his wife, DAFFNEY, a negro woman belonging to Reuben E. Phillips. I will give the above reward if taken out of the county, and $200 if taken in the county; in either case to be lodged in Cambridge Jail.
October 25, 1857.   LEVI D. TRAVERSE.

* A paw is a weapon with iron prongs, four inches long, to be grasped with the hand and used in close encounter.

To fully understand the Rev. Mr. Traverse's authority for taking the liberty he did with Aaron's good name, it may not be amiss to give briefly a paragraph of private information from Aaron, relative to his master. The Rev. Mr. Traverse belonged to the Methodist Church, and was described by Aaron as a " bad young man; rattle-brained; with the appearance of not having good sense,—not enough to manage the great amount of property (he had been left wealthy) in his possession." Aaron's servitude commenced under this spiritual protector in May prior to the escape, immediately after the death of his old master. His deceased master, William D. Traverse, by the way, was the father-in-law, and at the same time own uncle of Aaron's reverend owner. Though the young master, for marrying his own cousin and uncle's daughter, had been for years the subject of the old gentleman's wrath, and was not allowed to come near his house, or to entertain any reasonable hope of getting any of his father-in-law's estate, nevertheless, scarcely had the old man breathed his last, ere the young preacher seized upon the inheritance, slaves and all; at least he claimed two-thirds, allowing for the widow one-third. Unhesitatingly he had taken possession of all the slaves (some thirty head), and was making them feel his power to the fullest extent. To Aaron this increased oppression was exceedingly crushing, as he had been hoping at the death of his old master to be free. Indeed, it was understood that the old man had his will made, and freedom provided for the slaves. But, strangely enough, at his death no will could be found. Aaron was firmly of the conviction that the Rev. Mr. Traverse knew what became of it. Between the widow and the son-in-law, in consequence of his aggressive steps, existed much hostility, which strongly indicated the approach of a law-suit; therefore, except by escaping, Aaron could not see the faintest hope of freedom. Under his old master, the favor of hiring his time had been granted him. He had also been allowed by his wife's mistress (Miss Jane Carter, of Baltimore), to have his wife and children home with him—that is, until his children would grow to the age of eight and ten years, then they would be taken away and hired out at twelve or fifteen dollars a year at first. Her oldest boy, sixteen, hired the year he left for forty dollars. They had had ten children; two had died, two they were compelled to leave in chains; the rest they brought away. Not one dollar's expense had they been to their mistress. The industrious Aaron not only had to pay his own hire, but was obliged to do enough over-work to support his large family.

Though he said he had no special complaint to make against his old master, through whom he, with the rest of the slaves, hoped to obtain freedom, Aaron, nevertheless, spoke of him as a man of violent temper, severe on his slaves, drinking hard, etc., though he was a man of wealth and stood high in the community. One of Aaron's brothers, and others, had been sold South by him. It was on account of his inveterate hatred of his son-in-law, who, he declared, should never have his property (having no other heir but his niece, except his widow), that the slaves relied on his promise to free them. Thus, in view of the facts referred to, Aaron was led to commit the unpardonable sin of running away with his wife Daffney, who, by the way, looked like a woman fully capable of taking care of herself and children, instead of having them stolen away from her, as though they were pigs.

JOSEPH VINEY and family—Joseph was "held to service or labor," by Charles Bryant, of Alexandria, Va. Joseph had very nearly finished paying for himself. His wife and children were held by Samuel Pattison, Esq., a member of the Methodist Church, "a great big man," " with red eyes, bald head, drank pretty freely," and in the language of Joseph, "wouldn't bear nothing." Two of Joseph's brothers-in-law had been sold by his master. Against Mrs. Pattison his complaint was, that "she was mean, sneaking, and did not want to give half enough to eat."

For the enlightenment of all Christendom, and coming posterity especially, the following advertisement and letter are recorded, with the hope that they will have an important historical value. The writer was at great pains to obtain these interesting documents, directly after the arrival of the memorable Twenty-Eight; and shortly afterwards furnished to the New York *Tribune*, in a prudential manner, a brief sketch of these very passengers, including the advertisements, but not the letter. It was safely laid away for history—

 $2,000 REWARD.—Ran away from the subscriber on Saturday night, the 24th inst, FOURTEEN HEAD OF NEGROES, viz: Four men, two women, one boy and seven children. KIT is about 35 years of age, five feet six or seven inches high, dark chestnut color, and has a scar on one of his thumbs. JOE is about 30 years old, very black, his teeth are very white, and is about five feet eight inches high. HENRY is about 22 years old, five feet ten inches high, of dark chestnut color and large front teeth. JOE is about 20 years old, about five feet six inches high, heavy built and black. TOM is about 16 years old, about five feet high, light chestnut color. SUSAN is about 35 years old, dark chestnut color, and rather stout built; speaks rather slow, and has with her FOUR CHILDREN, varying from one to seven years of age. LEAH is about 28 years old, about five feet high, dark chestnut color, with THREE CHILDREN, two boys and one girl, from one to eight years old.

I will give $1,000 if taken in the county, $1,500 if taken out of the county and in the State, and $2,000 if taken out of the State; in either case to be lodged in Cambridge (Md.) Jail, so that I can get them again; or I will give a fair proportion of the above reward if any part be secured.   SAMUEL PATTISON,
    October 26, 1857.   Near Cambridge, Md.

P. S.—Since writing the above, I have discovered that my negro woman, SARAH JANE, 25 years old, stout built and chestnut color, has also run off.   S. P.

CAMBRIDGE, Nov. 16th, 1857.

L. W. THOMPSON :—SIR, this morning I received your letter wishing an accurate description of my Negroes which ran away on the 24th of last month and the amt of reward offered &c &c. The description is as follows. *Kit* is about 35 years old, five feet, six or seven inches high, dark chestnut color and has a scar on one of his thumbs, he has a very quick step and walks very straight, and can read and write. *Joe*, is about 30 years old, very black and about five feet eight inches high, has a very pleasing appearance, he has a free wife who left with him she is a light molatoo, she has a child not over one year old. *Henry* is about 22 years old, five feet, ten inches high, of dark chestnut coller and large front teeth, he stoops a little in his walk and has a downward look. *Joe* is about 20 years old, about five feet six inches high, heavy built, and has a grum look and voice dull, and black. *Tom* is about 16 years old about five feet high light chestnut coller, smart active boy, and swagers in his walk. Susan is about 35 years old, dark chesnut coller and stout built, speaks rather slow and has with her *four children, three boys* and one *girl*—the girl has a thumb or finger on her left hand (part of it) cut off, the children are from 9 months to 8 years old. (the youngest a boy 9 months and the oldest whose name is Lloyd is about 8 years old) The husband of Susan (Joe Viney) started off with her, he is a slave, belonging to a gentleman in Alexandria D. C. he is about 40 years old and dark chesnut coller rather slender built and about five feet seven or eight inches high, he is also the Father of Henry, Joe and Tom. A *reward* of $400. will be given for his apprehension. *Leah* is about 28 years old about five feet high dark chesnut coller, with three children. 2 Boys and 1 girl, they are from one to eight years old, the oldest boy is called Adam, Leah is the wife of Kit, the first named man in the list. *Sarah Jane* is about 25 years old, stout built and chesnut coller, quick and active in her walk. Making in all 15 head, men, women and children belonging to me, or 16 head including Joe Viney, the husband of my woman Susan.

A Reward of $2250. will be given for my negroes if taken out of the State of Maryland and lodged in Cambridge or Baltimore Jail, so that I can get them or a fair proportion for any part of them. And including Joe Viney's reward $2650 00.

At the same time eight other negroes belonging to a neighbor of mine ran off, for which a reward of $1400 00 has been offered for them.

If you should want any information, witnesses to prove or indentify the negroes, write immediately on to me. Or if you should need any information with regard to proving the negroes, before I could reach Philadelphia, you can call on Mr. Burroughs at Martin & Smith's store, Market Street, No 308. Phila and he can refer you to a gentleman who knows the negroes. Yours &c Saml. Pattison.

This letter was in answer to one written in Philadelphia and signed, "L. W. Thompson." It is not improbable that Mr. Pattison's loss had produced such a high state of mental excitement that he was hardly in a condition for cool reflection, or he would have weighed the matter a little more carefully before exposing himself to the U. G. R. R. agents. But the letter possesses two commendable features, nevertheless. It was tolerably well written and prompt.

Here is a wonderful exhibition of affection for his contented and happy negroes. Whether Mr. Pattison suspended on suddenly learning that he was minus fifteen head, the writer cannot say. But that there was a great slave hunt in every direction there is no room to doubt. Though much more might be said about the parties concerned, it must suffice to add that they came to the Vigilance Committee in a very sad plight—in tattered garments, hungry, sick, and penniless; but they were kindly clothed, fed, doctored, and sent on their way rejoicing.

Daniel Stanly, Nat Amby, John Scott, Hannah Peters, Henrietta Dobson, Elizabeth Amby, Josiah Stanly, Caroline Stanly, Daniel Stanly, jr.,

TWENTY-EIGHT FUGITIVES ESCAPING FROM THE EASTERN SHORE OF MARYLAND.

John Stanly and Miller Stanly (arrival from Cambridge.) Daniel is about 35, well-made and wide-awake. Fortunately, in emancipating himself, he also, through great perseverance, secured the freedom of his wife and six children ; one child he was compelled to leave behind. Daniel belonged to Robert Calender, a farmer, and, "except when in a passion," said to be "pretty clever." However, considering as a father, that it was his "duty to do all he could" for his children, and that all work and no play makes Jack a dull boy, Daniel felt bound to seek refuge in Canada. His wife and children were owned by "Samuel Count, an old, bald-headed, bad man," who "had of late years been selling and buying slaves as a business," though he stood high and was a "big bug in Cambridge." The children were truly likely-looking.

Nat is no ordinary man. Like a certain other Nat known to history, his honest and independent bearing in every respect was that of a natural hero. He was full black, and about six feet high ; of powerful physical proportions, and of more than ordinary intellectual capacities. With the strongest desire to make the Port of Canada safely, he had resolved to be "carried back," if attacked by the slave hunters, "only as a dead man." He was held to service by John Muir, a wealthy farmer, and the owner of 40 or 50 slaves. "Muir would drink and was generally devilish." Two of Nat's sisters and one of his brothers had been "sold away to Georgia by him." Therefore, admonished by threats and fears of having to pass through the same fiery furnace, Nat was led to consider the U. G. R. R. scheme. It was through the marriage of Nat's mistress to his present owner that he came into Muir's hands. "Up to the time of her death," he had been encouraged to "hope" that he would be "free ;" indeed, he was assured by her "dying testimony that the slaves were not to be sold." But regardless of the promises and will of his departed wife, Muir soon extinguished all hopes of freedom from that quarter. But not believing that God had put one man here to "be the servant of another—to work," and get none of the benefit of his labor, Nat armed himself with a good pistol and a big knife, and taking his wife with him, bade adieu forever to bondage. Observing that Lizzie (Nat's wife) looked pretty decided and resolute, a member of the committee remarked, "Would your wife fight for freedom?" "I have heard her say she would wade through blood and tears for her freedom," said Nat, in the most serious mood.

The following advertisement from *The Cambridge Democrat* of Nov. 4, speaks for itself—

$300 REWARD.—Ran away from the subscriber, on Saturday night last, 17th inst., my negro woman Lizzie, about 28 years old. She is medium sized, dark complexion, good-looking, with rather a down look. When spoken to, replies quickly. She was well dressed, wearing a red and green blanket shawl, and carried with her a variety of clothing. She ran off in company with her husband, Nat Amby (belonging to John Muir, Esq.), who is about 6 feet in height, with slight impediment in his speech, dark chestnut color, and a large scar on the side of his neck.

I will give the above reward if taken in this County, or one-half of what she sells for if taken out of the County or State. In either case to be lodged in Cambridge Jail.

　　Cambridge, Oct. 21, 1857.　　　　　　　　　　　ALEXANDER H. BAYLY.

P. S.—For the apprehension of the above-named negro man Nat, and delivery in Cambridge Jail, I will give $500 reward.　　　　　　　　　　JOHN MUIR.

Now since Nat's master has been introduced in the above order, it seems but appropriate that Nat should be heard too; consequently the following letter is inserted for what it is worth:

　　　　　　　　　　　　　　　　　　　　　　AUBURN, June 10th, 1858.

MR. WILLIAM STILL:—Sir, will you be so Kind as to write a letter to affey White in straw berry alley in Baltimore city on the point Say to her at nat Ambey that I wish to Know from her the Last Letar that Joseph Ambie and Henry Ambie two Brothers and Ann Warfield a couisin of them two boys I state above I would like to hear from my mother sichy Ambie you will Please write to my mother and tell her that I am well and doing well and state to her that I perform my Relissius dutys and I would like to hear from her and want to know if she is performing her Relissius dutys yet and send me word from all her children I left behind say to affey White that I wish her to write me a Letter in Hast my wife is well and doing well and my nephew is doing well Please tell affey White when she writes to me to Let me know where Joseph and Henry Ambie is

Mr. Still Please Look on your Book and you will find my name on your Book They was eleven of us children and all when we came through and I feal interrested about my Brothers I have never heard from them since I Left home you will Please Be Kind annough to attend to this Letter When you send the answer to this Letter you will Please send it to P. R. Freeman Auburn City Cayuga County New York

　　　　　　　　Yours Truly　　　　　　　　　　　　NAT AMBIE.

WILLIAM is 25, complexion brown, intellect naturally good, with no favorable notions of the peculiar institution. He was armed with a formidable dirk-knife, and declared he would use it if attacked, rather than be dragged back to bondage.

HANNAH is a hearty-looking young woman of 23 or 24, with a countenance that indicated that liberty was what she wanted and was contending for, and that she could not willingly submit to the yoke. Though she came with the Cambridge party, she did not come from Cambridge, but from Marshall Hope, Caroline County, where she had been owned by Charles Peters, a man who had distinguished himself by getting "drunk, scratching and fighting, etc.," not unfrequently in his own family even. She had no parents that she knew of. Left because they used her "so bad, beat and knocked" her about.

"JACK SCOTT." Jack is about thirty-six years of age, substantially built, dark color, and of quiet and prepossessing manners. He was owned by David B. Turner, Esq., a dry goods merchant of New York. By birth, Turner was a Virginian, and a regular slave-holder. His slaves were kept hired out by the year. As Jack had had but slight acquaintance with his New York owner, he says but very little about him. He was moved to leave simply because he had got tired of working for the "white people for nothing." Fled from Richmond, Va. Jack went to Canada direct. The following letter furnishes a clew to his whereabouts, plans, etc.

MONTREAL, September 1st 1859.

DEAR SIR:—It is with extreme pleasure that I set down to inclose you a few lines to let you know that I am well & I hope when these few lines come to hand they may find you & your family in good health and prosperity I left your house Nov. 3d, 1857, for Canada I Received a letter here from James Carter in Peters burg, saying that my wife would leave there about the 28th or the first September and that he would send her on by way of Philadelphia to you to send on to Montreal if she come on you be please to send her on and as there is so many boats coming here all times a day I may not know what time she will. So you be please to give her this direction, she can get a cab and go to the Donegana Hotel and Edmund Turner is there he will take you where I lives and if he is not there cabman take you to Mr Taylors on Durham St. nearly opposite to the Methodist Church. Nothing more at present but Remain your well wisher   JOHN SCOTT.

C. HITCHENS.—This individual took his departure from Milford, Del., where he was owned by Wm. Hill, a farmer, who took special delight in having "fighting done on the place." This passenger was one of our least intelligent travelers. He was about 22.

MAJOR ROSS.—Major fled from John Jay, a farmer residing in the neighborhood of Havre de Grace, Md. But for the mean treatment received from Mr. Jay, Major might have been foolish enough to have remained all his days in chains. "It's an ill wind that blows nobody any good."

HENRY OBERNE.—Henry was to be free at 28, but preferred having it at 21, especially as he was not certain that 28 would ever come. He is of chestnut color, well made, &c., and came from Seaford, Md.

PERRY BURTON.—Perry is about twenty-seven years of age, decidedly colored, medium size, and only of ordinary intellect. He acknowledged John R. Burton, a farmer on Indian River, as his master, and escaped because he wanted "some day for himself."

ALFRED HUBERT, Israel Whitney and John Thompson. Alfred is of powerful muscular appearance and naturally of a good intellect. He is full dark chestnut color, and would doubtless fetch a high price. He was owned by Mrs. Matilda Niles, from whom he had hired his time, paying $110 yearly. He had no fault to find with his mistress, except he observed she had a young family growing up, into whose hands he feared he might unluckily fall some day, and saw no way of avoiding it but by flight. Being only twenty-eight, he may yet make his mark.

ISRAEL was owned by Elijah Money. All that he could say in favor of his master was, that he treated him "respectfully," though he "drank hard." Israel was about thirty-six, and another excellent specimen of an able-bodied and wide-awake man. He hired his time at the rate of $120 a year, and had to find his wife and child in the bargain. He came from Alexandria, Va.

INTERESTING LETTER FROM ISRAEL.

HAMILTON, Oct. 16, 1858.

WILLIAM STILL—*My Dear Friend:*—I saw Carter and his friend a few days ago, and they told me, that you was well. On the seventh of October my wife came to Hamilton. Mr. A. Hurberd, who came from Virginia with me, is going to get married the 20th of

November, next. I wish you would write to me how many of my friends you have seen since October, 1857. Montgomery Green keeps a barber shop in Cayuga, in the State of New York. I have not heard of Oscar Ball but once since I came here, and then he was well and doing well. George Carroll is in Hamilton. The times are very dull at present, and have been ever since I came here. Please write soon. Nothing more at present, only I still remain in Hamilton, C. W.   ISRAEL WHITNEY.

JOHN is nineteen years of age, mulatto, spare made, but not lacking in courage, mother wit or perseverance. He was born in Fauquier county, Va., and, after experiencing Slavery for a number of years there—being sold two or three times to the "highest bidder"—he was finally purchased by a cotton planter named Hezekiah Thompson, residing at Huntsville, Alabama. Immediately after the sale Hezekiah bundled his new "purchase" off to Alabama, where he succeeded in keeping him only about two years, for at the end of that time John determined to strike a blow for liberty. The incentive to this step was the inhuman treatment he was subjected to. Cruel indeed did he find it there. His master was a young man, "fond of drinking and carousing, and always ready for a fight or a knock-down." A short time before John left his master whipped him so severely with the "bull whip" that he could not use his arm for three or four days. Seeing but one way of escape (and that more perilous than the way William and Ellen Craft, or Henry Box Brown traveled), he resolved to try it. It was to get on the top of the car, instead of inside of it, and thus ride of nights, till nearly daylight, when, at a stopping-place on the road, he would slip off the car, and conceal himself in the woods until under cover of the next night he could manage to get on the top of another car. By this most hazardous mode of travel he reached Virginia.

It may be best not to attempt to describe how he suffered at the hands of his owners in Alabama; or how severely he was pinched with hunger in traveling; or how, when he reached his old neighborhood in Virginia, he could not venture to inquire for his mother, brothers or sisters, to receive from them an affectionate word, an encouraging smile, a crust of bread, or a drink of water.

Success attended his efforts for more than two weeks; but alas, after having got back north of Richmond, on his way home to Alexandria, he was captured and put in prison; his master being informed of the fact, came on and took possession of him again. At first he refused to sell him; said he "had money enough and owned about thirty slaves;" therefore wished to "take him back to make an example of him." However, through the persuasion of an uncle of his, he consented to sell. Accordingly, John was put on the auction-block and bought for $1,300 by Green McMurray, a regular trader in Richmond. McMurray again offered him for sale, but in consequence of hard times and the high price demanded, John did not go off, at least not in the way the trader desired to dispose of him, but did, nevertheless, succeed in going off on the Underground Rail Road. Thus once more he reached his old home, Alexandria.   His mother was in one place, and his six brothers and sisters evidently scattered, where he knew not.   Since he was five years of age, not one of them had he seen.

If such sufferings and trials were not entitled to claim for the sufferer the honor of a hero, where in all Christendom could one be found who could prove a better title to that appellation ?

It is needless to say that the Committee extended to him brotherly kindness, sympathized with him deeply, and sent him on his way rejoicing.

Of his subsequent career the following extract from a letter written at London shows that he found no rest for the soles of his feet under the Stars and Stripes in New York :

I hope that you will remember John Thompson, who passed through your hands, I think, in October, 1857, at the same time that Mr. Cooper, from Charleston, South Carolina, came on.   I was engaged at New York, in the barber business, with a friend, and was doing very well, when I was betrayed and obliged to sail for England very suddenly, my master being in the city to arrest me.   (LONDON, December 21st, 1860.)

JEREMIAH COLBURN.—Jeremiah is a bright mulatto, of prepossessing appearance, reads and writes, and is quite intelligent.   He fled from Charleston, where he had been owned by Mrs. E. Williamson, an old lady about seventy-five, a member of the Episcopal Church, and opposed to Freedom. As far as he was concerned, however, he said, she had treated him well ; but, knowing that the old lady would not be long here, he judged it was best to look out in time.   Consequently, he availed himself of an Underground Rail Road ticket, and bade adieu to that hot-bed of secession, South

Carolina. Indeed, he was fair enough to pass for white, and actually came the entire journey from Charleston to this city under the garb of a white gentleman. With regard to gentlemanly bearing, however, he was all right in this particular. Nevertheless, as he had been a slave all his days, he found that it required no small amount of nerve to succeed in running the gauntlet with slave-holders and slave-catchers for so long a journey.

The following pointed epistle, from Jeremiah Colburn alias William Cooper, beautifully illustrates the effects of Freedom on many a passenger who received hospitalities at the Philadelphia depot—

SYRACUSE, June 9th, 1858.

MR. STILL :—*Dear Sir :*—One of your Underground R. R. Passenger Drop you these few Lines to let you see that he have not forgoten you one who have Done so much for him well sir I am still in Syracuse, well in regard to what I am Doing for a Living I no you would like to hear, I am in the Painting Business, and have as much at that as I can do, and enough to Last me all the Summer, I had a knolledge of Painting Before I Left the South, the Hotell where I was working Last winter the Proprietor fail & shot up in the Spring and I Loose evry thing that I was working for all Last winter. I have Ritten a Letter to my Friend P. Christianson some time a goo & have never Received an Answer, I hope this wont Be the case with this one, I have an idea sir, next winter iff I can this summer make Enough to Pay Expenses, to goo to that school at McGrowville & spend my winter their. I am going sir to try to Prepair myself for a Lectuer, I am going sir By the Help of god to try and Do something for the Caus to help my Poor Breathern that are suffering under the yoke. Do give my Respect to Mrs Stills & Perticular to Miss Julia Kelly, I supose she is still with you yet, I am in great hast you must excuse my short letter. I hope these few Lines may fine you as they Leave me quite well. It will afford me much Pleasure to hear from you.

yours Truly, WILLIAM COOPER.

John Thompson is still here and Doing well.

It will be seen that this young Charlestonian had rather exalted notions in his head. He was contemplating going to McGrawville College, for the purpose of preparing himself for the lecturing field. Was it not rather strange that he did not want to return to his "kind-hearted old mistress?"

THOMAS HENRY, NATHAN COLLINS AND HIS WIFE MARY ELLEN.—Thomas. is about twenty-six, quite dark, rather of a raw-boned make, indicating that times with him had been other than smooth. A certain Josiah Wilson owned Thomas. He was a cross, rugged man, allowing not half enough to eat, and worked his slaves late and early. Especially within the last two or three months previous to the escape, he had been intensely savage, in consequence of having lost, not long before, two of his servants. Ever since that misfortune, he had frequently talked of "putting the rest in his pocket." This distressing threat made the rest love him none the more; but, to make assurances doubly sure, after giving them their supper every evening, which consisted of delicious "skimmed milk, corn cake and a herring each," he would very carefully send them up in the loft over the kitchen, and there "lock them up," to remain until called the next morning at three or four o'clock to go to work again. Destitute of money, clothing, and a knowledge of the way, situated as they were they concluded to make an effort for Canada.

NATHAN was also a fellow-servant with Thomas, and of course owned by Wilson. Nathan's wife, however, was owned by Wilson's son, Abram. Nathan was about twenty-five years of age, not very dark. He had a remarkably large head on his shoulders and was the picture of determination, and apparently was exactly the kind of a subject that might be desirable in the British possessions, in the forest or on the farm.

His wife, Mary Ellen, is a brown-skinned, country-looking young woman, about twenty years of age. In escaping, they had to break jail, in the dead of night, while all were asleep in the big house; and thus they succeeded. What Mr. Wilson did, said or thought about these "shiftless" creatures we are not prepared to say; we may, notwithstanding, reasonably infer that the Underground has come in for a liberal share of his indignation and wrath. The above travelers came from near New Market, Md. The few rags they were clad in were not really worth the price that a woman would ask for washing them, yet they brought with them about all they had. Thus they had to be newly rigged at the expense of the Vigilance Committee.

The Cambridge Democrat, of Nov. 4, 1857, from which the advertisements were cut, said—

" At a meeting of the people of this county, held in Cambridge, on the 2d of November, to take into consideration the better protection of the interests of the slave-owners; among other things that were done, it was resolved to enforce the various acts of Assembly * * * * relating to servants and slaves.

" The act of 1715, chap. 44, sec. 2, provides 'that from and after the publication thereof no servant or servants whatsoever, within this province, whether by indenture or by the custom of the counties, or hired for wages shall travel by land or water ten miles from the house of his, her or their master, mistress or dame, without a note under their hands, or under the hands of his, her or their overseer, if any be, under the penalty of being taken for a runaway, and to suffer such penalties as hereafter provided against runaways.' The Act of 1806, chap. 81, sec. 5, provides, 'That any person taking up such runaway, shall have and receive $6,' to be paid by the master or owner. It was also determined to have put in force the act of 1825, chap. 161, and the act of 1839, chap. 320, relative to idle, vagabond, free negroes, providing for their sale or banishment from the State. All persons interested, are hereby notified that the aforesaid laws, in particular, will be enforced, and all officers failing to enforce them will be presented to the Grand Jury, and those who desire to avoid the penalties of the aforesaid statutes are requested to conform to these provisions."

As to the modus operandi by which so many men, women and children were delivered and safely forwarded to Canada, despite slave-hunters and the fugitive slave law, the subjoined letters, from different agents and depots, will throw important light on the question.

Men and women aided in this cause who were influenced by no oath of secrecy, who received not a farthing for their labors, who believed that God had put it into the hearts of all mankind to love liberty, and had commanded men to "feel for those in bonds as bound with them," "to break every yoke and let the oppressed go free." But here are the letters, bearing at least on some of the travelers :

WILMINGTON, 10th Mo. 31st, 1857.

ESTEEMED FRIEND WILLIAM STILL :—I write to inform thee that we have either 17 or 27, I am not certain which, of that large Gang of God's poor, and I hope they are safe. The man who has them in charge informed me there were 27 safe and one boy lost during last night, about 14 years of age, without shoes ; we have felt some anxiety about him, for fear he may be taken up and betray the rest. I have since been informed there are but 17 so that I cannot at present tell which is correct. I have several looking out for the lad ; they will be kept from Phila. for the present. My principal object in writing thee at this time is to inform thee of what one of our constables told me this morning ; he told me that a colored man in Phila. who professed to be a great friend of the colored people was a traitor ; that he had been written to by an Abolitionist in Baltimore, to keep a look out for those slaves that left Cambridge this night week, told him they would be likely to pass through Wilmington on 6th day or 7th day night, and the colored man in Phila. had written to the master of part of them telling him the above, and the master arrived here yesterday in consequence of the information, and told one of our constables the above ; the man told the name of the Baltimore writer, which he had forgotten, but declined telling the name of the colored man in Phila. I hope you will be able to find out who he is, and should I be able to learn the name of the Baltimore friend, I will put him on his Guard, respecting his Phila. correspondents. As ever thy friend, and the friend of Humanity, without regard to color or clime. THOS. GARRETT.

How much truth there was in the "constable's" story to the effect, "that a colored man in Philadelphia, who professed to be a great friend of the colored people, was a traitor, etc.," the Committee never learned. As a general thing, colored people were true to the fugitive slave ; but now and then some unprincipled individuals, under various pretenses, would cause us great anxiety.

LETTER FROM JOHN AUGUSTA.

NORRISTOWN Oct 18th 1857 2 o'clock P M

DEAR SIR :—There is Six men and women and Five children making Eleven Persons. If you are willing to Receve them write to me imediately and I will bring them to your To morrow Evening I would not Have wrote this But the Times are so much worse Financialy that I thought It best to hear From you Before I Brought such a Crowd Down Pleas Answer this and Oblige JOHN AUGUSTA.

This document has somewhat of a military appearance about it. It is short and to the point. Friend Augusta was well known in Norristown as a first-rate hair-dresser and a prompt and trustworthy Underground Rail Road agent. Of course a speedy answer was returned to his note, and he was instructed to bring the eleven passengers on to the Committee in Brotherly Love.

LETTER FROM MISS G. LEWIS ABOUT A PORTION OF THE SAME "MEMORABLE
TWENTY-EIGHT."

SUNNYSIDE, Nov. 6th, 1857.

DEAR FRIEND:—Eight more of the large company reached our place last night, direct from Ercildown. The eight constitute one family of them, the husband and wife with four children under eight years of age, wish tickets for Elmira. Three sons, nearly grown, will be forwarded to Phila., probably by the train which passes Phœnixville at seven o'clock of to-morrow evening the seventh. It would be safest to meet them there. We shall send them to Elijah with the request for them to be sent there. And I presume they will be. If they should not arrive you may suppose it did not suit Elijah to send them.

We will send the money for the tickets by C. C. Burleigh, who will be in Phila. on second day morning. If you please, you will forward the tickets by to-morrow's mail as we do not have a mail again till third day. Yours hastily,　　　　G. LEWIS.

Please give directions for forwarding to Elmira and name the price of tickets.

At first Miss Lewis thought of forwarding only a part of her fugitive guests to the Committee in Philadelphia, but on further consideration, all were safely sent along in due time, and the Committee took great pains to have them made as comfortable as possible, as the cases of these mothers and children especially called forth the deepest sympathy.

In this connection it seems but fitting to allude to Captain Lee's sufferings on account of his having brought away in a skiff, by sea, a party of four, alluded to in the beginning of this single month's report.

Unfortunately he was suspected, arrested, tried, convicted, and torn from his wife and two little children, and sent to the Richmond Penitentiary for twenty-five years. Before being sent away from Portsmouth, Va., where he was tried, for ten days in succession in the prison five lashes a day were laid heavily on his bare back. The further sufferings of poor Lee and his heart-broken wife, and his little daughter and son, are too painful for minute recital. In this city the friends of Freedom did all in their power to comfort Mrs. Lee, and administered aid to her and her children; but she broke down under her mournful fate, and went to that bourne from whence no traveler ever returns.

Captain Lee suffered untold misery in prison, until he, also, not a great while before the Union forces took possession of Richmond, sank beneath the severity of his treatment, and went likewise to the grave. The two children for a long time were under the care of Mr. Wm. Ingram of Philadelphia, who voluntarily, from pure benevolence, proved himself to be a father and a friend to them. To their poor mother also he had been a true friend.

The way in which Captain Lee came to be convicted, if the Committee were correctly informed and they think they were, was substantially in this wise: In the darkness of the night, four men, two of them constables, one of the other two, the owner of one of the slaves who had been aided away by Lee, seized the wife of one of the fugitives and took her to the woods, where the fiends stripped every particle of clothing from her person, tied her to a tree, and armed with knives, cowhides and a shovel, swore vengeance against her, declaring they would kill her if she did not testify against Lee. At first she refused to reveal the secret; indeed she knew but little to reveal; but her savage tormentors beat her almost to death. Under this barbarous infliction she was constrained to implicate Captain Lee, which was about all the evidence the prosecution had against him. And in reality her evidence, for two reasons, should not have weighed a straw, as it was contrary to the laws of the State of Virginia, to admit the testimony of colored persons against white; then again for the reason that this testimony was obtained wholly by brute force.

But in this instance, this woman on whom the murderous attack had been made, was brought into court on Lee's trial and was bid to simply make her statement with regard to Lee's connection with the escape of her husband. This she did of course. And in the eyes of this chivalric court, this procedure "was all right." But thank God the events since those dark and dreadful days, afford abundant proof that the All-seeing Eye was not asleep to the daily sufferings of the poor bondman.

A SLAVE GIRL'S NARRATIVE.

CORDELIA LONEY, SLAVE OF MRS. JOSEPH CAHELL (WIDOW OF THE LATE HON. JOSEPH CAHELL, OF VA.), OF FREDERICKSBURG, VA.—CORDELIA'S ESCAPE FROM HER MISTRESS IN PHILADELPHIA.

Rarely did the peculiar institution present the relations of mistress and maid-servant in a light so apparently favorable as in the case of Mrs. Joseph Cahell (widow of the late Hon. Jos Cahell, of Va.), and her slave, Cordelia. The Vigilance Committee's first knowledge of either of these memorable personages was brought about in the following manner.

About the 30th of March, in the year 1859, a member of the Vigilance Committee was notified by a colored servant, living at a fashionable boarding-house on Chestnut street that a lady with a slave woman from Fredericksburg, Va., was boarding at said house, and, that said slave woman desired to receive counsel and aid from the Committee, as she was anxious to secure her freedom, before her mistress returned to the South. On further consultation about the matter, a suitable hour was named for the meeting of the Committee and the Slave at the above named boarding-house. Finding that the woman was thoroughly reliable, the Committee told her "that two modes of deliverance were open before her. One was to take her trunk and all her clothing and quietly retire." The other was to "sue out a writ of habeas corpus, and bring the mistress before the Court, where she would be required, under the laws of Pennsylvania, to show cause why she restrained this woman of her freedom." Cordelia concluded to adopt the former expedient, provided the Committee would protect her. Without hesitation the Committee answered her, that to the extent of their ability, she should have their aid with pleasure, without delay. Consequently a member of the Committee was directed to be on hand at a given hour that evening, as Cordelia would certainly be ready to leave her mistress to take care of herself. Thus, at the appointed hour, Cordelia, very deliberately, accompanied the Committee away from her "kind hearted old mistress."

In the quiet and security of the Vigilance Committee Room, Cordelia related substantially the following brief story touching her relationship as a slave to Mrs. Joseph Cahell. In this case, as with thousands and tens of thousands of others, as the old adage fitly expresses it, "All is not gold that glitters." Under this apparently pious and noble-minded lady, it will be seen, that Cordelia had known naught but misery and sorrow.

Mrs. Cahell, having engaged board for a month at a fashionable private boarding-house on Chestnut street, took an early opportunity to caution Cordelia against going into the streets, and against having anything to say or do with "free niggers in particular"; withal, she appeared unusually kind, so much so, that before retiring to bed in the evening, she would call Cordelia to her chamber, and by her side would take her Prayer-book and Bible, and go through the forms of devotional service. She stood very high both as a church communicant and a lady in society.

For a fortnight it seemed as though her prayers were to be answered, for Cordelia apparently bore herself as submissively as ever, and Madame received calls and accepted invitations from some of the *elite* of the city, without suspecting any intention on the part of Cordelia to escape. But Cordelia could not forget how her children had all been sold by her mistress!

Cordelia was about fifty-seven years of age, with about an equal proportion of colored and white blood in her veins; very neat, respectful and prepossessing in manner.

From her birth to the hour of her escape she had worn the yoke under Mrs. C., as her most efficient and reliable maid-servant. She had been at her mistress' beck and call as seamstress, dressing-maid, nurse in the sick-room, etc., etc., under circumstances that might appear to the casual observer uncommonly favorable for a slave. Indeed, on his first interview with her, the Committee man was so forcibly impressed with the belief, that her condition in Virginia had been favorable, that he hesitated to ask her if she did not desire her liberty. A few moments' conversation with her, however, con-

8

vinced him of her good sense and decision of purpose with regard to this matter. For, in answer to the first question he put to her, she answered, that "As many creature comforts and religious privileges as she had been the recipient of under her 'kind mistress,' still she 'wanted to be free,' and 'was bound to leave,' that she had been 'treated very cruelly;' that her children had 'all been sold away' from her; that she had been threatened with sale herself 'on the first insult,'" etc.

She was willing to take the entire responsibility of taking care of herself. On the suggestion of a friend, before leaving her mistress, she was disposed to sue for her freedom, but, upon a reconsideration of the matter, she chose rather to accept the hospitality of the Underground Rail Road, and leave in a quiet way and go to Canada, where she would be free indeed. Accordingly she left her mistress and was soon a free woman.

The following sad experience she related calmly, in the presence of several friends, an evening or two after she left her mistress:

Two sons and two daughters had been sold from her by her mistress, within the last three years, since the death of her master. Three of her children had been sold to the Richmond market and the other in Nelson county.

Paulina was the first sold, two years ago last May. Nat was the next; he was sold to Abram Warrick, of Richmond. Paulina was sold before it was named to her mother that it had entered her mistress's mind to dispose of her. Nancy, from infancy, had been in poor health. Nevertheless, she had been obliged to take her place in the field with the rest of the slaves, of more rugged constitution, until she had passed her twentieth year, and had become a mother. Under these circumstances, the overseer and his wife complained to the mistress that her health was really too bad for a field hand and begged that she might be taken where her duties would be less oppressive. Accordingly, she was withdrawn from the field, and was set to spinning and weaving. When too sick to work her mistress invariably took the ground, that "nothing was the matter," notwithstanding the fact, that her family physician, Dr. Ellsom, had pronounced her "quite weakly and sick."

In an angry mood one day, Mrs. Cahell declared she would cure her; and again sent her to the field, "with orders to the overseer, to whip her every day, and make her work or kill her." Again the overseer said it was "no use to try, for her health would not stand it," and she was forthwith returned. The mistress then concluded to sell her.

One Sabbath evening a nephew of hers, who resided in New Orleans, happened to be on a visit to his aunt, when it occurred to her, that she had "better get Nancy off if possible." Accordingly, Nancy was called in for examination. Being dressed in her "Sunday best" and "before a poor candle-light," she appeared to good advantage; and the nephew concluded to start with her on the following Tuesday morning. However, the next morning, he happened to see her by the light of the sun, and in her working garments, which satisfied him that he had been grossly deceived; that she would barely live to reach New Orleans; he positively refused to carry out the previous evening's contract, thus leaving her in the hands of her mistress, with the advice, that she should "doctor her up."

The mistress, not disposed to be defeated, obviated the difficulty by selecting a little boy, made a lot of the two, and thus made it an inducement to a purchaser to buy the sick woman; the boy and the woman brought $700.

In the sale of her children, Cordelia was as little regarded as if she had been a cow.

"I felt wretched," she said, with emphasis, "when I heard that Nancy had been sold," which was not until after she had been removed. "But," she continued, "I was not at liberty to make my grief known to a single white soul. I wept and couldn't help it." But remembering that she was liable, "on the first insult," to be sold herself, she sought no sympathy from her mistress, whom she describes as "a woman who shows as little kindness towards her servants as any woman in the States of America. She neither likes to feed nor clothe well."

With regard to flogging, however, in days past, she had been up to the mark. "A many a slap and blow" had Cordelia received since she arrived at womanhood, directly from the madam's own hand.

One day smarting under cruel treatment, she appealed to her mistress in the following strain: "I stood by your mother in all her sickness and nursed her till she died!" "I waited on your niece, night and day for months, till she died." "I waited upon your husband all my life—in his sickness especially, and shrouded him in death, etc., yet I am treated cruelly." It was of no avail.

Her mistress, at one time, was the owner of about five hundred slaves, but within the last few years she had greatly lessened the number by sales.

She stood very high as a lady, and was a member of the Episcopal Church.

To punish Cordelia, on several occasions, she had been sent to one of the plantations to work as a field hand. Fortunately, however, she found the overseers more compassionate than her mistress, though she received no particular favors from any of them.

Asking her to name the overseers, etc., she did so. The first was "Marks, a thin-visaged, poor-looking man, great for swearing." The second was "Gilbert Brower, a very rash, portly man." The third was "Buck Young, a stout man, and very sharp." The fourth was "Lynn Powell, a tall man with red whiskers, very contrary and spiteful." There was also a fifth one, but his name was lost.

Thus Cordelia's experience, though chiefly confined to the "great house," extended occasionally over the corn and tobacco fields, among the overseers and field hands generally. But under no circumstances could she find it in her heart to be thankful for the privileges of Slavery.

After leaving her mistress she learned, with no little degree of pleasure, that a perplexed state of things existed at the boarding-house; that her mistress was seriously puzzled to imagine how she would get her shoes and stockings on and off; how she would get her head combed, get dressed, be attended to in sickness, etc., as she (Cordelia), had been compelled to discharge these offices all her life.

Most of the boarders, being slave-holders, naturally sympathized in her affliction; and some of them went so far as to offer a reward to some of the colored servants to gain a knowledge of her whereabouts. Some charged the servants with having a hand in her leaving, but all agreed that " she had left a very kind and indulgent mistress," and had acted very foolishly in running out of Slavery into Freedom.

A certain Doctor of Divinity, the pastor of an Episcopal church in this city and a friend of the mistress, hearing of her distress, by request or voluntarily, undertook to find out Cordelia's place of seclusion. Hailing on the street a certain colored man with a familiar face, who he thought knew nearly all the colored people about town, he related to him the predicament of his lady friend from the South, remarked how kindly she had always treated her servants, signified that Cordelia would rue the change, and be left to suffer among the " miserable blacks down town," that she would not be able to take care of herself; quoted Scripture justifying Slavery, and finally suggested that he (the colored man) would be doing a duty and a kindness to the fugitive by using his influence to " find her and prevail upon her to return."

It so happened that the colored man thus addressed, was Thomas Dorsey, the well-known fashionable caterer of Philadelphia, who had had the experience of quite a number of years as a slave at the South,—had himself once been pursued as a fugitive, and having, by his industry in the condition of Freedom, acquired a handsome estate, he felt entirely qualified to reply to the reverend gentleman, which he did, though in not very respectful phrases, telling him that Cordelia had as good a right to her liberty as he had, or her mistress either; that God had never intended one man to be the slave of another; that it was all false about the slaves being better off than the free colored people; that he would find as many "poor, miserably degraded," of his own color " down-town," as among the " degraded blacks"; and concluded by telling him that he would "rather give her a hundred dollars to help her off, than to do aught to make known her whereabouts, if he knew ever so much about her."

What further steps were taken by the discomfited divine, the mistress, or her boarding-house sympathizers, the Committee was not informed.

But with regard to Cordelia: she took her departure for Canada, in the midst of the Daniel Webster (fugitive) trial, with the hope of being permitted to enjoy the remainder of her life in Freedom and peace. Being a member of the Baptist Church, and professing to be a Christian, she was persuaded that, by industry and assistance of the Lord, a way would be opened to the seeker of Freedom even in a strange land and among· strangers.

This story appeared in part in the *N. Y. Evening Post*, having been furnished by the writer, without his name to it. It is certainly none the less interesting now, as it may be read in the light of Universal Emancipation.

ARRIVAL OF JACKSON, ISAAC AND EDMONDSON TURNER FROM PETERSBURG.

TOUCHING SCENE ON MEETING THEIR OLD BLIND FATHER AT THE U. G. R. R. DEPOT. LETTERS AND WARNING TO SLAVEHOLDERS.

About the latter part of December, 1857, Isaac and Edmondson, brothers, succeeded in making their escape together from Petersburg, Va. They barely escaped the auction block, as their mistress, Mrs. Ann Colley, a widow, had just completed arrangements for their sale on the coming first day of January. In this kind of property, however, Mrs. Colley had not largely invested. In the days of her prosperity, while all was happy and contented, she could only boast of "four head :" these brothers, Jackson, Isaac and Edmondson and one other. In May, 1857, Jackson had fled and was received by the Vigilance Committee, who placed him upon their books briefly in the following light :

"RUNAWAY—*Fifty Dollars Reward,*—Ran away some time in May last, my *Servant-man*, who calls himself *Jackson Turner.* He is about 27 years of age, and has one of his front teeth out. He is quite black, with thick lips, a little bow-legged, and looks down when spoken to. I will give a reward of Fifty dollars if taken out of the city, and twenty five Dollars if taken within the city. I forewarn all masters of vessels from harboring or employing the said slave ; all persons who disregard this Notice will be punished as the law directs. ANN COLLEY.
Petersburg, June 8th, 1857."

JACKSON is quite dark, medium size, and well informed for one in his condition. In Slavery, he had been "pressed hard." His hire, "ten dollars per month" he was obliged to produce at the end of each month, no matter how much he had been called upon to expend for "doctor bills, &c." The woman he called mistress went by the name of Ann Colley, a widow, living near Petersburg. "She was very quarrelsome," although a "member of the Methodist Church." Jackson seeing that his mistress was yearly growing "harder and harder," concluded to try and better his condition if possible." Having a free wife in the North, who was in the habit of communicating with him, he was kept fully awake to the love of Freedom. The Underground Rail Road expense the Committee gladly bore. No further record of Jackson was made. Jackson found his poor old father here, where he had resided for a number of years in a state of almost total blindness, and of course in much parental anxiety about his boys in chains. On the arrival of Jackson, his heart overflowed with joy and gratitude not easily described, as the old man had hardly been able to muster faith enough to believe that he should ever look with his dim eyes upon one of his sons in Freedom. After a day or two's tarrying, Jackson took his departure for safer and more healthful localities,—her "British Majesty's possessions." The old man remained only to feel more keenly than ever, the pang of having sons still toiling in hopeless servitude.

In less than seven months after Jackson had shaken off the yoke, to the unspeakable joy of the father, Isaac and Edmondson succeeded in following their brother's example, and were made happy partakers of the benefits and blessings of the Vigilance Committee of Philadelphia. On first meeting his two boys, at the Underground Rail Road Depot, the old man took each one in his arms, and as looking through a glass darkly, straining every nerve of his almost lost sight, exclaiming, whilst hugging them closer and closer to his bosom for some minutes, in tears of joy and wonder, "My son Isaac, is this you? my son Isaac, is this you, &c.?" The scene was calculated to awaken the deepest emotion and to bring tears to eyes not accustomed to weep. Little had the old man dreamed in his days of sadness, that he should share such a feast of joy over the deliverance of his sons. But it is in vain to attempt to picture the affecting scene at this reunion, for that would be impossible. Of their slave life, the records contain but a short notice, simply as follows :

"ISAAC is twenty-eight years of age, hearty-looking, well made, dark color and intelligent. He was owned by Mrs. Ann Colley, a widow, residing near Petersburg, Va. Isaac and Edmondson were to have been sold, on New Year's day ; a few days hence. How sad her disappointment must have been on finding them gone, may be more easily imagined than described."

EDMONDSON is about twenty-five, a brother of Isaac, and a smart, good-looking young man, was owned by Mrs. Colley also. "This is just the class of fugitives to make good subjects for John Bull," thought the Committee, feeling pretty well assured that they would make good reports after having enjoyed free air in Canada for a short time. Of course, the Committee enjoined upon them very earnestly "not to forget their brethren left behind groaning in fetters ; but to prove by their industry, uprightness, economy, sobriety and thrift, by the remembrance of their former days of oppression and their obligations to their God, that they were worthy of the country to which they were going, and so to help break the bands of the oppressors, and undo the heavy burdens of the oppressed." Similar advice was impressed upon the minds of all travelers passing over this branch of the Underground Rail Road. From hundreds thus admonished, letters came affording the most gratifying evidence that the counsel of the Committee was not in vain. The appended letter from the youngest brother, written with his own hand, will indicate his feelings and views in Canada:

HAMILTON, CANADA WEST Mar. 1, 1858.

MR. STILL, DEAR SIR :—I have taken the oppertunity to enform you yur letter came to hand 27th I ware glad to hear from you and yer famly i hope this letter May fine you and the famly Well i am Well my self My Brother join me in Love to you and all the frend. I ware sorry to hear of the death of Mrs freaman. We all must die sune or Late this a date we all must pay we must Perpar for the time she ware a nise lady dear sir the all is well and san thar love to you Emerline have Ben sick But is better at this time. I saw the hills the war well and san thar Love to you. I war sory to hear that My brother war sol i am glad that i did come away when i did god works all the things for the Best he is young he may get a long in the wole May god Bless hem ef you have any News from Petersburg Va Plas Rite me a word when you anser this Letter and ef any person came form home Letter Me know. Please sen me one of your Paper that had the under grands R wrod give My Love to Mr Careter and his family I am Seving with a barber at this time he have promust to give me the trad ef i can lane it he is much of a gentman. Mr Still sir i have writing a letter to Mr Brown of Petersburg Va Pleas reed it and ef you think it right Plas sen it by the Mail or by hand you wall see how i have writen it the will know how sent it by the way this writing ef the ancer it you can sen it to Me i have tol them direc to yor care for Ed. t. Smith Philadelphia i hope it may be right i promorst to rite to hear Please rite to me sune and let me know ef you do sen it on write wit you did with that ma a bught the cappet Bage do not fergit to rite tal John he mite rite to Me. I am doing as well is i can at this time but i get no wagges But my Bord but is satfid at that thes hard time and glad that i am Hear and in good helth. Northing More at this time   yor truly   EDMUND TURNER.

The same writer sent to the Corresponding Secretary the following "Warning to Slave-holders." At the time these documents were received, Slave-holders were never more defiant. The right to trample on the weak in oppression was indisputable. "Cinnamon and odors, and ointments, and frankincense, and wine, and oil, and fine flour and wheat, and beasts, and sheep, and horses, and chariots, and slaves, and souls of men," slave-holders believed doubtless were theirs by Divine Right. Little dreaming that in less than three short years—"Therefore shall her plagues come in one day, death, and mourning, and famine." In view of the marvelous changes which have been wrought by the hand of the Almighty, this warning to slave-holders from one who felt the sting of Slavery, as evincing a particular phase of simple faith and Christian charity is entitled to a place in these records.

A WARNING TO SLAVE-HOLDERS.

Well may the Southern slaveholder say, that holding their Fellow men in Bondage is no (sin, because it is their delight as the Egyptians, so do they; but nevertheless God in his own good time will bring them out by a mighty hand, as it is recorded in the sacred oracles of truth, that Ethiopia shall soon stretch out her hands to God, speaking in the positive (shall). And my prayer is to you, oh, slaveholder, in the name of that God who in the beginning said, Let there be light, and there was light. Let my People go that they may serve me; thereby good may come unto thee and to thy children's children. Slave-holder have you seriously thought upon the condition yourselves, family and slaves; have you read where Christ has enjoined upon all his creatures to read his word, thereby that they may have no excuse when coming before his judgment seat? But you say he shall not read his word, consequently his sin will be upon your head. I think every man has as much as he can do to answer for his own sins. And now my dear slave-holder, who with you are bound and fast hastening to judgment? As one that loves your soul repent ye, therefore, and be converted, that your sins may be blotted out when the time of refreshing shall come from the presence of the Lord.

In the language of the poet:

> Stop, poor sinner, stop and think,
>   Before you further go;
> Think upon the brink of death
>   Of everlasting woe.
> Say, have you an arm like God,
>   That you his will oppose?
> Fear you not that iron rod
>   With which he breaks his foes?

Is the prayer of one that loves your souls.   EDMUND TURNER.

N. B. The signature bears the name of one who knows and felt the sting of Slavery; but now, thanks be to God, I am now where the poisonous breath taints not our air, but every one is sitting under his own vine and fig tree, where none dare to make him ashamed or afraid.   EDMUND TURNER, formerly of Petersburg, Va.

HAMILTON, June 22d, 1858, C. W.

To MR. WM. STILL, DEAR SIR:—A favorable opportunity affords the pleasure of acknowledging the receipt of letters and papers; certainly in this region they were highly appreciated, and I hope the time may come that your kindness will be reciprocated we are al well at present, but times continue dull. I also deeply regret the excitement recently on the account of those slaves, you will favor me by keeping me posted upon the subject. Those words written to slaveholder is the thought of one who had sufferd, and now I thought it a duty incumbent upon me to cry aloud and spare not, &c., by sending these few lines where the slaveholder may hear. You will still further oblige your humble servant also, to correct any inaccuracy. My respects to you and your family and all inquiring friends.

Your friend and well wisher,   EDMUND TURNER.

The then impending judgments seen by an eye of faith as set forth in this "Warning," soon fell with crushing weight upon the oppressor, and Slavery died. But the old blind father of Jackson, Isaac and Edmondson, still lives and may be seen daily on the streets of Philadelphia; and though "halt, and lame, and blind, and poor," doubtless resulting from his early oppression, he can thank God and rejoice that he has lived to see Slavery abolished.

CROSSING THE RIVER ON HORSEBACK IN THE NIGHT.

ROBERT BROWN, ALIAS THOMAS JONES.

CROSSING THE RIVER ON HORSEBACK IN THE NIGHT.

In very desperate straits many new inventions were sought after by deep-thinking and resolute slaves, determined to be free at any cost. But it must here be admitted, that, in looking carefully over the more perilous methods resorted to, Robert Brown, alias Thomas Jones, stands second to none, with regard to deeds of bold daring. This hero escaped from Martinsburg, Va., in 1856. He was a man of medium size, mulatto, about thirty-eight years of age, could read and write, and was naturally sharp-witted. He had formerly been owned by Col. John F. Franic, whom Robert charged with various offences of a serious domestic character.

Furthermore, he also alleged, that his "mistress was cruel to all the slaves," declaring that "they (the slaves), could not live with her," that "she had to hire servants," etc.

In order to effect his escape, Robert was obliged to swim the Potomac river on horseback, on Christmas night, while the cold, wind, storm, and darkness were indescribably dismal. This daring bondman, rather than submit to his oppressor any longer, perilled his life as above stated. Where he crossed the river was about a half a mile wide. Where could be found in history a more noble and daring struggle for Freedom?

The wife of his bosom and his four children, only five days before he fled, were sold to a trader in Richmond, Va., for no other offence than simply "because she had resisted" the lustful designs of her master, being "true to her own companion." After this poor slave mother and her children were cast into prison for sale, the husband and some of his friends tried hard to find a purchaser in the neighborhood; but the malicious and brutal master refused to sell her—wishing to gratify his malice to the utmost, and to punish his victims all that lay in his power, he sent them to the place above named.

In this trying hour, the severed and bleeding heart of the husband resolved to escape at all hazards, taking with him a daguerreotype likeness of his wife which he happened to have on hand, and a lock of hair from her head, and from each of the children, as mementoes of his unbounded (though sundered) affection for them.

After crossing the river, his wet clothing freezing to him, he rode all night, a distance of about forty miles. In the morning he left his faithful horse tied to a fence, quite broken down. He then commenced his dreary journey on foot—cold and hungry—in a strange place, where it was quite unsafe to make known his condition and wants. Thus for a day or two, without food or shelter, he traveled until his feet were literally worn out, and in this condition he arrived at Harrisburg, where he found friends. Passing over many of the interesting incidents on the road, suffice it to say, he arrived safely in this city, on New Year's night, 1857, about two hours before day break (the telegraph having announced his coming from Harrisburg), having been a week on the way. The night he arrived was very cold; besides, the Underground train, that morning, was about three hours behind time; in waiting for it, entirely out in the cold, a member of the Vigilance Committee thought he was frosted. But when he came to listen to the story of the Fugitive's sufferings, his mind changed.

Scarcely had Robert entered the house of one of the Committee, where he was kindly received, when he took from his pocket his wife's likeness, speaking very touchingly while gazing upon it and showing it. Subsequently, in speaking of his family, he showed the locks of hair referred to, which he had carefully rolled up in paper separately. Unrolling them, he said, "this is my wife's;" "this is from my oldest daughter, eleven years old;" "and this is from my next oldest;" "and this from the next," "and this from my infant, only eight weeks old." These mementoes he cherished with the utmost care as the last remains of his affectionate family. At the sight of these locks of hair so tenderly preserved, the member of the Committee could fully appreciate the resolution of the fugitive in plunging into the Potomac, on the back of a dumb beast, in order to flee from a place and people who had made such barbarous havoc in his household.

His wife, as represented by the likeness, was of fair complexion, prepossessing, and good looking—perhaps not over thirty-three years of age.

ANTHONY LONEY, alias WILLIAM ARMSTEAD.

ANTHONY had been serving under the yoke of Warring Talvert, of Richmond, Va. Anthony was of a rich black complexion, medium size, about twenty-five years of age. He was intelligent, and a member of the Baptist Church. His master was a member of the Presbyterian Church and held family prayers with the servants. But Anthony believed seriously, that his master was no more than a "whitened sepulchre," one who was fond of saying, "Lord, Lord," but did not do what the Lord bade him, consequently Anthony felt, that before the Great Judge his "master's many prayers" would not benefit him, as long as he continued to hold his fellow-men in bondage. He left a father, Samuel Loney, and mother, Rebecca also, one sister and four brothers. His old father had bought himself and was free; likewise his mother, being very old, had been allowed to go free. Anthony escaped in May, 1857.

CORNELIUS SCOTT.

Cornelius took passage *per* the Underground Rail Road, in March, 1857, from the neighborhood of Salvington, Stafford county, Va. He stated that he had been claimed by Henry L. Brooke, whom he declared to be a "hard drinker and a hard swearer." Cornelius had been very much bleached by the Patriarchal Institution, and he was shrewd enough to take advantage of this circumstance. In regions of country where men were less critical and less experienced than Southerners, as to how the bleaching process was brought about, Cornelius Scott would have had no difficulty whatever in passing for a white man of the most improved Anglo-Saxon type. Although a young man only twenty-three years of age, and quite stout, his fair complexion was decidedly against him. He concluded, that for this very reason, he would not have been valued at more than five hundred dollars in the market. He left his mother (Ann Stubbs, and half brother, Isaiah), and traveled as a white man.

SAMUEL WILLIAMS, ALIAS JOHN WILLIAMS.

This candidate for Canada had the good fortune to escape the clutches of his mistress, Mrs. Elvina Duncans, widow of the late Rev. James Duncans, who lived near Cumberland, Md. He had very serious complaints to allege against his mistress, "who was a member of the Presbyterian Church." To use his own language, "the servants in the house were treated worse than dogs." John was thirty-two years of age, dark chestnut color, well made, prepossessing in appearance, and he "fled to keep from being sold." With the Underground Rail Road he was "highly delighted." Nor was he less pleased with the thought, that he had caused his mistress, who was "one of the worst women who ever lived," to lose twelve hundred dollars by him. He escaped in March, 1857. He did not admit that he loved slavery any the better for the reason that his master was a preacher, or that his mistress was the wife of a preacher. Although a common farm hand, Samuel had common sense, and for a long time previous had been watching closely the conduct of his mistress, and at the same time had been laying his plans for escaping on the Underground Rail Road the first chance.

$100 REWARD!—My negro man Richard has been missing since Sunday night, March 22d. I will give $100 to any one who will secure him or deliver him to me. Richard is thirty years old, but looks older; very short legs, dark, but rather bright color, broad cheek bones, a respectful and serious manner, generally looks away when spoken to, small moustache and beard (but he may have them off). He is a remarkably intelligent man, and can turn his hand to anything. He took with him a bag made of Brussels carpet, with my name written in large, rough letters on the bottom, and a good stock of coarse and fine clothes, among them a navy cap and a low-crowned hat. He has been seen about New Kent C. H., and on the Pamunky river, and is no doubt trying to get off in some vessel bound North.

April 18th, 1857.   J. W. RANDOLPH, Richmond, Va.

Even at this late date, it may perhaps afford Mr. R. a degree of satisfaction to know what became of Richard; but if this should not be the case, Richard's children, or mother, or father, if they are living, may possibly see these pages, and thereby be made glad by learning of Richard's wisdom as a traveler, in the terrible days of slave-hunting. Consequently here is what was recorded of him, April 3d, 1857, at the Underground Rail Road Station, just before a free ticket was tendered him for Canada. "Richard is thirty-three years of age, small of stature, dark color, smart and resolute. He was owned by Captain Tucker, of the United States Navy, from whom he fled." He was "tired of serving, and wanted to marry," was the cause of his escape. He had no complaint of bad treatment to make against his owner; indeed he said, that he had been "used well all his life." Nevertheless, Richard felt that this Underground Rail Road was the "greatest road he ever saw."

When the war broke out, Richard girded on his knapsack and went to help Uncle Sam humble Richmond and break the yoke.

BARNABY GRIGBY, ALIAS JOHN BOYER, AND MARY ELIZABETH, HIS WIFE; FRANK WANZER, ALIAS ROBERT SCOTT; EMILY FOSTER, ALIAS ANN WOOD.

(TWO OTHERS WHO STARTED WITH THEM WERE CAPTURED.)

All these persons journeyed together from Loudon Co., Va. on horseback and in a carriage for more than one hundred miles. Availing themselves of a holiday and their master's horses and carriage, they as deliberately started for Canada, as though they had never been taught that it was their duty, as servants, to "obey their masters." In this particular showing a most utter disregard of the interest of their "kind-hearted and indulgent owners." They left home on Monday, Christmas Eve, 1855, under the leadership of Frank Wanzer, and arrived in Columbia the following Wednesday at one o'clock. As willfully as they had thus made their way along, they had not found it smooth sailing by any means. The biting frost and snow rendered their travel anything but agreeable. Nor did they escape the gnawings of hunger, traveling day and night. And whilst these "articles" were in the very act of running away with themselves and their kind master's best horses and carriage—when about one hundred miles from home, in the neighborhood of Cheat river, Maryland, they were attacked by "six white men, and a boy," who, doubtless, supposing that their intentions were of a "wicked and unlawful character" felt it to be their duty in kindness to their masters, if not to the travelers to demand of them an account of themselves. In other words, the assailants

A BOLD STROKE FOR FREEDOM.

positively commanded the fugitives to "show what right" they possessed, to be found in a condition apparently so unwarranted.

The *spokesman* amongst the fugitives, affecting no ordinary amount of dignity, told their assailants plainly, that "no gentleman would interfere with persons riding along civilly"—not allowing it to be supposed that they were slaves, of course. These "gentlemen," however, were not willing to accept this account of the travelers, as their very decided steps indicated. Having the law on their side, they were for compelling the fugitives to surrender without further parley.

At this juncture, the fugitives verily believing that the time had arrived for the practical use of their pistols and dirks, pulled them out of their concealment—the young women as well as the young men—and declared they would not be "taken!" One of the white men raised his gun, pointing the muzzle directly towards one of the young women, with the threat that he would "shoot," etc. "Shoot! shoot!! shoot!!!" she exclaimed, with a double barrelled pistol in one hand and a long dirk knife in the other, utterly unterrified and fully ready for a death struggle. The male *leader* of the fugitives by this time had "pulled back the hammers" of his "pistols," and was about to fire! Their adversaries seeing the weapons, and the unflinching determination on the part of the *runaways* to stand their ground, "spill blood, kill, or die," rather than be "taken," very prudently "sidled over to the other side of the road," leaving at least four of the victors to travel on their way.

At this moment the four in the carriage lost sight of the two on horseback. Soon after the separation they heard firing, but what the result was, they knew not. They were fearful, however, that their companions had been captured.

The following paragraph, which was shortly afterwards taken from a Southern paper, leaves no room to doubt, as to the fate of the two.

☞ Six fugitive slaves from Virginia were arrested at the Maryland line, near Hood's Mill, on Christmas day, but, after a severe fight, four of them escaped and have not since been heard of. They came from Loudoun and Fauquier counties.

Though the four who were successful, saw no "severe fight," it is not unreasonable to suppose, that there was a fight, nevertheless; but not till after the number of the fugitives had been reduced to two, instead of six. As chivalrous as slave-holders and slave-catchers were, they knew the value of their precious lives and the fearful risk of attempting a capture, when the numbers were equal.

The party in the carriage, after the conflict, went on their way rejoicing.

The young men, one cold night, when they were compelled to take rest in the woods and snow, in vain strove to keep the feet of their female companions from freezing by lying on them; but the frost was merciless and bit them severely, as their feet very plainly showed. The following disjointed report was cut from the *Frederick (Md.) Examiner*, soon after the occurrence took place:

"Six slaves, four men and two women, fugitives from Virginia, having with them two spring wagons and four horses, came to Hood's Mill, on the Baltimore and Ohio Railroad, near the dividing line between Frederick and Carroll counties, on Christmas day. After feeding their animals, one of them told a Mr. Dixon whence they came; believing them to be fugitives, he spread the alarm, and some eight or ten persons gathered round to arrest them; but the negroes drawing revolvers and bowie-knives, kept their assailants at bay, until five of the party succeeded in escaping in one of the wagons, and as the last one jumped on a horse to flee, he was fired at, the load taking effect in the small of the back. The prisoner says he belongs to Charles W. Simpson, Esq., of Fauquier county, Va., and ran away with the others on the preceding evening."

This report from the *Examiner*, while it is not wholly correct, evidently relates to the fugitives above described. Why the reporter made such glaring mistakes, may be accounted for on the ground that the bold stand made by the fugitives was so bewildering and alarming, that the "assailants" were not in a proper condition to make correct statements. Nevertheless the *Examiner's* report was preserved with other records, and is here given for what it is worth.

These victors were individually noted on the Record thus: Barnaby was owned by William Rogers, a farmer, who was considered a "moderate slaveholder," although of late "addicted to intemperance." He was the owner of about one "dozen head of slaves," and had besides a wife and two children.

Barnaby's chances for making extra "change" for himself were never favorable; sometimes of "nights" he would manage to earn a "trifle." He was prompted to escape because he "wanted to live by the sweat of his own brow," believing that all men ought so to live. This was the only reason he gave for fleeing.

Mary Elizabeth had been owned by Townsend McVee (likewise a farmer), and in Mary's judgment, he was "severe," but she added, "his wife made him so." McVee owned about twenty-five slaves; "he hardly allowed them to talk—would not allow them to raise chickens," and "only allowed Mary three dresses a year;" the rest she had to get as she could. Sometimes McVee would sell slaves—last year he sold two. Mary said that she could not say anything good of her mistress. On the contrary, she declared that her mistress "knew no mercy nor showed any favor."

It was on account of this "domineering spirit," that Mary was induced to escape.

Frank was owned by Luther Sullivan, "the meanest man in Virginia," he said; he treated his people just as bad as he could in every respect. "Sullivan," added Frank, "would 'lowance the slaves and stint them to save food and get rich," and "would sell and whip," etc. To Frank's knowledge, he had sold some twenty-five head. "He sold my mother and her two children to Georgia some four years previous." But the motive which hurried Frank to make his flight was his laboring under the apprehension that his master had some "pretty heavy creditors who might come on him at any time." Frank, therefore, wanted to be from home in Canada when these gentry should make their visit. My poor mother has been often flogged by master, said Frank. As to his mistress, he said she was "tolerably good."

Ann Wood was owned by McVee also, and was own sister to Elizabeth. Ann very fully sustained her sister Elizabeth's statement respecting the character of her master.

The above-mentioned four, were all young and likely. Barnaby was twenty-six years of age, mulatto, medium size, and intelligent — his wife was about twenty-four years of age, quite dark, good-looking, and of pleasant appearance. Frank was twenty-five years of age, mulatto, and very smart; Ann was twenty-two, good-looking, and smart. After their pressing wants had been met by the Vigilance Committee, and after partial recuperation from their hard travel, etc., they were forwarded on to the Vigilance Committee in New York. In Syracuse, Frank (the leader), who was engaged to Emily, concluded that the knot might as well be tied on the U. G. R. R., although penniless, as to delay the matter a single day longer. Doubtless, the bravery, struggles, and trials of Emily throughout the journey, had, in his estimation, added not a little to her charms. Thus after consulting with her on the matter, her approval was soon obtained, she being too prudent and wise to refuse the hand of one who had proved himself so true a friend to Freedom, as well as so devoted to her. The twain were accordingly made one at the U. G. R. R. Station, in Syracuse, by Superintendent—Rev. J. W. Loguen. After this joyful event, they proceeded to Toronto, and were there gladly received by the Ladies' Society for aiding colored refugees.

The following letter from Mrs. Agnes Willis, wife of the distinguished Rev. Dr. Willis, brought the gratifying intelligence that these brave young adventurers, fell into the hands of distinguished characters and warm friends of Freedom:

TORONTO, 28th January, Monday evening, 1856.

MR. STILL, DEAR SIR:—I have very great pleasure in making you aware that the following respectable persons have arrived here in safety without being annoyed in any way after you saw them. The women, two of them, viz: Mrs. Greegsby and Mrs. Graham, have been rather ailing, but we hope they will very soon be well. They have been attended to by the Ladies' Society, and are most grateful for any attention they have received. The solitary person, Mrs. Graves, has also been attended to; also her box will be looked after. She is pretty well, but rather dull; however, she will get friends and feel more at home by and bye. Mrs. Wanzer is quite well; and also young William Henry Sanderson. They are all of them in pretty good spirits, and I have no doubt they will succeed in whatever business they take up. In the mean time the men are chopping

wood, and the ladies are getting plenty sewing. We are always glad to see our colored refugees safe here. I remain, dear sir, yours respectfully,   AGNES WILLIS,
Treasurer to the Ladies' Society to aid colored refugees.

For a time Frank enjoyed his newly won freedom and happy bride with bright prospects all around; but the thought of having left sisters and other relatives in bondage was a source of sadness in the midst of his joy. He was not long, however, in making up his mind that he would deliver them or "die in the attempt." Deliberately forming his plans to go South, he resolved to take upon himself the entire responsibility of all the risks to be encountered. Not a word did he reveal to a living soul of what he was about to undertake. With "twenty-two dollars" in cash and "three pistols" in his pockets, he started in the lightning train from Toronto for Virginia. On reaching Columbia in this State, he deemed it not safe to go any further by public conveyance, consequently he commenced his long journey on foot, and as he neared the slave territory he traveled by night altogether. For two weeks, night and day, he avoided trusting himself in any house, consequently was compelled to lodge in the woods. Nevertheless, during that space of time he succeeded in delivering one of his sisters and her husband, and another friend in the bargain. You can scarcely imagine the Committee's amazement on his return, as they looked upon him and listened to his "noble deeds of daring" and his triumph. A more brave and self-possessed man they had never seen.

He knew what Slavery was and the dangers surrounding him on his mission, but possessing true courage unlike most men, he pictured no alarming difficulties in a distance of nearly one thousand miles by the mail route, through the enemy's country, where he might have in truth said, "I could not pass without running the gauntlet of mobs and assassins, prisons and penitentiaries, bailiffs and constables, &c." If this hero had dwelt upon and magnified the obstacles in his way he would most assuredly have kept off the enemy's country, and his sister and friends would have remained in chains.

The following were the persons delivered by Frank Wanzer. They were his trophies, and this noble act of Frank's should ever be held as a memorial and honor. The Committee's brief record made on their arrival runs thus:

"August 18, 1856. Frank Wanzer, Robert Stewart, alias Gasberry Robison, Vincent Smith, alias John Jackson, Betsey Smith, wife of Vincent Smith, alias Fanny Jackson. They all came from Alder, Loudon county, Virginia."

Robert is about thirty years of age, medium size, dark chestnut color, intelligent and resolute. He was held by the widow Hutchinson, who was also the owner of about one hundred others. Robert regarded her as a "very hard mistress" until the death of her husband, which took place the Fall previous to his escape. That sad affliction, he thought, was the cause of a considerable change in her treatment of her slaves. But yet " nothing was said about freedom," on her part. This reticence Robert understood to mean, that she was still unconverted on this great cardinal principle at least. As he could see no prospect of freedom through her agency, when Frank approached him with a good report from Canada and his friends there, he could scarcely wait to listen to the glorious news; he was so willing and anxious to get out of slavery. His dear old mother, Sarah Davis, and four brothers and two sisters, William, Thomas, Frederick and Samuel, Violet and Ellen, were all owned by Mrs. Hutchinson. Dear as they were to him, he saw no way to take them with him, nor was he prepared to remain a day longer under the yoke; so he decided to accompany Frank, let the cost be what it might.

Vincent is about twenty-three years of age, very "likely-looking," dark color, and more than ordinarily intelligent for one having only the common chances of slaves.

He was owned by the estate of Nathan Skinner, who was "looked upon," by those who knew him, "as a good slave-holder." In slave property, however, he was only interested to the number of twelve head. Skinner "neither sold nor emancipated." A year and a half before Vincent escaped, his master was called to give an account of his stewardship, and there in the spirit land Vincent was willing to let him remain, without much more to add about him.

Vincent left his mother, Judah Smith, and brothers and sisters, Edwin, Angeline, Sina Ann, Adaline Susan, George, John and Lewis, all belonging to the estate of Skinner.

Vincent was fortunate enough to bring his wife along with him. She was about twenty-seven years of age, of a brown color, and smart, and was owned by the daughter of the widow Hutchinson. This mistress was said to be a " clever woman."

WILLIAM JORDON, ALIAS WILLIAM PRICE.

Under Governor Badger, of North Carolina, William had experienced Slavery in its most hateful form. True, he had only been twelve months under the yoke of this high functionary. But William's experience in this short space of time, was of a nature very painful.

Previous to coming into the governor's hands, William was held as the property of Mrs. Mary Jordon, who owned large numbers of slaves. Whether the governor was moved by this consideration, or by the fascinating charms of Mrs. Jordon, or both, William was not able to decide. But the governor offered her his hand, and they became united in wedlock. By this circumstance, William was brought into his unhappy relations with the Chief Magistrate of the State of North Carolina. This was the third time

9

the governor had been married. Thus it may be seen, that the governor was a firm believer in wives as well as slaves. Commonly he was regarded as a man of wealth. William being an intelligent piece of property, his knowledge of the governor's rules and customs was quite complete, as he readily answered such questions as were propounded to him. In this way a great amount of interesting information was learned from William respecting the governor, slaves, on the plantation, in the swamps, etc. The governor owned large plantations, and was interested in raising cotton, corn, and peas, and was also a practical planter. He was willing to trust neither overseers nor slaves any further than he could help.

The governor and his wife were both equally severe towards them; would stint them shamefully in clothing and food, though they did not get flogged quite as often as some others on neighboring plantations. Frequently, the governor would be out on the plantation from early in the morning till noon, inspecting the operations of the overseers and slaves.

In order to serve the governor, William had been separated from his wife by sale, which was the cause of his escape. He parted not with his companion willingly. At the time, however, he was promised that he should have some favors shown him;—could make over-work, and earn a little money, and once or twice in the year, have the opportunity of making visits to her. Two hundred miles was the distance between them.

He had not been long on the governor's plantation before his honor gave him distinctly to understand that the idea of his going two hundred miles to see his wife was all nonsense, and entirely out of the question. "If I said so, I did not mean it," said his honor, when the slave, on a certain occasion, alluded to the conditions on which he consented to leave home, etc.

Against this cruel decision of the governor, William's heart revolted, for he was warmly attached to his wife, and so he made up his mind, if he could not see her "once or twice a year even," as he had been promised, he had rather "die," or live in a "cave in the wood," than to remain all his life under the governor's yoke. Obeying the dictates of his feelings, he went to the woods. For ten months before he was successful in finding the Underground Road, this brave-hearted young fugitive abode in the swamps—three months in a cave—surrounded with bears, wild cats, rattle-snakes and the like.

While in the swamps and cave, he was not troubled, however, about ferocious animals and venomous reptiles. He feared only man!

From his own story there was no escaping the conclusion, that if the choice had been left to him, he would have preferred at any time to have encountered at the mouth of his cave a ferocious bear than his master, the governor of North Carolina. How he managed to subsist, and ultimately effected his escape, was listened to with the deepest interest, though the recital of these incidents must here be very brief.

After night he would come out of his cave, and, in some instances, would succeed in making his way to a plantation, and if he could get nothing else, he would help himself to a "pig," or anything else he could conveniently convert into food. Also, as opportunity would offer, a friend of his would favor him with some meal, etc. With this mode of living he labored to content himself until he could do better. During these ten months he suffered indescribable hardships, but he felt that his condition in the cave was far preferable to that on the plantation, under the control of his Excellency, the Governor. All this time, however, William had a true friend, with whom he could communicate; one who was wide awake, and was on the alert to find a reliable captain from the North, who would consent to take this "property," or "freight," for a consideration. He heard at last of a certain Captain, who was then doing quite a successful business in an Underground way. This good news was conveyed to William, and afforded him a ray of hope in the wilderness. As Providence would have it, his hope did not meet with disappointment ; nor did his ten months' trial, warring against the barbarism of Slavery, seem too great to endure for Freedom. He was about to leave his cave and his animal and reptile neighbors,—his heart swelling with gladness,—but the thought of soon being beyond the reach of his mistress and master thrilled him with inexpressible delight. He was brought away by Captain F., and turned over to the Committee, who were made to rejoice with him over the signal victory he had gained in his martyr-like endeavors to throw off the yoke, and of course they took much pleasure in aiding him. William was of a dark color, stout made physically, and well knew the value of Freedom, and how to hate and combat Slavery. It will be seen by the appended letter of Thomas Garrett, that William had the good luck to fall into the hands of this tried friend, by whom he was aided to Philadelphia :

WILMINGTON, 12th mo., 19th, 1855.

DEAR FRIEND, WILLIAM STILL :—The bearer of this is one of the twenty-one that I thought had all gone North ; he left home on Christmas day, one year since, wandered about the forests of North Carolina for about ten months, and then came here with those forwarded to New Bedford, where he is anxious to go. I have furnished him with a pretty good pair of boots, and gave him money to pay his passage to Philadelphia. He has been at work in the country near here for some three weeks, till taken sick ; he is, by no means, well, but thinks he had better try to get further North, which I hope his friends in Philadelphia will aid him to do. I handed this morning Captain Lambson's* wife twenty dollars to help fee a lawyer to defend him. She leaves this morning, with her child, for Norfolk, to be at the trial before the Commissioner on the 24th instant. Passmore Williamson agreed to raise fifty dollars for him. As none came to hand, and a good chance to send it by his wife, I thought best to advance that much.

Thy friend, THOS. GARRETT.

* Captain Lambson had been suspected of having aided in the escape of slaves from the neighborhood of Norfolk, and was in prison awaiting his trial.

JOSEPH GRANT AND JOHN SPEAKS.

It is to be regretted that, owing to circumstances, the account of these persons has not been fully preserved. Could justice be done them, probably their narratives would not be surpassed in interest by any other in the history of fugitives. In 1857, when these remarkable travelers came under the notice of the Vigilance Committee, as Slavery seemed likely to last for generations, and there was but little expectation that these records would ever have the historical value which they now possess, care was not always taken to prepare and preserve them. Besides, the cases coming under the notice of the Committee, were so numerous and so interesting, that it seemed almost impossible to do them anything like justice. In many instances the rapt attention paid by friends, when listening to the sad recitals of such passengers, would unavoidably consume so much time that but little opportunity was afforded to make any record of them. Particularly was this the case with regard to the above-mentioned individuals. The story of each was so long and sad, that a member of the Committee in attempting to write it out, found that the two narratives would take volumes. That all traces, of these heroes might not be lost, a mere fragment is all that was preserved.

The original names of these adventurers, were Joseph Grant and John Speaks. Between two and three years before escaping, they were sold from Maryland to John B. Campbell a negro trader, living in Baltimore, and thence to Campbell's brother, another trader in New Orleans, and subsequently to Daniel McBeans and Mr. Henry, of Harrison county, Mississippi.

Though both had to pass through nearly the same trial, and belonged to the same masters, this recital must be confined chiefly to the incidents in the career of Joseph. He was about twenty-seven years of age, well made, quite black, intelligent and self-possessed in his manner.

He was owned in Maryland by Mrs. Mary Gibson, who resided at St. Michael's on the Eastern Shore. She was a *nice woman* he said, but her property was under mortgage and had to be sold, and he was in danger of sharing the same fate.

Joseph was a married man, and spoke tenderly of his wife. She "promised" him when he was sold that she would "never marry," and earnestly entreated him, if he "ever met with the luck, to come and see her." She was unaware perhaps at that time of the great distance that was to divide them; his feelings on being thus sundered need not be stated. However, he had scarcely been in Mississippi three weeks, ere his desire to return to his wife, and the place of his nativity constrained him to attempt to return;

accordingly he set off, crossing a lake eighty miles wide in a small boat, he reached Kent Island. There he was captured by the watchman on the Island, who with *pistols, dirk and cutlass* in hand, threatened if he resisted that death would be his instant doom. Of course he was returned to his master.

He remained there a few months, but could content himself no longer to endure the ills of his condition. So he again started for home, walked to Mobile, and thence he succeeded in stowing himself away in a steamboat and was thus conveyed to Montgomery, a distance of five hundred and fifty miles through solid slave territory. Again he was captured and returned to his owners; one of whom always went for immediate punishment, the other being mild thought persuasion the better plan in such cases. On the whole, Joseph thus far had been pretty fortunate, considering the magnitude of his offence.

A third time he summoned courage and steered his course homewards towards Maryland, but as in the preceding attempts, he was again unsuccessful.

In this instance Mr. Henry, the harsh owner, was exasperated, and the mild one's patience so exhausted that they concluded that nothing short of stern measures would cause Joe to reform. Said Mr. Henry; "*I had rather lose my right arm than for him to get off without being punished, after having put us to so much trouble.*"

Joseph will now speak for himself.

"He (master) sent the overseer to tie me. I told him I would not be tied. I ran and stayed away four days, which made Mr. Henry very anxious. Mr. Beans told the servants if they saw me, to tell me to come back and I should not be hurt. Thinking that Mr. Beans had always stood to his word, I was over persuaded and came back. He sent for me in his parlor, talked the matter over, sent me to the steamboat (perhaps the one he tried to escape on.) After getting cleverly on board the captain told me, I am sorry to tell you, you have to be tied. I was tied and Mr. Henry was sent for. He came; 'Well, I have got you at last, beg my pardon and promise you will never run away again and I will not be so hard on you.' I could not do it. He then gave me three hundred lashes well laid on. I was stripped entirely naked, and my flesh was as raw as a piece of beef. He made John (the companion who escaped with him) hold one of my feet which I broke loose while being whipped, and when done made him bathe me in salt and water.

"Then I resolved to 'go or die' in the attempt. Before starting, one week, I could not work. On getting better we went to Ship Island; the sailors, who were Englishmen, were very sorry to hear of the treatment we had received, and counselled us how we might get free."

The counsel was heeded, and in due time they found themselves in Liverpool. There their stay was brief. Utterly destitute of money, education, and in a strange land, they very naturally turned their eyes again in the direction of their native land. Accordingly their host, the keeper of a sailor's boarding-house, shipped them to Philadelphia.

But to go back, Joseph saw many things in New Orleans and Mississippi of a nature too horrible to relate, among which were the following:

I have seen Mr. Beans whip one of his slaves to death, at the tree to which he was tied.

Mr. Henry would make them lie down across a log, stripped naked, and with every stroke would lay the flesh open. Being used to it, some would lie on the log without being tied.

In New Orleans, I have seen women stretched out just as naked as my hand, on boxes, and given one hundred and fifty lashes, four men holding them. I have helped hold them myself: when released they could hardly sit or walk. This whipping was at the " *Fancy House.*"

The "chain-gangs" he also saw in constant operation. Four and five slaves chained together and at work on the streets, cleaning, &c., was a common sight. He could hardly tell Sunday from Monday in New Orleans, the slaves were kept so constantly going.

WILLIAM N. TAYLOR.

ONE HUNDRED DOLLARS REWARD.—Ran away from Richmond City on Tuesday, the 2d of June, a negro man named WM. N. TAYLOR, belonging to Mrs. Margaret Tyler of Hanover county.

Said negro was hired to Fitzhugh Mayo, Tobacconist; is quite black, of genteel and easy manners, about five feet ten or eleven inches high, has one front tooth broken, and is about 35 years old.

He is supposed either to have made his escape North, or attempted to do so. The above reward will be paid for his delivery to Messrs. Hill and Rawlings, in Richmond, or secured in jail, so that I get him again.

JAS. G. TYLER, Trustee for Margaret Tyler.

June 8th &c2t—   *Richmond Enquirer, June 9, 57.*

William unquestionably possessed a fair share of common sense, and just enough distaste to Slavery to arouse him most resolutely to seek his freedom.

The advertisement of James G. Tyler was not altogether accurate with regard to his description of William; but notwithstanding, in handing William down to posterity, the description of Tyler has been adopted instead of the one engrossed in the records by the Committee. But as a simple matter of fair play, it seems fitting, that the description given by William, while on the Underground Rail Road, of his master, &c., should come in just here.

William acknowledged that he was the property of Walter H. Tyler, brother of EX-PRESIDENT TYLER, who was described as follows: " He (master) was about sixty-five years of age; was a barbarous man, very intemperate, horse racer, chicken-cock fighter and gambler. He had owned as high as forty head of slaves, but he had gambled them all away. He was a doctor, circulated high amongst southerners, though he never lived agreeably with his wife, would curse her and call her all kinds of names that he should not call a lady. From a boy of nine up to the time I was fifteen or sixteen, I don't reckon he whipped me less than a hundred times. He shot at me once with a double-barrelled gun.

"What made me leave was because I worked for him all my life-time and he never gave me but two dollars and fifteen cents in all his life. I was hired out this year for two hundred dollars, but when I would go to him to make complaints of hard treatment from the man I was hired to, he would say: "G—d d——n it, don't come to me, all I want is my money."

Mr. Tyler was a thin raw-boned man, with a long nose, the picture of the president. His wife was a tolerably well-disposed woman in some instances —she was a tall, thin-visaged woman, and stood high in the community. Through her I fell into the hands of Tyler. At present she owns about fifty slaves. His own slaves, spoken of as having been gambled away, came by his father—he has been married the second time."

Twice William had been sold and bought in, on account of his master's creditors, and for many months had been expecting to be sold again, to meet pressing claims in the hands of the sheriff against Tyler. He, by the way, "now lives in Hanover county, about eighteen miles from Richmond, and for fear of the sheriff, makes himself very scarce in that city."

At fourteen years of age, William was sold for eight hundred dollars; he would have brought in 1857, probably twelve hundred and fifty dollars; he was a member of the Baptist Church in good and regular standing.

LOUISA BROWN.

Louisa is a good-looking, well-grown, intelligent mulatto girl of sixteen years of age, and was owned by a widow woman of Baltimore, Md. To keep from being sold, she was prompted to try her fortune on the U. G. R. R., for Freedom in Canada, under the protection of the British Lion.

JACOB WATERS AND ALFRED GOULDEN.

Jacob is twenty-one years of age, dark chestnut color, medium size, and of prepossessing manners. Fled from near Frederick, Md., from the clutches of a farmer by the name of William Dorsey, who was described as a severe master, and had sold two of Jacob's sisters, South, only three years prior to his escape. Jacob left three brothers in chains.

ALFRED is twenty-three years of age, in stature quite small, full black, and bears the marks of ill usage. Though a member of the Methodist Church, his master, Fletcher Jackson, "thought nothing of taking the shovel to Alfred's head; or of knocking him, and stamping his head with the heels of his boots." Repeatedly, of late, he had been shockingly beaten. To escape those terrible visitations, therefore, he made up his mind to seek a refuge in Canada.

ARRIVAL FROM BALTIMORE.

JEFFERSON PIPKINS, ALIAS DAVID JONES, LOUISA PIPKINS, ELIZABETH BRIT, HAR-
RIET BROWN, ALIAS JANE WOOTON, GRACY MURRY, ALIAS SOPHIA SIMS,
EDWARD WILLIAMS, ALIAS HENRY JOHNSON, CHAS. LEE, ALIAS
THOMAS BUSHIER.

Six very clever-looking passengers, all in one party from Baltimore, Md., the first Sunday in April, 1853. Baltimore used to be in the days of Slavery one of the most difficult places in the South for even free colored people to get away from, much more for slaves. The rule forbade any colored person leaving there by rail road or steamboat, without such applicant had been weighed, measured, and then given a bond signed by unquestionable signatures, well known. Baltimore was rigid in the extreme, and was a never-failing source of annoyance, trouble and expense to colored people generally, and not unfrequently to slave-holders too, when they were travel- ing North with "colored servants." Just as they were ready to start, the "Rules" would forbid colored servants until the law was complied with. Parties hurrying on would on account of this obstruction "have to wait until their hurry was over." As this was all done in the interest of Slavery, the matter was not very loudly condemned. But, notwithstanding all this weighing, measuring and requiring of bonds, many travelers by the Under- ground Rail Road took passage from Baltimore.

The enterprising individual, whose name stands at the head of this nar- rative, came directly from this stronghold of Slavery. The widow Pipkins held the title deed for Jefferson. She was unfortunate in losing him, as she was living in ease and luxury off of Jefferson's sweat and labor. Louisa, Harriet and Grace owed service to Geo. Stewart of Baltimore; Edward was owned by Chas. Moondo, and Chas. Lee by the above Stewart.

Those who would have taken this party for stupid, or for know-nothings, would have found themselves very much mistaken. Indeed they were far from being dull or sleepy on the subject of Slavery at any rate. They had considered pretty thoroughly how wrongfully they, with all others in similar circumstances, had been year in and year out subjected to unrequited toil so resolved to leave masters and mistresses to shift for themselves, while they would try their fortunes in Canada.

Four of the party ranged in age from twenty to twenty-eight years of age, and the other two from thirty-seven to forty. The Committee on whom they called, rendered them due aid and advice, and forwarded them to the Committee in New York.

The following letter from Jefferson, appealing for assistance on behalf of his children in Slavery, was peculiarly touching, as were all similar letters. But the mournful thought that these appeals, sighs, tears and prayers would continue in most cases to be made till death, that nothing could be done directly for the deliverance of such sufferers was often as painful as the escape from the auction block was gratifying.

LETTER FROM JEFFERSON PIPKINS.

Sept. 28, 1856.

To Wm. Still. Sir:—I take the liberty of writing to you a few lines concerning my children, for I am very anxious to get them and I wish you to please try what you can do for me. Their names are Charles and Patrick and are living with Mrs. Joseph G. Wray Murphysborough Hartford county, North Carolina; Emma lives with a Lawyer Baker in Gatesville North Carolina and Susan lives in Portsmouth Virginia and is stopping with Dr. Collins sister a Mrs. Nash you can find her out by enquiring for Dr. Collins at the ferry boat at Portsmouth, and Rose a coloured woman at the Crawford House can tell where she is. And I trust you will try what you think will be the best way. And you will do me a great favour. Yours Respectfully,   Jefferson Pipkins.

P. S. I am living at Yorkville near Toronto Canada West. My wife sends her best respects to Mrs. Still.

SEVERAL ARRIVALS FROM DIFFERENT PLACES.

In order to economize time and space, with a view to giving an account of as many of the travelers as possible, it seems expedient, where a number of arrivals come in close proximity to each other, to report them briefly, under one head.

Henry Anderson, *alias* William Anderson. In outward appearance Henry was uninteresting. As he asserted, and as his appearance indicated, he had experienced a large share of " rugged " usage. Being far in the South, and in the hands of a brutal " Captain of a small boat," chances of freedom or of moderate treatment, had rarely ever presented themselves in any aspect. On the 3d of the preceding March he was sold to a negro trader—the thought of having to live under a trader was so terrible, he was moved to escape, leaving his wife, to whom he had only been married three months. Henry was twenty-five years of age, quite black and a little below the medium size.

He fled from Beaufort, North Carolina. The system of slavery in all the region of country whence Henry came, exhibited generally great brutality and cruelty.

CHARLES CONGO AND WIFE, MARGARET. Charles and his wife were fortunate in managing to flee together. Their attachment to each other was evidently true. They were both owned by a farmer, who went by the name of David Stewart, and resided in Maryland. As Charles' owner did not require their services at home, as he had more of that kind of stock than he had use for—he hired them out to another farmer—Charles for $105 per annum; how much for the wife they could not tell. She, however, was not blessed with good health, though she was not favored any more on that account. Charles' affection for his wife, on seeing how hard she had to labor when not well, aroused him to seek their freedom by flight. He resolved to spare no pains, to give himself no rest until they were both free. Accordingly the Underground Rail Road was sought and found. Charles was twenty-eight, with a good head and striking face, as well as otherwise well made; chestnut color and intelligent, though unable to read. Left two sisters in bondage. Margaret was about the same age as her husband, a nice-looking brown-skinned woman; worth $500. Charles was valued at $1200.

The atmosphere throughout the neighborhood where Charles and Margaret had lived and breathed, and had their existence, was heavily oppressed with slavery. No education for the freeman of color, much less for the slave. The order of the day was literally, as far as colored men were concerned : " No rights which white men were bound to respect."

CHASKEY BROWN, Wm. Henry Washington, James Alfred Frisley, and Charles Henry Salter. Chaskey is about twenty-four years of age, quite black, medium size, sound body and intelligent appearance, nevertheless he resembled a " farm hand " in every particular. His master was known by the name of Major James H. Gales, and he was the owner of a farm with eighteen men, women and children, slaves to toil for him. The Major in disposition was very abusive and profane, though old and grey-headed. His wife was pretty much the same kind of a woman as he was a man ; one who delighted in making the slaves tremble at her bidding. Chaskey was a member of the " Still Pond church," of Kent county, Md. Often Chaskey was made to feel the lash on his back, notwithstanding his good standing in the church. He had a wife and one child. In escaping, he was obliged to leave them both. Chaskey was valued at $1200.

WILLIAM HENRY was about 20 years of age, and belonged to Doctor B. Crain, of Baltimore, who hired him out to a farmer. Not relishing the idea of having to work all his life in bondage, destitute of all privileges, he resolved to seek a refuge in Canada. He left his mother, four sisters and two brothers.

JAMES is twenty-four years of age, well made, quite black and pretty shrewd. He too was unable to see how it was that he should be worked, and flogged, and sold, at the pleasure of his master and "getting nothing;" he "had rather work for himself." His master was a "*speckled-faced—pretty large stomach man*, but was not very abuseful." He only owned one other.

CHARLES HENRY is about thirty years of age, of good proportion, nice-looking and intelligent; but to rough usage he was no stranger. To select his own master was a privilege not allowed; privileges of all kinds were rare with him. So he resolved to flee. Left his mother, three sisters and five brothers in slavery. He was a member of "Albany Chapel," at Massey's Cross Roads, and a slave of Dr. B. Crain. Charles left his wife Anna, living near the head of Sassafras, Md. The separation was painful, as was everything belonging to the system of Slavery.

These were all gladly received by the Vigilance Committee, and the hand of friendship warmly extended to them; and the best of counsel and encouragement was offered; material aid, food and clothing were also furnished as they had need, and they were sent on their way rejoicing to Canada.

STEPHEN TAYLOR, Charles Brown, Charles Henry Hollis, and Luther Dorsey. Stephen was a fine young man, of twenty years of age; he fled to keep from being sold. He "supposed his master wanted money." His master was a "tall, spare-faced man, with long whiskers, very wicked and very quick-tempered," and was known by the name of James Smithen, of Sandy Hook, Harford county, Md. His wife was also a very "close woman." They had four children growing up to occupy their places as oppressors. Stephen was not satisfied to serve either old or young masters any longer, and made up his mind to leave the first opportunity. Before this watchful and resolute purpose the way opened, and he soon found it comparatively easy to find his way from Maryland to Pennsylvania, and likewise into the hands of the Vigilance Committee, to whom he made known fully the character of the place and people whence he had fled, the dangers he was exposed to from slave-hunters, and the strong hope he cherished of reaching free land soon. Being a young man of promise, Stephen was advised earnestly to apply his mind to seek an education, and to use every possible endeavor to raise himself in the scale of manhood, morally, religiously and intellectually; and he seemed to drink in the admonitions thus given with a relish. After recruiting, and all necessary arrangements had been made for his comfort and passage to Canada, he was duly forwarded. "One more slave-holder is minus another slave worth at least $1200, which is something to rejoice over," said Committee. Stephen's parents were dead; one brother was the only near relative he left in chains.

CHARLES BROWN was about twenty-five years of age, quite black, and bore the marks of having been used hard, though his stout and hearty appearance would have rendered him very desirable to a trader. He fled from William Wheeling, of Sandy Hook, Md. He spoke of his master as a "pretty bad man," who was "always quarreling," and "would drink, swear and lie." Left simply because he "never got anything for his labor." On taking his departure for Canada, he was called upon to bid adieu to his mother and three brothers, all under the yoke. His master he describes thus—

"His face was long, cheek-bones high, middling tall, and about twenty-six years of age." With this specimen of humanity, Charles was very much dissatisfied, and he made up his mind not to stand the burdens of Slavery a day longer than he could safely make his way to the North. And in making an effort to reach Canada, he was quite willing to suffer many things. So the first chance Charles got, he started, and Providence smiled upon his resolution; he found himself a joyful passenger on the Underground Rail Road, being entertained free, and receiving attentions from the Company all along the line through to her British Majesty's boundlessly free territory in the Canadas.

True, the thought of his mother and brothers, left in the prison house, largely marred his joy, as it did also the Committee's, still the Committee felt that Charles had gained his Freedom honorably, and at the same time, had left his master a poorer, if not a wiser man, by at least $1200.

CHARLES HENRY was a good-looking young man, only twenty years of age, and appeared to possess double as much natural sense as he would require to take care of himself. John Webster of Sandy Hook, claimed Charles' time, body and mind, and this was what made Charles unhappy. Uneducated as he was, he was too sensible to believe that Webster had any God-given right to his manhood. Consequently, he left because his master "did not treat him right." Webster was a tall man, with large black whiskers, about forty years of age, and owned Charles' two sisters. Charles was sorry for the fate of his sisters, but he could not help them if he remained. Staying to wear the yoke, he felt would rather make it worse instead of better for all concerned.

LUTHER DORSEY is about nineteen years of age, rather smart, black, well made and well calculated for a Canadian. He was prompted to escape purely from the desire to be "*free.*" He fled from a "very insulting man," by the name of Edward Schriner, from the neighborhood of Sairsville Mills, Frederick Co., Md. This Schriner was described as a "low chunky·man, with grum look, big mouth, etc.," and was a member of the German Reformed Church. "Don't swear, though might as well; he was so bad other ways."

LUTHER was a member of the Methodist church at Jones Hill. Left his father in chains; his mother had wisely escaped to Canada years back, when he was but a boy. Where she was then, he could not tell, but hoped to meet her in Canada.

ARRIVAL FROM RICHMOND.

JEREMIAH W. SMITH AND WIFE JULIA.

Richmond was a city noted for its activity and enterprise in slave trade. Several slave pens and prisons were constantly kept up to accommodate the trade. And slave auctions were as common in Richmond as dress goods auctions in Philadelphia; notwithstanding this fact, strange as it may seem, the Underground Rail Road brought away large numbers of passengers from Richmond, Petersburg and Norfolk, and not a few of them lived comparatively within a hair's breadth of the auction block. Many of those from these localities were amongst the most intelligent and respectable slaves in the South, and except at times when disheartened by some grave disaster which had befallen the road, as, for instance, when some friendly captain or conductor was discovered in aiding fugitives, many of the thinking bondmen were daily manœuvering and watching for opportunities to escape or aid their friends so to do. This state of things of course made the naturally hot blood of Virginians fairly boil. They had preached long and loudly about the contented and happy condition of the slaves,—that the chief end of the black man was to worship and serve the white man, with joy and delight, with more willingness and obedience indeed than he would be expected to serve his Maker. So the slave-holders were utterly at a loss to account for the unnatural desire on the part of the slaves to escape to the North where they affirmed they would be far less happy in freedom than in the hands of those so "kind and indulgent towards them." Despite all this, daily the disposition increased, with the more intelligent slaves, to distrust the statements of their masters especially when they spoke against the North. For instance if the master was heard to curse Boston the slave was then satisfied that Boston was just the place he would like to go to; or if the master told the slave that the blacks in Canada were freezing and starving to death by hundreds, his hope of trying to reach Canada was made tenfold stronger; he was willing to risk all the starving and freezing that the country could afford; his eagerness to find a conductor then would become almost painful.

The situations of Jeremiah and Julia Smith, however, were not considered very hard, indeed they had fared rather better than most slaves in Virginia, nevertheless it will be seen that they desired to better their condition, to keep off of the auction-block at least. Jeremiah could claim to have no mixture in his blood, as his color was of such a pure black; but with the way of the world, in respect to shrewdness and intelligence, he had evidently been actively conversant. He was about twenty-six years of age, and in stature only medium, with poor health.

The name of James Kinnard, whom he was obliged to call master and serve, was disgusting to him. Kinnard, he said, was a "close and severe man." At the same time he was not considered by the community "a hard man." From the age of fifteen years Jeremiah had been hired out, for which his owner had received from $50 to $130 per annum. In consequence of his master's custom of thus letting out Jeremiah, the master had avoided doctors' bills, &c. For the last two years prior to his escape, however, Jeremiah's health had been very treacherous, in consequence of which the master had been compelled to receive only $50 a year, sick or well. About one month before Jeremiah left, he was to have been taken on his master's farm, with the hope that he could be made more profitable there than he was in being hired out.

His owner had thought once of selling him, perhaps fearing that Jeremiah might unluckily die on his hands. So he put him in prison and advertised; but as he had the asthma pretty badly at that time, he was not saleable, the traders even declined to buy him.

While these troubles were presenting themselves to Jeremiah, Julia, his wife, was still more seriously involved, which added to Jeremiah's perplexities, of course.

Julia was of a dark brown color, of medium size, and thirty years of age. Fourteen years she had been the slave of A. Judson Crane, and under him she had performed the duties of nurse, chamber-maid, etc., "faithfully and satisfactorily," as the certificate furnished her by this owner witnessed. She actually possessing a certificate, which he, Crane, gave her to enable her to find a new master, as she was then about to be sold. Her master had experienced a failure in business. This was the reason why she was to be sold.

Mrs. Crane, her mistress, had always promised Julia that she should be free at her death. But, unexpectedly, as Mrs. Crane was on her journey home from Cape May, where she had been for her health the summer before Julia escaped, she died suddenly in Philadelphia. Julia, however, had been sold twice before her mistress' death; once to the trader, Reed, and afterwards to John Freeland, and again was on the eve of being sold. Freeland, her last owner, thought she was unhappy because she was denied the privilege of going home of nights to her husband, instead of being on hand at the beck and call of her master and mistress day and night. So the very day Julia and her husband escaped, arrangements had been made to put her up at auction a third time. But both Julia and her husband had seen enough of Slavery to leave no room to hope that they could ever find peace or rest so long as they remained. So there and then, they resolved to strike for Canada, via the Underground Rail Road. By a little good management, berths were procured for them on one of the Richmond steamers (berths not known to the officers of the boat), and they were safely landed in the hands of the Vigilance Committee, and a most agreeable interview was had.

The Committee extended to them the usual hospitalities, in the way of board, accommodations, and free tickets Canadaward, and wished them a safe and speedy passage. The passengers departed, exceedingly light-hearted, Feb. 1, 1854.

EIGHT ARRIVALS:

JAMES MASSEY, PERRY HENRY TRUSTY, GEORGE RHOADS, JAMES RHOADS,
GEORGE WASHINGTON, SARAH ELIZABETH RHOADS AND CHILD,
MARY ELIZABETH STEVENSON.

Doubtless there was a sensation in "the camp," when this gang was found missing.

JAMES was a likely-looking young man of twenty years of age, dark, tall, and sensible; and worth, if we may judge, about $1,600. He was owned by a farmer named James Pittman, a "crabid kind of a man," grey-headed, with a broken leg; drank very hard, at which times he would swear that he would "sell them all to Georgia;" this threat was always unpleasant to the ears of James, but it seemed to be a satisfaction to the master. Fearing that it would be put into execution, James thought he had better let no time be lost in getting on towards Canada, though he was entitled to his Freedom at the age of twenty-five. Left his father, four brothers and two sisters. Also left his wife, to whom he had been married the previous Christmas.

His master's further stock of slaves consisted of two women, a young man and a child. The name of his old mistress was Amelia. She was "right nice," James admitted. One of James' brothers had been sold to Georgia by Pittman, although he was also entitled to his Freedom at the age of twenty-five.

His near relatives left in bondage lived near Level Square, Queen Ann's county, Maryland. His wife's name was Henrietta. "She was free."

Interesting letter from James Massey to his wife. It was forwarded to the corresponding secretary, to be sent to her, but no opportunity was afforded so to do, safely.

ST. CATHARINES, C. W., April 24, 1857.

DEAR WIFE—I take this opertunity to inform you that I have Arive in St. Catharines this Eving, After Jorney of too weeks, and now find mysilf on free ground and wish that you was here with me But you are not here, when we parted I did not know that I should come away so soon as I did, But for that of causin you pain I left as I did, I hope that you will try to come. But if you cannot, write to me as soon as you can and tell me all that you can But dont be Desscuredged I was sorry to leave you, and I could not help it for you know that I promest see you to sister, But I was persuaded By Another man go part with it grived mutch, you must not think that I did not care for you. I cannot tell how I come, for I was some times on the earth and some times under the earth Do not Bee afraid to come But start and keep trying, if you are afrid fitch your tow sister with you for compeny and I will take care of you and treat you like a lady so long as you live. The talk of cold in this place is all a humbug, it is wormer here than it was there when I left, your father and mother has allways treated me like their own child I have no fault to find in them. I send my Respects to them Both and I hope that they will remember me in Prayer, if you make a start come to Philidelpa tell father and mother that I am safe and hope that they will not morn after me I shall ever Remember them. No more at present But yours in Body and mind, and if we no meet on Earth I hope that we shall meet in heven. Your husbern. Good night.

JAME MASEY.

PERRY was about thirty-one years of age, round-made, of dark complexion, and looked quite gratified with his expedition, and the prospect of becoming a British subject instead of a Maryland slave. He was not free, however, from the sad thought of having left his wife and three children in the *"prison house,"* nor of the fact that his own dear mother was brutally stabbed to the heart with a butcher knife by her young master, while he (Perry) was a babe; nor of a more recent tragedy by which a fellow-servant, only a short while before he fled, was also murdered by a stab in the groin from another young master. "Powerful bad" treatment, and "no pay," was the only reward poor Perry had ever received for his life services. Perry could only remember his having received from his master, in all, eleven cents. Left a brother and sister in Slavery. Perry was worth $1200 perhaps.

PERRY was compelled to leave his wife and three children—namely, Hannah (wife), Perry Henry, William Thomas and Alexander, who were owned by John McGuire, of Caroline county, Maryland. Perry was a fellow-servant of James Massey, and was held by the same owner who held James. It is but just, to say, that it was not in the Pittman family that his mother and his fellow-servant had been so barbarously murdered. These occurrences took place before they came into the hands of Pittman.

The provocation for which his fellow-servant was killed, was said to be very trifling. In a moment of rage, his young master, John Piper, plunged the blade of a small knife into Perry's groin, which resulted in his death twenty-six hours afterwards. For one day only the young master kept himself concealed, then he came forward and said he "did it in self-defense," and there the matter ended. The half will never be told of the barbarism of Slavery.

PERRY's letter subjoined, explains where he went, and how his mind was occupied with thoughts of his wife, children and friends.

ST. CATHARINES, C. W. June 21, 1857.

DEAR SIR.—I take this opportunity to inform you that I am well at present, and hope that these few lines may find you injoying the same Blessing, I have Been for some time now, But have not written to you Before, But you must Excuse me. I want you to give my Respects to all my inquiring friends and to my wife, I should have let you know But I was afraid and all three of .my little children too, P. H. Trusty if he was mine Wm. T. Trusty and to Alexander I have been A man agge But was assurd nuthin, H. Trusty, a hard grand citt. I should lic know how times is, Henry Turner if you get this keep it and read it to yourself and not let any one else But yourself, tell ann Henry, Samuel Henry, Jacob Bryant, Wm Claton, Mr James at Almira Receved at Mr Jones house the Best I could I have Been healthy since I arrived here. My Best Respect to all and my thanks for past favours. No more at present But Remain youre obedented Servent &c.

HENRY TRUSTY.

Please send me an answer as son as you get this, and oblige yours,

MR TRUSTY.

GEORGE RHOADS is a young man of twenty-five years of age, chestnut color, face round, and hating Slavery heartily. He had come from under the control of John P. Dellum a farmer, and a crabbed master, who "would swear very much when crossed, and would drink moderately every day," except sometimes he would " take a *spree*," and would then get pretty high. Withal he was a member of the Presbyterian church at Perryville, Maryland; he was a single man and followed farming. Within the last two or three years, he had sold a man and woman; hence, George thought it was time to take warning. Accordingly he felt it to be his duty to try for Canada, via Underground Rail Road. As his master had always declared that if one run off, he would sell the rest to Georgia, George very wisely concluded that as an effort would have to be made, they had better leave· their master with as " few as possible to be troubled with selling." Consequently, a consultation was had between the brothers, which resulted in the exit of a party of eight. The market price for George would be about $1400. A horrid example professed Christians set before the world, while holding slaves and upholding Slavery.

JAMES RHOADS, brother of George, was twenty-three years of age, medium size, dark color, intelligent and manly, and would doubtless have brought, in the Richmond market, $1700. Fortunately he brought his wife and child with him. James was also held by the same task-master who held George. Often had he been visited with severe stripes, and had borne his full share of suffering from his master.

GEORGE WASHINGTON, one of the same party, was only about fifteen years of age; he was tall enough, however, to pass for a young man of twenty. George was of an excellent, fast, dark color. Of course, mentally he was undeveloped, nevertheless, possessed of enough mother-wit to make good his escape. In the slave market he might have been valued at $800. George was claimed as the lawful property of Benjamin Sylves—a Presbyterian, who owned besides, two men, three girls, and a boy. He was "tolerable good " sometimes, and sometimes "bad." Some of the slaves supposed themselves to be on the eve of being emancipated about the time George left; but of this there was no certainty. George, however, was not among this hopeful number, consequently, he thought that he would start in time, and would be ready to shout for Freedom quite as soon as any other of his fellow-bondmen. George left a father and three sisters. Sarah Elizabeth Rhoads, wife of James Rhoads, was seventeen years of age, a tall, dark,

10

young woman, who had had no chances for mental improvement, except such as were usual on a farm, stocked with slaves, where learning to read the Bible was against the "rules." Sarah was a young slave mother with a babe (of course a slave) only eight months old. She was regarded as having been exceedingly fortunate in having rescued herself and child from the horrid fate of slaves.

MARY ELIZABETH STEPHENSON is a promising-looking young woman, of twenty years of age, chestnut color, and well made. Hard treatment had been her lot. Left her mother, two sisters and four brothers in bondage. Worth $1100.

Although these travelers were of the "field hand" class, who had never been permitted to see much off of the farm, and had been deprived of hearing intelligent people talk, yet the spirit of Freedom, so natural to man, was quite uppermost with all of them. The members of the Committee who saw them, were abundantly satisfied that these candidates for Canada would prove that they were able to "take care of themselves."

Their wants were attended to in the usual manner, and they were sent on their way rejoicing, the Committee feeling quite a deep interest in them. It looked like business to see so many passing over the Road.

CHARLES THOMPSON,

CARRIER OF "THE NATIONAL AMERICAN," OFF FOR CANADA.

The subjoined "pass" was brought to the Underground Rail Road station in Philadelphia by Charles, and while it was interesting as throwing light upon his escape, it is important also as a specimen of the way the "pass" system was carried on in the dark days of Slavery in Virginia:

> "NAT. AMERICAN OFFICE,
> Richmond, July 20th, 1857.
>
> Permit Charles to pass and repass from this office to the residence of Rev. B. Manly's on Clay St., near 11th, at any hour of the night for one month. WM. W. HARDWICK."

It is a very short document, but it used to be very unsafe for a slave in Richmond, or any other Southern city, to be found out in the evening without a legal paper of this description. The penalties for being found unprepared to face the police were fines, imprisonment and floggings. The satisfaction it seemed always to afford these guardians of the city to find either males or females trespassing in this particular, was unmistakable. It gave them (the police) the opportunity to prove to those they served (slaveholders), that they were the right men in the right place, guarding their interests. Then again they got the fine for pocket money, and likewise the still greater pleasure of administering the flogging. Who would want an office, if no opportunity should turn up whereby proof could be adduced of adequate qualifications to meet emergencies? But Charles was too wide awake to be caught without his pass day or night. Consequently he hung on to it, even after starting on his voyage to Canada. He, however, willingly surrendered it to a member of the Committee at his special request.

But in every way Charles was quite a remarkable man. It afforded. the Committee great pleasure to make his acquaintance, and much practical and useful information was gathered from his story, which was felt to be truthful.

The Committee feeling assured that this " chattel " must have been the subject of much inquiry and anxiety from the nature of his former position, as a prominent piece of property, as a member of the Baptist church, as taking " first premiums " in making tobacco, and as a paper carrier in the National American office, felt called upon to note fully his movements before and after leaving Richmond.

In stature he was medium size, color quite dark, hair long and bushy— rather of a raw-boned and rugged appearance, modest and self-possessed ; with much more intelligence than would be supposed from first observation. On his arrival, ere he had " shaken hands with the (British) Lion's paw," (which he was desirous of doing), or changed the habiliments in which he escaped, having listened to the recital of his thrilling tale, and wishing to get it word for word as it flowed naturally from his brave lips, at a late hour of the night a member of the Committee remarked to him, with pencil in hand, that he wanted to take down some account of his life. " Now," said he, " we shall have to be brief. Please answer as correctly as you can the following questions :" " How old are you ?" " Thirty-two years old the 1st day of last June." " Were you born a slave ?" " Yes." " How have you been treated ?" " Badly all the time for the last twelve years." " What do you mean by being treated badly ?" " Have been whipped, and they never give me anything ; some people give their servants at Christmas a dollar and a half and two dollars, and some five, but my master would never give me anything." " What was the name of your master ?" " Fleming Bibbs." " Where did he live ?" " In Caroline county, fifty miles above Richmond." " What did he do ?" " He was a farmer." " Did you ever live with him ?" " Never did ; always hired me out, and then I couldn't please him." " What kind of a man was he ?" " A man with a very severe temper ; would drink at all times, though would do it slyly." " Was he a member of any church ?" " Baptist church—would curse at his servants as if he wern't in any church." " Were his family members of church, too ?" " Yes." " What kind of family had he ?" " His wife was a tolerable fair woman, but his sons were dissipated, all of them *rowdies* and *gamblers. His sons has had children by the servants. One of his daughters had a child by his grandson last April.* They are traders, buy and sell."

"How many slaves did he own?" "Sam, Richmond, Henry, Dennis, Jesse, Addison, Hilliard, Jenny, Lucius, Julia, Charlotte, Easte, Joe, Taylor, Louisa, two more small children and Jim." Did any of them know that you were going to leave? "No, I saw my brother Tuesday, but never told him a word about it." "What put it into your head to leave?" "It was bad treatment; for being put in jail for sale the 7th of last January; was whipped in jail and after I came out the only thing they told me was that I had been selling newspapers about the streets, and was half free."

"Where did you live then?" "In Richmond, Va.; for twenty-two years I have been living out." "How much did your master receive a year for your hire?" "From sixty-five to one hundred and fifty dollars." "Did you have to find yourself?" "The people who hired me found me. The general rule is in Richmond, for a week's board, seventy-five cents is allowed; if he gets any more than that he has got to find it himself." "How about Sunday clothing?" "Find them yourself?" "How about a house to live in?" "Have that to find yourself." "Suppose you have a wife and family." "It makes no difference, they don't allow you anything for that at all." "Suppose you are sick who pays your doctor's bill?" "He (master) pays that." "How do you manage to make a little extra money?" "By getting up before day and carrying out papers and doing other jobs, cleaning up single men's rooms and the like of that." "What have you been employed at in Richmond?" "Been working in tobacco factory in general; this year I was hired at a printing-office. The National American. I carried papers." "Had you a wife?" "I did, but her master was a very bad man and was opposed to me, and was against my coming to his place to see my wife, and he persuaded her to take another husband in preference to me; being in his hands she took his advice." "How long ago was that?" "Very near twelve months; she got married last fall." "Had you any children?" "Yes." "How many?" "Five." "Where are they?" "Three are with Joel Luck, her master, one with his sister Eliza, and the other belongs to Judge Hudgins, of Bowling Green Court House." "Do you ever expect to see them again?" "No, not till the day of the Great I am!" "Did you ever have any chance of schooling?" "Not a day in my life." "Can you read?" "No, sir, nor write my own name." "What do you think of Slavery any how?" "I think it's a great curse, and I think the *Baptists* in *Richmond* will go to the deepest hell, if there is any, for they are so wicked they will work you all day and part of the night, and *wear cloaks and long faces,* and try to get all the work out of you they can by telling you about Jesus Christ. All the extra money you make they think you will give to hear talk about Jesus Christ. Out of their extra money they have to pay a white man *Five hundred dollars a year for preaching.*" "What kind of preaching does he give them?" "He tells them if they die in their sins they will go to hell; don't tell them any thing about their elevation; he would tell them to obey their masters and mistresses, for good servants make good masters." "Did you belong to the Baptist Church?" "Yes, Second Baptist Church." "Did you feel that the preaching you heard was the true Gospel?" "One part of it, and one part burnt me as bad as ever insult did. They would tell us that we must take money out of our pockets to send it to Africa, to enlighten the African race. I think that we were about as blind in Richmond as the African race is in Africa. All they want you to know, is to have sense enough to say master and mistress, and *run* like lightning, when they speak to you, to do exactly what they want you to do." "When you made up your mind to escape, where did you think you would go to?" "I made up my mind not to stop short of the British protection; to shake hands with the *Lion's* paw." "Were you not afraid of being captured on the way, of being devoured by the abolitionists, or of freezing and starving in Canada?" "Well, I had often thought that I would be in a bad condition to come here, without money and clothes, but I made up my mind to come, live or die." "What are your impressions from what little you have seen of Freedom?" "I think it is intended for all men, and all men ought to have it." "Suppose your master was to appear before you, and offer you the privilege of returning to Slavery or death on the spot, which would be your choice?" "*Die right there.* I made up my mind before I started." "Do you think that many of the slaves are anxious about their Freedom?" "The third part of them ain't anxious about it, because the white people have *blinded* them, telling about the North,—they *can't live here;* telling them that the people are worse off than they are there; they say that the 'niggers' in the North have no houses to live in, stand about freezing, dirty, no clothes to wear. They all would be very glad to get their time, but want to stay where they are." Just at this point of the interview, the hour of midnight admonished us that it was time to retire. Accordingly, said Mr. Thompson, "I guess we had better close," adding, if he "could only write, he could give seven volumes!" Also, said he, "give my best respects to Mr. W. W. Hardwicke, and Mr. Perry in the National American office, and tell them *I wish they will pay the two boys who carry the papers for me, for they are as ignorant of this matter as you are.*"

Charles was duly forwarded to Canada to shake hands with the Lion's paw, and from the accounts which came from him to the Committee, he was highly delighted. The following letter from him afforded gratifying evidence, that he neither forgot his God nor his friends in freedom:

DETROIT, Sept. 17, 1862.

DEAR BROTHER IN CHRIST :—It affords me the greatest pleasure imaginable in the time I shall occupy in penning these few lines to you and your dear loving wife; not because I can write them to you myself, but for the love and regard I have for you, for I never can forget a man who will show kindness to his neighbor when in distress. I remember when I was in distress and out of doors, you took me in; I was hungry, and you fed me; for these things God will reward you, dear brother. I am getting along as well as I can expect. Since I have been out here, I have endeavored to make every day tell for itself, and I can say, no doubt, what a great many men cannot say, that I have made good use of all the time that God has given me, and not one week has been spent in idleness. Brother William, I expect to visit you some time next summer to sit and have a talk with you and Mrs. Still. I hope to see that time, if it is God's will. You will remember me, with my wife, to Mrs. Still. Give my best respects to all inquiring friends, and believe me to be yours forever. Well wishes both soul and body. Please write to me sometimes.   C. W. THOMPSON.

BLOOD FLOWED FREELY.

ABRAM GALLOWAY AND RICHARD EDEN, TWO PASSENGERS SECRETED IN A VESSEL
LOADED WITH SPIRITS OF TURPENTINE. SHROUDS PREPARED TO PREVENT
BEING SMOKED TO DEATH.

The Philadelphia branch of the Underground Rail Road was not fortunate in having very frequent arrivals from North Carolina. Of course such of her slave population as managed to become initiated in the mysteries of traveling North by the Underground Rail Road were sensible enough to find out nearer and safer routes than through Pennsylvania. Nevertheless the Vigilance Committee of Philadelphia occasionally had the pleasure of receiving some heroes who were worthy to be classed among the bravest of the brave, no matter who they may be who have claims to this distinction.

In proof of this bold assertion the two individuals whose names stand at the beginning of this chapter are presented. Abram was only twenty-one years of age, mulatto, five feet six inches high, intelligent and the picture of good health. "What was your master's name?" inquired a member of the Committee. "Milton Hawkins," answered Abram. "What business did Milton Hawkins follow?" again queried said member. "He was chief engineer on the Wilmington and Manchester Rail Road" (not a branch of the Underground Rail Road), responded Richard. "Describe him," said the member. "He was a slim built, tall man with whiskers. He was a man of very good disposition. I always belonged to him; he owned three. He always said he would sell before he would use a whip. His wife was a very mean woman; she would whip contrary to his orders." "Who was your father?" was further inquired. "John Wesley Galloway," was the prompt response. "Describe your father?" "He was captain of a government vessel; he recognized me as his son, and protected me as far as he was allowed so to do; he lived at Smithfield, North Carolina. Abram's master, Milton Hawkins, lived at Wilmington, N. C." "What prompted you to escape?" was next asked. "Because times were hard and I could not come up with my wages as I was required to do, so I

HON. ABRAM GALLOWAY.

(Secreted in a vessel loaded with turpentine.)

thought I would try and do better." At this juncture Abram explained substantially in what sense times were hard, &c. In the first place he was not allowed to own himself; he, however, preferred hiring his time to serving in the usual way. This favor was granted Abram; but he was compelled to pay $15 per month for his time, besides finding himself in clothing, food, paying doctor bills, and a head tax of $15 a year.

Even under this master, who was a man of very good disposition, Abram was not contented. In the second place, he "always thought Slavery was wrong," although he had "never suffered any personal abuse." Toiling month after month the year round to support his master and not himself, was the one intolerable thought. Abram and Richard were intimate friends, and lived near each other. Being similarly situated, they could venture to communicate the secret feelings of their hearts to each other. Richard was four years older than Abram, with not quite so much Anglo-Saxon blood in his veins, but was equally as intelligent, and was by trade, a "fashionable barber," well-known to the ladies and gentlemen of Wilmington. Richard owed service to Mrs. Mary Loren, a widow. "She was very kind and tender to all her slaves." "If I was sick," said Richard, "she would treat me the same as a mother would." She was the owner of twenty, men, women and children, who were all hired out, except the children too young for hire. Besides having his food, clothing and doctor's expenses to meet, he had to pay the "very kind and tender-hearted widow" $12.50 per month, and head tax to the State, amounting to twenty-five cents per month. It so happened, that Richard at this time, was involved in a matrimonial difficulty. Contrary to the laws of North Carolina, he had lately married a free girl, which was an indictable offence, and for which the penalty was then in soak for him—said penalty to consist of thirty-nine lashes, and imprisonment at the discretion of the judge.

So Abram and Richard put their heads together, and resolved to try the Underground Rail Road. They concluded that liberty was worth dying for, and that it was their duty to strike for Freedom even if it should cost them their lives. The next thing needed, was information about the Underground Rail Road. Before a great while the captain of a schooner turned up, from Wilmington, Delaware. Learning that his voyage extended to Philadelphia, they sought to find out whether this captain was true to Freedom. To ascertain this fact required no little address. It had to be done in such a way, that even the captain would not really understand what they were up to, should he be found untrue. In this instance, however, he was the right man in the right place, and very well understood his business.

Abram and Richard made arrangements with him to bring them away; they learned when the vessel would start, and that she was loaded with tar, rosin, and spirits of turpentine, amongst which the captain was to secrete them. But here came the difficulty. In order that slaves might not be secreted in vessels, the slave-holders of North Carolina had procured the enactment of a law requiring all vessels coming North to be smoked.

To escape this dilemma, the inventive genius of Abram and Richard soon devised a safe-guard against the smoke. This safe-guard consisted in silk oil cloth shrouds, made large, with drawing strings, which, when pulled over their heads, might be drawn very tightly around their waists, whilst the process of smoking might be in operation. A bladder of water and towels were provided, the latter to be wet and held to their nostrils, should there be need. In this manner they had determined to struggle against death for liberty. The hour approached for being at the wharf. At the appointed time they were on hand ready to go on the boat; the captain secreted them, according to agreement. They were ready to run the risk of being smoked to death; but as good luck would have it, the law was not carried into effect in this instance, so that the "smell of smoke was not upon them." The effect of the turpentine, however, of the nature of which they were totally ignorant, was worse, if possible, than the smoke would have been. The blood was literally drawn from them at every pore in frightful quantities. But as heroes of the bravest type they resolved to continue steadfast as long as a pulse continued to beat, and thus they finally conquered.

The invigorating northern air and the kind treatment of the Vigilance Committee acted like a charm upon them, and they improved very rapidly from their exhaustive and heavy loss of blood. Desiring to retain some memorial of them, a member of the Committee begged one of their silk shrouds, and likewise procured an artist to take the photograph of one of them ; which keepsakes have been valued very highly. In the regular order of arrangements the wants of Abram and Richard were duly met by the Committee, financially and otherwise, and they were forwarded to Canada. After their safe arrival in Canada, Richard addressed a member of the Committee thus:

KINGSTON, July 20, 1857.

MR. WILLIAM STILL—*Dear Friend :*—I take the opertunity of wrighting a few lines to let you no that we air all in good health hoping thos few lines may find you and your family engoying the same blessing. We arived in King all saft Canada West Abram Galway gos to work this morning at $1 75 per day and John pediford is at work for mr george mink and i will opne a shop for my self in a few days My wif will send a daug-retipe to your cair whitch you will pleas to send on to me Richard Edons to the cair of George Mink Kingston C W   Yours with Respect,   RICHARD EDONS.

Abram, his comrade, allied himself faithfully to John Bull until Uncle Sam became involved in the contest with the rebels. In this hour of need Abram hastened back to North Carolina to help fight the battles of Freedom. How well he acted his part, we are not informed. We only know that, after the war was over, in the reconstruction of North Carolina, Abram was promoted to a seat in its Senate. He died in office only a few months since. The portrait is almost a "fac-simile."

JOHN PETTIFOOT.

Anglo-African and Anglo-Saxon were about equally mixed in the organization of Mr. Pettifoot. His education, with regard to books, was quite limited. He had, however, managed to steal the art of reading and writing, to a certain extent. Notwithstanding the Patriarchal Institution of the South, he was to all intents and purposes a rebel at heart, consequently he resolved to take a trip on the Underground Rail Road to Canada. So, greatly to the surprise of those whom he was serving, he was one morning inquired for in vain. No one could tell what had become of Jack no more than if he had vanished like a ghost. Doubtless Messrs. McHenry and McCulloch were under the impression that newspapers and money possessed great power and could, under the circumstances, be used with entire effect. The following advertisement is evidence, that Jack was much needed at the tobacco factory.

$100 REWARD—For the apprehension and delivery to us of a MULATTO MAN, named John Massenberg, or John Henry Pettifoot, who has been passing as free, under the name of Sydney. He is about 5 feet 6 or 8 inches high, spare made, bright, with a bushy head of hair, curled under and a small moustache. Absconded a few days ago from our Tobacco Factory.   McHENRY & McCULLOCH.
ju 16 3t.

Jack was aware that a trap of this kind would most likely be set for him, and that the large quantity of Anglo-Saxon blood in his veins would not save him. He was aware, too, that he was the reputed son of a white gentleman, who was a professional dentist, by the name of Dr. Peter Cards. The Doctor, however, had been called away by death, so Jack could see no hope or virtue in having a white father, although a "chivalric gentleman," while living, and a man of high standing amongst slave-holders. Jack was a member of the Baptist church, too, and hoped he was a good Christian; but he could look for no favors from the Church, or sympathy on the score of his being a Christian. He knew very well were it known, that he had the love of freedom in his heart, or the idea of the Underground Rail Road in his head, he would be regarded as having committed the "unpardonable sin." So Jack looked to none of these "broken reeds" in Richmond in the hour of his trial, but to Him above, whom he had not seen, and to the Underground Rail Road. He felt pretty well satisfied, that if Providence would aid him, and he could get a conductor to put him on the right road to Canada, he would be all right. Accordingly, he acted up to his best light, and thus he succeeded admirably, as the sequel shows.

"JOHN HENRY PETTIFOOT. John is a likely young man, quite bright in color and in intellect also. He was the son of Peter Cards, a dentist by profession, and a white man by complexion. As a general thing, he had been used 'very well;' had no fault to find, except this year, being hired to

McHenry & McCulloch, tobacconists, of Petersburg, Va., whom he found rather more oppressive than he agreed for, and supposing that he had 'no right' to work for any body for nothing, he 'picked up his bed and walked.' His mistress had told him that he was '*willed* free,' at her death, but John was not willing to wait her "motions to die."

He had a wife in Richmond, but was not allowed to visit her. He left one sister and a step-father in bondage. Mr. Pettifoot reached Philadelphia by the Richmond line of steamers, stowed away among the pots and cooking utensils. On reaching the city, he at once surrendered himself into the hands of the Committee, and was duly looked after by the regular acting members.

EMANUEL T. WHITE.

EMANUEL was about twenty-five years of age, with seven-eighths of white blood in his veins, medium size, and a very smart and likely-looking piece of property generally. He had the good fortune to escape from Edward H. Hubbert, a ship timber merchant of Norfolk, Va. Under Hubbert's yoke he had served only five years, having been bought by him from a certain Aldridge Mandrey, who was described as a "very cruel man," and would "rather fight than eat." "I have licks that will carry me to my grave, and will be there till the flesh rots off my bones," said Emanuel, adding that his master was a "*devil*," though a member of the Reformed Methodist Church. But his mistress, he said, was a "right nice little woman, and kept many licks off me." "If you said you were sick, he would whip it out of you." From Mandrey he once fled, and was gone two months, but was captured at Williamsburg, Va., and received a severe flogging, and carried home. Hubbert finally sold Emanuel to a Mr. Grigway of Norfolk; with Emanuel Mr. G. was pretty well suited, but his wife was not—he had "too much white blood in him" for her. Grigway and his wife were members of the Episcopal Church.

In this unhappy condition Emanuel found a conductor of the Underground Rail Road. A secret passage was secured for him on one of the Richmond steamers, and thus he escaped from his servitude. The Committee attended to his wants, and forwarded him on as usual. From Syracuse, where he was breathing quite freely under the protection of the Rev. J. W. Loguen, he wrote the following letter:

SYRACUSE, July 29, 1857.

MY DEAR FRIEND, MR. STILL:—I got safe through to Syracuse, and found the house of our friend, Mr. J. W. Loguen. Many thanks to you for your kindness to me. I wish to say to you, dear sir, that I expect my clothes will be sent to Dr. Landa, and I wish, if you please, get them and send them to the care of Mr. Loguen, at Syracuse, for me. He will be in possession of my whereabouts and will send them to me. Remember me to Mr. Landa and Miss Millen Jespan, and much to you and your family.

Truly Yours, MANUAL T. WHITE.

THE ESCAPE OF A CHILD FOURTEEN MONTHS OLD.

There is found the following brief memorandum on the Records of the Underground Rail Road Book, dated July, 1857 :

" A little child of fourteen months old was conveyed to its mother, who had been compelled to flee without it nearly nine months ago."

While the circumstances connected with the coming of this slave child were deeply interesting, no further particulars than the simple notice above were at that time recorded. Fortunately, however, letters from the good friends, who plucked this infant from the jaws of Slavery, have been preserved to throw light on this little one, and to show how true-hearted sympathizers with the Slave labored amid dangers and difficulties to save the helpless bondman from oppression. It will be observed, that both these friends wrote from Washington, D. C., the seat of Government, where, if Slavery was not seen in its worst aspects, the Government in its support of Slavery appeared in a most revolting light.

LETTER FROM " J. B."

WASHINGTON, D. C., July 12, 1857.

DEAR SIR :—Some of our citizens, I am told, lately left here for Philadelphia, three of whom were arrested and brought back.

I beg you will inform me whether two others—(I., whose wife is in Philadelphia, was one of them), ever reached your city.

To-morrow morning Mrs. Weems, *with her baby,* will start for Philadelphia and see you probably over night.   Yours Truly,   J. B.

" J. B." was not only a trusty and capable conductor of the Underground Rail Road in Washington, but was also a practical lawyer, at the same time. His lawyer-like letter, in view of the critical nature of the case, contained but few words, and those few naturally enough were susceptible of more than one construction.

Doubtless those styled " our citizens,"—" three of whom were arrested and brought back,"—were causing great anxiety to this correspondent, not knowing how soon he might find himself implicated in the " running off," etc. So, while he felt it to be his duty, to still aid the child, he was determined, if the enemy intercepted his letter, he should not find much comfort or information. The cause was safe in such careful hands. The following letters, bearing on the same case, are also from another good conductor, who was then living in Washington.

LETTERS FROM E. L. STEVENS.

WASHINGTON, D. C., July 8, 1857.

MY DEAR SIR :—I write you now to let you know that the children of E. are yet well, and that Mrs. Arrah Weems will start with one of them for Philadelphia to-morrow or next day. She will be with you probably in the day train. She goes for the purpose of making an effort to redeem her last child, now in Slavery. The whole amount necessary is raised, except about $300. She will take her credentials with her, and you can place the most implicit reliance on her statements. The story in regard to the Weems' family was published in Frederick Douglass' paper two years ago. Since then the two middle boys have been redeemed and there is only one left in Slavery, and he is in Alabama. The master has agreed to take for him just what he gave, $1100. Mr. Lewis Tappan has his letter and the money, except the amount specified. There were about $5000 raised in England to redeem this family, and they are now all free except this one. And there never was a more excellent and worthy family than the Weems' family. I do hope, that Mrs. W. will find friends who can advance the amount required.

Truly Yours,   E. L. STEVENS.

WASHINGTON, D. C., July 13th, 1857.

MY FRIEND:—Your kind letter in reply to mine about Arrah was duly received. As she is doubtless with you before this, she will explain all. I propose that a second journey be made by her or some one else, in order to take the other. They have been a great burden to the good folks here and should have been *at home* long ere this. Arrah will explain everything. I want, however, to say a word in her behalf. If there is a person in the world, that deserves the hearty co-operation of every friend of humanity, that person is Arrah Weems, who now, after a long series of self-sacrificing labor to aid others in their struggle for their God-given rights, solicits a small amount to redeem the last one of her own children in Slavery. Never have I had my sympathies so aroused in behalf of any object as in behalf of this most worthy family. She can tell you what I have done. And I do hope, that our friends in Philadelphia and New York will assist her to make up the full amount required for the purchase of the boy.

After she does what she can in P., will you give her the proper direction about getting to New York and to Mr. Tappan's? Inform him of what she has done, &c.

Please write me as soon as you can as to whether she arrived safely, &c. Give me your opinion, also, as to the proposal about the other. Had you not better keep the little one in P. till the other is taken there? Inform me also where E. is, how she is getting along, &c., who living with, &c.   Yours Truly,   E. L. S.

In this instance, also, as in the case of "J. B.," the care and anxiety of other souls, besides this child, crying for deliverance, weighed heavily on the mind of Mr. Stevens, as may be inferred from certain references in his letters. Mr. Stevens' love of humanity, and impartial freedom, even in those dark days of Slavery, when it was both unpopular and unsafe to allow the cries of the bondman to awaken the feeling of humanity to assist the suffering, was constantly leading him to take sides with the oppressed, and as he appears in this correspondence, so it was his wont daily to aid the helpless, who were all around him. Arrah Weems, who had the care of the child, alluded to so touchingly by Mr. Stevens, had known, to her heart's sorrow, how intensely painful it was to a mother's feelings to have her children torn from her by a cruel master and sold. For Arrah had had a number of children sold, and was at that very time striving diligently to raise money to redeem the last one of them. And through such kind-hearted friends as Mr. Stevens, the peculiar hardships of this interesting family of Weems' were brought to the knowledge of thousands of philanthropists in this country and England, and liberal contributions had already been made by friends of the Slave on both sides of the ocean. It may now be seen, that while this child had not been a conscious sufferer from the wicked system of Slavery, it had been the object of very great anxiety and suffering to several persons, who had individually perilled their own freedom for its redemption. This child, however, was safely brought to the Vigilance Committee, in Philadelphia, and was duly forwarded, *via* friends in New York, to its mother, in Syracuse, where she had stopped to work and wait for her little one, left behind at the time she escaped.

ESCAPE OF A YOUNG SLAVE MOTHER.

LEFT HER LITTLE BABY-BOY, LITTLE GIRL AND HUSBAND BEHIND.

She anxiously waits their coming in Syracuse, N. Y. Not until after the foregoing story headed, the " Escape of a Child," etc., had been put into the hands of the printer and was in type, was the story of the mother discovered, although it was among the records preserved. Under changed names, in many instances, it has been found to be no easy matter to cull from a great variety of letters, records and advertisements, just when wanted, all the particulars essential to complete many of these narratives. The case of the child, alluded to above, is a case in point. Thus, however, while it is impossible to introduce the mother's story in its proper place, yet, since it has been found, it is too important and interesting to be left out. It is here given as follows:

$300 REWARD.—RAN AWAY from the subscriber on Saturday, the 30th of August, 1856, my SERVANT WOMAN, named EMELINE CHAPMAN, about 25 years of age; quite dark, slender built, speaks short, and stammers some; with two children, one a female about two and a half years old; the other a male, seven or eight months old, bright color. I will give the above reward if they are delivered to me in Washington. MRS. EMILY THOMPSON, s23-TU, Th&st Capitol Hill, Washington, D. C.

Emeline Chapman, so particularly described in the " Baltimore Sun" of the 23d of September, 1856, arrived by the regular Underground Rail Road train from Washington. In order to escape the responsibility attached to her original name, she adopted the name of Susan Bell. Thus for freedom she was willing to forego her name, her husband, and even her little children. It was a serious sacrifice; but she had been threatened with the auction block, and she well understood what that meant. With regard to usage, having lived away from her owner, Emeline did not complain of any very hard times. True, she had been kept at work very constantly, and her owner had very faithfully received all her hire. Emeline had not even been allowed enough of her hire to find herself in clothing, or anything for the support of her two children—for these non-essentials, her kind mistress allowed her to seek elsewhere, as best she could. Emeline's husband was named John Henry; her little girl she called Margaret

Ann, and her babe she had named after its father, all with the brand of Slavery upon them. The love of freedom, in the breast of this spirited young Slave-wife and mother, did not extinguish the love she bore to her husband and children, however otherwise her course, in leaving them, as she did, might appear. For it was just this kind of heroic and self-sacrificing struggle, that appealed to the hearts of men and compelled attention. The letters of Biglow and Stevens, relative to the little child, prove this fact, and additional testimony found in the appended letter from Rev. J. W. Loguen conclusively confirms the same. Indeed, who could close his eyes and ears to the plaintive cries of such a mother? Who could refrain from aiding on to freedom children honored in such a heroic parent?

SYRACUSE, Oct. 5, 1856.

DEAR FRIEND STILL :—I write to you for Mrs. Susan Bell, who was at your city some time in September last. She is from Washington city. She left her dear little children behind (two children). She is stopping in our city, and wants to hear from her children very much indeed. She wishes to know if you have heard from Mr. Biglow, of Washington city. She will remain here until she can hear from you. She feels very anxious about her children, I will assure you. I should have written before this, but I have been from home much of the time since she came to our city. She wants to know if Mr. Biglow has heard anything about her husband. If you have not written to Mr. Biglow, she wishes you would. She sends her love to you and your dear family. She says that you were all kind to her, and she does not forget it. You will direct your letter to me, dear brother, and I will see that she gets it.

Miss F. E. Watkins left our house yesterday for Ithaca, and other places in that part of the State. Frederick Douglass, Wm. J. Watkins and others were with us last week ; Gerritt Smith with others. Miss Watkins is doing great good in our part of the State. We think much indeed of her. She is such a good and glorious speaker, that we are all charmed with her. We have had thirty-one fugitives in the last twenty-seven days; but you, no doubt, have had many more than that. I hope the good Lord may bless you and spare you long to do good to the hunted and outraged among our brethren.

Yours truly,   J. W. LOGUEN,
                    Agent of the Underground Rail Road.

SAMUEL W. JOHNSON.

ARRIVAL FROM THE "DAILY DISPATCH" OFFICE.

"SAM" was doing Slave labor at the office of the Richmond "Daily Dispatch," as a carrier of that thoroughly pro-slavery sheet. "Sam" had possessed himself somehow of a knowledge of reading and writing a little, and for the news of the day he had quite an itching ear. Also with regard to his freedom he was quite solicitous. Being of an ambitious turn of mind, he hired his time, for which he paid his master $175 per annum in regular quarterly payments. Besides paying this amount, he had to find himself in board, clothing, and pay doctor's expenses. He had had more than one owner in his life. The last one, however, he spoke of thus: "His name is

James B. Foster, of Richmond, a very hard man. He owns three more Slaves besides myself." In escaping, "Sam" was obliged to leave his wife, who was owned by Christian Bourdon. His attachment to her, judging from his frequent warm expressions of affection, was very strong. But, as strong as it was, he felt that he could not consent to remain in slavery any longer. "Sam" had luckily come across a copy of Uncle Tom's Cabin, and in perusing it, all his notions with regard to "Masters and Servants," soon underwent an entire change, and he began to cast his eyes around him to see how he might get his freedom. One who was thoroughly awake as he was to the idea of being free, with a fair share of courage, could now and then meet with the opportunity to escape by the steamers or schooners coming North. Thus Samuel found the way open and on one of the steamers came to Philadelphia. On arriving, he was put at once in the charge of the Committee. While in their hands he seemed filled with astonishment at his own achievements, and such spontaneous expressions as naturally flowed from his heart thrilled and amazed his new found friends, and abundant satisfaction was afforded, that Samuel Washington Johnson would do no discredit to his fugitive comrades in Canada. So the Committee gladly aided him on his journey.

After arriving in Canada, Samuel wrote frequently and intelligently. The subjoined letter to his wife shows how deeply he was attached to her, and, at the same time, what his views were of Slavery. The member of the Committee to whom it was sent with the request, that it should be forwarded to her, did not meet with the opportunity of doing so. A copy of it was preserved with other Underground Rail Road documents.

LETTER FROM SAMUEL W. JOHNSON TO HIS WIFE.

My Dear Wife I now embrace this golden opportunity of writing a few Lines to inform you that I am well at present engoying good health and hope that these few lines may find you well also My dearest wife I have Left you and now I am in a foreign land about fourteen hundred miles from you but though my wife my thoughts are upon you all the time My dearest Frances I hope you will remember me now gust as same as you did when I were there with you because my mind are with you night and day the Love that I bear for you in my breast is greater than I thought it was if I had thought I had so much Love for you I dont think I ever could Left being I have escape I and has fled into a land of freedom I can but stop and look over my past Life and say what a fool I was for staying in bondage as Long My dear wife I dont want you to get married before you send me some letters because I never shall get married until I see you again My mind dont deceive and it appears to me as if I shall see you again at my time of writing this letter I am desitute of money I have not got in no business yet but when I do get into business I shall write you and also remember you Tell my Mother and Brother and all enquiring friends that I am now safe in free state I cant tell where I am at present but Direct your Letters to Mr. William Still in Philadelphia and I will get them Answer this as soon as you can if you please for if you write the same day you receive it it will take a fortnight to reach me No more to relate at present but still remain your affectionate husband Mr. Still please defore this piece out if you please

SAMUEL WASHINGTON JOHNSON.

Whether Samuel ever met with the opportunity of communicating with his wife, the writer cannot say. But of all the trials which Slaves had to endure, the separations of husbands and wives were the most difficult to bear up under. Although feeling keenly the loss of his wife, Samuel's breast swelled with the thought of freedom, as will be seen from the letter which he wrote immediately after landing in Canada:

ST. CATHARINE, UPPER CANADA WEST.

MR. WILLIAM STILL :—I am now in safety   I arrived at home safe on the 11th inst at 12 o'clock M.   So I hope that you will now take it upon yourself to inform me something of that letter I left at your house that night when I left there and write me word how you are and how is your wife   I wish you may excuse this letter for I am so full that I cannot express my mind at all   I am only got $1.50 and I feel as if I had an independent fortune but I dont want you to think that I am going to be idle because I am on free ground and I shall always work though I am not got nothing to do at present   Direct your letter to the post office as soon as possible.

SAMUEL W. JOHNSON.

FAMILY FROM BALTIMORE.

STEPHEN AMOS, *alias* HENRY JOHNSON, HARRIET, *alias* MARY JANE JOHNSON (man and wife), and their four children, ANN REBECCA, WM. H., ELIZABETH and MARY ELLEN. Doubtless, in the eyes of a Slaveholder, a more "likely-looking" family could not readily be found in Baltimore, than the one to be now briefly noticed. The mother and her children were owned by a young slave-holder, who went by the name of William Giddings, and resided in Prince George's county, Md. Harriet acknowledged, that she had been treated "tolerably well in earlier days" for one in her condition; but, as in so many instances in the experience of Slaves, latterly, times had changed with her and she was compelled to serve under a new master who oft-times treated her "very severely." On one occasion, seven years previously, a brother of her owner for a trifling offence struck and kicked her so brutally, that she was immediately thrown into a fit of sickness, which lasted "all one summer"—from this she finally recovered.

On another occasion, about one year previous to her escape, she was seized by her owner and thrust into prison to be sold. In this instance the interference of the Uncle of Harriet's master saved her from the auction block. The young master, was under age, and at the same time under the guardianship of his Uncle. The young master had early acquired an ardent taste for fast horses, gambling, etc. Harriet felt, that her chances for the future in the hands of such a brutal master could not be other than miserable. Her husband had formerly been owned by John S. Giddings, who was said to have been a "mild man." He had allowed Stephen (her husband) to buy himself, and for eighteen months prior to the flight, he had been what was called a free man. It should also be further stated in justice to Stephen's master, that he was so disgusted with the manner in which Stephen's wife was treated, that he went so far as to counsel Stephen to escape with his wife and children. Here at least is one instance where a Maryland slave-holder lends his influence to the Underground Rail Road cause. The counsel was accepted, and the family started on their perilous flight. And although they necessarily had manifest trials and difficulties to discourage and beset them, they battled bravely with all these odds and reached the Vigilance Committee safely. Harriet was a bright mulatto, with marked features of character, and well made, with good address and quite intelligent. She was about twenty-six years of age. The children also were remarkably fine-looking little creatures, but too young to know the horrors of Slavery. The Committee at once relieved them of their heavy load of anxiety by cheering words and administering to their necessities with regard to food, money, etc. After the family had somewhat recovered from the fatigue and travel-worn condition in which they arrived, and were prepared to resume their journey, the Committee gave them the strictest caution with regard to avoiding slave-hunters, and also in reference to such points on the road where they would be most in danger of going astray from a lack of knowledge of the way. Then, with indescribable feelings of sympathy, free tickets were tendered them, and they having been conducted to the depot, were sent on their way rejoicing.

ELIJAH HILTON.

FROM RICHMOND.

After many years of hard toiling for the support of others, the yoke pressed so heavily upon Elijah's shoulders, that he could not endure Slave life any longer. In the hope of getting rid of his bondage, by dexterous management and a resolute mind, which most determined and thoughtful men exercise when undertaking to accomplish great objects, he set about contriving to gain his freedom. In proof of Elijah's truthfulness, the advertisement of Mr. R. J. Christians is here offered, as taken from a Richmond paper, about the time that Elijah passed through Philadelphia on the Underground Rail Road, in 1857.

 RAN AWAY—$500 REWARD.—Left the Tobacco Factory of the subscriber, on the 14th inst., on the pretence of being sick, a mulatto man, named ELIJAH, the property of Maj. Edward Johnson, of Chesterfield county. He is about 5 feet 8 or 10 inches high, spare made, bushy hair, and very genteel appearance; he is supposed to be making his way North. The above reward will be paid if delivered at my factory.   Ro. J. CHRISTIANS.
jy 21—ts.

From his infancy up to the hour of his escape, not a breath of free air

11

had he ever been permitted to breathe. He was first owned by Mrs. Caroline Johnson, "a stingy widow, the owner of about fifty slaves, and a member of Dr. Plummer's church." Elijah, at her death, was willed to her son, Major Johnson, who was in the United States service. Elijah spoke of him as a "favorable man," but added, "I'd rather be free. I believe I can treat myself better than he can or anybody else." For the last nineteen years he had been hired out, sometimes as waiter, sometimes in a tobacco factory, and for five years in the *Coal Mines.*

At the mines he was treated very brutally, but at Cornelius Hall's Tobacco factory, the suffering he had to endure seems almost incredible. The poor fellow, with the scars upon his person and the unmistakable earnestness of his manner, only needed to be seen and heard to satisfy the most incredulous of the truth of his story. For refusing to be flogged, one time at Hall's Factory, the overseer, in a rage, "took up a hickory club" and laid his head "open on each side." Overpowered and wounded, he was stripped naked and compelled to receive THREE HUNDRED LASHES, by which he was literally excoriated from head to foot. For six months afterwards he was "laid up." Last year he was hired out for "one hundred and eighty dollars," out of which he "received but five dollars." This year he brought "one hundred and ninety dollars." Up to the time he escaped, he had received "two dollars," and the promise of "more at Christmas." Left brothers and sisters, all ignorant of his way of escape. The following pass brought away by Elijah speaks for itself, and will doubtless be interesting to some of our readers who are ignorant of what used to be Republican usages in the "land of the Free."

RICHMOND, July 3d, 1857.

Permit the Bearer *Elijah* to pass to and from my FACTORY, to *Frederick Williams,*
　　In the Vallie,
for one month, untill 11 o'clock at night.
　　　　　　　　　　　　　　　　　　　　By *A. B. Wells,*
　　　　　　　　　　　　　　　　　　　　R. J. CHRISTIAN.

[PINE APPLE FACTORY.]

As usual, the Vigilance Committee tendered aid to Elijah, and forwarded him on to Canada, whence he wrote back as follows:

TORONTO, Canada West, July 28.

Dear friend in due respect to your humanity and nobility I now take my pen in hand to inform you of my health I am enjoying a reasonable proportion of health at this time and hope when these few lines come to hand they may find you and family the same dear Sir I am in Toronto and are working at my ole branch of business with meny of my friends I want you to send those to toronto to Mr Tueharts on Edward St what I have been talking about is my Clothes I came from Richmond Va and expect my things to come to you So when they come to you then you will send them to Jesse Tuehart Edward St no 43.

I must close by saying I have no more at present I still remain your brother,
　　　　　　　　　　　　　　　　　　　　ELIJAH HILTON.

SOLOMON BROWN.

ARRIVED PER CITY OF RICHMOND.

This candidate for Canada managed to secure a private berth on the steam-ship City of Richmond. He was thus enabled to leave his old mistress, Mary A. Ely, in Norfolk, the place of her abode, and the field of his servi-tude. Solomon was only twenty-two years of age, rather under the medium size, dark color, and of much natural ability. He viewed Slavery as a great hardship, and for a length of time had been watching for an opportunity to free himself. He had been in the habit of hiring his time of his mistress, for which he , paid ten dollars per month. This amount failed to satisfy the mistress, as she was inclined to sell him to North Carolina, where Slave stock, at that time, was commanding high prices. The idea of North Carolina and a new master made Solomon rather nervous, and he was thereby prompted to escape. On reaching the Committee he manifested very high appreciation of the attention paid him, and after duly resting for a day, he was sent on his way rejoicing. Seven days after leaving Phila-delphia, he wrote back from Canada as follows:

ST. CATHARINES, Feb. 20th, 1854.

MR. STILL—DEAR SIR :—It is with great pleasure that I have to inform you, that I have arrived safe in a land of freedom. Thanks to kind friends that helped me here. Thank God that I am treading on free soil. I expect to go to work to-morrow in a steam factory.

I would like to have you, if it is not too much trouble, see Mr. Minhett, the steward on the boat that I came out on, when he gets to Norfolk, to go to the place where my clothes are, and bring them to you, and you direct them to the care of Rev. Hiram Wilson, St. Catharines, Niagara District, Canada West, by rail-road via Suspension Bridge. You men-tioned if I saw Mr. Foreman. I was to deliver a message—he is not here. I saw two yesterday in church, from Norfolk, that I had known there. You will send my name, James Henry, as you knew me by that name; direct my things to James Henry. My love to your wife and children.

Yours Respectfully, SOLOMON BROWN.

WILLIAM HOGG, ALIAS JOHN SMITH.

TRAVELER FROM MARYLAND.

WILLIAM fled from Lewis Roberts, who followed farming in Baltimore county, Md. In speaking of him, William gave him the character of being a "fierce and rough man," who owned nine head of slaves. Two of Wil-liam's sisters were held by Roberts, when he left. His excuse for running away was, "ill-treatment." In traveling North, he walked to Columbia (in Pennsylvania), and there took the cars for Philadelphia. The Committee took charge of him, and having given him the usual aid, sent him hopefully on his way. After safely reaching Canada, the thought of his wife in a land of bondage, pressed so deeply upon his mind, that he was prompted to make an effort to rescue her. The following letter, written on his behalf by the Rev. H. Wilson, indicates his feelings and wishes with regard to her:

St. Catharines, Canada West, 24th July, 1854.

Dear Friend, William Still:—Your encouraging letter, to John Smith, was duly received by him, and I am requested to write again on his behalf. His colored friend in Baltimore county, who would favor his designs, is Thomas Cook, whom he wishes you to address, Baltimore post-office, care of Mr. Thomas Spicer.

He has received a letter from Thomas Cook, dated the 6th of June, but it was a long time reaching him. He wishes you to say to Cook, that he got his letter, and that he would like to have him call on his wife and make known to her, that he is in good health, doing well here, and would like to have her come on as soon as she can.

As she is a free woman, there will, doubtless, be no difficulty in her coming right through. He is working in the neighborhood of St. Catharines, but twelve miles from Niagara Falls. You will please recollect to address Thomas Cook, in the care of Thomas Spicer, Baltimore Post-office. Smith's wife is at, or near the place he came from, and, doubtless, Thomas Cook knows all about her condition and circumstances. Please write again to John Smith, in my care, if you please, and request Thomas Cook to do the same.

Very respectfully yours in the cause of philanthropy.　　　　Hiram Wilson.

TWO FEMALE PASSENGERS FROM MARYLAND.

As the way of travel, *via* the Underground Rail Road, under the most favorable circumstances, even for the sterner sex, was hard enough to test the strongest nerves, and to try the faith of the bravest of the brave, every woman, who won her freedom, by this perilous undertaking, deserves commemoration. It is, therefore, a pleasure to thus transfer from the old Record book the names of Ann Johnson and Lavina Woolfley, who fled from Maryland in 1857. Their lives, however, had not been in any way very remarkable. Ann was tall, and of a dark chestnut color, with an intelligent countenance, and about twenty-four years of age. She had filled various situations as a Slave. Sometimes she was required to serve in the kitchen, at other times she was required to toil in the field, with the plow, hoe, and the like. Samuel Harrington, of Cambridge District, Maryland, was the name of the man for whose benefit Ann labored during her younger days. She had no hesitation in saying, that he was a very " ill-natured man ;" he however, was a member of the "old time Methodist Church." In Slave property he had invested only to the extent of some five or six head. About three years previous to Ann's escape, one of her brothers fled and went to Canada. This circumstance so enraged the owner, that he declared he would " sell all " he owned. Accordingly Ann was soon put on the auction block, and was bought by a man who went by the name of William Moore. Moore was a married man, who, with his wife, was addicted to intemperance and carousing. Ann found that she had simply got " out of the fire into the frying-pan." She was really at a loss to tell when her lot was the harder, whether under the " rum drinker," or the old time Methodist. In this state of mind she decided to leave all and go to Canada, the refuge for the fleeing bondman. Lavina, Ann's companion, was the wife of James Woolfley. She and her husband set out together, with six others, and were of the party of eight who were betrayed into Dover jail, as has already been described in these pages. After fighting their way out of the jail, they separated (for prudential reasons). The husband of Lavina, immediately after the conflict at the jail, passed on to Canada, leaving his wife under the protection of friends. Since that time several months had elapsed, but of each other nothing had been known, before she received information on her arrival at Philadelphia. The Committee was glad to inform her, that her husband had safely passed on to Canada, and that she would be aided on also, where they could enjoy freedom in a free country.

CAPTAIN F. AND THE MAYOR OF NORFOLK.

TWENTY-ONE PASSENGERS SECRETED IN A BOAT. NOVEMBER, 1855.

CAPTAIN F. was certainly no ordinary man. Although he had been living a sea-faring life for many years, and the marks of this calling were plainly enough visible in his manners and speech, he was, nevertheless, unlike the great mass of this class of men, not addicted to intemperance and profanity. On the contrary, he was a man of thought, and possessed, in a large measure, those humane traits of character which lead men to sympathize with suffering humanity wherever met with.

It must be admitted, however, that the first impressions gathered from a hasty survey of his rough and rugged appearance, his large head, large mouth, large eyes, and heavy eye-brows, with a natural gift at keeping concealed the inner-workings of his mind and feelings, were not calculated to inspire the belief, that he was fitted to be entrusted with the lives of unprotected females, and helpless children; that he could take pleasure in risking his own life to rescue them from the hell of Slavery; that he could deliberately enter the enemy's domain, and with the faith of a martyr, face the dread slave-holder, with his Bowie-knives and revolvers—Slave-hunters, and blood-hounds, lynchings, and penitentiaries, for humanity's sake. But his deeds proved him to be a true friend of the Slave; whilst his skill, bravery, and success stamped him as one of the most daring and heroic Captains ever connected with the Underground Rail Road cause.

At the time he was doing most for humanity in rescuing bondsmen from

Slavery, Slave-laws were actually being the most rigidly executed. To show mercy, in any sense, to man or woman, who might be caught assisting a poor Slave to flee from the prison-house, was a matter not to be thought of in Virginia. This was perfectly well understood by Captain F.; indeed he did not hesitate to say, that his hazardous operations might any day result in the "sacrifice" of his life. But on this point he seemed to give himself no more concern than he would have done to know which way the wind would blow the next day. He had his own convictions about dying and the future, and he declared, that he had "no fear of death," however it might come. Still, he was not disposed to be reckless or needlessly to imperil his life, or the lives of those he undertook to aid. Nor was he averse to receiving compensation for his services. In Richmond, Norfolk, Petersburg, and other places where he traded, many slaves were fully awake to their condition. The great slave sales were the agencies that served to awaken a large number. Then the various mechanical trades were necessarily given to the Slaves, for the master had no taste for "greasy, northern mechanics." Then, again, the stores had to be supplied with porters, draymen, etc., from the slave population. In the hearts of many of the more intelligent amongst the slaves, the men, as mechanics, etc., the women, as dress-makers, chamber-maids, etc., notwithstanding all the opposition and hard laws, the spirit of Freedom was steadily burning. Many of the slaves were half brothers, and sisters, cousins, nephews, and nieces to their owners, and of course "blood would tell."

It was only necessary for the fact to be made known to a single reliable and intelligent slave, that a man with a boat running North had the love of Freedom for all mankind in his bosom to make that man an object of the greatest interest. If an angel had appeared amongst them doubtless his presence would not have inspired greater anxiety and hope than did the presence of Captain F. The class most anxious to obtain freedom could generally manage to acquire some means which they would willingly offer to captains or conductors in the South for such assistance as was indispensable to their escape. Many of the slaves learned if they could manage to cross Mason and Dixon's line, even though they might be utterly destitute and penniless, that they would then receive aid and protection from the Vigilance Committee. Here it may be well to state that, whilst the Committee gladly received and aided all who might come or be brought to them, they never employed agents or captains to go into the South with a view of enticing or running off slaves. So when captains operated, they did so with the full understanding that they alone were responsible for any failures attending their movements.

The way is now clear to present Captain F. with his schooner lying at the wharf in Norfolk, loading with wheat, and at the same time with twenty-one fugitives secreted therein. While the boat was thus lying at her moor-

THE MAYOR AND POLICE OF NORFOLK SEARCHING CAPT. FOUNTAIN'S SCHOONER.

(Twenty-eight fugitives were concealed in this vessel.)

ing, the rumor was flying all over town that a number of slaves had escaped, which created a general excitement a degree less, perhaps, than if the citizens had been visited by an earthquake. The mayor of the city with a posse of officers with axes and long spears repaired to Captain F.'s boat. The fearless commander received his Honor very coolly, and as gracefully as the circumstances would admit. The mayor gave him to understand who he was, and by what authority he appeared on the boat, and what he meant to do. "Very well," replied Captain F., "here I am and this is my boat, go ahead and search." His Honor with his deputies looked quickly around, and then an order went forth from the mayor to "spear the wheat thoroughly." The deputies obeyed the command with alacrity. But the spears brought neither blood nor groans, and the sagacious mayor obviously concluded that he was "barking up the wrong tree." But the mayor was not there for nothing. "Take the axes and go to work," was the next order; and the axe was used with terrible effect by one of the deputies. The deck and other parts of the boat were chopped and split; no greater judgment being exercised when using the axe than when spearing the wheat; Captain F. all the while wearing an air of utter indifference or rather of entire composure. Indeed every step they took proved conclusively that they were wholly ignorant with regard to boat searching. At this point, with remarkable shrewdness, Captain F. saw wherein he could still further confuse them by a bold strategical move. As though about out of patience with the mayor's blunders, the captain instantly reminded his Honor that he had "stood still long enough" while his boat was being "damaged, chopped up," &c. "Now if you want to search," continued he, "give me the axe, and then point out the spot you want opened and I will open it for you very quick." While uttering these words he presented, as he was capable of doing, an indignant and defiant countenance, and intimated that it mattered not where or when a man died provided he was in the right, and as though he wished to give particularly strong emphasis to what he was saying, he raised the axe, and brought it down edge foremost on the deck with startling effect, at the same time causing the splinters to fly from the boards. The mayor and his posse seemed, if not dreadfully frightened, completely confounded, and by the time Captain F. had again brought down his axe with increased power, demanding where they would have him open, they looked as though it was time for them to retire, and in a few minutes after they actually gave up the search and left the boat without finding a soul. Daniel in the lions' den was not safer than were the twenty-one passengers secreted on Captain F.'s boat. The law had been carried out with a vengeance, but did not avail with this skilled captain. The "five dollars" were paid for being searched, the amount which was lawfully required of every captain sailing from Virginia. And the captain steered direct for the City of Brotherly Love. The wind of heaven favoring the good cause, he arrived safely in due time, and delivered his precious freight in the vicinity of Philadelphia within the reach of the Vigilance Committee. The names of the passengers were as follows:

ALAN TATUM, DANIEL CARR, MICHAEL VAUGHN, THOMAS NIXON, FREDERICK NIXON, PETER PETTY, NATHANIEL GARDENER, JOHN BROWN, THOMAS FREEMAN, JAMES FOSTER, GODFREY SCOTT, WILLIS WILSON, NANCY LITTLE, JOHN SMITH, FRANCIS HAINES, DAVID JOHNSON, PHILLIS GAULT, ALICE JONES, NED WILSON, and SARAH ·C. WILSON, and one other, who subsequently passed on, having been detained on account of sickness. These passengers were most "likely-looking articles;" a number of them, doubtless, would have commanded the very highest prices in the Richmond market. Among them were some good mechanics—one excellent dress-maker, some "prime" waiters and chamber-maids;—men and women with brains, some of them evincing remarkable intelligence and decided bravery, just the kind of passengers that gave the greatest satisfaction to the Vigilance Committee. The interview with these passengers was extremely interesting. Each one gave his or her experience of Slavery, the escape, etc., in his or her own way, deeply impressing those who had the privilege of seeing and hearing them, with the fact of the growing spirit of Liberty, and the wonderful perception and intelligence possessed by some of the sons of toil in the South. While all the names of these passengers were duly entered on the Underground Rail Road records, the number was too large, and the time they spent with the Committee too short, in which to write out even in the briefest manner more than a few of the narratives of this party. The following sketches, how-ever, are important, and will, doubtless, be interesting to those at least who were interested in the excitement which existed in Norfolk at the time of this memorable escape:

ALAN TATUM. Alan was about thirty years of age, dark, intelligent, and of a good physical organization. For the last fourteen years he had been owned by Lovey White, a widow and the owner of nine slaves, from whom she derived a comfortable support. This slave-holding madam was a mem-ber of the Methodist Church, and was considered in her general deportment a "moderate slave-holder." For ten years prior to his escape, Alan had been hiring his time,—for this privilege he paid his mistress, the widow, $120 per annum. If he happened to be so unfortunate as to lose time by sickness within the year, he was obliged to make that up. In addition to these items of expenditure, he had his own clothes, etc., to find. Although Alan had at first stated, that his mistress was "moderate," further on in his story, as he recounted the exactions above alluded to, his tune turned, and he declared, that he was prompted to leave because he disliked his mistress; that "she was mean and without principle." Alan left three sisters, one brother, and a daughter. The names of the sisters and brother were as follows: Mary Ann, Rachel and William—the daughter, Mary.

DANIEL CARR. Daniel was about thirty-eight years of age, dark mulatto, apparently of sound body,—good mind and manly. The man to whom he had been compelled to render hard and unpaid labor and call master, was known by the name of John C. McBole. McBole lived at Plymouth, North Carolina, and was in the steam-mill business. McBole had bought Daniel in Portsmouth, where he had been raised, for $1150, only two years previously to his escape. Twice Daniel had been sold on the auction-block. A part of his life he had been treated hard. Two unsuccessful attempts to escape were made by Daniel, after being sold to North Carolina; for this offence, he was on one occasion stripped naked, and flogged severely. This did not cure him. Prior to his joining Captain F.'s party, he had fled to the swamps, and dwelt there for three months, surrounded with wild animals and reptiles, and it was this state of solitude that he left directly before finding Captain F. Daniel had a wife in Portsmouth, to whom he succeeded in paying a private visit, when, to his unspeakable joy, he made the acquaintance of the noble Captain F., whose big heart was delighted to give him a passage North. Daniel, after being sold, had been allowed, within the two years, only one opportunity of visiting his wife; being thus debarred he resolved to escape. His wife, whose name was Hannah, had three children—slaves—their names were Sam, Dan, and "baby." The name of the latter was unknown to him.

MICHAEL VAUGHN. Michael was about thirty-one years of age, with superior physical proportions, and no lack of common sense. His color was without paleness—dark and unfading, and his manly appearance was quite striking. Michael belonged to a lady, whom he described as a "very disagreeable woman." "For all my life I have belonged to her, but for the last eight years I have hired my time. I paid my mistress $120 a year; a part of the time I had to find my board and all my clothing." This was the direct, and unequivocal testimony that Michael gave of his slave life, which was the foundation for alleging that his mistress was a "very disagreeable woman."

Michael left a wife and one child in Slavery; but they were not owned by his mistress. Before escaping, he felt afraid to lead his companion into the secret of his contemplated movements, as he felt, that there was no possible way for him to do anything for her deliverance; on the other hand, any revelation of the matter might prove too exciting for the poor soul;—her name was Esther. That he did not lose his affection for her whom he was obliged to leave so unceremoniously, is shown by the appended letter:

NEW BEDFORD, August 22d, 1855.

DEAR SIR :—I send you this to inform you that I expect my wife to come that way. If she should, you will direct her to me. When I came through your city last Fall, you took my name in your office, which was then given you, Michael Vaughn ; since then my name is William Brown, No. 130 Kempton street. Please give my wife and child's name to Dr. Lundy, and tell him to attend to it for me. Her name is Esther, and the child's name Louisa.   Truly yours,   WILLIAM BROWN.

Michael worked in a foundry. In church fellowship he was connected with the Methodists—his mistress with the Baptists.

THOMAS NIXON was about nineteen years of age, of a dark hue, and quite intelligent. He had not much excuse to make for leaving, except, that he was "tired of staying" with his "owner," as he "feared he might be sold some day," so he "thought" that he might as well save him the trouble. Thomas belonged to a Mr. Bockover, a wholesale grocer, No. 12 Brewer street. Thomas left behind him his mother and three brothers. His father was sold away when he was an infant, consequently he never saw him. Thomas was a member of the Methodist Church; his master was of the same persuasion.

FREDERICK NIXON was about thirty-three years of age, and belonged truly to the wide-awake class of slaves, as his marked physical and mental appearance indicated. He had a more urgent excuse for escaping than Thomas; he declared that he fled because his owner wanted "to work him hard without allowing him any chance, and had treated him rough." Frederick was also one of Mr. Bockover's chattels; he left his wife, Elizabeth, with four children in bondage. They were living in Eatontown, North Carolina. It had been almost one year since he had seen them. Had he remained in Norfolk he had not the slightest prospect of being reunited to his wife and children, as he had been already separated from them for about three years. This painful state of affairs only increased his desire to leave those who were brutal enough to make such havoc in his domestic relations.

PETER PETTY was about twenty-four years of age, and wore a happy countenance; he was a person of agreeable manners, and withal pretty smart. He acknowledged, that he had been owned by Joseph Boukley, Hair Inspector. Peter did not give Mr. Boukley a very good character, however; he said, that Mr. B. was "rowdyish in his habits, was deceitful and sly, and would sell his slaves any time. Hard bondage—something like the children of Israel," was his simple excuse for fleeing. He hired his time of his master, for which he was compelled to pay $156 a year. When he lost time by sickness or rainy weather, he was required to make up the deficiency, also find his clothing. He left a wife—Lavinia—and one child, Eliza, both slaves. Peter communicated to his wife his secret intention to leave, and she acquiesced in his going. He left his parents also. All his sisters and brothers had been sold. Peter would have been sold too, but his owner was under the impression, that he was "too good a Christian" to violate the laws by running away. Peter's master was quite a devoted Methodist, and was attached to the same Church with Peter. While on the subject of religion, Peter was asked about the kind and character of preaching that he had been accustomed to hear; whereupon he gave the following graphic specimen: "Servants obey your masters; good servants make good masters;

when your mistress speaks to you don't pout out your mouths ; when you want to go to church ask your mistress and master," etc., etc. Peter declared, that he had never heard but one preacher speak against slavery, and that "one was obliged to leave suddenly for the North." He said, that a Quaker lady spoke in meeting against Slavery one day, which resulted in an outbreak, and final breaking up of the meeting.

PHILLIS GAULT. Phillis was a widow, about thirty years of age ; the blood of two races flowed in about equal proportions through her veins. Such was her personal appearance, refinement, manners, and intelligence, that had the facts of her slave life been unknown, she would have readily passed for one who had possessed superior advantages. But the facts in her history proved, that she had been made to feel very keenly the horrifying effects of Slavery ; not in the field, for she had never worked there ; nor as a common drudge, for she had always been required to fill higher spheres ; she was a dress-maker—but not without fear of the auction block. This dreaded destiny was the motive which constrained her to escape with the twenty others ; secreted in the hold of a vessel expressly arranged for bringing away slaves. Death had robbed her of her husband at the time that the fever raged so fearfully in Norfolk. This sad event deprived her of the hope she had of being purchased by her husband, as he had intended. She was haunted by the constant thought of again being sold, as she had once been, and as she had witnessed the sale of her sister's four children after the death of their mother.

Phillis was, to use her own striking expression in a state of "great horror ;" she felt, that nothing would relieve her but freedom. After having fully pondered the prospect of her freedom and the only mode offered by which she could escape, she consented to endure bravely whatever of suffering and trial might fall to her lot in the undertaking—and as was the case with thousands of others, she succeeded. She remained several days in the family of a member of the Committee in Philadelphia, favorably impressing all who saw her. As she had formed a very high opinion of Boston, from having heard it so thoroughly reviled in Norfolk, she desired to go there. The Committee made no objections, gave her a free ticket, etc. From that time to the present, she has ever sustained a good Christian character, and as an industrious, upright, and intelligent woman, she has been and is highly respected by all who know her. The following letter is characteristic of her :

BOSTON, March 22, 1858.

MY DEAR SIR—I received your photograph by Mr Cooper and it afforded me much pleasure to do so i hope that these few lines may find you and your family well as it leaves me and little Dicky at present i have no interesting news to tell you more than there is a great revival of religion through the land i all most forgoten to thank you for your kindness and our little Dick he is very wild and goes to school and it is my desire and prayer for him to grow up a useful man i wish you would try to gain some information from Norfolk and write me word how the times are there for i am afraid to write i wish yoo would see the Doctor for me and ask him if he could carefully find out any way that we could steal little Johny for i think to raise nine or ten hundred dollars for such a child is outraigust just at this time i feel as if i would rather steal him than to buy him give my kinde regards to the Dr and his family tell Miss Margret and Mrs Landy that i would like to see them out here this summer again to have a nice time in Cambridge Miss Walker that spent the evening with me in Cambridge sens much love to yoo and Mrs. Landy give my kindes regards to Mrs Still and children and receive a portion for yoo self i have no more to say at present but remain yoor respectfully.

FLARECE P. GAULT.

When you write direct yoo letters Mrs. Flarece P. Gault, No 62 Pinkney St.

ARRIVALS FROM DIFFERENT PLACES.

MATILDA MAHONEY,—DR. J. W. PENNINGTON'S BROTHER AND SONS CAPTURED AND CARRIED BACK.

While many sympathized with the slave in his chains, and freely wept over his destiny, or gave money to help buy his freedom, but few could be found who were willing to take the risk of going into the South, and standing face to face with Slavery, in order to conduct a panting slave to freedom. The undertaking was too fearful to think of in most cases. But there were instances when men and women too, moved by the love of freedom, would take their lives in their hands, beard the lion in his den, and nobly rescue the oppressed. Such an instance is found in the case of Matilda Mahoney, in Baltimore.

The story of Matilda must be very brief, although it is full of thrilling interest. She was twenty-one years of age in 1854, when she escaped and came to Philadelphia, a handsome young woman, of a light complexion, quite refined in her manners, and in short, possessing great personal attractions. But her situation as a slave was critical, as will be seen.

Her claimant was Wm. Rigard, of Frederick, Md., who hired her to a Mr. Reese, in Baltimore; in this situation her duties were general housework and nursing. With these labors, she was not, however, so much dissatisfied as she was with other circumstances of a more alarming nature: her old master was tottering on the verge of the grave, and his son, a trader in New Orleans. These facts kept Matilda in extreme anxiety. For two years prior to her escape, the young trader had been trying to influence his father to let him have her for the Southern market; but the old man had not consented. Of course the trader knew quite well, that an "article" of her appearance would command readily a very high price in the New Orleans market. But Matilda's attractions had won the heart of a young man in the North, one who had known her in Baltimore in earlier days, and this lover was willing to make desperate efforts to rescue her from her perilous situation. Whether or not he had nerve enough to venture down to Baltimore to accompany his intended away on the Underground Rail Road, his presence would not have aided in the case. He had, however, a friend who consented to go to Baltimore on this desperate mission. The friend was James Jefferson, of Providence, R. I. With the strategy of a skilled soldier, Mr. Jefferson hurried to the Monumental City, and almost under the eyes of the slave-holders and slave-catchers, despite of pro-slavery breastworks, seized his prize and speeded her away on the Underground Railway, before her owner was made acquainted with the fact of her intended escape. On Matilda's arrival at the station in Philadelphia, several other passengers from different points, happened to come to hand just at that time, and gave great solicitude and anxiety to the Committee. Among these were a man and his wife and their four children, (noticed elsewhere), from Maryland. Likewise an interesting and intelligent young girl who had been almost miraculously rescued from the prison-house at Norfolk, and in addition to these, the brother of J. W. Pennington, D. D., with his two sons.

While it was a great gratification to have travelers coming along so fast, and especially to observe in every countenance, determination, rare manly and womanly bearing, with remarkable intelligence, it must be admitted, that the acting committee felt at the same time, a very lively dread of the slave-hunters, and were on their guard. Arrangements were made to send the fugitives on by different trains, and in various directions. Matilda and all the others with the exception of the father and two sons (relatives of Dr. Pennington) successfully escaped and reached their longed-for haven in a free land. The Penningtons, however, although pains had been taken to apprize the Doctor of the good news of the coming of his kin, whom he had not seen for many, many years, were captured after being in New York some twenty-four hours. In answer to an advisory letter from the secretary of the Committee the following from the Doctor is explicit, relative to his wishes and feelings with regard to their being sent on to New York.

29 6th AVENUE, NEW YORK, May 24th, 1854.

MY DEAR MR. STILL :—Your kind letter of the 22d inst has come to hand and I have to thank you for your offices of benevolence to my bone and my flesh, I have had the pleasure of doing a little for your brother Peter, but I do not think it an offset. My burden has been great about these brethren. I hope they have started on to me. Many thanks, my good friend. Yours Truly.

J. W. C. PENNINGTON.

This letter only served to intensify the deep interest which had already been awakened for the safety of all concerned. At the same time also it made the duty of the Committee clear with regard to forwarding them to N. Y. Immediately, therefore, the Doctor's brother and sons were furnished with free tickets and were as carefully cautioned as possible with regard to slave-hunters, if encountered on the road. In company with several other Underground Rail Road passengers, under the care of an intelligent guide, all were sent off in due order, looking quite as well as the most respectable of their race from any part of the country. The Committee in New York, with the Doctor, were on the look out of course; thus without difficulty all arrived safely in the Empire City.

It would seem that the coming of his brother and sons so overpowered the Doctor that he forgot how imminent their danger was. The meeting and interview was doubtless very joyous. Few perhaps could realize, even in imagination, the feelings that filled their hearts, as the Doctor and his brother reverted to their boyhood, when they were both slaves together in Maryland; the separation—the escape of the former many years previous— the contrast, one elevated to the dignity of a Doctor of Divinity, a scholar and noted clergyman, and as such well known in the United States, and Great Britain, whilst, at the same time, his brother and kin were held in chains, compelled to do unrequited labor, to come and go at the bidding of another. Were not these reflections enough to incapacitate the Doctor for the time being, for cool thought as to how he should best guard against the enemy? Indeed, in view of Slavery and its horrid features, the wonder is, not that more was not done, but that any thing was done, that the victims were not driven almost out of their senses. But time rolled on until nearly twenty-four hours had passed, and while reposing their fatigued and weary limbs in bed, just before day-break, hyena-like the slave-hunters pounced upon all three of them, and soon had them hand-cuffed and hurried off to a United States' Commissioner's office. Armed with the Fugitive Law, and a strong guard of officers to carry it out, resistance would have been simply useless. Ere the morning sun arose the sad news was borne by the telegraph wires to all parts of the country of this awful calamity on the Underground Rail Road.

Scarcely less painful to the Committee was the news of this accident, than the news of a disaster, resulting in the loss of several lives, on the Camden and Amboy Road, would have been to its managers. This was the first accident that had ever taken place on the road after passengers had reached the Philadelphia Committee, although, in various instances, slave-hunters had been within a hair's breadth of their prey.

All that was reported respecting the arrest and return of the Doctor's kin, so disgraceful to Christianity and civilization, is taken from the Liberator, as follows:

THREE FUGITIVE SLAVES ARRESTED IN NEW YORK, AND GIVEN UP TO THEIR OWNERS.

NEW YORK, May 25th.

About three o'clock this morning, three colored men, father and two sons, known as Jake, Bob, and Stephen Pennington, were arrested at the instance of David Smith and Jacob Grove, of Washington Co., Md., who claimed them as their slaves. They were taken before Commissioner Morton, of the United States Court, and it was understood that they would be examined at 11 o'clock; instead of that, however, the case was heard at once, no persons being present, when the claimnants testified that they were the owners of said slaves and that they escaped from their service at Baltimore, on Sunday last.

From what we can gather of the proceedings, the fugitives acknowledged themselves to be slaves of Smith and Grove. The commissioner considering the testimony sufficient, ordered their surrender, and they were accordingly given up to their claimants, who hurried them off at once, and they are now on their way to Baltimore. A telegraph despatch has been sent to Philadelphia, as it is understood an attempt will be made to rescue the parties, when the cars arrive. There was no excitement around the commissioner's office, owing to a misunderstanding as to the time of examination. The men were traced to this city by the claimants, who made application to the United States Court, when officers Horton and De Angeles were deputed by the marshal to effect their arrest, and those officers, with deputy Marshal Thompson scoured the city, and finally found them secreted in a house in Broome St. They were brought before Commissioner Morton this morning. No counsel appeared for the fugitives. The case being made out, the usual affidavits of fear of rescue were made, and the warrants thereupon issued, and the three fugitives were delivered over to the U. S. Marshal, and hurried off to Maryland. They were a father and his two sons, father about forty-five and sons eighteen or nineteen. The evidence shows them to have recently escaped. The father is the brother of the Rev. Dr. Pennington, a highly respected colored preacher of this city.

NEW YORK, May 28.

Last evening the church at the corner of Prince and Marion streets was filled with an intelligent audience of white and colored people, to hear Dr. Pennington relate the circumstance connected with the arrest of his brother and nephews. He showed, that he attempted to afford his brother the assistance of counsel, but was unable to do so, the officers at the Marshal's office having deceived him in relation to the time the trial was to take place before the Commissioners. Hon. E. F. Culver next addressed the audience, showing, that a great injustice had been done to the brother of Dr. Pennington, and though he, up to that time, had advocated peace, he now had the spirit to tear down the building over the Marshal's head. Intense interest was manifested during the proceedings, and much sympathy in behalf of Dr. Pennington.

THE FUGITIVE SLAVES IN BALTIMORE.

The U. S. Marshal, A. T. Hillyer, Esq., received a dispatch this morning from officers Horton and Dellugelis, at Baltimore, stating, that they had arrived there with the three slaves, arrested here yesterday (the Penningtons), the owners accompanying them. The officers will return to New York, this evening.—*N. Y. Express, 27th.*

NEW YORK, May 30.

The Rev. Dr. Pennington has received a letter from Mr. Grove, the claimant of his brother, who was recently taken back from this city, offering to sell him to Dr. Pennington, should he wish to buy him, and stating, that he would await a reply, before "selling him to the slave-drivers." Mr. Groce, who accompanied his "sweet heart," Matilda, in the same train which conveyed the Penningtons to New York, had reason to apprehend danger to all the Underground Rail Road passengers, as will appear from his subjoined letter:

ELMIRA, May 28th.

DEAR LUKE:—I arrived home safe with my precious charge, and found all well. I have just learned, that the Penningtons are taken. Had he done as I wished him he would never have been taken. Last night our tall friend from Baltimore came, and caused great excitement here by his information. The lady is perfectly safe now in Canada. I will write you and Mr. Still as soon as I get over the excitement. This letter was first intended for Mr. Gains, but I now send it to you. Please let me hear their movements. Yours truly,

C. L. GROCE.

But sadly as this blow was felt by the Vigilance Committee, it did not cause them to relax their efforts in the least. Indeed it only served to stir them up to renewed diligence and watchfulness, although for a length of time afterwards the Committee felt disposed, when sending, to avoid New York as much as possible, and in lieu thereof, to send *viâ* Elmira, where there was a depot under the agency of John W. Jones. Mr. Jones was a true and prompt friend of the fugitive, and wide awake with regard to Slavery and slave-holders, and slave hunters, for he had known from sad experience in Virginia every trait of character belonging to these classes.

In the midst of the Doctor's grief, friends of the slave soon raised money to purchase his brother, about $1,000; but the unfortunate sons were doomed to the auction block and the far South, where, the writer has never exactly learned.

"FLEEING GIRL OF FIFTEEN," IN MALE ATTIRE.

PROFESSORS H. AND T. OFFER THEIR SERVICES—CAPTAINS B. ALSO ARE ENLISTED
—SLAVE-TRADER GRASPING TIGHTLY HIS PREY, BUT SHE IS RESCUED—
LONG CONFLICT, BUT GREAT TRIUMPH—ARRIVAL ON THANKSGIVING
DAY, NOV. 25, 1855.

It was the business of the Vigilance Committee, as it was clearly understood by the friends of the Slave, to assist all needy fugitives, who might in
any way manage to reach Philadelphia, but, for various reasons, not to
send agents South to incite slaves to run away, or to assist them in so doing.
Sometimes, however, this rule could not altogether be conformed to. Cases,
in some instances, would appeal so loudly and forcibly to humanity, civilization, and Christianity, that it would really seem as if the very stones
would cry out, unless something was done. As an illustration of this point,
the story of the young girl, which is now to be related, will afford the most
striking proof. At the same time it may be seen how much anxiety, care,
hazard, delay and material aid, were required in order to effect the deliverance of some who were in close places, and difficult of access. It will be
necessary to present a considerable amount of correspondence in this case,
to bring to light the hidden mysteries of this narrative. The first letter, in
explanation, is the following:

LETTER FROM J. BIGELOW, ESQ.

WASHINGTON, D. C., June 27, 1854.

MR. WM. STILL—*Dear Sir:*—I have to thank you for the prompt answer you had the
kindness to give to my note of 22d inst. Having found a correspondence so quick and
easy, and withal so very flattering, I address you again more fully.

The liberal appropriation for *transportation* has been made chiefly on account of a female
child of ten or eleven years old, for whose purchase I have been authorized to offer $700
(refused), and for whose sister I have paid $1,600, and some $1,000 for their mother, &c.

This child sleeps in the same apartment with its master and mistress, which adds to the
difficulty of removal. She is some ten or twelve miles from the city, so that really the
chief hazard will be in bringing her safely to town, and in secreting her until a few days of
storm shall have abated. All this, I think, is now provided for with entire safety.

The child has two cousins in the immediate vicinity; a young man of some twenty-two
years of age, and his sister, of perhaps seventeen—*both Slaves,* but bright and clear-headed
as anybody. The young man I have seen often—the services of *both* seem indispensable
to the main object suggested; but having once rendered the service, they cannot, and
ought not return to Slavery. They look for *freedom* as the reward of what they shall
now do.

Out of the $300, cheerfully offered for the whole enterprise, I must pay some reasonable
sum for transportation to the city and sustenance while here. It cannot be much; for the
balance, I shall give a draft, which will be *promptly paid* on their arrival in New York.

If I have been understood to offer the whole $300, *it shall be paid,* though I have meant
as above stated. Among the various ways that have been suggested, has been that of

12

taking *all of them* into the cars here; that, I think, will be found impracticable. I find so much vigilance at the depot, that I would not deem it safe, though in any kind of carriage they might leave in safety at any time.

All the rest I leave to the experience and sagacity of the gentleman who maps out the enterprise.

Now I will thank you to reply to this and let me know that it reaches you in safety, and is not put in a careless place, whereby I may be endangered; and state also, whether all my propositions are understood and acceptable, and whether, (pretty quickly after I shall inform you that *all things are ready*), the gentleman will make his appearance?

I live alone. My office and bed-room, &c., are at the corner of E. and 7th streets, opposite the east end of the General Post Office, where any one may call upon me.

It would, of course, be imprudent, that this letter, or any other *written* particulars, be in his pockets for fear of accident.   Yours very respectfully,   J. BIGELOW.

While this letter clearly brought to light the situation of things, its author, however, had scarcely begun to conceive of the numberless difficulties which stood in the way of success before the work could be accomplished. The information which Mr. Bigelow's letter contained of the painful situation of this young girl was submitted to different parties who could be trusted, with a view of finding a person who might possess sufficient courage to undertake to bring her away. Amongst those consulted were two or three captains who had on former occasions done good service in the cause. One of these captains was known in Underground Rail-Road circles as the "powder boy."* He was willing to undertake the work, and immediately concluded to make a visit to Washington, to see how the "land lay." Accordingly in company with another Underground Rail Road captain, he reported himself one day to Mr. Bigelow with as much assurance as if he were on an errand for an office under the government. The impression made on Mr. Bigelow's mind may be seen from the following letter; it may also be seen that he was fully alive to the necessity of precautionary measures.

SECOND LETTER FROM LAWYER BIGELOW.

WASHINGTON, D. C., September 9th, 1855.

MR. WM. STILL, DEAR SIR:—I strongly hope the little matter of business so long pending and about which I have written you so many times, will take a move now. I have the promise that the merchandize shall be delivered in this city to-night. Like so many other promises, this also may prove a failure, though I have reason to believe that it will not. I shall, however, know before I mail this note. In case the goods arrive here I shall hope to see your long-talked of "Professional gentleman" in Washington, as soon as possible. He will find-me by the enclosed card, which shall be a satisfactory introduction for him. You have never given me his name, nor am I anxious to know it. But on a pleasant visit made last fall to friend Wm. Wright, in Adams Co., I suppose I accidentally learned it to be a certain Dr. H—. Well, let him come.

I had an interesting call a week ago from two gentlemen, masters of vessels, and

---

* He had been engaged at different times in carrying powder in his boat from a powder magazine, and from this circumstance, was familiarly called the "Powder Boy."

brothers, one of whom, I understand, you know as the "powder boy." I had a little light freight for them; but not finding enough other freight to ballast their craft, they went down the river looking for wheat, and promising to return soon. I hope to see them often.

I hope this may find you returned from your northern trip,* as your time proposed was out two or three days ago.

I hope if the whole particulars of Jane Johnson's case † are printed, you will send me the copy as proposed.

I forwarded some of her things to Boston a few days ago, and had I known its importance in court, I could have sent you one or two witnesses who would prove that her freedom was intended by her before she left Washington, and that a man was *engaged* here to go on to Philadelphia the same day with her to give notice there of her case, though I think he failed to do so. It was beyond all question her purpose, *before leaving Washington and provable too,* that if Wheeler should make her a free woman by taking her to a free state "*to use it rather.*"

Tuesday, 11th September. The attempt was made on Sunday to forward the merchandize, but failed through no fault of any of the parties that I now know of. It will be repeated soon, and you shall know the result.

"Whorra for Judge Kane." I feel so indignant at the man, that it is not easy to write the foregoing sentence, and yet who is helping our cause like Kane and Douglas, not forgetting Stringfellow. I hope soon to know that this reaches you in safety.

It often happens that light freight would be offered to Captain B., but the owners cannot by possibility *advance* the amount of freight. I wish it were possible in some such extreme cases, that after advancing *all they have,* some public fund should be found to pay the balance or at least lend it.

[I wish here to caution you against the supposition that I would do any act, or say a word towards helping servants to escape. Although I hate slavery so much, I keep my hands clear of any such wicked or illegal act.] Yours, very truly, J. B.

Will you recollect, hereafter, that in any of my future letters, in which I may use [   ] whatever words may be within the brackets are intended to have no signification whatever to you, only to blind the eyes of the uninitiated. You will find an example at the close of my letter.

Up to this time the chances seemed favorable of procuring the ready services of either of the above mentioned captains who visited Lawyer Bigelow for the removal of the merchandize to Philadelphia, providing the shipping master could have it in readiness to suit their convenience. But as these captains had a number of engagements at Richmond, Petersburg, &c., it was not deemed altogether safe to rely upon either of them, consequently in order to be prepared in case of an emergency, the matter was laid before two professional gentlemen who were each occupying chairs in one of the medical colleges of Philadelphia. They were known to be true friends of the slave, and had possessed withal some experience in Underground Rail Road matters. Either of these professors was willing to undertake the operation, provided arrangements could be completed in time to be carried out during the vacation. In this hopeful, although painfully indefinite position the

---

* Mr. Bigelow's correspondent had been on a visit to the fugitives to Canada.
† Jane Johnson of the Passmore Williamson Slave Case.

matter remained for more than a year; but the correspondence and anxiety increased, and with them disappointments and difficulties multiplied. The hope of Freedom, however, buoyed up the heart of the young slave girl during the long months of anxious waiting and daily expectation for the hour of deliverance to come. Equally true and faithful also did Mr. Bigelow prove to the last; but at times he had some painfully dark seasons to encounter, as may be seen from the subjoined letter:

WASHINGTON, D. C., October 6th, 1855.

MR. STILL, DEAR SIR:—I regret exceedingly to learn by your favor of 4th instant, that all things are not ready. Although I cannot speak of any immediate and positive danger. [*Yet it is well known that the city is full of incendiaries.*]

Perhaps you are aware that any colored citizen is liable at any hour of day or night without any show of authority to have his house ransacked by constables, and if others do it and commit the most outrageous depredations none but white witnesses can convict them. ᐧ Such outrages are always common here, and no kind of property exposed to colored protection only, can be considered safe. [I don't say that *much liberty* should not be given to constables on account of numerous runaways, but it don't always work for good.] Before advertising they go round and offer rewards to sharp colored men of perhaps *one or two hundred dollars*, to betray runaways, and having discovered their hiding-place, seize them and then cheat their informers out of the money.

[*Although a law abiding man,*] I am anxious in this case of *innocence* to raise no conflict or suspicion. [*Be sure that the manumission is full and legal.*] And as I am *powerless* without your aid, *I pray you* don't lose a moment in giving me relief. The idea of waiting yet for weeks seems dreadful; do reduce it to days if possible, and give me notice of the *earliest possible time.*

The property is not yet advertised, but will be, [and if we delay too long, may be sold and lost.]

It was a great misunderstanding, though not your fault, that so much delay would be necessary. [I repeat again that I must have the thing done legally, therefore, please get a good lawyer to draw up the deed of manumission.] Yours Truly, J. BIGELOW.

Great was the anxiety felt in Washington. It is certainly not too much to say, that an equal amount of anxiety existed in Philadelphia respecting the safety of the merchandise. At this juncture Mr. Bigelow had come to the conclusion that it was no longer safe to write over his own name, but that he would do well to henceforth adopt the name of the renowned Quaker, Wm. Penn, (he was worthy of it) as in the case of the following letter.

WASHINGTON, D. C., November 10th, 1855.

DEAR SIR:—Doctor T. presented my card last night about half past eight which I instantly recognized. I, however, soon became suspicious, and afterwards confounded, to find the doctor using your name and the well known names of Mr. McK. and Mr. W. and yet, neither he nor I; could conjecture the object of his visit.

The doctor is agreeable and sensible, and doubtless a true-hearted man. He seemed to see the whole matter as I did and was embarrassed. He had nothing to propose, no information to give of the "P. Boy," or of any substitute, and seemed to want no particular information from me concerning my anxieties and perils, though I stated them to him, but found him as powerless as myself to give me relief. I had an agreeable interview with the doctor till after ten, when he left, intending to take the cars at six, as I suppose he did do, this morning.

This morning after eight, I got your letter of the 9th, but it gives me but little enlightenment or satisfaction. You simply say that the doctor is a *true man*, which I cannot doubt, that you thought it best we should have an interview, and that you supposed I would meet the expenses. You informed me also that the " P. Boy " left for Richmond, on Friday, the 2d, to be gone *the length of time named in your last*, I must infer that to be *ten days* though in your last *you assured me* that the " P. Boy " would certainly start for *this place* (not Richmond) in two or three days, though the difficulty about freight might cause delay, and the whole enterprise might not be accomplished under ten days, &c., &c. That time having elapsed and I having agreed to an extra fifty dollars to ensure promptness. I have scarcely left my office since, except for my hasty meals, awaiting his arrival. You now inform me he has gone to Richmond, to be gone ten days, which will expire tomorrow, but you do not say he will return here or to Phila., or where, at the expiration of that time, and Dr. T. could tell me nothing whatever about him. Had he been able to tell me that this *best plan*, which I have so long rested upon, would fail, or was abandoned, I could then understand it, but he says no such thing, and you say, as you have twice before said, " ten days more."

Now, my dear sir, after this recapitulation, can you not see that I have reason for great embarrassment? I have given assurances, both here and in New York, founded on your assurances to me, and caused my friends in the latter place great anxiety, so much that I have had no way to explain my own letters but by sending your last two to Mr. Tappan.

I cannot doubt, I do not, but that you wish to help me, and the cause too, for which both of us have made many and large sacrifices with no hope of reward in this world. If in this case I have been very urgent since September Dr. T. can give you some of my reasons, they have not been selfish.

The whole matter is in a nutshell. Can I, in your opinion, depend on the " P. Boy," and when?

If he promises to come here next trip, will he come, or go to Richmond? This I think is the best way. Can I depend on it?

Dr. T. promised to write me some explanation and give some advice, and at first I thought to await his letter, but on second thought concluded to tell you how I feel, as I have done.

Will you answer my questions with some explicitness, and without delay?

I forgot to inquire of Dr. T. who is the head of your Vigilance Committee, whom I may address concerning other and further operations? Yours very truly, WM. PENN.

P. S. I ought to say, that I have no doubt but there were good reasons for the P. Boy's going to Richmond instead of W.; *but what can they be?*

Whilst there are a score of other interesting letters, bearing on this case, the above must suffice, to give at least, an idea of the perplexities and dangers attending its early history. Having accomplished this end, a more encouraging and pleasant phase of the transaction may now be introduced. Here the difficulties, at least very many of them, vanish, yet in one respect, the danger became most imminent. The following letter shows that the girl had been successfully rescued from her master, and that a reward of five hundred dollars had been offered for her.

WASHINGTON, D. C., October 12, 1855.

MR. WM. STILL:—AS YOU PICK UP ALL THE NEWS THAT IS STIRRING, I CONTRIBUTE A FEW SCRAPS TO YOUR STOCK, GOING TO SHOW THAT THE POOR SLAVE-HOLDERS HAVE THEIR TROUBLES AS WELL AS OTHER PEOPLE.

Four heavy losses on one small scrap cut from a single number of the "Sun!" How vexatious! How provoking! On the other hand, think of the poor, timid, breathless, flying child of fifteen! FIVE HUNDRED DOLLARS REWARD! Oh, for succor! To whom in all this wide land of Freedom shall she flee and find safety? Alas!—Alas!—The law points to no one!

Is she still running with bleeding feet?* Or hides she in some cold cave, to rest and starve? "$500 reward." Yours, for the weak and the poor. PERISH the reward.   J. B.

Having thus succeeded in getting possession of, and secreting this fleeing child of fifteen, as best they could, in Washington, all concerned were compelled to "possess their souls in patience," until the storm had passed. Meanwhile, the "child of fifteen" was christened "Joe Wright," and dressed in male attire to prepare for traveling as a lad. As no opportunity had hitherto presented itself, whereby to prepare the "package" for shipment, from Washington, neither the "powder boy" nor Dr. T.,† was prepared to attend to the removal, at this critical moment. The emergency of the case, however, cried loudly for aid. The other professional gentleman (Dr. H.), was now appealed to, but his engagements in the college forbade his absence before about Thanksgiving day, which was then six weeks off. This fact was communicated to Washington, and it being the only resource left, the time named was necessarily acquiesced in. In the interim, "Joe" was to perfect herself in the art of wearing pantaloons, and all other male rig. Soon the days and weeks slid by, although at first the time for waiting seemed long, when, according to promise, Dr. H. was in Washington, with his horse and buggy prepared for duty. The impressions made by Dr. H., on William Penn's mind, at his first interview, will doubtless be interesting to all concerned, as may be seen in the following letter:

Washington, D. C., November 26, 1855.

My Dear Sir:—A recent letter from my friend, probably has led you to expect this from me. He was delighted to receive yours of the 23d, stating that the boy was *all right*. He found the "Prof. gentleman" a *perfect gentleman;* cool, quiet, thoughtful, and *perfectly competent to execute his undertaking.* At the first three minutes of their interview, he felt assured that all would be right. He, and all concerned, give you and that gentleman sincere thanks for what you have done. May the blessings of Him, who cares for the poor, be on your heads.

The especial object of this, is to inform you that there is a half dozen or so of packages here, *pressing for transportation;* twice or thrice that number are also pressing, but less so than the others. Their aggregate means will average, say, $10 each; besides these, we know of a few, say three or four, *able and smart*, but utterly destitute, and kept so purposely by their oppressors. For all these, we feel deeply interested; $10 each would not be enough for the "powder boy." Is there any fund from which a pittance could be spared to help these poor creatures? I don't doubt but that they would honestly repay

---

* At the time this letter was written, she was then under Mr. B.'s protection in Washington, and had to be so kept for six weeks. His question, therefore, "is she still running with bleeding feet," etc., was simply a precautionary step to blind any who might perchance investigate the matter.

† Dr. T. was one of the professional gentlemen alluded to above, who had expressed a willingness to act as an agent in the matter.

MARIA WEEMS ESCAPING IN MALE ATTIRE.

a small loan as soon as they could earn it. I know full well, that if you begin with such cases, there is no boundary at which you can stop. For years, one half at least, of my friend's time here has been gratuitously given to cases of distress among this class. He never expects or desires to do less; he literally has the *poor always with him.* He knows that it is so with you also, therefore, he only states the case, being especially anxious for at least those to whom I have referred.

I think a small lot of hard coal might always be sold here *from the vessel* at a profit. Would not a like lot of Cumberland coal always sell in Philadelphia?

My friend would be very glad to see the powder boy here again, and if he brings coal, there are those here, who would try to help him sell.

Reply to your regular correspondent as usual. WM. PENN.

By the presence of the Dr., confidence having been reassured that all would be right, as well as by the "inner light," William Penn experienced a great sense of relief. Everything having been duly arranged, the doctor's horse and carriage stood waiting before the White House (William Penn preferred this place as a starting point, rather than before his own office door). It being understood that "Joe" was to act as coachman in passing out of Washington, at this moment he was called for, and in the most polite and natural manner, with the fleetness of a young deer, he jumped into the carriage, took the reins and whip, whilst the doctor and William Penn were cordially shaking hands and bidding adieu. This done, the order was given to Joe, "drive on." Joe bravely obeyed. The faithful horse trotted off willingly, and the doctor sat in his carriage as composed as though he had succeeded in procuring an honorable and lucrative office from the White House, and was returning home to tell his wife the good news. The doctor had some knowledge of the roads, also some acquaintances in Maryland, through which State he had to travel; therefore, after leaving the suburbs of Washington, the doctor took the reins in his own hands, as he felt that he was more experienced as a driver than his young coachman. He was also mindful of the fact, that, before reaching Pennsylvania, his faithful beast would need feeding several times, and that they consequently would be obliged to pass one or two nights at least in Maryland, either at a tavern or farm-house.

In reflecting upon the matter, it occurred to the doctor, that in earlier days, he had been quite intimately acquainted with a farmer and his family (who were slave-holders), in Maryland, and that he would about reach their house at the end of the first day's journey. He concluded that he could do no better than to renew his acquaintance with his old friends on this occasion. After a very successful day's travel, night came on, and the doctor was safely at the farmer's door with his carriage and waiter boy; the doctor was readily recognized by the farmer and his family, who seemed glad to see him; indeed, they made quite a "fuss" over him. As a matter of strategy, the doctor made quite a "fuss" over them in return; nevertheless, he did not fail to assume airs of importance, which were calculated to lead them to think that he had grown older and wiser than when they knew him in his younger days. In casually referring to the manner of his traveling, he alluded to the fact, that he was not very well, and as it had been a considerable length of time since he had been through that part of the country, he thought that the drive would do him good, and especially the sight of old familiar places and people. The farmer and his family felt themselves exceedingly honored by the visit from the distinguished doctor, and manifested a marked willingness to spare no pains to render his night's lodging in every way comfortable.

The Dr. being an educated and intelligent gentleman, well posted on other questions besides medicine, could freely talk about farming in all its branches, and "niggers" too, in an emergency, so the evening passed off pleasantly with the Dr. in the parlor, and "Joe" in the kitchen. The Dr., however, had given "Joe" precept upon precept, "here a little, and there a little," as to how he should act in the presence of master white people, or slave colored people, and thus he was prepared to act his part with due exactness. Before the evening grew late, the Dr., fearing some accident, intimated, that he was feeling a "little languid," and therefore thought that he had better "retire." Furthermore he added, that he was "liable to vertigo," when not quite well, and for this reason he must have his boy "Joe" sleep in the room with him. "Simply give him a bed quilt and he will fare well enough in one corner of the room," said the Dr. The proposal was readily acceded to, and carried into effect by the accommodating host. The Dr. was soon in bed, sleeping soundly, and "Joe," in his new coat and pants, wrapped up in the bed quilt, in a corner of the room quite comfortably.

The next morning the Dr. arose at as early an hour as was prudent for a gentleman of his position, and feeling refreshed, partook of a good breakfast, and was ready, with his boy, "Joe," to prosecute their journey. Face, eyes, hope, and steps, were set as flint, Pennsylvania-ward. What time the following day or night they crossed Mason and Dixon's line is not recorded on the Underground Rail Road books, but at four o'clock on Thanksgiving Day, the Dr. safely landed the "fleeing girl of fifteen" at the residence of the writer in Philadelphia. On delivering up his charge, the Dr. simply remarked to the writer's wife, "I wish to leave this young lad with you a short while, and I will call and see further about him." Without further explanation, he stepped into his carriage and hurried away, evidently anxious to report himself to his wife, in order to relieve her mind of a great weight of anxiety on his account. The writer, who happened to be absent from home when the Dr. called, returned soon afterwards. "The Dr. has been here" (he was the family physician), "and left this 'young lad,' and said, that he would call again and see about him," said Mrs. S. The "young lad" was sitting quite composedly in the dining-room, with his cap on. The writer turned to him and inquired, "I suppose you are the person that the Dr. went to Washington after, are you not?" "No," said "Joe." "Where are you from then?" was the next question. "From York, sir." "From York? Why then did the Dr. bring you here?" was the next query, "the Dr. went expressly to Washington after a young girl, who was to be brought away dressed up as a boy, and I took you to be the person." Without replying "the lad" arose and walked out of the house. The querist, somewhat mystified, followed him, and then when the two were alone, "the lad" said, "I am the one the Dr. went after." After congratulating her, the writer asked why she had said, that she was not from Washington, but from York. She explained, that the Dr. had strictly charged her not to own to any person, except the writer, that she was from Washington, but from York. As there were persons present (wife, hired girl, and a fugitive woman), when the questions were put to her, she felt that it would be a violation of her pledge to answer in the affirmative. Before this examination, neither of the individuals present for a moment entertained the slightest doubt but that she was a "lad," so well had she acted her part in every particular. She was dressed in a new suit, which fitted her quite nicely, and with her unusual amount of common sense, she appeared to be in no respect lacking. To send off a prize so rare and remarkable, as she was, without affording some of the stockholders and managers of the Road the pleasure of seeing her, was not to be thought of. In addition to the Vigilance Committee, quite a number of persons were invited to see her, and were greatly astonished. Indeed it was difficult to realize, that she was not a boy, even after becoming acquainted with the facts in the case.

The following is an exact account of this case, as taken from the Underground Rail Road records:

"THANKSGIVING DAY, Nov., 1855.

Arrived, Ann Maria Weems, *alias* 'Joe Wright,' *alias* 'Ellen Capron,' from Washington, through the aid of Dr. H. She is about fifteen years of age; bright mulatto, well grown, smart and good-looking. For the last three years, or about that length of time, she has been owned by Charles M. Price, a negro trader, of Rockville, Maryland. Mr. P. was given to 'intemperance,' to a very great extent, and gross 'profanity.' He buys and sells many slaves in the course of the year. 'His wife is cross and peevish.' She used to take great pleasure in 'torturing' one 'little slave boy.' He was the son of his master (and was owned by him); this was the chief cause of the mistress' spite."

Ann Maria had always desired her freedom from childhood, and although not thirteen, when first advised to escape, she received the suggestion without hesitation, and ever after that time waited almost daily, for more than two years, the chance to flee. Her friends were, of course, to aid her, and make arrangements for her escape. Her owner, fearing that she might escape, for a long time compelled her to sleep in the chamber with " her master and mistress;" indeed she was so kept until about three weeks before she fled. She left her parents living in Washington. Three of her brothers had been sold South from their parents. Her mother had been purchased for $1,000, and one of her sisters for $1,600 for freedom. Before Ann Maria was thirteen years of age $700 was offered for her by a friend, who desired to procure her freedom, but the offer was promptly refused, as were succeeding ones repeatedly made. The only chance of procuring her freedom, depended upon getting her away on the Underground Rail Road. She was neatly attired in male habiliments, and in that manner came all the way from Washington. After passing two or three days with her new friends in Philadelphia, she was sent on (in male attire) to Lewis Tappan, of New York, who had likewise been deeply interested in her case from the beginning, and who held himself ready, as was understood, to cash a draft for three hundred dollars to compensate the man who might risk his own liberty in bringing her on from Washington. After having arrived safely in New York, she found a home and kind friends in the family of the Rev. A. N. Freeman, and received quite an ovation characteristic of an Underground Rail Road.

After having received many tokens of esteem and kindness from the friends of the slave in New York and Brooklyn, she was carefully forwarded on to Canada, to be educated at the " Buxton Settlement."

An interesting letter, however, from the mother of Ann Maria, conveying the intelligence of her late great struggle and anxiety in laboring to free her last child from Slavery is too important to be omitted, and hence is inserted in connection with this narrative.

LETTER FROM THE MOTHER.

WASHINGTON, D. C., September 19th, 1857.

WM. STILL, ESQ., Philadelphia, Pa. SIR:—I have just sent for my son Augustus, in Alabama. I have sent eleven hundred dollars which pays for his body and some thirty dollars to pay his fare to Washington. I borrowed one hundred and eighty dollars to make out the eleven hundred dollars. I was not very successful in Syracuse. I collected only twelve dollars, and in Rochester only two dollars. I did not know that the season was so unpropitious. The wealthy had all gone to the springs. They must have returned by this time. I hope you will exert yourself and help me get a part of the money I owe, at least. I am obliged to pay it by the 12th of next month. I was unwell when I returned through Philadelphia, or I should have called. I had been from home five weeks.

My son Augustus is the last of the family in Slavery. I feel rejoiced that he is soon to be free and with me, and of course feel the greatest solicitude about raising the one hundred and eighty dollars I have borrowed of a kind friend, or who has borrowed it for me at bank. I hope and pray you will help me as far as possible. Tell Mr. Douglass to remember me, and if he can, to interest his friends for me.

You will recollect that five hundred dollars of our money was taken to buy the sister of Henry H. Garnett's wife. Had I been able to command this I should not be necessitated to ask the favors and indulgences I do.

I am expecting daily the return of Augustus, and may Heaven grant him a safe deliverance and smile propitiously upon you and all kind friends who have aided in his return to me.

Be pleased to remember me to friends, and accept yourself the blessing and prayers of your dear friend, EARRO WEEMS.

P. S. Direct your letter to E. L. Stevens, in Duff Green's Row, Capitol Hill, Washington, D. C.

E. W.

That William Penn who worked so faithfully for two years for the deliverance of Ann Maria may not appear to have been devoting all his time and sympathy towards this single object it seems expedient that two or three additional letters, proposing certain grand Underground Rail Road plans, should have a place here. For this purpose, therefore, the following letters are subjoined.

LETTERS FROM WILLIAM PENN.

WASHINGTON, D. C., Oct. 3, 1854.

DEAR SIR :—I address you to-day chiefly at the suggestion of the Lady who will hand you my letter, and who is a resident of your city.

After stating to you, that the case about which I have previously written, remains just as it was when I wrote last—full of difficulty—I thought I would call your attention to another enterprise ; it is this : to find a man with a large heart for doing good to the oppressed, who will come to Washington to live, and who will *walk out to Penn'a., or a part of the way there, once or twice a week.* He will find parties who will *pay him for doing so.* Parties of say, two, three, five or so, who will pay him *at least* $5 each, for the privilege of following him, but *will never speak to him ;* but will keep just in sight of him and obey any sign he may give ; say, he takes off his hat and scratches his head as a sign for them to go to some barn or wood to rest, &c. No living being shall be found to say he ever spoke to them. A white man would be best, and then even parties led out by him could not, if they would, testify to any *understanding* or anything else against a white man. I think he might make a good living at it. Can it not be done ?

If one or two safe stopping-places could be found on the way—such as a barn or shed, they could walk quite safely all night and then sleep all day—about two, or *easily* three nights would convey them to a place of safety. The traveler might be a peddler or huckster, with an old horse and cart, and bring us in eggs and butter if he pleases.

Let him once plan out his route, and he might then take ten or a dozen at a time, and they are often able and willing to pay $10 a piece.

I have a hard case now on hand ; a brother and sister 23 to 25 years old, whose mother lives in your city. They are cruelly treated; they want to go, they *ought* to go ; but they are utterly destitute. Can nothing be done for such cases ? If you can think of anything let me know it. I suppose you know me ?

WASHINGTON, D. C., April 3, 1856.

DEAR SIR :—I sent you the recent law of Virginia, under which all vessels are to be searched for fugitives within the waters of that State.

It was long ago suggested by a sagacious friend, that the " powder boy " might find a better port in the Chesapeake bay, or in the Patuxent river to communicate with this vicinity, than by entering the Potomac river, even were there no such law.

Suppose he opens a trade with some place south-west of Annapolis, 25 or 30 miles from here, or less. He might carry wood, oysters, &c., and all his customers from this vicinity might travel in *that direction* without any of the suspicions that might attend their journeyings *towards this city.* In this way, doubtless, a good business might be carried on without interruption or competition, and provided the plan was conducted without affecting the inhabitants along that shore, no suspicion would arise as to the manner or magnitude of his business operations. How does this strike you? What does the "powder boy" think of it?

I heretofore intimated a *pressing necessity* on the part of several females—they are variously situated—two have children, say a couple each; some have none—of the latter, one can raise $50, another, say 30 or 40 dollars—another who was gazetted last August (a copy sent you), can raise, through her friends, 20 or 30 dollars, &c., &c. None of these can walk so far or so fast as scores of *men* that are constantly leaving. I cannot shake off my anxiety for these poor creatures. Can you think of anything for any of these? Address your other correspondent in answer to this at your leisure. Yours,

WM. PENN.

P. S.—April 3d. Since writing the above, I have received yours of 31st. I am rejoiced to hear that business is so successful and prosperous—may it continue till *the article* shall cease to be merchandize.

I spoke in my last letter of the departure of a "few friends." I have since heard of their good health in Penn'a. Probably you may have seen them.

In reference to the expedition of which you think you can "hold out some little encouragement," I will barely remark, that I shall be glad, if it is undertaken, to have all the notice of the *time and manner* that is possible, so as to make ready.

A friend of mine says, anthracite coal will always pay here from Philadelphia, and thinks a small vessel might run often—that she never would be searched in the Potomac, unless she went outside.

You advise caution towards Mr. P. I am precisely of your opinion about him, that he is a "queer stick," and while I advised him carefully in reference to his own undertakings, I took no counsel of him concerning mine. Yours,

W. P.

WASHINGTON, D. C., April 23d, 1856.

DEAR SIR:—I have to thank you for your last two encouraging letters of 31st of March and 7th April. I have seen nothing in the papers to interest you, and having bad health and a press of other engagements, I have neglected to write you.

Enclosed is a list of persons referred to in my last letter, all most anxious to travel—all meritorious. In some of these I feel an especial interest for what they have done to help others in distress.

I suggest for yours and the "powder boy's" consideration the following plan: that he shall take in coal for Washington and come directly here—sell his coal and go to Georgetown for freight, and *wait* for it. If any fancy articles are sent on board, *I understand he has a place* to put them in, and *if he has* I suggest that he lies still, still waiting for freight till the first anxiety is over. Vessels that have *just left* are the ones that will be inquired after, and perhaps chased. If he lays still a day or two all suspicion will be prevented. If there shall be occasion to refer to any of them hereafter, it may be by their numbers in the list.

The family—5 to 11—will be missed and inquired after soon and urgently; 12 and 13 will also be soon missed, but *none of the others.*

JOHN HENRY HILL.

Page 189.

If all this can be done, some little time or notice must be had to get them all ready. They tell me they can pay the sums marked to their names. The aggregate is small, but as I told you, they are poor. Let me hear from you when convenient.

Truly Yours, Wм. Penn.

1. A woman, may be 40 years old, ... $40.00
2. " " 40 " with 3 children, say 4, 6, and 8,* 15.00
3. A sister of the above, younger 10.00
4. A very genteel mulatto girl about 22 .... 25.00
5. A woman, say 45,   ⎫ These are all one   ⎫
6. A daughter, 18,   ⎪ family, either of   ⎪
7. A son, 16,   ⎪ them leaving   ⎪
8. A son, 14,   ⎬ alone, they think, ⎬ 50.00
9. A daughter, 12,   ⎪ would cause the   ⎪
10. A son, say 22,   ⎪ balance to be sold. ⎪
11. A man, the Uncle, 40, ⎭   ⎭
12. A very genteel mulatto girl, say 23 .... 25.00
13. "   "   "   "   24 .... 25.00

FIVE YEARS AND ONE MONTH SECRETED.

JOHN HENRY, HEZEKIAH, AND JAMES HILL.—JOHN MAKES A DESPERATE RESISTANCE
AT THE SLAVE AUCTION AND ESCAPES AFTER BEING SECRETED NINE MONTHS.
HEZEKIAH ESCAPED FROM A TRADER AND WAS SECRETED THIRTEEN MONTHS
BEFORE HIS FINAL DELIVERANCE.—JAMES WAS SECRETED THREE YEARS
IN A PLACE OF GREAT SUFFERING, AND ESCAPED. IN ALL FIVE
YEARS AND ONE MONTH.

Many letters from JOHN HENRY show how incessantly his mind ran out towards the oppressed, and the remarkable intelligence and ability he displayed with the pen, considering that he had no chance to acquire book knowledge. After having fled for refuge to Canada and having become a partaker of impartial freedom under the government of Great Britain, to many it seemed that the fugitive should be perfectly satisfied. Many appeared to think that the fugitive, having secured freedom, had but little occasion for anxiety or care, even for his nearest kin. "Change your name." "Never tell any one how you escaped." "Never let any one know where you came from." "Never think of writing back, not even to your wife; you can do your kin no good, but may do them harm by writing." "Take care of yourself." "You are free, well, be satisfied then." "It will do you no good to fret about your wife and children; that will not get them out of Slavery." Such was the advice often given to the fugitive. Men who had been slaves themselves, and some who had aided in the escape of individuals, sometimes urged these sentiments on men and women whose hearts were almost breaking over the thought that their dearest and best friends were in chains in the prison-house. Perhaps it was thoughtlessness

* The children might be left behind.

on the part of some, and a wish to inspire due cautiousness on the part of others, that prompted this advice. Doubtless some did soon forget their friends. They saw no way by which they could readily communicate with them. Perhaps Slavery had dealt with them so cruelly, that little hope or aspiration was left in them.

It was, however, one of the most gratifying facts connected with the fugitives, the strong love and attachment that they constantly expressed for their relatives left in the South; the undying faith they had in God as evinced by their touching appeals on behalf of their fellow-slaves. But few probably are aware how deeply these feelings were cherished in the breasts of this people. Forty, fifty, or sixty years, in some instances elapsed, but this ardent sympathy and love continued warm and unwavering as ever. Children left to the cruel mercy of slave-holders, could never be forgotten. Brothers and sisters could not refrain from weeping over the remembrance of their separation on the auction block: of having seen innocent children, feeble and defenceless women in the grasp of a merciless tyrant, pleading, groaning, and crying in vain for pity. Not to remember those thus bruised and mangled, it would seem alike unnatural, and impossible. Therefore it is a source of great satisfaction to be able, in relating these heroic escapes, to present the evidences of the strong affections of this greatly oppressed race.

JOHN HENRY never forgot those with whom he had been a fellow-sufferer in Slavery; he was always fully awake to their wrongs, and longed to be doing something to aid and encourage such as were striving to get their Freedom. He wrote many letters in behalf of others, as well as for himself, the tone of which, was always marked by the most zealous devotion to the slave, a high sense of the value of Freedom, and unshaken confidence that God was on the side of the oppressed, and a strong hope, that the day was not far distant, when the slave power would be " suddenly broken and that without remedy."

Notwithstanding the literary imperfections of these letters, they are deemed well suited to these pages Of course, slaves were not allowed book learning. Virginia even imprisoned white women for teaching free colored children the alphabet. Who has forgotten the imprisonment of Mrs. Douglass for this offense? In view of these facts, no apology is needed on account of Hill's grammar and spelling.

In these letters, may be seen, how much liberty was valued, how the taste of Freedom moved the pen of the slave; how the thought of fellow-bondmen, under the heel of the slave-holder, aroused the spirit of indignation and wrath; how importunately appeals were made for help from man and from God; how much joy was felt at the arrival of a fugitive, and the intense sadness experienced over the news of a failure or capture of a slave. Not only are the feelings of John Henry Hill represented in these epistles, but the feelings of very many others amongst the intelligent fugitives all over the country are also represented to the letter.   It is more with a view of doing justice to a brave, intelligent class, whom the public are ignorant of, than merely to give special prominence to John and his relatives as individuals, that these letters are given.

ESCAPE OF JOHN HENRY HILL FROM THE SLAVE AUCTION IN RICHMOND, ON THE
FIRST DAY OF JANUARY, 1853.

JOHN HENRY at that time, was a little turned of twenty-five years of age, full six feet high, and remarkably well proportioned in every respect. He was rather of a brown color, with marked intellectual features.   John was by trade, a carpenter, and was considered a competent workman.   The year previous to his escape, he hired his time, for which he paid his owner $150.   This amount John had fully settled up the last day of the year. As he was a young man of steady habits, a husband and father, and withal an ardent lover of Liberty; his owner, John Mitchell, evidently observed these traits in his character, and concluded that he was a dangerous piece of property to keep; that his worth in money could be more easily managed than the man.   Consequently, his master unceremoniously, without intimating in any way to John, that he was to be sold, took him to Richmond, on the first day of January (the great annual sale day), and directly to the slave-auction.   Just as John was being taken into the building, he was invited to submit to hand-cuffs.   As the thought flashed upon his mind that he was about to be sold on the auction-block, he grew terribly desperate. "Liberty or death" was the watchword of that awful moment.   In the twinkling of an eye, he turned on his enemies, with his fist, knife, and feet, so tiger-like, that he actually put four or five men to flight, his master among the number.   His enemies thus suddenly baffled, John wheeled, and, as if assisted by an angel, strange as it may appear, was soon out of sight of his pursuers, and securely hid away.   This was the last hour of John Henry's slave life, but not, however, of his struggles and sufferings for freedom, for before a final chance to escape presented itself, nine months elapsed.   The mystery as to where, and how he fared, the following account, in his own words, must explain—

Nine months I was trying to get away. I was secreted for a long time in a kitchen of a merchant near the corner of Franklyn and 7th streets, at Richmond, where I was well taken care of, by a lady friend of my mother. When I got Tired of staying in that place, I wrote myself a pass to pass myself to Petersburg, here I stopped with a very prominent Colored person, who was a friend to Freedom stayed here until two white friends told other friends if I was in the city to tell me to go at once, and stand not upon the order of going, because they had hard a plot.   I wrot a pass, started for Richmond, Reached Manchester, got off the Cars walked into Richmond, once more got back into the same old Den, Stayed here from the 16th of Aug. to 12th Sept. On the 11th of Sept. 8 o'clock P. M. a message came to me that there had been a State Room taken on the steamer City of Richmond for my benefit, and I assured the party that it would be occupied if

God be willing. Before 10 o'clock the next morning, on the 12th, a beautiful Sept. day, I arose early, wrote my pass for Norfolk left my old Den with a many a good bye, turned out the back way to 7th St., thence to Main, down Main behind 4 night waich to old Rockett's and after about 20 minutes of delay I succeed in Reaching the State Room. My Conductor was very much Excited, but I felt as Composed as I do at this moment, for I had started from my Den that morning for Liberty or for Death providing myself with a Brace of Pistels.   Yours truly J. H. HILL.

A private berth was procured for him on the steamship City of Richmond, for the amount of $125, and thus he was brought on safely to Philadelphia. While in the city, he enjoyed the hospitalities of the Vigilance Committee, and the greetings of a number of friends, during the several days of his sojourn. The thought of his wife, and two children, left in Petersburg, however, naturally caused him much anxiety. Fortunately, they were free, therefore, he was not without hope of getting them; moreover, his wife's father (Jack McCraey), was a free man, well known, and very well to do in the world, and would not be likely to see his daughter and grandchildren suffer. In this particular, Hill's lot was of a favorable character, compared with that of most slaves leaving their wives and children.

FIRST LETTER

ON ARRIVING IN CANADA.

TORONTO, October 4th, 1853.

DEAR SIR:—I take this method of informing you that I am well, and that I got to this city all safe and sound, though I did not get here as soon as I expect. I left your city on Saterday and I was on the way untel the Friday following. I got to New York the same day that I left Philadelphia, but I had to stay there untel Monday evening. I left that place at six o'clock. I got to Albany next morning in time to take the half past six o'clock train for Rochester, here I stay untel Wensday night. The reason I stay there so long Mr. Gibbs given me a letter to Mr Morris at Rochester. I left that place Wensday, but I only got five miles from that city that night. I got to Lewiston on Thurday afternoon, but too late for the boat to this city. I left Lewiston on Friday at one o'clock, got to this city at five. Sir I found this to be a very handsome city. I like it better than any city I ever saw. It are not as large as the city that you live in, but it is very large place much more so than I expect to find it. I seen the gentleman that you given me letter to. I think him much of a gentleman. I got into work on Monday. The man whom I am working for is name Myers; but I expect to go to work for another man by name of Tinsly, who is a master workman in this city. He says that he will give me work next week and everybody advises me to work for Mr. Tinsly as there more surity in him.

Mr. Still, I have been looking and looking for my friends for several days, but have not seen nor heard of them. I hope and trust in the Lord Almighty that all things are well with them. My dear sir I could feel so much better sattisfied if I could hear from my wife. Since I reached this city I have talagraphed to friend Brown to send my thing to me, but I cannot hear a word from no one at all. I have written to Mr. Brown two or three times since I left the city. I trust that he has gotten my wife's letters, that is if she has written. Please direct your letters to me, near the corner Sarah and Edward street, until I give you further notice. You will tell friend B. how to direct his letters, as I forgotten it when I writt to him, and ask him if he has heard anything from Virginia. Please to let me hear from him without delay for my very soul is trubled about my friends whom I expected to of seen here before this hour. Whatever you do please to write. I shall look for you paper shortly. Believe me sir to be your well wisher.

JOHN H. HILL.

SECOND LETTER.

Expressions of gratitude—The Custom House refuses to charge him duty—He is greatly concerned for his wife

TORONTO, October 30th, 1853.

MY DEAR FRIEND :—I now write to inform you that I have received my things all safe and sound, and also have shuck hand with the friend that you send on to this place one of them is stopping with me. His name is Chas. Stuert, he seemes to be a tolerable smart fellow. I Rec'd my letters. I have taken this friend to see Mr. Smith. However will give him a place to board untell he can get to work. I shall do every thing I can for them all that I see the gentleman wish you to see his wife and let her know that he arrived safe, and present his love to her and to all the friend. Mr. Still, I am under ten thousand obligation to you for your kindness when shall I ever repay ? S. speek very highly of you. I will state to you what Custom house master said to me. He ask me when he Presented my efects are these your efects. I answered yes. He then ask me was I going to settle in Canada. I told him I was. He then ask me of my case. I told all about it. He said I am happy to see you and all that will come. He ask me how much I had to pay for my Paper. I told him half dollar. He then told me that I should have my money again. He a Rose from his seat and got my money. So my friend you can see the people and tell them all this is a land of liberty and believe they will find friends here. My best love to all.

My friend I must call upon you once more to do more kindness for me that is to write to my wife as soon as you get this, and tell her when she gets ready to come she will pack and consign her things to you. You will give her some instruction, but not to your expenses but to her own.

When you write direct your letter to Phillip Ubank, Petersburg, Va. My Box arrived here the 27th.

My dear sir I am in a hurry to take this friend to church, so I must close by saying I am your humble servant in the cause of liberty and humanity. JOHN H. HILL.

THIRD LETTER.

Canada is highly praised—The Vigilance Committee is implored to send all the Fugitives there—" Farmers and Mechanics wanted "—" No living in Canada for Negroes," as argued by " Masters," flatly denied, &c., &c., &c.

So I ask you to send the fugitives to Canada. I don't know much of this Province but I beleaves that there is Rome enough for the colored and whites of the United States. We wants farmers mechanic men of all qualification &c, if they are not made we will make them, if we cannot make the old, we will make our children.

Now concerning the city toronto this city is Beautiful and Prosperous Levele city. Great many wooden codages more than what should be but I am in hopes there will be more of the Brick and Stonn. But I am not done about your Republicanism. Our masters have told us that there was no living in Canada for a Negro but if it may Please your gentlemanship to publish these facts that we are here able to earn our bread and money enough to make us comftable. But I say give me freedom, and the United States may have all her money and her Luxtures, yeas give Liberty or Death. I'm in America, but not under Such a Government that I cannot express myself, speak, think or write So as I am able, and if my master had allowed me to have an education I would make them American Slave-holders feel me, Yeas I would make them tremble when I spoke, and when I

13

take my Pen in hand their knees smote together. My Dear Sir suppose I was an educated man. I could write you something worth reading, but you know we poor fugitives whom has just come over from the South are not able to write much on no subject whatever, but I hope by the aid of my God I will try to use my midnight lamp, untel I can have some influence upon the American Slavery. If some one would say to me, that they would give my wife bread untel I could be Educated I would stoop my trade this day and take up my books.

But a crisis is approaching when assential requisite to the American Slaveholders when blood Death or Liberty will be required at their hands. I think our people have depened too long and too much on false legislator let us now look for ourselves. It is true that England however the Englishman is our best friend but we as men ought not to depened upon her Remonstrace with the Americans because she loves her commercial trade as any Nations do. But I must say, while we look up and acknowledge the Power greatness and honor of old England, and believe that while we sit beneath the Silken folds of her flag of Perfect Liberty, we are secure, beyond the reach of the aggressions of the Blood hounds and free from the despotism that would wrap around our limbs by the damable Slave-holder. Yet we would not like spoiled childeren depend upon her, but upon ourselves and as one means of strengthening ourselves, we should agitate the emigration to Canada. I here send you a paragraph which I clipted from the weekly Glob. I hope you will pub-lish so that Mr. Williamson may know that men are not chattel here but reather they are men and if he wants his chattle let him come here after it or his thing. I wants you to let the whole United States know we are satisfied here because I have seen more Pleasure since I came here then I saw in the U. S. the 24 years that I served my master. Come Poor distress men women and come to Canada where colored men are free. Oh how sweet the word do sound to me yeas when I contemplate of these things, my very flesh creaps my heart thrub when I think of my beloved friends whom I left in that cursid hole. Oh my God what can I do for them or shall I do for them. Lord help them. Suffer them to be no longer depressed beneath the Bruat Creation but may they be looked upon as men made of the Bone and Blood as the Anglo-Americans. May God in his mercy Give Lib-erty to all this world. I must close as it am late hour at night. I Remain your friend in the cause of Liberty and humanity,

JOHN H. HILL, a fugitive.

If you know any one who would give me an education write and let me know for I am in want of it very much.   Your with Respect,

J. H. H.

If the sentiments in the above letter do not indicate an uncommon degree of natural intelligence, a clear perception of the wrongs of Slavery, and a just appreciation of freedom, where shall we look for the signs of intellect and manhood?

FOURTH LETTER.

Longs for his wife—In hearing of the return of a Fugitive from Philadelphia is made sorrowful—His love of Freedom increases, &c., &c.

TORONTO, November 12th, 1853.

MY DEAR STILL :—Your letter of the 3th came to hand thursday and also three copes all of which I was glad to Received they have taken my attention all together Every Time I got them. I also Rec'd. a letter from my friend Brown. Mr. Brown stated to me that he had heard from my wife but he did not say what way he heard. I am looking for my wife every day. Yes I want her to come then I will be better sattisfied. My friend I am a free man and feeles alright about that matter. I am doing tolrable well in my line of business, and think I will do better after little. I hope you all will never stop any of our Brotheran that makes their Escep from the South but send them on to this Place where they can be free man and woman. We want them here and not in your State where they can be taken away at any hour. Nay but let him come here where he can Enjoy the Rights of a human being and not to be trodden under the feet of men like themselves. All the People that comes here does well. Thanks be to God that I came to this place. I would like very well to see you all but never do I expect to see you in the United States. I want you all to come to this land of Liberty where the bondman can be free. Come one come all come to this place, and I hope my dear friend you will send on here. I shall do for them as you all done for me when I came on here however I will do the best I can for them if they can they shall do if they will do, but some comes here that can't do well because they make no efford. I hope my friend you will teach them such lessons as Mrs. Moore Give me before I left your city. I hope she may live a hundred years longer and enjoy good health. May God bless her for the good cause which she are working in. Mr. Still you ask me to remember you to Nelson. I will do so when I see him, he are on the lake so is Stewart. I received a letter to-day for Stewart from your city which letter I will take to him when he comes to the city. He are not stoping with us at this time. I was very sorry a few days ago when I heard that a man was taken from your city.

Send them over here, then let him come here and take them away and I will try to have a finger in the Pie myself. You said that you had written to my wife ten thousand thanks for what you have done and what you are willing to do. My friend whenever you hear from my wife please write to me. Whenever she come to your city please give instruction how to travel. I wants her to come the faster way. I wish she was here now. I wish she could get a ticket through to this place. I have mail a paper for you to day.

We have had snow but not to last long. Let me hear from you. My Respect friend Brown. I will write more when I have the opportunity.   Yours with Respect,

JOHN H. HILL.

P. S. My dear Sir. Last night after I had written the above, and had gone to bed, I heard a strange voice in the house, Saying to Mr. Myers to come quickly to one of our colod Brotheran out of the street. We went and found a man a Carpenter laying on the side walk woltun in his Blood. Done by some unknown Person as yet but if they stay on the earth the law will deteck them. It is said that party of colord people done it, which party was seen to come out an infame house.

Mr. Myers have been down to see him and Brought the Sad news that the Poor fellow was dead. Mr. Scott for Henry Scott was the name, he was a fugitive from Virginia he came here from Pittsburg Pa. Oh, when I went where he laid what a shock, it taken my Sleep altogether night. When I got to Sopt his Body was surrounded by the Policeman. The law has taken the woman in cusidy. I write and also send you a paper of the case when it comes out.   J. H. HILL.

FIFTH LETTER.

He rejoices over the arrival of his wife—but at the same time. his heart is bleeding over a dear friend whom he had promised to help before he left Slavery.

TORONTO, December 29th, 1853.

MY DEAR FRIEND:—It affords me a good deel of Pleasure to say that my wife and the Children have arrived safe in this City. But my wife had very bad luck. She lost her money and the money that was belonging to the children, the whole amount was 35 dollars. She had to go to the Niagara falls and Telegraph to me come after her. She got to the falls on Sat'dy and I went after her on Monday. We saw each other once again after so long an Abstance, you may know what sort of metting it was, joyful times of corst. My wife are well Satisfied here, and she was well Pleased during her stay in your city. My Trip to the falls cost Ten Eighty Seven and half. The things that friend Brown Shiped to me by the Express costed $24¼. So you can see fiting out a house Niagara falls and the cost for bringing my things to this place, have got me out of money, but for all I am a free man.

The weather are very cold at Present, the snow continue to fall though not as deep here as it is in Boston. The people haves their own Amousements, the weather as it is now, they don't care for the snow nor ice, but they are going from Ten A. M. until Twelve P. M., the hous that we have open don't take well because we don't Sell Spirits, which we are trying to avoid if we can.

Mr. Still, I hold in my hand A letter from a friend of South, who calls me to promise that I made to him before I left. My dear Sir, this letter have made my heart Bleed, since I Received it, he also desires of me to remember him to his beloved Brethren and then to Pray for him and his dear friends who are in Slavery. I shall Present his letter to the churches of this city. I forward to your care for Mrs. Moore, a few weeks ago. Mrs. Hill sends her love to your wife and yourself.

Please to write, I Sincerely hope that our friends from Petersburg have reached your city before this letter is dated. I must close by saying, that I Sir, remain humble and obedient Servant, J. H. H.

SIXTH LETTER.

He is now earnestly appealing in behalf of a friend in Slavery, with a view to procuring aid and assistance from certain parties, by which this particular friend in bondage might be rescued.

TORONTO, March 8th, 1854.

My DEAR FRIEND STILL :—We will once more truble you opon this great cause of freedom, as we know that you are a man, that are never fatuged in Such a glorious cause. Sir, what I wish to Say is this. Mr. Forman has Received a letter from his wife dated the 29th ult. She States to him that She was Ready at any time, and that Everything was Right with her, and she hoped that he would lose no time in sending for her for she was Ready and awaiting for him. Well friend Still, we learnt that Mr. Minkens could not bring her the account of her child. We are very sorry to hear Such News, however, you will please to read this letter with care, as we have learnt that Minkens Cannot do what we wishes to be done; we perpose another way. There is a white man that Sale from Richmond to Boston, that man are very Safe, he will bring F's wife with her child. So you will do us a favour will take it upon yourself to transcribe from this letter what we shall write. I. E. this there is a Colored gen. that workes on the basin in R—d this man's name is Esue Foster, he can tell Mrs. forman all about this Saleor. So you can place the letter in the hands of M. to take to forman's wife, She can read it for herself. She will find Foster at ladlum's warehouse on the Basin, and when you write call my name to him and he will trust it. this foster are a member of the old Baptist Church. When you have done all you can do let us know what you have done, if you hears anything of my uncle let me know.

SEVENTH LETTER.

He laments over his uncle's fate, who was suffering in a dungeon-like place of concealment daily waiting for the opportunity to escape.

TORONTO, March 18th, 1864.

My DEAR STILL :—Yours of the 15th Reached on the 11th, found myself and family very well, and not to delay no time in replying to you, as there was an article in your letter which article Roused me very much when I read it; that was you praying to me to be cautious how I write down South. Be so kind as to tell me in your next letter whether you have at any time apprehended any danger in my letters however, in those bond southward; if there have been, allow me to beg ten thousand pardon before God and man, for I am not design to throw any obstacle in the way of those whom I left in South, but to aide them in every possible way. I have done as you Requested, that to warn the friends of the dager of writing South. I have told all you said in yours that Mr. Minkins would be in your city very soon, and you would see what you could do for me, do you mean or do speak in reference to my dear uncle. I am hopes that you will use every ifford to get him from the position in which he now stand. I know how he feels at this time, for I have felt the same when I was a runway. I was bereft of all participation with my family for nearly nine months, and now that poor fellow are place in same position. Oh God help I pray, what a pitty it is that I cannot do him no good, but I sincerely hope that you will not get fatigued at doing good in such cases, nay, I think other wises of you, however, I Say no more on this subject at present, but leave it for you to judge.

On the 13th inst. you made Some Remarks concerning friend Forman's wife, I am Satisfied that you will do all you can for her Release from Slavery, but as you said you feels for them, so do I, and Mr. Foreman comes to me very often to know if I have heard anything from you concerning his wife, they all comes to for the same.

God Save the Queen. All my letters Southward have passed through your hands with an exception of one. JOHN H. HILL.

EIGHTH LETTER.

Death has snatched away one of his children and he has cause to mourn. In his grief he recounts his struggles for freedom, and his having to leave his wife and children. He acknowledges that he had to "work very hard for comforts," but he declares that he would not " exchange with the comforts of ten thousand slaves."

TORONTO Sept 14th 1854

MY DEAR FRIEND STILL :—this are the first oppertunity that I have had to write you since I Recd your letter of the 20th July. there have been sickness and Death in my family since your letter was Recd. our dear little Child have been taken from us one whom we loved so very Dear. but the almighty God knows what are best for us all.

Louis Henry Hill, was born in Petersburg Va May 7th 1852. and Died Toronto August 19th 1854 at five o'clock P. M.

Dear Still I could say much about the times and insidince that have taken place since the coming of that dear little angle jest spoken of. it was 12 months and 3 days from the time that I took departure of my wife and child to proceed to Richmond to awaite a conveyance up to the day of his death.

it was thursday the 13th that I lift Richmond. it was saturday the 15th that I land to my great joy in the city of Phila. then I put out for Canada. I arrived in this city on Friday the 30th and to my great satisfaction. I found myself upon Briton's free land. not only free for the white man bot for all.

this day 12 months I was not out of the reach the slaveholders, but this 14th day of Sept. I am as Free as your President Pearce. only I have not been free so long However the 30th of the month I will have been free only 12 months.

It is true that I have to work very hard for comfort but I would not exchange with ten thousand slave that are equel with their masters. I am Happy, Happy.

Give love to Mrs. Still. My wife laments her child's death too much. wil you be so kind as to see Mr. Brown and ask him to write to me, and if he have heard from Petersburg Va. Yours truely J. H. HILL.

NINTH LETTER.

He is anxiously waiting for the arrival of friends from the South. Hints that slave-holders would be very unsafe in Canada, should they be foolish enough to visit that country for the purpose of enticing slaves back.

TORONTO, Jan. 19th 1854.

MY DEAR STILL:—Your letter of the 16th came to hand just in time for my perpose I perceivs by your statement that the money have not been to Petersburg at all done just what was right and I would of sent the money to you at first, but my dear friend I have called upon you for so many times that I have been ashamed of myself to call any more So you may perceive by the above written my obligations to you, you said that you had written on to Petersburg, you have done Right which I believes is your general way of doing your business. the money are all right I only had to pay a 6d on the Ten dollars. this money was given to by a friend in the city N. york, the friend was from Richmond Virginia (a white man) the amount was fifteen dollars, I forward a letter to you yesterday which letter I forgot to date. my friend I wants to hear from virginia the worst of all things. you know that we expect some freneds on and we cannot hear any thing from them which makes us uneasy for fear that they have attempt to come away and been detected. I have ears open at all times, listen at all hours expecting to hear from them Please to see friend Brown and know from him if he has heard anything from our friends, if he have not. tell him write and inquiare into the matter why it is that they have not come over, then let me hear from you all.

We are going to have a grand concert &c I mean the Abolisnous Socity. I will attend myself and also my wife if the Lord be willing you will perceive in previous letter that I mension something concerning Mr Forman's wife if there be any chance whatever please to proceed, Mr Foreman sends his love to you Requested you to do all you can to get his wife away from Slavery.

Our best respects to your wife. You promissed me that you would write somthing concerning our arrival in Canada but I suppose you have not had the time as yet, I would be very glad to read your opinion on that matter

I have notice several articles in the freeman one of the Canada weaklys concerning the Christiana prisoners respecting Castnor Hanway and also Mr. Rauffman. if I had one hundred dollars to day I would give them five each, however I hope that I may be able to subscribe something for their Relefe. in Regards to the letters have been writteu from Canada to the South the letters was not what they thought them to be and if the slave-holders know when they are doing well they had better keep their side for if they comes over this side of the lake I am under the impression they will not go back with somethin that their mother boned them with whether thiar slaves written for them or not. I know some one here that have written his master to come after him, but not because he expect to go with him home but because he wants to retaleate upon his persecutor, but I would be sorry for man that have written for his master expecting to return with him because the people here would kill them. Sir I cannot write enough to express myself so I must close by saying I Remain yours.   JOHN H. HILL.

TENTH LETTER.

Great joy over an arrival — Twelve months praying for the deliverance of an Uncle groaning in a hiding-place, while the Slave-hunters are daily expected—Strong appeals for aid, &c., &c.

TORONTO, January 7th, 1855.

MY DEAR FRIEND:—It is with much pleasure that I take this opportunity of addressing you with these few lines hoping when they reeches you they may find yourself and family enjoying good health as they leaves us at present.

And it is with much happiness that I can say to you that Mrs. Mercer arrived in this city on yesterday. Mr. Mercer was at my house late in the evening, and I told him that when he went home if hear anything from Virginia, that he must let me know as soon as possible. He told me that if he went home and found any news there he would come right back and inform me thereof. But little did he expect to find his dearest there. You may judge what a meeting there was with them, and may God grant that there may be some more meetings with our wives and friends. I had been looking for some one from the old sod for several days, but I was in good hopes that it would be my poor Uncle. But poor fellow he are yet groaning under the sufferings of a horrid sytam, Expecting every day to Receive his Doom. Oh, God, what shall I do, or what can I do for him? I have prayed for him more than 12 months, yet he is in that horrid condition. I can never hear anything Directly from him or any of my people.

Once more I appeal to your Humanity. Will you act for him, as if you was in slavery yourself, and I sincerely believe that he will come out of that condition? Mrs. M. have told me that she given some directions how he could be goten at, but friend Still, if this conductor should not be successfull this time, will you mind him of the Poor Slave again. I hope you will as Mrs. Mercer have told the friend what to do I cannot do more, therefore I must leve it to the Mercy of God and your Exertion.

The weather have been very mile Ever since the 23rd of Dec. I have thought considerable about our condition in this country Seeing that the weather was so very faverable to us. I was thinking a few days ago, that nature had giving us A country & adopted all things Sutable.

You will do me the kindness of telling me in your next whether or not the ten slaves have been Brought out from N. C.

I have not hard from Brown for Nine month he have done some very Bad letting me alone, for what cause I cannot tell Give my Best Respect to Mr. B. when you see him. I wish very much to hear from himself and family. You will please to let me hear from you. My wife Joines me in love to yourself and family.

Yours most Respectfully,

JOHN H. HILL.

P. S. Every fugitive Regreated to hear of the Death of Mrs. Moore. I myself think that there are no other to take her Place. yours J. H. H.

ELEVENTH LETTER.

[EXTRACT.]

Rejoices at hearing of the success of the Underground Rail Road—Inquires particularly after the "fellow" who "cut off the Patrol's head in Maryland."

HAMILTON, August 15th, 1856.

DEAR FRIEND :—I am very glad to hear that the Underground Rail Road is doing such good business, but tell me in your next letter if you have seen the heroic fellow that cut off the head of the Patrol in Maryland. We wants that fellow here, as John Bull has a great deal of fighting to do, and as there is a colored Captain in this city, I would seek to have that fellow Promoted, Provided he became a soldier.

Great respect, JOHN H. HILL.

P. S.—Please forward the enclosed to Mr. McCray.

TWELFTH LETTER.

[EXTRACT.]

Believes in praying for the Slave—but thinks "fire and sword" would be more effective with Slave-holders.

HAMILTON, Jan. 5th, 1857.

MR. STILL:—Our Pappers contains long details of insurrectionary movements among the slaves at the South and one paper adds that a great Nomber of Generals, Captains with other officers had being arrested. At this day four years ago I left Petersburg for Richmond to meet the man whom called himself my master, but he wanted money worser that day than I do this day, he took me to sell me, he could not have done a better thing for me for I intended to leave any how by the first convaiance. I hard some good Prayers put up for the suffers on last Sunday evening in the Baptist Church. Now friend still I beleve that Prayers affects great good, but I beleve that the fire and sword would affect more good in this case. Perhaps this is not your thoughts, but I must acknowledge this to be my Polacy. The world are being turned upside down, and I think we might as well take an active part in it as not. We must have something to do as other people, and I hope this moment among the Slaves are the beginning. I wants to see something go on while I live.

Yours truly,   JOHN H. HILL.

THIRTEENTH LETTER.

Sad tidings from Richmond—Of the arrest of a Captain with Slaves on board as Underground Rail Road passengers.

HAMILTON, June 5th, 1858.

DEAR FRIEND STILL:—I have just heard that our friend Capt. B. have being taken Prisoner in Virginia with slaves on board of his vessel. I hard this about an hour ago. the Person told me of this said he read it in the newspaper, if this be so it is awfull. You will be so kind as to send me some information. Send me one of the Virginia Papers. Poor fellow if they have got him, I am sorry, sorry to my heart. I have not heard from my Uncle for a long time if have heard or do hear anything from him at any time you will oblige me by writing. I wish you to inquire of Mr. Anderson's friends (if you know any of them), if they have heard anything from him since he was in your city. I have written to him twice since he was here according to his own directions, but never received an answer. I wants to hear from my mother very much, but cannot hear one word. You will present my best regards to the friend. Mrs. Hill is quite sick.

Yours truly,   J. H. HILL.

P. S.—I have not received the Anti-Slavery Standard for several weeks. Please forward any news relative to the Capt.   J. H. H.

THE ESCAPE OF HEZEKIAH HILL.

(UNCLE OF JOHN HENRY HILL.)

Impelled by the love of freedom Hezekiah resolved that he would work no longer for nothing; that he would never be sold on the auction block; that he no longer would obey the bidding of a master, and that he would die rather than be a slave. This decision, however, had only been entertained by him a short time prior to his escape. For a number of years Hezekiah had been laboring under the pleasing thought that he should succeed in obtaining freedom through purchase, having had an understanding with his owner with this object in view. At different times he had paid on account for himself nineteen hundred dollars, six hundred dollars more than he was to have paid according to the first agreement. Although so shamefully defrauded in the first instance, he concluded to bear the disappointment as patiently as possible and get out of the lion's mouth as best he could.

He continued to work on and save his money until he had actually come within one hundred dollars of paying two thousand. At this point instead of getting his free papers, as he firmly believed that he should, to his surprise one day he saw a notorious trader approaching the shop where he was at work. The errand of the trader was soon made known. Hezekiah simply requested time to go back to the other end of the shop to get his coat, which he seized and ran. He was pursued but not captured. This occurrence took place in Petersburg, Va., about the first of December, 1854. On the night of the same day of his escape from the trader, Hezekiah walked to Richmond and was there secreted under a floor by a friend. He was a tall man, of powerful muscular strength, about thirty years of age just in the prime of his manhood with enough pluck for two men.

A heavy reward was offered for him, but the hunters failed to find him in this hiding-place under the floor. He strongly hoped to get away soon; on several occasions he made efforts, but only to be disappointed. At different times at least two captains had consented to afford him a private passage to Philadelphia, but like the impotent man at the pool, some one always got ahead of him. Two or three times he even managed to reach the boat upon the river, but had to return to his horrible place under the floor. Some were under the impression that he was an exceedingly unlucky man, and for a time captains feared to bring him. But his courage sustained him unwaveringly.

Finally at the expiration of thirteen months, a private passage was procured for him on the steamship Pennsylvania, and with a little slave boy, seven years of age, (the son of the man who had secreted him) though placed in a very hard berth, he came safely to Philadelphia, greatly to the astonishment of the Vigilance Committee, who had waited for him so long that they had despaired of his ever coming.

The joy that filled Hezekiah's bosom may be imagined but never described. None but one who had been in similar straits could enter into his feelings.

He had left his wife Louisa, and two little boys, Henry and Manuel. His passage cost one hundred dollars.

Hezekiah being a noted character, a number of the true friends were invited to take him by the hand and to rejoice with him over his noble struggles and his triumph; needing rest and recruiting, he was made welcome to stay, at the expense of the committee, as long as he might feel disposed so to do. He remained several days, and then went on to Canada rejoicing. After arriving there he returned his acknowledgment for favors received, &c., in the following letter:

TORONTO Jan 24th 1856.

MR. STILL:—this is to inform you that Myself and little boy, arrived safely in this city this day the 24th, at ten o'clock after a very long and pleasant trip. I had a great deal of attention paid to me while on the way.

I owes a great deel of thanks to yourself and friends, I will just say hare that when I arrived at New York, I found Mr. Gibbs sick and could not be attended to there. However, I have arrived alright.

You will please to give my respects to your friend that writes in the office with you, and to Mr Smith, also Mr Brown, and the friends, Mrs Still in particular.

Friend Still you will please to send the enclosed to John Hill Petersburg I want him to send some things to me you will be so kind as to send your direction to them, so that the things to your care. if you do not see a convenient way to send it by hands, you will please direct your letter to Phillip Ubank Petersburg. Yours Respectfully H HILL.

JAMES—(BROTHER OF JOHN HENRY HILL).

For three years James suffered in a place of concealment, before he found the way opened to escape. When he resolved on having his freedom he was much under twenty-one years of age, a brave young man, for three years, with unfailing spirit, making resistance in the city of Richmond to the slave Power!

Such heroes in the days of Slavery, did much to make the infernal system insecure, and to keep alive the spirit of freedom in liberty-loving hearts the world over, wherever such deeds of noble daring were made known. But of his heroism, but little can be reported here, from the fact, that such accounts as were in the possession of the Committee, were never transferred from the loose slips of paper on which they were first written, to the regular record book. But an important letter from the friend with whom he was secreted, written a short while before he escaped (on a boat), gives some idea of his condition:

RICHMOND, VA., February 16th, 1861.

DEAR BROTHER STILL:—I received a message from brother Julius anderson, asking me to send the bundle on but I has no way to send it, I have been waiting and truly hopeing that you would make some arrangement with some person, and send for the parcel. I have no way to send it, and I cannot communicate the subject to a stranger there is a Way by the N. y. line, but they are all strangers to me, and of course I could not approach them With this subject for I would be indangered myself greatly. this business is left to you and to you alone to attend to in providing the way for me to send on the parcel, if you only make an arrangement with some person and let me know the said person and the article which they is to be sent on then I can send the parcel. unless you do make an arrangement with some person, and assure them that they will receive the funs for delivering the parcel this Business cannot be accomplished. it is in your power to try to make some provision for the article to be sent but it is not in my power to do so, the bundle has been on my hands now going on 3 years, and I have suffered a great deal of danger, and is still suffering the same. I have understood Sir that there were no difficul about the mone that you had it in your possession Ready for the bundle whenever it is delivered. But Sir as I have said I can do nothing now. Sir I ask you please through sympathy and feelings on my part & his try to provide a way for the bundle to be sent and relieve me of the danger in which I am in. you might succeed in making an arrangement with those on the New york Steamers for they dose such things but please let me know the man that the arrangement is made with—please give me an answer by the bearer.   yours truly friend   C. A.

At last, the long, dark night passed away, and this young slave safely made his way to freedom, and proceeded to Boston, where he now resides. While the Committee was looked to for aid in the deliverance of this poor fellow, it was painful to feel that it was not in their power to answer his prayers—not until after his escape, was it possible so to do. But his escape to freedom gave them a satisfaction which no words can well express. At present, John Henry Hill is a justice of the peace in Petersburg. Hezekiah resides at West Point, and James in Boston, rejoicing that all men are free in the United States, at last.

FROM VIRGINIA, MARYLAND AND DELAWARE.

ARCHER BARLOW, ALIAS EMIT ROBINS.

This passenger arrived from Norfolk, Va. in 1853. For the last four years previous to escaping, he had been under the yoke of Dr. George Wilson. Archer declared that he had been "very badly treated" by the Doctor, which he urged as his reason for leaving. True, the doctor had been good enough to allow him to hire his time, for which he required Archer to pay the moderate sum of $120 per annum. As Archer had been "sickly" most of the time, during the last year, he complained that there was "no reduction" in his hire on this account. Upon reflection, therefore, Archer thought, if he had justice done him, he would be in possession of this "one hundred and twenty" himself, and all his other rights, instead of having to toil for another without pay ; so he looked seriously into the matter of master and slave, and pretty soon resolved, that if others chose to make no effort to get away, for himself he would never be contented, until he was free. When a slave reached this decision, he was in a very hopeful state. He was near the Underground Rail Road, and was sure to find it, sooner or later. At this thoughtful period, Archer was thirty-one years of age, a man of medium size, and belonged to the two leading branches of southern humanity, *i. e.*, he was half white and half colored—a dark mulatto. His arrival in Philadelphia, per one of the Richmond steamers, was greeted with joy by the Vigilance Committee, who extended to him the usual aid and care, and forwarded him on to freedom. For a number of years, he has been a citizen of Boston.

SAMUEL BUSH, ALIAS WILLIAM OBLEBEE.

This "piece of property" fled in the fall of 1853. As a specimen of this article of commerce, he evinced considerable intelligence. He was a man of dark color, although not totally free from the admixture of the "superior" southern blood in his veins; in stature, he was only ordinary. For leaving, he gave the following reasons : " I found that I was working for my master, for his advantage, and when I was sick, I had to pay just as much as if I were well—$7 a month. But my master was cross, and said that he intended to sell me—to do better by me another year. Times grew worse and worse, constantly. I thought, as I had heard, that if I could raise thirty dollars I could come away." He at once saw the value of money. To his mind it meant liberty from that moment. Thenceforth he decided to treasure up every dollar he could get hold of until he could accumulate at least enough to get out of "Old Virginia." He was a married man, and thought he had a wife and one child, but on reflection, he found out that they did not actually belong to him, but to a carpenter, by the name of Bailey. The man whom Samuel was compelled to call master was named Hoyle.

The Committee's interview with Samuel was quite satisfactory, and they cheerfully accorded to him brotherly kindness and material aid at the same time.

JOHN SPENCER AND HIS SON WILLIAM, AND JAMES ALBERT.

These individuals escaped from the eastern shore of Maryland, in the Spring of 1853, but were led to conclude that they could enjoy the freedom they had aimed to find, in New Jersey. They procured employment in the neighborhood of Haddonfield, some six or eight miles from Camden, New Jersey, and were succeeding, as they thought, very well.

Things went on favorably for about three months, when to their alarm " slave-hunters were discovered in the neighborhood," and sufficient evidence was obtained to make it quite plain that, John, William and James were the identical persons, for whom the hunters were in " hot pursuit." When brought to the Committee, they were pretty thoroughly alarmed and felt very anxious to be safely off to Canada. While the Committee always rendered in such cases immediate protection and aid, they nevertheless, felt, in view of the imminent dangers existing under the fugitive slave law, that persons disposed to thus stop by the way, should be very plainly given to understand, that if they were captured they would have themselves the most to blame. But the dread of Slavery was strong in the minds of these fugitives, and they very fully realized their folly in stopping in New Jersey. The Committee procured their tickets, helped them to disguise themselves as much as possible, and admonished them not to stop short of Canada.

HETTY SCOTT ALIAS MARGARET DUNCANS AND DAUGHTER PRISCILLA.

This mother and daughter had been the "chattels personal" of Daniel Coolby of Harvard, Md. Their lot had been that of ordinary slaves in the country, on farms, &c. The motive which prompted them to escape was the fact that their master had "threatened to sell" them. He had a right to do so; but Hetty was a little squeamish on this point and took great umbrage at her "kind master." In this "disobedient" state of mind, she determined, if hard struggling would enable her, to defeat the threats of Mr. Daniel Coolby, that he should not much longer have the satisfaction of enjoying the fruit of the toil of herself and offspring. She at once began to prepare for her journey.

She had three children of her own to bring, besides she was intimately acquainted with a young man and a young woman, both slaves, to whom she felt that it would be safe to confide her plans with a view of inviting them to accompany her. The young couple were ready converts to the eloquent speech delivered to them by Hetty on Freedom, and were quite willing to accept her as their leader in the emergency. Up to the hour of setting out on their lonely and fatiguing journey, arrangements were being carefully completed, so that there should be no delay of any kind. At the appointed hour they were all moving northward in good order.

Arriving at Quakertown, Pa., they found friends of the slave, who welcomed them to their homes and sympathy, gladdening the hearts of all concerned. For prudential reasons it was deemed desirable to separate the party, to send some one way and some another. Thus safely, through the kind offices and aid of the friends at Quakertown, they were duly forwarded on to the Committee in Philadelphia. Here similar acts of charity were extended to them, and they were directed on to Canada.

ROBERT FISHER.

ROBERT was about thirty years of age, dark color, quite tall, and in talking with him a little while, it was soon discovered that Slavery had not crushed all the brains out of his head by a good deal. Nor was he so much attached to his "kind-hearted master," John Edward Jackson, of Anne Arundel, Md., or his old fiddle, that he was contented and happy while in bondage. Far from it. The fact was, that he hated Slavery so decidedly and had such a clear common sense-like view of the evils and misery of the system, that he declared he had as a matter of principle refrained from marrying, in order that he might have no reason to grieve over having added to the woes of slaves. Nor did he wish to be encumbered, if the opportunity offered to escape. According to law he was entitled to his freedom at the age of twenty-five.

But what right had a negro, which white slave-holders were "bound to respect?" Many who had been willed free, were held just as firmly in Slavery, as if no will had ever been made. Robert had too much sense to suppose that he could gain anything by seeking legal redress. This method, therefore, was considered out of the question. But in the meantime he was growing very naturally in favor of the Underground Rail Road. From his experience Robert did not hesitate to say that his master was "mean," "a very hard man," who would work his servants early and late, without allowing them food and clothing sufficient to shield them from the cold and hunger. Robert certainly had unmistakable marks about him, of having been used roughly. He thought very well of Nathan Harris, a fellow-servant belonging to the same owner, and he made up his mind, if Nathan would join him, neither the length of the journey, the loneliness of night travel, the coldness of the weather, the fear of the slave-hunter, nor the scantiness of their means should deter him from making his way to freedom. Nathan listened to the proposal, and was suddenly converted to freedom, and the two united during Christmas week, 1854, and set out on the Underground Rail Road. It is needless to say that they had trying difficulties to encounter. These they expected, but all were overcome, and they reached the Vigilance Committee, in Philadelphia safely, and were cordially welcomed. During the interview, a full interchange of thought resulted, the fugitives were well cared for, and in due time both were forwarded on, free of cost.

HANSEL WAPLES.

This traveler arrived from Millsboro, Indian River, Delaware, where he was owned by Wm. E. Burton. While Hansel did not really own himself, he had the reputation of having a wife and six children. In June, some six months prior to her husband's arrival, Hansel's wife had been allowed by her mistress to go out on a begging expedition, to raise money to buy herself; but contrary to the expectation of her mistress she never returned. Doubtless the mistress looked upon this course as a piece of the most high-handed stealing. Hansel did not speak of his owner as being a hard man, but on the contrary he thought that he was about as "good" as the best that he was acquainted with. While this was true, however, Hansel had quite good ground for believing that his master was about to sell him. Dreading this fate he made up his mind to go in pursuit of his wife to a Free state. Exactly where to look or how to find her he could not tell.

The Committee advised him to "search in Canada." And in order to enable him to get on quickly and safely, the Committee aided him with money, &c., in 1853.

ROSE ANNA TONNELL ALIAS MARIA HYDE.

She fled from Isaac Tonnell of Georgetown, Delaware, in Christmas week, 1853. A young woman with a little boy of seven years of age accompanied Rose Anna. Further than the simple fact of their having thus safely arrived, except the expense incurred by the Committee, no other particulars appear on the records.

MARY ENNIS ALIAS LICIA HEMMIN.

Mary arrived with her two children in the early Spring of 1854.

The mother was a woman of about thirty-three years of age, quite tall, with a countenance and general appearance well fitted to awaken sympathy at first sight. Her oldest child was a little girl seven years of age, named Lydia; the other was named Louisa Caroline, three years of age, both promising in appearance. They were the so called property of John Ennis, of Georgetown, Delaware. For their flight they chose the dead of Winter. After leaving they made their way to West Chester, and there found friends and security for several weeks, up to the time they reached Philadelphia. Probably the friends with whom they stopped thought the weather too inclement for a woman with children dependent on her support to travel. Long before this mother escaped, thoughts of liberty filled her heart. She was ever watching for an opportunity, that would encourage her to hope for safety, when once the attempt should be made. Until, however, she was convinced that her two children were to be sold, she could not quite muster courage to set out on the journey. This threat to sell proved in multitudes of instances, " the last straw on the camel's back." When nothing else would start them this would. Mary and her children were the only slaves owned by this Ennis, consequently her duties were that of " Jack of all trades ; " sometimes in the field and sometimes in the barn, as well as in the kitchen, by which, it is needless to say, that her life was rendered servile to the last degree.

To bind up the broken heart of such a poor slave mother, and to aid such tender plants as were these little girls, from such a wretched state of barbarism as existed in poor little Delaware, was doubly gratifying to the Committee.

"SAM," "ISAAC," "PERRY," "CHARLES," AND "GREEN."

 ONE THOUSAND DOLLARS REWARD.—Ran away on Saturday night, the 20th September, 1856, from the subscriber, living in the ninth district of Carroll county, Maryland, two Negro Men, SAM and ISAAC. Sam calls himself Samuel Sims; he is very black ; shows his teeth very much when he laughs ; no perceptible marks ; he is 5 feet 8 inches high, and about thirty years of age, but has the appearance of being much older.

Isaac calls himself Isaac Dotson he is about nineteen years of age, stout made, but rather chunky; broad across his shoulders, he is about five feet five or six inches high, always appears to be in a good humor ; laughs a good deal, and runs on with a good deal of foolishness ; he is of very light color, almost yellow, might be called a yellow boy ; has no perceptible marks.

They have such a variety of clothing that it is almost useless to say anything about them. No doubt they will change their names.

I will give the above reward for them, of one thousand dollars, or five hundred dollars for either of them, if taken and lodged in any jail in Maryland. so that I get them again.

Also two of Mr. Dade's, living in the neighborhood, went the same time ; no doubt they are all in company together.   THOMAS B. OWINGS.

s24–6t Wit*‖

These passengers reached the Philadelphia station, about the 24th of September, 1856, five days after they escaped from Carroll county. They were in fine spirits, and had borne the fatigue and privation of travel bravely. A free and interesting interview took place, between these passengers and the Committee, eliciting much information, especially with regard to the workings of the system on the farms, from which they had the good luck to flee. Each of the party was thoroughly questioned, about how time had passed with them at home, or rather in the prison house, what kind of men their masters were, how they fed and clothed, if they whipped, bought or sold, whether they were members of church, or not, and many more questions needless to enumerate bearing on the domestic relation which had existed between themselves and their masters. These queries they answered in their own way, with intelligence. Upon the whole, their lot in Slavery had been rather more favorable than the average run of slaves.

No record was made of any very severe treatment. In fact, the notices made of them were very brief, and, but for the elaborate way in which they were described in the "Baltimore Sun," by their owners, their narratives would hardly be considered of sufficient interest to record. The heavy rewards, beautiful descriptions, and elegant illustrations in the "Sun," were very attractive reading. The Vigilance Committee took the "Sun," for nothing else under the sun but for this special literature, and for this purpose they always considered the "Sun" a cheap and reliable paper.

A slave man or woman, running for life, he with a bundle on his back or she with a babe in her arms, was always a very interesting sight, and should always be held in remembrance. Likewise the descriptions given by slaveholders, as a general rule, showed considerable artistic powers and a most thorough knowledge of the physical outlines of this peculiar property. Indeed, the art must have been studied attentively for practical purposes. When the advertisements were received in advance of arrivals, which was always the case, the descriptions generally were found so lifelike, that the Committee preferred to take them in preference to putting themselves to the labor of writing out new ones, for future reference. This we think, ought not to be complained of by any who were so unfortunate as to lose wayward servants, as it is but fair to give credit to all concerned. True, sometimes some of these beautiful advertisements were open to gentle criticism. The one at the head of this report, is clearly of this character. For instance, in describing Isaac, Mr. Thomas B. Owings, represents him as being of a "very light color," "almost yellow," "might be called a yellow boy." In the next breath he has no perceptible marks. Now, if he is "very light," that is a well-known southern mark, admitted everywhere. A hint to the wise is sufficient. However, judging from what was seen of Isaac in Philadelphia, there was more cunning than "foolishness" about him. Slaves sometimes, when wanting to get away, would make their owners believe that they were very happy and contented. And, in using this kind of foolishness, would keep up appearances until an opportunity offered for an escape. So Isaac might have possessed this sagacity, which appeared like nonsense to his master. That slave-holders, above all others, were in the habit of taking special pains to encourage foolishness, loud laughing, banjo playing, low dancing, etc., in the place of education, virtue, self-respect and manly carriage, slave-holders themselves are witnesses.

As Mr. Robert Dade was also a loser, equally with Mr. Thomas B. Owings, and as his advertisement was of the same liberality and high tone, it seems but fitting that it should come in just here, to give weight and com-

14

pleteness to the story. Both Owings and Dade showed a considerable degree of southern chivalry in the liberality of their rewards. Doubtless, the large sums thus offered awakened a lively feeling in the breasts of old slave-hunters. But it is to be supposed that the artful fugitives safely reached Philadelphia before the hunters got even the first scent on their track. Up to the present hour, with the owners all may be profound mystery; if so, it is to be hoped, that they may feel some interest in the solution of these wonders. The articles so accurately described must now be permitted to testify in their own words, as taken from the records.

GREEN MODOCK acknowledges that he was owned by William Dorsey, Perry by Robert Dade, Sam and Isaac by Thomas Owings, all farmers, and all "tough" and "pretty mean men." Sam and Isaac had other names with them, but not such a variety of clothing as their master might have supposed. Sam said he left because his master threatened to sell him to Georgia, and he believed that he meant so to do, as he had sold all his brothers and sisters to Georgia some time before he escaped.

But this was not all. Sam declared his master had threatened to shoot him a short while before he left. This was the last straw on the camel's back. Sam's heart was in Canada ever after that. In traveling he resolved that nothing should stop him. Charles offered the same excuse as did Sam. He had been threatened with the auction-block. He left his mother free, but four sisters he left in chains. As these men spoke of their tough owners and bad treatment in Slavery, they expressed their indignation at the idea that Owings, Dade and Dorsey had dared to rob them of their God-given rights. They were only ignorant farm hands. As they drank in the free air, the thought of their wrongs aroused all their manhood. They were all young men, hale and stout, with strong resolutions to make Canada their future home. The Committee encouraged them in this, and aided them for humanity's sake.—Mr. Robert Dade's advertisement speaks for itself as follows:

RAN AWAY—On Saturday night, 20th inst., from the subscriber, living near Mount Airy P. O., Carroll county, two Negro men, PERRY and CHARLES. Perry is quite dark, full face; is about 5 feet 8 or 9 inches high; has a scar on one of his hands, and one on his legs, caused by a cut from a scythe; 25 years old. Charles is of a copper color, about 5 feet 9 or 10 inches high; round shouldered, with small whiskers; has one crooked finger that he cannot straighten, and a scar on his right leg, caused by the cut of a scythe; 22 years old. I will give two hundred and fifty dollars each, if taken in the State and returned to me, or secured in some jail so that I can get them again, or a $1,000 for the two, or $500 each, if taken out of the State, and secured in some jail in this State so that I can get them again.   ROBERT DADE.
s23–3f.

FROM RICHMOND AND NORFOLK, VA.

WILLIAM B. WHITE, SUSAN BROOKS AND WILLIAM HENRY ATKINS.—STOWED AWAY
IN THE STEAMSHIP CITY OF RICHMOND.

But for their hope of liberty, their uncomfortable position could hardly have been endured by these fugitives. William had been compelled to dig and delve, to earn bread and butter, clothing and luxuries, houses and land, education and ease for H. B. Dickinson, of Richmond. William smarted frequently; but what could he do? Complaint from a slave was a crime of the deepest dye. So William dug away mutely, but continued to think, nevertheless. He was a man of about thirty-six years of age, of dark chestnut color, medium size, and of pleasant manners to say the least. His owner was a tobacco manufacturer, who held some thirty slaves in his own right, besides hiring a great many others. William was regularly employed by day in his master's tobacco factory. He was likewise employed, as one of the carriers of the Richmond Dispatch; the time allotted to fill the duties of this office, was however, before sunrise in the morning. It is but just to state, in favor of his master, that William was himself the receiver of a part of the pay for this night work. It was by this means William procured clothing and certain other necessaries.

From William's report of his master, he was by no means among the worst of slave-holders in Richmond; he did not himself flog, but the overseer was allowed to conduct this business, when it was considered necessary. For a long time William had cherished a strong desire to be free, and had gone so far on several occasions as to make unsuccessful attempts to accomplish this end. At last he was only apprised of his opportunity to carry his wishes into practice a few moments before the hour for the starting of the Underground Rail Road train.

Being on the watch, he hailed the privilege, and left without looking back.

True he left his wife and two children, who were free, and a son also who was owned by Warner Toliver, of Gloucester county, Va. We leave the reader to decide for himself, whether William did right or wrong, and who was responsible for the sorrow of both husband and wife caused by the husband's course. The Committee received him as a true and honest friend of freedom, and as such aided him.

SUSAN BROOKS.

Susan was also a passenger on the same ship that brought Wm. B. White. She was from Norfolk. Her toil, body and strength were claimed by Thomas Eckels, Esq., a man of wealth and likewise a man of intemperance.

With those who regarded Slavery as a "divine institution," intemperance was scarcely a mote, in the eyes of such. For sixteen years, Susan had been in the habit of hiring her time, for which she was required to pay five dollars per month. As she had the reputation of being a good cook and chambermaid, she was employed steadily, sometimes on boats. This sum may therefore be considered reasonable.

Owing. to the death of her husband, about a year previous to her escape, she had suffered greatly, so much so, that on two or three occasions, she had fallen into alarming fits,—a fact by no means agreeable to her owner, as he feared that the traders on learning her failing health would underrate her on this account. But Susan was rather thankful for these signs of weakness, as she was thereby enabled to mature her plans and thus to elude detection.

Her son having gone on ahead to Canada about six months in advance of her, she felt that she had strong ties in the goodly land. Every day she remained in bondage, the cords bound her more tightly, and "weeks seemed like months, and months like years," so abhorrent had the peculiar institution become to her in every particular. In this state of mind, she saw no other way, than by submitting to be secreted, until an opportunity should offer, via the Underground Rail Road.

So for four months, like a true and earnest woman, she endured a great "fight of affliction," in this horrible place. But the thought of freedom enabled her to keep her courage up, until the glad news was conveyed to her that all things were ready, providing that she could get safely to the boat, on which she was to be secreted. How she succeeded in so doing the record book fails to explain.

One of the methods, which used to succeed very well, in skillful and brave hands, was this: In order to avoid suspicion, the woman intending to be secreted, approached the boat with a clean ironed shirt on her arm, bare headed and in her usual working dress, looking good-natured of course, and as if she were simply conveying the shirt to one of the men on the boat. The attention of the officer on the watch would not for a moment be attracted by a custom so common as this. Thus safely on the boat, the man whose business it was to put this piece of property in the most safe Underground Rail Road place, if he saw that every thing looked favorable, would quickly arrange matters without being missed from his duties. In numerous instances, officers were outwitted in this way.

As to what Susan had seen in the way of hardships, whether in relation to herself or others, her story was most interesting; but it may here be passed in order to make room for others. She left one sister, named Mary Ann Tharagood, who was wanting to come away very much. Susan was a woman of dark color, round built, medium height, and about forty years of age when she escaped in 1854.

WILLIAM HENRY ATKINS.

William Henry was also a fellow-passenger on the same boat with William B. White and Susan Cooke. These might be set down, as first-class Underground Rail Road travelers.

Henry was a very likely-looking article. He was quite smart, about six feet high, a dark mulatto, and was owned by a Baptist minister.

For some cause not stated on the books, not long before leaving, Henry had received a notice from his owner, (the Baptist Minister) that he might hunt himself a new master as soon as possible. This was a business that Henry had no relish for. The owner he already had, he concluded bad enough in all conscience, and it did not occur to him that hunting another would mend the matter much. So in thinking over the situation, he was "taken sick." He felt the need of a little time to reflect upon matters of very weighty moment involving his freedom. So when he was called upon one day to go to his regular toil, the answer was, "I am sick, I am not able to budge hardly." The excuse took and Henry attended faithfully to his "sick business," for the time being, while on the other hand, the Baptist Minister waited patiently all the while for William to get well enough for hunting a new master. What had to be done, needed to be done quickly, before his master's patience was exhausted. William soon had matters arranged for traveling North. He had a wife, Eliza, for whom he felt the greatest affection; but as he viewed matters at that time, he concluded that he could really do more for her in Canada than he could in Norfolk. He saw no chance, either under the Baptist minister, or under a new master. His wife was owned by Susan Langely. When the hour arrived to start, as brave men usually do, Henry, having counted all the cost, was in his place on the boat with his face towards Canada.

How he looked at matters on John Bull's side of the house, letters from Henry will abundantly reveal as follows:

ST. CATHARINES, August 4, 1854.

MY DEAR SIR:—It is with plesure that I now take my pen to inform you that I am well at present and I hope that these few lines may find you injoying good health, and will you plese to be so kind as to send a leter down home for me if you plese to my wife, the reason that I beg the favor of you I have written to you several times and never recieve no answer, she don't no whar I am at I would like her to no, if it is posible elizeran Actkins, and when you write will you plese to send me all the news, give my respect to all the fambley and allso to Mr lundey and his fambley and tell him plese to send me those books if you plese the first chance you can git. Mrs. Wood sends her love to Mr. Still answer this as soon as on hand, the boys all send their love to all, the reason why i sends for a answer write away i expect to live this and go up west nex mounth not to stay to git some land, i have no more at present, i remain your friend.

W. H. ACTKINS.

ST. CATHARINES, C. W., October 5th, 1854.

MR. WILLIAM STILL :—*Dear Friend:*—I take the liberty to address to you a few lines in behalf of my wife, who is still at Norfolk, Va. I have heard by my friend Richmond Bohm, who arrived lately, that she was in the hands of my friend Henry Lovey (the same who had me in hand at the time I started). I understood that she was about to make her start this month, and that she was only waiting for me to send her some means. I would like for you to communicate the substance of this letter to my wife, through my friend Henry Lovey, and for her to come on as soon as she can. I would like to have my wife write to me a few lines by the first opportunity. She could write to you in Philadelphia, 31 North Fifth street. I wish to send my love to you & your family & would like for you to answer this letter with the least possible delay in the care of Hiram Wilson.   Very respectfully yours,   W. H. ATKINS.

P. S. I would like for my friend Henry Lovey to send my wife right on to Philadelphia; not to stop for want of means, for I will forward means on to my friend Wm Still. My love to my father & mother, my friend Lovey & to all my inquiring friends. If you cannot find it convenient to write, please forward this by the Boat.   H. W. A.

FOUR ARRIVALS.

CHARLOTTE AND HARRIET ESCAPE IN DEEP MOURNING—MASTER IN THE SAME CAR HUNTING FOR THEM, SEES THEM, BUT DOES NOT KNOW THEM—WHITE LADY AND CHILD WITH A COLORED COACHMAN, TRAVELING—AT CHAMBERSBURG AT A HOTEL, THE PROPRIETOR DETECTS THEM AS U. G. R. R. PASSENGERS—THREE "LIKELY" YOUNG MEN FROM BALTIMORE—"FOUR LARGE AND TWO SMALL HAMS"—POLICE OFFICER IMPARTING INFORMATION AT THE ANTI-SLAVERY OFFICE—U. G. R. R. PASSENGERS TRAVELING WITH THEIR MASTERS' HORSES AND CARRIAGES—"BREAK DOWN"—CONFLICT WITH WHITE MEN—SIX PASSENGERS RIDING TWO HORSES, &c.

About the 31st of May, 1856, an exceedingly anxious state of feeling existed with the active Committee in Philadelphia. In the course of twenty-four hours four arrivals had come to hand from different localities. The circumstances connected with the escape of each party, being so unusual, there was scarcely ground for any other conclusion than that disaster was imminent, if not impossible to be averted.

It was a day long to be remembered. Aside from the danger, however, a more encouraging hour had never presented itself in the history of the Road. The courage, which had so often been shown in the face of great danger, satisfied the Committee that there were heroes and heroines among these passengers, fully entitled to the applause of the liberty-loving citizens of Brotherly Love. The very idea of having to walk for days and nights in succession, over strange roads, through by-ways, and valleys, over mountains, and marshes, was fitted to appal the bravest hearts, especially where women and children were concerned.

Being familiar with such cases, the Committee was delighted beyond measure to observe how wisely and successfully each of these parties had managed to overcome these difficulties.

Party No. 1 consisted of Charlotte Giles and Harriet Eglin, owned by Capt. Wm. Applegarth and John Delahay. Neither of these girls had any great complaint to make on the score of ill-treatment endured.

So they contrived each to get a suit of mourning, with heavy black veils, and thus dressed, apparently absorbed with grief, with a friend to pass them to the Baltimore depot (hard place to pass, except aided by an individual well known to the R. R. company), they took a direct course for Philadelphia.

While seated in the car, before leaving Baltimore (where slaves and masters both belonged), who should enter but the master of one of the girls! In a very excited manner, he hurriedly approached Charlotte and Harriet, who were apparently weeping. Peeping under their veils, "What is your name," exclaimed the excited gentleman. "Mary, sir," sobbed Charlotte. "What is your name?" (to the other mourner) "Lizzie, sir," was the faint reply. On rushed the excited gentleman as if moved by steam—through the cars, looking for his property; not finding it, he passed out of the cars, and to the delight of Charlotte and Harriet soon disappeared. Fair business men would be likely to look at this conduct on the part of the two girls in the light of a "sharp practice." In military parlance it might be regarded as excellent strategy. Be this as it may, the Underground Rail Road passengers arrived safely at the Philadelphia station and were gladly received.

A brief stay in the city was thought prudent lest the hunters might be on the pursuit. They were, therefore, retained in safe quarters.

In the meantime, Arrival No. 2 reached the Committee. It consisted of a colored man, a white woman and a child, ten years old. This case created no little surprise. Not that quite a number of passengers, fair enough to pass for white, with just a slight tinge of colored blood in their veins, even sons and daughters of some of the F. F. V., had not on various occasions come over the U. G. R. R. But this party was peculiar. An explanation was sought, which resulted in ascertaining that the party was from Leesburg, Virginia; that David, the colored man, was about twenty-seven years of age, intelligent, and was owned, or claimed by Joshua Pusey. David had no taste for Slavery, indeed, felt that it would be impossible for him to adapt himself to a life of servitude for the special benefit of others; he had, already, as he thought, been dealt with very wrongfully by Pusey, who had deprived him of many years of the best part of his life, and would continue thus to wrong him, if he did not make a resolute effort to get away. So after thinking of various plans, he determined not to run off as a slave with his "budget on his back," but to "travel as a coachman," under the "protection of a white lady." In planning this pleasant scheme, David was not blind to the fact that neither himself nor the "white lady," with whom he proposed to travel, possessed either horse or carriage.

But his master happened to have a vehicle that would answer for the occasion. David reasoned that as Joshua, his so called master, had deprived him of his just dues for so many years, he had a right to borrow, or take without borrowing, one of Joshua's horses for the expedition. The plan was submitted to the lady, and was approved, and a mutual understanding here entered into, that she should hire a carriage, and take also her little girl with them. The lady was to assume the proprietorship of the horse, carriage and coachman. In so doing all dangers would be, in their judgment, averted. The scheme being all ready for execution, the time for departure was fixed, the carriage hired, David having secured his master Joshua's horse, and off they started in the direction of Pennsylvania. White people being so accustomed to riding, and colored people to driving, the party looked all right. No one suspected them, that they were aware of, while passing through Virginia.

On reaching Chambersburg, Pa., in the evening, they drove to a hotel, the lady alighted, holding by the hand her well dressed and nice-looking little daughter, bearing herself with as independent an air as if she had owned twenty such boys as accompanied her as coachman. She did not hesitate to enter and request accommodations for the night, for herself, daughter, coachman, and horse. Being politely told that they could be accommodated, all that was necessary was, that the lady should show off to the best advantage possible. The same duty also rested with weight upon the mind of David.

The night passed safely and the morning was ushered in with bright hopes which were overcast but only for a moment, however. Breakfast having been ordered and partaken of, to the lady's surprise, just as she was in the act of paying the bill, the proprietor of the hotel intimated that he thought that matters "looked a little suspicious," in other words, he said plainly, that he "believed that it was an Underground Rail Road movement;" but being an obliging hotel-keeper, he assured her at the same time, that he "would not betray them." Just here it was with them as it would have been on any other rail road when things threaten to come to a stand; they could do nothing more than make their way out of the peril as best they could. One thing they decided to do immediately, namely, to "leave the horse and carriage," and try other modes of travel. They concluded to take the regular passenger cars. In this way they reached Philadelphia. In Harrisburg, they had sought and received instructions how to find the Committee in Philadelphia.

What relations had previously existed between David and this lady in Virginia, the Committee knew not. It looked more like the time spoken of in Isaiah, where it is said, "And a little child shall lead them," than any thing that had ever been previously witnessed on the Underground Rail Road. The Underground Rail Road never practised the proscription governing other roads, on account of race, color, or previous condition. All were welcome to its immunities, white or colored, when the object to be gained favored freedom, or weakened Slavery. As the sole aim apparent in this case was freedom for the slave the Committee received these travellers as Underground Rail Road passengers.

Arrival No. 3. Charles H. Ringold, Robert Smith, and John Henry Richards, all from Baltimore. Their ages ranged from twenty to twenty-four years. They were in appearance of the class most inviting to men who were in the business of buying and selling slaves. Charles and John were owned by James Hodges, and Robert by Wm. H. Normis, living in Baltimore. This is all that the records contain of them. The exciting and hurrying times when they were in charge of the Committee probably forbade the writing out of a more detailed account of them, as was often the case.

With the above three arrivals on hand, it may be seen how great was the danger to which all concerned were exposed on account of the bold and open manner in which these parties had escaped from the land of the peculiar institution. Notwithstanding, a feeling of very great gratification existed in view of the success attending the new and adventurous modes of traveling. Indulging in reflections of this sort, the writer on going from his dinner that day to the anti-slavery office, to his surprise found an officer awaiting his coming. Said officer was of the mayor's police force. Before many moments had been allowed to pass, in which to conjecture his errand, the officer, evidently burdened with the importance of his mission, began to state his business substantially as follows:

" I have just received a telegraphic despatch from a slave-holder living in Maryland, informing me that six slaves had escaped from him, and that he had reason to believe that they were on their way to Philadelphia, and would come in the regular train direct from Harrisburg; furthermore I am requested to be at the depot on the arrival of the train to arrest the whole party, for whom a reward of $1300 is offered. Now I am not the man for this business. I would have nothing to do with the contemptible work of arresting fugitives. I'd rather help them off. What I am telling you is confidential. My object in coming to the office is simply to notify the Vigilance Committee so that they may be on the look-out for them at the depot this evening and get them out of danger as soon as possible. This is the way I feel about them ; but I shall telegraph back that I will be on the look-out."

While the officer was giving this information he was listened to most attentively, and every word he uttered was carefully weighed. An air of truthfulness, however, was apparent; nevertheless he was a stranger and there was cause for great cautiousness. During the interview an unopened telegraphic despatch which had come to hand during the writer's absence, lay on the desk. Impressed with the belief that it might shed light on the officer's story, the first opportunity that offered, it was seized, opened, and it read as follows : (Copied from the original.)

HARRISBURG, May 31st, 1856.

WM. STILL, N. 5th St. :—I have sent via at two o'clock four large and two small hams.
JOS. C. BUSTILL.

Here there was no room for further doubt, but much need for vigilance. Although the despatch was not read to the officer, not that his story was doubted, but purely for prudential reasons, he was nevertheless given to understand, that it was about the same party, and that they would be duly looked after. It would hardly have been understood by the officer, had he been permitted to read it, so guardedly was it worded, it was indeed dead language to all save the initiated. In one particular especially, relative to the depot where they were expected to arrive, the officer was in the dark, as his despatch pointed to the regular train, and of course to the depot at Eleventh and Market streets. The Underground Rail Road despatch on the contrary pointed to Broad and Callowhill streets "Via," *i. e.* Reading.

As notified, that evening the "four large and two small hams" arrived, and turned out to be of the very finest quality, just such as any trader would have paid the highest market price for. Being mindful of the great danger of the hour, there was felt to be more occasion just then for anxiety and watchfulness, than for cheering and hurrahing over the brave passengers. To provide for them in the usual manner, in view of the threatening aspect of affairs, could not be thought of. In this critical hour it devolved upon a member of the Committee, for the safety of all parties, to find new and separate places of accommodation, especially for the six known to be pursued. To be stored in other than private families would not answer. Three or four such were visited at once; after learning of the danger much sympathy was expressed, but one after another made excuses and refused. This was painful, for the parties had plenty of house room, were identified with the oppressed race, and on public meeting occasions made loud professions of devotion to the cause of the fugitive, &c. The memory of the hour and circumstances is still fresh.

Accommodations were finally procured for a number of the fugitives with a widow woman, (Ann Laws) whose opportunities for succor were far less than at the places where refusals had been met with. But Mrs. L. was kind-hearted, and nobly manifested a willingness to do all that she could for their safety. Of course the Committee felt bound to bear whatever expense might necessarily be incurred. Here some of the passengers were kept for several days, strictly private, long enough to give the slave-hunters full opportunity to tire themselves, and give up the chase in despair. Some belonging to the former arrivals had also to be similarly kept for the same reasons. Through careful management all were succored and cared for. Whilst much interesting information was obtained from these several arrivals: the incidents connected with their lives in Slavery, and when escaping were but briefly written out. Of this fourth arrival, however, the following intelligence will doubtless be highly gratifying to the friends of freedom, wherever the labors of the Underground Rail Road may be appreciated. The people round about Hagerstown, Maryland, may like to know how these "articles" got off so successfully, the circumstances of their escape having doubtless created some excitement in that region of the country.

Arrival No. 4. Charles Bird, George Dorsey, Angeline Brown, Albert Brown, Charles Brown and Jane Scott.

CHARLES was twenty-four years of age, quite dark, of quick motion, and ready speech, and in every way appearing as though he could take care of

himself. He had occupied the condition of a farm laborer. This calling he concluded to forsake, not because he disliked farming, but simply
to get rid of David Clargart, who professed to own him, and compelled
him to work without pay, "for nothing." While Charles spoke favorably of Clargart as a man, to the extent, at all events, of testifying that
he was not what was called a hard man, nevertheless Charles was so
decidedly opposed to Slavery that he felt compelled to look. out for himself.
Serving another man on the no pay principle, at the same time liable to be
flogged, and sold at the pleasure of another, Charles felt was worse than
heathenish viewed in any light whatsoever. He was prepared therefore, to
leave without delay. He had four sisters in the hands of Clargart, but what
could he do for them but leave them to Providence.

The next on the list was GEORGE DORSEY, a comrade of Charles. He was
a young man, of medium size, mixed blood, intelligent, and a brave fellow
as will appear presently.

This party in order to get over the road as expeditiously as possible, availed themselves of their master's horses and wagon and moved off civilly and
respectably. About nine miles from home on the road, a couple of white
men, finding their carriage broken down approached them, unceremoniously
seized the horses by the reins and were evidently about to assume authority,
supposing that the boys would surrender at once. But instead of so doing,
the boys struck away at them with all their might, with their large clubs,
not even waiting to hear what these superior individuals wanted. The

effect of the clubs brought them prostrate in the road, in an attitude resembling two men dreaming, (it was in the night.) The victorious passengers, seeing that the smashed up carriage could be of no further use to them, quickly conceived the idea of unhitching and attempting further pursuit on horseback. Each horse was required to carry three passengers. So up they mounted and off they galloped with the horses' heads turned directly towards Pennsylvania. No further difficulty presented itself until after they had traveled some forty miles. Here the poor horses broke down, and had to be abandoned. The fugitives were hopeful, but of the difficulties ahead they wot not; surely no flowery beds of ease awaited them. For one whole week they were obliged to fare as they could, out in the woods, over the mountains, &c. How they overcame the trials in this situation we cannot undertake to describe. Suffice it to say, at the end of the time above mentioned they managed to reach Harrisburg and found assistance as already intimated.

GEORGE and Angeline, (who was his sister) with her two boys had a considerable amount of white blood in their veins, and belonged to a wealthy man by the name of George Schaeffer, who was in the milling business. They were of one mind in representing him as a hard man. " He would often threaten to sell, and was very hard to please." George and Angeline left their mother and ten brothers and sisters.

JANE was a well-grown girl, smart, and not bad-looking, with a fine brown skin, and was also owned by Schaeffer.

Letters from the enterprising Charlotte and Harriet (arrival No. 1), brought the gratifying intelligence, that they had found good homes in Western New York, and valued their freedom highly. Three out of quite a number of letters received from them from time to time are subjoined.

SENNETT, June, 1856.

MR. WILLIAM STILL :—*Dear Sir:*—I am happy to tell you that Charlotte Gildes and myself have got along thus far safely. We have had no trouble and found friends all the way along, for which we feel very thankful to you and to all our friends on the road since we left. We reached Mr. Loguen's in Syracuse, on last Tuesday evening & on Wednesday two gentlemen from this community called and we went with them to work in their families. What I wish you would do is to be so kind as to send our clothes to this place if they should fall into your hands. We hope our uncle in Baltimore will get the letter Charlotte wrote to him last Sabbath, while we were at your house, concerning the clothes. Perhaps the best would be to send them to Syracuse to the *care of Mr. Loguen* and he will send them to us. This will more certainly ensure our getting them. If you hear anything that would be interesting to Charlotte or me from Baltimore, please direct a letter to us to this place, to the care of Revd. Chas. Anderson, Sennett, Cayuga Co., N. Y. Please give my love and Charlotte's to Mrs. Still and thank her for her kindness to us while at your house. Your affectionate friend,

HARRIET EGLIN.

SECOND LETTER.

SENNETT, July 31st, 1856.

MR. WM. STILL:—*My Dear Friend:*—I have just received your note of 29th inst. and allow me dear sir, to assure you that the only letter I have written, is the one you received, an answer to which you sent me. I never wrote to Baltimore, nor did any person write for me there, and it is with *indescribable grief,* that I hear what your letter communicates to me, of those who you say have gotten into difficulty on my account. My Cousin Charlotte who came with me, got into a good place in this vicinity, but she could not content herself to stay here but just *one week*—she then went to Canada—and she is the one who by writing (if any one), has brought this trouble upon those to whom you refer in Baltimore.

She has written me two letters from Canada, and by neither of them can I ascertain *where she lives*—her letters are mailed at Suspension Bridge, but she does not live there as her letters show. In the first she does not even sign her name. She has evidently employed some person to write, who is nearly as ignorant as herself. If I knew where to find her I would find out *what* she has written.

I don't know but she has told where I live, and may yet get me and my friends here, in trouble too, as she has some in other places. I don't wish to have you trouble yourself about my clothes, I am in a place where I can get all the clothes I want or need. Will you please write me when convenient and tell me what you hear about those who I fear are suffering as the result of their kindness to me? May God, in some way, grant them deliverance. Oh the misery, the sorrow, which this cursed system of Slavery is constantly bringing upon millions in this land of boasted freedom!

Can you tell me where Sarah King is, who was at your house when I was there? She was going to Canada to meet her husband. Give my love to Mrs. Still & accept the same yourself. Your much indebted & obliged friend,   HARRIET EGLIN.

The "difficulty" about which Harriet expressed so much regret in the above letter, had reference to a letter supposed to have been written by her friend Charlotte to Baltimore about her clothing It had been intercepted, and in this way, a clue was obtained by one of the owners as to how they escaped, who aided them, etc. On the strength of the information thus obtained, a well-known colored man, named Adams, was straightway arrested and put in prison at the instance of one of the owners, and also a suit was at the same time instituted against the Rail Road Company for damages—by which steps quite a huge excitement was created in Baltimore. As to the colored man Adams, the prospect looked simply hopeless. Many hearts were sad in view of the doom which they feared would fall upon him for obeying a humane impulse (he had put the girls on the cars). But with the Rail Road Company it was a different matter; they had money, power, friends, etc., and could defy the courts. In the course of a few months, when the suit against Adams and the Rail Road Company came up, the Rail Road Company proved in court, in defense, that the prosecutor entered the cars in search of his runaway, and went and spoke to the two young women in "mourning" the day they escaped, looking expressly for the identical parties, for which he was seeking damages before the court, and that he declared to the conductor, on leaving the cars, that the said "two girls in mourning, were not the ones he was looking after," or in other words, that "neither" belonged to him. This positive testimony satisfied the jury, and the Rail Road Company and poor James Adams escaped by the verdict not guilty. The owner of the lost property had the costs to pay of course, but whether he was made a wiser or better man by the operation was never ascertained.

THIRD LETTER.

SENNETT, October 28th, 1856.

DEAR MR. STILL:—I am happy to tell you that I am well and happy. I still live with Rev. Mr. Anderson in this place, I am learning to read and write. I do not like to trouble you too much, but I would like to know if you have heard anything more about my friends in Baltimore who got into trouble on our account. Do be pleased to write me if you can give me any information about them. I feel bad that they should suffer for me. I wish all my brethren and sisters in bondage, were as well off as I am. The girl that came with me is in Canada, near the Suspension Bridge. I was glad to see Green Murdock, a colored young man, who stopped at your house about six weeks ago, he knew my folks at the South. He has got into a good place to work in this neighborhood. Give my love to Mrs Still, and believe me your obliged friend,   HARRIET EGLIN.

P. S. I would like to know what became of Johnson,* the man whose foot was smashed by jumping off the cars, he was at your house when I was there.   H. E.

FROM VIRGINIA, MARYLAND, DELAWARE, NORTH CARO-LINA, WASHINGTON, D. C., AND SOUTH CAROLINA.

JAMES BURRELL, DANIEL WIGGINS, WM. ROBINSON, EDWARD PEADEN, AND WIFE, ALEX. BOGGS, SAMUEL STATER, HARRISON BELL AND DAUGHTER, HARRIET ANN, DANIEL DAVIS, *alias* DAVID SMITH, JAMES STEWART, *alias* WILLIAM JACKSON, HARRIET HALEY, *alias* ANN RICHARDSON, BENJ. DUNCANS, *alias* GEORGE SCOTT, MOSES WINES, SARAH SMITH, *alias* MILDRETH PAGE, LUCY GARRETT, *alias* JULIA WOOD, ELLEN FORMAN, *alias* ELIZABETH YOUNG, WM. WOODEN, *alias* WM. NEL-SON, JAMES EDWARD HANDY, *alias* DENNIS CANNON, JAMES HENRY DELANY *alias* SMART STANLEY, JAMES HENRY BLACKSON, GEORGE FREELAND, MILES WHITE, LOUISA CLAYTON, LEWIS SNOWDEN, *alias* LEWIS WILLIAMS, WM. JOHNSON, JOHN HALL *alias* JOHN SIMPSON.

In order to keep this volume within due limits, in the cases to be noticed in this chapter, it will be impossible to state more than a few of the interesting particulars that make up these narratives. While some of these passengers might not have been made in the prison house to drink of the bitter cup as often as others, and in their flight might not have been called upon to pass through as severe perils as fell to the lot of others, nevertheless

---

* Johnson was an unfortunate young fugitive, who, while escaping, beheld his master or pursuer in the cars, and jumped therefrom, crushing his feet shockingly by the bold act.

justice seems to require, that, as far as possible, all the passengers passing over the Philadelphia Underground Rail Road shall be noticed.

JAMES BURRELL. James was certainly justifiable in making his escape, if for no other reason than on the score of being nearly related to the chivalry of the South. He was a mulatto (the son of a white man evidently), about thirty-two years of age, medium size, and of an agreeable appearance. He was owned by a maiden lady, who lived at Williamsburg, but not requiring his services in her own family, she hired him out by the year to a Mr. John Walker, a manufacturer of tobacco, for which she received $120 annually. This arrangement was not satisfactory to James. He could not see why he should be compelled to wear the yoke like an ox. The more he thought over his condition, the more unhappy was his lot, until at last he concluded, that he could not stand Slavery any longer. He had witnessed a great deal of the hardships of the system of Slavery, and he had quite enough intelligence to portray the horrors thereof in very vivid colors. It was the auction-block horror that first prompted him to seek freedom. While thinking how he would manage to get away safely, his wife and children were ever present in his mind. He felt as a husband should towards his " wife Betsy," and likewise loved his " children, Walter and Mary ;" but these belonged to another man, who lived some distance in the country, where he had permission to see them only once a week. This had its pleasure, it also had its painful influence. The weekly partings were a never-failing source of unhappiness. So when James' mind was fully made up to escape from Slavery, he decided that it would not be best to break the secret to his poor wife and children, but to get off to Canada, and afterwards to try and see what he could do for their deliverance. The hour fixed to leave Virginia arrived, and he started and succeeded in reaching Philadelphia, and the Committee. On arriving he needed medicine, clothing, food, and a carriage for his accommodation, all which were furnished freely by the Committee, and he was duly forwarded to Canada. From Canada, with his name changed, he wrote as follows:

TORONTO, March 28th, 1854.

SIR, MR. STILL—It does me pleasure to forward you this letter hopeing when this comes to hand it may find your family well, as they leaves me at present. I will also say that the friends are well. Allow me to say to you that I arrived in this place on Friday last safe and sound, and feeles well. under my safe arrival. Its true that I have not been employed as yet but I lives hopes to be at work very shortly. I likes this city very well, and I am in hopes that there a living here for me as much so as there for any one else. You will be please to write. I am bording at Mr. Phillip's Centre Street.

I have nothing more at present. Yours most respectfull. W. BOURAL.

DANIEL WIGGINS, *alias* DANIEL ROBINSON. Daniel fled from Norfolk, Va., where he had been owned by the late Richard Scott. Only a few days before Daniel escaped, his so-called owner was summoned to his last account.

While ill, just before the close of his career, he often promised D. his freedom and also promised, if restored, that he would make amends for the past, by changing his ways of living. His son, who was very reckless, he would frequently allude to and declared, " that he," the son, " should not have his ' property.' " These dying sentiments filled Daniel with great hopes that the day of his enslavement was nearly at an end. Unfortunately, however, death visited the old master, ere he had made provision for his slaves. At all events, no will was found. That he might not fall a prey to the reckless son, he felt, that he must nerve himself for a desperate struggle to obtain his freedom in some other way, by traveling on the Underground Rail Road. While he had always been debarred from book learning, he was, nevertheless, a man of some intelligence, and by trade was a practical Corker.

He was called upon in this trying hour to leave his wife with three children, but they were, fortunately, free. Coming to the Committee in want, they cheerfully aided him, and forwarded him on to Canada. Thence, immediately on his arrival, he returned the following grateful letter:

NEW BEDFORD, Mass., March 22d, 1854.

DEAR SIR :—I am happy to inform you that I arrived in this place this morning well and cheerful. I am, sir, to you and others under more obligations for your kindly protection of me than I can in any way express at present. May the Lord preserve you unto eternal life. Remember my respects to Mr. Lundy and family. Should the boat lay up please let me know. Yours respectfully, DAVID ROBINSON.

Please forward to Dr. H. Lundy, after you have gotten through. With respects, &c.
D. R.

WM. ROBINSON, *alias* THOS. HARRED. William gave satisfactory evidence, at first sight, that he was opposed to the unrequited labor system *in toto*, and even hated still more the flogging practices of the chivalry. Although he had reached his twenty-eighth year, and was a truly fair specimen of his race, considering his opportunities, a few days before William left, the overseer on the plantation attempted to flog him, but did not succeed. William's manhood was aroused, and he flogged the overseer soundly, if what he averred was true. The name of William's owner was John G. Beale, Esq., of Fauquier county, Va. Beale was considered to be a man of wealth, and had invested in Slave stock to the number of seventy head. According to William's account of Beale, he was a " hard man and thought no more of his black people than he did of dogs." When William entered upon the undertaking of freeing himself from Beale's barbarism, he had but one dollar and twenty-five cents in his possession ; but he had physical strength and a determined mind, and being heartily sick of Slavery, he was willing to make the trial, even at the cost of life. Thus hopeful, he prosecuted his journey with suc-

15

cess through strange regions of country, with but little aid or encouragement before reaching Philadelphia. This feat, however, was not performed without getting lost by the way. On arriving, his shoes were gone, and his feet were severely travel-worn. The Committee rendered needed aid, etc., and sent William on to Canada to work for himself, and to be recognized as a subject of Great Britain.

EDWARD PEADEN AND WIFE HARRIET, AND SISTER CELIA. This man and his wife and wife's sister were a nice-looking trio, but they brought quite a sad story with them: the sale of their children, six in number. The auction block had made such sad havoc among them, that no room was left to hope, that their situation would ever be improved by remaining. Indeed they had been under a very gloomy cloud for some time previous to leaving, fearing that the auction block was shortly to be their doom. To escape this fate, they were constrained to "secrete themselves for one month," until an opportunity offered them to secure a passage on a boat coming to Philadelphia. Edward (the husband), was about forty-four years of age, of a dark color, well made, full face, pleasant countenance, and talked fluently. Dr. Price claimed him as his personal property, and exacted all his hire and labor. For twelve years he had been hired out for $100 per annum. Harriet, the wife of Edward, belonged to David Baines, of Norfolk. Her general appearance indicated, that nature had favored her physically and mentally, although being subjected to the drudgery of Slave life, with no advantages for development, she was simply a living testimony to the crushing influence of Slavery— with a heart never free from the saddened recollection of the auction block, on which all of her children had been sacrificed, "one by one." Celia, the sister, also belonged to D. Baines, and was kept hired out—was last in the service of the Mayor of Norfolk. Of her story nothing of any moment was recorded. On their arrival in Philadelphia, as usual they were handed over to the Committee, and their wants were met.

WILLIAM DAVIS. All that the records contain of William is as follows: He left Emmitsburg, Md., the previous Friday night, where he had been held by Dr. James Shoul. William is thirty-two years of age, dark color, rather below medium stature. With regard to his slave life, he declared that he had been "roughly used." Besides, for some time before escaping, he felt that his owner was in the "notion of trading" him off. The fear that this apprehended notion would be carried into execution, was what prompted him to leave his master.

ALEXANDER BOGGS, alias JOHNSON HENSON. This subject was under the ownership of a certain John Emie, who lived about three miles from Baltimore. Mr. Emie had only been in possession of the wayward Alexander three weeks, having purchased him of a trader named Dennit, for $550. This was not the first time, however, that he had experienced the trouble of changing masters, in consequence of having been sold. Previously to his being disposed of by the trader Dennit, he had been owned by Senator Merrick, who had the misfortune to fail in business, in consequence whereof, his slaves had all to be sold and Alexander with the rest, away from his wife, Caroline, and two children, James and Eliezer.

This was a case that appealed for sympathy and aid, which were cheerfully rendered by the Committee. Alexander was about fifty years of age, of dark color. On the Records no account of cruel treatment is found, other than being sold, &c.

JOHN BROWN, alias JACOB WILLIAMS, arrived from Fredericktown, Md., where he had been working under the yoke of Joseph Postly. John was a young man of twenty-nine years of age. Up to the hour of his escape, his lot had been that of an ordinary slave. Indeed, he had much less to complain of with reference to usage than most slaves; the only thing in this respect the records contain, is simply a charge, that his master threatened to sell him. But this did not seem to have been the motive which prompted John to take leave of his master. Although untutored, he had mind enough to comprehend that Postly had no right to oppress him, and wrong him out of his hire. John concluded that he would not stand such treatment any longer, and made up his mind to leave for Canada. After due examination the Committee, finding his story reasonable, gave him the usual assistance, advice and instruction, and sent him on Canada-ward.

SAMUEL SLATER, alias PATTERSON SMITH, came from a place called Power Bridge, Md. He gave a satisfactory account of himself, and was commended for having wisely left his master, William Martin, to earn his bread by the sweat of his own brow. Martin had held up the vision of the auction-block before Sam; this was enough. Sam saw that it was time for him to be getting out of danger's way without delay, so he presumed, if others could manage to escape, he could too. And he succeeded. He was a stout man, about twenty-nine years of age, of dark complexion. No particular mention of ill treatment is found on the Records.

After arriving in Canada, his heart turned with deep interest and affection to those left in the prison-house, as the following letter indicates.

ST. CATHRINES Oct 29th.

MY DEAR FRIEND :—yours of the 15th came to hand and I was glad to hea from you and your dear family were well and the reason that I did not write sooner I expected get a letter from my brother in pennsylvania but I have not received any as yet when I wrote last I directed my letter to philip scott minister of the asbury church baltimore and that was the reason that I thought it strange I did not get an answer but I did not put my brother name to it I made arrangements before I left home with a family of smiths that I was to write to and the letter that I enclose in this I want you to direct it to D Philip scott in his care for mrs cassey Jackson Duke Jacksons wife and she will give to Priana smith or Sarah Jane Smith those are the persons I wish to write to I wish you to write on as quick as you can and let them know that there is a lady coming on by the name of mrs Holonsworth and she will call and see you and you will find her a very interesting and inteligent person one worthy of respect and esteem and a high reputation I must now bring my letter to a close no more at present but remain your humble servant

PATTERSON SMITH

In my letters I did not write to my friends how they shall write to me but in the letter that you write you will please to tell them how they shall write to me.

HARRISON BELL AND DAUGHTER HARRIET ANN. Father and daughter were fortunate enough to escape together from Norfolk, Va.

HARRISON was just in the prime of life, forty years of age, stout made, good features, but in height was rather below medium, was a man of more than ordinary shrewdness, by trade he was a chandler. He alleged that he had been used hard.

HARRIET ANN was a well-grown girl of pleasant appearance, fourteen years of age. Father and daughter had each different owners, one belonged to James Snyder, the other to John G. Hodgson.

Harrison had been informed that his children were to be sold; to prevent this shocking fate, he was prompted to escape. Several months previous to finding a chance to make a safe flight, he secreted himself with his children in Norfolk, and so remained up to the day he left, a passage having been secured for them on one of the boats coming to Philadelphia. While the records contain no definite account of other children, it is evident that there were others, but what became of them is not known.

If at the time of their arrival, it had been imagined that the glorious day of universal freedom was only about eight years off, doubtless much fuller records would have been made of these struggling Underground Rail Road passengers. If Harrison's relatives and friends, who suddenly missed him and his daughter Harriet Ann, in the Spring of 1854, are still ignorant of his whereabouts, this very brief account of their arrival in Philadelphia, may be of some satisfaction to all concerned, not excepting his old master, whom he had served so faithfully.

The Committee finding them in need, had the pleasure of furnishing them with food, material aid and a carriage, with cheering words and letters of introduction to friends on the road to Canada.

DANIEL DAVIS, ALIAS DAVID SMITH, ADAM NICHOLSON, ALIAS JOHN WYNKOOP, REUBEN BOWLES, ALIAS CUNNIGAN, ARRIVED FROM HEDGEVILLE, VA.

DANIEL was only about twenty, just at a capital age to make a bold strike for freedom. The appearance and air of this young aspirant for liberty indicated that he was not of the material to be held in chains. He was a man of medium size, well-built, dark color, and intelligent. Hon. Charles J. Fortner, M. C. was the reputed owner of this young fugitive, but the honorable gentleman having no use for his services, or because he may have profited more by hiring him out, Daniel was placed in the employ of a farmer, by the name of Adam Quigley. It was at this time he resolved that he would not be a slave any longer. He declared that Quigley was a " very mean man," one for whom he had no respect whatever. Indeed he felt that the system of Slavery was an abomination in any form it might be viewed. While he was yet so young, he had pretty clear views with regard to Slavery, and remembered with feelings of deep indignation, how his father had been sold when he himself was a boy, just as a horse might have been sold; and how his mother was dragging her chains in Slavery, up to the hour he fled. Thus in company with his two companions he was prepared for any sacrifice.

ADAM's tale is soon told; all that is on the old record in addition to his full name, is in the following words: "Adam is dark, rugged and sensible, and was owned by Alexander Hill, a drunkard, gambler, &c."

REUBEN had been hired out to John Sabbard near Hedgeville. Startled at hearing that he was to be sold, he was led to consider the propriety of seeking flight via the Underground Rail Road. These three young men were all fine specimens of farm hands, and possessed more than average common sense, considering the oppression they had to labor under. They walked the entire distance from Hedgeville, Va., to Greenville, Pa. There they took the cars and walked no more. They appeared travel-worn, garments dirty, and forlorn; but the Committee had them cleanly washed, hair cut and shaved, change of clothing furnished, &c., which at once made them look like very different men. Means were appropriated to send them on free of cost.

JAMES STEWART, *alias* WM. JACKSON. James had been made acquainted with the Peculiar Institution in Fauquier county, Va. Being of sound judgment and firm resolution, he became an enemy to Slavery at a very early age; so much so, that by the time he was twenty-one he was willing to put into practice his views of the system by leaving it and going where all men are free. Very different indeed were these notions, from those held by his owner, Wm. Rose, who believed in Slavery for the black man. So as James could neither enjoy his freedom nor express his opinion in Virginia, he determined, that he had better get a passage on the Underground Rail Road, and leave the land of Slavery and the obnoxious sentiments of his master. He, of course, saw formidable difficulties to be encountered all the way along in escaping, but these, he considered, would be more easy for him to overcome than it would be for him to learn the lesson—" Servants, obey your masters." The very idea made James sick. This, therefore, was the secret of his escape.

HARRIET HALEY, *alias* ANN RICHARDSON, AND ELIZABETH HALEY, *alias* SARAH RICHARDSON. These travelers succeeded in escaping from Geo. C. Davis, of Harford county, Md. In order to carry out their plans, they took advantage of Whitsuntide, a holiday, and with marked ingenuity and perseverance, they managed to escape and reach Quakertown Underground Rail Road Station without obstruction, where protection and assistance were rendered by the friends of the cause. After abiding there for a short time, they were forwarded to the Committee in Philadelphia. Their ages ranged from nineteen to twenty-one, and they were apparently "servants" of a very superior order. The pleasure it afforded to aid such young women in escaping from a condition so loathsome as that of Slavery in Maryland, was unalloyed.

BENJAMIN DUNCANS, *alias* GEORGE SCOTT. This individual was in bonds under Thomas Jeffries, who was a firm believer in the doctrine: "Servants, obey your masters," and, furthermore, while laboring "pretty hard" to make Benjamin a convert to this idea, he had made Benjamin's lot anything else than smooth. This treatment on the part of the master made a wise and resolute man of the Slave. For as he looked earnestly into the fact, that he was only regarded by his owner in the light of an ox, or an ass, his manhood rebelled straightway, and the true light of freedom told him, that he must be willing to labor, and endure suffering for the great prize, liberty. So, in company with five others, at an appointed time, he set out for freedom, and succeeded. The others, alluded to, passed on to Canada direct. Benjamin was induced to stop a few months in Pennsylvania, during which time he occupied himself in farming. He looked as if he was well able to do a full day's work at this occupation. He was about twenty-five years of age, of unmixed blood, and wore a pleasant countenance.

MOSES WINES. Portsmouth, Va., lost one of her most substantial laborers in the person of Moses, and Madam Abigail Wheeler, a very "likely article" of merchandise. "No complaint" as to "ill treatment" was made by Moses against "Miss Abigail." The truth was, he admitted, that he had been used in a "mild way." With some degree of pride, he stated that he "had never been flogged." But, for the "last fifteen years, he had been favored with the exalted privilege of 'hiring' his time at the 'reasonable' sum of $12 per month." As he stood pledged to have this amount always ready, "whether sick or well," at the end of the month, his mistress "never neglected to be in readiness to receive it" to the last cent. In this way Moses was taught to be exceedingly punctual. Who would not commend such a mistress for the punctuality, if nothing more? But as smoothly as matters seemed to be going along, the mischievous idea crept into Moses' head, that he ought to have some of the money claimed by his "kind" mistress, and at the same time, the thought would often forcibly press upon his mind that he might any day be sold. In addition to this unpleasant prospect, Virginia had just about that time passed a law "prohibiting Slaves from hiring their time"—also, a number of "new Police rules with reference to Slaves and free colored people," all of which, the "humane Slave-holders" of that "liberal State," regarded as highly essential both for the "protection and safety of Master and Slave." But the stupid-headed Moses was not pleased with these arrangements. In common with many of the Slaves, he smarted severely under his heavy oppression, and felt that it was similar to an old rule, which had been once tried under Pharaoh—namely, when the children of Israel were required to "make bricks without straw." But Moses was not a fit subject to submit to be ruled so inhumanly.

Despite the beautiful sermons he had often listened to in favor of Slavery, and the many wise laws, above alluded to, he could not reconcile himself to his condition. The laws and preaching were alike as "sounding brass, and tinkling cymbals" to him. He made up his mind, therefore, that he must try a free country; that his manhood required him to make the effort at once, even at the risk of life. Father and husband, as he was, and loving his wife, Grace, and son, Alphonso, tenderly as he did, he nevertheless felt himself to be in chains, and that he could do but little for them by remaining. He conceived that, if he could succeed in gaining his freedom, he might possibly aid them away also. With this hope in him, he contrived to secure a private passage on the steamship City of Richmond, and in this way reached Philadelphia, but not without suffering fearfully the entire journey through, owing to the narrowness of the space into which he was obliged to be stowed in order to get away.

Moses was a man of medium size, quite dark, and gave promise of being capable of taking care of himself in freedom. He had seen much of the cruelties of Slavery inflicted upon others in various forms, which he related in a way to make one shudder; but these incidents were not recorded in the book at the time.

SARAH SMITH, alias MILDRETH PAGE, and her daughter, nine years of age. Sarah and her child were held to service by the Rev. A. D. Pollock, a resident of Wilmington, Del. Until about nine months before she escaped from the Reverend gentleman, she was owned by Mrs. Elizabeth Lee of Fauquier Co., Va., who had moved with Sarah to Wilmington. How Mr. Pollock came by Sarah is not stated on the records; perhaps by marriage; be that as it may, it was owing to ill treatment from her mistress that Sarah "took out" with her child. Sarah was a woman of becoming manners, of a dark brown complexion, and looked as though she might do a fair share of housework, if treated well. As it required no great effort to escape from Wilmington, where the watchful Garrett lived, she reached the Committee in Philadelphia without much difficulty, received assistance and was sent on her way rejoicing.

LUCY GARRETT, alias JULIA WOOD. John Williams, who was said to be a "very cruel man," residing on the Western Shore of Va., claimed

Lucy as his chattel personal. Julia, having a lively sense of his meanness stood much in fear of being sold; having seen her father, three sisters, and two brothers, disposed of at auction, she was daily on the look-out for her turn to come next. The good spirit of freedom made the way plain to her by which an escape could be effected. Being about nineteen years of age, she felt that she had served in Slavery long enough. She resolved to start immediately, and did so, and succeeded in reaching Pennsylvania. Her appearance recommended her so well, that she was prevailed upon to remain and accept a situation in the family of Joseph A. Dugdale, so well known in reformatory circles, as an ardent friend of humanity. While in his family she gave great satisfaction, and was much esteemed for uprightness and industry. But this place was not Canada, so, when it was deemed best, she was sent on.

ELLEN FORMAN, alias ELIZABETH YOUNG. Ellen had formerly been owned by Dr. Thomas, of the Eastern Shore of Maryland, but about one year before escaping, she was bought by a lady living in Baltimore known by the name of Mrs. Johnson. Ellen was about thirty years of age, of slender stature, and of a dark brown complexion. The record makes no mention of cruel treatment or very hard usage, as a slave. From traveling, probably, she had contracted a very heavy cold, which threatened her with consumption. The Committee cheerfully rendered her assistance.

WILLIAM WOODEN, alias WILLIAM NELSON. While Delaware was not far from freedom, and while Slavery was considered to exist there comparatively in a mild form, nevertheless, what with the impenetrable ignorance in which it was the wont of pro-slavery whites to keep the slaves, and the unwillingness on the part of slave-holders generally to conform to the spirit of progress going on in the adjacent State of Pennsylvania, it was wonderful how the slaves saw through the thick darkness thus prevailing, and how wide-awake they were to escape.

It was from this State, that William Wooden fled. True, William was said to belong to Judge Wooden, of Georgetown, Del., but, according to the story of his "chattel," the Judge was not of the class who judged righteously. He had not only treated William badly, but he had threatened to sell him. This was the bitter pill which constrained William to "take out." The threat seemed hard at first, but its effect was excellent for this young man; it was the cause of his obtaining his freedom at the age of twenty-three. William was a tall, well-built man, of dark complexion and promising. No further particulars concerning him are on the records.

JAMES EDWARD HANDY, *alias* DANIEL CANON. At Seaford, Delaware, James was held in bonds under a Slave-holder called Samuel Lewis, who followed farming. Lewis was not satisfied with working James hard and keeping all his earnings, but would insolently talk occasionally of handing him "over to the trader." This "stirred James' blood" and aroused his courage to the "sticking point." Nothing could induce him to remain. He had the name of having a wife and four children, but according to the Laws of Delaware, he only had a nominal right in them. They were "legally the property of Capt. Martin." Therefore they were all left in the hands of Capt. Martin. The wife's name was Harriet Delaney, *alias* Smart Stanley. James Henry Delaney came as a fellow-traveler with James Edward. He had experienced oppression under Capt. Martin, and as a witness, was prepared to testify, that Martin "ill-treated his Slaves, especially with regard to the diet, which was very poor." Nevertheless James was a stout, heavy-built young man of twenty-six years of age, and looked as if he might have a great deal of valuable work in him. He was a single man.

JAMES HENRY BLACKSON. James Henry had only reached twenty-five, when he came to the "conclusion, that he had served long enough under bondage for the benefit of Charles Wright." This was about all of the excuse he seemed to have for escaping. He was a fine specimen of a man, so far as physical strength and muscular power were concerned. Very little was recorded of him.

GEORGE FREELAND. It was only by the most indomitable resolution and perseverance, that Freeland threw off the yoke. Capt. John Pollard of Petersburg, Va., held George to service. As a Slave-holder, Pollard belonged to that class, who did not believe in granting favors to Slaves. On the contrary, he was practically in favor of wringing every drop of blood from their bodies.

George was a spare-built man, about twenty-five years of age, quite dark, but had considerable intelligence. He could read and write very well, but how he acquired these arts is not known. In testifying against his master, George used very strong language. He declared that Pollard "thought no more of his servants than if they had been dogs. He was very mean. He gave nothing to his servants. He has given me only one pair of shoes the last ten years." After careful inquiry, George learned that he could get a private passage on the City of Richmond, if he could raise the passage money. This he could do cheerfully. He raised "sixty dollars" for the individual who was to "secrete him on the boat." In leaving the land of Slave auctions, whips and chains, he was obliged to leave his mother and father and two brothers in Petersburg. Pollard had been offered $1,500 for George. Doubtless he found, when he discovered George had gone, that he had "overstood the market." This was what produced action prompt and decisive on the part of George. So the old adage, in this case, was verified—"It's an ill wind that blows nobody any good."

On arriving in Canada, George did not forget to express gratitude to those who aided him on his road there, as the following note will show:

SINCATHANS, canada west.

Brother Still :—I im brace this opportunity of pening you a few lines to in form you that I am well at present & in hopes to find you & family well also I hope that god Will Bless you & and your family & if I never should meet you in this world I hope to meet you in glory Remember my love to Brother Brown & tell him that I am well & hearty tell him to writ Thomas word that I am well at present you must excuse me I will Rite when I return from the west.   GEORGE W. FREELAND.

Send your Letters in the name of John Anderson.

MILES WHITE. This passenger owed service to Albert Kern, of Elizabeth City, N. C. At least Kern, through the oppressive laws of that State, claimed Miles as his personal property. Miles, however, thought differently, but he was not at liberty to argue the case with Kern ; for on the "side of the oppressor there was strength." So he resolved, that he would adopt the Underground Rail Road plan. As he was only about twenty-one years of age, he found it much easier to close his affairs with North Carolina, than it would have been had he been encumbered with a family. In fact, the only serious difficulty he had to surmount was to find a captain with whom he could secure a safe passage North. To his gratification it was not long before his efforts in this direction were crowned with success. A vessel was being loaded with shingles, the captain of which was kind enough to allow Miles to occupy a very secure hiding-place thereon. In course of time, having suffered to the extent usual when so closely conveyed, he arrived in Philadelphia, and being aided, was duly forwarded by the Committee.

JOHN HALL, *alias* JOHN SIMPSON. John fled from South Carolina. In this hot-bed of Slavery he labored and suffered up to the age of thirty-two. For a length of time before he escaped, his burdens were intolerable ; but he could see no way to rid himself of them, except by flight. Nor was he by any means certain that an effort in this direction would prove successful. In planning the route which he should take to travel North he decided, that if success was for him, his best chance would be to wend his way through North Carolina and Virginia. Not that he hoped to find friends or helpers in these States. He had heard enough of the cruelties of Slavery in these regions to convince him, that if he should be caught, there would be no sympathy or mercy shown. Nevertheless the irons were piercing him so severely, that he felt constrained to try his luck, let the consequences be what they might, and so he set out for freedom or death. Mountains of difficulties, and months of suffering and privations by land and water, in the woods, and swamps of North Carolina and Virginia, were before him, as his experience in traveling proved. But the hope of final victory and his daily sufferings before he started, kept him from faltering, even when starvation and death seemed to be staring him in the face. For several months he was living in dens and caves of the earth.

Ultimately, however, the morning of his ardent hopes dawned. How he succeeded in finding a captain who was kind enough to afford him a secret hiding-place on his boat, was not noted on the records. Indeed the incidents of his story were but briefly written out. Similar cases of thrilling interest seemed almost incredible, and the Committee were constrained to doubt the story altogether until other testimony could be obtained to verify the statement. In this instance, before the Committee were fully satisfied, they felt it necessary to make inquiry of trustworthy Charlestonians to ascertain if John were really from Charleston, and if he were actually owned by the man that he represented as having owned him, Dr. Philip Mazyck, by name; and furthermore, to learn if the master was really of the brutal character given him. The testimony of thoroughly reliable persons, who were acquainted with master and slave, so far as this man's bondage in Charleston was concerned, fully corroborated his statement, and the Committee could not but credit his story; indeed they were convinced, that he had been one of the greatest of sufferers and the chief of heroes. Nevertheless his story was not written out, and can only be hinted at. Perhaps more time was consumed in its investigation and in listening to a recital of his sufferings than could well be spared; perhaps it was thought, as was often the case, unless full justice could be given him, the story would be spoiled; or perhaps the appalling nature of his sufferings rendered the pen powerless, and made the heart too sick for the task. Whether it was so or not in this case, it was not unfrequently so in other instances, as is well remembered. It will be necessary, in the subsequent pages of this work, to omit the narratives of a great many who, unfortunately, were but briefly noted on the books at the time of their arrival. In the eyes of some, this may prove disappointing, especially in instances where these pages are turned to with the hope of gaining a clue to certain lost ones. As all, however, cannot be mentioned, and as the general reader will look for incidents and facts which will most fittingly bring out the chief characteristics in the career and escape of bondmen, the reasonableness of this course must be obvious to all.

CHARLES GILBERT.

FLEEING FROM DAVIS A NEGRO TRADER, SECRETED UNDER A HOTEL, UP A TREE, UNDER A FLOOR, IN A THICKET, ON A STEAMER.

In 1854 Charles was owned in the city of Richmond by Benjamin Davis, a notorious negro trader. Charles was quite a "likely-looking article," not too black or too white, but rather of a nice "ginger-bread color." Davis was of opinion that this "article" must bring him a tip-top price. For two or three months the trader advertised Charles for sale in the papers, but for some reason or other Charles did not command the high price demanded.

While Davis was thus daily trying to sell Charles, Charles was contemplating how he might escape. Being uncommonly shrewd he learned something about a captain of a schooner from Boston, and determined to approach him with regard to securing a passage. The captain manifested a disposition to accommodate him for the sum of ten dollars, provided Charles could manage to get to Old Point Comfort, there to embark. The Point was about one hundred and sixty miles distant from Richmond.

A man of ordinary nerve would have declined this condition unhesitatingly. On the other hand it was not Charles' intention to let any offer slide ; indeed he felt that he must make an effort, if he failed. He could not see how his lot could be made more miserable by attempting to flee. In full view of all the consequences he ventured to take the hazardous step, and to his great satisfaction he reached Old Point Comfort safely. In that locality he was well known, unfortunately too well known, for he had been raised partly there, and, at the same time, many of his relatives and acquaintances were still living there. These facts were evidently well known to the trader, who unquestionably had snares set in order to entrap Charles should he seek shelter among his relatives, a reasonable supposition. Charles had scarcely reached his old home before he was apprised of the fact that the hunters and watch dogs of Slavery were eagerly watching for him. Even his nearest relatives, through fear of consequences had to hide their faces as it were from him. None dare offer him a night's lodging, scarcely a cup of water, lest such an act might be discovered by the hunters, whose fiendish hearts would have found pleasure in meting out the most dire punishments to those guilty of thus violating the laws of Slavery. The prospect, if not utterly hopeless, was decidedly discouraging. The way to Boston was entirely closed. A "reward of $200" was advertised for his capture. For the first week after arriving at Old Point he entrusted himself to a young friend by the name of E. S. The fear of the pursuers drove him from his hiding-place at the expiration of the week. Thence he sought shelter neither with kinfolks, Christians, nor infidels, but in this hour of his calamity he made up his mind that he would try living under a large hotel for a while. Having watched his opportunity, he managed to reach Higee hotel, a very large house without a cellar, erected on pillars three or four feet above the ground. One place alone, near the cistern, presented some chance for a hiding-place, sufficient to satisfy him quite well under the circumstances. This dark and gloomy spot he at once willingly occupied rather than return to Slavery. In this refuge he remained four weeks. Of course he could not live without food ; but to communicate with man or woman would inevitably subject him to danger. Charles' experience in the neighborhood of his old home left no ground for him to hope that he would be likely to find friendly aid anywhere under the shadow of Slavery. In consequence of these fears he received his food from the "slop tub," securing this diet in the darkness of night after all was still and quiet around the hotel. To use his own language, the meals thus obtained were often " sweet " to his taste.

One evening, however, he was not a little alarmed by the approach of an Irish boy who came under the hotel to hunt chickens. While prowling around in the darkness he appeared to be making his way unconsciously to the very spot where Charles was reposing. How to meet the danger was to Charles' mind at first very puzzling, there was no time now to plan. As quick as thought he feigned the bark of a savage dog accompanied with a furious growl and snarl which he was confident would frighten the boy half out of his senses, and cause him to depart quickly from his private apartment. The trick succeeded admirably, and the emergency was satisfactorily met, so far as the boy was concerned, but the boy's father hearing the attack of the dog, swore that he would kill him. Charles was a silent listener to the threat, and he saw that he could no longer remain in safety in his present quarter. So that night he took his de-

parture for Bay Shore; here he decided to pass a day in the woods, but the privacy of this place was not altogether satisfactory to Charles' mind; but where to find a more secure retreat he could not,—dared not venture to ascertain that day. It occurred to him, however, that he would be much safer up a tree than hid in the bushes and undergrowth. He therefore climbed up a large acorn tree and there passed an entire day in deep meditation. No gleam of hope appeared, yet he would not suffer himself to think of returning to bondage. In this dilemma he remembered a poor washer-woman named Isabella, a slave who had charge of a wash-house. With her he resolved to seek succor.

Leaving the woods he proceeded to the wash-house and was kindly received by Isabella, but what to do with him or how to afford him any protection she could see no way whatever. .The schooling which Charles had been receiving a number of weeks in connection with the most fearful looking-for of the threatened wrath of the trader made it much easier for him than for her to see how he could be provided for. A room and comforts he was not accustomed to. Of course he could not expect such comforts now. Like many another escaping from the relentless tyrant, Charles could contrive methods which to his venturesome mind would afford hope, however desperate they might appear to others. He thought that he might be safe under the floor. To Isabella the idea was new, but her sympathies were strongly with Charles, and she readily consented to accommodate him under the floor of the wash-house. Isabella and a friend of Charles, by the name of John Thomas, were the only persons who were cognizant of this arrangement. The kindness of these friends, manifested by their willingness to do anything in their power to add to the comfort of Charles, was proof to him that his efforts and sufferings had not been altogether in vain. He remained under the floor two weeks, accessible to kind voices and friendly ministrations. At the end of this time his repose was again sorely disturbed by reports from without that suspicion had been awakened towards the wash-house. How this happened neither Charles nor his friends could conjecture. But the arrival of six officers whom he could hear talking very plainly in the house, whose errand was actually to search for him, convinced him that he had never for a single moment been in greater danger. The officers not only searched the house, but they offered his friend John Thomas $25 if he would only put them on Charles' track. John professed to know nothing; Isabella was equally ignorant. Discouraged with their efforts on this occasion, the officers gave up the hunt and left the house. Charles, however, had had enough of the floor accommodations. He left that night and returned to his old quarters under the hotel. Here he stayed one week, at the expiration of which time the need of fresh air was so imperative, that he resolved to go out at night to Allen's cottage and spend a day in the woods. He had knowledge of a place where the undergrowth and bushes were almost impenetrable. To rest and refresh himself in this thicket he felt would be a great comfort to him. Without serious difficulty he reached the thicket, and while pondering over the all-absorbing matter as to how he should ever manage to make his escape, an old man approached. Now while Charles had no reason to think that he was sought by the old intruder, his very near approach admonished him that it would neither be safe nor agreeable to allow him to come nearer. Charles remembering that his trick of playing the dog, when previously in danger under the hotel, had served a good end, thought that it would work well in the thicket. So he again tried his power at growling and barking hideously for a moment or two, which at once caused the man to turn his course. Charles could hear him distinctly retreating, and at the same time cursing the dog. The owner of the place had the reputation of keeping "bad dogs," so the old man poured out a dreadful threat against "Stephens' dogs," and was soon out of the reach of the one in the thicket.

Notwithstanding his success in frightening off the old man, CHARLES felt that the thicket was by no means a safe place for him. He concluded to make another change. This time he sought a marsh; two hours' stay there was sufficient to satisfy him, that that too was no place to tarry in, even for a single night. He, therefore, left immediately. A third time, he returned to the hotel, where he remained only two days. His appeals had at last reached the heart of his mother—she could no longer bear to see him struggling, and suffering, and not render him aid, whatever the consequences might be. If she at first feared to lend him a helping hand, she now resolutely worked with a view of saving money to succor him. Here the prospect began to brighten.

A passage was secured for him on a steamer bound for Philadelphia. One more day, and night must elapse, ere he could be received on board. The joyful anticipations which now filled his breast left no room for fear; indeed, he could scarcely contain himself; he was drunk with joy. In this state of mind he concluded that nothing would afford him more pleasure before leaving, than to spend his last hours at the wash house, "under the floor." To this place he went with no fear of hunters before his eyes. Charles had scarcely been three hours in this place, however, before three officers came in search of him. Two of them talked with Isabella, asked her about her "boarders," etc.; in the meanwhile, one of them uninvited, made his way up stairs. It so happened, that Charles was in this very portion of the house. His case now seemed more hopeless than ever. The officer up stairs was separated from him simply by a thin curtain. Women's garments hung all around. Instead of fainting or surrendering, in the twinkling of an eye, Charles' inventive intellect, led him to enrobe himself in female attire. Here, to use his own language, a "thousand thoughts" rushed into his mind in a minute. The next instant he was going down stairs in the presence of the officers, his old calico dress, bonnet and rig, attracting no further attention than simply to elicit the following simple questions: "Whose gal are you?" "Mr. Cockling's, sir." "What is your name?" "Delie, sir." "Go on then!" said one of the officers, and on Charles went to avail himself of the passage on the steamer which his mother had procured for him for the sum of thirty dollars.

In due time, he succeeded in getting on the steamer, but he soon learned, that her course was not direct to Philadelphia, but that some stay would be made in Norfolk, Va. Although disappointed, yet this being a step in the right direction, he made up his mind to be patient. He was delayed in Norfolk four weeks. From the time Charles first escaped, his owner (Davis the negro trader), had kept a standing reward of $550 advertised for his recovery. This showed that Davis was willing to risk heavy expenses for Charles as well as gave evidence that he believed him still secreted either about Richmond, Petersburg, or Old Point Comfort. In this belief he was not far from being correct, for Charles spent most of his time in either of these three places, from the day of his escape until the day that he finally embarked. At last, the long looked-for hour arrived to start for Philadelphia.

He was to leave his mother, with no hope of ever seeing her again, but she had purchased herself and was called free. Her name was Margaret Johnson. Three brothers likewise were ever in his thoughts, (in chains), " Henry," " Bill," and " Sam," (half brothers). But after all the hope of freedom outweighed every other consideration, and he was prepared to give up all for liberty. To die rather than remain a slave was his resolve.

Charles arrived per steamer, from Norfolk, on the 11th day of November, 1854. The Richmond papers bear witness to the fact, that Benjamin Davis advertised Charles Gilbert, for months prior to this date, as has been stated in this narrative. As to the correctness of the story, all that the writer has to say is, that he took it down from the lips of Charles, hurriedly, directly after his arrival, with no thought of magnifying a single incident. On the contrary, much that was of interest in the story had to be omitted. Instead of being overdrawn, not half of the particulars were recorded. Had the idea then been entertained, that the narrative of this young slave-warrior was to be brought to light in the manner and time that it now is, a far more thrilling account of his adventures might have been written. Other colored men who knew both Davis and Charles, as well as one man ordinarily knows another, rejoiced at seeing Charles in Philadelphia, and they listened with perfect faith to his story. So marvellous were the incidents of his escape, that his sufferings in Slavery, previous to his heroic struggles to throw off the yoke, were among the facts omitted from the records. While this may be regretted it is, nevertheless, gratifying on the whole to have so good an account of him as was preserved. It is needless to say, that the Committee took especial pleasure in aiding him, and listening to so remarkable a story narrated so intelligently by one who had been a slave.

LIBERTY OR DEATH.

JIM BOW-LEGS, *alias* BILL PAUL.

In 1855 a traveler arrived with the above name, who, on examination, was found to possess very extraordinary characteristics. As a hero and adventurer some passages of his history were most remarkable. His schooling had been such as could only be gathered on plantations under brutal overseers;—or while fleeing,—or in swamps,—in prisons,—or on the auction-block, etc.; in which condtion he was often found. Nevertheless in these circumstances his mind got well stored with vigorous thoughts—neither books nor friendly advisers being at his command. Yet his native intelligence as it regarded human nature, was extraordinary. His resolution and perseverance never faltered. In all respects he was a remarkable man. He was a young man, weighing about one hundred and eighty pounds, of uncommon muscular strength. He was born in the State of Georgia, Oglethorpe county, and was owned by Dr. Thomas Stephens, of Lexington. On reaching the Vigilance Committee in Philadelphia, his story was told many times over to one and another. Hour after hour was occupied by friends in listening to the simple narrative of his struggles for freedom. A very full account of " Jim," was forwarded in a letter to M. A. Shadd, the then Editress of the " Provincial Freeman." Said account has been carefully preserved, and is here annexed as it appeared in the columns of the above named paper :

"I must now pass to a third adventurer. The one to whom I allude, is a young man of twenty-six years of age, by the name of 'Jim,' who fled from near Charleston, S. C. Taking all the facts and circumstances into consideration respecting the courageous career of this successful adventurer for freedom, his case is by far more interesting than any I have yet referred to. Indeed, for the good of the cause, and the honor of one who gained his liberty by periling his life so frequently :—shot several times,—making six unsuccessful attempts to escape from the far South,—numberless times chased by bloodhounds,—captured, imprisoned and sold repeatedly,—living for months in the woods, swamps and caves, subsisting mainly on parched corn and berries, &c., &c., his narrative ought, by all means, to be published, though I doubt very much whether many could be found who could persuade themselves to believe one-tenth part of this marvellous story.

Though this poor Fugitive was utterly ignorant of letters, his natural good sense and keen perception qualified him to arrest the attention and interest the heart in a most remarkable degree.

His master finding him not available, on account of his absconding propensities, would gladly have offered him for sale. He was once taken to Florida, for that purpose ; but, generally, traders being wide awake, on inspecting him, would almost invariably pronounce him a 'd—n rascal,' because he would never fail to eye them sternly, as they inspected him. The obedient and submissive slave is always recognized by hanging his head and looking on the ground, when looked at by a slave-holder. This lesson Jim had never learned, hence he was not to be trusted.

His head and chest, and indeed his entire structure, as solid as a rock, indicated that he was physically no ordinary man ; and not being under the

16

influence of the spirit of "non-resistance," he had occasionally been found to be a rather formidable customer.

His father was a full-blooded Indian, brother to the noted Indian Chief, Billy Bowlegs; his mother was quite black and of unmixed blood.

For five or six years, the greater part of Jim's time was occupied in trying to escape, and in being in prison for sale, to punish him for running away.

His mechanical genius was excellent, so were his geographical abilities. He could make shoes or do carpenter's work very handily, though he had never had the chance to learn. As to traveling by night or day, he was always road-ready and having an uncommon memory, could give exceedingly good accounts of what he saw, etc.

When he entered a swamp, and had occasion to take a nap he took care first to decide upon the posture he must take, so that if come upon unexpectedly by the hounds and slave-hunters, he might know in an instant which way to steer to defeat them. He always carried a liquid, which he had prepared, to prevent hounds from scenting him, which he said had never failed. As soon as the hounds came to the place where he had rubbed his legs and feet with said liquid, they could follow him no further, but howled and turned immediately.

Quite a large number of the friends of the slave saw this noble-hearted fugitive, and would sit long and listen with the most undivided attention to his narrative—none doubting for a moment, I think, the entire truthfulness of his story. Strange as his story was, there was so much natural simplicity in his manner and countenance, one could not refrain from believing him."

SALT-WATER FUGITIVE.

This was an exceptional case, as this passenger did not reach the Vigilance Committee of Philadelphia, yet to exclude him on this account, would be doing an injustice to history.

The facts in his case were incontestably established in the Philadelphia Register in April, 1854, from which the following thrilling account is taken:

The steamship, Keystone State, which arrived at this port on Saturday morning, had just entered Delaware Bay, when a man was discovered secreted outside of the vessel and under the guards. When brought from his hiding-place, he was found to be a Fugitive Slave, who had secreted himself there before the vessel left Savannah on Wednesday, and had remained in that place from the time of starting!

His position was such, that the water swept over and around him almost constantly. He had some bread in his pocket, which he had intended for subsistence until he could reach a land of liberty. It was saturated with sea-water and dissolved to a pulp.

When our readers remember the high winds of Friday, and the sudden change to cold during that night, and the fact that the fugitive had remained in that situation for three days and nights, we think it will be conceded that he fully earned his liberty, and that the "institution," which was so intolerable that he was willing to run the risk of almost certain death to escape from it had no very great attractions for him. But the poor man was doomed to disappointment. The captain ordered the vessel to put into Newcastle, where, the fugitive, hardly able to stand, was taken on shore and incarcerated, and where he now awaits the order of his owner in Savannah. The following additional particulars are from the same paper of the 21st.

The Keystone State case.—Our article yesterday morning brought us several letters of inquiry and offers of contributions to aid in the purchase from his master of the unfortunate inmate of Newcastle jail. In answer to the former, we would say, that the steamer Keystone State, left Savannah, at 9 A. M., last Wednesday. It was about the same hour next morning that the men engaged in heaving lead, heard a voice from under the guards imploring help. A rope was procured, and the man relieved from his dangerous and suffering situation. He was well cared for immediately ; a suit of dry clothes was furnished him, and he was given his share of the contents of the boat pantry. On arriving at Newcastle, the captain had him placed in jail, for the purpose, as we are informed, of taking him back to Savannah.

To those who have offered contributions so liberally, we answer, that the prospect is, that only a small amount will be needed—enough to fee a lawyer to sue out a writ of habeas corpus. The salt water fugitive claims to be a free man, and a native of Philadelphia. He gives his name as Edward Davis, and says that he formerly lived at No. 5 Steel's court, that he was a pupil in Bird's school, on Sixth St. above Lombard, and that he has a sister living at Mr. Diamond's, a distiller, on South St. We are not informed why he was in Georgia, from which he took such an extraordinary means to effect his escape. If the above assertion be true, we apprehend little trouble in restoring the man to his former home. The claim of the captain to take him back to Savannah, will not be listened to for a moment by any court. The only claim the owners of the "Keystone State" or the captain can have on salt water Davis, is for half passenger fare ; he came half the way as a fish. A gentleman who came from Wilmington yesterday, assures us that the case is in good hands at Newcastle.

FULL PARTICULARS OF THE ABDUCTION, ENSLAVING AND ESCAPE OF DAVIS.
ATTEMPT TO REDUCE HIM TO SLAVERY AGAIN.

The case of the colored man Davis, who made such a bold stroke to regain his liberty, by periling his life on board the steamer Keystone State, has excited very general attention. He has given a detailed account of his abduction and sale as a slave in the State of Maryland and Georgia, and some of his adventures up to the time of reaching Delaware. His own story is substantially as follows:

He left Philadelphia on the 15th of September, 1851, and went to Harrisburg, intending to go to Hollidaysburg; took a canal boat for Havre de Grace, where he arrived next day. There he hired on board the schooner Thomas and Edward (oyster boat), of Baltimore. Went from Havre de Grace to St. Michael's, for oysters, thence to Baltimore, and thence to Havre de Grace again.

He then hired to a Mr. Sullivan, who kept a grocery store, to do jobs. While there, a constable, named Smith, took him before a magistrate named Graham, who fined him fifteen or twenty dollars for violating the law in relation to free negroes coming into the State. This fine he was not able to pay, and Smith took him to Bell Air prison. Sheriff Gaw wrote to Mr. Maitland in Philadelphia, to whom he referred, and received an answer that Mr. Maitland was dead and none of the family knew him. He remained in that prison nearly two months. He then had a trial in court before a Judge Grier (most unfortunate name), who sentenced him to be sold to pay his fine and expenses, amounting to fifty dollars.

After a few days and *without being offered at public sale*, he was taken out of jail at two o'clock in the morning and carried to Campbell's slave pen, in Baltimore, where he remained several months. While there, he was employed to cook for some fifty or sixty slaves, being told that he was working out his fine and jail fees. After being there about six months, he was taken out of prison, handcuffed by one Winters, who took him and two or three others to Washington and thence to Charleston, S. C. Here Winters left them, and they were taken by steamboat to Savannah. While on board the boat, he learned that himself and the other two had been sold to Mr. William Dean, of Macon, where he stayed two days, and was taken from that place to the East Valley Railroad.

Subsequently he was sent to work on the Possum Tail Railroad. Here he was worked so hard, that in one month he lost his health. The other two men taken on with him, failed before he did. He was then sent to Macon, and thence to the cotton plantation again.

During the time he worked on the railroad he had allowed him for food, one peck of corn meal, four pounds of bacon, and one quart of molasses per week. He cooked it himself at night, for the next day's use. He worked at packing cotton for four or five months, and in the middle of November, 1852, was sent back to the railroad, where he was again set to wheeling.

He worked at "task work" two months, being obliged to wheel *sixteen* square yards per day. At the end of two months he broke down again, and was sick. They tried one month to cure him, but did not succeed. In July, 1853, he was taken to an infirmary in Macon. Dr. Nottinghan and Dr. Harris, of that institution, both stated that his was the worst case of the kind they ever had. He remained at the infirmary two months and partially recovered. He told the story of his wrongs to these physicians, who tried to buy him. One of his legs was drawn up so that he could not walk well, and they offered four hundred dollars for him, which his master refused. The doctors wanted him to attend their patients, (mostly slaves). While in Georgia he was frequently asked where he came from, being found more intelligent than the common run of slaves.

On the 12th of March he ran away from Macon and went to Savannah. There he hid in a stable until Tuesday afternoon at six o'clock, when he secreted himself on board the Keystone State. At 9 o'clock the next morning the Keystone State left with Davis secreted, as we have before stated. With his imprisonment in Newcastle, after being pronounced free, our readers are already familiar. We subjoin the documents on which he was discharged from his imprisonment in Newcastle, and his subsequent re-committal on the oath of Capt. Hardie.

COPY OF FIRST ORDER OF COMMITMENT.

New Castle county, ss., State of Delaware.—To Wm. R. Lynam, Sheriff of said county.————————Davis (Negro) is delivered to your custody for further examination and hearing for traveling without a pass, and supposed to be held a Slave to some person in the State of Georgia.

[Seal]. Witness the hand and seal of John Bradford, one of the Justices of the Peace for the county of Newcastle, the 17th day of March, 1854.

JOHN BRADFORD, J. P.

COPY OF DISCHARGE.

To Wm. R. Lynam, Sheriff of Newcastle county: You will discharge ————————Davis from your custody, satisfactory proof having been made before me that he is a free man. JOHN BRADFORD, J. P.

Witnesses—Joanna Diamond, John H. Brady, Martha C. Maguire.

COPY OF ORDER OF RE-COMMITMENT.

New Castle county, ss., the State of Delaware to Wm. R. Lynam, and to the Sheriff or keeper of the Common Jail of said county, Whereas ——— Davis hath this day been brought before me, the subscriber, one of the Justices of the Peace, in and for the said county, charged upon the oath of Robert Hardie with being a runaway slave, and also as a suspicious person, traveling without a pass, these are therefore to command you, the said Wm. R. Lynam, forthwith to convey and deliver into the custody of the said Sheriff, or keeper of the said jail, the body of the said Davis, and you the said Sheriff or receiver of the body of the said Davis into your custody in the said jail, and him there safely keep until he be thence delivered by due course of the law.

Given under my hand and seal at New Castle this 21st day of March, A. D., 1854.   JOHN BRADFORD, J. P.

On the fourth of April, the Marshal of Macon called at the jail in Newcastle, and demanded him as a fugitive slave, but the Sheriff refused to give him up until a fair hearing could be had according to the laws of the State of Delaware. The Marshal has returned to Georgia, and will probably bring the claimant on the next trip of the Keystone State. The authorities of Delaware manifest no disposition to deliver up a man whose freedom has been so clearly proved ; but every effort will be made to reduce him again to slavery by the man who claims him, in which, it seems, he has the hearty co-operation of Capt. Hardie. A trial will be had before U. S. Commissioner Guthrie, and we have every reason to suppose it will be a fair one. The friends of right and justice should remember that such a trial will be attended with considerable expense, and that the imprisoned man has been too long deprived of his liberty to have money to pay for his own defence.

SAMUEL GREEN alias WESLEY KINNARD, August 28th, 1854.

TEN YEARS IN THE PENITENTIARY FOR HAVING A COPY OF UNCLE TOM'S CABIN.

The passenger answering to the above name, left Indian Creek, Chester Co., Md., where he had been held to service or labor, by Dr. James Muse. One week had elapsed from the time he set out until his arrival in Philadelphia. Although he had never enjoyed school privileges of any kind, yet he was not devoid of intelligence. He had profited by his daily experience as a slave, and withal, had managed to learn to read and write a little, despite law and usage to the contrary. Sam was about twenty-five years of age and by trade, a blacksmith. Before running away, his general character for sobriety, industry, and religion, had evidently been considered good, but in coveting his freedom and running away to obtain it, he had sunk far below the utmost limit of forgiveness or mercy in the estimation of the slave-holders of Indian Creek.

During his intercourse with the Vigilance Committee, while rejoicing over his triumphant flight, he gave, with no appearance of excitement, but calmly, and in a common-sense like manner, a brief description of his master, which was entered on the record book substantially as follows: "Dr. James Muse is thought by the servants to be the worst man in Maryland, inflicting whipping and all manner of cruelties upon the servants."

While Sam gave reasons for this sweeping charge, which left no room for doubt, on the part of the Committee, of his sincerity and good judgment, it was not deemed necessary to make a note of more of the doctor's character than seemed actually needed, in order to show why "Sam" had taken passage on the Underground Rail Road. For several years, "Sam" was hired out by the doctor at blacksmithing; in this situation, daily wearing the yoke of unrequited labor, through the kindness of Harriet Tubman (sometimes called "Moses"), the light of the Underground Rail Road and Canada suddenly illuminated his mind. It was new to him, but he was quite too intelligent and liberty-loving, not to heed the valuable information which this sister of humanity imparted. Thenceforth he was in love with Canada, and likewise a decided admirer of the U. R. Road. Harriet was herself, a shrewd and fearless agent, and well understood the entire route from that part of the country to Canada. The spring previous, she had paid a visit to the very neighborhood in which "Sam" lived, expressly to lead her own brothers out of "Egypt." She succeeded. To "Sam" this was cheering and glorious news, and he made up his mind, that before a great while, Indian Creek should have one less slave and that Canada should have one more citizen. Faithfully did he watch an opportunity to carry out his resolution. In due time a good Providence opened the way, and to "Sam's" satisfaction he reached Philadelphia, having encountered no peculiar difficulties. The Committee, perceiving that he was smart, active, and promising, encouraged his undertaking, and having given him friendly advice, aided him in the usual manner. Letters of introduction were given him, and he was duly forwarded on his way. He had left his father, mother, and one sister behind. Samuel and Catharine were the names of his parents. Thus far, his escape would seem not to affect his parents, nor was it apparent that there was any other cause why the owner should revenge himself upon them.

The father was an old local preacher in the Methodist Church—much esteemed as an inoffensive, industrious man; earning his bread by the sweat of his brow, and contriving to move along in the narrow road allotted colored people bond or free, without exciting a spirit of ill will in the proslavery power of his community. But the rancor awakened in the breast of slave-holders in consequence of the high-handed step the son had taken, brought the father under suspicion and hate. Under the circumstances, the eye of Slavery could do nothing more than watch for an occasion to pounce upon him. It was not long before the desired opportunity presented itself. Moved by parental affection, the old man concluded to pay a visit to his boy, to see how he was faring in a distant land, and among strangers. This resolution he quietly carried into effect. He found his son in Canada, doing well; industrious; a man of sobriety, and following his father's footsteps religiously. That the old man's heart was delighted with what his eyes saw and his ears heard in Canada, none can doubt. But in the simplicity of his imagination, he never dreamed that this visit was to be made the means of his destruction. During the best portion of his days he had faithfully worn the badge of Slavery, had afterwards purchased his freedom, and thus become a free man. He innocently conceived the idea that he was doing no harm in availing himself not only of his God-given rights, but of the rights that he had also purchased by the hard toil of his own hands. But the enemy was lurking in ambush for him—thirsting for his blood. To his utter consternation, not long after his return from his visit to his son "a party of gentlemen from the New Market district, went at night to Green's house and made search, whereupon was found a copy of Uncle Tom's Cabin, etc." This was enough—the hour had come, wherein to wreak vengeance upon poor Green. The course pursued and the result, may be seen in the following statement taken from the Cambridge (Md.), "Democrat," of April 29th, 1857, and communicated by the writer to the "Provincial Freeman."

SAM GREEN.

The case of the State against Sam Green (free negro) indicted for having in his possession, papers, pamphlets and pictorial representations, having a tendency to create discontent, etc., among the people of color in the State, was tried before the court on Friday last.

This case was of the utmost importance, and has created in the public mind a great deal of interest—it being the first case of the kind ever having occurred in our country.

It appeared, in evidence, that this Green has a son in Canada, to whom Green made a visit last summer. Since his return to this county, suspicion has fastened upon him, as giving aid and assisting slaves who have since absconded and reached Canada, and several weeks ago, a party of gentlemen from New Market district, went at night, to Green's house and made search, whereupon was found a volume of "Uncle Tom's Cabin," a map of Canada, several schedules of routes to the North, and a letter from his son in Canada, detailing the pleasant trip he had, the number of friends he met with on the way, with plenty to eat, drink, etc., and concludes with a request to his father, that he shall tell certain other slaves, naming them, to come on, which slaves, it is well known, did leave shortly afterwards, and have reached Canada. The case was argued with great ability, the counsel on both sides displaying a great deal of ingenuity, learning and eloquence. The first indictment was for the having in possession the letter, map and route schedules.

Notwithstanding the mass of evidence given, to show the prisoner's guilt, in unlawfully having in his possession these documents, and the nine-tenths of the community in which he lived, believed that he had a hand in the running away of slaves, it was the opinion of the court, that the law under which he was indicted, was not applicable to the case, and that he must, accordingly, render a verdict of not guilty.

He was immediately arraigned upon another indictment, for having in possession "Uncle Tom's Cabin," and tried ; in this case the court has not yet rendered a verdict, but holds it under *curia* till after the Somerset county court. It is to be hoped, the court will find the evidence in this case sufficient to bring it within the scope of the law under which the prisoner is indicted (that of 1842, chap. 272), and that the prisoner may meet his due reward—be that what it may.

That there is something required to be done by our Legislators, for the protection of slave property, is evident from the variety of constructions put upon the statute in this case, and we trust, that at the next meeting of the Legislature there will be such amendments, as to make the law on this subject, perfectly clear and comprehensible to the understanding of every one.

In the language of the assistant counsel for the State, " Slavery must be protected or it must be abolished."

From the same sheet, of May 20th, the terrible doom of Samuel Green, is announced in the following words:

In the case of the State against Sam Green, (free negro) who was tried at the April term of the Circuit Court of this county, for having in his possession abolition pamphlets, among which was " Uncle Tom's Cabin," has been found guilty by the court, and sentenced to the penitentiary for the term of ten years—until the 14th of May, 1867.

The son, a refugee in Canada, hearing the distressing news of his father's sad fate in the hands of the relentless " gentlemen," often wrote to know if there was any prospect of his deliverance. The subjoined letter is a fair sample of his correspondence :

SALFORD, 22, 1857.

Dear Sir I take my pen in hand to Request a faver of you if you can by any means without duin InJestus to your self or your Bisness to grant it as I Bleve you to be a man that would Sympathize in such a ones Condition as my self I Reseved a letter that Stats to me that my Fater has ben Betraed in the act of helping sum frend to Canada and the law has Convicted and Sentanced him to the Stats prison for 10 yeares his White Frands ofered 2 thousen Dollers to Redem him but they would not short three thousen. I am in Canada and it is a Dificult thing to get a letter to any of my Frands in Maryland so as to get prop per infermation abot it—if you can by any means get any in telligence from Baltimore City a bot this Event Plese do so and Rit word and all so all the inform mation that you think prop per as Regards the Evant and the best mathod to Redeme him and so Plese Rite soon as you can You will oblige your sir Frand and Drect your letter to Salford P. office C. W. SAMUEL GREEN.

In this dark hour the friends of the Slave could do but little more than sympathize with this heart-stricken son and grey-headed father. The aged follower of the Rejected and Crucified had like Him to bear the "reproach of many," and make his bed with the wicked in the Penitentiary. Doubtless there were a few friends in his neighborhood who sympathized with him, but they were powerless to aid the old man. But thanks to a kind Providence, the great deliverance brought about during the Rebellion by which so many captives were freed, also unlocked Samuel Green's prison-doors and he was allowed to go free.

After his liberation from the Penitentiary, we had from his own lips narrations of his years of suffering—of the bitter cup, that he was compelled to drink, and of his being sustained by the Almighty Arm—but no notes were taken at the time, consequently we have nothing more to add concerning him, save quite a faithful likeness.

AN IRISH GIRL'S DEVOTION TO FREEDOM.

IN LOVE WITH A SLAVE—GETS HIM OFF TO CANADA—FOLLOWS HIM—MARRIAGE, &C.

Having dwelt on the sad narratives of Samuel Green and his son in the preceding chapter, it is quite a relief to be able to introduce a traveler whose story contains incidents less painful to contemplate. From the record book the following brief account is taken:

"April 27, 1855. John Hall arrived safely from Richmond, Va., per schooner, (Captain B). One hundred dollars were paid for his passage. In Richmond he was owned by James Dunlap, a merchant. John had been sold several times, in consequence of which, he had possessed very good opportunities of experiencing the effect of change of owners. Then, too, the personal examination made before sale, and the gratification afforded his master when he (John), brought a good price—left no very pleasing impressions on his mind.

By one of his owners, named Burke, John alleged that he had been "cruelly used." When quite young, both he and his sister, together with their mother, were sold by Burke. From that time he had seen neither mother nor sister—they were sold separately. For three or four years the desire to seek liberty had been fondly cherished, and nothing but the want of a favorable opportunity had deterred him from carrying out his designs. He considered himself much "imposed upon" by his master, particularly as he was allowed "no choice about living" as he "desired." This was indeed ill-treatment as John viewed the matter. John may have wanted too much. He was about thirty-five years of age, light complexion—tall—rather handsome-looking, intelligent, and of good manners. But notwithstanding these prepossessing features, John's owner valued him at only $1,000. If he had been a few shades darker and only about half as intelligent as he was, he would have been worth at least $500 more. The idea of having had a white father, in many instances, depreciated the pecuniary value of male slaves, if not of the other sex. John emphatically was one of this injured class; he evidently had blood in his veins which decidedly warred against submitting to the yoke. In addition to the influence which such rebellious blood exerted over him, together with a considerable amount of intelligence, he was also under the influence and advice of a daughter of old Ireland. She was heart and soul with John in all his plans which looked Canada-ward. This it was that "sent him away."

It is very certain, that this Irish girl was not annoyed by the kinks in John's hair. Nor was she overly fastidious about the small percentage of colored blood visible in John's complexion. It was, however, a strange occurrence and very hard to understand. Not a stone was left unturned until John was safely on the Underground Rail Road. Doubtless she helped to earn the money which was paid for his passage. And when he was safe off, it is not too much to say, that John was not a whit more delighted than was his intended Irish lassie, Mary Weaver. John had no sooner reached Canada than Mary's heart was there too. Circumstances, however, required that she should remain in Richmond a number of months for the purpose of winding up some of her affairs. As soon as the way opened for her, she followed him. It was quite manifest, that she had not let a single opportunity slide, but seized the first chance and arrived partly by means of the Underground Rail Road and partly by the regular train. Many difficulties were surmounted before and after leaving Richmond, by which they earned their merited success. From Canada, where they anticipated entering upon the matrimonial career with mutual satisfaction, it seemed to afford them great pleasure to write back frequently, expressing their heartfelt gratitude for assistance, and their happiness in the prospect of being united under the favorable auspices of freedom. At least two or three of these letters, bearing on particular phases of their escape, etc., are too valuable not to be published in this connection:

FIRST LETTER.

HAMILTON, March 25th, 1856.

MR. STILL :—Sir and Friend—I take the liberty of addressing you with these few lines hoping that you will attend to what I shall request of you.

I have written to Virginia and have not received an answer yet. I want to know if you can get any one of your city to go to Richmond for me. If you can, I will pay the expense of the whole. The person that I want the messenger to see is a white girl. I expect you know who I allude to, it is the girl that sent me away. If you can get any one to go, you will please write right away and tell me the cost, &c. I will forward the money and a letter. Please use your endeavors.   Yours Respectfully,   JOHN HALL.

Direct yours to Mr. Hill.

SECOND LETTER.

HAMILTON, Sept. 15th, 1856.

To MR. STILL, DEAR SIR :—I take this opportunity of addressing these few lines to you hoping to find you in good health I am happy to inform you that Miss Weaver arrived here on Tuesday last, and I can assure you it was indeed a happy day. As for your part that you done I will not attempt to tell you how thankful I am, but I hope that you can imagine what my feelings are to you. I cannot find words sufficient to express my gratitude to you, I think the wedding will take place on Tuesday next, I have seen some of the bread from your house, and she says it is the best bread she has had since she has been in America. Sometimes she has impudence enough to tell me she would rather be where you are in Philadelphia than to be here with me. I hope this will be no admiration to you for no honest hearted person ever saw you that would not desire to be where you are, No flattery, but candidly speaking, you are worthy all the praise of any person who has ever been with you, I am now like a deserted Christian, but yet I have asked so much, and all has been done yet I must ask again, My love to Mrs. Still. Dear Mr. Still I now ask you please to exercise all your influence to get this young man Willis Johnson from Richmond for me It is the young man that Miss Weaver told you about, he is in Richmond I think he is at the corner of Fushien Street, & Grace in a house of one Mr. Rutherford, there is several Rutherford in the neighborhood, there is a church call'd the third Baptist Church, on the R. H. side going up Grace street, directly opposite the Baptist church at the corner, is Mrs. Meads Old School at one corner, and Mr. Rutherfords is at the other corner. He can be found out by seeing Fountain Tombs who belongs to Mr. Rutherford and if you should not see him, there is James Turner who lives at the Governors, Please to see Captain Bayliss and tell him to take these directions and go to John Hill, in Petersburgh, and he may find him. Tell Captain Bayliss that if he ever did me a friendly thing in his life which he did do one friendly act, if he will take this on himself, and if money should be lacking I will forward any money that he may require, I hope you will sympathize with the poor young fellow, and tell the captain to do all in his power to get him and the costs shall be paid. He lies now between death or victory, for I know the man he belongs to would just as soon kill him as not, if he catches him, I here enclose to you a letter for Mr. Wm. C. Mayo, and please to send it as directed. In this letter I have asked him to send a box to you for me, which you will please pay the fare of the express upon it, when you get it please to let me know, and I will send you the money to pay the expenses of the carriage clear through. Please to let Mr. Mayo know how to direct a box to you, and the best way to send it from Richmond to Philadelphia. You will greatly oblige me by so doing. In this letter I have enclosed a trifle for postage which you will please to keep on account of my letters I hope you wont think hard of me but I simply send it because I know you have done enough, and are now doing more, without imposing in the matter I have done it a great many more of our people who you have done so much fore. No more from your humble and oldest servant.

JOHN HALL, Norton's Hotel, Hamilton.

THIRD LETTER.

MONDAY, Sept. 29, 56.

SIR:—I take this opportunity of informing you that we are in excellent health, and hope you are the same, I wrote a letter to you about 2 weeks ago and have not yet had an answer to it I wish to inform you that the wedding took place on Tuesday last, and Mrs. Hall now sends her best love to you, I enclose a letter which I wish you to forward to Mr. Mayo, you will see in his letter what I have said to him and I wish you would furnish him with such directions as it requires for him to send them things to you. I have told him not to pay for them but to send them to you so when you get them write me word what the cost of them are, and I will send you the money for them. Mary desires you to give her love to Mrs. Still. If any letters come for me please to send to me at Nortons Hotel, Please to let me know if you had a letter from me about 12 days ago. You will please Direct the enclosed to Mr. W. C. Mayo, Richmond, Va. Let me know if you have heard anything of Willis Johnson Mr. & Mrs. Hill send their kind love to you, they are all well, no more at present from your affect.,

JOHN HALL Nortons Hotel.

FOURTH LETTER.

HAMILTON, December 23d, 1856.

DEAR SIR:—I am happy to inform you that we are both enjoying good health and hope you are the same. I have been expecting a letter from you for some time but I suppose your business has prevented you from writing. I suppose you have not heard from any of my friends at Richmond. I have been longing to hear some news from that part, you may think " Out of sight and out of mind," but I can assure you, no matter how far I may be, or in what distant land, I shall never forget you, if I can never reach you by letters you may be sure I shall always think of you. I have found a great many friends in my life, but I must say you are the best one I ever met with, except one, you must know who that is, 'tis one who if I did not consider a friend, I could not consider any other person a friend, and that is Mrs. Hall. Please to let me know if the navigation between New York & Richmond is closed. Please to let me know whether it would be convenient to you to go to New York if it is please let me know what is the expense. Tell Mrs Still that my wife would be very happy to receive a letter from her at some moment when she is at leisure, for I know from what little I have seen of domestic affairs it keeps her pretty well employed, And I know she has not much time to write but if it were but two lines, she would be happy to receive it from her, my reason for wanting you to go to New York, there is a young man named Richard Myers and I should like for you to see him. He goes on board the Orono to Richmond and is a particular friend of mine and by seeing him I could get my clothes from Richmond, I expect to be out of employ in a few days, as the hotel is about to close on the 1st January and I hope you will write to me soon I want you to send me word how you and all the family are and all the news you can, you must excuse my short letter, as it is now near one o'clock and I must attend to business, but I have not written half what I intended to, as time is short, hoping to hear from you soon I remain yours sincerely,   JOHN HALL.

Mr. and Mrs. Hill desire their best respects to you and Mrs. Still.

It cannot be denied that this is a most extraordinary occurrence. In some respects it is without a parallel. It was, however, no uncommon thing for white men (slave-holders) in the South to have colored wives and children whom they did not hesitate to live with and acknowledge by their actions, with their means, and in their wills as the rightful heirs of their substance. Probably there is not a state in the Union where such relations have not existed. Seeing such usages, Mary might have reasoned that she had as good a right to marry the one she loved most as anybody else, particularly as she was in a "free country."

"SAM" NIXON ALIAS DR. THOMAS BAYNE.

THE ESCAPE OF A DENTIST ON THE U. G. R. R.—HE IS TAKEN FOR AN IMPOSTOR— ELECTED A MEMBER OF CITY COUNCIL IN NEW BEDFORD—STUDYING MEDICINE, ETC.

But few could be found among the Underground Rail Road passengers who had a stronger repugnance to the unrequited labor system, or the recognized terms of "master and slave," than Dr. Thomas Bayne. Nor were many to be found who were more fearless and independent in uttering their sentiments. His place of bondage was in the city of Norfolk, Va., where he was held to service by Dr. C. F. Martin, a dentist of some celebrity. While with Dr. Martin, "Sam" learned dentistry in all its branches, and was often required by his master, the doctor, to fulfil professional engagements, both at home and at a distance, when it did not suit his pleasure or convenience to appear in person. In the mechanical department, especially, "Sam" was called upon to execute the most difficult tasks. This was not the testimony of "Sam" alone; various individuals who were with him in Norfolk, but had moved to Philadelphia, and were living there at the time of his arrival, being invited to see this distinguished professional piece of property, gave evidence which fully corroborated his. The master's professional practice, according to "Sam's" calculation, was worth $3,000 per annum. Full $1,000 of this amount in the opinion of "Sam" was the result of his own fettered hands. Not only was "Sam" serviceable to the doctor in the mechanical and practical branches of his profession, but as a sort of ready reckoner and an apt penman, he was obviously considered by the doctor, a valuable "article." He would frequently have "Sam" at his books instead of a book-keeper. Of course, "Sam" had never received, from Dr. M., an hour's schooling in his life, but having perceptive faculties naturally very large, combined with much self-esteem, he could hardly help learning readily. Had his master's design to keep him in ignorance been ever so great, he would have found it a labor beyond his power. But there is no reason to suppose that Dr. Martin was opposed to Sam's learning to read and write. We are pleased to note that no charges of ill-treatment are found recorded against Dr. M. in the narrative of "Sam."

True, it appears that he had been sold several times in his younger days, and had consequently been made to feel keenly, the smarts of Slavery, but nothing of this kind was charged against Dr. M., so that he may be set down as a pretty fair man, for aught that is known to the contrary, with the exception of depriving "Sam" of the just reward of his labor, which, according to St. James, is pronounced a "fraud." The doctor did not keep "Sam" so closely confined to dentistry and book-keeping that he had no time to attend occasionally to outside duties. It appears that he was quite active and successful as an Underground Rail Road agent, and rendered important aid in various directions. Indeed, Sam had good reason to suspect that the slave-holders were watching him, and that if he remained, he would most likely find himself in "hot water up to his eyes." Wisdom dictated that he should "pull up stakes" and depart while the way was open. He knew the captains who were then in the habit of taking similar passengers, but he had some fears that they might not be able to pursue the business much longer. In contemplating the change which he was about to make, "Sam" felt it necessary to keep his movements strictly private. Not even was he at liberty to break his mind to his wife and child, fearing that it would do them no good, and might prove his utter failure. His wife's name was Edna and his daughter was called Elizabeth; both were slaves and owned by E. P. Tabb, Esq., a hardware merchant of Norfolk.

No mention is made on the books, of ill-treatment, in connection with his wife's servitude; it may therefore be inferred, that her situation was not remarkably hard. It must not be supposed that "Sam" was not truly attached to his wife. He gave abundant proof of true matrimonial devotion, notwithstanding the secrecy of his arrangements for flight. Being naturally hopeful, he concluded that he could better succeed in securing his wife after obtaining freedom himself, than in undertaking the task beforehand.

The captain had two or three other Underground Rail Road male passengers to bring with him, besides "Sam," for whom, arrangements had been previously made—no more could be brought that trip. At the appointed time, the passengers were at the disposal of the captain of the schooner which was to bring them out of Slavery into freedom. Fully aware of the dangerous consequences should he be detected, the captain, faithful to his promise, secreted them in the usual manner, and set sail northward. Instead of landing his passengers in Philadelphia, as was his intention, for some reason or other (the schooner may have been disabled), he landed them on the New Jersey coast, not a great distance from Cape Island. He directed them how to reach Philadelphia. Sam knew of friends in the city, and straightway used his ready pen to make known the distress of himself and partners in tribulation. In making their way in the direction of their destined haven, they reached Salem, New Jersey, where they were discovered to be strangers and fugitives, and were directed to Abigail Goodwin, a Quaker lady, an abolitionist, long noted for her devotion to the cause of freedom, and one of the most liberal and faithful friends of the Vigilance Committee of Philadelphia.

This friend's opportunities of witnessing fresh arrivals had been rare, and perhaps she had never before come in contact with a "chattel" so smart as "Sam." Consequently she was much embarrassed when she heard his story, especially when he talked of his experience as a "Dentist." She was inclined to suspect that he was a "shrewd impostor" that needed "watching" instead of aiding. But her humanity forbade a hasty decision on this point. She was soon persuaded to render him some assistance, notwithstanding her apprehensions. While tarrying a day or two in Salem, "Sam's" letter was received in Philadelphia. Friend Goodwin was written to in the meantime, by a member of the Committee, directly with a view of making inquires concerning the stray fugitives, and at the same time to inform her as to how they happened to be coming in the direction found by her. While the mind of the friend was much relieved by the letter she received, she was still in some doubt, as will be seen by the appended extract from a letter on the subject:

LETTER FROM A. GOODWIN.

SALEM, 3 mo , 25, '55.

DEAR FRIEND :—Thine of the 22d came to hand yesterday noon.

*   *   *   *   *   *   *   *

I do not believe that any of them are the ones thee wrote about, who wanted Dr. Lundy to come for them, and promised they would pay his expenses. They had no money, the minister said, but were pretty well off for clothes. I gave him all I had and more, but it seemed very little for four travelers—only a dollar for each—but they will meet with friends and helpers on the way. He said they expected to go away to-morrow. I am afraid, it's so cold, and one of them had a sore foot, they will not get away—it's dangerous staying here. There has been a slave-hunter here lately, I was told yesterday, in search of a woman; he tracked her to our Alms-house—she had lately been confined and was not able to go—he will come back for her and his infant—and will not wait long I expect. I want much to get her away first—and if one had a C. C. Torney here no doubt it would be done; but she will be well guarded. How much I wish the poor thing could be secreted in some safe place till she is able to travel Northward; but where that could be it's not easy to see. I presume the Carolina freed people have arrived ere now. I hope they will meet many friends, and be well provided for. Mary Davis will be then paid—her cousins have sent her twenty-four dollars, as it was not wanted for the purchase money—it was to be kept for them when they arrive. I am glad thee did keep the ten for the fugitives.

Samuel Nixon is now here, just come—a smart young man—they will be after him soon. I advise him to hurry on to Canada; he will leave here to-morrow, but don't say that he will go straight to the city. I would send this by him if he did. I am afraid he will loiter about and be taken—do make them go on fast—he has left. I could not hear much he said—some who did don't like him at all—think him an impostor—a great brag—said he was a dentist ten years. He was asked where he came from, but would not tell till he looked at the letter that lay on the table and that he had just brought back. I don't feel much confidence in him—don't believe he is the one thee alluded to. He was asked his name—he looked at the letter to find it out. Says nobody can make a better set of teeth than he can. He said they will go on to-morrow in the stage—he took down the number and street of the Anti-slavery office—you will be on your guard against imposition—he kept the letter thee sent from Norfolk. I had then no doubt of him, and had no objection to it. I now rather regret it. I would send it to thee if I had it, but perhaps it is of no importance.

He wanted the names taken down of nine more who expected to get off soon and might come here. He told us to send them to him, but did not seem to know where he was going to. He was well dressed in fine broad-cloth coat and overcoat, and has a very active tongue in his head.

But I have said enough—don't want to prejudice thee against him, but only be on thy guard, and do not let him deceive thee, as I fear he has some of us here.

With kind regards,   A. GOODWIN.

In due time Samuel and his companions reached Philadelphia, where a cordial welcome awaited them. The confusion and difficulties into which they had fallen, by having to travel an indirect route, were fully explained, and to the hearty merriment of the Committee and strangers, the dilemma of their good Quaker friend Goodwin at Salem was alluded to. After a sojourn of a day or two in Philadelphia, Samuel and his companions left for New Bedford. Canada was named to them as the safest place for all Refugees; but it was in vain to attempt to convince "Sam" that Canada or any other place on this Continent, was quite equal to New Bedford. His heart was there, and there he was resolved to go—and there he did go too, bearing with him his resolute mind, determined, if possible, to work his way up to an honorable position at his old trade, Dentistry, and that too for his own benefit.

Aided by the Committee, the journey was made safely to the desired haven, where many old friends from Norfolk were found. Here our hero was known by the name of Dr. Thomas Bayne—he was no longer "Sam." In a short time the Dr. commenced his profession in an humble way, while, at the same time, he deeply interested himself in his own improvement, as well as the improvement of others, especially those who had escaped from Slavery as he himself had. Then, too, as colored men were voters and, therefore, eligible to office in New Bedford, the Doctor's naturally ambitious and intelligent turn of mind led him to take an interest in politics, and before he was a citizen of New Bedford four years, he was duly elected a member of the City Council. He was also an outspoken advocate of the

17

cause of temperance, and was likewise a ready speaker at Anti-slavery meetings held by his race. Some idea of his abilities, and the interest he took in the Underground Rail Road, education, etc., may be gathered from the appended letters:

NEW BEDFORD, June 23d, 1855.

W. STILL:—Sir—I write you this to inform you that I has received my things and that you need not say any thing to Bagnul about them—I see by the Paper that the under ground Rail Road is in operation. Since 2 weeks a go when Saless Party was betrayed by that Capt whom we in mass. are so anxious to Learn his name—There was others started last Saturday night—They are all my old friends and we are waiting their arrival, we hope you will look out for them they may come by way of Salem, N. J. if they be not overtaken. They are from Norfolk—Times are very hard in Canada 2 of our old friends has left Canada and come to Bedford for a living. Every thing are so high and wages so low They cannot make a living (owing to the War) others are Expected shortly—let me hear from Sales and his Party. Get the Name of the Capt. that betrayed him let me know if Mrs. Goodwin of Salem are at the same place yet—John Austin are with us. C. Lightfoot is well and remembers you and family. My business increases more since I has got an office. Send me a Norfolk Paper or any other to read when convenient.

Let me hear from those People as soon as possible. They consist of woman and child 2 or 3 men belonging to Marsh Bottimore, L. Slosser and Herman & Co—and Turner—all of Norfolk, Va.　　　　Truly yours,　　　　THOS. BAYNE.

Direct to Box No. 516, New Bedford, Mass. Don't direct my letters to my office. Direct them to my Box 516. My office is 66½ William St. The same street the Post office is near the city market.

The Doctor, feeling his educational deficiency in the enlightened city of New Bedford, did just what every uncultivated man should, devoted himself assiduously to study, and even applied himself to abstruse and hard subjects, medicine, etc., as the following letters will show:

NEW BEDFORD, Jan., 1860. ⎫
No. 22, Cheapside, opposite City Hall. ⎭

MY DEAR FRIEND:—Yours of the 3d inst. reached me safely in the midst of my misfortune. I suppose you have learned that my office and other buildings burned down during the recent fire. My loss is $550, insured $350.

I would have written you before, but I have been to R. I. for some time and soon after I returned before I examined the books, the fire took place, and this accounts for my delay. In regard to the books I am under many obligations to you and all others for so great a piece of kindness, and shall ever feel indebted to you for the same. I shall esteem them very highly for two reasons, first, The way in which they come, that is through and by your Vigilance as a colored man helping a colored man to get such knowledge as will give the lie to our enemies. Secondly—their contents being just the thing I needed at this time. My indebtedness to you and all concerned for me in this direction is inexpressible. There are some books the Doctor says I must have, such as the Medical Dictionary, Physician's Dictionary, and a work on Anatomy. These I will have to get, but any work that may be of use to a student of anatomy or medicine will be thankfully received. You shall hear from me again soon.　　　　Truly Yours,　　　　THOS. BAYNE.

NEW BEDFORD, March 18th, 1861.

MR. WM. STILL :—Dear Sir—Dr. Powell called to see me and informed me that you had a medical lexicon (Dictionary) for me. If you have such a book for me, it will be very thankfully received, and any other book that pertains to the medical or dental profession. I am quite limited in means as yet and in want of books to prosecute my studies. The books I need most at present is such as treat on midwifery, anatomy, &c. But any book or books in either of the above mentioned cases will be of use to me. You can send them by Express, or by any friend that may chance to come this way, but by Express will be the safest way to send them. Times are quite dull. This leaves me well and hope it may find you and family the same. My regards to your wife and all others.

Yours, &c.,   THOMAS BAYNE,
22 Cheapside, opposite City Hall.

Thus the doctor continued to labor and improve his mind until the war removed the hideous institution of Slavery from the nation; but as soon as the way opened for his return to his old home, New Bedford no longer had sufficient attractions to retain him. With all her faults he conceived that "Old Virginia" offered decided inducements for his return. Accordingly he went directly to Norfolk, whence he escaped. Of course every thing was in the utmost confusion and disorder when he returned, save where the military held sway. So as soon as the time drew near for reorganizing, elections, &c., the doctor was found to be an aspirant for a seat in Congress, and in "running" for it, was found to be a very difficult candidate to beat. Indeed in the first reports of the election his name was amongst the elected; but subsequent counts proved him to be among the defeated by only a very slight majority.

At the time of the doctor's escape, in 1855, he was thirty-one years of age, a man of medium size, and about as purely colored, as could readily be found, with a full share of self-esteem and pluck.

SUNDRY ARRIVALS

FROM LOUDON CO , VA., NORFOLK, BALTIMORE, MD., PETERSBURG, VA., &C., ABOUT THE MONTH OF JUNE, 1855.

Arrival 1st. David Bennett and family.

Arrival 2d. Henry Washington, alias Anthony Hanly, and Henry Stewart.

Arrival 3d. William Nelson and wife, William Thomas, Louisa Bell, and Elias Jasper.

Arrival 4th. Maria Joiner.

Arrival 5th. Richard Green and his brother George.

Arrival 6th. Henry Cromwell.

Arrival 7th. Henry Bohm.

Arrival 8th. Ralph Whiting, James H. Forman, Anthony Atkinson, Arthur
        Jones, Isaiah Nixon, Joseph Harris, John Morris, Henry
        Hodges.
Arrival 9th. Robert Jones and wife.

The first arrival to be here noticed consisted of David Bennett, and his
wife Martha, with their two children, a little boy named George, and a
nameless babe one month old. This family journeyed from Loudon county,
Va. David, the husband, had been in bonds under Captain James Taylor.
Martha, the wife, and her two children were owned by George Carter.
Martha's master was represented as a very barbarous and cruel man to the
slaves. He made a common practice of flogging females when stripped
naked. This was the emphatic testimony of Martha. Martha declared that
she had been so stripped, and flogged by him after her marriage. The story
of this interesting young mother, who was about twenty-seven years of age,
was painful to the ear, particularly as the earnestness and intelligence of this
poor, bruised, and mangled soul bore such strong evidence to the truthfulness of her statements. During the painful interview the mind would in-
voluntarily picture this demon, only as the representative of thousands in
the South using the same relentless sway over men and women ; and this
fleeing victim and her little ones, before escaping, only as sharers of a common lot with many other mothers and children, whose backs were daily
subjected to the lash. If on such an occasion it was hard to find fitting
words of sympathy, or adequate expressions of indignation, the pleasure of
being permitted to give aid and comfort to such was in part a compensation
and a relief. David, the husband of this woman, was about thirty-two
years of age. No further notice was made of him.

ARRIVAL No. 2 consisted of Henry Washington, alias Anthony Hanly,
and Henry Stewart. Henry left Norfolk and a " very mild master," known
by the name of " Seth March," out of sheer disgust for the patriarchal institution. Directly after speaking of his master in such flattering terms he
qualified the " mild," &c. by adding that he was excessively close in money
matters. In proof of this assertion, Henry declared, that out of his hire
he was only allowed $1.50 per week to pay his board, clothe himself, and
defray all other expenses ; leaving no room whatever for him to provide for
his wife. It was, therefore, a never-failing source of unhappiness to be thus
debarred, and it was wholly on this account that he " took out," as he did,
and at the time that he did. His wife's name was " Sally." She too was
a slave, but " had not been treated roughly."

For fifty long years Henry had been in the grasp of this merciless
system—constrained to toil for the happiness of others, to make them comfortable, rich, indolent, and tyrannical. To say that he was like a bird out
of a cage, conveys in no sense whatever the slightest idea of his delight in

escaping from the prison house. And yet, his pleasure was sadly marred by the reflection that his bosom companion was still in bondage in the gloomy prison-house. Henry was a man of dark color, well made, and of a reflective turn of mind. On arriving in Canada, he manifested his gratitude through Rev. H. Wilson, as follows—

St. Catharines, Aug. 20th, 1855.

Dear Br. Still :—I am requested by Henry Washington to inform you that he got through safe, and is here in good business. He returns to you his sincere thanks for your attention to him on his way. I had the pleasure of receiving seven fugitives last week. Send them on, and may God speed them in the flight. I would like to have a miracle-working power, that I could give wings to them all so that they could come faster than by Railroads either underground or above. Yours truly, Hiram Wilson.

While he was thus hopefully succeeding in Canada, separated from his companion by many hundreds of miles, death came and liberated her from the yoke, as the subjoined letter indicates—

St. Catharines, C. W. Nov. 12, 1855.

Mr. William Still :—*Dear Sir :*—I have received a letter from Joseph G. Selden a friend in Norfolk, Va., informing me of the death of my wife, who deceased since I saw you here; he also informs me that my clothing will be forwarded to you by Jupiter White, who now has it in his charge. You will therefore do me a great favor, if you will be so good as to forward them to me at this place St. Catharines, C. W.

The accompanying letter is the one received from Mr. Selden which I send you, that you may see that it is all right. You will please give my respects to Mrs. Still and family. Most respectfully yours, Henry Washington.

Henry Stewart, who accompanied the above mentioned traveler to Canada, had fled a short while before from Plymouth, North Carolina. James Monroe Woodhouse, a farmer, claimed Stewart as his property, and "hired him out" for $180 per annum. As a master, Woodhouse was considered to be of the "moderate" type, according to Stewart's judgment. But respecting money matters (when his slaves wanted a trifle), "he was very hard. He did not flog, but would not give a slave a cent of money upon any consideration."

It was by procuring a pass to Norfolk, that Henry managed to escape. Although a father and a husband, having a wife (Martha) and two children (Mary Ann and Susan Jane), he felt that his lot as a slave utterly debarred him from discharging his duty to them; that he could exercise no rights or privileges whatever, save as he might obtain permission from his master. In the matter of separation, even although the ties of husband and wife, parents and children were most closely knit, his reason dictated that he would be justified in freeing himself if possible; indeed, he could not endure the pressure of Slavery any longer. Although only twenty-three years of age, the burdens that he had been called upon to bear, made his naturally intelligent mind chafe to an unusual degree, especially when reflecting upon a continued life of Slavery. When the time decided upon for his flight arrived, he said nothing to his wife on the subject, but secured his pass and took his departure for Norfolk. On arriving there, he sought out an Underground Rail Road captain, and arranged with him to bring him to Philadelphia. Whether the sorrow-stricken wife ever afterwards heard of her husband, or the father of his two little children, the writer is unable to say. It is possible that this narrative may reveal to the mother and her offspring (if they are still living), the first ray of light concerning the missing one. Indeed it is not unreasonable to suppose, that thousands of anxious wives, husbands and children, who have been scattered in every direction by Slavery, will never be able to learn as much of their lost ones as is contained in this brief account of Henry Stewart.

ARRIVAL NO. 3, brought William Nelson, his wife, Susan, and son, William Thomas, together with Louisa Bell, and Elias Jasper. These travelers availed themselves of the schooner of Captain B. who allowed them to embark at Norfolk, despite the search laws of Virginia. It hardly need be said, however, that it was no trifling matter in those days, to evade the law. Captains and captives, in order to succeed, found that it required more than ordinary intelligence and courage, shrewdness and determination, and at the same time, a very ardent appreciation of liberty, without which, there could be no success. The simple announcement then, that a party of this number had arrived from Norfolk, or Richmond, or Petersburg, gave the Committee unusual satisfaction. It made them quite sure that there was pluck and brain somewhere.

These individuals, in a particularly marked degree, possessed the qualities that greatly encouraged the efforts of the Committee. William Nelson, was a man of a dark chestnut color, medium size, with more than an ordinary degree of what might be termed "mother wit." Apparently, William possessed well settled convictions, touching the questions of morals and religion, despite the overflowing tide of corruption and spurious religious teachings consequent on the existing pro-slavery usages all around him. He was a member of the Methodist Church, under the charge of the Rev. Mr. Jones. For twenty years, William had served in the capacity of a "packer" under Messrs. Turner and White, who held a deed for William as their legal property. While he declared that he had been very "tightly worked" he nevertheless admitted that he had been dealt with in a mild manner in some respects.

For his board and clothing, William had been allowed $1.50 per week. Truly a small sum for a hard-working man with a family—yet this was far more than many slaves received from their masters. In view of receiving this small pittance, he had toiled hard—doing over-work in order to make "buckle and strap meet." Once he had been sold on the auction-block. A sister of his had also shared the same fate. While seriously contemplating his life as a slave, he was soon led to the conclusion that it was his duty to bend his entire energies towards freeing himself and his family if possible. The idea of not being able to properly provide for his family rendered him quite unhappy; he therefore resolved to seek a passage North, via the Underground Rail Road. To any captain who would aid him in the matter, he resolved to offer a large reward, and determined that the amount should only be limited by his inability to increase it. Finally, after much anxious preparation, agreement was entered into with Captain B., on behalf of himself, wife, child, and Louisa Bell, which was mutually satisfactory to all concerned, and afforded great hope to William. In due time the agreement was carried into effect, and all arrived safely and were delivered into the hands of the Committee in Philadelphia. The fare of the four cost $240, and William was only too grateful to think, that a Captain could be found who would risk his own liberty in thus aiding a slave to freedom.

The Committee gladly gave them aid and succor, and agreed with William that the Captain deserved all that he received for their deliverance. The arrival of William, wife, and child in Canada was duly announced by the agent at St. Catharines, Rev. H. Wilson, as follows:

St. Catharines, C. W., June 28th, 1855.

Mr. Wm. Still:—*My Dear Friend:*—I am happy to announce the safe arrival of Thomas Russell with his wife and child. They have just arrived. I am much pleased with their appearance. I shall do what I can for their comfort and encouragement. They stopt at Elmira from Monday night till this morning, hoping that Lucy Bell would come up and join them at that place. They are very anxious to hear from her, as they have failed of meeting with her on the way or finding her here in advance of them. They wish to hear from you as soon as you can write, and would like to know if you have forwarded Lucy on, and if so, what route you sent her. They send their kind respects to you and your family and many thanks for your kindness to them.

They wish you to inquire after Lucy if any harm has befallen her after her leaving Philadelphia. Please write promptly in my care.

Yours truly in the love of freedom, Hiram Wilson.

The man who came to us as Wm. Nelson, is now known only as "Thomas Russell." It may here be remarked, that, owing to the general custom of changing names, as here instanced, it is found difficult to tell to whom the letters severally refer. Where the old and new names were both carefully entered on the book there is no difficulty, of course, but it was not always thus.

Susan Bell, the wife of William, was about thirty years of age, of a dark color, rather above medium size, well-made, good-looking, and intelligent— quite equal to her husband, and appeared to have his affections undividedly. She was owned by Thomas Baltimore, with whom she had lived for the last seven years. She stated that during a part of her life she had been treated in a "mild manner." She had no complaint to make until after the marriage of her master. Under the new wife and mistress, Susan found a very marked change for the worse. She fared badly enough then. The mistress, on every trifling occasion for complaint, was disposed to hold the auction-block up to Susan, and would likewise influence her husband to do the same. From the fact, that four of Susan's sisters had been sold away to "parts unknown," she was not prepared to relish these almost daily threats from her irritable mistress, so she became as anxious for a trip on the Underground Rail Road as was her husband.

About one hundred miles away in the country, her father, mother, three brothers, and one sister were living; but she felt that she could not remain a slave on their account. Susan's owner had already fixed a price on her and her child, twenty-two months old, which was one thousand dollars. From this fate she was saved only by her firm resolution to seek her freedom.

LOUISA BELL was also of Wm. Nelson's party, and a fair specimen of a nice-looking, wide awake woman; of a chestnut color, twenty-eight years of age. She was the wife of a free man, but the slave of L. Stasson, a confectioner. The almost constant ringing in her ears of the auction-block, made her most miserable, especially as she had once suffered terribly by being sold, and had likewise seen her mother, and five sisters placed in the same unhappy situation, the thought of which never ceased to be most painful. In reflecting upon the course which she was about to pursue in order to free herself from the prison-house, she felt more keenly than ever for her little children, and readily imagined how sadly she would mourn while thinking of them hundreds of miles distant, growing up only to be slaves. And particularly would her thoughts dwell upon her boy, six years of age; full old enough to feel deeply the loss of his mother, but without hope of ever seeing her again.

Heart-breaking as were these reflections, she resolved to leave Robert and Mary in the hands of God, and escape, if possible from her terrible thraldom. Her plan was submitted to her husband; he acquiesced fully and promised to follow her as soon as an opportunity might present itself. Although the ordeal that she was called upon to pass through was of the most trying nature she bravely endured the journey through to Canada. On her arrival there the Rev. H. Wilson wrote on behalf of herself, and the cause as follows:

St. Catherines, C. W. July 6th, 1855.

DEAR BR. STILL :—I have just received your letters touching U. G. R. R. operations. All is right. Jasper and Mrs. Bell got here on Saturday last, and I think I dropt you a line announcing the fact. I write again thus soon because two more by name of Smith, John and Wm., have arrived the present week and were anxious to have me inform you that they are safely landed and free in this refuge land. They wish me to communicate their kind regards to you and others who have aided them. They have found employment and are likely to do well. The 5 of last week have gone over to Toronto. I gave them letters to a friend there after furnishing them as well as I could with such clothing as they required. I am afraid that I am burdening you too much with postage, but can't help doing so unless I fail to write at all, as my means are not half equal to the expenses to which I am subject.   Faithfully and truly yours,   HIRAM WILSON.

ELIAS JASPER, who was also a fellow-passenger with Wm. Nelson and Co., was noticed thus on the Underground Rail Road: Age thirty-two years, color dark, features good, and gifted both with his tongue and hands. He had worked more or less at the following trades: Rope-making, carpentering, engineering, and photographing. It was in this latter calling that he was engaged when the Underground Rail Road movement first arrested his attention, and so continued until his departure.

For several years he had been accustomed to hire his time, for which he had been required to pay $10 per month. In acquiring the above trades he had been at no expense to his master, as he had learned them solely by his own perseverance, endowed as he was with a considerable share of genius. Occasionally he paid for lessons, the money being earned by his over-work. His master, Bayham, was a "retired gentleman."

Elias had been sold once, and had suffered in various other ways, particularly from being flogged. He left his wife, Mary, but no child. Of his intention to leave Elias saw not how to impart to his wife, lest she should in some way let the "cat out of the bag." She was owned by a Miss Portlock, and had been treated " tolerably well," having had the privilege of hiring her time. She had $55 to pay for this favor, which amount she raised by washing, etc. Elias was a member of the Methodist Church, as were all of his comrades, and well did they remember the oft-repeated lesson, " Servants obey your masters," etc. They soon understood this kind of preaching after breathing free air. The market value of Elias was placed at $1200.

ARRIVAL No. 4. Maria Joiner. Captain F. arrived, from Norfolk, with the above named passenger, the way not being open to risk any other on that occasion. This seemed rather slow business with this voyager, for he was usually accustomed to bringing more than one. However, as this arrival was only one day later than the preceding one noticed, and came from the same place, the Committee concluded, that they had much reason for rejoicing nevertheless. As in the case of a great number among the oppressed of the South, when simply looking at Maria, no visible marks of ill usage in any way were discernible. Indeed, as she then appeared at the age of thirty-three, a fine, fresh, and healthy-looking mulatto woman, nine out of every ten would have been impressed with the idea, that she had never been subjected to hard treatment; in other words, that she had derived her full share of advantages from the " Patriarchal Institution." The appearance of just such persons in Southern cities had often led Northerners, when traveling in those parts, to regard the lot of slaves as quite comfortable. But the story of Maria, told in an earnest and intelligent manner, was at once calculated to dissipate the idea of a "comfortable" existence in a state of bondage. She frankly admitted, however, that prior to the death of her old master, she was favorably treated, compared with many others; but, unfortunately, after his death, she had fallen into the hands of one of the old man's daughters, from whom, she declared, that she had received continued abuse, especially when said daughter was under the influence of liquor. At such times she was very violent. Being spirited, Maria could not consent to suffer on as a slave in this manner. Consequently she began to cogitate how she might escape from her mistress (Catharine Gordon), and reach a free State. None other than the usual trying and hazardous ways could be devised— which was either to be stowed away in the hold of a schooner, or concealed amongst the rubbish of a steamer, where, for the time being, the extreme suffering was sure to tax every nerve even of the most valiant-hearted men. The daily darkening prospects constrained her to decide, that she was willing to suffer, not only in adopting this mode of travel, but on the other hand, that she had better be dead than remain under so cruel a woman as her mistress. Maria's husband and sister (no other relatives are noticed), were naturally formidable barriers in the way of her escape. Notwithstanding her attachment to them, she fully made up her mind to be free. Immediately she took the first prerequisite step, which was to repair to a place of concealment with a friend in the city, and there, like the man at the pool, wait until her turn came to be conveyed thence to a free State. In this place she was obliged to wait eight long months, enduring daily suffering in various ways, especially during the winter season. But, with martyr-like faith, she endured to the end, and was eventually saved from the hell of Slavery. Maria was appraised at $800.

ARRIVAL No. 5. Richard Green, alias Wm. Smith, and his brother George. These young brothers fled from George Chambers of Baltimore. The elder brother was twenty-five, the younger twenty-three. Both were tall and well made and of a chestnut color, and possessed a good degree of natural ability. When desiring to visit their parents, their request was positively refused by their owner. Taking offence at this step, both mutually resolved to run away at the earliest opportunity. Thus in accordance with well premeditated plans, they set out and unobstructedly arrived in Philadelphia. At first it was simply very pleasant to take them by the hand and welcome them; then to listen for a few moments to their intelligent narration of how they escaped, the motives that prompted them, etc. But further inquiries soon brought out incidents of the most thrilling and touching nature—not with regard to hardships which they had personally experienced, but in relation to outrages which had been perpetrated upon their mother. Such simple facts as were then written are substantially as follows: Nearly thirty years prior to the escape of Richard and his brother their mother was in very bad health, so much so that physicians regarded her incurable. Her owner was evidently fully impressed with the belief that instead of being profitable to him, she might be an expense, which he could not possibly obviate, while he retained her as a slave. Now there was a way to get out of this dilemma. He could emancipate her and throw the responsibility of her support upon herself. Accordingly he drew up papers, called for his wife's mother to witness them, then formally put them into the hands of the invalid slave woman (Dinah), assuring her at the same time, that she was free— being fully released as set forth in her papers. "Take notice I have no more claim on you nor you on me from this time." Marvellous liberality! After working the life out of a woman, in order that he should not have her to bury, he becomes hastily in favor of freedom. He is, however, justified by the laws of Maryland. Complaint, therefore, would simply amount to nothing. In the nature of the case Dinah was now free, but she was not wholly alone in the world. She had a husband, named Jacob Green, who was owned by Nathan Childs for a term of years only, at the expiration of which time he was to be free. All lived then in Talbot county, Md. At the appointed time Jacob's bondage ended, and he concluded that he might succeed better by moving to Baltimore. Indeed the health of his wife was so miserable that nothing in his old home seemed to offer any inducement in the way of a livelihood. So off they moved to Baltimore. After a time, under careful and kind treatment, the faithful Jacob was greatly encouraged by perceiving that the health of his companion was gradually improving— signs indicated, that she might yet become a well woman. The hopes of husband and wife, in this particular, were, in the lapse of time, fully realized. Dinah was as well as ever, and became the mother of another child— a little boy. Everything seemed to be going on happily, and they had no apparent reason to suspect any troubles other than such as might naturally have to be encountered in a state of poverty and toil.

The unfettered boy was healthy, and made rapid advance in a few years. That any one should ever claim him was never for a moment feared.

The old master, however, becoming tired of country life, had also moved to Baltimore. How, they knew not, but he had heard of the existence of this boy.

That he might satisfy himself on this point, he one day very slyly approached the house with George. No sooner was the old man within the enclosures than he asked Dinah, " Whose child is that ?" pointing to the boy. " Ask Jacob," was the reply of the mother. The question was then put to Jacob, the father of the boy. " I did not think that you would ask such a question, or that you would request anything like that," Jacob remarked, naturally somewhat nervous, but he added, " I have the privilege of having any one. I please in my house." " Where is he from ?" again demanded the master. The father repeated, "I have a right to have," etc., "I am my own man," etc. "I have found out whose he is," the hunter said. "I am going presently to take him home with me." At this juncture he seized the little fellow, at the same time calling out, "Dinah, put his clothes on." By this time the father too had seized hold of the child. Mustering courage, the father said, "Take notice that you are not in the country, pulling and hauling people about." "I will have him or I will leave my heart's blood in the house," was the savage declaration of the master. In his rage he threatened to shoot the father. In the midst of the excitement George called in two officers to settle the trouble. "What are you doing here?" said the officers to the slave-holder. "I am after my property—this boy," he exclaimed. "Have you ever seen it before?" they inquired. "No," said the slave-holder. "Then how do you know that he belongs to you?" inquired the officers. "I believe he is mine," replied the slave-holder.

All the parties concerned were then taken by the officers before an Alderman. The father owned the child but the mother denied it. The Alderman then decided that the child should be given to the father.

The slave-holder having thus failed, was unwilling, nevertheless, to relinquish his grasp. Whereupon he at once claimed the mother. Of course he was under the necessity of resorting to the Courts in order to establish his claim. Fortunately the mother had securely preserved the paper given her by her master so many years before, releasing her. Notwithstanding this the suit was pending nearly a year before the case was decided. Everything was so clear the mother finally gained the suit. This decision was rendered only about two months prior to the escape of Richard and George.

ARRIVAL No. 6. Henry Cromwell. This passenger fled from Baltimore county, Md. The man that he escaped from was a farmer by the name of William Roberts, who also owned seven other young slaves. Of his treatment of his slaves nothing was recorded.

Henry was about six feet high, quite black, visage thin, age twenty-five. He left neither wife, parents, brothers nor sisters to grieve after him. In making his way North he walked of nights from his home to Harrisburg, Pa., and there availed himself of a passage on a freight car coming to Philadelphia.

ARRIVAL No. 7. Henry Bohm. Henry came from near Norfolk, Va. He was about twenty-five years of age, and a fair specimen of a stout man, possessed of more than ordinary physical strength. As to whom he fled from, how he had been treated, or how he reached Philadelphia, the record book is silent. Why this is the case cannot now be accounted for, unless the hurry of getting him off forbade sufficient delay to note down more of the particulars.

ARRIVAL No. 8. Ralph Whiting, James H. Forman, Anthony Atkinson, Arthur Jones, Isaiah Nixon, Joseph Harris, John Morris, and Henry

Hodges. A numerous party like this had the appearance of business. They were all young and hopeful, and belonged to the more intelligent and promising of their race. They were capable of giving the best of reasons for the endeavors they were making to escape to a free country.

They imparted to the Committee much information respecting their several situations, together with the characters of their masters in relation to domestic matters, and the customs and usages under which they had been severally held to service—all of which was listened to with deep interest. But it was not an easy matter, after having been thus entertained, to write out the narratives of eight such persons. Hundreds of pages would hardly have contained a brief account of the most interesting portion of their histories. It was deemed sufficient to enter their names and their forsaken homes, etc., as follows:

"Ralph was twenty-six years of age, five feet ten inches high, dark, well made, intelligent, and a member of the Methodist Church. He was claimed by Geo. W. Kemp, Esq., cashier of the Exchange Bank of Norfolk, Va. Ralph gave Mr. Kemp the credit of being a 'moderate man' to his slaves. Ralph was compelled to leave his wife, Lydia, and two children, Anna Eliza, and Cornelius."

"James was twenty-three years of age, dark mulatto, nearly six feet high, and of prepossessing appearance. He fled from James Saunders, Esq. Nothing, save the desire to be free, prompted James to leave his old situation and master. His parents and two sisters he was obliged to leave in Norfolk."

Two brief letters from James, one concerning his "sweet-heart," whom he left in Norfolk, the other giving an account of her arrival in Canada and marriage thereafter will, doubtless, be read with interest. They are here given as follows:

NIAGARA FALLS, June 5th, 1856.

MR. STILL:—Sir—I take my pen in hand to write you theas few lines to let you know that I am well at present and hope theas few lines may find you the same. Sir my object in writing to you is that I expect a young Lady by the name of Miss Mariah Moore, from Norfolk, Virginia. She will leave Norfolk on the 13th of this month in the Steamship Virginia for Philadelphia you will oblige me very much by seeing her safely on the train of cars that leaves Philadelphia for the Suspension Bridge Niagara Falls pleas to tell the Lady to telegraph to me what time she will leave Philadelphia so i may know what time to meet her at the Suspension Bridge my Brother Isaac Forman send his love also his family to you and your family they are all well at present pleas to give my respects to Mr. Harry Londay, also Miss Margaret Cunigan, no more at present.

I remain your friend, JAMES H. FORMAN.

When you telegraph to me direct to the International Hotel, Niagara Falls, N. Y.

NIAGARA FALLS, July 24th, 1856.

DEAR SIR:—I take this opportunity of writing these few lines to you hoping that they may find you enjoying good health as these few lines leave me at present. I thank you for your kindness. Miss Moore arrived here on the 30th of June and I was down to the cars to receive her. I thought I would have written to you before, but I thought I would wait till I got married. I got married on the 22d of July in the English Church Canada about 11 o'clock my wife sends all her love to you and your wife and all enquiring friends please to kiss your two children for her and she says she is done crying and I am glad to hear she enjoyed herself so well in Philadelphia give my respects to Miss Margaret Cuningham and I am glad to hear her sister arrived my father sends his respects to you no more at present but remain your friend,   JAMES H. FORMAN.

Direct your letter to the International Hotel, Niagara Falls.

ANTHONY was thirty-six years of age, and by blood, was quite as nearly related to the Anglo-Saxon as the Anglo-African. He was nevertheless, physically a fine specimen of a man. He was about six feet high, and bore evidence of having picked up a considerable amount of intelligence considering his opportunities. He had been sold three times. Anthony was decidedly opposed to having to pass through this ordeal a fourth time, therefore, the more he meditated over his condition, the more determined he became to seek out an Underground Rail Road agent, and make his way to Canada.

Concluding that Josiah Wells, who claimed him, had received a thousand times too much of his labor already, Anthony was in a fit state of mind to make a resolute effort to gain his freedom. He had a wife, but no children. His father, one sister, and two brothers were all dear to him, but all being slaves "one could not help the other," Anthony reasoned, and wisely too. So, at the command of the captain, he was ready to bear his part of the suffering consequent upon being concealed in the hold of a vessel, where but little air could penetrate.

ARTHUR was forty-one years of age, six feet high—chestnut color, well made, and possessed good native faculties needing cultivation. He escaped from a farmer, by the name of John Jones, who was classed, as to natural temperament, amongst "moderate slave-holders."

"I wanted my liberty," said Arthur promptly and emphatically, and he declared that was the cause of his escape. He left his mother, two sisters, and three brothers in Slavery.

ISAIAH was about twenty-two, small of stature, but smart, and of a substantially black complexion. He had been subjected to very hard treatment under Samuel Simmons who claimed him, and on this account he was first prompted to leave. His mother and three brothers he left in bondage.

JOSEPH was twenty-three years of age, and was, in every way, "likely-looking." According to the laws of Slavery, he was the property of David Morris, who was entitled to be ranked amongst the more compassionate slave-holders of the South. Yet, Joseph was not satisfied, deprived of his freedom. He had not known hardships as many had, but it was not in him notwithstanding, to be contented as a slave. In leaving, he had to "tear himself away" from his parents, three brothers, and two sisters.

HENRY escaped from S. Simmons of Plymouth, North Carolina, and was a fellow-servant with Isaiah. Simmons was particularly distinguished for his tyrannical rule and treatment of his slaves—so Henry and Isaiah had the good sense to withdraw from under his yoke, very young in life; Henry being twenty-three.

JOHN was about twenty-one years of age, five feet eight inches high, dark color, and well-grown for his years. Before embarking, he had endured seven months of hard suffering from being secreted, waiting for an opportunity to escape. It was to keep his master from selling him, that he was thus induced to secrete himself. After he had remained away some months, he resolved to suffer on until his friends could manage to procure him a passage on the Underground Rail Road. With this determined spirit he did not wait in vain.

ARRIVAL No. 9. Robert Jones and wife:—In the majority of cases, in order to effect the escape of either, sad separations between husbands and wives were unavoidable. Fortunately, it was not so in this case. In journeying from the house of bondage, Robert and his wife were united both in sympathies and in struggles. Robert had experienced "hard times" just in what way, however, was not recorded; his wife had been differently treated, not being under the same taskmaster as her husband. At the time of their arrival all that was recorded of their bondage is as follows—

August 2d, 1855, Robert Jones and wife, arrived from Petersburg, Va. Robert is about thirty-five, chestnut color, medium size, of good manners, intelligent, had been owned by Thomas N. Lee, "a very hard man." Robert left because he "wanted his liberty—always had from a boy." Eliza, his wife, is about forty years of age, chestnut color, nice-looking, and well-dressed. She belonged to Eliza H. Richie, who was called a "moderate woman" towards her slaves. Notwithstanding the limited space occupied in noting them on the record book, the Committee regarded them as being among the most worthy and brave travelers passing over the Underground Rail Road, and felt well satisfied that such specimens of humanity would do credit in Canada, not only to themselves, but to their race.

Robert had succeeded in learning to read and write tolerably well, and had thought much over the condition and wrongs of the race, and seemed to be eager to be where he could do something to lift his fellow-sufferers up to a higher plane of liberty and manhood. After an interview with Robert and his wife, in every way so agreeable, they were forwarded on in the usual manner, to Canada. While enjoying the sweets of freedom in Canada, he was not the man to keep his light under a bushel. He seemed to have a high appreciation of the potency of the pen, and a decidedly clear idea that colored men needed to lay hold of many enterprises with resolution, in order to prove themselves qualified to rise equally with other branches of the human family. Some of his letters, embracing his views, plans and suggestions, were so encouraging and sensible, that the Committee was in the habit of showing them to friendly persons, and indeed, extracts of some of his letters were deemed of sufficient importance to publish. One alone, taken from many letters received from him, must here suffice to illustrate his intelligence and efforts as a fugitive and citizen in Canada.

HAMILTON, C. W., August 9th, 1856.

MR. WM. STILL :—*Dear Friend:*—I take this opportunity of writing you these few lines to inform you of my health, which is good at present, &c.   *   *   *   *

I was talking to you about going to Liberia, when I saw you last, and did intend to start this fall, but I since looked at the condition of the colored people in Canada. I thought I would try to do something for their elevation as a nation, to place them in the proper position to stand where they ought to stand. In order to do this, I have undertaken to get up a military company amongst them. They laughed at me to undertake such a thing; but I did not relax my energies. I went and had an interview with Major J. T. Gilepon, told him what my object was, he encouraged me to go on, saying that he would do all he could for the accomplishment of my object. He referred to *Sir Allan McNab*, &c.   *   *   *   I took with me Mr. J. H. Hill to see him—he told me that it should be done, and required us to write a petition to the *Governor General*, which has been done.   *   *   *   The company is already organized. Mr. Howard was elected Captain ; J. H. Hill, 1st Lieutenant; Hezekiah Hill, Ensign ; Robert Jones, 1st Sergeant. The company's name is, Queen Victoria's Rifle Guards. You may, by this, see what I have been doing since I have been in Canada. When we receive our appointments by the Government. I will send by express, my daguerreotype in uniform.

My respects, &c. &c.,   ROBERT JONES.

HEAVY REWARD.

 TWO THOUSAND SIX HUNDRED DOLLARS REWARD.—Ran away from the subscriber, on Saturday night, November 15th, 1856, Josiah and William Bailey, and Peter Pennington. Joe is about 5 feet 10 inches in height, of a chestnut color, bald head, with a remarkable scar on one of his cheeks, not positive on which it is, but think it is on the left, under the eye, has intelligent countenance, active, and well-made. He is about 28 years old. Bill is of a darker color, about 5 feet 8 inches in height, stammers a little when confused, well-made, and older than Joe, well dressed, but may have pulled kearsey on over their other clothes. Peter is smaller than either the others, about 25 years of age, dark chestnut color, 5 feet 7 or 8 inches high.

A reward of fifteen hundred dollars will be given to any person who will apprehend the said Joe Bailey, and lodge him safely in the jail at Easton, Talbot Co., Md., and $300 for Bill and $800 for Peter.   W. R. HUGHLETT,
           JOHN C. HENRY,
           T. WRIGHT.

When this arrival made its appearance, it was at first sight quite evident that one of the company was a man of more than ordinary parts, both physically and mentally. Likewise, taking them individually, their appearance and bearing tended largely to strengthen the idea that the spirit of freedom was rapidly gaining ground in the minds of the slaves, despite the efforts of the slave-holders to keep them in darkness. In company with the three men, for whom the above large reward was offered, came a woman by the name of Eliza Nokey.

As soon as the opportunity presented itself, the Active Committee feeling an unusual desire to hear their story, began the investigation by inquiring as to the cause of their escape, etc., which brought simple and homely but earnest answers from each. These answers afforded the best possible means of seeing Slavery in its natural, practical workings—of obtaining such testimony and representations of the vile system, as the most eloquent orator or able pen might labor in vain to make clear and convincing, although this arrival had obviously been owned by men of high standing. The fugitives themselves innocently stated that one of the masters, who was in the habit of flogging adult females, was a "moderate man." Josiah Bailey was the leader of this party, and he appeared well-qualified for this position. He was about twenty-nine years of age, and in no particular physically, did he seem to be deficient. He was likewise civil and polite in his manners, and a man of good common sense. He was held and oppressed by William H. Hughlett, a farmer and dealer in ship timber, who had besides invested in slaves to the number of forty head. In his habits he was generally taken for a "moderate" and "fair" man, "though he was in the habit of flogging the slaves—females as well as males," after they had arrived at the age of maturity. This was not considered strange or cruel in Maryland. Josiah was the "foreman" on the place, and was entrusted with the management of hauling the ship-timber, and through harvesting and busy seasons was required to lead in the fields. He was regarded as one of the most valuable hands in that part of the country, being valued at $2,000. Three weeks before he escaped, Joe was "stripped naked," and "flogged" very cruelly by his master, simply because he had a dispute with one of the fellow-servants, who had stolen, as Joe alleged, seven dollars of his hard earnings. This flogging, produced in Joe's mind, an unswerving determination to leave Slavery or die: to try his luck on the Underground Rail Road at all hazards. The very name of Slavery, made the fire fairly burn in his bones. Although a married man, having a wife and three children (owned by Hughlett), he was not prepared to let his affection for them keep him in chains—so Anna Maria, his wife, and his children Ellen, Anna Maria, and Isabella, were shortly widowed and orphaned by the slave lash.

WILLIAM BAILEY was owned by John C. Henry, a large slave-holder, and a very "hard" one, if what William alleged of him was true. His story certainly had every appearance of truthfulness. A recent brutal flogging had "stiffened his back-bone," and furnished him with his excuse for not being willing to continue in Maryland, working his strength away to enrich his master, or the man who claimed to be such. The memorable flogging, however, which caused him to seek flight on the Underground Rail Road, was not administered by his master or on his master's plantation. He was hired out, and it was in this situation that he was so barbarously treated. Yet he considered his master more in 'fault than the man to whom he was hired, but redress there was none, save to escape.

The hour for forwarding the party by the Committee, came too soon to allow time for the writing of any account of Peter Pennington and Eliza Nokey. Suffice it to say, that in struggling through their journey, their spirits never flagged; they had determined not to stop short of Canada. They truly had a very high appreciation of freedom, but a very poor opinion of Maryland.

SLAVE TRADER HALL IS FOILED.

ROBERT M'COY *alias* WILLIAM DONAR.

In October, 1854, the Committee received per steamer, directly from Norfolk, Va., Robert McCoy and Elizabeth Saunders. Robert had constantly been in the clutches of the negro-trader Hall, for the last sixteen years, previous to his leaving, being owned by him. He had, therefore, possessed very favorable opportunities for varied observation and experience relative to the trader's conduct in his nefarious business, as well as for witnessing the effects of the auction-block upon all ages—rending asunder the dearest ties, despite the piteous wails of childhood or womanhood, parental or conjugal relations. But no attempt will be made to chronicle the deeds of this dealer in human flesh. Those stories fresh from the lips of one who had just escaped, were painful in the extreme, but in the very nature of things some of the statements are too revolting to be published. In lieu of this fact, except the above allusions to the trader's business, this sketch will only refer to Robert's condition as a slave, and finally as a traveler on the Underground Rail Road.

Robert was a man of medium size, dark mulatto, of more than ordinary intelligence. His duties had been confined to the house, and not to the slave pen. As a general thing, he had managed, doubtless through much shrewdness, to avoid very severe outrages from the trader. On the whole, he had fared " about as well " as the generality of slaves.

Yet, in order to free himself from his " miserable " life, he was willing, as he declared, to suffer almost any sacrifice. Indeed, his conduct proved the sincerity of this declaration, as he had actually been concealed five months in a place in the city, where he could not possibly avoid daily suffering of the most trying kind. His resolve to be free was all this while maturing. The trader had threatened to sell Robert, and to prevent it Robert (thus) " took out." Successfully did he elude the keen scent and grasp of the hunters, who made diligent efforts to recapture him. Although a young man—only about twenty-eight years of age, his health was by no means good. His system had evidently been considerably shattered by Slavery, and symptoms of consumption, together with chronic rheumatism, were making rapid headway against the physical man. Under his various ills, he declared, as did many others from the land of bondage, that his faith in God afforded him comfort and hope. He was obliged to leave his wife, Eliza, in bonds, not knowing whether they should ever meet again on earth, but he was somewhat hopeful that the way would open for her escape also.

After reaching Philadelphia, where his arrival had long been anticipated by the Vigilance Committee, his immediate wants were met, and in due order he was forwarded to New Bedford, where, he was led to feel, he would be happy in freedom.

Scarcely had he been in New Bedford one month, before his prayers and hopes were realized with regard to the deliverance of his wife. On hearing of the good news of her coming he wrote as follows—

NEW BEDFORD, Nov. 3, 1859.

DEAR SIR:—i embrace this opertunity to inform you that i received your letter with pleasure, i am enjoying good health and hope that these few lines will find you enjoying the same blessing. i rejoise to hear from you i feel very much indetted to you for not writing before but i have been so bissy that is the cause, i rejoise to heare of the arrival of my wife, and hope she is not sick from the roling of the sea and if she is not, pleas to send her on here Monday with a six baral warlian and a rifall to gard her up to my residance i thank you kindly for the good that you have don for me. Give my respects to Mrs. Still, tell her i want to see her very bad and you also i would come but i am afraid yet to venture, i received your letter the second, but about the first of spring i hope to pay you a visit or next summer. i am getting something to do every day. i will write on her arrivall and tell you more. Mr. R. White sends his love to you and your famerly and says that he is very much indetted to you for his not writing and all so he desires to know wheather his cloths has arived yet or not, and if they are please to express them on to him or if at preasant by Mrs. Donar. Not any more at preasant. i remain your affectionate brother,   WILLIAM DONAR.

By the same arrival, and similarly secreted, Elizabeth Frances, alias Ellen Saunders, had the good luck to reach Philadelphia. She was a single young woman, about twenty-two, with as pleasant a countenance as one would wish to see. Her manners were equally agreeable. Perhaps her joy over her achieved victory added somewhat to her personal appearance. She had, however, belonged to the more favored class of slaves. She had neither been over-worked nor badly abused. Elizabeth was the property of a lady a few shades lighter than herself, (Elizabeth was a mulatto) by the name of Sarah Shephard, of Norfolk. In order the more effectually to profit by Elizabeth's labor, the mistress resorted to the plan of hiring her out for a given sum per month. Against this usage Elizabeth urged no complaint. Indeed the only very serious charge she brought was to the effect, that her mistress sold her mother away from her far South, when she was a child only ten years old. She had also sold a brother and sister to a foreign southern market. The reflections consequent upon the course that her mistress had thus pursued, awakened Elizabeth to much study relative to freedom, and by the time that she had reached womanhood she had very decided convictions touching her duty with regard to escaping. Thus growing to hate slavery in every way and manner, she was prepared to make a desperate effort to be free. Having saved thirty-five dollars by rigid economy, she was willing to give every cent of it (although it was all she possessed), to be aided from Norfolk to Philadelphia. After reaching the city, having suffered severely while coming, she was invited to remain until somewhat recruited. In the healthy air of freedom she was soon fully restored, and ready to take her departure for New Bedford, which place she reached without difficulty and was cordially welcomed. The following letter, expressive of her obligations for aid received, was forwarded soon after her arrival in New Bedford :

New Bedford, Mass., October 16th, 1854.

Mr. Still :—Dear Sir—I now take my pen in my hand to inform you of my health which is good at present all except a cold I have got but I hope when these few lines reach you you may be enjoying good health. I arrived in New Bedford Thursday morning safely and what little I have seen of the city I like it very much my friends were very glad to see me. I found my sister very well. Give my love to Mrs. Still and also your dear little children. I am now out at service. I do not think of going to Canada now. I think I shall remain in this city this winter. Please tell Mrs. Still I have not met any person who has treated me any kinder than she did since I left. I consider you both to have been true friends to me. I hope you will think me the same to you. I feel very thankful to you indeed. It might been supposed, out of sight out of mind, but it is not so. I never forget my friends. Give my love to Florence. If you come to this city I would be very happy to see you. Kiss your dear little children for me. Please to answer this as soon as possible, so that I may know you received this. No more at present. I still remain your friend,

Ellen Saunders.

Eliza McCoy—the wife of Robert McCoy, whose narrative has just been given—and who was left to wait in hope when her husband escaped— soon followed him to freedom. It is a source of great satisfaction to be able to present her narrative in so close proximity to her husband's. He arrived about the first of October—she about the first of November, following. From her lips testimony of much weight and interest was listened to by several friends relative to her sufferings as a slave—on the auction-block, and in a place of concealment seven months, waiting and praying for an opportunity to escape. But it was thought sufficient to record merely a very brief outline of her active slave life, which consisted of the following noticeable features.

Eliza had been owned by Andrew Sigany, of Norfolk—age about thirty-eight—mulatto, and a woman whose appearance would readily command attention and respect anywhere outside of the barbarism of Slavery. She stated that her experience as a sufferer in cruel hands had been very trying, and that in fretting under hardships, she had "always wanted to be free." Her language was unmistakable on this point. Neither mistress nor servant was satisfied with each other; the mistress was so "queer" and "hard to please," that Eliza became heartily sick of trying to please her—an angel would have failed with such a woman. So, while matters were getting no better, but, on the contrary, were growing worse and worse, Eliza thought she would seek a more pleasant atmosphere in the North. In fact she felt that it would afford her no little relief to allow her place to be occupied by another. When she went into close quarters of concealment, she fully understood what was meant and all the liabilities thereto. She had pluck enough to endure unto the end without murmuring. The martyrs in olden times who dwelt in " dens and caves of the earth," could hardly have fared worse than some of these way-worn travelers.

After the rest, needed by one who had suffered so severely until her arrival in Philadelphia, she was forwarded to her anxiously waiting husband in New Bedford, where she was gladly received.

From the frequent arrivals from Virginia, especially in steamers, it may be thought that no very stringent laws or regulations existed by which offenders, who might aid the Underground Rail Road, could be severely punished—that the slave-holders were lenient, indifferent and unguarded as to how this property took wings and escaped. In order to enlighten the reader with regard to this subject, it seems necessary, in this connection, to publish at least one of the many statutes from the slave laws of the South bearing directly on the aid and escape of slaves by vessels. The following enactment is given as passed by the Legislature of Virginia in 1856:

THE PROTECTION OF SLAVE PROPERTY IN VIRGINIA.

A BILL PROVIDING ADDITIONAL PROTECTION FOR THE SLAVE PROPERTY OF CITIZENS OF THIS COMMONWEALTH.

(1.) Be it enacted, by the General Assembly, that it shall not be lawful for any vessel, of any size or description, whatever, owned in whole, or in part, by any citizen or resident of another State, and about to sail or steam for any port or place in this State, for any port or place north of and beyond the capes of Virginia, to depart from the waters of this commonwealth, until said vessel has undergone the inspection hereinafter provided for in this act, and received a certificate to that effect. If any such vessel shall depart from the State without such certificate of inspection, the captain or owner thereof, shall forfeit and pay the sum of five hundred dollars, to be recovered by any person who will sue for the same, in any court of record in this State, in the name of the Governor of the Commonwealth.

Pending said suit, the vessel of said captain or owner shall not leave the State until bond be given by the captain or owner, or other person for him, payable to the Governor, with two or three sureties satisfactory to the court, in the penalty of one thousand dollars, for the payment of the forfeit or fine, together with the cost and expenses incurred in enforcing the same; and in default of such bond, the vessel shall be held liable. Provided that nothing contained in this section, shall apply to vessels belonging to the United States Government, or vessels, American or foreign, bound direct to any foreign country other than the British American Provinces.

(2.) The pilots licensed under the laws of Virginia, and while attached to a vessel regularly employed as a pilot boat, are hereby constituted inspectors to execute this act, so far as the same may be applicable to the Chesapeake Bay, and the waters tributary thereto, within the jurisdiction of this State, together with such other inspectors as may be appointed by virtue of this act.

(3.) The branch or license issued to a pilot according to the provisions of the 92d chapter of Code, shall be sufficient evidence that he is authorized and empowered to act as inspector as aforesaid.

(4.) It shall be the duty of the inspector, or other person authorized to act under this law, to examine and search all vessels hereinbefore described, to see that no slave or person held to service or labor in this State, or person charged with the commission of any crime within the State, shall be concealed on board said vessel. Such inspection shall be made within twelve hours of the time of departure of such vessel from the waters of Virginia, and may be made in any bay, river, creek, or other water-course of the State, provided, however, that steamers plying as regular packets, between ports in Virginia and those north of, and outside of the capes of Virginia, shall be inspected at the port of departure nearest Old Point Comfort.

(5.) A vessel so inspected and getting under way, with intent to leave the waters of the State, if she returns to an anchorage above Back River Point, or within Old Point Comfort, shall be again inspected and charged as if an original case. If such vessel be driven back by stress of weather to seek a harbor, she shall be exempt from payment of a second fee, unless she holds intercourse with the shore.

(6.) If, after searching the vessel, the inspector see no just cause to detain her, he shall give to the captain a certificate to that effect. If, however, upon such inspection, or in any other manner, any slave or person held to service or labor, or any person charged with any crime, be found on board of any vessel whatever, for the purpose aforesaid, or said vessel be detected in the act of leaving this commonwealth with any such slave or person on board, or otherwise violating the provisions of this act, he shall attach said vessel, and arrest all persons on board, to be delivered up to the sergeant or sheriff of the nearest port in this commonwealth, to be dealt with according to law.

(7.) If any inspector or other officer be opposed, or shall have reason to suspect that he will be opposed or obstructed in the discharge of any duty required of him under this act, he shall have power to summon and command the force of any county or corporation to aid him in the discharge of such duty, and every person who shall resist, obstruct, or refuse to aid any inspector or other officer in the discharge of such duty, shall be deemed guilty of a misdemeanor, and, upon conviction thereof, shall be fined and imprisoned as in other cases of misdemeanor.

(8.) For every inspection of a vessel under this law, the inspector, or other officer shall be entitled to demand and receive the sum of five dollars; for the payment of which such vessel shall be liable, and the inspector or other officer may seize and hold her until the same is paid, together with all charges incurred in taking care of the vessel, as well as in enforcing the payment of the same. Provided, that steam packets trading regularly between the waters of Virginia and ports north of and beyond the capes of Virginia, shall pay not more than five dollars for each inspection under the provisions of this act; provided, however, that for every inspection of a vessel engaged in the coal trade, the inspector shall not receive a greater sum than two dollars.

(9.) Any inspector or other person apprehending a slave in the act of escaping from the state, on board a vessel trading to or belonging to a non-slave-holding state, or who shall give information that will lead to the recovery of any slave, as aforesaid, shall be entitled to a reward of One Hundred Dollars, to be paid by the owner of such slave, or by the fiduciary having charge of the estate to which such slave belongs; and if the vessel be forfeited under the provisions of this act, he shall be entitled to one-half of the proceeds arising from the sale of the vessel; and if the same amounts to one hundred dollars, he shall not receive from the owner the above reward of one hundred dollars.

(10.) An inspector permitting a slave to escape for the want of proper exertion, or by neglect in the discharge of his duty, shall be fined One Hundred Dollars; or if for like causes he permit a vessel, which the law requires him to inspect, to leave the state without inspection, he shall be fined not less than twenty, nor more than fifty dollars, to be recovered by warrant by any person who will proceed against him.

(11.) No pilot acting under the authority of the laws of the state, shall pilot out of the jurisdiction of this state any such vessel as is described in this act, which has not obtained and exhibited to him the certificate of inspection hereby required; and if any pilot shall so offend, he shall forfeit and pay not less than twenty, or more than fifty dollars, to be recovered in the mode prescribed in the next preceding section of this act.

(12.) The courts of the several counties or corporations situated on the Chesapeake Bay, or its tributaries, by an order entered on record, may appoint one or more inspectors, at such place or places within their respective districts as they may deem necessary, to prevent the escape or for the recapture of slaves attempting to escape beyond the limits of the state, and to search or otherwise examine all vessels trading to such counties or corporations. The expenses in such cases to be provided for by a levy on negroes now taxed by law; but no inspection by county or corporation officers thus appointed, shall supersede the inspection of such vessels by pilots and other inspectors, as specially provided for in this act.

(13.) It shall be lawful for the county court of any county, upon the application of five or more slave-holders, residents of the counties where the application is made, by an order of record, to designate one or more police stations in their respective counties, and a captain and three or more other persons as a police patrol on each station, for the recapture of fugitive slaves; which patrol shall be in service at such times, and such stations as the court shall direct by their order aforesaid; and the said court shall allow a reasonable compensation, to be paid to the members of such patrol; and for that purpose, the said court may from time to time direct a levy on negroes now taxed by law, at such rate per capita as the court may think sufficient, to be collected and accounted for by the sheriff as other county levies, and to be called, "The fugitive slave tax." The owner of each fugitive slave in the act of escaping beyond the limits of the commonwealth, to a non-slave-holding state, and captured by the patrol aforesaid, shall pay for each slave over fifteen, and under forty-five years old, a reward of One Hundred dollars; for each slave over five, and under fifteen years old, the sum of sixty dollars; and for all others, the sum of forty dollars. Which reward shall be divided equally among the members of the patrol retaking the slave and actually on duty at the time; and to secure the payment of said reward, the said patrol may retain possession and use of the slave until the reward is paid or secured to them.

(14.) The executive of this State may appoint one or more inspectors for the Rappahannock and Potomac rivers, if he shall deem it expedient, for the due execution of this act. The inspectors so appointed to perform the same duties, and to be invested with the same powers in their respective districts, and receive the same fees, as pilots acting as inspectors in other parts of the State. A vessel subject to inspection under this law, departing from any of the above-named counties or rivers on her voyage to sea, shall be exempted from the payment of a fee for a second inspection by another officer, if provided with a certificate from the proper inspecting officer of that district; but if, after proceeding on her voyage, she returns to the port or place of departure, or enters any other port, river, or roadstead in the State, the said vessel shall be again inspected, and pay a fee of five dollars, as if she had undergone no previous examination and received no previous certificate.

If driven by stress of weather to seek a harbor, and she has no intercourse with the shore, then, and in that case, no second fee shall be paid by said vessel.

(15.) For the better execution of the provisions of this act, in regard to the inspection of vessels, the executive is hereby authorized and directed to appoint a chief inspector, to reside at Norfolk, whose duty it shall be, to direct and superintend the police, agents, or inspectors above referred to. He shall keep a record of all vessels engaged in the piloting business, together with a list of such persons as may be employed as pilots and inspectors under this law. The owner or owners of each boat shall make a monthly report to him, of all vessels inspected by persons attached to said pilot boats, the names of such vessels, the owner or owners thereof, and the places where owned or licensed, and where trading to or from, and the business in which they are engaged, together with a list of their crews. Any inspector failing to make his report to the chief inspector, shall pay a fine of twenty dollars for each such failure, which fine shall be recovered by warrant, before a justice of the county or corporation. The chief inspector may direct the time and station for the cruise of each pilot boat, and perform such other duty as the Governor may designate, not inconsistent with the other provisions of this act. He shall make a quarterly return to the executive of all the transactions of his department, reporting to him any failure or refusal on the part of inspectors to discharge the duty assigned to them, and the Governor, for sufficient cause, may suspend or remove from office any delinquent inspector. The chief inspector shall receive as his compensation, ten per cent. on all the fees and fines received by the inspectors acting under his authority, and may be removed at the pleasure of the executive.

(16.) All fees and forfeitures imposed by this act, and not otherwise specially provided for, shall go one half to the informer, and the other be paid into the treasury of the State, to constitute a fund, to be called the "fugitive slave fund," and to be used for the payment of rewards awarded by the Governor, for the apprehension of runaway slaves, and to pay other expenses incident to the execution of this law, together with such other purposes as may hereafter be determined on by the General Assembly.

(17.) This act shall be in force from its passage.

ESCAPING IN A CHEST.

$150 REWARD. Ran away from the subscriber, on Sunday night, 27th inst., my NEGRO GIRL, Lear Green, about 18 years of age, black complexion, round-featured, good-looking and ordinary size; she had on and with her when she left, a tan-colored silk bonnet, a dark plaid silk dress, a light mouslin delaine, also one watered silk cape and one tan colored cape. I have reason to be confident that she was per-

suaded off by a negro man named Wm. Adams, black, quick spoken, 5 feet 10 inches high, a large scar on one side of his face, running down in a ridge by the corner of his mouth, about 4 inches long, barber by trade, but works mostly about taverns, opening oysters, &c. He has been missing about a week; he had been heard to say he was going to marry the above girl and ship to New York, where it is said his mother resides. The above reward will be paid if said girl is taken out of the State of Maryland and delivered to me; or fifty dollars if taken in the State of Maryland.　　　　　　　　　　　　　JAMES NOBLE,
　m26–3t.　　　　　　　　　　　　　　　　　　　　　　　No. 153 Broadway, Baltimore.

LEAR GREEN, so particularly advertised in the "Baltimore Sun" by "James Noble," won for herself a strong claim to a high place among the heroic women of the nineteenth century. In regard to description and age the advertisement is tolerably accurate, although her master might have added, that her countenance was one of peculiar modesty and grace. Instead of being "black," she was of a "dark-brown color." Of her bondage she made the following statement: She was owned by "James Noble, a Butter Dealer " of Baltimore. He fell heir to Lear by the will of his wife's mother, Mrs. Rachel Howard, by whom she had previously been owned. Lear was but a mere child when she came into the hands of Noble's family. She, therefore, remembered but little of her old mistress. Her young mistress, however, had made a lasting impression upon her mind; for she was very exacting and oppressive in regard to the tasks she was daily in the habit of laying upon Lear's shoulders, with no disposition whatever to allow her any liberties. At least Lear was never indulged in this respect. In this situation a young man by the name of William Adams proposed marriage to her. This offer she was inclined to accept, but disliked the idea of being encumbered with the chains of slavery and the duties of a family at the same time.

After a full consultation with her mother and also her intended upon the matter, she decided that she must be free in order to fill the station of a wife and mother. For a time dangers and difficulties in the way of escape seemed utterly to set at defiance all hope of success. Whilst every pulse was beating strong for liberty, only one chance seemed to be left, the trial of which required as much courage as it would to endure the cutting off the right arm or plucking out the right eye. An old chest of substantial make, such as sailors commonly use, was procured. A quilt, a pillow, and a few articles of raiment, with a small quantity of food and a bottle of water were put in it, and Lear placed therein; strong ropes were fastened around the chest and she was safely stowed amongst the ordinary freight on one of the Ericson line of steamers. Her intended's mother, who was a free woman, agreed to come as a passenger on the same boat. How could she refuse? The prescribed rules of the Company assigned colored passengers to the deck. In this instance it was exactly where this guardian and mother desired to be—as near the chest as possible. Once or twice, during the silent watches of the night, she was drawn irresisti-

bly to the chest, and could not refrain from venturing to untie the rope and raise the lid a little, to see if the poor child still lived, and at the same time to give her a breath of fresh air. Without uttering a whisper, that frightful moment, this office was successfully performed. That the silent prayers of this oppressed young woman, together with her faithful protector's, were momentarily ascending to the ear of the good God above, there can be no question. Nor is it to be doubted for a moment but that some ministering angel aided the mother to unfasten the rope, and at the same time nerved the heart of poor Lear to endure the trying ordeal of her perilous situation. She declared that she had no fear.

After she had passed eighteen hours in the chest, the steamer arrived at the wharf in Philadelphia, and in due time the living freight was brought off the boat, and at first was delivered at a house in Barley street, occupied by particular friends of the mother. Subsequently chest and freight were removed to the residence of the writer, in whose family she remained several days under the protection and care of the Vigilance Committee.

Such hungering and thirsting for liberty, as was evinced by Lear Green, made the efforts of the most ardent friends, who were in the habit of aiding fugitives, seem feeble in the extreme. Of all the heroes in Canada, or out of it, who have purchased their liberty by downright bravery, through perils the most hazardous, none deserve more praise than Lear Green.

She remained for a time in this family, and was then forwarded to Elmira. In this place she was married to William Adams, who has been

previously alluded to. They never went to Canada, but took up their permanent abode in Elmira. The brief space of about three years only was
allotted her in which to enjoy freedom, as death came and terminated her
career. About the time of this sad occurrence, her mother-in-law died in
this city. The impressions made by both mother and daughter can never be
effaced. The chest in which Lear escaped has been preserved by the writer
as a rare trophy, and her photograph taken, while in the chest, is an excellent likeness of her and, at the same time, a fitting memorial.

ISAAC WILLIAMS, HENRY BANKS, AND KIT NICKLESS.

MONTHS IN A CAVE.—SHOT BY SLAVE-HUNTERS.

Rarely were three travelers from the house of bondage received at the
Philadelphia station whose narratives were more interesting than those of
the above-named individuals. Before escaping they had encountered difficulties of the most trying nature. No better material for dramatic effect
could be found than might have been gathered from the incidents of their
lives and travels. But all that we can venture to introduce here is the brief
account recorded at the time of their sojourn at the Philadelphia station
when on their way to Canada in 1854. The three journeyed together. They
had been slaves together in the same neighborhood. Two of them had
shared the same den and cave in the woods, and had been shot, captured, and
confined in the same prison; had broken out of prison and again escaped;
consequently their hearts were thoroughly cemented in the hope of reaching
freedom together.

ISAAC was a stout-made young man, about twenty-six years of age,
possessing a good degree of physical and mental ability. Indeed his
intelligence forbade his submission to the requirements of Slavery, rendered
him unhappy and led him to seek his freedom. He owed services to D.
Fitchhugh up to within a short time before he escaped. Against Fitchhugh
he made grave charges, said that he was a "hard, bad man." It is but fair
to add that Isaac was similarly regarded by his master, so both were dissatisfied with each other. But the master had the advantage of Isaac, he could
sell him. Isaac, however, could turn the table on his master, by running
off. But the master moved quickly and sold Isaac to Dr. James, a negro
trader. The trader designed making a good speculation out of his invest-
ment: Isaac determined that he should be disappointed; indeed that he
should lose every dollar that he paid for him. So while the doctor was
planning where and how he could get the best price for him, Isaac was
planning how and where he might safely get beyond his reach. The time
for planning and acting with Isaac was, however, exceedingly short. He

was daily expecting to be called upon to take his departure for the South. In this situation he made known his condition to a friend of his who was in a precisely similar situation; had lately been sold just as Isaac had to the same trader James. So no argument was needed to convince his friend and fellow-servant that if they meant to be free they would have to set off immediately.

That night Henry Banks and Isaac Williams started for the woods together, preferring to live among reptiles and wild animals, rather than be any longer at the disposal of Dr. James. For two weeks they successfully escaped their pursuers. The woods, however, were being hunted in every direction, and one day the pursuers came upon them, shot them both, and carried them to King George's Co. jail. The jail being an old building had weak places in it; but the prisoners concluded to make no attempt to break out while suffering badly from their wounds. So they remained one month in confinement. All the while their brave spirits under suffering grew more and more daring. Again they decided to strike for freedom, but where to go, save to the woods, they had not the slightest idea. Of course they had heard, as most slaves had, of cave life, and pretty well understood all the measures which had to be resorted to for security when entering upon so hazardous an undertaking. They concluded, however, that they could not make their condition any worse, let circumstances be what they might in this respect. Having discovered how they could break jail, they were not long in accomplishing their purpose, and were out and off to the woods again. This time they went far into the forest, and there they dug a cave, and with great pains had every thing so completely arranged as to conceal the spot entirely. In this den they stayed three months. Now and then they would manage to secure a pig. A friend also would occasionally serve them with a meal. Their sufferings at best were fearful; but great as they were, the thought of returning to Slavery never occurred to them, and the longer they stayed in the woods, the greater was their determination to be free. In the belief that their owner had about given them up they resolved to take the North Star for a pilot, and try in this way to reach free land.

KIT, an old friend in time of need, having proved true to them in their cave, was consulted. He fully appreciated their heroism, and determined that he would join them in the undertaking, as he was badly treated by his master, who was called General Washington, a common farmer, hard drinker, and brutal fighter, which Kit's poor back fully evinced by the marks it bore. Of course Isaac and Henry were only too willing to have him accompany them.

In leaving their respective homes they broke kindred ties of the tenderest nature. Isaac had a wife, Eliza, and three children, Isaac, Estella, and Ellen, all owned by Fitchhugh. Henry was only nineteen, single, but left parents, brothers, and sisters, all owned by different slave-holders. Kit had a wife, Matilda, and three children, Sarah Ann, Jane Frances, and Ellen, slaves.

SEPTEMBER 28, 1856.

ARRIVAL OF FIVE FROM THE EASTERN SHORE OF MARYLAND.

CYRUS MITCHELL, *alias* JOHN STEEL; JOSHUA HANDY, *alias* HAMBLE-TON HAMBY; CHARLES DULTON, *alias* WILLIAM ROBINSON; EPHRAIM HUDSON, *alias* JOHN SPRY; FRANCIS MOLOCK, *alias* THOMAS JACKSON; all in "good order" and full of hope.

The following letter from the fearless friend of the slave, Thomas Garrett, is a specimen of his manner of dispatching Underground Rail Road business. He used Uncle Sam's mail, and his own name, with as much freedom as though he had been President of the Pennsylvania Central Rail Road, instead of only a conductor and stock-holder on the Underground Rail Road.

9 mo. 26th, 1856.

RESPECTED FRIEND:—WILLIAM STILL, I send on to thy care this evening by Rail Road, 5 able-bodied men, on their way North; receive them as the Good Samaritan of old and oblige thy friend, THOMAS GARRETT.

The "able-bodied men" duly arrived, and were thus recorded on the Underground Rail Road books as trophies of the success of the friends of humanity.

CYRUS is twenty-six years of age, stout, and unmistakably dark, and was owned by James K. Lewis, a store-keeper, and a "hard master." He kept slaves for the express purpose of hiring them out, and it seemed to afford him as much pleasure to receive the hard-earned dollars of his bondmen as if he had labored for them with his own hands. "It mattered not, how mean a man might be," if he would pay the largest price, he was the man whom the store-keeper preferred to hire to. This always caused Cyrus to dislike him. Latterly he had been talking of moving into the State of Virginia. Cyrus disliked this talk exceedingly, but he "said nothing to the white people" touching the matter. However, he was not long in deciding that such a move would be of no advantage to him; indeed, he had an idea if all was true that he had heard about that place, he would be still more miserable there, than he had ever been under his present owner. At once, he decided that he would move towards Canada, and that he would be fixed in his new home before his master got off to Virginia, unless he moved sooner than Cyrus expected him to do. Those nearest of kin, to whom he felt most tenderly allied, and from whom he felt that it would be hard to part, were his father and mother. He, however, decided that he should have to leave them. Freedom, he felt, was even worth the giving up of parents.

Believing that company was desirable, he took occasion to submit his plan to certain friends, who were at once pleased with the idea of a trip on the Underground Rail Road, to Canada, etc; and all agreed to join him. At first, they traveled on foot; of their subsequent travel, mention has already been made in friend Garrett's epistle.

JOSHUA is about twenty-seven years of age, quite stout, brown color, and would pass for an intelligent farm hand. He was satisfied never to wear the yoke again that some one else might reap the benefit of his toil. His master, Isaac Harris, he denounced as a "drunkard." His chief excuse for escaping, was because Harris had "sold" his "only brother." He was obliged to leave his father and mother in the hands of his master.

CHARLES is twenty-two years of age, also stout, and well-made, and apparently possessed all the qualifications for doing a good day's work on a farm. He was held to service by Mrs. Mary Hurley. Charles gave no glowing account of happiness and comfort under the rule of the female sex, indeed, he was positive in saying that he had "been used rough." During the present year, he was sold for $1200.

EPHRAIM is twenty-two years of age, stout and athletic, one who appears in every way fitted for manual labor or anything else that he might be privileged to learn. John Campbell Henry, was the name of the man whom he had been taught to address as master, and for whose benefit he had been compelled to labor up to the day he "took out." In considering what he had been in Maryland and how he had been treated all his life, he alleged that John Campbell Henry was a "bad man." Not only had Ephraim been treated badly by his master but he had been hired out to a man no better than his master, if as good. Ephraim left his mother and six brothers and sisters.

FRANCIS is twenty-one, an able-bodied "article," of dark color, and was owned by James A. Waddell. All that he could say of his owner, was, that he was a "hard master," from whom he was very glad to escape.

SUNDRY ARRIVALS, ABOUT AUGUST 1st, 1855.

Arrival 1st. Frances Hilliard.
Arrival 2d. Louisa Harding, alias Rebecca Hall.
Arrival 3d. John Mackintosh.
Arrival 4th. Maria Jane Houston.

Arrival 5th. Miles Hoopes.
Arrival 6th. Samuel Miles, alias Robert King.
Arrival 7th. James Henson, alias David Caldwell.
Arrival 8th. Laura Lewis.
Arrival 9th. Elizabeth Banks.
Arrival 10th. Simon Hill.
Arrival 11th. Anthony and Albert Brown.
Arrival 12th. George Williams and Charles Holladay.
Arrival 13th. William Govan.

While none in this catalogue belonged to the class whose daring adventures rendered their narratives marvellous, nevertheless they represented a very large number of those who were continually on the alert to get rid of their captivity. And in all their efforts in this direction they manifested a marked willingness to encounter perils either by land or water, by day or by night, to obtain their God-given rights. Doubtless, even among these names, will be found those who have been supposed to be lost, and mysteries will be disclosed which have puzzled scores of relatives longing and looking many years in vain to ascertain the whereabouts of this or that companion, brother, sister, or friend. So, if impelled by no other consideration than the hope of consoling this class of anxious inquirers, this is a sufficient justification for not omitting them entirely, notwithstanding the risk of seeming to render these pages monotonous.

ARRIVAL No. 1. First on this record was a young mulatto woman, twenty-nine years of age—orange color, who could read and write very well, and was unusually intelligent and withal quite handsome. She was known by the name of Frances Hilliard, and escaped from Richmond, Va., where she was owned by Beverly Blair. The owner hired her out to a man by the name of Green, from whom he received seventy dollars per annum. Green allowed her to hire herself for the same amount, with the understanding that Frances should find all her own clothes, board herself and find her own house to live in. Her husband, who was also a slave, had fled nearly one year previous, leaving her widowed, of course. Notwithstanding the above mentioned conditions, under which she had the privilege of living, Frances said that she "had been used well." She had been sold four times in her life. In the first instance the failure of her master was given as the reason of her sale. Subsequently she was purchased and sold by different traders, who designed to speculate upon her as a "fancy article." They would dress her very elegantly, in order to show her off to the best advantage possible, but it appears that she had too much regard for her husband and her honor, to consent to fill the positions which had been basely assigned her by her owners.

Frances assisted her husband to escape from his owner—Taits—and was never contented until she succeeded in following him to Canada. In escaping, she left her mother, Sarah Corbin, and her sister, Maria. On reaching the Vigilance Committee she learned all about her husband. She was conveyed from Richmond secreted on a steamer under the care of one of the colored hands on the boat. From here she was forwarded to Canada at the expense of the Committee. Arriving in Toronto, and not finding her hopes fully realized, with regard to meeting her husband, she wrote back the following letter:

TORONTO, CANADA, U. C., October 15th, 1855.

MY DEAR MR. STILL:—Sir—I take the opportunity of writing you a few lines to inform you of my health. I am very well at present, and hope that when these few lines reach you they may find you enjoying the same blessing. Give my love to Mrs. Still and all the children, and also to Mr. Swan, and tell him that he must give you the money that he has, and you will please send it to me, as I have received a letter from my husband saying that I must come on to him as soon as I get the money from him. I cannot go to him until I get the money that Mr. Swan has in hand. Please tell Mr. Caustle that the clothes he spoke of my mother did not know anything about them. I left them with Hinson Brown and he promised to give them to Mr. Smith. Tell him to ask Mr. Smith to get them from Mr. Brown for me, and when I get settled I will send him word and he can send them to me. The letters that were sent to me I received them all. I wish you would send me word if Mr. Smith is on the boat yet—if he is please write me word in your next letter. Please send me the money as soon as you possibly can, for I am very anxious to see my husband. I send to you for I think you will do what you can for me. No more at present, but remain   Yours truly,   FRANCES HILLIARD.

Send me word if Mr. Caustle had given Mr. Smith the money that he promised to give him.

For one who had to steal the art of reading and writing, her letter bears studying.

ARRIVAL No. 2. Louisa Harding, alias Rebecca Hall. Louisa was a mulatto girl, seventeen years of age. She reported herself from Baltimore, where she had been owned by lawyer Magill. It might be said that she also possessed great personal attractions as an "article" of much value in the eye of a trader. All the near kin whom she named as having left behind, consisted of a mother and a brother.

ARRIVAL No. 3. John Mackintosh. John's history is short. He represented himself as having arrived from Darien, Georgia, where he had seen "hard times." Age, forty-four. This is all that was recorded of John, except the expenses met by the Committee.

ARRIVAL No. 4. Maria Jane Houston. The little State of Delaware lost in the person of Maria, one of her nicest-looking bond-maids. She had just arrived at the age of twenty-one, and felt that she had already been sufficiently wronged. She was a tall, dark, young woman, from the neighborhood of Cantwell's Bridge. Although she had no horrible tales of suffering to relate, the Committee regarded her as well worthy of aid.

19

ARRIVAL No. 5. Miles Hooper. This subject came from North Carolina; he was owned by George Montigue, who lived at Federal Mills, was a decided opponent to the no-pay system, to flogging, and selling likewise. In fact nothing that was auxiliary to Slavery was relished by him. Consequently he concluded to leave the place altogether. At the time that Miles took this stand he was twenty-three years of age, a dark-complexioned man, rather under the medium height, physically, but a full-grown man mentally. "My owner was a hard man," said Miles, in speaking of his characteristics. His parents, brothers, and sisters were living, at least he had reason to believe so, although they were widely scattered.

ARRIVAL No. 6. Samuel Miles, alias Robert King. Samuel was a representative of Revel's Neck, Somerset Co., Md. His master he regarded as a "very fractious man, hard to please." The cause of the trouble or unpleasantness, which resulted in Samuel's Underground adventure, was traceable to his master's refusal to allow him to visit his wife. Not only was Samuel denied this privilege, but he was equally denied all privileges. His master probably thought that Sam had no mind, nor any need of a wife. Whether this was really so or not, Sam was shrewd enough to "leave his old master with the bag to hold," which was sensible. Thirty-one years of Samuel's life were passed in Slavery, ere he escaped. The remainder of his days he felt bound to have the benefit of himself. In leaving home he had to part with his wife and one child, Sarah and little Henry, who were fortunately free.

On arriving in Canada Samuel wrote back for his wife, &c., as follows:

ST. CATHARINES, C. W., Aug. 20th, 1855.

To MR. WM. STILL, DEAR FRIEND:—It gives me pleasure to inform you that I have had the good fortune to reach this northern Canaan. I got here yesterday and am in good health and happy in the enjoyment of Freedom, but am very anxious to have my wife and child here with me.

I wish you to write to her immediately on receiving this and let her know where I am you will recollect her name Sarah Miles at Baltimore on the corner of Hamburg and Eutaw streets. Please encourage her in making a start and give her the necessary directions how to come. She will please to make the time as short as possible in getting through to Canada. Say to my wife that I wish her to write immediately to the friends that I told her to address as soon as she hears from me. Inform her that I now stop in St. Catharines near the Niagara Falls that I am not yet in business but expect to get into business very soon—That I am in the enjoyment of good health and hoping that this communication may find my affectionate wife the same. That I have been highly favored with friends throughout my journey I wish my wife to write to me as soon as she can and let me know how soon I may expect to see her on this side of the Niagara River. My wife had better call on Dr. Perkins and perhaps he will let her have the money he had in charge for me but that I failed of receiving when I left Baltimore. Please direct the letter for my wife to Mr. George Lister, in Hill street between Howard and Sharp. My compliments to all enquiring friends. Very respectfully yours, SAMUEL MILES.

P. S. Please send the thread along as a token and my wife will understand that all is right. S. M.

ARRIVAL No. 7. James Henson, alias David Caldwell. James fled from Cecil Co., Md. He claimed that he was entitled to his freedom according to law at the age of twenty-eight, but had been unjustly deprived of it. Having waited in vain for his free papers for four years, he suspected that he was to be dealt with in a manner similar to many others, who had been willed free or who had bought their time, and had been shamefully cheated out of their freedom. So in his judgment he felt that his only hope lay in making his escape on the Underground Rail Road. He had no faith whatever in the man who held him in bondage, Jacob Johnson, but no other charges of ill treatment, &c., have been found against said Johnson on the books, save those alluded to above.

James was thirty-two years of age, stout and well proportioned, with more than average intelligence and resolution. He left a wife and child, both free.

ARRIVAL No. 8. Laura Lewis. Laura arrived from Louisville, Kentucky. She had been owned by a widow woman named Lewis, but as lately as the previous March her mistress died, leaving her slaves and other property to be divided among her heirs. As this would necessitate a sale of the slaves, Laura determined not to be on hand when the selling day came, so she took time by the forelock and left. Her appearance indicated that she had been among the more favored class of slaves. She was about twenty-five years of age, quite stout, of mixed blood, and intelligent, having traveled considerably with her mistress. She had been North in this capacity. She left her mother, one brother, and one sister in Louisville.

ARRIVAL No. 9. Elizabeth Banks, from near Easton, Maryland. Her lot had been that of an ordinary slave. Of her slave-life nothing of interest was recorded. She had escaped from her owner two and a half years prior to coming into the hands of the Committee, and had been living in Pennsylvania pretty securely as she had supposed, but she had been awakened to a sense of her danger by well grounded reports that she was pursued by her claimant, and would be likely to be captured if she tarried short of Canada. With such facts staring her in the face she was sent to the Committee for counsel and protection, and by them she was forwarded on in the usual way. She was about twenty-five years of age, of a dark, and spare structure.

ARRIVAL No. 10. Simon Hill. This fugitive had escaped from Virginia. The usual examination was made, and needed help given him by the Committee, who felt satisfied that he was a poor brother who had been shamefully wronged, and that he richly deserved sympathy. He was aided and directed Canada-ward. He was a very humble-looking specimen of the peculiar institution, about twenty-five years of age, medium size, and of a dark hue.

ARRIVAL No. 11. Anthony and Albert Brown (brothers), Jones Anderson and Isaiah.

This party escaped from Tanner's Creek, Norfolk, Virginia, where they had been owned by John and Henry Holland, oystermen. As slaves they alleged that they had been subjected to very brutal treatment from their profane and ill-natured owners. Not relishing this treatment, Albert and Anthony came to the conclusion that they understood boating well enough to escape by water. They accordingly selected one of their master's small oyster-boats, which was pretty-well rigged with sails, and off they started for a Northern Shore. They proceeded on a part of their voyage merely by guess work, but landed safely, however, about twenty-five miles north of Baltimore, though, by no means, on free soil. They had no knowledge of the danger that they were then in, but they were persevering, and still determined to make their way North, and thus, at last, success attended their efforts. Their struggles and exertions having been attended with more of the romantic and tragical elements than had characterized the undertakings of any of the other late passengers, the Committee felt inclined to make a fuller notice of them on the book, yet failed to do them justice in this respect.

The elder brother was twenty-nine, the younger twenty-seven. Both were mentally above the average run of slaves. They left wives in Norfolk, named Alexenia and Ellen. While Anthony and Albert, in seeking their freedom, were forced to sever their connections with their companions, they did not forget them in Canada.

How great was their delight in freedom, and tender their regard for their wives, and the deep interest they felt for their brethren and friends generally, may be seen from a perusal of the following letters from them:

HAMELTON, March 7th 1856.

MR. WM. STILL :—*Sir :*—I now take the opportunity of writting you a few lins hoping to find yourself and famly well as thes lines leves me at present, myself and brother, Anthony & Albert brown's respects. We have spent quite agreeable winter, we ware emploied in the new hotel name Anglo american, wheare we wintered and don very well, we also met with our too frends ho came from home with us, Jonas anderson and Izeas, now we are all safe in hamilton, I wish to cale you to youre prommos, if convenient to write to Norfolk, Va., for me, and let my wife mary Elen Brown, no where I am, and my brothers wife Elickzener Brown, as we have never heard a word from them since we left, tel them that we found our homes and situation in canady much better than we expected, tel them not to think hard of us, we was boun to flee from the rath to come, tel them we live in the hopes of meting them once more this side of the grave, tel them if we never more see them, we hope to meet them in the kingdom of heaven in pece, tel them to remember my love to my cherch and brethren, tel them I find there is the same prayer-hearing God heare as there is in old Va ; tel them to remember our love to all the enquiring frends, I have written sevrel times but have never reseived no answer, I find a gret meny of my old accuaintens from Va., heare we are no ways lonesom, Mr. Still, I have written to you once before, but reseve no answer. Pleas let us hear from you by any means. Nothing more at present, but remane youre frends,

ANTHONY & ALBERT BROWN.

HAMILTON June 26th, 1856.

MR. WM. STILL:—*kine Sir:*—I am happy to say to you that I have jus reseved my letter dated 5 of the present month, but previeously had bin in form las night by Mr. J. H. Hall, he had jus reseved a letter from you stating that my wife was with you, oh my I was so glad it case me to shed tears.

Mr. Still, I cannot return you the thanks for the care of my wife, for I am so Glad that I dont now what to say, you will pleas start her for canaday. I am yet in hamilton, C. W, at the city hotel, my brother and Joseph anderson is at the angle american hotel, they send there respects to you and family my self also, and a greater part to my wife. I came by the way of syracruse remember me to Mrs. logins, tel her to writ back to my brothers wife if she is living and tel her to com on tel her to send Joseph Andersons love to his mother.

i now send her 10 Dollers and would send more but being out of employment some of winter it pulls me back, you will be so kine as to forward her on to me, and if life las I will satisfie you at some time, before long. Give my respects and brothers to Mr. John Dennes, tel him Mr. Hills famly is wel and send there love to them, I now bring my letter to a close, And am youre most humble Servant,   ANTHONY BROWN.

P. S. I had given out the notion of ever seeing my wife again, so I have not been attending the office, but am truly sorry I did not, you mention in yours of Mr. Henry lewey, he has left this city for Boston about 2 weeks ago, we have not herd from him yet.
          A. BROWN.

ARRIVAL No. 12. George Williams and Charles Holladay. These two travelers were about the same age. They were not, however, from the same neighborhood—they happened to meet each other as they were traveling the road. George fled from St. Louis, Charles from Baltimore. George "owed service" to Isaac Hill, a planter; he found no special fault with his master's treatment of him ; but with Mrs. Hill, touching this point, he was thoroughly dissatisfied. She had treated him "cruelly," and it was for this reason that he was moved to seek his freedom.

Charles, being a Baltimorean, had not far to travel, but had pretty sharp hunters to elude.

His claimant, F. Smith, however, had only a term of years claim upon him, which was within about two years of being out. This contract for the term of years, Charles felt was made without consulting him, therefore he resolved to break it without consulting his master. He also declined to have anything to do with the Baltimore and Wilmington R. R. Co., considering it a proscriptive institution, not worthy of his confidence. He started on a fast walk, keeping his eyes wide open, looking out for slave-hunters on his right and left. In this way, like many others, he reached the Committee safely and was freely aided, thenceforth traveling in a first class Underground Rail Road car, till he reached his journey's end.

ARRIVAL No. 13. William Govan. Availing himself of a passage on the schooner of Captain B., William left Petersburg, where he had been owned by "Mark Davis, Esq., a retired gentleman," rather, a retired negro trader.

William was about thirty-three years of age, and was of a bright orange color. Nothing but an ardent love of liberty prompted him to escape. He was quite smart, and a clever-looking man, worth at least $1,000.

DEEP FURROWS ON THE BACK.

THOMAS MADDEN.

Of all the passengers who had hitherto arrived with bruised and mangled bodies received at the hands of slave-holders, none brought a back so shamefully lacerated by the lash as Thomas Madden. Not a single spot had been exempted from the excoriating cow-hide. A most bloody picture did the broad back and shoulders of Thomas present to the eye as he bared his wounds for inspection. While it was sad to think, that millions of men, women, and children throughout the South were liable to just such brutal outrages as Thomas had received, it was a satisfaction to think, that this outrage had made a freeman of him.

He was only twenty-two years of age, but that punishment convinced him that he was fully old enough to leave such a master as E. Ray, who had almost murdered him. But for this treatment, Thomas might have remained in some degree contented in Slavery. He was expected to look after the fires in the house on Sunday mornings. In a single instance desiring to be absent, perhaps for his own pleasure, two boys offered to be his substitute. The services of the boys were accepted, and this gave offence to the master. This Thomas declared was the head and front of his offending. His simple narration of the circumstances of his slave life was listened to by the Committee with deep interest and a painful sense of the situation of slaves under the despotism of such men as Ray.

After being cared for by the Committee he was sent on to Canada. When there he wrote back to let the Committee know how he was faring, the narrow escape he had on the way, and likewise to convey the fact, that one named " Rachel," left behind, shared a large place in his affections. The subjoined letter is the only correspondence of his preserved :

STANFORD, June 1st, 1855, Niagara districk.

DEAR SIR :—I set down to inform you that I take the liberty to rite for a frend to inform you that he is injoying good health and hopes that this will finde you the same he got to this cuntry very well except that in Albany he was vary neig taking back to his oald home but escaped and when he came to the suspention bridg he was so glad that he run for freadums shore and when he arived it was the last of october and must look for sum wourk for the winter he choped wood until Feruary times are good but money is scarce he thinks a great deal of the girl he left behind him he thinks that there is non like her here non so hansom as his Rachel right and let him hear from you as soon as convaniant no more at presant but remain yours, ALBERT METTER.

"PETE MATTHEWS," ALIAS SAMUEL SPARROWS.

"I MIGHT AS WELL BE IN THE PENITENTIARY, &C."

Up to the age of thirty-five "Pete" had worn the yoke steadily, if not patiently under William S. Matthews, of Oak Hall, near Temperanceville, in the State of Virginia. Pete said that his "master was not a hard man," but the man to whom he "was hired, George Matthews, was a very cruel man." "I might as well be in the penitentiary as in his hands," was his declaration.

One day, a short while before Pete "took out," an ox broke into the truck patch, and helped himself to choice delicacies, to the full extent of his capacious stomach, making sad havoc with the vegetables generally. Peter's attention being directed to the ox, he turned him out, and gave him what he considered proper chastisement, according to the mischief he had done. At this liberty taken by Pete, the master became furious. "He got his gun and threatened to shoot him." "Open your mouth if you dare, and I will put the whole load into you," said the enraged master. "He took out a large dirk-knife, and attempted to stab me, but I kept out of his way," said Pete. Nevertheless the violence of the master did not abate until he had beaten Pete over the head and body till he was weary, inflicting severe injuries. A great change was at once wrought in Pete's mind. He was now ready to adopt any plan that might hold out the least encouragement to escape. Having capital to the amount of four dollars only, he felt that he could not do much towards employing a conductor, but he had a good pair of legs, and a heart stout enough to whip two or three slave-catchers, with the help of a pistol. Happening to know a man who had a pistol for sale, he went to him and told him that he wished to purchase it. For one dollar the pistol became Pete's property. He had but three dollars left, but he was determined to make that amount answer his purposes under the circumstances. The last cruel beating maddened him almost to desperation, especially when he remembered how he had been compelled to work hard night and day, under Matthews. Then, too, Peter had a wife, whom his master prevented him from visiting; this was not among the least offences with which Pete charged his master. Fully bent on leaving, the following Sunday was fixed by him on which to commence his journey.

The time arrived and Pete bade farewell to Slavery, resolved to follow the North Star, with his pistol in hand ready for action. After traveling about two hundred miles from home he unexpectedly had an opportunity of using his pistol. To his astonishment he suddenly came face to face with a former master, whom he had not seen for a long time. Pete desired no friendly intercourse with him whatever; but he perceived that his old master recognized him and was bent upon stopping him. Pete held on to his pistol, but moved as fast as his wearied limbs would allow him, in an opposite direction. As he was running, Pete cautiously, cast his eye over his shoulder, to see what had become of his old master, when to his amazement, he found that a regular chase was being made after him. Need of redoubling his pace was quite obvious. In this hour of peril, Pete's legs saved him.

After this signal leg-victory, Pete had more confidence in his "understandings," than he had in his old pistol, although he held on to it until he reached Philadelphia, where he left it in the possession of the Secretary of the Committee. Considering it worth saving simply as a relic of the Underground Rail Road, it was carefully laid aside. Pete was now christened Samuel Sparrows. Mr. Sparrows had the rust of Slavery washed off as clean as possible and the Committee furnishing him with clean clothes, a ticket, and letters of introduction, started him on Canada-ward, looking quite respectable. And doubtless he felt even more so than he looked; free air had a powerful effect on such passengers as Samuel Sparrows.

The unpleasantness which grew out of the mischief done by the ox on George Matthews' farm took place the first of October, 1855. Pete may be described as a man of unmixed blood, well-made, and intelligent.

"MOSES" ARRIVES WITH SIX PASSENGERS.

"Not allowed to seek a master;"—"Very devilish;"—father "leaves two little sons;"—"Used hard;"—"Feared falling into the hands of young heirs," etc. John Chase, alias Daniel Floyd; Benjamin Ross, alias James Stewart; Henry Ross, alias Levin Stewart; Peter Jackson, alias Staunch Tilghman; Jane Kane, alias Catharine Kane, and Robert Ross.

The coming of these passengers was heralded by Thomas Garrett as follows:

THOMAS GARRETT'S LETTER.

WILMINGTON, 12 mo. 29th, 1854.

Esteemed Friend, J. Miller McKim:—We made arrangements last night, and sent away Harriet Tubman, with six men and one woman to Allen Agnew's, to be forwarded across the country to the city. Harriet, and one of the men had worn their shoes off their feet, and I gave them two dollars to help fit them out, and directed a carriage to be hired at my expense, to take them out, but do not yet know the expense. I now have two more from the lowest county in Maryland, on the Peninsula, upwards of one hundred miles. I will try to get one of our trusty colored men to take them to-morrow morning to the Anti-slavery office. You can then pass them on. Thomas Garrett.

Harriet Tubman had been their "Moses," but not in the sense that Andrew Johnson was the "Moses of the colored people." She had faithfully gone down into Egypt, and had delivered these six bondmen by her own heroism. Harriet was a woman of no pretensions, indeed, a more ordinary specimen of humanity could hardly be found among the most unfortunate-looking farm hands of the South. Yet, in point of courage, shrewdness and disinterested exertions to rescue her fellow-men, by making personal visits to Maryland among the slaves, she was without her equal.

Her success was wonderful. Time and again she made successful visits to Maryland on the Underground Rail Road, and would be absent for weeks, at a time, running daily risks while making preparations for herself and passengers. Great fears were entertained for her safety, but she seemed wholly devoid of personal fear. The idea of being captured by slave-hunters or slave-holders, seemed never to enter her mind. She was apparently proof against all adversaries. While she thus manifested such utter personal indifference, she was much more watchful with regard to those she was piloting. Half of her time, she had the appearance of one asleep, and would actually sit down by the road-side and go fast asleep when on her errands of mercy through the South, yet, she would not suffer one of her party to whimper once, about "giving out and going back," however wearied they might be from hard travel day and night. She had a very short and pointed rule or law of her own, which implied death to any who talked of giving out and going back. Thus, in an emergency she would give all to understand that "times were very critical and therefore no foolishness would be indulged in on the road." That several who were rather weak-kneed and faint-hearted were greatly invigorated by Harriet's blunt and positive manner and threat of extreme measures, there could be no doubt.

After having once enlisted, "they had to go through or die." Of course Harriet was supreme, and her followers generally had full faith in her, and would back up any word she might utter. So when she said to them that "a live runaway could do great harm by going back, but that a dead one could tell no secrets," she was sure to have obedience. Therefore, none had to die as traitors on the "middle passage." It is obvious enough, however, that her success in going into Maryland as she did, was attributable to her adventurous spirit and utter disregard of consequences. Her like it is probable was never known before or since. On examining the six passengers who came by this arrival they were thus recorded :

December 29th, 1854—John is twenty years of age, chestnut color, of spare build and smart. He fled from a farmer, by the name of John Campbell Henry, who resided at Cambridge, Dorchester Co., Maryland. On being interrogated relative to the character of his master, John gave no very amiable account of him. He testified that he was a "hard man" and that he "owned about one hundred and forty slaves and sometimes he would sell," etc. John was one of the slaves who were "hired out." He "desired to have the privilege of hunting his own master." His desire was not granted. Instead of meekly submitting, John felt wronged, and made this his reason for running away. This looked pretty spirited on the part of one so young as John. The Committee's respect for him was not a little increased, when they heard him express himself.

BENJAMIN was twenty-eight years of age, chestnut color, medium size, and shrewd. He was the so-called property of Eliza Ann Brodins, who lived near Buckstown, in Maryland. Ben did not hesitate to say, in unqualified terms, that his mistress was "very devilish." He considered his charges, proved by the fact that three slaves (himself one of them) were required to work hard and fare meagerly, to support his mistress' family in idleness and luxury. The Committee paid due attention to his ex parte statement, and was obliged to conclude that his argument, clothed in common and homely language, was forcible, if not eloquent, and that he was well worthy of aid. Benjamin left his parents besides one sister, Mary Ann Williamson, who wanted to come away on the Underground Rail Road.

HENRY left his wife, Harriet Ann, to be known in future by the name of "Sophia Brown." He was a fellow-servant of Ben's, and one of the supports of Eliza A. Brodins.

HENRY was only twenty-two, but had quite an insight into matters and things going on among slaves and slave-holders generally, in country life. He was the father of two small children, whom he had to leave behind.

PETER was owned by George Wenthrop, a farmer, living near Cambridge, Md. In answer to the question, how he had been used, he said "hard." Not a pleasant thought did he entertain respecting his master, save that he was no longer to demand the sweat of Peter's brow. Peter left parents, who were free; he was born before they were emancipated, consequently, he was retained in bondage.

JANE, aged twenty-two, instead of regretting that she had unadvisedly left a kind mistress and indulgent master, who had afforded her necessary comforts, affirmed that her master, "Rash Jones, was the worst man in the country." The Committee were at first disposed to doubt her sweeping statement, but when they heard particularly how she had been treated, they thought Catharine had good ground for all that she said. Personal abuse and hard usage, were the common lot of poor slave girls.

ROBERT was thirty-five years of age, of a chestnut color, and well made. His report was similar to that of many others. He had been provided with plenty of hard drudgery—hewing of wood and drawing of water, and had hardly been treated as well as a gentleman would treat a dumb brute. His feelings, therefore, on leaving his old master and home, were those of an individual who had been unjustly in prison for a dozen years and had at last regained his liberty.

The civilization, religion, and customs under which Robert and his companions had been raised, were, he thought, " very wicked." Although these travelers were all of the field-hand order, they were, nevertheless, very promising, and they anticipated better days in Canada. Good advice was proffered them on the subject of temperance, industry, education, etc. Clothing, food and money were also given them to meet their wants, and they were sent on their way rejoicing.

ESCAPED FROM "A WORTHLESS SOT."

JOHN ATKINSON.

John was a prisoner of hope under James Ray, of Portsmouth, Va., whom he declared to be "a worthless sot." This character was fully set forth, but the description is too disgusting for record. John was a dark mulatto, thirty-one years of age, well-formed and intelligent. For some years before escaping he had been in the habit of hiring his time for $120 per annum. Daily toiling to support his drunken and brutal master, was a hardship that John felt keenly, but was compelled to submit to up to the day of his escape.

A part of John's life he had suffered many abuses from his oppressor, and only a short while before freeing himself, the auction-block was held up before his troubled mind. This caused him to take the first daring step towards Canada,—to leave his wife, Mary, without bidding her good-bye, or saying a word to her as to his intention of fleeing.

John came as a private passenger on one of the Richmond steamers, and was indebted to the steward of the boat for his accommodations. Having been received by the Committee, he was cared for and sent on his journey Canada-ward. There he was happy, found employment and wanted for nothing but his wife and clothing left in Virginia. On these two points he wrote several times with considerable feeling.

Some slaves who hired their time in addition to the payment of their monthly hire, purchased nice clothes for themselves, which they usually valued highly, so much so, that after escaping they would not be contented until they had tried every possible scheme to secure them. They would write back continually, either to their friends in the North or South, hoping thus to procure them.

Not unfrequently the persons who rendered them assistance in the South, would be entrusted with all their effects, with the understanding, that such valuables would be forwarded to a friend or to the Committee at the earliest opportunity. The Committee strongly protested against fugitives writing back to the South (through the mails) on account of the liability of getting parties into danger, as all such letters were liable to be intercepted in order to the discovery of the names of such as aided the Underground Rail Road. To render needless this writing to the South the Committee often submitted to be taxed with demands to rescue clothing as well as wives, etc., belonging to such as had been already aided.

The following letters are fair samples of a large number which came to the Committee touching the matter of clothing, etc. :

St. Catharines, Sept. 4th.

DEAR SIR:—I now embrace this favorable opportunity of writing you a few lines to inform you that I am quite well and arrived here safe, and I hope that these few lines may find you and your family the same. I hope you will intercede for my clothes and as soon as they come please to send them to me, and if you have not time, get Dr. Lundy to look out for them, and when they come be very careful in sending them. I wish you would copy off this letter and give it to the Steward, and tell him to give it to Henry Lewy and tell him to give it to my wife. Brother sends his love to you and all the family and he is overjoyed at seeing me arrive safe, he can hardly contain himself; also he wants to see his wife very much, and says when she comes he hopes you will send her on as soon as possible. Jerry Williams' love, together with all of us. I had a message for Mr. Lundy, but I forgot it when I was there. No more at present, but remain your ever grateful and sincere friend, JOHN ATKINSON.

St. Catharines, C. W., Oct. 5th, 1854.

MR. WM. STILL :—Dear Sir—I have learned of my friend, Richmond Bohm, that my clothes were in Philadelphia. Will you have the kindness to see Dr. Lundy and if he has my clothes in charge, or knows about them, for him to send them on to me immediately, as I am in great need of them. I would like to have them put in a small box, and the overcoat I left at your house to be put in the box with them, to be sent to the care of my friend, Hiram Wilson. On receipt of this letter, I desire you to write a few lines to my wife, Mary Atkins, in the care of my friend, Henry Lowey, stating that I am well and hearty and hoping that she is the same. Please tell her to remember my love to her mother and her cousin, Emelin, and her husband, and Thomas Hunter; also to my father and mother. Please request her to write to me immediately, for her to be of good courage, that I love her better than ever. I would like her to come on as soon as she can, but for her to write and let me know when she is going to start. Affectionately Yours,

JOHN ATKINS.

W. H. ATKINSON, Fugitive, Oct., 1854.

WILLLIAM BUTCHER, ALIAS WILLIAM T. MITCHELL.

"HE WAS ABUSEFUL."

This passenger reported himself from Massey's Cross-Roads, near George-town, Maryland. William gave as his reason for being found destitute, and under the necessity of asking aid, that a man by the name of William Boyer, who followed farming, had deprived him of his hard earnings, and also claimed him as his property; and withal that he had abused him for years, and recently had "threatened to sell" him. This threat made his yoke too intolerable to be borne.

He here began to think and plan for the future as he had never done before. Fortunately he was possessed with more than an average amount of mother wit, and he soon comprehended the requirements of the Underground Rail Road. He saw exactly that he must have resolution and self-dependence, very decided, in order to gain the victory over Boyer. In his hour of trial his wife, Phillis, and child, John Wesley, who were free, caused him much anxiety; but his reason taught him that it was his duty to throw off the yoke at all hazards, and he acted accordingly. Of course he left behind his wife and child. The interview which the Committee held with William was quite satisfactory, and he was duly aided and regularly despatched by the name of William T. Mitchell. He was about twenty-eight years of age, of medium size, and of quite a dark hue.

"WHITE ENOUGH TO PASS."

JOHN WESLEY GIBSON represented himself to be not only the slave, but also the son of William Y. Day, of Taylor's Mount, Maryland. The faintest shade of colored blood was hardly discernible in this passenger. He relied wholly on his father's white blood to secure him freedom. Having resolved to serve no longer as a slave, he concluded to "hold up his head and put on airs." He reached Baltimore safely without being discovered or suspected of being on the Underground Rail Road, as far as he was aware of. Here he tried for the first time to pass for white; the attempt proved a success beyond his expectation. Indeed he could but wonder how it was that he had never before hit upon such an expedient to rid himself of his unhappy lot. Although a man of only twenty-eight years of age, he was foreman of his master's farm, But he was not particularly favored in any way on this account. His master and father endeavored to hold the reins very tightly upon him. Not even allowing him the privilege of visiting around on neighboring plantations. Perhaps the master thought the family likeness was rather too discernible. John believed that on this account all privileges were denied him, and he resolved to escape. His mother, Harriet, and sister, Frances, were named as near kin whom he had left behind. John was quite smart, and looked none the worse for having so much of his master's blood in his veins. The master was alone to blame for John's escape, as he passed on his (the master's) color.

ESCAPING WITH MASTER'S CARRIAGES AND HORSES.

HARRIET SHEPHARD, AND HER FIVE CHILDREN, WITH FIVE OTHER PASSENGERS.

One morning about the first of November, in 1855, the sleepy, slave-holding neighborhood of Chestertown, Maryland, was doubtless deeply excited on learning that eleven head of slaves, four head of horses, and two carriages were missing. It is but reasonable to suppose that the first report must have produced a shock, scarcely less stunning than an earthquake. Abolitionists, emissaries, and incendiaries were farther below par than ever. It may be supposed that cursings and threatenings were breathed out by a deeply agitated community for days in succession.

Harriet Shephard, the mother of five children, for whom she felt of course a mother's love, could not bear the thought of having her offspring compelled to wear the miserable yoke of Slavery, as she had been compelled to do. By her own personal experience, Harriet could very well judge what their fate would be when reaching man and womanhood. She declared that she had never received "kind treatment." It was not on this account, however, that she was prompted to escape. She was actuated by a more disinterested motive than this. She was chiefly induced to make the bold effort to save her children from having to drag the chains of Slavery as she herself had done.

Anna Maria, Edwin, Eliza Jane, Mary Ann, and John Henry were the names of the children for whom she was willing to make any sacrifice. They were young, and unable to walk, and she was penniless, and unable to hire a conveyance, even if she had known any one who would have been willing to risk the law in taking them a night's journey. So there was no hope in these directions. Her rude intellect being considered, she was entitled to a great deal of credit for seizing the horses and carriages belonging to her master, as she did it for the liberation of her children.

Knowing others at the same time, who were wanting to visit Canada, she consulted with five of this class, males and females, and they mutually decided to travel together.

It is not likely that they knew much about the roads, nevertheless they reached Wilmington, Delaware, pretty direct, and ventured up into the heart of the town in carriages, looking as innocent as if they were going to meeting to hear an old-fashioned Southern sermon—"Servants, obey your masters." Of course, the distinguished travelers were immediately reported to the noted Thomas Garrett, who was accustomed to transact the affairs of the Underground Rail Road in a cool masterly way. But, on this occasion, there was but little time for deliberation, but much need of haste to meet the emergency. He at once decided, that they must immediately be separated from the horses and carriages, and got out of Wilmington as quickly as possible. With the courage and skill, so characteristic of Garrett, the fugitives, under escort, were soon on their way to Kennett Square (a hot-bed of abolitionists and stock-holders of the Underground Rail Road), which place they reached safely. It so happened, that they reached Long Wood meeting-house in the evening, at which place a fair circle had convened. Being invited, they stayed awhile in the meeting, then, after remaining all night with one of the Kennett friends, they were brought to Downingtown early in the morning and thence, by daylight, within a short distance of Kimberton, and found succor with friend Lewis, at the old headquarters of the fugitives.

[A letter may be found from Miss G. A. Lewis, on page thirty-nine, throwing much light on this arrival]. After receiving friendly aid and advice while there, they were forwarded to the Committee in Philadelphia. Here further aid was afforded them, and as danger was quite obvious, they were completely divided and disguised, so that the Committee felt that they might safely be sent on to Canada in one of the regular trains considered most private.

Considering the condition of the slave mother and her children and friends, all concerned rejoiced, that they had had the courage to use their master's horses and vehicles as they did.

EIGHT AND A HALF MONTHS SECRETED.

WASHINGTON SOMLOR, ALIAS JAMES MOORE.

But few could tell of having been eye-witnesses to outrages more revolting and disgraceful than Washington Somlor. He arrived per steamer Pennsylvania (secreted), directly from Norfolk, Virginia, in 1855. He was thirty-two years of age—a man of medium size and quite intelligent. A merchant by the name of Smith owned Washington.

Eight and a half months before escaping, Washington had been secreted in order to shun both master and auction-block. Smith believed in selling, flogging, cobbing, paddling, and all other kinds of torture, by which he could inflict punishment in order to make the slaves feel his power. He thus tyrannized over about twenty-five head.

Being naturally passionate, when in a brutal mood, he made his slaves suffer unmercifully. Said Washington, "On one occasion, about two months before I was secreted, he had five of the slaves (some of them women) tied across a barrel, lashed with the cow-hide and then cobbed—this was a common practice."

Such treatment was so inhuman and so incredible, that the Committee hesitated at first to give credence to the statement, and only yielded when facts and evidences were given which seemed incontestible.

The first effort to come away was made on the steamship City of Richmond. Within sixty miles of Philadelphia, in consequence of the ice obstruction in the river, the steamer had to go back. How sad Washington felt at thus having his hopes broken to pieces may be imagined but cannot be described. Great as was his danger, when the steamer returned to Norfolk, he was safely gotten off the boat and under the eye of officers walked away. Again he was secreted in his old doleful quarters, where he waited patiently for the Spring. It came. Again the opportunity for another trial was presented, and it was seized unhesitatingly. This time, his tried faith was rewarded with success. He came through safely to the Committee's satisfaction as well as his own. The recital of his sufferings and experience had a very inspiring effect on those who had the pleasure of seeing Wash. in Philadelphia.

Although closely secreted in Norfolk, he had, through friends, some little communication with the outside world. Among other items of information which came to his ears, was a report that his master was being pressed by his creditors, and had all his slaves advertised for sale. An item still more sad also reached his ear, to the effect that his wife had been sold away to North Carolina, and thus separated from her child, two years old. The child was given as a present to a niece of the master. While this is only a meagre portion of his interesting story, it was considered at the time sufficient to identify him should the occasion ever require it. We content ourselves, therefore, simply with giving what was recorded on the book. Wash. spent a short while in Philadelphia in order to recruit, after which, he went on North, where colored men were free.

ARTHUR FOWLER, alias BENJAMIN JOHNSON.

ARTHUR came from Spring Hill, Maryland. Edward Fowler held Arthur in fetters and usurped authority over him as his lord and master. Arthur saw certain signs connected with his master's family which presaged to him that the day was not far distant, when somebody would have to be sold to raise money to pamper the appetites of some of the superior members of the patriarchal institution. Among these provocations were indulgence in a great deal of extravagance, and the growing up of a number of young masters and mistresses. Arthur would often look at the heirs, and the very thought of their coming into possession, would make him tremble. Nothing so affected Arthur's mind so much in moving him to make a bold stroke for freedom as these heirs.

Under his old master, the usage had been bad enough, but he feared that it would be a great deal worse under the sons and daughters. He therefore wisely concluded to avoid the impending danger by availing himself of the Underground Rail Road. After completing such arrangements as he deemed necessary, he started, making his way along pretty successfully, with the exception of a severe encounter with Jack Frost, by which his feet were badly bitten. He was not discouraged, however, but was joyful over his victory and hopeful in view of his prospects in Canada. Arthur was about thirty years of age, medium size, and of a dark color. The Committee afforded him needed assistance, and sent him off.

SUNDRY ARRIVALS.

About the 1st of June, 1855, the following arrivals were noted in the record book:

EMORY ROBERTS, *alias* WILLIAM KEMP, Talbot Co., Maryland; DANIEL PAYNE, Richmond, Virginia; HARRIET MAYO, JOHN JUDAH, and RICHARD BRADLEY, Petersburg and Richmond; JAMES CRUMMILL, SAMUEL JONES, TOLBERT JONES, and HENRY HOWARD, Haverford Co., Maryland; LEWIS CHILDS, Richmond, DANIEL BENNETT, *alias* HENRY WASHINGTON, and wife (MARTHA,) and two children (GEORGE and a nameless babe).

20

The road at this time, was doing a fair business, in a quiet way. Passengers were managing to come, without having to suffer in any very violent manner, as many had been called upon to do in making similar efforts. The success attending some of these passengers was partly attributable to the intelligence of individuals, who, for years, had been planning and making preparations to effect the end in view. Besides, the favorableness of the weather tended also to make travel more pleasant than in colder seasons of the year.

While matters were thus favorable, the long stories of individual suffering and of practices and customs among young and old masters and mistresses, were listened to attentively, although the short summer nights hardly afforded sufficient opportunity for writing out details.

EMORY arrived safely from Talbot county. As a slave, he had served Edward Lloyd. He gave his master the character of treating his slaves with great severity. The "lash" was freely used "on women as well as men, old and young." In this kind of property Lloyd had invested to the extent of "about five hundred head," so Emory thought. Food and clothing for this large number were dealt out very stintedly, and daily suffering was the common lot of slaves under Lloyd.

EMORY was induced to leave, to avoid a terrible flogging, which had been promised him for the coming Monday. He was a married man, but exercised no greater control over his wife than over himself. She was hired on a neighboring plantation; the way did not seem open for her to accompany him, so he had to leave her behind. His mother, brothers, and sisters had to be left also. The ties of kindred usually strong in the breasts of slaves, were hard for Emory to break, but, by a firm resolution, that he would not stay on Lloyd's plantation to endure the impending flogging, he was nerved to surmount every obstacle in the way of carrying his intention into execution. He came to the Committee hungry and in want of clothing, and was aided in the usual way.

DANIEL PAYNE. This traveler was a man who might be said to be full of years, infirm, and well-nigh used up under a Virginia task-master. But within the old man's breast a spark was burning for freedom, and he was desirous of reaching free land, on which to lay his body when life's toil ended. So the Committee sympathized with him, aided him and sent him on to Canada. He was owned by a man named M. W. Morris, of Richmond, whence he fled.

HARRIET MAYO, John Judah, and Richard Bradley were the next who brought joy and victory with them.

HARRIET was a tall, well-made, intelligent young woman, twenty-two years of age. She spoke with feelings of much bitterness against her master, James Cuthbert, saying that he was a "very hard man," at the same time, adding that his "wife was still worse." Harriet "had been sold once."

She admitted however, having been treated kindly a part of her life. In escaping, she had to leave her "poor old mother" with no hope of ever seeing her again; likewise she regretted having to leave three brothers, who kindly aided her to escape. But having her heart bent on freedom, she resolved that nothing should deter her from putting forth efforts to get out of Slavery.

JOHN was a mulatto, of genteel address, well clothed, and looked as if he had been "well fed." Miss Eliza Lambert had the honor of owning John, and was gracious enough to allow him to hire his time for one hundred and ten dollars per annum. After this sum was punctually paid, John could do what he pleased with any surplus earnings. Now, as he was fond of nice clothing, he was careful to earn a balance sufficient to gratify this love. By similar means, many slaves were seen in southern cities elegantly dressed, and, strangers and travelers from the North gave all the credit to "indulgent masters," not knowing the facts in the case.

John accused his mistress of being hard in money matters, not caring how the servants fared, so she got "plenty of money out of them." For himself, however, he admitted that he had never experienced as great abuses as many had. He was fortunate in being wedded to a free wife, who was privy to all his plans and schemes looking forth to freedom, and fully acquiesced in the arrangement of matters, promising to come on after he should reach Canada. This promise was carried out in due time, and they were joyfully re-united under the protection of the British Lion.

RICHARD was about twenty-seven. For years the hope of freedom had occupied his thoughts, and many had been the longing desires to see the way open by which he could safely get rid of oppression. He was sufficiently intelligent to look at Slavery in all its bearings, and to smart keenly under even ordinarily mild treatment. Therefore, he was very happy in the realization of his hopes. In the recital of matters touching his slave life, he alluded to his master, Samuel Ball, as a "very hard man," utterly unwilling to allow his servants any chance whatever. For reasons which he considered judicious, he kept the matter of his contemplated escape wholly private, not even revealing it to his wife. Probably he felt that she would not be willing to give him up, not even for freedom, as long as she could not go too. Her name was Emily, and she belonged to William Bolden. How she felt when she learned of her husband's escape is for the imagination to picture. These three interesting passengers were brought away snugly secreted in Captain B's. schooner.

JAMES CRUMMILL, SAMUEL and TOLBERT JONES and HENRY HOWARD. This party united to throw off the yoke in Haverford county, Md.

JAMES, SAMUEL and TOLBERT had been owned by William Hutchins. They agreed in giving Hutchins the character of being a notorious "frolicker," and a " very hard master." Under him, matters were growing " worse and worse." Before the old master's death times were much better.

HENRY did not live under the same authority that his three companions were subjected to, but belonged to Philip Garrison. The continual threat to sell harassed Henry so much, that he saw no chance of peace or happiness in the future. So one day the master laid the "last straw on the camel's back," and not another day would Henry stay. Many times it required a pretty heavy pressure to start off a number of young men, but in this instance they seemed unwilling to wait to be worn out under the yoke and violent treatment, or to become encumbered with wives and children before leaving. All were single, with the exception of James, whose wife was free, and named Charlotte; she understood about his going to Canada, and, of course, was true to him.

These young men had of course been reared under circumstances altogether unfavorable to mental development. Nevertheless they had fervent aspirations to strike for freedom.

LEWIS GILES belonged, in the prison-house of bondage, in the city of Richmond, and owed service to a Mr. Lewis Hill, who made it a business to keep slaves expressly to hire out, just as a man keeps a livery stable. Lewis was not satisfied with this arrangement; he could see no fair play in it. In fact, he was utterly at variance with the entire system of Slavery, and, a long time before he left, had plans laid with a view of escaping. Through one of the Underground Rail Road Agents the glad tidings were borne to him that a passage might be procured on a schooner for twenty-five dollars. Lewis at once availed himself of this offer, and made his arrangements accordingly. He, however, made no mention of this contemplated movement to his wife, Louisa; and, to her astonishment, he was soon among the missing. Lewis was a fine-looking " article," six feet high, well proportioned, and of a dark chestnut color, worth probably $1200, in the Richmond market. Touching his slave life, he said that he had been treated " pretty well," except that he " had been sold several times." Intellectually he was above the average run of slaves. He left on the twenty-third of April, and arrived about the second of June, having, in the meantime, encountered difficulties and discouragements of various kinds. His safe arrival, therefore, was attended with unusual rejoicing.

DANIEL BENNETT and his wife and children were the next in order. A woman poorly clad with a babe just one month old in her arms, and a little boy at her side, who could scarcely toddle, together with a husband who had never dared under penalty of the laws to protect her or her little ones, presented a most painfully touching picture. It was easy enough to see, that they had been crushed. The husband had been owned by Captain James Taylor—the wife and children by George Carter.

The young mother gave Carter a very bad character, affirming, that it was a "common practice with him to flog the slaves, stripped entirely naked "— that she had herself been so flogged, since she had been a married woman. How the husband was treated, the record book is silent. He was about thirty-two—the wife about twenty-seven. Especial pains were taken to provide aid and sympathy to this family in their destitution, fleeing under such peculiarly trying circumstances and from such loathsome brutality. They were from Aldie P. O., Loudon County, Virginia, and passed through the hands of the Committee about the 11th of June. What has been their fate since is not known.

SUNDRY ARRIVALS ABOUT JANUARY FIRST, 1855.

VERENEA MERCER.

The steamship Pennsylvania, on one of her regular trips from Richmond, brought one passenger, of whom the Captain had no knowledge; no permission had been asked of any officer of the boat. Nevertheless, Verenea Mercer managed, by the most extraordinary strategy, to secrete herself on the steamer, and thus succeeded in reaching Philadelphia. She was following her husband, who escaped about nine months before her.

Verenea was about forty-one years of age, of a dark chestnut color, prepossessing in manners, intelligent and refined. She belonged to the slave population of Richmond, and was owned by Thomas W. Quales. According to her testimony, she had not received severe treatment during the eight and a half years that she had been in his hands. Previous to his becoming the owner of Verenea, it might have been otherwise, although nothing is recorded in proof of this inference, except that she had the misfortune to lose her first husband by a sale. Of course she was left a widow, in which state she remained nine years, at the expiration of which period, she married a man by the name of James Mercer, whose narrative may be found on p. 54.

How James got off, and where he went, Verenea knew quite well; consequently, in planning to reach him, she resorted to the same means by which he achieved success. The Committee rendered her the usual aid, and sent her on direct to her husband in Canada. Without difficulty of any kind she reached there safely, and found James with arms wide open to embrace her. Frequent tidings reached the Committee, that they were getting along quite well in Toronto.

On the same day (January 1st), PETER DERRICKSON and CHARLES PURNELL arrived from Berlin, Worcester county, Maryland. Both were able-bodied young men, twenty-four and twenty-six years of age, just the kind that a trader, or an experienced slave-holder in the farming business, would be most likely to select for doing full days' work in the field, or for bringing high prices in the market.

Peter toiled and toiled, with twenty others, on John Derrickson's farm. And although Derrickson was said to be a "mild master," Peter decidedly objected to working for him for nothing. He thought over his situation a great deal, and finally came to the conclusion, that he must get from under the yoke, if possible, before entering another New Year. His friend Charles he felt could be confided in, therefore he made up his mind, that he would broach the question of Canada and the Underground Rail Road to him. Charles was equally ready and willing to enter into any practical arrangements by which he could get rid of his no-pay task-master, and be landed safely in Canada. After taking into account the dangers likely to attend such a struggle, they concluded that they would risk all and try their luck, as many had done before them.

" What made you leave, Charles?" said a member of the Committee.

" I left because I wanted my time and money for myself."

No one could gainsay such a plain common-sense answer as that. The fact, that he had to leave his parents, three brothers, and five sisters, all in slavery, brought sad reflections.

LLOYD HACKET, alias Perry Watkins and WILLIAM HENRY JOHNSON, alias John Wesley.

No weather was too cold for travel, nor way too rough, when the slave was made to feel by his heartless master, that he was going to sell him or starve him to death.

Lloyd had toiled on until he had reached fifty-five, before he came to the conclusion, that he could endure the treatment of his master, John Griffin, no longer, simply because " he was not good to feed and clothe," and was a " great fighter." Moreover, he would " never suffer his slaves to stop work on account of bad weather." Not only was his master cruel in these particulars, but he was equally cruel with regard to selling. Georgia was continually held up to the slaves with a view of producing a wholesome fear, but in this instance, as in many similar ones, it only awakened desires to seek flight via the Underground Rail Road.

Lloyd, convinced by experience, that matters with him would be no better, but worse and worse, resolved that he would start with the opening of the New Year to see if he could not find a better country than the one that he was then in.

He consulted William, who, although a young man of only twenty-four years of age, had the hate of slavery exceedingly strong in his heart, and was at once willing to accompany Lloyd—ready to face cold weather and start on a long walk if freedom could be thus purchased, and his master, John Hall, thus defeated. So Lloyd took a heroic leave of his wife, Mary Ann, and their little boy, one brother, one sister, and two nieces, and at once set out with William, like pilgrims and strangers seeking a better country—where they would not have to go "hungry" and be "worked hard in all weather," threatened with the auction-block, and brutally flogged if they merely seemed unwilling to endure a yoke too grievous to be borne. Both these travelers were mulattoes, and but for the crushing influences that they had lived under would have made smart men—as it was they showed plainly, that they were men of shrewd sense.

Inadvertently at the time of their arrival, the names of the State and place whence they fled were not entered on the book.

In traveling they suffered severely from hunger and the long distance they had to walk, but having succeeded victoriously they were prepared to rejoice all the more.

DAVID EDWARDS. John J. Slater, coachmaker of Petersburg, Virginia, if he is still living, and should see these items, may solve what may have been for years a great mystery to him—namely, that David, his man-servant, was enjoying himself in Philadelphia about the first week in January, 1855, receiving free accommodations and obtaining letters of introduction to friends in Canada. Furthermore, that David alleged that he was induced to escape because he (the coachmaker) was a very hard man, who took every dollar of his earnings, from which he would dole out to him only one dollar a week for board, etc., a sum less than David could manage to get along with.

David was thirty years of age, black, weighed one hundred and forty-five pounds, and was worth one thousand dollars. He left his wife behind.

BEVERLY GOOD and GEORGE WALKER, alias Austin Valentine. These passengers came from Petersburg, per steamship Pennsylvania. Richard Perry was lording it over Beverly, who was a young man of twenty-four years of age, dark, medium size, and possessed of a quick intellect—just the man that an Underground Rail Road agent in the South could approach with assurance with questions such as these—"What do you think of Slavery?" "Did you ever hear of the Underground Rail Road?" "How would you like to be free?" "Would you be willing to go to Canada if you could get off safely," etc., etc.

Such questions at once kindled into a flame the sparks of freedom lying dormant in the heart. Although uttered in a whisper, they had a wondrous ring about them, and a wide-awake bondman instantly grasped their meaning. Beverly was of this class; he needed no arguments to prove that he was daily robbed of his rights—that Slavery was merciless and freedom the God-given right of all mankind. Of him, therefore, there was no fear that he would betray his trust or flinch too soon when cramped up in his hiding-place on the steamer.

His comrade, George, was likewise of the same mettle, and was aided in the same way. George, however, had more age on his side, being about forty-three. He was about six feet high, with marked physical and mental abilities, but Slavery had had its heel upon his neck. And who could then have risen?

Eliza Jones held the deed for George, and by her he was hired as foreman in a tobacco factory, in which position his duties were onerous—especially to one with a heavy, bleeding heart, throbbing daily for freedom, while, at the same time, mournfully brooding over past wrongs. Of these wrongs one incident must suffice. He had been married twice, and had been the father of six children by his first wife; at the command of his owner the wedded relations were abruptly broken, and he was obliged to seek another wife. In entering this story on the book at the time of the arrival, the concluding words were written thus: "This story is thrilling, but time will not allow its being penned."

Although safely under the protection of the British Lion, George's heart was in Virginia, where his wife was retained. As he could not return for her deliverance, he was wise enough to resort to the pen, hoping in this way to effect his grand object, as the following letter will show:

TORONTO, January 25th, 1855.

DEAR FRIEND STILL:—George Walker, of Petersburg, Va., is now in my office, and requests me to write a letter to you, and request you to write to his wife, after or according to the instructions he gave to his friend, John Brown, in your city, with whom he says you are acquainted. You will understand, of course, his reason for wanting the letter wrote and posted at Philadelphia. You will please attend to it and address a letter to him (Walker) in my care. He and Beverly Good, his comrade, tender much love to you. Send them on; we are prepared for them. Yours in great haste, J. B. SMITH.

P. S.—Be sure and follow the directions given to Brown.

ADAM BROOKS, alias William Smith. Hardtown, Montgomery county, Maryland, lost a rather promising "article of merchandise," in the person of Adam. The particulars of his going are on this wise: John Phillips, his so-called master, believed in selling, and practiced accordingly, to the extent at least of selling Adam's mother, brother, and sister only two years before his escape.

If Adam had known nothing else against Phillips, this was enough in all conscience to have awakened his deadly hate; but, added to this, Phillips was imprudent in his habit of threatening to "sell," etc. This kept the old wound in Adam's heart continually bleeding and forced him to the conclusion, that his master was not only a hard man, as a driver on the farm, but that at heart he was actually a bad man. Furthermore, that it was his duty to break his fetters and seek his freedom in Canada.

In thus looking at his situation, his mind was worked up to fever heat, and he resolved that, let the consequences be what they might, go he must. In this promising state of mind he started, at an appointed time, for Pennsylvania, and, sure enough, he succeeded. Having the appearance of a desirable working-hand, a Pennsylvania farmer prevailed on him to stop for a time. It was not long before the folly of this halt was plainly discernible, as his master had evidently got wind of his whereabouts, and was pretty hot in pursuit. Word reached Adam, however, barely in time for him to make his escape through the aid of friends.

In coming into the hands of the Committee he needed no persuading to go to Canada; he was occupied with two interesting problems, to go back or to go forward. But he set his face hopefully towards Canada, and had no thought of stopping short thereof. In stature, he was small; color, black; countenance, pleasant, and intellect, medium. As to his fitness for making a good citizen in Canada the Committee had no doubt.

SARAH A. DUNAGAN. Having no one to care for her, and, having been threatened with the auction-block, Sarah mustered pluck and started out in search of a new home among strangers beyond the borders of slave territory. According to her story, she "was born free" in the State of Delaware, but had been "bound out" to a man by the name of George Churchman, living in Wilmington. Here she averred, that she "had been flogged repeatedly," and had been otherwise ill-treated, while no one interfered to take her part. Consequently she concluded, that although she was born free, she would not be likely to be benefited thereby unless she made her escape on the Underground Rail Road. This idea of freedom continued to agitate Sarah's mind until she decided to leave forthwith. She was a young mulatto woman, single, and told her story of hardships and of the dread of being sold, in a manner to elicit much sympathy. She had a mother living in New Castle, named Ann Eliza Kingslow. It was no uncommon thing for free-born persons in slave States to lose their birth-right in a manner similar to that by which Sarah feared that she had lost hers.

"Arrived JOSEPH HALL, JR., son of Joseph Hall, of Norfolk, Virginia." This is all that is recorded of this passenger, yet it is possible that this item of news may lead to the recognition of Joseph, should he still happen to be of the large multitude of fugitives scattered over the land amongst the living.

ISAAC D. DAVIS. In fleeing from bondage, in Maryland, Davis was induced to stop, as many others were, in Pennsylvania. Not comprehending the Fugitive Slave Law he fancied that he would be safe so long as he kept matters private concerning his origin. But in this particular he labored under a complete delusion—when he least dreamed of danger the slave-catchers were scenting him close. Of their approach, however, he was fortunate enough to be notified in time to place himself in the hands of the Committee, who soon held out Canada to him, as the only sure refuge for him, and all others similarly situated. His fears of being carried back opened his eyes, and understanding, so that he could readily see the force of this argument, and accepting the proffered aid of the Committee was sent on his way rejoicing.   He had been away from his master eighteen months, and in the meanwhile had married a wife in Pennsylvania. What became of them after this flight the book contains no record.

JACOB MATTHIAS BOYER left at about the age of twenty.   He had no idea of working in the condition of a slave, but if he had not been threatened with the auction-block, he might have remained much longer than he did.   He had been owned by Richard Carman, cashier of one of the Annapolis banks, and who had recently died.   Jacob fled from Annapolis.   Very little record was made of either master or slave.   Probably no incidents were related of sufficient importance, still the Committee felt pleased to receive one so young.   Indeed, it always afforded the Committee especial satisfaction to see children, young people, and females escaping from the prison-house.   Jacob was of a dark hue, a little below medium stature.

ZECHARIAH MEAD, alias John Williams.   This traveler had been in the house of bondage in Maryland, doing service for Charles C. Owens, to whom he belonged.   According to Zechariah's statement, his mistress had been very unfortunate with her slave property, having lost fifteen head out of twenty in a similar manner to that by which she lost Zechariah.   Thus she had been considerably reduced in circumstances.   But Zechariah had no compassion on her whatever, but insisted that she was a hard mistress.   Doubtless Zechariah was prompted to flee by the "bad" example of others who had succeeded in making good their escape, before he had made up his mind to leave.   He was not yet quite twenty-one, but was wide-awake, and it appeared from his conversation, that he had done some close thinking before he started for freedom.   He left his father, mother, and three brothers, all slaves except his father.

SLAVE–HOLDER IN MARYLAND WITH THREE COLORED WIVES.

JAMES GRIFFIN ALIAS THOMAS BROWN.

JAMES was a tiller of the soil under the yoke of Joshua Hitch, who lived on a farm about seventeen miles from Baltimore.   James spoke rather favorably of him; indeed, it was through a direct act of kindness on the part of his master that he procured the opportunity to make good his escape.   It appeared from his story, that his master's affairs had become particularly embarrassed, and the Sheriff was making frequent visits to his house.   This sign was interpreted to mean that James, if not others, would have to be sold before long.   The master was much puzzled to decide which way to turn.   He owned but three other adult slaves besides James, and they were females. One of them was his chief housekeeper, and with them all his social relations were of such a nature as to lead James and others to think and say that they "were all his wives." Or to use James's own language, "he had three slave women; two were sisters, and he lived with them all as his wives; two of them he was very fond of," and desired to keep them from being sold if possible. The third, he concluded he could not save, she would have to be sold. In this dilemma, he was good enough to allow James a few days' holiday, for the purpose of finding him a good master. Expressing his satisfaction and gratification, James, armed with full authority from his master to select a choice specimen, started for Baltimore.

On reaching Baltimore, however, James carefully steered clear of all slave-holders, and shrewdly turned his attention to the matter of getting an Underground Rail Road ticket for Canada. After making as much inquiry as he felt was safe, he came to the conclusion to walk of nights for a long distance. He examined his feet and legs, found that they were in good order, and his faith and hope strong enough to remove a mountain. Besides several days still remained in which he was permitted to look for a new master, and these he decided could be profitably spent in making his way towards Canada. So off he started, at no doubt a very diligent pace, for at the end of the first night's journey, he had made much headway, but at the expense of his feet.

His faith was stronger than ever. So he rested next day in the woods, concealed, of course, and the next evening started with fresh courage and renewed perseverance. Finally, he reached Columbia, Pennsylvania, and there he had the happiness to learn, that the mountain which at first had tried his faith so severely, was removed, and friendly hands were reached out and a more speedy and comfortable mode of travel advised. He was directed to the Vigilance Committee in Philadelphia, from whom he received friendly aid, and all necessary information respecting Canada and how to get there.

James was thirty-one years of age, rather a fine-looking man, of a chestnut color, and quite intelligent. He had been a married man, but for two years before his escape, he had been a widower—that is, his wife had been sold away from him to North Carolina, and in that space of time he had received only three letters from her; he had given up all hope of ever seeing her again. He had two little boys living in Baltimore, whom he was obliged to leave. Their names were Edward and William. What became of them afterwards was never known at the Philadelphia station.

James's master was a man of about fifty years of age—who had never been lawfully married, yet had a number of children on his place who were of great concern to him in the midst of other pressing embarrassments. Of course, the Committee never learned how matters were settled after James left, but, in all probability, his wives, Nancy and Mary (sisters), and Lizzie, with all the children, had to be sold.

CAPTAIN F. ARRIVES WITH NINE PASSENGERS.

PETER HEINES, Eatontown, North Carolina; MATTHEW BODAMS, Plymouth, North Carolina; JAMES MORRIS, South End, North Carolina; CHARLES THOMPSON, CHARITY THOMPSON, NATHANIEL BOWSER, and THOMAS COOPER, Portsmouth, Virginia; GEORGE ANDERSON, Elkton, Maryland.

Their arrival was announced by Thomas Garrett as follows:

WILMINGTON, 7th mo., 19th, 1856.

RESPECTED FRIEND, WILLIAM STILL :—I now have the pleasure of consigning to thy care four able-bodied human beings from North Carolina, and five from Virginia, one of which is a girl twelve or thirteen years of age, the rest all men. After thee has seen and conversed with them, thee can determine what is best to be done with them. I am assured they are such as can take good care of themselves. Elijah Pennypacker, some time since, informed me he could find employment in his neighborhood for two or three good hands. I should think that those from Carolina would be about as safe in that neighborhood as any place this side of Canada. Wishing our friends a safe trip, I remain thy sincere friend,   THOS. GARRETT.

After conferring with Harry Craige, we have concluded to send five or six of them to-night in the cars, and the balance, if those go safe, to-morrow night, or in the steam-boat on Second day morning, directed to the Anti-Slavery office.

There was much rejoicing over these select passengers, and very much interesting information was elicited from them.

PETER was only twenty-one years of age, composed of equal parts of Anglo-Saxon and Anglo-African blood—rather a model-looking "article," with a fair share of intelligence. As a slave, he had fared pretty well— he had neither been abused nor stinted of food or clothing, as many others had been. His duties had been to attend upon his master (and reputed father), Elias Heines, Esq., a lawyer by profession in North Carolina.

No charges whatever appear to have been made against Mr. Heines, according to the record book; but Peter seemed filled with great delight at the prospects ahead, as well as with the success that had attended his efforts thus far in striking for freedom.

JAMES was twenty-seven years of age. His experience had been quite different from that of Peter's. The heel of a woman, by the name of Mrs. Ann McCourt, had been on James's neck, and she had caused him to suffer severely. As James recounted his grievances, while under the rule, he by no means gave her a very flattering character, but, on the contrary, he plainly stated, that she was a "desperate woman"—that he had "never known any good of her," and that he was moved to escape to get rid of her. In other words she had threatened to sell him; this well nigh produced a frenzy in James's mind, for too well did he remember, that he had already been sold three times, and in different stages of his bondage had been treated quite cruelly. In the change of masters he was positive in saying, that he had not found a good one, and, besides, he entertained the belief that such personages were very rare.

Those of the Committee who listened to James were not a little amazed at his fluency, intelligence and earnestness, and acknowledged that he dealt unusually telling blows against the Patriarchal Institution.

MATTHEW was twenty-three years of age, very stout—no fool—a man of decided resolution, and of the very best black complexion produced in the South. Matthew had a very serious bill of complaints against Samuel Simmons, who professed to own him (Matthew), both body and mind, while in this world at least. Among these complaints was the charge of ill-treatment. Nevertheless Matthew's joy and pleasure were matchless over his Underground Rail Road triumph, and the prospect of being so soon out of the land and reach of Slavery, and in a land where he could enjoy his freedom as others enjoyed theirs. Indeed the entire band evinced similar feelings. Matthew left a brother in Martin county.

Further sketches of this interesting company were not entered on the book at the time, perhaps on account of the great press of Underground Rail Road business which engaged the attention of the acting Committee. However, they were all duly cared for, and counselled to go to Canada, where their rights would be protected by a strong and powerful government, and they could enjoy all the rights of citizenship in common with " all the world and the rest of mankind." And especially were they advised to get education; to act as men, and remember those still in bonds as bound with them, and that they must not forget to write back, after their arrival in Canada, to inform their friends in Philadelphia of their prospects, and what they thought of the "goodly land." Thus, with the usual Underground Rail Road passports, they were again started Canada-ward. Without difficulty of any kind they duly reached Canada, and a portion of them wrote back as follows:

"TORONTO, C. W., Aug. 17th, 1856.

MR. STILL:—Dear Sir—These few lines may find you as they leave us, we are well at present and arrived safe in Toronto. Give our respects to Mrs. S.—— and daughter. Toronto is a very extensive place. We have plenty of pork, beef and mutton. There are five market houses and many churches. Female wages is 62½ cents per day, men's wages is $1 and york shilling. We are now boarding at Mr. George Blunt's, on Centre street, two doors from Elm, back of Lawyer's Hall, and when you write to us, direct your letter to the care of Mr. George Blunt, &c. (Signed), James Monroe, Peter Heines, Henry James Morris, and Matthew Bodams."

This intelligence was very gratifying, and most assuredly added to the pleasurable contemplation of having the privilege of holding out a helping hand to the fleeing bondman. From James Morris, one of this company, however, letters of a painful nature were received, touching his wife in bonds, setting forth her "awful" situation and appealing to the Committee to use their best endeavors to rescue her, with her child, from Slavery. One of these letters, so full of touching sentiments of affection and appeal on behalf of his wife, is as follows:

TORONTO, Canada West, upper, 18th day of the 9th mo., 1856.

MR. WILLIAM STILL:—Dear Sir—I hope these lines may find you and your family as they leave me give my respects to little Caroline and her mother.

Dear Sir, I have received two letters from my wife since I saw you, and the second was awful. I am sorry to say she says she has been treated awful since I left, and she told the lady she thought she was left free and she told her she was as much slave as ever she was that the state was not to be settled until her death and it would be a meracle if she and her child got it then and that her master left a great many relations and she diden no what they would do. Mr. Still dear sir I am very sorry to hear my wife and child are slaves if you please dear sir inform me what to do for my dear wife and child. She said she has been threatened to be put in jail three times since I left also she tells me that she is wash-ing for the captain of a vesel that use to run to Petersburg but now he runs to Baltimore and he has promas to take her to Delaware or New York for 50 dollars and she had not the money, she sent to me and I sent her all I had which was 5 dollars dear sir can you inform me what to do with a case of this kind the captains name is Thomas.

My wife is name lucy an morris my child is name lot, if you please dear sir answer me as soon as you can posable.   HENRY JAMES MORRIS, Toronto C. W.

Henry James Morris in care of Wm. George Blunt, Centre st., 2 doors from Elam.

This sad letter made a mournful impression, as it was not easy to see how her deliverance was to be effected. One feature, however, about this epistle afforded much satisfaction, namely, to know, that James did not forget his poor wife and child, who were in the prison-house. Many months after this first letter came to hand, Mrs. Dr. Willis, one of the first ladies in Toronto, wrote on his behalf as follows:

TORONTO, 15th June, Monday morning, 1857.

To MR. STILL, DEAR SIR:—I write you this letter for a respectable young man (his name is James Morris), he passed through your hands July of last year (1856), and has just had a letter from his wife, whom he left behind in Virginia, that she and her child are likely to be sold. He is very anxious about this and wishful that she could get away by some vessel or otherwise. His wife's name is Lucy Morris; the child's name is Lot Mor-ris; the lady's name she lives with is a Mrs. Hine (I hope I spell her name right, Hine), at the corner of Duke street and Washington street, in Norfolk city, Virginia. She is hired out to this rich old widow lady. James Morris wishes me to write you—he has saved forty dollars, and will send it to you whenever it is required, to bring her on to Toronto, Canada West. It is in the bank ready upon call. Will you please, sir, direct your letter in reply to this, to a Mrs. Ringgold, Centre street, two doors from Elam street, Toronto, Canada West, as I will be out of town. I write this instead of Mr. Thomas Henning, who is just about leaving for England. Hoping you will reply soon, I remain, sir,

Respectfully yours,   AGNES WILLIS.

Whether James ever succeeded in recovering his wife and child, is not known to the writer. Many similarly situated were wont to appeal again and again, until growing entirely hopeless, they would conclude to marry.

Here it may be remarked, with reference to marrying, that of the great number of fugitives in Canada, the male sex was largely in preponderance over the female, and many of them were single young men. This class found themselves very acceptable to Irish girls, and frequently legal alliances were the result. And it is more than likely, that there are white women in Canada to-day, who are married to some poor slave woman's fugitive husband.

Verily, the romantic and tragic phases of the Underground Rail Road are without number, if not past finding out.

Scarcely had the above-mentioned nine left the Philadelphia depot, ere the following way-worn travelers came to hand:

PERRY SHEPHARD, and ISAAC REED, Eastern Shore, Maryland; GEORGE SPERRYMAN, *alias* THOMAS JOHNSON, Richmond; VALENTINE SPIRES, near Petersburg; DANIEL GREEN, *alias* GEORGE TAYLOR, Leesburg, Virginia; JAMES JOHNSON, *alias* WILLIAM GILBERT and wife HARRIET, Prince George's county, Maryland; HENRY COOPER, and WILLIAM ISRAEL SMITH, Middletown, Delaware ; ANNA DORSEY, Maryland.

Although starting from widely separated localities without the slightest communication with each other in the South, each separate passenger earnestly bent on freedom, had endured suffering, hunger, and perils, by land and water, sustained by the hope of ultimate freedom.

PERRY SHEPHARD and ISAAC REED reported themselves as having fled from the Eastern Shore of Maryland ; that they had there been held to service or Slavery by Sarah Ann Burgess, and Benjamin Franklin Houston, from whom they fled. No incidents of slave life or travel were recorded, save that Perry left his wife Milky Ann, and two children, Nancy and Rebecca (free). Also Isaac left his wife, Hester Ann Louisa, and the following named children : Philip Henry, Harriet Ann and Jane Elizabeth.

GEORGE SPERRYMAN's lot was cast amongst the oppressed in the city of Richmond, Va. Of the common ills of slave life, George could speak from experience ; but little of his story, however, was recorded at the time. He had reached the Committee through the regular channel—was adjudged worthy of aid and encouragement, and they gave it to him freely. Nickless Templeman was the loser in this instance; how he bore the misfortune the Committee was not apprised. Without question, the property was delighted with getting rid of the owner.

VALENTINE SPIRES came a fellow-passenger with George, having "took out" the previous Christmas, from a place called Dunwoody, near Petersburg. He was held to service in that place by Dr. Jesse Squires. Under his oppressive rules and demands, Valentine had been convinced that there could be no peace, consequently he turned his attention to one idea—freedom and the Underground Rail Road, and with this faith, worked his way through to the Committee, and was received, and aided of course.

DAVID GREEN, fled from Warrington, near Leesburg. Elliott Curlett so alarmed David by threatening to sell him, that the idea of liberty immediately took possession in David's mind. David had suffered many hardships at the hands of his master, but when the auction-block was held up to him, that was the worst cut of all. He became a thinker right away. Although he had a wife and one child in Slavery, he decided to flee for his freedom at all hazards, and accordingly he carried out his firm resolution.

JAMES JOHNSON. This "article" was doing unrequited labor as the slave of Thomas Wallace, in Prince George county, Maryland. He was a stout and rugged-looking man, of thirty-five years of age. On escaping, he was fortunate enough to bring his wife, Harriet with him. She was ten years younger than himself, and had been owned by William T. Wood, by whom she said that she had "been well treated." But of late, this Wood had taken to liquor, and she felt in danger of being sold. She knew that rum ruined the best of slave-holders, so she was admonished to get out of danger as soon as possible.

CHARLES HENRY COOPER and WILLIAM ISRAEL SMITH. These passengers were representatives of the peculiar Institution of Middletown, Delaware. Charles was owned by Catharine Mendine, and William by John P. Cather. According to their confession, Charles and William it seemed had been thinking a good deal over the idea of "working for nothing," of being daily driven to support others, while they were rendered miserable thereby. So they made up their minds to try the Underground Rail Road, "hit or miss." This resolution was made and carried into effect (on the part of Charles at least), at the cost of leaving a mother, three brothers, and three sisters in Slavery, without hope of ever seeing them again. The ages of Charles and William were respectively twenty-two and twenty-one. Both stout and well-made young men, with intellects well qualified to make the wilderness of Canada bud and blossom as the rose, and thitherward they were dispatched.

ANNA DORSEY became tired of Slavery in Maryland, where she reported that she had been held to service by a slave-holder, known by the name of Eli Molesworth. The record is silent as to how she was treated. As a slave, she had been brought up a seamstress, and was quite intelligent. Age twenty-two, mulatto.

OWEN AND OTHO TAYLOR'S FLIGHT WITH HORSES, Etc.

THREE BROTHERS, TWO OF THEM WITH WIVES AND CHILDREN.

About the latter part of March, 1856, Owen Taylor and his wife, Mary Ann, and their little son, Edward, together with a brother and his wife and two children, and a third brother, Benjamin, arrived from near Clear

Springs, nine miles from Hagerstown, Maryland. They all left their home, or rather escaped from the prison-house, on Easter Sunday, and came *via* Harrisburg, where they were assisted and directed to the Vigilance Committee in Philadelphia. A more interesting party had not reached the Committee for a long time.

The three brothers were intelligent, and heroic, and, in the resolve to obtain freedom, not only for themselves, but for their wives and children desperately in earnest. They had counted well the cost of this struggle for liberty, and had fully made up their minds that if interfered with by slave-catchers, somebody would have to bite the dust. That they had pledged themselves never to surrender alive, was obvious. Their travel-worn appearance, their attachment for each other, the joy that the tokens of friendship afforded them, the description they gave of incidents on the road, made an impression not soon to be effaced.

In the presence of a group like this Sumner's great and eloquent speech on the Barbarism of Slavery, seemed almost cold and dead,—the mute appeals of these little ones in their mother's arms—the unlettered language of these young mothers, striving to save their offspring from the doom of Slavery—the resolute and manly bearing of these brothers expressed in words full of love of liberty, and of the determination to resist Slavery to the death, in defence of their wives and children—this was Sumner's speech enacted before our eyes.

OWEN was about thirty-one years of age, but had experienced a deal of trouble. He had been married twice, and both wives were believed to be living. The first one, with their little child, had been sold in the Baltimore market, about three years before, the mother was sent to Louisiana, the child to South Carolina. Father, mother, and child, parted with no hope of ever seeing each other again in this world. After Owen's wife was sent South, he sent her his likeness and a dress; the latter was received, and she was greatly delighted with it, but he never heard of her having received his likeness. He likewise wrote to her, but he was not sure that she received his letters. Finally, he came to the conclusion that as she was forever dead to him, he would do well to marry again. Accordingly he took to himself another partner, the one who now accompanied him on the Underground Rail Road.

Omitting other interesting incidents, a reference to his handiwork will suffice to show the ability of Owen. Owen was a born mechanic, and his master practically tested his skill in various ways ; sometimes in the blacksmith shop—at other times as a wheelwright—again at making brushes and brooms, and at leisure times he would try his hand in all these crafts. This Jack-of-all-trades was, of course, very valuable to his master. Indeed his place was hard to fill.

Henry Fiery, a farmer, "about sixty-four years of age, a stout, crusty old
21

fellow," was the owner of Owen and his two brothers. Besides slaves, the old man was in possession of a wife, whose name was Martha, and seven children, who were pretty well grown up. One of the sons owned Owen's wife and two children. Owen declared, that they had been worked hard, while few privileges had been allowed them. Clothing of the poorest texture was only sparingly furnished. Nothing like Sunday raiment was ever given them; for these comforts they were compelled to do over-work of nights. For a long time the idea of escape had been uppermost in the minds of this party. The first of January, past, was the time "solemnly" fixed upon to "took out," but for some reason or other (not found on the record book), their strategical minds did not see the way altogether clear, and they deferred starting until Easter Sunday.

On that memorable evening, the men boldly harnessed two of Mr. Fiery's steeds and placing their wives and children in the carriage, started off *via* Hagerstown, in a direct line for Chambersburg, Pennsylvania, at a rate that allowed no grass to grow under the horses' feet. In this manner they made good time, reached Chambersburg safely, and ventured up to a hotel where they put up their horses. Here they bade their faithful beasts good-bye and "took out" for Harrisburg by another mode of travel, the cars. On their arrival they naturally fell into the hands of the Committee, who hurried them off to Philadelphia, apprising the Committee there of their approach by a dispatch sent ahead. Probably they had scarcely reached Philadelphia ere the Fierys were in hot haste after them, as far as Harrisburg, if not farther.

It hardly need be hinted, that the community in which the Fierys lived was deeply agitated for days after, as indeed it was along the entire route to Chambersburg, in consequence of this bold and successful movement. The horses were easily captured at the hotel, where they were left, but, of course, they were mute as to what had become of their drivers. The furious Fierys probably got wind of the fact, that they had made their way to Harrisburg. At any rate they made very diligent search at this point. While here prosecuting his hunting operations, Fiery managed to open communication with at least one member of the Harrisburg Committee, to whom his grievances were made known, but derived little satisfaction.

After the experience of a few weeks, the pursuers came to the conclusion, that there was no likelihood of recovering them through these agencies, or through the Fugitive Slave Law. In their despair, therefore, they resorted to another "dodge." All at once they became "sort-o'-friendly"—indeed more than half disposed to emancipate. The member of the Committee in Harrisburg had, it is probable, frequently left room for their great delusion, if he did not even go so far as to feed their hopes with plausible suggestions, that some assistance might be afforded by which an amicable settlement might be made between masters and slaves.

The following extract, from the Committee's letter, relative to this matter, is open to this inference, and may serve to throw some light on the subject:

HARRISBURG, April 28, '56.

FRIEND STILL :—Your last came to hand in due season, and I am happy to hear of the safe arrival of those gents.   *   *   *   *   *   *   *

I have before me the Power of Attorney of Mr. John S. Fiery, son of Mr. Henry Fiery, of Washington county, Md., the owner of those three men, two women and three children, who arrived in your town on the 24th or 25th of March. He graciously condescends to liberate the oldest in a year, and the remainder in proportional time, if they will come back ; or to sell them their time for $1300. He is sick of the job, and is ready to make any conditions. Now, if you personally can get word to them and get them to send him a letter, in my charge, informing him of their whereabouts and prospects, I think it will be the best answer I can make him. He will return here in a week or two, to know what can be done. He offers $500 to see them.

Or if you can send me word where they are, I will endeavor to write to them for his special satisfaction ; or if you cannot do either, send me your latest information, for I intend to make him spend a few more dollars, and if possible get a little sicker of this bad job. Do try and send him a few bitter pills for his weak nerves and disturbed mind.

Yours in great haste,   Jos. C. BUSTILL.

A subsequent letter from Mr. Bustill contains, besides other interesting Underground Rail Road matter, an item relative to the feeling of disappointment experienced by Mr. Fiery on learning that his property was in Canada.

HARRISBURG, May 26, '56.

FRIEND STILL :—I embrace the opportunity presented by the visit of our friend, John F. Williams, to drop you a few lines in relation to our future operations.

The Lightning Train was put on the Road on last Monday, and as the traveling season has commenced and this is the Southern route for Niagara Falls, I have concluded not to send by way of Auburn, except in cases of great danger ; but hereafter we will use the Lightning Train, which leaves here at 1½ and arrives in your city at 5 o'clock in the morning, and I will telegraph about 5½ o'clock in the afternoon, so it may reach you before you close. These four are the only ones that have come since my last. The woman has been here some time waiting for her child and her beau, which she expects here about the first of June. If possible, please keep a knowledge of her whereabouts, to enable me to inform him if he comes.   *   *   *   *   *   *   *

I have nothing more to send you, except that John Fiery has visited us again and much to his chagrin received the information of their being in Canada.

Yours as ever,   Jos. C. BUSTILL.

Whilst the Fierys were working like beavers to re-enslave these brave fugitives, the latter were daily drinking in more and more of the spirit of freedom and were busy with schemes for the deliverance of other near kin left behind under the galling yoke.

Several very interesting letters were received from Otho Taylor, relative to a raid he designed making expressly to effect the escape of his family. The two subjoined must suffice, (others, much longer, cannot now be produced, they have probably been loaned and not returned.)

APRIL 15th, 1857.

SIR—We arrived here safely. Mr. Syrus and his lady is well situated. They have a place for the year round 15 dollars per month. We are all well and hope that you are all the same. Now I wish to know whether you would please to send me some money to go after those people. Send it here if you please.   Yours truly,   OTHO TAYLOR.

WILLIAM STILL.

ST. CATHARINES, Jan. 26, 1857.

MR. WM. STILL :—Dear Sir—I write at this time in behalf of Otho Taylor. He is very anxious to go and get his family at Clear Spring, Washington county, Md. He would like to know if the Society there would furnish him the means to go after them from Philadelphia, that you will be running no risk in doing this. If the Society can do this, he would not be absent from P. more than three days.

He is so anxious to get his family from slavery that he is willing to do almost anything to get them to Canada. You may possibly recollect him—he was at your place last August. I think he can be trusted. If you can do something for him, he has the means to take him to your place.

Please let me know immediately if you can do this.   Respectfully yours,

M. A. H. WILSON.

Such appeals came very frequently from Canada, causing much sadness, as but little encouragement could be held out to such projects. In the first place, the danger attendant upon such expeditions was so fearful, and in the second place, our funds were so inadequate for this kind of work, that, in most cases, such appeals had to be refused. Of course, there were those whose continual coming, like the poor widow in the Gospel, could not be denied.

HEAVY REWARD.

THREE HUNDRED DOLLARS REWARD.—Ran away from the subscriber, residing near Bladensburg, Prince George's county, Maryland, on Saturday night, the 22d of March, 1856, my negro man, Tom Matthews, aged about 25 years, about 5 feet 9 or 10 inches high, dark copper color, full suit of bushy hair, broad face, with high cheek bones, broad and square shoulders, stands and walks very erect, though quite a sluggard in action, except in a dance, at which he is hard to beat. He wore away a black coat and brown pantaloons. I will give the above reward if taken and brought home, or secured in jail, so that I get him.

E. A. JONES, near Bladensburg, Md.

As Mr. Jones may be unaware which way his man Tom traveled, this item may inform him that his name was entered on the Underground Rail Road book April 4th, 1856, at which date he appeared to be in good health and full of hope for a safe sojourn in Canada. He was destitute, of course, just as anybody else would have been, if robbers had stripped him of every dollar of his earnings; but he felt pretty sure, that he could take care of himself in her Majesty's dominion.

The Committee, encouraged by his efforts, reached him a helping hand and sent him on to swell the goodly number in the promised land—Canada.

On the same day that Tom arrived, the Committee had the pleasure of taking JAMES JONES by the hand. He was owned by Dr. William Stewart, of King George's Court House, Maryland. He was not, however, in the service of his master at the time of his escape but was hired out in Alexandria. For some reason, not noticed in the book, James became dissatisfied, changed his name to Henry Rider, got an Underground Rail Road pass and left the Dr. and his other associations in Maryland. He was one of the well-cared for "articles," and was of very near kin to the white people, at least a half-brother (mulatto, of course). He was thirty-two years of age, medium size, hard-featured and raw-boned, but "no marks about him."

James looked as if he had had pretty good health, still the Committee thought that he would have much better in Canada. After hearing a full description of that country and of the great number of fugitives there from Maryland and other parts of the South, "Jim" felt that that was just the place he wanted to find, and was soon off with a free ticket, a letter of introduction, etc.

CAPTAIN F. ARRIVES WITH FOURTEEN "PRIME ARTI-CLES" ON BOARD.

Thomas Garrett announced this in the following letter:

WILMINGTON, 3d mo., 23d, 1856.

DEAR FRIEND, WILLIAM STILL:—Captain Fountain has arrived all safe, with the human cargo thee was inquiring for, a few days since. I had men waiting till 12 o'clock till the Captain arrived at his berth, ready to receive them; last night they then learned, that he had landed them at the Rocks, near the old Swedes church, in the care of our efficient Pilot, who is in the employ of my friend, John Hillis, and he has them now in charge. As soon as my breakfast is over, I will see Hillis and determine what is best to be done in their case. My own opinion is, we had better send them to Hook and there put them in the cars to-night and send a pilot to take them to thy house. As Marcus Hook is in Pennsylvania, the agent of the cars runs no risk of the fine of five hundred dollars our State imposes for assisting one of God's poor out of the State by steamboat or cars. As ever thy friend, THOS. GARRETT.

NAMES OF THE "ARTICLES."

Rebecca Jones, and her three daughters, Sarah Frances, Mary, and Rebecca; Isaiah Robinson, Arthur Spence, Caroline Taylor, and her two daughters, Nancy, and Mary; Daniel Robinson; Thomas Page; Benjamin Dickinson; David Cole and wife.

From the tenor of Thomas Garrett's letter, the Committee was prepared for a joyful reception, knowing that Captain F. was not in the habit of doing things by the halves—that he was not in the habit of bringing numb-skulls; indeed he brought none but the bravest and most intelligent. Yet notwithstanding our knowledge of his practice in this respect, when he arrived we were surprised beyond measure. The women outnumbered the men. The two young mothers, with their interesting, hearty and fine-looking children representing in blood the two races about equally—pre-sented a very impressive spectacle.

The men had the appearance of being active, smart, and well disposed, much above the generality of slaves; but, compared with those of the oppo-site sex, their claims for sympathy were very faint indeed. No one could possibly avoid the conclusion, that these mothers, with their handsome daughters, were valued on the Ledger of their owners at enormously high prices; that lustful traders and sensualists had already gloated over the thought of buying them in a few short years. Probably not one of those beautiful girls would have brought less than fifteen hundred or two thousand dollars at the age of fifteen. It was therefore a great satisfaction to think, that their mothers, who knew full well to what a fate such slave girls were destined, had labored so heroically to snatch them out of this danger ere the critical hour arrived.

Rebecca Jones was about twenty-eight years of age; mulatto, good-looking, considerably above medium size, very intelligent, and a true-born heroine.

The following reward, offered by the notorious negro-trader, Hall, proved that Rebecca and her children were not to be allowed to go free, if slave-hunters could be induced by a heavy pecuniary consideration to recapture them:

$300 Reward is offered for the apprehension of negro woman, REBECCA JONES and her three children, and man ISAIAH, belonging to W. W. Davidson, who have disappeared since the 20th inst. The above reward will be paid for the apprehension and delivery of the said Negroes to my Jail, by the attorney in fact of the owner, or the sum of $250 for the man alone, or $150 for the woman and three children alone.   Wm. W. Hall, for the Attorney.
feb. 1.

Years before her escape, her mistress died in England; and as Rebecca had always understood, long before this event, that all the slaves were to be freed at the death of her mistress, she was not prepared to believe any other report. It turned out, however, as in thousands of other instances, that no will could be found, and, of course, the administrators retained the slave property, regardless of any verbal expressions respecting freeing, etc. Rebecca closely watched the course of the administrators, and in the meanwhile firmly resolved, that neither she nor her children should ever serve another master. Rather than submit, she declared that she would take the lives of her children and then her own. Notwithstanding her bold and decided stand, the report went out that she was to be sold, and that all the slaves were still to be held in bondage. Rebecca's sympathizers and friends advised her, as they thought for the best, to get a friend or gentleman to purchase her for herself. To this she replied: "Not three cents would I give, nor do I want any of my friends to buy me, not if they could get me for three cents. It would be of no use," she contended, "as she was fully bent on dying, rather than remain a slave." The slave-holders evidently understood her, and were in no hurry about bringing her case to an issue—they rather gave her time to become calm. But Rebecca was inflexible.

Six years before her arrival, her husband had escaped, in company with the noted fugitive, "Shadrach." For a time after he fled, she frequently received letters from him, but for a long while he had ceased to write, and of late she had heard nothing from him.

In escaping stowed away in the boat, she suffered terribly, but faithfully endured to the end, and was only too happy when the agony was over. After resting and getting thoroughly refreshed in Philadelphia, she, with others, was forwarded to Boston, for her heart was there. Several letters were received from her, respecting her prospects, etc., from which it appears that she had gained some knowledge of her husband, although not of a satisfactory nature. At any rate she decided that she could not receive him back again. The following letter has reference to her prospects, going to California, her husband, etc.:

PARKER HOUSE, School street, Boston, Oct. 18th, '56.

MY DEAR SIR:—I can hardly express the pleasure I feel at the receipt of your kind letter; but allow me to thank you for the same.

And now I will tell you my reasons for going to California. Mrs. Tarrol, a cousin of my husband, has sent for me. She says I can do much better there than in Boston. And as I have my children's welfare to look to, I have concluded to go. Of course I shall be just as likely to hear from home *there* as *here*. Please tell Mr. Bagnale I shall expect one letter from him before I leave here.

I should like to hear from my brothers and sisters once more, and let me hear every particular. You never can know how anxious I am to hear from them; do please impress this upon their minds.

I have written two letters to Dr. Lundy and never received an answer. I heard Mrs. Lundy was dead, and thought that might possibly be the reason he had not replied to me. Please tell the Doctor I should take it as a great favor if he would write me a few lines.

I suppose you think I am going to live with my husband again. Let me assure you 'tis no such thing. My mind is as firm as ever. And believe me, in going away from Boston, I am going away from him, for I have heard he is living somewhere near. He has been making inquiries about me, but that can make no difference in my feelings to him. I hope that yourself, wife and family are all quite well. Please remember me to them all. Do me the favor to give my love to all inquiring friends. I should be most happy to have any letters of introduction you may think me worthy of, and I trust I shall ever remain   Yours faithfully,   REBECCA JONES.

P. S.—I do not know if I shall go this Fall, or in the Spring. It will depend upon the letter I receive from California, but whichever it may be, I shall be happy to hear from you very soon.

ISAIAH, who was a fellow-servant with Rebecca, and was included in the reward offered by Hall for Rebecca, etc., was a young man about twenty-three years of age, a mulatto, intelligent and of prepossessing manners. A purely ardent thirst for liberty prompted him to flee; although he declared that he had been treated very badly, and had even suffered severely from being shamefully "beaten." He had, however, been permitted to hire his time by the year, for which one hundred and twenty dollars were regularly demanded by his owner. Young as he was, he was a married man, with a wife and two children, to whom he was devoted. He had besides two brothers and two sisters for whom he felt a warm degree of brotherly affection; yet when the hour arrived for him to accept a chance for freedom at the apparent sacrifice of these dearest ties of kindred, he was found heroic enough for this painful ordeal, and to give up all for freedom.

CAROLINE TAYLOR, and her two little children, were also from Norfolk, and came by boat. Upon the whole, they were not less interesting than Rebecca Jones and her three little girls. Although Caroline was not in her person half so stately, nor gave such promise of heroism as Rebecca—for Caroline was rather small of stature—yet she was more refined, and quite as intelligent as Rebecca, and represented considerably more of the Anglo-Saxon blood. She was a mulatto, and her children were almost fair enough to pass for white—probably they were quadroons, hardly any one would have suspected that they had only one quarter of colored blood in their veins. For ten years Caroline had been in the habit of hiring her time at the rate of seventy-five dollars per year, with the exception of the last year, when her hire was raised to eighty-four dollars. So anxious was she to have her older girl (eleven years old) at home with her, that she also hired her time by the year, for which she was compelled to pay twenty-four dollars. As her younger child was not sufficiently grown to hire out for pay, she was permitted to have it at home with her on the conditions that she would feed, clothe and take good care of it, permitting no expense whatever to fall upon the master.

Judging from the appearance and manners of the children, their mother had, doubtless, been most faithful to them, for more handsome, well-behaved, intelligent and pleasing children could not easily be selected from either race or any station of life. The younger, Mary by name, nine years of age, attracted very great attention, by the deep interest she manifested in a poor fugitive (whom she had never seen before), at the Philadelphia station, confined to the bed and suffering excruciating pain from wounds he had received whilst escaping. Hours and hours together, during the two or three days of their sojourn, she spent of her own accord, by his bed-side, manifesting almost womanly sympathy in the most devoted and tender manner. She thus, doubtless, unconsciously imparted to the sufferer a great deal of comfort. Very many affecting incidents had come under the observation of the acting Committee, under various circumstances, but never before had they witnessed a sight more interesting, a scene more touching.

Caroline and her children were owned by Peter March, Esq., late of Norfolk, but at that time, he was living in New York, and was carrying on the iron business. He came into possession of them through his wife, who was the daughter of Caroline's former master, and almost the only heir left, in consequence of the terrible fever of the previous summer. Caroline was living under the daily fear of being sold; this, together with the task of supporting herself and two children, made her burden very grievous. Not a great while before her escape, her New York master had been on to Norfolk, expressly with a view of selling her, and asked two thousand dollars for her. This, however, he failed to get, and was still awaiting an offer.

These ill omens aroused Caroline to think more seriously over the condition of herself and children than she had ever done before, and in this state of mind she came to the conclusion, that she would strive to save herself and children by flight on the Underground Rail Road. She knew full well, that it was no faint-hearted struggle that was required of her, so she had nerved herself with the old martyr spirit to risk her all on her faith in God and Freedom, and was ready to take the consequences if she fell back into the hands of the enemy. This noble decision was the crowning act in the undertakings of thousands similarly situated. Through this faith she gained the liberty of herself and her children. Quite a number of the friends of the slave saw these interesting fugitives, and wept, and rejoiced with them.

Col. A. Cummings, in those days Publisher of the "Evening Bulletin," for the first time, witnessed an Underground Rail Road arrival. Some time previous, in conversation with Mr. J. M. McKim, the Colonel had expressed views not altogether favorable to the Underground Rail Road indeed he was rather inclined to apologize for slavery, if not to defend the Fugitive Slave Law. While endeavoring somewhat tenaciously to maintain his ground, Mr. McKim opposed to him not only the now well established Anti-Slavery doctrines, but also offered as testimony Underground Rail Road facts—the results of personal knowledge from daily proofs of the heroic struggles, marvellous faith, and intense earnestness of the fugitives.

In all probability the Colonel did not feel prepared to deny wholly Mr. McKim's statement, yet, he desired to see "some" for himself. "Well," said Mr. McK., "you shall see some." So when this arrival came to hand, true to his promise, Mr. McK. called on the Colonel and invited him to accompany him to the Underground Rail Road station. He assured the

Colonel that he did not want any money from him, but simply wanted to convince him of his error in the recent argument that they had held on the subject. Accordingly the Colonel accompanied him, and found that twenty-two passengers had been on hand within the past twenty-four hours, and at least sixteen or seventeen were then in his presence. It is needless to say, that such a sight admitted of no contradiction—no argument —no doubt. The facts were too self-evident. The Colonel could say but little, so complete was his amazement; but he voluntarily attested the thoroughness of his conversion by pulling out of his pocket and handing to Mr. McK. a twenty dollar gold piece to aid the passengers on to freedom.

In these hours of rest and joyful anticipation the necessities of both large and small were administered to according to their needs, before forwarding them still further. The time and attention required for so many left but little opportunity, however, for the Secretary to write their narratives. He had only evening leisure for the work. Ten or twelve of that party had to be sent off without having their stories recorded. Daniel Robertson was one of this number ; his name is simply entered on the roll, and, but for letters received from him, after he passed on North, no further knowledge would have been obtained. In Petersburg, whence he escaped, he left his wife, for whose deliverance he felt bound to do everything that lay in his power, as the subjoined letters will attest :

HAVANA, August 11, 1856, Schuylkill Co., N. Y.

MR. WM. STILL—Dear Sir :—I came from Virginia in March, and was at your office the last of March. My object in writing you, is to inquire what I can do, or what can be done to help my wife to escape from the same bondage that I was in. You will know by your books that I was from Petersburg, Va., and that is where my wife now is. I have received two or three letters from a lady in that place, and the last one says, that my wife's mistress is dead, and that she expects to be sold. I am very anxious to do what I can for her before it is too late, and beg of you to devise some means to get her away. Capt. the man that brought me away, knows the colored agent at Petersburg, and knows he will do all he can to forward my wife. The Capt. promised, that when I could raise one hundred dollars for him that he would deliver her in Philadelphia. Tell him that I can now raise the money, and will forward it to you at any day that he thinks that he can bring her. Please see the Captain and find when he will undertake it, and then let me know when to forward the money to you. I am at work for the Hon. Charles Cook, and can send the money any day. My wife's name is Harriet Robertson, and the agent at Petersburg knows her.

Please direct your answer, with all necessary directions, to N. Coryell, of this village, and he will see that all is right. Very respectfully, DANIEL ROBERTSON.

HAVANA, Aug. 18, 1856.

MR. WM. STILL—Dear Sir :—Yours of the 18th, for D. Robertson, was duly received. In behalf of Daniel, I thank you kindly for the interest you manifest in him. The letters that have gone from him to his friends in Virginia, have been written by me, and sent in such a manner as we thought would best ensure safety. Yet I am well aware of the risk of writing, and have restrained him as far as possible, and the last one I wrote was to be the last, till an effort was made to reclaim his wife. Daniel is a faithful, likely man, and is well liked by all who know him. He is industrious and prudent, and is bending his whole energies toward the reclaiming his wife. He can forward to you the one hundred dollars at any day that it may be wanted, and if you can do anything to forward his interests it will be very gratefully received as an additional favor on your part. He asks for no money, but your kindly efforts, which he regards more highly than money.

Very respectfully,   N. CORYELL.

The letters that have been written for him were dated "Niagara Falls, Canada West," and his friends think he is there—none of them know to the contrary—it is important that they never do know.   N. C.

HAVANA, Sept. 29, 1856.

MR. WM. STILL—Dear Sir:—I enclose herewith a draft on New York, payable to your order, for $100, to be paid on the delivery at Philadelphia of Daniel Robertson's wife.

You can readily see that it has been necessary for Daniel to work almost night and day to have laid up so large an amount of money, since the first of April, as this one hundred dollars. Daniel is industrious and prudent, and saves all of his earnings, above his most absolute wants. If the Captain is not successful in getting Daniel's wife, you, of course, will return the draft, without charge, as you said. I hope success will attend him, for Daniel deserves to be rewarded, if ever man did.   Yours, &c.   N. CORYELL.

HAVANA, Jan. 2, 1857.

DEAR SIR:—Your favor containing draft on N. York, for Daniel Robertson, came to hand on the 31st ult. Daniel begs to tender his acknowledgments for your kind interest manifested in his behalf, and says he hopes you will leave no measure untried which has any appearance of success, and that the money shall be forthcoming at a moment's notice. Daniel thinks that since Christmas, the chances for his wife's deliverance are fewer than before, for at that time he fears she was disposed of and possibly went South.

The paper sent me, with your well-written article, was received, and on reading it to Daniel, he knew some of the parties mentioned in it—he was much pleased to hear it read. Daniel spent New Year's in Elmira, about 18 miles from this place, and there he met two whom he was well acquainted with.   Yours, &c.,   N. CORYELL.

WM. STILL, Esq., Phila.

Such devotion to freedom, such untiring labor, such appeals as these letters contained awakened deep interest in the breasts of Daniel's new friends, which spoke volumes in favor of the Slave and against slave-holders. But, alas, nothing could be done to relieve the sorrowing mind of poor Daniel for the deliverance of his wife in chains. The Committee sympathized deeply with him, but could do no more. What other events followed, in Daniel's life as a fugitive, were never made known to the Committee.

ARTHUR SPENCE also deserves a notice. He was from North Carolina, about twenty-four years of age, and of pleasing appearance, and was heart and soul in sympathy with the cause of the Underground Rail Road. In North Carolina he declared that he had been heavily oppressed by being compelled to pay $175 per annum for his hire. In order to get rid of this heavy load, by shrewd management he gained access to the kind-hearted Captain and procured an Underground Rail Road ticket. In leaving bondage, he was obliged to leave his mother, two brothers and one sister. He appeared to be composed of just the kind of material for making a good British subject.

BEN DICKINSON. Ben was also a slave in North Carolina—located at Eatontown, being the property of "Miss Ann Blunt, who was very hard." In slave property Miss Blunt was interested to the number of about "ninety head." She was much in the habit of hiring out servants, and in thus disposing of her slaves Ben thought she was a great deal more concerned in getting good prices for herself than good places for them. Indeed he declared that "she did not care how mean the place was, if she could only get her price." For three years Ben had Canada and the Underground Rail Road in view, having been "badly treated." At last the long-looked for time arrived, and he conferred neither with master nor mistress, but "picked himself up" and "took out." Age twenty-eight, medium size, quite dark, a good carpenter, and generally intelligent. Left two sisters, etc.

Of this heroic and promising party we can only mention, in conclusion, one more passenger, namely:

TOM PAGE. At the time of his arrival, his name only was enrolled on the book. Yet he was not a passenger soon to be forgotten—he was but a mere boy, probably eighteen years of age; but a more apt, ready-witted, active, intelligent and self-reliant fellow is not often seen.

Judging from his smartness, under slavery, with no chances, it was easy to imagine how creditably he might with a white boy's chances have climbed the hill of art and science. Obviously he had intellect enough, if properly cultivated, to fill any station within the ordinary reach of intelligent American citizens. He could read and write remarkably well for a slave, and well did he understand his advantages in this particular; indeed if slave-holders had only been aware of the growing tendency of Tom's mind, they would have rejoiced at hearing of his departure for Canada; he was a most dangerous piece of property to be growing up amongst slaves.

After leaving the Committee and going North his uncaged mind felt the need of more education, and at the same time he was eager to make money, and do something in life. As he had no one to depend on, parents and relatives being left behind in Norfolk, he felt that he must rely upon himself, young as he was. He first took up his abode in Boston, or New Bedford, where most of the party with whom he escaped went, and where he had an aunt, and perhaps some other distant kin. There he worked and was a live young man indeed—among the foremost in ideas and notions about freedom, etc., as many letters from him bore evidence. After spending a year or more in Massachusetts, he had a desire to see how the fugitives were doing in Upper and Lower Canada, and if any better chances existed in these parts for men of his stamp.

Some of his letters, from different places, gave proof of real thought and close observation, but they were not generally saved, probably were loaned to be read by friendly eyes. Nevertheless the two subjoined will, in a measure, suffice to give some idea of his intelligence, etc.

BOSTON, Mass., Feb. 25th, 1857.

WILLIAM STILL, Esq.:—Dear Sir—I have not heard from you for some time. I take this opportunity of writing you a few lines to let you and all know that I am well at present and thank God for it. Dear Sir, I hear that the under ground railroad was in operation. I am glad to hear that. Give my best respects to your family and also to Dr. L., Mr. Warrick, Mr. Camp and familys, to Mr. Fisher, Mr. Taylor to all Friends names too numerous to mention. Please to let me know when the road arrived with another cargo. I want to come to see you all before long, if nothing happens and life lasts. Mrs. Gault requested me to learn of you if you ask Mr. Bagnal if he will see father and what he says about the children. Please to answer as soon as possible. No more at present from a friend, THOMAS F. PAGE.

NIAGARA FALLS, N. Y., Oct. 6th, '58.

DEAR SIR:—I received your kind letter and I was very glad to hear from you and your family. This leaves me well, and I hope when this comes to hand it may find you the same. I have seen a large number of your U. G. R. R. friends in my travels through the Eastern as well as the Western States. Well there are a good many from my own city who I know—some I talk to on private matters and some I wont. Well around here there are so many—Tom, Dick and Harry—that you do not know who your friend is. So it don't hurt any one to be careful. Well, somehow or another, I do not like Canada, or the Provinces. I have been to St. John, N. B., Lower Province, or Lower Canada, also St. Catharines, C. W., and all around the Canada side, and I do not like it at all. The people seem to be so queer—though I suppose if I had of went to Canada when I first came North to live, I might like it by this time. I was home when Aunt had her Ambrotype taken for you. She often speaks of your kindness to her. There are a number of your friends wishes you well. My little brother is going to school in Boston. The lady, Mrs. Hillard, that my Aunt lives with, thinks a good deal of him. He is very smart and I think, if he lives, he may be of some account. Do you ever see my old friend, Capt. Fountain? Please to give my love to him, and tell him to come to Boston, as there are a number of his friends that would like to see him. My best respects to all friends. I must now bring my short epistle to a close, by saying I remain your friend truly,

THOMAS F. PAGE.

While a portion of the party, on hand with him, came as passengers with Capt. F., another portion was brought by Capt. B., both parties arriving within twelve hours of each other; and both had likewise been frozen up on the route for weeks with their respective live freight on board.

The sufferings for food, which they were called upon to endure, were beyond description. They happened to have plenty of salt fat pork, and perhaps beans, Indian meal and some potatoes for standing dishes; the more delicate necessaries did not probably last longer than the first or second week of their ice-bondage.

Without a doubt, one of these Captains left Norfolk about the twentieth of January, but did not reach Philadelphia till about the twentieth of

March, having been frozen up, of course, during the greater part of that time. Men, women and children were alike sharers in the common struggle for freedom—were alike an hungered, in prison, naked, and sick, but it was a fearful thing in those days for even women and children to whisper their sad lamentations in the city of Philadelphia, except to those friendly to the Underground Rail Road.

Doubtless, if these mothers, with their children and partners in tribulation, could have been seen as they arrived direct from the boats, many hearts would have melted, and many tears would have found their way down many cheeks. But at that time cotton was acknowledged to be King—the Fugitive Slave Law was supreme, and the notorious decision of Judge Taney, that "black men had no rights which white men were bound to respect," echoed the prejudices of the masses too clearly to have made it safe to reveal the fact of their arrival, or even the heart-rending condition of these Fugitives.

Nevertheless, they were not turned away empty, though at a peril they were fed, aided, and comforted, and sent away well clothed. Indeed, so bountifully were the women and children supplied, that as they were being conveyed to the Camden and Amboy station, they looked more like a pleasuring party than like fugitives. Some of the good friends of the slave sent clothing, and likewise cheered them with their presence.

[Before the close of this volume, such friends and sympathizers will be more particularly noticed in an appropriate place.]

SUNDRY ARRIVALS—LATTER PART OF DECEMBER, 1855, AND BEGINNING OF JANUARY, 1856.

Joseph Cornish, Dorchester Co., Md.; Lewis Francis, *alias* Lewis Johnson, Harford Co., Md.; Alexander Munson, Chestertown, Md.; Samuel and Ann Scott, Cecil Cross-Roads, Md.; Wm. Henry Laminson, Del.; Isaac Stout, *alias* George Washington, Caroline Graves, Md.; Henry and Eliza Washington, Alexandria, Va.; Henry Chambers, John Chambers, Samuel Fall, and Thomas Anderson, Md.

Joseph Cornish was about forty years of age when he escaped. The heavy bonds of Slavery made him miserable. He was a man of much natural ability, quite dark, well-made, and said that he had been "worked very hard." According to his statement, he had been an "acceptable preacher in the African Methodist Church," and was also "respected

by the respectable white and colored people in his neighborhood." He would
not have escaped but for fear of being sold, as he had a wife and five children to whom he was very much attached, but had to leave them behind.
Fortunately they were free.

Of his ministry and connection with the Church, he spoke with feelings
of apparent solemnity, evidently under the impression that the little flock
he left would be without a shepherd. Of his master, Captain Samuel Le
Count, of the U. S. Navy, he had not one good word to speak; at least
nothing of the kind is found on the Record Book; but, on the contrary,
he declared that "he was very hard on his servants, allowing them no
chance whatever to make a little ready money for themselves." So in turning his face towards the Underground Rail Road, and his back against
slavery, he felt that he was doing God service.

The Committee regarded him as a remarkable man, and was much impressed with his story, and felt it to be a privilege and a pleasure to aid him.

LEWIS FRANCIS was a man of medium size, twenty-seven years of age,
good-looking and intelligent. He stated that he belonged to Mrs. Delinas,
of Abingdon, Harford Co., Md., but that he had been hired out from a boy
to a barber in Baltimore. For his hire his mistress received eight dollars
per month.

To encourage Lewis, his kind-hearted mistress allowed him out of his
own wages the sum of two dollars and fifty cents per annum! His clothing he got as best he could, but nothing did she allow him for that purpose.
Even with this arrangement she had been dissatisfied of late years, and
thought she was not getting enough out of Lewis; she, therefore, talked
strongly of selling him. This threat was very annoying to Lewis,
so much so, that he made up his mind that he would one day let her see,
that so far as he was concerned, it was easier to talk of selling than it would
be to carry out her threat.

With this growing desire for freedom he gained what little light he could
on the subject of traveling, Canada, etc., and at a given time off he started
on his journey and found his way to the Committee, who imparted substantial aid as usual.

ALEXANDER MUNSON, alias Samuel Garrett. This candidate for Canada
was only eighteen years of age; a well-grown lad, however, and had the
one idea that "all men were born free" pretty deeply rooted in his mind.
He was quite smart, and of a chestnut color. By the will of his original
owner, the slaves were all entitled to their freedom, but it appeared, from
Alexander's story, that the executor of the estate did not regard this freedom
clause in the will. He had already sold some of the slaves, and others—
he among them—were expecting to be sold before coming into possession of
their freedom. Two of them had been sold to Alabama, therefore, with
these evil warnings, young Alexander resolved to strike out at once for

Canada, despite Maryland slave-holders. With this bold and manly spirit he succeeded, of course.

ANNA SCOTT and husband, Samuel Scott. This couple escaped from Cecil Cross-Roads, Md. The wife, in this instance, evidently took the lead, and acted the more manly part in striking for freedom; therefore, our notice of this arrival will chiefly relate to her.

Anna was owned by a widow, named Mrs. Ann Elizabeth Lushy, who resided on a farm of her own. Fifteen slaves, with other stock, were kept on the place. She was accustomed to rule with severity, being governed by a "high temper," and in nowise disposed to allow her slaves to enjoy even ordinary privileges, and besides, would occasionally sell to the Southern market. She was calculated to render slave life very unhappy. Anna portrayed her mistress's treatment of the slaves with much earnestness, especially when referring to the sale of her own brother and sister. Upon the whole, the mistress was so hateful to Anna, that she resolved not to live in the house with her. During several years prior to her escape, Anna had been hired out, where she had been treated a little more decently than her mistress was wont to do; on this account she was less willing to put up with any subsequent abuse from her mistress.

To escape was the only remedy, so she made up her mind, that she would leave at all hazards. She gave her husband to understand, that she had resolved to seek a home in Canada. Fortunately, he was free, but slavery had many ways of putting the yoke on the colored man, even though he might be free; it was bound to keep him in ignorance, and at the same time miserably abject, so that he would scarcely dare to look up in the presence of white people.

SAM, apparently, was one of the number who had been greatly wronged in this particular. He had less spirit than his wife, who had been directly goaded to desperation. He agreed, however, to stand by her in her struggles while fleeing, and did so, for which he deserves credit. It must be admitted, that it required some considerable nerve for a free man even to join his wife in an effort of this character. In setting out, Anna had to leave her father (Jacob Trusty), seven sisters and two brothers. The names of the sisters were as follows: Emeline, Susan Ann, Delilah, Mary Eliza, Rosetta, Effie Ellender and Elizabeth; the brothers—Emson and Perry. For the commencement of their journey they availed themselves of the Christmas holidays, but had to suffer from the cold weather they encountered. Yet they got along tolerably well, and were much cheered by the attention and aid they received from the Committee.

WILLIAM HENRY LAMINSON came from near Newcastle, Delaware. He was smart enough to take advantage of the opportunity to escape at the age of twenty-one. As he had given the matter his fullest attention for a long time, he was prepared to make rapid progress when he did start, and as he had no great distance to travel it is not unlikely, that while his master was one night sleeping soundly, this young piece of property (worth at least $1,000 in the market), was crossing Mason and Dixon's Line, and steering directly for Canada. Francis Harkins was the name of the master. William did not give him a very bad character.

GEORGE WASHINGTON GOOSEBERRY, alias Isaac Stout, also took advantage of the holidays to separate from his old master, Anthony Rybold, a farmer living near Newcastle, Delaware. Nothing but the desire to be free moved George to escape. He was a young man about twenty-three years of age, of a pure black color, in stature, medium size, and well-made. Nothing remarkable is noted in the book in any way connected with his life or escape.

CAROLINE GRAVES. Caroline was of the bond class belonging to the State of Maryland. Having reached the age of forty without being content, and seeing no bright prospect in the future, she made up her mind to break away from the bonds of Slavery and seek a more congenial atmosphere among strangers in Canada. She had had the privilege of trying two masters in her life-time; the first she admitted was "kind" to her, but the latter was "cruel." After arriving in Canada, she wrote back as follows:

TORONTO, Jan. 22, 1856.

DEAR SIR:—WILLIAM STILL—I have found my company they arrived here on monday eving I found them on tusday evening. Please to be so kind as to send them boxes we are here without close to ware we have some white frendes is goin to .pay for them at this end of the road. The reason that we send this note we are afraid the outher one woudent go strait because it wasent derected wright. Please to send them by the express then thay wont be lost. Please to derect these boxes for Carline Graives in the car of mrs. Brittion. Please to send the bil of the boxes on with them. Mrs. Brittion, Lousig street near young street.

GEORGE GRAHAM and wife, Jane, alias Henry Washington and Eliza. The cold weather of January was preferred, in this instance, for traveling. Indeed matters were so disagreeable with them that they could not tarry in their then quarters any longer. George was twenty-four years of age, quite smart, pleasant countenance, and of dark complexion.

He had experienced "rough usage" all the way along through life, not unfrequently from severe floggings. Twice, within the last year, he had been sold. In order to prevent a renewal of these inflictions he resorted to the Underground Rail Road with his wife, to whom he had only been married six months.

In one sense, they appeared to be in a sad condition, it being the dead of winter, but their condition in Alexandria, under a brutal master and mistress which both had the misfortune to have, was much sadder. To give all their due, however, George's wife acknowledged, that she had

22

been "well treated under her old mistress," but through a change, she had fallen into the hands of a "new one," by whom her life had been rendered most "miserable ;" so much so, that she was willing to do almost anything to get rid of her, and was, therefore, driven to join her husband in running away.

HENRY CHAMBERS, John Chambers, Samuel Fall, and Jonathan Fisher. This party represented the more promising-looking field-hand slave population of Maryland. Henry and John were brothers, twenty-four and twenty-six years of age, stout made, chestnut color, good-looking, but in height not quite medium. Henry "owed service or labor," to a fellow-man by the name of William Rybold, a farmer living near Sassafras Neck, Md. Henry evidently felt, that he did master Rybold no injustice in testifying that he knew no good of him, although he had labored under him like a beast of burden all his days. He had been "clothed meanly," and "poorly fed." He also alleged, that his mistress was worse than his master, as she would "think nothing of knocking and beating the slave women for nothing." John was owned by Thomas Murphy. From that day to this, Thomas may have been troubling his brain to know why his man John treated him so shabbily as to leave him in the manner that he did. Jack had a good reason for his course, nevertheless. In his corn field-phrase he declared, that his master Murphy would not give you half clothes, and besides he was a " hard man," who kept Jack working out on hire. Therefore, feeling his wrongs keenly, Jack decided, with his other friends, to run off and be free.

SAM, another comrade, was also owned by William Rybold. Sam had just arrived at his maturity (twenty-one), when he was invited to join in the plot to escape. At first, it might be thought strange, why one so young should seek to escape. A few brief words from Sam soon explained the mystery. It was this: his master, as he said, had been in the habit of tying him up by the hands and flogging him unmercifully; besides, in the allowance of food and clothing, he always "stinted the slaves yet worked them very hard." Sam's chances for education had been very unfavorable, but he had mind enough to know that liberty was worth struggling for. He was willing to make the trial with the other boys. He was of a dark chestnut color, and of medium size.

JONATHAN belonged to A. Rybold, and was only nineteen years of age. All that need be said in relation to his testimony, is, that it agreed with his colleague's and fellow-servant's, Samuel. Before starting on their journey, they felt the need of new names, and in putting their wits together, they soon fixed this matter by deciding to pass in future by the following names: James and David Green, John Henry, and Jonathan Fisher.

In the brief sketches given in this chapter, some lost ones, seeking information of relatives, may find comfort, even if the general reader should fail to be interested.

PART OF THE ARRIVALS IN DECEMBER, 1855.

THOMAS JERVIS GOOSEBERRY and WILLIAM THOMAS FREEMAN, *alias* EZEKIEL CHAMBERS; HENRY HOOPER; JACOB HALL, *alias* HENRY THOMAS, and wife, HENRIETTA and child; Two men from near Chestertown, Md.; FENTON JONES; MARY CURTIS; WILLIAM BROWN; CHARLES HENRY BROWN; OLIVER PURNELL and ISAAC FIDGET.

THOMAS JERVIS GOOSEBERRY and WILLIAM THOMAS FREEMAN. The coming of this party was announced in the subjoined letter:

SCHUYLKILL, 11th Mo., 29th, 1855.

WILLIAM STILL: DEAR FRIEND:—Those boys will be along by the last Norristown train to-morrow evening. I think the train leaves Norristown at 6 o'clock, but of this inform thyself. The boys will be sent to a friend at Norristown, with instructions to assist them in getting seats in the last train that leaves Norristown to-morrow evening. They are two of the eleven who left some time since, and took with them some of their master's horses; I have told them to remain in the cars at Green street until somebody meets them. E. F. PENNYPACKER.

Having arrived safely, by the way and manner indicated in E. F. Pennypacker's note, as they were found to be only sixteen and seventeen years of age, considerable interest was felt by the Acting Committee to hear their story. They were closely questioned in the usual manner. They proved to be quite intelligent, considering how young they were, and how the harrow of Slavery had been upon them from infancy.

They escaped from Chestertown, Md., in company with nine others (they being a portion of the eleven who arrived in Wilmington, with two carriages, etc., noticed on page 302), but, for prudential reasons they were separated while traveling. Some were sent on, but the boys had to be retained with friends in the country. Many such separations were inevitable. In this respect a great deal of care and trouble had to be endured for the sake of the cause.

THOMAS JERVIS, the elder boy, was quite dark, and stammered somewhat, yet he was active and smart. He stated that Sarah Maria Perkins was his mistress in Maryland. He was disposed to speak rather favorably of her, at least he said that she was "tolerably kind" to her servants. She, however, was in the habit of hiring out, to reap a greater revenue for them, and did not always get them places where they were treated as well as she herself treated them. Tom left his father, Thomas Gooseberry, and three sisters, Julia Ann, Mary Ellen, and Katie Bright, all slaves.

EZEKIEL, the younger boy, was of a chestnut color, clever-looking, smart, and well-grown, just such an one as a father enjoying the blessings of education and citizenship, might have felt a considerable degree of pride in. He was owned by a man called John Dwa, who followed "farming and drinking," and when under the influence of liquor, was disposed to ill-treat the slaves. Ezekiel had not seen his mother for many years, although she was living in Baltimore, and was known by the name of "Dorcas Denby." He left no brothers nor sisters.

The idea of boys, so young and inexperienced as they were, being thrown on the world, gave occasion for serious reflection. Still the Committee were rejoiced that they were thus early in life, getting away from the "Sum of all villanies." In talking with them, the Committee endeavored to impress them with right ideas as to how they should walk in life, aided them, of course, and sent them off with a double share of advice. What has been their destiny since, is not known.

HENRY HOOPER, a young man of nineteen years of age, came from Maryland, in December, in a subsequent Underground Rail Road arrival. That he came in good order, and was aided and sent off, was fully enough stated on the book, but nothing else; space, however was left for the writing out of his narrative, but it was never filled up. Probably the loose sheet on which the items were jotted down, was lost.

JACOB HALL, alias Henry Thomas, wife Henrietta, and child, were also among the December passengers. On the subject of freedom they were thoroughly converted. Although Jacob was only about twenty years of age, he had seen enough of Slavery under his master, "Major William Hutchins," whom he described as a "farmer, commissioner, drunkard, and hard master," to know that no hope could be expected from him, but if he remained, he would daily have to be under the "harrow." The desire to work for himself was so strong, that he could not reconcile his mind to the demands of Slavery. While meditating upon freedom, he concluded to make an effort with his wife and child to go to Canada.

His wife, Henrietta, who was then owned by a woman named Sarah Ann McGough, was as unhappily situated as himself. Indeed Henrietta had come to the conclusion, that it was out of the question for a servant to please her mistress, it mattered not how hard she might try; she also said, that her mistress drank, and that made her "wus."

Besides, she had sold Henrietta's brother and sister, and was then taking steps to sell her,—had just had her appraised with this view. It was quite easy, therefore, looking at their condition in the light of these plain facts, for both husband and wife to agree, that they could not make their condition any worse, even if they should be captured in attempting to escape. Henrietta also remembered, that years before her mother had escaped, and got off to Canada, which was an additional encouragement. Thus, as her own faith was strengthened, she could strengthen that of her husband.

Their little child they resolved to cling to through thick and thin; so, in order that they might not have so far to carry him, father and mother each bridled a horse and "took out" in the direction of the first Underground Rail Road station. Their faithful animals proved of incalculable service, but they were obliged to turn them loose on the road without even having the opportunity or pleasure of rewarding them with a bountiful feed of oats.

Although they had strange roads, woods and night scenes to pass through, yet they faltered not. They found friends and advisers on the road, however, and reached the Committee in safety, who was made to rejoice that such promising-looking "property" could come out of Ladies' Manor, Maryland. The Committee felt that they had acted wisely in taking the horses to assist them the first night.

The next arrival is recorded thus: "Dec. 10, 1855. Arrived, two men from near Chestertown, Md. They came to Wilmington in a one horse wagon, and through aid of T. G. they were sent on." (Further account at the time, written on a loose piece of paper, is among the missing).

FENTON JONES escaped from Frederick, Md. After arriving in the neighborhood of Ercildoun, Pa., he was induced to tarry awhile for the purpose of earning means to carry him still farther. But he was soon led to apprehend danger, and was advised and directed to apply to the Vigilance Committee of Philadelphia for the needed aid, which he did, and was dispatched forthwith to Canada.

About the same time a young woman arrived, calling herself Mary Curtis. She was from Baltimore, and was prompted to escape to keep from being sold. She was nineteen years of age, small size, dark complexion. No special incidents in her life were noted.

WILLIAM BROWN came next. If others had managed to make their way out of the prison-house without great difficulties, it was far from William to meet with such good luck, as he had suffered excessively for five weeks while traveling. It was an easy matter for a traveler to get lost, not knowing the roads, nor was it safe to apply to a stranger for information or direction—therefore, in many instances, the journey would either have to be given up, or be prosecuted, suffering almost to the death.

In the trying circumstances in which William found himself, dark as everything looked, he could not consent to return to his master, as he felt persuaded, that if he did, there would be no rest on earth for him. He well remembered, that, because he had resisted being flogged (being high spirited), his master had declined to sell him for the express purpose of making an example of him—as a warning to the other slaves on the place. William was as much opposed to being thus made use of as he was to being flogged. His reflections and his stout heart enabled him to endure five weeks of severe suffering while fleeing from oppression. Of course, when he did succeed, the triumph was unspeakably joyous. Doubtless, he had thought a great deal during this time, and being an intelligent fugitive, he interested the Committee greatly.

The man that he escaped from was called William Elliott, a farmer, living in Prince George's county, Md. William Elliott claimed the right to flog and used it too. William, however, gave him the character of being among the moderate slave-holders of that part of the country. This was certainly a charitable view. William was of a chestnut color, well made, and would have commanded, under the "hammer," a high price, if his apparent intelligence had not damaged him. He left his father, grand-mother, four sisters and two brothers, all living where he fled from.

CHARLES HENRY BROWN. This "chattel" was owned by Dr. Richard Dorsey, of Cambridge, Maryland. Up to twenty-seven years of age, he had experienced and observed how slaves were treated in his neighborhood, and he made up his mind that he was not in favor of the Institution in any form whatever. Indeed he felt, that for a man to put his hand in his neighbor's pocket and rob him, was nothing compared to the taking of a man's hard earnings from year to year. Really Charles reasoned the case so well, in his uncultured country phrases, that the Committee was rather surprised, and admired his spirit in escaping. He was a man of not quite medium size, with marked features of mind and character.

OLIVER PURNELL and ISAAC FIDGET arrived from Berlin, Md. Each had different owners. Oliver stated that Mose Purnell had owned him, and that he was a tolerably moderate kind of a slave-holder, although he was occasionally subject to fractious turns. Oliver simply gave as his reason for leaving in the manner that he did, that he wanted his "own earnings." He felt that he had as good a right to the fruit of his labor as anybody else. Despite all the pro-slavery teachings he had listened to all his life, he was far from siding with the pro-slavery doctrines. He was about twenty-six years of age, chestnut color, wide awake and a man of promise; yet it was sadly obvious that he had been blighted and cursed by slavery even in its mildest forms He left his parents, two brothers and three sisters all slaves in the hands of Purnell, the master whom he deserted.

ISAAC, his companion, was about thirty years of age, dark, and in intellect about equal to the average passengers on the Underground Rail Road. He had a very lively hope of finding his wife in freedom, she having escaped the previous Spring; but of her whereabouts he was ignorant, as he had had no tidings of her since her departure. A lady by the name of Mrs. Fidget held the deed for Isaac. He spoke kindly of her, as he thought she treated her slaves quite as well at least as the best of slave-holders in his neighborhood.   His view was a superficial one, it meant only that they had not been beaten and starved half to death.

As the heroic adventures and sufferings of Slaves struggling for freedom, shall be read by coming generations, were it not for unquestioned statutes upholding Slavery in its dreadful heinousness, people will hardly be able to believe that such atrocities were enacted in the nineteenth century, under a highly enlightened, Christianized, and civilized government.   Having already copied a statute enacted by the State of Virginia, as a sample of Southern State laws, it seems fitting that the Fugitive Slave Bill, enacted by the Congress of the United States, shall be also copied, in order to commemorate that most infamous deed, by which, it may be seen, how great were the bulwarks of oppression to be surmounted by all who sought to obtain freedom by flight.

THE FUGITIVE SLAVE BILL OF 1850.

"AN ACT RESPECTING FUGITIVES FROM JUSTICE, AND PERSONS ESCAPING FROM THE SERVICE OF THEIR MASTERS."

Be it enacted by the Senate and House of Representatives of the United States of America in Congress assembled:

That the persons who have been, or may hereafter be appointed commissioners, in virtue of any Act of Congress, by the circuit courts of the United States, and who, in consequence of such appointment, are authorized to exercise the powers that any justice of the peace or other magistrate of any of the United States, may exercise in respect to offenders for any crime or offence against the United States, by arresting, imprisoning, or bailing the same under and by virtue of the thirty-third section of the act of the twenty-fourth of September, seventeen hundred and eighty-nine, entitled, "An act to establish the judicial courts of the United States," shall be, and are hereby authorized and required to exercise and discharge all the powers and duties conferred by this act.

Sec. 2. And be it further enacted: That the superior court of each organized territory of the United States, shall have the same power to appoint commissioners to take acknowledgments of bail and affidavit, and to take depositions of witnesses in civil causes, which is now possessed by the circuit courts of the United States, and all commissioners, who shall hereafter be appointed for such purposes, by the superior court of any organized territory of the United States, shall possess all the powers, and exercise all the duties conferred by law, upon the commissioners appointed by the circuit courts of the United States for similar purposes, and shall, moreover, exercise and discharge all the powers and duties conferred by this act.

SEC. 3. And be it further enacted: That the circuit courts of the United States, and the superior courts of each organized territory of the United States, shall, from time to time, enlarge the number of Commissioners, with a view to afford reasonable facilities to reclaim fugitives from labor, and to the prompt discharge of the duties imposed by this act.

SEC. 4. And be it further enacted, that the commissioners above named, shall have concurrent jurisdiction with the judges of the circuit and district courts of the United States, in their respective circuits and districts within the several States, and the judges of the superior courts of the Territories severally and collectively, in term time and vacation; and shall grant certificates to such claimants, upon satisfactory proof being made, with authority to take and remove such fugitives from service or labor, under the restrictions herein contained, to the State or territory from which such persons may have escaped or fled.

SEC. 5. And be it further enacted: That it shall be the duty of all marshals and deputy marshals, to obey and execute all warrants and precepts issued under the provisions of this act, when to them directed; and should any marshal or deputy marshal refuse to receive such warrant or other process when tendered, or to use all proper means diligently to execute the same, he shall, on conviction thereof, be fined in the sum of one thousand dollars to the use of such claimant, on the motion of such claimant by the circuit or district court for the district of such marshal; and after arrest of such fugitive by the marshal, or his deputy, or whilst at any time in his custody, under the provisions of this act, should such fugitive escape, whether with or without the assent of such marshal or his deputy, such marshal shall be liable, on his official bond, to be prosecuted, for the benefit of such claimant, for the full value of the service or labor of said fugitive in the State, Territory or district whence he escaped; and the better to enable the said commissioners, when thus appointed, to execute their duties faithfully and efficiently, in conformity with the requirements of the Constitution of the United States, and of this act, they are hereby authorized and empowered, within their counties respectively, to appoint in writing under their hands, any one or more suitable persons, from time to time, to execute all such warrants and other process as may be issued by them in the lawful performance of their respective duties, with an authority to such commissioners, or the persons to be appointed by them, to execute process as aforesaid, to summon and call to their aid the bystanders or posse comitatus, of the proper county, when necessary to insure a faithful observance of the clause of the Constitution referred to, in conformity with the provisions of this act; and all good citizens are hereby commanded to aid and assist in the prompt and efficient execution of this law, whenever their services may be required, as aforesaid, for that purpose; and said warrants shall run and be executed by said officers anywhere in the State within which they are issued.

SEC. 6. And be it further enacted, That when a person held to service or labor in any State or Territory of the United States, has heretofore, or shall hereafter escape into another State or Territory of the United States, the person or persons to whom such service or labor may be due, or his, her or their agent or attorney, duly authorized, by power of attorney, in writing, acknowledged and certified under the seal of some legal office or court of the State or Territory, in which the same may be executed, may pursue and re-claim such fugitive person, either by procuring a warrant from some one of the courts, judges, or commissioners aforesaid, of the proper circuit, district or county, for the apprehension of such fugitive from service or labor, or by seizing and arresting such fugitive, where the same can be done without process, and by taking, or causing such person to be taken, forthwith, before such court, judge or commissioner, whose duty it shall be to hear and deter-mine the case of such claimant in a summary manner, and upon satisfactory proof being made, by deposition or affidavit, in writing, to be taken and certified by such court, judge or commissioner, or by other satisfactory testi-mony, duly taken and certified by some court, magistrate, justice of the peace, or other legal officer authorized to administer an oath and take depo-sitions under the laws of the State or Territory from which such person owing service or labor may have escaped, with a certificate of such magis-trate, or other authority, as aforesaid, with the seal of the proper court or officer thereto attached, which seal shall be sufficient to establish the com-petency of the proof, and with proof also, by affidavit, of the identity of the person whose service or labor is claimed to be due, as aforesaid, that the person so arrested does in fact owe service or labor to the person or persons claiming him or her, in the State or Territory from which such fugitive may have escaped, as aforesaid, and that said person escaped, to make out and deliver to such claimant, his or her agent or attorney, a certificate setting forth the substantial facts as to the service or labor due from such fugitive to the claimant, and of his or her escape from the State or Territory in which such service or labor was due, to the State or Territory, in which he or she was arrested, with authority to such claimant, or his or her agent or attorney, to use such reasonable force and restraint as may be necessary, under the circumstances of the case, to take and remove such fugitive person back to the State or Territory from whence he or she may have escaped, as aforesaid. In no trial or hearing, under this act, shall the testimony of such alleged fugitives be admitted in evidence, and the certificates in this and the first section mentioned, shall be conclusive of the right of the person or per-sons in whose favor granted to remove such fugitives to the State or Ter-ritory from which they escaped, and shall prevent all molestation of said person or persons by any process issued by any court, judge, magistrate, or other person whomsoever.

SEC. 7. And be it further enacted, That any person who shall knowingly and willfully obstruct, hinder, or prevent such claimant, his agent, or attorney, or any person or persons lawfully assisting him, her or them from arresting such a fugitive from service or labor, either with or without process, as aforesaid, or shall rescue, or attempt to rescue, such fugitive from service or labor, or from the custody of such claimant, his or her agent, or attorney, or other person or persons lawfully assisting, as aforesaid, when so arrested, pursuant to the authority herein given and declared, or shall aid, abet, or assist such person, so owing service or labor, as aforesaid, directly or indirectly, to escape from such claimant, his agent or attorney, or other person or persons legally authorized, as aforesaid, or shall harbor or conceal such fugitive, so as to prevent the discovery and arrest of such person, after notice or knowledge of the fact that such person was a fugitive from service or labor, as aforesaid, shall, for either of said offences, be subject to a fine not exceeding one thousand dollars, and imprisonment not exceeding six months, by indictment and conviction before the District Court of the United States, for the district in which such offence may have been committed, or before the proper court of criminal jurisdiction, if committed within any one of the organized Territories of the United States ; and shall, moreover, forfeit and pay, by way of civil damages, to the party injured by such illegal conduct, the sum of one thousand dollars for each fugitive so lost, as aforesaid, to be recovered by action of debt in any of the District or Territorial Courts aforesaid, within whose jurisdiction the said offence may have been committed.

SEC. 8. And be it further enacted, That the Marshals, their deputies, and the clerks of the said districts and territorial courts, shall be paid for their services the like fees as may be allowed to them for similar services in other cases ; and where such services are rendered exclusively in the arrest, custody, and delivery of the fugitives to the claimant, his or her agent, or attorney, or where such supposed fugitive may be discharged out of custody from the want of sufficient proof, as aforesaid, then such fees are to be paid in the whole by such complainant, his agent or attorney, and in all cases where the proceedings are before a Commissioner, he shall be entitled to a fee of ten dollars in full for his services in each case, upon the delivery of the said certificate to the claimant, his or her agent or attorney ; or a fee of five dollars in cases where proof shall not, in the opinion of said Commissioner, warrant such certificate and delivery, inclusive of all services incident to such arrest and examination, to be paid in either case, by the claimant, his or her agent or attorney. The person or persons authorized to execute the process to be issued by such Commissioners for the arrest and detention of fugitives from service or labor, as aforesaid, shall also be entitled to a fee of five dollars each for each person he or they may arrest and take before any such Commissioners, as aforesaid, at the instance and request of such claimant, with such other fees as may be deemed reasonable by such Commissioner for such other additional services as may be necessarily performed by him or them ; such as attending to the examination, keeping the fugitive in custody, and providing him with food and lodgings during his detention, and until the final determination of such Commissioner ; and in general for performing such other duties as may be required by such claimant, his or her attorney or agent or commissioner in the premises ; such fees to be made up in conformity with the fees usually charged by the officers of the courts of justice within the proper district or county as far as may be practicable, and paid by such claimants, their agents or attorneys, whether such supposed fugitive from service or labor be ordered to be delivered to such claimants by the final determination of such Commissioners or not.

Sec. 9. And be it further enacted, That upon affidavit made by the claimant of such fugitive, his agent or attorney, after such certificate has been issued, that he has reason to apprehend that such fugitive will be rescued by force from his or their possession before he can be taken beyond the limits of the State in which the arrest is made, it shall be the duty of the officer making the arrest to retain such fugitive in his custody, and to remove him to the State whence he fled, and there to deliver him to said claimant, his agent or attorney. And to this end the officer aforesaid is hereby authorized and required to employ so many persons as he may deem necessary, to overcome such force, and to retain them in his service so long as circumstances may require ; the said officer and his assistants, while so employed, to receive the same compensation, and to be allowed the same expenses as are now allowed by law for the transportation of criminals, to be certified by the judge of the district within which the arrest is made, and paid out of the treasury of the United States.

Sec. 10. And be it further enacted, That when any person held to service or labor in any State or Territory, or in the District of Columbia, shall escape therefrom, the party to whom such service or labor shall be due, his, her, or their agent, or attorney may apply to any court of record therein, or judge thereof in vacation, and make such satisfactory proof to such court or judge in vacation, of the escape aforesaid, and that the person escaping owed service or labor to such party. Thereupon the court shall cause a record to be made of the matters so proved, and also a personal description of the person so escaping, with such convenient certainty as may be ; and a transcript of such record, authenticated by the attestation of the clerk, and of the seal of said court being produced in any other State, Territory or District in which the person so escaping may be found, and being exhibited to any judge, commissioner, or other officer authorized by the law of the United States to cause persons escaping from service or labor to be delivered up, shall be held and taken to be full and conclusive evidence of the fact of escape, and that the service or labor of the person escaping is due to the party in such record mentioned. And upon the production, by the said party, of other and further evidence, if necessary, either oral or by affidavit, in addition to what is contained in said record of the identity of the person escaping, he or she shall be delivered up to the claimant. And said court, commissioners, judge, or other persons authorized by this act to grant certificates to claimants of fugitives, shall, upon the production of the record and other evidence aforesaid, grant to such claimant a certificate of his right to take any such person, identified and proved to be owing service or labor as aforesaid, which certificate shall authorize such claimant to seize, or arrest, and transport such person to the State or Territory from which he escaped : Provided, That nothing herein contained shall be construed as requiring the production of a transcript of such record as evidence as aforesaid, but in its absence, the claim shall be heard and determined upon other satisfactory proofs competent in law.

THE SLAVE–HUNTING TRAGEDY IN LANCASTER COUNTY, IN SEPTEMBER, 1851.

"TREASON AT CHRISTIANA."

Having inserted the Fugitive Slave Bill in these records of the Underground Rail Road, one or two slave cases will doubtless suffice to illustrate the effect of its passage on the public mind, and the colored people in particular. The deepest feelings of loathing, contempt and opposition were manifested by the opponents of Slavery on every hand. Anti-slavery papers, lecturers, preachers, etc., arrayed themselves boldly against it on the ground of its inhumanity and violation of the laws of God.

On the other hand, the slave-holders South, and their pro-slavery adherents in the North demanded the most abject obedience from all parties, regardless of conscience or obligation to God. In order to compel such obedience, as well as to prove the practicability of the law, unbounded zeal daily marked the attempt on the part of slave-holders and slave-catchers to refasten the fetters on the limbs of fugitives in different parts of the North, whither they had escaped.

In this dark hour, when colored men's rights were so insecure, as a matter of self-defence, they felt called upon to arm themselves and resist all kidnapping intruders, although clothed with the authority of wicked law. Among the most exciting cases tending to justify this course, the following may be named :

JAMES HAMLET was the first slave case who was summarily arrested under the Fugitive Slave Law, and sent back to bondage from New York.

WILLIAM and ELLEN CRAFT were hotly pursued to Boston by hunters from Georgia.

ADAM GIBSON, a free colored man, residing in Philadelphia, was arrested, delivered into the hands of his alleged claimants, by commissioner Edward D. Ingraham, and hurried into Slavery.

EUPHEMIA WILLIAMS (the mother of six living children),—her case excited much interest and sympathy.

SHADRACH was arrested and rescued in Boston.

HANNAH DELLUM and her child were returned to Slavery from Philadelphia.

THOMAS HALL and his wife were pounced upon at midnight in Chester county, beaten and dragged off to Slavery, etc.

And, as if gloating over their repeated successes, and utterly regardless of all caution, about one year after the passage of this nefarious bill, a party of slave-hunters arranged for a grand capture at Christiana.

One year from the passage of the law, at a time when alarm and excitement were running high, the most decided stand was taken at Christiana, in the State of Pennsylvania, to defeat the law, and defend freedom. Fortunately for the fugitives the plans of the slave-hunters and officials leaked out while arrangements were making in Philadelphia for the capture, and, information being sent to the Anti-slavery office, a messenger was at once dispatched to Christiana to put all persons supposed to be in danger on their guard.

Among those thus notified, were brave hearts, who did not believe in running away from slave-catchers. They resolved to stand up for the right of self-defence. They loved liberty and hated Slavery, and when the slave-catchers arrived, they were prepared for them. Of the contest, on that bloody morning, we have copied a report, carefully written at the time, by C. M. Burleigh, editor of the "Pennsylvania Freeman," who visited the scene of battle, immediately after it was over, and doubtless obtained as faithful an account of all the facts in the case, as could then be had.

"Last Thursday morning, (the 11th inst.), a peaceful neighborhood in the borders of Lancaster county, was made the scene of a bloody battle, resulting from an attempt to capture seven colored men as fugitive slaves. As the reports of the affray which came to us were contradictory, and having good reason to believe that those of the daily press were grossly one-sided and unfair, we repaired to the scene of the tragedy, and, by patient inquiry and careful examination, endeavored to learn the real facts. To do this, from the varying and conflicting statements which we encountered, scarcely two of which agreed in every point, was not easy ; but we believe the account we give below, as the result of these inquiries, is substantially correct.

Very early on the 11th inst. a party of slave-hunters went into a neighborhood about two miles west of Christiana, near the eastern border of Lancaster county, in pursuit of fugitive slaves. The party consisted of Edward Gorsuch, his son, Dickerson Gorsuch, his nephew, Dr. Pearce, Nicholas Hutchins, and others, all from Baltimore county, Md., and one Henry H. Kline, a notorious slave-catching constable from Philadelphia, who had been deputized by Commissioner Ingraham for this business. At about day-dawn they were discovered lying in an ambush near the house of one William Parker, a colored man, by an inmate of the house, who had started for his work. He fled back to the house, pursued by the slave-hunters, who entered the lower part of the house, but were unable to force their way into the upper part, to which the family had retired. A horn was blown from an upper window; two shots were fired, both, as we believe, though we are not certain, by the assailants, one at the colored man who fled into the house, and the other at the inmates, through the window. No one was wounded by either. A parley ensued. The slave-holder demanded his slaves, who he said were concealed in the house. The colored men presented themselves successively at the window, and asked if they were the slaves claimed; Gorsuch said, that neither of them was his slave. They told him that they were the only colored men in the house, and were determined never to be taken alive as slaves. Soon the colored people of the neighborhood, alarmed by the horn, began to gather, armed with guns, axes, corn-cutters, or clubs. Mutual threatenings were uttered by the two parties. The slave-holders told the blacks that resistance would be useless, as they had a party of thirty men in the woods near by. The blacks warned them again to leave, as they would die before they would go into Slavery.

From an hour to an hour and a half passed in these parleyings, angry conversations, and threats; the blacks increasing by new arrivals, until they probably numbered from thirty to fifty, most of them armed in some way. About this time, Castner Hanaway, a white man, and a Friend, who resided in the neighborhood, rode up, and was soon followed by Elijah Lewis, another Friend, a merchant, in Cooperville, both gentlemen highly esteemed as worthy and peaceable citizens. As they came up, Kline, the deputy marshal, ordered them to aid him, as a United States officer, to capture the fugitive slaves. They refused of course, as would any man not utterly destitute of honor, humanity, and moral principle, and warned the assailants that it was madness for them to attempt to capture fugitive slaves there, or even to remain, and begged them if they wished to save their own lives, to leave the ground. Kline replied, "Do you really think so?" "Yes," was the answer, "the sooner you leave, the better, if you would prevent bloodshed." Kline then left the ground, retiring into a very safe distance into a corn-field, and toward the woods. The blacks were so exasperated by his threats, that, but for the interposition of the two white Friends, it is very doubtful whether he would have escaped without injury. Messrs. Hanaway and

THE CHRISTIANA TRAGEDY.

Lewis both exerted their influence to dissuade the colored people from violence, and would probably have succeeded in restraining them, had not the assailing party fired upon them. Young Gorsuch asked his father to leave, but the old man refused, declaring, as it is said and believed, that he would "go to hell, or have his slaves."

Finding they could do nothing further, Hanaway and Lewis both started to leave, again counselling the slave-hunters to go away, and the colored people to peace, but had gone but a few rods, when one of the inmates of the house attempted to come out at the door. Gorsuch presented his revolver, ordering him back. The colored man replied, "You had better go away, if you don't want to get hurt," and at the same time pushed him aside and passed out. Maddened at this, and stimulated by the question of his nephew, whether he would "take such an insult from a d—d nigger," Gorsuch fired at the colored man, and was followed by his son and nephew, who both fired their revolvers. The fire was returned by the blacks, who made a rush upon them at the same time. Gorsuch and his son fell, the one dead the other wounded. The rest of the party after firing their revolvers, fled precipitately through the corn and to the woods, pursued by some of the blacks. One was wounded, the rest escaped unhurt. Kline, the deputy marshal, who now boasts of his miraculous escape from a volley of musket-balls, had kept at a safe distance, though urged by young Gorsuch to stand by his father and protect him, when he refused to leave the ground. He of course came off unscathed. Several colored men were wounded, but none severely. Some had their hats or their clothes perforated with bullets; others had flesh wounds. They said that the Lord protected them, and they shook the bullets from their clothes. One man found several shot in his boot, which seemed to have spent their force before reaching him, and did not even break the skin. The slave-holders having fled, several neighbors, mostly Friends and anti-slavery men, gathered to succor the wounded and take charge of the dead. We are told that Parker himself protected the wounded man from his excited comrades, and brought water and a bed from his own house for the invalid, thus showing that he was as magnanimous to his fallen enemy as he was brave in the defence of his own liberty. The young man was then removed to a neighboring house, where the family received him with the tenderest kindness and paid him every attention, though they told him in Quaker phrase, that "they had no unity with his cruel business," and were very sorry to see him engaged in it. He was much affected by their kindness, and we are told, expressed his regret that he had been thus engaged, and his determination, if his life was spared, never again to make a similar attempt. His wounds are very severe, and it is feared mortal. All attempts to procure assistance to capture the fugitive slaves failed, the people in the neighborhood either not relishing the business of slave-catching, or at least, not choosing to risk their lives in it.

There was a very great reluctance felt to going even to remove the body and the wounded man, until several abolitionists and Friends had collected for that object, when others found courage to follow on. The excitement caused by this most melancholy affair is very great among all classes. The abolitionists, of course, mourn the occurrence, while they see in it a legitimate fruit of the Fugitive Slave Law, just such a harvest of blood as they had long feared that the law would produce, and which they had earnestly labored to prevent. We believe that they alone, of all classes of the nation, are free from responsibility for its occurrence, having wisely foreseen the danger, and faithfully labored to avert it by removing its causes, and preventing the inhuman policy which has hurried on the bloody convulsion.

The enemies of the colored people, are making this the occasion of fresh injuries, and a more bitter ferocity toward that defenceless people, and of new misrepresentation and calumnies against the abolitionists.

The colored people, though the great body of them had no connection with this affair, are hunted like partridges upon the mountains, by the relentless horde which has been poured forth upon them, under the pretense of arresting the parties concerned in the fight. When we reached Christiana, on Friday afternoon, we found that the Deputy-Attorney Thompson, of Lancaster, was there, and had issued warrants, upon the depositions of Kline and others, for the arrest of all suspected persons. A company of police were scouring the neighborhood in search of colored people, several of whom were seized while at their work near by, and brought in.

CASTNER HANAWAY and Elijah Lewis, hearing that warrants were issued against them, came to Christiana, and voluntarily gave themselves up, calm and strong in the confidence of their innocence. They, together with the arrested colored men, were sent to Lancaster jail that night.

The next morning we visited the ground of the battle, and the family where young Gorsuch now lives, and while there, we saw a deposition which he had just made, that he believed no white persons were engaged in the affray, beside his own party. As he was on the ground during the whole controversy, and deputy Marshall Kline had discreetly run off into the corn-field, before the fighting began, the hireling slave-catcher's eager and confident testimony against our white friends, will, we think, weigh lightly with impartial men.

On returning to Christiana, we found that the United States Marshal from the city, had arrived at that place, accompanied by Commissioner Ingraham, Mr. Jones, a special commissioner of the United States, from Washington, the U. S. District Attorney Ashmead, with forty-five U. S. Marines from the Navy Yard, and a posse of about forty of the City Marshal's police, together with a large body of special constables, eager for such a man-hunt, from Columbia and Lancaster and other places. This crowd divided into parties, of from ten to twenty-five, and scoured the country, in every direction, for miles around, ransacking the houses of the colored people, and captured every colored man they could find, with several colored women, and two other white men. Never did our heart bleed with deeper pity for the peeled and persecuted colored people, than when we saw this troop let loose upon them, and witnessed the terror and distress which its approach excited in families, wholly innocent of the charges laid against them."

On the other hand, a few extracts from the editorials of some of the leading papers, will suffice to show the state of public feeling at that time, and the dreadful opposition abolitionists and fugitives had to contend with.

From one of the leading daily journals of Philadelphia, we copy as follows:

" There can be no difference of opinion concerning the shocking affair which occurred at Christiana, on Thursday, the resisting of a law of Congress by a band of armed negroes, whereby the majesty of the Government was defied and life taken in one and the same act. There is something more than a mere ordinary, something more than even a murderous, riot in all this. It is an act of insurrection, we might, considering the peculiar class and condition of the guilty parties, almost call it a servile insurrection—if not also one of treason. Fifty, eighty, or a hundred persons, whether white or black, who are deliberately in arms for the purpose of resisting the law, even the law for the recovery of fugitive slaves, are in the attitude of levying war against the United States ; and doubly heavy becomes the crime of murder in such a case, and doubly serious the accountability of all who have any connection with the act as advisers, suggesters, countenancers, or accessories in any way whatever."

In those days, the paper from which this extract is taken, represented the Whig party and the more moderate and respectable class of citizens.

The following is an extract from a leading democratic organ of Philadelphia:

" We will not, however, insult the reader by arguing that which has not been heretofore doubted, and which is not doubted now, by ten honest men in the State, and that is that the abolitionists are implicated in the Christiana murder. All the ascertained facts go to show that they were the real, if not the chief instigators. White men are known to harbor fugitives, in the neighborhood of Christiana, and these white men are known to be abolitionists, known to be opposed to the Fugitive Slave Law, and *known* to be the warm friends of William F. Johnston, (Governor of the State of Pennsylvania). And, as if to clinch the argument, no less than three white men are now in the Lancaster prison, and were arrested as accomplices in the dreadful affair on the morning of the eleventh. And one of these white men was committed on a charge of high treason, on Saturday last, by United States Commissioner Ingraham."

Another daily paper of opposite politics thus spake:

23

"The unwarrantable outrage committed last week, at Christiana, Lancaster county, is a foul stain upon the fair name and fame of our State. We are pleased to see that the officers of the Federal and State Governments are upon the tracks of those who were engaged in the riot, and that several arrests have been made.

We do not wish to see the poor misled blacks who participated in the affair, suffer to any great extent, for they were but tools. The men who are really chargeable with treason against the United States Government, and with the death of Mr. Gorsuch, an estimable citizen of Maryland, are unquestionably *white*, with hearts black enough to incite them to the commission of any crime equal in atrocity to that committed in Lancaster county. Pennsylvania has now but one course to pursue, and that is to aid, and warmly aid, the United States in bringing to condign punishment, every man engaged in the riot. She owes it to herself and to the Union. Let her in this resolve, be just and fearless."

From a leading neutral daily paper the following is taken: "One would suppose from the advice of forcible resistance, so familiarly given by the abolitionists, that they are quite unaware that there is any such crime as treason recognized by the Constitution, or punished with death by the laws of the United States. We would remind them, that not only is there such a crime, but that there is a solemn decision of the Supreme Court, that all who are concerned in a conspiracy which ripens into treason, whether present or absent from the scene of actual violence, are involved in the same liabilities as the immediate actors. If they engage in the conspiracy and stimulate the treason, they may keep their bodies from the affray without saving their necks from a halter.

It would be very much to the advantage of society, if an example could be made of some of these persistent agitators, who excite the ignorant and reckless to treasonable violence, from which they themselves shrink, but who are, not only in morals, but in law, equally guilty and equally amenable to punishment with the victims of their inflammatory counsels."

A number of the most influential citizens represented the occurrence to the Governor as follows:

"To the Governor of Pennsylvania:

The undersigned, citizens of Pennsylvania, respectfully represent:

That citizens of a neighboring State have been cruelly assassinated by a band of armed outlaws at a place not more than three hours' journey distant from the seat of Government and from the commercial metropolis of the State:

That this insurrectionary movement in one of the most populous parts of the State has been so far successful as to overawe the local ministers of justice and paralyze the power of the law:

That your memorialists are not aware that 'any military force' has been sent to the seat of insurrection, or that the civil authority has been strengthened by the adoption of any measures suited to the momentous crisis.

They, therefore, respectfully request the chief executive magistrate of Pennsylvania to take into consideration the necessity of vindicating the outraged laws, and sustaining the dignity of the Commonwealth on this important and melancholy occasion."

Under this high pressure of public excitement, threatening and alarm breathed so freely on every hand, that fugitive slaves and their friends in this region of Pennsylvania at least, were compelled to pass through an hour of dreadful darkness—an ordeal extremely trying. The authorities of the United States, as well as the authorities of the State of Pennsylvania and Maryland, were diligently making arrests wherever a suspected party could be found, who happened to belong in the neighborhood of Christiana.

In a very short time the following persons were in custody: J. Castner Hanaway, Elijah Lewis, Joseph Scarlett, Samuel Kendig, Henry Spins, George Williams, Charles Hunter, Wilson Jones, Francis Harkins, Benjamin Thomson, William Brown (No. 1), William Brown (No. 2), John Halliday, Elizabeth Mosey, John Morgan, Joseph Berry, John Norton, Denis Smith, Harvey Scott, Susan Clark, Tansy Brown, Eliza Brown, Eliza Parker, Hannah Pinckney, Robert Johnson, Miller Thompson, Isaiah Clark, and Jonathan Black.

These were not all, but sufficed for a beginning; at least it made an interesting entertainment for the first day's examination; and although there were two or three non-resistant Quakers, and a number of poor defenceless colored women among those thus taken as prisoners, still it seemed utterly impossible for the exasperated defenders of Slavery to divest themselves of the idea, that this heroic deed, in self-defence, on the part of men who felt that their liberties were in danger, was anything less than actually levying war against the United States.

Accordingly, therefore, the hearing gravely took place at Lancaster. On the side of the Commonwealth, the following distinguished counsel appeared on examination: Hon. John L. Thompson, District Attorney; Wm. B. Faulney, Esq.; Thos. E. Franklin, Esq., Attorney-General of Lancaster county; George L. Ashmead, Esq., of Philadelphia, representative of the United States authorities; and Hon. Robert Brent, Attorney-General of Maryland.

For the defence—Hon. Thaddeus Stevens, Reah Frazer, Messrs. Ford, Cline, and Dickey, Esquires.

From a report of the first day's hearing we copy a short extract, as follows:

"The excitement at Christiana, during yesterday, was very great. Several hundred persons were present, and the deepest feeling was manifested against the perpetrators of the outrage. At two o'clock yesterday afternoon, the United States Marshal, Mr. Roberts, United States District Attorney, J. H. Ashmead, Esq., Mr. Commissioner Ingraham, and Recorder Lee, accompanied by the United States Marines, returned to the city. Lieut. Johnson, and officers Lewis S. Brest, Samuel Mitchell, Charles McCully, Samuel Neff, Jacob Albright, Robert McEwen, and — Perkenpine, by direction of the United States Marshal, had charge of the following named prisoners, who were safely lodged in Moyamensing prison, accompanied by the Marines:—Joseph Scarlett, (white), William Brown, Ezekiel Thompson, Isaiah Clarkson, Daniel Caulsberry, Benjamin Pendergrass, Elijah Clark, George W. H. Scott, Miller Thompson, and Samuel Hanson, all colored. The last three were placed in the debtors' apartment, and the others in the criminal apartment of the Moyamensing prison to await their trial for treason, &c."

In alluding to the second day's doings, the Philadelphia Ledger thus represented matters at the field of battle:

"The intelligence received last evening, represents the country for miles around, to be in as much excitement as at any time since the horrible deed was committed. The officers sent there at the instance of the proper authorities are making diligent search in every direction, and securing every person against whom the least suspicion is attached. The police force from this city, amounting to about sixty men, are under the marshalship of Lieut. Ellis. Just as the cars started east, in the afternoon, five more prisoners who were secured at a place called the Welsh Mountains, twelve miles distant, were brought into Christiana. They were placed in custody until such time as a hearing will take place."

Although the government had summoned its ablest legal talent and the popular sentiment was as a hundred to one against William Parker and his brave comrades who had made the slave-hunter "bite the dust," most nobly did Thaddeus Stevens prove that he was not to be cowed, that he believed in the stirring sentiment so much applauded by the American people, "Give me liberty, or give me death," not only for the white man but for all men. Thus standing upon such great and invulnerable principles, it was soon discovered that one could chase a thousand, and two put ten thousand to flight in latter as well as in former times.

At first even the friends of freedom thought that the killing of Gorsuch was not only wrong, but unfortunate for the cause. Scarcely a week passed, however, before the matter was looked upon in a far different light, and it was pretty generally thought that, if the Lord had not a direct hand in it, the cause of Freedom at least would be greatly benefited thereby.

And just in proportion as the masses cried, Treason! Treason! the hosts of freedom from one end of the land to the other were awakened to sympathize with the slave. Thousands were soon aroused to show sympathy who had hitherto been dormant. Hundreds visited the prisoners in their cells to greet, cheer, and offer them aid and counsel in their hour of sore trial.

The friends of freedom remained calm even while the pro-slavery party were fiercely raging and gloating over the prospect, as they evidently thought of the satisfaction to be derived from teaching the abolitionists a lesson from the scaffold, which would in future prevent Underground Rail Road passengers from killing their masters when in pursuit of them.

Through the efforts of the authorities three white men, and twenty-seven colored had been safely lodged in Moyamensing prison, under the charge of treason. The authorities, however, had utterly failed to catch the hero, William Parker, as he had been sent to Canada, *via* the Underground Rail Road, and was thus "sitting under his own vine and fig tree, where none dared to molest, or make him afraid."

As an act of simple justice it may here be stated that the abolitionists and prisoners found a true friend and ally at least in one United States official, who, by the way, figured prominently in making arrests, etc., namely: the United States Marshal, A. E. Roberts. In all his intercourse with the prisoners and their friends, he plainly showed that all his sympathies were on the side of Freedom, and not with the popular pro-slavery sentiment which clamored so loudly against traitors and abolitionists.

Two of his prisoners had been identified in the jail as fugitive slaves by their owners. When the trial came on these two individuals were among the missing. How they escaped was unknown; the Marshal, however, was strongly suspected of being a friend of the Underground Rail Road, and to add now, that those suspicions were founded on fact, will, doubtless, do him no damage.

In order to draw the contrast between Freedom and Slavery, simply with a view of showing how the powers that were acted and judged in the days of the reign of the Fugitive Slave Law, unquestionably nothing better could be found to meet the requirements of this issue than the charge of Judge Kane, coupled with the indictment of the Grand Jury. In the light of the Emancipation and the Fifteenth Amendment, they are too transparent to need a single word of comment. Judge and jury having found the accused chargeable with Treason, nothing remained, so far as the men were concerned, but to bide their time as best they could in prison. Most of them were married, and had wives and children clinging to them in this hour of fearful looking for of judgment.

THE LAW OF TREASON, AS LAID DOWN BY JUDGE KANE.

The following charge to the Grand Jury of the United States District Court, in reference to the Slave-hunting affray in Lancaster county, and preparatory to their finding bills of indictment against the prisoners, was delivered on Monday, September 28, by Judge Kane:

"Gentlemen of the Grand Jury:—It has been represented to me, that since we met last, circumstances have occurred in one of the neighboring counties in our District, which should call for your prompt scrutiny, and perhaps for the energetic action of the Court. It is said, that a citizen of the State of Maryland, who had come into Pennsylvania to reclaim a fugitive from labor, was forcibly obstructed in the attempt by a body of armed men, assaulted, beaten and murdered; that some members of his family, who had accompanied him in the pursuit, were at the same time, and by the same party maltreated and grievously wounded; and that an officer of justice, constituted under the authority of this Court, who sought to arrest the fugitive, was impeded and repelled by menaces and violence, while proclaiming his character, and exhibiting his warrant. It is said, too, that the time and manner of these outrages, their asserted object, the denunciations by which they were preceded, and the simultaneous action of most of the guilty parties, evinced a combined purpose forcibly to resist and make nugatory a constitutional provision, and the statutes enacted in pursuance of it: and it is added, in confirmation of this, that for some months back, gatherings of people, strangers, as well as citizens, have been held from time to time in the vicinity of the place of the recent outbreaks, at which exhortations were made and pledges interchanged to hold the law for the recovery of fugitive slaves as of no validity, and to defy its execution. Such are some of the representations that have been made in my hearing, and in regard to which, it has become your duty, as the Grand Inquest of the District, to make legal inquiry. Personally, I know nothing of the facts, or the evidence relating to them. As a member of the Court, before which the accused persons may hereafter be arraigned and tried, I have sought to keep my mind altogether free from any impressions of their guilt or innocence, and even from an extra-judicial knowledge of the circumstances which must determine the legal character of the offence that has thus been perpetrated. It is due to the great interests of public justice, no less than to the parties implicated in a criminal charge, that their cause should be in no wise and in no degree pre-judged. And in referring, therefore, to the representations which have been made to me, I have no other object than to point you to the reasons for my addressing you at this advanced period of our sessions, and to enable you to apply with more facility and certainty the principles and rules of law, which I shall proceed to lay before you.

If the circumstances, to which I have adverted, have in fact taken place, they involve the highest crime known to our laws. Treason against the United States is defined by the Constitution, Art. 3, Sec. 3, cl. 1, to consist in "levying war against them, or adhering to their enemies, giving them aid and comfort." This definition is borrowed from the ancient Law of England, Stat. 25, Edw. 3, Stat. 5, Chap. 2, and its terms must be understood, of course, in the sense which they bore in that law, and which obtained here when the Constitution was adopted. The expression, "levying war," so regarded, embraces not merely the act of formal or declared war, but any combination forcibly to prevent or oppose the execution or enforcement of a provision of the Constitution, or of a public Statute, if accompanied or followed by an act of forcible opposition in pursuance of such combination. This, in substance, has been the interpretation given to these words by the English Judges, and it has been uniformly and fully recognized and adopted in the Courts of the United States. (See Foster, Hale, and Hawkins, and the opinions of Iredell, Patterson, Chase, Marshall, and Washington, J. J., of the Supreme Court, and of Peters, D. J., in U. S. vs. Vijol, U. S. vs. Mitchell, U. S. vs. Fries, U. S. vs. Bollman and Swartwout, and U. S. vs. Burr).

The definition, as you will observe, includes two particulars, both of them indispensable elements of the offence. There must have been a combination or conspiring together to oppose the law by force, and some actual force must have been exerted, or the crime of treason is not consummated. The highest, or at least the direct proof of the combination may be found in the declared purposes of the individual party before the actual outbreak; or it may be derived from the proceedings of meetings, in which he took part openly; or which he either prompted, or made effective by his countenance or sanction,—commending, counselling and instigating forcible resistance to the law. I speak, of course, of a conspiring to resist a law, not the more limited purpose to violate it, or to prevent its application and enforcement in a particular case, or against a particular individual. The combination must be directed against the law itself. But such direct proof of this element of the offence is not legally necessary to establish its existence. The concert of purpose may be deduced from the concerted action itself, or it may be inferred from facts occurring at the time, or afterwards, as well as before. Besides this, there must be some act of violence, as the result or consequence of the combining.

But here again, it is not necessary to prove that the individual accused was a direct, personal actor in the violence. If he was present, directing, aiding, abetting, counselling, or countenancing it, he is in law guilty of the forcible act. Nor is even his personal presence indispensable. Though he be absent at the time of its actual perpetration, yet, if he directed the act, devised, or knowingly furnished the means for carrying it into effect, instigated others to perform it, he shares their guilt.

In treason there are no accessories. There has been, I fear, an erroneous impression on this subject, among a portion of our people. If it has been thought safe, to counsel and instigate others to acts of forcible oppugnation to the provisions of a statute, to inflame the minds of the ignorant by appeals to passion, and denunciations of the law as oppressive, unjust, revolting to the conscience, and not binding on the actions of men, to represent the constitution of the land as a compact of iniquity, which it were meritorious to violate or subvert, the mistake has been a grievous one; and they who have fallen into it may rejoice, if peradventure their appeals and their counsels have been hitherto without effect. The supremacy of the constitution, in all its provisions, is at the very basis of our existence as a nation. He, whose conscience, or whose theories of political or individual right, forbid him to support and maintain it in its fullest integrity, may relieve himself from the duties of citizenship, by divesting himself of its rights. But while he remains within our borders, he is to remember, that successfully to instigate treason, is to commit it. I shall not be supposed to imply in these remarks, that I have doubts of the law-abiding character of our people. No one can know them well, without the most entire reliance on their fidelity to the constitution. Some of them may differ from the mass, as to the rightfulness or the wisdom of this or the other provision that is found in the federal compact, they may be divided in sentiment as to the policy of a particular statute, or of some provision in a statute; but it is their honest purpose to stand by the engagements, all the engagements, which bind them to their brethren of the other States. They have but one country; they recognize no law of higher social obligation than its constitution and the laws made in pursuance of it; they recognize no higher appeal than to the tribunals it has appointed; they cherish no patriotism that looks beyond the union of the States. That there are men here, as elsewhere, whom a misguided zeal impels to violations of law; that there are others who are controlled by false sympathies, and some who yield too readily and too fully to sympathies not always false, or if false, yet pardonable, and become criminal by yielding, that we have, not only in our jails and almshouses, but segregated here and there in detached portions of the State, ignorant men, many of them without political rights, degraded in social position, and instinctive of revolt, all this is true. It is proved by the daily record of our police courts, and by the ineffective labors of those good men among us, who seek to detach want from temptation, passion from violence, and ignorance from crime.

But it should not be supposed that any of these represent the sentiment of Pennsylvania, and it would be to wrong our people sorely, to include them in the same category of personal, social, or political morals. It is declared in the article of the constitution, which I have already cited, that 'no person shall be convicted of treason, unless on the testimony of two witnesses to the same overt act, or on confession in open court.' This and the corresponding language in the act of Congress of the 30th of April, 1790, seem to refer to the proofs on the trial, and not to the preliminary hearing before the committing magistrate, or the proceeding before the grand inquest. There can be no conviction until after arraignment on bill found. The previous action in the case is not a trial, and cannot convict, whatever be the evidence or the number of witnesses. I understand this to have been the opinion entertained by Chief Justice Marshall, 1 Burr's Trial, 195, and though it differs from that expressed by Judge Iredell on the indictment of Fries, (1 Whart. Am. St. Tr. 480), I feel authorized to recommend it to you, as within the terms of the Constitution, and involving no injustice to the accused. I have only to add that treason against the United States, may be committed by any one resident or sojourning within its territory, and under the protection of its laws, whether he be a citizen or an alien. (Fost. C. L. 183, 5.—1 Hale 59, 60, 62. 1 Hawk. ch. 17, § 5, Kel. 38).

Besides the crime of treason, which I have thus noticed, there are offences of minor grades, against the Constitution and the State, some or other of which may be apparently established by the evidence that will come before you. These are embraced in the act of Congress, on the 30th of Sept., 1790, Ch. 9, Sec. 22, on the subject of obstructing or resisting the service of legal process,—the act of the 2d of March, 1831, Chap. 99, Sec. 2, which secures the jurors, witnesses, and officers of our Courts in the fearless, free, and impartial administration of their respective functions,—and the act of the 18th of September, 1850, Ch. 60, which relates more particularly to the rescue, or attempted rescue of a fugitive from labor. These Acts were made the subject of a charge to the Grand Jury of this Court in November last, of which I shall direct a copy to be laid before you; and I do not deem it necessary to repeat their provisions at this time.

Gentlemen of the Grand Jury: You are about to enter upon a most grave and momentous duty. You will be careful in performing it, not to permit your indignation against crime, or your just appreciation of its perilous consequences, to influence your judgment of the guilt of those who may be charged before you with its commission. But you will be careful, also, that no misguided charity shall persuade you to withhold the guilty from the retributions of justice. You will inquire whether an offence has been committed, what was its legal character, and who were the offenders,—and this done, and this only, you will make your presentments according to the evidence and the law. Your inquiries will not be restricted to the conduct of the people belonging to our own State. If in the progress of them, you shall find, that men have been among us, who, under whatever mask of conscience or of peace, have labored to incite others to treasonable violence, and who, after arranging the elements of the mischief, have withdrawn themselves to await the explosion they had contrived, you will feel yourselves bound to present the fact to the Court,—and however distant may be the place in which the offenders may have sought refuge, we give you the pledge of the law, that its far-reaching energies shall be exerted to bring them up for trial,—if guilty, to punishment. The offence of treason is not triable in this Court; but by an act of Congress, passed on the 8th of August, 1845, Chap. 98, it is made lawful for the Grand Jury, empanelled and sworn in the District Court, to take cognizance of all the indictments for crimes against the United States within the jurisdiction of either of the Federal Courts of the District. There being no Grand Jury in attendance at this time in the Circuit Court, to pass upon the accusations I have referred to in the first instance, it has fallen to my lot to assume the responsible office of expounding to you the law in regard to them. I have the satisfaction of knowing, that if the views I have expressed are in any respect erroneous, they must undergo the revision of my learned brother of the Supreme Court, who presides in this Circuit, before they can operate to the serious prejudice of any one; and that if they are doubtful even, provision exists for their re-examination in the highest tribunal of the country."

On the strength of Judge Kane's carefully-drawn up charge the Grand Jury found true bills of indictment against forty of the Christiana offenders, charged with treason. James Jackson, an aged member of the Society of Friends (a Quaker), and a well-known non-resistant abolitionist, was of this number. With his name the blanks were filled up; the same form (with regard to these bills) was employed in the case of each one of the accused. The following is a

COPY OF THE INDICTMENT.

Eastern District of Pennsylvania, ss.:

The Grand Inquest of the United States of America, inquiring for the Eastern District of Pennsylvania, on their oaths and affirmations, respectfully do present, that James Jackson, yeoman of the District aforesaid, owing allegiance to the United States of America, wickedly devising and intending the peace and tranquility of said United States, to disturb, and prevent the execution of the laws thereof within the same, to wit, a law of the United States, entitled "An act respecting fugitives from justice and persons escaping from the service of their masters," approved February twelfth, one thousand seven hundred and ninety-three, and also a law of the United States, entitled "An act to amend, and supplementary to, the act entitled, An act respecting fugitives from justice and persons escaping from the service of their masters, approved February the twelfth, one thousand seven hundred and ninety-three," which latter supplementary act was approved September eighteenth, one thousand eight hundred and fifty, on the eleventh day of September, in the year of our Lord, one thousand eight hundred and fifty-one, in the county of Lancaster, in the State of Pennsylvania and District aforesaid, and within the jurisdiction of this Court, wickedly and traitorously did intend to levy war against the United States within the same. And to fulfill and bring to effect the said traitorous intention of him, the said James Jackson, he, the said James Jackson afterward, to wit, on the day and year aforesaid, in the State, District and County aforesaid, and within the jurisdiction of this Court, with a great multitude of persons, whose names, to this Inquest are as yet unknown, to a great number, to wit, to the number of one hundred persons and upwards, armed and arrayed in a war-like manner, that is to say, with guns, swords, and other warlike weapons, as well offensive as defensive, being then and there unlawfully and traitorously assembled, did traitorously assemble and combine against the said United States, and then and there, with force and arms, wickedly and traitorously, and with the wicked and traitorous intention to oppose and prevent, by means of intimidation and violence, the execution of the said laws of the United States within the same, did array and dispose themselves in a war-like and hostile manner against the said United States, and then and there, with force and arms, in pursuance of such their traitorous intention, he, the said James Jackson, with the said persons so as aforesaid, wickedly and traitorously did levy war against the United States.

And further, to fulfill and bring to effect the said traitorous intention of him, the said James Jackson, and in pursuance and in execution of the said wicked and traitorous combination to oppose, resist and prevent the said laws of the United States from being carried into execution, he, the said James Jackson, afterwards, to wit, on the day and year first aforesaid, in the State, District and county aforesaid, and within the jurisdiction aforesaid, with the said persons whose names to this Inquest are as yet unknown, did, wickedly and traitorously assemble against the said United States, with the avowed intention by force of arms and intimidation to prevent the execution of the said laws of the United States within the same; and in pursuance and execution of such their wicked and traitorous combination, he, the said James Jackson, then and there with force and arms, with the said persons to a great number, to wit, the number of one hundred persons and upwards, armed and arrayed in a warlike manner, that is to say, with guns, swords, and other warlike weapons, as well offensive as defensive, being then and there, unlawfully and traitorously assembled, did wickedly, knowingly, and traitorously resist and oppose one Henry H. Kline, an officer, duly appointed by Edward D. Ingraham, Esq., a commissioner, duly appointed by the Circuit Court of the United States, for the said district, in the execution of the duty of the office of the said Kline, he, the said Kline, being appointed by the said Edward Ingraham, Esq., by writing under his hand, to execute warrants and other process issued by him, the said Ingraham, in the performance of his duties as Commissioner, under the said laws of the United States, and then and there, with force and arms, with the said great multitude of persons, so as, aforesaid, unlawfully and traitorously assembled, and armed and arrayed in manner as aforesaid, he, the said, James Jackson, wickedly and traitorously did oppose and resist, and prevent the said Kline, from executing the lawful process to him directed and delivered by the said commissioner against sundry persons, then residents of said county, who had been legally charged before the said commissioner as being persons held to service or labor in the State of Maryland, and owing such service or labor to a certain Edward Gorsuch, under the laws of the said State of Maryland, had escaped therefrom, into the said Eastern district of Pennsylvania; which process, duly issued by the said commissioner, the said Kline then and there had in his possession, and was then and there proceeding to execute, as by law he was bound to do; and so the grand inquest, upon their respective oaths and affirmations aforesaid, do say, that the said James Jackson, in manner aforesaid, as much as in him lay, wickedly and traitorously did prevent, by means of force and intimidation, the execution of the said laws of the United States, in the said State and District. And further, to fulfill and bring to effect, the said traitorous intention of him, the said James Jackson, and in further pursuance, and in the execution of the said wicked and traitorous combination to expose, resist, and prevent the execution of the said laws of the said United States, in the State and District aforesaid, he, the said James Jackson, afterwards, to wit, on the day and year first aforesaid, in the State, county, and district aforesaid, and within the jurisdiction of this court, with the said persons whose names to the grand inquest aforesaid, are as yet unknown, did, wickedly and traitorously assemble against the said United States with the avowed intention, by means of force and intimidation, to prevent the execution of the said laws of the United States in the State and district aforesaid, and in pursuance and execution of such, their wicked and traitorous combination and intention, then and there to the State, district, and county aforesaid, and within the jurisdiction of this court, with force and arms, with a great multitude of persons, to wit, the number of one hundred persons and upwards, armed and arrayed in a warlike manner, that is to say, with guns, swords, and other warlike weapons, as well offensive as defensive, being then and there unlawfully and traitorously assembled, he, the said James Jackson, did, knowingly, and unlawfully assault the said Henry H. Kline, he, the said Kline, being an officer appointed by writing, under the hand of the said Edward D. Ingraham, Esq., a commissioner under said laws, to execute warrants and other process, issued by the said commissioner in the performance of his duties as such; and he, the said James Jackson, did, then and there, traitorously, with force and arms, against the will of the said Kline, liberate and take out of his custody, persons by him before that time arrested, and in his lawful custody, then and there being, by virtue of lawful process against them issued by the said commissioner, they being legally charged with being persons held to service or labor in the State of Maryland, and owing such service or labor to a certain Edward Gorsuch, under the laws of the said State of Maryland, who had escaped therefrom into the said district; and so the grand inquest aforesaid, upon their oaths and affirmations, aforesaid, do say, that he, the said James Jackson, as much as in him lay, did, then and there, in pursuance and in execution of the said wicked and traitorous combination and intention, wickedly and traitorously, by means of force and intimidation, prevent the execution of the said laws of the United States, in the said State and district.

And further to fulfill and bring to effect, the said traitorous intention of him, the said James Jackson, and in pursuance and in execution of the said wicked and traitorous combination to oppose, resist and prevent the said laws of the United States from being carried into execution, he, the said James Jackson, afterwards, to wit, on the day and year first aforesaid, and on divers other days, both before and afterwards in the State and district aforesaid, and within the jurisdiction of this court, with the said persons to this inquest as yet unknown, maliciously and traitorously did meet, conspire, consult, and agree among themselves, further to oppose, resist, and prevent, by means of force and intimidation, the execution of the said laws herein before specified.

And further to fulfill, perfect, and bring to effect the said traitorous intention of him the said James Jackson, and in pursuance and execution of the said wicked and traitorous combination to oppose and resist the said laws of the United States from being carried into execution, in the State and district aforesaid, he, the said James Jackson, together with the other persons whose names are to this inquest as yet unknown, on the day and year first aforesaid, and on divers other days and times, as well before and after, at the district aforesaid, within the jurisdiction of said court, with force and arms, maliciously and traitorously did prepare and compose, and did then and there maliciously and traitorously cause and procure to be prepared and composed, divers books, pamphlets, letters, declarations, resolutions, addresses, papers and writings, and did then and there maliciously and traitorously publish and disperse and cause to be published and dispersed, divers other books and pamphlets, letters, declarations, resolutions, addresses, papers and writings ; the said books, pamphlets, letters, declarations, resolutions, addresses, papers and writings, so respectively prepared, composed, published and dispersed, as last aforesaid, containing therein, amongst other things, incitements, encouragements, and exhortations, to move, induce and persuade persons held to service in any of the United States, by the laws thereof, who had escaped into the said district, as well as other persons, citizens of said district, to resist, oppose, and prevent, by violence and intimidation, the execution of the said laws, and also containing therein, instructions and directions how and upon what occasion, the traitorous purposes last aforesaid, should and might be carried into effect, contrary to the form of the act of Congress in such case made and provided, and against the peace and dignity of the United States.

JOHN W. ASHMEAD,
Attorney of the U. S. for the Eastern District of Pennsylvania.

The abolitionists were leaving no stone unturned in order to triumphantly meet the case in Court. During the interim many tokens of kindness and marks of Christian benevolence were extended to the prisoners by their friends and sympathizers; among these none deserve more honorable mention than the noble act of Thomas L. Kane (son of Judge Kane, and now General), in tendering all the prisoners a sumptuous Thanksgiving dinner, consisting of turkey, etc., pound cake, etc., etc. The dinner for the white prisoners, Messrs. Hanaway, Davis, and Scarlett, was served in appropriate style in the room of Mr. Morrison, one of the keepers. The U. S. Marshal, A. E. Roberts, Esq., several of the keepers, and Mr. Hanes, one of the prison officers, dined with the prisoners as their guests. Mayor Charles Gilpin was also present and accepted an invitation to test the quality of the luxuries, thus significantly indicating that he was not the enemy of Freedom.

Mrs. Martha Hanaway, the wife of the " traitor " of that name, and who had spent most of her time with her husband since his incarceration, served each of the twenty-seven colored " traitors " with a plate of the delicacies, and the supply being greater than the demand, the balance was served to outsiders in other cells on the same corridor.

The pro-slavery party were very indignant over the matter, and the Hon. Mr. Brent thought it incumbent upon him to bring this high handed procedure to the notice of the Court, where he received a few crumbs of sympathy, from the pro-slavery side, of course. But the dinner had been so handsomely arranged, and coming from the source that it did, it had a very telling effect. Long before this, however, Mr. T. L. Kane had given abundant evidence that he approved of the Underground Rail Road, and was a decided opponent of the Fugitive Slave Law; in short, that he believed in freedom for all men, irrespective of race or color.

Castnor Hanaway was first to be tried; over him, therefore, the great contest was to be made. For the defence of this particular case, the abolitionists selected J. M. Read, Thaddeus Stevens, Joseph S. Lewis and Theodore Cuyler, Esqs. On the side of the Fugitive Slave Law, and against the " traitors," were U. S. District Attorney, John W. Ashmead, Hon. James

Cooper, James R. Ludlow, Esq., and Robert G. Brent, Attorney General of Maryland. Mr. Brent was allowed to act as "overseer" in conducting matters on the side of the Fugitive Slave Law. On this infamous enactment, combined with a corrupted popular sentiment, the pro-slavery side depended for success. The abolitionists viewed matters in the light of freedom and humanity, and hopefully relied upon the justice of their cause and the power of truth to overcome and swallow up all the Pharaoh's rods of serpents as fast as they might be thrown down.

The prisoners having lain in their cells nearly three months, the time for their trial arrived. Monday morning, November 24th, the contest began. The first three days were occupied in procuring jurors. The pro-slavery side desired none but such as believed in the Fugitive Slave Law and in "Treason" as expounded in the Judge's charge and the finding of the Grand Jury.

The counsel for the "Traitors" carefully weighed the jurors, and when found wanting challenged them; in so doing, they managed to get rid of most all of that special class upon whom the prosecution depended for a conviction. The jury having been sworn in, the battle commenced in good earnest, and continued unabated for nearly two weeks. It is needless to say, that the examinations and arguments would fill volumes, and were of the most deeply interesting nature.

No attempt can here be made to recite the particulars of the trial other than by a mere reference. It was, doubtless, the most important trial that ever took place in this country relative to the Underground Rail Road passengers, and in its results more good was brought out of evil than can easily be estimated. The pro-slavery theories of treason were utterly demolished, and not a particle of room was left the advocates of the peculiar institution to hope, that slave-hunters in future, in quest of fugitives, would be any more safe than Gorsuch. The tide of public sentiment changed—Hanaway, and the other "traitors," began to be looked upon as having been greatly injured, and justly entitled to public sympathy and honor, while confusion of face, disappointment and chagrin were plainly visible throughout the demoralized ranks of the enemy. Hanaway was victorious.

An effort was next made to convict Thompson, one of the colored "traitors." To defend the colored prisoners, the old Abolition Society had retained Thaddeus Stevens, David Paul Brown, William S. Pierce, and Robert P. Kane, Esqs., (son of Judge Kane). Stevens, Brown and Pierce were well-known veterans, defenders of the slave wherever and whenever called upon so to do. In the present case, they were prepared for a gallant stand and a long siege against opposing forces. Likewise, R. P. Kane, Esq., although a young volunteer in the anti-slavery war, brought to the work great zeal, high attainments, large sympathy and true pluck, while, in view of all the circumstances, the committee of arrangements felt very much gratified to have him in their ranks.

By this time, however, the sandy foundations of "overseer" Brent and Co., (on the part of slavery), had been so completely swept away by the Hon. J. M. Read and Co., on the side of freedom, that there was but little chance left to deal heavy blows upon the defeated advocates of the Fugitive Slave Law. Thompson was pronounced "not guilty." The other prisoners, of course, shared the same good luck. The victory was then complete, equally as much so as at Christiana. Underground Rail Road stock arose rapidly, and a feeling of universal rejoicing pervaded the friends of freedom from one end of the country to the other.

Especially were slave-holders taught the wholesome lesson, that the Fugitive Slave Law was no guarantee against "red hot shot," nor the charges of U. S. Judges and the findings of Grand Juries, together with the superior learning of counsel from slave-holding Maryland, any guarantee that "traitors" would be hung. In every respect, the Underground Rail Road made capital by the treason. Slave-holders from Maryland especially were far less disposed to hunt their runaway property than they had hitherto been. The Deputy Marshal likewise considered the business of catching slaves very unsafe.

WILLIAM AND ELLEN CRAFT.
FEMALE SLAVE IN MALE ATTIRE, FLEEING AS A PLANTER, WITH HER HUSBAND AS HER BODY SERVANT.

A quarter of a century ago, William and Ellen Craft were slaves in the State of Georgia. With them, as with thousands of others, the desire to be free was very strong. For this jewel they were willing to make any sacrifice, or to endure any amount of suffering. In this state of mind they commenced planning. After thinking of various ways that might be tried, it occurred to William and Ellen, that one might act the part of master and the other the part of servant.

Ellen being fair enough to pass for white, of necessity would have to be transformed into a young planter for the time being. All that was needed, however, to make this important change was that she should be dressed elegantly in a fashionable suit of male attire, and have her hair cut in the style usually worn by young planters. Her profusion of dark hair offered a fine opportunity for the change. So far this plan looked very tempting. But it occurred to them that Ellen was beardless. After some mature reflection, they came to the conclusion that this difficulty could be very readily obviated by having the face muffled up as though the young planter was suffering badly with the face or toothache; thus they got rid of this trouble. Straightway, upon further reflection, several other very serious difficulties

WILLIAM CRAFT.

ELLEN CRAFT.

stared them in the face. For instance, in traveling, they knew that they would be under the necessity of stopping repeatedly at hotels, and that the custom of registering would have to be conformed to, unless some very good excuse could be given for not doing so.

Here they again thought much over matters, and wisely concluded that the young man had better assume the attitude of a gentleman very much indisposed. He must have his right arm placed carefully in a sling; that would be a sufficient excuse for not registering, etc. Then he must be a little lame, with a nice cane in the left hand; he must have large green spectacles over his eyes, and withal he must be very hard of hearing and dependent on his faithful servant (as was no uncommon thing with slave-holders), to look after all his wants.

William was just the man to act this part. To begin with, he was very "likely-looking;" smart, active and exceedingly attentive to his young master—indeed he was almost eyes, ears, hands and feet for him. William knew that this would please the slave-holders. The young planter would have nothing to do but hold himself subject to his ailments and put on a bold air of superiority; he was not to deign to notice anybody. If, while traveling, gentlemen, either politely or rudely, should venture to scrape acquaintance with the young planter, in his deafness he was to remain mute; the servant was to explain. In every instance when this occurred, as it actually did, the servant was fully equal to the emergency—none dreaming of the disguises in which the Underground Rail Road passengers were traveling.

They stopped at a first-class hotel in Charleston, where the young planter and his body servant were treated, as the house was wont to treat the chivalry. They stopped also at a similar hotel in Richmond, and with like results.

They knew that they must pass through Baltimore, but they did not know the obstacles that they would have to surmount in the Monumental City. They proceeded to the depot in the usual manner, and the servant asked for tickets for his master and self. Of course the master could have a ticket, but "bonds will have to be entered before you can get a ticket," said the ticket master. "It is the rule of this office to require bonds for all negroes applying for tickets to go North, and none but gentlemen of well-known responsibility will be taken," further explained the ticket master.

The servant replied, that he knew "nothing about that"—that he was "simply traveling with his young master to take care of him—he being in a very delicate state of health, so much so, that fears were entertained that he might not be able to hold out to reach Philadelphia, where he was hastening for medical treatment," and ended his reply by saying, "my master can't be detained." Without further parley, the ticket master very obligingly waived the old "rule," and furnished the requisite tickets. The mountain being

24

thus removed, the young planter and his faithful servant were safely in the cars for the city of Brotherly Love.

Scarcely had they arrived on free soil when the rheumatism departed —the right arm was unslung—the toothache was gone—the beardless face was unmuffled—the deaf heard and spoke—the blind saw—and the lame leaped as an hart, and in the presence of a few astonished friends of the slave, the facts of this unparalleled Underground Rail Road feat were fully established by the most unquestionable evidence.

The constant strain and pressure on Ellen's nerves, however, had tried her severely, so much so, that for days afterwards, she was physically very much prostrated, although joy and gladness beamed from her eyes, which bespoke inexpressible delight within.

Never can the writer forget the impression made by their arrival. Even now, after a lapse of nearly a quarter of a century, it is easy to picture them in a private room, surrounded by a few friends—Ellen in her fine suit of black, with her cloak and high-heeled boots, looking, in every respect, like a young gentleman; in an hour after having dropped her male attire, and assumed the habiliments of her sex the feminine only was visible in every line and feature of her structure.

Her husband, William, was thoroughly colored, but was a man of marked natural abilities, of good manners, and full of pluck, and possessed of perceptive faculties very large.

It was necessary, however, in those days, that they should seek a permanent residence, where their freedom would be more secure than in Philadelphia; therefore they were advised to go to headquarters, directly to Boston. There they would be safe, it was supposed, as it had then been about a generation since a fugitive had been taken back from the old Bay State, and through the incessant labors of William Lloyd Garrison, the great pioneer, and his faithful coadjutors, it was conceded that another fugitive slave case could never be tolerated on the free soil of Massachusetts. So to Boston they went.

On arriving, the warm hearts of abolitionists welcomed them heartily, and greeted and cheered them without let or hindrance. They did not pretend to keep their coming a secret, or hide it under a bushel; the story of their escape was heralded broadcast over the country—North and South, and indeed over the civilized world. For two years or more, not the slightest fear was entertained that they were not just as safe in Boston as if they had gone to Canada. But the day the Fugitive Bill passed, even the bravest abolitionist began to fear that a fugitive slave was no longer safe anywhere under the stars and stripes, North or South, and that William and Ellen Craft were liable to be captured at any moment by Georgia slave hunters. Many abolitionists counselled resistance to the death at all hazards. Instead of running to Canada, fugitives generally armed themselves and thus said, "Give me liberty or give me death."

William and Ellen Craft believed that it was their duty, as citizens of Massachusetts, to observe a more legal and civilized mode of conforming to the marriage rite than had been permitted them in slavery, and as Theodore Parker had shown himself a very warm friend of their's, they agreed to have their wedding over again according to the laws of a free State. After performing the ceremony, the renowned and fearless advocate of equal rights (Theodore Parker), presented William with a revolver and a dirk-knife, counselling him to use them manfully in defence of his wife and himself, if ever an attempt should be made by his owners or anybody else to re-enslave them.

But, notwithstanding all the published declarations made by abolitionists and fugitives, to the effect, that slave-holders and slave-catchers in visiting Massachusetts in pursuit of their runaway property, would be met by just such weapons as Theodore Parker presented William with, to the surprise of all Boston, the owners of William and Ellen actually had the effrontery to attempt their recapture under the Fugitive Slave Law. How it was done, and the results, taken from the *Old Liberator*, (William Lloyd Garrison's organ), we copy as follows :

From the "Liberator," Nov. 1, 1850.

SLAVE-HUNTERS IN BOSTON.

Our city, for a week past, has been thrown into a state of intense excitement by the appearance of two prowling villains, named Hughes and Knight, from Macon, Georgia, for the purpose of seizing William and Ellen Craft, under the infernal Fugitive Slave Bill, and carrying them back to the hell of Slavery. Since the day of '76, there has not been such a popular demonstration on the side of human freedom in this region. The humane and patriotic contagion has infected all classes. Scarcely any other subject has been talked about in the streets, or in the social circle. On Thursday, of last week, warrants for the arrest of William and Ellen were issued by Judge Levi Woodbury, but no officer has yet been found ready or bold enough to serve them. In the meantime, the Vigilance Committee, appointed at the Faneuil Hall meeting, has not been idle. Their number has been increased to upwards of a hundred " good men and true," including some thirty or forty members of the bar; and they have been in constant session, devising every legal method to baffle the pursuing bloodhounds, and relieve the city of their hateful presence. On Saturday placards were posted up in all directions, announcing the arrival of these slave-hunters, and describing their persons. On the same day, Hughes and Knight were arrested on the charge of slander against William Craft. The Chronotype says, the damages being laid at $10,000 ; bail was demanded in the same sum, and was promptly furnished. By whom? is the question. An immense crowd was assembled in front of the Sheriff's office, while the bail matter was being arranged. The reporters were not admitted. It was only known that Watson Freeman, Esq., who once declared his readiness to hang any number of negroes remarkably cheap, came in, saying that the arrest was a shame, all a humbug, the trick of the damned abolitionists, and proclaimed his readiness to stand bail. John H. Pearson was also sent for, and came— the same John H. Pearson, merchant and Southern packet agent, who immortalized himself by sending back, on the 10th of September, 1846, in the bark Niagara, a poor fugitive slave, who came secreted in the brig Ottoman, from New Orleans—being himself judge, jury and executioner, to consign a fellow-being to a life of bondage—in obedience to the law of a slave State, and in violation of the law of his own. This same John H. Pearson, not contented with his previous infamy, was on hand. There is a story that the slave-hunters have been his table-guests also, and whether he bailed them or not, we don't know. What we know is, that soon after Pearson came out from the back room, where he and Knight and the Sheriff had been closeted, the Sheriff said that Knight was bailed—he would not say by whom. Knight being looked after, was not to be found. He had slipped out through a back door, and thus cheated the crowd of the pleasure of greeting him—possibly with that rough and ready affection which Barclay's brewers bestowed upon Haynau. The escape was very fortunate every way. Hughes and Knight have since been twice arrested and put under bonds of $10,000 (making $30,000 in all), charged with a conspiracy to kidnap and abduct William Craft, a peaceable citizen of Massachusetts, etc. Bail was entered by Hamilton Willis, of Willis & Co., 25 State street, and Patrick Riley, U. S. Deputy Marshal.

The following (says the Chronotype), is a *verbatim et literatim* copy of the letter sent by Knight to Craft, to entice him to the U. S. Hotel, in order to kidnap him. It shows, that the school-master owes Knight more "service and labor" than it is possible for Craft to:

BOSTON, Oct. 22, 1850, 11 Oclk P. M.

Wm. Craft—Sir—I have to leave so Eirley in the moring that I cold not call according to promis, so if you want me to carry a letter home with me, you must bring it to the United States Hotel to morrow and leave it in box 44, or come your self to morro eavening after tea and bring it. let me no if you come your self by sending a note to box 44 U. S. Hotel so that I may know whether to wate after tea or not by the Bearer. If your wife wants to see me you cold bring her with you if you come your self.

JOHN KNIGHT.

P. S. I shall leave for home eirley a Thursday moring.   J. K.

At a meeting of colored people, held in Belknap Street Church, on Friday evening, the following resolutions were unanimously adopted :

Resolved, That God willed us free; man willed us slaves. We will as God wills ; God's will be done.

Resolved, That our oft repeated determination to resist oppression is the same now as ever, and we pledge ourselves, at all hazards, to resist unto death any attempt upon our liberties.

Resolved, That as South Carolina seizes and imprisons colored seamen from the North, under the plea that it is to prevent insurrection and rebellion among her colored population, the authorities of this State, and city in particular, be requested to lay hold of, and put in prison, immediately, any and all fugitive slave-hunters who may be found among us, upon the same ground, and for similar reasons.

Spirited addresses, of a most emphatic type, were made by Messrs. Remond, of Salem, Roberts, Nell, and Allen, of Boston, and Davis, of Plymouth. Individuals and highly respectable committees of gentlemen have repeatedly waited upon these Georgia miscreants, to persuade them to make a speedy departure from the city. After promising to do so, and repeatedly falsifying their word, it is said that they left on Wednesday afternoon, in the express train for New York, and thus (says the Chronotype), they have " gone off with their ears full of fleas, to fire the solemn word for the dissolution of the Union !"

Telegraphic intelligence is received, that President Fillmore has announced his determination to sustain the Fugitive Slave Bill, at all hazards. Let him try ! The fugitives, as well as the colored people generally, seem determined to carry out the spirit of the resolutions to their fullest extent.

ELLEN first received information that the slave-hunters from Georgia were after her through Mrs. Geo. S. Hilliard, of Boston, who had been a good friend to her from the day of her arrival from slavery. How Mrs. Hilliard obtained the information, the impression it made on Ellen, and where she was secreted, the following extract of a letter written by Mrs. Hilliard, touching the memorable event, will be found deeply interesting:

" In regard to William and Ellen Craft, it is true that we received her at our house when the first warrant under the act of eighteen hundred and fifty was issued.

Dr. Bowditch called upon us to say, that the warrant must be for William and Ellen, as they were the only fugitives here known to have come from Georgia, and the Dr. asked what we could do. I went to the house of the Rev. F. T. Gray, on Mt. Vernon street, where Ellen was working with Miss Dean, an upholsteress, a friend of ours, who had told us she would teach Ellen her trade. I proposed to Ellen to come and do some work for me, intending not to alarm her. My manner, which I supposed to be indifferent and calm, *betrayed* me, and she threw herself into my arms, sobbing and weeping. She, however, recovered her composure as soon as we reached the street, and was *very firm* ever after.

My husband wished her, by all means, to be brought to our house, and to remain under his protection, saying: 'I am perfectly willing to meet the penalty, should she be found here, but will never give her up.' The penalty, you remember, was six months' imprisonment and a thousand dollars fine. William Craft went, after a time, to Lewis Hayden. He was at first, as Dr. Bowditch told us, ' barricaded in his shop on Cambridge street.' I saw him there, and he said, ' Ellen must not be left at your house.' 'Why? William,' said I, ' do you think we would give her up ?' ' Never,' said he, ' but Mr. Hilliard is not only our friend, but he is a U. S. Commissioner, and should Ellen be found in his house, he must resign his office, as well as incur the penalty of the law, and I will not subject a friend to such a punishment for the sake of our safety.' Was not this noble, when you think how small was the penalty that any one could receive for aiding slaves to escape, compared to the fate which threatened them in case they were captured ? William C. made the same objection to having his wife taken to Mr. Ellis Gray Loring's, he also being a friend and a Commissioner."

This deed of humanity and Christian charity is worthy to be commemorated and classed with the act of the good Samaritan, as the same spirit is shown in both cases. Often was Mrs. Hilliard's house an asylum for fugitive slaves.

After the hunters had left the city in dismay, and the storm of excitement had partially subsided, the friends of William and Ellen concluded that they had better seek a country where they would not be in daily fear of slave-catchers, backed by the Government of the United States. They were, therefore, advised to go to Great Britain. Outfits were liberally provided for them, passages procured, and they took their departure for a habitation in a foreign land.

Much might be told concerning the warm reception they met with from the friends of humanity on every hand, during a stay in England of nearly a score of years, but we feel obliged to make the following extract suffice :

EXTRACT OF A LETTER FROM WM. FARMER, ESQ., OF LONDON, TO WM. LLOYD GARRISON, JUNE 26, 1851—"FUGITIVE SLAVES AT THE GREAT EXHIBITION."

Fortunately, we have, at the present moment, in the British Metropolis, some specimens of what were once American "chattels personal," in the persons of William and Ellen Craft, and William W. Brown, and their friends resolved that they should be exhibited under the world's huge glass case, in order that the world might form its opinion of the alleged mental inferiority of the African race, and their fitness or unfitness for freedom. A small party of anti-slavery friends was accordingly formed to accompany the fugitives through the Exhibition. Mr. and Mrs. Estlin, of Bristol, and a lady friend, Mr. and Mrs. Richard Webb, of Dublin, and a son and daughter, Mr. McDonnell, (a most influential member of the Executive Committee of the National Reform Association—one of our unostentatious, but highly efficient workers for reform in this country, and whose public and private acts, if you were acquainted with, you would feel the same esteem and affection for him as is felt towards him by Mr. Thompson, myself and many others)—these ladies and gentlemen, together with myself, met at Mr. Thompson's house, and, in company with Mrs. Thompson, and Miss Amelia Thompson, the Crafts and Brown, proceeded from thence to the Exhibition. Saturday was selected, as a day upon which the largest number of the aristocracy and wealthy classes attend the Crystal Palace, and the company was, on this occasion, the most distinguished that had been gathered together within its walls since its opening day. Some fifteen thousand, mostly of the upper classes, were there congregated, including the Queen, Prince Albert, and the royal children, the anti-slavery Duchess of Sutherland, (by whom the fugitives were evidently favorably regarded), the Duke of Wellington, the Bishops of Winchester and St. Asaph, a large number of peers, peeresses, members of Parliament, merchants and bankers, and distinguished men from almost all parts of the world, surpassing, in variety of tongue, character and costume, the description of the population of Jerusalem on the day of Pentecost—a season of which it is hoped the Great Exhibition will prove a type, in the copious outpouring of the holy spirit of brotherly union, and the consequent diffusion, throughout the world, of the anti-slavery gospel of good will to all men.

In addition to the American exhibitors, it so happened that the American visitors were particularly numerous, among whom the experienced eyes of Brown and the Crafts enabled them to detect slave-holders by dozens. Mr. McDonnell escorted Mrs. Craft, and Mrs. Thompson; Miss Thompson, at her own request, took the arm of Wm. Wells Brown, whose companion she elected to be for the day; Wm. Craft walked with Miss Amelia Thompson and myself. This arrangement was purposely made in order that there might be no appearance of patronizing the fugitives, but that it might be shown that we regarded them as our equals, and honored them for their heroic escape from Slavery. Quite contrary to the feeling of ordinary visitors, the American department was our chief attraction. Upon arriving at Powers' Greek Slave, our glorious anti-slavery friend, Punch's 'Virginia Slave' was produced. I hope you have seen this production of our great humorous moralist. It is an admirably-drawn figure of a female slave in chains, with the inscription beneath, 'The Virginia Slave, a companion for Powers' Greek Slave.' The comparison of the two soon drew a small crowd, including several Americans, around and near us. Although they refrained from any audible expression of feeling, the object of the comparison was evidently understood and keenly felt. It would not have been prudent in us to have challenged, in words, an anti-slavery discussion in the World's Convention; but everything that we could with propriety do was done to induce them to break silence upon the subject. We had no intention, verbally, of taking the initiative in such a discussion; we confined ourselves to speaking at them, in order that they might be led to speak to us; but our efforts were of no avail. The gauntlet, which was unmistakably thrown down by our party, the Americans were too wary to take up. We spoke, among each other of the wrongs of Slavery; it was in vain. We discoursed freely upon the iniquity of a professedly Christian Republic holding three millions of its population in cruel and degrading bondage; you might as well have preached to the winds. Wm. Wells Brown took 'Punch's Virginia Slave' and deposited it within the enclosure by the 'Greek Slave,' saying audibly, 'As an American fugitive slave, I place this 'Virginia Slave' by the side of the 'Greek Slave,' as its most fitting companion.' Not a word, or reply, or remonstrance from Yankee or Southerner. We had not, however, proceeded many steps from the place before the 'Virginia Slave' was removed. We returned to the statue, and stood near the American by whom it had been taken up, to give him an opportunity of making any remarks he chose upon the matter. Whatever were his feelings, his policy was to keep his lips closed. If he had felt that the act was wrongful, would he not have appealed to the sense of justice of the British bystanders, who are always ready to resist an insult offered to a foreigner in this country? If it was an insult, why not resent it, as became high-spirited Americans? But no; the chivalry of the South tamely allowed itself to be plucked by the beard; the garrulity of the North permitted itself to be silenced by three fugitive slaves. . . . . We promenaded the Exhibition between six and seven hours, and visited nearly every portion of the vast edifice. Among the thousands whom we met in our perambulations, who dreamed of any impropriety in a gentleman of character and standing, like Mr. McDonnell, walking arm-in-arm with a colored woman; or an elegant and accomplished young lady, like Miss Thompson, (daughter of the Hon. George Thompson, M. C.), becoming the promenading companion of a colored man? Did the English peers or peeresses? Not the most aristocratic among them. Did the representatives of any other country have their notions of propriety shocked by the matter? None but Americans. To see the arm of a beautiful English young lady passed through that of 'a nigger,' taking ices and other refreshments with him, upon terms of the most perfect equality, certainly was enough to 'rile,' and evidently did 'rile' the slave-holders who beheld it; but there was no help for it. Even the New York Broadway bullies would not have dared to utter a word of insult, much less lift a finger against Wm. Wells Brown, when walking with his fair companion in the World's Exhibition. It was a circumstance not to be forgotten by these Southern Bloodhounds. Probably, for the first time in their lives, they felt themselves thoroughly muzzled; they dared not even to bark, much less bite. Like the meanest curs, they had to sneak through the Crystal Palace, unnoticed and uncared for; while the victims who had been rescued from their jaws, were warmly greeted by visitors from all parts of the country.

* * * * * * * *

Brown and the Crafts have paid several other visits to the Great Exhibition, in one of which, Wm. Craft succeeded in getting some Southerners "out" upon the Fugitive Slave Bill, respecting which a discussion was held between them in the American department. Finding themselves worsted at every point, they were compelled to have recourse to lying, and unblushingly denied that the bill contained the provisions which Craft alleged it did.

Craft took care to inform them who and what he was. He told them that there had been too much information upon that measure diffused in England for lying to conceal them. He has subsequently met the same parties, who, with contemptible hypocrisy, treated " the nigger " with great respect.

In England the Crafts were highly respected. While under her British Majesty's protection, Ellen became the mother of several children, (having had none under the stars and stripes). These they spared no pains in educating for usefulness in the world. Some two years since William and Ellen returned with two of their children to the United States, and after visiting Boston and other places, William concluded to visit Georgia, his old home, with a view of seeing what inducement war had opened up to enterprise, as he had felt a desire to remove his family thither, if encouraged. Indeed he was prepared to purchase a plantation, if he found matters satisfactory. This visit evidently furnished the needed encouragement, judging from the fact that he did purchase a plantation somewhere in the neighborhood of Savannah, and is at present living there with his family.

The portraits of William and Ellen represent them at the present stage of life, (as citizens of the U. S.)—of course they have greatly changed in appearance from what they were when they first fled from Georgia. Obviously the Fugitive Slave Law in its crusade against William and Ellen Craft, reaped no advantages, but on the contrary, liberty was greatly the gainer.

ARRIVALS FROM RICHMOND.

LEWIS COBB AND NANCY BRISTER.

No one Southern city furnished a larger number of brave, wide-awake and likely-looking Underground Rail Road passengers than the city of Richmond. Lewis and Nancy were fair specimens of the class of travelers coming from that city. Lewis was described as a light yellow man, medium size, good-looking, and intelligent. In referring to bondage, he spoke with great earnestness, and in language very easily understood ; especially when speaking of Samuel Myers, from whom he escaped, he did not hesitate to give him the character of being a very hard man, who was never satisfied, no matter how hard the slaves might try to please him.

Myers was engaged in the commission and forwarding business, and was a man of some standing in Richmond. From him Lewis had received very severe floggings, the remembrance of which he would not only carry with him to Canada, but to the grave. It was owing to abuse of this kind that he was awakened to look for a residence under the protection of the British

Lion. For eight months he longed to get away, and had no rest until he found himself on the Underground Rail Road.

His master was a member of the Century Methodist Church, as was also his wife and family; but Lewis thought that they were strangers to practical Christianity, judging from the manner that the slaves were treated by both master and mistress. Lewis was a Baptist, and belonged to the second church. Twelve hundred dollars had been offered for him. He left his father (Judville), and his brother, John Harris, both slaves. In view of his prospects in Canada, Lewis' soul overflowed with pleasing anticipations of freedom, and the Committee felt great satisfaction in assisting him.

NANCY was also from Richmond, and came in the same boat with Lewis. She represented the most "likely-looking female bond servants." Indeed her appearance recommended her at once. She was neat, modest, and well-behaved—with a good figure and the picture of health, with a countenance beaming with joy and gladness, notwithstanding the late struggles and sufferings through which she had passed. Young as she was, she had seen much of slavery, and had, doubtless, profited by the lessons thereof. At all events, it was through cruel treatment, having been frequently beaten after she had passed her eighteenth year, that she was prompted to seek freedom. It was so common for her mistress to give way to unbridled passions that Nancy never felt safe. Under the severest infliction of punishment she was not allowed to complain. Neither from mistress nor master had she any reason to expect mercy or leniency—indeed she saw no way of escape but by the Underground Rail Road.

It was true that the master, Mr. William Bears, was a Yankee from Connecticut, and his wife a member of the Episcopal Church, but Nancy's yoke seemed none the lighter for all that. Fully persuaded that she would never find her lot any better while remaining in their hands, she accepted the advice and aid of a young man to whom she was engaged; he was shrewd enough to find an agent in Richmond, with whom he entered into a covenant to have Nancy brought away. With a cheerful heart the journey was undertaken in the manner aforesaid, and she safely reached the Committee. Her mother, one brother and a sister she had to leave in Richmond. One thousand dollars were lost in the departure of Nancy.

Having been accommodated and aided by the Committee, they were forwarded to Canada. Lewis wrote back repeatedly and expressed himself very gratefully for favors received, as will be seen by the appended letters from him:

TORONTO, April 25, 1857.

To MR. WM. STILL—Dear Sir:—I take this opportunity of addressing these few lines to inform you that I am well and hope that they may find you and your family enjoying the same good health. Please to give my love to you and your family. I had a very pleasant trip from your house that morning. Dear sir, you would oblige me much, if you have not sent that box to Mr. Robinson, to open it and take out the little yellow box that I tied up in the large one and send it on by express to me in Toronto. Lift up a few of the things and you will find it near the top. All the clothes that I have are in that box and I stand in need of them. You would oblige me much by so doing. I stopped at Mr. Jones' in Elmira, and was very well treated by him while there. I am now in Toronto and doing very well at present. I am very thankful to you and your family for the attention you paid to me while at your house. I wish you would see Mr. Ormsted and ask him if he has not some things for Mr. Anthony Loney, and if he has, please send them on with my things, as we are both living together at this time. Give my love to Mr. Anthony, also to Mr. Ormsted and family. Dear sir, we both would be very glad for you to attend to this, as we both do stand very much in need of them at this time. Dear sir, you will oblige me by giving my love to Miss Frances Watkins, and as she said she hoped to be out in the summer, I should like to see her. I have met with a gentleman here by the name of Mr. Truehart, and he sends his best love to you and your family. Mr. Truehart desires to know whether you received the letter he sent to you, and if so, answer it as soon as possible. Please answer this letter as soon as possible. I must now come to a close by saying that I remain your beloved friend,   Lewis Cobb.

The young man who was there that morning, Mr. Robinson, got married to that young lady.

Toronto, June 2d, 1857.

To Mr. Wm. Still—Dear Sir :—I received yours dated May 6th, and was extremely happy to hear from you. You may be surprised that I have not answered you before this, but it was on account of not knowing anything concerning the letter being in the post-office until I was told so by a friend. The box, of which I had been inquiring, I have received, and am infinitely obliged to you for sending it. Mr. and Mrs. Renson are living in Hamilton, C. W. They send their best love to you and your family. I am at present residing in Toronto, C. W. Mr. Anthony Loney has gone on to Boston, and is desirous of my coming on to him ; and as I have many acquaintances there, I should like to know from you whether it would be advisable or not. Give, if you please, my best love to your family and accept the same for yourself, and also to Mr. James Ormsted and family. Tell James Ormsted I would be glad if he would send me a pair of thick, heavy boots, for it rains and hails as often out here in the summer, as it does there in the winter. Tell him to send No. 9, and anything he thinks will do me good in this cold country. Please to give to Mr. James Ormsted to give to Mr. Robert Seldon, and tell him to give it to my father. Mr. and Mrs. Truehart send their love to you and your family. If the gentleman, Mr. R. S., is not running on the boat now, you can give directions to Ludwill Cobb, in care of Mr. R. Seldon, Richmond, Va. Tell Mr. Ormsted not to forget my boots and send them by express. No more at present, but remain yours very truly,

Please write soon.   Lewis Cobb.

PASSENGERS FROM NORTH CAROLINA.

[BY SCHOONER.]

MAJOR LATHAM, WILLIAM WILSON, HENRY GORHAM, WILEY MADDISON, AND ANDREW SHEPHERD.

The above named passengers were delivered into the hands of Thomas Garrett by the Captain who brought them, and were aided and forwarded to the Committee in Philadelphia, as indicated by the subjoined letter :

WILMINGTON, 11th mo., 6th, 1856.

RESPECTED FRIEND:—WILLIAM STILL:—Thine of yesterday, came to hand this morning, advising me to forward those four men to thee, which I propose to send from here in the steam boat, at two o'clock, P. M. to day to thy care; one of them thinks he has a brother and cousin in New Bedford, and is anxious to get to them, the others thee can do what thee thinks best with, after consulting with them, we have rigged them up pretty comfortably with clothes, and I have paid for their passage to Philadelphia, and also for the passage of their pilot there and back; he proposed to ask thee for three dollars, for the three days time he lost with them, but that we will raise here for him, as one of them expects to have some money brought from Carolina soon, that belongs to him, and wants thee when they are fixed, to let me know so that I may forward it to them. I will give each of them a card of our firm. Hoping they may get along safe, I remain as ever, thy sincere friend,   THOS. GARRETT.

The passengers by this arrival were above the ordinary plantation or farm hand slave, as will appear from a glance at their condition under the yoke.

MAJOR LATHAM was forty-four years of age, mulatto, very resolute, with good natural abilities, and a decided hater of slavery. John Latham was the man whom he addressed as "master," which was a very bitter pill for him to swallow. He had been married twice, and at the time of his escape he was the husband of two wives. The first one, with their three children, in consequence of changes incident to slave life, was sold a long distance from her old home and husband, thereby ending the privilege of living together; he could think of them, but that was all; he was compelled to give them up altogether. After a time he took to himself another wife, with whom he lived several years. Three more children owned him as father—the result of this marriage. During his entire manhood Major had been brutally treated by his master, which caused him a great deal of anguish and trouble of mind.

Only a few weeks before he escaped, his master, in one of his fits of passion, flogged him most cruelly. From that time the resolution was permanently grounded in his mind to find the way to freedom, if possible, before many more weeks had passed. Day and night he studied, worked and planned, with freedom uppermost in his mind. The hour of hope arrived and with it Captain F.

WILLIAM, a fellow-passenger with Major, was forty-two years of age, just in the prime of life, and represented the mechanics in chains, being a blacksmith by trade. Dr. Thomas Warren, who followed farming in the neighborhood of Eatontown, was the owner of William. In speaking of his slave life William said: "I was sold four times; twice I was separated from my wives. I was separated from one of my wives when living in Portsmouth, Virginia," etc.

In his simple manner of describing the trials he had been called upon to endure, it was not to be wondered at that he was willing to forsake all and run fearful risks in order to rid himself not only of the "load on his back," but the load on his heart. By the very positive character of William's testimony against slavery, the Committee felt more than ever justified in encouraging the Underground Rail Road.

HENRY GORHAM was thirty-four years of age, a "prime," heavy, dark, smart, "article," and a good carpenter. He admitted that he had never felt the lash on his back, but, nevertheless, he had felt deeply on the subject of slavery. For years the chief concern with him was as to how he could safely reach a free State. Slavery he hated with a perfect hatred. To die in the woods, live in a cave, or sacrifice himself in some way, he was bound to do, rather than remain a slave. The more he reflected over his condition the more determined he grew to seek his freedom. Accordingly he left and went to the woods; there he prepared himself a cave and resolved to live and die in it rather than return to bondage. Before he found his way out of the prison-house eleven months elapsed. His strong impulse for freedom, and intense aversion to slavery, sustained him until he found an opportunity to escape by the Underground Rail Road.

One of the tried Agents of the Underground Rail Road was alone cognizant of his dwelling in the cave, and regarding him as a tolerably safe passenger (having been so long secreted), secured him a passage on the schooner, and thus he was fortunately relieved from his eleven months' residence in his den. No rhetoric or fine scholarship was needed in his case to make his story interesting. None but hearts of stone could have listened without emotion.

ANDREW, another fellow-passenger, was twenty-six years of age, and a decidedly inviting-looking specimen of the peculiar institution. He filled the situation of an engineer. He, with his wife and one child, belonged to a small orphan girl, who lived at South End, Camden county, N. C. His wife and child had to be left behind. While it seemed very hard for a husband thus to leave his wife, every one that did so weakened slavery and encouraged and strengthened anti-slavery.

Numbered with these four North Carolina passengers is found the name of WILEY MADDISON, a young man nineteen years of age, who escaped from Petersburg on the cars as a white man. He was of promising appearance, and found no difficulty whatever on the road. With the rest, however, he concluded himself hardly safe this side of Canada, and it afforded the Committee special pleasure to help them all.

THOMAS CLINTON, SAUNEY PRY AND BENJAMIN DUCKET.

PASSED OVER THE U. G. R. R., IN THE FALL OF 1856.

THOMAS escaped from Baltimore. He described the man from whom he fled as a " rum drinker" of some note, by the name of Benjamin Walmsly, and he testified that under him he was neither " half fed nor clothed," in consequence of which he was dissatisfied, and fled to better his condition. Luckily Thomas succeeded in making his escape when about twenty-one years of age. His appearance and smartness indicated resolution and gave promise of future success. He was well made and of a chestnut color.

SAUNEY PRY came from Loudon Co., Va. He had been one of the " well-cared for," on the farm of Nathan Clapton, who owned some sixty or seventy slaves. Upon inquiry as to the treatment and character of his master, Sauney unhesitatingly described him as a " very mean, swearing, blustering man, as hard as any that could be started." It was on this account that he was prompted to turn his face against Virginia and to venture on the Underground Rail Road. Sauney was twenty-seven years of age, chestnut color, medium size, and in intellect was at least up to the average.

BENJAMIN DUCKET came from Bell Mountain, Prince George's Co., Maryland. He stated to the Committee that he escaped from one Sicke Perry, a farmer. Of his particular master he spoke thus: "He was one of the baddest men about Prince George; he would both fight and kill up."

These characteristics of the master developed in Ben very strong desires to get beyond his reach. In fact, his master's conduct was the sole cause of his seeking the Underground Rail Road. At the time that he came to Philadelphia, he was recorded as twenty-three years of age, chestnut color, medium size, and wide awake. He left his father, mother, two brothers, and three sisters, owned by Marcus Devoe.

About the same time that the passengers just described received succor, ELIZABETH LAMBERT, with three children, reached the Committee. The names of the children were, Mary, Horace, and William Henry, quite marketable-looking articles.

They fled from Middletown, Delaware, where they had been owned by Andrew Peterson. The poor mother's excuse for leaving her " comfortable home, free board, and kind-hearted master and mistress," was simply because she was tired of such " kindness," and was, therefore, willing to suffer in order to get away from it.

HILL JONES, a lad of eighteen, accompanied Elizabeth with her children from Middletown. He had seen enough of Slavery to satisfy him that he could never relish it. His owner was known by the name of John Cochran, and followed farming. He was of a chestnut color, and well-grown.

ARRIVALS IN APRIL, 1856.

CHARLES HALL, JAMES JOHNSON, CHARLES CARTER, GEORGE, AND JOHN LOGAN, JAMES HENRY WATSON, ZEBULON GREEN, LEWIS, AND PETER BURRELL, WILLIAM WILLIAMS, AND HIS WIFE—HARRIET TUBMAN, WITH FOUR PASSENGERS.

CHARLES HALL. This individual was from Maryland, Baltimore Co., where " black men had no rights which white men were bound to respect," according to the decision of the late Chief Justice Taney of the Supreme Court of the United States.

Charles was owned by Atwood A. Blunt, a farmer, much of whose time was devoted to card playing, rum-drinking and fox-hunting, so Charles stated. Charles gave him the credit of being as mild a specimen of a slave-holder as that region of country could claim when in a sober mood, but when drunk every thing went wrong with him, nothing could satisfy him.

Charles testified, however, that the despotism of his mistress was much worse than that of his master, for she was all the time hard on the slaves. Latterly he had heard much talk about selling, and, believing that matters would soon have to come to that, he concluded to seek a place where colored men had rights, in Canada.

JAMES JOHNSON. James fled from Deer Creek, Harford Co., Md., where he was owned by William Rautty. " Jim's " hour had come. Within one day of the time fixed for his sale, he was handcuffed, and it was evidently supposed that he was secure. Trembling at his impending doom he resolved to escape if possible. He could not rid himself of the handcuffs. Could he have done so, he was persuaded that he might manage to make his way along safely. He resolved to make an effort with the handcuffs on.

With resolution his freedom was secured. What Master Rautty said when he found his property gone with the handcuffs, we know not.

The next day after Jim arrived, Charles Carter, George and John Logan came to hand.

CHARLES had been under the yoke in the city of Richmond, held to service by Daniel Delaplain, a flour inspector. Charles was hired out by the flour inspector for as much as he could command for him, for being a devoted lover of money, ordinary wages hardly ever satisfied him. In other respects Charles spoke of his master rather favorably in comparison with slaveholders generally.

A thirty years' apprenticeship as a slave had not, however, won him over to the love of the system ; he had long since been convinced that it was non-sense to suppose that such a thing as happiness could be found even under the best of masters. He claimed to have a wife and four little children living in Alexandria Va. ; the name of the wife was Lucinda. In the estimation of slave-holders, the fact of Charles having a family might have offered no cause for unhappiness, but Charles felt differently in relation to the matter. Again, for reasons best known to the owner, he talked of selling Charles. On this point Charles also felt quite nervous, so he began to think that he had better make an attempt to get beyond the reach of·buyers and sellers. He knew that many others similarly situated had got out of bondage simply by hard struggling, and he felt that he could do likewise. When he had thus determined the object was half accomplished. True, every step that he should take was liable to bring trouble upon himself, yet with the hope of freedom buoying him up he resolved to run the risk. Charles was about thirty years of age, likely-looking, well made, intelligent, and a mulatto.

GEORGE was twenty-three years of age, quite dark, medium size, and bore the marks of a man of considerable pluck. He was the slave of Mrs. Jane Coultson. No special complaint of her is recorded on the book. She might have been a very good mistress, but George was not a very happy and contented piece of property, as was proved by his course in escaping. The cold North had many more charms for him than the sunny South.

JOHN has been already described in the person of his brother George. He was not, however, the property of Mrs. Coultson, but was owned by Miss Cox, near Little Georgetown, Berkeley Co., Va. These three individuals were held as slaves by that class of slave-holders, known in the South as the most kind-hearted and indulgent, yet they seemed just as much delighted with the prospects of freedom as any other passengers.

The next day following the arrival of the party just noticed JAMES HENRY WATSON reached the Committee. He was in good condition, the spring weather having been favorable, and the journey made without any serious difficulty.

He was from Snowhill, Worcester county, Md., and had escaped from James Purnell, a farmer of whom he did not speak very favorably. Yet James admitted that his master was not as hard on his slaves as some others.

For the benefit of James' kinsfolk, who may still perchance be making searches for him, not having yet learned whither he went or what became of him, we copy the following paragraph as entered on our book April 11th, 1856:

JAMES HENRY is twenty years of age, dark, well-made, modest, and seems fearful of apprehension; was moved to escape in order to obtain his freedom. He had heard of others who had run away and thus secured their freedom; he thought he could do the same. He left his father, mother, three brothers and five sisters owned by Purnell. His father's name was Ephraim, his mother's name Mahala. The names of his sisters and brothers were as follows: Hetty, Betsy, Dinah, Catharine and Harriet; Homer, William and James.

ZEBULON GREEN was the next traveler. He arrived from Duck Creek, Md. John Appleton, a farmer, was chargeable with having deprived Zeb of his rights. But, as Zeb was only about eighteen years of age when he made his exit, Mr. Appleton did not get much the start of him In answer to the question as to the cause of his escape, he replied "bad usage." He was smart, and quite dark. In traveling, he changed his name to Samuel Hill. The Committee endeavored to impress him thoroughly, with the idea that he could do much good in the world for himself and fellow-men, by using his best endeavors to acquire education, etc., and forwarded him on to Canada.

LEWIS BURRELL and his brother PETER arrived safely from Alexandria, Virginia, April 21, 1856. Lewis had been owned by Edward M. Clark, Peter by Benjamin Johnson Hall. These passengers seemed to be well posted in regard to Slavery, and understood full well their responsibilities in fleeing from "kind-hearted" masters. All they feared was that they might not reach Canada safely, although they were pretty hopeful and quite resolute. Lewis left a wife, Winna Ann, and two children, Joseph and Mary, who were owned by Pembroke Thomas, at Culpepper, Va., nearly a hundred miles distant from him. Once or twice in the year, was the privilege allowed him to visit his wife and little ones at this long distance. This separation constituted his daily grief and was the cause of his escape. Lewis and Peter left their father and mother in bondage, also one brother (Reuben), and three sisters, two of whom had been sold far South.

After a sojourn in freedom of nearly three years, Lewis wrote on behalf of his wife as follows:

TORONTO, C. W., Feb. 2, 1859.

MR. WM. STILL:

DEAR SIR:—It have bin two years since I war at your house, at that time I war on my way to cannadia, and I tould you that I had a wife and had to leave her behind, and you promiest me that you would healp me to gait hir if I ever heaird from hir, and I think my dear frend, that the time is come for me to strick the blow, will you healp me, according to your promis. I recived a letter from a frend in Washington last night and he says that my wife is in the city of Baltimore, and she will come away if she can find a frend to healp hir, so I thought I would writ to you as you are acquanted with foulks theare to howm you can trust with such matthas. I could write to Mr Noah davis in Baltimore, who is well acquanted with my wife, but I do not think that he is a trew frend, and I could writ to Mr Samual Maden in the same city, but I am afread that a letter coming from cannada might be dedteced, but if you will writ to soume one that you know, and gait them to see Mr Samual Maden he will give all the information that you want, as he is acquanted with my wife, he is a preacher and belongs to the Baptis church. My wifes name is Winne Ann Berrell, and she is oned by one Dr. Tams who is on a viset to Baltimore, now Mr Still will you attend to this thing for me, fourthwith, if you will I will pay you four your truble, if we can dow any thing it must be don now, as she will leave theare in the spring, and if you will take the matter in hand, you mous writ me on to reseption of this letter, whether you will or not. Yours truly,

LEWIS BURRELL.

No. 49 Victoria St., Toronto, C. W.

25

As in the case of many others, the way was so completely blocked that nothing could be done for the wife's deliverance. Until the day when the millions of fetters were broken, nothing gave so much pain to husbands and wives as these heart-breaking separations.

William Williams and his wife were the next who arrived. They came from Haven Manor, Md. They had been owned by John Peak, by whom, according to their report, they had been badly treated, and the Committee had no reason to doubt their testimony.

The next arrival numbered four passengers, and came under the guidance of "Moses" (Harriet Tubman), from Maryland. They were adults, looking as though they could take care of themselves very easily, although they had the marks of Slavery on them. It was no easy matter for men and women who had been ground down all their lives, to appear as though they had been enjoying freedom. Indeed, the only wonder was that so many appeared to as good advantage as they did, after having been crushed down so long.

The paucity of the narratives in the month of April, is quite noticeable. Why fuller reports were not written out, cannot now be accounted for; probably the feeling existed that it was useless to write out narratives, except in cases of very special interest.

FIVE FROM GEORGETOWN CROSS ROADS.

MOTHER AND CHILD FROM NORFOLK, VA., ETC.

Abe Fineer, Sam Davis, Henry Saunders, Wm. Henry Thompson and Thomas Parker arrived safely from the above named place. Upon inquiry, the following information was gleaned from them.

Abe spoke with feelings of some bitterness of a farmer known by the name of George Spencer, who had deprived him of the hard earnings of his hands. Furthermore, he had worked him hard, stinted him for food and clothing and had been in the habit of flogging him whenever he felt like it. In addition to the above charges, Abe did not hesitate to say that his master meddled too much with the bottle, in consequence of which, he was often in a "top-heavy" state. Abe said, however, that he was rich and stood pretty high in the neighborhood—stinting, flogging and drinking were no great disadvantages to a man in Georgetown, Maryland.

Abe was twenty-three years of age, pure black, ordinary size, and spirited, a thorough convert to the doctrine that all men are born free, and although he had been held in bondage up to the hour of his escape, he gave much reason for believing that he would not be an easy subject to manage under the yoke, if ever captured and carried back.

SAM was about thirty years of age, genuine black, common size, and a hater of slavery; he was prepared to show, by the scars he bore about his person, why he talked as he did. Forever will he remember James Hurst, his so-called master, who was a very blustering man oft-times, and in the habit of abusing his slaves. Sam was led to seek the Underground Rail Road, in order to get rid of his master and, at the same time, to do better for himself than he could possibly do in Slavery. He had to leave his wife, Phillis, and one child.

WILLIAM HENRY was about twenty-four years of age, and of a chestnut color. He too talked of slave-holders, and his master in particular, just as any man would talk who had been shamefully robbed and wronged all his life.

TOM, likewise, told the same story, and although they used the corn-field vernacular, they were in earnest and possessed an abundance of mother-wit, so that their testimony was not to be made light of.

The following letter from Thomas Garrett speaks for itself:

WILMINGTON, 5 mo. 11th, 1856.

ESTEEMED FRIENDS—McKim and Still:—I purpose sending to-morrow morning by the steamboat a woman and child, whose husband, I think, went some nine months previous to New Bedford. She was furnished with a free passage by the same line her husband came in. She has been away from the person claiming to be her master some five months; we, therefore, think there cannot be much risk at present. Those four I wrote thee about arrived safe up in the neighborhood of Longwood, and Harriet Tubman followed after in the stage yesterday. I shall expect five more from the same neighborhood next trip. Captain Lambdin is desirous of having sent him a book, or books, with the strongest arguments of the noted men of the South against the institution of slavery, as he wishes to prepare to defend himself, as he has little confidence in his attorney. Cannot you send to me something that will be of benefit to him, or send it direct to him? Would not W. Goodell's book be of use? His friends here think there is no chance for him but to go to the penitentiary. They now refuse to let any one but his attorney see him.

As ever your friend,   THOS. GARRETT.

The woman and child alluded to were received and noted on the record book as follows:

WINNIE PATTY, and her daughter, ELIZABETH, arrived safely from Norfolk, Va. The mother is about twenty-two years of age, good-looking and of chestnut color, smart and brave. From the latter part of October, 1855, to the latter part of March, 1856, this young slave mother, with her child, was secreted under the floor of a house. The house was occupied by a slave family, friends of Winnie. During the cold winter weather she suffered severely from wet and cold, getting considerably frosted, but her faith failed not, even in the hour of greatest extremity. She chose rather to suffer thus than endure slavery any longer, especially as she was aware that the auction-block awaited her. She had already been sold three times; she knew therefore what it was to be sold.

Jacob Shuster was the name of the man whom she spoke of as her tormentor and master, and from whom she fled. He had been engaged in the farming business, and had owned quite a large number of slaves, but from time to time he had been selling off, until he had reduced his stock considerably.

Captain Lambdin, spoken of in Thomas Garrett's letter, had, in the kindness of his heart, brought away in his schooner some Underground Rail Road passengers, but unfortunately he was arrested and thrust into prison in Norfolk, Va., to await trial. Having no confidence in his attorney there he found that he would have to defend himself as best he could, consequently he wanted books, etc. He was in the attitude of a drowning man catching at a straw. The Committee was powerless to aid him, except with some money; as the books that he desired had but little effect in the lions' den, in which he was. He had his trial, and was sent to the penitentiary, of course.

 ONE HUNDRED DOLLARS REWARD.—Ran away from the subscriber, living in Rockville, Montgomery county, Md., on Saturday, 31st of May last, NEGRO MAN, ALFRED, about twenty-two years of age; five feet seven inches high; dark copper color, and rather good looking.

He had on when he left a dark blue and green plaid frock coat, of cloth, and lighter colored plaid pantaloons.

I will give the above reward if taken out of the county, and in any of the States, or fifty dollars if taken in the county or the District of Columbia, and secured so that I get him again. JOHN W. ANDERSON.

j6–1w W2.

A man calling himself Alfred Homer, answering to the above description, came to the Vigilance Committee in June, 1856. As a memorial we transferred the advertisement of John W. Anderson to our record book, and concluded to let that suffice. Alfred, however, gave a full description of his master's character, and the motives which impelled him to seek his freedom. He was listened to attentively, but his story was not entered on the book.

PASSENGERS FROM MARYLAND, 1857.

WILLIAM HENRY MOODY, BELINDA BIVANS, ETC.

WILLIAM was about twenty years of age, black, usual size, and a lover of liberty. He had heard of Canada, had formed a very favorable opinion of the country and was very desirous of seeing it. The man who had habitually robbed him of his hire, was a "stout-built, ill-natured man," a farmer, by the name of William Hyson.

To meet the expenses of an extensive building enterprise which he had undertaken, it was apparent that Hyson would have to sell some of his property. William and some six others of the servants got wind of the fact that they would stand a chance of being in the market soon. Not relishing the idea of going further South they unanimously resolved to emigrate to Canada. Accordingly they borrowed a horse from Dr. Wise, and another from H. K. Tice, and a carriage from F. J. Posey, and Joseph P. Mong's buggy (so it was stated in the Baltimore Sun, of May 27th), and off they started for the promised land. The horses and carriages were all captured at Chambersburg, a day or two after they set out, but the rest of the property hurried on to the Committee. How Mr. Hyson raised the money to carry out his enterprise, William and his "ungrateful" fellow-servants seemed not to be concerned.

BELINDA BIVANS. Belinda was a large woman, thirty years of age, wholly black, and fled from Mr. Hyson, in company with William, and those above referred to, with the idea of reaching Canada, whither her father had fled eight years before.

She was evidently pleased with the idea of getting away from her ill-natured mistress, from poor fare and hard work without pay. She had experienced much hardship, and had become weary of her trial in bondage. She had been married, but her husband had died, leaving her with two little girls to care for, both of whom she succeeded in bringing away with her.

In reference to the church relations of her master and mistress, she represented the former as a backslider, and added that money was his church; of the latter she said, "she would go and take the sacrament, come back and the old boy would be in her as big as a horse." Belinda could see but little difference between her master and mistress.

JOSEPH WINSTON. In the Richmond Dispatch, of June 9th, the following advertisement was found:

RUNAWAY —$200 REWARD will be given if taken in the state, and $500 if taken out of the state.

Run away, my negro boy JOE, sometimes called JOE WINSTON ; about 23 years old, a little over 5 feet high, rather stout-built, dark ginger-bread color, small moustache, stammers badly when confused or spoken to; took along two or three suits of clothes, one a blue dress coat with brass buttons, black pants, and patent leather shoes, white hat, silver watch with gold chain ; was last seen in this city on Tuesday last, had a pass to Hanover county, and supposed to be making his way towards York River, for the purpose of getting on board some coasting vessel.

SAMUEL ELLIS.

The passenger above described reached the Underground Rail Road station, June 6th, 1857.

"Why did you leave your master?" said a member of the Committee to Joe. "I left because there was no enjoyment in slavery for colored people." After stating how the slaves were treated he added, "I was working all the time for master and he was receiving all my money for my daily labor." "What business did your master follow?" inquired the Committee. "He was a carpenter by trade." "What kind of a looking man was he?" again inquired the Committee. "He was a large, stout man, don't swear, but lies and cheats." Joe admitted that he had been treated very well all his life, with the exception of being deprived of his freedom. For eight years prior to his escape he had been hired out, a part of the time as porter in a grocery store, the remainder as bar-tender in a saloon. At the time of his escape he was worth twenty-two dollars per month to his master. Joe had to do over-work and thus procure clothing for himself.

When a small boy he resolved, that he never would work all his days as a slave for the white people. As he advanced in years his desire for free-dom increased. An offer of fifteen hundred dollars was made for Joe, so he was informed a short time before he escaped; this caused him to move promptly in the matter of carrying out his designs touching liberty.

His parents and three brothers, slaves, were to be left; but when the decisive hour came he was equal to the emergency. In company with William Naylor secreted in a vessel, he was brought away and delivered to the Committee for aid and counsel, which he received, and thus ended his bondage. The reward offered by his master, Samuel Ellis, proved of no avail.

ARRIVAL FROM MARYLAND.

WILLIAM SCOTT. William was about twenty-four years of age, well made, though not very heavy—stammered considerably when speaking—wide awake and sensible nevertheless. For two years the fear of being sold had not been out of his mind. To meet a security agreement, which had been contracted by his mistress—about which a law-suit had been pending for two years—was what he feared he should be sold for. About the first of May he found himself in the hands of the sheriff. On being taken to Stafford Court-House Jail, however, the sheriff permitted him to walk a "little ways." It occurred to William that then was his only chance to strike for freedom and Canada, at all hazards. He soon decided the matter, and the sheriff saw no more of him.

Susan Fox was the name of the person he was compelled to call mistress. She was described as a "large, portly woman, very gross, with a tolerably severe temper, at times." William's mother and one of his brothers had been sold by this woman—an outrage to be forever remembered. His grandmother, one sister, with two children, and a cousin with five children, all attached by the sheriff, for sale, were left in the hands of his mistress. He was married the previous Christmas, but in the trying hour could do nothing for his wife, but leave her to the mercy of slave-holders. The name of the sheriff that he outgeneralled was Walter Cox. William was valued at $1,000.

Perhaps, after all, but few appreciated the sorrow that must have filled the hearts of most of those who escaped. Though they succeeded in gaining their own liberty — they were not insensible to the oppression of their friends and relatives left in bondage. On reaching Canada and tasting the sweets of freedom, the thought of dear friends in bondage must have been acutely painful.

William had many perils to encounter. On one occasion he was hotly chased, but proved too fleet-footed for his pursuers. At another time, when straitened, he attempted to swim a river, but failed. His faith remained strong, nevertheless, and he succeeded in reaching the Committee.

ARRIVAL FROM WASHINGTON, D. C., etc., 1857.

GEORGE CARROLL, RANDOLPH BRANSON, JOHN CLAGART, AND WILLIAM ROYAN.

These four journeyed from "Egypt" together—but did not leave the same "kind protector."

GEORGE was a full black, ordinary size, twenty-four years of age, and a convert to the doctrine that he had a right to himself. For years the idea of escape had been daily cherished. Five times he had proposed to buy himself, but failed to get the consent of his "master," who was a merchant, C. C. Hirara, a man about sixty years of age, and a member of the Methodist Church. His property in slaves consisted of two men, two women, two girls and a boy.

Three of George's brothers escaped to Canada many years prior to his leaving—there he hoped on his arrival to find them in the possession of good farms. $1,300 walked off in the person of George.

RANDOLPH, physically, was a superior man. He was thirty-one years of age and of a dark chestnut color. Weary with bondage he came to the conclusion that he had served a master long enough "without privileges." Against his master, Richard Reed, he had no hard things to say, however. He was not a "crabbed, cross man"—had but "little to say," but "didn't believe in freedom."

Three of his brothers had been sold South. Left his father, two sisters and one brother. Randolph was worth probably $1,700.

JOHN was a well-made yellow man, twenty-two years of age, who had counted the cost of slavery thoroughly, besides having experienced the effects of it. Accordingly he resolved to "be free or die," "to kill or be killed, in trying to reach free land somewhere!"

Having "always been hired out amongst very hard white people," he was "unhappy." His owner, George Coleman, lived near Fairfax, Va., and was a member of the Methodist Church, but in his ways was "very sly," and "deadly against anything like freedom." He held fifteen of his fellow-men in chains.

For John's hire he received one hundred and fifty dollars a year. He was, therefore, ranked with first-class "stock," valued at $1,500.

WILLIAM was about thirty-five years of age, neat, and pleasing in his manners. He would be the first selected in a crowd by a gentleman or a lady, who might want a very neat-looking man to attend to household affairs. Though he considered Captain Cunningham, his master, a "tolerable fair man," he was not content to be robbed of his liberty and earnings. As he felt that he "could take care of himself," he decided to let the Captain have the same chance—and so he steered his course straight for Canada.

ARRIVAL FROM UNIONVILLE, 1857.

ISRAEL TODD, AND BAZIL ALDRIDGE.

ISRAEL was twenty-three years of age, yellow, tall, well made and intelligent. He fled from Frederick county, Md. Through the sweat of his brow, Dr. Greenberry Sappington and his family had been living at ease. The doctor was a Catholic, owning only one other, and was said to be a man of "right disposition." His wife, however, was "so mean that nobody could stay with her." Israel was prompted to escape to save his wife, (had lately been married) and her brother from being sold south. His detestation of slavery in every shape was very decided. He was a valuable man, worth to a trader fifteen hundred dollars, perhaps.

BAZIL was only seventeen years of age. About as near a kin to the "white folks" as to the colored people, and about as strong an opponent of slavery as any "Saxon" going of his age. He was a brother-in-law of Israel, and accompanied him on the Underground Rail Road. Bazil was held to service or labor by Thornton Pool, a store-keeper, and also farmer, and at the same time an ardent lover of the "cretur," so much so that "he kept about half-drunk all the time." So Bazil affirmed. The good spirit moved two of Bazil's brothers to escape the spring before. A few months afterwards a brother and sister were sold south. To manage the matter smoothly, previous to selling them, the master pretended that he was "only going to hire them out a short distance from home." But instead of doing so he sold them south. Bazil might be put down at nine hundred dollars.

ARRIVAL FROM MARYLAND, 1857.

ORDEE LEE, AND RICHARD J. BOOCE.

Both of these passengers came from Maryland. ORDEE was about thirty-five years of age, gingerbread color, well made, and intelligent. Being allowed no chances to make anything for himself, was the excuse offered for his escape. Though, as will appear presently, other causes also helped to make him hate his oppression.

The man who had daily robbed him, and compelled him to call him master, was a notorious "gambler," by the name of Elijah Thompson, residing in Maryland. " By his bad habits he had run through with his property, though in society he stood pretty tolerably high amongst some people ; then again some didn't like him, he was a mean man, all for himself. He was a man that didn't care anything about his servants, except to get work out of them. When he came where the servants were working, he would snap and bite at them and if he said anything at all, it was to hurry the work on."

" He never gave me," said Ordee, " a half a dollar in his life. Didn't more than half feed, said that meat and fish was too high to eat. As for clothing, he never gave me a new hat for every day, nor a Sunday rag in his life." Of his mistress, he said, " She was stingy and close,—made him (his master) worse than what he would have been." Two of his brothers were sold to Georgia, and his uncle was cheated out of his freedom. Left three brothers and two sisters in chains. Elijah Thompson had at least fifteen hundred dollars less to sport upon by this bold step on the part of Ordee.

RICHARD was about twenty-two years of age, well grown, and a very likely-looking article, of a chestnut color, with more than common intelligence for a slave.

His complaints were that he had been treated " bad," allowed "no privileges" to make anything, allowed "no Sunday clothing," &c. So he left the portly-looking Dr. Hughes, with no feeling of indebtedness or regret. And as to his " cross and ill-natured " mistress, with her four children, they might whistle for his services and support. His master had, however, some eighteen or twenty others to rob for the support of himself and family, so they were in no great danger of starving.

" Would your owner be apt to pursue you ?" said a member of the Committee. " I don't think he will. He was after two uncles of mine, one time, saw them, and talked with them, but was made to run."

Richard left behind his mother, step-father, two sisters, and one brother. As a slave, he would have been considered cheap at sixteen hundred dollars. He was a fine specimen.

ARRIVAL FROM CAMBRIDGE, 1857.

SILAS LONG and SOLOMON LIGHT.   Silas and Solomon both left together from Cambridge, Md.

SILAS was quite black, spare-built and about twenty-seven years of age. He was owned by Sheriff Robert Bell, a man about "sixty years of age, and had his name up to be the hardest man in the county." "The Sheriff's wife was about pretty much such a woman as he was a man—there was not a pin's point of difference between them." The fear of having to be sold caused this Silas to seek the Underground Rail Road. Leaving his mother, one brother and one cousin, and providing himself with a Bowie-knife and a few dollars in money, he resolved to reach Canada, "or die on the way." Of course, when slaves reached this desperate point, the way to Canada was generally found.

SOLOMON was about twenty-three years of age, a good-natured-looking "article," who also left Cambridge, and the protection of a certain Willis Branick, described as an "unaccountable mean man." "He never gave me any money in his life," said Sol., "but spent it pretty freely for liquor." "He would not allow enough to eat, or clothing sufficient." And he sold Sol.'s brother the year before he fled, "because he could not whip him." The fear of being sold prompted Sol. to flee. The very day he escaped he had a serious combat with two of his master's sons. The thumb of one of them being "badly bit," and the other used roughly—the ire of the master and sons was raised to a very high degree—and the verdict went forth that "Sol. should be sold to-morrow." Unhesitatingly, he started for the Underground Rail Road and Canada — and his efforts were not in vain. Damages, $1,500.

"THE MOTHER OF TWELVE CHILDREN."

OLD JANE DAVIS—FLED TO ESCAPE THE AUCTION-BLOCK.

The appended letter, from Thomas Garrett, will serve to introduce one of the most remarkable cases that it was our privilege to report or assist:

WILMINGTON, 6 mo., 9th, 1857.

ESTEEMED FRIEND—WILLIAM STILL:—We have here in this place, at Comegys Munson's an old colored woman, the mother of twelve children, one half of which has been sold South. She has been so ill used, that she was compelled to leave husband and children behind, and is desirous of getting to a brother who lives at Buffalo. She was nearly naked. She called at my house on 7th day night, but being from home, did not see her till last evening. I have procured her two under garments, one new; two skirts, one new ; a good frock with cape ; one of my wife's bonnets and stockings, and gave her five dollars in gold, which, if properly used, will put her pretty well on the way. I also gave her a letter to thee. Since I gave them to her she has concluded to stay where she is till 7th day night, when Comegys Munson says he can leave his work and will go with her to thy house. I write this so that thee may be prepared for them ; they ought to arrive between 11 and 12 o'clock. Perhaps thee may find some fugitive that will be willing to accompany her. With desire for thy welfare and the cause of the oppressed, I remain thy friend, THOS. GARRETT.

Jane did not know how old she was. She was probably sixty or seventy. She fled to keep from being sold. She had been " whipt right smart," poorly fed and poorly clothed, by a certain Roger McZant, of the New Market District, Eastern Shore of Maryland. His wife was a " bad woman too." Just before escaping, Jane got a whisper that her " master " was about to sell her; on asking him if the rumor was true, he was silent. He had been asking " one hundred dollars " for her.

Remembering that four of her children had been snatched away from her and sold South, and she herself was threatened with the same fate, she was willing to suffer hunger, sleep in the woods for nights and days, wandering towards Canada, rather than trust herself any longer under the protection of her " kind " owner. Before reaching a place of repose she was *three weeks in the woods*, almost wholly without nourishment.

JANE, doubtless, represented thousands of old slave mothers, who, after having been worn out under the yoke, were frequently either offered for sale for a trifle, turned off to die, or compelled to eke out their existence on the most stinted allowance.

BENJAMIN ROSS, AND HIS WIFE HARRIET.

FLED FROM CAROLINE COUNTY, EASTERN SHORE OF MARYLAND, JUNE, 1857.

This party stated that Dr. Anthony Thompson had claimed them as his property. They gave the Committee a pretty full report of how they had been treated in slavery, especially under the doctor. A few of the interesting points were noted as follows : The doctor owned about twenty head of slaves when they left; formerly he had owned a much larger number, but circumstances had led him to make frequent sales during the few years previous to their escape, by which the stock had been reduced. As well as having been largely interested in slaves, he had at the same time been largely interested in real estate, to the extent of a dozen farms at least. But in consequence of having reached out too far, several of his farms had slipped out of his hands.

Upon the whole, Benjamin pronounced him a rough man towards his slaves, and declared, that he had not given him a dollar since the death of his (the master's) father, which had been at least twenty years prior to Benjamin's escape. But Ben. did not stop here, he went on to speak of the religious character of his master, and also to describe him physically; he was a Methodist preacher, and had been "pretending to preach for twenty years." Then the fact that a portion of their children had been sold to Georgia by this master was referred to with much feeling by Ben and his wife; likewise the fact that he had stinted them for food and clothing, and led them a rough life generally, which left them no room to believe that he was anything else than "a wolf in sheep's clothing." They described him as a "spare-built man, bald head, wearing a wig."

These two travelers had nearly reached their three score years and ten under the yoke. Nevertheless they seemed delighted at the idea of going to a free country to enjoy freedom, if only for a short time. Moreover some of their children had escaped in days past, and these they hoped to find. Not many of those thus advanced in years ever succeeded in getting to Canada.

ARRIVAL FROM VIRGINIA, 1857.

WILLIAM JACKSON.

WILLIAM was about fifty years of age, of usual size, of good address, and intelligent. He was born the property of a slaveholder, by the name of Daniel Minne, residing in Alexandria in Virginia. His master was about eighty-four years of age, and was regarded as kind, though he had sold some of his slaves and was in favor of slavery. He had two sons, Robert and Albert, "both dissipated, would lay about the tippling taverns, and keep low company, so much so that they were not calculated to do any business for their father." William had to be a kind of a right hand man to his master. The sons seeing that the "property" was trusted instead of themselves, very naturally hated it, so the young men resolved that at the death of their father, William should be sent as far south as possible. Knowing that the old man could not stand it much longer, William saw that it was his policy to get away as fast as he could. He was the husband of a free wife, who had come on in advance of him.

For thirty years William had been foreman on his old master's plantation, and but for the apprehension caused by the ill-will of his prospective young masters, he would doubtless have remained in servitude at least until the death of the old man. But when William reflected, and saw what he had been deprived of all his life by being held in bondage, and when he began to breathe free air, with the prospect of ending his days on free land, he rejoiced that his eyes had been opened to see his danger, and that he had been moved to make a start for liberty.

ARRIVAL FROM DELAWARE, 1857.

JOHN WRIGHT AND WIFE, ELIZABETH ANN, AND CHARLES CONNOR.

This party arrived from Sussex county. John was about thirty years of age, ordinary size, full black and clear-headed. In physical appearance he would have readily passed for a superior laborer. The keenness of his eyes and quickness of his perception, however, would doubtless have rendered him an object of suspicion in some parts of the South. The truth was that the love of liberty was clearly indicated in his expressive countenance. William S. Phillips, a farmer, had been " sucking " John's blood, and keeping him poor and ignorant for the last eight years at least; before that, Phillips' father had defrauded him of his hire.

Under the father and son John had found plenty of hard work and bad usage, severe and repeated floggings not excepted. Old master and mistress and young master and mistress, including the entire family, belonged to what was known as the " Farmer church," at Portsville. Outwardly they were good Christians. " Occasionally," John said, " the old man would have family prayers," and to use John's own words, " in company he would try to moralize, but out of company was as great a rowdy as ever was." In further describing his old master, he said that he was a large man, with a red face and blunt nose, and was very quick and fiery in his temper; would drink and swear—and even his wife, with åll hands, would have to run when he was " raised."

Of his young master he said: " He was quite a long-bodied, thin-faced man, weighing over one hundred and fifty pounds. In temper just like his father, though he did not drink—that is all the good quality that I can recommend in him." John said also that his master, on one occasion, in a most terribly angry mood, threatened that he would " wade up to his knees in his (John's) blood." It so happened that John's blood was up pretty high just at that time; he gave his master to understand that he would rather go South (be sold) than submit to the scourging which was imminent. John's pluck probably had the effect of allaying the master's fire ; at any rate the storm subsided after awhile, and until the day that he took the Underground Rail Road car the servant managed to put up with his master. As John's wife was on the eve of being sold he was prompted to leave some time sooner than he otherwise would have done.

THE WIFE'S STATEMENT.

She was thirty-two years of age, of good physical proportions, and a promising-looking person, above the ordinary class of slaves belonging to Delaware. She was owned by Jane Cooper, who lived near Laurel, in Sussex county. She had been more accustomed to field labor than house-work; ploughing, fencing, driving team, grubbing, cutting wood, etc., were well understood by her. During "feeding times" she had to assist in the house. In this respect, she had harder times than the men. Her mistress was also in the habit of hiring Elizabeth out by the day to wash. On these occasions she was required to rise early enough to milk the cows, get breakfast, and feed the hogs before sunrise, so that she might be at her day's washing in good time.

It is plainly to be seen, that Elizabeth had not met with the "ease" and kindness which many claimed for the slave. Elizabeth was sensible of the wrongs inflicted by her Delaware mistress, and painted her in very vivid colors. Her mistress was a widow, "quite old," but "very frisky," and "wore a wig to hide her gray hairs." At the death of her husband, the slaves believed, from what they had heard their master say, that they would be freed, each at the age of thirty. But no will was found, which caused Elizabeth, as well as the rest of the slaves, to distrust the mistress more than ever, as they suspected that she knew something of its disappearance.

Her mistress belonged to the Presbyterian Church, but would have "family prayers only when the minister would stop;" Elizabeth thought that she took greater pains to please the minister than her Maker. Elizabeth had no faith in such religion.

Both Elizabeth and her husband were members of the Methodist Church. Neither had ever been permitted to learn to read or write, but they were naturally very smart. John left his mother and one sister in bondage. One of his brothers fled to Canada fifteen years before their escape. His name was Abraham.

CHARLES CONNOR, the third person in the party, was twenty-seven years of age—fast color, and a tough-looking "article," who would have brought twelve hundred dollars or more in the hands of a Baltimore trader. The man from whom Charles fled was known by the name of John Chipman, and was described as "a fleshy man, with rank beard and quick temper, very hard—commonly kept full of liquor, though he would not get so drunk that he could not go about." For a long time Charles had been the main dependence on his master's place, as he only owned two other slaves. Charles particularly remarked, that no weather was too bad for them to be kept at work in the field. Charles was a fair specimen of the "corn-field hand," but thought that he could take care of himself in Canada.

ARRIVAL FROM ALEXANDRIA, 1857.

OSCAR D. BALL, AND MONTGOMERY GRAHAM.

FOUR HUNDRED DOLLARS REWARD.—Ran away from the owner in Alexandria, Va., on the night of the 13th inst., two young negro men, from twenty to twenty-five years of age. MONTGOMERY is a very bright mulatto, about five feet, six inches in height, of polite manners, and smiles much when speaking or spoken to. OSCAR is of a tawny complexion, about six feet high, sluggish in his appearance and movements, and of awkward manners.

One hundred dollars each will be paid for the delivery of the above slaves if taken in a slave state, or two hundred dollars each if taken in a free state. One or more slaves belonging to other owners, it is supposed, went in their company.

Address :   JOHN T. GORDON,
Alexandria, Va.

Although the name of John T. Gordon appears signed to the above advertisement, he was not the owner of Montgomery and Oscar. According to their own testimony they belonged to a maiden lady, by the name of Miss Elizabeth Gordon, who probably thought that the business of advertising for runaway negroes was rather beneath her.

While both these passengers manifested great satisfaction in leaving their mistress they did not give her a bad name. On the contrary they gave her just such a character as the lady might have been pleased with in the main. They described her thus : " Mistress was a spare woman, tolerably tall, and very kind, except when sick, she would not pay much attention then. She was a member of the Southern Methodist Church, and was strict in her religion."

Having a good degree of faith in his mistress, Oscar made bold one day to ask her how much she would take for him. She agreed to take eight hundred dollars. Oscar wishing to drive a pretty close bargain offered her seven hundred dollars, hoping that she would view the matter in a religious light, and would come down one hundred dollars. After reflection instead of making a reduction, she raised the amount to one thousand dollars, which Oscar concluded was too much for himself. It was not, however, as much as he was worth according to his mistress' estimate, for she declared that she had often been offered fifteen hundred dollars for him. Miss Gordon raised Oscar from a child and had treated him as a pet. When he was a little "shaver" seven or eight years of age, she made it a practice to have him sleep with her, showing that she had no prejudice.

Being rather of a rare type of slave-holders she is entitled to special credit. Montgomery the companion of Oscar could scarcely be distinguished from the white folks. In speaking of his mistress, however, he did not express himself in terms quite so complimentary as Oscar. With regard to giving " passes," he considered her narrow, to say the least. But he was in such perfectly good humor with everybody, owing to the fact that he had succeeded in getting his neck out of the yoke, that he evidently had no desire to say hard things about her.

Judging from his story he had been for a long time desiring his freedom, and looking diligently for the Underground Rail Road, but he had had many things to contend with when looking the matter of escape in the face. Arriving in Philadelphia, and finding himself breathing free air, receiving aid and encouragement in a manner that he had never known before, he was one of the happiest of creatures.

Oscar left his wife and one child, one brother and two sisters. Montgomery left one sister, but no other near kin.

Instead of going to Canada, Oscar and his comrade pitched their tents in Oswego, N. Y., where they changed their names, and instead of returning themselves to their kind mistress they were wicked enough to be plotting as to how some of their friends might get off on the Underground Rail Road, as may be seen from the appended letters from Oscar, who was thought to be sluggish, etc.

Oswego, Oct 25th, 1857.

Dear Sir:—I take this opportunity of writing you these few lines to inform you that I am well and hope these few lines will find you the same (and your family you must excuse me for not writing to you before. I would have written to you before this but I put away the card you gave me and could not find it until a few days sins. I did not go to Canada for I got work in Oswego, but times are very dull here at present. I have been out of employ about five weeks I would like to go to Australia. Do you know of any gentleman that is going there or any other place, except south that wants a servant to go there with him to wait on him or do any other work, I have a brother that wants to come north. I received a letter from him a few days ago. Can you tell me of any plan that I can fix to get him give my respects to Mrs. Still and all you family. Please let me know if you hear of any berth of that kind. Nothing more at present I remain your obedient servant, Oscar D. Ball.

But my name is now John Delaney. Direct your letter to John Delaney Oswego N. Y. care of R. Oliphant.

Oswego, Nov. 21st, 1857.

Mr. William Still, Esq. Dear Sir:—Your letter of the 19th came duly to hand I am glad to hear that the Underground Rail Road is doing so well I know those three well that you said come from alex I broke the ice and it seems as if they are going to keep the track open. but I had to stand and beg of those two that started with me to come and even give one of them money and then he did not want to come. I had a letter from my brother a few days ago, and he says if he lives and nothing happens to him he will make a start for the north and there is many others there that would start now but they are afraid of getting frost bitten, there was two left alex about five or six weeks ago. ther names are as follows Lawrence Thornton and Townsend Derrit. have they been to philadelphia from what I can learn they will leave alex in mourning next spring in the last letter I got from my brother he named a good many that wanted to come when he did and the are all sound men and can be trusted. he reads and writes his own letters. William Triplet and Thomas Harper passed through hear last summer from my old home which way did those three that you spoke of go times are very dull here at present and I can get nothing to do. but thank God have a good boarding house and will be sheltered from the weather this winter give my respects to your family Montgomery sends his also Nothing more at presant Yours truly John Delaney.

N. W. DEPEE.

JACOB C. WHITE.

CHARLES WISE,

TREASURER.

EDWIN H. COATES.

MEMBERS OF THE ACTING COMMITTEE.

ARRIVAL FROM UNIONVILLE, 1857.

CAROLINE ALDRIDGE AND JOHN WOOD.

CAROLINE was a stout, light-complexioned, healthy-looking young woman of twenty-three years of age. She fled from Thornton Poole, of Unionville, Md. She gave her master the character of being a "very mean man; with a wife meaner still." "I consider them mean in every respect," said Caroline. No great while before she escaped, one of her brothers and a sister had been sent to the Southern market. Recently she had been apprized that herself and a younger brother would have to go the same dreadful road. She therefore consulted with the brother and a particular young friend, to whom she was "engaged," which resulted in the departure of all three of them. Though the ordinary steps relative to marriage, as far as slaves were allowed, had been complied with, nevertheless on the road to Canada, they availed themselves of the more perfect way of having the ceremony performed, and went on their way rejoicing.

Since the sale of Caroline's brother and sister, just referred to, her mother and three children had made good their exit to Canada, having been evidently prompted by said sale. Long before that time, however, three other brothers fled on the Underground Rail Road. They were encouraged to hope to meet each other in Canada.

JOHN WOOD. John was about twenty-eight years of age, of agreeable manners, intelligent, and gave evidence of a strong appreciation of liberty. Times with John had "not been very rough," until within the last year of his bondage. By the removal of his old master by death, a change for the worse followed. The executors of the estate—one of whom owed him an old grudge—made him acquainted with the fact, that amongst certain others, he would have to be sold. Judge Birch (one of the executors), "itching" to see him "broke in," "took particular pains" to speak to a notorious tyrant by the name of Boldin, to buy him. Accordingly on the day of sale, Boldin was on hand and the successful bidder for John. Being familiar with the customs of this terrible Boldin,—of the starving fare and cruel flogging usual on his farm, John mustered courage to declare at the sale, that he "*would not serve him.*" In the hearing of his new master, he said, "*before I will serve him I will* CUT *my throat!*" The master smiled, and simply asked for a rope; "had me tied and delivered into the hands of a constable," to be sent over to the farm. Before reaching his destination, John managed to untie his hands and feet and flee to the woods. For three days he remained secreted. Once or twice he secretly managed to get an interview with his mother and one of his sisters, by whom he was persuaded to return to his master. Taking their advice, he commenced service under circumstances, compared with which, the diet, labor and comforts of an

26

ordinary penitentiary would have been luxurious. The chief food allowed the slaves on the plantation consisted of the pot liquor in which the pork was boiled, with Indian-meal bread. The merest glance at what he experienced during his brief stay on the plantation must suffice. In the field where John, with a number of others was working, stood a hill, up which they were repeatedly obliged to ascend, with loads on their backs, and the overseer at their heels, with lash in hand, occasionally slashing at first one and then another; to keep up, the utmost physical endurance was taxed. John, though a stout young man, and having never known any other condition than that of servitude, nevertheless found himself quite unequal to the present occasion. " I was surprised," said he, " to see the expertness with which all flew up the hill." " *One woman, quite* LUSTY, *unfit to be out of the house, on* RUNNING UP THE HILL, fell; in a moment she was up again with her brush on her back, and an hour afterwards the overseer was whipping her." " MY turn came." " What is 'the reason you can't get up the hill faster?" exclaimed the overseer, at the same time he struck me with a cowhide. " I told him I would not stand it." " Old Uncle George Washington never failed to get a whipping every day."

So after serving at this only a few days, John made his last solemn vow to be free or die; and off he started for Canada. Though he had to contend with countless difficulties he at last made the desired haven. He hailed from one of the lower counties of Maryland.

JOHN was not contented to enjoy the boon alone, but like a true lover of freedom he remembered those in bonds as bound with them, and so was scheming to make a hazardous " adventure " South, on the express errand of delivering his " family," as the subjoined letter will show:

GLANDFORD, August 15th, 1858.

DEAR SIR :—I received your letter and was glad to hear that your wife and family was all well and I hope it will continue so. I am glad to inform you that this leaves me well. Also, Mr. Wm. Still, I want for you to send me your opinion respecting my circumstances. I have made up my mind to make an adventure after my family and I want to get an answer from you and then I shall know how to act and then I will send to you all particulars respecting my starting to come to your house. Mr. Still I should be glad to know whare Abraham Harris is, as I should be as glad to see him as well as any of my own brothers. His wife and my wife's mother is sisters. My wife belongs to Elson Burdel's estate. Abraham's wife belongs to Sam Adams. Mr. Still you must not think hard of me for writing you these few lines as I cannot rest until I release my dear family. I have not the least doubt but I can get through without the least trouble.

So no more at present from your humble servant,

JOHN B. WOODS.

ARRIVAL FROM NEW ORLEANS, 1857.

JAMES CONNER, SHOT IN DIFFERENT PARTS OF THE BODY.

James stated to the Committee that he was about forty-three years of age, that he was born a slave in Nelson county, Ky., and that he was first owned by a widow lady by the name of Ruth Head. " She (mistress) was like a mother to me," said Jim. " I was about sixteen years old when she died ; the estate was settled and I was sold South to a man named Vincent Turner, a planter, and about the worst man, I expect, that ever the sun shined on. His slaves he fairly murdered ; two hundred lashes were merely a promise for him. He owned about three hundred slaves. I lived with Turner until he died. After his death I still lived on the plantation with his widow, Mrs. Virginia Turner." About twelve years ago (prior to Jim's escape) she was married to a Mr. Charles Parlange, "a poor man, though a very smart man, bad-hearted, and very barbarous."

Before her second marriage cotton had always been cultivated, but a few years later sugar had taken the place of cotton, and had become the principal thing raised in that part of the country. Under the change sugar was raised and the slaves were made to experience harder times than ever ; they were allowed to have only from three to three and a half pounds of pork a week, with a peck of meal ; nothing else was allowed. They commenced work in the morning, just when they could barely see ; they quit work in the evening when they could not see to work longer.

Mistress was a large, portly woman, good-looking, and pretty well liked by her slaves. The place where the plantation was located was at Point Copee, on Falls River, about one hundred and fifty miles from New Orleans. She also owned property and about twenty slaves in the city of New Orleans.

" I lived there and hired my time for awhile. I saw some hard times on the plantation. Many a time I have seen slaves whipped almost to death— well, I tell you I have seen them whipped to death. A slave named Sam was whipped to death tied to the ground. Joe, another slave, was whipped to death by the overseer : running away was the crime.

" Four times I was shot. Once, before I would be taken, all hands, young and old on the plantation were on the chase after me. I was strongly armed with an axe, tomahawk, and butcher knife. I expected to be killed on the spot, but I got to the woods and stayed two days. At night I went back to the plantation and got something to eat. While going back to the woods I was shot in the thigh, legs, back and head, was badly wounded, my mind was to die rather than be taken. I ran a half mile after I was shot, but was taken. I have shot in me now. Feel here on my head, feel my back, feel buck shot in my thigh. I shall carry shot in me to my grave. I have been shot four different times. I was shot twice by a fellow-servant; it was my master's orders. Another time by the overseer. Shooting was no uncommon thing in Louisiana. At one time I was allowed to raise hogs. I had twenty-five taken from me without being allowed the first copper.

"My mistress promised me at another time forty dollars for gathering honey, but when I went to her, she said, by and by, but the by and by never came. In 1853 my freedom was promised; for five years before this time I had been overseer; during four years of this time a visit was made to France by my owners, but on their return my freedom was not given me. My mistress thought I had made enough money to buy myself. They asked eleven hundred and fifty dollars for me. I told them that I hadn't the money. Then they said if I would go with them to Virginia after a number of slaves they wished to purchase, and would be a good boy, they would give me my freedom on the return of the trip. We started on the 8th of June, 1857. I made fair promises wishing to travel, and they placed all confidence in me. I was to carry the slaves back from Virginia.

"They came as far as Baltimore, and they began to talk of coming farther North, to Philadelphia. They talked very good to me, and told me that if they brought me with them to a free State that I must not leave them; talked a good deal about giving me my freedom, as had been promised before starting, etc. I let on to them that I had no wish to go North; that Baltimore was as far North as I wished to see, and that I had rather be going home than going North. I told them that I was tired of this country. In speaking of coming North, they made mention of the Alleghany mountains. I told them that I would like to see that, but nothing more. They hated the North, and I made believe that I did too. Mistress said, that if I behaved myself I could go with them to France, when they went again, after they returned home—as they intended to go again.

"So they decided to take me with them to Philadelphia, for a short visit, before going into Virginia to buy up their drove of slaves for Louisiana. My heart leaped for joy when I found we were going to a free State; but I did not let my owners know my feelings.

"We reached Philadelphia and went to the Girard Hotel, and there I made up my mind that they should go back without me. I saw a colored man who talked with me, and told me about the Committee. He brought me to the anti-slavery office," etc., etc., etc.

The Committee told Jim that he could go free immediately, without saying a word to anybody, as the simple fact of his master's bringing him into the State was sufficient to establish his freedom before the Courts. At the same time the Committee assured him if he were willing to have his master arrested and brought before one of the Judges of the city to show cause why he held him a slave in Pennsylvania, contrary to the laws of the State, that he should lack neither friends nor money to aid him in the matter; and, moreover, his freedom would be publicly proclaimed.

JIM thought well of both ways, but preferred not to meet his " kindhearted " master and mistress in Court, as he was not quite sure that he would have the courage to face them and stand by his charges.

This was not strange. Indeed not only slaves cowed before the eye of slave-holders. Did not even Northern men, superior in education and wealth, fear to say their souls were their own in the same presence ?

JIM, therefore, concluded to throw himself upon the protection of the Committee and take an Underground Rail Road ticket, and thereby spare himself and his master and mistress the disagreeableness of meeting under such strange circumstances. The Committee arranged matters for him to the satisfaction of all concerned, and gave him a passport for her British majesty's possession, Canada.

The unvarnished facts, as they were then recorded substantially from the lips of Jim, and as they are here reproduced, comprise only a very meagre part of his sadly interesting story. At the time Jim left his master and mistress so unceremoniously in Philadelphia, some excitement existed at the attempt of his master to recover him through the Police of Philadelphia, under the charge that he (Jim) had been stealing, as may be seen from the following letter which appeared in the " National Anti-Slavery Standard :"

ANOTHER SLAVE HUNT IN PHILADELPHIA.

Philadelphia, Monday, July 27, 1857.

Yesterday afternoon a rumor was afloat that a negro man named Jim, who had accompanied his master (Mr. Charles Parlange), from New Orleans to this city, had left his master for the purpose of tasting the sweets of freedom. It was alleged by Mr. Parlange that the said "Jim" had taken with him two tin boxes, one of which contained money. Mr. Parlange went, on his way to New York, *via* the Camden and Amboy Railroad, and upon his arrival at the Walnut street wharf, with two ladies, "Jim" was missing. Mr. Parlange immediately made application to a Mr. Wallace, who is a Police officer stationed at the Walnut street depot. Mr. Wallace got into a carriage with Mr. Parlange and the two ladies, and, as Mr. Wallace stated, drove back to the Girard House, where "Jim" had not been heard of since he had left for the Walnut street wharf.

A story was then set afloat to the effect, that a negro of certain, but very particular description (such as a Louisiana nigger-driver only can give), had stolen two boxes as stated above. A notice signed "Clarke," was received at the Police Telegraph Office by the operator (David Wunderly) containing a full description of Jim, also offering a reward of $100 for his capture. This notice was telegraphed to all the wards in every section. This morning Mr. Wunderly found fault with the reporters using the information, and, in presence of some four or five persons, said the notice signed "Clarke," was a private paper, and no reporter had a right to look at it; at the same time asserting, that if he knew where the nigger was he would give him up, as $100 did not come along every day. The policeman, Wallace, expressed the utmost fear lest the name of Mr. Parlange should transpire, and stated, that he was an intimate friend of his. It does not seem that the matter was communicated to the wards by any official authority whatever, and who the "Clarke" is, whose name was signed to the notice, has not yet transpired. Some of the papers noticed it briefly this morning, which has set several of the officers on their tips. There is little doubt, that "Jim" has merely exercised his own judgment about remaining with his master any longer, and took this opportunity to betake himself to freedom. It is assumed, that he was to precede his master to Walnut street wharf with the baggage; but, singular enough to say, no complaint has been made about the baggage being missed, simply the two tin boxes, and particularly the one containing money. This is, doubtless, a ruse to engage the services of the Philadelphia police in the interesting game of nigger hunting. Mr. Parlange, if he is sojourning in your city, will doubtless be glad to learn that the matter of his man "Jim" and the two tin boxes has received ample publicity. W. H.

Rev. Hiram Wilson, the Underground Rail Road agent at St. Catharines, C. W., duly announced his safe arrival as follows:

BUFFALO, Aug. 12th, 1857.

MY DEAR FRIEND—WM. STILL:—I take the liberty to inform you, that I had the pleasure of seeing a man of sable brand at my house in St. C. yesterday, by name of James Connor, lately from New Orleans, more recently from the city of Brotherly love, where he took French leave of his French master. He desired me to inform you of his safe arrival in the glorious land of Freedom, and to send his kind regards to you and to Mr. Williamson; also to another person, (the name I have forgotten). Poor Malinda Smith, with her two little girls and young babe is with us doing well.

Affectionately yours, HIRAM WILSON.

ARRIVAL FROM WASHINGTON, D. C.

HARRISON CARY.

The passenger bearing this name who applied to the Committee for assistance, was a mulatto of medium size, with a prepossessing countenance, and a very smart talker. With only a moderate education he might have raised himself to the "top round of the ladder," as a representative of the down-trodden slave. Seeking, as usual, to learn his history, the subjoined questions and answers were the result of the interview:

Q. "How old are you?"

A. "Twenty-eight years of age this coming March."

Q. " To whom did you belong?"

A. " Mrs. Jane E. Ashley."

Q. " What kind of a woman was she?"

A. " She was a very clever woman; never said anything out of the way."

Q. " How many servants had she?"

A. " She had no other servants."

Q. " Did you live with her?"

A. " No. I hired my time for twenty-two dollars a month."

Q. " How could you make so much money?"

A. " I was a bricklayer by trade, and ranked among the first in the city."

As Harrison talked so intelligently, the member of the Committee who was examining him, was anxious to know how he came to be so knowing, the fact that he could read being very evident.

Harrison proceeded to explain how he was led to acquire the art both of reading and writing: " Slaves caught out of an evening without passes from their master or mistress, were invariably arrested, and if they were unable to raise money to buy themselves off, they were taken and locked up in a place known as the ' cage,' and in the morning the owner was notified, and after paying the fine the unfortunate prisoner had to go to meet his fate at the hands of his owner."

Often he or she found himself or herself sentenced to take thirty-nine or more lashes before atonement could be made for the violated law, and the fine sustained by the enraged owner.

Harrison having strong aversion to both of the " wholesome regulations " of the peculiar institution above alluded to, saw that the only remedy that he could avail himself of was to learn to write his own passes. In possessing himself of this prize he knew that the law against slaves being taught, would have to be broken, nevertheless he was so anxious to succeed, that he was determined to run the risk. Consequently he grasped the boon with but very little difficulty or assistance. Valuing his prize highly, he improved more and more until he could write his own passes satisfactorily. The "cage" he denounced as a perfect "hog hole," and added, "it was more than I could bear."

He also spoke with equal warmth on the pass custom, " the idea of working hard all day and then being obliged to have a pass," etc.,—his feelings sternly revolted against. Yet he uttered not a disrespectful word against the individual to whom he belonged. Once he had been sold, but for what was not noted on the record book.

His mother had been sold several times. His brother, William Henry Cary, escaped from Washington, D. C., when quite a youth. What became of him it was not for Harrison to tell, but he supposed that he had made his way to a free State, or Canada, and he hoped to find him. He had no knowledge of any other relatives.

In further conversation with him, relative to his being a single man, he said, that he had resolved not to entangle himself with a family until he had obtained his freedom.

He had found it pretty hard to meet his monthly hire, consequently he was on the look-out to better his condition as soon as a favorable opportunity might offer. Harrison's mistress had a son named John James Ashley, who was then a minor. On arriving at majority, according to the will of this lad's father, he was to have possession of Harrison as his portion. Harrison had no idea of having to work for his support—he thought that, if John could not take care of himself when he grew up to be a man, there was a place for all such in the poor-house.

Harrison was also moved by another consideration. His mistress' sister had been trying to influence the mistress to sell him ; thus considering himself in danger, he made up his mind that the time had come for him to change his habitation, so he resolved to try his fortune on the Underground Rail Road.

ARRIVAL FROM VIRGINIA, 1857.

JOE ELLIS.

The subject of this sketch was one of two hundred slaves, owned by Bolling Ellis, who possessed large plantations at Cabin Point, Surrey Co., Va. Joe pictured his master, overseers, and general treatment of slaves in no favorable light.

The practice of punishing slaves by putting them in the stocks and by flogging, was dwelt upon in a manner that left no room to doubt but that Joe had been a very great sufferer under his master's iron rule. As he described the brutal conduct of overseers in resorting to their habitual modes of torturing men, women, and children, it was too painful to listen to with composure, much more to write down.

Joe was about twenty-three years of age, full black, slender, and of average intellect, considering the class which he represented. On four occasions previous to the final one he had made fruitless efforts to escape from his tormentors in consequence of brutal treatment. Although he at last succeeded, the severe trials through which he had to pass in escaping, came very near costing him his life. The effects he will always feel ; prostration and sickness had already taken hold upon him in a serious degree.

During Joe's sojourn under the care of the Committee, time would not admit of the writing out of further details concerning him.

ARRIVAL FROM MARYLAND.

CHRISTOPHER GREEN AND WIFE, ANN MARIA, AND SON NATHAN.

CHRISTOPHER had a heavy debt charged against Clayton Wright, a commission merchant, of Baltimore, who claimed him as his property, and was in the habit of hiring him out to farmers in the country, and of taking all his hire except a single dollar, which was allotted him every holiday.

The last item in his charge against Wright, suggested certain questions: "How have you been used?" was the first query. "Sometimes right smart, and then again bad enough for it," said Christopher. Again he was asked, "What kind of a man was your master?" "He was only tolerable, I can't say much good for him. I got tired of working and they getting my labor and I getting nothing for my labor." At the time of his escape, he was employed in the service of a man by the name of Cook. Christopher described him as "a dissatisfied man, who couldn't be pleased at nothing and his wife was like him."

This passenger was quite black, medium size, and in point of intellect, about on a par with ordinary field hands. His wife, Ann, in point of go-ahead-ativeness, seemed in advance of him. Indeed, she first prompted her husband to escape.

ANN bore witness against one James Pipper, a farmer, whom she had served as a slave, and from whom she fled, saying that "he was as mean a man as ever walked—a dark-complected old man, with gray hair." With great emphasis she thus continued her testimony : "He tried to work me to death, and treated me as mean as he could, without killing me; he done so much I couldn't tell to save my life. I wish I had as many dollars as he has whipped me with sticks and other things. His wife will do tolerable." "I left because he was going to sell me and my son to Georgia; for years he had been threatening; since the boys ran away, last spring, he was harder than ever. One was my brother, Perry, and the other was a young man by the name of Jim." "David, my master, drank all he could get, poured it down, and when drunk, would cuss, and tear, and rip, and beat. He lives near the nine bridges, in Queen Ann county."

ANN was certainly a forcible narrator, and was in every way a wide-awake woman, about thirty-seven years of age. Among other questions they were asked if they could read, etc. "Read," said Ann. "I would like to see anybody (slave) that could read our way ; to see you with a book in your hand they would almost cut your throat."

ANN had one child only, a son, twenty years of age, who came in company with his parents. This son belonged to the said Pipper already described. When they started from the land of bondage they had large hopes, but not much knowledge of the way ; however, they managed to get safely on the Underground Rail Road track, and by perseverance they reached the Committee and were aided in the usual manner.

ARRIVAL FROM GEORGETOWN CROSS-ROADS, 1857.

LEEDS WRIGHT AND ABRAM TILISON.

For three years Leeds had been thirsting for his liberty ; his heart was fixed on that one object. He got plenty to eat, drink, and wear, but was nevertheless dissatisfied.

The name of his master was Rev. John Wesley Pearson, who was engaged in school teaching and preaching, and belonged to the more moderate class of slave-holders. Once when a boy Leeds had been sold, but being very young, he did not think much about the matter.

For the last eight or ten years previous to his escape he had not seen his relatives, his father (George Wright) having fled to Canada, and the remainder of the family lived some fifty miles distant, beyond the possibility of intercourse ; therefore, as he had no strong ties to break, he could look to the time of leaving the land of bondage without regret.

ABRAM, the companion of Leeds, had been less comfortably situated. His lot in Slavery had been cast under Samuel Jarman, by whom he had been badly treated.

Abram described him as a "big, tall, old man, who drank and was a real wicked man ; he followed farming ; had thirteen children. His wife was different ; she was a pretty fine woman, but the children were all bad ; the young masters followed playing cards." No chance at all had been allowed them to learn to read, although Abram and Leeds both coveted this knowledge. As they felt that they would never be able to do anything for their improvement by remaining, they decided to follow the example of Abram's father and others and go to Canada.

ARRIVAL FROM ALEXANDRIA.

WILLIAM TRIPLETT AND THOMAS HARPER.

RAN AWAY from the subscriber, on Saturday night, 22d instant, WILLIAM TRIPLETT, a dark mulatto, with whiskers and mustache, 23 to 26 years of age ; lately had a burn on the instep of his right foot, but perhaps well enough to wear a boot or shoe. He took with him very excellent clothing, both summer and winter, consisting of a brown suit in cloth, summer coats striped, check cap, silk hat, &c. $50 reward will be paid if taken within thirty miles of Alexandria or in the State of Virginia, and $150 and necessary expenses if taken out of the State and secured so that I get him again. He is the property of Mrs. A. B. Fairfax, of Alexandria, and is likely to make his way to Cincinnati, where he has friends, named Hamilton and Hopes, now living.   ROBT. W. WHEAT.

WILLIAM, answering to the above description, arrived safely in company with Thomas Harper, about six days after the date of their departure from the house of bondage.

Mrs. A. B. Fairfax was the loser of this "article." William spoke rather favorably of her. He said he did not leave because he was treated badly, but simply because he wanted to own himself—to be free. He also said that he wanted to be able to take care of his family if he should see fit to marry.

As to Slavery, he could see no justice in the system; he therefore made up his mind no longer to yield submission thereto. Being a smart "chattel," he reasoned well on the question of Slavery, and showed very conclusively that even under the kindest mistress it had no charms for him—that at best, it was robbery and an outrage.

THOMAS HARPER, his comrade, fled from John Cowling, who also lived near Alexandria. His great trouble was, that he had a wife and family, but could do nothing for them. He thought that it was hard to see them in want and abused when he was not at liberty to aid or protect them. He grew very unhappy, but could see no remedy except in flight.

Cowling, his master, was an Englishman by birth, and followed blacksmithing for a living. He was a man in humble circumstances, trying to increase his small fortune by slave-labor.

He allowed Thomas to hire himself for one hundred dollars a year, which amount he was required to raise, sick or well. He did not complain, however, of having received any personal abuse from his blacksmith master. It was the system which was daily grinding the life out of him, that caused him to suffer, and likewise escape. By trade Thomas was also a blacksmith. He left a wife and three children.

ARRIVAL FROM MARYLAND.

HARRY WISE.

 $100 REWARD.—Ran away, on the 11th inst., negro man, Harry Wise. He is about 24 years of age, and 5 feet 4 inches high; muscular, with broad shoulders, and black or deep copper color; roundish, smooth face, and rather lively expression. He came from Harford county, and is acquainted about Belair market, Baltimore. I will pay $50 reward for him, if taken in this or Prince George's county, or $100 if arrested elsewhere.

ELLIOTT BURWELL,
West River, Anne Arundel county.

a29-eo3t*

HARRY reached the station in Philadelphia, the latter part of August, 1857. His excuse for leaving and seeking a habitation in Canada, was as follows:

"I was treated monstrous bad; my master was a very cross, crabbed man, and his wife was as cross as he was. The day I left they had to tie me to beat me, what about I could not tell; this is what made me leave. I escaped right out of his hands the day he had me; he was going with me to the barn to tie me across a hogshead, but I broke loose from him and ran. He ran and got the gun to shoot me, but I soon got out of his reach, and I have not seen him since."

HARRY might never have found the Underground Rail Road, but for this deadly onslaught upon him by his master. His mind was wrought up to a very high state of earnestness, and he was deemed a very fitting subject for Canada.

ARRIVAL FROM NORFOLK, VA.
ABRAM WOODERS.

Although slave-holders had spared no pains to keep Abram in the dark and to make him love his yoke, he proved by his actions, that he had no faith in their doctrines. Nor did he want for language in which to state the reasons for his actions. He was just in the prime of life, thirty-five years of age, chestnut color, common size, with a scar over the left eye, and another on the upper lip.

Like many others, he talked in a simple, earnest manner, and in answer to queries as to how he had fared, the following is his statement:

"I was held as the property of the late Taylor Sewell, but when I escaped I was in the service of W. C. Williams, a commission merchant. My old master was a very severe man, but he was always very kind to me. He had a great many more colored folks, was very severe amongst them, would get mad and sell right away. He was a drinking man, dissipated and a gambler, a real sportsman. He lived on Newell Creek, about twelve miles from Norfolk. For the last eight years I was hired to W. C. Williams, for $150 a year—if I had all that money, it might do me some good. I left because I wanted to enjoy myself some. I felt if I staid and got old no one would care for me, I wouldn't be of no account to nobody."

"But are not the old slaves well cared for by their masters?" a member of the Committee here remarked. "Take care of them! no!" Abram replied with much earnestness, and then went on to explain how such property was left to perish. Said Abram, "There was an old man named Ike, who belonged to the same estate that I did, he was treated like a dog; after they could get no more work out of him, they said, 'let him die, he is of no service; there is no use of getting a doctor for him.' Accordingly there could be no other fate for the old man but to suffer and die with creepers in his legs."

It was sickening to hear him narrate instances of similar suffering in the case of old slaves. Abram left two sisters and one brother in bondage.

ARRIVAL FROM WASHINGTON, D. C.

GEORGE JOHNSON, THOMAS AND ADAM SMITH.

$300 REWARD.—Ran away from Kalorama, near Washington City, D. C., on Saturday night, the 22d of August, 1857, negro man, George Johnson, aged about 25 years. Height about six feet; of dark copper color; bushy hair; erect in stature and polite in his address.

I will give the above reward if taken in a free State; $100 if taken within the District of Columbia, or $200 if taken in Maryland. In either case he must be secured so that I get him.   MISS ELEANOR J. CONWAY, Baltimore, Md., or OLIVER DUFOUR, Washington City, D. C.

sl–eod 2w.

"Polite in his address" as George was, he left his mistress, Eleanor J. Conway, without bidding her good-bye, or asking for a pass. But he did not leave his young mistress in this way without good reasons for so doing.

In his interview with the Committee about five days after his departure from his old home, he stated his grievances as follows: "I was born the slave of a Mr. Conway, of Washington, D. C." Under this personage George admitted that he had experienced slavery in rather a mild form until death took the old man off, which event occurred when George was quite young. He afterwards served the widow Conway until her death, and lastly he fell into the hands of Miss Eleanor J. Conway, who resided in Baltimore, and derived her support from the labor of slaves whom she kept hired out as was George. Of the dead, George did not utter very hard things, but he spoke of his young mistress as having a "very mean principle." Said George, "She has sold one of my brothers and one of my cousins since last April, and she was very much opposed to freedom."

Judging from the company that she kept she might before a great while change her relations in life. George thought, however agreeable to her, it might not be to him. So he made up his mind that his chances for freedom would not be likely to grow any better by remaining. In the neighborhood from which he fled he left his father, mother and two sisters, each having different owners. Two brothers had been sold South. Whether they ever heard what had become of the runaway George is not known.

THOMAS, the companion of George, was of a truly remarkable structure; physically and mentally he belonged to the highest order of the bond class. His place of chains was in the city of Washington, and the name of the man for whom he had been compelled to do unrequited labor was William Rowe, a bricklayer, and a " pretty clever fellow,—always used me well," said Thomas. "Why did you leave then?" asked a member of the Committee. He replied, "I made a proposition to my master to buy myself for eight hundred dollars, but he refused, and wanted a thousand. Then I made up my mind that I would make less do." Thomas had been hired out at the National Hotel for thirty dollars a month.

Adam was well described in the following advertisement taken from the *Baltimore Sun:*

 $300 REWARD.—Ran away from the subscriber, near Beltsville, Prince George's county, Md., on Saturday night, the 22d of August, 1857, Negro Man, Adam Smith, aged about 30. Height 5 feet 4 or 5 inches; black bushy hair, and well dressed. He has a mother living at Mr. Hamilton's, on Capitol Hill, Washington, D. C.

I will give the above reward if taken in a free State; $50 if taken in the District of Columbia or counties of Montgomery and Prince George's, or $100 if taken elsewhere and secured so that I get him. ISAAC SCAGGS.

a27–6t*

With his fellow-passengers, George and Thomas, he greatly enjoyed the hospitalities of the Underground Rail Road in the city of Brotherly Love, and had a very high idea of Canada, as he anticipated becoming a British subject at an early day. The story which Adam related concerning his master and his reasons for escaping ran thus:

"My master was a very easy man, but would work you hard and never allow you any chance night or day; he was a farmer, about fifty, stout, full face, a real country ruffian; member of no church, a great drinker and gambler; will sell a slave as quick as any other slave-holder. He had a great deal of cash, but did not rank high in society. His wife was very severe; hated a colored man to have any comfort in the world. They had eight adult and nine young slaves."

ADAM left because he "didn't like the treatment." Twice he had been placed on the auction-block. He was a married man and left a wife and one child.

FOUR ABLE-BODIED "ARTICLES" IN ONE ARRIVAL, 1857.

EDWARD, AND JOSEPH HAINES, THOMAS HARRIS, AND JAMES SHELDON.

"This certainly is a likely-looking party," are the first words which greet the eye, on turning to the record, under which their brief narratives were entered at the Philadelphia station, September 7th, 1857.

EDWARD was about forty-four years of age, of unmixed blood, and in point of natural ability he would rank among the most intelligent of the oppressed class. Without owing thanks to any body he could read and write pretty well, having learned by his own exertions.

Tabby and Eliza Fortlock, sisters, and single women, had been deriving years of leisure, comfort, and money from the sweat of Edward's brow. The maiden ladies owned about eighteen head of this kind of property, far more than they understood how to treat justly or civilly. They bore the name of being very hard to satisfy. They were proverbially "stingy." They were members of the Christ Episcopal Church.

Edward, however, remembered very sensibly that his own brother had been sold South by these ladies; and not only he, but others also, had been sent to the auction-block, and there made merchandise of. Edward, therefore, had no faith in these lambs of the flock, and left them because he thought there was reason in all things. " Yearly my task had been increased and made heavier and heavier, until I was pressed beyond what I could bear." Under this pressure no hope, present or future, could be discerned, except by escaping on the Underground Rail Road.

JOSEPH was also one of the chattels belonging to the Misses Portlock. A more active and wide-awake young man of twenty years of age, could not easily be found among the enslaved; he seemed to comprehend Slavery in all its bearings. From a small boy he had been hired out, making money for the "pious ladies" who owned him. His experience under these protectors had been similar to that of Edward given above. Joseph was of a light brown color, (some of his friends may be able to decide by this simple fact whether he is a relative, etc.).

TOM, a full-faced, good-natured-looking young man, was also of this party. He was about twenty-seven years of age, and was said to be the slave of John Hatten, Esq., Cashier of the Virginia Bank of Portsmouth. Tom admitted that he was treated very well by Mr. Hatten and his family, except that he was not allowed his freedom; besides he felt a little tired of having to pay twelve dollars a month for his hire, as he hired his time of his master. Of course he was not insensible to the fact also that he was liable to be sold any day.

In pondering over these slight drawbacks, Tom concluded that Slavery was no place for a man who valued his freedom, it mattered not how kind masters or mistresses might be. Under these considerations he made up his mind that he would have to let the cashier look out for himself, and he would do the same. In this state of mind he joined the party for Canada.

JAMES was another associate passenger, and the best-looking "article" in the party; few slaves showed a greater degree of intelligence and shrewdness. He had acquired the art of reading and writing very well, and was also a very ready talker. He was owned by Mrs. Maria Hansford of New York. When he was quite small he remembered seeing his mistress, but not since. He was raised with her sister, who resided in Norfolk, the place of James' servitude.

James confessed that he had been treated very kindly, and had been taught to read by members of the family. This was an exceptional case, worthy of especial note.

Notwithstanding all the kindness that James had received, he hated Slavery, and took a deep interest in the Underground Rail Road, and used his intelligence and shrewdness to good purpose in acting as an Underground Rail Road agent for a time. James was a young man, about twenty-five years of age, well made, and of a yellow complexion.

Although none of this party experienced brutal treatment personally, they had seen the "elephant" quite to their satisfaction in Norfolk and vicinity.

ARRIVAL FROM ARLINGTON, Md. 1857.

JOHN ALEXANDER BUTLER, WILLIAM HENRY HIPKINS, JOHN HENRY MOORE AND GEORGE HILL.

This party made, at first sight, a favorable impression; they represented the bone and sinew of the slave class of Arlington, and upon investigation the Committee felt assured that they would carry with them to Canada industry and determination such as would tell well for the race.

JOHN ALEXANDER BUTLER was about twenty-nine years of age, well made, dark color, and intelligent. He assured the Committee that he had been hampered by Slavery from his birth, and that in consequence thereof he had suffered serious hardships. He said that a man by the name of Wm. Ford, belonging to the Methodist Church at Arlington, had defrauded him of his just rights, and had compelled him to work on his farm for nothing; also had deprived him of an education, and had kept him in poverty and ignorance all his life.

In going over the manner in which he had been treated, he added that not only was his master a hard man, but that his wife and children partook of the same evil spirit; "they were all hard." True, they had but three slaves to oppress, but these they spared not.

John was a married man, and spoke affectionately of his wife and children, whom he had to leave behind at Cross-Roads.

WILLIAM HENRY, who was heart and soul in earnest with regard to reaching Canada, and was one of this party, was twenty-three years of age, and was a stout, yellow man with a remarkably large head, and looked as if he was capable of enjoying Canada and caring for himself.

In speaking of the fettered condition from which he had escaped, the name of Ephraim Swart, "a gambler and spree'r" was mentioned as the individual who had wronged him of his liberty most grievously.

Against Swart he expressed himself with much manly feeling, and judging from his manner he appeared to be a dangerous customer for master Swart to encounter north of Mason and Dixon's line.

WILLIAM complained that Swart "would come home late at night drunk, and if he did not find us awake he would not attempt to wake us, but would begin cutting and slashing with a cowhide. He treated his wife very bad too; sometimes when she would stand up for the servants he would knock her down. Many times at midnight she would have to leave the house and go to her mother's for safety; she was a very nice woman, but he was the very old Satan himself."

While William Henry was debarred from learning letters under his brutal overseer, he nevertheless learned how to plan ways and means by which to escape his bondage. He left his old mother and two brothers wholly ignorant of his movements.

JOHN HENRY MOORE, another one of the Arlington party, was about twenty-four years of age, a dark, spare-built man. He named David Mitchell, of Havre-de-Grace, as the individual above all others who had kept his foot on his neck. Without undertaking to give John Henry's description of Mitchell in full, suffice it to give the following facts: "Mitchell would go off and get drunk, and come home, and if the slaves had not as much work done as he had tasked them with, he would go to beating them with clubs or anything he could get in his hand. He was a tall, spare-built man, with sandy hair. He had a wife and family, but his wife was no better than he was." When charges or statements were made by fugitives against those from whom they escaped, particular pains were taken to find out if such statements could be verified; if the explanation appeared valid, the facts as given were entered on the books.

JOHN HENRY could not read, but greatly desired to learn, and he looked as though he had a good head for so doing. Before he left there had been some talk of selling him South. This rumor had a marked effect upon John Henry's nervous system; it also expanded his idea touching traveling, the Underground Rail Road, etc. As he had brothers and sisters who had been sold to Georgia he made up his mind that his master was not to be trusted for a single day; he was therefore one of the most willing-hearted passengers in the party.

GEORGE HILL, also a fellow-passenger, was about twenty-four years of age, quite black, medium size, and of fair, natural mother wit. In looking back upon his days of bondage, his mind reverted to Dr. Savington, of Harford county, as the person who owed him for years of hard and unrequited toil, and at the same time was his so-called owner.

The Doctor, it seemed, had failed to treat George well, for he declared that he had never received enough to eat the whole time that he was with him. "The clothes I have on I got by overwork of nights. When I started I hadn't a shoe on my foot, these were given to me. He was an old man, but a very wicked man, and drank very hard."

George had been taught field work pretty thoroughly, but nothing in the way of reading and writing.

George explained why he left as follows: "I left because I had got along with him as well as I could. Last Saturday a week he was in a great rage

27

and drunk. He shot at me. He never went away but what he would come home drunk, and if any body made him angry out from home, he would come home and take his spite out of his people."

He owned three grown men, two women and six children. Thus hating Slavery heartily, George was enthusiastically in favor of Canada.

FIVE PASSENGERS, 1857.

ELIZA JANE JOHNSON, HARRIET STEWART, AND HER DAUGHTER MARY ELIZA, WILLIAM COLE, AND HANSON HALL.

ELIZA JANE was a tall, dark, young woman, about twenty-three years of age, and had been held to service by a widow woman, named Sally Spiser, who was "anything but a good woman." The place of her habitation was in Delaware, between Concord and Georgetown.

Eliza Jane's excuse for leaving was this : She charged her mistress with trying to work her to death, and with unkind treatment generally. When times became so hard that she could not stand her old mistress "Sally" any longer, she "took out."

HARRIET did not come in company with Eliza Jane, but by accident they met at the station in Philadelphia. Harriet and daughter came from Washington, D. C.

Harriet had treasured up a heavy account against a white man known by the name of William A. Linton, whom she described as a large, red-faced man, who had in former years largely invested in slave property, but latterly he had been in the habit of selling off, until only seven remained, and among them she and her child were numbered ; therefore, she regarded him as one who had robbed her of her rights, and daily threatened her with sale.

Harriet was a very likely-looking woman, twenty-nine years of age, medium size, and of a brown color, and far from being a stupid person. Her daughter also was a smart, and interesting little girl of eight years of age, and seemed much pleased to be getting out of the reach of slave-holders. The mother and daughter, however, had not won their freedom thus far, without great suffering, from the long and fatiguing distance which they were obliged to walk. Sometimes the hardness of the road made them feel as though they would be compelled to give up the journey, whether or not ; but they added to their faith, patience, and thus finally succeeded.

Heavy rewards were offered through advertisements in the Baltimore Sun, but they availed naught. The Vigilance Committee received them safely, fully cared for them, and safely sent them through to the land of refuge. Harriet's daring undertaking obliged her to leave her husband,

John Stewart, behind; also one sister, a slave in Georgetown. One brother had been sold South. Her mother she had laid away in a slave's grave: but her father she hoped to find in Canada, he having escaped thither when she was a small girl; at least it was supposed that he had gone there.

ARRIVAL FROM HOWARD CO., MD., 1857.

BILL COLE AND HANSON.

$500 REWARD.—Ran away on Saturday night, September 5th, Bill Cole, aged about 37 years, of copper complexion, stout built, ordinary height, walks very erect, earnest but squint look when spoken to.

Also, Hanson, copper complexion, well made, sickly look, medium height, stoops when walking, quick when spoken to; aged about 30 years.

Three hundred dollars will be paid for the apprehension and delivery of Bill, if caught out of the State, and two hundred if in the State. Two hundred dollars for Hanson if out of the State, and one hundred dollars if in the State.

W. BAKER DORSEY,
HAMMOND DORSEY,

Savage P. O., Howard county, Md.

Such notoriety as was given them by the above advertisement, did not in the least damage Bill and Hanson in the estimation of the Committee. It was rather pleasing to know that they were of so much account as to call forth such a public expression from the Messrs. Dorsey. Besides it saved the Committee the necessity of writing out a description of them, the only fault found with the advertisement being in reference to their ages. Bill, for instance, was put down ten years younger than he claimed to be. Which was correct, Bill or his master? The Committee were inclined to believe Bill in preference to his master, for the simple reason that he seemed to account satisfactorily for his master's making him so young: he (the master) could sell him for much more at thirty-seven than at forty-seven. Unscrupulous horse-jockies and traders in their fellow-men were about on a par as to that kind of sharp practice.

HANSON, instead of being only thirty, declared that he was thirty-seven the fifteenth of February. These errors are noticed and corrected because it is barely possible that Bill and Hanson may still be lost to their relatives, who may be inquiring and hunting in every direction for them, and as many others may turn to these records with hope, it is, therefore, doubly important that these descriptions shall be as far as possible, correct, especially as regards ages.

HANSON laughed heartily over the idea that he looked "sickly." While on the Underground Rail Road, he looked very far from sickly; on the contrary, a more healthy, fat, and stout-looking piece of property no one need wish to behold, than was this same Hanson. He confessed, however, that for some time previous to his departure, he had feigned sickness,—told his master that he was "sick all over." "Ten times a day Hanson said they would ask him how he was, but was not willing to make his task much lighter." The following description was given of his master, and his reason for leaving him:

"My master was a red-faced farmer, severe temper, would curse, and swear, and drink, and sell his slaves whenever he felt like it. My mistress was a pretty cross, curious kind of a woman too, though she was a member of the Protestant Church. They were rich, and had big farms and a good many slaves. They didn't allow me any provisions hardly; I had a wife, but they did not allow me to go see her, only once in a great while."

BILL providentially escaped from a well-known cripple, whom he undertook to describe as a "very sneaking-looking man, medium size, smooth face; a wealthy farmer, who owned eighteen or twenty head of slaves, and was Judge of the Orphans' Court." "He sells slaves occasionally." "My mistress was a very large, rough, Irish-looking woman, with a very bad disposition; it appeared like as if she hated to see a 'nigger,' and she was always wanting her husband to have some one whipped, and she was a member of the Methodist Church. My master was a trustee in the Episcopal Church."

In consequence of the tribulation Bill had experienced under his Christian master and mistress, he had been led to disbelieve in the Protestant faith altogether, and declared that he felt persuaded that it was all a "pretense," and added that he "never went to Church; no place was provided in church for 'niggers' except a little pen for the coachmen and waiters."

BILL had been honored with the post of "head man on the place," but of this office he was not proud.

ARRIVAL FROM PRINCE GEORGE'S COUNTY, MD.

"JIM BELLE."

$100 REWARD.—Ran away from the subscriber on Saturday night, Negro Man JIM BELLE. Jim is about five feet ten inches high, black color, about 26 years of age; has a down look; speaks slow when spoken to; he has large, thick lips, and a mustache. He was formerly owned by Edward Stansbury, late of Baltimore county, and purchased by Edward Worthington, near Reisterstown, in Baltimore county, at the late Stansbury's sale, who sold him to B. M. and W. L. Campbell, of Baltimore city, of whom I purchased Jim on the 13th of June last. His wife lives with her mother, Ann Robertson, in Corn Alley, between Lee and Hill streets, Baltimore city, where he has other relations, and where he is making his way. I will give the above reward, no matter where taken, so he is brought home or secured in jail so I get him again. ZACHARIAH BERRY, of W.,
j28–6t. near Upper Marlboro', Prince George's county, Md.

Mr. Zachariah Berry, who manifested so much interest in Jim, may be until this hour in ignorance of the cause of his running off without asking leave, etc. Jim stated, that he was once sold and flogged unmercifully simply for calling his master "Mr.," instead of master, and he alleged that this was the secret of his eyes being opened and his mind nerved to take advantage of the Underground Rail Road.

While it may not now do Zachariah Berry much good to learn this secret, it may, nevertheless, be of some interest to those who were of near kin to Jim to glean even so small a ray of light.

ARRIVAL FROM RAPPAHANNOCK COUNTY, 1857.

PASCAL QUANTENCE.

PASCAL fled from Virginia, and accused Bannon and Brady of doing violence to his liberty. He had, however, been in their clutches only a short while before escaping, but that short while seemed almost an age, as he was treated so meanly by them compared with the treatment which he had experienced under his former master.

According to Pascal's story, which was evidently true, his previous master was his own father (John Quantence), who had always acknowledged Pascal as his child, whom he did not scruple to tell people he should set free; that he did not intend that he should serve anybody else. But, while out riding one day, he was thrown from his horse and instantly killed. Naturally enough, no will being found, his effects were all administered upon and Pascal was sold with the farm. Bannon and Brady were the purchasers, at least of Pascal. In their power, immediately the time of trouble began with Pascal, and so continued until he could no longer endure it. "Hoggishness," according to Pascal's phraseology, was the most predominant trait in the character of his new masters. In his mournful situation and grief he looked toward Canada and started with courage and hope, and thus succeeded. Such deliverances always afforded very great joy to the Committee.

ARRIVAL FROM NORTH CAROLINA, 1857.

HARRY GRIMES, GEORGE UPSHER, AND EDWARD LEWIS.

FEET SLIT FOR RUNNING AWAY, FLOGGED, STABBED, STAYED IN THE HOLLOW OF
A BIG POPLAR TREE, VISITED BY A SNAKE, ABODE IN A CAVE.

The coming of the passengers here noticed was announced in the subjoined
letter from Thomas Garrett:

WILMINGTON, 11th Mo. 25th, 1857.

RESPECTED FRIEND, WILLIAM STILL:—I write to inform thee, that Captain Fountain
has arrived this evening from the South with three men, one of which is nearly naked,
and very lousy. He has been in the swamps of Carolina for eighteen months past. One
of the others has been some time out. I would send them on to-night, but will have to
provide two of them with some clothes before they can be sent by rail road. I have forgotten the number of thy house. As most likely all are more or less lousy, having been
compelled to sleep together, I thought best to write thee so that thee may get a suitable
place to take them to, and meet them at Broad and Prime streets on the arrival of the
cars, about 11 o'clock to-morrow evening. I have engaged one of our men to take them
to his house, and go to Philadelphia with them to-morrow evening. Johnson who will
accompany them is a man in whom we can confide. Please send me the number of thy
house when thee writes.   THOMAS GARRETT.

This epistle from the old friend of the fugitive, Thomas Garrett, excited
unusual interest. Preparation was immediately made to give the fugitives
a kind reception, and at the same time to destroy their plagues, root and
branch, without mercy.

They arrived according to appointment. The cleansing process was
carried into effect most thoroughly, and no vermin were left to tell the
tale of suffering they had caused. Straightway the passengers were made
comfortable in every way, and the spirit of freedom seemed to be burning
like "fire shut up in the bones." The appearance alone of these men indicated their manhood, and wonderful natural ability. The examining Committee were very desirous of hearing their story without a moment's delay.

As Harry, from having suffered most, was the hero of this party, and
withal was an intelligent man, he was first called upon to make his statement as to how times had been with him in the prison house, from his
youth up. He was about forty-six years of age, according to his reckoning,
full six feet high, and in muscular appearance was very rugged, and in his
countenance were evident marks of firmness. He said that he was born a
slave in North Carolina, and had been sold three times. He was first sold
when a child three years of age, the second time when he was thirteen years
old, and the third and last time he was sold to Jesse Moore, from whom he
fled. Prior to his coming into the hands of Moore he had not experienced

any very hard usage, at least nothing more severe than fell to the common lot of slave-boys, therefore the period of his early youth was deemed of too little interest to record in detail. In fact time only could be afforded for noticing very briefly some of the more remarkable events of his bondage. The examining Committee confined their interrogations to his last task-master.

"How did Moore come by you?" was one of the inquiries. "He bought me," said Harry, "of a man by the name of Taylor, nine or ten years ago; he was as bad as he could be, couldn't be any worse to be alive. He was about fifty years of age, when I left him, a right red-looking man, big bellied old fellow, weighs about two hundred and forty pounds. He drinks hard, he is just like a rattlesnake, just as cross and crabbed when he speaks, seems like he could go through you. He flogged Richmond for not plough-ing the corn good, that was what he pretended to whip him for. Richmond ran away, was away four months, as nigh as I can guess, then they cotched him, then struck him a hundred lashes, and then they split both feet to the bone, and split both his insteps, and then master took his knife and stuck it into him in many places; after he done him that way, he put him into the barn to shucking corn. For a long time he was not able to work; when he did partly recover, he was set to work again."

We ceased to record anything further concerning Richmond, although not a fourth part of what Harry narrated was put upon paper. The account was too sickening and the desire to hear Harry's account of himself too great to admit of fur-ther delay; so Harry confined him-self to the sufferings and adventures which had marked his own life. Briefly he gave the following facts: "I have been treated bad. One day we were grubbing and master said we didn't do work enough. 'How came there was no more work done that day?' said master to me. I told him I did work. In a more stormy manner he 'peated the ques-tion. I then spoke up and said: 'Massa, I don't know what to say.' At once massa plunged his knife into my neck causing me to stagger. Massa was drunk. He then drove

me down to the black folk's houses (cabins of the slaves). He then got his gun, called the overseer, and told him to get some ropes. While he was gone I said, 'Massa, now you are going to tie me up and cut me all to pieces for nothing. I would just as leave you would take your gun and shoot me down as to tie me up and cut me all to pieces for nothing.' In a great rage he said 'go.' I jumped, and he put up his gun and snapped both barrels at me. He then set his dogs on me, but as I had been in the habit of making much of them, feeding them, &c., they would not follow me, and I kept on straight to the woods. My master and the overseer cotched the horses and tried to run me down, but as the dogs would not follow me they couldn't make nothing of it. It was the last of August a year ago. The devil was into him, and he flogged and beat four of the slaves, one man and three of the women, and said if he could only get hold of me he wouldn't strike me, 'nary-a-lick,' but would tie me to a tree and empty both barrels into me.

In the woods I lived on nothing, you may say, and something too. I had bread, and roasting ears, and 'taters. I stayed in the hollow of a big poplar tree for seven months; the other part of the time I stayed in a cave. I suffered mighty bad with the cold and for something to eat. Once I got me some charcoal and made me a fire in my tree to warm me, and it liked to killed me, so I had to take the fire out. One time a snake come to the tree, poked its head in the hollow and was coming in, and I took my axe and chopped him in two. It was a poplar leaf moccasin, the poisonest kind of a snake we have. While in the woods all my thoughts was how to get away to a free country."

Subsequently, in going back over his past history, he referred to the fact, that on an occasion long before the cave and tree existence, already noticed, when suffering under this brutal master, he sought protection in the woods and abode twenty-seven months in a cave, before he surrendered himself, or was captured. His offence, in this instance, was simply because he desired to see his wife, and "stole" away from his master's plantation and went a distance of five miles, to where she lived, to see her. For this grave crime his master threatened to give him a hundred lashes, and to shoot him; in order to avoid this punishment, he escaped to the woods, etc. The lapse of a dozen years and recent struggles for an existence, made him think lightly of his former troubles and he would, doubtless, have failed to recall his earlier conflicts but for the desire manifested by the Committee to get all the information out of him they could.

He was next asked, "Had you a wife and family?" "Yes, sir," he answered, "I had a wife and eight children, belonged to the widow Slade." Harry gave the names of his wife and children as follows: Wife, Susan, and children, Oliver, Sabey, Washington, Daniel, Jonas, Harriet, Moses and Rosetta, the last named he had never seen. "Between my mistress and my master there was not much difference."

Of his comrades time admitted of writing out only very brief sketches, as follows:

EDWARD LEWIS.

$100 REWARD.—Ran away from the subscriber, on the 7th of November, negro slave, EDGAR. He is 36 years old, 6 feet high, of dark brown complexion, very high forehead, is a little bald, and is inclined to stoop in the shoulders. Edgar says he was raised in Norfolk county, has worked about Norfolk several years. I bought him at the Auction house of Messrs. Pulliam & Davis, the 20th of July, 1856. The bill of sale was signed by W. Y. Miliner for Jas. A. Bilisoly, administrator of G. W. Chambers, dec'd. He told one of my negroes he was going to Norfolk to sell some plunder he had there, then go to Richmond, steal his wife, get on board a boat about Norfolk, and go to a free State. He can read and write well, and I have no doubt he has provided himself with papers of some kind. He may have purchased the papers of some free negro. I will give the above reward of One Hundred Dollars to any person who will arrest and confine him, so I can get him.

C. H. GAY.

My Post office is Laurel, N. C.   no. 21.

The above advertisement, which was cut from a Southern paper, brought light in regard to one of the passengers at least. It was not often that a slave was so fortunate as to get such a long sketch of himself in a newspaper. The description is so highly complimentary, that we simply endorse it as it stands. The sketch as taken for the record book is here transcribed as follows:

"Edward reported himself from Franklin county, N. C., where, according to statement, a common farmer by the name of Carter Gay owned him, under whose oppression his life was rendered most unhappy, who stinted him daily for food and barely allowed him clothing enough to cover his nakedness, who neither showed justice nor mercy to any under his control, the 'weaker vessels' not excepted; therefore Edward was convinced that it was in vain to hope for comfort under such a master. Moreover, his appetite for liquor, combined with a high temper, rendered him a being hard to please, but easy to excite to a terrible degree. Scarcely had Edward lived two years with this man (Gay) when he felt that he had lived with him long enough. Two years previous to his coming into the hands of Gay, he and his wife were both sold; the wife one day and he the next. She brought eleven hundred and twenty-five dollars, and he eight hundred and thirty-five dollars; thus they were sold and resold as a matter of speculation, and husband and wife were parted.

After the fugitives had been well cared for by the Committee, they were forwarded on North; but for some reason they were led to stop short of Canada, readily finding employment and going to work to take care of themselves. How they were received and in what way they were situated, the subjoined letter from Edward will explain:

SKANEATELES, Dec. 17, 1857.

DEAR SIR:—As I promised to let you hear from me as soon as I found a home, I will now fulfill my promise to you and say that I am alive and well and have found a stopping place for the winter.

When we arrived at Syracuse we found Mr. Loguen ready to receive us, and as times are rather hard in Canada he thought best for us not to go there, so he sent us about twenty miles west of Syracuse to Skaneateles, where George Upshur and myself soon found work. Henry Grimes is at work in Garden about eight miles from this place.

If you should chance to hear any of my friends inquiring for me, please direct them to Skaneateles, Onondaga county, N. Y.

If you can inform me of the whereabouts of Miss Alice Jones I shall be very much obliged to you, until I can pay you better. I forgot to ask you about her when I was at your house. She escaped about two years ago.

Please not to forget to inquire of my wife, Rachel Land, and if you should hear of her, let me know immediately. George Upshur and myself send our best respects to you and your family. Remember us to Mrs. Jackson and Miss Julia. I hope to meet you all again, if not on earth may we so live that we shall meet in that happy land where tears and partings are not known.

Let me hear from you soon. This from your friend and well wisher,

EDWARD LEWIS,
formerly, but now WILLIAM BRADY.

GEORGE UPSHER.—The third in this arrival was also a full man. Slavery had robbed him shamefully it is true; nevertheless he was a man of superior natural parts, physically and intellectually. Despite the efforts of slave-holders to keep him in the dark, he could read and write a little. His escape in the manner that he did, implied a direct protest against the conduct of Dr. Thomas W. Upsher, of Richmond, Va., whom, he alleged, deprived him of his hire, and threatened him with immediate sale. He had lived in North Carolina with the doctor about two years. As a slave, his general treatment had been favorable, except for a few months prior to his flight, which change on the part of his master led him to fear that a day of sale was nigh at hand. In fact the seventh of July had been agreed upon when he was to be in Richmond, to take his place with others in the market on sale day; his hasty and resolute move for freedom originated from this circumstance. He was well-known in Norfolk, and had served almost all his days in that city. These passengers averaged about six feet, and were of uncommonly well-developed physical structure.

The pleasure of aiding such men from the horrors of Carolina Slavery was great.

ALFRED HOLLON, GEORGE AND CHARLES N. RODGERS.

The loss of this party likewise falls on Maryland. With all the efforts exerted by slave-holders, they could not prevent the Underground Rail Road from bringing away passengers.

ALFRED was twenty-eight years of age, with sharp features, dark color, and of medium size. He charged one Elijah J. Johnson, a commissioner of Baltimore Co., with having deprived him of the fruits of his labor. He had looked fully into his master's treatment of him, and had come to the conclusion that it was wrong in every respect, for one man to make another work and then take all his wages from him; thus decided, Alfred, desiring liberty, whereby he could do better for himself felt that he must "took out" and make his way to Canada. Nevertheless, he admitted that he had been "treated pretty well" compared with others. True, he had "not been fed very well;" Elijah, his master, was an old man with a white head, tall and stout, and the owner of fifteen head of slaves. At the same time, a member of St. John's church.

ALFRED had treasured up the sad remembrance against him of the sale of his mother from him when a little boy, only three years old. While he was then too young to have retained her features in his memory, the fact had always been a painful one to reflect upon.

GEORGE was twenty-six years of age, stout, long-faced, and of dark complexion. He looked as though he might have eagerly grasped education if the opportunity had been allowed him. He too belonged to Elijah J. Johnson, against whom he entertained much more serious objections than Alfred. Indeed, George did not hesitate to say with emphasis, that he neither liked his old master, mistress, nor any of the family. Without recording his grievances in detail, a single instance will suffice of the kind of treatment to which he objected, and which afforded the pretext for his becoming a patron of the Underground Rail Road.

It was this, said George: "I went into the corn-field and got some corn. This made my master and mistress very mad, and about it Dr. Franklin Rodgers, my young mistress' husband, struck me some pretty heavy blows, and knocked me with his fist, etc." Thus, George's blood was raised, and he at once felt that it was high time to be getting away from such patriarchs. It was only necessary to form a strong resolution and to start without delay.

There were two others who, he believed, could be trusted, so he made known his intentions to them, and finding them sound on the question of freedom he was glad of their company. For an emergency, he provided himself with a pair of pistols and a formidable-looking knife, and started, bent on reaching Canada; determined at least, not to be taken back to bondage alive. Charles was twenty-four years of age, a very dark-colored individual, and also belonged to said Johnson.

CHARLES was well acquainted with his old master and mistress, and made very quick work of giving his experience. After hearing him, from the manner in which he expressed himself, no one could doubt his earnestness and veracity. His testimony ran substantially thus:

" For the last three years I have been treated very hard. In the presence of the servants, old Johnson had me tied, stripped, and with his own hands, flogged me on the naked back shamefully. The old mistress was cross too." It was some time before the smarting ceased, but it was not long ere the suffering produced very decided aspirations to get over to John Bull's Dominions. He resolved to go, at all hazards. In order that he might not be surprised on the Underground Rail Road without any weapons of defense, determined as he was to fight rather than be dragged back, he provided himself with a heavy, leaden ball and a razor. They met, however, with no serious difficulty, save from hard walking and extreme hunger. In appearance, courage, and mother-wit, this party was of much promise.

ARRIVAL FROM KENT COUNTY, 1857.

SAMUEL BENTON, JOHN ALEXANDER, JAMES HENRY, AND SAMUEL TURNER.

These passengers journeyed together from the land of whips and chains.

SAM BENTON was about twenty-six years of age, medium size, pretty dark color, and possessed a fair share of intelligence. He understood very well how sadly Slavery had wronged him by keeping him in ignorance and poverty.

He stated as the cause of his flight that William Campbell had oppressed him and kept him closely at hard labor without paying him, and at the same time "did not give him half enough to eat, and no clothing."

JOHN ALEXANDER was about forty-four years of age, a man of ordinary size, quite black, and a good specimen of a regular corn-field hand.

"Why did you leave, John?" said a member of the Committee. He coolly replied that "Handy (his master was named George Handy) got hold of me twice, and I promised my Lord that he should never get hold of me another time."

Of course it was the severity of these two visitations that made John a thinker and an actor at the same time. The evil practices of the master produced the fruits of liberty in John's breast.

JAMES HENRY, the third passenger, was about thirty-two years of age, and quite a spirited-looking "article." A few months before he fled he had been sold, at which time his age was given as "only twenty." He had suffered considerably from various abuses; the hope of Canada however tended to make him joyful.

The system of oppression from which these travelers fled had afforded them no privileges in the way of learning to read. All that they had ever known of civilization was what they perchance picked up in the ordinary routine of the field.

Notice of the fourth passenger unfortunately is missing.

ARRIVAL FROM BALTIMORE COUNTY, 1857.

ELIZABETH WILLIAMS.

ELIZABETH fled in company with her brother the winter previous to her arrival at the Philadelphia station. Although she reached free land the severe struggle cost her the loss of all her toes. Four days and nights out in the bitter cold weather without the chance of a fire left them a prey to the frost, which made sad havoc with their feet especially—particularly Elizabeth's. She was obliged to stop on the way, and for seven months she was unable to walk.

ELIZABETH was about twenty years of age, chestnut color, and of considerable natural intellect. Although she suffered so severely as the result of her resolution to throw off the yoke, she had no regrets at leaving the prison-house; she seemed to appreciate freedom all the more in consequence of what it cost her to obtain the prize.

In speaking of the life she had lived, she stated that her mistress was "good enough," but her "master was a very bad man." His name was Samuel Ward; he lived in Baltimore county, near Wrightstown. Elizabeth left her mother, four brothers and one sister under the yoke.

MARY COOPER AND MOSES ARMSTEAD, 1857.

MARY arrived from Delaware, Moses from Norfolk, Virginia, and happened to meet at the station in Philadelphia.

MARY was twenty years of age, of a chestnut color, usual size, and well disposed. She fled from Nathaniel Herne, an alderman. Mary did not find fault with the alderman, but she could not possibly get along with his wife; this was the sole cause of her escape.

MOSES was twenty-four years of age, of a chestnut color, a bright-looking young man. He fled from Norfolk, Virginia, having been owned by the estate of John Halters. Nothing but the prevailing love of liberty in the breast of Moses moved him to seek his freedom. He did not make one complaint of bad treatment.

ARRIVAL FROM NEAR WASHINGTON, D. C.

JOHN JOHNSON AND LAWRENCE THORNTON.

JOHN escaped from near Washington. He stated that he was owned by an engraver, known by the name of William Stone, and added that himself and seven others were kept working on the farm of said Stone for nothing. John did not, however, complain of having a hard master in this hard-named personage, (Stone); for, as a slave, he confessed that he had seen good times. Yet he was not satisfied; he felt that he had a right to his freedom, and that he could not possibly be contented while deprived of it, for this reason, therefore, he dissolved his relationship with his kind master.

John was about twenty-seven years of age, smart, possessed good manners, and a mulatto.

LAWRENCE was about twenty-three years of age, tall and slender, of dark complexion, but bright intellectually. With Lawrence times had been pretty rough. Dr. Isaac Winslow of Alexandria was accused of defrauding Lawrence of his hire. "He was anything else but a gentleman," said Lawrence. "He was not a fair man no way, and his wife was worse than he was, and she had a daughter worse than herself."

"Last Sunday a week my master collared me, for my insolence he said, and told me that he would sell me right off. I was tied and put up stairs for safe keeping. I was tied for about eight hours. I then untied myself, broke out of prison, and made for the Underground Rail Road immediately."

Lawrence gave a most interesting account of his life of bondage, and of the doctor and his family. He was overjoyed at the manner in which he had defeated the doctor, and so was the Committee.

HON. L. McLANE'S PROPERTY, SOON AFTER HIS DEATH, TRAVELS *via* THE UNDERGROUND RAIL ROAD.—WILLIAM KNIGHT, Esq., LOSES A SUPERIOR "ARTICLE."

JIM SCOTT, TOM PENNINGTON, SAM SCOTT, BILL SCOTT, ABE BACON, AND JACK WELLS.

An unusual degree of pleasure was felt in welcoming this party of young men, not because they were any better than others, or because they had suffered more, but simply because they were found to possess certain knowledge and experience of slave life, as it existed under the government of the chivalry; such information could not always be obtained from those whose lot had been cast among ordinary slave-holders. Consequently the Committee interviewed them closely, and in point of intellect found them to be above the average run of slaves. As they were then entered on the record, so in like manner are the notes made of them transferred to these pages.

Jim was about nineteen years of age, well grown, black, and of prepossessing appearance. The organ of hope seemed very strong in him. Jim had been numbered with the live stock of the late Hon. L. McLane, who had been called to give an account of his stewardship about two months before Jim and his companions "took out."

As to general usage, he made no particular charge against his distinguished master; he had, however, not been living under his immediate patriarchal government, but had been hired out to a farmer by the name of James Dodson, with whom he experienced life "sometimes hard and sometimes smooth," to use his own words. The reason of his leaguing with his fellow-servants to abandon the old prison-house, was traceable to the rumor, that he and some others were to appear on the stage, or rather the auction-block, in Baltimore, the coming Spring.

TOM, another member of the McLane institution, was about twenty-five years of age, of unmixed blood, and a fair specimen of a well-trained field-hand. He conceived that he had just ground to bring damages against the Hon. L. McLane for a number of years of hard service, and for being deprived of education. He had been compelled to toil for the Honorable gentleman, not only on his own place, but on the farms of others. At the time that Tom escaped, he was hired for one hundred dollars per annum (and his clothes found him), which hire McLane had withheld from him contrary to all justice and fair dealing; but as Tom was satisfied, that he could get no justice through the Maryland courts, and knew that an old and intimate friend of his master had already proclaimed, that "negroes had no rights which white men are bound to respect;" also, as his experience tended to confirm him in the belief, that the idea was practically carried out in the courts of Maryland; he thought, that it would be useless to put in a plea for justice in Maryland. He was not, however, without a feeling of some satisfaction, that his old master, in giving an account of his stewardship at the Bar of the Just One, would be made to understand the amount of his indebtedness to those whom he had oppressed. With this impression, and the prospects of equal rights and Canada, under her British Majesty's possessions, he manifested as much delight as if he was traveling with a half million of dollars in his pocket.

SAM, another likely-looking member of this party, was twenty-two years of age, and a very promising-looking young fugitive, having the appearance of being able to take education without difficulty. He had fully made up his mind, that slavery was never intended for man, and that he would never wear himself out working for the "white people for nothing." He wanted to work for himself and enjoy the benefits of education, etc.

BILL SCOTT, another member of the McLane party, was twenty-one years of age, "fat and slick," and fully satisfied, that Canada would agree with him in every particular. Not a word did he utter in favor of Maryland, but said much against the manner in which slaves were treated, how he had felt about the matter, etc.

ABE was also from the McLane estate. He possessed apparently more general intelligence than either of his companions. He was quite bright-witted, a ready talker, and with his prospects he was much satisfied. He was twenty-two years of age, black, good-looking, and possessed very good manners. He represented, that his distinguished master died, leaving thirteen head of slaves. His (Abe's) father, Tom's mother and the mother of the Scotts were freed by McLane. Strong hopes were entertained that before the old man's death he would make provision in his will for the freedom of all the other slaves; when he died, the contrary was found to be the fact; they were still left in chains. The immediate heirs consisted of six sons and five daughters, who moved in the first circle, were "very wealthy and aristocratic." Abe was conversant with the fact, that his master, the "Hon. L. McLane, was once Secretary under President Jackson;" that he had been "sent to England on a mission for the Government," and that he had "served two terms in Congress." Some of the servants, Abe said, were "treated pretty well, but some others could not say anything in the master's favor." Upon the whole, however, it was manifest that the McLane slaves had not been among the number who had seen severe hardships. They came from his plantation in Cecil county, Maryland, where they had been reared.

In order to defend themselves on the Underground Rail Road, they were strongly armed. Sam had a large horse pistol and a butcher knife; Jack had a revolver; Abe had a double-barrelled pistol and a large knife; Jim had a single-barrelled pistol and counted on "blowing a man down if any one touched" him. Bill also had a single-barrelled pistol, and when he started resolved to "come through or die."

Although this party was of the class said to be well fed, well clothed, and not over-worked, yet to those who heard them declare their utter detestation of slavery and their determination to use their instruments of death, even to the taking of life, rather than again be subjected to the yoke, it was evident that even the mildest form of slavery was abhorrent. They left neither old nor young masters, whom they desired to serve any longer or look up to for care and support.

JACK, who was not of the McLane party, but who came with them, had been kept in ignorance with regard to his age. He was apparently middle-aged, medium size, dark color, and of average intelligence. He accused William Knight, a farmer, of having enslaved him contrary to his will or wishes, and averred that he fled from him because he used him badly and kept mean overseers. Jack said that his master owned six farms and kept three overseers to manage them. The slaves numbered twenty-one head. The names of the overseers were given in the following order: "Alfred King, Jimmy Allen, and Thomas Brockston." In speaking of their habits, Jack said, that they were "very smart when the master was about, but as soon as he was gone they would instantly drop back." "They were all mean, but the old boss was meaner than them all," and "the overseers were 'fraider' of him than what I was," said Jack.

His master (Mr. Knight), had a wife and seven children, and was a member of the Episcopal Church, in "good and regular standing." He was rich, and, with his family, moved in good society. "His wife was too

28

stingy to live, and if she was to die, she would die holding on to something," said Jack. Jack had once had a wife and three children, but as they belonged to a slave-holder ("Jim Price") Jack's rights were wholly ignored, and he lost them.

ARRIVAL FROM HARFORD CO., 1857.

JOHN MYERS.

JOHN fled from under the yoke of Dr. Joshua R. Nelson. Until within two years of "Jack's" flight, the doctor "had been a very fine man," with whom Jack found no fault. But suddenly his mode of treatment changed; he became very severe. Nothing that Jack could do, met the approval of the doctor. Jack was constantly looked upon with suspicion.

The very day that Jack fled, four men approached him (the doctor one of them), with line in hand; that sign was well understood, and Jack resolved that they should not get within tying distance of him. "I dodged them," said Jack. Never afterwards was Jack seen in that part of the country, at least as long as a fetter remained.

The day that he "dodged" he also took the Underground Rail Road, and although ignorant of letters, he battled his way out of Maryland, and succeeded in reaching Pennsylvania and the Committee. He was obliged to leave four children behind—John, Abraham, Jane and Ellen.

JACK'S wife had been freed and had come to Philadelphia two years in advance of him. His master evidently supposed that Jack would be mean enough to wish to see his wife, even in a free State, and that no slave, with such an unnatural desire, could be tolerated or trusted, that the sooner such "articles" were turned into cash the better. This in substance, was the way Jack accounted for the sudden change which had come over his master. In defense of his course, Jack referred to the treatment which he had received while in servitude under his old master, in something like the following words: "I served under my young master's father, thirty-five years, and from him received kind treatment. I was his head man on the place, and had everything to look after."

ARRIVAL FROM MARYLAND, 1857.

WILLIAM LEE, SUSAN JANE BOILE AND AMARIAN LUCRETIA RISTER.

Although these three passengers arrived in Philadelphia at the same time, they did not come from Maryland together.

WILLIAM LEE found himself under the yoke on a farm in the possession of Zechariah Merica, who, Wm. said, was a "low ignorant man, not above a common wood-chopper, and owned no other slave property than William." Against him, however, William brought no accusation of any very severe treatment; on the contrary, his master talked sometimes "as though he wanted to be good and get religion, but said he could not while he was trying to be rich." Everything looked hopeless in William's eyes, so far as the master's riches and his own freedom were concerned. He concluded that he would leave him the "bag to hold alone." William therefore laid down "the shovel and the hoe," and, without saying a word to his master, he took his departure, under the privacy of the night, for Canada. William represented the white and colored races about equally; he was about twenty-seven years of age, and looked well fitted for a full day's work on a farm.

SUSAN JANE came from New Market, near Georgetown Cross-Roads, where she had been held to unrequited labor by Hezekiah Masten, a farmer. Although he was a man of fair pretensions, and a member of the Methodist Church, he knew how to draw the cords very tightly, with regard to his slaves, keeping his feet on their necks, to their sore grievance. Susan endured his bad treatment as long as she could, then left, destitute and alone. Her mother and father were at the time living in Elkton, Md. Whether they ever heard what became of their daughter is not known.

AMARIAN was twenty-one years of age, a person of light color, medium size, with a prepossessing countenance and smart; she could read, write, and play on the piano. From a child, Amarian had been owned by Mrs. Elizabeth Key Scott, who resided near Braceville, but at the time of her flight she was living at Westminster, in the family of a man named "Boile," said to be the clerk of the court. In reference to treatment, Amarian said: "I have always been used very well; have had it good all my life, etc." This was a remarkable case, and, at first, somewhat staggered the faith of the Committee, but they could not dispute her testimony, consequently they gave her the benefit of the doubt. She spoke of having a mother living in Hagerstown, by the name of Amarian Ballad, also three sisters who were slaves, and two who were free; she also had a brother in chains in Mississippi.

ARRIVAL FROM NORFOLK, VA. 1857.

WILLIAM CARNEY AND ANDREW ALLEN.

WILLIAM was about fifty-one years of age, a man of unmixed blood. Physically he was a superior man, and his mental abilities were quite above the average of his class.

He belonged to the estate of the late Mrs. Sarah Twyne, who bore the reputation of being a lady of wealth, and owned one hundred and twelve slaves. Most of her slave property was kept on her plantation not far from Old Point Comfort. According to William's testimony " of times Mrs. Twyne would meddle too freely with the cup, and when under its influence she was very desperate, and acted as though she wanted to kill some of the slaves."

After the evil spirit left her and she had regained her wonted composure, she would pretend that she loved her " negroes," and would make a great fuss over them. Not infrequently she would have very serious difficulty with her overseers. Having license to do as they pleased, they would of course carry their cruelties to the most extreme verge of punishment. If a slave was maimed or killed under their correction, it was no loss of theirs. " One of the overseers by the name of Bill Anderson once shot a young slave man called Luke and wounded him so seriously that he was not expected to live." " At another time one of the overseers beat and kicked a slave to death." This barbarity caused the mistress to be very much " stirred up," and she declared that she would not have any more white overseers; condemned them for everything, and decided to change her policy in future and to appoint her overseers from her own slaves, setting the property to watch the property. This system was organized and times were somewhat better.

WILLIAM had been hired out almost his entire life. For the last twelve or fifteen years he had been accustomed to hire his time for one hundred and thirty dollars per annum. In order to meet this demand he commonly resorted to oystering. By the hardest toil he managed to maintain himself and family in a humble way.

For the last twenty years (prior to his escape) the slaves had constantly been encouraged by their mistress' promises to believe that at her death all would be free, and transported to Liberia, where they would enjoy their liberty and be happy the remainder of their days.

With full faith in her promises year by year the slaves awaited her demise with as much patience as possible, and often prayed that her time might be shortened for the general good of the oppressed. Fortunately, as the slaves thought, she had no children or near relatives to deprive them of their just and promised rights.

In November, previous to William's escape, her long looked-for dissolution took place. Every bondman who was old enough to realize the nature and import of the change felt a great anxiety to learn what the will of their old mistress said, whether she had actually freed them or not. Alas! when the secret was disclosed, it was ascertained that not a fetter was broken, not a bond unloosed, and that no provision whatever had been made looking towards freedom. In this sad case, the slaves could imagine no other fate than soon to be torn asunder and scattered. The fact was soon made known that the High Sheriff had administered on the estate of the late mistress; it was therefore obvious enough to William and the more intelligent slaves that the auction block was near at hand.

The trader, the slave-pen, the auction-block, the coffle gang, the rice swamp, the cotton plantation, bloodhounds, and cruel overseers loomed up before him, as they had never done before. Without stopping to consider the danger, he immediately made up his mind that he would make a struggle, cost what it might. He knew of no other way of escape than the Underground Rail Road. He was shrewd enough to find an agent, who gave him private instructions, and to whom he indicated a desire to travel North on said road. On examination he was deemed reliable, and a mutual understanding was entered into between William and one of the accommodating Captains running on the Richmond and Philadelphia Line, to the effect that he, William, should have a first class Underground Rail Road berth, so perfectly private that even the law-officers could not find him.

The first ties to be severed were those which bound him to his wife and children, and next to the Baptist Church, to which he belonged. His family were slaves, and bore the following names: his wife, Nancy, and children, Simon Henry, William, Sarah, Mary Ann, Elizabeth, Louis, and Cornelius. It was no light matter to bid them farewell forever. The separation from them was a trial such as rarely falls to the lot of mortals; but he nerved himself for the undertaking, and when the hour arrived his strength was sufficient for the occasion.

Thus in company with Andrew they embarked for an unknown shore, their entire interests entrusted to a stranger who was to bring them through difficulties and dangers seen and unseen.

ANDREW was about twenty-four years of age, very tall, quite black, and bore himself manfully. He too was of the same estate that William belonged to. He had served on the farm as a common farm laborer. He had had it "sometimes rough and sometimes smooth," to use his own language. The fear of what awaited the slaves prompted Andrew to escape. He too was entangled with a wife and one child, with whom he parted only as a friend parts with a companion when death separates them. Catharine was the name of Andrew's wife; and Anna Clarissa the name of his child left in chains.

ARRIVAL FROM HOOPESVILLE, MD., 1857.

JAMES CAIN, "GENERAL ANDREW JACKSON," AND ANNA PERRY.

These passengers came from the field where as slaves very few privileges had been afforded them.

JIM was about thirty-five years of age, a dark brown skin with average intellect for one in his condition. He had toiled under John Burnham, in Dorchester county, from whom he had received hard treatment, but harder still from his mistress. He averred that she was the cause of matters being so hard with the slaves on the place. Jim contented himself under his lot as well as he could until within a short time of his escape when he learned that measures were on foot to sell him. The fear of this change brought him directly to meditate upon a trip to Canada. Being a married man he found it hard to leave his wife, Mary, but as she was also a slave, and kept in the employment of her owners at some distance from where he lived, he decided to say nothing to her of his plans, but to start when ready and do the best he could to save himself, as he saw no chance of saving her.

"GENERAL ANDREW JACKSON." When the above "article" gave the Committee his name they were amused and thought that he was simply jesting, having done a smart thing in conquering his master by escaping; but on a fuller investigation they found that he really bore the name, and meant to retain it in Canada. It had been given him when a child, and in Slavery he had been familiarly called "Andy," but since he had achieved his freedom he felt bound to be called by his proper name.

General Andrew was about twenty-seven years of age, a full black, and a man of extraordinary muscular powers, with coarse hard features, such as showed signs that it would not be safe for his master to meddle with him when the General's blood was up.

He spoke freely of the man who claimed him as a slave, saying that his name was Shepherd Houston, of Lewistown, Delaware, and that he owned seven head of "God's poor," whom he compelled to labor on his farm without a cent of pay, a day's schooling, or an hour's freedom; furthermore, that he was a member of the Ebenezer Methodist Church, a class-leader, and an exhorter, and in outward show passed for a good Christian. But in speaking of his practical dealings with his slaves, General said that he worked them hard, stinted them shamefully for food, and kept them all the time digging.

Also when testifying with regard to the "weaker vessel," under whose treatment he had suffered much, the General said that his master's wife had a meaner disposition than he had; she pretended to belong to church too, said General, but it was nothing but deceit.

This severe critic could not read, but he had very clear views on the ethics of his master and mistress, agreeing with Scripture concerning whited sepulchres, etc.

The question of Christian slave-holders, for a great while, seriously puzzled the wise and learned, but for the slave it was one of the easiest of solution. All the slaves came to the same conclusion, notwithstanding the teaching of slave-holders on the one idea, that "servants should obey their masters," etc.

General had a brother in Baltimore, known by the name of Josephus, also two sisters Anna and Annie; his father was living at Cannon's Ferry.

ANNA PERRY was the intended of General. She was about nineteen years of age, of a dark brown color, and came from the same neighborhood. According to law Anna was entitled to her freedom, but up to the time of her escape she had not been permitted to enjoy the favor. She found that if she would be free she would have to run for it.

JOHN SMITH. A better specimen of one who had been ill treated, and in every way uncared for, could not be easily found. In speech, manners, and whole appearance he was extremely rude. He was about twenty years of age, and in color was of a very dark hue.

That John had received only the poorest kind of " corn-field fare " was clearly evidenced both by body and mind. Master George H. Morgan was greatly blamed for John's deficiencies; it was on his farms, under mean overseers that John had been crushed and kept under the harrow.

His mother, Mary Smith, he stated, his master had sold away to New Orleans, some two years before his escape. The sad effect that this cruel separation had upon him could only be appreciated by hearing him talk of it in his own untutored tongue. Being himself threatened with the auction-block, he was awakened to inquire how he could escape the danger, and very soon learned that by following the old methods which had been used by many before him, resolution and perseverance, he might gain the victory over master and overseers. As green as he seemed he had succeeded admirably in his undertaking.

ARRIVAL FROM MARYLAND, 1858.

GEORGE RUSSELL AND JAMES HENRY THOMPSON.

JAMES, for convenience' sake, was supplied with two other names (Milton Brown and John Johnson), not knowing exactly how many he would need in freedom or which would be the best adapted to keep his whereabouts the most completely veiled from his master.

GEORGE reported that he fled from Henry Harris, who lived near Baltimore on the Peach Orchard Road, and that he had lived with said Harris all his life. He spoke of him as being a " blustering man, who never liked the slaves to make anything for themselves." George bore witness that the usage which he had received had been hard; evidently his intellect had been seriously injured by what he had suffered under his task-master. George was of a very dark hue, but not quite up to medium size.

JAMES HENRY THOMPSON did not accompany George, but met him at the station in Philadelphia. He contrasted favorably with George, being about twenty-eight years of age, with a countenance indicative of intelligence and spirit. He was of a chestnut color and of average size. He charged one Dennis Mannard, of Johnsonville, with being his personal enemy as an oppressor, and added that he could "say nothing good of him." He could say, however, that Mannard was bitterly opposed to a slave's learning how to read, would not listen to the idea of giving them any privileges, and tried to impress them with the idea that they needed to know nothing but simply how to work hard for the benefit of their masters and mistresses; in fulfilling these conditions faithfully the end for which they had been designed would be accomplished according to his doctrine.

Notwithstanding so much pains had been resorted to throughout the South to impress these ideas upon the slaves, no converts were made.

JAMES thought that the doctrine was infamous, and that it was dangerous to live with such a man as his master; that freedom was as much his right as it was his master's; and so he resolved to leave for Canada as soon as he could see any chance for escape.

ARRIVAL FROM QUEEN ANN COUNTY, 1858.

CATHARINE JONES AND SON HENRY, ETNA ELIZABETH DAUPHUS, AND GEORGE NELSON WASHINGTON.

These passengers, although interesting, and manifesting a strong desire to be free, had no remarkable tales of personal suffering to relate; their lot had evidently been cast among the more humane class of slave-holders, who had acted towards their slaves with some moderation.

CATHARINE was twenty-four years of age, of a dark chestnut color, possessed a fair share of mother wit, and was fitted to make a favorable impression. In no degree whatever did she think well of slavery; she had had, as she thought, sufficient experience under Joshua Duvall (who professed to own her) to judge as to the good or evil of the system. While he was by no means considered a hard man, he would now and then buy and sell a slave. She had no fault to find with her mistress.

ETNA was about twenty years of age, of a "ginger-bread" color, modest in demeanor, and appeared to have a natural capacity for learning. She was also from under the Duvall yoke. In setting forth her reasons for escaping she asserted that she was tired of slavery and an unbeliever in the doctrine that God made colored people simply to be slaves for white people; besides, she had a strong desire to "see her friends in Canada."

GEORGE also escaped from Duvall; happily he was only about nineteen years of age, not too old to acquire some education and do well by himself. He was greatly elated at the prospect of freedom in Canada.

WILLIAM HENRY was a plump little fellow only two years of age. At the old price (five dollars per pound) he was worth something, fat as he was. Being in the hands of his mother, the Committee considered him a lucky child.

ARRIVAL FROM BALTIMORE.

ELIJAH BISHOP AND WILLIAM WILLIAMSON.

ELIJAH represented to the Committee that he had been held under the enthrallment of a common "gambler and drunkard," who called himself by the name of Campbell, and carried on his sporting operations in Baltimore.

Under this gambler Elijah had been wronged up to the age of twenty-eight years, when he resolved to escape. Having had several opportunities of traveling through the United States and South America with his sporting master, he managed to pick up quite an amount of information. For the benefit of Elijah's relatives, if any should have occasion to look for particulars concerning this lost individual, we add, that he was a spare-built man of a dark color.

WILLIAM WILLIAMSON fled from Mrs. Rebecca Davidge, of Perryman-ville. He declared that he had been used badly—had been worked hard and had been fed and clothed but poorly. Under such treatment he had reached his twenty-fourth year. Being of a resolute and determined mind, and feeling considerably galled by the burdens heaped upon him, he resolved that he would take his chances on the Underground Rail Road. The only complaint that he had to make against his mistress was, that she hired him to a man named Smith, a farmer, and a slave-holder of the meanest type, in William's opinion. For many a day William will hold her responsible for abuses he received from him.

ARRIVAL FROM DUNWOODY COUNTY, 1858.

DARIUS HARRIS.

One of the most encouraging signs connected with the travel *via* the Underground Rail Road was, that passengers traveling thereon were, as a general thing, young and of determined minds. Darius, the subject of this sketch, was only about twenty-one when he arrived. It could be seen in his looks that he could not be kept in the prison-house unless constantly behind bars. His large head and its formation indicated a large brain. He stated that "Thomas H. Hamlin, a hard case, living near Dunwoody," had professed to own him. Darius alleged that this same Hamlin, who had thus stripped him of every cent of his earnings was doing the same thing by sixty others, whom he held in his grasp.

With regard to " feeding and clothing" Darius set Hamlin down as " very hoggish ;" he also stated that he would sell slaves whenever he could. He (Darius), had been hired out in Petersburg from the age of ten ; for the last three years previous to his escape he had been bringing one hundred and fifty dollars a year into the coffers of his owners. Darius had not been ignorant of the cruelties of the slave system up to the time of his escape, for the fetters had been galling his young limbs for several years ; especially had the stringent slave laws given him the horrors. Loathing the system of slavery with his whole heart, he determined to peril his all in escaping there-from ; seeking diligently, he had found means by which he could carry his designs into execution.

In the way of general treatment, however, Darius said that bodily ·he had escaped " abuses tolerably well." He left in slavery his father and mother, four brothers and one sister. He arrived by one of the Richmond boats.

ARRIVED FROM ALEXANDRIA, Va., 1857.

TOWNSEND DERRIX.

The above-named escaped from a "Dutchman" by the name of Gallipap-pick, who was in the confectionery business. For the credit of our German citizens, it may be said, that slave-holders within their ranks were very few. This was a rare case. The Committee were a little curious to know how the German branch of civilization conducted when given unlimited control over human beings.

In answering the requisite questions, and in making his statement, Towns-end gave entire satisfaction. His German master he spoke of as being a tolerably fair man, " considering his origin." At least he (Townsend), had not suffered much from him ; but he spoke of a woman, about sixty, who had been used very badly under this Dutchman. He not only worked her very hard, but, at the same time, he would beat her over the head, and that in the most savage manner. His mistress was also " Dutch," a " great swabby, fat woman," with a very ill disposition. Master and mistress were both members of the Episcopal Church. " Mistress drank, that was the reason she was so disagreeable."

Townsend had been a married man for about seven months only. In his effort to obtain his own freedom he sought diligently to deliver his young wife. They were united heart and hand in the one great purpose to reach free land, but unfortunately the pursuers were on their track ; the wife was captured and carried back, but the husband escaped.   It was particularly with a view of saving his poor wife that Townsend was induced to peril his life, for she (the wife) was not owned by the same party who owned Townsend, and was on the eve of being taken by her owners some fifty miles distant into the country, where the chances for intercourse between husband and wife would no longer be favorable.   Rather than submit to such an outrage, Townsend and his wife made the attempt aforementioned.

ARRIVAL FROM MARYLAND, 1858.

EDWARD CARROLL.

EDWARD, a youthful passenger about twenty-one years of age, slow of speech, with a stammering utterance, and apparently crushed in spirits, claimed succor and aid of the Committee.   At first the Committee felt a little puzzled to understand, how one, apparently so deficient, could succeed in surmounting the usual difficulties consequent upon traveling, via the Underground Rail Road; but in conversing with him, they found him possessed of more intelligence than they had supposed; indeed, they perceived that he could read and write a little, and that what he lacked in aptness of speech, he supplied as a thinker, and although he was slow he was sure. He was owned by a man named John Lewis, who also owned about seventy head of slaves, whom he kept on farms near the mouth of the Sassafras River, in Sussex county.

Lewis had not only held Edward in bondage, but had actually sold him, with two of his brothers, only the Saturday before his escape, to a Georgia trader, named Durant, who was to start south with them on the subsequent Monday.   Moved almost to desperation at their master's course in thus selling them, the three brothers, after reflection, determined to save themselves if possible, and without any definite knowledge of the journey, they turned their eyes towards the North Star, and under the cover of night they started for Pennsylvania, not knowing whether they would ever see the goodly land of freedom.   After wandering for about two weeks, having been lost often and compelled to lie out in all weathers, a party of pursuers suddenly came upon them.   Both parties were armed; the fugitives therefore resolved to give their enemies battle, before surrendering.   Edward felt certain that one of the pursuers received a cut from his knife, but the extent of the injury was unknown to him.   For a time the struggle was of a very serious character; by using his weapons skillfully, however, Edward managed to keep the hand-cuff off of himself, but was at this point separated from his two brothers.   No further knowledge of them did he possess; nevertheless, he trusted that they succeeded in fighting their way through to freedom. How any were successful in making their escape under such discouraging circumstances is a marvel.

EDWARD took occasion to review his master's conduct, and said that he "could not recommend him," as he would "drink and gamble," both of which, were enough to condemn him, in Edward's estimation, even though he were passable in other respects. But he held him doubly guilty for the way that he acted in selling him and his brothers.

So privately had his master transacted business with the trader, that they were within a hair's breadth of being hand-cuffed, ere they knew that they were sold. Probably no outrage will be remembered with feelings of greater bitterness, than this proceeding on the part of the master; yet, when he reflected that he was thereby prompted to strike for freedom, Edward was disposed to rejoice at the good which had come out of the evil.

ARRIVAL FROM PETERSBURG, 1858.

JAMES MASON.

This passenger brought rare intelligence respecting the manner in which he had been treated in Slavery. He had been owned by a lady named Judith Burton, who resided in Petersburg, and was a member of the Baptist Church. She was the owner of five other slaves. James said that she had been "the same as a mother" to him; and on the score of how he came to escape, he said: "I left for no other cause than simply to get my liberty." This was an exceptional case, yet he had too much sense to continue in such a life in preference to freedom. When he fled he was only twenty-four years of age. Had he remained, therefore, he might have seen hard times before he reached old age; this fact he had well considered, as he was an intelligent young man.

ARRIVAL FROM MARYLAND.

ROBERT CARR.

$300 REWARD.—Ran away from the subscriber, on the 26th December, 1857, Negro Man ROBERT CARR. He had on when last seen on West River, a close-bodied blue cloth coat with brass buttons, drab pantaloons, and a low crown and very narrow brim beaver hat; he wore a small goatee, is pleasant when spoken to, and very polite; about five feet ten inches high; copper-colored. I will give $125 if taken in Anne Arundel, Prince George's, Calvert or Montgomery county, $150 if taken in the city of Baltimore; or $300 if taken out of the State and secured so that I get him again.

THOS. J. RICHARDSON,

j13-w& s3w   West River, Anne Arundel county, Maryland.

ROBERT was too shrewd to be entrapped by the above reward. He sat down and counted the cost before starting; then with his knowledge of slave-holders when traveling he was cautious enough not to expose himself by day or night where he was liable to danger.

He had reached the age of thirty, and despite the opposition he had had to encounter, unaided he had learned to read, which with his good share of native intelligence, he found of service.

Whilst Robert did not publish his mistress, he gave a plain statement of where he was from, and why he was found in the city of Brotherly Love in the dead of Winter in a state of destitution. He charged the blame upon a woman, whose name was Richardson, who, he said, was quite a "fighter, and was never satisfied, except when quarreling and fighting with some of the slaves." He also spoke of a certain T. J. Richardson, a farmer and a "very driving man" who was in the habit of oppressing poor men and women by compelling them to work in his tobacco, corn, and wheat fields without requiting them for their labor. Robert felt if he could get justice out of said Richardson he would be the gainer to the amount of more than a thousand dollars in money besides heavy damages for having cheated him out of his education.

In this connection, he recalled the fact of Richardson's being a member of the church, and in a sarcastic manner added that his "religious pretensions might pass among slave-holders, but that it would do him no good when meeting the Judge above." Being satisfied that he would there meet his deserts Robert took a degree of comfort therefrom.

ARRIVAL OF A PARTY OF SIX, 1858.

PLYMOUTH CANNON, HORATIO WILKINSON, LEMUEL MITCHELL, JOSIAH MITCHELL, GEORGE HENRY BALLARD, AND JOHN MITCHELL.

Thomas Garrett announced the coming of this party in the subjoined letter:

WILMINGTON, 2 MO. 5TH, 1858.

ESTEEMED FRIEND:—WILLIAM STILL:—I have information of 6 able-bodied men that are expected here to-morrow morning; they may, to-morrow afternoon or evening, take the cars at Chester, and most likely reach the city between 11 and 12 at night; they will be accompanied by a colored man that has lived in Philadelphia and is free; they may think it safer to walk to the city than to go in the cars, but for fear of accident it may be best to have some one at the cars to look out for them. I have not seen them yet, and cannot certainly judge what will be best. I gave a man 3 dollars to bring those men 15 miles to-night, and I have been two miles in the country this afternoon, and gave a colored man 2 dollars to get provisions to feed them. Hoping all will be right, I remain thy friend,   HUMANITAS.

Arriving as usual in due time these fugitives were examined, and all found to be extra field hands.

PLYMOUTH was forty-two years of age, of a light chestnut color, with keen eyes, and a good countenance, and withal possessed of shrewdness enough to lead double the number that accompanied him. He had a strong desire to learn to read, but there was no possible way of his gaining the light; this he felt to be a great drawback.

The name of the man who had made merchandise of Plymouth was Nat Horsey, of Horsey's Cross Roads. The most striking characteristic in Horsey's character, according to Plymouth's idea was, that he was very "hard to please, did not know when a slave did enough, had no idea that they could get tired or that they needed any privileges." He was the owner of six slaves, was engaged in farming and mercantile pursuits, and the postmaster of the borough in which he lived.

When Plymouth parted with his wife with a "full heart," he bade her good-night, without intimating to her that he never expected to see her again in this world; she evidently supposed that he was going home to his master's place as usual, but instead he was leaving his companion and three children to wear the yoke as hitherto. He sympathized with them deeply, but felt that he could render them no real good by remaining; he could neither live with his wife nor could he have any command over one of his children. Slavery demanded all, but allowed nothing.

Notwithstanding, Plymouth admitted that he had been treated even more favorably than most slaves. The family thus bound consisted of his wife Jane, and four children, as follows: Dorsey, William Francis, Mary Ellen, and baby.

HORATIO was a little in advance of Plymouth in years, being forty-four years of age. His physical outlines gave him a commanding appearance for one who had worn the yoke as he had for so many years. He was of a yellow complexion, and very tall.

As a slave laborer he had been sweating and toiling to enrich a man by the name of Thomas J. Hodgson, a farmer on a large scale, and owning about a dozen slaves.

HORATIO gave him the character of being "a man of a hidden temper," and after the election of Buchanan he considered him a great deal worse than ever. HORATIO told of a visit which his master made to Canada, and which, on his return, he had taken much pains to report to the slaves to the effect that he had been there the previous summer, and saw the country for himself, adding in words somewhat as follows: "Canada is the meanest part of the globe that I ever found or heard of;"—did not see but one black or colored person in Canada,—inquired at the custom-house to know what became of all the blacks from the South, and was told that they shipped them off occasionally and sent them round Cape Horn and sold them." In addition to this report he said that "the suffering from deep snows and starvation was fearful," all of which Horatio believed "to be a lie." Of course he concealed this opinion from his master. Many such stories were sounded in the ears of slaves but without much effect.

LEMUEL, John and Josiah were brothers. Lemuel was thirty-five, and might be called a jet-black. He was uncommonly stout, with a head indicative of determination of purpose, just suited to an Underground Rail Road passenger. He fled from James R. Lewis, "a tall, stout man, very wealthy and close." Lemuel said that he fed and clothed the slaves pretty well. He had invested to the extent of twelve head. No money or privileges were allowed, and for a small offence the threat to sell was made. It was Lemuel's opinion that his master's wife made him worse than he otherwise would have been.

JOHN was twenty-four years of age, of unmixed blood, and of a quiet demeanour. He belonged to Miss Catharine Cornwell, of Viana. John described her as "tolerable good-looking, but real bad." His sister and one other slave besides himself comprised her entire stock (of slaves).

According to John's story, his mistress was in the habit of telling her slaves that she did not "intend that any of them should be free if she could help it;" this sentiment was uttered so "scornfully" that it "insulted" Jack very much. Indeed, it was this that put the idea of Canada into his mind. The more she kept the idea of perpetual Slavery before the slaves, the more Jack resolved to make her arrogance cost her one slave at least.

Miss Cornwell was not only a warm advocate of Slavery, but was likewise a member of the Methodist church, under the pastoral charge of the Rev. J. C. Gregg. On one occasion, when the minister was visiting Miss C., the subject of Slavery was introduced in John's hearing. The reverend gentleman took the ground that it was not right to hold slaves,—said there were none in Pennsylvania, etc. The young mistress showed little or no sign of thinking otherwise while he remained, "but, after he was gone, she raved and went on in a great way, and told her brother if he (the minister), ever married her, he would have to come out of his notions about freedom." It was John's opinion that the subject of matrimony was then under consideration between them. For himself, he was highly delighted with the minister's "notions of freedom," as he had heard so many high notions of Slavery.

In reference to the labor usage under the young mistress, John said that they had been "worked very hard, and especially last, and the present year." "Last year," he stated, "they had hardly any meat, but were fed chiefly on herring. Seeing that it was going to be the same thing this year too, I thought that if I could make my escape to Canada, I would do it." He had strong parental and kindred ties to break, but resolved to break them rather than remain under Miss Cornwell.

JOSIAH was twenty-three. A more promising-looking subject to represent the fugitives in Canada, was not readily to be found. His appearance indicated that he was a young man of extra physical powers, at least, one not likely to turn his face again towards Egypt.

JOSIAH'S gain was the loss of Thomas J. Hodgson (above alluded to). For full three years this desire and determination to be free had been in Josiah's heart. The denial of his manhood nerved him to seek for refuge in a foreign clime.

GEORGE, the last named in this party, gave his age as twenty-six. In appearance he was not behind any of his comrades. He fled from a farmer, (the late William Jackson), who owned, it was said, "sixteen head." He had recently died, leaving all his slaves in bondage. Seeing that the settlement of the estate might necessitate the sale of some of the slaves, George thought that he had better not wait for the division of the property or anything else, but push ahead with the first train for Canada. Slavery, as he viewed it, was nothing more nor less than downright robbery. He left his mother, one sister, and other near kin. After George went to Canada, his heart yearned tenderly after his mother and sister, and, as the following letter will show, he was prepared to make commendable exertions in their behalf:

ST. CATHARINES, JULY 19th, 1858.

DEAR SIR :—With pleasure I now inform you that I am well, and hope this may find you and yours the same also. I hope kind sir you will please to see Mr. Paul Hammon, to know when he will try to get my Mother and Sister I wish him to send me word when he will go so I may meet him in Philadelphia.

And I will Endevor to meet him there With some money to assist him in getting them. Let me know when you start for them so I may be able to meet you there, please after this letter passes from you sir, give it to John Camper tell him to give it to his Mother, so that my Mother can get it, be careful and not let no white man get hold of it. I am now living with my cousin Leven Parker, near Saint Catharines, $10 a month. No more at present, from your friend,   GEORGE BALLARD.

The inquiry may arise, as to how such passengers managed to get through Maryland and Delaware. But it cannot be expected that the manner in which each arrival traveled should be particularly described. It might not be prudent even now, to give the names of persons still living in the South, who assisted their fellow-men in the dark days of Slavery. In order, however, that some idea may be gathered as to the workings of one branch of the road in Delaware (with names suppressed) we insert the following original letter for what it may be worth.

CAMDEN, June 13, 1858.

MR. STILL :—I writ to inform you that we stand in need of help if ever we wonted help it is in theas day, we have Bin trying to rais money to By a hors but there is so few here that we can trust our selves with for fear that they may serve us as tom otwell served them when he got them in dover Jail. But he is dun for ever, i wont to no if your friends can help us, we have a Road that more than 100 past over in 1857. it is one we made for them, 7 in march after the lions had them there is no better in the State, we are 7 miles from Delaware Bay. you may understand what i mean. I wrote last december to the anti Slavery Society for James Mot and others concerning of purchasing a horse for this Bisnes if your friends can help us the work must stil go on for ther is much frait pases over this Road, But ther has Ben but 3 conductors for sum time. you may no that there is but few men, sum talks all dos nothing, there is horses owned by Collard peopel but not for this purpose. We wont one for to go when called for, one of our best men was nigh Cut By keeping of them too long, By not having means to convay them tha must Be convad if they pass over this Road safe tha go through in 2 nights to Wilmington, for i went there with 28 in one gang last November, tha had to ride for when thea com to us we go 15 miles, it is hard Road to travel i had sum conversation with mr. Evens and wos down here on a visit. pleas try what you can do for us this is the place we need help, 12 mile i live from mason and Dixson Line. I wod have come but cant have time, as yet there has been some fuss about a boy ho lived near Camden, he has gone away, he ses me and my brother nose about it but he dont.

There is but 4 slaves near us, never spoke to one of them but wonce she never gos out pleas to tri and help, you can do much if you will it will be the means of saving ourselves and others. Ancer this letter.

Pleas to writ let me no if you can do anything for us. I still remain your friend.

ARRIVAL FROM RICHMOND, 1858.

EBENEZER ALLISON.

"Eb" was a bright mulatto, handsome, well-made, and barely twenty years of age. He reported that he fled from Mr. John Tilghman Foster, a farmer, living in the vicinity of Richmond. His master, Ebenezer unhesitatingly declared, was a first-rate man. "I had no right to leave him in the world, but I loved freedom better than Slavery." After fully setting forth the kind treatment he had been accustomed to receive under his master, a member of the Committee desired to know of him if he could read, to which he answered that he could, but he admitted that what knowledge he had obtained in this direction was the result of efforts made stealthily, not through any license afforded by his master. John Tilghman Foster held deeds for about one hundred and fifty head of slaves, and was a man of influence.

Ebenezer had served his time in the barber's shop. On escaping he forsook his parents, and eight brothers and sisters. As he was so intelligent, the Committee believed he would make his mark in life some time.

ARRIVAL FROM RICHMOND, 1858.

JOHN THOMPSON CARR, ANN MOUNTAIN AND CHILD, AND WILLIAM BOWLER.

John was a sturdy-looking chattel, but possessed far less intelligence than the generality of passengers. He was not too old, however, to improve. The fact that he had spirit enough to resent the harsh treatment

29

of one Albert Lewis, a small farmer, who claimed to own him, showed that he was by no means a hopeless case. With all his apparent stupidity he knew enough to give his master the name of a " free whiskey drinker," likewise of " beating and fighting the slaves." It was on this account that John was compelled to escape.

ANN MOUNTAIN arrived from Delaware with her child about the same time that John did, but not in company with him; they met at the station in Philadelphia. That Slavery had crippled her in every respect was very discernible; this poor woman had suffered from cuffing, etc., until she could no longer endure her oppression. Taking her child in her arms, she sought refuge beyond the borders of slave territory. Ann was about twenty-two years of age, her child not quite a year old. They were considered entitled to much pity.

WILLIAM was forty-one years of age, dark, ordinary size, and intelligent. He fled from Richmond, where he had been held by Alexander Royster, the owner of fifteen slaves, and a tobacco merchant. William said that his master was a man of very savage temper, short, and crabbed. As to his social relations, William said that he was " a member of nothing now but a liquor barrel."

Knowing that his master and mistress labored under the delusion that he was silly enough to look up to them as kind-hearted slave-holders, to whom he should feel himself indebted for everything, William thought that they would be sadly puzzled to conjecture what had become of him. He was sure that they would be slow to believe that he had gone to Canada. Until within the last five years he had enjoyed many privileges as a slave, but he had since found it not so easy to submit to the requirements of Slavery. He left his wife, Nancy, and two children.

ARRIVAL FROM BALTIMORE, 1858.

ROBERTA TAYLOR.

The subject of this sketch was a young mulatto woman, twenty-three years of age, who fled from the City of Baltimore. Both before and after her escape Roberta appeared to appreciate her situation most fully. Her language concerning freedom had in it the ring of common sense, as had her remarks touching her slave life.

In making her grievances known to the Committee she charged Mr. and Mrs. McCoy with having done great violence to her freedom and degrading her womanhood by holding her in bonds contrary to her wishes. Of Mr. McCoy, however, she spoke less severely than she did of his " better half." Indeed she spoke of some kind traits in his character, but said that his wife was one of "the torn down, devilish dispositions, all the time quarreling and fighting, and would swear like an old sailor." It was in consequence of these evil propensities that her ladyship was intolerable to Roberta. Without being indebted to her owners for any privileges, she had managed to learn to read a little, which knowledge she valued highly and meant to improve in Canada.

Roberta professed to be a Christian, and was a member of the Bethel Methodist Church. Her servitude, until within four years of her escape, had been passed in Virginia, under Mrs. McCoy's father, when to accommodate the daughter she was transferred to Baltimore. Of her parentage or relatives no note was made on the book. It was sad to see such persons destitute and homeless, compelled to seek refuge among strangers, not daring to ask the slightest favor, sympathy or prayer to aid her, Christian as she was, from any Christian of Baltimore, wearing a fair skin.

ARRIVAL FROM HIGHTSTOWN, 1858.

ROBERT THOMPSON (A PREACHER).

Slavery exempted from the yoke no man with a colored skin no matter what his faith, talent, genius, or worth might be. The person of Christ in a black skin would scarcely have caused it to relinquish its tyrannical grasp; neither God nor man was regarded by men who dealt in the bodies and souls of their fellow-men. Robert stated to the Committee that he fled from "John R. Laten, a very harsh kind of a farmer, who drank right smart," that on the morning he "took out," while innocent of having committed any crime, suddenly in a desperate fit of passion, his master took him "by the collar," at the same time calling loudly to "John" for "ropes." This alarming assault on the part of his master made the preacher feel as though his Satanic majesty had possession of him. In such a crisis he evidently felt that preaching would do no good; he was, however, constrained to make an effort. To use his own words, he said: "I gave a sudden jerk and started off on a trot, leaving my master calling, 'stop! stop!' but I kept on running, and was soon out of sight."

The more he thought over the brutal conduct of his master the more decided he became never to serve him more, and straightway he resolved to try to reach Canada. Being in the prime of his life (thirty-nine years of age) and having the essential qualifications for traveling over the Underground Rail Road, he was just the man to endure the trials consequent upon such an undertaking.

Said Robert: "I always thought slavery hard, a very dissipated life to live. I always thought we colored people ought to work for ourselves and wives and children like other people. The Committee saw that Robert's views were in every word sound doctrine, and for further light asked him some questions respecting the treatment he had received at the hands of his mistress, not knowing but that he had received kindness from the "weaker vessel," while enduring suffering under his master; but Robert assured them in answer to this inquiry that his mistress was a very "ill, dissipated woman," and "was not calculated to sympathize with a poor slave." Robert was next interviewed with regard to religious matters, when it was ascertained that he bore the name of being a "local preacher of the gospel of the Bethel Methodist denomination." Thus in leaving slavery he had to forsake his wife and three children, kinfolks and church, which arduous task but for the brutal conduct of the master he might have labored in vain for strength to perform.

As he looked calmly back upon the past, and saw how he and the rest of the slaves had been deprived of their just rights he could hardly realize how Providence could suffer slave-holders to do as they had been doing in trampling upon the poor and helpless slaves. Yet he had strong faith that the Almighty would punish slave-holders severely for their wickedness.

ARRIVAL FROM VIRGINIA, 1858.

ALFRED S. THORNTON.

The subject of this sketch was a young man about twenty-two years of age, of dark color, but bright intellectually. Alfred found no fault with the ordinary treatment received at the hands of his master; he had evidently been on unusually intimate terms with him. Nor was any fault found with his mistress, so far as her treatment of him was concerned; thus, comparatively, he was "happy and contented," little dreaming of trader or a change of owners. One day, to his utter surprise, he saw a trader with a constable approaching him. As they drew nearer and nearer he began to grow nervous. What further took place will be given, as nearly as possible, in Alfred's own words as follows:

"William Noland (a constable), and the trader was making right up to me almost on my heels, and grabbed at me, they were so near. I flew, I took off my hat and run, took off my jacket and run harder, took off my vest and doubled my pace, the constable and the trader both on the chase hot foot. The trader fired two barrels of his revolver after me, and cried out as loud as he could call, G–d d–n, etc., but I never stopped running, but run for my master. Coming up to him, I cried out, Lord, master, have you sold me? 'Yes,' was his answer. 'To the trader,' I said. 'Yes,' he answered. 'Why couldn't you sold me to some of the neighbors?' I said. 'I don't know,' he said, in a dry way. With my arms around my master's neck, I begged and prayed him to tell me why he had sold me. The trader and constable was again pretty near. I let go my master and took to my heels to save me. I run about a mile off and run into a mill dam up to my head in water. I kept my head just above and hid the rest part of my body for more than two hours. I had not made up my mind to escape until I had got into the water. I run only to have little more time to

breathe before going to Georgia or New Orleans; but I pretty soon made up my mind in the water to try and get to a free State, and go to Canada and make the trial anyhow, but I didn't know which way to travel."

Such great changes in Alfred's prospects having been wrought in so short a while, together with such a fearful looking-for of a fate in the far South more horrid than death, suddenly, as by a miracle, he turns his face in the direction of the North. But the North star, as it were, hid its face from him. For a week he was trying to reach free soil, the rain scarcely ceasing for an hour. The entire journey was extremely discouraging, and many steps had to be taken in vain, hungry and weary. But having the faith of those spoken of in the Scriptures, who wandered about in dens and caves of the earth, being destitute, afflicted and tormented, he endured to the end and arrived safely to the Committee.

He left his father and mother, both slaves, living near Middleburg, in Virginia, not far from where he said his master lived, who went by the name of C. E. Shinn, and followed farming. His master and mistress were said to be members of the "South Baptist Church," and both had borne good characters until within a year or so previous to Alfred's departure. Since then a very serious disagreement had taken place between them, resulting in their separation, a heavy lawsuit, and consequently large outlays. It was this domestic trouble, in Alfred's opinion, that rendered his sale indispensable. Of the merits of the grave charges made by his master against his mistress, Alfred professed to have formed no opinion; he knew, however, that his master blamed a school-master, by the name of Conway, for the sad state of things in his household. Time would fail to tell of the abundant joy Alfred derived from the fact, that his "heels" had saved him from a Southern market. Equally difficult would it be to express the interest felt by the Committee in this passenger and his wonderful hair-breadth escape.

ARRIVAL FROM BELLEAIR.

JULIUS SMITH, WIFE MARY, AND BOY JAMES, HENRY AND EDWARD SMITH, AND
JACK CHRISTY.

While this party was very respectable in regard to numbers and enlisted much sympathy, still they had no wounds or bruises to exhibit, or very hard reports to make relative to their bondage. The treatment that had been meted out to them was about as tolerant as Slavery could well afford; and the physical condition of the passengers bore evidence that they had been used to something better than herring and corn cake for a diet.

JULIUS, who was successful enough to bring his wife and boy with him, was a wonderful specimen of muscular proportions. Although a young man, of but twenty-five, he weighed two hundred and twenty-five pounds; he was tall and well-formed from the crown of his head to the soles of his feet. Nor was he all muscle by a great deal; he was well balanced as to mother wit and shrewdness.

In looking back into the pit from whence he had been delivered he could tell a very interesting story of what he had experienced, from which it was evident that he had not been an idle observer of what had passed relative to the Peculiar Institution; especially was it very certain that he had never seen anything lovely or of good report belonging to the system. So far as his personal relations were concerned, he acknowledged that a man named Mr. Robert Hollan, had assumed to impose himself upon him as master, and that this same man had also wrongfully claimed all his time, denied him all common and special privileges; besides he had deprived him of an education, etc., which looked badly enough before he left Maryland, but in the light of freedom, and from a free State stand-point, the idea that "man's inhumanity to man" should assume such gigantic proportions as to cause him to seize his fellow-man and hold him in perpetual bondage, was marvellous in the extreme.

JULIUS had been kept in the dark in Maryland, but on free soil, the light rushed in upon his astonished vision to a degree almost bewildering. That his master was a man of "means and pretty high standing"—Julius thought was not much to his credit since they were obtained from unpaid labor. In his review allusion was made not only to his master, but also to his mistress, in which he said that she was "a quarrelsome and crabbed woman, middling stout." In order to show a reason why he left as he did, he stated that "there had been a fuss two or three times" previous to the escape, and it had been rumored "that somebody would have to be sold soon." This was what did the mischief so far as the "running away" was concerned. Julius' color was nearly jet black, and his speech was very good considering his lack of book learning; his bearing was entirely self-possessed and commendable.

His wife and boy shared fully in his affections, and seemed well pleased to have their faces turned Canada-ward. It is hardly necessary to say more of them here.

HENRY was about twenty-three years of age, of an active turn, brown skin, and had given the question of freedom his most serious attention, as his actions proved. While he could neither read nor write, he could think. From the manner in which he expressed himself, with regard to Robert Hollan, no man in the whole range of his recollections will be longer remembered than he; his enthralment while under Hollan will hardly ever be forgotten. Any being who had been thus deprived of his rights, could hardly fail to command sympathy; in cases like this, however, the sight and language of such an one was extremely impressive.

Of this party, Edward, a boy of seventeen, called forth much sympathy; he too was claimed by Hollan. He was of a good physical make-up, and seemed to value highly the great end he had in view, namely, a residence in Canada.

ARRIVAL FROM MARYLAND, 1858.

JOHN WESLEY COMBASH, JACOB TAYLOR, AND THOMAS EDWARD SKINNER.

The revelations made by these passengers were painful to listen to, and would not have been credited if any room had existed for doubt.

JOHN WESLEY was thirty-two years of age, of a lively turn, pleasant countenance, dark color, and ordinary size. In unburdening his mind to the Committee the all-absorbing theme related to the manner in which he had been treated as a slave, and the character of those who had oppressed him. He stated that he had been the victim of a man or party, named Johnson, in whose family John had been a witness to some of the most high-handed phases of barbarism; said he, " these Johnsons were notorious for abusing their servants. A few years back one of their slaves, a coachman, was kept on the coach box one cold night when they were out at a ball until he became almost frozen to death, in fact he did die in the infirmary from the effects of the frost about one week afterwards."

Another case was that of a slave woman in a very delicate state, who was one day knocked down stairs by Mrs. Johnson herself, and in a few weeks after, the poor woman died from the effects of the injury thus received. The doctor who attended the injured creature in this case was simply told that she slipped and fell down stairs as she was coming down. Colored witnesses had no right to testify, and the doctor was mute, consequently the guilty escaped wholly unpunished." "Another case," said John Wesley, " was a little girl, half-grown, who was washing windows up stairs one day, and unluckily fell asleep in the window, and in this position was found by her mistress; in a rage the mistress hit her a heavy slap, knocked her out of the window, and she fell to the pavement, and died in a few hours from the effects thereof. The mistress professed to know nothing about it, simply said, 'she went to sleep and fell out herself.' As usual nothing was done in the way of punishment."

These were specimens of the inner workings of the peculiar institution. John, however, had not only observed Slavery from a domestic stand-point, he had also watched master and mistress abroad as visitors and guests in other people's houses, noticed not only how they treated white people, but also how they treated black people. "These Johnsons thought that they were first-rate to their servants. When visiting among their friends they were usually very polite, would bow and scrape more than a little, even to colored people, knowing that their names were in bad odor, on account of their cruelty, for they had been in the papers twice about how they abused their colored people."

As to advertising him, John gave it as his opinion that they would be ashamed to do it from the fact that they had already rendered themselves more notorious than they had bargained for, on account of their cruelty towards their slaves; they were wealthy, and courted the good opinion of society. Besides they were members of the Presbyterian Church, and John thought that they were very willing that people should believe that they were great saints. On the score of feeding and clothing John gave them credit, saying that "the clothing was good enough, they liked to see the house servants dressed;" he spoke too of the eating as being all right, but added, that "very often time was not allowed them to finish their meals." Respecting work, John bore witness that they were very sharp.

With John's intelligence, large observation, good memory, and excellent natural abilities, with the amount of detail that he possessed, nothing more would have been needed for a thrilling book than the facts and incidents of slave life, as he had been conversant with it under the Johnsons in Maryland.

As the other two companions of John Wesley were advertised in the *Baltimore Sun*, we avail ourselves of the light thus publicly afforded:

$ 200 REWARD.—Ran away from the subscriber, living on the York Turnpike, eight miles from Baltimore city, on Sunday, April 11th, my negro man, JACOB, aged 20 years : 5 feet 10 inches high ; chestnut color ; spare made ; good features. I will give $50 reward if taken in Baltimore city or county, and $200 if taken out of the State and secured in jail so that I get him again.
          a13–3t*‖   WM. J. B. PARLETT.

" JACOB," answering to the description in Mr. Wm. J. B. Parlett's advertisement, gave his views of the man who had enslaved him. His statement is here transferred from the record book : " My master," said Jacob, " was a farmer, a very rough man, hard to satisfy. I never knew of but one man who could ever please him. He worked me very hard ; he wanted to be beating me all the time." This was a luxury which Jacob had no appetite for, consequently he could not resist signifying his unwillingness to yield, although resistance had to be made at some personal risk, as his master had " no more regard for a colored man than he had for a stone under his feet." With him the following expression was common : " The niggers are not worth a d–n." Nor was his wife any better, in Jacob's opinion. "She was a cross woman, and as much of a boss as he was." "She would take a club and with both hands would whack away as long as you would stand it." "She was a large, homely woman ; they were common white people, with no reputation in the community." Substantially this was Jacob's unvarnished description of his master and mistress.

As to his age, and also the name of his master, Jacob's statement varied somewhat from the advertisement. For instance, Jacob Taylor was noticed on the record book as being twenty-three years of age, and the name of his master was entered as " William Pollit ;" but as Jacob had never been allowed to learn to read, he might have failed in giving a correct pronunciation of the name.

When asked what first prompted him to seek his freedom, he replied, " Oh my senses ! I always had it in my mind to leave, but I was 'jubus ', (dubious?) of starting. I didn't know the way to come. I was afraid of being overtaken on the way." He fled from near Baltimore, where he left brothers and other relatives in chains.

$ 20 REWARD.—Ran away at the same time and in company with the above negro man, a bright mulatto boy named THOMAS SKINNER, about 18 years old, 5 feet 8 inches high and tolerable stout made ; he only has a term of years to serve. I will pay $ 20 reward if delivered to me or lodged in jail so I can get him again.   GEO. H. CARMAN,
          a13–3t*‖.   Towsontown, Baltimore county, Md.

About the same time that this advertisement came to hand a certain young aspirant for Canada was entered on the Underground Rail Road Book thus:

"THOMAS EDWARD SKINNER, a bright mulatto, age eighteen years, well formed, good-looking, and wide awake; says, that he fled from one G. H. Carman, Esq., head Clerk of the County Court." He bore voluntary testimony to Carman in the following words: "He was a very good man; he fed and clothed well and gave some money too occasionally." Yet Thomas had no idea of remaining in Slavery under any circumstances. He hated everything like Slavery, and as young as he was, he had already made five attempts to escape. On this occasion, with older and wiser heads, he succeeded.

ARRIVAL FROM NEW MARKET, 1858.

ELIJAH SHAW.

This "article" reported himself as having been deprived of his liberty by Dr. Ephraim Bell, of Baltimore County, Maryland. He had no fault to find with the doctor, however; on the contrary, he spoke of him as a "very clever and nice man, as much so as anybody need to live with;" but of his wife he could not speak so favorably; indeed, he described her as a most tyrannical woman. Said Elijah, "she would make a practice of rapping the broomstick around the heads of either men, women, or children when she got raised, which was pretty often. But she never rapped me, for I wouldn't stand it; I shouldn't fared any better than the rest if I hadn't been resolute. I declared over and over again to her that I would scald her with the tea kettle if she ever took the broomstick to me, and I meant it. She took good care to keep the broomstick from about my head. She was as mischievous and stingy as she could live; wouldn't give enough to eat or wear. These facts and many more were elicited from Elijah, when in a calm state of mind and when feeling much elated with the idea that his efforts in casting off the yoke were met with favor by the Committee, and that the accommodations and privileges on the road were so much greater than he had ever dreamed of. Such luck on the road was indeed a matter of wonder and delight to passengers generally. They were delighted to find that the Committee received them and forwarded them on "without money and without price." Elijah was capable of realizing the worth of such friendship. He was a young man twenty-three years of age, spare made, yellow complexion, of quick motion and decidedly collected in his bearing. In short, he was a man well adapted to make a good British subject.

ARRIVAL FROM VIRGINIA, 1858.

MARY FRANCES MELVIN, ELIZA HENDERSON, AND NANCY GRANTHAM.

MARY FRANCES hailed from Norfolk; she had been in servitude under Mrs. Chapman, a widow lady, against whom she had no complaint to make; indeed, she testified that her mistress was very kind, although fully allied to slavery. She said that she left, not on account of bad treatment, but simply because she wanted her freedom. Her calling as a slave had been that of a dress-maker and house servant. Mary Frances was about twenty-three years of age, of mixed blood, refined in her manners and somewhat cultivated.

ELIZA HENDERSON, who happened at the station at the same time that Frances was on hand, escaped from Richmond. She was twenty-eight years of age, medium size, quite dark color, and of pleasant countenance. Eliza alleged that one William Waverton had been wronging her by keeping her down-trodden and withholding her hire. Also, that this same Waverton had, on a late occasion, brought his heavy fist violently against her "jaws," which visitation, however "kindly" intended by her chivalrous master, produced such an unfavorable impression on the mind of Eliza that she at once determined not to yield submission to him a day longer than she could find an Underground Rail Road conductor who would take her North.

The blow that she had thus received made her almost frantic; she had however thought seriously on the question of her rights before this outrage.

In Waverton's household Eliza had become a fixture as it were, especially with regard to his children; she had won their affections completely, and she was under the impression that in some instances their influence had saved her from severe punishment; and for them she manifested kindly feelings. In speaking of her mistress she said that she was "only tolerable."

It would be useless to attempt a description of the great satisfaction and delight evinced by Eliza on reaching the Committee in Philadelphia.

NANCY GRANTHAM also fled from near Richmond, and was fortunate in that she escaped from the prison-house at the age of nineteen. She possessed a countenance peculiarly mild, and was good-looking and interesting, and although evidently a slave her father belonged strictly to the white man's party, for she was fully half white. She was moved to escape simply to shun her master's evil designs; his brutal purposes were only frustrated by the utmost resolution. This chivalric gentleman was a husband, the father of nine children, and the owner of three hundred slaves. He belonged to a family bearing the name of Christian, and was said to be an M. D. "He was an old man, but very cruel to all his slaves." It was said that Nancy's sister was the object of his lust, but she resisted, and the result was that she was sold to New Orleans. The auction-block was not the only punishment she was called upon to endure for her fidelity to her womanhood, for resistance to her master, but before being sold she was cruelly scourged.

NANCY'S sorrows first commenced in Alabama. Five years previous to her escape she was brought from a cotton plantation in Alabama, where she had been accustomed to toil in the cotton-field. In comparing and contrasting the usages of slave-holders in the two States in which she had served, she said she had " seen more flogging under old Christian " than she had been accustomed to see in Alabama ; yet she concluded, that she could hardly tell which State was the worst; her cup had been full and very bitter in both States.

Nancy said, " the very day before I escaped, I was required to go to his (her master's) bed-chamber to keep the flies off of him as he lay sick, or pretended to be so. Notwithstanding, in talking with me, he said that he was coming to my pallet that night, and with an oath he declared if I made a noise he would cut my throat. I told him I would not be there. Accordingly he did go to my room, but I had gone for shelter to another room. At this his wrath waxed terrible. Next morning I was called to account for getting out of his way, and I was beaten awfully." This outrage moved Nancy to a death-struggle for her freedom, and she succeeded by dressing herself in male attire.

After her harrowing story was told with so much earnestness and intelligence, she was asked as to the treatment she had received at the hand of Mrs. Christian (her mistress). In relation to her, Nancy said, " Mrs. Christian was afraid of him (master); if it hadn't been for that I think she would have been clever; but I was often threatened by her, and once she undertook to beat me, but I could not stand it. I had to resist, and she got the worst of it that time."

All that may now be added, is, that the number of young slave girls shamefully exposed to the base lusts of their masters, as Nancy was—truly was legion. Nancy was but one of the number who resisted influences apparently overpowering. All honor is due her name and memory !

She was brought away secreted on a boat, but the record is silent as to which one of the two or three Underground Rail Road captains (who at that time occasionally brought passengers), helped her to escape. It was hard to be definite concerning minor matters while absorbed in the painful reflections that her tale of suffering had naturally awakened. If one had arisen from the dead the horrors of Slavery could scarcely have been more vividly pictured ! But in the multitude of travelers coming under the notice of the Committee, Nancy's story was soon forgotten, and new and marvellous narratives were told of others who had shared the same bitter cup, who had escaped from the same hell of Slavery, who had panted for the same freedom and won the same prize.

ARRIVAL FROM RICHMOND, 1858.

ORLANDO J. HUNT.

When ORLANDO escaped from Richmond the Underground Rail Road business was not very brisk. A disaster on the road, resulting in the capture of one or two captains, tended to damp the ardor of some who wanted to come, as well as that of sympathizers. The road was not idle, however. Orlando's coming was hailed with great satisfaction. He was twenty-nine years of age, full black, possessed considerable intelligence, and was fluent in speech ; fully qualified to give clear statements as to the condition of Slavery in Richmond, etc. While the Committee listened to his narrations with much interest, they only took note of how he had fared, and the character of the master he was compelled to serve. On these points the substance of his narrations may be found annexed:

"I was owned by High Holser, a hide sorter, a man said to be rich, a good Catholic, though very disagreeable; he was not cruel, but was very driving and abusive in his language towards colored people. I have been held in bondage about eighteen years by Holser, but have failed, so far, to find any good traits in his character. I purchased my mother for one hundred dollars, when she was old and past labor, too old to earn her hire and find herself; but she was taken away by death, before I had finished paying for her ; twenty-five dollars only remained to be paid to finish the agreement. Owing to her unexpected death, I got rid of that much, which was of some consequence, as I was a slave myself, and had hard work to raise the money to purchase her."

Thus, finding the usages of Slavery so cruel and outlandish, he resolved to leave " old Virginny " and " took out," via the Underground Rail Road. He appeared to be of a religious turn of mind, and felt that he had "a call to preach."

After his arrival in Canada, the following letter was received from him:

ST. CATHARINES, C. W., May 6th, 1858.

MY DEAR FRIEND :—WM. STILL:—Mr. Orlando J. Hunt, who has just arrived here from Richmond, Va., desires me to address to you a line in his behalf. Mr. Hunt is expecting his clothing to come from Richmond to your care, and if you have received them, he desires you to forward them immediately to St. Catharines, in my care, in the safest and most expeditious way in your power. Mr. Hunt is much pleased with this land of freedom, and I hope he may do well for himself and much good to others. He preached here in the Baptist church, last evening.

He sends his kind regards and sincere thanks to you and your family, and such friends as have favored him on his way. Very respectfully yours,

HIRAM WILSON, for ORLANDO HUNT.

ARRIVAL FROM NORFOLK, VA., 1858.

WILLIAM MACKEY.

WILLIAM made no complaint against his master of a serious nature touching himself. True, he said his "master was a frolicker, and fond of drink," but he was not particularly unkind to him. His name was Tunis; he was a military man, and young; consequently William had not been in his hands long. Prior to his being owned by the young master, he had lived with old mistress Tunis. Concerning her the following is one of William's statements:

"My sister about the first of this month, three weeks after her confinement, had word sent to her by her mistress, Mrs. Tunis, that she thought it was time for her to come out and go to work, as she had been laying by long enough." In reply to this message, William said that "his sister sent word to her mistress, that she was not well enough, and begged that her mistress would please send her some tea and sugar, until she got well enough to go to work. The mistress' answer was to the effect that she did not intend to give her anything until she went to work, and at the same time she sent word to her, that she had better take her baby down to the back of the garden and throw it away, adding 'I will sell her, etc.' "

It was owing to the cruelty of Mrs. Tunis that William was moved to flee. According to his statement, which looked reasonable and appeared truthful, he had been willed free by his master, who died at the time that the plague was raging in Norfolk. At the same time his mistress also had the fever, and was dreadfully frightened, but recovered. Not long after this event it was William's belief that the will was made away with through the agency of a lawyer, and in consequence thereof the slaves were retained in bondage.

ARRIVAL FROM NEAR BALTIMORE, 1858.

HENRY TUCKER.

HENRY fled from Baltimore county; disagreement between him and his so-called master was the cause of his flight. Elias Sneveley, a farmer, known on the Arabella Creek Place as a "hard swearer," an "old bachelor," and a common tormentor of all around him, was the name of the man that Harry said he fled from. Not willing to be run over at the pleasure of Sneveley, on two occasions just before his escape serious encounters had arisen between master and slave.

HENRY being spirited and hungering for freedom, while his master was old and hardened in his habits, very grave results had well nigh happened;

it was evident, therefore, in Harry's opinion that the sooner he took his departure for Canada the better. His father's example was ever present to encourage him, for he had escaped when Henry was a little boy; (his name was Benjamin Tucker). A still greater incentive, however, moved him, which was that his mother had been sold South five years prior to his escape, since which time he had heard of her but once, and that vaguely.

Although education was denied him, Henry had too much natural ability to content himself under the heel of Slavery. He saw and understood the extent of the wrongs under which he suffered, and resolved not to abide in such a condition, if, by struggling and perseverance, he could avoid it. In his resolute attempt he succeeded without any very severe suffering. He was not large, rather below the ordinary size, of a brown color, and very plucky.

ARRIVAL FROM VIRGINIA, 1858.

PETER NELSON. (RESEMBLED AN IRISHMAN.)

The coming of this strange-looking individual caused much surprise, representing, as he did, if not a full-blooded Irishman, a man of Irish descent. He was sufficiently fair to pass for white anywhere, with his hat on—with it off, his hair would have betrayed him; it was light, but quite woolly. Nor was he likely to be called handsome; he was interesting, nevertheless. It was evident, that the "white man's party" had damaged him seriously. He represented that he had been in the bonds of one James Ford, of Stafford county, Virginia, and that this "Ford was a right tough old fellow, who owned about two dozen head." "How does he treat them?" he was asked. "He don't treat them well no way," replied the passenger. "Why did you leave?" was the next question. "Because of his fighting, knocking and carrying on so," was the prompt answer. The Committee fully interviewed him, and perceived that he had really worn the fetters of Slavery, and that he was justified in breaking his bonds and fleeing for refuge to Canada, and was entitled to aid and sympathy. Peter was about twenty-four years of age. He left nine brothers and sisters in bondage.

ARRIVAL FROM WASHINGTON, 1858.

MARY JONES AND SUSAN BELL.

These "weaker vessels" came from the seat of government. Mary confessed that she had been held to service as the property of Mrs. Henry Harding, who resided at Rockville, some miles out of Washington. Both Mr.

and Mrs. Harding she considered "bad enough," but added, "if it had not been for the young set I could get along with them; they can't be pleased." Yet Mary had not fared half so hard under the Hardings as many slaves had under their claimants. Intellectually, she was quite above the average; she was tall, and her appearance was such as to awaken sympathy. Through the permission of her claimant she had been in the habit of hiring her time for three dollars per month and find herself; she was also allowed to live in Washington. Such privileges, with wages at so low a rate, were thought to be extra, and could only be obtained in exceptional cases.

"In nine years," said Mary, "I have not even as much as received an apron from them," (her owners). The meanness of the system under which she had been required to live, hourly appeared clearer and clearer to her, as she was brought into contact with sympathizing spirits such as she had never known before.

SUSAN, who was in Mary's charge, was an invalid child of four years of age, who never walked, and whose mother had escaped to Canada about three years before under circumstances which obliged her to leave this child, then only a year old.

Susan had been a great sufferer, and so had her mother, who had been a long time anxiously looking and praying for her coming, as she had left her in charge of friends who were to take care of her until the way might open for her safe delivery to her mother. Many letters, fitted to awaken very deep feelings came from the mother about this child. It was a satisfaction to the Committee to feel that they could be the medium in aiding in the reunion of mother and child.

ARRIVAL FROM VIRGINIA, 1858.

WILLIAM CARPENTER.

Escaped from the Father of the Fugitive Slave Law—Senator Mason.

It was highly pleasing to have a visit from a "chattel" belonging to the leading advocate of the infamous Fugitive Slave Bill. He was hurriedly interviewed for the sake of reliable information.

That William possessed a fair knowledge of slave life under the Senator there was no room to doubt, although incidents of extreme cruelty might not have been so common on Mason's place as on some others. While the verbal interchange of views was quite full, the hour for the starting of the Underground Rail Road train arrived too soon to admit of a full report for the record book. From the original record, however, the following statement is taken as made by William, and believed to be strictly true. We give it as it stands on the old Underground Rail Road book : " I belonged to Senator Mason. The Senator was down on colored people. He owned about eighty head—was very rich and a big man, rich enough to lose all of them. He kept terrible overseers ; they would beat you with a stick the same as a dog. The overseers were poor white trash ; he would give them about sixty dollars a year."

The Fugitive Slave Law and its Father are both numbered with the " Lost Cause," and the " Year of Jubilee has come."

ARRIVAL FROM THE OLD DOMINION.

NINE VERY FINE "ARTICLES." LEW JONES, OSCAR PAYNE, MOSE WOOD, DAVE DIGGS, JACK, HEN, AND BILL DADE, AND JOE BALL.

The coming of this interesting party was as gratifying, as their departure must have been disagreeable to those who had been enjoying the fruits of their unpaid labor. Stockholders of the Underground Rail Road, conductors, etc., about this time were well pleased with the wonderful success of the road, especially as business was daily increasing.

Upon inquiry of these passengers individually, the following results were obtained :

LEWIS was about fifty-two years of age, a man of superior stature, six feet high, with prominent features, and about one third of Anglo-Saxon blood in his veins. The apparent solidity of the man both with respect to body and mind was calculated to inspire the idea that he would be a first-rate man to manage a farm in Canada.

Of his bondage and escape the following statement was obtained from him : " I was owned by a man named Thomas Sydan, a Catholic, and a farmer. He was not a very hard man, but was very much opposed to black folks having their liberty. He owned six young slaves not grown up. It was owing to Sydan's mother's estate that I came into his hands ; before her death I had hoped to be free for a long time as soon as she died. My old mistress' name was Nancy Sydan ; she was lame for twenty years, and couldn't walk a step without crutches, and I was her main support. I was foreman on the farm ; sometimes no body but me would work, and I was looked up to for support. A good deal of the time I would have to attend to her. If she was going to ride, I would have to pick her up in my arms and put her in the carriage, and many times I would have to lift her in her sick room. No body couldn't wait upon her but me. She had a husband, and he had a master, and that was rum ; he drank very hard, he killed himself drinking. He was poor support. When he died, fifteen years ago, he left three sons, Thomas, James, and Stephen, they were all together then,

30

only common livers. After his death about six years mistress died. I felt sure then I would be free, but was very badly disappointed. I went to my young masters and asked them about my freedom; they laughed at me and said, no such thought had entered their heads, that I was to be free. The neighbors said it was a shame that they should keep me out of my freedom, after I had been the making of the family, and had behaved myself so faithful. One gentleman asked master John what he would take for me, and offered a thousand dollars; that was three months before I ran away, and massa John said a thousand dollars wouldn't buy one leg. I hadn't anything to hope for from them. I served them all my life, and they didn't thank me for it. A short time before I come away my aunt died, all the kin I had, and they wouldn't let me go to the funeral. They said 'the time couldn't be spared.'" This was the last straw on the camel's back.

In Lewis' grief and disappointment he decided that he would run away the first chance that he could get, and seek a home in Canada. He held counsel with others in whom he could confide, and they fixed on a time to start, and resolved that they would suffer anything else but Slavery. Lewis was delighted that he had managed so cunningly to leave master Tom and mistress Margaret, and their six children to work for their own living. He had an idea that they would want Lew for many things; the only regret he felt was that he had served them so long, that they had received his substance and strength for half a century. Fortunately Lewis' wife escaped three days in advance of him, in accordance with a mutual understanding. They had no children. The suffering on the road cost Lewis a little less than death, but the joy of success came soon to chase away the effects of the pain and hardship which had been endured.

Oscar, the next passenger, was advertised as follows:

$200 Reward.—Ran away from the service of the Rev. J. P. McGuire, Episcopal High School, Fairfax county, Va., on Saturday, 10th inst., Negro Man, Oscar Payne, aged 30 years, 5 feet 4 inches in height, square built, mulatto color, thick, bushy suit of hair, round, full face, and when spoken to has a pleasant manner—clothes not recollected.

I will give $200 for his recovery if taken out of the State, or $150 if taken in the State, and secured that I can get him.

T. D. Fendall.   jy17-6t.

Such announcements never frightened the Underground Rail Road Committee; indeed, the Committee rather preferred seeing the names of their passengers in the papers, as, in that case, they could all the more cautiously provide against Messrs. slave-hunters. Oscar was a " prime, first-class article," worth $1800. The above description of him is endorsed. His story ran thus:

" I have served under Miss Mary Dade, of Alexandria—Miss Dade was a very clever mistress; she hired me out. When I left I was hired at the Episcopal school—High School of Virginia. With me times had been very well. No privilege was allowed me to study books. I cannot say that I left for any other cause than to get my freedom, as I believe I have been used as well as any slave in the District. I left no relatives but two cousins; my two brothers ran away, Brooks and Lawrence, but where they went I can't tell, but would be pleased to know. Three brothers and one sister have been sold South, can't tell where they are." Such was Oscar's brief narrative ; that he was truthful there was no room to doubt.

The next passenger was MOSES or "Mose," who looked as though he had been exceedingly well-cared for, being plump, fat, and extra-smart. He declared that General Briscoe, of Georgetown, D. C., had been defrauding him out of thirteen dollars per month, this being the amount for which he was hired, and, instead of being allowed to draw it for himself, the general pocketed it. For this "kind treatment" he summed up what seemed to be a true bill for ten years against the general. But he made another charge of a still graver character : he said that the general professed to own him. But as he (Moses) was thoroughly tired, and believed that Slavery was no more justifiable than murder, he made up his mind to leave and join the union party for Canada. He stated that the general owned a large number of slaves, which he hired out principally. Moses had no special fault to find with his master, except such as have been alluded to, but as to mistress Briscoe, he said, that she was pretty rough. Moses left four sisters in bondage.

DAVID, the next member of this freedom-loving band, was an intelligent man ; his manners and movements were decidedly prepossessing. He was about thirty-seven years of age, dark, tall, and rather of a slender stature, possessing very large hopes. He charged Dr. Josiah Harding of Rockville, Montgomery county, with having enslaved him contrary to his wish or will.

As a slave, David had been required at one time to work on a farm, and at another time to drive carriage, of course, without pay. Again he had been bound as a waiter on the no pay system, and again he had been called into the kitchen to cook, all for the benefit of the Doctor—the hire going into the Dr.'s pocket. This business David protested against in secret, but when on the Underground Rail Road his protestations were " over and above board."

Of the Doctor, David said, that " he was clever, but a Catholic ;" he also said, that he thought his wife was " tolerable clever," although he had never been placed under her where he would have had an opportunity of learning her bad traits if she had any.

The Doctor had generously bargained with David, that he could have himself by paying $1000 ; he had likewise figured up how the money might be paid, and intimated what a nice thing it would be for " Dave " to wake up some morning and find himself his own man. This was how it was to be accomplished : Dave was to pay eighty-five dollars annually, and in about twelve years he would have the thousand, and a little over, all made up. On this principle and suggestion Dave had been digging faithfully and hard, and with the aid of friends he had nearly succeeded. Just when he was within sight of the grand prize, and just as the last payment was about to be made, to Dave's utter surprise the Doctor got very angry one day about some trifling matter (all pretension) and in his pretended rage he said there were too many " free niggers " going about, and he thought that Dave would do better as a slave, etc.

After that, all the satisfaction that he was able to get out of the Doctor, was simply to the effect, that he had hired him to Mr. Morrison for one hundred and fifty dollars a year. After his " lying and cheating " in this way, David resolved that he would take his chances on the Underground Rail Road. Not a spark of faith did he have in the Doctor. For a time, however, before the opportunity to escape offered, he went to Mr. Morrison as a waiter, where it was his province to wait on six of the Judges of the Supreme Court of the United States. In the meantime his party matured arrangements for their trip, so Dave " took out " and left the Judges without a waiter. The more he reflected over the nature of the wrongs he had suffered under, the less he thought of the Doctor.

JOE, who also came with this band, was half Anglo-Saxon; an able-bodied man, thirty-four years of age. He said, that " Miss Elizabeth Gordon, a white woman living in Alexandria," claimed him. He did not find much fault with her. She permitted him to hire his time, find his own clothing, etc., by which regulation Joe got along smoothly. Nevertheless he declared, that he was tired of wearing the yoke, and felt constrained to throw it off as soon as possible. Miss Gordon was getting old, and Joe noticed that the young tribe of nephews and nieces was multiplying in large numbers. This he regarded as a very bad sign ; he therefore, gave the matter of the Underground Rail Road his serious attention, and it was not long ere he was fully persuaded that it would be wisdom for him to tarry no longer in the prison-house. Joe had a wife and four children, which were as heavy weights to hold him in Virginia, but the spirit of liberty prevailed. Joe, also, left two sisters, one free, the other a slave. His wife belonged to the widow Irwin. She had assured her slaves, that she had " provided for them in her will," and that at her death all would be freed. They were daily living on the faith thus created, and obviously thought the sooner the Lord relieved the old mistress of her earthly troubles the better.

Although Joe left his wife and children, he did not forget them, but had strong faith they would be reunited. After going to Canada, he addressed several letters to the Secretary of the Committee concerning his family, and as will be seen by the following, he looked with ardent hopes for their arrival :

TORONTO, Nov. 7th, 1857.

DEAR MR. STILL :—As I must again send you a letter fealing myself oblidge to you for all you have done and your kindness. Dear Sir my wife will be on to Philadelphia on the 8th 7th, and I would you to look out for her and get her an ticket and send her to me Toronto. Her name are May Ball with five children. Please send her as soon as you can.

Yours very truly, JOSEPH BALL.

Will you please to telegrape to me, No. 31 Dummer st.

JAKE, another member of the company of nine, was twenty-two years of age, of dark hue, round-made, keen eyes, and apparently a man of superior intelligence. Unfortunately his lot had been of such a nature that no helping opportunity had been afforded for the cultivation of his mind.

He condemned in very strong terms a man by the name of Benjamin B. Chambers, who lived near Elkton, but did not there require the services of Jake, hiring Jake out just as he would have hired a horse, and likewise keeping his pay. Jake thought that if justice could have been awarded him, Chambers would either have had to restore that of which he had wronged him, or expiate the wrong in prison.

Jake, however, stood more in awe of a young master, who was soon likely to come into power, than he did of the old master. This son had already given Jake to understand that once in his hands it "wouldn't be long before he would have him jingling in his pocket," signifying, that he would sell him as soon as his father was gone.

The manner of the son stirred Jake's very blood to boiling heat it seemed. His suffering, and the suffering of his fellow-bondsmen had never before appeared so hard. The idea that he must work, and be sold at the pleasure of another, made him decide to "pull up stakes," and seek refuge elsewhere. Such a spirit as he possessed could not rest in servitude.

MARY ANN, the wife of Jake, who accompanied him, was a pleasant-looking bride. She said that she was owned by "Elias Rhoads, a farmer, and a pretty fair kind of a man." She had been treated very well.

JOHN AND HENRY DADE, ages twenty and twenty-five years, were from Washington. They belonged to the class of well-cared for slaves ; at least they said that their mistress had not dealt severely with them, and they never would have consented to pass through the severe sufferings encountered on their journey, but for the strong desire they had to be free. From Canada John wrote back as follows :

ST. CATHARINES, Canada.

MR. STILL, SIR :—I ar rivd on Friday evenen bot I had rite smart troble for my mony gave out at the bridge and I had to fot et to St. Catherin tho I went rite to worke at the willard house for 8 dolor month bargend for to stae all the wentor bot I havent eny clouse nor money please send my tronke if et has come. Derate et to St. Catharines to the willard house to John Dade and if et ant come plice rite for et soon as posable deract your letter to Rosenen Dade Washington send your deraction please tend to this rite a way for I haf made a good start I think that I can gate a longe en this plase. If my brother as well send him on for I haf a plase for him ef he ant well please dont send him for this as no plase for a sik possan. The way I got this plase I went to see a fran of myen from Washington. Dan al well and he gave me werke. Pleas ancer this as soon as you gat et you must excues this bad riting for my chance wars bot small to line this mouch,

JOHN H. DADE.

If you haf to send for my tronke to Washington send the name of John Trowharte. Sir please rite as soon as you gat this for et as enporten.   JOHN H. DADE.

ARRIVAL FROM DELAWARE, 1858.

GEORGE LAWS AND COMRADE—TIED AND HOISTED WITH BLOCK AND TACKLE, TO BE COWHIDED.

GEORGE represented the ordinary young slave men of Delaware. He was of unmixed blood, medium size and of humble appearance. He was destitute of the knowledge of spelling, to say nothing of reading. Slavery had stamped him unmistakably for life. To be scantily fed and clothed, and compelled to work without hire, George did not admire, but had to submit without murmuring; indeed, he knew that his so-called master, whose name was Denny, would not be likely to hear complaints from a slave; he therefore dragged his chain and yielded to his daily task.

One day, while hauling dirt with a fractious horse, the animal manifested an unwillingness to perform his duty satisfactorily. At this procedure the master charged George with provoking the beast to do wickedly, and in a rage he collared George and bade him accompany him "up stairs" (of the soap house). Not daring to resist, George went along with him. Ropes being tied around both his wrists, the block and tackle were fastened thereto, and George soon found himself hoisted on tip-toe with his feet almost clear of the floor.

The "kind-hearted master" then tore all the poor fellow's old shirt off his back, and addressed him thus: "You son of a b—h, I will give you pouting around me; stay there till I go up town for my cowhide."

George begged piteously, but in vain. The fracas caused some excitement, and it so happened that a show was to be exhibited that day in the town, which, as is usual in the country, brought a great many people from a distance; so, to his surprise, when the master returned with his cowhide, he found that a large number of curiosity-seekers had been attracted to the soap house to see Mr. Denny perform with his cowhide on George's back, as he was stretched up by his hands. Many had evidently made up their minds that it would be more amusing to see the cowhiding than the circus.

The spectators numbered about three hundred. This was a larger number than Mr. Denny had been accustomed to perform before, consequently he was seized with embarrassment; looking confused he left the soap house and went to his office, to await the dispersion of the crowd.

The throng finally retired, and left George hanging in mortal agony. Human nature here made a death-struggle; the cords which bound his wrists were unloosed, and George was then prepared to strike for freedom at the mouth of the cannon or point of the bayonet. How Denny regarded the matter when he found that George had not only cheated him out of the anticipated delight of cowhiding him, but had also cheated him out of himself is left for the imagination to picture.

George fled from Kent; he was accompanied by a comrade whose name inadvertently was not recorded; he, however, was described as a dark, round, and full-faced, stout-built man, with bow legs, and bore the appearance of having been used hard and kept down, and in ignorance, &c. Hard usage constrained him to flee from his sore oppression.

ARRIVAL FROM DELAWARE, 1858.

JOHN WEEMS, ALIAS JACK HERRING.

Although Jack was but twenty-three years of age, he had tasted the bitter cup of Slavery pretty thoroughly under Kendall B. Herring, who was a member of the Methodist Church, and in Jack's opinion a "mere pretender, and a man of a very bad disposition." Jack thought that he had worked full long enough for this Herring for nothing. When a boy twelve years of age, his mother was sold South; from that day, until the hour that he fled he had not heard a word from her. In making up his mind to leave Slavery, the outrage inflicted upon his mother only tended to increase his resolution.

In speaking of his mistress, he said that "she was a right fine woman." Notwithstanding all his sufferings in the Kendall family, he seemed willing to do justice to his master and mistress individually. He left one sister free and one brother in the hands of Herring. Jack was described as a man of dark color, stout, and well-made.

ARRIVAL FROM MARYLAND, 1858.

RUTH HARPER, GEORGE ROBINSON, PRISCILLA GARDENER, AND JOSHUA JOHN ANDERSON.

RUTHIE'S course in seeking her freedom left John McPherson a woman less to work for him, and to whip, sell, or degrade at his pleasure. It is due to candor, however, to say that she admitted that she had not been used very roughly by Mr. McPherson. Ruth was rather a nice-looking young woman, tall, and polite in her manners. She came from Frederick, Maryland.

GEORGE ROBINSON stated that he came from a place about one and a half miles from the Chesapeake Bay, one mile from Old town, and five miles from Elkton, and was owned by Samuel Smith, a farmer, who was "pretty cross and an ill man." George's excuse for withdrawing his valuable services from Mr. Smith at the time that he did, was attributable to the fact, that he entertained fears that they were about to sell him. Having cautiousness largely developed he determined to reach Canada and keep out of danger. George was only twenty-one, passable-looking in appearance, and of a brown color, and when speaking, stammered considerably.

PRISCILLA GARDENER fled from the widow Hilliard. Her master departed to his long home not a great while before she left. Priscilla was a young woman of about thirty years of age, ordinary size, and of a ginger-bread color; modest in demeanor. She first commenced her bondage in Richmond, under the late Benjamin Hilliard, of whom she said that he was "a very bad man, who could never be pleased by a servant," and was constantly addicted to fighting not only with others, but also with herself. So cruelly had Priscilla been treated, that when he died she did not hesitate to say that she was glad. Soon after this event, sick of Slavery and unwilling to serve the widow any longer, she determined to escape, and succeeded.

JOSHUA JOHN ANDERSON fled from a farmer who was said to be a poor man, by the name of Skelton Price, residing in Baltimore county, near a little village called Alexandria, on the Harford county turn-pike road. Price, not able to own a farm and slaves too, rented one, and was trying to "get up in the world." Price had a wife and family, but in the way of treatment, Joshua did not say anything very hard against him. As his excuse for leaving them, he said, coolly, that he had made up his mind that he could get along better in freedom than he could in Slavery, and that no man had a right to his labor without paying him for it. He left his mother and also three brothers and two sisters owned by Price. Joshua was about twenty-two years of age, of a coarse make, and a dark hue; he had evidently held but little intercourse with any class, save such as he found in the corn-field and barn-yard.

ARRIVAL FROM NORTH CAROLINA AND DELAWARE.

"DICK BEESLY," MURRAY YOUNG AND CHARLES ANDREW BOLDEN.

Physically, Dick was hardly up to the ordinary stature of slaves, but mentally he had the advantage of the masses; he was too sharp to be kept in Slavery. His hue was perfect, no sign of white about him, if that were any advantage.

From Dick's story, it appeared that he had seen hard times in North Carolina, under a man he designated by the name of Richard Smallwood. He was a farmer, living near Wheldon. One of the faults that he found with Smallwood was, that he was a "tough, drinking man"—he also charged him with holding "two hundred and sixty slaves in bonds," the most of whom he came in possession of through his wife. "She," Dick thought "was pretty fair." He said that no slave had any reason to look for any other than hard times under his master, according to what he had seen and known since he had been in the "institution," and he fancied that his chances for observation had been equally as good as the great majority of slaves. Young as he was, Dick had been sold three times already, and didn't know how much oftener he might have to submit to the same fate if he remained; so, in order to avoid further trouble, he applied his entire skill to the grand idea of making his way to Canada.

Manfully did he wrestle with difficulty after difficulty, until he finally happily triumphed and reached Philadelphia in a good condition—that is, he was not sick, but he was without money—home—education or friends, except as he found them among strangers. He was hopeful, nevertheless.

MURRAY YOUNG was also of the unmixed-blood class, and only twenty-one years of age. The spirit of liberty in him was pretty largely developed. He entertained naught against Dr. Lober, of Newcastle, but rather against the Doctor's wife. He said that he could get along pretty well with the Doctor, but, he could not get along with Mrs. Lober. But the very idea of Slavery was enough for him. He did not mean to work for any body for nothing.

ANDREW BOLDEN was still younger than Charles Murray, being only eighteen years of age, but he was very well grown, and on the auction-block he would, doubtless, have brought a large price. He fled from Newark. His story contained nothing of marked importance.

ARRIVAL FROM MARYLAND.

JOHN JANNEY, TALBOT JOHNSON, SAM GROSS, PETER GROSS, JAMES HENRY JACK-
SON, AND SAM SMITH.

$1.000 REWARD.—Ran away from the subscriber, August 14th, two negro men, viz :

BILL HUTTON,

aged 48 or 50 years, dark brown, round face, 5 feet 7 or 8 inches high, rather stout, has a waddling walk, and small bald spot on the top of his head.

TALBOT JOHNSON,

aged about 35, is black, spare, and lean-visaged, about 5 feet 10 inches high, has lost some of his front teeth, leans forward as he walks.

If taken in a slave State I will give $200 each for their recovery. For their recovery from a free State I will give one-half their value.   B. D. BOND, Port Republic, Md.

RAN AWAY at the same time and in company, negro man

SAM GROSS,

aged about 33, is 5 feet 8 or 9 inches high, black color, rather bad teeth. For his recovery, if taken in a slave State, I will give $200. For his recovery from a free State, I will give half his value.   GEO. IRELAND, Port Republic, Md.

RAN AWAY at the same time and in company, two negro men, viz :

PETER GROSS,

aged 33, is light-brown color, 5 feet 9 or 10 inches high, has a small scar over his right eyebrow, usually wears a goatee, has a pleasant countenance.

JOHN JANNEY, aged 22, light-brown color, 5 feet 6 or seven inches high, broad across the shoulders, has one of his front upper teeth broken, has a scar upon one of his great toes from the cut of an axe. For their recovery, if taken in a slave State, I will give $200 each. For their recovery from a free State I will give half their value.

JOS. GRIFFISS, St. Leonards, Calvert county, Md.

Refer to N. E. BERRY, No. 63 Pratt street, Baltimore.

So far as Messrs. Bond, Ireland, and Griffiss may be concerned (if they are still living), they may not care to have the reward kept in view, or to hear anything about the "ungrateful" fellows. It may be different, however, with other parties concerned. This company, some of whom bore names agreeing with those in the above advertisement, are found described in the record book as follows :

"Sept. 10th, 1858. JOHN JANNEY is a fine specimen of the peculiar institution; color brown, well-formed, self-possessed and intelligent. He says that he fled from master Joseph Griffiss of Culbert county, Maryland; that he has been used to "tight work," "allowed no chances," and but "half fed." His reason for leaving was partly "hard treatment," and partly because he could "get along better in freedom than in slavery." He found fault with his master for not permitting him to "learn to read," etc. He referred to his master as a man of "fifty years of age, with a wife and three children." John said that "she was a large, portly woman, with an evil disposition, always wanted to be quarreling and fighting, and was stingy." He said, however, that his "master's children, Ann Rebecca, Dorcas, and Joe were not allowed to meddle with the slaves on the farm." Thirty head of slaves belonged on the place.

PETER GROSS says that he too was owned by Joseph Griffiss. Peter is, he thinks, thirty-nine years of age,—tall, of a dark chestnut color, and in intellect mediocre. He left his wife and five children behind. He could not bring them with him, therefore he did not tell them that he was about to leave. He was much dissatisfied with Slavery and felt that he had been badly dealt with, and that he could do better for himself in Canada.

TALBOT JOHNSON, is thirty-five years of age, quite dark, and substantially built. He says that he has been treated very badly, and that Duke Bond was the name of the "tyrant" who held him. He pictured his master as "a lean-faced man—not stout—of thirty-eight or thirty-nine years of age, a member of the Episcopal Church." "He had a wife and two children; his last wife was right pleasant—he was a farmer, and was rich, had sold slaves, and was severe when he flogged." Talbot had been promised a terrible beating on the return of his master from the Springs, whither he had gone to recruit his health, "as he was poorly." This was the sole cause of Talbot's flight.

SAM GROSS is about forty, a man of apparent vigor physically, and wide awake mentally. He confesses that he fled from George Island, near Port Republic, Md. He thought that times with him had been bad enough all his life, and he would try to get away where he could do better. In referring to his master and mistress, he says that "they are both Episcopalians, hard to please, and had as bad dispositions as could be,—would try to knock the slaves in the head sometimes." This spirit Sam condemned in strong terms, and averred that it was on account of such treatment that he was moved to seek out the Underground Rail Road. Sam left his wife, Mary Ann, and four children, all under bonds. His children, he said, were treated horribly. They were owned by Joseph Griffiss spoken of above.

JAMES HENRY JACKSON is seventeen years of age; he testifies that he fled from Frederica, Delaware, where he had been owned by Joseph Brown. Jim does not make any serious complaint against his master, except that he had him in the market for sale. To avert this fate, Jim was moved to flee. His mother, Ann Jackson, lived nine miles from Milford, and was owned by Jim Loflin, and lived on his place. Of the going of her son she had no knowledge.

These narratives have been copied from the book as they were hastily recorded at the time. During their sojourn at the station, the subjoined letter came to hand from Thomas Garrett, which may have caused anxiety and haste:

WILMINGTON, 9th mo. 6th, 1858.

ESTEEMED FRIENDS, J. M. McKIM AND WM. STILL:—I have a mixture of good and bad news for you. Good in having passed five of God's poor safely to Jersey, and Chester county, last week; and this day sent on four more, that have caused me much anxiety. They were within twenty miles of here on sixth day last, and by agreement I had a man out all seventh day night watching for them, to pilot them safely, as 1,000 dollars reward was offered for four of the five; and I went several miles yesterday in the country to try to learn what had become of them, but could not hear of them. A man of tried integrity just called to say that they arrived at his house last night, about midnight, and I employed him to pilot them to a place of safety in Pennsylvania, to-night, after which I trust they will be out of reach of their pursuers. Now for the bad news. That old scoundrel, who applied to me some three weeks since, pretending that he wished me to assist him in getting his seven slaves into a free state, to avoid the sheriff, and which I agreed to do, if he would bring them here; but positively refused to send for them. Ten days since I received another letter from him, saying that the sheriff had been there, and taken away two of the children, which he wished me to raise money to purchase and set free, and then closed by saying that his other slaves, a man, his wife, and three children had left the same evening and he had no doubt I would find them at a colored man's house, he named, here, and wished me to ascertain at once and let him know. I at once was convinced he wished to know so as to have them arrested and taken back. I found the man had arrived; but the woman and children had given out, and he left them with a colored family in Cecil. I wrote him word the family had not got here, but said nothing of the man being here. On seventh day evening I saw a colored woman from the neighborhood; she told me that the owner and sheriff were out hunting five days for them before they found them, and says there is not a greater hypocrite in that part of the world. I wrote him a letter yesterday letting him know just what I thought of him. Your Friend, THOS. GARRETT.

ARRIVAL FROM MARYLAND.

BIRTH-DAY PRESENT FROM THOMAS GARRETT.

WILMINGTON, 8th mo. 21st, 1858.

ESTEEMED FRIEND:—WILLIAM STILL:—This is my 69th birth-day, and I do not know any better way to celebrate it in a way to accord with my feelings, than to send to thee two fugitives, man and wife; the man has been here a week waiting for his wife, who is expected in time to leave at 9 this evening in the cars for thy house with a pilot, who knows where thee lives, but I cannot help but feel some anxiety about the woman, as there is great commotion just now in the neighborhood where she resides. There were 4 slaves betrayed near the Maryland line by a colored man named Jesse Perry a few nights since. One of them made a confidant of him, and he agreed to pilot them on their way, and had several white men secreted to take them as soon as they got in his house; he is the scoundrel that was to have charge of the 7 I wrote you about two weeks since; their master was to take or send them there, and he wanted me to send for them. I have since been confirmed it was a trap set to catch one of our colored men and me likewise, but it was no go. I suspected him from the first, but afterwards was fully confirmed in my suspicions. We have found the two Rust boys, John and Elsey Bradley, who the villain of a Rust took out of jail and sold to a trader of the name of Morris, who sold them to a trader who took them to Richmond, Virginia, where they were sold at public sale two days before we found them, for $2600, but fortunately the man had not paid for them ; our Attorney had them by habeas corpus before a Judge, who detained them till we can prove their identity and freedom; they are to have a hearing on 2d day next, when we hope to have a person on there to prove them. In haste, thine, THOS. GARRETT.

Unfortunately all the notice that the record contains of the two passengers referred to, is in the following words : " Two cases not written out for want of time."

The "boys" alluded to as having been "found" &c., were free-born, but had been kidnapped and carried south and sold.

Three days after the above letter, the watchful Garrett furnished further light touching the hair-breadth escape of the two that he had written about, and at the same time gave an interesting account of the efforts which were made to save the poor kidnapped boys, &c.

SECOND LETTER FROM THOMAS GARRETT.

WILMINGTON, 8th mo. 25th, 1858.

ESTEEMED FRIEND :—WILLIAM STILL :—Thine was received yesterday. Those two I wrote about to be with thee last 7th day evening, I presume thee has seen before this. A. Allen had charge of them; he had them kept out of sight at the depot here till the cars should be ready to start, in charge of a friend, while he kept a lookout and got a ticket. When the Delaware cars arrived, who should step out but the master of both man and woman, (as they had belonged to different persons); they knew him, and he knew them. He left in a different direction from where they were secreted, and got round to them and hurried them off to a place of safety, as he was afraid to take them home for fear they would search the house. On 1st day morning the boat ran to Chester to take our colored people to the camp at Media; he had them disguised, and got them in the crowd and went with them; when he got to Media, he placed them in care of a colored man, who promised to hand them over to thee on 2d day last; we expect 3 more next 7th day night, but how we shall dispose of them we have not yet determined; it will depend on circumstances. Judge Layton has been on with a friend to Richmond, Virginia, and fully identified the two Bradley boys that were kidnapped by Clem Rust. He has the assurance of the Judge there that they will be tried and their case decided by Delaware Laws, by which they must be declared free and returned here. We hope to be able to bring such proof against both Rust and the man he sold them to, who took them out of the State, to teach them a lesson they will remember. Thy friend,

THOS. GARRETT.

ARRIVAL FROM THE DISTRICT OF COLUMBIA, 1858.

REBECCA JACKSON AND DAUGHTER, AND ROBERT SHORTER.

The road to Washington was doing about this time a marvellously large business. "William Penn" and other friends in Washington were most vigilant, and knew where to find passengers who were daily thirsting for deliverance.

REBECCA JACKSON was a woman of about thirty-seven years of age, of a yellow color, and of bright intellect, prepossessing in her manners. She had pined in bondage in Georgetown under Mrs. Margaret Dick, a lady of wealth and far advanced in life, a firm believer in slavery and the Presbyterian Church, of which she was a member.

Rebecca had been her chief attendant, knew all her whims and ways to perfection. According to Rebecca's idea, "she was a peevish, fretful, ill-natured, but kind-hearted creature." Being very tired of her old mistress and heartily sick of bondage, and withal desiring to save her daughter, she ascertained the doings of the Underground Rail Road,—was told about Canada, &c. She therefore resolved to make a bold adventure. Mrs. Dick had resided a long time in Georgetown, but owned three large plantations in the country, over which she kept three overseers to look after the slaves. Rebecca had a free husband, but she was not free to serve him, as she had to be digging day and night for the "white people." Robert, a son of the mistress, lived with his mother. While Rebecca regarded him as "a man with a very evil disposition," she nevertheless believed that he had "sense enough to see that the present generation of slaves would not bear so much as slaves had been made to bear the generation past."

ARRIVAL FROM HONEY BROOK TOWNSHIP, 1858.

FRANK CAMPBELL.

FRANK was a man of blunt features, rather stout, almost jet black, and about medium height and weight. He was not certain about his age, rather thought that he was between thirty and forty years. He had been deprived of learning to read or write, but with hard treatment he had been made fully acquainted under a man named Henry Campbell, who called himself Frank's master, and without his consent managed to profit by his daily sweat and toil. This Campbell was a farmer, and was said to be the owner of about one hundred head of slaves, besides having large investments in other directions. He did not hesitate to sell slaves if he could get his price. Every now and then one and another would find it his turn to be sold. Frank resolved to try and get out of danger before times were worse. So he struck out resolutely for freedom and succeeded.

ARRIVAL FROM ALEXANDRIA, VA., 1858.

RICHARD BAYNE, CARTER DOWLING AND BENJAMIN TAYLOR.

RICHARD stated that a man named "Rudolph Massey, a merchant tailor, hard rum-drinker, card player, etc." claimed to own him, and had held him, up to the time of his escape, as with bands of brass.

Richard said, "I was hired out for ten dollars a month, but I never suffered like many—didn't leave because I have been abused, but simply to keep from falling into the hands of some heirs that I had been willed to." In case of a division, Richard did not see how he could be divided without being converted into money. Now, as he could have no fore-knowledge as to the place or person into whose hands he might be consigned by the auctioneer, he concluded that he could not venture to risk himself in the hands of the young heirs. Richard began to consider what Slavery was, and his eyes beheld chains, whips, hand-cuffs, auction-blocks, separations and countless sufferings that had partially been overlooked before; he felt the injustice of having to toil hard to support a drunkard and gambler. At the age of twenty-three Richard concluded to "lay down the shovel and the hoe," and look out for himself. His mother was owned by Massey, but his father belonged to the "superior race" or claimed so to do, and if anything could be proved by appearances it was evident that he was the son of a white man. Richard was endowed with a good share of intelligence. He not only left his mother but also one sister to clank their chains together.

CARTER, who accompanied Richard, had just reached his majority. He stated that he escaped from a "maiden lady" living in Alexandria, known by the name of Miss Maria Fitchhugh, the owner of twenty-five slaves. Opposed to Slavery as he was, he nevertheless found no fault with his mistress, but on the contrary, said that she was a very respectable lady, and a member of the Episcopal Church. She often spoke of freeing her servants when she died; such talk was too uncertain for Carter, to pin his faith to, and he resolved not to wait. Such slave-holders generally lived a great while, and when they did die, they many times failed to keep their promises. He concluded to heed the voice of reason, and at once leave the house of bondage. His mother, father, five brothers and six sisters all owned by Miss Fitchhugh, formed a strong tie to keep him from going; he "conferred not with flesh and blood," but made a determined stroke for freedom.

BENJAMIN, the third in this company, was only twenty years of age, but a better-looking specimen for the auction-block could hardly be found. He fled from the Meed estate; his mistress had recently died leaving her affairs, including the disposal of the slaves, to be settled at an early date. He spoke of his mistress as "a very clever lady to her servants," but since her death he had realized the danger that he was in of being run off south with a coffle gang. He explained the course frequently resorted to by slave-holders under similar circumstances thus: "frequently slaves would be snatched up, hand cuffed and hurried off south on the night train without an hour's notice." Fearing that this might be his fate, he deemed it prudent to take a northern train via the Underground Rail Road without giving any notice.

He left no parents living, but six brothers and four sisters, all slaves with the exception of one brother who had bought himself. In order to defend themselves if molested on the road, the boys had provided themselves with pistols and dirks, and declared that they were fully bent on using them rather than be carried back to slavery.

ARRIVAL FROM THE SEAT OF GOVERNMENT.

HANSON WILLIAMS, NACE SHAW, GUSTA YOUNG, AND DANIEL M'NORTON SMITH.

$200 REWARD.—Ran away from the subscriber, (Levi Pumphrey,) two NEGRO MEN—one, named "Hanson," about forty years old, with one eye out, about 5 feet 4 inches in height, full, bushy hair and whiskers and copper color. "Gusta" is about 21 years or 22 years of age, smooth face and thick lips, and stoops in his walk; black color, about 5 feet 5 or 6 inches in height; took away sundry articles of clothing.

I will give one hundred dollars for each of them, if secured in jail so that I can get them.   LEVI PUMPHREY,
s14–6t.   Washington City, D. C.

These four fugitives were full of enthusiasm for Canada, although by no means among the worst abused of their class.

Hanson was about forty years of age, with apparently a good degree of intellect, and of staid principles.

In the above advertisement clipped from the Baltimore Sun, he is more fully described by Mr. Levi Pumphrey; it can now be taken for what it is worth. But, as Hanson left home suddenly without apprising his owner, or any of his owner's intimate white friends, of the circumstances which led him to thus leave, his testimony and explanation, although late, may not be wholly uninteresting to Mr. Levi Pumphrey and others who took an interest in the missing "Hanson." "How have you had it in slavery?" he was asked. "I have had it pretty rough," answered Hanson. "Who held you in bondage, and how have you been treated?" "I was owned by Levi Pumphrey, an old man with one eye, a perfect savage; he allowed no privileges of any kind, Sunday or Monday."

Gusta, who was also described in Pumphrey's advertisement, was a rugged-looking specimen, and his statement tended to strengthen Hanson's in every particular. It was owing to the bad treatment of Pumphrey, that Gusta left in the manner that he did.

After deciding to take his departure for Canada, he provided himself with a Colt's revolver, and resolved that if any man should attempt to put his hand on him while he was on the "King's highway," he would shoot him down, not excepting his old master.

$150 REWARD.—Ran away from the subscriber, living near Upper Marlboro', Prince George's county, Md., on the 11th day of September, 1858, a negro man, "Nace," who calls himself "Nace Shaw;" is forty-five years of age, about five feet 8 or 9 inches high, of a copper color, full suit of hair, except a bald place upon the top of his head. He has a mother living in Washington city, on South B street, No. 212 Island.

I will pay the above reward no matter where taken, if secured in jail so that I get him again. SARAH ANN TALBURTT.
s15-eotf.

NACE, advertised by Miss Sarah Ann Talburtt, was a remarkably good-natured looking piece of merchandise. He gave a very interesting account of his so called mistress, how he came to leave her, etc. Said Nace: "My mistress was an old maid, and lived on a farm. I was her foreman on the farm. She lived near Marlborough Forest, in Prince George's county, Md., about twelve miles from Washington ; she was a member of the Episcopal Church. She fed well, and quarrelled a caution, from Monday morning till Saturday night, not only with the slaves, but among the inmates of the big house. My mistress had three sisters, all old maids living with her, and a niece besides ; their names were Rebecca, Rachel, Caroline, and Sarah Ann, and a more disagreeable family of old maids could not be found in a year's time. To arise in the morning before my mistress, Sarah Ann, was impossible." Then, without making it appear that he or other of the slaves had been badly treated under Miss Talburtt, he entered upon the cause of escape, and said ; " I left simply because I wanted a chance for my life ; I wanted to die a free man if it pleased God to have it so." His wife and a grown-up son he was obliged to leave, as no opportunity offered to bring them away with him.

DAN was also of this party. He was well tinctured with Anglo-Saxon blood. His bondage had been in Alexandria, with a mill-wright, known by the name of James Garnett. Dan had not been in Garnett's hands a great while. Mr. Garnett's ways and manners were not altogether pleasing to him; besides, Dan stated that he was trying to sell him, and he made up his mind that at an early opportunity, he would avail himself of a ticket for Canada, via the Underground Rail Road. He left his mother and brothers all scattered.

CROSSING THE BAY IN A SKIFF.

WILLIAM THOMAS COPE, JOHN BOICE GREY, HENRY BOICE AND ISAAC WHITE.

These young bondmen, whilst writhing under the tortures heaped upon them, resolved, at the cost of life, to make a desperate trial for free land ; to rid themselves of their fetters, at whatever peril they might have to encounter. The land route presented less encouragement than by water ; they knew but little, however, concerning either way. After much

31

anxious reflection, they finally decided to make their Underground Rail
Road exit by water. Having lived all their lives not far from the bay,
they had some knowledge of small boats, skiffs in particular, but of course
they were not the possessors of one. Feeling that there was no time to lose,
they concluded to borrow a skiff, though they should never return it. So
one Saturday evening, toward the latter part of January, the four young
slaves stood on the beach near Lewes, Delaware, and cast their longing
eyes in the direction of the Jersey shore. A fierce gale was blowing, and
the waves were running fearfully high; not daunted, however, but as one
man they resolved to take their lives in their hands and make the bold
adventure.

With simple faith they entered the skiff; two of them took the oars, manfully to face uncertain dangers from the waves. But they remained steadfast,
oft as they felt that they were making the last stroke with their oars, on the
verge of being overwhelmed with the waves. At every new stage of
danger they summoned courage by remembering that they were escaping
for their lives.

Late on Sunday afternoon, the following day, they reached their much
desired haven, the Jersey shore. The relief and joy were unspeakably
great, yet they were strangers in a strange land. They knew not which way
to steer. True, they knew that New Jersey bore the name of being a Free
State; but they had reason to fear that they were in danger. In this
dilemma they were discovered by the captain of an oyster boat whose
sense of humanity was so strongly appealed to by their appearance that he
engaged to pilot them to Philadelphia. The following account of them was
recorded:

WILLIAM THOMAS was a yellow man, twenty-four years of age, and
possessing a vigorous constitution. He accused Shepherd P. Houston of
having restrained him of his liberty, and testified that said Houston was a
very bad man. His vocation was that of a farmer, on a small scale; as a
slave-holder he was numbered with the "small fry." Both master and

mistress were members of the Methodist Church. According to William Thomas' testimony his mistress as well as his master was very hard on the slaves in various ways, especially in the matter of food and clothing. It would require a great deal of hard preaching to convince him that such Christianity was other than spurious.

JOHN stated that David Henry Houston, a farmer, took it upon himself to exercise authority over him. Said John, "If you didn't do the work right, he got contrary, and wouldn't give you anything to eat for a whole day at a time; he said a 'nigger and a mule hadn't any feeling.'" He described his stature and circumstances somewhat thus: "Houston is a very small man; for some time his affairs had been in a bad way; he had been broke, some say he had bad luck for killing my brother. My brother was sick, but master said he wasn't sick, and he took a chunk, and beat on him, and he died a few days after." John firmly believed that his brother had been the victim of a monstrous outrage, and that he too was liable to the same treatment.

John was only nineteen years of age, spare built, chestnut color, and represented the rising mind of the slaves of the South.

HENRY was what might be termed a very smart young man, considering that he had been deprived of a knowledge of reading. He was a brother of John, and said that he also had been wrongfully enslaved by David Houston, alluded to above. He fully corroborated the statement of his brother, and declared, moreover, that his sister had not long since been sold South, and that he had heard enough to fully convince him that he and his brother were to be put up for sale soon.

Of their mistress John said that she was a "pretty easy kind of a woman, only she didn't want to allow enough to eat, and wouldn't mend any clothes for us."

ISAAC was twenty-two, quite black, and belonged to the "rising" young slaves of Delaware. He stated that he had been owned by a "blacksmith, a very hard man, by the name of Thomas Carper." Isaac was disgusted with his master's ignorance, and criticised him, in his crude way, to a considerable extent. Isaac had learned blacksmithing under Carper. Both master and mistress were Methodists. Isaac said that he "could not recommend his mistress, as she was given to bad practices," so much so that he could hardly endure her. He also charged the blacksmith with being addicted to bad habits. Sometimes Isaac would be called upon to receive correction from his master, which would generally be dealt out with a "chunk of wood" over his "no feeling" head. On a late occasion, when Isaac was being *chunked* beyond measure, he resisted, but the persistent blacksmith did not yield until he had so far disabled Isaac that he was rendered helpless for the next two weeks. While in this state he pledged himself to freedom and Canada, and resolved to win the prize by crossing the Bay.

While these young passengers possessed brains and bravery of a rare order, at the same time they brought with them an unusual amount of the soil of Delaware; their persons and old worn-out clothing being full of it. Their appearance called loudly for immediate cleansing. A room—free water—free soap, and such other assistance as was necessary was tendered them in order to render the work as thorough as possible. This healthy process over, clean and comfortable clothing were furnished, and the change in their appearance was so marked, that they might have passed as strangers, if not in the immediate corn-fields of their masters, certainly among many of their old acquaintances, unless subjected to the most careful inspection. Raised in the country and on farms, their masters and mistresses had never dreamed of encouraging them to conform to habits of cleanliness; washing their persons and changing their garments were not common occurrences. The coarse garment once on would be clung to without change as long as it would hold together. The filthy cabins allotted for their habitations were in themselves incentives to personal uncleanliness. In some districts this was more apparent than in others. From some portions of Maryland and Delaware, in particular, passengers brought lamentable evidence of a want of knowledge and improvement in this direction. But the master, not the slave, was blameworthy. The master, as has been intimated, found but one suit for working (and sometimes none for Sunday), consequently if Tom was set to ditching one day and became muddy and dirty, and the next day he was required to haul manure, his ditching suit had to be used, and if the next day he was called into the harvest-field, he was still obliged to wear his barn-yard suit, and so on to the end. Frequently have such passengers been thoroughly cleansed for the first time in their lives at the Philadelphia station. Some needed practical lessons before they understood the thoroughness necessary to cleansing. Before undertaking the operation, therefore, in order that they might be made to feel the benefit to be derived therefrom, they would need to have the matter brought home to them in a very gentle way, lest they might feign to fear taking cold, not having been used to it, etc.

It was customary to say to them: " We want to give you some clean clothing, but you need washing before putting them on. It will make you feel like a new man to have the dirt of slavery all washed off. Nothing that could be done for you would make you feel better after the fatigue of travel than a thorough bath. Probably you have not been allowed the opportunity of taking a good bath, and so have not enjoyed one since your mother bathed you. Don't be afraid of the water or soap—the harder you rub yourself the better you will feel. Shall we not wash your back and neck for you? We want you to look well while traveling on the Underground Rail Road, and not forget from this time forth to try to take care of yourself," &c., &c. By this course the reluctance where it existed would be overcome and the proposition would be readily acceded to, if the water was not too cool; on the other hand, if cool, a slight shudder might be visible, sufficient to raise a hearty laugh. Yet, when through, the candidate always expressed a hearty sense of satisfaction, and was truly thankful for this attention.

ARRIVAL FROM KENT COUNTY, Md., 1858.

ASBURY IRWIN, EPHRAIM ENNIS, AND LYDIA ANN JOHNS.

The party whose narratives are here given brought grave charges against a backsliding member of the Society of Friends—a renegade Quaker.

Doubtless rare instances may be found where men of the Quaker persuasion, emigrating from free and settling in slave States and among slaveholders, have deserted their freedom-loving principle and led captive by the force of bad examples, have linked hands with the oppressor against the oppressed. It is probable, however, that this is the only case that may turn up in these records to the disgrace of this body of Christians in whom dwelt in such a signal degree large sympathy for the slave and the fleeing bondman. Many fugitives were indebted to Friends who aided them in a quiet way, not allowing their left hand to know what their right hand did, and the result was that Underground Rail Road operations were always pretty safe and prosperous where the line of travel led through "Quaker settlements." We can speak with great confidence on this point especially with regard to Pennsylvania, where a goodly number might be named, if necessary, whose hearts, houses, horses, and money were always found ready and willing to assist the fugitive from the prison-house. It is with no little regret that we feel that truth requires us to connect the so-called owner of Asbury, Ephraim, and Lydia with the Quakers.

ASBURY was first examined, and his story ran substantially thus: "I run away because I was used bad; three years ago I was knocked dead with an axe by my master; the blood run out of my head as if it had been poured out of a tumbler; you can see the mark plain enough—look here," (with his finger on the spot). I left Millington, at the head of Chester in Kent County, Maryland, where I had been held by a farmer who called himself Michael Newbold. He was originally from Mount Holly, New Jersey, but had been living in Maryland over twenty years. He was called a Hickory Quaker, and he had a real Quaker for a wife. Before he was in Maryland five years he bought slaves, became a regular slave-holder, got to drinking and racing horses, and was very bad—treated all hands bad, his wife too, so that she had to leave him and go to Philadelphia to her kinsfolks. It was because he was so bad we all had to leave," &c.

While Asbury's story appeared truthful and simple, a portion of it was too shocking to morality and damaging to humanity to be inserted in these pages.

Asbury was about forty years of age, a man of dark hue, size and height about mediocrity, and mental ability quite above the average.

EPHRAIM was a fellow-servant and companion of Asbury. He was a man of superior physical strength, and from all outward appearance, he possessed qualities susceptible of ready improvement. He not only spoke of Newbold in terms of strong condemnation but of slave-holders and slavery everywhere. The lessons he had learned gave him ample opportunity to speak from experience and from what he had observed in the daily practices of slave-holders; consequently, with his ordinary gifts, it was impossible for him to utter his earnest feelings without making a deep impression.

LYDIA also fled from Michael Newbold. She was a young married woman, only twenty-two years of age, of a chestnut color and a pleasant countenance. Her flight for liberty cost her her husband, as she was obliged to leave him behind. What understanding was entered into between them prior to her departure we failed to note at the time. It was very clear that she had decided never to wear the yoke again.

ARRIVAL FROM WASHINGTON, 1858.

JOSEPHINE ROBINSON.

Many reasons were given by Josephine for leaving the sunny South. She had a mistress, but was not satisfied with her—hadn't a particle of love for her; "she was all the time fussing and scolding, and never could be satisfied." She was very well off, and owned thirteen or fourteen head of slaves. She was a member of the Methodist Church, was stingy and very mean towards her slaves. Josephine having lived with her all her life, professed to have a thorough knowledge of her ways and manners, and seemed disposed to speak truthfully of her. The name of her mistress was Eliza Hambleton, and she lived in Washington. Josephine had fully thought over the matter of her rights, so much so, that she was prompted to escape. So hard did she feel her lot to be, that she was compelled to resign her children, uncle and aunt to the cruel mercy of slavery. What became of the little ones, David, Ogden and Isaiah, is a mystery.

ARRIVAL FROM CECIL COUNTY, 1858.

ROBERT JOHNS AND HIS WIFE "SUE ANN."

Fortunately, in this instance, man and wife succeeded in making their way out of Slavery together. Robert was a man of small stature, and the farthest shade from white. In appearance and intellect he represented the ordinary Maryland slave, raised on a farm, surrounded with no refining influences or sympathy. He stated that a man by the name of William Cassey had claimed the right to his labor, and that he had been kept in bondage on his farm.

For a year or more before setting out for freedom, Robert had watched his master pretty closely, and came to the conclusion, that he was "a monstrous blustery kind of a man; one of the old time fellows, very hard and rash—not fit to own a dog." He owned twelve slaves; Robert resolved that he would make one less in a short while. He laid the matter before his wife, "Sue," who was said to be the property of Susan Flinthrew, wife of John Flinthrew, of Cecil county, Maryland. "Sue" having suffered severely, first from one and then another, sometimes from floggings, and at other times from hunger, and again from not being half clothed in cold weather, was prepared to consider any scheme that looked in the direction of speedy deliverance. The way that they were to travel, and the various points of danger to be passed on the road were fully considered; but Robert and Sue were united and agreed that they could not fare much worse than they had fared, should they be captured and carried back. In·this state of mind, as in the case of thousands of others, they set out for a free State, and in due time reached Pennsylvania and the Vigilance Committee, to whom they made known the facts here recorded, and received aid and comfort in return.

SUE was a young woman of twenty-three, of a brown color, and somewhat under medium size.

ARRIVAL FROM GEORGETOWN, D. C., 1858.

PERRY CLEXTON, JIM BANKS AND CHARLES NOLE.

This party found no very serious obstacles in their travels, as their plans were well arranged, and as they had at least natural ability sufficient for ordinary emergencies.

PERRY reported that he left "a man by the name of John M. Williams, of Georgetown, D. C., who was in the wood business, and kept a wharf." As to treatment, he said that he had not been used very hard, but had been worked hard and allowed but few privileges. The paltry sum of twenty-five cents a week, was all that was allowed him out of his hire. With a wife and one child this might seem a small sum, but in reality it was a liberal outlay compared with what many slaves were allowed. Perry being a ready-witted article, thought that it was hardly fair that Mr. Williams should live by the sweat of his brow instead of his own; he was a large, portly man, and able to work for himself in Perry's opinion. For a length of time, the notion of leaving and going to Canada' was uppermost in his heart; probably he would have acted with more promptness but for the fact that his wife and child rested with great weight on his mind. Finally the pressure became so great that he felt that he must leave at all hazards, forsaking wife and child, master and chains. He was a young man, of about twenty-five years of age, of a dark shade, ordinary build, and full of grit. His wife was named Amelia; whether she ever afterwards heard from her husband is a question.

JIM, who accompanied Perry, brought the shoe-making art with him. He had been held a slave under John J. Richards, although he was quite as much a white man as he was black. He was a mulatto, twenty-nine years of age, well-made, and bore a grum countenance, but a brave and manly will to keep up his courage on the way. He said that he had been used very well, had no fault to find with John J. Richards, who was possibly a near relative of his. He forsook his mother, four brothers and three sisters with no hope of ever seeing them again.

CHARLES bore strong testimony in favor of his master, Blooker W. Hansborough, a farmer, a first-rate man to his servants, said Charles. "I was used very well, can't complain." "Why did you not remain then?" asked a member of the Committee. "I left," answered C., "because I was not allowed to live with my wife. She with our six children, lived a long distance from my master's place, and he would not hire me out where I could live near my wife, so I made up my mind that I would try and do better. I could see no enjoyment that way." As the secret of his master's treatment is here brought to light, it is very evident that Charles, in speaking so highly in his favor, failed to take a just view of him, as no man could really be first-rate to his servants, who would not allow a man to live with his wife and children, and who would persist in taking from another what he had no right to take. Nevertheless, as Charles thought his master "first-rate," he shall have the benefit of the opinion, but it was suspected that Charles was not disposed to find fault with his kin, as it was very likely that the old master claimed some of the white blood in his veins.

ARRIVAL FROM SUSSEX COUNTY, 1858.

JACOB BLOCKSON, GEORGE ALLIGOOD, JIM ALLIGOOD, AND GEORGE LEWIS.

The coming of Jacob and his companions was welcomed in the usual way. The marks of Slavery upon them were evident; however they were subjected to the usual critical examination, which they bore with composure, and without the least damage. The following notes in the main were recorded from their statements:

JACOB was a stout and healthy-looking man, about twenty-seven years of age, with a countenance indicative of having no sympathy with Slavery. Being invited to tell his own story, describe his master, etc., he unhesitatingly relieved himself somewhat after this manner; " I escaped from a man by the name of Jesse W. Paten; he was a man of no business, except drinking whiskey, and farming. He was a light complected man, tall large, and full-faced, with a large nose. He was a widower. He belonged to no society of any kind. He lived near Seaford, in Sussex county, Delaware."

" I left because I didn't want to stay with him any longer. My master was about to be sold out this Fall, and I made up my mind that I did not want to be sold like a horse, the way they generally sold darkies then; so when I started I resolved to die sooner than I would be taken back; this was my intention all the while.

" I left my wife, and one child; the wife's name was Lear, and the child was called Alexander. I want to get them on soon too. I made some arrangements for their coming if I got off safe to Canada."

GEORGE was next called upon to give his statement concerning where he was from, etc. I " 'scaped " from Sussex too, from a man by the name of George M. Davis, a large man, dark-complected, and about fifty years of age; he belonged to the old side Methodist Church, was a man with a family, and followed farming, or had farming done by me and others. Besides he was a justice of the peace. I always believed that the Master above had no wish for me to be held in bondage all my days; but I thought if I made up my mind to stay in Slavery, and not to make a desperate trial for my freedom, I would never have any better times. I had heard that my old mistress had willed me to her children, and children's children. I thought at this rate there was no use of holding on any longer for the good time to come, so here I said, I am going, if I die a trying. I got me a dagger, and made up my mind if they attempted to take me on the road, I would have one man. As for my part, I have not had it so slavish as many, but I have never had any privileges to learn to read, or to go about anywhere. Now and then they let me go to church. My master belonged to church, and so did I.

For a young man, being only twenty-two years of age, who had been kept from the light of freedom, as much as he had, his story was thought to be exceedingly well told throughout.

JAMES, a brother of George, said: " I came from Horse's Cross-Roads, not far from where my brother George came from. William Gray, rail road ticket agent at Bridgewater, professed to own me. He was a tolerable sized man, with very large whiskers, and dark hair; he was rather a steady kind of a man, he had a wife, but no child. The reason I left, I thought I had served Slavery long enough, as I had been treated none the best. I did not believe in working my life out just to support some body else. My master had as many hands and feet as I have, and is as able to work for his bread as I am; and I made up my mind that I wouldn't stay to be a slave under him any longer, but that I would go to Canada, and be my own master."

James left his poor wife, and three children, slaves perhaps for life. The wife's name was Esther Ann, the children were called Mary, Henry, and Harriet. All belonged to Jesse Laten.

GEORGE LEWIS had more years than any of his companions, being about forty years of age. He had been kept in as low a state of ignorance as the ingenuity of a slave-holder of Delaware could keep one possessed of as much mother-wit as he was, for he was not quite so ignorant as the interests of the system required. His physical make and mental capacity were good. He was decidedly averse to the peculiar institution in every particular. He stated, that a man named Samuel Laws had held him in bondage—that this " Laws was a man of no business—just sat about the house and went about from store to store and sat ; that he was an old man, pretty grey, very long hair. He was a member of a church in the neighborhood, which was called Radical." Of this church and its members he could give but little account, either of their peculiarities or creed ; he said, however, that they worshipped a good deal like the Methodists, and allowed their members to swear heartily for slavery.

"Something told" George that he had worked long enough as a slave, and that he should be man enough to take the Underground Rail Road and go off to a free country. Accordingly George set out. When he arrived at the station he was so highly delighted with his success and the prospect before him, that he felt very sorry that he hadn't started ten years sooner. He said that he would have done so, but he was afraid, as slave-holders were always making the slaves believe that if they should ever escape they would catch them and bring them back and sell them down South, certain ; that they always did catch every one who ran off, but never brought them home, but sold them right off where they could never run away any more, or get to see their relatives again. This threat, George said, was continually rung in the ears of the slaves, and with the more timid it was very effective.

JACOB BLOCKSON, after reaching Canada, true to the pledge that he made to his bosom companion, wrote back as follows :

SAINT CATHARINES. Cannda West, Dec. 26th, 1858.

DEAR WIFE :—I now infom you I am in Canada and am well and hope you are the same, and would wish you to be here next august, you come to suspension bridge and from there to St. Catharines, write and let me know. I am doing well working for a Butcher this winter, and will get good wages in the spring I now get $2,50 a week.

I Jacob Blockson, George Lewis, George Alligood and James Alligood are all in St. Catharines, and met George Ross from Lewis Wright's, Jim Blockson is in Canada West, and Jim Delany, Plunnoth Connon. I expect you my wife Lea Ann Blockson, my son

Alexander & Lewis and Ames will all be here and Isabella also, if you cant bring all bring Alexander surely, write when you will come and I will meet you in Albany. Love to you all, from your loving Husband,   JACOB BLOCKSON. fare through $12,30 to here.

MR. STILL : SIR:—you will please Envelope this and send it to John Sheppard Bridgeville P office in Sussex county Delaware, seal it in black and oblige me, write to her to come to you.

SUNDRY ARRIVALS IN 1859.

SARAH ANN MILLS, Boonsborough; CAROLINE GASSWAY, Mt. Airy; LEVIN HOLDEN, Laurel; WILLIAM JAMES CONNER, with his wife, child, and four brothers; JAMES LAZARUS, Delaware; RICHARD WILLIAMS, Richmond, Virginia; SYDNEY HOPKINS and HENRY WHEELER, Havre de Grace.

SARAH MILLS set out for freedom long before she reached womanhood ; being about sixteen years of age. She stated that she had been very cruelly treated, that she was owned by a man named Joseph O'Neil, " a tax collector and a very bad man." Under said O'Neil she had been required to chop wood, curry horses, work in the field like a man, and all one winter she had been compelled to go barefooted. Three weeks before Sarah fled, her mistress was called away by death ; nevertheless Sarah could not forget how badly she had been treated by her while living. According to Sarah's testimony the mistress was no better than her husband. Sarah came from Boonsborough, near Hagerstown, Md., leaving her mother and other relatives in that neighborhood.

It was gratifying to know that such bond-women so early got beyond the control of slave-holders; yet girls of her age from having had no pains taken for their improvement, appealed loudly for more than common sympathy and humanity, but rarely ever found it ; on the contrary, their paths were beset with great danger.

CAROLINE GASSWAY, after being held to service by Summersett Walters, until she had reached her twenty-seventh year, was forced, by hard treatment and the love of freedom, to make an effort for deliverance. Her appearance at once indicated, although she was just out of the prison-house, that she possessed more than an ordinary share of courage, and that she had had a keen insight into the system under which she had been oppressed. She was of a dark chestnut color, well-formed, with a large and high forehead, indicative of intellect. She had much to say of the ways and practices of slave-holders; of the wrongs of the system. She dwelt especially upon her own situation as a slave, and the character of her master ; she told not only of his ill treatment of her, but described his physical appearance as well. " He was a spare-made man, with a red head and quick temper: he would go off in a flurry like a flash of powder, and would behave shamefully towards the slaves when in these fits of passion." His wife, however, Caroline confessed was of a different temper, and was a pretty good kind of a woman. If he had been anything like his wife in disposition, most likely Caroline would have remained in bondage. Fortunately, Caroline was a single woman. She left her mother.

LEVIN HOLDEN, having been sold only a few weeks prior to his escape, was so affected by the change which awaited him, that he was irresistibly led to seek the Underground Rail Road. Previous to being sold he was under a master by the name of Jonathan Bailey, who followed farming in the neighborhood of Laurel, Delaware, and, as a master, was considered a moderate man—was also well to do in the world; but the new master he could not endure, as he had already let the secret out that Levin was to be sent South. Levin had a perfect horror of a more Southern latitude; he made up his mind that he would try his luck for Canada. Levin was a man of twenty-seven years of age, smart, dark color, and of a good size for all sorts of work.

WILLIAM JAMES CONNER, his wife, child, and four brothers came next. The brothers were hale-looking fellows, and would have commanded high prices in any market South of Mason and Dixon's Line. It was said, that they were the property of Kendall Major Lewis, who lived near Laurel, Delaware. It was known, however, that he never had any deed from the Almighty, but oppressed them without any just right so to do; they were perfectly justifiable in leaving Kendall Major Lewis, and all his sympathizers, to take care of themselves as best they could.

No very serious charges were made against Lewis, but on the contrary they said, that he had been looked upon as a " moderate slave-holder ;" they also said, that " he had been a member of the Methodist Episcopal Church for fifty years, and stood high in that body." Furthermore they stated, that he sold slaves occasionally. Eight had been sold by him some time before this party escaped (two of them to Georgia); besides William James had been sold and barely found opportunity to escape. Wm. James, Major Lewis, Dennis Betts, Peter, and Lazarus, with the wife and child of the former, not only found themselves stripped from day to day of their hard earnings, but fearful forebodings of the auction-block were ever uppermost in their minds. While they spoke of Lewis as " moderate," etc., they all said that he allowed no privileges to his slaves.

RICHARD WILLIAMS gave a full account of himself, but only a meagre report was recorded. He said that he came from Richmond, and left because he was on the point of being sold by John A. Smith, who owned him. He gave Smith credit for being a tolerable fair kind of a slave-holder, but added, that " his wife was a notoriously hard woman ;" she had made a very deep impression on Richard's mind by her treatment of him. In finding himself on free ground, however, with cheering prospects ahead, he did not stop to brood over the ills that he had suffered, but rejoiced heartily. He left his wife, Julia, who was free.

SYDNEY HOPKINS and HENRY WHEELER. These young men made their way out of Slavery together. While Sydney lives he will forever regard Jacob Hoag, of Havre-de-Grace, as the person who cheated him out of himself, and prevented him from becoming enlightened and educated.

HENRY, his companion, was also from Havre De Grace. He had had trouble with a man by the name of Amos Barnes, or in other words Barnes claimed to own him, just as he owned a horse or a mule, and daily controlled him in about the same manner that he would manage the animals above alluded to. Henry could find no justification for such treatment. He suffered greatly under the said Barnes, and finally his eyes were open to see that there was an Underground Rail Road for the benefit of all such slavery-sick souls as himself. So he got a ticket as soon as possible, and came through without accident, leaving Amos Barnes to do the best he could for a living. This candidate for Canada was twenty-one years of age, and a likely-looking boy.

JOSEPH HENRY HILL. The spirit of freedom in this passenger was truly the "one idea" notion. At the age of twenty-eight his purpose to free himself by escaping on the Underground Rail Road was successfully carried into effect, although not without difficulty. Joseph was a fair specimen of a man physically and mentally, could read and write, and thereby keep the run of matters of interest on the Slavery question.

James Thomas, Jr., a tobacco merchant, in Richmond, had Joe down in his ledger as a marketable piece of property, or a handy machine to save labor, and make money. To Joe's great joy he heard the sound of the Underground Rail Road bell in Richmond,—had a satisfactory interview with the conductor,—received a favorable response, and was soon a traveler on his way to Canada. He left his mother, a free woman, and two sisters in chains. He had been sold twice, but he never meant to be sold again.

ARRIVAL FROM RICHMOND, 1859.

CORNELIUS HENRY JOHNSON. FACE CANADA-WARD FOR YEARS.

Quite an agreeable interview took place between Cornelius and the Committee. He gave his experience of Slavery pretty fully, and the Committee enlightened him as to the workings of the Underground Rail Road, the value of freedom, and the safety of Canada as a refuge.

Cornelius was a single man, thirty-six years of age, full black, medium size, and intelligent. He stated that he had had his face set toward Canada for a long-while. Three times he had made an effort to get out of the prison-house. "Within the last four or five years, times have gone pretty hard with me. My mistress, Mrs. Mary F. Price, had lately put me in charge of her brother, Samuel M. Bailey, a tobacco merchant of Richmond. Both believed in nothing as they did in Slavery; they would sooner see a black man dead than free. They were about second class in society. He and his sister own well on to one hundred head, though within the last few years he has been thinning off the number by sale. I was allowed one dollar a week for my board; one dollar is the usual allowance for slaves in my situation. On Christmas week he allowed me no board money, but made me a present of seventy-five cents; my mistress added twenty-five cents, which was the extent of their liberality. I was well cared for. When the slaves got sick he doctored them himself, he was too stingy to employ a physician. If they did not get well as soon as he thought they should, he would order them to their work, and if they did not go he would beat them. My cousin was badly beat last year in the presence of his wife, and he was right sick. Mr. Bailey was a member of St. James' church, on Fifth street, and my mistress was a communicant of the First Baptist church on Broad Street. She let on to be very good."

"I am one of a family of sixteen; my mother and eleven sisters and brothers are now living; some have been sold to Alabama, and some to Tennessee, the rest are held in Richmond. My mother is now old, but is still in the service of Bailey. He promised to take care of her in her old age, and not compel her to labor, so she is only required to cook and wash for a dozen slaves. This they consider a great favor to the old 'grand-mother.' It was only a year ago he cursed her and threatened her with a flogging. I left for nothing else but because I was dissatisfied with Slavery. The threats of my master caused me to reflect on the North and South. I had an idea that I was not to die in Slavery. I believed that God would assist me if I would try. I then made up my mind to put my case in the hands of God, and start for the Underground Rail Road. I bade good-bye to the old tobacco factory on Seventh street, and the First African Baptist church on Broad street (where he belonged), where I had so often heard the minister preach 'servants obey your masters;' also to the slave pens, chain-gangs, and a cruel master and mistress, all of which I hoped to leave forever. But to bid good-bye to my old mother in chains, was no easy job, and if my desire for freedom had not been as strong as my desire for life itself, I could never have stood it; but I felt that I could do her no good; could not help her if I staid. As I was often threatened by my master, with the auction-block, I felt I must give up all and escape for my life."

Such was substantially the story of Cornelius Henry Johnson. He talked for an hour as one inspired, and as none but fugitive slaves could talk.

ARRIVAL FROM DELAWARE, 1858.

THEOPHILUS COLLINS, ANDREW JACKSON BOYCE, HANDY BURTON AND ROBERT JACKSON.

A DESPERATE, BLOODY STRUGGLE—GUN, KNIFE AND FIRE SHOVEL, USED BY AN INFURIATED MASTER.

Judged from their outward appearance, as well as from the fact that they were from the neighboring State of Delaware, no extraordinary revelations were looked for from the above-named party. It was found, however, that one of their number, at least, had a sad tale of outrage and cruelty to relate. The facts stated are as follows :

THEOPHILUS is twenty-four years of age, dark, height and stature hardly medium, with faculties only about average compared with ordinary fugitives from Delaware and Maryland. His appearance is in no way remarkable. His bearing is subdued and modest; yet he is not lacking in earnestness. Says Theophilus, " I was in servitude under a man named Houston, near Lewes, Delaware; he was a very mean man, he didn't allow you enough to eat, nor enough clothes to wear. He never allowed a drop of tea, or coffee, or sugar, and if you didn't eat your breakfast before day he wouldn't allow you any, but would drive you out without any. He had a wife ; she was mean, too, meaner than he was. Four years ago last Fall my master cut my entrails out for going to meeting at Daniel Wesley's church one Sabbath night. Before day, Monday morning, he called me up to whip me; called me into his dining-room, locked the doors, then ordered me to pull off my shirt. I told him no, sir, I wouldn't; right away he went and got the cowhide, and gave me about twenty over my head with the butt. He tore my shirt off, after I would not pull it off; he

ordered me to cross my hands. I didn't do that. After I wouldn't do that he went and got his gun and broke the breech of that over my head. He then seized up the fire-tongs and struck me over the head ever so often. The next thing he took was the parlor shovel and he beat on me with that till he broke the handle; then he took the blade and stove it at my head with all his might. I told him that I was bound to come out of that room. He run up to the door and drawed his knife and told me if I ventured to the door he would stab me. I never made it any better or worse, but aimed straight for the door; but before I reached it he stabbed me, drawing the knife (a common pocket knife) as hard as he could rip across my stomach; right away he began stabbing me about my head," (marks were plainly to be seen). After a desperate struggle, Theophilus succeeded in getting out of the building.

"I started," said he, "at once for Georgetown, carrying a part of my entrails in my hands for the whole journey, sixteen miles. I went to my young masters, and they took me to an old colored woman, called Judah Smith, and for five days and nights I was under treatment of Dr. Henry Moore, Dr. Charles Henry Richards, and Dr. William Newall; all these attended me. I was not expected to live for a long time, but the Doctors cured me at last."

ANDREW reported that he fled from Dr. David Houston. "I left because of my master's meanness to me; he was a very mean man to his servants," said Andrew, "and I got so tired of him I couldn't stand him any longer." Andrew was about twenty-six years of age, ordinary size; color, brown, and was entitled to his freedom, but knew not how to secure it by law, so resorted to the Underground Rail Road method.

HANDY, another of this party, said that he left because the man who claimed to be his master "was so hard." The man by whom he had been wronged was known where he came from by the name of Shepherd Burton, and was in the farming business. "He was a churchman," said Handy, "but he never allowed me to go to church a half dozen times in my life."

ROBERT belonged to Mrs. Mary Hickman, at least she had him in her possession and reaped the benefit of his hire and enjoyed the leisure and ease thereof while he toiled. For some time prior to his leaving, this had been a thorn in his side, hard to bear; so when an opening presented itself by which he thought he could better his condition, he was ready to try the experiment. He, however, felt that, while she would not have him to look to for support, she would not be without sympathy, as she was a member of the Episcopal Church; besides she was an old-looking woman and might not need his help a great while longer.

ARRIVAL FROM RICHMOND, 1859.

STEPNEY BROWN.

Stepney was an extraordinary man, his countenance indicating great goodness of heart, and his gratitude to his heavenly Father for his deliverance proved that he was fully aware of the Source whence his help had come. Being a man of excellent natural gifts, as well as of religious fervor and devotion to a remarkable degree, he seemed admirably fitted to represent the slave in chains, looking up to God with an eye of faith, and again the fugitive in Canada triumphant and rejoicing with joy unspeakable over his deliverance, yet not forgetting those in bonds, as bound with them. The beauty of an unshaken faith in the good Father above could scarcely have shone with a brighter lustre than was seen in this simple-hearted believer.

STEPNEY was thirty-four years of age, tall, slender, and of a dark hue. He readily confessed that he fled from Mrs. Julia A. Mitchell, of Richmond; and testified that she was decidedly stingy and unkind, although a member of St. Paul's church. Still he was wholly free from acrimony, and even in recounting his sufferings was filled with charity towards his oppressors. He said, "I was moved to leave because I believed that I had a right to be a free man."

He was a member of the Second Baptist church, and entertained strong faith that certain infirmities, which had followed him through life up to within seven years of the time of his escape, had all been removed through the Spirit of the Lord. He had been an eye-witness to many outrages inflicted on his fellow-men. But he spoke more of the sufferings of others than his own.

His stay was brief, but interesting. After his arrival in Canada he turned his attention to industrial pursuits, and cherished his loved idea that the Lord was very good to him. Occasionally he would write to express his gratitude to God and man, and to inquire about friends in different localities, especially those in bonds.

The following letters are specimens, and speak for themselves:

CLIFTON HOUSE, NIAGARA FALLS, August the 27.

DEAR BROTHER :—It is with pleasure i take my pen in hand to write a few lines to inform you that i am well hopeing these few lines may fine you the same i am longing to hear from you and your family i wish you would say to Julis Anderson that he must realy excuse me for not writing but i am in hopes that he is doing well. i have not heard no news from Virgina. plese to send me all the news say to Mrs. Hunt an you also forever pray for me knowing that God is so good to us. i have not seen brother John Dungy for 5 months, but we have corresponded together but he is doing well in Brandford. i am now at the falls an have been on here some time an i shall with the help of the lord locate myself somewhere this winter an go to school excuse me for not annser your letter sooner

32

knowing that i cannot write well you please to send me one of the earliest papers send me word if any of our friends have been passing through i know that you are very busy but ask your little daughter if she will annser this letter for you i often feel that i cannot turn god thanks enough for his blessings that he has bestoueth upon me. Say to brother suel that he must not forget what god has consighn to his hand, to do that he must pray in his closet that god might teach him. say to mr. Anderson that i hope he have retrad an has seeked the lord an found him precious to his own soul for he must do it in this world for he cannot do it in the world to come. i often think about the morning that i left your house it was such a sad feeling but still i have a hope in crist do you think it is safe in boston my love to all i remain your brother, STEPNEY BROWN.

BRANTFORD, March 3d, 1860.

MR. WILLIAM STILL, DEAR SIR :—I now take the pleasure of writing to you a few lines write soon hoping to find you enjoying perfect health, as I am the same.

My joy within is so great that I cannot find words to express it. When I met with my friend brother Dungy who stopped at your house on his way to Canada after having a long chase after me from Toronto to Hamilton he at last found me in the town of Brant-ford Canada West and ought we not to return Almighty God thanks for delivering us from the many dangers and trials that beset our path in this wicked world we live in.

I have long been wanting to write to you but I entirely forgot the number of your house Mr. Dungy luckily happened to have your directions with him.

Religion is good when we live right may God help you to pray often to him that he might receive you at the hour of your final departure. Yours most respectfully.

STEPNEY BROWN, per Jas. A. Walk.

P. S. Write as soon as possible for I wish very much to hear from you. I understand that Mrs, Hunt has been to Richmond, Va. be so kind as to ask her if she heard anything about that money. Give my love to all inquiring friends and to your family especially. I now thank God that I have not lost a day in sickness since I came to Canada.

Kiss the baby for me. I know you are busy but I hope you will have time to write a few lines to me to let me know how you and your family are getting on. No more at present, but I am yours very truly, STEPNEY BROWN, per Jas. A. Walkinshaw.

BRANTFORD, Oct. 25, '60

DEAR SIR :—I take the pleasure of dropping you a few lines, I am yet residing in Brantford and I have been to work all this summer at the falls and I have got along re-markably well, surely God is good to those that put their trust in him I suppose you have been wondering what has become of me but I am in the lands of living and long to hear from you and your family. I would have wrote sooner, but the times has been such in the states I have not but little news to send you and I'm going to school again this winter and will you be pleased to send me word what has become of Julius Anderson and the rest of my friends and tell him I would write to him if I knew where to direct the letter, please send me word whether any body has been along lately that knows me. I know that you are busy but you must take time and answer this letter as I am anxious to hear from you, but nevertheless we must not forget our maker, so we cannot pray too much to our lord so I hope that mr. Anderson has found peace with God for me myself really appreciate that hope that I have in Christ, for I often find myself in my slumber with you and I hope we will meet some day. Mr. Dungy sends his love to you I suppose you are aware that he is married, he is luckier than I am or I must get a little foothold before I do marry if I ever do. I am in a very comfortable room all fixed for the winter and we have had one snow. May the lord be with you and all you and all your house-hold. I remain forever your brother in Christ, STEPNEY BROWN.

ARRIVAL FROM MARYLAND, 1859.

JIM KELL, CHARLES HEATH, WILLIAM CARLISLE, CHARLES RINGGOLD, THOMAS
MAXWELL, AND SAMUEL SMITH.

On the evening of the Fourth of July, while all was hilarity and rejoicing the above named very interesting fugitives arrived from the troubled district, the Eastern shore of Maryland, where so many conventions had been held the previous year to prevent escapes; where the Rev. Samuel Green had been convicted and sent to the penitentiary for ten years for having a copy of Uncle Tom's Cabin in his humble home; where so many parties, on escaping, had the good sense and courage to secure their flight by bringing their masters' horses and carriages a good way on their perilous journey.

SAM had been tied up and beat many times severely. WILLIAM had been stripped naked, and frequently and cruelly cowhided. THOMAS had been clubbed over his head more times than a few. JIM had been whipped with clubs and switches times without number. Charles had had five men on him at one time, with cowhides, his master in the lead.

CHARLES HEATH had had his head cut shockingly, with a club, in the hands of his master; this well cared-for individual in referring to his kind master, said: " I can give his character right along, he was a perfect devil. The night we left, he had a woman tied up—God knows what he done. He was always blustering, you could never do enough for him no how. First thing in the morning and last thing at night, you would hear him cussing—he would cuss in bed. He was a large farmer, all the time drunk. He had a good deal of money but not much character. He was a savage, bluff, red face-looking concern." Thus, in the most earnest, as well as in an intelligent manner, Charles described the man (Aquila Cain), who had hitherto held him under the yoke.

JAMES left his mother, Nancy Kell, two brothers, Robert and Henry, and two sisters, Mary and Annie; all living in the neighborhood whence he fled. Besides these, he had eight brothers and sisters living in Baltimore and elsewhere, under the yoke. He was twenty-four years of age, of a jet color, but of a manly turn. He fled from Thomas Murphy, a farmer, and regular slave-holder. Charles Heath was twenty-five years of age, medium size, full black, a very keen-looking individual.

WILLIAM was also of unmixed blood, shrewd and wide-awake for his years,—had been ground down under the heel of Aquila Cain. He left his mother and two sisters.

CHARLES RINGGOLD was eighteen years of age; no white blood showed itself in the least in this individual. He fled from Dr. Jacob Preston, a member of the Episcopal Church, and a practical farmer with twenty head of slaves. "He was not so bad, but his wife was said to be a 'stinger.'" Charles left his mother and father behind, also four sisters.

THOMAS was of pure blood, with a very cheerful, healthy-looking countenance,—twenty-one years of age, and was to "come free" at twenty-five, but he had too much good sense to rely upon the promises of slave-holders in matters of this kind. He too belonged to Cain who, he said, was constantly talking about selling, etc. He left his father and mother.

After being furnished with food, clothing, and free tickets, they were forwarded on in triumph and full of hope.

SUNDRY ARRIVALS, 1859.

JOHN EDWARD LEE, JOHN HILLIS, CHARLES ROSS, JAMES RYAN, WILLIAM JOHNSTON, EDWARD WOOD, CORNELIUS FULLER AND HIS WIFE HARRIET, JOHN PINKET, ANSAL CANNON, AND JAMES BROWN.

JOHN came from Maryland, and brought with him a good degree of pluck. He satisfied the Committee that he fully believed in freedom, and had proved his faith by his works, as he came in contact with pursuers, whom he put to flight by the use of an ugly-looking knife, which he plunged into one of them, producing quite a panic; the result was that he was left to pursue his Underground Rail Road journey without further molestation. There was nothing in John's appearance which would lead one to suppose that he was a blood-thirsty or bad man, although a man of uncommon muscular powers; six feet high, and quite black, with resolution stamped on his countenance. But when he explained how he was enslaved by a man named John B. Slade, of Harford Co., and how, in some way or other, he became entitled to his freedom, and just as the time arrived for the consummation of his long prayed-for boon, said Slade was about to sell him,—after this provocation, it was clear enough to perceive how John came to use his knife.

JOHN HILLIS was a tiller of the ground under a widow lady (Mrs. Louisa Le Count), of the New Market District, Maryland. He signified to the mistress, that he loved to follow the water, and that he would be just as safe on water as on land, and that he was discontented. The widow heard John's plausible story, and saw nothing amiss in it, so she consented that he should work on a schooner. The name of the craft was "Majestic." The hopeful John endeavored to do his utmost to please, and was doubly happy when he learned that the "Majestic" was to make a trip to Philadelphia. On arriving John's eyes were opened to see that he owed Mrs. Le Count nothing, but that she was largely indebted to him for years of unrequited toil; he could not, therefore, consent to go back to her. He was troubled to think of his poor wife and children, whom he had left in the hands of Mrs. Harriet Dean, three quarters of a mile from New Market; but it was easier for him to imagine plans by which he could get them off than to incur the hazard of going back to Maryland; therefore he remained in freedom.

CHARLES ROSS was clearly of the opinion that he was free-born, but that he had been illegally held in Slavery, as were all his brothers and sisters, by a man named Rodgers, a farmer, living near Greensborough, in Caroline county, Md. Very good reasons were given by Charles for the charge which he made against Rodgers, and it went far towards establishing the fact, that "colored men had no rights which white men were bound to respect," in Maryland. Although he was only twenty-three years of age, he had fully weighed the matter of his freedom, and appeared firmly set against Slavery.

WILLIAM JOHNSON was owned by a man named John Bosley, a farmer, living near Gun Powder Neck, Maryland. One morning he, unexpectedly to William, gave him a terrible cowhiding, which, contrary to the master's designs, made him a firm believer in the doctrine of immediate abolition, and he thought, that from that hour he must do something against the system—if nothing more than to go to Canada. This determination was so strong, that in a few weeks afterwards he found himself on the Underground Rail Road. He left one brother and one sister; his mother was dead, and of his father's whereabouts he knew nothing. William was nineteen years of age, brown color, smart and good-looking.

EDWARD WOOD was a "chattel" from Drummerstown, Accomac county, Virginia, where he had been owned by a farmer, calling himself James White; a man who "drank hard and was very crabbed," and before Edward left owned eleven head of slaves. Edward left a wife and three children, but the strong desire to be free, which had been a ruling passion of his being from early boyhood, rendered it impossible for him to stay, although the ties were very hard to break. Slavery was crushing him hourly, and he felt that he could not submit any longer.

CORNELIUS FULLER, and his wife, HARRIET, escaped together from Kent county, Maryland. They belonged to separate masters; Cornelius, it was said, belonged to the Diden Estate; his wife to Judge Chambers, whose Honor lived in Chestertown. "He is no man for freedom, bless you," said Harriet. "He owned more slaves than any other man in that part of the country; he sells sometimes, and he hired out a great many; would hire them to any kind of a master, if he half killed you." Cornelius and Harriet were obliged to leave their daughter Kitty, who was thirteen years of age.

JOHN PINKET and Ansal Cannon took the Underground Rail Road cars at New Market, Dorchester county, Maryland.

JOHN was a tall young man, of twenty-seven years of age, of an active turn of mind and of a fine black color. He was the property of Mary Brown, a widow, firmly grounded in the love of Slavery; believing that a slave had no business to get tired or desire his freedom. She sold one of John's sisters to Georgia, and before John fled, had still in her possession nine head of slaves. She was a member of the Methodist church at East New Market. From certain movements which looked very suspicious in John's eyes, he had been allotted to the Southern Market, he therefore resolved to look out for a habitation in Canada. He had a first-rate corn-field education, but no book learning. Up to the time of his escape, John had shunned entangling himself with a wife.

ANSAL was twenty-five years of age, well-colored, and seemed like a good-natured and well-behaved article. He escaped from Kitty Cannon, another widow, who owned nine chattels. "Sometimes she treated her slaves pretty well," was the testimony of Ansal. He ran away because he did not get pay for his services. In thus being deprived of his hire, he concluded that he had no business to stay if he could get away.

ARRIVAL FROM MARYLAND, 1859.

JAMES BROWN.

A more giant-like looking passenger than the above named individual had rarely ever passed over the road. He was six feet three inches high, and in every respect, a man of bone, sinew and muscle. For one who had enjoyed only a field hand's privileges for improvement, he was not to be despised.

JIM owed service to Henry Jones; at least he admitted that said Jones claimed him, and had hired him out to himself for seven dollars per month. While this amount seemed light, it was much heavier than Jim felt willing to meet solely for his master's benefit. After giving some heed to the voice of freedom within, he considered that it behooved him to try and make his way to some place where men were not guilty of wronging their neighbors out of their just hire. Having heard of the Underground Rail Road running to Canada, he concluded to take a trip and see the country, for himself; so he arranged his affairs with this end in view, and left Henry Jones with one less to work for him for nothing. The place that he fled from was called North Point, Baltimore county. The number of fellow-slaves left in the hands of his old master, was fifteen.

ARRIVAL FROM DELAWARE, 1859.

EDWARD, JOHN, AND CHARLES HALL.

The above named individuals were brothers from Delaware. They were young; the eldest being about twenty, the youngest not far from seventeen years of age.

EDWARD was serving on a farm, under a man named Booth. Perceiving that Booth was "running through his property" very fast by hard drinking, Edward's better judgment admonished him that his so-called master would one day have need of more rum money, and that he might not be too good to offer him in the market for what he would bring. Charles resolved that when his brothers crossed the line dividing Delaware and Pennsylvania, he would not be far behind.

The mother of these boys was freed at the age of twenty-eight, and lived in Wilmington, Delaware. It was owing to the fact that their mother had been freed that they entertained the vague notion that they too might be freed; but it was a well established fact that thousands lived and died in such a hope without ever realizing their expectations. The boys, more shrewd and wide awake than many others, did not hearken to such "stuff." The two younger heard the views of the elder brother, and expressed a willingness to follow him. Edward, becoming satisfied that what they meant to do must be done quickly, took the lead, and off they started for a free State.

JOHN was owned by one James B. Rodgers, a farmer, and "a most every kind of man," as John expressed himself; in fact John thought that his owner was such a strange, wicked, and cross character that he couldn't tell himself what he was. Seeing that slaves were treated no better than dogs and hogs, John thought that he was none too young to be taking steps to get away.

CHARLES was held by James Rodgers, Sr., under whom he said that he had served nine years with faint prospects of some time becoming free, but when, was doubtful.

ARRIVAL FROM VIRGINIA, 1859.

JAMES TAYLOR, ALBERT GROSS, AND JOHN GRINAGE.

To see mere lads, not twenty-one years of age, smart enough to outwit the very shrewdest and wisest slave-holders of Virginia was very gratifying. The young men composing this arrival were of this keen-sighted order.

JAMES was only a little turned of twenty, of a yellow complexion, and intelligent. A trader, by the name of George Ailer, professed to own James. He said that he had been used tolerable well, not so bad as many had been used. James was learning the carpenter trade; but he was anxious to obtain his freedom, and finding his two companions true on the main question, in conjunction with them he contrived a plan of escape, and 'took out.' His father and mother, Harrison and Jane Taylor, were left at Fredericksburg to mourn the absence of their son.

ALBERT was in his twentieth year, the picture of good health, not homely by any means, although not of a fashionable color. He was under the patriarchal protection of a man by the name of William Price, who carried on farming in Cecil county, Maryland. Albert testified that he was a bad man.

JOHN GRINAGE was only twenty, a sprightly, active young man, of a brown color. He came from Middle Neck, Cecil county, where he had served under William Flintham, a farmer.

SUNDRY ARRIVALS FROM MARYLAND (1859)

AND OTHER PLACES.

JAMES ANDY WILKINS, and wife LUCINDA, with their little boy, CHARLES, CHARLES HENRY GROSS, A WOMAN with her TWO CHILDREN—one in her arms—JOHN BROWN, JOHN ROACH, and wife LAMBY, and HENRY SMALLWOOD.

The above-named passengers did not all come from the same place, or exactly at the same time; but for the sake of convenience they are thus embraced under a general head.

JAMES ANDY WILKINS "gave the slip" to a farmer, by the name of George Biddle, who lived one mile from Cecil, Cecil county, Maryland. While he hated Slavery, he took a favorable view of his master in some respects at least, as he said that he was a "moderate man in talk;" but "sly in action." His master provided him with two pairs of pantaloons in the summer, and one in the winter, also a winter jacket, no vest, no cap, or hat. James thought the sum total for the entire year's clothing would not amount to more than ten dollars. Sunday clothing he was compelled to procure for himself by working of nights; he made axe handles, mats, etc., of evenings, and caught musk rats on Sunday, and availed himself of their hides to procure means for his most pressing wants. Besides these liberal privileges his master was in the habit of allowing him two whole days every harvest, and at Christmas from twenty-five cents to as high as three dollars and fifty cents, were lavished upon him.

His master was a bachelor, a man of considerable means, and "kept tolerable good company," and only owned two other slaves, Rachel Ann Dumbson and John Price.

LUCINDA, the companion of James, was twenty-one years of age, good-looking, well-formed and of a brown color. She spoke of a man named George Ford as her owner. He, however, was said to be of the "moderate class" of slave-holders; Lucinda being the only slave property he possessed, and she came to him through his wife (who was a Methodist). The master was an outsider, so far as the Church was concerned. Once in a great while Lucinda was allowed to go to church, when she could be spared from her daily routine of cooking, washing, etc. Twice a week she was permitted the special favor of seeing her husband. These simple privations not being of a grave character, no serious fault was found with them ; yet Lucinda was not without a strong ground of complaint. Not long before escaping, she had been threatened with the auction-block ; this fate she felt bound to avert, if possible, and the way she aimed to do it was by escaping on the Underground Rail Road. Charley, a bright little fellow only three years of age, was " contented and happy " enough. Lucinda left her father, Moses Edgar Wright, and two brothers, both slaves. One belonged to " Francis Crookshanks," and the other to Capt. Jim Mitchell. Her mother, who was known by the name of Betsy Wright, escaped when she (Lucinda) was seven years of age. Of her whereabouts nothing further had ever been heard. Lucinda entertained strong hopes that she might find her in Canada.

CHARLES HENRY GROSS began life in Maryland, and was made to bear the heat and burden of the day in Baltimore, under Henry Slaughter, proprietor of the Ariel Steamer. Owing to hard treatment, Charles was induced to fly to Canada for refuge.

A woman with two children, one in her arms, and the other two years of age (names, etc., not recorded), came from the District of Columbia. Mother and children, appealed loudly for sympathy.

JOHN BROWN, being at the beck of a man filling the situation of a common clerk (in the shoe store of McGrunders), became dissatisfied. Asking himself what right Benjamin Thorn (his professed master) had to his hire, he was led to see the injustice of his master, and made up his mind, that he would leave by the first train, if he could get a genuine ticket *via* the Underground Rail Road. He found an agent and soon had matters all fixed. He left his father, mother and seven sisters and one brother, all slaves. John was a man small of stature, dark, with homely features, but he was very determined to get away from oppression.

JOHN and LAMBY ROACH had been eating bitter bread under bondage near Seaford. John was the so-called property of Joshua O'Bear, "a fractious, hard-swearing man, and when mad would hit one of his slaves with anything he could get in his hands." John and his companion made the long journey on foot. The former had been trained to farm labor and the common drudgery of slave life. Being a man of thirty-three years of age, with more than ordinary abilities, he had given the matter of his bondage considerable thought, and seeing that his master "got worse the older he got," together with the fact, that his wife had recently been sold, he was strongly stirred to make an effort for Canada. While it was a fact, that his wife had already been sold, as above stated, the change of ownership was not to take place for some months, consequently John "took out in a hurry."

His wife was the property of Dr. Shipley, of Seaford, who had occasion to raise some money for which he gave security in the shape of this wife and mother. Horsey was the name of the gentleman from whom it was said that he obtained the favor; so when the time was up for the payment to be made, the Dr. was not prepared. Horsey, therefore, claimed the collateral (the wife) and thus she had to meet the issue, or make a timely escape to Canada with her husband. No way but walking was open to them. Deciding to come this way, they prosecuted their journey with uncommon perseverance and success. Both were comforted by strong faith in God, and believed that He would enable them to hold out on the road until they should reach friends.

HENRY SMALLWOOD saw that he was working every day for nothing, and thought that he would do better. He described his master (Washington Bonafont) as a sort of a rowdy, who drank pretty hard, leaving a very unfavorable impression on Henry's mind, as he felt almost sure such conduct would lead to a sale at no distant day. So he was cautious enough to "take the hint in time." Henry left in company with nine others; but after being two days on the journey they were routed and separated by their pursuers. At this point Henry lost all trace of the rest. He heard afterwards that two of them had been captured, but received no further tidings of the others. Henry was a fine representative for Canada; a tall, dark, and manly-looking individual, thirty-six years of age. He left his father and mother behind.

ARRIVAL FROM RICHMOND, 1859.

HENRY JONES AND TURNER FOSTER.

HENRY was left free by the will of his mistress (Elizabeth Mann), but the heirs were making desperate efforts to overturn this instrument. Of this, there was so much danger with a Richmond court, that Henry feared that the chances were against him; that the court was not honest enough to do him justice. Being a man of marked native foresight, he concluded that the less he talked about freedom and the more he acted the sooner he would be out of his difficulties. He was called upon, however, to settle certain minor matters, before he could see his way clear to move in the direction of Canada; for instance, he had a wife on his mind to dispose of in some way, but how he could not tell. Again, he was not in the secret of the Underground Rail Road movement; he knew that many got off, but how they managed it he was ignorant. If he could settle these two points satisfactorily, he thought that he would be willing to endure any sacrifice for the sake of his freedom. He found an agent of the Underground Rail Road, and after surmounting various difficulties, this point was settled. As good luck would have it, his wife, who was a free woman, although she heard the secret with great sorrow, had the good sense to regard his step for the best, and thus he was free to contend with all other dangers on the way.

He encountered the usual suffering, and on his arrival experienced the wonted pleasure. He was a man of forty-one years of age, spare made, with straight hair, and Indian complexion, with the Indian's aversion to Slavery.

TURNER, who was a fellow-passenger with Henry, arrived also from Richmond. He was about twenty-one, a bright, smart, prepossessing young man. He fled from A. A. Mosen, a lawyer, represented to be one of the first in the city, and a firm believer in Slavery. Turner differed widely with his master with reference to this question, although, for prudential reasons, he chose not to give his opinion to said Mosen.

ARRIVAL FROM MARYLAND.

TWO YOUNG MOTHERS, EACH WITH BABES IN THEIR ARMS—ANNA ELIZABETH YOUNG AND SARAH JANE BELL—WHIPPED TILL THE BLOOD FLOWED.

The appearance of these young mothers at first produced a sudden degree of pleasure, but their story of suffering quite as suddenly caused the most painful reflections. It was hardly possible to listen to their tales of outrage and wrong with composure. Both came from Kent county, Maryland, and reported that they fled from a man by the name of Massey; a man of low stature, light-complexioned, with dark hair, dark eyes, and very quick temper; given to hard swearing as a common practice; also, that the said Massey had a wife, who was a very tall woman, with blue eyes, chestnut-colored hair, and a very bad temper; that, conjointly, Massey and his wife were in the habit of meting out cruel punishment to their slaves, without regard to age or sex, and that they themselves, (Anna Elizabeth and Sarah Jane), had received repeated scourgings at the hands of their master. Anna and Sarah were respectively twenty-four and twenty-five years of age; Anna was of a dark chestnut color, while Sarah was two shades lighter; both had good manners, and a fair share of intelligence, which afforded a hopeful future for them in freedom. Each had a babe in her arms.

SARAH had been a married woman for three years; her child, a boy, was eight months old, and was named Garrett Bell. Elizabeth's child was a girl, nineteen months old, and named Sarah Catharine Young. Elizabeth had never been married. They had lived with Massey five years up to the last March prior to their escape, having been bought out of the Baltimore slave-pen, with the understanding that they were to be free at the expiration of five years' service under him. The five years had more than expired, but no hope or sign of freedom appeared. On the other hand, Massey was talking loudly of selling them again. Threats and fears were so horrifying to them, that they could not stand it; this was what prompted them to flee. "As often as six or seven times," said Elizabeth, "I have been whipped by master, once with the carriage whip, and at other times with a raw hide trace. The last flogging I received from him, was about four weeks before last Christmas; he then tied me up to a locust tree standing before the door, and whipped me to his satisfaction."

SARAH had fared no better than Elizabeth, according to her testimony. "Three times," said she, "I have been tied up; the last time was in planting corn-time, this year. My clothing was all stripped off above my waist, and then he whipped me till the blood ran down to my heels." Her back was lacerated all over. She had been ploughing with two horses, and unfortunately had lost a hook out of her plough; this, she declared was the head and front of her offending, nothing more. Thus, after all their suffering, utterly penniless, they reached the Committee, and were in every respect, in a situation to call for the deepest commiseration. They were helped and were thankful.

ARRIVAL FROM MARYLAND, VIRGINIA, AND THE DISTRICT OF COLUMBIA.

JOHN WESLEY SMITH, ROBERT MURRAY, SUSAN STEWART, AND JOSEPHINE SMITH.

Daniel Hubert was fattening on John Wesley's earnings contrary to his, John's, idea of right. For a long time John failed to see the remedy, but as he grew older and wiser the scales fell from his eyes and he perceived that the Underground Rail Road ran near his master's place, Cambridge, Md., and by a very little effort and a large degree of courage and perseverance he might manage to get out of Maryland and on to Canada, where slave-holders had no more rights than other people. These reflections came seriously into John's mind at about the age of twenty-six; being about this time threatened with the auction-block he bade slavery good-night, jumped into the Underground Rail Road car and off he hurried for Pennsylvania. His mother, Betsy, one brother, and one sister were left in the hands of Hubert. John Wesley could pray for them and wish them well, but nothing more.

ROBERT MURRAY became troubled in mind about his freedom while living in Loudon county, Virginia, under the heel of Eliza Brooks, a widow woman, who used him bad, according to his testimony. He had been

" knocked about a good deal." A short while before he fled, he stated that he had been beat brutally, so much so that the idea of escape was beat into him. He had never before felt as if he dared hope to try to get out of bondage, but since then his mind had undergone such a sudden and powerful change, he began to feel that nothing could hold him in Virginia; the place became hateful to him. He looked upon a slave-holder as a kind of a living, walking, talking "Satan, going about as a roaring lion seeking whom he may destroy." He left his wife, with one child; her name was Nancy Jane, and the name of the offspring was Elizabeth. As Robert had possessed but rare privileges to visit his wife, he felt it less a trial to leave than if it had been otherwise. William Seedam owned the wife and child.

SUSAN STEWART and JOSEPHINE SMITH fled together from the District of Columbia. Running away had been for a long time a favorite idea with Susan, as she had suffered much at the hands of different masters. The main cause of her flight was to keep from being sold again; for she had been recently threatened by Henry Harley, who "followed droving," and not being rich, at any time when he might be in want of money she felt that she might have to go. When a girl only twelve years of age, her young mind strongly revolted against being a slave, and at that youthful period she tried her fortune at running away. While she was never caught by her owners, she had the misfortune to fall into the hands of another slave-holder no better than her old master, indeed she thought that she found it even worse under him, so far as severe floggings were concerned. Susan was of a bright brown color, medium size, quick and active intellectually and physically, and although she had suffered much from Slavery, as she was not far advanced in years, she might still do something for herself. She left no near kin that she was aware of.

JOSEPHINE fled from Miss Anna Maria Warren, who had previously been deranged from the effects of paralysis. Josephine regarded this period of her mistress' sickness as her opportunity for planning to get away before her mistress came to her senses.

SUNDRY ARRIVALS FROM MARYLAND AND VIRGINIA.

HENRY FIELDS, CHARLES RINGGOLD, WILLIAM RINGGOLD, ISAAC NEWTON AND JOSEPH THOMAS.

["Five other cases were attended to by Dillwyn Parish and J. C. White"—other than this no note was made of them.]

HENRY FIELDS took the benefit of the Underground Rail Road at the age of eighteen. He fled from the neighborhood of Port Deposit while being "broke in" by a man named Washington Glasby, who was wicked enough to claim him as his property, and was also about to sell him. This chattel was of a light yellow complexion, hearty-looking and wide awake.

CHARLES RINGGOLD took offence at being whipped like a dog, and the prospect of being sold further South; consequently in a high state of mental dread of the peculiar institution, he concluded that freedom was worth suffering for, and although he was as yet under twenty years of age, he determined not to remain in Perrymanville, Maryland, to wear the chains of Slavery for the especial benefit of his slave-holding master (whose name was inadvertently omitted).

WILLIAM RINGGOLD fled from Henry Wallace, of Baltimore. A part of the time William said he "had had it pretty rough, and a part of the time kinder smooth," but never had had matters to his satisfaction. Just before deciding to make an adventure on the Underground Rail Road his owner had been talking of selling him. Under the apprehension that this threat would prove no joke, Henry began to study what he had better do to be saved from the jaws of hungry negro traders. It was not long before he came to the conclusion that he had best strike out upon a venture in a Northern direction, and do the best he could to get as far away as possible from the impending danger threatened by Mr. Wallace. After a long and weary travel on foot by night, he found himself at Columbia, where friends of the Underground Rail Road assisted him on to Philadelphia. Here his necessary wants were met, and directions given him how to reach the land of refuge, where he would be out of the way of all slave-holders and slave-traders. Six of his brothers had been sold; his mother was still in bondage in Baltimore.

ISAAC NEWTON hailed from Richmond, Virginia. He professed to be only thirty years of age, but he seemed to be much older. While he had had an easy time in slavery, he preferred that his master should work for himself, as he felt that it was his bounden duty to look after number one; so he did not hesitate about leaving his situation vacant for any one who might desire it, whether white or black, but made a successful "took out."

JOSEPH THOMAS was doing the work of a so-called master in Prince George's county, Maryland. For some cause or other the alarm of the auction-block was sounded in his ears, which at first distracted him greatly; upon sober reflection it worked greatly to his advantage. It set him to thinking seriously on the subject of immediate emancipation, and what a miserable hard lot of it he should have through life if he did not "pick up" courage and resolution to get beyond the terror of slave-holders; so under these reflections he found his nerves gathering strength, his fears leaving him, and he was ready to venture on the Underground Rail Road. He came through without any serious difficulty. He left his father and mother, Shadrach and Lucinda Thomas.

ARRIVAL FROM SEAFORD, 1859.

ROBERT BELL AND TWO OTHERS.

ROBERT came from Seaford, where he had served under Charles Wright, a farmer, of considerable means, and the owner of a number of slaves, over whom he was accustomed to rule with much rigor.

Although Robert's master had a wife and five children, the love which Robert bore them was too weak to hold him; and well adapted as the system of Slavery might be to render him happy in the service of young and old masters, it was insufficient for him. Robert found no rest under Mr. Wright; no privileges, scantily clad, poor food, and a heavy yoke, was the policy of this "superior." Robert testified, that for the last five years, matters had been growing worse and worse; that times had never been so bad before. Of nights, under the new regime, the slaves were locked up and not allowed to go anywhere; flogging, selling, etc., were of every-day occurrence throughout the neighborhood. Finally, Robert became sick of such treatment, and he found that the spirit of Canada and freedom was uppermost in his heart. Slavery grew blacker and blacker, until he re-solved to "pull up stakes" upon a venture. The motion was right, and succeeded.

Two other passengers were at the station at the same time, but they had to be forwarded without being otherwise noticed on the book.

ARRIVAL FROM TAPPS' NECK, MD., 1859.

LEWIS WILSON, JOHN WATERS, ALFRED EDWARDS, AND WILLIAM QUINN.

LEWIS' grey hairs signified that he had been for many years plodding under the yoke. He was about fifty years of age, well set, not tall, but he had about him the marks of a substantial laborer. He had been brought up on a farm under H. Lynch, whom Lewis described as "a mean man when drunk, and very severe on his slaves." The number that he ruled over as his property, was about twenty. Said Lewis, about two years ago, he shot a free man, and the man died about two hours afterwards; for this offence he was not even imprisoned. Lynch also tried to cut the throat of John Waters, and succeeded in making a frightful gash on his left shoulder (mark shown), which mark he will carry with him to the grave; for this he was not even sued. Lewis left five children in bondage, Horace, John, Georgiana, Louisa and Louis, Jr., owned by Bazil and John Benson.

JOHN was forty years of age, dark, medium size, and another of Lynch's "articles." He left his wife Anna, but no children; it was hard to leave her, but he felt that it would be still harder to live and die under the usage that he had experienced on Lynch's farm.

ALFRED was twenty-two years of age; he was of a full dark color, and quite smart. He fled from John Bryant, a farmer. Whether he deserved it or not, Alfred gave him a bad character, at least, with regard to the treatment of his slaves. He left his father and mother, six brothers and sisters. Traveling under doubts and fears with the thought of leaving a large family of his nearest and dearest friends, was far from being a pleasant undertaking with Alfred, yet he bore up under the trial and arrived in peace.

" WILLIAM is twenty-two, black, tall, intelligent, and active," are the words of the record.

ARRIVAL FROM MARYLAND, 1859.

ANN MARIA JACKSON AND HER SEVEN CHILDREN—MARY ANN, WILLIAM HENRY, FRANCES SABRINA, WILHELMINA, JOHN EDWIN, EBENEZER THOMAS, AND WILLIAM ALBERT.

The coming of the above named was duly announced by Thomas Garrett:

WILMINGTON, 11th mo., 21st, 1858.

DEAR FRIENDS—MCKIM AND STILL:—I write to inform you that on the 16th of this month, we passed on four able bodied men to Pennsylvania, and they were followed last night by a woman and her six children, from three or four years of age, up to sixteen years; I believe the whole belonged to the same estate, and they were to have been sold at public sale, I was informed yesterday, but preferred seeking their own master; we had some trouble in getting those last safe along, as they could not travel far on foot, and could not safely cross any of the bridges on the canal, either on foot or in carriage. A man left here two days since, with carriage, to meet them this side of the canal, but owing to spies they did not reach him till 10 o'clock last night; this morning he returned, having seen them about one or two o'clock this morning in a second carriage, on the border of Chester county, where I think they are all safe, if they can be kept from Philadelphia. If you see them they can tell their own tales, as I have seen one of them. May He, who feeds the ravens, care for them. Yours,

THOS. GARRETT.

The fire of freedom obviously burned with no ordinary fervor in the breast of this slave mother, or she never would have ventured with the burden of seven children, to escape from the hell of Slavery.

ANN MARIA was about forty years of age, good-looking, pleasant countenance, and of a chestnut color, height medium, and intellect above the average. Her bearing was humble, as might have been expected, from the fact that she emerged from the lowest depths of Delaware Slavery. During the Fall prior to her escape, she lost her husband under most trying circumstances: he died in the poor-house, a raving maniac. Two of his children had been taken from their mother by her owner, as was usual with slave-holders, which preyed so severely on the poor father's mind that it drove him into a state of hopeless insanity. He was a "free man" in the eye of Delaware laws, yet he was not allowed to exercise the least authority over his children.

Prior to the time that the two children were taken from their mother, she had been allowed to live with her husband and children, independently of her master, by supporting herself and them with the white-wash brush, wash-tub, etc. For this privilege the mother doubtless worked with double energy, and the master, in all probability, was largely the gainer, as the children were no expense to him in their infancy; but when they began to be old enough to hire out, or bring high prices in the market, he snatched away two of the finest articles, and the powerless father was immediately rendered a fit subject for the mad-house; but the brave hearted mother looked up to God, resolved to wait patiently until in a good Providence the way might open to escape with her remaining children to Canada.

Year in and year out she had suffered to provide food and raiment for her little ones. Many times in going out to do days' work she would be compelled to leave her children, not knowing whether during her absence they would fall victims to fire, or be carried off by the master. But she possessed a well tried faith, which in her flight kept her from despondency. Under her former lot she scarcely murmured, but declared that she had never been at ease in Slavery a day after the birth of her first-born. The desire to go to some part of the world where she could have the control and comfort of her children, had always been a prevailing idea with her. "It almost broke my heart," she said, "when he came and took my children away as soon as they were big enough to hand me a drink of water. My

33

husband was always very kind to me, and I had often wanted him to run away with me and the children, but I could not get him in the notion; he did not feel that he could, and so he stayed, and died broken-hearted, crazy. I was owned by a man named Joseph Brown; he owned property in Milford, and he had a place in Vicksburg, and some of his time he spends there, and some of the time he lives in Milford. This Fall he said he was going to take four of my oldest children and two other servants to Vicksburg. I just happened to hear of this news in time. My master was wanting to keep me in the dark about taking them, for fear that something might happen. My master is very sly; he is a tall, slim man, with a smooth face, bald head, light hair, long and sharp nose, swears very hard, and drinks. He is a widower, and is rich.

On the road the poor mother, with her travel-worn children became desperately alarmed, fearing that they were betrayed. But God had provided better things for her; her strength and hope were soon fully restored, and she was lucky enough to fall into the right hands. It was a special pleasure to aid such a mother. Her arrival in Canada was announced by Rev. H. Wilson as follows:

NIAGARA CITY, Nov. 30th, 1858.

DEAR BRO. STILL:—I am happy to inform you that Mrs. Jackson and her interesting family of seven children arrived safe and in good health and spirits at my house in St. Catharines, on Saturday evening last. With sincere pleasure I provided for them comfortable quarters till this morning, when they left for Toronto. I got them conveyed there at half fare, and gave them letters of introduction to Thomas Henning, Esq., and Mrs. Dr. Willis, trusting that they will be better cared for in Toronto than they could be at St. Catharines. We have so many coming to us we think it best for some of them to pass on to other places. My wife gave them all a good supply of clothing before they left us. James Henry, an older son is, I think, not far from St. Catharine, but has not as yet reunited with the family. Faithfully and truly yours, HIRAM WILSON.

SUNDRY ARRIVALS FROM VIRGINIA, MARYLAND AND DELAWARE.

LEWIS LEE, ENOCH DAVIS, JOHN BROWN, THOMAS EDWARD DIXON, AND WILLIAM OLIVER.

Slavery brought about many radical changes, some in one way and some in another. Lewis Lee was entirely too white for practical purposes. They tried to get him to content himself under the yoke, but he could not see the point. A man by the name of William Watkins, living near Fairfax, Virginia, claimed Lewis, having come by his title through marriage. Title or no title, Lewis thought that he would not serve him for nothing, and that he had been hoodwinked already a great while longer than he should have allowed himself to be. Watkins had managed to keep him in the dark and doing hard work on the no-pay system up to the age of twenty-five. In Lewis' opinion, it was now time to "strike out on his own hook;" he took his last look of Watkins (he was a tall, slim fellow, a farmer, and a hard drinker), and made the first step in the direction of the North. He was sure that he was about as white as anybody else, and that he had as good a right to pass for white as the white folks, so he decided to do so with a high head and a fearless front. Instead of skulking in the woods, in thickets and swamps, under cover of the darkness, he would boldly approach a hotel and call for accommodations, as any other southern gentleman. He had a little money, and he soon discovered that his color was perfectly orthodox. He said that he was "treated first-rate in Washington and Baltimore;" he could recommend both of these cities. But destitute of education, and coming among strangers, he was conscious that the shreds of slavery were still to be seen upon him. He had, moreover, no intention of disowning his origin when once he could feel safe in assuming his true status. So as he was in need of friends and material aid, he sought out the Vigilance Committee, and on close examination they had every reason to believe his story throughout, and gave him the usual benefit.

ENOCH DAVIS came from within five miles of Baltimore, having been held by one James Armstrong, "an old grey-headed man," and a farmer, living on Huxtown Road. Judged from Davis' stand-point, the old master could never be recommended, unless some one wanted a very hard place and a severe master. Upon inquiry, it was ascertained that Enoch was moved to leave on account of the "riot," (John Brown's Harper's Ferry raid), which he feared would result in the sale of a good many slaves, himself among the number; he, therefore, "laid down the shovel and the hoe," and quit the place.

JOHN BROWN (this was an adopted name, the original one not being preserved), left to get rid of his connection with Thomas Stevens, a grocer, living in Baltimore. John, however, did not live in the city with said Stevens, but on the farm near Frederick's Mills, Montgomery county, Maryland. This place was known by the name of "White Hall Farm;" and was under the supervision of James Edward Stevens, a son of the above-named Stevens. John's reasons for leaving were not noted on the book, but his eagerness to reach Canada spoke louder than words, signifying that the greater the distance that separated him from the old "White Hall Farm" the better.

THOMAS EDWARD DIXON arrived from near the Trap, in Delaware. He was only about eighteen years of age, but as tall as a man of ordinary height;—dark, with a pleasant countenance. He reported that he had had trouble with a man known by the name of Thomas W. M. McCracken, who had treated him "bad;" as Thomas thought that such trouble and bad treatment might be of frequent occurrence, he concluded that he had better go away and let McCracken get somebody else to fill his place, if he did not choose to fill it himself. So off Thomas started, and as if by instinct, he came direct to the Committee. He passed a good examination and was aided.

WILLIAM OLIVER, a dark, well-made, young man with the best of country manners, fled from Mrs. Marshall, a lady living in Prince George's county, Maryland. William had recently been in the habit of hiring his time at the rate of ten dollars per month, and find himself everything. The privilege of living in Georgetown had been vouchsafed him, and he preferred this locality to his country situation. Upon the whole he said he had been treated pretty well. He was, nevertheless, afraid that times were growing "very critical," and as he had a pretty good chance, he thought he had better make use of it, and his arrangements were wisely made. He had reached his twenty-sixth year, and was apparently well settled. He left one child, Jane Oliver, owned by Mrs. Marshall.

ARRIVAL FROM DIFFERENT POINTS.

JACOB BROWN, JAMES HARRIS, BENJAMIN PINEY, JOHN SMITH, ANDREW JACKSON, WILLIAM HUGHES, WESLEY WILLIAMS, ROSANNA JOHNSON, JOHN SMALLWOOD, AND HENRY TOWNSEND.

JACOB BROWN was eating the bread of Slavery in North Carolina. A name-sake of his by the name of Lewis Brown, living in Washington, according to the slave code of that city had Jacob in fetters, and was exercising about the same control over him that he exercised over cattle and horses. While this might have been a pleasure for the master, it was painful for the slave. The usage which Jacob had ordinarily received made him anything but contented.

At the age of twenty, he resolved that he would run away if it cost him his life. This purpose was made known to a captain, who was in the habit of bringing passengers from the South to Philadelphia. With an unwavering faith he took his appointed place in a private part of the vessel, and as fast as wind and tide would bring the boat he was wafted on his way Canada-ward. Jacob was a dark man, and about full size, with hope large.

JAMES HARRIS escaped from Delaware. A white woman, Catharine Odine by name, living near Middletown, claimed James as her man; but James did not care to work for her on the unrequited labor system. He resolved to take the first train on the Underground Rail Road that might pass that way. It was not a great while ere he was accommodated, and was brought safely to Philadelphia. The regular examination was made and he passed creditably. He was described in the book as a man of yellow complexion, good-looking, and intelligent. After due assistance, he was regularly forwarded on to Canada. This was in the month of November, 1856. Afterwards nothing more was heard of him, until the receipt of the following letter from Prof. L. D. Mansfield, showing that he had been reunited to his wife, under amusing, as well as touching circumstances:

AUBURN, Dec. 15th, '56.

DEAR BRO. STILL :—A very pleasant circumstance has brought you to mind, and I am always happy to be reminded of you, and of the very agreeable, though brief acquaintance which we made at Philadelphia two years since. Last Thursday evening, while at my weekly prayer meeting, our exercises were interrupted by the appearance of Bro. Loguen, of Syracuse, who had come on with Mrs. Harris in search of her husband, whom he had sent to my care three weeks before. I told Bro. L. that no such man had been at my house, and I knew nothing of him. But I dismissed the meeting, and went with him immediately to the African Church, where the colored brethren were holding a meeting. Bro. L. looked through the door, and the first person whom he saw was Harris. He was called out, when Loguen said, in a rather reproving and excited tone, "What are you doing here; didn't I tell you to be off to Canada? Don't you know they are after you? Come get your hat, and come with us, we'll take care of you." The poor fellow was by this time thoroughly frightened, and really thought he had been pursued. We conducted him nearly a mile, to the hotel where his wife was waiting for him, leaving him still under the impression that he was pursued and that we were conducting him to a place of safety, or were going to box him up to send him to Canada. Bro. L. opened the door of the parlor, and introduced him; but he was so frightened that he did not know his wife at first, until she called him James, when they had a very joyful meeting. She is now a servant in my family, and he has work, and doing well, and boards with her. We shall do all we can for them, and teach them to read and write, and endeavor to place them in a condition to take care of themselves. Loguen had a fine meeting in my Tabernacle last night, and made a good collection for the cause of the fugitives.

I should be happy to hear from you and your kind family, to whom remember me very cordially. Believe me ever truly yours, L. D. MANSFIELD.

Mr. and Mrs. Harris wish to be gratefully remembered to you and yours.

BENJAMIN PINEY reported that he came from Baltimore county, Maryland, where he had been held in subjection to Mary Hawkins. He alleged that he had very serious cause for grievance; that she had ill-treated him for a long time, and had of late, threatened to sell him to Georgia. His brothers and sisters had all been sold, but he meant not to be if he could help himself. The sufferings that he had been called upon to endure had opened his eyes, and he stood still to wait for the Underground Rail Road car, as he anxiously wished to travel north, with all possible speed. He waited but a little while, ere he was on the road, under difficulties it is true, but he arrived safely and was joyfully received. He imagined his mistress in a fit of perplexity, such as he might enjoy, could he peep at her from Canada, or some safe place. He however did not wish her any evil, but he was very decided that he did not want any more to do with her. Benjamin was twenty years of age, dark complexion, size ordinary, mental capacity, good considering opportunities.

JOHN SMITH was a yellow boy, nineteen years of age, stout build, with marked intelligence. He held Dr. Abraham Street responsible for treating him as a slave. The doctor lived at Marshall District, Harford county, Maryland. John frankly confessed, to the credit of the doctor, that he got "a plenty to eat, drink and wear," yet he declared that he was not willing to remain a slave, he had higher aims; he wanted to be above that condition. "I left," said he, " because I wanted to see the country. If he had kept me in a hogshead of sugar, I wouldn't stayed," said the bright-minded slave youth. "They told me anything—told me to obey my master, but I didn't mind that. I am going off to see the Scriptures," said John.

ANDREW JACKSON "took out" from near Cecil, Delaware, where he had been owned by a man calling himself Thomas Palmer, who owned seven or eight others. His manners were by no means agreeable to Andrew; he was quite too "blustery," and was dangerous when in one of his fits. Although Andrew was but twenty-three years of age, he thought that Palmer had already had much more of his valuable services than he was entitled to, and he determined, that if he (the master), ever attempted to capture him, he would make him remember him the longest day he lived.

WILLIAM HUGHES was an Eastern Shore "piece of property" belonging to Daniel Cox. William had seen much of the dark doings of Slavery, and his mind had been thoroughly set against the system. True, he had been but twenty-two years under the heel of his master, but that was sufficient.

WESLEY WILLIAMS, on his arrival from Warrick, Maryland, testified that he had been in the hands of a man known by the name of Jack Jones, from whom he had received almost daily floggings and scanty food. Jones was his so-called owner. These continual scourgings stirred the spirit of freedom in Wesley to that degree, that he was compelled to escape for his life. He left his mother (a free woman), and one sister in Slavery.

ROSANNA JOHNSON, alias CATHARINE BRICE. The spot that Rosanna looked upon with most dread and where she had suffered as a slave, under a man called Doctor Street, was near the Rock of Deer Creek, in Harford county, Maryland.

In the darkness in which Slavery ordinarily kept the fettered and "free niggers," it was a considerable length of time ere Rosanna saw how barbarously she and her race were being wronged and ground down—driven to do unrequited labor—deprived of an education, obliged to receive the cuffs, kicks, and curses of old or young, who might happen to claim a title to them. But when she did see her true condition, she was not content until she found herself on the Underground Rail Road.

Rosanna was about thirty years of age, of a dark color, medium stature, and intelligent. She left two brothers and her father behind. The Committee forwarded her on North. From Albany Rose wrote back to inquire after particular friends, and to thank those who had aided her—as follows:

ALBANY, Jan. the 30, 1858.

MRS. WILLIAM STILL :—i sit don to rite you a fue lines in saying hav you herd of John Smith or Bengernin Pina i have cent letters to them but i hav know word from them John Smith was oned by Doker abe Street Bengermin oned by Mary hawkings i wish to kno if you kno am if you will let me know as swon as you get this. My lov to Mis Still i am much oblige for those articales. My love to mrs george and verry thankful to her Rosean Johnson oned by docter Street when you cend the letter rite it Cend it 63 Gran St in the car of andrue Conningham rite swon dela it not write my name Cathrin Brice.

Let me know swon as you can.

SMALLWOOD reported that he came from Ellicott's Mills, Maryland; that he had been restrained of his liberty all his life, by one Samuel Simons, who had treated him "bad" all the time that he had held him in his possession. He had, therefore, persuaded himself that Ellicott's Mills was a poor neighborhood for a colored man who wanted his freedom, and that all Maryland was no better. He had heard but little of Canada, but what he had heard pleased him. As to how he should get there, he knew not; a whisper pointed him to the Underground Rail Road, and told him to be fearless and take the first train. Sam considered the matter carefully and concluded that that would be the only way to get off. Unfortunately his mother and two brothers were left behind in the hands of Simons.

HENRY TOWNSEND ran away from Caroline county, near Purnell P. O., Maryland. The name of his reputed owner, according to his statement, was E. Townsend, a farmer. Against him Henry harbored a very heavy grudge, and will long hold said Townsend in remembrance for the injury he had received at his hands on his naked back. The back was shown, and a most frightful picture was presented; it had been thoroughly cut in all directions.

HENRY was about twenty-one years of age, dark chesnut color, build substantial. He left behind two brothers and one sister in Slavery. The Committee comforted him with the usual hospitality.

These passengers arrived the latter part of 1856 and the beginning of 1857.

SUNDRY ARRIVALS FROM MARYLAND, 1860.

WILLIAM CHION AND HIS WIFE, EMMA, EVAN GRAFF, AND FOUR OTHERS.

WILLIAM AND EMMA came from Dorchester county, Maryland. The cords of Slavery had been tightly drawn around them. William was about twenty-seven years of age, of a dark hue, and of a courageous bearing. On the score of treatment he spake thus: "I have been treated as bad as a man could be." Emma, his wife, had seen about the same number of years that he had, and her lot had been similar to his. Emma said, "My master never give me the second dress, never attempted such a thing." The master was called Bushong Blake. William was owned by a Mr.

Tubman. After leaving Slavery, William changed his last name to Williams, and if he and his wife are now living, they are known only by their adopted names.

EVAN GRAFF was of square solid build, dark, and smart, age twenty-five. He fled in company with four others (whose narratives were not written), from Frederick county, Maryland. Henry Heart, residing at Sam's Creek, exercised authority over Evan. With this master, said Evan, I have known hard times. I have been treated as bad as a man could be. I have been married three years and have not received five dollars in money since, towards supporting my family. "How have you lived then?" inquired one who sympathized. "My wife has kept house for a colored gentleman, and got her board for her services," said Evan. "In what other particulars have you been treated hard?" was next asked. "Sometimes I hadn't half clothes enough to keep me warm, through all weathers," answered Evan. "What put it into your head to leave?" was the third query. "Well, sir," said Evan, "I thought to try and do better." How did you make up your mind to leave your wife and child in Slavery? "Well, sir, I was very loth to leave my wife and child, but I just thought in this way: I had a brother who was entitled to his freedom, but he fell out with one of his young masters, and was just taken up and sold South, and I thought I might be taken off too, so I thought I would stand as good a chance in leaving, as if I stayed." Had you a mother and father, brothers and sisters? inquired a member of the Committee. "Yes, sir," was the prompt reply. Evan then gave their names thus: "My father's name was Sam Graff, my mother's name was Becky." Ruth Ann Dorsey, Isaac Hanson (and two brothers of Evan), Grafton and Allen accompanied him in his flight. James, Harriet, Charles Albert, Thomas Ephraim, Adeline Matilda, John Israel and Daniel Buchanan (brothers and sisters of Evan), were all left in Slavery.

Polly Pool was their mistress, rather had owned them up to within a short time before the flight of Evan and his comrades, but she had lately been unfortunate in business, which resulted in a thorough scattering of the entire family. Some fell into the hands of the mistress' children, and some into the hands of the grandchildren. In Evan's opinion she was a tolerable good mistress; his opportunities of judging, however, had not been very favorable, as he had not been in her hands a great while.

LUKE GOINES came from Harper's Ferry, where he was owned by Mrs. Carroll. Luke first made his way to Baltimore and afterwards to Philadelphia.

HENSON KELLY was owned by Reason Hastell, of Baltimore. Slavery did not agree with him, and he left to better his condition.

STAFFORD SMITH fled from Westmoreland county, Virginia, where he was owned by Harriet Parker, a single woman, advanced in years, and the owner of many slaves. "As a mistress, she was very hard. I have been hired to first one and then another, bad man all along. My mistress was a Methodist, but she seemed to know nothing about goodness. She was not in the habit of allowing the slaves any chance at all."

ARRIVAL FROM VIRGINIA, 1860.

JENNY BUCHANAN.

A KIND MASTER; JENNY CHASTISED ONE OF HIS SONS FOR AN INSULT, AND AS A PUNISHMENT SHE WAS SOLD—SEIZED FOR DEBT—SOLD A SECOND TIME.

JENNY was about forty-five years of age, a dark mulatto, stature medium, manners modest and graceful; she had served only in high life; thus she had acquired a great deal of information. She stated that she was born a slave, under John Bower, of Rockbridge, Virginia, and that he was the owner of a large plantation, with a great number of slaves. He was considered to be a good man to his servants, and was generally beloved by them. Suddenly, however, he was taken ill with paralysis, which confined him to his bed. During this illness one of the sons, a young gentleman, offered an insult to Jenny, for which she felt justified in administering to him, a severe chastisement. For this grave offence she was condemned to be sold to a trader by the name of William Watts, who owned a place in Mississippi. The conditions of sale were that she was to be taken out of the state and never to be allowed to return. It so happened, however, before she was removed that Watts, the trader, failed in order to cheat his creditors it was supposed. Governor McDowell, of Virginia, was one of those to whom he was largely indebted for a number of slaves which he, the Governor, had placed in his hands for disposal, some time before the trader took the benefit. Therefore, as the Governor was anxious to recover his loss as much as possible, he seized on Jenny. It was through this interference that the condition relative to her being sent out of the state was broken.

"The Governor," said Jenny, "was a very fine gentleman, as good as I could expect of Virginia. He allowed his slaves to raise fowl and hogs, with many privileges of one kind and another; besides he kept them all together; but he took sick and died. There was a great change shortly after that. The slaves were soon scattered like the wind. The Governor had nine sons and daughters.

After his death Mrs. McDowell, alias Mrs. Sally Thomas, took possession, and employed an overseer, by the name of Henry Morgan. He was a very good man in his looks, but a very rascally man; would get drunk, and sell her property to get whisky. Mrs. McDowell would let him do just as he pleased. For the slightest complaint the overseer might see fit to make against any of the slaves, she would tell him to sell them—"Sell, Mr. Morgan." "He would treat them worse than he would any dog; would beat them over the head with great hickory sticks, the same as he would beat an ox. He would pasture cows and horses on the plantation, and keep the money. We slaves all knew it, and we told her; but our words would not go in court against a white man, and until she was told by Mr. White, and her cousin, Dr. Taylor, and Mr. Barclay, she would not believe how shamefully this overseer was cheating her. But at last she was convinced, and discharged him, and hired another by the name of John Moore. The new one, if anything, was worse than the old one, for he could do the most unblushing acts of cruelty with pleasure. He was a demon."

Finally the estate had to be settled, and the property divided. At this time it was in the hands of the oldest daughter, Mistress Sally, who had been married to Frank Thomas, the Governor of Maryland. But the Governor had discarded her for some reason or other, and according to his published account of her it might seem that he had good reason for doing so. It was understood that he gave her a divorce, so she was considered single for life. It was also understood that she was to buy in the homestead at a moderate price, with as many slaves as she might desire.

Said Jenny, "I was sold at this settlement sale, and bought in by the 'grass widow' for four hundred dollars." The place and a number of slaves were bought in on terms equally as low. After this the widow became smitten with a reverend gentleman, by the name of John Miller, who had formerly lived North; he had been a popular preacher. After a courtship, which did not last very long, they were married, This took place three years ago, prior to the writing of this narrative. After the marriage, Rev. Mr. Miller took up his abode on the old homestead, and entered upon his duties as a slave-holder in good earnest.

"How did you like him?" inquired a member of the Committee.

"I despised him," was Jenny's prompt answer.

"Why did you despise him?"

"Because he had such mean ways with him," said Jenny. She then went on to remark as follows:—"Coming there, taking so much authority over other people's servants. He was so mean that he broke up all the privileges the servants had before he came. He stopped all hands from raising chickens, pigs, etc. He don't like to see them hold up their heads above their shoulders." Didn't he preach? she was asked. "Yes, but I never heard him preach; I have heard him pray though. On Thursday nights, when he would not want the servants to go into town to meeting, he would keep up until it would be too late for them to go. He is now carrying on the farm, and follows butchering. He has not yet sold any of the slaves, but has threatened to sell all hands to the trader."

Jenny once had a husband, but he went to Canada, and that was all she could tell about him, as she had never had a letter or any direct information from him since he left. That she was childless, she regarded as a matter of great satisfaction, considering all the circumstances.

ARRIVAL FROM BALTIMORE, 1860.

WILLIAM BROWN, AND JAMES HENSON

Considering themselves trampled upon by their fellow-men, unitedly resolved to seek a better country.

WILLIAM was pained with the idea that so much of his time had already been used up, as he was then thirty-six years of age. Yet he thought that it would do no good to mourn over the past, but do what he intended to do quickly. The master whom he had served, he called, "Master Lynchum." He was a farmer, and knew full well how to use severity with the slaves; but had never practiced showing favors, or allowing privileges of any kind. True he did not flog, but he resorted to other means of punishment when he desired to make the slaves feel that he was master. William left his mother, Harriet Brown, three sisters, and one brother,—Francis, Mary, Eliza, and Robert. They were all free but Eliza.

Seven weeks William and James were under the painful anxiety of trying to escape, but conscious of the snares and dangers on the road, and desirous of success, they did not feel at liberty to move, save as they saw their way clear. This well-exercised sagacity was strongly marked in the intellectual region of William's head.

JAMES HENSON was a man of rather slender build. From exposure in traveling he took a severe cold and was suffering with sore throat. He and Mrs. Maria Thomas disagreed. She set herself up to be "Jim's" mistress and owner. For some cause or other Jim was unwilling to fill this station longer. He had been hired out by his mistress, who received one hundred dollars per annum; and, for aught Jim knew, she was pretty well pleased with him and the money also. She coolly held eleven others in the same predicament. While Jim found no fault with the treatment received at the hands of his mistress, he went so far as to say that "she was a right fine woman," yet, the longer he lived her slave, the more unhappy he became. Therefore, he decided that he would try and do better, and accordingly, in company with William he started, success attending their efforts. James left three sisters and one brother, Charlotte, Susan, Ellen and Johnson, all slaves.

ARRIVAL FROM MARYLAND.

PHILIP STANTON, RANDOLPH NICHOLS, AND THOMAS DOUGLASS.

PHILIP had a master by the name of John Smith, whom he was very anxious to get rid of, but hardly knew how. For a long time, Philip was annoyed in various ways. Being the only slave on the place, there was no rest for him. Said Smith was a bachelor, and his mother, who kept house for him, was quite aged; "she was worse than the old boy wanted her to be, a more contrary woman never was; she was bad in this way, she was quarrelsome, and then again she would not give you as much to eat as you ought to have, and it was pretty rough; nothing but corn bread and the fattest pork, that was about all. She was a Catholic, and was known by the name of Mary Eliza Smith." This was Philip's testimony against his master and mistress. Working on a farm, driving carriage, etc., had been Philip's calling as a slave. His father and mother were free. His father had been emancipated, and afterwards had purchased his wife. One sister, however, was still in Slavery. Philip had scarcely reached his twenty-second year; he was nevertheless wide-awake and full of courage.

RANDOLPH was still younger; he had only just reached his twentieth year; was nearly six feet high, athletic, and entertained quite favorable notions of freedom. He was owned by Mrs. Caroline Brang, a widow; he had never lived with her, however. Notwithstanding the fact that he had been held in such unpleasant relations, Randolph held the opinion, that "she was a tolerable good woman." He had been hired out under Isaac Howard, a farmer, who was described by Randolph as "a rough man to everybody around him; he was the owner of slaves, and a member of the Methodist Church, in the bargain." As if actuated by an evil spirit continually, he seemed to take delight in "knocking and beating the slaves," and would compel them to "be out in all weathers not fit to be out in." Randolph declared that "he had never been allowed a day's schooling in his life. On the contrary, he had often been threatened with sale, and his mind had finally become so affected by this fearful looking-for of evil, that he thought he had better make tracks."

He left his mother, Louisa, three brothers and three sisters, namely: Andrew, Mary, Charity, Margaret, Lewis and Samuel, all slaves. His desire to escape brought the thought home to his mind with great emphasis, that he was parting with his kinsfolk, to see them perhaps, no more on earth; that however, happily he might be situated in freedom, he would have the painful reflection ever present with him, that those he most loved in this world, were slaves—"knocked and beat about—and made to work out in all weathers." It was this that made many falter and give up their purpose to gain their freedom by flight, but Randolph was not one of this class. His young heart loved freedom too well to waver. True to his love of liberty, he left all, followed the north star, and was delivered.

THOMAS, an older companion of Philip and Randolph, was twenty-five years of age, full black, and looked as if he could appreciate the school-room and books, and take care of himself in Canada or any other free country. Mary Howard was the name of the individual that he was com-pelled to address as "mistress." He said, however, that·"she was a very good woman to her servants," and she had a great many. She had sons, but they turned out to be drunkards, and followed no business; at one time, each of them had been set up in business, but as they would not attend to it, of course they failed. Money was needed more than ever, through their intem-perate course, consequently the mistress was induced to sell her large house-hold, as well as her plantation slaves, to Georgia. Thomas had seen the most of them take up their sorrowful march for said State, and the only reason that he was not among them, was attributable to the fact, that he had once been owned and thought pretty well of by the brother of his mistress, who interceded in Thomas' behalf. This interference had the desired effect, and Thomas was not sold. Still, his eyes were fairly opened to see his danger and to learn a valuable lesson at the same time; he, there-fore, profited by it in escaping the first chance. He left his mother Ann Williams, and one brother, James Douglass, both slaves.

ARRIVAL FROM FREDERICKSBURG, 1860.

HENRY TUDLE AND WIFE, MARY WILLIAMS.

HENRY affirmed, that for the last twenty years, his freedom had been promised him, and during all these long years, hardly a month had passed, that he had not fixed his hopes upon a definite time, when his bondage would end and his freedom commence. But he had been trusting the word of a slave-holder, who had probably adopted this plan simply with a view of drawing more willing toil out of him than he could have accom-plished in any other way.

MARY complained that she had suffered severely for food, and likewise for privileges. Ezra Houpt was the name of Henry's master, and the name of his mistress was Catharine, she was hasty and passionate; slaves were shown no quarter under her. Mary was owned by Christian Thomas. He was said to be not so hard, but his wife was very hard, so much so, that she would rule both master and slaves. Her name was Mary Elizabeth.

SUNDRY ARRIVALS FROM MARYLAND, 1860.

SAM ARCHER, LEWIS PECK, DAVID EDWARDS, EDWARD CASTING, JOE HENRY, GEORGE
AND ALBERT WHITE, JOSEPH C. JOHNSON, DAVID SNIVELY, AND HENRY
DUNMORE.

SAM ARCHER was to "become free at thirty-five years of age." He had
already served thirty years of this time; five years longer seemed an age to
him. The dangers from other sources presented also a frightful aspect.
Sam had seen too many who had stood exactly in the same relations to
Slavery and freedom, and not a few were held over their time, or cheated
out of their freedom altogether. He stated that his own mother was "kept
over her time," simply "that her master might get all her children." Two
boys and two girls were thus gained, and were slaves for life. These
facts tended to increase Sam's desire to get away before his time was out;
he, therefore, decided to get off via the Underground Rail Road. He grew
very tired of Bell Air, Harford county, Maryland, and his so-called owner,
Thomas Hayes. He said that Hayes had used him "rough," and he was
"tired of rough treatment." So when he got his plans arranged, one
morning when he was expected to go forth to an unrequited day's labor, he
could not be found. Doubtless, his excited master thought Sam a great
thief, to take himself away in the manner that he did, but Sam was not concerned on this point; all that concerned him was as to how he could get to
Canada the safest and the quickest. When he reached the Philadelphia
station, he felt that the day dawned, his joy was full, despite the Fugitive
Slave Law.

LEWIS PECK was a man six feet high, and of the darkest hue. He
reported that he fled from Joseph Bryant, a farmer, who lived near Patapsco
River. Bryant was in the habit of riding around to look after the slaves.
Lewis had become thoroughly disgusted with this manner of superintending.
"I got tired of having Bryant riding after me, working my life out of me,"
said Lewis. He was also tired of Bryant's wife; he said "she was always
making mischief, and he didn't like a mischief maker."

Thus he complained of both master and mistress, seeming not to understand that he "had no rights which they were bound to respect."

DAVID EDWARDS broke away from the above named Bryant, at the age
of twenty-four. His testimony fully corroborated that of his comrade,
Lewis Peck. He was also a man of the darkest shade, tall, intellect good,
and wore a pleasant countenance. The ordinary difficulties were experienced, but all were surmounted without serious harm.

EDWARD CASTING and JOSEPH HENRY were each about seventeen years
of age. Boys, as they were, with no knowledge of the world, they had
wisely resolved not to remain in that condition. Edward fled from Robert
Moore, who lived at Duck Creek. He gave his master the name of being a

"bad man," and refused to recommend him for anything. Being a likely-looking chattel, he would have doubtless brought seven hundred dollars in the market.

JOSEPH HENRY came from Queen Ann county, Maryland. He was a well-grown lad, and showed traces of having been raised without proper care, or training. For deficiencies in this direction, he charged Greenberry Parker, his claimant, who he said had treated him "bad." Friends had helped these boys along.

GEORGE and ALBERT WHITE were brothers. They fled from Cecil county, Maryland. They escaped from William Parker. "What kind of a man was William Parker?" they were asked. "He was a big, bad man, no goodness in him," quickly replied one of the brothers. Their lot in Slavery had not been different from that of numbers coming from that section of the State.

JOSEPH G. JOHNSON fled from William Jones of Baltimore. He said that his master kept a grocery store in Pratt street, and owned six head of slaves; that he was a "good man, and always treated his servants very well," until about three weeks before he escaped. For some reason unknown to Joseph, within the time just alluded to, he had sold all his slaves, with the exception of himself. Joseph was far from being at ease, as he hourly felt oppressed with the fear that he was to be sold at an early day.

Summoning courage he started by the Baltimore and Wilmington Rail Road. In this way he reached Wilmington where he unfortunately fell into the hands of his master's son, who resided in Wilmington, and happened to discover Joseph in the cars, (most likely he had been telegraphed to) and had him arrested and returned. But Joseph did not allow a week to pass over him before he was ready to make even a still more daring adventure for his liberty. This time he concluded to try the water; by great economy he had saved up twenty-five dollars. This was a great deal to him, but he resolved to give it all willingly to any man who would secrete him, or procure him a passage to Philadelphia. The right man was soon found, and Joseph was off again. Good luck attended him, and he reached the Committee safely. He was in his twenty-third year, a man of medium size, copper-colored, and of a prepossessing countenance.

DAVID SNIVELY ran away from Frederick, Maryland. He was moved to escape solely by the love of freedom. His services had been required in the blacksmith shop, and on the farm under Charles Preston, who claimed to own him. He had been sold once and brought nine hundred dollars; he resolved that a similar fate should never overtake him, unless his owner moved very suddenly in that direction. While Joseph was working daily in the blacksmith shop, he was planning how to make good his escape. No way was open but the old route, which led "hard by" many dangers, and was only accessible now and then through regions where friends were few and far between. Howbeit he possessed the faith requisite, and was victorious.

Joseph was twenty-six years of age, of unmixed blood, ordinary size, and had a commendable share of courage and intellect. He could recommend no good traits as his master's.

HENRY DUNMORE had served as a slave up to the age of thirty-five, and was then on the eve of being sold. As he had endured severe hardship under his old master John Maldon he was unwilling to try another. While he gave Maldon credit for being a member of the Methodist Church, he charged him with treating himself in a most unchristian-like manner. He testified that Maldon did not allow him half enough to eat; and once he kept him out in the cold until his toes were frozen off. Consequently it was not in the heart of Henry to give his master any other than a bad name. He lived about sixteen miles from Elkton, near Charleston, Maryland. He was of a dark chestnut color, well-made, and active.

CROSSING THE BAY IN A BATTEAU.

SHARP CONTEST WITH PURSUERS ON WATER.   FUGITIVES VICTORIOUS.

THOMAS SIPPLE, and his wife, MARY ANN, HENRY BURKETT, and ELIZABETH, his wife, JOHN PURNELL, and HALE BURTON. This party

were slaves, living near Kunkletown, in Worcester county, Maryland, and had become restive in their fetters. Although they did not know a letter of the alphabet, they were fully persuaded that they were entitled to their freedom. In considering what way would be safest for them to adopt, they concluded that the water would be less dangerous than any other route. As the matter of freedom had been in their minds for a long time, they had frequently counted the cost, and had been laying by trifling sums of money which had fallen perchance into their hands. Among them all they had about thirty dollars. As they could not go by water without a boat, one of their number purchased an old batteau for the small sum of six dollars. The Delaware Bay lay between them and the Jersey shore, which they desired to reach. They did not calculate, however, that before leaving the Delaware shore they would have to contend with the enemy. That in crossing, they would lose sight of the land they well understood. They managed to find out the direction of the shore, and about the length of time that it might take them to reach it. Undaunted by the perils before them the party repaired to the bay, and at ten o'clock, P. M. embarked direct for the other shore.

Near Kate's Hammock, on the Delaware shore, they were attacked by five white men in a small boat. One of them seized the chain of the fugitives' boat, and peremptorily claimed it. "This is not your boat, we bought this boat and paid for it," spake one of the brave fugitives. "I am an officer, and must have it," said the white man, holding on to the chain. Being armed, the white men threatened to shoot. Manfully did the black men stand up for their rights, and declare that they did not mean to give up their boat alive. The parties speedily came to blows. One of the white men dealt a heavy blow with his oar upon the head of one of the black men, which knocked him down, and broke the oar at the same time. The blow was immediately returned by Thomas Sipple, and one of the white men was laid flat on the bottom of the boat. The white men were instantly seized with a panic, and retreated; after getting some yards off they snapped their guns at the fugitives several times, and one load of small shot was fired into them. John received two shot in the forehead, but was not dangerously hurt. George received some in the arms, Hale Burton got one about his temple, and Thomas got a few in one of his arms; but the shot being light, none of the fugitives were seriously damaged. Some of the shot will remain in them as long as life lasts. The conflict lasted for several minutes, but the victorious bondmen were only made all the more courageous by seeing the foe retreat. They rowed with a greater will than ever, and landed on a small island. Where they were, or what to do they could not tell. One whole night they passed in gloom on this sad spot. Their hearts were greatly cast down; the next morning they set out on foot to see what they could see. The young women were very sick, and the men were tried to the last extremity; however, after walking about one mile, they came across the captain of an oyster boat. They perceived that

34

he spoke in a friendly way, and they at once asked directions with regard to Philadelphia. He gave them the desired information, and even offered to bring them to the city if they would pay him for his services. They had about twenty-five dollars in all. This they willingly gave him, and he brought them according to agreement. When they found the captain they were not far from Cape May light-house.

Taking into account the fact that it was night when they started, that their little boat was weak, combined with their lack of knowledge in relation to the imminent danger surrounding them, any intelligent man would have been justified in predicting for them a watery grave, long before the bay was half crossed. But they crossed safely. They greatly needed food, clothing, rest, and money, which they freely received, and were afterwards forwarded to John W. Jones, Underground Rail Road agent, at Elmira. The subjoined letter giving an account of their arrival was duly received:

ELMIRA, June 6th, 1860.

FRIEND WM. STILL :—All six came safe to this place. The two men came last night, about twelve o'clock; the man and woman stopped at the depot, and went east on the next train, about eighteen miles, and did not get back till to-night, so that the two men went this morning, and the four went this evening.

> O, old master don't cry for me,
> For I am going to Canada where colored men are free.

P. S. What is the news in the city? Will you tell me how many you have sent over to Canada? I would like to know. They all send their love to you. I have nothing new to tell you. We are all in good health. I see there is a law passed in Maryland not to set any slaves free. They had better get the consent of the Underground Rail Road before they passed such a thing. Good night from your friend,　　　　JOHN W. JONES.

ARRIVAL FROM DORCHESTER CO., 1860.

HARRIET TUBMAN'S LAST "TRIP" TO MARYLAND.

STEPHEN ENNETS and wife, MARIA, with three children, whose names were as follows: HARRIET, aged six years; AMANDA, four years, and a babe (in the arms of its mother), three months old.

The following letter from Thomas Garrett throws light upon this arrival:

WILMINGTON, 12th mo., 1st, 1860.

RESPECTED FRIEND :—WILLIAM STILL :—I write to let thee know that Harriet Tubman is again in these parts. She arrived last evening from one of her trips of mercy to God's poor, bringing two men with her as far as New Castle. I agreed to pay a man last evening, to pilot them on their way to Chester county; the wife of one of the men, with two or three children, was left some thirty miles below, and I gave Harriet ten dollars, to hire a man with carriage, to take them to Chester county. She said a man had offered for that sum, to bring them on. I shall be very uneasy about them, till I hear they are safe.

There is now much more risk on the road, till they arrive here, than there has been for several months past, as we find that some poor, worthless wretches are constantly on the look out on two roads, that they cannot well avoid more especially with carriage, yet, as it is Harriet who seems to have had a special angel to guard her on her journey of mercy, I have hope.   Thy Friend,   THOMAS GARRETT.

N. B.   We hope all will be in Chester county to-morrow.

These slaves from Maryland, were the last that Harriet Tubman piloted out of the prison-house of bondage, and these "came through great tribulation."

STEPHEN, the husband, had been a slave of John Kaiger, who would not allow him to live with his wife (if there was such a thing as a slave's owning a wife.) She lived eight miles distant, hired her time, maintained herself, and took care of her children (until they became of service to their owner), and paid ten dollars a year for her hire. She was owned by Algier Pearcy. Both mother and father desired to deliver their children from his grasp. They had too much intelligence to bear the heavy burdens thus imposed without feeling the pressure a grievous one.

Harriet Tubman being well acquainted in their neighborhood, and knowing of their situation, and having confidence that they would prove true, as passengers on the Underground Rail Road, engaged to pilot them within reach of Wilmington, at least to Thomas Garrett's. Thus the father and mother, with their children and a young man named John, found aid and comfort on their way, with Harriet for their "Moses." A poor woman escaping from Baltimore in a delicate state, happened to meet Harriet's party at the station, and was forwarded on with them. They were cheered with clothing, food, and material aid, and sped on to Canada. Notes taken at that time were very brief; it was evidently deemed prudent in those days, not to keep as full reports as had been the wont of the secretary, prior to 1859. The capture of John Brown's papers and letters, with names and plans in full, admonished us that such papers and correspondence as had been preserved concerning the Underground Rail Road, might perchance be captured by a pro-slavery mob. For a year or more after the Harper's Ferry battle, as many will remember, the mob spirit of the times was very violent in all the principal northern cities, as well as southern ("to save the Union.") Even in Boston, Abolition meetings were fiercely assailed by the mob. During this period, the writer omitted some of the most important particulars in the escapes and narratives of fugitives. Books and papers were sent away for a long time, and during this time the records were kept simply on loose slips of paper.

ARRIVAL FROM MARYLAND, 1860.

JERRY MILLS, AND WIFE, DIANA, SON, CORNELIUS, AND TWO DAUGHTERS, MARGARET, AND SUSAN.

The father of this family was sixty-five years of age, and his working days were apparently well nigh completed. The mother was fifty-seven years of age; son twenty-seven; daughters seventeen and fifteen years of age.

The old man was smart for his years, but bore evidence that much hard labor had been wrung out of him by Slavery. Diana said that she had been the mother of twelve children; five had escaped to Canada, three were in their graves, and three accompanied her; one was left in Maryland. They had seen hard times, according to the testimony of the old man and his companion, especially under David Snively, who, however, had been "removed by the Lord" a number of years prior to their escape; but the change proved no advantage to them, as they found Slavery no better under their mistress, the widow, than under their master. Mistress Snively was said to be close and stingy, and always unfriendly to the slave. "She never thought you were doing enough." For her hardness of heart they were sure she would repent some time, but not while she could hold slaves. The belief was pretty generally entertained with the slaves that the slaveholder would have to answer for his evil doings in another world.

TWELVE MONTHS IN THE WOODS, 1860.

HENRY COTTON.

As a slave, subjected to the whims and passions of his master, Henry made up his mind that he could not stand it longer. The man who mastered it over him was called Nathaniel Dixon, and lived in Somerset Co., near Newtown. This Dixon was not content with his right to flog and abuse Henry as he saw fit, but he threatened to sell him, as he would sell a hog.

At this time Henry was about twenty-four years of age, but a man of more substantial parts physically was rarely to be seen. Courage was one of his prominent traits. This threat only served to arouse him completely. He had no friends save such as were in the same condition with himself, nevertheless he determined not to be sold. How he should escape this fate did not at first present itself. Every thing looked very gloomy; Slavery he considered as death to him; and since his master had threatened him, he looked upon him as his greatest enemy, and rather than continue a slave he preferred living in the swamps with wild animals. Just one year prior to the time that he made his way North, determined not to be a slave any longer, he fled to a swamp and made his way to the most secluded spot that he could find,—to places that were almost impenetrable so dense were the trees and undergrowth. This was all the better for Henry, he wanted to get safety; he did not wish company. He made known his plans to a dear brother, who engaged to furnish him occasionally with food. Henry passed twelve months in this way, beholding no human soul save his brother. His brother faithfully took him food from time to time. The winter weather of 1859 was very hard, but it was not so hard to bear as his master Nathaniel Dixon. The will of Henry's old master entitled him to his freedom, but the heirs had rendered said will null and void; this act in addition to the talk of selling had its effect in driving him to the woods. For a time he hid in the hollow of a tree, which went very hard with him, yet he was willing to suffer anything rather than go back to his so-called master. He managed finally to make good his escape and came to the Committee for aid and sympathy, which he received.

ARRIVAL FROM MARYLAND.

WILLIAM PIERCE.

But few passengers expressed themselves in stronger terms in regard to their so-called masters, than William Pierce, from Long Green. "I fled," said he, "from John Hickol, a farmer, about fifty years old, grey-headed and drinks whiskey very hard—was always a big devil—ill-grained. He owned fifteen head; he owns three of my brothers. He has a wife, a big devil, red head; her servants, she wouldn't feed 'em none, except on corn bread; she would fight and swear too, when she got ready. She and her husband would quarrel too. A slave man, a deceitful fellow, who had been put up to watch on one occasion, when the rest of the slaves had helped themselves to a chicken, and cooked and ate it about midnight, though he was allowed to share a portion of the feast, was ready enough to betray them by times next morning. This made master and mistress 'cuss' all hands at a great rate, and master beat all hands except the one that told. I was caned so badly that it laid me up for several weeks. I am a little lame yet from the beating."

Such was William's story. He was twenty-three years of age, of a light brown color, well-made. Judging from his expressions and apparent feelings against his master and mistress, he would be willing to endure many years of suffering in Canada snows, before he would apply to them for care and protection.

A SLAVE CATCHER CAUGHT IN HIS OWN TRAP.

GEORGE F. ALBERTI PERSONATED BY A MEMBER OF THE VIGILANCE COMMITTEE—
A LADY FRIGHTENED BY A PLACARD.

One afternoon, the quiet of the Anti-Slavery Office was suddenly agitated by the contents of a letter, privately placed in the hands of J. Miller McKim by one of the clerks of the Philadelphia Ledger office. Said letter it would seem, had been dropped into the box of the Ledger office, instead of the U. S. box (one of which, was also in the Ledger office), through a mistake, and seeing that it bore the name of a well-known slave-catcher, Alberti, the clerk had a great desire to know its import. Whether it was or was not sealed, the writer cannot say, it certainly was not sealed when it reached the Anti-Slavery office. It stated that a lady from Maryland was then in Philadelphia, stopping at a boarding-house on Arch Street, and that she was very desirous of seeing the above-mentioned Alberti, with a view of obtaining his services to help catch an Underground Rail Road sojourner, whom she claimed as her property. That she wrote the letter could not be proved, but that it was sent by her consent, there was no doubt. In order to save the poor fellow from his impending doom, it seemed that nothing would avail but a bold strategical movement. Mr. McKim proposed to find some one who would be willing to answer for Alberti. Cyrus Whitson, a member of the Committee, in Mr. McKim's judgment, could manage the matter successfully. At that time, C. Whitson was engaged in the Free Labor store, at the corner of Fifth and Cherry streets, near the Anti-Slavery office. On being sent for, he immediately answered the summons, and Mr. McKim at once made known to him his plan, which was to save a fellow-man from being dragged back to bondage, by visiting the lady, and ascertaining from her in conversation the whereabouts of the fugitives, the names of the witnesses, and all the particulars. Nothing could have delighted the shrewd Whitson better; he saw just how he could effect the matter, without the slightest probable failure. So off he started for the boarding-house.

Arriving, he rang the bell, and when the servant appeared, he asked if Miss Wilson, from Maryland, was stopping there. "She is," was the answer. "I wish to see her." "Walk in the parlor, sir." In went Mr. W., with his big whiskers. Soon Miss Wilson entered the parlor, a tall, and rather fine-looking well dressed lady. Mr. Whitson bowing, politely addressed her, substantially thus:

"I have come to see you instead of Mr. Geo. F. Alberti, to whom you addressed a note, this morning. Circumstances, over which Mr. A. had no control, prevented his coming, so I have come, madam, to look after your business in his place. Now, madam, I wish it to be distinctly understood in the outset, that whatever transpires between us, so far as this business is concerned, must be kept strictly confidential, by no means, must this matter be allowed to leak out; if it does, the darned abolitionists (excuse me), may ruin me; at any rate we should not be able to succeed in getting your slave. I am particular on this point, remember.'

"You are perfectly right, Sir, indeed I am very glad that your plan is to conduct this matter in this manner, for I do not want my name mixed up with it in any way."

"Very well, madam, I think we understand each other pretty well; now please give me the name of the fugitive, his age, size, and color, and where he may be found, how long he has been away, and the witness who can be relied on to identify him after he is arrested."

Miss Wilson carefully communicated these important particulars, while Mr. Whitson faithfully penciled down every word. At the close of the interview he gave her to understand that the matter should be attended to immediately, and that he thought there would be no difficulty in securing the fugitive. "You shall hear from me soon, madam, good afternoon."

In five minutes after this interview Whitson was back to the Anti-slavery Office with all Miss Wilson's secrets. The first thing to be attended was to send a messenger to the place where the fugitive was at work, with a view of securing his safety; this was a success. The man was found, and, frightened almost out of his wits, he dropped all and followed the messenger, who bore him the warning. In the meanwhile Mr. McKim was preparing, with great dispatch, the subjoined document for the enlightenment and warning of all.

TO WHOM IT MAY CONCERN:

BEWARE OF SLAVE-CATCHERS.

Miss Wilson, of Georgetown Cross Roads, Kent county, Md., is now in the city in pursuit of her alleged slave man, Butler. J. M. Cummings and John Wilson, of the same place, are understood to be here on a similar errand, This is to caution Butler and his friends to be on their guard. Let them keep clear of the above-named individuals. Also, let them have an eye on all persons known to be friends of Dr. High, of Georgetown Cross Roads, and Mr. D. B. Cummings, who is not of Georgetown Cross Roads.

It is requested that all parties to whom a copy of this may be sent will post it in a public place, and that the friends of Freedom and Humanity will have the facts herein contained openly read in their respective churches.

"Hide the outcast; bewray not him that wandereth." Isaiah xvi. 3.

"Thou shalt not deliver unto his master the servant that has escaped from his master unto thee." Deut. xxiii. 15.

This document printed as a large poster, about three feet square, and displayed in large numbers over the city, attracted much attention and comment, which facts were quickly conveyed to Miss Wilson, at her boarding-house. At first, as it was understood, she was greatly shocked to find herself in everybody's mouth. She unhesitatingly took her baggage and started for "My Maryland." Thus ended one of the most pleasant interviews that ever took place between a slave-hunter and the Vigilance Committee of Philadelphia.

ARRIVAL FROM RICHMOND, 1858.

HENRY LANGHORN *alias* WM. SCOTT.

THIS "chattel" from Richmond, Virginia, was of a yellow complexion, with some knowledge of the arts of reading and writing; he was about twenty-three years of age and considered himself in great danger of being subjected to the auction-block by one Charles L. Hobson. Hobson and Henry had grown up from boyhood together; for years they had even occupied the same room,—Henry as a servant-boy and protector of his prospective young master. Under these relations quite strong affinities were cemented between them, and Henry succeeded in gaining a knowledge of the alphabet with an occasional lesson in spelling. Both reached their majority. William was hired out at the American Hotel, and being a "smart, likely-looking boy," commanded good wages for his young master's benefit, who had commenced business as a tobacco merchant, with about seven head of slaves in his possession. A year or two's experiment proved that the young master was not succeeding as a merchant, and before the expiration of three years he had sold all his slaves except Henry. From such indications, Henry was fully persuaded that his time was well nigh at hand, and great was his anxiety as he meditated over the auction-block. "In his heart" he resolved time and again that he would never be sold. It behooved him, therefore, to avert that ill fate. He at first resolved to buy himself, but in counting the cost he found that he would by no means be able to accumulate as much money as his master would be likely to demand for him; he, therefore, abandoned this idea and turned his attention straightway to the Underground Rail Road, by which route he had often heard of slaves escaping. He felt the need of money and that he must make and save an extra quarter whenever he could; he soon learned to be a very rigid economist, and being exceedingly accommodating in waiting upon gentlemen at the hotel and at the springs, he found his little "pile" increasing weekly. His object was to have enough to pay for a private berth on one of the Richmond steamers and also to have a little left to fall back on after landing in a strange land and among strangers. He saved about two hundred dollars in cash; he was then ready to make a forward move, and he arranged all his plans with an agent in Richmond to leave by one of the steamers during the Christmas holidays. "You must come down to the steamer about dark," said the agent "and if all is right you will see the Underground Rail Road agent come out with some ashes as a signal, and by this you may know that all is ready."

"I will be there certain," said Henry. Christmas week he was confident would be granted as usual as a holiday week; a few days before Christmas he went to his master and asked permission to spend said holiday with his mother, in Cumberland county, adding that he would need some spending money, enough at least to pay his fare, etc. Young master freely granted his request, wrote him a pass, and doled him out enough money to pay his fare thence, but concluded that Henry could pay his way back out of his extra change. Henry expressed his obligations, etc., and returned to the American Hotel. The evening before the time appointed for starting on his Underground Rail Road voyage, he had occasion to go out to see the Underground Rail Road agent, and asked the clerk to give him a pass. This favor was peremptorily refused. Henry, "not willing to give it up so," sat down to write a pass for himself; he found it all that was necessary, and was thus enabled to accomplish his business satisfactorily. Next day his Christmas holiday commenced, but instead of his enjoying the sight of his mother, he felt that he had seen her for the last time in the flesh. It was a sad reflection. That evening at dark, he was at the wharf, according to promise. The man with the ashes immediately appeared and signalled him. In his three suits of clothing (all on his back), he walked on the boat, and was conducted to the coal covering, where Egyptian darkness prevailed. The appointed hour for the starting of the steamer, was ten o'clock the following morning. By the aid of prayer, he endured the suffering that night. No sooner had the steamer got under way, than a heavy gale was encountered; for between three and four days the gale and fog combined, threatened the steamer with a total loss. All the freight on deck, consisting of tobacco and cotton, had to be thrown overboard, to save the passengers.

HENRY, in his state of darkness, saw nothing, nor could he know the imminent peril that his life was in. Fortunately he was not sea-sick, but slept well and long on the voyage. The steamer was five days coming. On landing at Philadelphia, Henry could scarcely see or walk; the spirit of freedom, however, was burning brightly in the hidden man, and the free gales of fresh air and a few hours on free soil soon enabled him to overcome the difficulties which first presented themselves, and he was soon one of the most joyful mortals living. He tarried two days with his friends in Philadelphia, and then hastened on to Boston. After being in Boston two months, he was passing through the market one day, when, to his surprise, he espied his young master, Charles L. Hobson. Henry was sure, however, that he was not recognized, but suspected that he was hunted. Instantly, Henry pulled up his coat collar, and drew his hat over his face to disguise himself as much as possible; but he could not wholly recover from the shock he had thus sustained. He turned aside from the market and soon met a friend formerly from Richmond, who had been in servitude in the tobacco factory owned by his master. Henry tried to prevail on him to spot out said Hobson, in the market, and see if there possibly could be any mistake. Not a step would his friend take in that direction. He had been away for several years, still he was a fugitive, and didn't like the idea of renewing his acquaintance with old or new friends with a white skin from Virginia. Henry, however, could not content himself until he had taken another good look at Mr. Hobson. Disguising himself he again took a stroll through the market, looking on the right and left as he passed along; presently he saw him seated at a butcher's stall. He examined him to his satisfaction, and then went speedily to headquarters (the Anti-Slavery Office), made known the fact of his discovery, and stated that he believed his master had no other errand to Boston than to capture him. Measures were at once taken to ascertain if such a man as Charles L. Hobson was booked at any of the hotels in Boston.

On finding that this was really a fact, Henry was offered and accepted private quarters with the well-known philanthropist and friend of the fugitive, Francis Jackson. His house as well as his purse was always open to the slave. While under the roof of Mr. Jackson, as Hobson advertised and described Henry so accurately, and offered a reward of two hundred and fifty dollars for him, Henry's friends thought that they would return him the compliment by publishing him in the Boston papers quite as accurately if not with as high a reward for him; they advertised him after this manner: "Charles L. Hobson, twenty-two years of age, six feet high, with a slouched hat on, mixed coat, black pants, with a goatee, is stopping at the Tremont Hotel," &c., &c. This was as a bomb-shell to Mr. Hobson, and he immediately took the hint, and with his trunks steered for the sunny South. In a day or two afterwards Henry deemed it advisable to visit Canada. After arriving there he wrote back to his young master, to let him know where he was, and why he left, and what he was doing. How his letter was received Henry was never informed. For five years he lived in Boston and ran on a boat trading to Canada East. He saved up his money and took care of himself creditably. He was soon prepared to go into some business that would pay him better than running on the boat. Two of his young friends agreed with him that they could do better in Philadelphia than in Boston, so they came to the City of Brotherly Love and opened a first-class dining-saloon near Third and Chestnut streets. For a time they carried on the business with enterprise and commendable credit, but one of the partners, disgusted with the prejudices of the city passenger railway cars, felt that he could no longer live here. Henry, known after leaving Slavery only by the name of Wm. Scott, quitted the restaurant business and found employment as a messenger under Thomas A.

Scott, Esq., Vice-President of the Pennsylvania Central Rail Road, where he has faithfully served for the last four years, and has the prospect of filling the office for many years to come. He is an industrious, sober, steady, upright, and intelligent young man, and takes care of his wife and child in a comfortable three story brick house of his own.

ARRIVAL FROM RICHMOND, 1859.

MILES ROBINSON was the slave of Mrs. Roberts, a widow lady living in York County, Virginia. He did not live with her, however, but was hired out in the city of Richmond. He had been fortunate in falling into hands that had not treated him harshly. He was not contented, however. Much of the leisure falling incidentally to his lot from hours of duty, he devoted to the banjo. As a player on this instrument he had become quite gifted, but music in Richmond was not liberty. The latter he craved, and in thought was often far beyond Mason and Dixon's line, enjoying that which was denied him in Virginia. Although but twenty-two years of age, Miles was manly, and determination and intelligence were traits strongly marked in his unusually well-shaped visage. Hearing that he was to be sold, he conferred not with his mother, brothers, or sisters, (for such he had living as slaves in Richmond) but resolved to escape by the first convenience. Turning his attention to the Underground Rail Road, he soon found an agent who communicated his wishes to one of the colored women running as cook or chambermaid on one of the Philadelphia and Richmond steamers, and she was bold enough to take charge of him, and found him a safe berth in one of the closets where the pots and other cooking utensils belonged. It was rather rough and trying, but Miles felt that it was for liberty, and he must pass through the ordeal without murmuring, which he did, until success was achieved and he found himself in Philadelphia. Boston being the haven on which his hopes were fixed, after recruiting a short while in the city he steered for said place. Finding liberty there as sweet as he had fondly hoped to find it, he applied himself unceasingly to industrial pursuits, economy, the improvement of his mind and the elevation of his race. Four years he passed thus, under the shadow of Bunker Hill, at the end of which time he invested the earnings, which he had saved, in a business with two young friends in Philadelphia. All being first-class waiters and understanding catering, they decided to open a large dining-saloon. Miles was one of the two friends mentioned in Wm. Scott's narrative, and as his success and consequent fortunes have been already referred to, it will suffice here to mention him simply in connection with two contests that he sustained with the prejudice that sought to drive colored people from the passenger cars.

At the corner of Fourth and Walnut streets Miles, in company with two other young men, Wallace and Marshall, one evening in a most orderly manner, entered the cars and took their seats. The conductor ordered them on the front platform; they did not budge. He stopped the car and ordered them out; this did no good. He read rules, and was not a little embarrassed by these polite and well-dressed young men. Finally he called for the police, who arrested all three. Miles did not yield his seat without a struggle. In being pulled out his resistance was such that several window lights were broken in the car. The police being in strong force, however, succeeded in marching their prisoners to the Mayor's police station at the corner of Fifth and Chestnut streets where they were locked up to await further investigation. The prisoners thought they were back in "old Virginny" again. Miles gritted his teeth and felt very indignant, but what could he do? The infamous prejudice against which they had borne testimony was controlling all the lines of city passenger railways in Philadelphia. While Miles and his friends were willing to suffer for a principle, the dirt, filth, cold, and disagreeableness of the quarters that they most likely would be compelled to occupy all night and the following day (Sunday) forbade submission. Added to this Miles felt that his young wife would hardly be able to contain herself while he was locked up. They sent for the writer to intercede for them.

At a late hour of the night, after going from the alderman's boarding-house to a fire engine house and other places, where it was supposed that he might probably be found, on going a third time to his hotel, a little before midnight, he was discovered to be in bed, and it was then ascertained that he had not been out all the evening. The night was very stormy. We could not tell whether or not the fruitless chase on which we had been sent in search of the alderman, was in keeping with the spirit that had locked the men up, designed to mislead us; he condescended at last to appear, and accepted our offer to go bail for all of them, and finally issued a discharge. This was hastily delivered at the station, and the prisoners were released.

But Miles was not satisfied; he had breathed free air in Massachusetts for four years, and being a man of high spirit he felt that he must further test the prejudices of the cars. Consequently one very cold night, when a deep snow covered the pavements, he was out with his wife, and thought that he would ride; his wife being fair, he put her on the car at the corner of Third and Pine streets, and walked to the corner of Fourth and Pine streets, where he stepped into the car and took his seat. The conductor straightway ordered him out, on the plea of color. God had shaded him a little too much. "How is this, my wife is in this car," spake Miles. All eyes gazed around to see who his wife was. By this time the car had been stopped, and the wrath of the conductor was kindled prodigiously. He did not, however, lay violent hands upon Miles. A late decision in court nad taught the police that they had no right to interfere, except in cases where the peace was actually being broken; so in order to get rid of this troublesome customer, the car was run off the track, the shivering passengers all leaving it, as though flying from a plague, with the exception of Miles, his wife, and another colored gentleman, who got on with Miles. The conductor then hoisted all the windows, took out the cushions, and unhitched the horses. But Miles and his party stood it bravely; Miles burning all the time with indignation at this exhibition of prejudice in the city of Brotherly Love. The war was then raging fiercely, and as Miles then felt, he was almost prepared to say, he didn't care which beat, as the woman said, when she saw her husband and the bear wrestling. He was compelled to admit that this prejudice was akin to slavery, and gave to slavery its chief support.

The occupants of the horseless car, which was being aired so thoroughly, remained in it for a length of time, until they had sufficiently borne their testimony, and they too quietly forsook it.

Prior to this event, by his industry and hard-earned savings, Miles had become the owner of a comfortable brick house, and had made up his mind to remain a citizen of Philadelphia, but the spirit which prompted the aforesaid treatment called up within him reflections somewhat similar to those aroused by Slavery, and it was not a great while before he offered his property for sale, including his business stand, resolving to return to Boston. He received an offer for his property, accepted it, pulled up stakes, and again hopefully turned his face thitherward. The ambitious Miles commenced business in Chelsea, near Boston, where he purchased himself a comfortable home; and he has ever since been successfully engaged in the sale of kerosene oil. Instead of seeking pleasure in the banjo, as he was wont to do in Virginia, he now finds delight in the Baptist Church, Rev. Mr. Grimes', of which he is a prominent member, and in other fields of usefulness tending to elevate and better the condition of society generally.

ARRIVAL FROM RICHMOND.

JOHN WILLIAM DUNGY.—BROUGHT A PASS FROM EX. GOV. GREGORY.

"HE ought to be put in a cage and kept for a show," said Anna Brown, daughter of the hero, John Brown, at the house of the writer, where she happened to meet the above named Underground Rail Road passenger. He had then just returned from Canada, after being a Refugee four years. In the mean time through the war and the Proclamation of Father Abraham the fetters had been torn from the limbs of the slave, and the way to Rich-

mond was open to all. John William on this occasion was on his way thither to see how his brethren together with their old oppressors looked facing each other as freemen. Miss Anna Brown was *en route* to Norfolk, where she designed to teach a school of the unfettered bondmen. The return of the Refugee was as unexpected as it was gratifying. Scarcely had the cordial greetings of the writer and his family ended and the daughter of Brown been introduced before the writer was plying his Refugee guest with a multiplicity of questions relative to his sojourn in Canada, etc. "How have you been getting along in Canada? Do you like the country?" "First-rate," said John William. "You look as though you had neither been starved, nor frozen. Have you had plenty of work, made some money, and taken care of yourself?" "Yes." "When you were on the Underground Rail Road on your way to Canada you promised that you were going to keep from all bad habits; how about the 'crittur?' do you take a little sometimes?" "No, I have not drank a drop since I left the South" replied John William with emphasis. "Good! "I suppose you smoke and chew at any rate?" "No, neither. I never think of such a thing." "Now don't you keep late hours at night and swear occasionally?" "No, Sir. All the leisure that I have of evenings is spent over my books as a general thing; I have not fallen into the fashionable customs of young men." Miss Brown, who had been an attentive listener, remarked: "HE OUGHT TO BE PUT IN A CAGE, ETC."

He was twenty-seven years of age when he first landed in Philadelphia, in the month of February, 1860, per steamer Pennsylvania, in which he had been stowed away in a store-room containing a lot of rubbish and furniture; in this way he reached City Point; here a family of Irish emigrants, very dirty, were taken on board, and orders were given that accommodations should be made for them in the room occupied by J. W. Here was trouble, but only for a moment. Those into whose charge he had been consigned on the boat knew that the kettle and pot-closet had often been used for Underground Rail Road purposes, and he was safely conducted to quarters among the pots. The room was exceedingly limited; but he stood it bravely. On landing he was not able to stand. It required not only his personal efforts but the help of friends to get him in a condition to walk. No sooner had he stepped on shore, however, than he began to cry aloud for joy. "Thank God!" rang out sonorously from his overflowing soul. Alarmed at this indication of gratitude his friends immediately told him that that would never do; that all hands would be betrayed; that he was far from being safe in Philadelphia. He suppressed his emotion. After being delivered into the hands of the Acting Committee, where he was in more private quarters, he gave full vent to the joy he experienced on reaching this city. He said that he had been trying earnestly for five years to obtain his freedom. For this special object he had saved up sixty-eight dollars and fifteen cents, all of which but the fifteen cents he willingly paid for his passage on the boat. Fifteen cents, the balance of his entire capital, was all that he had when he landed in Philadelphia.

Before leaving the South he was hired in the family of Ex-Governor Gregory. Of the Governor and his wife he spoke very highly,—said that they were kind to him and would readily favor him whenever he solicited them to do so. He stated that after making his arrangements to start, in order that he might be away several days before being missed, he told Mrs. Gregory that he would be glad to spend a week with his mother, (she lived some distance in the country). As he was not feeling very well she kindly acceded to his request, and told him to ask the Governor for a pass and some money. The Governor was busy writing, but he at once granted the prayer, wrote him a pass, gave John five dollars, adding that he was sorry that he had no more in his pocket, &c. John bowed and thanked the Governor, and soon got ready for his visit; but his route lay in a far different direction than that contemplated by the Governor and his lady. He was aiming for the Underground Rail Road. As has already been intimated, he was not owned by the Governor, but by the Ferrell heirs—five children who had moved from Virginia to Alabama years back. "Every Ferrell that lives is down on slaves; they are very severe," said John. Yet he had not suffered as many others had who belonged to them, as he had been a dining-room servant. At one time they had owned large numbers of slaves, but latterly they had been selling them off. Contrary to John's wishes his Alabama owners had notified him as well as the Governor, that in a short while he was to be taken to Alabama. This induced John to act with great promptness in leaving at the time that he did.

After passing several years in Canada as has been already noticed, he returned to Richmond and paid a visit to his old home.

He found that the governor and his wife had both departed, but two of the daughters (young ladies), still lived. They were both glad to see him; the younger especially; she told him that she was glad that he escaped, and that she "prayed for him." The elder remarked that she had always thought that he was too "good a Christian to run away." Another thing which she referred to, apparently with much feeling, was this: On his way to Canada, he wrote to the governor, from Rochester, "that he need put himself to no trouble in hunting him up, as he had made up his mind to visit Canada." She thought that John was rather "naughty," to write thus to her "papa," nevertheless, she was disposed to forgive him, after she had frankly spoken her mind.

JOHN found Richmond, which so long had held him in chains, fully humbled, and her slave power utterly cast down. His wondering eyes gazed until he was perfectly satisfied that it was the Lord's doings, and it was marvellous in his eyes. He was more than ever resolved to get an education, and go back to Virginia, to help teach his brethren who had been so long denied the privilege. It was not long before he was at Oberlin College, a faithful student, commanding the highest respect from all the faculty for his good deportment and studious habits.

After advancing rapidly there, the way opened more fully to pursue his studies with greater facilities and less expense at a college in one of the Eastern States. He accepted the favors of friends who offered him assistance, with a view of preparing him for a mission among the freedmen, believing that he possessed in a high degree, the elements for a useful worker, preacher, organizer and teacher. As the friends alluded to, were about taking measures to start a college at Harper's Ferry, especially for the benefit of the Freedmen, they anticipated making this latitude the field of his future endeavors, at least for a time. Ere he graduated in view of the fact that the harvest in the South so urgently called for laborers, he was solicited to be an agent for the Storer College,* and subsequently to enter upon a mission under the auspices of the Free-Will Baptists, in Martinsburg, Virginia. For three or four years he labored in this field with commendable zeal and acceptably, gathering young and old in day and Sunday-schools, and also organizing churches. By his constant labors his health

---

* The appended extract from an official circular, issued by the Board of Instruction of Storer College, will throw light upon this Institution :

STORER COLLEGE, HARPER'S FERRY, WEST VIRGINIA.

This Institution, deriving its name from John Storer, Esq., late of Sanford, Me., who gave ten thousand dollars to aid in its establishment, is located at Harper's Ferry, West Va., and has been chartered with full powers by a special act of the Legislature. The Corporation has been regularly organized, about thirty thousand dollars in money has been obtained, a large tract of land has been purchased, ample buildings have been secured, and a Normal School has been in successful operation during the last eighteen months. The U. S. authorities have repeatedly expressed their confidence in and sympathy with this undertaking, by liberal grants of money and buildings, and the agent for the distribution of the Peabody Fund, has pledged pecuniary aid to the best of the pupils in attendance, who may be in need of such assistance.

REV. J. CALDER, D. D., *Pres.*,
Harrisburg, Penna.
Harper's Ferry, West Va., March 1, 1869.

REV. N. C. BRACKETT, *Act. Sec'y.*,
Harper's Ferry, West Va.

became impaired; receiving a call from a church in Providence, he accepted, not without knowing, however, that his mission was to be left in faithful hands, to carry on the good work.

There is still need of efficient laborers in the Shenandoah Valley. According to the testimony of Mr. Dungy, scores of places may still be found where the children have no school privileges, and where many, both old and young, have never had the opportunity of entering a meeting-house or church since the war, as the spirit of the white Christians in these regions is greatly embittered against the colored people, owing to the abolition of Slavery; and they do not invite them to either church or school. Indeed, the churches are closed against them. At different times, Mr. Dungy has eloquently represented the condition of the colored churches of the South, in the city of Philadelphia. As a speaker, Mr. Dungy is able and interesting, of good address, remarkably graceful in his manners, and possessing much general information.

The subjoined letters received from him, while a fugitive in Canada, are characteristic of the man, and will repay a perusal.

BRANTFORD, March 3d, 1860.

MR. WM. STILL, DEAR SIR:—I have seated myself this evening to write you a few lines to inform you that I have got through my journey, and landed safely in Brantford, where I found my friend, Stepney Brown, and we expressed great joy at meeting each other, and had a great shaking of hands, and have not got done talking yet of the old times we had in Virginia.

I thank God I am enjoying vigorous health, and hope you all are well, as it is written in the first Psalm, "Blessed is the man that walketh not in the counsel of the ungodly, nor standeth in the way of sinners, nor sitteth in the seat of the scornful."

I wish you may think of me often and pray for me that I may grow a man, one of the followers of our meek and lowly Saviour Give my love to Mrs. Still, and family, and the Rev. Mr. Gibbs, that was residing with you when I was there.

I must now inform you a little about Canada, at least as much of it as I have seen and heard. I arrived in the city of Hamilton, on the 15th February, 1860, at nine o'clock in the evening, and the weather was dreary and cold, and the cars laid over there until ten o'clock next day, and I went up into the city and saw a portion of it. I then started for Toronto, arrived there same day at 12 o'clock. There I met friends from Richmond, remained there several days; during the time we had a very extensive snow storm, and I took the opportunity of walking around the city looking at the elephants, and other great sights. I liked it very much; but upon hearing that my friend and brother Stepney Brown was in Brantford, I became disatisfied and left for Brantford on the 21st February, 1860. I have found it a very pleasant, and have been told it is the prettiest place in Canada.

It is built upon the Grand River, which is two hundred miles long, and empties into Lake Erie. It rises to a great height every spring, and great masses of ice come down, bringing bridges, saw-logs, trees, and fairly sweeps everything before it. The people who live upon the flats are in great danger of being drowned in their houses.

I got a situation immediately at the Kerby House, by the influence of my friend and brother, Stepney Brown, who I must say has been very kind to me, as also have the peo-

35

ple of Brantford. The Kerbey House is the largest hotel in the town about 250 rooms, and a stable at the back, with a gas-house of its own. No more at present, but remain,

Yours very respectfully,   JOHN WILLIAM DUNGY.

P. S. Write at your earliest convenience, and oblige your friend,   J. W. D.

BRANTFORD, April 20th.

MR. STILL, DEAR SIR:—I feel myself quite lonesome this evening, and not hearing from you lately I take this oppertunity to drop you a few lines. I have not much to say, . brother Brown has left for the falls, and expects to return next winter. The weather is mild and warm at this time; the grass is putting up and begins to look like spring. I thank the Lord I am enjoying good health at this time. I hope this letter will find you and your family well, give my compliments to them all and Mr. Gibbs and the young lady that was at your house when I was there. Times has been hard this winter, but they are increasing for the better. I wrote to you a few days ago, I don't know whether you got my letter. I asked in my letter if Mr. Williams was on the pennsylvania, that runs from their to Richmond, Va. I should have written to him, but I did not know his number, I also named a friend of mine, Mr. Plumer if he arrives their pleas to tell him to come to Brantford, where I am for there are good chances for business I think a great deal about my colored brethren in the South but I hope to be a benefit to them one of these days. We have quite a melancholy affair about one of our colored brothers who made his escape from the South those who took him up have gone back to obtain witness to convict him for murder. These witness is to be here on Monday 23 inst but the defendence of the law says they shant take him back unless they bring good witness and men of truth I will write you more about it after the trial comes of. I must say a little about myself. I want to devote myself to study if I can for the next twelve months. I expect to leave the Kirby House on the 5th of may. I have taken a barber shop which is a very good situation and one hand employed with me. I would be much oblige to you if you would give me some advice what to do. I sent you the morning herald yesterday which contained a accident which occurd on the G. trunk R. W. you will see in it that we don't have much politics here. The late destructive fire we had I thought it would have kept brantford back this summer but it is increasing slowly I have nothing more to say at this time. I hope the Lord may bless you all and take care of you in this world, and after time receive you in his everlasting kingdom through Jesus Christ our Lord. Answer this as soon as convenient. Good bye.   Yours respectfully   J. W. DUNGY.

BRANTFORD, C. W., JANUARY 11th, 61.

MR. WM. STILL, DEAR SIR:—I take this opportunity to drop you a few lines to let you hear from me. I am well at this time, hoping this will find you the same.

I acknowledge my great neglectness of you with great regret that I have not answered your letter before this, I hope you will excuse me as I have succeeded in getting me a wife since I wrote to you last.

My mind has been much taken up in so doing for several months past. Give my compliments to your wife and your family, and Mr. Gibbs, also hoping they are all well. Tell Mrs. Still to pray for me that I may grow in grace and the knowledge of the truth as it is in Jesus.

I often think of you all. I pray that the time may come when we will all be men in the United States. We have read here of the great disturbance in the South. My prayer is that this may be a deathblow to Slavery. Do you ever have any Underground Rail Road passengers now? Times have been very prosperous in Canada this year.

The commercial trade and traffic on the railways has been very dull for these few months back. Business on the Buffalo and Lake Huron railway has been so dull that a great number of the hands have been discharged on account of the panic in the South.

Canada yet cries, Freedom! Freedom! Freedom!

I must now say a little about my friend and brother Stepney Brown, he lived about six months at the Niagara Falls and is now going to school here in Brantford, he sends his best respects to you all. He and I often sit together at night after the labor of the day is over talking about our absent friends wishing we could see them once more.

Mr. Brown and myself have been wishing for one or two of your slavery standards and would be much obliged to you if you would send some of the latest.

Please let me hear from you as soon as possible. I must now bring my letter to a close and remain your affectionate friend, J. W. DUNGY.

P. S. May the Lord be with you. J. W. DUNGY.

Address your letter to John W. Dungy, Brantford, C. W.

"AUNT HANNAH MOORE."

In 1854 in company with her so-called Mistress (Mary Moore) Aunt Hannah arrived in Philadelphia, from Missouri, being *en route* to California, where she with her mistress was to join her master, who had gone there years before to seek his fortune. The mistress having relatives in this city tarried here a short time, not doubting that she had sufficient control over Aunt Hannah to keep her from contact with either abolitionists or those of her own color, and that she would have no difficulty in taking her with her to her journey's end. If such were her calculations she was greatly mistaken. For although Aunt Hannah was destitute of book-learning she was nevertheless a woman of thought and natural ability, and while she wisely kept her counsel from her mistress she took care to make her wants known to an abolitionist. She had passed many years under the yoke, under different owners, and now seeing a ray of hope she availed herself of the opportunity to secure her freedom. She had occasion to go to a store in the neighborhood where she was stopping, and to her unspeakable joy she found the proprietor an abolitionist and a friend who inquired into her condition and proffered her assistance. The store-keeper quickly made known her condition at the Anti-slavery Office, and in double-quick time J. M. McKim and Charles Wise as abolitionists and members of the Vigilance Committee repaired to the stopping-place of the mistress and her slave to demand in the name of humanity and the laws of Pennsylvania that Aunt Hannah should be no longer held in fetters but that she should be immediately proclaimed free. In the eyes of the mistress this procedure was so extraordinary that she became very much excited and for a moment threatened them with the "broomstick," but her raving had no effect on Messrs. McKim and Wise, who did not rest contented until Aunt Hannah was safely in their hands.

She had lived a slave in Moore's family in the State of Missouri about ten years and said she was treated very well, had plenty to eat, plenty to wear, and a plenty of work. It was prior to her coming into the possession of Moore that Aunt Hannah had been made to drink the bitter waters of oppression. From this point, therefore, we shall present some of the incidents of her life, from infancy, and very nearly word for word as she related them:

"Moore bought me from a man named McCaully, who owned me about a year. I fared dreadful bad under McCaully. One day in a rage he undertook to beat me with the limb of a cherry-tree; he began at me and tried in the first place to snatch my clothes off, but he did not succeed. After that he beat the cherry-tree limb all to pieces over me. The first blow struck me on the back of my neck and knocked me down; his wife was looking on, sitting on the side of the bed crying to him to lay on. After the limb was worn out he then went out to the yard and got a lath, and he come at me again and beat me with that until he broke it all to pieces. He was not satisfied then; he next went to the fence and tore off a paling, and with that he took both hands, 'cursing' me all the time as hard as he could. With an oath he would say, 'now don't you love me?' 'Oh master, I will pray for you, I would cry, then he would 'cuss' harder than ever.' He beat me until he was tired and quit. I crept out of doors and throwed up blood; some days I was hardly able to creep. With this beating I was laid up several weeks. Another time Mistress McCaully got very angry. One day she beat me as bad as he did. She was a woman who would get very mad in a minute. One day she began scolding and said the kitchen wasn't kept clean. I told her the kitchen was kept as clean as any kitchen in the place; she spoke very angry, and said she didn't go by other folks but she had rules of her own. She soon ordered me to come in to her. I went in as she ordered me; she met me with a mule-rope, and ordered me to cross my hands. I crossed my hands and she tied me to the bedstead. Here her husband said, 'my dear, now let me do the fighting.' In her mad fit she said he shouldn't do it, and told him to stand back and keep out of the way or I will give you the cowhide she said to him. He then 'sot' down in a 'cheer' and looked like a man condemned to be hung; then she whipped me with the cowhide until I sunk to the floor. He then begged her to quit. He said to his wife she has begged and begged and you have whipped her enough. She only raged 'wus;' she turned the butt end of the cowhide and struck me five or six blows over my head as hard as she could; she then throwed the cowhide down and told a little girl to untie me. The little girl was not able to do it; Mr. McCaully then untied me himself. Both times that I was beat the blood run down from my head to my feet.

"They wouldn't give you anything to eat hardly. McCaully bore the name of coming by free colored children without buying them, and selling them afterwards. One boy on the place always said that he was free but had been kidnapped from Arkansas. He could tell all about how he was kidnapped, but could not find anybody to do anything for him, so he had to content himself.

"McCaully bought me from a man by the name of Landers. While in Landers' hands I had the rheumatism and was not able to work. He was afraid I was going to die, or he would lose me, and I would not be of any service to him, so he took and traded me off for a wagon. I was something better when he traded me off; well enough to be about. My health remained bad for about four years, and I never got my health until Moore bought me. Moore took me for a debt. McCaully owed Moore for wagons. I was not born in Missouri but was born in Virginia. From my earliest memory I was owned by Conrad Hackler; he lived in Grason County. He was a very poor man, and had no other slave but me. He bought me before I was quite four years old, for one hundred dollars. Hackler bought me from a man named William Scott. I must go back by good rights to the beginning and tell all: Scott bought me first from a young man he met one day in the road, with a bundle in his arms. Scott, wishing to know of the young man what he had in his bundle, was told that he had a baby. 'What are you going to do with it?' said Scott. The young man said that he was going to take it to his sister; that its mother was dead, and it had nobody to take care of it. Scott offered the young man a horse for it, and the young man took him up. This is the way I was told that Scott came by me. I never knowed anything about my mother or father, but I have always believed that my mother was a white woman, and that I was put away to save her character; I have always thought this. Under Hackler I was treated more like a brute than a human being. I was fed like the dogs; had a trough dug out of a piece of wood for a plate. After I growed up to ten years old they made me sleep out in an old house standing off some distance from the main house where my master and mistress lived. A bed of straw and old rags was made for me in a big trough called the tan trough (a trough having been used for tanning purposes). The cats about the place came and slept with me, and was all the company I had. I had to work with the hoe in the field and help do everything in doors and out in all weathers. The place was so poor that some seasons he would not raise twenty bushels of corn and hardly three bushels of wheat. As for shoes I never knowed what it was to have a pair of shoes until I was grown up. After I growed up to be a woman my master thought nothing of taking my clothes off, and would whip me until the blood would run down to the ground. After I was twenty-five years old they did not treat me so bad; they both professed to get religion about that time; and my master said he would never lay the weight of his finger on me again. Once after that mistress wanted him to whip me, but he didn't do it, nor never whipped me any more. After awhile my master died; if they had gone according to law I would have been hired out or sold, but my mistress wanted to keep me to carry on the place for her support. So I was kept for seven or eight years after his death. It was understood between my mistress, and her children, and her friends, who all met after master died, that I was to take care of mistress, and after mistress died I should not serve anybody else. I done my best to keep my mistress from suffering. After a few years they all became dissatisfied, and moved to Missouri. They scattered, and took up government land. Without means they lived as poor people commonly live, on small farms in the woods. I still lived with my mistress. Some of the heirs got dissatisfied, and sued for their rights or a settlement; then I was sold with my child, a boy."

Thus Aunt Hannah reviewed her slave-life, showing that she had been in the hands of six different owners, and had seen great tribulation under each of them, except the last; that she had never known a mother's or a father's care; that Slavery had given her one child, but no husband as a protector or a father. The half of what she passed through in the way of suffering has scarcely been hinted at in this sketch. Fifty-seven years were passed in bondage before she reached Philadelphia. Under the good Providence through which she came in possession of her freedom, she found a kind home with a family of Abolitionists, (Mrs. Gillingham's), whose hearts had been in deep sympathy with the slave for many years. In this situation Aunt Hannah remained several years, honest, faithful, and obliging, taking care of her earnings, which were put out at interest for her by her friends. Her mind was deeply imbued with religious feeling, and an unshaken confidence in God as her only trust; she connected herself with the A. M. E. Bethel Church, of Philadelphia, where she has walked, blameless and exemplary up to this day. Probably there is not a member in that large congregation whose simple faith and whose walk and conversation are more commendable than Aunt Hannah's. Although she has passed through so many hardships she is a woman of good judgment and more than average intellect; enjoys good health, vigor, and peace of mind in her old days, with a small income just sufficient to meet her humble wants without having to live at service. After living in Philadelphia for several years, she was married to a man of about her own age, possessing all her good qualities; had served a life-time in a highly respectable Quaker family of this city, and had so won the esteem of his kind employer that at his death he left him a comfortable house for life, so that he was not under the necessity of serving another. The name of the recipient of the good Quaker friend's bounty and Aunt Hannah's companion, was Thomas Todd. After a few years of wedded life, Aunt Hannah was called upon to be left alone again in the world by the death of her husband, whose loss was mourned by many friends, both colored and white, who knew and respected him.

KIDNAPPING OF RACHEL AND ELIZABETH PARKER— MURDER OF JOSEPH C. MILLER IN 1851 AND 1852.

Those who were interested in the Anti-Slavery cause, and who kept posted with reference to the frequent cases of kidnapping occurring in different Free States, especially in Pennsylvania, during the twenty years previous to emancipation, cannot fail to remember the kidnapping of Rachel and Elizabeth Parker, and the murder of Joseph C. Miller, who resided in West Nottingham township, Chester county, Pennsylvania, in the latter part of 1851, and the beginning of 1852.

Both the kidnapping and the murder at the time of the occurrence shocked and excited the better thinking and humane classes largely, not only in Pennsylvania, but to a considerable extent over the Northern States. It may be said, without contradiction, that Chester county, at least, was never more aroused by any one single outrage that had taken place within her borders, than by these occurrences. For a long while the interest was kept alive, and even as lately as the past year (1870), we find the case still agitating the citizens of Chester county. Judge Benjamin I. Passmore, of said county, in defence of truth in an exhaustive article published in the "Village Record," West Chester, Oct. 12th, 1870, gives a reliable version of the matter, from beginning to end, which we feel constrained to give in full, as possessing great historical value, bearing on kidnapping in general, especially in Pennsylvania.

TOM M'CREARY.

FRIEND EVANS:—I noticed in the "Village Record," a short time since, an article taken from the Delaware "Transcript," an obituary notice of the death of the noted character, whose name heads this article, in which false statements were made, relative to the outrage he committed in kidnapping Rachel and Elizabeth Parker, two colored girls who were then, 1851, residing in the southern portion of Chester county. In your paper of the 13th ult., I also read an answer to the charges and insinuations made in the "Transcript," against Joseph C. Miller, (whose life was basely destroyed), and other citizens of Chester county ; as the occurrence took place in my immediate neighborhood, and I was familiar with all the facts and circumstances, I propose to give a truthful history of that vile and wicked transaction.

In the winter of 1851, the said McCreary in some unexplained way, took Elizabeth Parker, one of the said colored girls, from the house of one Donally (not McDonald), in the township of East Nottingham, where she was living ; but little was said about it by Donally, or any one else. Soon after, McCreary with two or three others of like proclivities, called at the house of Joseph C. Miller, in West Nottingham, where Rachel was living, and seized her, gagged her, and placed her in a carriage and drove off. The screams of Mrs. Miller and her children, soon brought the husband and father to the rescue; he pursued them on foot, and at a short distance overtook them in a narrow private road, disputing with James Pollock, the owner of the land, whose wagon prevented them from passing. They turned and took another road, and came out at Stubb's Mill, making for the Maryland line with all possible speed; they arrived at Perryville before the train for Baltimore. Eli Haines and a young man named Wiley, who lived near Rising Sun, Maryland, about two miles from Joseph C. Miller's, arrived at the same place soon after, intending to go to Philadelphia. Mr. Haines knew Rachel, and seeing McCreary there, and her so overwhelmed in sorrow, at once guessed the situation of affairs, and he and Wiley changed their intentions of going to Philadelphia, and went in the same car with McCreary and his victim, to Baltimore, and quietly watched what disposition would be made of her, as they felt certain pursuit would be made.

As soon as possible, after McCreary had escaped from West Nottingham, Joseph C. Miller, William Morris, Abner Richardson, Jesse B. Kirk, and H. G. Coates, started in pursuit on horseback; when they arrived at Perryville, the train had gone, with the kidnapper and the girl; they followed in the next train. Soon after they arrived in Baltimore, they were met by Haines and Wiley, who had been on the lookout for a pursuing party, and they gave the information that Rachel was deposited in Campbell's slave-pen. They were directed by an acquaintance of one of the party, to Francis S. Cochran, a prominent member of the Society of Friends. Francis informed them he was well acquainted with Campbell, and he at once accompained them. Campbell assured Friend Cochran that whilst he approved of Slavery and catching runaway slaves, he despised kidnapping and kidnappers; and on the arrival of McCreary, he ordered him to remove Rachel forthwith, which he proceeded to do. Friend Cochran insisted on going with them, and saw the girl deposited in jail to await a legal investigation. By this time it was evening, and the Chester county men all went home with Cochran, where they had their suppers; the excitement being great, Friend Cochran did not consider it safe for them to go to the depot direct; he procured their tickets and had them driven by a circuitous route to the depot, charging them to keep together, and take their seats in the cars at once. Soon after they were seated and before the cars started, Miller stepped out on the platform to smoke, against the expostulations of his friends. Jesse B. Kirk, his brother-in-law and Abner Richardson followed immediately, and although they were right at his heels, he was gone; they called him by name, and stepped down into the crowd, but soon became alarmed for their own safety, and returned to their seats. A consultation was held, and it was agreed that Wiley, who was least known, and not directly identified with the affair, should pass through the train when it started, and see if Miller had not mistakenly got into another car. At Stemen's Run station, Wiley returned to the party with the sad tidings that Joseph C. Miller was not in that train. On consultation, it was agreed that Jesse B. Kirk and Abner Richardson should return from Perryville in the next train, and prosecute further search for Miller. They did so return, and McCreary also returned to Baltimore in the same car, he having left Baltimore in the car in the evening with the Chester county men; they arrived late in the night, and locked themselves up in a room in the first hotel they came to. Their search was fruitless, and they were forced to return home with the sad tidings that Miller could not be found. This intelligence aroused the whole neighborhood; public meetings were held to consult about what was best to be done. The writer presided at one of those meetings, which was largely attended, and it was with difficulty that the people could be restrained from organizing an armed force to kidnap and lynch McCreary. Better counsels, however, finally prevailed and it was resolved to send a party to Baltimore to prosecute further the search for Miller. About twenty men volunteered for the service; I went to the house of Joseph C. Miller, the morning they were to start, but they had met at Lewis Mellrath's, a brother-in-law of Miller. I was there endeavoring to console the aged mother and distracted wife and children of Joseph C. Miller, when word came that he had been found hanging to a limb in the bushes near Stemen's Run station, and such a scene of distress I hope may never again be my lot to witness; it was heart-rending in the extreme.

The party went to Baltimore, and such was the excitement that it was considered unsafe for the party to go out in a body in day-time. Levi K. Brown, who then resided in Baltimore, went with them by moonlight, and they disinterred the body, which they found about two feet under ground, in a rough box, with a narrow lid that freely admitted the dirt to surround his body in the box. No undertaker in Baltimore could be found that would allow the body left at his place of business whilst a coffin was prepared, and it was deposited in "Friends'" vault; a coffin was finally procured and William Morris and Abner Richardson started with it for his home. When they arrived at Perryville no one would render them any assistance, and they were compelled to leave the corpse in an old saw mill, and walk up to Port Deposit, a distance of five miles, in the night, the weather being extremely cold, and a deep snow on the ground. There they procured horses and a sled and started with the body, but when within a short distance of the Pennsylvania line they were overtaken by a messenger with a requisition from the Governor of Maryland to return the body to Baltimore county, in order that an inquisition and post-mortem examination might be held in legal form. With sorrowful hearts they turned back; (one of these young men told me that at no place south of Port Deposit could they get any one to assist them in handling the corpse). By this time the affair had created a great excitement, both in Chester county and the City of Baltimore. Rev. John M. Dickey, Hon. Henry S. Evans, then a member of the Senate, Brinton Darlington, then Sheriff of Chester county, and very many of the leading men took a deep interest in the matter; we all did our part. The Society of Friends in Baltimore took the matter in hand, and many other worthy citizens belonging to the Presbyterian Church and others lent their aid and influence. Hon. Henry S. Evans, who was then in the Senate of Pennsylvania, brought the matter before the Legislature, and the result was that the Governor appointed Judges Campbell and Bell, the latter of our county, to defend these two poor colored girls thus foully kidnapped.

The body of Miller underwent a post-mortem examination in Baltimore county, at which a great number of rowdies attended, who occupied their time drinking whisky and cursing the Pennsylvania Abolitionists; the body finally reached its distressed home for interment. Drs. Hutchinson and Dickey were called upon to make an examination, at which I was present, and all were clearly of opinion that he had been foully murdered. His wrists and ankles bore the unmistakable marks of manacles; across the abdomen was a black mark as if made by a rope or cord; the end of his nose bore marks as if held by some instrument of torture. His funeral took place, and his remains were followed to the grave by an immense concourse of sympathizing friends and neighbors.

Such, however, was the excitement, that the public demanded a further examination; he was disinterred again, and the same two eminent physicians made a thorough post-mortem examination, and one of them told the writer that there were not two ounces of contents in his stomach and bowels, and that there was abundant evidence of the presence of arsenic. His remains were again interred and suffered to remain undisturbed.

The theory of his friends was that he had been suddenly snatched from the platform of the car in the Baltimore Depot, gagged, stripped, and lashed down by the ankles and wrists, and a rope across his abdomen, that his nose had been held by some instrument, and that he was in this situation drenched with arsenic, and puked and purged to death, and that McCreary, or some one for him, had heard Wiley repeat at Stemen's Run Station, that he was not on the train, conceived the idea of taking his body there and hanging it to a tree to convey the idea that he had committed suicide at that place, and such was the statement published by some of the Maryland newspapers. His companions said he eat a very hearty supper that evening at Francis S. Cochran's, which with the other facts that his clothing were not soiled, and his stomach and bowels were empty, goes strongly to substantiate the theory that he had been stripped and foully murdered, as above indicated. Never was there a more false assertion than that the "broad brimmed Quakers in Pennsylvania were accomplices of McCreary," as it is well known that opposition to slavery has been a cardinal principle of the Society of Friends for a century. And that Joseph C. Miller committed suicide because of his being implicated in the kidnapping is a base fabrication. I knew Joseph C. Miller from boyhood intimately, and I here take pleasure in saying that he was an honest, unassuming man, of good moral character and stern integrity, and would have spurned the idea of any complication, directly or indirectly, with slavery or kidnapping.

It appears his foul murder was not sufficient to satisfy the friends of slavery and kidnapping, but an attempt is now made, after the victim has slumbered near twenty years in the grave, to blast his good name by insinuating that he was a party, or implicated in the vile transactions here narrated.

Rachel remained in jail; Elizabeth, who had been sold to parties in New Orleans, was sent for by Campbell, ample security having been given that she should be returned if proved to be a slave. Their trial finally came on, and after a long and tedious investigation they were both proven, by hosts of respectable witnesses to be free. They returned to their mother, in Chester county, who was still living.

The Grand Jury of Chester county found a true bill against McCreary for kidnapping, a requisition was obtained, and B. Darlington, Esq., then High Sheriff, proceeded with it to Annapolis; but the Governor of Maryland refused to allow McCreary to be arrested in that State.

Thus terminated this terrible affair, which cost the State of Pennsylvania nearly $3000, as well as a heavy expense to many citizens of Baltimore, and those of this county who took an active part, and whilst it is to be hoped that the principal actor in this sad transaction fully atoned for his evil deeds, whilst living, and his friends may have had a right to eulogize him after death, they should not have gone out of their way to traduce other parties, dead and alive, whose reputations were known by living witnesses, to be beyond reproach.   JUSTICE.

ARRIVAL FROM VIRGINIA, 1854.

TUCKER WHITE.

TUCKER reported that he fled from Major Isaac Roney, of Dinwiddie Court-House, Virginia, in the Christmas week prior to his arrival; that he reached Petersburg and then encountered difficulties of the most trying nature; he next stopped at City Point, and was equally unfortunate there. From exposure in the cold he was severely frost-bitten. While suffering from the frost he was kept in the poor-house. After partial recovery he made his way to Baltimore and thence to Philadelphia. Once or twice he was captured and carried back. The Committee suspected that he was a cunning impostor who had learned how to tell a tale of suffering simply to excite the sympathies of the benevolent; yet, with the map of Virginia before them, he proved himself familiar with localities adjacent to the neighborhood in which he was raised. Although not satisfied with his statement, the Committee decided to aid him.

Passmore Williamson, who had taken a deep interest in the examination of his case, in order to ascertain the facts, addressed the following note to Major Roney, using as his signature the name of his friend, Wm. J. Canby:

PHILADELPHIA, June 24, 1854.

MAJOR ISAAC RONEY:

DEAR SIR :—Within a few days past a colored man has been traversing the streets of this city, exciting the sympathies of the benevolent by the recital of a tale of the hardships he has lately passed through. He represents himself to be Tucker White, your slave, a carpenter by trade, and that he escaped from your service last Christmas. He is quite dark in complexion, rather over the medium size, and a little lame; the latter, probably, from the effects of frost on his feet, from which, he alleges, he suffered severely.

He seems to be well acquainted with the adjoining localities, but altogether his narrative is almost incredible, and I am therefore induced to make the inquiry whether such a man has escaped from your service or lately left your neighborhood. We are perfectly flooded with such vagrants. It would be a great relief if some measures could be resorted to to keep them under legal restraint. An answer addressed to No. 73 South 4th Street, above Walnut, will reach me, and oblige,   Yours, &c.   WM. J. CANBY.

Weeks passed, but no answer came from the Major. All hope was abandoned of obtaining a more satisfactory clue to the history of Tucker White. About three months, however, after Mr. Williamson had written, the appended note came as an answer:

MR. CANBY:

Major Roney received a letter from you relative to his boy, Tucker White, and has sent me here to inquire of you his whereabouts now. If you know anything concerning him and will give me such information so I can get him, you will be rewarded for your trouble. You will please address,

No. 147 American Hotel.

The Major would have sent on sooner but he has been sick, and the letter laid in Office several days.

Mr. Canby was at the time ill, and no attention was paid to the communication. After a day's delay the following note came to hand, but, as in the former instance, no answer was returned.

MR. CANBY:

You will confer a great favor on me by writing me whether you were really the author of a letter to Major Isaac Roney, of Dinwiddie Court House, Va., relative to his boy Tucker White, and if you were the author, please let me know when you last saw him, and where. I called at your office yesterday to see you, but your cousin (I think he said he was) told me you had the cholera, and if you felt well enough you were going to the country to-morrow. I hope you will excuse my writing to you to-day, on that account. I would not know where to direct a letter if I were to wait until to-morrow. If you know anything concerning him and will let me know it, so that I can find and arrest him, you will very much oblige   Yours, &c.,   I. M. TUCKER,

No. 147 American Hotel.

Please write me an answer to-day, so I may know how to proceeed to-morrow. If I find him I will be very happy to see you before I leave in behalf of Major Roney, in whose business I am now engaged.   I. M. T.

Some one, however, who had a hand in the first letter, referred the Major to Passmore Williamson, Seventh and Arch Streets. To Mr. Williamson's surprise the individual who had addressed Mr. C. appeared at his office with the identical letter in his hand that had been addressed him by Mr. W. (with W. J. C.'s signature.) On addressing Mr. W. he held out the letter and inquired: "Are you the author of this letter, sir?" Mr. W. looked at it and remarked that it appeared to have been written by a man named Canby. "My name is Williamson, but if you will walk in and take a seat I will attend to you in a few moments." Accordingly, after occupying a little time in adjusting some papers, he signified to the stranger that he was ready to answer any of his questions. Said Mr. W., "I say frankly that I am the author of that letter." He then paused for a reply. The stranger then said, "I have come from Virginia in behalf of Major Roney, in search of his boy, Tucker White; the Major was very anxious to recover him, and he would gladly reward Mr. W. or anybody else who would aid him in the matter." He then asked Mr. W. if he knew anything of his whereabouts. Mr. W. replied: "I do not at present; for a long time I have heard nothing of him. I must tell you that I am very sorry that Major Roney gave himself the trouble to send all the way to Philadelphia to re-capture his 'boy Tucker White,' and with regard to giving information or assistance, I know of but one or two men in this city who would be mean enough to stoop to do such dirty work. Geo. F. Alberti, a notorious kidnapper, and E. D. Ingraham, equally as notorious as a counsel of slave-hunters whom everybody here despises, might have served you in this matter. I know no others to recommend; if anybody can find the 'boy,' they can. But should they find him they will be obliged to take legal steps in arresting him before they can proceed. In such a case, instead of assisting Major Roney, I should feel bound to assist Tucker White by throwing every obstacle that .I possibly could in the way of his being carried back to Virginia; and to close the matter I wish it to be understood that I do not desire to hold any further correspondence with Major Roney, of Dinwiddie, Virginia, about his 'boy,' Tucker White."

ARRIVAL FROM NORFOLK.

MARY MILLBURN, *alias* LOUISA F. JONES, ESCAPED IN MALE ATTIRE.

Neither in personal appearance, manners, nor language, were any traces of the Peculiar Institution visible in Mary Millburn. On the contrary, she represented a young lady, with a passable education, and very refined in her deportment. She had eaten the white bread of Slavery, under the Misses Chapman, and they had been singularly kind to her, taking special pains with her in regard to the company she should keep, a point important to young girls, so liable to exposure as were the unprotected young females of the South. She being naturally of a happy disposition, obliging, competent, there was but little room for any jars in the household, so far as Mary was concerned. Notwithstanding all this, she was not satisfied; Slavery in its most dreaded aspect, was all around her, continually causing the heart to bleed and eyes to weep of both young and old. The auction-block and slave-pen were daily in view. Young girls as promising as herself, she well knew, had to be exposed, examined, and sold to the vilest slave-holders living.

With her knowledge of the practical wickedness of the system, how could she be satisfied? It was impossible! She determined to escape. She could be accommodated, but with no favored mode of travel. No flowery beds of ease could be provided in her case, any more than in the case of others. Mary took the Underground Rail Road enterprise into consideration. The opportunity of a passage on a steamer was before her to accept or refuse. The spirit of freedom dictated that she should accept the offer and leave by the first boat. Admonished that she could reach the boat and also travel more safely in male attire she at once said, "Any way so I succeed." It is not to be supposed for a moment, that the effort could be made without encountering a great "fight of affliction." When the hour arrived for the boat to start, Mary was nicely secreted in a box (place), where she was not discovered when the officers made their usual search. On arriving in Philadelphia, she mingled her rejoicings with the Committee in testifying to the great advantage of the Underground Rail Road, and to the carefulness of its agents in guarding against accidents. After remaining a short time in Philadelphia, she made choice of Boston as her future residence, and with a letter of introduction to William Lloyd Garrison, she proceeded thitherward. How she was received, and what she thought of the place and people, may be gleaned from this letter (written by herself.)

BOSTON, May 15th, 1858.

DEAR FRIEND :—I have selected this oppotunity to write you a few lines, hopeing thay may find you and yours enjoying helth and happiness. I arrived hear on Thirsday last, and had a lettor of intoduction giving to me by one of the gentlemen at the Antoslavery office in New York, to Mr. Garrison in Boston, I found him and his lady both to bee very clever. I stopped with them the first day of my arrivel hear, since that Time I have been living with Mrs. Hilliard I have met with so menny of my acquaintances hear, that I all most immagion my self to bee in the old country. I have not been to Canaday yet, as you expected. I had the pleasure of seeing the lettor that you wrote to them on the subject. I suffored much on the road with head ake but since that time I have no reason to complain, please do not for git to send the degarritips in the Shaimpain basket with Dr. Lundys, Mr. Lesley said he will send them by express. tell Julia kelly, that through mistake, I took one of her pocket handkerchift, that was laying on the table, but I shall keep it in remembranc of the onner. I must bring my lettor to a close as I have nothing more to say, and believe me to be your faithfull friend.   LOUISA F. JONES.

P. S. Remember me to each and every member of your familly and all Enquiring Friends.

Being of an industrious turn she found a situation immediately, and from that day to the present, she has sustained an excellent character in every respect, and as a fashionable dressmaker does a good business.

ARRIVAL OF FIFTEEN FROM NORFOLK, VIRGINIA.

PER SCHOONER—TWICE SEARCHED—LANDED AT LEAGUE ISLAND.

ISAAC FORMAN, HENRY WILLIAMS, WILLIAM SEYMOUR, HARRIET TAYLOR, MARY BIRD, MRS. LEWEY, SARAH SAUNDERS, SOPHIA GRAY, HENRY GRAY, MARY GRAY, WINFIELD SCOTT, and three children.

About the 4th of July, 1856, a message reached the Secretary that a schooner containing fifteen Underground Rail Road passengers, from Norfolk, Virginia, would be landed near League Island, directly at the foot of Broad street, that evening at a late hour, and a request accompanied the message, to the effect that the Committee would be on hand to receive them. Accordingly the Secretary procured three carriages, with trustworthy drivers, and between ten and eleven o'clock at night arrived on the banks of the Schuylkill, where all was quiet as a " country grave-yard." The moon was shining and soon the mast of a schooner was discovered. No sign of any other vessel was then in sight. On approaching the bank, in the direction of the discovered mast, the schooner was also discovered. The hearts of those on board were swelling with unutterable joy; yet even at that dead hour of night, far away from all appearance of foes, no one felt at liberty to give vent to his feelings other than in a whisper. The name of the captain and schooner being at once recognized, the first impulse was to jump down on the deck. Upon second view it was seen that the descent was too great to admit of such a feat. In a moment we concluded that we could pull them up the embankment from the deck by taking hold of their hands as they stood on tip toe.

One after another was pulled up, and warmly greeted, until it came the turn of a large object, weighing about two hundred and sixty pounds, full large enough to make two ordinary women. The captain, who had experienced much inconvenience with her on the voyage, owing to the space she required chuckled over the fact that the Committee would have their hands full for once. Poor Mrs. Walker, however, stretched out her large arms, we seized her hands vigorously; the captain laughing heartily as did the other passengers at the tug now being made. We pulled with a will, but Mrs. Walker remained on the deck. A one horse power was needed. The pullers took breath, and again took hold, this time calling upon the captain to lay-to a helping hand; the captain prepared to do so, and as she was being raised, he having a good foot-hold, placed himself in a position for pushing to the full extent of his powers, and thus she was safely landed. All being placed in the carriages, they were driven to the station and comfortably provided for.

On the voyage they had encountered more than the usual dangers. Indeed troubles began with them before they had set sail from Norfolk. The first indication of danger manifested itself as they stood on the bank of the river awaiting the arrival of a small boat which had been engaged to row them to the schooner. Although they had sought as they supposed a safe place, sufficiently far from the bounds usually traversed by the police; still, in the darkness, they imagined they heard watchmen coming. Just on the edge of the river, opposite where they were waiting, a boat under repairs was in the stocks. In order to evade the advancing foe, they all marched into the river, the water being shallow, and with the vessel for a breastwork hiding them from the shore, there they remained for an hour and a half. They were thoroughly soaked if nothing more. However, about ten o'clock a small oyster boat came to their relief, and all were soon placed aboard the schooner, which was loaded with corn, etc. All, with the exception of the large woman above referred to, and one other female, were required to enter a hole apparently leading through the bottom of the boat, but in reality only a department which had been expressly con-

HEAVY WEIGHTS—ARRIVAL OF A PARTY AT LEAGUE ISLAND.

(Fifteen escaped in this Schooner.)

structed for the Underground Rail Road business, at the expense of the captain, and in accordance with his own plan.

The entrance was not sufficiently large to admit Mrs. Walker, so she with another female who was thought "too fat" to endure the close confinement, was secreted behind some corn back of the cabin, a place so secluded that none save well-experienced searchers would be likely to find it. In this way the Captain put out to sea. After some fifteen hours he deemed it safe to bring his passengers up on deck where they could inhale pure air which was greatly needed, as they had been next-door to suffocation and death. The change of air had such an effect on one of the passengers (Scott) that, in his excitement, he refused to conform to the orders required; for prudential reasons the Captain, threatened to throw him over-board. Whereupon Scott lowered his tone. Before reaching the lock the Captain supposing that they might be in danger from contact with boats, men, etc., again called upon them "to go into their hole" under the deck. Not even the big woman was excused now. She pleaded that she could not get through, her fellow-sufferers said that she must be got through urging the matter on the ground that they would have great danger to face. The big woman again tried to effect an entrance, but in vain. Said one of the more resolute sisters "she must take off her clothes then, it will never do to have her staying up on deck to betray all the rest;" thus this resolute stand being unanimous, the poor woman had to comply, and except a single garment she was as destitute of raiment as was Mother Eve before she induced Adam to eat of the forbidden fruit in the garden of Eden. With the help of passengers below, she was squeezed through, but not without bruising and breaking the skin considerably where the rub was severest. All were now beneath the deck, the well-fitting oil-cloth was put over the hole covering the cabin-floor snugly, and a heavy table was set over the hole. They are within sight of the lock, but no human beings are visible about the schooner save the Captain, the mate and a small boy, the son of the Captain. At the lock not unexpectedly three officers came on board of the boat and stopped her. The Captain was told that they had received a telegraphic dispatch from Norfolk to the effect that his boat was suspected of having slaves secreted thereon. They talked with the Captain and mate separately for a considerable while, and more closely did they examine the boy, but gained no information except that "the yellow-fever had been raging very bad in Norfolk." At this fever-news the officers were not a little alarmed, and they now lost no time in attending to their official errand. They searched the cabin where the two fat women were first secreted, and other parts of the boat pretty thoroughly. They then commenced taking up the hatchways, but the place seemed so shockingly perfumed with foul air that the men started back and declared that nobody could live in such a place, and swore that it smelt like the yellow-fever;

36

the Captain laughed at them, and signified that they were perfectly welcome to search to their hearts' content. The officers concluded that there were no slaves on that boat, that nobody could live there, etc., etc., asked for their charges ($3), and discharged the Captain. The children had been put under the influence of liquor to keep them still, so they made no noise; the others endured their hour of agony patiently until the lock was safely passed, and the river reached. Fresh air was then allowed them, and the great danger was considered overcome. The Captain, however, far from deeming it advisable to land his live cargo at the wharves of Philadelphia, delivered them at League Island. The passengers testified that Captain B. was very kind. They were noticed thus:

ISAAC, was about fifty years of age, dark, tall, well-made, intelligent, and was owned by George Brown, who resided at Deep Creek. Isaac testified that said Brown had invariably treated him cruelly. For thirty years Isaac had hired his time, found himself in food, clothing, and everything, yet as he advanced in years, neither his task, nor his hire was diminished, but on the contrary his hire of late years had been increased. He winced under the pressure, and gave himself up to the study of the Underground Rail Road. While arrangements for fleeing were pending, he broke the secret to his wife, Polly, in whom he trusted; she being true to freedom, although sorrowing to part with him, threw no obstacle in his way. Besides his wife, he had also two daughters, Amanda A. and Mary Jane, both slaves. Nevertheless, having made up his mind not to die a slave, he resolved to escape at all hazards.

HENDERSON belonged to the estate of A. Briggs, which was about to be settled, and knowing that he was accounted on the inventory as personal property, he saw that he too would be sold with the rest of the movables, if he was not found among the missing.

He began to consider what he had endured as a slave, and came to the conclusion that he had had a "rugged road to hoe all the way along" and that he might have it much worse if he waited to be sold. The voice of reason admonished him to escape for his life. In obeying this call he suffered the loss of his wife, Julia, and two children, who were fortunately free. Henderson was about thirty-one years of age, stout, and of healthy appearance, worth in cash perhaps $1200.

WILLIAM was thirty-four years of age, of a chestnut color, substantial physical structure, and of good faculties. The man who professed to own him he called William Taylor, and "he was a very hard man, one of the kind which could not be pleased, nor give a slave a pleasant answer one time in fifty." Being thoroughly sick of William Taylor, he fell in love with the Underground Rail Road and Canada.

MRS. WALKER, the big fat woman, was thirty-eight years of age, and a pleasant-looking person, of a very dark hue. Besides the struggles already alluded to, she was obliged to leave her husband. Of her master she declared that she could "say nothing good." His name was Arthur Cooper, of Georgetown; she had never lived with him, however; for twenty years she had hired her time, paying five dollars per month. When young she scarcely thought of the gross wrongs that were heaped upon her; but as she grew older, and thought more about her condition, she scouted the idea that God had designed her to be a slave, and decided that she would be one to leave Dixey in the first Underground Rail Road train that might afford her the chance. She determined not to remain even for the sake of her husband, who was a slave. With such a will, therefore, she started. Upon leaving Philadelphia, she went with the most of her company to Boston, and thence to New Bedford, where she was living when last heard from.

REBECCA LEWEY was the wife of a man, who was familiarly known by the name of "Blue Beard," his proper name being Henry Lewey. For a long time, although a slave himself, he was one of the most dexterous managers in the Underground Rail Road agency in Norfolk. No single chapter in this work could be more interesting than a chapter of his exploits in this respect.

The appearing of Mrs. Lewey, was a matter of unusual interest. Although she had worn the yoke, she was gentle in her manners, and healthy-looking, so much so that no life insurance agent would have had need to subject her to medical examination before insuring her. She was twenty-eight years of age, but had never known personal abuse as a slave; she was none the less anxious, however, to secure her freedom. Her husband, Blue Beard, judging from certain signs, that he was suspected by slave-holders, and might at any time be caged, (indeed he had recently been in the lions' den, but got out); in order to save his wife, sent her on in advance as he had decided to follow her soon in a similar manner. Rebecca was not without hope of again meeting her husband. This desire was gratified before many months had passed, as he was fortunate enough to make his way to Canada.

MARY KNIGHT was a single woman, twenty-six years of age, dark, stout, and of pleasing manners; she complained of having been used hard.

SARAH SAUNDERS had been claimed as the property of Richard Gatewood, a clerk in the naval service. According to Sarah he was a very clever slave-holder, and had never abused her. Nor was she aware that he had ever treated any of his servants cruelly. Sarah, however, had not lived in Gatewood's immediate family, but had been allowed to remain with her grandmother, rather as a privileged character. She was young, fair, and prepossessing. Having a sister living in Philadelphia, who was known to the agent in Norfolk, Sarah was asked one day if she would not like to see her sister. She at once answered "Yes." After further conversation the agent told her that if she would keep the matter entirely private, he would arrange for her to go by the Underground Rail Road. Being willing and anxious to go, she promised due obedience to the rules; she was not told, however, how much she would have to pass through on the way, else, according to her own admission, she never would have come as she did; her heart would have failed her. But when the goal was gained, like all others, she soon forgot her sufferings, and rejoiced heartily at getting out of Slavery, even though her condition had not been so bad as that of many others.

SOPHIA GRAY, with her son and daughter, Henry and Mary, was from Portsmouth. The mother was a tall, yellow woman, with well cut features, about thirty-three years of age, with manners indicative of more than ordinary intelligence. The son and daughter were between twelve and fourteen years of age; well-developed for their age, modest, and finely-formed mulattoes. All the material necessary for a story of great interest, might have readily been found in the story of the mother and her children. They were sent with others to New Bedford, Massachusetts. It was not long after being in New Bedford, before the boy was put to a trade, and the daughter was sent to Boston, where she had an aunt (a fugitive), living in the family of the Hon. George S. Hilliard. Mr. and Mrs. Hilliard were so impressed by Mary's intelligent countenance and her appearance generally, that they decided that she must have a chance for an education, and opened their hearts and home to her.

On a visit to Boston, in 1859, the writer found Mary at Mr. Hilliard's, and in an article written for the "Anti-Slavery Standard," upon the condition of fugitive slaves in Boston and New Bedford, allusion was made particularly to her and several others, under this hospitable roof, in the following paragraph:

"On arriving in Boston, the first persons I had the pleasure to converse with, were four or five uncommonly interesting Underground Rail Road passengers, who had only been out of bondage between three and five years. Their intelligent appearance contradicted the idea that they had ever been an hour in Slavery, or a mile on an Underground Rail Road. Two of them were filling trustworthy posts, where they were respected and well paid for their services. Two others were young people (one two, and the other three years out of Slavery), a girl of fifteen, and a boy of twelve, whose interesting appearance induced a noble-hearted Anti-Slavery lady to receive them into her own family, expressly to educate them; and thus, almost ever since their arrival, they have been enjoying this lady's kindness, as well as the excellent equal Free School privileges of Boston. The girl, in the Grammar School (chiefly composed of whites), has already distinguished herself, having received a diploma, with an excellent certificate of character; and the boy, naturally very apt, has made astonishing progress.

The "boy of twelve," alluded to, was not Mary's brother. He was quite a genius of his age, who had escaped from Norfolk, stowed away in a schooner and was known by the name of "Dick Page."

On arriving in Philadelphia, Dick was delivered, as usual, into the hands of the Committee. The extraordinary smartness of the little fellow (only ten years old), astonished all who saw him. The sympathies of a kind-hearted gentleman and his wife, living in Philadelphia, had been deeply awakened in his behalf, through their relative and friend, Mrs. Hilliard, in whose family, as has been already stated, the boy's aunt lived. So much were these friends interested to secure Dick's freedom, that they often contemplated buying him, although they did not like the idea of buying, as the money would go into the pocket of the master, who they considered had no just right to deprive any individual of his freedom. So when Dick arrived the Committee felt that it was as little as they could do, to give these friends the pleasure of seeing the little Underground Rail Road passenger. He was therefore conveyed to the residence of Prof. J. P. Lesley. He could not have been sent to a house in the great city of Brotherly Love, where he would have found a more cordial and sincere reception. After passing an hour or so with them, Dick was brought away, but he had been so touched by their kindness, that he felt that he must see them again, before leaving the city; so just before sundown, one evening, he was missed; search was made for him, but in vain. Great anxiety was felt for him, fearing that he was lost. During the early part of the evening, the writer, with a bell in hand, passed up one street and down another, in quest of the stranger, but no one could give any information of him. Finally about ten o'clock, the mayor's office was visited with a view of having the police stations telegraphed. Soon the mystery was solved ; one of the policemen stated that he had noticed a strange colored boy with Professor Lesley's children. Hastening to the residence of the professor, sure enough, Dick was there, happy in bed and asleep.

From that time to this, it has been a mystery to know how a boy, a perfect stranger, could make his way alone, (having passed over the route but once), without getting lost, so circuitous was the road that he had to travel, in order to reach Professor Lesley's house. Having said this much, the way is now open to refer to him again, in Boston at school. He was generously assisted through his education and trade, and was prepared to commence life at his majority, an intelligent mechanic, and a man of promise.

THE CASE OF EUPHEMIA WILLIAMS,

CLAIMED AS A FUGITIVE SLAVE UNDER THE FUGITIVE SLAVE-LAW AFTER HAVING
LIVED IN PENNSYLVANIA FOR MORE THAN TWENTY YEARS.

Scarcely had the infamous statute been in existence six months, ere the worst predictions of the friends of the slave were fulfilled in different Northern States. It is hardly too much to say, that Pennsylvania was considered wholly unsafe to nine-tenths of her colored population. The kidnapper is fully shown in the case of Rachel and Elizabeth Parker as he appeared on the soil of Pennsylvania, doing his vile work in the dead of night, entering the homes of unprotected females and children, therefore:

The case of Euphemia Williams will serve to represent the milder form of kidnapping in open day, in the name of the law, by professed Christians in the city of Brotherly Love, and the home of William Penn.

February 6, 1851, Euphemia Williams, the mother of six children, the youngest at the breast, was arrested in the upper part of the city (Philadelphia), and hurried before Edward D. Ingraham, a United States commissioner, upon the charge of being a fugitive from labor. She was claimed by William T. J. Purnell, of Worcester county, Maryland, who admitted that she had been away from him for twenty-two years, or since 1829. Her offspring were born on the soil of Pennsylvania, and the eldest daughter was seventeen years of age.

EUPHEMIA was living in her own house, and had been a member of church, in good and regular standing, for about seventeen years, and was about forty years of age. When the arrest was made, Euphemia had just risen from her bed, and was only partly dressed, when a little after daylight, several persons entered her room, and arrested her. Murder! murder! was cried lustily, and awakened the house. Her children screamed lamentably, and her eldest daughter cried "They've got my mother! they've got my mother!" "For God's sake, save me," cried Euphemia, to a woman in the second story, who was an eye-witness to this monstrous outrage. But despite the piteous appeals of the mother and children, the poor woman was hastened into a cab, and borne to the marshall's office.

Through the vigilance of J. M. McKim and Passmore Williamson, a writ of habeas corpus returnable forthwith was obtained at about one o'clock. The heart-broken mother was surrounded by five of her children, three of whom were infants. It was a dark and dreadful hour. When her children were brought into the room where she was detained, great drops of sweat standing on her face plainly indicated her agony.

By mutual arrangement between the claimants and the prisoner's counsel the hearing was fixed for the next day, at the hour of three o'clock. According to said arrangement, at three o'clock Euphemia was brought face to face with her claimant, William T. J. Purnell. The news had already gone out that the trial would come off at the time fixed; hence a multitude were on hand to witness the proceedings in the case. The sympathy of anti-slavery ladies was excited, and many were present in the court-room to manifest their feelings in behalf of the stricken woman. The eloquent David Paul Brown (the terror of slave-hunters) and William S. Pierce, Esqrs., appeared for Euphemia, R. C. McMurtrie, Esq., for the claimant.

Mr. McMurtrie in the outset, arose and said, that it was with extreme regret that he saw an attempt to influence the decision of this case by tumult and agitation. The sympathy shown by so many friendly ladies, was not a favorable sign for the slave-holder. Notwithstanding, Mr. McMurtrie said that he would "prove that Mahala, sometimes called Mahala Purnell, was born and bred a slave of Dr. George W. Purnell, of Worcester county, Maryland, who was in the habit of hiring her to the neighbors, and while under a contract of hiring, she escaped with a boy, with whom she had taken up, belonging to the person who hired her." The present claimant claimed her as the administrator of Dr. George W. Purnell.

In order to sustain this claim many witnesses and much positive swearing were called forth. Robert F. Bowen, the first witness, swore that he knew both Mahala and her master perfectly well, that he had worked as a carpenter in helping to build a house for the latter, and also had hired the former directly from her owner.

Definite time and circumstances were all harmoniously fixed by this leading witness. One of the important circumstances which afforded him ground for being positive was, as he testified on cross-examination, that he was from home at a camp-meeting (when she run away); "our camp-meetings," said the witness, "are held in the last of August or the first of September; the year I fix by founding it upon knowledge; the year before she ran away, I professed religion; I have something at home to fix the year; she was with me a part of a year. I hired her for the year 1848 as a house servant; I hired her directly from Dr. George W. Purnell. When she ran away I proceeded after her. I advertised, in Delware in written advertisements, in Georgetown, Milford and Millsborough, and described her and the boy; her general features. I have not the advertisement and can't tell how she was described; Dr. George Purnell united with me in the advertisement. I followed her to Delaware City; that's all I have done since, about inquiring after them. I came, after twenty-two years' absence, to seek my own rights, and as an evidence for my friend. I have not seen her more than once since she ran away, until she was arrested; I saw her two or three times in court. I saw her first in a wretched-looking room, at Fifth and Germantown Road; it was yesterday morning; it was the evening before at

Congress Hall; I arrived here last Tuesday a week; a man told me where she was"—"I beg the court,"—here Mr. McMurtrie interposed an objection to his mentioning the person. The court, however, said the question could be put.

Witness.—I was pledged not to tell the name; the person signed her name Louisa Truit; the information was got by letter; the reason I did not tell, because I thought she might be murdered; I have not the letters, and can't tell the contents; the letter that I received required a pledge that I would not tell: I was directed to send my letter to the post-office without any definite place; the representative of Louisa Truit was a man; I saw him in Market street between Third and Fourth, at Taylor and Paulding's store, in the course of last week; I was brought into contact with the representative of Louisa by appointment in the letter, to get the information; I never heard him tell his name; he was neither colored nor white; we call them with us mixed blood; (I should take you to be colored, said the witness to Mr. Brown.) I suppose he lives somewhere up there; I saw him at my room the next morning; I did not learn from him who wrote the letter; he did not describe the person of the woman in the letter written to me, only her general appearance; Purnell said he burnt the letter.

Mr. Brown demanded the letter, or the proof of its destruction.

I never wrote myself, but my friend, Mr. Henry did; he said so; I never received a letter; it was written to Robert J. Henry; part of the letter was written to me, but not directed to me; the Louisa Truit, who wrote, stated, that for the information he wanted $100 for one of the fugitives; he was referred to the store of Taylor & Paulding, and Mr. Henry would meet him there; when I got to the store, some of the concern let Mr. Henry know that a man wanted to see him; I heard this at the store the man was there; he was a mulatto man, middle-aged, and middling tall; he is not here, that I know of; can't tell when I last saw him. His name I understood to be Gloucester.

Under the severe cross-examination that the witness had been subjected to under D. P. Brown, he became very faint, and called for water. Large drops of sweat stood upon his forehead, and he was obliged to sit down, lest he should fall down. "Take a seat," said Mr. Brown tauntingly, "and enjoy yourself, while I proceed with my interrogations." But the witness was completely used up, and was allowed to withdraw to another room, where fresh air was more plentiful. The cause of the poor slave woman was greatly strengthened by this failure.

Another witness, named Zachariah Bowen, for the claimants, swore positively that he knew the prisoner well, that she had been hired to his brother for three years by Dr. Purnell, whose slave she was; also he swore that he knew her parents, who were slaves to the said Doctor P.; that he last saw her in 1827, etc. On cross-examination he swore thus: "I last saw her in 1827, she was about sixteen or seventeen; she was about an ordinary size, not the smallest size, nor the largest; she was neither thick nor thin; there was nothing remarkable in her more than is common; nothing in her speech; she was about the same color as the woman here; I never saw a great deal of change in a nigger, from sixteen to thirty-five or forty, sometimes they grow fatter, and sometimes leaner. As to recognizing her in Philadelphia, he had not the slightest difficulty. He went on to swear, that he first saw her in a cab, in the city; I knew her yesterday; if you could see the rest of the family you could pick her out yourself in thirty : I knew her by her general favor, and have no particular mark ; I would not attempt to describe features; her favor is familiar to me; I never saw any marks upon her."

Here Mr. Brown said he would not examine this witness further until he had concluded the examination of the witness, who had become sick. The court then adjourned till nine o'clock the next morning.

The avenues to the court were filled with anxious persons, and in the front and rear of the state house the crowd was very great.

The next morning, at an early hour, the court-room, and all the avenues to it were densely crowded by people interested in behalf of the woman whose case was under trial. A large number of respectable ladies formed a part of the large gathering.

Robert F. Bowen, the witness, who became sick, was recalled.

Witness.—" I saw the colored person, who gave the information, the next evening; after I saw him in Market street, at Congress Hall, in our room; the gentleman who keeps the hotel we did not wish to place under any responsibility, as he might be accused of carrying on the business. (Of kidnapping, suggested Mr. Brown.) No, said witness, that is what you call it; the woman would have run away if it had gone out; I heard his name was Gloucester, that gave the information; I saw him three times; once on the street; I have never been in his house; I have been to a house where I heard he lived; I gave a pledge not to disclose the matter; I made a personal pledge to Gloucester in our room last week at Congress Hall; he said he was afraid of being abused by the population of his own color for telling that this girl run away from Dr. Purnell; I understood that Louisa Truit was Gloucester's wife.

Under this searching cross-examination, Mr. Brown constrained him not only to tell all and more than he knew in favor of his friend, the claimant, but wrung from him the secrets which he stood pledged never to disclose.

Witness.—I know no marks; she was in the condition of a married woman when she left me; it was the particular favor of her father and mother that made me recognize her; nothing else; she was pretty well built for her size."

While this witness remembered every thing so accurately occurring in relation to the life and escape of the girl of sixteen, and was prepared to swear to her identity simply "by her favor," as he termed it, he was found sadly deficient in memory touching the owner, whom he had known much longer, and more intimately than he had the girl, as will be seen from the following facts in this witness' testimony:

Witness.—"I don't know when Dr. P. died; I can't tell the year; I should suppose about fourteen years ago; I was at the funeral, and helped to make his coffin; it was in the fall, I think; it was after the camp-meeting I spoke of; at that time I went regularly, but not of late; I have no certain recollection of the year he died; I kept a record of the event of my conversion, and have referred to it often. It has been a reference every year, and perhaps a thousand times a year; it was in the Bible, and I was in the habit of looking into it; I was in the habit of turning over the leaves of this precious book; I think it was eighteen years ago; can't say I'm certain; can't say it was more than twelve years; Dr. P. left six children; two remain in our country, and one in Louisiana, and the one, who is here, making four; I have no interest in the fugitive; I made no contract in regard to this case; there was an offer; are you waiting for an answer? the offer was this, that I was to come on after my fugitive, and if I did not get him they were to pay my expenses; I hesitated about coming; it was a long time before I made up my mind; they said they would pay my expenses if I didn't succeed in getting mine out of prison."

In this way the above witness completely darkened counsel, and added to the weakness of his cause in a marked degree.

THE OVERSEER IS NOW EXAMINED.

Zachariah Bowen recalled.—"I didn't come here on any terms; I hardly understand what you mean by terms; I made no contract; I came upon my own hook; there was no contract; I have no expectations; I don't know that Dr. P. ever manumitted any female slaves; I never knew that she was in the family way when she ran away; I heard of it about that time; she ran off in the fall of 1828. Dr. P. told me so; in the fall of 1828; in 1825, '26, '27, she lived with my brother; in 1825 I lived there; in 1827 and '28 I lived with Dr. P. I moved there and was overseer for him; I was overseer for fifteen years for him; two years at his house; I ceased to be his overseer in 1841, I think; he was living in 1841; I am certain of that year, I think; Dr. Purnell died in 1844, I feel certain; I said to Mr. Purnell that I did not know what ailed the other Mr. Bowen, for the doctor died in 1844; he died in the latter part of the Spring of 1844; Mr. Bowen made a mistake in saying it was eighteen years ago; if you recall him he will rectify the mistake, I think; several slaves escaped from Dr. Purnell; a boy, that lived with my brother, ran away in 1827; the others were not hired to my brother; I don't know that I could tell the exact time, nor the year; the doctor used to say to us, there is another of my niggers ran away; the reason that I can tell when Mahala ran away, is because she took a husband and ran away; I was married that year; the reason I cannot tell about the others is, because they went at different times in five years; the first who ran away before Mahala, was named Grace; she went in 1827; I don't know when the last went, or who it was.

*   *   *   *   *   *   *   *

Gloucester said they had raised a mob on him, on account of this case, and he would have to leave the city; the case of this woman or these proceedings was not spoken of there; he staid but a short time; he said one of the witnesses had betrayed him in court, yesterday, and they attacked him last night; I asked him how he escaped from so many; he said very few were in the city who could outrun him; I asked him where he was going, he replied he had a notion to put for Canada; some of the gentlemen proposed his going to Baltimore; he said that would not do, as the laws of Maryland would catch him; he was going to get a boat and go to New Jersey, and then to New York; Mr. Purnell gave him just thirty-five dollars last night; he paused a while, and Mr. P. told him to hand it back; he then took out his money and put some more to it, and said: "Here is fifty dollars." Mr. P. said that if he got the slave he would leave fifty dollars more with a person in the city.

*   *   *   *   *   *   *   *

Question by the judge.—"You have spoken of a conversation in which Mr. P. told you of certain letters or correspondence, and that they had reference to this alleged fugitive. I want you to give me, to the best of your recollection, everything he said the letters contained."

Witness.—Mr P. told me when he first mentioned it to me, he said that he was going to mention something to me, that he did not want anything said, in regard to some negroes that had run away from his father; he said he wanted me to come on here, and he did not want me to tell any person before we left our county; that if the negroes heard of it, they could get information to the parties before he could get here; I told him I would not tell any person except my wife; he then said he had correspondence with a person here, for a month or two, and he had no doubt but that several of his negroes were here, from what he had heard from his correspondent; he asked me if I could recognize the favor of this Mahala? I told him I didn't know; he then said if anybody would know her, I would, as she had lived with my brother three years; he then said that he would want to start the next week, but he would see me again at that time; that was all he said at that time, only we turned into a hotel, and he said don't breathe this to anybody; on Saturday before we left home, he came to my house, and said: well, I shall want you to start for Philadelphia, on Monday morning; I suppose you will go? I told him I would rather not, if he could do without me; but as I told him before, I would go, if he still requested it, I would go; that's all, sir, except that I said I would be along in the stage.

*   *   *   *   *   *   *   *

J. T. Hammond was then called, a young man who admitted he had never seen the respondent till he came to the court-house, but was ready to swear that he would have known her by her resemblance to Dr. Purnell's set of negroes. " His whole set?" said Mr. Brown. " Yes, sir." (Derisive laughter).

*   *   *   *   *   *   *   *

Mr. McMurtrie offered to prove, by persons who had known the two witnesses who had testified in this case, from their youth, that they were respectable and worthy men. D. P. Brown, said that if the gentleman found it necessary to sustain his witnesses' reputation, in consequence of the peculiar dilemma they had got into, he would object, and if he supposed that he was about to contradict them in some point in the defence, he certainly was right, but as the case could not be concluded to-day, he would like to have the matter adjourned over until Tuesday next.

Mr. McMurtrie objected, by saying, that his client was anxious to have the matter disposed of as soon as possible, as he had been subjected to numerous insults since the matter had been before the court.

Judge Kane intimated that no weight was to be attached to this consideration, as the full power of the court was at his disposal for the purpose of protecting his client from insult.

Mr. McMurtrie replied that he did not know whether words spoken came within the meaning of the act of Congress, in such matters.

The court took a recess until a quarter to three o'clock.

The court met again at a quarter to three o'clock.

Mr. McMurtrie asked that the witnesses for the defence be excluded from the court room, except the one upon the stand.

This was objected to by Mr. Brown, as the witnesses for the prosecution had not been required so to do; but he afterwards withdrew his objections, and notified Mr. McMurtrie that he would require any witnesses he might have in addition, should retire also; as he would object to any of them being heard if they remained.

The Defence.——Mr. Pierce opened the case by saying that the testimony for the defence would be clear and conclusive; that the witnesses for the prosecution are mistaken in the identity of the alleged fugitive. That at the time they allege her to have been in Maryland, on the plantation of Dr. Purnell, she was in Chester county, and in the year Lafayette visited this country, she was in this city. He would confine the testimony exclusively to these two counties, and show that she is not the alleged slave.

Henry C. Cornish, sworn. I live in this city, and am a shoemaker; I came here in the year 1830; before that I lived in Chester county, East

Whiteland township, with Wm. Latta; my father lived with Mr. Latta six or eight years; I lived there three years before that time, and was familiar with the place for more than six years before 1830; I saw the alleged fugitive some five years before 1830, at George Amos', in Uwchland township, some eight or ten miles from our house; I fix the time from a meeting being held on the Valley Hill by a minister, named Nathan D. Tierney; that must have been in 1825; I am positive it was before the beginning of the year 1828; I have not the least doubt; I joined church about that time; it was the first of my uniting with the church; it was in 1825; I joined the Methodist Episcopal Church; before they built a church they held meetings alternately at people's houses; I met her at Amos' house, I recollect my father going to dig the foundation of the church: I saw her there before the church was built; I knew her before she was married; and since I left there I have met her at the annual meetings of the church; I have kept up the acquaintance ever since; I knew that she had two children, that were buried as long as twenty-one or twenty-two years ago; if the boy had lived he would have been twenty-three or twenty-four years old; he was the oldest; she was not married when I first saw her in 1827; she did not appear to be anything but a girl, and was not married, and she of course could not be in the condition of a married woman; I was not at her wedding; if I had not continued to know her, I would not now know her; she was then a small person; age and flesh would change her a little; her complexion has not changed; I think she worked for Mrs. Amos; a church record is now kept very correct; but when I first went into the church, colored men could not read and write; I acted as the clerk of the church; I united with the church after I first saw her; I have seen her very often since I left Chester; five hundred times to speak safely; I worship down town and she up in Brown street; to the best of my recollection they moved over Schuylkill about twelve years ago; she has lived here about nine years; she has six children, I have heard; I have seen five; the oldest is eighteen or nineteen; the youngest a sucking babe; I have visited her house since I have been here; I was not sent for by my uncle, who was employed by Joseph Smith & Co., next to the Girard Bank; I was with Edward Biddle for four years, until he was elected President of the Morris Canal and Banking Company, and then I went to learn shoemaking under instructions, since which time I have been in business for myself; my father burnt limestone for Mr. Latta; he and his wife are dead; I was there a day or two ago for witnesses to testify in this case.

Cross-examined.—I was born in 1814, and am thirty-seven years of age; when I first knew her I suppose she was fifteen years old; she was married about three years afterwards; her husband's name is Micajah Williams; I heard he was in prison for stealing; her name before marriage was Phamie Coates; I didn't know her husband before they were married; don't know whether they came from Maryland; I never knew of Mahala Richardson before last evening in court; the difference in her appearance is a natural one, that every body is acquainted with; I mean that a little boy is not a man, and a growing girl is not a woman; age and flesh and size make a difference; if I had not conversed with her during the twenty-one years, I would not have known her; I never changed a word with her about the case, except to say I was sorry to see her here; I knew her the moment I saw her; her arrest could not have been in the newspapers of the morning as she was not arrested until seven o'clock that day; I went to Chester to look for witnesses; I came to the court because I am a vigilant man, and my principle is to save any person whose liberty is in danger; I had heard that a woman was arrested; her business is to get work wherever she can.

Deborah Ann Boyer, sworn. I was thirty-three last January; I live within one mile of West Chester; I am a married woman; I have lived there since 1835. I went there with my mother; I can read; I have seen the alleged fugitive before this; I first knew her at Downingtown, when she came to my mother's house; that was before I had gone to West Chester with my mother; you can tell how long it was, for it was in 1826; my brother was born in that year; I was quite small then; don't know how she came there; she was with my mother during her confinement; my brother is dead; it is written down in our Testament; and I took an epitaph from it to put on the tombstone; the last time I saw it was when the fellow killed the school-mistress. I looked because about 1830, a man killed a woman, and was hung, and I wanted to see how long ago it was. I have seen her more or less ever since, until within two years. I don't remember when she went from mother, but I saw her at Mr. Latta's afterwards. I have no doubt she is the woman; she was then a slim, tall girl, larger than myself; she is not darker now, but heavier set every way.

*   *   *   *   *   *   *   *

Sarah Gayly affirmed.—I am between forty-seven and forty-eight years of age. I live in the city at this time. I was raised in Chester county, in 1824, and have been here about five years. I lived in Downingtown nine or ten years. I lived awhile in West Chester, and lived in Chester county until about five years ago. I know the alleged fugitive. I first saw her in the neighborhood of Downingtown, at a place they call Downing's old stage office; she worked in the house with me; it was somewhere near 1824, just before Lafayette came about; she worked off and on days' work, to wash dishes; she was a small girl then, very thin, and younger than me. I met with her, as near as I can tell you, down in the valley, at a place called the Valley Inn. I used to see her off and on at church, in 1826. I visited her at Mr. Latta's, after she lived at the Valley Inn. I don't know when she left that county. I know the alleged fugitive is the same person; she belonged to the same church, Ebenezer. I know the brothers Cornish, and have whipped them many a time. I lived with Latta myself, and the Cornish, who is now a minister, lived there; he lived there before I did, and so did the alleged fugitive. I was then between twenty-three and twenty-five years old; she was a strip of a girl; she was not in the family way when she came there.

Cross-examined.—I have not seen her since 1826, until I saw her here in the court-room; I recognized her when I first saw her here without anybody pointing her out, and she recognized me; I have reason to know her, because she has the same sort of a scar on her forehead that I have; we used to make fun of each other about the marks; she went by the name of Fanny Coates. I know nothing about her husband; she did not do the work of a woman in 1826; she washed dishes, scrubbed, etc. I heard her say her father and mother were dead, and that they lived somewhere in that neighborhood; she at that time made her home with a family named Amos.

The Judge asked to see the scar on the witness' forehead and that on the forehead of the respondent. They were brought near the bench, and the marks inspected, which were plainly seen on both. During this time the infant of the respondent was entrusted to another colored woman. The child, who, up to this time, had been quiet, raised a piteous cry and would not be pacified. The whole scene excited a great sensation.

*   *   *   *   *   *   *   *

Mr. Brown then rose in reply to the plaintiff's counsel, and said: If I consulted my own views, I should not say one syllable, in answer to the arguments of the learned counsel upon the other side, and relying as I do upon the evidence, and out of respect to the convenience of your honor, I shall say very little as it is. The views of the counsel it appears to me, are most extraordinary indeed. He seems to take it for granted that everything that is said on the part of the witnesses for the claimant is gospel, and that what is said on the part of the witnesses for the respondent, is to be considered matter of suspicion. Now I rate no man by his size, color, or position, but I appeal to you in looking at the testimony that has been produced here, on the different sides of the question, and judging it by its intrinsic worth, whether there is the slightest possible comparison between the witnesses on the part of the plaintiff, and those of the defendant, either in intelligence, memory, language, thought, or anything else. This is a fine commentary upon the disparagement of color! Looking at the men as they are, as you will, I say that the testimony exhibited on the part of the. respondent would outweigh a whole theatre of such men as are exhibited on the part of the complainant. I say nothing here about their respectability. It would have been proper for the learned counsel on the part of the plaintiff, if he thought the witnesses on the part of the respondent unworthy of belief, to have proved them so; but instead of that, he attempts to bolster up men, who, whether respectable or otherwise, from their inconsistency, involutions and tergiversations in regard to this case, produce no possible effect upon the judicial mind, but that which is unfavorable to themselves. Impartial men, are they? How do they appear before you? They appear under cover from first to last; standing upon their right to resist inquiries legitimately propounded to them; burning up letters since they have arrived, calculated to shed light upon this subject; and before they come here, corresponding with and deriving information from a man, an evident kidnapper, who dare not sign his name and gets his wife to sign hers. This is the character these men exhibit here before you; clandestinely meeting together at the tavern, and that to consult in regard to the identity of a person about whom they know nothing. Can they refer to any marks by which to identify this person? Nothing at all of the kind. Do they, with the exception of the first witness examined, state even the time when she left? Have they produced the letter written by this kidnapper, showing how he described her? Why, let me ask, is not the full light allowed to shine on this case? But even with the light they have shed upon it, I would have been perfectly content to have rested it, relying upon their testimony alone, for a just decision.

*　　*　　*　　*　　*　　*　　*　　*

Now, what man among them, professes to have seen this woman for twenty-one years? Not one. The learned gentleman attempts to sustain his case, because one of our witnesses, certainly not more than one, has not seen this woman for about the same length of time: but don't you perceive, that in this case they all lived in the same State, if not in the same county— they had intercourse with persons mutually acquainted with her, and three out of four of them, met her for several months at the same church; and one witness, who had long been in her society, and in close association with her, knew she had a mark upon her forehead corresponding to the one she bore on her own. And by dint of all these matters, this long continued acquaintance only reviving the impressions received in early life, they had no doubt of the identity of the person. Was there ever a more perfect train of evidence exhibited to prove the identity of a person, than on the present occasion?

*　　*　　*　　*　　*　　*　　*　　*

We have called witnesses on this point alone, and have more than counter-poised the evidence produced upon the opposite side. And we have not only made it manifest that she was a free woman, but we have confirmed her charter by separate proof. What does the gentleman say further? Do I understand him to say we have no right to determine this matter judicially? Now what is all this about? Why is it before you, taking your time day after day? According to this argument, you have nothing to do but to give the master the flesh he claims. But you are to be satisfied that you have sufficient reason to believe that these claims are well founded. And if you leave that matter in a state of doubt, it does not require a single witness to be called on the part of the respondent, to prove on the opposite side of the question. But we have come in with a weight of evidence demolishing the structure he has raised, restoring the woman to her original position in the estimation of the law. " Well," says the gentleman, " it is like the case of a fugitive from justice." But it is not, and if it were, it would not benefit his case. The case of a fugitive from justice is one in which the prisoner is remanded to the custody of the law, handed over for legal purposes. The case of a fugitive from labor is a case in which the individual is handed over sometimes to a merciless master, and very rarely to a charitable one. Does the counsel mean to say that in the case of a fugitive from justice he is not bound to satisfy the judge before whom the question is heard? He should prove our witnesses unworthy of belief. As Judge Grier said, upon a former occasion, " You can choose your own time ; you have full and abundant opportunities on every side to prepare against any contingency." Why don't they do so? He is not to come here and force on a case, and say, I suppose you take every thing for granted. He is to come prepared to prove the justice of his claim before the tribunal who is to decide upon it. That he has not done successfully, and I would, therefore, ask your Honor, after the elaborate argument on the part of the plaintiff, to discharge this woman : for after such an abundance of testimony unbroken and incontestable as that we have exhibited here, it would be a monstrous perversion of reason to suppose that anything more could be required.

Mr. McMurtrie replied by reasserting his positions. It was a grave question for the court to consider what evidence was required. He thought that this decision might be the turning case to show whether the act of Congress would be carried out or whether we were to return in fact to the state of affairs under the old laws.

Judge Kane said, in reference to the remarks at the close of Mr. McMurtrie's speech : So long as I retain my seat on this bench, I shall endeavor to enforce this law without reference to my own sympathies, or the sympathies and opinions of others. I do not think, in the cases under this act of Congress, or a treaty, or constitutional, or legal provision for the extradition of fugitives from justice, that it is possible to imagine that conclusive proof of identity could be established by depositions. From the nature of the case and the facts to be proved, proof cannot be made in anticipation of the identity of the party. That being established, it is the office of the judge, to determine whether a *prima facie* case indicates the identity of the party charged, with the party before him.

*　　*　　*　　*　　*　　*　　*　　*

On the other hand, the evidence of the claimant has been met, and regarding the bearing of the witnesses for the respondent, met by witnesses who testified, with apparent candor and great intelligence. If they are

37

believed, then the witnesses for the claimant are mistaken. The question is, whether two witnesses for the claimant, who have not seen the respondent for twenty-three, one for twenty-four years, are to be believed in preference to four witnesses on the other side, three of whom have seen her frequently since 1826, and known her as Euphemia Williams, and the fourth, who has not seen her for a quarter of a century, but testifies that when they were children, they used to jest each other about scars, which they still bear upon their persons ; I am bound to say that the proof by the four witnesses has not been overthrown by the contrary evidence of the two who only recognized her when they called on her with the marshall. One says he called her Mahala Purnell as soon as he saw her. He might be mistaken. He inferred he would find her at the place to which he went. There were three persons in the room, one was Mahala Richardson, whom he knew, a young girl, and the prisoner. If she had been alone, his recognition would have been of no avail. The fact is obvious to this court, that the respondent has no peculiar physiognomy or gait. It has been shown she has no peculiarity of voice; I cannot but feel that the fact alleged by the claimant is very doubtful, when the witnesses, without mark or peculiarity, testify that they can readily recognize the girl of fifteen in the woman of forty. The prisoner is therefore discharged.

A slight attempt at applause in the court room was promptly suppressed. The intelligence of the discharge of the woman, was quickly spread to those without, who raised shouts of joy. The woman, with her children, were hurried into a carriage, which was driven first to the Anti-slavery office and then to the Philadelphia Institute, in Lombard Street above Seventh. Here she was introduced to a large audience of colored people, who hailed her appearance with lively joy; several excited speeches were made, and great enthusiasm was manifested in and outside of the building and the adjacent streets. When Euphemia came out, the horses were taken out of the carriage, and a long rope was attached, which was taken by as many colored people as could get hold of it, and the woman and her children thus conveyed to her home.

The procession was accompanied by several hundreds of men, women and boys. They dragged the carriage past the residence of the counsel for the respondent, cheering them by huzzas of the wildest kind, and then took the vehicle and its contents to the residence of the woman, Germantown Road near Fifth street, beguiling the way with songs and shouts. The whole scene was one of wild, ungovernable excitement, produced by exuberance of joy.

The masterly management of abolitionists in connection with the counsel, saved poor Euphemia from being dragged from her children into hopeless bondage. While the victory was a source of great momentary rejoicing on the part of the friends of the slave it was nevertheless quite manifest that she was only released by the "skin of her teeth." "A scar on her forehead" saved her. Relative to this important mark, a few of Euphemia's friends enjoyed a very pleasing anecdote, which, at the time, they were obliged to withhold from the public; it is too good to be kept any longer. For a time, Euphemia was kept in durance vile, up in the dome of Independence Hall, partly in the custody of Lieutenant Gouldy of the Mayor's police, (who was the right man in the right place), whose sympathies were secretly on the side of the slave. While his pitying eyes gazed on Euphemia's sad face, he observed a very large scar on her forehead, and was immediately struck with the idea that that old scar might be used with damaging effect by the witnesses and counsel against her. At once he decided that the scar must be concealed, at least, until after the examination of the claimant's witnesses. Accordingly a large turban was procured and placed on Euphemia's head in such a manner as to hide the scar completely, without exciting the least suspicion in the minds of any. So when the witnesses against her swore that she had no particular mark, David Paul Brown made them clinch this part of their testimony irrevocably. Now, when Sarah Gayly affirmed (on the part of the prisoner) that " I have reason to know her because she has the same sort of a scar on her forehead that I have, we used to make fun of each other about the marks," etc., if it was not evident to all, it was to some, that she had "stolen their thunder," as the "chop-fallen" countenances of the slave-holder's witnesses indicated in a moment. Despair was depicted on all faces sympathizing with the pursuers.

With heavy pecuniary losses, sad damage of character, and comfortless, the unhappy claimant and his witnesses were compelled to return to Maryland, wiser if not better men. The account of this interesting trial, we have condensed from a very careful and elaborate report of it published in the " Pennsylvania Freeman," January 13th, 1857.

Apparently, the vigilance of slave-hunters was not slackened by this defeat, as the records show that many exciting cases took place in Philadelphia and Pennsylvania, and if the records of the old Abolitionist Society could be published, as they should be, it would appear that many hard-fought battles have taken place between Freedom and Slavery on this soil.

Here in conclusion touching the Fugitive Slave Law, arrests under it, etc., as a fitting sequel we copy two extracts from high authority. The first is from the able and graphic pen of James Miller McKim, who was well known to stand in the front ranks of both the Anti-slavery Society and the Underground Rail Road cause through all the long and trying contest, during which the country was agitated by the question of immediate emancipation, and shared the full confidence and respect of Abolitionists of all classes throughout the United States and Great Britain.

The letter from which we have made this extract was written to Hon.

George Thompson, the distinguished abolitionist of England, and speaks for itself. The other quotation is from the pen of a highly respectable and intelligent lady, belonging to the Society of Friends, or Quakers, and a most devoted friend of the slave, whose statement obviously is literally true.

From Mr. McKim to George Thompson, 1851.

" The accompanying parcel of extracts will give you a full account of the different slave cases tried in this city, under the new Fugitive Slave Law up to this time. Full and accurate as these reports are, they will afford you but a faint idea of the anguish and confusion that have been produced in this part of the country by this infamous statute. It has turned Southeastern Pennsylvania into another Guinea Coast, and caused a large portion of the inhabitants to feel as insecure from the brutal violence and diabolical acts of the kidnapper, as are the unhappy creatures who people the shores of Africa. Ruffians from the other side of the Slave-line, aided by professional kidnappers on our own soil, a class of men whose 'occupation' until lately, had been 'gone,' are continually prowling through the community, and every now and then seizing and carrying away their prey. As a specimen of the boldness, though fortunately, not of the success always with which these wretches prosecute their nefarious trade, read the enclosed article, which I cut from the *Freeman*, of January 2d, and bear in mind that in no respect are the facts here mentioned over-stated.

This affair occurred in Chester county, one of the most orderly and intelligent counties in the State, a county settled principally by Quakers. A week or two after this occurrence, and not far from the same place, a farmhouse was entered by a band of armed ruffians, in the evening, and at a time when all the able-bodied occupants, save one, were known to be absent. This was a colored man, who was seated by the kitchen fire, and in the act of taking off his shoes. He was instantly knocked down and gagged; but, still resisting, he was beaten most unmercifully. There was a woman, and also a feeble old man, in the house, who were attracted to the spot by the scuffle; but they could neither render any assistance, nor (the light being put out), could they recognize the parties engaged in it. The unhappy victim being fairly overcome, was dragged like a slain beast to a wagon, which was about a hundred yards distant, waiting to receive him. In this he was placed, and conveyed across the line, which was about twenty miles further south; and that was the last, so far as I know, that has ever been heard of him. The alarm was given, of course, as soon as possible, and the neighbors were quickly in pursuit; but the kidnappers had got the start of them. The next morning the trail between the house, and the place where the wagon stood, was distinctly visible, and deeply marked with blood.

About a fortnight since, a letter was brought to our office, from a well-known friend, the contents of which were in substance as follows: A case of kidnapping had occurred in the vicinity of West Caln Township, Chester county, at about half past one on Sunday morning, the 16th March. A black man, by the name of Thomas Hall, an honest, sober, and industrious individual, living in the midst of a settlement of farmers, had been stolen by persons who knocked at his door, and told him that his nearest neighbor wanted him to come to his house, one of his children being sick. Hall, not immediately opening his door, it was burst in, and three men rushed into his house; Hall was felled by the bludgeons of the men. His wife received several severe blows, and on making for the door was told, that if she attempted to go out or halloo, she would have her brains blown out. She, however, escaped through a back window, and gave the alarm; but before any person arrived upon the ground, they had fled with their victim. He was taken without any clothing, except his night clothes. A six-barrelled revolver, heavily loaded, was dropped in the scuffle, and left; also a silk handkerchief, and some old advertisement of a bear bait, that was to take place in Emmittsburg, Maryland. In how many cases the persons stolen are legally liable to capture, it is impossible to state. The law, you know, authorizes arrests to be made, with or without process, and nothing is easier under such circumstances than to kidnap persons who are free born.

The very same day that I received the above mentioned letter, and while our hearts were still aching over its contents, another was brought us from Thomas Garrett, of Wilmington, Delaware, announcing the abduction, a night or two before, of a free colored man of that city. The outrage was committed by an ex-policeman, who, pretending to be acting under the commission which he had been known to hold, entered, near the hour of midnight, the house of the victim, and alleging against him some petty act of disorder, seized him, handcuffed him in the presence of his dismayed family, and carried him off to Maryland. The cheat that had been practised was not discovered by the family until next evening; but it was too late, the man was gone.

At the time Mr. Garrett's letter was handed to me, narrating the foregoing case of man stealing, I was listening to the sad tales of two colored women, who had come to the office for advice and assistance. One of them was an elderly person, whose son had been pursued by the marshal's deputies, and who had just escaped with 'the skin of his teeth.' She did not come on her own account, however; her heart was too full of joy for that. She came to accompany the young woman who was with her. This young woman was a remarkably intelligent, lady-like person, and her story made a strong appeal to my feelings. She is a resident of Washington, and her errand here was, to procure the liberation of a sister-in-law, who is confined in that city, under very peculiar circumstances. The sister-in-law had absconded from her mistress about nine months since, and was secreted in the room of an acquaintance, who was cook in a distinguished slave-holding family in Washington; her intention being, there to wait until all search should be over, and an opportunity offer of escape to the North. But, as yet, no such opportunity had presented itself; at least none that was available, and for nine long months had that poor girl been confined in the narrow limits of the cook's chamber, watched over day and night by that faithful friend with a vigilance as sleepless as it was disinterested. The time had now come, however, when something must be done. The family in whose house she is hid is about to be broken up, and the house to be vacated, and the girl must either be rescued from her peril, or she, and all her accomplices must be exposed. What to do under these circumstances was the question which brought this woman to Philadelphia. I advised her to the best of my ability, and sent her away hopeful, if not rejoicing.

But in many of these cases we can render no aid whatever. All we can do is to commend them to the God of the oppressed, and labor on for the day of general deliverance. But, oh! the horrors of this hell-born system, and the havoc made by this, its last foul offspring, the Fugitive Slave law. The anguish, the terror, the agony inflicted by this infamous statute, must be witnessed to be fully appreciated. You must hear the tale of the broken-hearted mother, who has just received tidings that her son is in the hands of man-thieves. You must listen to the impassioned appeal of the wife, whose husband's retreat has been discovered, and whose footsteps are dogged by the blood-hounds of Slavery. You must hear the husband, as I did, a few weeks ago, himself bound and helpless, beg you for God's sake to save his wife. You must see such a woman as Hannah Dellam, with her noble-looking boy at her side, pleading in vain before a pro-slavery judge, that she is of right free; that her son is entitled to his freedom; and above all, that her babe, about to be born, should be permitted to open its eyes upon the light of liberty. You must hear the judge's decision, remorselessly giving up the woman with her children born and unborn, into the hands of their claimants—by them to be carried to the slave prison, and thence to be sold to a returnless distance from the remaining but scattered fragments of her once happy family. These things you must see and hear for yourself before you can form any adequate idea of the bitterness of this cup which the unhappy children of oppression along this southern border are called upon to drink. Manifestations like these have we been obliged either to witness ourselves, or hear the recital of from others, almost daily, for weeks together. Our aching hearts of late, have known but little respite. A shadow has been cast over our home circles, and a check been given to the wonted cheerfulness of our families. One night, the night that the woman and the boy and the unborn babe received their doom, my wife, long after midnight, literally wept herself to sleep. For the last fortnight we have had no new cases; out even now, when I go home in the evening, if I happen to look more serious than usual, my wife notices it, and asks: "Is there another slave case?" and my little girls look up anxiously for my reply.

From Miss MARY B. THOMAS.

Daring outrage! burglary and kidnapping! The following letter tells its own startling and most painful story. Every manly and generous heart must burn with indignation at the villainy it describes, and bleed with sympathy for the almost broken-hearted sufferers.

"DOWNINGTOWN, 19th, 4th mo., 1848.

"MY DEAR FRIEND:—This morning our family was aroused by the screams of a young colored girl, who has been living with us nearly a year past; but we were awakened only in time to see her borne off by three white men, ruffians indeed, to a carriage at our door, and in an instant she was on her way to the South. I feel so much excited by the attendant circumstances of this daring and atrocious deed, as scarcely to be able to give you a coherent account of it, but I know that it is a duty to make it known, and, I therefore write this immediately.

"As soon as the house was opened in the morning, these men who were lurking without, having a carriage in waiting in the street, entered on their horrid errand. They encountered no one in their entrance, except a colored boy, who was making the fire ; and who, being frightened at their approach, ran and hid himself; taking a lighted candle from the kitchen, and carrying it up stairs, they went directly to the chamber in which the poor girl lay in a sound sleep. They lifted her from her bed and carried her down stairs. In the entry of the second floor they met one of my sisters, who, hearing an unusual noise, had sprung from her bed. Her screams, and those of the poor girl, who was now thoroughly awakened to the dreadful truth, aroused my father, who hurried undressed from his chamber, on the ground floor. My father's efforts were powerless against the three ; they threw him off, and with frightful imprecations hurried the girl to the carriage. Quickly as possible my father started in pursuit, and reached West Chester only to learn that the carriage had driven through the borough at full speed, about half an hour before. They had two horses to their vehicle, and there were three men besides those in the house. These particulars we gather from the colored boy Ned, who, from his hiding-place, was watching them in the road.

"Can anything be done for the rescue of this girl from the kidnappers? We are surprised and alarmed ! This deliberate invasion of our house, is a thing unimagined. There must be some informer, who is acquainted with our house and its arrangements, or they never would have come so boldly through. Truly, there is no need to preach about Slavery in the abstract, this individual case combines every wickedness by which human nature can be degraded.   Truly, thy friend,

MARY B. THOMAS."

In a subsequent letter, our friend says: " As to detail, the whole transaction was like a flash to those who saw the miserable ending. I was impelled to write without delay, by the thought that it would be in time for the 'Freeman,' and that any procrastination on my part, might jeopard others of these suffering people, who are living, as was this poor girl, in fancied security. Our consternation was inexpressible; our sorrow and indignation deepen daily, as the thought returns of the awful announcement with which we were awakened: they have carried Martha to the South. To do what will be of most service to the cause—not their cause—ours— that of our race, is our burning desire."

HELPERS AND SYMPATHIZERS AT HOME AND ABROAD— INTERESTING LETTERS.

The necessities of the Committee for the relief of the destitute and way-worn travelers bound freedom-ward, were met mainly by friends of the cause in Philadelphia. Generous-hearted abolitionists nobly gave their gold in this work. They gave not only material, but likewise whole-souled aid and sympathy in times of need, to a degree well worthy of commemoration while the name of slave is remembered. The Shipleys, Hoppers, Parrishes, Motts, Whites, Copes, Wistars, Pennocks, Sellers, Davis, Prices, Hallowells, Sharpless, Williams, Coates, Morris, Browns, Townsends, Taylors, Jones, Grews, Wises, Lindseys, Barkers, Earles, Pughs, Rogers, Whartons, Barnes, Willsons, Wrights, Peirces, Justices, Smiths, Cavenders, Stackhouses, Nealls, Dawsons, Evans, Lees, Childs, Clothiers, Harveys, Laings, Middletons, etc., are among the names well-known in the days which tried men's souls, as being most true to the bondman, whether on the Underground Rail Road, before a Fugitive Slave-Law Court, or on a rice or cotton plantation in the South. Nor would we pass over the indefatigable labors of the Ladies' Anti-slavery Societies and Sewing Circles of Philadelphia, whose surpassing fidelity to the slave in the face of prejudice, calumny and reproach, year in and year out, should be held in lasting remembrance. In the hours of darkness they cheered the cause. While we thus honor the home-guards and coadjutors in our immediate neighborhood, we cannot forget other earnest and faithful friends of the slave, in distant parts of the country and the world, who volunteered timely aid and sympathy to the Vigilance Committee of Philadelphia. Not to mention any of this class would be to fail to bestow honor where honor is due. We have only to allow the friends to whom we allude, to speak for themselves through their correspondence when their hearts were stirred in the interest of the escaping slave, and they were practically doing unto others as they would have others do unto them.

Here, truly, is pure philanthropy, that vital Christianity, that True and Undefiled Religion before God and the Father, which is to visit the fatherless and widow in their affliction, and to undo the heavy burden, and let the oppressed go free. The posterity of the oppressed at least, will need such evidences of tender regard and love as here evinced. In those days, such expressions of Christian benevolence were cheering in the extreme. From his able contribution to Anti-slavery papers, and his fearless and eloquent advocacy of the cause of the down-trodden slave in the pulpit, on the platform, and in the social circle, the name of Rev. N. R. Johnston, Reformed Presbyterian (of the old Covenanter faith), will be familiar to many. But we think it safe to say that his fidelity and devotion to the slave are nowhere more fully portrayed than in the appended Underground Rail Road letters.

TOPSHAM, VT., September 1st, 1855.

WM. STILL, MY DEAR FRIEND :—I have the heart, but not the time, to write you a long letter. It is Saturday evening, and I am preparing to preach to-morrow afternoon from Heb. xiii. 3, " Remember them that are in bonds as bound with them." This will be my second sermon from this text. Sabbath before last I preached from it, arguing and illustrating the proposition, deduced from it, that " the great work to which we are now called is the abolition of Slavery, or the emancipation of the slave," showing our duty as *philanthropists*. To-morrow I intend to point out our duty as *citizens*. Some to whom I minister, I know, will call it a political speech ; but I have long since determined to speak for the dumb what is in my heart and in my Bible, let men hear or forbear. I am accountable to the God of the oppressed, not to man. If I have his favor, why need I regard man's disfavor. Many besides the members of my own church come out regularly to hear me. Some of them are pro-slavery politicians. The consequence is, I preach much on the subject of Slavery. And while I have a tongue to speak, and lips to pray, they shall never be sealed or silent so long as millions of dumb have so few to speak for them.

But poor Passmore Williamson is in bonds. Let us also remember him, as bound with him. He has many sympathizers. I am glad you did not share the same fate. For some reasons I am sorry you have fallen into the hands of thieves. For some others I am glad. It will make you more devoted to your good work. Persecution always brightens the Christian, and gives more zeal to the true philanthropist. I hope you will come off victorious. I pray for you and your co-laborers and co-sufferers.

My good brother, I am greatly indebted to you for your continued kindness. The Lord reward you.

I have a scholarship in an Ohio College, Geneva Hall, which will entitle me—any one I may send—to six years tuition. It is an Anti-slavery institution, and wholly under Anti-slavery control and influence. They want colored students to prepare them for the great field of labor open to men of talent and piety of that class. When I last saw you I purposed talking to you about this matter, but was disappointed very much in not getting to take tea with you, as I partly promised. Have you a son ready for college? or for the grammar school? Do you know any promising young man who would accept my scholarship? Or would your brother's son, Peter or Levin, like to have the benefit of it? If so, you are at liberty to promise it to any one whom you think I would be willing to educate. Write me at your earliest convenience, about this matter.

* * * * * * * *

I presume the Standard will contain full accounts of the Norristown meeting, the Williamson case, and your own and those connected. If it does not, I will thank you to write me fully.

* * * * * * * *

What causes the delay of that book, the History of Peter Still's Family, etc.? I long to see it.

The Lord bless you in your labors for the slave.

Yours, etc., N. R. JOHNSTON.

TOPSHAM, VT., December 26th, 1855.

WM. STILL, MY DEAR FRIEND:—I wrote to you some two or three weeks ago, enclosing the letter to the care of a friend in Philadelphia, whom I wished to introduce to you. I have had no answer to that letter, and I am afraid you have not received it, or that you have written me, and I have not received yours. In that letter I wished to receive information respecting the best way to expend money for the aid of fugitives. Lest you may not have received it, I write you again, though briefly.

A few of the Anti-slavery friends, mostly ladies, in our village have formed an Anti-slavery Society and sewing circle, the proceeds of which are to go to aid needy or destitute fugitive slaves. They have appointed me corresponding secretary. In obedience to my instructions, and that I may fulfill my promises, I want to find out from you the desired information. We want to give the little money raised, in such a way that fugitives who are really needy will be benefited by it. Write me as soon as possible, where and to whom we should send the funds when raised. I have thought that you of the Vigilance Committee, in Philadelphia had need of it. Or, if not, you can tell us where money is needed. Probably you know of some one in Canada who acts for the needy there. So many impositions have been palmed off upon charitable abolitionists, I am afraid to act in such a case without the directions of one who knows all about these things. Is money needed to help those escaping? If so, should we send to New York, Philadelphia, or where else? When I was in New York last, a young man from Richmond, Va., assuming the name of Robert Johnston, who had come by steamboat to Philadelphia, and whom you had directed to the Anti-slavery office in New York, had only one dollar in money. His fare had to be paid by a friend there, the treasurer of the fund being absent. I know that they nearly all need money, or clothing. We want to send our money wherever it is most needed, to help the destitute, or those in danger, and where it will be faithfully applied. Write me fully, giving specific directions; and I will read your letter to the society. . And as I have been waiting anxiously, for some two weeks or more, for an answer to my previous letter, but am disappointed unless you have written very recently, I will be much obliged if you will write on the reception of this. Any information you may communicate, respecting the doing of your section of the Underground Railway will be read before the society with much interest.

If you know the address of any one in Canada, who would be a good correspondent respecting this matter, please give me his name.

  * * * * * * * *

My dear brother, go on in your good work; and the God of the oppressed sustain and reward you, is my earnest prayer.

   Yours, fraternally, in our common cause, N. R. JOHNSTON.

       TOPSHAM, VT., December 18th, 1856.

WM. STILL, VERY DEAR FRIEND:—I will be much pleased to hear from you and our common cause in Pennsylvania. I am so far removed, away here in Yankeedom, that I hear nothing from that quarter but by the public prints. And as for the Underground Railway, of course, I hear nothing, except now and then. I would be greatly pleased if you would write me the state of its funds and progress. Whatever you write will be interesting.

The Topsham Sewing Circle has begun its feeble operations again. Owing to much opposition, a very few attend, consequently little is made. The ladies, however, have some articles on hand unsold, which will bring some money ere long. I wish you would write me another long letter in detail of interesting fugitives, etc., such as you wrote last winter, and I will have it read before the circle. Your letter last winter was heard by the ladies with great interest. You are probably not aware that fugitives are never seen here. Indeed the one half of the people have never seen more than a half-dozen of colored people. There are none in all this region.

I am lending Peter Still—the book—to my neighbors. It is devoured with great interest. It does good. I think, however, if I had been writing such a book, I would have wedged in much more testimony against slavery and its horrid accompaniments and consequences.

I would be glad to hear how Peter and his family are prospering.

Do you see my friends, Mr. Orr and Rev. Willson, now-a-days? Do they help in the good cause?

If the ladies here should make up fine shirts for men, or children's clothes of various kinds, would they be of use at Philadelphia, or New York, to fugitives? Or would it not be advisable to send them there? The ladies here complain that they cannot sell what they make.

My dear brother, be not discouraged in your work, your labor of love. The prospect before the poor slave is indeed dark, dark! But the power shall not always be on the side of the oppressor. God reigns. A day of vengeance will come, and that soon.

Mrs. Stowe makes Dred utter many a truth. Would that God would write it indelibly on the heart of the nation. But the people will not hear, and the cup of iniquity will soon fill to overflowing; and whose ears will not be made to tingle when the God of Sabaoth awakes to plead the cause of the dumb? Yours, very sincerely, N. R. JOHNSTON.

P. S. When I was in New York last Fall, October, I was in the Anti-Slavery office one day, when a friend in the office showed me a dispatch just received from Philadelphia, signed W. S., which gave notice of "six parcels" coming by the train, etc. And before I left the office the "parcels" came in, each on two legs. Strange parcels, that would run away on legs.

My heart leaped for joy at seeing these rescued ones. O that God would arise and break the yoke of oppression! Let us labor on and ever, until our work is done, until all are free.

Since the late Republican farce has closed I hope to get some more subscribers for the Standard. Honest men's eyes will be opened after a while, and the standard of right and expediency be elevated. Let us "hope on and ever." Yours, for the right, N. R. J.

Topsham, Vt., April 3d, 1858.

DEAR FRIEND STILL :—I entreat you not to infer from my tardiness or neglect, that I am forgetful of my dear friend in Philadelphia. For some time past I have done injustice to many of my friends, in not paying my debts in epistolary correspondence. Some of my dearest friends have cause to censure me. But you must pardon me. I have two letters of yours on hand, unanswered. One of them I read to the Sewing Circle; and part of the other. For them I most heartily thank you. You are far kinder to me than I deserve. May God reward you.

I long to see you. My head and heart is full of the cause of the slave.

I fear I give the subject too much relative importance. Is this possible? I preach, lecture, and write for the slave continually. And yet I don't do enough. Still I fear I neglect the great concerns of religion at home, in my own heart, in my congregation, and in the community.

I wish we were located near to each other. We are far separated. I am almost isolated. You are surrounded by many friends of the cause. Still we are laboring on the same wall, though far apart. Are we not near in spirit?

You see by the papers that we have been trying to do something in our Green Mountain State. The campaign has fairly begun. We will carry the battle to the gate.

I see our friend, Miss Watkins, is still pleading for the dumb. Noble girl! I love her for her devotedness to a good cause. Oh, that her voice could be heard by the millions! I hope that we can have her again in Vermont.

Give my kind regards to our mutual friend, Miller McKim. Will I not see him and you at the anniversary in New York?

Do you ever see Rev. Willson? Is he doing anything for the cause? I wish I could peep into your house to-night, and see if there are any "packages" on hand. God bless you in your labors of love.

Yours, truly, for the slave,

N. R. JOHNSTON.

While it was not in the power of Mr. Johnston and his coadjutors, to render any great amount of material aid to the Committee, as they had not been largely blessed with this world's goods, nevertheless, the sympathy shown was as highly valued, as if they had given thousands of dollars. Not unfrequently has the image of this singularly faithful minister entered the writer's mind as he once appeared when visiting the Synod of his church in Philadelphia. Having the Underground Rail Road cause at heart, he brought with him—all the way from Vermont—his trunk well filled with new shirts and under-clothing for the passengers on that Road. It was characteristic of the man, and has ever since been remembered with pleasure.

From another quarter, hundreds of miles from Philadelphia, similar tokens of interest in the cause of the fleeing bondmen were manifested by a Ladies' Anti-slavery Society, in Western New York, which we must here record. As the proffered aid was wholly unsolicited, and as the Committee had no previous knowledge whatever of the existence of the society, or any of its members, and withal, as the favors conferred, came at times when the cause was peculiarly in need (the Committee oft-times being destitute of clothing or money), the idea that the Underground Rail Road was providentially favored, in this respect, was irresistible.

We therefore take great pleasure in commemorating the good deeds of the society, by copying the following letters from its president, Mrs. Dr. Brooks:

ELLINGTON, Nov. 21st, 1859.

MR. WILLIAM STILL:—Dear Sir:—In the above-named place, some five years since there was formed a Ladies' Anti-slavery Society, which has put forth its feeble endeavors to aid the cause of "breaking every yoke and letting the oppressed go free," and we trust, through our means, others have been made glad of heart. Every year we have sent a box of clothing, bedding, etc., to the aid of the fugitive, and wishing to send it where it would be of the most service, we have it suggested to us, to send to you the box we have at present. You would confer a favor upon the members of our society, by writing us, giving a detail of that which would be the most service to you, and whether or no it would be more advantageous to you than some nearer station, and we will send or endeavor to, that which would benefit you most.

William Wells Brown visited our place a short time since, recommending us to send to you in preference to Syracuse, where we sent our last box.

Please write, letting me know what most is needed to aid you in your glorious work, a work which will surely meet its reward. Direct, Ellington, Chautauqua county, N. Y.　　　Your sister, in the cause,

MRS. M. BROOKS.

ELLINGTON, Chautauqua Co., N. Y., Dec. 7th, 1859.

MR. STILL:—Dear Sir:—Yours of the 29th, was duly and gratefully received, although the greater portion of your epistle, of a necessity, portrayed the darker side of the picture, yet we have great reason to be thankful for the growing interest there is for the cause throughout the free States, for it certainly is on the increase, even in our own locality. There are those who, five years since, were (ashamed, must I say it!) to bear the appellation of "*Anti-slavery,*" who can now manfully bear the one then still more repellant of *Abolitionist.* All this we wish to feel thankful for, and wish their number may never grow less.

The excitement relative to the heroic John Brown, now in his grave, has affected the whole North, or at least every one who has a heart in his breast, particularly this portion of the State, which is so decidedly Anti-slavery.

At a meeting of our Society, to-day, at which your letter was read, it was thought best that I should reply to it, a request with which I cheerfully comply. We would like to hear from you, and learn the directions to be given to our box, which will be ready to send as soon as we can hear from you. Please give us all necessary information, and oblige our Society.

You have the kind wishes and prayers of all the members, that you may be the instrument of doing much good to those in bonds, and may God speed the time when every yoke shall be broken, and let the oppressed go free.　　　Yours, truly,　　　MRS. DR. BROOKS.

P. S. I have just learned that John Brown's body passed through Dunkirk, a few miles from this place, yesterday. A funeral sermon is to be preached in this place one week from next Sabbath, for the good old man.

Mrs. DR. B.

ELLINGTON, Jan. 2d, 1860.

WILLIAM STILL:—Dear Sir:—Enclosed are $2,00, to pay freightage on the box of bedding, wearing apparel, etc., that has been sent to your address. It has been thought best to send you a schedule of the contents of said box. Trusting it will be acceptable, and be the means of assisting the poor fugitive on his perilous way, you have the prayers of our Society, that you may be prospered in your work of mercy, and you surely will meet with your reward according to your merciful acts.

Two bed quilts, 32, $8,00; five bed quilts, 24, $15,00; one bed quilt, 28, $3,50; two pairs cotton socks, 3, 75 cents; three pairs cotton stockings, 4, $1,50; one pair woolen stockings, 6, 75 cents; one pair woolen stockings, 4, 50 cents; three pair woolen socks, 2, 75 cents; five pair woolen socks, 3, $1,88; eight chemise, 32, $4,50; thirteen men's shirts, 66 cents, $8,58; one pair pants, 12, $1,50; six pair overall pants, 80 cents, $4,80; three pair pillow cases, $1,00; three calico aprons, 2, 75 cents; three sun-bonnets, 2, 75 cents; two small aprons, 1, 25 cents; one alpaca cape, 8, $1,00; two capes, 1, 25 cents; one black shawl, 4, 50 cents. Total, $56,51.

The foregoing is a correct list of the articles and the appraisal of the same. Please acknowledge the receipt of the letter and box, and oblige the Antislavery Society of Ellington.

Mrs. DR. BROOKS.

The road was doing a flourishing business during the short time that this station received aid and sympathy from the Ladies' Anti-slavery Society of Ellington, and little did we dream that its existence would so soon be rendered null and void by the utter overthrow of Slavery.

We have great pleasure in stating that beyond our borders also, across the ocean, there came help to a laudable degree in the hour of need. The numbers of those who aided in this special work, however, were very few and far between, a hundred per cent. less (so far as the receipts of the Philadelphia Committee were concerned), than was supposed by slave-holders and their sympathizers, judging from their oft repeated allegations on this subject.

It is true, that the American Anti-slavery Society and kindred associations, received liberal contributions from a few warm-hearted and staunch abolitionists abroad, to aid the great work of abolishing Slavery. In reference to the Philadelphia Vigilance Committee, we are safe in saying, that, except from a few sources, no direct aid came. How true this was of other stations, we do not pretend to know or speak, but in the directions above alluded to, we feel that the cause was placed under lasting obligations. The Webbs of

Dublin, and the Misses Wighams, of Scotland, representatives of the Edinburgh Ladies' Emancipation Society, were constantly in correspondence with
leading abolitionists in different parts of the country, manifesting a deep
interest in the general cause, and were likewise special stockholders of the
Underground Rail Road of Philadelphia.   In common with stockholders
at home, these trans-atlantic investors were willing to receive their shares of
dividends in the answer of a good conscience, or, in other words, from the
satisfaction and pleasure derivable from a consciousness of having done what
they could to alleviate the sufferings of the oppressed struggling to be free.
Having thus shown their faith by their works it would be unjust not to
make honorable mention of them.

Last, though not least, at the risk of wounding the feelings of one who
preferred not to let the left hand know what the right hand doeth, we may
contemplate the philanthropic labors of one, whose generosity and benevolence knew no bounds; whose friendship devotion and liberality, were felt
in all the principal stations of the Underground Rail Road; whose heart
went out after the millions in fetters, the fleeing fugitive, the free, proscribed,
the ignorant deprived of education; whose house was the home of the advocate of the slave from the United States, especially if he wore a colored skin
or had been a slave.   We would not venture to say how many of the
enslaved this kind hand helped to purchase (Frederick Douglass and many
others, being of the number.)

How many were assisted in procuring an education, how many who pined
in slave prisons were aided, how many fleeing over the perilous Underground Rail Road were benefited, the All-seeing Eye alone knoweth;
nevertheless, we are happy to be able to give our readers some idea of
the unwearied labors of the friend to whom we allude.   Here again we
are compelled to resort to private correspondence which took place when
Cotton was King, and the Slave-power of the South could boastingly say,
in the language of the apocalyptic woman, "I sit as a queen, and shall
see no sorrow," when that power was maddened to desperation, by the heroism of the martyr, John Brown, and the fettered bondmen were ever and
anon traveling over the Underground Rail Road.   In this "darkest hour,
just before the break of day," the heart of the friend of whom we speak,
was greatly moved to consider the wants of the oppressed in various
directions.

How worthily and successfully her labors gave evidence of an earnest
devotion to freedom, the mode and measures adopted by her, to awaken
sympathy in the breast of the benevolent of her own countrymen, and how
noble her example, may be learned from a small pamphlet and explanatory
letters which, when written, were intended especially for private use, but
which we now feel constrained to copy from a sense of justice to disinterested
philanthropy.

PAMPHLET, AND LETTERS

FROM MRS. ANNA H. RICHARDSON, OF NEWCASTLE, ENGLAND.

TO THE FRIENDS OF THE SLAVE.

DEAR FRIENDS —For some months past my dear husband and I have wished very gratefully to thank you for having so kindly assisted us in various Anti-Slavery efforts, and we now think it quite time to give an account of our stewardship, and also to lay before you several items of interesting intelligence received from different parts of the United States. We will thank you to look upon this intelligence as private, and must request you to guard against any portion of it being reprinted.

WILLIAM S. BAILEY.—We have had great pleasure in forwarding £222 to our valued correspondent, William S. Bailey, of Newport, Kentucky; £160 of this sum in response to a circular issued at Newcastle in the summer of last year, and received by our friend, David Oliver, who acted as treasurer, and the remainder chiefly collected by our dear young friends in England and Ireland, after reading the account of his little daughter, "Laura." This money has been very thankfully acknowledged, with the exception of the last remittance just now on the road.

Most of our readers will be aware that W. S. Bailey's printing-office and premises were again ruthlessly attacked after the Harper's Ferry outbreak, on the unfounded assumption that he was meditating a similar proceeding, and that it was unsafe for a free press to be any longer tolerated in Kentucky. His forms and type were accordingly dragged through the streets of Newport, and a considerable portion of them flung by a mob (of "gentlemen") into the Ohio River. A few extracts from his own letters will pretty fully explain both his past and present position. The subscription list on his behalf is still open, and any further assistance for this heroic man and his noble-hearted family will be very gratefully received and forwarded.

"NEWPORT, KENTUCKY, Nov. 19th, 1859.

"From my letter of the 7th inst. you will have learned the sad intelligence that my printing-office has been destroyed by a brutal mob of Pro-Slavery men. Through the money I received from you and other friends in this country I was moving the cause of freedom in all parts of Kentucky. The people seemed to grasp our platform with eagerness, and the slaveholders became alarmed to see their wish to read and discuss its simple truths. Hence they plotted together to devise a stratagem by which they could destroy *The Free South*, and in the meantime the Harper's Ferry difficulty, by Mr. Brown, was seized upon to excite the people against me, and the most extravagant lies were told about me, as trying to excite slaves to

38

rebellion; intending to seize the United States barracks at this place, arm the negroes, and commence war upon slave-holders. All these lies were told as profound secrets to the people by the tools of the slave-power. But these lies have already exploded, and the people are resuming their common sense again.

"I tried your plan of non-resistance with all my power. I pleaded with all the earnestness of my soul, and so did my wife and daughters, but though I am certain many were moved in conscience against the savage outrage, and did their work with a stinging heart, yet they felt that they must stick to their party, and complete the destruction. Slavery, indeed, makes the most hardened savages the world ever knew. The savage war-whoop of the Indian never equalled their dastardly cry of 'shoot him,' 'cut his throat,' 'stab him,' and such like words most maliciously spoken."   *   *

"Slavery is the cause of this devilish spirit in men; but this outrage has gained me many friends, and will do much towards putting down Slavery in the state. It will also add many thousand votes to the republican presidential candidate in 1860. God grant it may work out a great good!"   *

*   *   *   "I want to get started again as soon as I possibly can. As soon as I can raise 1,000 dollars, I can make a beginning, and soon after you will see *The Free South* again, and I trust a much handsomer sheet than it was before."

NEWPORT, January 6th, 1860.

"Yours of 12mo. 17th, 1860, is received, containing a draft for £50, and another of the 'Little Laura' books, which, thank God, is doing some good in Newport and Covington, in the hands of two Christian friends. The renewed obligations under which the good people of England, through your instrumentality, place me and my abused people, call for expressions of gratitude from both me and them beyond my ability to pen. But you can imagine how we ought to feel in our trials and wants to such kind friends as you. Neither I nor my Anti-Slavery friends here can express our thankfulness in the elegant language your better educated countrymen may feel we should use, but, by the Omnipotent Judge of all hearts, I trust our feeble effort will be accepted, and you and yours be blessed and protected now and for ever. Such encouragement strengthens me in the belief that the Spirit of God is abroad in the hearts of the people, moving them to sympathize with the poor, subjected slave."   *   *   *   *   "I have the promise of abler pens to aid me when I get started again; and I am glad to see that a poor working-man and his family have been the means of calling the attention of men of letters to assist in raising from the dust a crushed race of men; and although the red clouds of war hover thick around us, and vengeance lurks in secret places, I trust, through the guidance of an All-wise Director, to steer safely through the angry tide that now so often ebbs and flows around me; but should I fall, I trust, dear lady, that my dear wife and family may be remembered by the good and true."

"NEWPORT, May 25th, 1860.

"I am glad to tell you that we feel it a great victory over the slave power to be able to rise again from our ruins, and in the face of slave-owning despots denounce their inhumanity and their sins. I trust that Almighty God will continue to be with me and my dear family in this good work." * * * "You cannot but see, I think, by the southern press, that slave-holders begin to fear and tremble for the safety of their 'peculiar institution.' The death of John Brown is yet to be atoned for, by the slave-holding oligarchy. His undying spirit haunts them by day and by night, and in the midst of their voluptuous enjoyments, the very thought of John Brown chills their souls and poisons their pleasures. Their tarring and feathering of good citizens; their riding them upon rails, and ducking them in dirty ponds; their destruction of liberty presses, and the hanging of John Brown and his friends, to intimidate men from the advocacy of freedom, will all come tumbling upon their own heads as a just retribution for their outrageous brutality. Only let us persevere, and oppressed humanity, bent in timid silence throughout the south, will rise and throw off the yoke of Slavery and rejoice in beholding itself *free!*"

"NEWPORT, August 18.

"I send you three copies of my paper. Since receiving your letter, I and my family have done all in our power to get it out, but we had to get old type from the foundry and sort it, to make the sheet the size you now see it. We hate to be put down by the influence of tyranny, and you cannot imagine our sorrow, anxiety, necessity and determination." * * *
"I have received, since the press was destroyed, 700 dollars in all, which has been spent in repairing and roofing our dwelling-house, and repairing the breaches made upon the office, together with mending the presses and procuring job type and some little for the paper, but nearly all the latter is old type. Our kindest thanks to the liberty-loving people of your country, Scotland, and Ireland, and tell them I shall never surrender the cause of freedom. A little money from all my friends, would soon reinstate me, and when they see my paper I trust it will cheer their hopes, and cause a new fire for liberty in Kentucky.

"I cannot but sometimes ask in my closet meditations: O God of mercy and love, why permittest Thou these things? But still I hope for a change of mind in my enemies, and shall press onward to accomplish the great task seemingly allotted to me upon Kentucky soil."

THE PERSECUTED BEREANS.—There is another call connected with Kentucky, which we wish to bring before our friends. At a village in that State, called Berea, (situated in Madison county), a little band of Christian men and women, had been pursuing their useful labors for some years past.

They avowedly held Anti-slavery sentiments, but this was the beginning and end of their offending. They possessed a farm and saw-mill, etc., and had established a flourishing school. These good people were quietly following their usual employments, when, in the early part of last winter, sixty-two armed Kentuckians rode upon horseback to their cottage doors, and summarily informed them that they must leave the State in ten days' time, or would be expelled from it forcibly. All pleading was hopeless, and any attempt at self-defence out of the question. They bowed before the storm, and hastily gathering up their garments, in three days' time were on their road to Ohio. Their three Christian pastors took the same course. One of the latter has since returned to Kentucky, to bury his youngest little boy, in a grave-yard attached to one of the churches there. He was enabled to preach to the people who assembled on the occasion, but was not allowed to remain in his native State.

Another of the exiles ventured to go back to Berea, but this immediately led to an outbreak of popular feeling, for his saw-mill was set on fire by the mob, and presently destroyed. The exiles are consequently still in Ohio, or wandering about in search of employment. We have been privileged in receiving two letters respecting them, from one of their excellent pastors, John G. Fee. This gentleman is himself, the son of a slave-holder, but gave up his earthly patrimony many years since for conscience' sake, and has since made it the business of his life to proclaim the gospel in its purity, and to use every available means for directing all to Christ.

When speaking of Berea, Mr. Fee remarks: "The land was poor, but the situation beautiful, with good water, and a favorable location, in some respects. We could have had locations more fertile and more easy of access, but more exposed to the slave-power. It was five miles from a turnpike road, with quite a population around it for a slave State."

In one of Mr. Fee's letters he introduces a subject which we wish especially to bring before our friends, feeling almost sure that many of them will respond to its importance:

"You ask, he says, if there are not noble-hearted young people in slave-holding families? There is one whom I desire to commend to your special prayer and regard, Elizabeth Rawlings, daughter of John H. Rawlings, of Madison county, Kentucky. He was once a slave-holder, but has twice been a delegate to our Free-soil National Conventions, and is a strong friend of freedom. His daughter has had small opportunities for acquiring knowledge, but was in our school at Berea, and making rapid progress. Our school was not only Anti-slavery, but avowedly Anti-caste. This made it the more odious. When Mr. Rogers and others were about to be driven away, she announced that she would continue the school on the same principles. Accordingly she went into the school-room after a few days, with a little band of small scholars, and has perseveringly kept it up. This noble and brave-hearted young woman is about twenty-two years of age; has a very vigorous mind; acquires knowledge very rapidly; is very modest; and is, I trust, a true believer in Christ. I desire to see her fitted for the post of teacher. One year's study would greatly benefit her. She has not gone beyond grammar and arithmetic. I have not means or would at once give her those advantages she needs. I once had a small patrimony, but expended it in freedom's cause, and now live on the small salary of a [Home] Missionary. I have a daughter of fifteen, as far advanced as Miss Rawlings. I want to train and educate them both for teaching, and had thought to educate the latter, and suggest to some one to educate the other. I do not urge, but simply suggest. This might be another cord binding the two continents. Lewis Tappan, of New York, would receive to transmit, and I would report."

Now if we may lay before you, dear friends, our hearts' inquiry, it is this: " Cannot we in England, raise £50 or £60 for one year's schooling for these two dear girls, Elizabeth Rawlings and J. G. Fee's daughter?" It seems to us, that the one deserves it from her noble daring, the other as a little tribute to her father's virtues. How delightful it would be if these two young people could become able teachers of our own rearing, and in days to come, be looked to as maintaining schools of an elevated character upon their native soil! We have laid the case before a few kind friends, and already had the pleasure of forwarding £8 to Mr. Fee's care, on behalf of his valued young friend, Elizabeth Rawlings.

CORNELIA WILLIAMS.—The next person to be referred to is Cornelia Williams, a bright young niece of our friend, Henry H. Garnet's, whom many of our friends kindly assisted to redeem from Slavery, in North Carolina, about three years since. We rejoice to say this dear girl is going on very satisfactorily. She has been diligently pursuing her studies in a school at Nantucket, and appears to be much esteemed by all who know her. She kindly sends us a little letter now and then, again returning her glowing thanks to all who assisted in procuring her freedom. Her mother, Dinah Williams (also a slave a few years since, and redeemed in part by the surplus of 'the Weims Ransom Fund),' has married an estimable Baptist minister within the last year, and Cornelia resides under their roof.

FREDERICK DOUGLASS.—It is known that our much-valued friend, Frederick Douglass, left this country suddenly for America last spring, chiefly on account of the decease of a most beloved little girl. Till quite recently he was intending to return to England very soon, but this is for the present delayed, on account of increasing and pressing engagements in the United States. We take the liberty of quoting an extract from one of his letters :

"ROCHESTER, July 2d, 1860.

"You hold up before me the glorious promises contained in the sacred Scriptures. These are needed by none more than by those who have presumed to put themselves to the work of accomplishing the abolition of Slavery in this country. There is scarcely one single interest, social, moral, religious, or physical, which is not in some way connected with this stupendous evil. On the side of the oppressor there is power, now as in the earlier days of the world. I find much comfort in the thought that I am but a passenger on board of this ship of life. I have not the management committed to me. I am to obey orders, and leave the rest to the great Captain whose wisdom is able to direct. I have only to go on in His fear and in His spirit, uttering with pen and tongue the whole truth against Slavery, leaving to Him the honor and the glory of destroying this mighty work of the devil. I long for the end of my people's bondage, and would give all I possess to witness the great jubilee; but God can wait, and surely I may. If He, whose pure eyes cannot look upon sin with allowance, can permit the day of freedom to be deferred, I certainly can work and wait. The times are just now a little brighter; but I will walk by faith, not by sight, for all grounds of hope founded on external appearance, have thus far signally failed and broken down under me. Twenty years ago, Slavery did really *seem* to be rapidly hastening to its fall, but ten years ago, the Fugitive Slave Bill, and the efforts to enforce it, changed the whole appearance of the struggle. Anti-slavery in an abolition sense, has been ever since battling against heavy odds, both in Church and State. Nevertheless, God reigns, and we need not despair, and I for one do not. I know, at any rate, no better work for me during the brief period I am to stay on the earth, than is found in pleading the cause of the down-trodden and the dumb.

"Since I reached home I have had the satisfaction of passing nearly a score on to Canada, only two women among them all. The constant meeting with these whip-scarred brothers will not allow me to become forgetful of the four millions still in bonds."

Our friends may, perhaps, remember that the cost of *Frederick Douglass' paper* is but five shillings per annum (with the exception of a penny per month at the door for postage.) It is a very interesting publication, and amply repays the trifling outlay. F. D. would be glad to increase the number of his British readers. He also continues gratefully to receive any aid from this country for the assistance of the fugitives who are so often taking refuge under his roof. Another letter of his remarks, when speaking of them: "They usually tarry with us only during the night, and are forwarded to Canada by the morning train. We give them supper, lodging, and breakfast; pay their expenses, and give them a half dollar over."

Fugitive Slaves.—We next turn to the communication of another warm friend to the fugitives in the State of ———. The following is an extract from a recent letter of his:

"We have had within the last week just nineteen Underground passengers. Fifteen came last Saturday, between the hours of six in the morning and eleven at night. Three only were females, wives of men in the parties, the rest were all able-bodied young men. That they were all likely-looking it needed no southern eye to decide, and that their hearts burned within them for freedom was apparent in every look of their countenances. But it is only of one arrival that my time will allow me to speak on the present occasion.

This consisted of two married couples, and two single young men. They had been a week on the way. To accomplish the desired object they could see no way so feasible as to cross the ——— Bay. By inquiry they gained instructions as to the direction they should steer to strike for the lighthouse on the opposite shore. Consequently they invested six dollars in a little boat, and at once prepared themselves for this most fearful adventure. To the water and their little bark they stealthily repaired, and off they started. For some distance they rowed not far from the shore. Being in sight of land, they were spied by the ever-watchful slave-holder or some one not favorable to their escape. Hence a small boat, containing four white men, soon put out after the fugitives. On overhauling them, stern orders were given to surrender. The boat the runaways were in was claimed, if not the party themselves. With determined words the fugitives declared that the boat was their own property, and that they would not give it up; they said they would die before they would do so. At this sign of resistance one of the white men, with an oar, struck the head of one of the fugitives, which knocked him down. At the same moment another white man seized the chain of their boat, and the struggle became fearful in the extreme for a few moments. However, the same spirit that prompted the effort to be free, moved one of the heroic black bondmen to apply the oar to the head of one of their pursuers, which straightway laid him prostrate. The whites, like old Apollyon in the Pilgrim's Progress, at this decided indication that their precious lives might not be spared if they did not avail themselves of an immediate retreat, suddenly parted from their antagonists. Not being contented, however, thus to give up the struggle, after getting some yards off, they fired a loaded gun in the midst of the fugitives, peppering two of them considerably about the head and face, and one about the arms. As the shot was light they were not much damaged, however, at any rate not discouraged. Not forgetting which way to steer across the bay, in the direction of the lighthouse, they rowed for that point with all possible speed, but their bark being light, and the wind and rough water by no means manageable,

ere they reached the desired shore they were carried a considerable distance off their course, in the immediate vicinity of a small island. Leaving their boat they went upon the island, the women sick, and there reposed without food, utterly ignorant of where they were for one whole day and night, without being able to conjecture when or where they should find free land for which they had so long and fervently prayed. However, after thus resting, feeling compelled to start on again, they set off on foot. They had not walked a mile ere, providentially, they fell in with an oyster man and a little boy waiting for the tide. With him they ventured to converse, and soon felt that he might be trusted with, at least, a hint of their condition. Accordingly they made him acquainted in part with their piteous story, and he agreed to bring them within fifteen miles of —— for twenty-five dollars, all the capital they had. Being as good as his word, he did not leave them fifteen miles off the city, but brought them directly to it." *   *   *   *
" How happy they were at finding themselves in the hands of friends, and surrounded with flattering prospects of soon reaching Canada you may imagine, but I could not describe."*

Thanks to the benevolent bounty of several kind donors, we had lately the pleasure of sending a few pounds to the writer of the foregoing letter. We omit his name and residence. He belongs, like Douglass, to the proscribed race. Who would not help these generous-hearted men, who are devoting their whole energies to the well-being of the crushed and down-trodden? We are the more encouraged to send out this little sheet, made up of thanks and requisitions, because occasional inquiries are reaching us of " What can we do for the slave? We are hearing but little about him, and do not know how to work on his behalf." Allow us to say to one and all, who may be thus circumstanced, that we do not look for great things, but that if they can levy a shilling a year from all who feel for the injured bondman, these little sums would soon mount up and prove of incalculable service to those who are struggling for freedom. As to the special destiny of these shillings or half-crowns, let the subscribers choose for themselves, and their kind aid will be sure to be truly welcome to the party receiving it. We do not ask for such contributions to be forwarded through Newcastle unless this be a matter of convenience to those concerned. If there be other modes of sending to the United States within the reach of the friends, who receive this paper, let them by all means be used. We are always happy to receive aid for the fugitives or for any other Anti-slavery cause, and consider it no trouble at all to send it on, but do not wish to be monopolizing. As far as Kentucky is concerned, that State being distant, and mob-law ram-

---

* In those days the writer in giving information enjoined the utmost secrecy, considering that the cause might be sadly damaged simply by being inadvertently exposed even by friends, thousands of miles away. The Pro-slavery-mob spirit at that time was also very rampant in Philadelphia and other northern cities, threatening abolitionists and all concerned in the work of aiding the slave.

pant there, we shall continue gratefully to receive assistance on its behalf, and to avail ourselves of the accustomed mode of reaching it, this having been proved to be both safe and easy.

FREE LABOR PRODUCE.—And lastly, as to the long-prized principle, to our minds the very alphabet of Anti-Slavery action, the importance of encouraging the growth and consumption of Free produce rather than that raised by the sweat and blood of the bondman. Our convictions of the righteousness of this course are as strong as they ever were ; but perhaps we hoped too much, relied too fondly on the conscientiousness of the British Anti-Slavery public, in supposing that a sufficient number of individuals could be found prepared to make a slight sacrifice for humanity's sake, and to keep the oppressed continually in mind by a little untiring pains-taking. We hardly supposed that the most strenuous efforts in this direction would be enough to affect the British market ; but we did believe, and believe still, that not only is there a consistency in a preference for free produce, but that this preference is encouraging to the free laborer, and that humanly speaking nothing is more calculated to nerve his hand and heart for vigorous effort. The principle of abstinence from slave produce may be smiled at, but we are quite sure it is an honest one, and, as a good old proverb observes, " It takes a great many bushels full of earth to bury a truth."

But while this self-denying protest has been going on in a few limited circles, how great is the advance that free labor has been making within the last two years ! Who is to say whether some of those quiet testimonies may not have contributed to erect that mighty machinery that is now adding to its wheels and springs from day to day, and which bids fair at no distant period to supersede slave labor and its long train of sorrow and oppression ?

Earnest lectures have just been delivered in Newcastle by our colored friend, Dr. M. R. Delany, lately engaged in a tour of observation in West Africa, where he longs to establish a flourishing colony of his people, whose express object shall be to put down the abominable Slave-trade and to cultivate free cotton and other tropical produce. We wish this brave man every encouragement in his noble enterprise. He has secured the confidence of " The African Aid Society," in London, one of whose earliest measures has been to assist him with funds. The present Secretary of the society is Frederick W. Fitzgerald, 7 Adam Street, Strand, London.

And who need speak of the Zambesi and Dr. Livingston, or of Central or Eastern Africa ; of India, or Australia, or of the prolific West India Islands?

As we prepare this little sheet, a kind letter has come in from Stephen Bourne, for many years a stipendiary magistrate in Jamaica, and now the ardent promoter of a cotton-growing company of that island. He says to us, when writing from London, on the 19th inst., " Our scheme embraces more than meets the eye, and to illustrate this, I send a map (with prospectus) of the proposed estate, by which you will see that we reckon on

obtaining cotton by free labor and by mechanical agency from Jamaica, at a price so far below that at which it can be produced by slave labor, that if we succeed, we shall put an end to the whole system, as no one will be able to afford to carry it on in competition with free labor." *   *   *
" Jamaica is much nearer and easier of access for fugitives from Cuba and Porto Rico, than Canada is to Georgia, Virginia, or Louisiana. If, therefore, we can offer them an asylum and profitable employment on the estate, we shall open up a new Underground Rail Road, or rather enable the slaves to escape from Cuba by getting into a boat, and in one night finding their way to freedom."   *   *   *   " There is no doubt they could do this at much less risk than slaves now incur, in order to obtain liberty in America."

The proposed estate in Jamaica consists of about one thousand acres, and the shares in this company are £10 each, £1 only to be called up immediately, the rest by instalments. The liability is limited. Full information may be obtained by addressing Stephen Bourne, Esq., 55 Charing Cross, London, or the Secretary of the "Jamaica Cotton-growing Company," C. W. Streatfield, Esq. We rejoice to see that this new company is being supported not only by benevolent philanthropists and capitalists in London, but by experienced Manchester manufacturers; among the rest by the excellent Thomas Clegg, so well known for his persevering efforts in West Africa, and by Thomas Bazley, M. P. for Manchester, and a most extensive cotton spinner. Their mills would alone, consume the cotton grown on three such estates as that which it is proposed to cultivate. There is abundant room, therefore, for cultivation of cotton by the emancipated freeholders.

Communications have also reached us from Demerara. Charles Rattray, a valuable Scotch missionary in that colony, was in England last spring, and went back to his adopted country with his mind full fraught with the importance of cotton growing within its borders. He happened to have small samples of Demerara cotton with him. These were shown to cotton-brokers and manufacturers in Liverpool and Manchester, and were pronounced to be most excellent—so much so, that specimen gins and a supply of cotton-seed were kindly presented to him at the latter place, before he left England. Mr. Rattray is now bringing the subject before his people, and is also intending to plant with cotton some ground belonging to the Mission station.

But we will not further enlarge. Commending our cause to Him, who has promised never to forget the poor and needy, and that in His own good time He will arise for their deliverance and "break every yoke."

I remain, sincerely and respectfully, your friend,

ANNA H. RICHARDSON.

54 *Westmoreland Terrace,*
Newcastle-on-Tyne, 9 *mo.,* 22, 1860.

P. S. Since writing the above, we have seen it stated in the *Principia*, a New York paper, that William S. Bailey has been arrested on a charge of publishing an incendiary paper, and held to bail in the sum of $1,000, to appear before the Circuit Court, in November next. It is further stated that one of the two magistrates by whom W. S. Bailey was examined, and held to bail on this charge, was the chosen leader of the mob that destroyed his type and printing press.

We have yet to see what will be the end of this cruel conflict. Let us not desert our suffering friend and his noble-hearted family.

LETTERS TO THE WRITER.

WESTMORELAND TERRACE, December 28, 1860.

MY ESTEEMED FRIEND :—I received thy touching letter of the 10th inst. a few days since, and hasten to assure thee of our heart-felt sympathy, and most lively interest in the present tremendous state of things around you. At the same time, I cannot tell thee how glad and thankful we feel, that with God's help thou art determined to persevere and not in any way flinch in this day of sore trial. " Be thou faithful unto death, and I will give thee a crown of life." " Be strong, fear not." " In the fear of the Lord is strong confidence ; and his children shall have a place of refuge." One thing, too, is sure, " that all things will work together for the good " of those who love their Lord, that He will never, never forsake them whatever their outward trials may be.

I think, dear friend, thou shouldst be careful not to be about alone, particularly in the evening. We heard from W. S. Bailey the other day, and he spoke of the advantage of several kind friends sticking close to him under recent circumstances at Alexandria, when he was exposed to the spite and rage of slave-holding bullies. Would it not be well to make a habit, in the evening in particular, of you, who are marked men, going about in little companies? Wicked men are generally cowards ; and I think would hesitate more to do a bad act in the presence of observers. I think thou wouldst receive a little letter from me a day or two after thine was written, through our friend Saml. Rhoads, enclosing £7 for the fugitives, £5 for thy own use, and £2 for the Vigilance Committee. This letter of mine was sent off about the 24th ult., but I conclude was not delivered till just after thine was written. It is well to keep us fully informed of your circumstances, whether favorable or more appalling. I do not intend to put anything of a private character into print; but private confidence is the creed in England, and thou needst not fear my abusing it. I enclose the only paper that we have printed that thou mayest see there was nothing to fear. Thou wilt observe there is no reference either to thy own name or to Philadelphia, and people here are not very familiar with American topography. I am sending W. S. Bailey one of the same papers by to-day's mail. We have merely a limited number of them printed. I cannot very well obtain money from my friends, (with numerous home claims constantly pressing on them), without having something to show. Some fugitives are now beginning to reach England. A gentleman in London wrote to me, a day or two ago, to know if we could find a berth for a fine fellow, who had just applied to him. He had arrived by steamer from New York, after residing there for three years. A police-man, in the street, good-naturedly whispered to him his own name, and then that of his masters. He was sure that peril was at hand, and that, having been branded for escaping before, he should be whipped to death if taken again, so he packed up his little wardrobe and embarked for England im-mediately.

Another poor fellow is in this town, recently from Charleston, whence he escaped, among some cotton bales to Greenock. He is getting fair wages in a saw-yard, and likes England very well, if it were not for the thought of his poor wife and children still in Slavery. We invited him, the other day to a working-men's tea party, where I had been asked to make tea for them; and he gave us quite an able account of his travels. The men kindly invited him to join their "Benefit Club," and told him they would like to have "a colored brother" amongst them.

Art thou not thinking, dear friend, of asking your people to emigrate to the African Coast, or the West India Islands? Two gentlemen in London are writing most warmly about this. I wrote Mr. Fitzgerald's address on the enclosed paper. Instead of being colonizationists, in the objectionable sense, he and Mrs. Bowen are burning with love to your people, and are fervently desirous of doing them all the good they can. I cannot see why little united parties should not promptly emigrate under the wing of these gentlemen. Assure those who think and feel with thee, dear friend, and are nobly determined to suffer rather than to sin, that according to our very small ability we will not desert them in their hour of trial and danger. We commend them to Him who can do for them a thousand times more, and better than we can either ask or think. With our united kindest remem-brance, sincerely, ANNA H. RICHARDSON.

WESTMORELAND TERRACE, NEWCASTLE-ON-TYNE, March 16, 1860.

We have lately read the life of thy brother and sister (Peter and Vina Still), dear friend, with the deepest interest. It is a most touching and beautiful book, and we think should be either reprinted in England or sent over here very largely. My husband and I are hardly acquainted with a volume more calculated to stir up the British mind on the subject of Slavery. Great Britain is just now getting really warm on the Anti-slavery subject, and is longing to shake herself from being so dependent as hitherto, on slave produce. Why, Oh! why should not the expatriated blacks go to free countries and grow produce for themselves and for everybody who requires it ? Why not, in time, become " merchants and princes," in those countries? I am told (as a secret) that this subject is likely, ere long, to be taken up in high quarters in England. We are feeling hopeful, dear friends, about thy crushed and persecuted people, for surely God is working for them by ways and means that we know not. I have been careful to keep it to private circles, but thy valuable letter of last July, has been read by many with the deepest interest. A dear young lady from Dublin is by my side, and has but this minute returned it to me. It is but a little, but I have gathered £4, by its perusal here and there. I am not able to forward so small a sum in this letter, but some way wish to send £2 of this amount for thy own use, and the other £2 to your Vigilance Committee. It so happens that we have not anything for the better from our own Anti-slavery Association this year. Very sincerely thy friend, my dear husband uniting in kind regards,

ANNA H. RICHARDSON.

WOOD HOUSE, near NEWCASTLE, May 3, 1860.

[An occasional rural residence of ours, five miles from home.]

To WILLIAM STILL :—I have again to thank thee, dear friend, for a kind letter and for the perusal of three letters from thy fugitive friends. It must be truly cheering to receive such, and their warm and affectionate gratitude must be as rich reward for many anxieties. I conclude that it is not necessary for those letters to be returned, but should it be so, let me know, and I will be on the lookout for some private opportunity of return- ing them to Philadelphia. Such occur now and then. We like to see such letters. They assist us to realize the condition of these poor wanderers. I am sorry for not having explained myself distinctly in my last. The promised £4 were *for the fugitives,* being gathered from various Christian friends, who gave it me for their particular use. But we wished half of that sum to be laid out (as on a previous occasion), at thy own discretion, irrespective of the Vigilance Committee. I have now another £1 to add to the latter half, and would gladly have enclosed a £5 note in this envelope, but we are rather afraid of sending the actual money in letters, and our London bankers do not like to remit small sums. I shall continue to watch for the first opportunity of forwarding the above.

Our valued friend, Samuel Rhoads, has been lately in heavy sorrow. I send this through his medium, but fear to add more lest I should make his letter too heavy. With our united kind regards, very truly, thy friend,

ANNA H. RICHARDSON.

54, WESTMORELAND TERRACE, June 8, 1860.

DEAR FRIEND :—WILLIAM STILL :—It is a good plan to send me these interesting communications. The letter to your coadjutor at Elmira, reached us a few days since. That depot must not be allowed to go down if it be possible for this to be prevented. Perhaps J. W. Jones might be encouraged by a gift from England, that is, by a little aid from this country, expressly for the fugitives, being put into his hands. If you think so, I am sure my friends would approve of this, and you can use your own discretion in giving him our gifts in one sum or by detached remittances. The greatest part of the money on hand, has come in from the private perusal of thy interesting letters, and my friends simply gave my husband and me their money for the fugitives, leaving the exact disposal of it to our own discretion. It has struck me of late, that if I may be allowed to print occasional extracts from thy letters (with other Anti-slavery information), it would greatly facilitate the obtaining of pecuniary aid. As it is, I can lend a private letter to a trustworthy friend, but if by any chance, this letter got lost, it would be awkward, and it is also impossible, of course, to lend the original in two quarters at once. Then, again, the mechanical trouble of making copies of letters, is not convenient; much sedentary employment does not suit my health, and I cannot manage it. I have been thinking of late, that if my friends in various parts of the country, could be supplied with a small quarto, an occasional printed paper, for private circulation, it would save a great deal of trouble, and probably bring in considerable aid. My husband and I have long been accustomed to preparing tracts and small periodicals for the press, so that I think we know exactly what ought to be made public and what not. If thou likest to give me this discretionary power, do so, and I will endeavor to exercise it wisely, and in a way that I feel almost certain would be in accordance with thy wishes.

The sum now remitted through our friend, Samuel Rhoads, is £8 (eight pounds). Of this, we should like £3 to be placed at thy own discretion, for the benefit of the fugitives, £3 (if you approve it) in a similar way, to be handed to J. W. Jones, and £2 as formerly, to be handed to the Philadelphia Vigilance Committee. The latter is not, however, as in past times, from the Newcastle Anti-slavery Society, for, I am sorry to say, it is not a sufficiently pains-taking and executive little body, but more apt to work by fits and starts, but from our private friends, who kindly place their money in our hands as their Anti-slavery stewards. My friend S. R. will therefore kindly hand for us: £3 for William Still, for fugitives; £3 for J. W. Jones, for fugitives; £2 for Philadelphia Vigilance Committee, for fugitives. Total £8.

We are very sorry for thee to have to incur so much persecution. Be of good cheer, the right will eventually triumph, if not in this world, in that day, when all shall be eventually righted on our Lord's right hand. Oh, for ability in the meantime, to love Him, trust Him, confide in Him implicitly!

Many thanks for the "Anti-slavery Standards." No one in this town, takes them in, consequently we only see them occasionally. Do any tidings reach you of our friend, Frederick Douglass? We heard from him from Portland, but are anxiously looking for another letter. He always spoke of thee, my friend, very kindly, and one day, when some money had been given to him for fugitives, said: "You shall have part of this if you like, for William Still," but I said, "No, I will try and get some elsewhere for him." Douglass left us in April, after losing his little Annie, but wished his visit to be kept private, and hoped to be able to return to England in August. My husband and I agree with F. D. in political matters. We are not disunionists, but want to mend your corrupted government. With kind regards, sincerely thy friend,   A. H. R.

Wé are well acquainted with William and Ellen Craft. They have just sent us their little book.

NEWCASTLE, 5th mo., 2, 1861.

W. STILL:—DEAR FRIEND:—That poor fellow, who was so long secreted, had been often in my thoughts, when laying this case of the fugitives before our friends. I should like thee to feel at liberty to replace the remainder of the twenty-five dollars from the accompanying ten pounds, which I have much pleasure in forwarding, but think it better to mention, that it may perhaps be the last remittance for some little time from this quarter, as I do not at present see any immediate opening for getting more. Our worthy friend, W. S. Bailey, has lately been here, and Dr. Cheever and W. H. Day, are expected in a week or two. From London too, there are very earnest appeals to assist the "African Anti-slavery Society." Thank thee for the newspapers and thy last kind note. I think thou rather over-rates my little services. What a crisis is coming! O, what will the end be? With our united best wishes, thy sincere friend,

ANNA H. RICHARDSON.

£7 of this money is from some personally unknown friend at Lancaster; £5 from two nice little children of my acquaintance.

54 WESTMORELAND TERRACE,
NEWCASTLE-ON-TYNE, Oct. 10, 1862.

I have pleasure, dear friend, in sending you £5 for your "contrabands," in response to your last letter of the 17th ult. It is not much, but may be a little help. It will be forwarded by our valued and mutual friend, H. H. Garnet, to whom I am sending a remittance for his "contrabands," by the same mail.

We shall be interested in any particulars you may like to send us, of these poor creatures, but at the same time, I dare not hold out any hopes of considerable assistance from England, for our own manufacturing districts are in a starving state, from the absence of the accustomed supply of cotton, and till this has been grown in other quarters, they will continue to have a strong claim on every thoughtful mind. Some of us would rather work with your colored people *in your own cause*, than with any one else, for we *do not like the war*, and do not at all approve of "the American churches" committing themselves to it so fearfully. If your President had but taken the step at first, he is taking now, what rivers of blood might have been stayed! It is remarkable, how you, as a people, have been preserved to each other, without having your own hands stained with blood. But as to expatriation, the very thought of it is foolish. You have been brought to America, not emigrated to it, and who on earth has any possible right to send you away? Some of us are almost as much displeased with the North, for talking of this, as with the South for holding you in Slavery. What can we say to you, but "watch and pray," "hope and wait," and surely, in His own good time, the Most High will make you a pathway out of trouble. We are delighted to hear of the good behaviour of your people, wherever they have a fair chance of acting (on the borders), as upright men and Christians.

Very sincerely, your friend,

To WILLIAM STILL.   ANNA H. RICHARDSON.

WOMAN ESCAPING IN A BOX, 1857.

SHE WAS SPEECHLESS.

In the winter of 1857 a young woman, who had just turned her majority, was boxed up in Baltimore by one who stood to her in the relation of a companion, a young man, who had the box conveyed as freight to the depot in Baltimore, consigned to Philadelphia. Nearly all one night it remained at the depot with the living agony in it, and after being turned upside down more than once, the next day about ten o'clock it reached Philadelphia. Her companion coming on in advance of the box, arranged with a hackman, George Custus, to attend to having it brought from the depot to a designated house, Mrs. Myers', 412 S. 7th street, where the resurrection was to take place.

Custus, without knowing exactly what the box contained, but suspecting from the apparent anxiety and instructions of the young man who engaged him to go after it, that it was of great importance, while the freight car still remained on the street, demanded it of the freight agent, not willing to wait the usual time for the delivery of freight. At first the freight agent declined delivering under such circumstances. The hackman insisted by saying that he wished to despatch it in great haste, said it is all right, you know me, I have been coming here for many years every day, and will be responsible for it. The freight-master told him to "take it and go ahead with it." No sooner said than done. It was placed in a one horse wagon at the instance of Custus, and driven to Seventh and Minster streets.

The secret had been intrusted to Mrs. M. by the young companion of the woman. A feeling of horror came over the aged woman, who had been thus suddenly entrusted with such responsibility. A few doors from her lived an old friend of the same religious faith with herself, well known as a brave woman, and a friend of the slave, Mrs. Ash, the undertaker or shrouder, whom every body knew among the colored people. Mrs. Myers felt that it would not be wise to move in the matter of this resurrection without the presence of the undertaker. Accordingly, she called Mrs. Ash in. Even her own family was excluded from witnessing the scene. The two aged women chose to be alone in that fearful moment, shuddering at the thought that a corpse might meet their gaze instead of a living creature. However, they mustered courage and pried off the lid. A woman was discovered in the straw but no sign of life was perceptible. Their fears seemed fulfilled. "Surely she is dead," thought the witnesses.

"Get up, my child," spake one of the women. With scarcely life enough to move the straw covering, she, nevertheless, did now show signs of life, but to a very faint degree. She could not speak, but being assisted arose. She was straightway aided up stairs, not yet uttering a word. After a short while she said, "I feel so deadly weak." She was then asked if she would not have some water or nourishment, which she declined. Before a great while, however, she was prevailed upon to take a cup of tea. She then went to bed, and there remained all day, speaking but a very little during that time. The second day she gained strength and was able to talk much better, but not with ease. The third day she began to come to herself and talk quite freely. She tried to describe her sufferings and fears while in the box, but in vain. In the midst of her severest agonies her chief fear was, that she would be discovered and carried back to Slavery. She had a pair of scissors with her, and in order to procure fresh air she had made a hole in the box, but it was very slight. How she ever managed to breathe and maintain her existence, being in the condition of becoming a mother, it was hard to comprehend. In this instance the utmost endurance was put to the test. She was obviously nearer death than Henry Box Brown, or any of the other box or chest cases that ever came under the notice of the Committee.

In Baltimore she belonged to a wealthy and fashionable family, and had been a seamstress and ladies' servant generally. On one occasion when sent of an errand for certain articles in order to complete arrangements for the Grand Opening Ball at the Academy of Music, she took occasion not to return, but was among the missing. Great search was made, and a large reward offered, but all to no purpose. A free colored woman, who washed for the family, was suspected of knowing something of her going, but they failing to get aught out of her, she was discharged.

Soon after the arrival of this traveler at Mrs. Myers' the Committee was

39

sent for and learned the facts as above stated. After spending some three or four days in Mrs. Myers' family she remained in the writer's family about the same length of time, and was then forwarded to Canada.

Mrs. Myers was originally from Baltimore, and had frequently been in the habit of receiving Underground Rail Road passengers; she had always found Thomas Shipley, the faithful philanthropist, a present help in time of need. The young man well knew Mrs. Myers would act with prudence in taking his companion to her house.

George Custus, the hackman, a colored man, was cool, sensible, and reliable in the discharge of his duty, as were the other parties, therefore every thing was well managed.

With this interesting case our narratives end, except such facts of a like kind as may be connected with some of the sketches of stockholders. A large number on the record book must be omitted. This is partly owing to the fact that during the first few years of our connection with the Underground Rail Road, so little was written out in the way of narratives, that would hardly be of sufficient interest to publish; and partly from the fact that, although there are exceptional cases even among those so omitted, that would be equally as interesting as many which have been inserted, time and space will not admit of further encroachment. If in any way we have erred in the task of furnishing facts and important information touching the Underground Rail Road, it has not been in overstating the sufferings, trials, perils, and marvellous escapes of those described, but on the contrary. In many instances after hearing the most painful narratives we had neither time nor inclination to write them out, except in the briefest manner, simply sufficient to identify parties, which we did, not dreaming that the dark cloud of Slavery was so soon to give way to the bright sunlight of Freedom.

ORGANIZATION OF THE VIGILANCE COMMITTEE.

MEETING TO FORM A VIGILANCE COMMITTEE.

As has already been intimated, others besides the Committee were deeply interested in The Road; indeed, the little aid actually rendered by the Committee, was comparatively insignificant, compared with the aid rendered by some who were not nominally members. To this latter class of friends, it seems meet that we should particularly allude. Before doing so, however, simple justice to all concerned, dictates that we should here copy the official proceedings of the first meeting and organization of the Philadelphia Vigilance Committee as it existed until the very day that the ever to be remembered Emancipation Proclamation of Abraham Lincoln, rendered the services of the organization and road no longer necessary. It reads as follows:

"PENNSYLVANIA FREEMAN," December 9, 1852.

Pursuant to the motion published in last week's "Freeman," a meeting was held in the Anti-slavery rooms, on the evening of the 2d inst., for the purpose of organizing a Vigilance Committee.

On motion Samuel Nickless was appointed chairman, and William Still secretary. J. M. McKim then stated at some length, the object of the meeting. He said, that the friends of the fugitive slave had been for some years past, embarrassed, for the want of a properly constructed active, Vigilance Committee; that the old Committee, which used to render effective service in this field of Anti-slavery labor, had become disorganized and scattered, and that for the last two or three years, the duties of this department had been performed by individuals on their own responsibility, and sometimes in a very irregular manner; that this had been the cause of much dissatisfaction and complaint, and that the necessity for a remedy of this state of things was generally felt. Hence, the call for this meeting. It was intended now to organize a committee, which should be composed of persons of known responsibility, and who could be relied upon to act systematically and promptly, and with the least possible expenditure of money in all cases that might require their attention.

James Mott and Samuel Nickless, expressed their hearty concurrence in what had been said, as did also B. N. Goines and N. W. Depee. The opinion was also expressed by one or more of these gentlemen, that the organization to be formed should be of the simplest possible character; with no more machinery or officers than might be necessary to hold it together and keep it in proper working order. After some discussion, it was agreed first to form a general committee, with a chairman, whose business it should be to call meetings when necessity should seem to require it, and to preside at the same; and a treasurer to take charge of the funds; and second, to appoint out of this general committee, an acting committee of four persons, who should have the responsibility of attending to every case that might require their aid, as well as the exclusive authority to raise the funds necessary for their purpose. It was further agreed that it should be the duty of the chairman of the Acting Committee to keep a record of all their doings, and especially of the money received and expended on behalf of every case claiming their interposition.

The following persons were appointed on the General Vigilance Committee:

GENERAL VIGILANCE COMMITTEE.

ROBERT PURVIS,	WILLIAM STILL,
CHARLES H. BUSTILL,	P. WILLIAMSON,
SAMUEL NICKLESS,	B. N. GOINES,
MORRIS HALL,	J. M. M'KIM,
NATHANIEL DEPEE,	ISAIAH C. WEARS,
CHARLES WISE,	JOHN D. OLIVER,
JACOB C. WHITE,	PROF. C. L. REASON,
CYRUS WHITSON,	HENRY GORDON,
J. ASHER,	W. H. RILEY.
J. P. BURR,	

Robert Purvis was understood to be Chairman of the General Committee, having been nominated at the head of the list, and Charles Wise was appointed treasurer. The Acting Committee was thus constituted :

William Still, chairman, N. W. Depee, Passmore Williamson, J. C. White. This Committee was appointed for the term of one year.

On motion, the proceedings of this meeting were ordered to be published in the " Pennsylvania Freeman."

(Adjourned.)

WILLIAM STILL, Secretary.   SAMUEL NICKLESS, Chairman.

The Committee having been thus organized, J. M. McKim, corresponding secretary and general agent of the Pennsylvania Anti-slavery Society, issued the subjoined notice, which was published shortly afterwards in the " Pennsylvania Freeman," and the colored churches throughout the city:

" We are pleased to see that we have at last, what has for some time been felt to be a desideratum in Philadelphia, a responsible and duly authorized Vigilance Committee. The duties of this department of Anti-slavery labor, have, for want of such an organization, been performed in a very loose and unsystematic manner. The names of the persons constituting the Acting Committee, are a guarantee that this will not be the case hereafter. They are—

WILLIAM STILL (Chairman), 31 North Fifth Street,

NATHANIEL W. DEPEE, 334 South Street,

JACOB C. WHITE, 100 Old York Road, and

PASSMORE WILLIAMSON, southwest cor. Seventh and Arch Streets.

We respectfully commend these gentlemen, and the cause in which they are engaged, to the confidence and co-operation of all the friends of the hunted fugitive. Any funds contributed to either of them, or placed in the hands of their Treasurer, Charles Wise, corner of Fifth and Market Streets, will be sure of a faithful and judicious appropriation.

PORTRAITS AND SKETCHES.

ESTHER MOORE.

For many years no woman living in Philadelphia was better known to the colored people of the city generally, than Esther Moore. No woman, white or colored, living in Philadelphia for the same number of years, left her home oftener, especially to seek out and aid the weary travelers escaping from bondage, than did this philanthropist. It is hardly too much to say that with her own hand she administered to hundreds. She begged of the Committee, as a special favor, that she might be duly notified of every fugitive reaching Philadelphia, and actually felt hurt if from any cause whatever this request was not complied with. For it was her delight to see the fugitives individually, take them by the hand and warmly welcome them to freedom. She literally wept with those who wept, while in tones of peculiar love, sincerity, and firmness, she lauded them for their noble daring, and freely expressed her entire sympathy with them, and likewise with all in the prison-house. She condemned Slavery in all its phases, as a "monster to be loathed as the enemy of God and man."

Often after listening attentively for hours together to recitals of a very harrowing nature, especially from females, her mind would seem to be filled with the sufferings of the slave and it was hard for her to withdraw from them even when they were on the eve of taking up their march for a more distant station; and she never thought of parting with them without showing her faith by her works putting a "gold dollar" in the hand of each passenger, as she knew that it was not in the power of the Committee to do much more than defray their expenses to the next station, to New York sometimes, to Elmira at other times, and now and then clear through to Canada. She desired that they should have at least one dollar to fall back upon, independent of the Committee's aid. This magnanimous rule of giving the gold dollar was adopted by her shortly after the passage of the Fugitive Slave Law, which daily vexed her righteous soul, and was kept up as long as she was able to leave her house, which was within a short time of her death.

Not only did Esther Moore manifest such marked interest in the fugitive but she likewise took an abiding interest in visiting the colored people in their religious meetings, schools, and societies, and whenever the way opened and the Spirit moved her she would take occasion to address them in the most affectionate manner, in regard to their present and future welfare, choosing for her theme the subjects of temperance, education, and slavery.

Nor did she mean that her labors in the interest of the oppressed should cease with her earthly existence, as the following extracts from her last will and testament will prove:

2d Item. I give and bequeath to my executors, hereinafter named, the sum of Twelve hundred dollars, in trust to invest in ground rent, or City of Philadelphia Loans at their disposal or discretion to pay the interest or income arising therefrom annually. To be applied, the interest of the Twelve hundred dollars above mentioned, for educational purposes alone, for children of both sexes of color, in Canada, apart from all sectarian or traditional dogmas, which is the only hope for the rising generation. The application of this money is intended to remain perpetual.

7th Item. I give and bequeath to my executors the sum of one hundred dollars, to be expended by them in educating and assisting to clothe Phaeton and Pliny J. Lock, the sons of Ishmael Lock, deceased, and Matilda Lock (his wife). My will is that it shall be given out discretionally by my executors for the purpose above mentioned.

17th Item. I give and bequeath to Oliver Johnson, editor of the Pennsylvania Freeman, one hundred dollars, if he be living at my death; if not living, to go with the remainder of my estate. My will is that if Oliver Johnson be not living at my death his bequest go with my estate.

18th Item. I give and bequeath to Cyrus Burleigh, lecturer and agent for the Pennsylvania Anti-slavery Society, one hundred dollars, if Cyrus be living at my death. If not living at my death, his bequest, Cyrus Burleigh's, I wish to go with the residue of my estate. The untiring vigilance of these two young men, in devoting the best of their days to the rescue and emancipation of the poor and down-trodden fugitives has obtained for them a warm place in my heart. And may heaven's richest blessings reward them. They have ministered more than " the cup of water."

Item 19th. I give and bequeath unto the Association for the care of Colored Orphans of Philadelphia, called the Shelter for the use and benefit of colored orphans of both sexes, to be paid into the hands of the treasurer for the time being, for the use of said Society all the rest and remainder of my estate.

I wish my Executors or Trustees *to carry out* my views in regard to the education of colored children in Canada, by paying over the interest arising annually from the twelve hundred dollars mentioned in the second item to such school or schools as in their judgment they may deem best. My desire being the benefit of such children who may be in the same neighborhood with them. The interest arising from the twelve hundred dollars mentioned in second item for the purpose of educating colored children in Canada is intended to remain perpetual.

* * * * * * * *

I give and bequeath to William Still, of Philadelphia, now employed in the Anti-slavery office, in Fifth St., Philadelphia, February 21, the sum of one hundred dollars; and request my executors and trustees to pay over that amount out of my estate.

Esther Moore was not rich in this world's goods, but was purely benevolent and rich in good works towards her fellow-men, hating every form of oppression and injustice, and an uncompromising witness against prejudice on account of color. Such a friend as was Esther Moore during these many dark years of kidnapping, slave-catching, mob violence, and bitter prejudice which the colored people were wont to encounter, should never be forgotten.

The legacy devised for educational purposes was applied in due time, after one of the executors in company with his wife, Dr. J. Wilson and Rachel Barker Moore, visited the various settlements of fugitives in Canada, expressly with a view of finding out where the fund would do the most good, in accordance with the testator's wishes. And although the testator has been dead seventeen years, her legacy is still doing its mission in her name, in a school, near Chatham, Canada West.

In order to complete this sketch, it is only necessary that we should copy the beautiful and just tribute to her memory, written by Oliver Johnson, editor of the "National Anti-slavery Standard," and published in the columns thereof, as follows:

DEATH OF A NOBLE WOMAN.

[From the "National Anti-Slavery Standard."]

Just as our paper is going to press, there comes to us intelligence of the death of our beloved and revered friend, Esther Moore, widow of the late Dr. Robert Moore, of Philadelphia. She expired on Tuesday morning, November 21st, 1854, of gout of the heart, after a short, but painful illness, in the eightieth year of her age.

The writer of this first became acquainted with her in 1836, and, at various times since then, has met her at Anti-slavery meetings, or in familiar intercourse at her own house. Her most remarkable traits of character were an intense hatred of oppression in all its forms, a corresponding love for the oppressed, an untiring devotion to their welfare, and a courage that never quailed before any obstacles, however formidable. Her zeal in behalf of the Anti-slavery cause, and especially in behalf of the fugitive, a zeal that absorbed all the powers of her noble nature, was a perpetual rebuke to the comparative coldness and indifference of those around her. We well remember how her soul was fired with a righteous indignation when upwards of thirty innocent persons, most of them colored people, were thrown into prison at Philadelphia, upon a charge of treason, for their alleged participation in the tragedy at Christiana. Day after day did she visit the prisoners in their cells, to minister to their wants, and cheer them in their sorrow;

and during the progress of Hanway's trial, her constant presence in the court-room, and her frequent interviews with the District Attorney, attested her deep anxiety as to the result of the impending struggle. When we last saw her, about a month since, she was engaged in collecting a large sum of money to ransom a family of slaves, whose peculiar condition had enlisted her deepest sympathy. Notwithstanding her age and infirmities, she had enlisted in this work with a zeal which, even in a younger person, would have been remarkable. For many days, perhaps for many weeks, she went from door to door, asking for the means whereby to secure the freedom and the happiness of an enslaved and plundered household.

As a member of the Society of Friends, she lamented the guilty supineness of that body, in regard to the question of Slavery, and often, in its meetings, as well as in private intercourse, felt herself constrained to utter the language of expostulation and rebuke. In this, as in other relations of life, she was obedient to the revelation of God in her own soul, and a worthy example of fidelity to her convictions of duty. Her step-son, J. Wilson Moore, in a letter to us announcing her decease, says:

Among the last injunctions she gave, was, "Write to Oliver Johnson, and tell him I die firm in the faith! MIND THE SLAVE!" She had enjoyed excellent health the last few years, and continued actively engaged in works of benevolence. During the last few weeks, she had devoted much time and labor to the collection of funds for the liberation of ten slaves in North Carolina, who had been promised their freedom at a comparatively small amount. Notwithstanding her great bodily suffering, her mind was clear to the last, expressing her full assurance of Divine approbation in the course she had taken.

This is all that we can now say of the life of our revered and never-to-be-forgotten friend. Perhaps some one who knew her more intimately than we did, and who is better acquainted with the history of her life and labors, will furnish us with a more complete sketch. If so, we shall publish it with great satisfaction.

> Happy! ay, happy! let her ashes rest;
> Her heart was honest, and she did her best;
> In storm and darkness, evil and dismay,
> The star of duty was her guiding ray.

Her injunction to "MIND THE SLAVE," comes to us as the dying admonition of one, whose life was a beautiful exemplification of the duty and the privilege thus enjoined. It imposes, indeed, no new obligation; but coming from such a source, it will linger in our memory while life and its scenes shall last, inspiring in us, we hope, a purer and a more ardent devotion to the cause of freedom and humanity. And may we not hope that others also, will catch a new inspiration from the dying message of our departed friend: "MIND THE SLAVE!"

ABIGAIL GOODWIN.

Contemporary with Esther Moore, and likewise an intimate personal friend of hers, Abigail Goodwin, of Salem, N. J., was one of the rare, true friends to the Underground Rail Road, whose labors entitle her name to be mentioned in terms of very high praise.

A. W. M. a most worthy lady, in a letter to a friend, refers to her in the following language:

"From my long residence under the same roof, I learned to know well her uncommon self-sacrifice of character, and to be willing and glad, whenever in my power, to honor her memory. But, yet I should not know what further to say about her than to give a very few words of testimony to her life of ceaseless and active benevolence, especially toward the colored people.

"Her life outwardly was wholly uneventful; as she lived out her whole life of seventy-three years in the neighborhood of her birth-place."

With regard to her portrait, which was solicited for this volume, the same lady thus writes: "No friend of hers would for a moment think of permitting that miserable caricature, the only picture existing meant to represent her, to be given to the public. I cannot even bear to give a place in my little album to so mournful and ridiculous a misrepresentation of her interesting face."   *   *   *   *   *   *

"You wonder why her sister, E., my loved and faithful friend, seems to be so much less known among anti-slavery people than Abbie? One reason is, that although dear Betsy's interest in the subject was quite equal in *earnestness*, it was not quite so absorbingly *exclusive*. Betsy economized greatly in order to give to the cause, but Abby denied herself even *necessary apparel*, and Betsy has often said that few beggars came to our doors whose garments were so worn, forlorn, and patched-up as Abby's. Giving to the colored people was a perfect *passion* with her; consequently she was known as a larger giver than Betsy.

"Another and greater reason why she was more known abroad than her sister E., was that she wrote with facility, and corresponded at intervals with many on these matters, Mr. McKim and others, and for many years."

        *   *   *   *   *   *   *   *

Abigail was emphatically of the type of the poor widow, who cast in all her living. She worked for the slave as a mother would work for her children. Her highest happiness and pleasure in life seemed to be derived from rendering acts of kindness to the oppressed. Letters of sympathy accompanied with bags of stockings, clothing, and donations of money were not unfrequent from her.

New Jersey contained a few well-tried friends, both within and without the Society of Friends, to which Miss Goodwin belonged; but among them all none was found to manifest, at least in the Underground Rail Road of Philadelphia, such an abiding interest as a co-worker in the cause, as did Abigail Goodwin.

The sympathy which characterized her actions is clearly evinced in her own words, as contained in the appended extracts from her letter, as follows:

"DEAR FRIEND:—I sent E. M. (Esther Moore) forty-one dollars more by half than I expected to when I set about it. I expect that abolitionists there are all opposed to buying slaves, and will not give anything. I don't like buying them, or giving money to slave-holders either; but this seems to be a peculiar case, can be had so cheap, and so many young ones that would be separated from their parents; slavery is peculiarly hard for children, that cannot do anything to protect themselves, nor can their parents, and the old too, it is hard for them; but it is a terrible thing altogether. The case of the fugitive thee mentioned was indeed truly affecting; it makes one ashamed as well as sad to read such things, that human beings, or any other beings should be so treated. I cannot but hope and believe that slavery will ere long cease. I have a strong impression that the colored people and the women are to have a day of prosperity and triumph over their oppressors. We must patiently wait and quietly hope; but not keep too much 'in the quiet.' Shall have to work our deliverance from bondage. 'Who would be free, themselves must strike the blow.'

"I regret very much that I have not more clothing to send than the stockings. I have not had time since I thought of it, to make anything; am ashamed that I was so inconsiderate of the poor runaways. I will go to work as soon as I have earned money to buy materials; have managed so as to spend my little annual allowance in nine months, and shall not be able to give you any money for some months, but if more stockings are wanted let me know, our benevolent society have plenty on hand; and I have some credit if not money; they will trust me till I have; they furnish work for poor women and sell it. I get them for fifty cents a pair.

"My sister says Lucretia (Mott) told her that there was not much clothing in the trunk, only a few old things. I think she told me there was nothing in it, she meant, I suppose, of any consequence.   *   *   *

"I should like to know if the fugitives are mostly large. I have an idea they are generally small in stature; that slavery stunts the body as well as mind. I want to know in regard to the clothes that I intend making; it's best to have them fit as well as can be. I shall work pretty much for women. I hope and expect there are many friends of the cause who furnish clothing in the city. They ought to be fitted out for Canada with strong, warm clothing in cold weather, and their sad fate alleviated as much as can be."   *   *   *   *   *   *   *

The forty-one dollars, referred to in the above letter, and sent to "E. M."

was to go especially towards buying an interesting family of ten slaves, who were owned in North Carolina by a slave-holder, whose rare liberality was signalized by offering to take $1,000 for the lot, young and old. In this exceptional case, while opposed to buying slaves, in common with abolitionists generally, she was too tender-hearted to resist the temptation so long as "they could be bought so cheap."

To rid men of their yoke was her chief desire. Such was her habit of making the sad lot of a slave a personal matter, that let her view him, in any light whatever, whether in relation to young ones that would be separated from their parents, or with regard to the old, the life of a slave was "peculiarly hard," "a terrible thing" in her judgment.

The longer she lived, and the more faithfully she labored for the slave's deliverance, the more firmly she became rooted in the soul-encouraging idea, that "Slavery will ere long cease." Whilst the great masses were either blind, or indifferent, she was nerved by this faith to bear cheerfully all the sacrifices she was called on to make. From another letter we copy as follows:

JANUARY 25th, 1855.

DEAR FRIEND:—The enclosed ten dollars I have made, earned in two weeks, and of course it belongs to the slave. It may go for the fugitives, or Carolina slaves, whichever needs it most. I am sorry the fugitives' treasury is not better supplied, if money could flow into it as it does into the Tract Fund; but that is not to be expected.   *   *   *

Thy answer in regard to impostors is quite satisfactory. No doubt you take great pains to arrive at the truth, but cannot at all times avoid being imposed on. Will that little boy of seven years have to travel on foot to Canada? There will be no safety for him here. I hope his father will get off. John Hill writes very well, considering his few advantages. If plenty of good schools could be established in Canada for the benefit of fugitives, many bright scholars and useful citizens would be added to society. I hope these will be in process of time.

It takes the most energetic and intelligent to make their way out of bondage from the most Southern States. It is rather a wonder to me that so many can escape, the masters are so continually watching them. The poor man that secreted himself so long, must, indeed, have suffered dreadfully, and been exceedingly resolute to brave dangers so long.   *   *   *

It was so characteristic of her to take an interest in everything that pertained to the Underground Rail Road, that even the deliverance of a little nameless boy was not beneath her notice. To her mind, his freedom was just as dear to him as if he had been the son of the President of the United States.

How they got on in Canada, and the question of education, were matters that concerned her deeply; hence, occasional letters received from Canada, evincing marked progress, such as the hero John H. Hill was in the habit of writing, always gave her much pleasure to peruse.

In the Wheeler slave-case, in which Passmore Williamson and others were engaged, her interest was very great. From a letter dated Salem, September 9, 1855, we quote the subjoined extract:

DEAR FRIEND :—I am truly rejoiced and thankful that the right has triumphed. But stranger had it been otherwise, in your intelligent community, where it must be apparent to all who inquire into it, that you had done nothing but what was deserving of high commendation, instead of blame and punishment; and shame on the jury who would bring in the two men guilty of assault and battery. They ought to have another trial; perhaps another jury would be more just. It is well for the credit of Philadelphia, that there is one upright judge, as Kelley seems to be, and his sentence will be a light one it is presumed, showing he considered the charge a mere pretence.

I hope and trust, that neither thyself nor the other men will have much if any of the expense to bear; your lawyers will not charge anything I suppose, and the good citizens will pay all else. It seems there are hopes entertained that Passmore Williamson will soon be set at liberty. It must be a great comfort to him and wife, in their trials, that it will conduce to the furtherance of the good cause.

If Philadelphians are not aroused now after this great stretch of power, to consider their safety, they must be a stupid set of people, but it must certainly do good. * * * You will take good care of Jane Johnson, I hope, and not let her get kidnapped back to Slavery. Is it safe for her to remain in your city or anywhere else in our "free land?" I have some doubts and fears for her; do try to impress her with the necessity of being very cautious and careful against deceivers, pretended friends. She had better be off to Canada pretty soon.

Thy wife must not sit up washing and ironing all night again. She ought to have help in her sympathy and labors for the poor fugitives, and, I should think there are many there who would willingly assist her.

I intended to be careful of trespassing upon thy time, as thee must have enough to do; the fugitives are still coming I expect. With kind regards, also to thy wife, your friend,

A. GOODWIN.

In another letter, she suggests the idea of getting up a committee of women to provide clothing for fugitive females; on this point she wrote thus:

"SALEM, 8th mo., 1st.

"Would it not be well to get up a committee of women, to provide clothes for fugitive females—a dozen women sewing a day, or even half a day of each week, might keep a supply always ready, they might, I should think, get the merchants or some of them, to give cheap materials—mention it to thy wife, and see if she cannot get up a society. I will do what I can here for it. I enclose five dollars for the use of fugitives. It was a good while that I heard nothing of your rail road concerns; I expected thee had gone to Canada, or has the journey not been made, or is it yet to be accomplished, or given up? I was in hopes thee would go and see with thy own eyes, how things go on in that region of fugitives, and if it's a goodly land to live in.

"This is the first of August, and I suppose you are celebrating it in Philadelphia, or some of you are, though I believe you are not quite as zealous as the Bostonians are in doing it. When will our first of August come? oh, that it might be soon, very soon! * * * It's high time the 'reign of oppression was over.'"

Ever alive to the work, she would appeal to such as were able among her friends, to take stock in the Underground Rail Road, and would sometimes succeed. In a letter dated July 30, 1856, she thus alludes to her efforts:

"I have tried to beg something for them, but have not got much; one of our neighbors, S. W. Acton, gave me three dollars for them; I added enough to make ten, which thee will find inside. I shall owe three more, to make my ten. I presume they are still coming every day almost, and I fear it comes rather hard on thee and wife to do for so many; but you no doubt feel it a satisfaction to do all you can for the poor sufferers."

February 10, 1858, she forwarded her willing contribution, with the following interesting remarks:

SALEM, February 10, 1858.

DEAR FRIEND:—Thee will find enclosed, five dollars for the fugitives, a little for so many to share it, but better than nothing; oh, that people, rich people, would remember them instead of spending so much on themselves; and those too, who are not called rich, might, if there was only a willing mind, give too of their abundance; how can they forbear to sympathize with those poor destitute ones—but so it is—there is not half the feeling for them there ought to be, indeed scarcely anybody seems to think about them. "Inasmuch as ye have *not* done it unto one of the least of these my brethren, ye have not done it unto me." Thy friend,

A. GOODWIN.

When the long looked-for day of emancipation arrived, which she had never expected to witness, the unbounded thankfulness of her heart found expression in the appended letter:

SALEM, September 23, 1862.

DEAR FRIEND:—Thy letter dated 17th, was not received till last night. I cannot tell where it has been detained so long. On the 22d, yesterday, Amy Reckless came here, after I began writing, and wished me to defer sending for a day or two, thinking she could get a few more dollars, and she has just brought some, and will try for more, and clothing. A thousand thanks to President Hamlin for his kindness to the contrabands; poor people! how deplorable their situation; where will they go to, when cold weather comes? so many of them to find homes for, but they must and will, I trust be taken care of, not by their former care-takers though.

I have read the President's proclamation of emancipation, with thankfulness and rejoicing; but upon a little reflection, I did not feel quite satisfied with it; three months seems a long time to be in the power of their angry and cruel masters, who, no doubt, will wreak all their fury and vengeance upon them, killing and abusing them in every way they can—and sell them to Cuba if they can. It makes me sad to think of it. Slavery, I fear, will be a long time in dying, after receiving the fatal stroke. What do abolitionists think of it? and what is thy opinion? I feel quite anxious to know something more about it. The "Daily Press" says, it will end the war and its cause. How can we be thankful enough if it should, and soon too. "Oh, praise and tanks," what a blessing for our country. I never expected to see the happy day. If thee answers this, thee will please tell me all about it, and what is thought of it by the wise ones; but I ought not to intrude on thy time, thee has so much on thy hands, nor ask thee to write. I shall know in time, if I can be patient to wait.

Enclosed are seventeen dollars; from Amy Reckless, $1,50; J. Bassett, $1; Jesse Bond, $1; Martha Reeve, $1; S. Woodnutt, $1; Hannah Wheeler, $1; a colored man, 25 cents; 25 cents thrown in, to make even; A. G., $10. Amy is very good in helping, and is collecting clothing, which she thinks, cannot be sent till next week. I will attend to sending it, as soon as can be, by stage driver. May every success attend thy labors for the poor sufferers.   *   *   *

With kind regards, thy friend,   A. GOODWIN.

Thus, until the last fetter was broken, with singular persistency, zeal, faith and labor, she did what she could to aid the slave, without hope of reward in this world. Not only did she contribute to aid the fugitives, but was, for years, a regular and liberal contributor to the Pennsylvania Anti-slavery Society, as well as a subscriber to the Anti-slavery papers, The "Liberator," "National Anti-Slavery Standard," "Pennsylvania Freeman," etc.

Having seen with joy, the desire of her heart, in the final emancipation of every bondman in the United States, she departed in peace, November 2, 1867, in the 74th year of her age.

ABIGAIL GOODWIN. See p. 617.

THOMAS GARRETT,

STATION MASTER. See p. 623.

DANIEL GIBBONS,

STATION MASTER. See p. 642.

LUCRETIA MOTT. See p. 649.

FAITHFUL WORKERS IN THE CAUSE.

THOMAS GARRETT.

The recent death of Thomas Garrett, called forth from the press, as well as from abolitionists and personal friends, such universal expressions of respect for his labors as a philanthropist, and especially as an unswerving friend of the Underground Rail Road, that we need only reproduce selections therefrom, in order to commemorate his noble deeds in these pages.

From the "Wilmington Daily Commercial," published by Jenkins and Atkinson (men fully inspired with the spirit of impartial freedom), we copy the following notice, which is regarded by his relatives and intimate anti-slavery friends as a faithful portraiture of his character and labors:

Thomas Garrett, who died full of years and honor, this morning, at the ripe age of eighty-one, was a man of no common character. He was an abolitionist from his youth up, and though the grand old cause numbered amongst its supporters, poets, sages, and statesmen, it had no more faithful worker in its ranks than Thomas Garrett.

He has been suffering for several years, from a disease of the bladder, which frequently caused him most acute anguish, and several times threatened his life. The severe pain attending the disease, and the frequent surgical operations it rendered necessary, undermined his naturally strong constitution, so that when he was prostrated by his last illness, grave fears were entertained of a fatal result. He continued in the possession of his faculties to the last, and frequently expressed his entire willingness to die.

Yesterday he was found to be sinking very rapidly. Just before midnight, last night, he commenced to speak, and some of those in attendance, went close to his bed-side. He was evidently in some pain, and said: "It is all peace, peace, peace, but no rest this side of the river." He then breathed calmly on for some time. About half an hour later, one of those in attendance ceased to hear his breathing, and bending over him, found that his soul had fled.

He retained a good deal of his strength through his illness, and was able to get up from his bed, every day, with the assistance of one person.

He will be buried in the Friends' grave-yard, corner of Fourth and West Streets, on Saturday next, at three o'clock, P. M., and in accordance with a written memorandum of an agreement made by him a year ago with them, the colored people will bear him to his grave, they having solicited of him that honor.

He was born of Quaker parents, in Upper Darby, Delaware county, Pa., on the 21st of August, 1789, on a farm still in the possession of the family. His father, though a farmer, had been a scythe and edge-tool maker, and Thomas learned of him the trade, and his knowledge of it afterwards proved of the utmost advantage to him.

He grew up and married at Darby, his wife being Sarah Sharpless, and in 1820 they came to Wilmington to live, bringing with them several children, most of whom still live here.

Some years after his arrival here, his wife died, and in course of time, he again married, his second wife being Rachel Mendenhall, who died in April, 1868, beloved and regretted by all who knew her.

His business career was one of vicissitude, but generally and ultimately successful, for he made the whole of the comfortable competence of which he died possessed, after he was sixty years of age. While in the beginning of his business career, as an iron merchant in this city, a wealthy rival house attempted to crush him, by reducing prices of iron to cost, but Mr. Garrett, nothing dismayed, employed another person to attend his store, put on his leather apron, took to his anvil, and in the prosecution of his trade, as an edge-tool maker, prepared to support himself as long as this ruinous rivalry was kept up. Thus in the sweat of the brow of one of the heroes and philanthropists of this age, was laid the foundation of one of the most extensive business houses that our city now boasts. His competitor saw that no amount of rivalry could crush a man thus self-supporting and gave up the effort.

Of course, Thomas Garrett is best known for his labors in behalf of the abolition of Slavery, and as a practical and effective worker for emancipation long before the nation commenced the work of liberation and justice.

Born a Quaker, he held with simple trust, the faith of the society that God moves and inspires men to do the work he requires of their hands, and throughout his life he never wavered in his conviction, that his Father had called him to work in the cause to which he devoted himself.

His attention was first directed to the iniquity of Slavery, while he was a young man of twenty-four or twenty five. He returned one day to his father's house, after a brief absence, and found the family dismayed and indignant at the kidnapping of a colored woman in their employ.

Thomas immediately resolved to follow the kidnappers, and so started in pursuit. Some peculiarity about the track made by their wagon, enabled him to trace them with ease, and he followed them by a devious course, from Darby, to a place near the Navy Yard, in Philadelphia, and then by inquiries, etc., tracked them to Kensington, where he found them, and, we believe, secured the woman's release.

During this ride, he afterwards assured his friends, he felt the iniquity and abomination of the whole system of Slavery borne in upon his mind so strongly, as to fairly appal him, and he seemed to hear a voice within him, assuring him that his work in life must be to help and defend this persecuted race.

From this time forward, he never failed to assist any fugitive from Slavery on the way to freedom, and, of course, after his removal to this city, his opportunities for this were greatly increased, and in course of time, his house became known as one of the refuges for fugitives. The sentiment of this community was, at that time, bitterly averse to any word or effort against Slavery, and Mr. Garrett had but half a dozen friends who stood by him. Nearly all others looked at him with suspicion, or positive aversion, and his house was constantly under the surveillance of the police, who then, sad to say, were always on the watch for any fugitives from bondage. Thomas was not disheartened or dismayed by the lack of popular sympathy or approval. He believed the Lord was on his side, and cared nothing for the adverse opinion of men.

Many and interesting stories are told of the men and women he helped away, some of them full of pathos, and some decidedly amusing. He told the latter which related to his ingenious contrivances for assisting fugitives to escape the police with much pleasure, in his later years. We would repeat many of them, but this is not the time or place. The necessity of avoiding the police was the only thing, however, which ever forced him into any secrecy in his operations, and in all other respects he was "without concealment and without compromise" in his opposition to Slavery. He was a man of unusual personal bravery, and of powerful physique, and did not present an encouraging object for the bullying intimidation by which the pro-slavery men of that day generally overawed their opponents. He seems to have scarcely known what fear was, and though irate slave-holders often called on him to learn the whereabouts of their slaves, he met them placidly, never denied having helped the fugitives on their way, positively refused to give them any information, and when they flourished pistols, or bowie-knives to enforce their demands, he calmly pushed the weapons aside, and told them that none but cowards resorted to such means to carry their ends.

He continued his labors, thus, for years, helping all who came to him, and making no concealment of his readiness to do so. His firmness and courage slowly won others, first to admire, and then to assist him, and the little band of faithful workers, of which he was chief, gradually enlarged and included in its number, men of all ranks, and differing creeds, and, singular as it may seem, even numbering some ardent Democrats in its ranks. He has, in conversation with the present writer and others, frequently acknowledged the valuable services of two Roman Catholics, of Irish birth, still living in this city, who were ever faithful to him, and will now be amongst those who most earnestly mourn his decease.

His efforts, of course, brought him much persecution and annoyance, but never culminated in anything really serious, until about the year 1846 or '47.

He then met, at New Castle, a man, woman, and six children, from down on the Eastern Shore of Maryland. The man was free, the woman had been a slave, and while in Slavery had had by her husband, two children. She was then set free, and afterwards had four children. The whole party ran away. They traveled several days, and finally reached Middletown, late

40

at night, where they were taken in, fed and cared for, by John Hunn, a wealthy Quaker, there. They were watched, however, by some persons in that section, who followed them, arrested them, and sent them to New Castle to jail. The sheriff and his daughter were Anti-slavery people, and wrote to Mr. Garrett to come over. He went over, had an interview, found from their statement, that four of the party were undoubtedly free, and returned to this city. On the following day, he and U. S. Senator Wales, went over and had the party taken before Judge Booth, on a writ of *habeas corpus*. Judge Booth decided that there was no evidence on which to hold them, that in the absence of evidence the *presumption was always in favor of freedom* and discharged them.

Mr. Garrett then said, here is this woman with a babe at her breast, the child suffering from a white swelling on its leg, is there any impropriety in my getting a carriage and helping them over to Wilmington? Judge Booth responded certainly not.

Mr. Garrett then hired the carriage, but gave the driver distinctly to understand that he only paid for the woman and the young children; the rest might walk. They all got in, however, and finally escaped, of course the two children born in slavery amongst the rest.

Six weeks afterwards the slave-holders followed them, and incited, it is said, by the Cochrans and James A. Bayard, commenced a suit against Mr. Garrett, claiming all the fugitives as slaves. Mr. Garrett's friends claim that the jury was packed to secure an adverse verdict. The trial came on before Chief Justice Taney and Judge Hall, in the May term (1848) of the U. S. Court, sitting at New Castle, Bayard representing the prosecutors, and Wales the defendant. There were four trials in all, lasting three days. We have not room here for the details of the trial, but the juries awarded even heavier damages than the plaintiffs claimed, and the judgments swept away every dollar of his property.

When the trials were concluded, Mr. Garrett arose, the court being adjourned, made a speech of an hour to the large crowd in the court-room, in the course of which he declared his intention to redouble his exertions, so help him God. His bold assertion was greeted with mingled cheers and hisses, and at the conclusion of his speech one of the jurors who had convicted him strode across the benches, grasped his hand, and begged his forgivenness.

Mr. Garrett kept his pledge and redoubled his exertions. The trial advertised him, and such was the demand on him for shelter, that he was compelled to put another story on his back buildings. His friends helped him to start again in business, and commencing anew in his sixtieth year with nothing, he again amassed a handsome competence, generously contributing all the while to every work in behalf of the down-trodden blacks or his suffering fellow-men of any color.

In time the war came, and as he remarked, the nation went into the business by the wholesale, so he quit his retail operations, having, after he commenced to keep a record, helped off over twenty-one hundred slaves, and no inconsiderable number before that time.

In time, too, he came to be honored instead of execrated for his noble efforts. Wilmington became an abolition city, and for once, at least, a prophet was not without honor in his own city. Mr. Garrett continued his interest in every reform up to his last illness, and probably his last appearance in any public capacity, was as president of a Woman Suffrage meeting, in the City Hall, a few months ago, which was addressed by Julia Ward Howe, Lucy Stone, and Henry B. Blackwell.

He lived to see the realization of his hopes for Universal Freedom, and in April last on the occasion of the great parade of the colored people in this city, he was carried through our streets in an open barouche, surrounded by the men in whose behalf he had labored so faithfully, and the guards around his carriage carrying banners, with the inscription, " Our Moses."

A Moses he was to their race; but unto him it was given to enter into the promised land toward which he had set his face persistently and almost alone for more than half a century.

He was beloved almost to adoration by his dusky-hued friends, and in the dark days of the beginning of the war, which every Wilmingtonian will remember with a shudder, in those days of doubt, confusion, and suspicion, without his knowledge or consent, Thomas Garrett's house was constantly surrounded and watched by faithful black men, resolved that, come weal come woe to them, no harm should come to the benefactor of their race.

He was a hero in a life-time fight, an upright, honest man in his dealings with men, a tender husband, a loving father, and above all, a man who loved his neighbor as himself, and righteousness and truth better than ease, safety, or worldly goods, and who never let any fear of harm to person or property sway him from doing his whole duty to the uttermost.

He was faithful among the faithless, upright and just in the midst of a wicked and perverse generation, and lived to see his labors rewarded and approved in his own life-time, and then with joy that the Right had triumphed by mightier means than his own; with thankfulness for the past, and with calm trust for the future, he passed to the reward of the just. He has fought a good fight, he has finished his course, he has kept the faith.

From the same paper, of January 30th, 1871, we extract an account of the funeral obsequies which took place on Saturday, January 28th.

FUNERAL SERVICE ON SATURDAY.

The funeral of Thomas Garrett, which took place on Saturday, partook almost of the character of a popular ovation to the memory of the deceased, though it was conducted with the plainness of form which characterizes the society of which he was a member.

There was no display, no organization, nothing whatever to distinguish this from ordinary funerals, except the outpouring of people of every creed, condition, and color, to follow the remains to their last resting-place.

There was for an hour or two before the procession started, a constant living stream of humanity passing into the house, around the coffin, and out at another door, to take a last look at the face of the deceased, the features of which displayed a sweetness and serenity which occasioned general remark. A smile seemed to play upon the dead lips.

Shortly after three o'clock the funeral procession started, the plain coffin, containing the remains, being carried by the stalwart arms of a delegation of colored men, and the family and friends of the deceased following in carriages with a large procession on foot, while the sidewalks along the line, from the house to the meeting-house, more than six squares, were densely crowded with spectators.

The Friends' Meeting House was already crowded, except the place reserved for the relatives of the deceased, and, though probably fifteen hundred people crowded into the capacious building, a greater number still were unable to gain admission.

The crowd inside was composed of all kinds and conditions of men, white and black, all uniting to do honor to the character and works of the deceased.

The coffin was laid in the open space in front of the gallery of ministers and elders, and the lid removed from it, after which there was a period of silence.

Presently the venerable Lucretia Mott arose and said that, seeing the gathering of the multitude there and thronging along the streets, as she had passed on her way to the meeting-house, she had thought of the multitude which gathered after the death of Jesus, and of the remark of the Centurion, who, seeing the people, said : " Certainly this was a righteous man." Looking at this multitude she would say surely this also was a righteous man. She was not one of those who thought it best always on occasions like this, to speak in eulogy of the dead, but this was not an ordinary case, and seeing the crowd that had gathered, and amongst it the large numbers of a once despised and persecuted race, for which the deceased had done so much, she felt that it was fit and proper that the good deeds of this man's life should be remembered, for the encouragement of others. She spoke of her long acquaintance with him, of his cheerful and sunny disposition, and his firm devotion to the truth as he saw it.

Aaron M. Powell, of New York, was the next speaker, and he spoke at length with great earnestness of the life-long labor of his departed friend in the abolition cause, of his cheerfulness, his courage, and his perfect consecration to his work.

He alluded to the fact, that deceased was a member of the Society of Friends, and held firmly to its faith that God leads and inspires men to do the work He requires of them, that He speaks within the soul of every man, and that all men are equally His children, subject to His guidance, and that all should be free to follow wherever the Spirit might lead. It was Thomas Garrett's recognition of this sentiment that made him an abolitionist, and inspired him with the courage to pursue his great work. He cared little for the minor details of Quakerism, but he was a true Quaker in his devotion to this great central idea which is the basis on which it rests. He urged the Society to take a lesson from the deceased, and recognizing the responsibility of their position, to labor with earnestness, and to consecrate their whole beings to the cause of right and reform. It is impossible for us to give any fair abstract of Mr. Powell's earnest and eloquent tribute to his friend, on whom he had looked, he said, as " a Father in Israel" from his boyhood.

William Howard Day, then came forward, saying, he understood that it would not be considered inappropriate for one of his race to say a few words on this occasion, and make some attempt to pay a fitting tribute to one to whom they owed so much. He did not feel to-day like paying such a tribute, his grief was too fresh upon him, his heart too bowed down, and he could do no more, than in behalf of his race, not only those here, but the host the deceased has befriended, and of the whole four millions to whom he had been so true a friend, cast a tribute of praise and thanks upon his grave.

Rev. Alfred Cookman, of Grace M. E. Church, next arose, and said that he came there intending to say nothing, but the scene moved him to a few words. He remembered once standing in front of St. Paul's Cathedral, in London, and seeing therein the name of the architect, Sir Christopher Wren, inscribed, and under it this inscription : " Stranger, if you would see his monument look about you." And the thought came to him that if you would see the monument of him who lies there, look about you and see it built in stones of living hearts. He thanked God for the works of this man ; he thanked Him especially for his noble character. He said that he felt that that body had been the temple of a noble spirit, aye the temple of God himself, and some day they would meet the spirit in the heavenly land beyond the grave

Lucretia Mott arose, and said she feared the claim might appear to be made that Quakerism alone held the great central principle which dominated this man's life; but she wished it understood that they recognized this " voice within " as leading and guiding all men, and they probably meant by it much the same as those differing from them meant by the Third person in their Trinity. She did not wish, even in appearance, to claim a belief in this voice for her own sect alone.

T. Clarkson Taylor then said, that the time for closing the services had arrived, and in a very few words commended the lesson of his life to those present, after which the meeting dissolved, and the body was carried to the grave-yard in the rear of the meeting-house, and deposited in its last resting-place.

THE TRIAL OF THE CASES, 1848.

To the Editor of the Commercial:

Your admirable and interesting sketch of the career of the late Thomas Garrett contains one or two statements, which, according to my recollection of the facts, are not entirely accurate, and are perhaps of sufficient importance to be corrected.

The proceedings in the U. S. Circuit Court were not public prosecutions or indictments, but civil suits instituted by the owners of the runaway slaves, who employed and paid counsel to conduct them. An act of Congress, then in force, imposed a penalty of five hundred dollars on any person who should knowingly harbor or conceal a fugitive from labor, to be recovered by and for the benefit of the claimant of such fugitive, in any Court proper to try the same; saving, moreover, to the claimant his right of action for or on account of loss, etc.; thus giving to the slave-owner two cases for action for each fugitive, one of debt for the penalty, and one of trespass for damages.

There were in all seven slaves, only the husband and father of the family being free, who escaped under the friendly help and guidance of Mr. Garrett, five of whom were claimed by E. N. Turner, and the remaining two by C. T. Glanding, both claimants being residents of Maryland.

In the suits for the penalties, Turner obtained judgment for twenty-five hundred dollars, and Glanding, one for one thousand dollars. In these cases the jury could give neither less nor more than the amount of the penalties, on the proper proof being made. Nor in the trespass case did the jury give "larger damages than were claimed." A jury sometimes does queer things, but it cannot make a verdict for a greater sum than the plaintiff demands; in the trespass cases, Glanding had a verdict for one thousand dollars damages, but in Turner's case only nine hundred dollars were allowed, though the plaintiff sued for twenty-five hundred.

It is hardly true to say that any one of the juries was *packed*, indeed, it would have been a difficult matter in that day for the Marshal to summon thirty sober, honest, and judicious men, fairly and impartially chosen from the three counties of Delaware, who would have found verdicts different from those which were rendered. The jury must have been fixed for the defendant to have secured any other result, on the supposition that the testimony admitted of any doubt or question, the anti-slavery men in the state being like Virgil's ship-wrecked mariners, very few in number and scattered over a vast space.

What most redounds to the honor and praise of Mr. Garrett, in this transaction, as a noble and disinterested philanthropist is, that after the fugitives
had been discharged from custody under the writ of *habeas corpus*, and
when he had been advised by his lawyer, who was also his personal friend,
to keep his hands off and let the party work their own passage to a haven of
freedom, not then far distant, or he might be involved in serious trouble, he
deliberately refused to abandon them to the danger of pursuit and capture.
The welfare and happiness of too many human beings were at stake to permit him to think of personal consequences, and he was ready and dared to
encounter any risk for himself, so that he could insure the safety of those
fleeing from bondage. It was this heroic purpose to protect the weak and
helpless at any cost, this fearless unselfish action, not stopping to weigh the
contingencies of individual gain or loss, that constitutes his best title to the
gratitude of those he served, and to the admiration and respect of all who
can appreciate independent conduct springing from pure and lofty motives.
He did what he thought and believed to be right, and let the consequences
take care of themselves. He never would directly or otherwise, entice a
slave to leave his master; but he never would refuse his aid to the hunted,
panting wretch that in the pursuit of happiness was seeking after liberty.
And who among us is now bold enough to say, that in all this he did not
see clearly, act bravely, do justly, and live up to the spirit of the sacred
text:—" Whatsoever ye would that men should do to you, do ye even so to
them?" W.

In a letter addressed to one of the sons, William Lloyd Garrison pays the
following beautiful and just tribute to his faithfulness in the cause of
freedom.

BOSTON, January 25th, 1871.

MY DEAR FRIEND:—I have received the intelligence of the death of
your honored and revered father, with profound emotions. If it were not
for the inclemency of the weather, and the delicate state of my health, I
would hasten to be at the funeral, long as the distance is; not indeed as a
mourner, for, in view of his ripe old age, and singularly beneficent life, there
is no cause for sorrow, but to express the estimation in which I held him, as
one of the best men who ever walked the earth, and one of the most beloved
among my numerous friends and co-workers in the cause of an oppressed
and down-trodden race, now happily rejoicing in their heavenly-wrought
deliverance. For to no one was the language of Job more strictly applicable
than to himself:—" When the ear heard me, then it blessed me, and when
the eye saw me, it gave witness to me ; because I delivered the poor that
cried, and the fatherless, and him that had none to help him. The blessing
of him that was ready to perish came upon me ; and I caused the widow's
heart to sing for joy. I put on righteousness, and it clothed me ; my judgment was as a robe and a diadem. I was eyes to the blind, and feet was I

to the lame. I was a father to the poor; and the cause which I knew not I searched out. And I brake the jaws of the wicked, and plucked the spoil out of his teeth." This is an exact portraiture of your father, a most comprehensive delineation of his character as a philanthropist and reformer. It was his meat and drink.

> " The poor to feed, the lost to seek,
>   To proffer life to death,
> Hope to the erring, to the weak
>   The strength of his own faith.
>
> " To plead the captive's right; remove
>   The sting of hate from law;
> And soften in the fire of love
>   The hardened steel of war.
>
> " He walked the dark world in the mild,
>   Still guidance of the light;
> In tear.ul tenderness a child,
>   A strong man in the right."

Did there ever live one who had less of that " fear of man which bringeth a snare," than himself? Or who combined more moral courage with exceeding tenderness of spirit? Or who adhered more heroically to his convictions of duty in the face of deadly peril and certain suffering? Or who gave himself more unreservedly, or with greater disinterestedness, to the service of bleeding humanity? Or who took more joyfully the spoiling of his goods as the penalty of his sympathy for the hunted fugitive? Or who more untiringly kept pace with all the progressive movements of the age, as though in the very freshness of adult life, while venerable with years? Or who, as a husband, father, friend, citizen, or neighbor, more nobly performed all the duties, or more generally distributed all the charities of life? He will leave a great void in the community. Such a stalwart soul appears only at rare intervals. Delaware, enslaved, treated him like a felon; Delaware, redeemed, will be proud of his memory.

> " Only the actions of the just
> Smell sweet and blossom in the dust."

His rightful place is conspicuously among the benefactors, saviours, martyrs of the human race.

His career was full of dramatic interest from beginning to end, and crowded with the experiences and vicissitudes of a most eventful nature. What he promised he fulfilled; what he attempted, he seldom, or never failed to accomplish; what he believed, he dared to proclaim upon the housetop; what he ardently desired, and incessantly labored for, was the reign of universal freedom, peace, and righteousness. He was among the manliest of men, and the gentlest of spirits. There was no form of human suffering that did not touch his heart; but his abounding sympathy was especially drawn out towards the poor, imbruted slaves of the plantation, and such of their number as sought their freedom by flight. The thousands that passed safely through his hands, on their way to Canada and the North, will never forget his fatherly solicitude for their welfare, or the dangers he unflinchingly encountered in their behalf. Stripped of all his property under the Fugitive Slave law, for giving them food, shelter, and assistance to continue their flight, he knew not what it was to be intimidated or disheartened, but gave himself to the same blessed work as though conscious of no loss. Greathearted philanthropist, what heroism could exceed thy own ?

> " For, while the jurist sitting with the slave-whip o'er him swung,
> From the tortured truths of freedom the lie of slavery wrung,
> And the solemn priest to Moloch, on each God-deserted shrine,
> Broke the bondman's heart for bread, poured the bondman's blood for wine—
> While the multitude in blindness to a far-off Saviour knelt,
> And spurned, the while, the temple where a present Saviour dwelt ;
> Thou beheld'st Him in the task-field, in the prison shadow dim,
> And thy mercy to the bondman, it was mercy unto Him ! "

I trust some one, well qualified to execute the pleasing task, will write his biography for the grand lessons his life inculcated. Yours, in full sympathy and trust, WM. LLOYD GARRISON.

A cotemporary who had known him long and intimately—who had appreciated his devotion to freedom, who had shared with him some of the perils consequent upon aiding the fleeing fugitives, and who belonged to the race with whom Garrett sympathized, and for whose elevation and freedom he labored so assiduously with an overflowing heart of tender regard and sympathy—penned the following words, touching the sad event :

CHATHAM, C. W., January 30, 1871.

To MR. HENRY GARRETT :—Dear Sir :—I have just heard, through the kindness of my friend, Mrs. Graves, of the death of your dear father ; the intelligence makes me feel sad and sorrowful ; I sincerely sympathize with you and all your brothers and sisters, in your mournful bereavement ; but you do not mourn without hope, for you have an assurance in his death that your loss is his infinite gain. For he was a good Christian, a good husband, a good father, a good citizen, and a truly good Samaritan, for his heart, his hand and his purse, were ever open to the wants of suffering humanity, wherever he found it ; irrespective of the country, religion, or complexion of the sufferer. Hence there are many more who mourn his loss, as well as yourselves ; and I know, verily, that many a silent tear was shed by his fellow-citizens, both white and colored, when he took his departure ; especially the colored ones ; for he loved them with a brother's love, not because they were colored, but because they were oppressed, and, like John Brown, he loved them to the last ; that was manifest by his request that they should be his bearers. I can better feel than I have language to express the mournful and sorrowing pride that must have stirred the inmost souls of those men of color, who had the honor conferred on them of bearing his mortal remains to their last resting-place, when they thought of what a sacred trust was committed to their hands. We are told to mark the perfect man, and behold the upright, for the end of that man is peace; and such was the end of your dear father, and he has gone to join the innumerable company of the spirits of the just, made perfect on the other side of the river, where there is a rest remaining for all the children of God. My brother, Abraham D. Shadd, and my sister Amelia, join their love and condolence with mine to you all, hoping that the virtues of your father may be a guiding star to you all, until you meet him again in that happy place, where parting will be no more, forever.

Your humble friend,   ELIZABETH J. WILLIAMS.

From the learned and the unlearned, from those in high places and from those in humble stations, many testimonials reached the family, respecting this great friend of the slave, but it is doubtful, whether a single epistle from any one, was more affectingly appreciated by the bereaved family, than the epistle just quoted from Elizabeth J. Williams.

The Slave's most eloquent advocate, Wendell Phillips, in the "National Standard," of February 4, 1871, in honor of the departed, bore the following pertinent testimony to his great worth in the cause of Liberty.

"I should not dare to trust my memory for the number of fugitive slaves this brave old friend has helped to safety and freedom — nearly three thousand, I believe. What a rich life to look back on! How skilful and adroit he was, in eluding the hunters! How patient in waiting days and weeks, keeping the poor fugitives hidden meanwhile, till it was safe to venture on the highway! What whole-hearted devotion, what unselfish giving of time, means, and everything else to this work of brotherly love! What house in Delaware, so honorable in history, as that where hunted men fled, and were sure to find refuge. It was the North Star to many a fainting heart. This century has grand scenes to show and boast of among its fellows. But few transcend that auction-block where the sheriff was selling all Garrett's goods for the crime (!) of giving a breakfast to a family of fugitive slaves. As the sale closed, the officer turns to Garrett, saying: 'Thomas, I hope you'll never be caught at this again.'

"'Friend,' was the reply, 'I haven't a dollar in the world, but if thee knows a fugitive who needs a breakfast, send him to me.'

"Over such a scene, Luther and Howard and Clarkson clapped their hands.

"Such a speech redeems the long infamy of the State. It is endurable, the having of such a blot as Delaware in our history, when it has once been the home of such a man. I remember well the just pride with which he told me, that after that sale, pro-slavery as Wilmington was, he could have a discount at the bank as readily as any man in the city. Though the laws robbed him, his fellow-citizens could not but respect and trust him, love and honor him.

" The city has never had, we believe, a man die in it worthy of a statue. We advise it to seize this opportunity to honor itself and perpetuate the good name of its worthiest citizen, by immortalizing some street, spot, shaft or building with his name.

" Brave, generous, high-souled, sturdy, outspoken friend of all that needed aid or sympathy, farewell for these scenes ! In times to come, when friendless men and hated ideas need champions, God grant them as gallant and successful ones as you have been, and may the State you honored grow worthy of you. WENDELL PHILLIPS."

Likewise in the " National Standard," the editor, Aaron M. Powell, who attended the funeral, paid the following glowing tribute to the moral, religious, and anti-slavery character of the slave's friend :

On the 24th inst., Thomas Garrett, in his eighty-second year, passed on to the higher life. A week previous we had visited him in his sick chamber, and, on leaving him felt that he must go hence ere long. He was the same strong, resolute man in spirit to the last. He looked forward to the welcome change with perfect serenity and peace of mind. And well he might, for he had indeed fought the good fight and been faithful unto the end.

He was most widely known for his services to fugitive slaves. Twenty-five hundred and forty five he had preserved a record of; and he had assisted somewhat more than two hundred prior to the commencement of the record. Picture to the mind's eye this remarkable procession of nearly three thousand men, women and children fleeing from Slavery. and finding in this brave, large-hearted man, a friend equal to their needs in so critical an emergency ! No wonder he was feared by the slave-holders, not alone of his own State, but of the whole South. If their human chattels once reached his outpost, there was indeed little hope of their reclamation. The friend and helper of fugitives from Slavery, truly their Moses, he was more than this, he was the discriminating, outspoken, uncompromising opponent of Slavery itself. He was one of the strongest pillars and one of the most efficient working-members of the American Anti-slavery Society. He was an abolitionist of the most radical and pronounced character, though a resident of a slave State, and through all the period wherein to be an abolitionist was to put in jeopardy, not only reputation and property, but life itself. Though he rarely addressed public meetings, his presence imparted much strength to others, was " weighty " in the best Quaker sense. He was of the rare type of character, represented by Francis Jackson and James Mott.

Thomas Garrett was a member of the Society of Friends, and as such, served by the striking contrast of his own life and character, with the average of the Society, to exemplify to the world the real, genuine Quakerism. It is not at all to the credit of his fellow-members, that it must be said of them, that when he was bearing the cross and doing the work for which he is now so universally honored, they, many of them, were not only not in sympathy with him, but would undoubtedly, if they had had the requisite vitality and courage, have cut him off from their denominational fellowship. He was a sincere, earnest believer in the cardinal point of Quakerism, the Divine presence in the human soul—this furnishes the key to his action through life. This divine attribute he regarded not as the birth-right of Friends alone, not of one race, sex or class, but of all mankind. Therefore was he an abolitionist; therefore was he interested in the cause of the Indians; therefore was he enlisted in the cause of equal rights for women; therefore was he a friend of temperance, of oppressed and needy working-men and women, world-wide in the scope of his philanthropic sympathy, and broadly catholic, and comprehensive in his views of religious life and duty. He was the soul of honor in business. His experience, when deprived at sixty, of every dollar of his property for having obeyed God rather than man, in assisting fugitives from Slavery, and the promptness with which his friends came forward with proffered co-operation, furnishes a lesson which all should ponder well. He had little respect for, or patience with shams of any kind, in religious, political or social life.

As we looked upon Thomas Garrett's calm, serene face, mature in a ripe old age, still shadowing forth kindliness of heart, firmness of purpose, discriminating intelligence, conscientious, manly uprightness, death never seemed more beautiful :

> " Why, what is Death but Life
> In other forms of being?   Life without
> The coarser attributes of men, the dull
> And momently decaying frame which holds
> The ethereal spirit in, and binds it down
> To brotherhood with brutes !   There's no
> Such thing as Death; what's so-called is but
> The beginning of a new existence. a fresh
> Segment of the eternal round of change."

A. M. P.

Another warm admirer of this Great Lover of humanity, in a letter to George W. Stone thus alludes to his life and death :

TAUNTON, MASS., June 25th, 1871.

DEAR STONE :—Your telegram announcing the death of that old soldier and saint, and my good friend, Thos. Garrett, reached me last evening at ten o'clock.

My first impulse was to start for Wilmington, and be present at his funeral ; but when I considered my work here, and my engagements for the next four days, I found it impossible to go.

I will be there in spirit, and bow my inmost soul before the All Loving One, his Father and ours, in humble thankfulness, that I ever knew him, and had the privilege of enjoying his friendship and witnessing his devotion to the interest of every good cause of benevolence and Reform.

I could write you many things of interest which I heard from him, and which I have noted on my memory and heart; but I cannot now. I think he was one of the remarkable men of the times, in faith, in holy boldness, in fearless devotion to the right, in uncompromising integrity, in unselfish benevolence, in love to God and man, and in unceasing, life-long efforts to do justly, to love mercy, and to walk humbly with God. We shall not soon look upon his like again.

If I was present at his funeral, I should take it as a privilege to pronounce his name, and say, as I never said before, " Blessed are the dead that die in the Lord; even so saith the Spirit; for they rest from their labors, and their works do follow them."

Do, at once, see his children and Clarkson Taylor, and give them my condolence, no, my *congratulation*, and assure them that they have a rich legacy in his noble life, and he has a glorious reward in the bosom of God.

Peace to his memory! Noble old man, so pure and peaceful, and yet so strong, firm, and fearless, so gentle, tender, and truthful, afraid and ashamed of nothing but sin, and in love and labor with every good work.

I could write on and fill many pages. But he desired no eulogy, and needs none. He lives, and will live for ever in many hearts and in the heaven of heavens above. T. Israel.

If it were necessary we might continue to introduce scores of editorials, communications, epistles, etc., all breathing a similar spirit of respect for the rare worth of this wonderful man, but space forbids. In conclusion, therefore, with a view of presenting him in the light of his own interesting letters, written when absorbed in his peculiar work, from a large number on file the following are submitted :

Wilmington, 11th mo. 21st, 1855.

Esteemed Friend, Wm. Still :—Thine of this date, inquiring for the twenty-one, and how they have been disposed of, has just been received. I can only answer by saying, when I parted with them yesterday forenoon, I gave the wife of the person, in whose house they were, money to pay her expenses to Philadelphia and back in the cars to pilot the four women to thy place. I gave her husband money to pay a pilot to start yesterday with the ten men, divided in two gangs; also a letter for thee. I hope they have arrived safe ere this. I had to leave town soon after noon yesterday to attend a brother ill with an attack of apoplexy, and to-day I have been very much engaged. The place they stayed here is a considerable distance off. I will make inquiry to-morrow morning, and in case any other disposition has been made of them than the above I will write thee. I should think they have stopped to-day, in consequence of the rain, and most likely will arrive safe to-morrow. In haste, thy friend, Thos. Garrett.

Although having " to attend a brother, ill with an attack of apoplexy," Garrett took time to attend to the interest of the " twenty-one," as the above letter indicates. How many other men in the United States, under similar circumstances, would have been thus faithful?

On another occasion deeply concerned for A FORWARDER OF SLAVES, he wrote thus:

Wilmington, 12th mo. 26th, 1855.

Esteemed Friend, Wm. Still :—The bearer of this, George Wilmer, is a slave, whose residence is in Maryland. He is a true man, and a forwarder of slaves. Has passed some twenty-five within four months. He is desirous of finding some of his relations, Wm. Mann and Thomas Carmichael, they passed here about a month since. If thee can give him any information where they can be found thee will much oblige him, and run no risk of their safety in so doing. I remain, as ever, thy sincere friend,

Thos. Garrett.

" Four able-bodied men," form the subject of the subjoined correspondence:

Wilmington, 11th mo., 4th, 1856.

Esteemed Friends, J. Miller McKim and William Still :—Captain F., has arrived here this day, with four able-bodied men. One is an engineer, and has been engaged in sawing lumber, a second, a good house-carpenter, a third a blacksmith, and the fourth a farm hand. They are now five hundred miles from their home in Carolina, and would be glad to get situations, without going far from here. I will keep them till to-morrow. Please inform me whether thee knows of a suitable place in the country where the mechanics can find employment at their trades for the winter; let me hear to-morrow, and oblige your friend, Thomas Garrett.

" What has become of Harriet Tubman?" (agent of the Underground Rail Road), is made a subject of special inquiry in the following note:

Wilmington, 3d mo., 27th, 1857.

Esteemed Friend, William Still :—I have been very anxious for some time past, to hear what has become of Harriet Tubman. The last I heard of her, she was in the State of New York, on her way to Canada with some friends, last fall. Has thee seen, or heard anything of her lately? It would be a sorrowful fact, if such a hero as she, should be lost from the Underground Rail Road. I have just received a letter from Ireland, making inquiry respecting her. If thee gets this in time, and knows anything respecting her, please drop me a line by mail to-morrow, and I will get it next morning if not sooner, and oblige thy friend.

I have heard nothing from the eighth man from Dover, but trust he is safe.   THOMAS GARRETT.

On being informed that Harriet was "all right," the following extract from a subsequent letter, expresses his satisfaction over the good news, and at the same time, indicates his sympathy for a "poor traveler," who had fallen a victim to the cold weather, and being severely frost-bitten, had died of lock-jaw, as related on page 52.

"I was truly glad to learn that Harriet Tubman was still in good health and ready for action, but I think there will be more danger at present than heretofore, there is so much excitement below in consequence of the escape of those eight slaves. I was truly sorry to hear of the fate of that poor fellow who had periled so much for liberty. I was in hopes from what thee told me, that he would recover with the loss perhaps of some of his toes.

THOMAS GARRETT."

In the next letter, an interesting anecdote is related of an encounter on the Underground Rail Road, between the fugitives and several Irishmen, and how one of the old countrymen was shot in the forehead, etc., which G. thought would make such opponents to the Road "more cautious."

WILMINGTON, 11th mo., 5th, 1857.

ESTEEMED FRIEND, WILLIAM STILL:—I have just written a note for the bearer to William Murphy Chester, who will direct him on to thy care; he left his home about a week since. I hear in the lower part of this State, he met with a friend to pilot him some twenty-five miles last night. We learn that one party of those last week were attacked with clubs by several Irishmen, and that one of them was shot in the forehead, the ball entering to the skull bone, and passing under the skin partly round the head. My informant says he is likely to recover, but it will leave an ugly mark it is thought, as long as he lives. We have not been able to learn, whether the party was on the look out for them, or whether they were rowdies out on a Hallow-eve frolic; but be it which it may, I presume they will be more cautious hereafter, how they trifle with such. Desiring thee prosperity and happiness, I remain thy friend,   THOMAS GARRETT.

FOUR OF GOD'S POOR.

The following letter shows the fearless manner in which he attended to the duties of his station:

WILMINGTON, 9th mo. 6th, 1857.

RESPECTED FRIEND, WM. STILL:—This evening I send to thy care four of God's poor. Severn Johnson, a true man, will go with them to-night by rail road to thy house. I have given Johnson five dollars, which will pay all expenses, and leave each twenty-five cents. We are indebted to Captain F–t–n for those. May success attend them in their efforts to maintain themselves. Please send word by Johnson whether or no, those seven arrived safe I wrote thee of ten days since. My wife and self were at Longwood to-day, had a pleasant ride and good meeting. We are, as ever, thy friend, THOS. GARRETT.

Quite a satisfactory account is given in the letter below of the "Irishman who was shot in the forehead;" also of one of the same kin, who in meddling with Underground Rail Road passengers, got his arm broken in two places, etc.

WILMINGTON, 11th mo. 14th, 1857.

ESTEEMED FRIEND, WM. STILL :—Thy favor of a few days since came to hand, giving quite a satisfactory account of the large company.

I find in the melee near this town, one of the Irishmen got his arm broken in two places. The one shot in the forehead is badly marked, but not dangerously injured. I learn to-day, that the carriage in that company, owing to fast driving with such a heavy load, is badly broken, and the poor horse was badly injured; it has not been able to do anything since.

Please say to my friend, Rebecca Hart, that I have heretofore kept clear of persuading, or even advising slaves to leave their masters till they had fully made up their minds to leave, knowing as I do there is great risk in so doing, and if betrayed once would be a serious injury to the cause hereafter. I had spoken to one colored man to try to see him, but he was not willing to risk it. If he has any desire to get away, he can, during one night, before they miss him, get out of the reach of danger. Booth has moved into New Castle, and left the two boys on the farm. If Rebecca Hart will write to me, and give me the name of the boy, and the name of his mother, I will make another effort. The man I spoke to lives in New Castle, and thinks the mother of the boy alluded to lives between here and New Castle. The young men's association here wants Wendell Phillips to deliver a lecture on the lost arts, and some of the rest of us wish him to deliver a lecture on Slavery. Where will a letter reach him soonest, as I wish to write him on the subject. I thought he could perhaps deliver two lectures, two nights in succession. If thee can give the above information, thee will much oblige—

GARRETT & SON.

In his business-like transactions, without concealment, he places matters in such a light that the wayfaring man, though a fool, need not err, as may here be seen.

WILMINGTON, 11th mo. 25th, 1857.

ESTEEMED FRIEND, WM. STILL:—I now send Johnson, one of our colored men, up with the three men I wrote thee about. Johnson has undertook to have them well washed and cleaned during the day. And I have provided them with some second-hand clothes, to make them comfortable, a new pair of shoes and stockings, and shall pay Johnson for taking care of them. I mention this so that thee may know. Thee need not advance him any funds. In the present case I shall furnish them with money to pay their fare to Philadelphia, and Johnson home again. Hoping they will get on safe, I remain thy friend, THOS. GARRETT.

FOUR FEMALES ON BOARD.

The fearless Garrett communicated through the mail, as usual, the following intelligence:

WILMINGTON, 8th mo. 25th, 1859.

ESTEEMED FRIEND, WM. STILL:—The brig Alvena, of Lewistown, is in the Delaware opposite here, with four females on board. The colored man, who has them in charge, was employed by the husband of one of them to bring his wife up. When he arrived here, he found the man had left. As the vessel is bound to Red Bank, I have advised him to take them there in the vessel, and to-morrow take them in the steamboat to the city, and to the Anti-slavery office. He says they owe the captain one dollar and fifty cents for board, and I gave him three dollars, to pay the captain and take them to your office. I have a man here, to go on to-night, that was nearly naked; shall rig him out pretty comfortably. Poor fellow, he has lost his left hand, but he says he can take care of himself. In haste, thy friend,

THOS. GARRETT.

While Father Abraham was using his utmost powers to put down the rebellion, in 1864, a young man who had "been most unrighteously sold for seven years," desirous of enlisting, sought advice from the wise and faithful Underground Rail Road manager, who gave him the following letter, which may be looked upon in the light of a rare anecdote, as there is no doubt but that the "professed non-resistant" in this instance, hoped to see the poor fellow "*snugly fixed in his regimentals*" doing service for "Father Abraham."

WILMINGTON, 1st mo. 23d, 1864.

RESPECTED FRIEND, WILLIAM STILL:—The bearer of this, Winlock Clark, has lately been most unrighteously sold for seven years, and is desirous of enlisting, and becoming one of Uncle Sam's boys; I have advised him to call on thee so that no land sharks shall get any bounty for enlisting him; he has a wife and several children, and whatever bounty the government or the State allows him, will be of use to his family. Please write me when he is snugly fixed in his regimentals, so that I may send word to his wife. By so doing, thee will much oblige thy friend, and the friend of humanity,

THOMAS GARRETT.

N. B. Am I naughty, being a professed non-resistant, to advise this poor fellow to serve Father Abraham? T. G.

We have given so many of these inimitable Underground Rail Road letters from the pen of the sturdy old laborer, not only because they will be new to the readers of this work, but because they so fittingly illustrate his practical devotion to the Slave, and his cheerfulness—in the face of danger and difficulty—in a manner that other pens might labor in vain to describe.

41

DANIEL GIBBONS.

A life as uneventful as the one whose story we are about to tell, affords little scope for the genius of the biographer or the historian, but being carefully studied, it cannot fail to teach a lesson of devotion and self-sacrifice, which should be learned and remembered by every succeeding age.

Daniel Gibbons, son of James and Deborah (Hoopes) Gibbons, was born on the banks of Mill Creek, in Lancaster county, Pennsylvania, on the 21st day of the 12th month (December), 1775. He was descended on his father's side from an English ancestor, whose name appears on the colonial records, as far back as 1683. John Gibbons evidently came with or before William Penn to this "goodly heritage of freedom." His earthly remains lie at Concord Friends' burying-ground, Delaware county, near where the family lived for a generation or two. The grandfather of Daniel Gibbons, who lived near where West Town boarding-school now is, in Chester county, bought for seventy pounds, "one thousand acres of land and allowances," in what is now Lancaster county, intending, as he ultimately did, to settle his three sons upon it. This purchase was made about the year 1715. In process of time, the eldest son, desiring to marry Deborah Hoopes, the daughter of Daniel Hoopes, of a neighboring township in Chester county, the young people obtained the consent of parents and friends, but it was a time of grief and mourning among young and old. The young Friends assured the intended bride, that they would not marry the best man in the Province and do what she was about to do; and the elder dames, so far relaxed the Puritanic rigidity of their rules, as to allow the invitation of an uncommonly large company of guests to the wedding, in order that a long and perhaps last farewell, might be said to the beloved daughter, who, with her husband, was about to emigrate to the "far West." Loud and long were the lamentations, and warm the embraces of these simple-minded Christian rustics, companions of toil and deprivation, as they parted from two of their number who were to leave their circle for the West; the West being then thirty-six miles distant. This was on the sixth day of the fifth month, 1756. More than a century has passed away; all the good people, eighty-nine in number, who signed the wedding certificate as witnesses, have passed away, and how vast is the change wrought in· our midst since that day!

Joseph Gibbons was so much pleased with the daring enterprise of his son and daughter-in-law, that he gave them one hundred acres of land in his Western possessions more than he reserved for his other and younger sons, and to it they immediately emigrated, and building first a cabin and the next year a store-house, began life for themselves in earnest.

It is interesting, in view of the long and consistent anti-slavery course which Daniel Gibbons pursued, to trace the influence that wrought upon him while his character was maturing, and the causes which led him to see the wickedness of the system which he opposed.

The Society of Friends in that day bore in mind the advice of their great founder, Fox, whose last words were: "Friends, mind the light." And following that guide which leads out of all evil and into all good, they viewed every custom of society with eyes undimmed by prejudice, and were influenced in every action of life by a belief in the common brotherhood of man, and a resolve to obey the command of Jesus, to love one another. This being the case, slavery and oppression of all kinds were unpopular, and indeed almost unknown amongst them.

James Gibbons was a republican, and an enthusiastic advocate of American liberty. Being a man of commanding presence, and great energy and determination, efforts were made during the Revolution to induce him to enlist as a cavalry soldier. He was prevented from so doing by the entreaties of his wife, and his own conscientious scruples as a Friend. About the time of the Revolution, or immediately after, he removed to the borough of Wilmington, Delaware, where, being surrounded by slavery, he became more than ever alive to its iniquities. He was interested during his whole life in getting slaves off. And being elected second burgess of Wilmington during his residence there, his official position gave him great opportunities to assist in this noble work. It is related that during his magistracy a slave-holder brought a colored man before him, whom he claimed as his slave. There being no evidence of the alleged ownership, the colored man was set at liberty. The pretended owner was inclined to be impudent; but James Gibbons told him promptly that nothing but silence and good behaviour on his part would prevent his commitment for contempt of court.

About the year 1790, James Gibbons came back to Lancaster county, where he spent twenty years in the practice of those deeds which will remain "in everlasting remembrance;" dying, full of years and honors, in 1810.

Born in the first year of the revolution and growing up surrounded by such influences, Daniel Gibbons could not have been other than he was, the friend of the down-trodden and oppressed of every nationality and color. In 1789 his father took him to see General Washington, then passing through Wilmington. To the end of his life he retained a vivid recollection of this visit, and would recount its incidents to his family and friends. During his father's residence in Wilmington, he spent his summers with kinsmen in Lancaster county, learning to be a farmer, and his winters in Wilmington going to school.

At the age of fourteen years he was bound an apprentice, as was the good custom of the day, to a Friend in Lancaster county to learn the tanning business. At this he served about six years, or until his master ceased to follow the business. During this apprenticeship he became accustomed to severe labor, so severe indeed that he never recovered from the effects thereof, having a difficulty in walking during the remainder of his life, which prevented him from taking the active part in Underground Rail Road business which he otherwise would have done. His father's estate being involved in litigation caused him to be put to this trade, farming being his favorite employment, and one which he followed during his whole life.

In 1805 he took a pedestrian tour, by way of New York, Albany, and Niagara Falls to the State of Ohio, then the far West, coming home by way of Pittsburg, and walking altogether one thousand three hundred and fifty miles. In this trip he increased the injury to his feet, so as to render himself virtually a cripple. Upon the death of his father, he settled upon the farm, on which he died.

About the year 1808 on going to visit some friends, who had removed to Adams county, Pennsylvania, he became acquanted with Hannah Wierman, whom he married on the fourth day of the fifth month, 1815. At this time Daniel Gibbons was about forty years old, and his wife about twenty-eight, she having been born on the ninth of the seventh month, 1787. A life of one after their union, would be incomplete without some notice of the other.

During a married life of thirty-seven years, Hannah Gibbons was the assistant of her husband in every good and noble work. Possessed of a warm heart, a powerful, though uncultivated intellect, an excellent judgment, and great sweetness of disposition, she was fitted both by nature and training to endure without murmuring the inconvenience and trouble incident to the reception and care of fugitives and to rejoice that to her was given the opportunity of assisting them in their efforts to be free.

The true measure of greatness in a human soul, is its willingness to suffer for its own good, or the good of its fellows, its self-sacrificing spirit. Granting the truth of this, one of the greatest souls was that of Hannah W. Gibbons. The following incident is a proof of this:

In 1836, when she was no longer a young woman, there came to her home, one of the poorest, most ignorant, and filthiest of mankind—a slave from the great valley of Virginia. He was foot-sore and weary, and could not tell how he came, or who directed him. He seemed indeed, a missive directed and sent by the hand of the Almighty. Before he could be cleansed or recruited, he was taken sick, and before he could be removed (even if he could have been trusted at the county poor house), his case was pronounced to be small-pox. For six long weeks did this good angel in human form, attend upon this unfortunate object. Reasons were found why no one else could do it, and with her own hands, she ministered to his wants, until he was restored to health. Such was her life. This is merely one case. She was always ready to do her duty. Her interest in good, never left her, for when almost dying, she aroused from her lethargy and asked if Abraham Lincoln was elected president of the United States, which he was a few days afterwards. She always predicted a civil war, in the settlement of the Slavery question.

During the last twenty-five years of her life she was an elder in the Society of Friends, of which she had always been an earnest, consistent, and devoted member. Her patience, self-denial, and warm affection were manifested in every relation of life. As a daughter, wife, mother, friend, and mistress of a family she was beloved by all, and to her relatives and friends who are left behind, the remembrance of her good deeds comes wafted like a perfume from beyond the golden gates. She survived her husband about eight years, dying on the sixteenth of the tenth month, 1860. Three children, sons, were born to their marriage, two of whom died in infancy and one still (1871) survives.

To give some idea of the course pursued by Daniel and Hannah Gibbons, I insert the following letter, containing an account of events which took place in 1821 :

"A short time since, I learned that my old friend, William Still, was about to publish a history of the Underground Rail Road. His own experience in the service of this road would make a large volume. I was brought up by Daniel Gibbons, and am asked to say what I know of him as an abolitionist. From my earliest recollection, he was a friend to the colored people, and often hired them and paid them liberal wages. His house was a depot for fugitives, and many hundreds has he helped on their way to freedom. Many a dark night he has sent me to carry them victuals and change their places of refuge, and take them to other people's barns, when not safe for him to go. I have known him start in the night and go fifty miles with them, when they were very hotly pursued. One man and his wife lived with him for a long time. Afterwards the man lived with Thornton Walton. The man was hauling lumber from Columbia. He was taken from his team in Lancaster, and lodged in Baltimore jail. Daniel Gibbons went to Baltimore, visited the jail and tried hard to get him released, but failed. I would add here, that Daniel Gibbons' faithful wife, one of the best women I ever knew, was always ready, day or night, to do all she possibly could, to help the poor fugitives on their way to freedom. Many interesting incidents occurred at the home of my uncle. I will relate one. He had living with him at one time, two colored men, Thomas Colbert and John Stewart. The latter was from Maryland ; John often said he would go back and get his wife. My uncle asked him if he was not afraid of his master's catching him. He said no, for his master knew if he undertook to take him, he would kill him. He did go and brought his wife to my uncle's.

While these two large men, Tom and John, were there, along came Robert (other name unknown), in a bad plight, his feet bleeding. Robert was put in the barn to thrash, until he could be fixed up to go again on his journey. But in a few days, behold, along came his master. He brought with him that notorious constable, Haines, from Lancaster, and one other man. They came suddenly upon Robert; as soon as he saw them he ran and jumped out of the "overshoot," some ten feet down. In jumping, he put one knee out of joint. The men ran around the barn and seized him. By this time, the two colored men, Tom and John, came, together with my uncle and aunt. Poor Robert owned his master, but John told them they should not take him away, and was going at them with a club. One of the men drew a pistol to shoot John, but uncle told him he had better not shoot him; this was not a slave State. Inasmuch as Robert had owned his master, Uncle told John he must submit, so they put Robert on a horse, and started with him. After they were gone John said: "Mr. Gibbons, just say the word, and I will bring Robert back." Aunt said: "Go, John, go!" So John ran to Joseph Rakestraw's and got a gun (without any lock), and ran across the fields, with Tom after him, and headed the party. The men all ran except Haines, who kept Robert between himself and John, so that John should not shoot him. But John called out to Robert to drop off that horse, or he would shoot him. This Robert did, and John and Tom brought him back in triumph. My aunt said: "John, thee is a good fellow, thee has done well." Robert was taken to Jesse Gilbert's barn, and Dr. Dingee fixed his knee. As soon as he was able to travel, he took a "bee-line" for the North star.

My life with my uncle and aunt made me an abolitionist. I left them in the winter of 1824, and came to Salem, Ohio, where I kept a small station on the Underground Rail Road, until the United States government took my work away. I have helped over two hundred fugitives on their way to Canada.　　Respectfully,　　DANIEL BONSALL,

Salem, Columbiana county, Ohio."

One day, in the winter of 1822, Thomas Johnson, a colored man, living with Daniel Gibbons, went out early in the morning, to set traps for musk-rats. While he was gone, a slave-holder came to the house and inquired for his slave. Daniel Gibbons said: "There is no slave here of that name." The man replied: "I know he is here. The man we're after, is a miserable, worthless, thieving scoundrel." "Oh! very well, then," said the good Quaker, "if that's the kind of man thee's after, then I know he is not here. We have a colored man here, but he is not that kind of a man." The slave-holder waited awhile, the man not making his appearance, then said: "Well, now, Mr. Gibbons, when you see that man next, tell him that we were here, and if he will come home, we will take good care of him, and be kind to him." "Very well," said Daniel, "I will tell him what thee says, but say to him at the same time, that he is a very great fool, if he does as thee requests." The colored man sought, having caught sight of the slave-holders, and knowing who they were, went off that night, under Daniel Gibbons' directions, and was never seen by his master again. Afterward, Daniel and his nephew, William Gibbons, went with this man to Adams county. With his master came the master of Mary, a girl with straight hair, and nearly white, who lived with Daniel Gibbons and his wife. Poor Mary was unfortunate. Her master caught her, and took her back with him into Slavery. She and a little girl, who was taken away about the year 1830, were the only ones ever taken back from the house of Daniel Gibbons.

Between the time of his marriage, when he began to keep a depot on the Underground Rail Road, and the year 1824, he passed more than one hundred slaves through to Canada, and between the latter time and his death, eight hundred more, making, in all nine hundred aided by him. He was ever willing to sacrifice his own personal comfort and convenience, in order to assist fugitives. In 1833, when on his way to the West, in a carriage, with his friend, Thomas Peart, also a most faithful friend of the colored man and interested in Underground Rail Road affairs, he found a fugitive slave, a woman, in Adams county, who was in immediate danger. He stopped his journey, and sent his horse and wagon back to his own home with the woman, that being the only safe way of getting her off. This was but a sample of his self-denial, in the cause of human freedom.

His want of ability to guide in person runaway slaves, or to travel with them, prevented him from taking active part in the wonderful adventures and hair-breadth escapes which his brain and tact rendered possible and successful. It is believed that no slave was ever recaptured that followed his directions. Sometimes the abolitionists were much annoyed by impostors, who pretended to be runaways, in order to discover their plans, and betray them to the slave-holders. Daniel Gibbons was possessed of much acuteness in detecting these people, but having detected them, he never treated them harshly or unkindly.

Almost from infancy, he was distinguished for the gravity of his deportment, and his utter heedlessness of small things. The writer has heard men preach the doctrine of the trifling value of the things of a present time, and of the tremendous importance of those of a never-ending eternity, but Daniel Gibbons is the only person she ever knew, who lived that doctrine. He believed in plainness of apparel as taught by Friends, not as a form or a rule of society, but as a principle; often quoting from some one who said that "the adornment of a vain and foolish world, would feed a starving one." He opposed extravagant fashions and all luxury of habit and life, as calculated to produce effeminacy and degrading sensuality, and as a bestowal of idolatrous attention upon that body which he would often say "was here but for a short time."

Looking only upon that as religion, which made men love each other and do good to each other in this world, he was little of a stickler for points of belief, and even when he did look into theological matters or denounce a man's religious opinions, it was generally because they were calculated to darken the mind and be entertained as a substitute for good works. Pursuing the even tenor of his way, he could as easily lead the flying fugitive slave by night out of the way of his powerful master, as one differently constituted could bestow his wealth upon the most popular charity in the land.

His faith was of the simplest kind—the Parable of the prodigal son, contains his creed. Discarding what are commonly called "plans of salvation," he believed in the light "which lighteth every man that cometh into the world," and that if people would follow this light, they would thus seek "the kingdom of Heaven and its righteousness and all other things needful would be added thereunto." He was a devoted member of the Society of Friends, in which he held the position of elder, during the last twenty-five years of his life. That peculiar doctrine of the Society, which repudiates systematic divinity and with it a paid ministry, he held in special reverence, finding confirmation of its truth in the general advocacy of Slavery, by the popular clergy of his day.

When he was quite advanced in years, and the Anti-slavery agitation grew warm, he was solicited to join an anti-slavery society, but on hearing the constitution read, and finding that it repudiated all use of physical force on the part of the oppressed in gaining their liberty, he said that he could not assent to that—that he had long been engaged in getting off slaves, and that he had always advised them to use force, although remonstrating against going to the extent of taking life, and that now he could not recede from that position, and he did not see how they could always be got off without the use of some force.

His faith in an overruling Providence was complete. He believed, even in the darkest days of freedom in our land, in the ultimate extinction of Slavery, and at times, although advanced in years, thought he would live to witness that glorious consummation. It is only in a man's own family and by his wife and children, that he is really known, and it is by those who best knew, and indeed, who only knew this good man, that his biographer is most anxious that he should be judged. As a parent, he was not excessively indulgent, as a husband, one more nearly a model is rarely found. But his kindness in domestic life, his love for his wife, his son and his grandchildren, and their reciprocal love and affection for him, no words can express.

It was in his father's household in his youth and in his own household in his mature years, that was fostered that wealth of love and affection, which, extending and widening, took in the whole race, and made him the friend of the oppressed everywhere, and especially of those whom it was a dangerous and unpopular task to befriend.

The tenderness and thoughtfulness of his disposition are well shown in the following incident : Upon one occasion, his son received a kick from a horse, which he was about to mount at the door. When he had recovered from the shock, and it was found that he was not seriously injured, the father still continued to look serious, and did not cease to shed tears. On being asked why he grieved, his answer was: "I was just thinking how it would have been with thee, had that stroke proved fatal." Such thoughts were at once the notes of his own preparation and a warning to others to be also ready.

A life consistent with his views, was a life of humility and universal benevolence, and such was his. It was a life, as it were in Heaven, while yet on earth, for it soared above and beyond the corrupt and slavish influences of earthly passions.

His interest in temperance never failed him. On his death-bed he would call persons to him, who needed such advice, and admonish them on the subject of using strong drinks, and his last expression of interest in any humanitarian movement, was an avowal of his belief in the great good to arise from a prohibitory liquor law.

To a friend, who entered his sick room, a few days before his death, he said : "Well, E., thee is preparing to go to the West." The friend replied: "Yes, and Daniel, I suppose thee is preparing to go to eternity." There was an affirmative reply, and E. inquired, "How does thee find it?" Daniel said : "I don't find much to do, I find that I have not got a hard master to deal with. Some few things which I have done, I find not entirely right." He quitted the earthly service of the Master, on the 17th day of the eighth month, 1852.

A young physician, son of one of his old friends, after attending his funeral, wrote to a friend, as follows : "To quote the words of Webster, 'We turned and paused, and joined our voices with the voices of the air, and bade him hail! and farewell!' Farewell, kind and brave old man! The voices of the oppressed whom thou hast redeemed, welcome thee to the Eternal City."

LUCRETIA MOTT.

Of all the women who served the Anti-slavery cause in its darkest days, there is not one whose labors were more effective, whose character is nobler, and who is more universally respected and beloved, than Lucretia Mott. You cannot speak of the slave without remembering her, who did so much to make Slavery impossible. You cannot speak of freedom, without recalling that enfranchised spirit, which, free from all control, save that of conscience and God, labored for absolute liberty for the whole human race. We cannot think of the partial triumph of freedom in this country, without rejoicing in the great part she took in the victory. Lucretia Mott is one of the noblest representatives of ideal womanhood. Those who know her, need not be told this, but those who only love her in the spirit, may be sure that they can have no faith too great in the beauty of her pure and Christian life.

This book would be incomplete without giving some account, however brief, of Lucretia Mott's character and labors in the great work to which her life has been devoted. To write it fully would require a volume. She was born in 1793, in the island of Nantucket, and is descended from the Coffins and Macys, on the father's side, and from the Folgers, on the mother's side, and through them is related to Dr. Benjamin Franklin. Her maiden name was Lucretia Coffin.

During the absence of her father on a long voyage, her mother was engaged in mercantile business, purchasing goods in Boston, in exchange for oil and candles, the staples of the island. Mrs. Mott says in reference to this employment: "The exercise of women's talent in this line, as well as the general care which devolved upon them in the absence of their husbands, tended to develop their intellectual powers, and strengthened them mentally and physically."

The family removed to Boston in 1804. Her parents belonged to the religious Society of Friends, and carefully cultivated in their children, the peculiarities as well as the principles of that sect. To this early training, we may ascribe the rigid adherence of Mrs. Mott, to the beautiful but sober costume of the Society.

When in London, in 1840, she visited the Zoological Gardens, and a gentleman of the party, pointing out the splendid plumage of some tropical birds, remarked: "You see, Mrs. Mott, our heavenly Father believes in bright colors. How much it would take from our pleasure, if all the birds were dressed in drab." "Yes;" she replied, "but immortal beings do not depend upon feathers for their attractions. With the infinite variety of the human face and form, of thought, feeling and affection, we do not need gorgeous apparel to distinguish us. Moreover, if it is fitting that woman should dress in every color of the rainbow, why not man also? Clergymen, with their black clothes and white cravats, are quite as monotonous as the Quakers." Whatever may be the abstract merit of this argument, it is certain that the simplicity of Lucretia Mott's nature, is beautifully expressed by her habitual costume.

In giving the principal events of Lucretia Mott's life, we prefer to use her own language whenever possible. In memoranda furnished by her to Elizabeth Cady Stanton, she says: "My father had a desire to make his daughters useful. At fourteen years of age, I was placed, with a younger sister, at the Friends' Boarding School, in Dutchess county, State of New York, and continued there for more than two years, without returning home. At fifteen, one of the teachers leaving the school, I was chosen as an assistant in her place. Pleased with the promotion, I strove hard to give satisfaction, and was gratified, on leaving the school, to have an offer of a situation as teacher if I was disposed to remain; and informed that my services should entitle another sister to her education, without charge. My father was at that time, in successful business in Boston, but with his views of the importance of training a woman to usefulness, he and my mother gave their consent to another year being devoted to that institution." Here is another instance of the immeasurable value of wise parental influence.

In 1809 Lucretia joined her family in Philadelphia, whither they had removed. "At the early age of eighteen," she says, "I married James Mott, of New York—an attachment formed while at the boarding-school." Mr. Mott entered into business with her father. Then followed commercial depressions, the war of 1812, the death of her father, and the family became involved in difficulties. Mrs. Mott was again obliged to resume teaching. "These trials," she says, "in early life, were not without their good effect in disciplining the mind, and leading it to set a just estimate on worldly pleasures."

To this early training, to the example of a noble father and excellent mother, to the trials which came so quickly in her life, the rapid development of Mrs. Mott's intellect is no doubt greatly due. Thus the foundation was laid, which has enabled her, for more than fifty years, to be one of the great workers in the cause of suffering humanity. These are golden words which we quote from her own modest notes : "I, however, always loved the good, in childhood desired to do the right, and had no faith in the generally received idea of human depravity." Yes, it was because she believed in human virtue, that she was enabled to accomplish such a wonderful work. She had the inspiration of faith, and entered her life-battle against Slavery with a divine hope, and not with a gloomy despair.

The next great step in Lucretia Mott's career, was taken at the age of twenty-five, when, "summoned by a little family and many cares, I felt called to a more public life of devotion to duty, and engaged in the ministry in our Society."

In 1827 when the Society was divided Mrs. Mott's convictions led her "to adhere to the sufficiency of the light within us, resting on the truth as authority, rather than 'taking authority for truth.'" We may find no better place than this to refer to her relations to Christianity. There are many people who do not believe in the progress of religion. They are right in one respect. God's truth cannot be progressive because it is absolute, immutable and eternal. But the human race is struggling up to a higher comprehension of its own destiny and of the mysterious purposes of God so far as they are revealed to our finite intelligence. It is in this sense that religion is progressive. The Christianity of this age ought to be more intelligent than the Christianity of Calvin. "The popular doctrine of human depravity," says Mrs. Mott, "never commended itself to my reason or conscience. I searched the Scriptures daily, finding a construction of the text wholly different from that which was pressed upon our acceptance. The highest evidence of a sound faith being the practical life of the Christian, I have felt a far greater interest in the moral movements of our age than in any theological discussion." Her life is a noble evidence of the sincerity of this belief. She has translated Christian principles into daily deeds.

That spirit of benevolence which Mrs. Mott possesses in a degree far above the average, of necessity had countless modes of expression. She was not so much a champion of any particular cause as of all reforms. It was said of Charles Lamb that he could not even hear the devil abused without trying to say something in his favor, and with all Mrs. Mott's intense hatred of Slavery we do not think she ever had one unkind feeling toward the slaveholder. Her longest, and probably her noblest work, was done in the anti-slavery cause. "The millions of down-trodden slaves in our land," she says, "being the greatest sufferers, the most oppressed class, I have felt bound to plead their cause, in season and out of season, to endeavor to put my soul in their soul's stead, and to aid, all in my power, in every right effort for their immediate emancipation." When in 1833, Wm. Lloyd Garrison took the ground of immediate emancipation and urged the duty of unconditional liberty without expatriation, Mrs. Mott took an active part in the movement. She was one of the founders of the Philadelphia Female Anti-Slavery Society in 1834. "Being actively associated in the efforts for the slave's redemption," she says, "I have traveled thousands of miles in this country, holding meetings in some of the slave states, have been in the midst of mobs and violence, and have shared abundantly in the odium attached to the name of an uncompromising modern abolitionist, as well as partaken richly of the sweet return of peace attendant on those who would 'undo the heavy burdens and let the oppressed go free, and break every yoke.'" In 1840 she attended the World's Anti-Slavery Convention in London. Because she was a woman she was not admitted as a delegate. All the female delegates, however, were treated with courtesy, though not with justice. Mrs. Mott spoke frequently in the liberal churches of England, and her influence outside of the Convention had great effect on the Anti-Slavery movement in Great Britain.

But the value of Mrs. Mott's anti-slavery work is not limited to what she individually did, great as that labor was. Her influence over others, and especially the young, was extraordinary. She made many converts, who went forth to spread the great ideas of freedom throughout the land. No one can of himself accomplish great good. He must labor through others, he must inspire them, convince the unbelieving, kindle the fires of faith in doubting souls, and in the unequal fight of Right with Wrong make Hope take the place of despair. This Lucretia Mott has done. Her example was an inspiration.

In the Temperance reform Mrs. Mott took an early interest, and for many years she has practiced total abstinence from intoxicating drinks In the cause of Peace she has been ever active, believing in the "ultra non-resistance ground, that no Christian can consistently uphold and actively engage in and support a government based on the sword." Yet this, we believe, did not prevent her from taking a profound interest in the great war for the Union; though she deplored the means, her soul must have exulted in the result. Through anguish and tears, blood and death America wrought out her salvation. Do we not believe that the United States leads the cause of human freedom? It follows then that the abolition of the gigantic system of human slavery in this country is the grandest event in modern history. Mrs. Mott has also been earnestly engaged in aid of the working classes, and has labored effectively for "a radical change in the system which makes the rich richer, and the poor poorer." In the Woman's Rights question she was early interested, and with Mrs. Elizabeth Cady Stanton, she organized, in 1848, a Woman's Rights' Convention at Seneca Falls, New York. At the proceedings of this meeting, "the nation was convulsed with laughter." But who laughs now at this irresistible reform?

The public career of Lucretia Mott is in perfect harmony with her private life. "My life in the domestic sphere," she says, "has passed much as that of other wives and mothers of this country. I have had six children. Not accustomed to resigning them to the care of a nurse, I was much confined to them during their infancy and childhood." Notwithstanding her devotion to public matters her private duties were never neglected. Many of our readers will no doubt remember Mrs. Mott at Anti-slavery meetings, her mind intently fixed upon the proceedings, while her hands were as busily engaged in useful sewing or knitting. It is not our place to inquire too closely into this social circle, but we may say that Mrs. Mott's history is a living proof that the highest public duties may be reconciled with perfect fidelity to private responsibilities. It is so with men, why should it be different with women?

In her marriage, Mrs. Mott was fortunate. James Mott was a worthy partner for such a woman. He was born in June, 1788, in Long Island. He was an anti-slavery man, almost before such a thing as anti-slavery was known. In 1812 he refused to use any article which was produced by slave labor. The directors of that greatest of all railway corporations, the Underground Rail Road, will never forget his services. He died, January 26, 1868, having nearly completed his 80th year. "Not only in regard to Slavery," said the "Philadelphia Morning Post," at the time, "but in all things was Mr. Mott a reformer, and a radical, and while his principles were absolute, and his opinions uncompromising, his nature was singularly generous and humane. Charity was not to him a duty, but a delight; and the benevolence, which, in most good men, has some touch of vanity or selfishness, always seemed in him pure, unconscious and disinterested. His life was long and happy, and useful to his fellow-men. He had been married for fifty-seven years, and none of the many friends of James and Lucretia Mott, need be told how much that union meant, nor what sorrow comes with its end in this world." Mary Grew pronounced his fitting epitaph when she said: " He was ever calm, steadfast, and strong in the fore front of the conflict."

In her seventy-ninth year, the energy of Lucretia Mott is undiminished, and her soul is as ardent in the cause to which her life has been devoted, as when in her youth she placed the will of a true woman against the impotence of prejudiced millions. With the abolition of Slavery, and the passage of the Fifteenth Amendment, her greatest life-work ended. Since then, she has given much of her time to the Female Suffrage movement, and so late as November, 1871, she took an active part in the Annual Meeting of the Pennsylvania Peace Society.

Since the great law was enacted, which made all men, black or white, equal in political rights—as they were always equal in the sight of God— Mrs. Mott has made it her business to visit every colored church in Philadelphia. This we may regard as the formal closing of fifty years of work in behalf of a race which she has seen raised from a position of abject servitude, to one higher than that of a monarch's throne. But though she may have ended this Anti-slavery work, which is but the foundation of the destiny of the colored race in America, her influence is not ended—*that* cannot die; it must live and grow and deepen, and generations hence the world will be happier and better that Lucretia Mott lived and labored for the good of all mankind.

JAMES MILLER McKIM.

More vividly than it is possible for the pen to portray, the subject of this sketch recalls the struggles of the worst years of Slavery, when the conflict was most exciting and interesting, when more minds were aroused, and more laborers were hard at work in the field; when more anti-slavery speeches were made, tracts, papers, and books, were written, printed and distributed; when more petitions were signed for the abolition of Slavery; in a word, when the barbarism of Slavery was more exposed and condemned than ever before, in the same length of time. Abolitionists were then intensely in earnest, and determined never to hold their peace or cease their warfare, until *immediate* and *unconditional* emancipation was achieved.

On the other hand, during this same period, it is not venturing too much to assert that the slave power was more oppressive than ever before;

slave enactments more cruel; the spirit of Slavery more intolerant; the fetters more tightly drawn; perilous escapes more frequent; slave captures and slave hunts more appalling; in short, the enslavers of the race had never before so defiantly assumed that negro Slavery was sanctioned by the Divine laws of God.

Thus, while these opposing agencies were hotly contesting the rights of man, James Miller McKim, as one of the earliest, most faithful, and ablest abolitionists in Pennsylvania, occupied a position of influence, labor and usefulness, scarcely second to Mr. Garrison.

For at least fourteen of the eventful years referred to, it was the writer's privilege to occupy a position in the Anti-slavery office with Mr. McKim, and the best opportunity was thus afforded to observe him under all circumstances while battling for freedom. As a helper and friend of the fleeing bondman, in numberless instances the writer has marked well his kind and benevolent spirit, before and after the formation of the late Vigilance Committee. At all times when the funds were inadequate, his aid could be counted upon for sure relief. He never failed the fugitive in the hour of need. Whether on the Underground Rail Road bound for Canada, or before a United States commissioner trying a fugitive case, the slave found no truer friend than Mr. McKim.

If the records of the Pennsylvania Society for Promoting the Abolition of Slavery, and the Pennsylvania Anti-slavery Society were examined and written out by a pen, as competent as Mr. McKim's, two or three volumes of a most thrilling, interesting, and valuable character could be furnished to posterity. But as his labors have been portrayed for these pages, by a hand much more competent than the writer's, it only remains to present it as follows:

The subject of this sketch was born in Carlisle, Pennsylvania, November 14, 1810, the oldest but one of eight children. On his father's side, he was of Scotch Irish, on his mother's (Miller) of German descent. He graduated at Dickinson College in 1828; and entering upon the study of medicine, attended one or more courses of lectures in the University of Pennsylvania. Before he was ready to take his degree, his mind was powerfully turned towards religion, and he relinquished medicine for the study of divinity, entering the Theological Seminary at Princeton, in the fall of 1831, and a year later, being matriculated at Andover. The death of his parents, however, and subsequently that of his oldest brother, made his connection with both these institutions a very brief one, and he was obliged, as the charge of the family now devolved upon him, to continue his studies privately at home, under the friendly direction of the late Dr. Duffield. An ardent and pronounced disciple of the "New School" of Presbyterians, belonging to a strongly Old School Presbytery; he was able to secure license and ordination only by transfer to another; and, in October, 1835, he accepted a pulpit in Womelsdorf, Berks County, Pa., where he preached for one year, to a Presbyterian congregation, to what purpose, and with what views, may be learned from the following passage taken from one of his letters, written more than twenty years afterwards, to the *National Anti-Slavery Standard.*

"The first settled pastor of this little flock was one sufficiently well-known to such of your readers as will be interested in this, to make mention of his name unnecessary. He had studied for the ministry with a strong desire, and a half formed purpose to become a missionary in foreign lands. Before he had proceeded far in his studies, however, he became alive to the claims of the 'perishing heathen' here at home. When he received his licensure, his mind was divided between the still felt impulse of his first purpose and the pressure of his later convictions. While yet unsettled on this point, the case of the little church at Womelsdorf was made known to him, followed by an urgent request from the people and from the Home Missionary Society to take charge of it. He acceded to the request and remained there one year, zealously performing the duties of his office to the best of his knowledge and ability. The people, earnest and simple-hearted, desired the 'sincere milk of the Word,' and receiving it 'grew thereby.' All the members of the church became avowed abolitionists. They showed their faith by their works, contributing liberally to the funds of the Anti-slavery Society. Many a seasonable donation has our Pennsylvania organization received from that quarter. For though their anti-slavery minister had left and had been followed by others of different sentiments and though he had withdrawn from the church with which they were in common connected, and that on grounds which subjected him to the imputation and penalties af heresy, these good people did not feel called upon to change their relations of personal friendship, nor did they make it a pretext, as others have done, for abandoning the cause."

In October, 1836, he accepted a lecturing agency under the American Anti-slavery Society, as one of the "seventy," gathered from all professions, whom Theodore D. Weld had by his eloquence inspired to spread the gospel of emancipation. Mr. McKim had long before this had his attention drawn to the subject of slavery, in the summer of 1832; and the reading of Garrison's "Thoughts on Colonization," at once made him an abolitionist. He was an appointed delegate to the Convention which formed the American Anti-slavery Society, and enjoyed the distinction of being the youngest member of that body.* Henceforth the object of the society, and of his ministry became inseparable in his mind.

* It may be a matter of some interest to state that the original draft of the Declaration of Sentiments adopted at this meeting, together with the autographs of the signers, is now in the keeping of the New York Historical Society.

In the following summer, 1834, he delivered in Carlisle two addresses in favor of immediate emancipation, which excited much discussion and bitter feeling in that border community, and gained him no little obloquy, which was of course increased when, as a lecturer, on the regular stipend of eight dollars a week and travelling expenses, ("pocket lined with British gold" was the current charge), he traversed his native state, among a people in the closest geographical, commercial, and social contact with the system of slavery. His fate was not different from that of his colleagues, in respect of interruptions of his meetings by mob violence, personal assaults with stale eggs and other more dangerous missiles, and a public sentiment which everywhere encouraged and protected the rioters.

Meantime, a radical change of opinion on theological questions, led Mr. McKim formally to sever his connection with the Presbyterian Church, and ministry. Being now free to act without sectarian constraint, he was, in the beginning of 1840, made Publishing Agent of the Pennsylvania Anti-slavery Society, which caused him to settle in Philadelphia, where he was married, in October, to Sarah A. Speakman, of Chester county. The chief duties of his office at first, were the publication and management of the *Pennsylvania Freeman*, including, for an interval after the retirement of John G. Whittier, the editorial conduct of that paper. In course of time his functions were enlarged, and under the title of Corresponding Secretary, he performed the part of a factotum and general manager, with a share in all the anti-slavery work, local and national. After the consolidation of the *Freeman* with the *Standard*, in 1854, he became the official correspondent of the latter paper, his letters serving to some extent as a substitute for the discontinued *Freeman*. The operations of the Underground Rail Road came under his review and partial control, as has already appeared in these pages, and the slave cases which came before the courts claimed a large share of his attention. After the passage of the Fugitive Slave Law, in 1851, his duties in this respect were arduous and various, as may be inferred from one of his private letters to an English friend, which found its way into print abroad, and which will be found in another place. (See p. 581).

During the John Brown excitement Mr. McKim had the privilege of accompanying Mrs. Brown in her melancholy errand to Harper's Ferry, to take her last leave of her husband before his execution, and to bring away the body. His companions on that painful but memorable journey, were his wife, and Hector Tyndale, Esq., afterwards honorably distinguished in the war as General Tyndale. Returning with the body of the hero and martyr, still in company with Mrs. Brown, Mr. McKim proceeded to North Elba, where he and Wendell Phillips, who had joined him in New York with a few other friends gathered from the neighborhood, assisted in the final obsequies.

When the war broke out, Mr. McKim was one of the first to welcome it

42

as the harbinger of the slave's deliverance, and the country's redemption. " A righteous war," he said, " is better than a corrupt peace. * * * When war can only be averted by consenting to crime, then welcome war with all its calamities." In the winter of 1862, after the capture of Port Royal, he procured the calling of a public meeting of the citizens of Philadelphia to consider and provide for the wants of the ten thousand slaves who had been suddenly liberated. One of the results of this meeting was the organization of the Philadelphia Port Royal Relief Committee. By request he visited the Sea Islands, accompanied by his daughter, and on his return made a report which served his associates as a basis of operations, and which was republished extensively in this country and abroad.

After the proclamation of emancipation, he advocated an early dissolution of the anti-slavery organization, and at the May Meeting of the American Anti-slavery Society, in 1864, introduced a proposition looking to that result. It was favorably received by Mr. Garrison and others, but no action was taken upon it at that time. When the question came up the following year, the proposition to disband was earnestly supported by Mr. Garrison, Mr. Quincy, Mr. May, Mr. Johnson, and others, but was strongly opposed by Wendell Phillips and his friends, among whom from Philadelphia were Mrs. Mott, Miss Grew, and Robert Purvis, and was decided by a vote in the negative.

Mr. McKim was an early advocate of colored enlistments, as a means of lifting up the blacks and putting down the rebellion. In the spring of 1863, he urged upon the Philadelphia Union League, of which he was a member, the duty of recruiting colored soldiers ; as the result, on motion of Thomas Webster, Esq., a movement was set on foot which led to the organization of the Philadelphia Supervisory Committee, and the subsequent establishment of Camp William Penn, with the addition to the national army, of eleven colored regiments.

When, in November, 1863, the Port Royal Relief Committee was enlarged into the Pennsylvania Freedman's Relief Association, Mr. McKim was made its corresponding secretary. He had previously resigned his place in the Anti-slavery Society, believing that that organization was near the end of its usefulness.

In the freedmen's work, he traveled extensively, and worked hard, establishing schools at the South and organizing public sentiment in the free States. In the spring of 1865, he was made corresponding secretary of the American Freedman's Commission, which he had helped to establish, and took up his residence in the city of New York. This association was afterwards amplified, in name and scope, into the American Freedman's Union Commission, and Mr. McKim continued with it as corresponding secretary, laboring for reconstruction by means of Freedman's schools, and impartial popular education. On the 1st of July, 1869, the Commission, by unani-

J. MILLER McKIM.

See p. 654.

REV. WILLIAM H. FURNESS.

See p. 659.

WILLIAM LLOYD GARRISON.

See p. 665.

LEWIS TAPPAN.

See p. 680.

EMINENT ANTI–SLAVERY MEN.

mous vote on his motion, disbanded, and handed over the funds in its treasury to its constituent State associations. Mr. McKim retired from his labors with impaired health, and has since taken no open part in public affairs. He is one of the proprietors of the New York *Nation*, in the establishment of which, he took an effective interest.

Mr. McKim's long and assiduous career in the anti-slavery cause, has given evidence of a peculiar fitness in him for the functions he successively discharged. His influence upon men and the times, has been less as a speaker, than as a writer, and perhaps still less as a writer than as an organizer, a contriver of ways and means; fertile in invention, prepared to take the initiative, and bringing to the conversion of others, an earnestness of purpose and a force of language that seldom failed of success. In an enterprise where theory and sentiment were fully represented, and business capacity, and what is called "practical sense," were comparatively rare, his talents were most usefully employed; while, in periods of excitement— and when were such wanting? his caution, sound judgment, and mental balance were qualities hardly less needed or less important.

WILLIAM H. FURNESS, D. D.

Among the Abolitionists of Pennsylvania no man stands higher than Dr. Furness; and no anti-slavery minister enjoys more universal respect. For more than thirty years he bore faithful witness for the black man; in season and out of season contending for his rights. When others deserted the cause he stood firm; when associates in the ministry were silent he spoke out. They defined their position by declaring themselves "as much opposed to slavery as ever, but without sympathy for the abolitionists." He defined his by showing himself more opposed to slavery than ever, and fraternizing with the most hated and despised anti-slavery people.

Dr. Furness came into the cause when it was in its infancy, and had few adherents. From that time till the day of its triumph he was one with it, sharing in all its trials and vicissitudes. In the operations of the Vigilance Committee he took the liveliest interest. Though not in form a member he was one of its chief co-laborers. He brought it material aid continually, and was one of its main reliances for outside support. His quick sympathies were easily touched and when touched were sure to prompt him to corresponding action. He would listen with moistened eyes to a tale of outrage, and go away saying never a word. But the story of wrong would work upon him; and through him upon others. His own feelings were communicated to his friends, and his friends would send gifts to the Committee's treasury. A wider spread sympathy would manifest itself in the community, and the general interests of the cause be visibly promoted. It was in the latter respect, that of moral co-operation, that Dr.

Furness's services were most valuable. After hearing a harrowing recital, whether he would or not, it became the burden of his next Sunday's sermon. Abundant proof of this may be found in his printed discourses. Take the following as an illustration. It is an extract from a sermon delivered on the 29th of May, 1854, a period when the slave oligarchy was at the height of its power and was supported at the North by the most violent demonstrations of sympathy. The text was, "Feed my Lambs:"

"And now brothers, sisters, children, give me your hearts, listen with a will to what I have to say. As heaven is my witness, I would not utter one word save for the dear love of Christ and of God, and the salvation of your own souls. Does it require any violent effort of the mind to suppose Christ to address each one of us personally the same question that He put to Peter, 'Lovest thou me?' * * * And at the hearing of His brief command, 'Feed my lambs,' so simple, so direct, so unqualified, are we prompted like the teacher of the law who, when Christ bade him love his neighbor as himself, asked, 'And who is my neighbor?' and in the parable of the good Samaritan, received an answer that the Samaritans whom he despised, just as we despise the African, was his neighbor, are we prompted in like manner to ask, 'Who are the lambs of Christ?' Who are His lambs? Behold that great multitude, more than three millions of men and feeble women and children, wandering on our soil; no not wandering, but chained down, not allowed to stir a step at their own free will, crushed and hunted with all the power of one of the mightiest nations that the world has yet seen, wielded to keep them down in the depths of the deepest degradation into which human beings can be plunged. These, then that we despise, are our neighbors, the poor, stricken lambs of Christ.

To cast one thought towards them, may well cause us to bow down our heads in the very dust with shame. No wonder that professing to love Christ and his religion, we do not like to hear them spoken of; for so far from feeding the lambs of Christ, we are exciting the whole associated power of this land, to keep them from being fed. 'Feed my lambs.' We might feed them with fraternal sympathy, with hope, with freedom, the imperishable bread of Heaven. We might lead them into green pastures and still waters, into the glorious liberty wherewith Christ died to make all men free, the liberty of the children of God. We might secure to them the exercise of every sacred affection and faculty, wherewith the Creator has endowed them. But we do none of those things. We suffer this great flock of the Lord Jesus to be treated as chattels, bought and sold, like beasts of burden, hunted and lacerated by dogs and wolves. I say we, we of these Free Northern communities, because it is by our allowance, signified as effectually by silence, as by active co-operation, that such things are. They could continue so, scarcely an hour, were not the whole moral, religious and physical power of the North pledged to their support. Are we not in closest league and union with those who claim and use the right to buy and sell human beings, God's poor, the lambs of Christ, a union, which we imagine brings us in as much silver and gold as compensates for the sacrifice of our humanity and manhood? Nay, are we not under a law to do the base work of bloodhounds, hunting the panting fugitives for freedom? I utter no word of denunciation. There is no need. For facts that have occurred only within the last week, transcend all denunciation. Only a few hours ago, there was a man with his two sons, hurried back into the inhuman bondage, from which they had just escaped, and that man, the brother, and those two sons, the nephews of a colored clergyman of New York, of such eminence in the New School Presbyterian Church, that he has received the honors of a European University, and has acted as Moderator in one of the Presbyteries of the same Church, when held in the city where he resides. Almost at the very moment the poor fugitive with his children, were dragged through our city, the General Assembly of that very branch of the Presbyterian Church, now in session here, after discussing for days the validity of Roman Catholic baptism, threw out as inexpedient to be discussed, the subject of that great wrong which was flinging back into the agony of Slavery, a brother of one of their own ordained ministers, and could not so much as breathe a word of condemnation against the false and cruel deed which has just been consummated at the capitol of the nation.

When such facts are occurring in the midst of us, we cannot be guiltless concerning the lambs of Christ. It is we, we who make up the public opinion of the North, we who consent that these free States shall be the hunting-ground, where these, our poor brothers and sisters, are the game; it is we that withhold from them the bread of life, the inalienable rights of man. As we withhold these blessings, so is it in our power to bestow them. The sheep then that Christ commands us, as we love Him, to feed, are those who are famishing for the lack of the food which it is in our power to supply. And we can help to feed and relieve and liberate them, by giving our hearty sympathy to the blessed cause of their emancipation, to the abolition of the crying injustice with which they are treated, by uttering our earnest protest against the increasing and flagrant outrages of the oppressor, by withholding all aid and countenance from the work of oppression."

To say that Dr. Furness, in his pleadings for the slave, was "instant in season and out of season," is not to exaggerate. So palpably was this true, that even some of his sympathizing friends intimated to him, that his zeal carried him beyond proper bounds, and that his discourses were needlessly reiterative. To these friends,—who, it is needless to say, did not fully comprehend the breadth and bearing of the question,—he would reply as he did in the following extract from a sermon delivered soon after the one above quoted:

"Again and again, I have had it said to me, with apparently the most perfect simplicity, 'Why do you keep saying so much about the slaves? Do you imagine that there is one among your hearers who does not agree with you? We all know that Slavery is very wrong. What is the use of harping upon this subject Sunday after Sunday? We all feel about it just as you do.' 'Feel about it just as I do.' Very likely, my friends. It is very possible that you all feel as much, and that many of you feel about it more than I do. God knows that my regret always has been not that I feel so much, but that I do not feel more. Would to Heaven that neither you nor I could eat or sleep for pity, pity for our poor down-trodden brothers and sisters. But the thing to which I implore your attention now, is, not what we know and feel, but the delusion which we are under, in confounding *knowing* with *doing*, in fancying that we are working to abolish Slavery because we know that it is wrong. This is what I would have you now to consider, the deception that we practise on ourselves, the dangerous error into which we fall, when we pass off the knowledge of our duty for the performance of it. These are two very distinct things. If you know what is right, happy are ye if ye do it.

Observe, my friends, what it is to which I am now entreating your consideration. It is not the wrongs nor the rights of the oppressed upon which I am now discoursing. It is our own personal exposure to a most serious mistake. It is a danger, which threatens our own souls, to which I would that our eyes should be open and on the watch.

And here, by the way, let me say that one great reason why I refer as often as I do, to that great topic of the day, which, in one shape or another, is continually shaking the land and marking the age in which we live, is not merely the righting of the wronged, but the instruction, the moral enlightenment, the religious edification of our own hearts, which this momentous topic affords. To me this subject involves infinitely more than a mere question of humanity. Its political bearing is the very least and most superficial part of it, scarcely worth noticing in comparison with its moral and religious relations. Once, deterred by its outside, political aspect, I shunned it as many do still, but the more it has pressed itself on my attention, the more I have considered it—the more and more manifest has it become to me, that it is a subject full of light and of guidance, of warning and inspiration for the individual soul. It is the most powerful means of grace and salvation appointed in the providence of Heaven, for the present day and generation, more religious than churches and Sabbaths. It is full of sermons. It is a perfect gospel, a whole Bible of mind-enlightening, heart-cleansing, soul-saving truth. How much light has it thrown for me on the page of the New Testament! What a profound significance has it disclosed in the precepts and parables of Jesus Christ! How do His words burst out with a new meaning! How does it help us to appreciate His trials and the God-like spirit with which He bore them!"

The dark winter of 1860 broke gloomily over all abolitionists; perhaps upon none did it press more heavily, than upon the small band in Philadelphia. Situated as that city is, upon the very edge of Slavery, and socially bound as it was, by ties of blood or affinity with the slave-holders of the South, to all human foresight it would assuredly be the first theatre of bloodshed in the coming deadly struggle. As Dr. Furness said in his sermon on old John Brown: "Out of the grim cloud that hangs over the South, a bolt has darted, and blood has flowed, and the place where the lightning struck, is wild with fear." The return stroke we all felt must soon follow, and Philadelphia, we feared, would be selected as the spot where Slavery would make its first mortal onslaught, and the abolitionists there, the first victims. Dr. Furness had taken part in the public meeting held on the day of John Brown's execution, to offer prayers for the heroic soul that was then passing away, and had gone with two or three others, to the rail-road station, to receive the martyr's body, when it was brought from the gallows by Mr. (afterwards General) Tyndale and Mr. McKim, and it was generally feared that he and his church would receive the brunt of Slavery's first blow. The air was thick with vague apprehension and rumor, so much so, that some of Dr. Furness's devoted parishioners, who followed his abolitionism but not his non-resistance, came armed to church, uncertain what an hour might bring forth, or in what shape of mob violence or assassination the blow would fall. Few of Dr. Furness's hearers will forget his sermon of December 16, 1860, so full was it of prophetic warning, and saddened by the thought of the fate which might be in store for him and his congregation. It was printed in the "Evening Bulletin," and made a deep impression on the public outside of his own church, and was reprinted in full, in the Boston "Atlas."

"But the trouble cannot be escaped. It must come. But we can put it off. By annihilating free speech; by forbidding the utterance of a word in the pulpit and by the press, for the rights of man; by hurling back into the jaws of oppression, the fugitive gasping for his sacred liberty; by recognizing the right of one man to buy and sell other men; by spreading the blasting curse of despotism over the whole soil of the nation, you may allay the brutal frenzy of a handful of southern slave-masters; you may win back the cotton States to cease from threatening you with secession, and to plant their feet upon your necks, and so evade the trouble that now menaces us. Then you may live on the few years that are left you, and perhaps—it is not certain—we may be permitted to make a little more money and die in our beds. But no, friends, I am mistaken. We cannot put the trouble off. Or, we put it off in its present shape, only that it may take another and more terrible form. If, to get rid of the present alarm, we concede all that makes it worth while to live—and nothing less will avail—perhaps those who can deliberately make such a concession, will not feel the degradation, but, stripped of all honor and manhood, they may eat as heartily and sleep as soundly as ever. But the degradation is not the less, but the greater, for our unconsciousness of it. The trouble which we shall then bring upon ourselves, is a trouble in comparison with which the loss of all things but honor is a glorious gain, and a violent death for right's sake on the scaffold, or by the hands of a mob, peace and joy and victory.

Since we are thus placed, and there is no alternative for us of the free States, but to meet the trouble that is upon us, or by base concessions and compromises to bring upon ourselves a far greater trouble, in the name of God, let us let all things go, and cleave to the right. Prepared to confront the crisis like men, let us with all possible calmness endeavor to take the measure of the calamity that we dread. God knows I have no desire to make light of it. But I affirm, that never since the world began, was there a grander cause for which to speak, to suffer and to die, than the cause of these free States, as against that of the States now rushing upon Secession. The great grievance of which they complain, is nothing more nor less than this: that we endanger the right they claim to treat human beings as beasts of burden. And they maintain this monstrous claim by measures inhuman and barbarous, listening not to the voice of reason or humanity, but treating every man who goes amongst them, suspected of not favoring their cause, or of the remotest connection with others who do not favor it, with a most savage and fiendish cruelty. It is the conflict between barbarism and civilization, between liberty and the most horrible despotism that ever cursed this earth, in which we are called to take part.

And all that is great and noble in the past, all the patriots and martyrs that have suffered in man's behalf, all the sacred instincts and hopes of the human soul are on our side, and the welfare of untold generations of men. Oh, if God, in his infinite bounty, grants us the grace to appreciate the transcendent worth of the cause which is now at stake, there is no trouble that can befall us, no, not the loss of property, of idolized parents or children, or life itself, that we shall not count a blessed privilege. To serve this dear cause of peace and liberty and love, we have no need to grasp the sword or any instrument of violence and death. But we must be ready without flinching, to confront the utmost that men can do, and amidst all the uproar and violence of human passions, still calmly to assert and to exercise our sacred and inalienable liberties, let who will frown and forbid, assured that no just and law-of-God-abiding people, will ever do otherwise than give us their sympathy and their aid.

Death is the worst that can befall us, if so be that we are faithful to the right. It is a solemn and a fearful thing to die, and mortality shrinks from facing that last great mystery. But we must all die, my friends, and the dying hour is not far distant from the youngest of us. To most of us it is very near. To many, only a few brief years remain. And for the sake of these few and uncertain years, shall we push off this present trouble upon our children, who have to stay here a little longer? There is nothing that can so sweeten the bitter cup of mortality when we shall be called to drink it, nothing that can so cheer us in the prospect of parting from all we love, nothing that can send such a blessed light on before us into the dark valley which we must enter, as the consciousness of fidelity to man and to God. And now in these times of great trouble which have come upon us, we have a peculiar and special opportunity of testifying our fidelity, and of enjoying a full experience of its power to support us. We may gather from this trouble, a sweetness that shall take away from all suffering its bitterness. We may kindle that light in our bosoms, which shall make death come to us as a radiant angel."

Four months after the above was uttered, on the 28th of April, 1861, after the attack on Fort Sumter, and the whole North had burst into a flame, people of all denominations flocked to Dr. Furness's church, as to that church which had shown that it was founded on a rock, and none can ever forget the long-drawn breath with which the sermon began: "The long agony is over!" It was the "*Te Deum*" of a life-time.

Dr. Furness's words and counsels were not wanting throughout the war, and his sermons were constantly printed in the daily press and in separate pamphlet form. And since its close he has continued his absorbing study of the historical accounts of Jesus.

Dr. Furness was born in Boston, in April, 1802, and was graduated at Harvard, in 1820, and five years later became the minister of the First Congregational Unitarian Christians, in this city, and is consequently the senior clergyman, here, on the score of length of pastorate.

Happy is the man, and enviable the gospel minister, who, looking back upon his course in the great anti-slavery contest, can recall as the chief charge brought against him, that of being over-zealous! That he spoke too often and said too much in favor of the slave! There are but few men, and still fewer ministers, who have a right to take comfort from such recollections! and yet it is to this small class that the cause is most indebted under God, for its triumph, and the country for its deliverance from Slavery.

WILLIAM LLOYD GARRISON.

The character and career of the leader of the movement for immediate emancipation in this country, are too well known to be dwelt on here; nor, in the space at our command, is it possible to give in full those facts of his life which have already appeared in print. His earliest biographer was Mary Howitt; and another even more famous authoress, Mrs. H. B. Stowe, in "Men of Our Times," has stood in the same relation to him, while his life-long friend, Oliver Johnson, has writen the best concise account of him, in "Appleton's New American Cyclopædia."

Mr. Garrison (the Cyclopædia is, on this point, in error) was born December 12, 1804, in Newburyport, Mass., his father, Abijah Garrison, being a ship-captain, trading with the West Indies, and his mother, Fanny Lloyd, a woman of remarkable beauty, as well as piety and force of character. Intemperate habits led the husband and father from home to a solitary and obscure end, leaving his family entirely dependent. William (or as he was always called, Lloyd), was the youngest but one of five children, and had not done with his schooling before he began to contribute to his own support; at first in Lynn, where he was set at shoemaking, at the age of eleven; afterwards in Newburyport, and finally, in 1818, at Haverhill, where he was apprenticed to a cabinet maker. Not finding these trades suited to his taste, the same year he was indentured to Ephraim W. Allen, editor of the " *Newburyport Herald*," and in the printing-office he completed his education, so far as he was to have any, with such early success, as soon to be an acceptable contributor to his employer's paper, while the authorship of his articles was still his own secret. As soon as his apprenticeship came to a close, in 1826, he became proprietor of the " *Free Press*," in his native city, but the paper failed of support. Seeking work as a journeyman, in Boston, he was engaged in 1827 to edit, in the interest of " total abstinence," the " *National Philanthropist*," the first paper of its kind ever published. On a change of proprietors in 1828, he was induced to join a friend in Bennington, Vt., in publishing the " *Journal of the Times*," which advocated the election of John Quincy Adams for president, besides being devoted to peace, temperance, anti-slavery and other reforms. In this town, Mr. Garrison began his agitation of the subject of Slavery, " in consequence of which there was transmitted to Congress an anti-slavery memorial, more numerously signed than any similar paper previously submitted to that body." It was in Bennington, too, that he received from Benjamin Lundy, who had met him the previous year at his boarding-house in Boston, an invitation to go to Baltimore, and aid him in editing the " *Genius of Universal Emancipation*."

Baltimore was no strange city to Mr. Garrison. Thither he had accompanied his mother, in 1815, serving as a chore-boy, and he had visited her just before her death, in 1823. He took leave of Boston in the fall of 1829, after having acted as the orator of the day, July 4th, in Park Street church, and surprised his hearers by the boldness of his utterances on the subject of Slavery. The causes of his imprisonment at Baltimore scarcely need to be repeated. For an alleged " gross and malicious libel " on a townsman (of Newburyport) whose ship was engaged in the coastwise slave-trade, and whom he accordingly denounced in the " *Genius*," he was tried and convicted, and sentenced to pay a fine of $50 and costs. The cell in which he was confined for forty-nine days, and from which he was liberated only by the spontaneous liberality of Arthur Tappan, a perfect stranger to him, he had the satisfaction of reseeking, after the close of the war, in company with Judge Bond, but the prison had been removed.

Compelled to part company with Lundy, to whom he has ever owned his moral indebtedness, Mr. Garrison at length started in Boston, in January 1831, his "*Liberator,*" with little else besides his "dauntless spirit and a press." The difficulties which beset the birth of this paper were never entirely overcome, and its publication was attended, through all the thirty-five years of its existence, with constant struggle and privation, and with personal labor, at the printer's case, and over the forms, which only an iron constitution could have endured. The "*Liberator*" was the organ of the editor alone, and he gave room in it to the numerous reforms which were, in his mind, only subordinate to abolition. In 1865 the last volume was issued, Mr. Garrison having already, in May, withdrawn from the American Anti-slavery Society, which he had helped to found, in 1833, and of which, as he drew up the Declaration of Sentiments, he may be supposed to have known something of the original aims and proper duration.

In September, 1834, Mr. Garrison was married to Helen Eliza, daughter of the venerable philanthropist, George Benson, of Providence, R. I., who had, even in the previous century, been an active member of a combined anti-slavery and freedmen's aid society in that city. In October, 1835, occurred the Boston riot, led by "gentlemen of property and standing," in which Mr. Garrison's life was imperilled, and which made him once more familiar with the interior of a jail—this time, a place of refuge. In 1832, he went to England, as an agent of the New England Anti-slavery Society, to awaken English sympathy for the anti-slavery movement, and to undeceive Clarkson and Wilberforce and their distinguished associates as to the nature and object of the Colonization Society, as to which he had already had occasion to undeceive himself. His mission was eminently successful in both its aspects, and resulted in the subsequent visits of George Thompson to this country, between whom and himself a strong personal attachment had arisen and has ever since continued. A second visit to England he made as a delegate to the World's Anti-slavery Convention, in which he refused to sit after his female colleagues had been rejected. A third visit, still in behalf of the cause, took place in 1846. Twenty years later—the war over and Slavery abolished—he again went abroad, to repair his health and renew old friendships, and for the first time passed over to the Continent. In England, he was greeted with cordial appreciation and hospitality by all classes. Numerous public receptions of a most flattering character were given to him, but without the effect of causing him to magnify his own merits or to forget the honor due to his associates in the anti-slavery struggle. At the London Breakfast, where John Bright presided, and John Stuart Mill, the Duke of Argyll, and others spoke, he said, when called upon to reply : " I disclaim, with all the sincerity of my soul, any special praise for anything I have done. I have simply tried to maintain the integrity of my soul before God, and to do my duty." In Edinburgh, the " freedom of the city " was conferred upon him with impressive ceremonies—he being the third American ever thus honored. In Paris he was also received with distinction, his special mission to that city being to attend the International Anti-slavery Convention, in the capacity of a delegate from the American Freedman's Union Commission, of which he was first vice-president.

The justice of the war on the part of the North, and its effect on the fate of Slavery at the South, were never subjects of doubt in the mind of Mr. Garrison, and he quickly recognized the force of events which had taken from the abolitionists the helm of direction, and reunited them with their countrymen in the irresistible flood which no man's hand guided, and no man's hand could stay. An agitator from conviction and not from choice, he was only too glad to lay down the heavy burden of a life-time, and retire to well-earned repose, after such a vision of faint hope realized as certainly no other reformer was ever blessed with. He had lived to see the disunion which he advocated on sacred principles, attempted by the South in the name of the sum of all villanies ; the uprising of the North ; the grand career of Lincoln ; the proclamation of emancipation ; the arming of the blacks—his own son among their officers ; the end of the rebellion ; and the consummation of his prayers and labors for the salvation of his country. He had taken part in the ceremonies at the recovery of Sumter, had walked the streets of Charleston, and received floral tokens of the gratitude of the emancipated. To him it seemed as if his work was done, and that he might, without suspicion or accusation, cease to be conspicuous, or to occupy the public attention in any way relating to the past and recalling his part in the anti-slavery struggle. Notoriety, no longer a necessity, was eagerly avoided ; and the physical rest which was now enjoined upon him the liberality of his friends having enabled him to secure, he settled down into the quiet life of a private citizen, whose great duty had become to him merely one of the duties which every man owes his country and his race. His sweet temper, his modesty, his unfailing cheerfulness, his rarely mistaken judgment of men and measures; his blameless and happy domestic life, and his hospitality ; his warm sympathy with all forms of human suffering— these and other qualities which cannot be enumerated here, will doubtless receive the just judgment of posterity.

As a fitting adjunct to the foregoing sketch, extracts from some of the speeches made at the London breakfast so magnanimously extended to Mr. Garrison in 1867, are here introduced. As presiding officer on the occasion, John Bright, M. P. spoke as follows :

SPEECH OF MR. BRIGHT, M. P.

The position in which I am placed this morning is one very unusual for me, and one that I find somewhat difficult; but I consider it a signal distinction to be permitted to take a prominent part in the proceedings of this day, which are intended to commemorate one of the greatest of the great triumphs of freedom, and to do honor to a most eminent instrument in the achievement of that freedom. (Hear, hear.) There may be, perhaps, those who ask what is this triumph of which I speak? To put it briefly, and, indeed, only to put one part of it, I may say that it is a triumph which has had the effect of raising 4,000,000 of human beings from the very lowest depths of social and political degradation to that lofty height which men have attained when they possess equality of rights in the first country on the globe. (Cheers.) More than this, it is a triumph which has pronounced the irreversible doom of slavery in all countries and for all time. (Renewed cheers.) Another question suggests itself—how has this great matter been accomplished? The answer suggests itself in another question. How is it that any great matter is accomplished? By love of justice, by constant devotion to a great cause, and by an unfaltering faith that that which is right will in the end succeed. (Hear, hear.)

When I look at this hall, filled with such an assembly; when I partake of the sympathy which runs from heart to heart at this moment in welcome to our guest of to-day, I cannot but contrast his present position with that which, not so far back but that many of us can remember, he occupied in his own country. It is not forty years ago, I believe about the year 1829, when the guest whom we honor this morning was spending his solitary days in a prison in the slave-owning city of Baltimore. I will not say that he was languishing in prison, for that I do not believe; he was sustained by a hope that did not yield to the persecution of those who thus maltreated him; and to show that the effect of that imprisonment was of no avail to suppress or extinguish his ardor, within two years after that he had the courage, the audacity—I dare say many of his countrymen used even a stronger phrase than that—he had the courage to commence the publication, in the city of Boston, of a newspaper devoted mainly to the question of the abolition of slavery. The first number of that paper, issued on the 1st January, 1831, contained an address to the public, one passage of which I have often read with the greatest interest, and it is a key to the future life of Mr. Garrison. He had been complained of for having used hard language, which is a very common complaint indeed, and he said in his first number: " I am aware that many object to the severity of my language, but is there not cause for such severity? I will be as harsh as truth, and as uncompromising as justice. I am in earnest, I will not equivocate, I will not excuse, I will not retract a single inch, and I will be heard." (Cheers.) And that, after all, expresses to a great extent the future course of his life.

But what was at that time the temper of the people amongst whom he lived, of the people who are glorying now, as they well may glory, in the abolition of slavery throughout their country? At that time it was very little better in the North than it was in the South. I think it was in the year 1835 that riots of the most serious character took place in some of the northern cities; during that time Mr. Garrison's life was in the most imminent peril; and he has never ascertained to this day how it was that he was left alive on the earth to carry on his great work. Turning to the South, a State that has lately suffered from the ravages of armies, the State of Georgia, by its legislature of House, Senate, and Governor, if my memory does not deceive me, passed a bill, offering ten thousand dollars reward, (Mr. Garrison here said five thousand) well, they seemed to think there were people who would do it cheap, (laughter) offered five thousand dollars, and zeal, doubtless, would make up the difference, for the capture of Mr. Garrison, or for adequate proof of his death. Now, these were menaces and perils such as we have not in our time been accustomed to in this country in any of our political movements, (hear, hear) and we shall take a very poor measure indeed of the conduct of the leaders of the emancipation party in the United States if we estimate them by any of those who have been concerned in political movements amongst us. But, notwithstanding all drawbacks, the cause was gathering strength, and Mr. Garrison found himself by and by surrounded by a small but increasing band of men and women who were devoted to this cause, as he himself was. We have in this country a very noble woman, who taught the English people much upon this question, about thirty years ago; I allude to Harriet Martineau. (Cheers.) I recollect well the impression with which I read a most powerful and touching paper which she had written, and which was published in the number of the *Westminster Review* for December, 1838. It was entitled "The Martyr Age of the United States." The paper introduced to the English public the great names which were appearing on the scene in connection with this cause in America. There was, of course I need not mention, our eminent guest of to-day; there was Arthur Tappan, and Lewis Tappan, and James G. Birney of Alabama, a planter and slave-owner, who liberated his slaves and came north, and became, as I think, the first presidential candidate upon abolition principles in the United States. (Hear, hear.) There were besides them, Dr. Channing, John Quincy Adams, a statesman and President of the United States, and father of the eminent man who is now Minister from that people amongst us. (Cheers.) Then there was Wendell Phillips, admitted to be by all who know him perhaps the most powerful orator who speaks the English language. (Hear, hear.) I might refer to others, to Charles Sumner, the well-known statesman, and

Horace Greeley, I think the first of journalists in the United States, if not the first of journalists in the world. (Hear, hear.) But besides these, there were of noble women not a few. There was Lydia Maria Child; there were the two sisters, Sarah and Angelina Grimke, ladies who came from South Carolina, who liberated their slaves, and devoted all they had to the service of this just cause; and Maria Weston Chapman, of whom Miss Martineau speaks in terms which, though I do not exactly recollect them, yet I know described her as noble-minded, beautiful and good. It may be that there are some of her family who are now within the sound of my voice. If it be so, all I have to say is, that I hope they will feel, in addition to all they have felt heretofore as to the character of their mother, that we who are here can appreciate her services, and the services of all who were united with her as co-operators in this great and worthy cause. But there was another whose name must not be forgotten, a man whose name must live for ever in history, Elijah P. Lovejoy, who in the free State of Illinois laid down his life for the cause. (Hear, hear.) When I read that article by Harriet Martineau, and the description of those men and women there given, I was led, I know not how, to think of a very striking passage which I am sure must be familiar to most here, because it is to be found in the Epistle to the Hebrews. After the writer of that epistle has described the great men and fathers of the nation, he says: "Time would fail me to tell of Gideon, of Barak, of Samson, of Jephtha, of David, of Samuel, and the Prophets, who through faith subdued kingdoms, wrought righteousness, obtained promises, stopped the mouths of lions, quenched the violence of fire, escaped the edge of the sword, out of weakness were made strong, waxed valiant in fight, turned to flight the armies of the aliens." I ask if this grand passage of the inspired writer may not be applied to that heroic band who have made America the perpetual home of freedom? (Enthusiastic cheering.)

Thus, in spite of all that persecution could do, opinion grew in the North in favor of freedom; but in the South, alas! in favor of that most devilish delusion that slavery was a Divine institution. The moment that idea took possession of the South war was inevitable. Neither fact nor argument, nor counsel, nor philosophy, nor religion, could by any possibility affect the discussion of the question when once the Church leaders of the South had taught their people that slavery was a Divine institution; for then they took their stand on other and different, and what they in their blindness thought higher grounds, and they said, "Evil! be thou my good;" and so they exchanged light for darkness, and freedom for bondage, and good for evil, and, if you like, heaven for hell. *   *   *   *

There was a universal feeling in the North that every care should be taken of those who had so recently and marvellously been enfranchised. Immediately we found that the privileges of independent labor were open to them, schools were established in which their sons might obtain an education that would raise them to an intellectual position never reached by their fathers ; and at length full political rights were conferred upon those who a few short years, or rather months, before, had been called chattels, and things to be bought and sold in any market. (Hear, hear.) And we may feel assured, that those persons in the Northern States who befriended the negro in his bondage will not now fail to assist his struggles for a higher position.   *   *   *   *   *   *   *

To Mr. Garrison more than any other man this is due ; his is the creation of that opinion which has made slavery hateful, and which has made freedom possible in America. (Hear, hear.) His name is venerated in his own country, venerated where not long ago it was a name of obloquy and reproach. His name is venerated in this country and in Europe wheresoever Christianity softens the hearts and lessens the sorrows of men ; and I venture to say that in time to come, near or remote I know not, his name will become the herald and the synonym of good to millions of men who will dwell on the now almost unknown continent of Africa. (Loud cheers.)   *   *   *

To Mr. Garrison, as is stated in one of the letters which has just been read, to William Lloyd Garrison it has been given, in a manner not often permitted to those who do great things of this kind, to see the ripe fruit of his vast labors. Over a territory large enough to make many realms, he has seen hopeless toil supplanted by compensated industry ; and where the bondman dragged his chain, there freedom is established for ever. (Loud cheers.) We now welcome him amongst us as a friend whom some of us have known long ; for I have watched his career with no common interest, even when I was too young to take much part in public affairs ; and I have kept within my heart his name, and the names of those who have been associated with him in every step which he has taken ; and in public debate in the halls of peace, and even on the blood-soiled fields of war, my heart has always been with those who were the friends of freedom. (Renewed cheering.) We welcome him then with a cordiality which knows no stint and no limit for him and for his noble associates, both men and women.

    *   *   *   *   *   *   *   *

After this eloquent and able speech by the chairman, the honor of proposing an address to Mr. Garrison devolved upon the Duke of Argyll, who introduced the subject in the following glowing speech :

SPEECH OF THE DUKE OF ARGYLL.

Mr. Chairman, Ladies, and Gentlemen :—It is hard to follow an address of such extraordinary beauty, simplicity and power ; but it now becomes my duty at your command, sir, to move an address of hearty congratulation to our distinguished guest, William Lloyd Garrison. (Cheers.) Sir, this country is from time to time honored by the presence of many distinguished, and of a few illustrious men; but for the most part we are contented to receive them with that private cordiality and hospitality with which, I trust, we shall always receive strangers who visit our shores. The people of this country are not pre-eminently an emotional people; they are not naturally fond of public demonstrations; and it is only upon rare occasions that we give, or can give, such a reception as that we see here this day. There must be something peculiar in the cause which a man has served, in the service which he has rendered, and in our own relations with the people whom he represents, to justify or to account for such a reception. (Hear, hear.) As regards the cause, it is not too much to say that the cause of negro emancipation in the United States of America has been the greatest cause which, in ancient or in modern times, has been pleaded at the bar of the moral judgment of mankind. (Cheers.) I know that to some this will sound as the language of exaggerated feeling; but I can only say that I have expressed myself in language which I believe conveys the literal truth. (Hear, hear.)

I have, indeed, often heard it said in deprecation of the amount of interest which was bestowed in this country on the cause of negro emancipation in America, that we are apt to forget the forms of suffering which are immediately at our own doors, over which we have some control, and to express exaggerated feeling as to the forms of suffering with which we have nothing to do, and for which we are not responsible. I have never objected to that language in so far as it might tend to recall us to the duties which lie immediately around us, and in so far as it might tend to make us feel the forgetfulness of which we are sometimes guilty, of the misery and poverty in our own country; but, on the other hand, I will never admit, for I think it would be confounding great moral distinctions, that the miseries which arise by way of natural consequence out of the poverty and the vices of mankind, are to be compared with those miseries which are the direct result of positive law and of a positive institution, giving to man property in man. (Loud cheers.) It is true, also, that there have been forms of servitude, meaning thereby compulsory labor, against which we do not entertain the same feelings of hostility and horror with which we have regarded slavery in America.

* * * * * * * *

It was a system of which it may be truly said, that it was twice cursed. It cursed him who served, and it cursed him that owned the slave. (Hear, hear.) When we recollect the insuperable temptations which that system held out to maintain in a state of degradation and ignorance a whole race of mankind; the horrors of the internal slave-trade, more widely demoralizing, in my opinion, than the foreign slave-trade itself; the violence which was done to the sanctities of domestic life; the corrupting effect which it was having upon the very churches of Christianity, when we recollect all these things, we can fully estimate the evil from which my distinguished friend

43

and his coadjutors have at last redeemed their country. (Cheers.) It was not only the Slave states which were concerned in the guilt of slavery; it had struck its roots deep in the free States of North America. * * *

We honor Mr. Garrison, in the first place, for the immense pluck and courage he displayed. (Cheers.) Sir, you have truly said that there is no comparison between the contests in which he had to fight and the most bitter contests of our own public life. In looking back, no doubt, to the contest which was maintained in this country some thirty-five years ago against slavery in our colonies, we may recollect that Clarkson and Wilberforce were denounced as fanatics, and had to encounter much opprobrium; but it must not be forgotten that, so far as regards the entwining of the roots of slavery into the social system, in the opinions and interests of mankind, there was no comparison whatever between the circumstances of that contest here and those which attended it in America. (Hear, hear.) The number of persons who in this country were enlisted on the side of slavery by personal interest was always comparatively few; whilst, in attacking slavery at its head-quarters in the United States, Mr. Garrison had to encounter the fiercest passions which could be roused. * * * *

Thank God, Mr. Garrison appears before us as the representative of the United States; freedom is now the policy of the government and the assured policy of the country, and we can to-day accept and welcome Mr. Garrison, not merely as the liberator of the slaves, but as the representative also of the American Government. (Cheers.) * * * *

THE ADDRESS TO WILLIAM LLOYD GARRISON, ESQ.

"Sir:—We heartily welcome you to England in the name of thousands of Englishmen who have watched with admiring sympathy your labors for the redemption of the negro race from slavery, and for that which is a higher object than the redemption of any single race, the vindication of the universal principles of humanity and justice; and who, having sympathized with you in the struggle, now rejoice with you in the victory.

"Forty years ago, when you commenced your efforts, slavery appeared to be rapidly advancing to complete ascendency in America. Not only was it dominant in the Southern States, but even in the Free States it had bowed the constituencies, society, and, in too many instances, even the churches to its will. Commerce, linked to it by interest, lent it her support. A great party, compactly organized and vigorously wielded, placed in its hands the power of the state. It bestowed political offices and honors, and was thereby enabled to command the apostate homage of political ambition. Other nations felt the prevalence in your national councils of its insolent and domineering spirit. There was a moment, most critical in the history of America and of the world, when it seemed as though that continent, with all its resources and all its hopes, was about to become the heritage of the slave power.

" But Providence interposes to prevent the permanent triumph of evil. It interposes, not visibly or by the thunderbolt, but by inspiring and sustaining high moral effort and heroic lives.

" You commenced your crusade against slavery in isolation, in weakness, and in obscurity. The emissaries of authority with difficulty found the office of the *Liberator* in a mean room, where its editor was aided only by a negro boy, and supported by a few insignificant persons (so the officers termed them) of all colors. You were denounced, persecuted, and hunted down by mobs of wealthy men alarmed for the interests of their class. You were led out by one of these mobs, and saved from their violence and the imminent peril of death, almost by a miracle. You were not turned from your path of devotion to your cause, and to the highest interests of your country, by denunciation, persecution, or the fear of death. You have lived to stand victorious and honored in the very stronghold of slavery ; to see the flag of the republic, now truly free, replace the flag of slavery on Fort Sumter ; and to proclaim the doctrines of the *Liberator* in the city, and beside the grave of Calhoun.

" Enemies of war, we most heartily wish, and doubt not that you wish as heartily as we do, that this deliverance could have been wrought out by peaceful means. But the fierce passions engendered by slavery in the slave-owner, determined it otherwise ; and we feel at liberty to rejoice, since the struggle was inevitable, that its issue has been the preservation, not the extinction, of all that we hold most dear. We are, however, not more thankful for the victories of freedom in the field than for the moderation and mercy shown by the victors, which have exalted and hallowed their cause and ours in the eyes of all nations.

" We shall now watch with anxious hope the development, amidst the difficulties which still beset the regeneration of the South, of a happier order of things in the States rescued from slavery, and the growth of free communities, in which your name, with the names of your fellow-workers in the same cause, will be held in grateful and lasting remembrance.

" Once more we welcome you to a country in which you will find many sincere admirers and warm friends."

EARL RUSSELL and JOHN STUART MILL, M. P., at the close of the address, followed with most eloquent speeches, conferring on the honored guest the highest praise for his life-long and successful labors in the cause of freedom. After these gentlemen had taken their seats, the Chairman proposed that the address should be passed unanimously.

The Chairman's call was responded to by the whole assemblage lifting up their hands ; and Mr. Garrison, presenting himself in front of the platform, was received with an enthusiastic burst of cheering, hats and handkerchiefs being waved by nearly all present.

SPEECH OF MR. GARRISON.

Mr. Garrison said:—Mr. Chairman, Ladies and Gentlemen,—For this marked expression of your personal respect, and appreciation of my labors in the cause of human freedom, and of your esteem and friendship for the land of my nativity, I offer you, one and all, my grateful acknowledgments. But I am so profoundly impressed by the formidable array of rank, genius, intellect, scholarship, and moral and religious worth which I see before me, that I fear I shall not be able to address you, except with a fluttering pulse and a stammering tongue. For me this is, indeed, an anomalous position. Assuredly, this is treatment with which I have not been familiar. For more than thirty years, I had to look the fierce and unrelenting hostility of my countrymen in the face, with few to cheer me onward. In all the South I was an outlaw, and could not have gone there, though an American citizen guiltless of wrong, and though that flag (here the speaker pointed to the United States ensign) had been over my head, except at the peril of my life; nay, with the certainty of finding a bloody grave. (Hear, hear.) In all the North I was looked upon with hatred and contempt. The whole nation, subjugated to the awful power of slavery, rose up in mobocratic tumult against any and every effort to liberate the millions held in bondage on its soil. And yet I demanded nothing that was not perfectly just and reasonable, in exact accordance with the Declaration of American Independence and the Golden Rule. I was not the enemy of any man living. I cherish no personal enmities; I know nothing of them in my heart. Even whilst the Southern slave-holders were seeking my destruction, I never for a moment entertained any other feeling toward them than an earnest desire, under God, to deliver them from a deadly curse and an awful sin. (Hear, hear.) It was neither a sectional nor a personal matter at all. It had exclusive reference to the eternal law of justice between man and man, and the rights of human nature itself.

Sir, I always found in America that a shower of brickbats had a remarkably tonic effect, materially strengthening to the back-bone. (Laughter.) But, sir, the shower of compliments and applause which has greeted me on this occasion would assuredly cause my heart to fail me, were it not that this generous reception is only incidentally personal to myself. (Hear, hear.) You, ladies and gentlemen, are here mainly to celebrate the triumph of humanity over its most brutal foes; to rejoice that universal emancipation has at last been proclaimed throughout the United States: and to express, as you have already done through the mouths of the eloquent speakers who have preceded me, sentiments of peace and of good-will toward the American Republic. Sure I am that these sentiments will be heartily reciprocated by my countrymen. (Cheers.)

I must here disclaim, with all sincerity of soul, any special praise for anything that I have done. I have simply tried to maintain the integrity of my soul before God, and to do my duty. (Cheers.) I have refused to go with the multitude to do evil. I have endeavored to save my country from ruin. I have sought to liberate such as were held captive in the house of bondage. But all this I ought to have done.

And now, rejoicing here with you at the marvellous change which has taken place across the Atlantic, I am unable to express the satisfaction I feel in believing that, henceforth, my country will be a mighty power for good in the world. While she held a seventh portion of her vast population in a state of chattelism, it was in vain that she boasted of her democratic principles and her free institutions; ostentatiously holding her Declaration of Independence in one hand, and brutally wielding her slave-driving lash in the other. Marvellous inconsistency and unparalleled assurance. But now, God be praised, she is free, free to advance the cause of liberty throughout the world. (Loud cheers.)

Sir, this is not the first time I have been in England. I have been here three times before on anti-slavery missions; and wherever I traveled, I was always exultantly told, "Slaves cannot breathe in England!" Now, at last, I am at liberty to say, and I came over with the purpose to say it, "Slaves cannot breathe in America!" (Cheers.) And so England and America stand side by side in the cause of negro emancipation; and side by side may they stand in all that is just and noble and good, leading the way gloriously in the world's redemption. (Loud cheers.)

I came to this country for the first time in 1833, to undeceive Wilberforce, Clarkson, and other eminent philanthropists, in regard to the real character, tendency, and object of the American Colonization Society. I am happy to say that I quickly succeeded in doing so. Before leaving, I had the pleasure of receiving a protest against that Society as an obstruction to the cause of freedom throughout the world, and, consequently, as undeserving of British confidence and patronage, signed by William Wilberforce, Thomas Fowell Buxton, Zachary Macaulay, and other illustrious philanthropists. On arriving in London I received a polite invitation by letter from Mr. Buxton to take breakfast with him. Presenting myself at the appointed time, when my name was announced, instead of coming forward promptly to take me by the hand, he scrutinized me from head to foot, and then inquired, somewhat dubiously, "Have I the pleasure of addressing Mr. Garrison, of Boston, in the United States?" "Yes, sir," I replied, "I am he; and I am here in accordance with your invitation." Lifting up his hands he exclaimed, "Why, my dear sir, I thought you were a black man. And I have consequently invited this company of ladies and gentlemen to be present to welcome Mr. Garrison, the black advocate of emancipation from the United States of America." (Laughter.) I have often said, sir, that that is the only compliment I have ever had paid to me that I care to remember or tell of. For Mr. Buxton had somehow or other supposed that no white American could plead for those in bondage as I had done, and therefore I must be black. (Laughter.)

It is indeed true, sir, that I have had no other rule by which to be guided than this. I never cared to know precisely how many stripes were inflicted on the slaves. I never deemed it necessary to go down into the Southern States, if I could have gone, for the purpose of taking the exact dimensions of the slave system. I made it from the start, and always, my own case, thus: Did I want to be a slave? No. Did God make me to be a slave? No. But I am only a man, only one of the human race; and if not created to be a slave, then no other human being was made for that purpose. My wife and children, dearer to me than my heart's blood, were they made for the auction-block? Never! And so it was all very easily settled here (pointing to his breast). (Great cheering.) I could not help being an uncompromising abolitionist.

Here allow me to pay a brief tribute to the American abolitionists. Putting myself entirely out of the question, I believe that in no land, at any time, was there ever a more devoted, self-sacrificing, and uncompromising band of men and women. Nothing can be said to their credit which they do not deserve. With apostolic zeal, they counted nothing dear to them for the sake of the slave, and him dehumanized. But whatever has been achieved through them is all of God, to whom alone is the glory due. Thankful are we all that we have been permitted to live to see this day, for our country's sake, and for the sake of mankind. Of course, we are glad that our reproach is at last taken away; for it is very desirable, if possible, to have the good opinions of our fellow-men; but if, to secure these, we must sell our manhood and sully our souls, then their bad opinions of us are to be coveted instead.

Sir, my special part in this grand struggle was in first unfurling the banner of immediate and unconditional emancipation, and attempting to make a common rally under it. This I did, not in a free State, but in the city of Baltimore, in the slave-holding State of Maryland. It was not long before I was arrested, tried, condemned by a packed jury, and incarcerated in prison for my anti-slavery sentiments. This was in 1830. In 1864 I went to Baltimore for the first time since my imprisonment. I do not think that I could have gone at an earlier period, except at the peril of my life; and then only because the American Government was there in force, holding the rebel elements in subserviency. I was naturally curious to see the old prison again, and, if possible, to get into my old cell; but when I went to the spot, behold! the prison had vanished; and so I was greatly disappointed, (Laughter.) On going to Washington, I mentioned to President Lincoln the disappointment I had met with. With a smiling countenance and a ready wit, he replied, "So, Mr. Garrison, the difference between 1830 and 1864 appears to be this: in 1830 you could not get out, and in 1864 you could not get in!" (Great laughter.) This was not only wittily said, but it truthfully indicated the wonderful revolution that had taken place in Maryland; for she had adopted the very doctrine for which she imprisoned me, and given immediate and unconditional emancipation to her eighty thousand slaves. (Cheers.)

I commenced the publication of the "*Liberator*" in Boston, on the 1st of January, 1831. At that time I was very little known, without allies, without means, without subscribers; yet no sooner did that little sheet make its appearance, than the South was thrown into convulsions, as if it had suddenly been invaded by an army with banners! Notwithstanding, the whole country was on the side of the slave power—the Church, the State, all parties, all denominations, ready to do its bidding! O the potency of truth, and the inherent weakness and conscious insecurity of great wrong! Immediately a reward of five thousand dollars was offered for my apprehension, by the State of Georgia. When General Sherman was making his victorious march through that State, it occurred to me, but too late, that I ought to have accompanied him, and in person claimed the reward—(laughter)—but I remembered, that, had I done so, I should have had to take my pay in Confederate currency, and therefore it would not have paid traveling expenses. (Renewed laughter.) Where is Southern Slavery now? (Cheers.) Henceforth, through all coming time, advocates of justice and friends of reform, be not discouraged; for you will, and you must succeed, if you have a righteous cause. No matter at the outset how few may be disposed to rally round the standard you have raised—if you battle unflinchingly and without compromise—if yours be a faith that cannot be shaken, because it is linked to the Eternal Throne—it is only a question of time when victory shall come to reward your toils. Seemingly, no system of iniquity was ever more strongly intrenched, or more sure and absolute in its sway, than that of American Slavery; yet it has perished.

> "In the earthquake God has spoken;
> He has smitten with His thunder
> The iron walls asunder,
> And the gates of brass are broken."

So it has been, so it is, so it ever will be throughout the earth, in every conflict for the right. (Great cheering.) * * * * * *

Ladies and gentlemen, I began my advocacy of the Anti-slavery cause at the North in the midst of brickbats and rotten eggs. I ended it on the soil of South Carolina, almost literally buried beneath the wreaths and flowers which were heaped upon me by her liberal bondmen. (Cheers.)

LEWIS TAPPAN

Was one of the warmest friends of the slave and of the colored man. He was very solicitous for their welfare, and that the colored people who were free should be enlightened and educated. He opened a Sunday-school for colored adults, which was numerously attended, in West Broadway, New York, and with a few others, devoted the most of the Sabbath to their teaching. When he and his brother Arthur, assembled the seventy anti-slavery agents, who were thereafter, like "firebrands," scattered all over the land, they held their meetings in this room. These agents were entertained by abolitionists in the city, and many of us had two or three of them in each of our families for a couple of weeks. They went out all over the land, and were instrumental in diffusing more truth, perhaps, about the dreadful system of American Slavery, than was accomplished in any other way. He also aided in establishing several periodicals, brimful of anti-slavery truth; among which, were the "*Anti-Slavery Record*," the "*Emancipator*," the "*Slave's Friend;*" the latter, to indoctrinate the children in Anti-slavery. The American Missionary Society, originally begun for the support of a mission in Africa, on the occasion of the return of the Amistad captors to their native land, and now doing so much for the freedmen of the South, was almost entirely established by his efforts. During the continuance of Slavery, much was done by this Society for the diffusion of an anti-slavery gospel.

The "Vigilance Committee," for aiding and befriending fugitives, of which I was treasurer for many years, had no better or warmer friend than he. He was almost always at their meetings, which were known only to "the elect," for we dared not hold them too publicly, as we almost always had some of the travelers toward the "north star" present, whose masters or their agents were frequently in the city, in hot pursuit. At first, we sent them to Canada, but after a while, sent them only to Syracuse, and the centre of the State.

In 1834, I think, was the first rioting, the sacking of Mr. Tappan's house, in Rose Street. The mob brought all his furniture out, and piling it up in the street, set it on fire. The family were absent at the time. Soon after, they stoned Rev. Mr. Ludlow's, and Dr. Cox's church, and the house of the latter. They threatened Arthur Tappan & Co's. store, in Pearl Street, but hearing that there were a few loaded muskets there, they *took it out in threats*. But their mercantile establishment was almost ostracised at this time, by the dry goods merchants; and country merchants in all parts of the country, north as well as south, did not dare to have it known that they bought goods of them; and when they did so, requested particularly, that the bundles or boxes, should not be marked "from A. Tappan & Co.," as was customary. Southern merchants especially, avoided them, and when, two or three years later, there was a general insolvency among them, occasionally large losses to New York merchants, and in some cases failure ; *the Tappans were saved by having no Southern debts !*

Through Mr. Tappan's influence and extensive correspondence abroad, many remittances came for the help of the "Vigilance Committee," from England and Scotland, and at one time, an extensive invoice of useful and fancy articles, in several large boxes, was received from the Glasgow ladies, sufficient to furnish a large bazaar or fair, which was held in Brooklyn, for the benefit of the Committee.

Although lately afflicted by disease, Mr. Tappan still lives in the enjoyment of all his faculties, and a good measure of health, and in his advanced years, sees now some of the great results of his life-long efforts for the restoration and maintenance of human rights.

Although still suffering under many of the evils which Slavery has inflicted upon him, the *American slave* no longer exists! Instead stands up in all our Southern States the *freedman*, knowing his rights, and, as a rule, enjoying them. Original American abolitionists, who met the scorn and odium, the imputed shame and obloquy, the frowns and cold-shoulders which they bore through all the dark days of Slavery, now see and feel their reward in some measure ; to be completed only, when they shall hear the plaudit: "Inasmuch as ye have done it to the least of these my brethren, ye have done it unto me."   Anthony Lane.

New York, Nov. 8, 1871.

Mr. Lane, Mr. Tappan's personal friend who labored with him in the Anti-Slavery Cause, and especially in the Vigilance Committee for many years, from serious affection of his eyes was not prepared to furnish as full a sketch of his (Mr. T.'s) labors as was desirable. Mr. Tappan was, therefore, requested to furnish a few reminiscences from his own store-house, which he kindly did as follows :

William Still, Esq., My dear Sir :—In answer to your request, that I would furnish an article for your forthcoming book, giving incidents within my personal knowledge, relating to the Underground Rail Road ; I have already apprized you of my illness and my consequent inability to write such an article as would be worthy of your publication. However, feeling somewhat relieved to-day, from my paralysis, owing to the cheering sunshine and the favor of my Almighty Preserver, I will try to do what I can, in dictating a few anecdotes to my amanuensis, which may afford you and your readers some gratification.

These facts I must give without reference to date, as I will not tax my memory with perhaps a vain attempt to narrate them in order.

As mentioned in my "Life of Arthur Tappan," some abolitionists (myself among the number), doubted the propriety of engaging in such measures as were contemplated by the conductors of the "Underground Rail Road," fearing that they would not be justified in aiding slaves to escape from their masters; but reflection convinced them that it was not only right to assist men in efforts to obtain their liberty, when unjustly held in bondage, but a DUTY.

Abolitionists, white and colored, both in slave and free States, entered into extensive correspondence, set their wits at work to devise various expedients for the relief from bondage and transmission to the free States and to Canada, of many of the most enterprising bondmen and bondwomen. They vied with each other in devising means for the accomplishment of this object. Those who had money contributed it freely, and those who were destitute of money, gave their time, saying with the Apostle: "Silver and gold have I none; but such as I have, give I thee."

1. I recollect that one morning on reaching my office (that of the treasurer of the American Missionary Association), my assistant told me that in the inner room were eighteen fugitives, men, women and children, who had arrived that morning from the South in one company. On going into the room, I saw them lying about on the bales and boxes of clothing destined for our various missionary stations, fatigued, as they doubtless were, after their sleepless and protracted struggle for freedom.

On inquiry, I learned that they had come from a southern city. After most extraordinary efforts, it seemed that they had while in Slavery, secretly banded together, and put themselves under the guidance of an intrepid conductor, whom they had hired to conduct them without the limits of the city, in the evening, when the police force was changed. They came through Pennsylvania and New Jersey to my office. The agent of the Underground Rail Road in New York, took charge of them, and forwarded them to Albany, and by different agencies to Canada.

2. I well remember that one morning as I entered the Sabbath-school,* one of the scholars, a Mrs. Mercy Smith, beckoned to me to come to her class, and there introduced to me a young girl of about fifteen, as a fugitive, who had arrived the day before. In answer to my inquiries, this girl told me the name of the southern city, and the names of the persons who had held her as a slave, and the mode of her escape, etc. " I was walking near the water," she said, " when a white sailor spoke to me, and after a few questions, offered to hide me on board his vessel and conduct me safely to New York, if I would come to him in the evening. I did so, and was hid and fed by him, and on landing at New York, he conducted me to Mrs. Smith's house, where I am now staying."

---

* For three years I superintended a Sabbath-school mostly composed of colored children and adults. Most of the teachers were warm-hearted abolitionists, and the whole number taught in this school during this period, was seven or eight hundred.

To my inquiry, have you parents living, and also brothers and sisters, she replied : "There is no child but myself." "Were not your parents kind to you, and did you not love them ?" "Yes I love them very much." "How were you treated by your master and mistress ?" "They treated me very well." "How then," said I, "could you put yourself in the care of that sailor, who was a stranger to you, and leave your parents ?" I shall never forget her heart-felt reply : *" He told me I should be free !"*

3. One Sunday morning, I received a letter, informing me that an officer belonging to Savannah, Ga., had started for New York, in pursuit of two young men, of nineteen or twenty, who had been slaves of one of the principal physicians of the place, and who had escaped and were supposed to be in New York. The letter requested me to find them and give them warning. As there was no time to be lost, I concluded to go over to New York, notwithstanding the doubtfulness of attempting to find them in so large a city. I wrote notices to be read in the colored churches and colored Sabbath-schools, which I delivered in person. I then went to the colored school, superintended by Rev. C. B. Bay. I stated my errand to him, with a description of the young men. "Why," said he, "I must have one of them in my school." He took me to a class where I found one of the young men, to whom I gave the needful information.

He told me that his father was Dr. ———, of Savannah, and that he had five children by the young man's mother, who was his slave. On his marriage to a white woman, he sent his five colored children and their mother to auction, to be sold for cash to the highest bidder. On being put upon the auction-block, this young man addressed the bystanders, and told them the circumstances of the case ; that his mother had long lived in the family of the doctor, that it was cruel to sell her and her children, and he warned the people not to bid for him, for he would no longer be a slave to any man, and if any one bought him, he would lose his money. He added, " I thought it right to say this." I then spoke to the crowd. "My father," said I, " has long been one of your first doctors, and do you think it right for him to sell my mother and his children in this way?"

" I was sold, and my brother also, and the rest, although my brother said to the crowd what I had said. We soon made our escape, and are now both in the city. I am a blacksmith, and have worked six months in one shop, in New York, with white journeymen, not one of whom believes, I suppose, that I am a colored man."

It was not surprising, for so fair was his complexion, that with the aid of a brown wig, after he had cut off his hair, he was completely disguised. He soon notified his brother, who lived in another part of the city, and both put themselves out of harm's way. They were remarkably fine young men, and it seemed a special Providence that I should find them in such a large city, and direct them to escape from their pursuer, within one hour after I left my house in Brooklyn. I felt it to be an answer to prayer.

4. One day, when I lived in New York City, a colored man came running to my house, and in a hurried manner, said: "Is this Mr. Tappan?" On replying in the affirmative, he said: "I have driven my master from Baltimore. He has just arrived, and the servants are taking off the baggage at the Astor House. I inquired of a person passing by, where you lived. He said, 80, White Street, and I have run here, to tell you that you may give notice to a man who has escaped from my master, to this city, that the object of this journey is to find him and take him back to Slavery."

The man hurried back, so that he need not be missed by his master, who believed that this coachman, who had lived years with him, was his confidential servant, and would be true to his interest.

I went immediately to the house of a colored friend, to describe the fugitive and see if we could not concert measures to protect him. "I think," said he, "that I know the man, by your description, and that he boards in this house. He will soon come in from South Street, where he has worked to-day." While we were consulting together, sure enough, the man came in, and was most glad to have the opportunity thus afforded, of secreting himself.

I have not strength to dictate much more, although many other instances occur to me of most remarkable providential occurrences, of the escape of fugitives within my knowledge. I used to say that I was the owner of *half-a-horse* that was in active service, near the Susquehanna River. This horse I owned jointly with another friend of the slave, dedicating the animal to the service of the Underground Rail Road.

It was customary for the agent at Havre de Grace, bringing a fugitive to the river, to kindle a fire (as it was generally in the night), to give notice to a person living on the opposite side of the river. This person well understood the signal, and would come across in his boat and receive the fugitive.

5. An aged colored couple, residing in Brooklyn, came over to my office, in New York City, and said that they had just heard from Wilmington, N. C., that their two sons (about twenty-five or twenty-six years of age), who were slaves, were about to be sold, for one thousand dollars each ; and they hoped I should be able and willing to assist them in raising the money.

I told them that I had scruples about putting money into the hands of slave-holders, but I would give them something that might be of as much value. I then pointed out a way by which their sons might reach the city.

In about three weeks, one of the young men came to my office. Give me, said I, some particulars of your escape. "I am," said he, "a builder, and planned and erected the hotel at Wilmington, and some other houses. I used to hire my time of my master, and was accustomed to ride about the country attending to my business. I borrowed a pass from a man about my size and complexion. I then went to the rail road office, and asked for a ticket for Fredericksburg. From there I came on directly to Washington. I had not been questioned before; but here, I was taken up and carried before a magistrate. He examined me by the description in my pass; complexion, height, etc., then read '*and a scar under his left knee.*' When I heard that, my heart sank within me; for I had no scar there that I knew. 'Pull up the boy's trowsers,' said the justice to the constable. He did so, and said 'here's a scar!' 'All right,' said the justice, 'no mistake, let him go.' Glad was I. I got a ticket for Baltimore, and there for another town, and finally reached here."

You asked me to give an account of the sums that I have expended for the Underground Rail Road, etc. I must be excused from doing this, as if I could now ascertain, I should not think it worth while to mention. I must now conclude my narrative, by giving, with some additions, an account of an interesting escape from Slavery, which was written by my wife, more than fifteen years ago, for Frederic Douglass' paper.

[On page 177 the narrative of "The Fleeing Girl of Fifteen" is so fully written out, that it precludes the necessity of reproducing a large portion of this story.]

In the evening a friend arrived, bringing with him a bright, handsome *boy*, whom he called Joe. Most heartily was "Joe" welcomed, and deep was the thrill which we felt, as we looked upon him and thought of the perils he had escaped. The next day was Thanksgiving-day, and my house was thronged with guests. In an upper room, with a comfortable fire, and the door locked, sat "Joe," still in boy's clothes, to be able to escape at the first intimation of danger, but with a smile and look of touching gratitude, whenever any one of the family who was in the secret, left the festive group to look in upon the interesting stranger. Not one of us can ever forget the deep abhorrence of Slavery, and thanksgiving to Almighty God, that we felt that day as we moved among the guests, who were wholly ignorant of the occupant of that upper room. Some curiosity was indeed excited among the little grandchildren, who saw slices of turkey and plum pudding sent up stairs. It was "Joe's" first Thanksgiving dinner in a free State.

As she brought nothing away with her, it was necessary, the next day, to procure a complete wardrobe for a girl, which was carefully packed for her to take with her.

The second day after "Joe's" arrival, the Rev. Mr. Freeman, pastor of a colored church in Brooklyn, agreed to accompany her to her uncle Brown's in Canada West, and we saw them depart, knowing the danger that would beset both on the way. The following is part of a letter from Mr. F., giving an account of their journey. After stating that they left New York, in the cars at five o'clock, P. M., and through the providence of God, went on their way safely and speedily, with none to molest or to make them afraid, he says:

"On reaching Rochester, I began to ask myself 'how shall we get over Niagara Falls?' I was not sure that the cars ran across the Suspension Bridge; besides, I felt that we were in more danger here, than we had been at any other place. Knowing that there was a large reward offered for Joe's apprehension, I feared there might be some lurking spy ready to pounce upon us. But when we arrived at the Bridge, the conductor said: 'Sit still; this car goes across.' You may judge of my joy and relief of mind, when I looked out and was sure that we were over! Thank God, I exclaimed, we are safe in Canada!

Having now a few minutes before the cars would start again, I sat down and hastily wrote a few lines, to inform friends at home of our safe arrival. As soon as possible, I ran to the post-office with my letter, paid the postage, and while I was waiting for my change, the car bell rang. I quickly returned, and in a few minutes, we were on our way to Chatham (200 miles West). That place we reached between seven and eight o'clock, Saturday evening. When we got out, we met a gentleman who asked me if I wanted a boarding-house. I said yes; and he invited me to go with him. I asked him if there was any way for us to get to Dresden that night. He answered, 'No, it is a dark night, and a muddy road, and no conveyance can be got to-night.' I soon found that we must stay in Chatham until Monday morning.

On our way to the boarding-house, the gentleman said to me: 'Is this your son with you?' I answered, no; and then I asked him, if he knew a man living in D., by the name of Bradley. He replied that he was very well acquainted with him, and then inquired if that young man was Mr. Bradley's brother. I said, no—not exactly a brother. He must have thought it strange that I did not give him a more definite answer to his question.

When we reached the house, we found several boarders in the sitting-room and a few neighbors. I had already told him my name, but with regard to Joe, I had not yet had a chance to explain. I, of course, was introduced to those who were in the room, but Joe—well, Joe took a seat, and did not seem to be troubled about an introduction. As the landlord was going out of the room, I asked permission to speak with him alone. He took me into another room, and I said to him: 'That young man, as you call him, is a young woman, and has come dressed in this manner, all the way from Washington City. She would be very glad now to be able to change her clothes.'

He was greatly surprised, and would hardly believe that it was so; but said, 'I will call my wife.' She came, and I guess all the women in the house came with her. They soon disappeared, and Joe with them, who, after being absent a while, returned, and was introduced as Miss Ann Maria Weems. The whole company were on their feet, shook hands, laughed, and rejoiced , declaring that this beat all they had ever seen before. Chatham contains, I was told, more than three thousand fugitives. The weather there, is not colder than in New York.

The next morning was the Sabbath, but this I must pass and hasten to D., the residence of Mr. Bradley. We started early Monday morning. As a part of the road was very bad, we did not reach there till a late hour. As we were passing along, and getting near to the place, we met two colored men who were talking together—one on horseback, and the other on foot. I inquired of them, if they could tell me how far it was to Mr. Bradley's. The man on horseback said it was about a mile further, and then proceeded to give directions. After he had done this, he said : 'I reckon I am the one that you want to find, my name is Bradley.' Well, I replied, probably you are the man. Just then Ann Maria turned her head around. As soon as he saw her face, he exclaimed : 'My Lord ! Maria, is that you ? Is that you ? My child, is it you ? We never expected to see you again ! We had given you up ; O, what will your aunt say ? It will kill her ! She will die ! It will kill her.'

I told him, that as I was obliged to leave again soon, I must proceed. 'Well,' said he, 'you go on ; I am just going over to M., and will be back in a few minutes.' We started for his house, and he towards M., but we had only gone a short distance, when he overtook us, exclaiming : 'I can't go to M.,' and began talking to Ann Maria, asking her all about her friends and relatives, whom they had left behind, and about his old master, and his wife's master, from whom they had run away four years before. As we approached the house, he said : 'I will go and open the gate, and have a good fire to warm you.' When he came up to the gate, he met his wife, who was returning from a store or neighbor's house, and he said to her, "That's Ann Maria coming yonder.' She stopped until we came to the gate; the tears were rolling from her eyes, and she exclaimed : 'Ann Maria, is it you ?' The girl leaped from the wagon, and they fell on each other's necks, weeping and rejoicing. Such a scene I never before witnessed. She, who had been given up as lost, was now found ! She, who but a short time. before, had been, as they supposed, a slave for life, was now free.

We soon entered the house, and after the first gush of feeling had somewhat subsided, they both began a general inquiry about the friends they had left behind. Every now and then, the aunt would break out : 'My child, you are here ! Thank God, you are free ! We were talking about you to-day, and saying, we shall never see you again ; and now here you are with us.' I remained about an hour and a half with them, took dinner, and then started for home, rejoicing that I had been to a land where colored men are free.

This Mr. Bradley, who ran away with himself and wife about four years ago from the land of whips and chains, is the owner of two farms, and is said to be worth three thousand dollars. Can slaves take care of themselves?"

You may well suppose that the receipt of this letter gave us great pleasure, and called forth heartfelt thanksgiving to Him, who had watched over this undertaking, and protected all concerned in it. A bright and promising girl had been rescued from the untold miseries of a slave woman's life, and found a good home, where she would have an opportunity to acquire an education and be trained for a useful and happy life. Mr. Bradley intended to send for her parents, and hoped to prevail on them to come and live with him.

Truly yours, LEWIS TAPPAN.

ELIJAH F. PENNYPACKER,

Whose name belongs to the history of the Underground Rail Road, owed his peculiarly fine nature to a mother of large physical proportions, and correspondingly liberal mental and spiritual endowments. She was a natural sovereign in the sphere in which she moved, and impressed her son with the qualities which made his Anti-slavery life nothing but an expression of the rules of conduct which governed him in all other particulars. Believing in his inmost soul in principles of rectitude, all men believed in him, his "yea," or "nay," passing current wherever he went. Tall, dignified, and commanding, he had that in his face which inspired immediate confidence. Said one who looked: "If that is not a good man, there is no use in the Lord writing His signature on human countenances." Even in early youth, honors which he never sought, were pressed upon him, as he gave assurance of ability commensurate with his worth. He was sent to the Legislature of Pennsylvania for five sessions, where he became the personal friend of the Governor, Joseph Ritner, and also of Thaddeus Stevens. At the request of the latter, he consented to occupy the position of Secretary to the Board of Canal Commissioners, and two years after, by the wishes of Mr. Ritner, took a seat in the Canal Board, becoming a co-worker with Thaddeus Stevens. Here ripened a friendship, which afterward became of national importance, for although a nature so positive as that of Thaddeus Stevens could scarcely be said to be under the influence of any other mind, still, if there were those who exercised a moral sway, sustaining this courageous republican leader, at a higher level than he might otherwise have attained, Elijah F. Pennypacker was surely amongst them. Almost antipodal as they were in certain respects, each recognized the genuine ring of the other, and admired and respected that which was most true and noble. The purity, simplicity and high-minded honor which distinguished the younger, had its effect on the elder, even while he smiled at the inflexibility which would not swerve one hair's breadth from the line of right. The story is often told, how, when this young man's conscience stood bolt upright in the way of what was deemed a desirable arrangement, Stevens one day exclaimed: "It don't do, Pennypacker, to be so d——d honest." Pennypacker stood his ground, and the life-long respect which Stevens ever after awarded, proved that *he* at least, thought it *did* do.

When it became clear to his mind, that a great battle was to be fought between Liberty and Slavery in America, Mr. Pennypacker felt it to be his duty to turn aside from the sunny paths of political preferment, into the shadows of obscure life, and ally himself with the misrepresented, despised and outcast Abolitionists, ever after devoting himself assiduously to the promotion of the cause of Freedom. Notwithstanding his natural modesty, here as elsewhere, he took a conspicuous position. At home, in the local Anti-slavery Society of his neighborhood, he was for many years chosen president, as he was also of the Chester county Anti-slavery Society, and of the Pennsylvania State Anti-slavery Society.

Soon after his retirement from public life, he united himself with the Society of Friends, but was much too radical to be an acceptable addition. For a long time he was endured rather than endorsed, and it was only when such anti-slavery feelings as he cherished became generally diffused throughout the Society, that he found the unity he desired and expected. Whatever may have been his trials here or elsewhere, he found a rich reward for his faithfulness in the intellectual and moral growth which he attained by association with the most advanced minds of the time, and he has often been heard to say that no part of his life has been more fully and generously compensated than that devoted to the Anti-slavery cause.

His home, near Phœnixville, Chester county, Pa., was an important station on the Underground Rail Road, the majority of fugitives proceeding through the southern rural districts of Eastern Pennsylvania, passing through his hands. At all times he was deeply interested in their welfare, and in his hospitality towards them, had the entire sympathy and co-operation of his family, they, like himself, being earnest abolitionists, but his more important duty of influencing public sentiment in favor of freedom, overshadowed his labors in this department. In steadfastness and integrity he stood beside Findley Coates and Thomas Whitson, a trio who will long be remembered in their native State.

So long as Dr. B. Fussell resided in the northern section of Chester county, he and Elijah F. Pennypacker, were companions in Anti-slavery and other reform labors, as well as in business on the Underground Rail Road. Differing widely in temperament and mental structure, these two men were harmonious in spirit, and a close bond of sympathy and affection existed between them. It was a mutual pleasure to work as brothers, and after-

44

ward to rejoice together in labor accomplished. One of the last visits which roused the flickering animation of the dying physician, was from this friend of more vigorous years, and the voice which gave fitting expression to the worth of the departed, at his funeral, was that of Elijah F. Pennypacker.

Like that of the highest grade of men everywhere, his appreciation of woman has ever been keen and true, and demanding the full rights of humanity, he makes no distinction, either on account of sex or color. In his own family, he has always encouraged the pursuit of any occupation congenial to the person choosing it; whether or not, it were a departure from the routine of custom, and in educational advantages he has ever demanded the widest possible culture for all. Wherever known, he is estimated as a pillar in the temperance cause. Gentle, modest, courteous and benignant, he combines, in a remarkable degree, strength and tenderness, courage and sympathy. At one time, holding at bay the powers of evil and baffling the most determined opponents by his manly adherence to right; at another he may be found yielding to impressions bidding him to seek the source of some hidden private sorrow, and with delicate touch, binding up a flowing wound, or offering himself as the defender and protector of such as may need his brotherly care. Obedient to these impressions, he rarely errs in his ministrations, and whether his errand be to remonstrate with the evil doer, setting his sins clearly and vividly before him, or to strengthen and encourage suffering innocence, he is alike successful. Men, whom he has warned in reproof when it cost the utmost bravery to do so, have become his confiding friends, and have been known afterward to entrust him with heavy pecuniary responsibilities, and to point him out to their children as an example worthy of imitation. Those whose griefs he has frequently softened, have laid upon his head a crown of blessing whiter than the honors which come with his silver hairs, and all with whom he comes in contact in business, in duty, or in social intercourse, acknowledge the presence, the wide usefulness and influence of the upright man.

The memories of the choice spirits he used to meet in the Anti-slavery gatherings; their mutual and kindly greetings; the holy resolves which animated them and made the time hours of exaltation, now serve to brighten the pathway of his declining years, and to throw a halo around the restfulness of his home, as in peace of mind he looks abroad over his beloved country, to see millions of enfranchised men beginning to avail themselves of its pecuniary, educational and political advantages, and beholds them starting on a career of material and spiritual prosperity, with a rapidity commensurate with the expansive force of the repressed energies of a race.

ELIJAH F. PENNYPACKER.

See p. 688

WILLIAM WRIGHT.

See p. 691.

DR. BARTHOLOMEW FUSSELL.

See p. 695.

ROBERT PURVIS.

See p. 711.

STATION MASTERS ON THE ROAD.

WILLIAM WRIGHT.

MEMORIAL.

WILLIAM WRIGHT, a distinguished abolitionist of Adams county, Pennsylvania, was born on the 21st of December, 1788. Various circumstances conspired to make this unassuming Quaker an earnest Abolitionist and champion of the oppressed in every land and of every nationality and color. His uncle, Benjamin Wright, and cousin, Samuel B. Wright, were active members of the old Pennsylvania Abolition Society, and at the time of the emancipation of the slaves in this state were often engaged in lawsuits with slave-holders to compel them to release their bondmen, according to the requirements of the law. William Wright grew up under the influence of the teachings of these relatives. Joined to this, his location caused him to take an extraordinary interest in Underground Rail Road affairs. He lived near the foot of the southern slope of the South Mountain, a spur of the Alleghenies which extends, under various names, to Chattanooga, Tennessee. This mountain was followed in its course by hundreds of fugitives until they got into Pennsylvania, and were directed to William Wright's house.

In November, 1817, William Wright married Phebe Wierman, (born on the 8th of February, 1790,) daughter of a neighboring farmer, and sister of Hannah W. Gibbons, wife of Daniel Gibbons, a notice of whom appears elsewhere in this work. Phebe Wright was the assistant of her husband in every good work, and their married life of forty-eight years was a long period of united and efficient labor in the cause of humanity. She still (1871) survives him. William and Phebe Wright began their Underground Rail Road labors about the year 1819. Hamilton Moore, who ran away from Baltimore county, Maryland, was the first slave aided by them. His master came for him, but William Wright and Joel Wierman, Phebe Wright's brother, who lived in the neighborhood, rescued him and sent him to Canada.

In the autumn of 1828, as Phebe Wright, surrounded by her little children, came out upon her back porch in the performance of some household duty, she saw standing before her in the shade of the early November morning, a colored man without hat, shoes, or coat. He asked if Mr. Wright lived there, and upon receiving an affirmative reply, said that he wanted work. The good woman, comprehending the situation at a glance, told him to come into the house, get warm, and wait till her husband came home. He was shivering with cold and fright. When William Wright came home the fugitive told his story. He came from Hagerstown, Maryland, having been taught the blacksmith's trade there. In this business it was his duty to keep an account of all the work done by him, which record he showed to his master at the end of the week. Knowing no written character but the figure 5 he kept this account by means of a curious system of hieroglyphics in which straight marks meant horse shoes put on, circles, cart-wheels fixed, etc. One day in happening to see his master's book he noticed that wherever five and one were added the figure 6 was used. Having practiced this till he could make it he ever after used it in his accounts. As his master was looking over these one day, he noticed the new figure and compelled the slave to tell how he had learned it. He flew into a rage, and said, "I'll teach you how to be learning new figures," and picking up a horse-shoe threw it at him, but fortunately for the audacious chattel, missed his aim. Notwithstanding his ardent desire for liberty, the slave considered it his duty to remain in bondage until he was twenty-one years old in order to repay by his labor the trouble and expense which his master had had in rearing him. On the evening of his twenty-first anniversary he turned his face toward the North star, and started for a land of freedom. Arriving at Reisterstown, a village on the Westminster turnpike about twenty-five miles from Baltimore and thirty-five miles from Mr. Wright's house, he was arrested and placed in the bar-room of the country tavern in care of the landlady to wait until his captors, having finished some work in which they were engaged, could take him back to his master. The landlady, being engaged in getting supper, set him to watch the cakes that were baking. As she was passing back and forth he ostentatiously removed his hat, coat, and shoes, and placed them in the bar-room. Having done this, he said to her, "I will step out a moment." This he did, she sending a boy to watch him. When the boy came out he appeared to be very sick and called hastily for water. The boy ran in to get it. Now was his golden opportunity. Jumping the fence he ran to a clump of trees which occupied low ground behind the house and concealing himself in it for a moment, ran and continued to run, he knew not whither, until he found himself at the toll gate near Petersburg, in Adams county. Before this he had kept in the fields and forests, but now found himself compelled to come out upon the road. The toll-gate keeper, seeing at once that he was a fugitive, said to him, "I guess you don't know the road." "I guess I can find it myself," was the reply. "Let me show you," said the man. "You may if you please," replied the fugitive. Taking him out behind his dwelling, he pointed across the fields to a new brick farm-house, and said, "Go there and inquire for Mr. Wright." The slave thanked him and did as he was directed.

He remained with William Wright until April, 1829. During this short time he learned to read, write, and cipher as far as the single rule of three, as it was then called, or simple proportion. During his residence with William Wright, nothing could exceed his kindness or gratitude to the whole family. He learned to graft trees, and thus rendered great assistance to William Wright in his necessary business. When working in the kitchen during the winter he would never allow Phebe Wright to perform any hard labor, always scrubbing the floor and lifting heavy burdens for her. Before he went away in the spring he assumed a name which his talents, perseverance, and genius have rendered famous in both hemispheres, that of James W. C. Pennington. The initial W. was for his benefactor's family, and C. for the family of his former master. From William Wright's he went to Daniel Gibbons', thence to Delaware county, Pennsylvania, and from there to New Haven, Conn., where, while performing the duties of janitor at Yale College, he completed the studies of the college course. After a few years, he went to Heidelberg, where the degree of D. D. was conferred upon him. He never forgot William Wright and his family, and on his return from Europe brought them each a present. The story of his escape and wonderful abilities was spread over England. An American acquaintance of the Wright family was astonished, on visiting an Anti-slavery fair in London many years ago, to see among the pictures for sale there, one entitled, "William and Phebe Wright receiving James W. C. Pennington." The Dr. died in Florida, in 1870, where he had gone to preach and assist in opening schools amongst the Freemen.

In 1842 a party of sixteen slaves came to York, Pa., from Baltimore county, Md. Here they were taken in charge by William Wright, Joel Fisher, Dr. Lewis, and William Yocum. The last named was a constable, and used to assist the Underground Rail Road managers by pretending to hunt fugitives with the kidnappers. Knowing where the fugitives were he was enabled to hunt them in the opposite direction from that in which they had gone, and thus give them time to escape. This constable and a colored man of York took this party one by one out into Samuel Willis' corn-field, near York, and hid them under the shocks. The following night Dr. Lewis piloted them to near his house, at Lewisburg, York county, on the banks of the Conewago. Here they were concealed several days, Dr. Lewis carrying provisions to them in his saddle-bags. When the search for them had been given up in William Wright's neighborhood, he went down to Lewisburg and in company with Dr. Lewis took the whole sixteen across the Conewago, they fording the river and carrying the fugitives across on their horses. It was a gloomy night in November. Every few moments clouds floated across the moon, alternately lighting up and shading the river, which, swelled by autumn rains, ran a flood. William Wright and Dr. Lewis mounted men or women behind and took children in their arms. When the last one got over, the doctor, who professed to be an atheist, exclaimed, "Great God! is this a Christian land, and are Christians thus forced to flee for their liberty?" William Wright guided this party to his house that night and concealed them in a neighboring forest until it was safe for them to proceed on their way to Canada.

Just in the beginning of harvest of the year 1851, four men came off from Washington county, Maryland. They were almost naked and seemed to have come through great difficulties, their clothing being almost entirely torn off. As soon as they came, William Wright went to the store and got four pair of shoes. It was soon heard that their masters and the officers had gone to Harrisburg to hunt them. Two of them, Fenton and Tom, were concealed at William Wright's, and the other two, Sam and one whose name has been forgotten, at Joel Wierman's. In a day or two, as William Wright, a number of carpenters, and other workmen, among whom were Fenton and Tom, were at work in the barn, a party of men rode up and recognized the colored men as slaves of one of their number. The colored men said they had left their coats at the house. William Wright looked earnestly at them and told them to go to the house and get their coats. They went off, and one of them was observed by one of the family to take his coat hastily down from where it hung in one of the outhouses, a few moments afterward. After conversing a few moments at the barn, William Wright brought the slave-holders down to the house, where he, his wife and daughters engaged them in a controversy on the subject of slavery which lasted about an hour. One of them seemed very much impressed, and labored hard to convince his host that he was a good master and would treat his men well. Finally one of the party asked William Wright to produce the men. He replied that he would not do that, that they might search his premises if they wished to, but they could not compel him to bring forth the fugitives. Seeing that they had been duped, they became very angry and proceeded forthwith to search the house and all the outhouses immediately around it, without, however, finding those whom they sought. As they left the house and went toward the barn, William Wright, waving his hand toward the former, said, "You see they are not anywhere there." They then went to the barn and gave it a thorough search. Between it and the house, a little away from the path, but in plain sight, stood the carriage-house, *which they passed by without seeming to notice.* After they had gone, poor Tom was found in this very house, curled up under the seats of the old-fashioned family carriage. He had never come to the house at all, but had heard the voices of his hunters from his hiding-place, during their whole search. About two o'clock in the morning, Fenton was found by William Wright out in the field. He had run along the bed of a small water course, dry at that time of year, until he came to a rye field amid whose high grain he hid himself until he thought the danger was past. From William Wright's the slave-catchers went to Joel Wierman's, where, despite all that could be done, they got poor Sam, took him off to Maryland and sold him to the traders to be taken far south.

In 1856 William Wright was a delegate from Adams county to the Convention at Philadelphia which nominated John C. Fremont for President of the United States. As the counties were called in alphabetical order, he responded first among the Pennsylvania delegation. It is thought that he helped away during his whole life, nearly one thousand slaves. During his latter years, he was aided in the good work by his children, who never hesitated to sacrifice their own pleasure in order to help away fugitives.

His convictions on the subject of slavery seem to have been born with him, to have grown with his growth, and strengthened with his strength. He could not remember when he first became interested in the subject.

William Wright closed his long and useful life on the 25th of October, 1865. More fortunate than his co-laborer, Daniel Gibbons, he lived to see the triumph of the cause in which he had labored all his life. His latter years were cheered by the remembrance of his good deeds in the cause of human freedom. Modest and retiring, he would not desire, as he does not need, a eulogy. His labors speak for themselves, and are such as are recorded upon the Lamb's Book of Life.

DR. BARTHOLOMEW FUSSELL.

Dr. Fussell, whose death occurred within the current year, was no ordinary man. He was born in Chester county, Pa., in 1794, his ancestors being members of the Society of Friends, principally of English origin, who arrived in America during the early settlement of Pennsylvania, some being of the number who, with William Penn, built their homes on the unbroken soil, where Philadelphia now stands.

He inherited all the bravery of these early pioneers, who left their homes for the sake of religious freedom, the governing principle of his life being a direct antagonism to every form of oppression. Removing in early manhood, to Maryland, where negro Slavery was legally protected, he became one of the most active opponents of the system, being a friend and co-laborer of Elisha Tyson, known and beloved as "Father Tyson," by all the 'slaves of the region, and to the community at large, as one of the most philanthropic of men.

While teaching school during the week, as a means of self-education, and reading medicine at night, the young student expended his surplus energy in opening a Sabbath-school for colored persons, teaching them the rudiments of knowledge, not for a few hours only, but for the whole day, and frequently finding as many as ninety pupils collected to receive the inestimable boon which gave them the power of reading the Bible for themselves. To the deeply religious nature of these Africans, this was the one blessing they prized above all others in his power to bestow, and the overflowing gratitude they gave in return, was a memory he cherished to the latest years of his life.

After his graduation in medicine, being at one time called upon to deliver an address before the Medical Society of Baltimore, in the midst of a pro-slavery audience, and before slave-holding professors and men of authority, Dr. Fussell, with a courage scarcely to be comprehended at this late day, denounced " the most preposterous and cruel practice of Slavery, as replete with the causes of disease," and expressed the hope that the day would come " when Slavery and cruelty should have no abiding place in the whole habitable earth ; when the philosopher and the pious Christian could use the salutation of ' brother,' and the physician and divine be as one man ; when the rich and the poor should know no distinction ; the great and the small be equal in dominion, and the *arrogant master* and *his menial slave* should make a truce of friendship with each other, all following the same law of reason, all guided by the same light of Truth !"

As a matter of course, a spirit so thoroughly awake to the welfare of humanity, would hail with joy and welcome as a brother, the appearance of such a devoted advocate of freedom, as Benjamin Lundy ; and, with all the warmth of his nature, would give love, admiration, and reverence to the later apostle of immediate emancipation, William Lloyd Garrison.

It was one of the pleasures of Dr. Fussell's life that he had been enabled to take the first number of the " *Liberator,*" and to continue a subscriber without intermission, until the battle being ended, the last number was announced.

He was himself, one of the most earnest workers in the Anti-slavery cause, never omitting in a fearless manner, to embrace an opportunity to protest against the encouragement of a pro-slavery spirit.

Returning to Pennsylvania, to practice his profession, his home became one of the havens where the hunted fugitive from Slavery found food, shelter and rest. Laboring in connection with the late Thomas Garrett, of Wilmington, Del., and with many others, at available points, about two thousand fugitives passed through his hands, on their way to freedom, and amongst these, he frequently had the delight of welcoming some of his old Sabbath-school pupils. The mutual recognition was sometimes touching in the extreme.

In later life, his anecdotes and reminiscences, told in the vivid style, resulting from a remarkably retentive memory, which could recall word, tone, and gesture, brought to life, some of the most interesting of his experiences with these fleeing bondmen, whose histories no romance could ever equal.

Being one of the signers of the " Declaration of Sentiments," issued by the American Anti-slavery Society in 1833, he had also the gratification of attending the last meeting of the Pennsylvania Anti-slavery Society, called to celebrate the downfall of Slavery in America, and the dissolution of an organization whose purpose was effected. There are those, who may remember how at that time, in perfect forgetfulness of self, the relation of the heroism of his friend, Elisha Tyson, seemed to recall for a moment, the vigor of youth to render the decrepitude of age almost majestic.

But it was not Slavery alone, which occupied the thoughts and attention of this large-hearted man. He was well known as an advocate of common school education, of temperance, and of every other interest, which, in his view, pertained to the welfare of man.

Unfortunately, he was addicted to the use of tobacco from his youth. Having become convinced that it was an evil, he, for the sake of consistency and as an example to others, resolutely abandoned the habit, at the age of seventy. He was fond of accrediting his resolve to a very aged relative, who, in remonstrating with him upon the subject, replied·to his remark, that a sudden cessation from a practice so long indulged in, might result in his death : " Well, die, then, and go to heaven decently."

As a practitioner of medicine, he was eminently successful, his intense sympathy with suffering, seeming to elevate his faculties and give them unwonted vigor in tracing the hidden causes of disease, and in suggesting to his mind alleviating agencies. His patients felt an unspeakable comfort in his presence, well knowing that the best possible remedy which his knowledge, his judgment or his experience suggested, would be selected, let the difficulty and inconvenience to himself be what it would. In cases where life hung trembling in the balance, he would watch night after night, feeding the flickering flame until he perceived it brighten, and this in the abode of misery just as freely as in the home of wealth. The life-long affection of those whom he recalled, was his reward where often none was sought or expected.

He believed in woman as only a thoroughly good man can, and from early youth, he had been impressed·with her peculiar fitness for the practice of medicine. The experience of a physician confirmed him in his sentiments, and it became one of his most earnest aspirations to open to her all the avenues to the study of medicine. In the year 1840, he gave regular instruction to a class of ladies, and it was through one of these pupils, that the first female graduate in America was interested in the study of medicine. In 1846 he communicated to a few liberal-minded professional men, a plan for the establishment of a college of the highest grade for the medical education of women. This long-cherished plan, hallowed to him by the approbation of a beloved wife, was well received. Others, with indomitable zeal, took up the work, and finally, after a succession of disappointments and discouragements from causes within and without, the Woman's College, on North College avenue, Philadelphia, starting from the germ of his thought, entered on the career of prosperity it is so well entitled to receive. Though never at any time connected with the college, he regarded its success with the most affectionate interest, considering its proposition as one of the most important results of his life.

Happy in having lived to see Slavery abolished, and believing in the speedy elevation of woman to her true dignity as joint sovereign with man, and in the mitigation of the evils of war, intemperance, poverty, and crime, which might be expected to follow such a result, he rested from his labors, and died in peace.

THOMAS SHIPLEY.*

Thomas Shipley, one of the foremost in the early generation of philanthropists who devoted their lives to the extinction of human slavery, was born in Philadelphia on the second of Fourth month, 1787. He was the youngest of five children of William and Margaret Shipley, his father having emigrated from Uttoxeter, in Staffordshire, England, about the year 1750. From a very early period in the history of the Society of Friends his ancestors had been members of that body, and he inherited from them the strong sense of personal independence, and the love of toleration and respect for the rights of others which have ever characterized that body of people.

Soon after his birth, his mother died, and he was thus early deprived of the fostering care of a pious and devoted parent, whose counsels are so important in forming the youthful mind, and in giving a direction to future life.

A few years after the death of his mother, his father was removed, and Thomas was left an orphan before he had attained his sixth year. After this affecting event he was taken into the family of Isaac Bartram, who had married his eldest sister. Here he remained for several years, acquiring the common rudiments of education, and at a suitable age was sent to Westtown school; after remaining there for a little more than a year, he met with an accident, which rendered it necessary for him to return home; and the effects of which prevented him from proceeding with his education. He fell from the top of a high flight of steps to the ground, and received an injury of the head, followed by convulsions, which continued at intervals for a considerable time, and rendered him incapable of any effort of mind or body.

He was, during childhood, remarkably fond of reading, and was distinguished among his friends and associates for uncommon perseverance in accomplishing anything he undertook, a trait which peculiarly marked him through life; his disposition is said to have been unusually amiable and docile, so as to endear him very strongly to his relatives and friends.

After his removal from Westtown, he was again taken into the family of his brother-in-law, and remained under the care of his sister, who was very

---

* This account of the Life of Thomas Shipley is abridged from a Memoir by Dr. Isaac Parrish, published in 1837.

much attached to him, until he was placed as an apprentice to the hardware business. While here, he was entirely relieved of the affliction caused by the fall, and was restored to sound health. About the age of twenty-one, he entered upon the pursuits of the business he had selected.

The exact time at which his attention was turned to the subject of slavery cannot be ascertained, but it is probable that a testimony against it was among his earliest impressions as a member of the religious Society of Friends. He joined the " Pennsylvania Society for the Promoting the Abolition of Slavery," etc., in 1817, and the ardent interest which he took in its objects, was evinced on many occasions within the recollection of many now living. He was for many years an active member of its Board of Education, and took a prominent part in extending the benefits of learning to colored children and youth.

The career of Thomas Shipley, as it was connected with the interests of the colored community, abounds in incidents which have rarely occurred in the life of any individual. Being universally regarded as their adviser and protector, he was constantly solicited for his advice on questions touching their welfare. This led him to investigate the laws relating to this class of persons, in all their extended ramifications. The knowledge he thus acquired, together with his practical acquaintance with the business and decisions of our courts, rendered his opinion peculiarly serviceable on all matters affecting their rights. Never did a merchant study more closely the varied relations of business, and their influence on his interests, than did Thomas Shipley all those questions which concerned the well-being of·those for whom he was so warmly interested. He had volunteered his services as their advocate, and they could not have been more faithfully served had they poured out the wealth of Crœsus at the feet of the most learned counsel.

On every occasion of popular commotion where the safety of the colored people was threatened, he was found at his post, fearlessly defending their rights, and exerting his influence with those in authority to throw around them the protection of the laws. In the tumultuous scenes which disgraced Philadelphia, in the summer of 1835, in which the fury of the mob was directed against the persons and property of the colored inhabitants, he acted with an energy and prudence rarely found combined in the same individual.

The mob had collected and organized to the number of several hundred, and were marching through the lower part of the city, dealing destruction in their course ; the houses of respectable and worthy colored citizens were broken in upon, the furniture scattered to the winds, all they possessed destroyed or plundered, and they themselves subjected to the most brutal and savage treatment. Defenceless infancy and decrepid age were alike disregarded in the general devastation which these ruffians had decreed should attend their course. The color of the skin was the mark by which their vengeance was directed, and the cries and entreaties of their innocent and defenceless victims were alike disregarded in the accomplishment of their ends. Already had several victims fallen before the fury of the ruthless band. Law and order were laid waste, and the officers of justice looked on, some perhaps with dismay, and others with indifference, while the rights of citizens were prostrated, and their peaceful and quiet homes invaded by the hand of violence. At such a time the voice of remonstrance or entreaty, would have been useless, and had the avowed friends of the colored man interfered in any public manner, the effect would probably have been to increase the fury of the storm, and to have directed the violence of the mob upon themselves.

Under these perilous circumstances, Thomas Shipley was determined to attempt an effort for their relief. He could not look on and see those for whom he was so deeply interested threatened almost with extermination without an effort for their preservation, and yet he was aware that his presence amongst the mob might subject him to assassination, without adding to the security of the objects of his solicitude. He, therefore, determined to disguise himself in such a manner as not to be recognized, and to mingle amongst the rioters in order to ascertain their objects, and if possible to convey such information to the proper authorities as might lead to the arrest of those most active in fomenting disorder. Accordingly he left his house late in the evening, attired so as to be completely disguised, and repaired to the scene of tumult. By this time much mischief had been done, and to add fresh fury to the multitude, and to incite them to new deeds of blood, nothing was wanting but some act of resistance on the part of their victims, who, during the whole period, had conducted themselves with a forbearance and patience highly creditable to them as good citizens and upright Christians. Such an occasion was about to occur, and was prevented by the admirable coolness and forethought of Thomas Shipley.

A number of colored men who had been driven to desperation by the acts of the mob, and who had relinquished the idea of protection from the civil authorities, determined to resort to arms, to defend themselves and their families from the further aggressions of their persecutors. They accordingly repaired to Benezet Hall, one of their public buildings in South Seventh Street, with a supply of fire arms and ammunition, determined to fire upon the assailants, and maintain their post or die in the attempt. This fact became known to the leaders of the mob, and the cry was raised to march for the hall, and make the attack. Thomas Shipley who had mingled· amongst the rioters, and apparently identified himself with them, was now perfectly aware of all their designs ; he knew their numbers, he had seen the implements of destruction which they were brandishing about them, and he was aware that the occurrence of such a conflict would be attended with the most disastrous results, and might be the beginning of hostilities which would terminate in the destruction of the weaker party, or at least in a dreadful effusion of human blood. Seeing the position in which the parties were now placed, he left the ranks of the rioters, and ran at the top of his speed to the house in which the colored people were collected, awaiting the approach of their enemy. As he drew near, they were about coming out to meet their assailants, highly excited by continued outrages, and determined to defend themselves or die. At this unexpected moment, their protector drew nigh ; he raised his voice aloud, and addressed the multitude. He deprecated the idea of a resort to physical force, as being calculated to increase their difficulties, and to plunge them into general distress, and entreated them to retire from the hall. His voice was immediately recognized ; the effect was electric ; the whole throng knew him as their friend ; their fierce passions were calmed by the voice of reason and admonition. They could not disregard his counsels ; he had come among them, at the dead hour of night, in the midst of danger and trial, to raise his warning voice against a course of measures they were about to pursue. They listened to his remonstrances, and retreated before the mob had reached the building. At this juncture the Mayor and his officers assembled in front of the hall, and by prompt and energetic action succeeded in dispersing the mob, and through the information received from Thomas Shipley, the ringleaders were secured and lodged in prison.

The part which Thomas Shipley acted in the trying scenes so often presented in our courts, during this unhappy period, has invested his character with a remarkable degree of interest. It is probable that his connection with the Pennsylvania Abolition Society was the means of enlisting his talents and exertions in this important service.

The energy and zeal of our friend in his efforts for the relief of those about to be deprived of their dearest rights, soon distinguished him as the most efficient member of the Society, in this department of its duties. So intense was his interest in all cases where the liberty of his fellow-man was at issue, that, during a period of many years, he was scarcely ever absent from the side of the unhappy victim, as he sat before our judicial tribunals, trembling for his fate. The promptings of interest, the pleasures and allurements of the world, the quiet enjoyment of a peaceful home, were all cheerfully sacrificed, when his services were demanded in these distressing cases. Often has he left the business, in which his pecuniary interests were materially involved, to stand by the unhappy fugitive in the hour of his extremity, with an alacrity and a spirit which could only be displayed by one animated by the loftiest principles and the purest philanthropy.

Who, that has ever witnessed one of these trying scenes, can forget his manly and honest bearing, as he stood before the unrelenting and arrogant claimant, watching with an eagle eye, every step of the process by which he hoped to gain his victim ? Who has not been struck with his expressive glances toward the judge, when a doubtful point arose in the investigation of the case? Who has not caught the lively expression of delight which beamed from his countenance, when a fact was disclosed which had a favorable bearing on the liberty of the captive? Who has not admired the sagacity with which his inquiries were dictated, and the tact and acumen with which he managed every part of his cause? His principle was unhesitatingly to submit to existing laws, however unjust their decrees might be, but to scan well the bearing of the facts and principles involved in each case, and to see that nothing was wanting in the chain of evidence, or in the legal points in question, fully to satisfy the requisitions of law. If a doubtful point arose, he was unwearied in investigating it, and devoted hours, days, and even weeks, in the collection of testimony which he thought would have a favorable influence on the prisoner.

Through his untiring vigilance, many victims have escaped from the hand of the oppressor, whose title to freedom, according to the laws of this commonwealth, was undoubted, and many others, whose enslavement was at least questionable.

The time and labor expended by Thomas Shipley in protecting the interests of his colored clients, would be almost incredible to those who were not aware of his extraordinary devotion to the cause. The only notice which can be found among his papers, of the various slave cases in which he was engaged, is contained in a memorandum book, which he commenced in the summer of 1835. In this book he has noted, in the order of their occurrence, such instances of difficulty or distress as demanded his interference, almost without a comment. I find from this book, that his advice and assistance were bestowed in twenty-five cases, from Seventh mo. 16th, to Eighth mo. 24th, 1836, a period of little more than a month. A number of these cases required the writing of letters to distant places; in some it was necessary for him to visit the parties interested; and others demanded his personal attendance at court. This perhaps, may be considered as a fair average of the amount of labor which he constantly expended in this department of his benevolent efforts; and when we consider the time occupied in the necessary duties of his ordinary avocations, it must be evident that he possessed not only extraordinary humanity, but uncommon activity and energy, to have accomplished so much.

In the memorandum book referred to, under date of Twelfth mo., 1835, I find the following note: Spent eighteen days in the trial of A. Hemsley, and his wife Nancy, and her three children, arrested at Mount Holly, the husband claimed by Goldsborough Price, executor of Isaac Boggs, of Queen Ann's county, Maryland, and the wife and children by Richard D. Cooper, of the same county. John Willoughby, agent for both claimants. B. R. Brown and B. Clarke, attorneys for the claimant, and D. P. Brown, J. R. Slack, E. B. Cannon, and G. W. Camblos, for defendants. After a full argument, in which a manumission was produced for Nancy, from R. D. Cooper's father, she and her children were discharged, but her husband was remanded; on which a certiorari was served on the judge, and a habeas corpus placed in the sheriff's hands."

" Alexander was discharged by the Supreme Court, at Trenton, Third mo. 5th. The circumstances of the case, were briefly the following: The woman and children had been regularly manumitted in Delaware by the father of the claimant, while the title of the father to freedom was less positive, though sufficiently clear to warrant a vigorous effort on his behalf.

The first object of the counsel on the part of the alleged fugitive, was to prove the manumission of the mother and children, and, as it was thought, the necessary documents for that purpose were collected and arranged. After the trial had proceeded, however, for a short time, the attorney for the defendants discovered a defect in the testimony on this point; the necessary papers, duly authenticated by the Governor or Chief Justice of Delaware, were missing, and without them it was impossible to make out the case. The fact was immediately communicated to Thomas Shipley—he saw that the papers must be had, and that they could not be procured without a visit to Dover, in Delaware. He at once determined to repair thither in person, and obtain them. Without the knowledge of the claimant's counsel, who might have taken advantage of the omission, and hurried the case to a decision; he started on the evening of the sixth day, and traveled as fast as possible to Dover, in the midst of a season unusually cold and inclement. On the next morning inquiries were made in all directions for friend Shipley; it was thought strange that he should desert his post in the midst of so exciting and momentous a trial, and at a time when his presence seemed to be particularly required. The counsel for the prisoners, who were aware of his movements, proceeded with the examination of witnesses as slowly as possible, in order to allow time for procuring this important link in the chain of testimony, and thus to procrastinate the period when they should be called upon to sum up the case.

Fortunately, on the evening of the day on which Thomas Shipley set out upon his journey, it was proposed to adjourn, and farther proceedings were postponed until Second day morning. At the meeting of the court, in the morning, the expected messenger was not there, and the ingenuity or the counsel was taxed still farther to procrastinate the important period. After three hours had been consumed in debate upon legal points, he, who was so anxiously looked for, came hurrying through the crowd, making his way toward the bench. His countenance and his movements soon convinced the wondering spectators that he was the bearer of gratifying news, and in a few minutes, the mystery of his absence was revealed, by the production of a document which was the fruit of his effort. The papers completely established the legal title of the mother and children to their freedom, and placed them out of the reach of further persecution. An attack of illness was the result of the extreme exertion and fatigue endured by this devoted man, in his earnest advocacy of the rights of these friendless beings.

The freedom of the husband and father, was, however, still in jeopardy. If the decision of the court should be against him, he would be torn from the bosom of his now joyful and emancipated family, and consigned to a life of bondage. To avert this calamity, the counsel for the prisoner suggested an expedient as humane as it was ingenious. He proposed that a writ of certiorari which would oblige the judge to remove the case to the Supreme Court and a habeas corpus from the Chief Justice of the State, should both be in readiness when the decision of the judge should be pronounced, in case that if it should be unfavorable, the writs might be at once served, and the prisoner remanded to the sheriff of the county, to be brought up before the Supreme Court at Trenton for another trial.

To procure these writs, it was necessary to obtain the signature of the chief justice of New Jersey, who resided at Newark, and again Thomas Shipley was ready to enter with alacrity into the service. He saw the importance of the measure, and that it would require prompt action, inasmuch as the decision of the judge would probably be pronounced on the following day. It fortunately happened that a friend was just about leaving for Newark, in his own conveyance, and feeling an interest in the case, he kindly invited friend Shipley to accompany him. They left in the afternoon, traveled all night, and arrived at Newark by daylight the following morning. The weary traveler was unwilling, however, to retire to bed, although the night was exceedingly cold and tempestuous, but he proceeded at once to the house of the chief justice. He called the worthy judge from his bed, offering the importance of his business, and the necessity of speedy action, as an apology for so unseasonable a visit. Chief Justice Hornblower, on being informed of the circumstances of the case, expressed his pleasure at having it in his power to accede to his wishes and treated him with a respect and kindness which the disinterested benevolence of his mission was calculated to inspire.

Having obtained the necessary papers, he left at once for Mount Holly, where he arrived on the following day, in time to place the writs in the hands of the sheriff, just before the decision of Judge H. was pronounced. Had he consulted his ease or convenience, and deferred his visit to Newark a few hours, or had he, as most men, under similar circumstances would have done, reposed his weary limbs, after a cold and dreary ride of eighty miles, in order to enable him to return with renewed strength, he would have arrived too late to render this meritorious effort effectual. As it was, he was there in time. The judge, according to the expectation of the friends of the colored man, gave his decision in favor of the slave-holders, and ordered poor Alexander to be given up to the tender mercies of the exasperated claimant. The decision sent a thrill of indignation through the anxious and excited multitude, which perhaps, was never equalled amongst the inhabitants of that quiet town. The friends of humanity had assembled from all parts of the country to witness the proceedings in the case. Many of them were personally acquainted with the prisoner; they knew him to be a man of intelligence and integrity; he was an industrious and orderly citizen, and was universally respected in the neighborhood. He was now about to be made a slave, and was declared to be the property of another. The father was about to be torn from his helpless children; the husband in defiance of the Divine command, was to be wrested from the fond embrace of his sorrowing wife, to spend his days in misery and toil. And this was to be done before the eyes of those who had a just regard for human rights, a hearty hatred of oppression. Is it wonderful, that under such circumstances, there should have been a deep abhorrence for the perpetrators of this outrage upon humanity, and a general sympathy for the innocent captive?

But it was decreed that those feelings of honest indignation should be speedily supplanted by the warm outpouring of public gratitude and joy. While the feeling of the spectators was in this state of intense interest and excitement, the judge, stern and inflexible in his purposes, and the clan of greedy claimants ready to seize upon their prey, the sheriff produced his writ of certiorari and handed it to the court. It was instantly returned, and the judge who sat unmoved, by a scene to which he was not unaccustomed, and conceiving, perhaps, that his official dignity was impugned, persisted in his determination that the prisoner should be handed over to the claimant. The prudence and foresight of Thomas Shipley and his friends had provided, however, for this anticipated difficulty. Happily for the prisoner, he was yet embraced under the provision of that constitution, which secured to him the protection of a habeas corpus, and this threw around him a shield which his enemies could not penetrate. A writ of habeas corpus, signed by the chief justice of the State and demanding the body of the prisoner, before the Supreme Court at its next term, was now produced!

The astonished judge found himself completely foiled. He had exercised his authority to its utmost limit, in support of the claims of his slave-holding friends, and had given the influence of his station and character, to bolster up the "patriarchal institution;" but it was all in vain. Just as they supposed they had achieved a victory, they were obliged with fallen crests, to succumb to the dictates of a higher tribunal, and to see their victim conveyed beyond their reach in the safe keeping of the sheriff.

In the Third month, (March,) the case was brought up before the Supreme Court for final adjudication. In the meantime, Thomas Shipley adopted vigorous measures to have the facts collected and arranged. He procured the aid of an intelligent and humane friend of the cause, who resided near

45

Trenton, to attend, personally to the case, and secured the legal services of Theodore Frelinghuysen, well known as one of the most gifted and virtuous statesmen of the age, and as a warm and zealous friend of the oppressed. Under these happy auspices, the case came before the Supreme Court, and gave rise to a highly interesting and important argument; in which the distinguished Frelinghuysen appeared as the disinterested advocate of the prisoner, and urged upon the court his claim to liberty, under the laws of New Jersey, in a speech which was one of his most brilliant and eloquent efforts, and added another to the many laurels which his genius and philanthropy have achieved.

The opinion of Chief Justice Hornblower was given at length, and is said to have displayed a soundness and extent of legal knowledge, with a spirit of mildness and humanity, well worthy of the highest judicial tribunal of New Jersey.

By this decision, Alexander Helmsley was declared to be a freeman, and returned with rejoicing into the bosom of his family, and to the enjoyment of the rights and privileges of a free citizen.

Thus terminated this interesting case, which for several months agitated the public mind of Burlington county, to an extent almost unequalled.

Such disinterested devotion to the defence of the rights of the oppressed, had it been displayed only in the instance recited, would be sufficient to enroll the name of Thomas Shipley on the list of the benefactors of his race; but when we consider that, for a period of twenty years, his history abounds in similar incidents, and that he uniformly stood forth as the unflinching advocate of the oppressed, regardless of the sacrifices which he was obliged to make on their behalf, we are disposed to view him as one of that noble band whose lives have been consecrated to deeds of charity and benevolence, and whose names will illumine the moral firmament, so long as virtue and truth shall command the homage of mankind.

Thomas Shipley was one of the founders of the American Anti-Slavery Society, and was an active agent in those stirring movements which soon aroused the nation to a full consideration of the enormities of Slavery. He was a prominent member of the Anti-slavery Convention, which assembled in this city in 1833, and a signer of their declaration of sentiments.

During the last few years of his life, he was more devotedly engaged in his abolition labors than at any previous period. It was his constant desire to diffuse the principles which had been so fearlessly proclaimed by the Convention, and to encourage the formation of Anti-slavery societies throughout the sphere of his influence. He was one of the most prominent members of the Philadelphia Anti-slavery Society, which was formed through much opposition, in 1835, and he steadily adhered to its meetings, notwithstanding the threats which were so loudly made by the enemies of public order.

In the midst of the popular commotions and tumults, which marked the progress of Anti-slavery principles, he stood calm and unmoved. Having been long known as a firm friend of the rights of the colored man, and being amongst the most efficient public advocates of his cause, he was of course subjected to the revilings which were so liberally heaped upon the Abolitionists at that time. His name was associated with that of Tappan, Birney, Green, Jay, Garrison, and other leading Abolitionists, who were singled out by slave-holders and their abettors as fit subjects for the merciless attacks of excited mobs.

In several attempts which were made in this city to stir up the passions of the ignorant against the advocates of human rights, his person and property were openly threatened with assault. Such menaces failed, however, to deter him from the steady performance of what he believed to be a solemn duty. Being fully satisfied of the truth of the principles which he had espoused, he relied with unwavering confidence upon Divine power for their ultimate triumph, and for the protection of those who advocated them. When his friends expressed their anxiety for his safety, he always allayed their apprehensions, and evinced by the firmness and benignity of his manner that he was divested of the fear of man, and acted under the influence of that spirit which is from above.

The active part which Thomas Shipley took in Anti-slavery movements, did not diminish his interest in the prosperity and usefulness of the old Pennsylvania Society. He was a steady attendant on its meetings, and exercised his wonted care on all subjects connected with its interests.

A short time previous to his death, his services were acknowledged by his fellow-members, by his election to the office of president.

The incessant and fatiguing labors in which he was engaged, had sensibly affected the vigor of a constitution naturally delicate, and rendered him peculiarly liable to the inroads of disease. He was seized in the autumn of 1836, with an attack of intermittent fever, which confined him to the house for ten or twelve days, and very much reduced his strength; while recovering from this attack, he experienced an accession of disease which terminated his life in less than twenty-four hours. But a few hours before his death, he inquired of his physicians as to the probable issue of his case; when informed of his critical condition, he received the intelligence with composure, and immediately requested Dr. Atlee, who was by his side, to take down some directions in regard to his affairs, on paper. In a few minutes after this, he quietly lapsed into the sleep of death, in the morning, on the 17th of Ninth month, 1836.

His last words were, " I die at peace with all mankind, and hope that my trespasses may be as freely forgiven, as I forgive those who have trespassed against me."

To all who knew him well, of whatever class in the community, the tidings of this unexpected event brought a personal sorrow. It was felt that a man of rare probity and virtue had gone to his reward. But to the colored people the intelligence of his death was at once startling and confounding. Their whole community was bowed down in public lamentation, for their warmest and most steadfast friend was gone.

They repaired in large numbers to the house of their benefactor to obtain a last glance at his lifeless body. Parents brought their little ones to the house of mourning, and as they gazed upon the features of the departed, now inanimate in death, they taught their infant minds the impressive lesson, that before them were the mortal remains of one who had devoted his energies to the disenthralment of their race, and whose memory they should ever cherish with gratitude and reverence. When the day arrived for committing his remains to the grave the evidence of deep and pervading sorrow among these wronged and outraged people was strikingly apparent.

Thousands, whose serious deportment and dejected countenances evinced that they were fully sensible of their loss, collected in the vicinity of his dwelling, anxious to testify their respect for his memory. Theirs was not the gaze of the indifferent crowd, which clusters around the abodes of fashion and splendor, to witness the pomp and circumstance attendant on the interment of the haughty or the rich. It was a solemn gathering, brought together by the impulse of feeling, to mingle their tears and lamentations at the grave of one whom they had loved and revered as a protector and a friend.

When the hearse arrived at the quiet burial place in Arch street, where the Friends for many generations have buried their dead, six colored men carried the body to its last resting-place, and the silent tear of the son of Africa over the grave of his zealous friend, was more expressive of real affection than all the parade which is sometimes brought so ostentatiously before the public eye. In the expressive words of the leading newspaper of the day, "Aaron Burr was lately buried with the honors of war. Thomas Shipley was buried with the honors of peace. Let the reflecting mind pause in the honorable contrast."

As a public speaker Thomas Shipley was clear, cogent, sometimes eloquent, and always impressive. He never attempted oratorical effect, or studied harangues. He generally spoke extemporaneously, on the spur of the occasion, and what he said came warm from the heart. It was the simple and unadorned expression of his sentiments and feelings. He was, however, argumentative and even logical, when the occasion required it. When intensely interested, his eye was full of deep and piercing expression.

Although his education had been limited, and his pursuits afforded him but little leisure time, yet he indulged his fondness for reading, and exhibited a refined literary taste in his selections. He has left amongst his books and papers eight manuscript volumes of about one hundred and fifty pages each, filled with selections, copied in his own handwriting, and culled from the writings of many of the most gifted authors, both in poetry and prose.

These extracts are generally of a moral and religious caste, and include scraps from Young, Milton, Addison, Burns, Cowper, Watts, Akenside, Pope, Byron, Hemans, and many others.

In the domestic and social circle, his conversation was animated and instructive, and always tempered by that kindness and amenity of manners which endeared him to his family and friends.

He was no bigot in religion. While a firm believer in the doctrines of the Gospel as maintained by the orthodox Society of Friends, he yet held that religion was an operative principle producing the fruits of righteousness and peace, in all of whatever name, who are sincere followers of our Lord Jesus Christ. In conclusion we may add, that more than most men he bore about with him the sentiment of that old Roman, "Nihil humanum alienum a me puto," while he added to it the higher thought of the Christian, that he who loveth God loveth his brother also. We need not dwell upon the life of such a man. To-day, after the lapse of more than a generation, his memory is fresh and green in the hearts of those who knew him, and who still survive to hand down to their children the story of the trials of that eventful period in our history.

To the Memory of

THOMAS SHIPLEY,

President of the Pennsylvania Abolition Society,

Who died on the 17th of Ninth mo., 1836, a devoted Christian and Philanthropist.

BY JOHN G. WHITTIER.

Gone to thy Heavenly Father's rest—
  The flowers of Eden round thee blowing!
And, on thine ear, the murmurs blest
  Of Shiloah's waters softly flowing!
Beneath that tree of life which gives
To all the earth its healing leaves—
In the white robe of angels clad,
  And wandering by that sacred river,
Whose streams of holiness make glad
  The city of our God forever!

Gentlest of spirits!—not for thee
  Our tears are shed, our sighs are given:
Why mourn to know thou art a free
  Partaker of the joys of Heaven?
Finished thy work, and kept thy faith
In Christian firmness unto death—
And beautiful as sky and earth,
  When Autumn's sun is downward going,
The blessed memory of thy worth
  Around thy place of slumber glowing!

But, wo for us!—who linger still
　　With feebler strength and hearts less lowly,
And minds less steadfast to the will
　　Of Him, whose every work is holy!
For not like thine, is crucified
The spirit of our human pride:
And at the bondman's tale of woe,
　　And for the outcast and forsaken,
Not warm like thine, but cold and slow,
　　Our weaker sympathies awaken!

Darkly upon our struggling way
　　The storm of human hate is sweeping;
Hunted and branded, and a prey,
　　Our watch amidst the darkness keeping!
Oh! for that hidden strength which can
Nerve unto death the inner man!
Oh—for thy spirit tried and true
　　And constant in the hour of trial—
Prepared to suffer or to do
　　In meekness and in self-denial.

Oh, for that spirit meek and mild,
　　Derided, spurned, yet uncomplaining—
By man deserted and reviled,
　　Yet faithful to its trust remaining.
Still prompt and resolute to save
From scourge and chain the hunted slave!
Unwavering in the truth's defence
　　E'en where the fires of hate are burning,
The unquailing eye of innocence
　　Alone upon the oppressor turning!

Oh, loved of thousands! to thy grave,
　　Sorrowing of heart, thy brethren bore thee!
The poor man and the rescued slave
　　Wept as the broken earth closed o'er thee—
And grateful tears, like summer rain,
Quickened its dying grass again!—
And there, as to some pilgrim shrine,
　　Shall come the outcast and the lowly,
Of gentle deeds and words of thine
　　Recalling memories sweet and holy!

Oh, for the death the righteous die!
　　An end, like Autumn's day declining,
On human hearts, as on the sky,
　　With holier, tenderer beauty shining!
As to the parting soul were given
　　The radiance of an opening heaven!
As if that pure and blessed light
　　From off the eternal altar flowing,
Were bathing in its upward flight
　　The spirit to its worship going!

ROBERT PURVIS

Was born in Charleston, S. C. on the 4th day of August, 1810. His father, William Purvis, was a native of Ross county, in Northumberland, England. His mother was a free-born woman, of Charleston. His maternal grandmother was a Moor; and her father was an Israelite, named Baron Judah. Robert Purvis and his two brothers were brought to the North by their parents in 1819. In Pennsylvania and New England he received his scholastic education, finishing it at Amherst College. Since that time his home has been in Philadelphia, or in the vicinity of that city.

His interest in the Anti-slavery cause began in his childhood, inspired by such books as "Sandford and Merton," and Dr. Toney's "Portraiture of Slavery," which his father put into his hands. His father, though resident in a slave state, was never a slaveholder; but was heartily an Abolitionist in principle. It was Robert Purvis' good fortune, before he attained his majority, to make the acquaintance of that earnest and self-sacrificing pioneer of freedom, Benjamin Lundy; and in conjunction with him, was an early laborer in the anti-slavery field. He was a member of the Convention held in Philadelphia in 1833, which formed the American Anti-slavery Society; and among the signatures to its Declaration of Sentiments, the name of Robert Purvis is to be seen ; a record of which his posterity to the latest generation may be justly proud. During the whole period of that Society's existence he was a member of it; and was also an active member and officer of The Pennsylvania Anti-slavery Society. To the cause of the slave's freedom he gave with all his heart his money, his time, his talents. Fervent in soul, eloquent in speech, most gracious in manner, he was a favorite on the platform of Anti-slavery meetings. High-toned in moral nature, keenly sensitive in all matters pertaining to justice and integrity, he was a most valuable coadjutor with the leaders of an unpopular reform ; and throughout the Anti-slavery conflict, he always received, as he always deserved, the highest confidence and warm personal regard of his fellow-laborers.

His faithful labors in aiding fugitive slaves cannot be recorded within the limits of this sketch. Throughout that long period of peril to all who dared to "remember those in bonds as bound with them," his house was a well-known station on the Underground Rail Road; his horses and carriages, and his personal attendance, were ever at the service of the travelers upon that road. In those perilous duties his family heartily sympathized with him, and cheerfully performed their share.

He has lived to witness the triumph of the great cause to which he devoted his youth and his manhood; to join in the jubilee song of the American slave; and the thanksgiving of the Abolitionists; and to testify that the work of his life has been one " whose reward is in itself."

JOHN HUNN.

Almost within the lions' den, in daily sight of the enemy, in the little slave-holding State of Delaware, lived and labored the freedom-loving, earnest and whole-souled Quaker abolitionist, John Hunn. His headquarters were at Cantwell's Bridge, but, as an engineer of the Underground Rail Road, his duties, like those of his fellow-laborer Thomas Garrett, were not confined to that section, but embraced other places, and were attended with great peril, constant care and expense. He was well-known to the colored people far and near, and was especially sought with regard to business pertaining to the Underground Rail Road, as a friend who would never fail to assist as far as possible in every time of need. Through his agency many found their way to freedom, both by land and water.

The slave-holders regarding him with much suspicion, watched him closely, and were in the habit of "breathing out threatenings and slaughter" very fiercely at times. But Hunn was too plucky to be frightened by their threats and menaces, and as one, commissioned by a higher power to remember those in bonds as bound with them he remained faithful to the slave. Men, women or children seeking to be unloosed from the fetters of Slavery, could not make their grievances known to John Hunn without calling forth his warmest sympathies. His house and heart were always open to all such. The slave-holders evidently concluded that Hunn could not longer be tolerated, consequently devised a plan to capture him, on the charge of aiding off a woman with her children.

[John Hunn and Thomas Garrett were conjointly prosecuted in this case, and in the sketch of the latter, the trial, conviction, etc., are so fully referred to, that it is unnecessary to do more than allude to it here].

These noted Underground Rail Road offenders being duly brought before the United States District Court, in May, 1848, Judge Taney, presiding, backed by a thoroughly pro-slavery sentiment, obviously found it a very easy matter to convict them, and a still easier matter to fine them to the extent of every dollar they possessed in the world. Thousands of dollars were swept from Hunn in an instant, and his family left utterly destitute; but he was by no means conquered, as he deliberately gave the court to understand in a manly speech, delivered while standing to receive his sentence. There and then he avowed his entire sympathy with the slave, and declared that in the future, as in the past, by the help of God, he would never withhold a helping hand from the down-trodden in the hour of distress. That this pledge was faithfully kept by Hunn, there can be no question, as he continued steadfast at his post until the last fetter was broken by the great proclamation of Abraham Lincoln.

He was not without friends, however, for even near by, dwelt a few well-tried Abolitionists. Ezekiel Jenkins, Mifflin Warner, and one or two others, whole-souled workers in the same cause with Hunn; he was therefore not forgotten in the hour of his extremity.

Wishing to produce a sketch worthy of this veteran, we addressed him on the subject, but failed to obtain all the desired material. His reasons, however, for withholding the information which we desired were furnished, and, in connection therewith, a few anecdotes touching Underground Rail Road matters coming under his immediate notice, which we here take great pleasure in transcribing.

BEAUFORT, S. C. 11th mo. 7th, 1871.

Wm. STILL, DEAR FRIEND:—In thy first letter thee asked for my photograph as well as for an opinion of the book about to be edited by thyself. I returned a favorable answer and sent likeness, as requested. I incidentally mentioned that, probably some of my papers might be of service to thee. The papers alluded to had no reference to myself; but consisted of anecdotes and short histories of some of the fugitives from the hell of American Slavery, who gave me a call, as engineer of the Underground Rail Road in the State of Delaware, and received the benefit of my advice and assistance.

I was twenty-seven years-old when I engaged in the Underground Rail Road business, and I continued therein diligently until the breaking up of that business by the Great Rebellion I then came to South Carolina to witness the uprising of a nation of slaves into the dignity and privileges of mankind.

Nothing can possibly have the same interest to me. Therefore, I propose to remain where this great problem is in the process of solution; and to give my best efforts to its successful accomplishment. In this matter the course that I have pursued thus far through life has given me solid satisfaction. I ask no other reward for any efforts made by me in the cause, than to feel that I have been of use to my fellow-men.

No other course would have brought peace to my mind; then why should any credit be awarded to me; or how can I count any circumstance that may have occurred to me, in the light of a sacrifice? If a man pursues the only course that will bring peace to his own mind, is he deserving of any credit therefor? Is not the reward worth striving for at any cost? Indeed it is, as I well know.

Would it be well for me, entertaining such sentiments, to sit down and write an account of my sacrifices? I think not. Therefore please hold me excused. I am anxious to see thy book, and will forward the price of one as soon as I can ascertain what it is.

Please accept my thanks for thy kind remembrance of me. I am now fifty-three years old, but I well remember thy face in the Anti-slavery Office in Fifth street, when I called on business of the Underground Rail Road. Our mutual friend, S. D. Burris, was the cause of much uneasiness to us in those times. It required much trouble, as well as expense to save him from the slave-traders. I stood by him on the auction-block; and when I stepped down, they thought they had him sure. Indeed he thought so himself for a little while. But we outwitted them at last, to their great chagrin. Those were stirring times, and the people of Dover, Delaware, will long remember the time when S. D. Burris was sold at public sale for aiding slaves, to escape from their masters, and was bought by the Pennsylvania Anti-slavery Society. I remain very truly thy friend, JOHN HUNN.

THE CASE OF MOLLY, A SLAVE, BELONGING TO R—— B——, OF SMYRNA, DELAWARE. BY JOHN HUNN, ENGINEER OF THE UNDERGROUND RAIL ROAD.

Molly escaped from her master's farm, in Cecil county, Maryland, and found a place of refuge in the house of my cousin, John Alston, near Middletown, Delaware. The man-hunters, headed by a constable with a search warrant, took her thence and lodged her in New Castle Jail. This fact was duly published in the county papers, and her master went after his chattel, and having paid the expenses of her capture took immediate possession thereof.

She was hand-cuffed, and, her feet being tied together, she was placed in the wagon. Before she left the jail, the wife of the sheriff gave her a piece of bread and butter, which her master kicked out of her hand, and swore that bread and butter was too good for her. After this act her master took a drink of brandy and drove off.

He stopped at a tavern about four miles from New Castle and took another drink of brandy. He then proceeded to Odessa, then called Cantwell's Bridge, and got his dinner and more brandy, for the day was a cold one. He had his horse fed, but gave no food to his human chattel, who remained in the wagon cold and hungry. After sufficient rest for himself and horse he started again. He was now twelve miles from home, on a good road, his horse was gentle, and he himself in a genial mood at the recovery of his bond-woman. He yielded to the influence of the liquor he had imbibed and fell into a sound sleep. Molly now determined to make another effort for her freedom. She accordingly worked herself gradually over the tail board of the wagon, and fell heavily upon the frozen ground. The horse and wagon passed on, and she rolled into the bushes, and waited for deliverance from her bonds. This came from a colored man who was passing that way. As he was neither a priest nor a Levite, he took the rope from her feet and guided her to a cabin near at hand, where she was kindly received. Her deliverer could not take the hand-cuffs off, but promised to bring a person, during the evening, who could perform that operation. He fulfilled his promise, and brought her that night to my house, which was in sight of the one whence she had been taken to New Castle Jail.

I had no fear for her safety, as I believed that her master would not think of looking for her so near to the place where she had been arrested. Molly remained with us nearly a month; but, seeing fugitives coming and going continually, she finally concluded to go further North. I wrote to my friend, Thomas Garrett, desiring him to get a good home for Molly. This he succeeded in doing, and a friend from Chester county, Pennsylvania, came to my house and took Molly with him. She remained in his family more than six months.

In the mean time the Fugitive Slave Law was passed by Congress, and several fugitives were arrested in Philadelphia and sent back to their masters. Molly, hearing of these doings, became uneasy, and finally determined to go to Canada. She arrived safely in the Queen's Dominions, and felt at last that she had escaped from the hell of American Slavery.

Molly described her master as an indulgent one when sober, but when he was on a "spree" he seemed to take great delight in tormenting her. He would have her beaten unmercifully without cause, and then have her stripes washed in salt water, then he would have her dragged through the horse pond until she was nearly dead. This last operation seemed to afford him much pleasure. When he became sober he would express regret at having treated her so cruelly. I frequently saw this master of Molly's, and was always treated respectfully by him. He would have his "sprees" after Molly left him.

AN ACCOUNT OF THE ESCAPE FROM SLAVERY OF SAMUEL HAWKINS AND FAMILY, OF QUEEN ANNE'S COUNTY, MARYLAND, ON THE UNDERGROUND RAIL ROAD, IN THE STATE OF DELAWARE. BY JOHN HUNN.

On the morning of the 27th of 12th month (December), 1845, as I was washing my hands at the yard pump of my residence, near Middletown, New Castle county, Delaware, I looked down the lane, and saw a covered wagon slowly approaching my house. The sun had just risen, and was shining brightly (after a stormy night) on the snow which covered the ground to the depth of six inches. My house was situated three quarters of a mile from the road leading from Middletown to Odessa, (then called Cantwell's Bridge.) On a closer inspection I noticed several men walking beside the wagon. This seemed rather an early hour for visitors, and I could not account for the circumstance. When they reached the yard fence I met them, and a colored man handed me a letter addressed to Daniel Corbit, John Alston or John Hunn; I asked the man if he had presented the letter to either of the others to whom it was addressed; he said, no, that he had not been able to see either of them. The letter was from my cousin, Ezekiel Jenkins, of Camden, Delaware, and stated that the travelers were fugitive slaves, under the direction of Samuel D. Burris (who handed me the note). The party consisted of a man and his wife, with their six children, and four fine-looking colored men, without counting the pilot, S. D. Burris, who was a free man, from Kent county, Delaware.

This was the first time that I ever saw Burris, and also the first time that I had ever been called upon to assist fugitives from the hell of American Slavery. The wanderers were gladly welcomed, and made as comfortable as possible until breakfast was ready for them. One man, in trying to pull his boots off, found they were frozen to his feet; he went to the pump and filled them with water, thus he was able to get them off in a few minutes.

This increase of thirteen in the family was a little embarrassing, but after breakfast they all retired to the barn to sleep on the hay, except the woman and four children, who remained in the house. They were all very weary, as they had traveled from Camden (twenty-seven miles), through a snow-storm; the woman and four children in the wagon with the driver, the others walking all the way. Most of them were badly frost-bitten, before they arrived at my house. In Camden, they were sheltered in the houses of their colored friends. Although this was my first acquaintance with S. D. Burris, it was not my last, as he afterwards piloted them himself, or was instrumental in directing hundreds of fugitives to me for shelter.

About two o'clock of the day on which these fugitives arrived at my house, a neighbor drove up with his daughter in a sleigh, apparently on a friendly visit. I noticed his restlessness and frequent looking out of the window fronting the road; but did not suppose, that he had come "to spy out the land."

The wagon and the persons walking with it, had been observed from his house, and he had reported the fact in Middletown. Accordingly, in half an hour, another sleigh came up, containing a constable of Middletown, William Hardcastle, of Queen Ann's county, Maryland, and William Chesnut, of the same neighborhood. I met them at the gate, and the constable handed me an advertisement, wherein one thousand dollars reward was offered for the recovery of three runaway slaves, therein described.

The constable asked me if they were in my house? I said they were not! He then asked me if he might search the house? I declined to allow him this privilege, unless he had a warrant for that purpose. While we stood thus conversing, the husband of the woman with the six children, came out of a house near the barn, and ran into the woods. The constable and his two companions immediately gave chase, with many halloos! After running more than a mile through the snow, the fugitive came toward the house; I went to meet him, and found him with his back against the barn-yard fence, with a butcher's knife in his hand. The man hunters soon came up, and the constable asked me to get the knife from the fugitive. This I declined, unless the constable should first give me his pistol, with which he was threatening to shoot the man. He complied with my request, and the fugitive handed me the knife. Then he produced a pass, properly authenticated, and signed by a magistrate of Queen Ann's county, Maryland, certifying that this man was free! and that his name was Samuel Hawkins.

William Hardcastle now advanced, and said that he knew the man to be free; but that he was accused of running away with his wife and children who were slaves. He also said, that this man had two boys with him, who belonged to a neighbor of his, named Charles Wesley Glanding, and that the four other children and mother belonged to Catharine Turner, of Queen Ann's county, Maryland. Hardcastle further expressed his belief, that this man knew where his wife and children were at that time, and insisted that he should go before a magistrate in Middletown, and be examined in regard thereto. He also expressed doubts as to the genuineness of this pass, and wished the man to go to Middletown on that account also. As there was no other course to pursue under the circumstances, I had my sleigh brought out, and we all went to Middletown, before my friend, William Streets, who was then in commission as a magistrate. It was now after dark of this short winter's day. Soon after our arrival at the office of William Streets, Hardcastle put his arm very lovingly around the neck of the colored man, Samuel Hawkins, and drew him into another room. In a short time, Samuel came out, and told me that Hardcastle had agreed, that if he, Hawkins, would give up his two older boys, who belonged to Charles Wesley Glanding; then he might pursue his journey with his wife and four children. I asked him if he believed Hardcastle would keep his promise? He replied: "Yes! I do not think master William would cheat me." I assured him that he would cheat him, and that the offer was made for the purpose of not only getting the two older boys (fourteen and sixteen years of age), but his wife and other children to the office, when all of them would be taken together to the jail, in New Castle. Samuel thought differently, and at his request, I wrote to my wife for the delivery of the family of Samuel Hawkins to the constable. They were soon forthcoming, and on their arrival at the office, a commitment was made out for the whole party. Samuel and his two older sons were hand-cuffed, amidst many tears and lamentations, and they all went off under charge of the man-hunters, to New Castle jail, a distance of eighteen miles.

William Streets committed the whole party as fugitives from Slavery, while the husband (Samuel), was a free man. This was done on account of the detestation of the wicked business, as much as on account of his friendship for me.

On their arrival at the jail, about midnight, the sheriff was aroused, and the commitment shown to him; after reading it, he asked Samuel if he was a slave? He said no, and showed his pass (which had been pronounced genuine by the magistrate). The sheriff hereupon told them, that the commitment was not legal, and would not hold them lawfully. It was now first day (Sunday), and the man-hunters were in a quandary.

The constable finally agreed to go back and get another commitment, if the sheriff would take the party into the jail until his return; Hardcastle also urged the sheriff to adopt this plan. Accordingly they were taken into the jail.

The sheriff's daughter had heard her father's conversation with the constable, accordingly she sent word on First-day morning, to my revered friend, Thomas Garrett, of Wilmington, five miles distant, in regard to the matter, inviting him to see the fugitives. Early on Second day morning (Monday), Thomas went over with John Wales, attorney at law. The latter soon obtained a writ of habeas corpus from Judge Booth of New Castle, which was served upon the sheriff; who, therefore, brought the whole party before Judge Booth, who discharged them at once, as being illegally detained by the sheriff. Thomas Garrett, with the consent of the judge, then hired a carriage to take the woman and four children over to Wilmington, Samuel and the two older boys walked, so they all escaped from the man-hunters. They went from Wilmington to Byberry, and settled near the farm of Robert Purvis. Samuel Hawkins and wife have since died, but their descendants still live in that neighborhood, under the name of Hackett.

Soon after the departure of the fugitives from New Castle jail, the constable arrived with new commitments from William Streets, and presented them in due form to the sheriff; who informed him that they had been liberated by order of Judge Booth! A few hours after, William Hardcastle arrived from Philadelphia, expecting to take Samuel Hawkins and his family to Queen Ann's county, Maryland. Judge of his disappointment at finding they were beyond his control—absolutely gone! They returned to Middletown in great anger, and threatened to prosecute William Streets for his participation in the affair.

After the departure of the Hawkins family from Middletown, I returned home to see what had become of S. D. Burris and his four men. I found them taking some solid refreshment, preparatory to taking a long walk in the snow. They left about nine P. M., for Wilmington. I sent by S. D. Burris a letter to Thomas Garrett, detailing the arrest and commitment of S. Hawkins and family to New Castle jail. They all arrived safely in Wilmington before daylight next morning. Burris waited to hear the result of the expedition to New Castle ; and actually had the pleasure of seeing S. Hawkins and family arrive in Wilmington.

Samuel Burris returned to my house early on Third day morning, with a letter from Thomas Garrett, giving me a description of the whole transaction. My joy on this occasion was great ! and I returned thanks to God for this wonderful escape of so many human beings from the charnel-house of Slavery.

Of course, this circumstance excited the ire of many pro-slavery editors in Maryland. I had copies of several papers sent me, wherein I was described as a man unfit to live in a civilized commnnity, and calling upon

JOHN HUNN,

CHIEF ENGINEER OF THE SOUTHERN END. See p. 712.

SAMUEL RHOADS,

STOCKHOLDER. See p. 719.

WILLIAM WHIPPER,

CONDUCTOR AT COLUMBIA. See p. 735.

SAMUEL D. BURRIS,

CONDUCTOR. See p. 746.

OFFICERS OF THE ROAD.

the inhabitants of Middletown to expel such a dangerous person from that neighborhood! They also told exactly where I lived, which enabled many a poor fugitive escaping from the house of bondage, to find a hearty welcome and a resting-place on the road to liberty. Thanks be to God! for His goodness to me in this respect.

The trial which ensued from the above, came off before Chief Justice Taney, at New Castle. My revered friend, Thomas Garrett, and myself, were there convicted of harboring fugitive slaves, and were fined accordingly, to the extent of the law; Judge Taney delivering the sentence. A detailed account of said trial, will fully appear in the memoirs of our deceased friend, Thomas Garrett.

SAMUEL RHOADS

Was born in Philadelphia, in 1806, and was through life a consistent member of the Society of Friends. His parents were persons of great respectability and integrity. The son early showed an ardent desire for improvement, and was distinguished among his young companions for warm affections, amiable disposition, and genial manners, rare purity and refinement of feeling, and a taste for literary pursuits. Preferring as his associates those to whom he looked for instruction and example, and aiming at a high standard, he won a position, both mentally and socially, superior to his early surroundings. With a keen sense of justice and humanity, he could not fail to share in the traditional opposition of his religious society to slavery, and to be quickened to more intense feeling as the evils of the system were more fully revealed in the Anti-slavery agitation which in his early manhood began to stir the nation.

A visit to England, in 1834, brought him into connection and friendship with many leading Friends in that country, who were actively engaged in the Anti-slavery movement, and probably had much to do with directing his attention specially to the subject. Once enlisted, he never wavered, but as long as slavery existed by law in our country his influence, both publicly and privately, was exerted against it. He was strengthened in his course by a warm friendship and frequent intercourse with the late Abraham L. Pennock, a man whose unbending integrity and firm allegiance to duty were equalled only by his active benevolence, broad charity, and rare clearness of judgment. Samuel Rhoads, like him, while sympathizing with other phases of the Anti-slavery movement, took especial interest in the subject of abstaining from the use of articles produced by slave labor. Believing that the purchase of such articles, by furnishing to the master the only possibility of pecuniary profit from the labor of his slaves, supplied one motive for holding them in bondage, and that the purchaser thus became, however unwittingly, a partaker in the guilt, he felt conscientiously bound to withhold his individual support as far as practicable, and to recommend the same course to others.

His practical action upon these views began about the year 1841, and was persevered in, at no small expense and inconvenience, till slavery ceased in this country to have a legal existence.   About this time he united with the American Free Produce Association, which had been formed in 1838, and in 1845 took an active part in the formation of the Free Produce Association of Friends of Philadelphia, Y. M. ; both associations having the object of promoting the production by free labor of articles usually grown by slaves, particularly of cotton.   Agents were sent into the cotton States, to make arrangements with small planters, who were growing cotton by the labor of themselves and their families without the help of slaves, to obtain their crops, which otherwise went into the general market, and could not be distinguished.   A manufactory was established for working this cotton, and a limited variety of goods were thus furnished.   In all these operations Samuel Rhoads aided efficiently by counsel and money.

In 1846, "The Non-slave-holder," a monthly periodical, devoted mainly to the advocacy of the Free Produce cause, was established in Philadelphia, edited by A. L. Pennock, S. Rhoads, and George W. Taylor.   It was continued five years, for the last two of which Samuel Rhoads conducted it alone.   He wrote also a pamphlet on the free labor question.   From July, 1856 to January, 1867 he was Editor of the "Friends' Review," a weekly paper, religious and literary, conducted in the interest of his own religious society, and in this position he gave frequent proofs of interest in the slave, keeping his readers well advised of events and movements bearing upon the subject.

While thus awake to all forms of anti-slavery effort, his heart and hand were ever open to the fugitive from bondage, who appealed to him, and none such were ever sent away empty.   Though not a member of the Vigilance Committee, he rendered it frequent and most efficient aid, especially during the dark ten years after the passage of the Fugitive Slave Law.

A second visit to England, in 1847, had enlarged his connection and correspondence with anti-slavery friends there, and in addition to his own contributions, very considerable sums of money were transmitted to him, especially through A. H. Richardson, for the benefit of the fugitives.   Often when the treasury of the Committee ran low, he came opportunely to their relief with funds sent by his English friends, while his sympathy and encouragement never failed.   The extent of his assistance in this direction was known to but few, but by them its value was gratefully acknowledged.   None rejoiced more than he in the overthrow of American slavery, though its end came in convulsion and bloodshed, at which his spirit revolted, not by the peaceful means through which he with others had labored to bring it about

He had some years before been active in preparing a memorial to Congress, asking that body to make an effort to put an end to slavery in the States, by offering from the national treasury, to any State or States which would emancipate the slaves therein, and engage not to renew the system, compensation for losses thus sustained. This proposition was made, not as admitting any *right* of the masters to compensation; but on the ground that the whole nation, having shared in the guilt of maintaining slavery, might justly share also in whatever pecuniary loss might follow its abandonment.

This memorial was sent to Congress, but elicited no response; and in the fulness of time, the nation paid even in money many times any possible price that could have been demanded under this plan. Samuel Rhoads died in 1868.

GEORGE CORSON

Was born in Plymouth township, Montgomery county, Pennsylvania, January 24th, 1803. He was the son of Joseph and Hannah Corson. He was married January 24th, 1832, to Martha, daughter of Samuel and Susanna Maulsby.

There were perhaps few more devoted men than George Corson to the interests of the oppressed everywhere. The slave, fleeting from his master, ever found a home with him, and felt while there that no slave-hunter would get him away until every means of protection should fail. He was ever ready to send his horse and carriage to convey them on the road to Canada, or elsewhere towards freedom. His home was always open to entertain the anti-slavery advocates, and being warmly supported in the cause by his excellent wife, everything which they could do to make their guests comfortable was done. The Burleighs, J. Miller McKim, Miss Mary Grew, F. Douglass, and others will not soon forget that hospitable home. It is to be regretted that he died before the emancipation of the slaves, which he had so long labored for, arrived. In this connection it may not be improper to state that simultaneously with his labors in the Anti-slavery cause, he was also laboring with zeal in the cause of Temperance. Of his efforts in that direction through nearly thirty years, our space will not allow us to speak. His life and labors were a daily protest against the traffic of rum. There is also another phase of his character which should be mentioned. Whenever he saw animals abused, horses beaten, he instantly interfered, often at great risk of personal harm from the brutal drivers about the lime quarries and iron ore diggings. So firm, so determined was he, that the cruellest ruffian felt that he must yield or confront the law. Take him all for all, there will rarely be found in one man more universal benevolence and justice than was possessed by the subject of this notice.

Hiram Corson, brother of the subject of this sketch, and a faithful co-

46

laborer in the cause, in response to a request that he would furnish a reminiscence touching his brother's agency in assisting fugitives, wrote as follows:

November 1st, 1871.

DEAR ROBERT:—Wm. Still wishes some account of the case of the negro slave taken from our neighborhood some years ago, after an attempt by my brother George to release him. (About thirty years ago.) George had been on a visit to our brother Charles, living at the fork of the Skippack and Per-kiomen Creeks, in this county, and on his return, late in the afternoon, while coming along an obscure road, not the main direct road, he came up to a man on horseback, who was followed at a distance of a few feet by a colored man with a rope tied around his neck, and the other end held by the person on horseback.

George had had experience with those slave-drivers before, as in the case of John and James Lewis, and withal had become deeply interested in the Anti-slavery cause. He, therefore, inquired of the mounted man, what the other had done that he was to be thus treated. He quietly remarked that he was his slave and had run away. He then asked by what authority he held him. He said by warrant from Esquire Vanderslice. Indignant at this great outrage, my brother hurried on to Norristown, and waited his arrival with a process to arrest him. The slave-master, confident in his rights, bold in the country of those pretended freemen, who were ever ready to kiss the rod of Slavery, came slowly riding into Norristown, just before sunset, with the rope still fast to the slave's neck. He was immediately taken before a Justice of the Peace, whose name I do not now remember. The people gathered around; anxious inquiries were made as to the person who had the audacity to question the right of this quiet, peaceable man to do with his slave as he pleased. Great scorn was expressed for the busy Abolitionists. Much sympathy given to the abused slave owner. It was soon decided, by the aid of a volunteer lawyer, whose sons have since fought the battle for freedom, that the slave-owner had a right to take his slave where-ever, and in whatever way he pleased, through the country, and not only that, but at his call for help it was the bounden duty of every man, called upon, to aid him; and the person who had the audacity to stop him was threatened with punishment.

But George's blood was up, so pained was he at the sight of a man, a poor man, a helpless man, being dragged through from Pennsylvania with a halter around his neck, that, amidst the jeers and insults of the debased crowd, he denounced Slavery, its aiders and abettors, in tones of scorn and loathing. But the man thief was left with his prey. Through the advice of those who stood by the slave laws and who knelt before the slave power, as personified by that hunter of slaves, the rope was taken from the neck, and the man guarded while the master regaled himself. That night he disappeared with his man.

I can also give a few particulars of the escape of the Gorsuch murderers, from Norristown on their way to Canada. There should be a portrait of Daniel Ross, and a history of his labors during twenty or more years. Hundreds were entertained in his humble home, and it was in his home that the Gorsuch murderer was secreted. He must not be left out. I can also get the whole history, escape, capture, trial, conviction and redemption of James and John Lewis, and one other. They were captured here within sight of our house. George Corson, Esq., published it all, about ten years ago. Respectfully,

Robert R. Corson.   Hiram Corson.

CHARLES D. CLEVELAND.

Mr. Still has asked me to record the part that my father bore in the Anti-slavery enterprise, as it began and grew in this city. I comply, because the history of that struggle would be very incomplete, if from it were omitted the peculiar work which my father's position here shaped for him. Yet I can only indicate his work, not portray it; tell some of its elements, and then leave them to the moral sympathies of the reader to upbuild. For, first, his labor for the love of man was evenly distributed through the mould and movements of his entire life; and from a perpetual current of nourishing blood, one cannot name those particular atoms that are busiest or richest to sustain vitality. And, further, if I could hear his voice, it would forbid any detailed account of what he accomplished and endured. It was all done unobtrusively in his life; bravely, defiantly, in regard of the evil to be met and mastered, but as unconsciously in regard of himself as every conviction works, when it is as broad as the entire spiritual life of a man and has his entire spiritual force to give it expression. I know, therefore, that while I should be permitted to mention so much of his service as the history of the conflict might demand, I should be forbidden all tale of sacrifice and labor that mere personal narrative would include; and I ask now only this: What peculiar influence did he exert for the furtherance of the cause which so largely absorbed his labor and life? Did he contribute anything to it stamped with the signature of so clear an individuality that no other man could have contributed quite the same? To this I maintain an affirmative answer; and in witness of its truth, I sketch the general course of his life, that through it we may find those elements of his character which intuitively ranged him on the side of the slave.

When my father came to Philadelphia in 1834, his sentiments in regard to Slavery were those held generally in the North—an easy-going wish to avoid direct issue with the South on a question supposed to be peculiarly theirs. But the winds of Heaven owned to no decorous limit in Mason and Dixon's line; and there were larger winds blowing than these—winds rising in the vast laboratories of the general human heart, and destined to sweep into all the vast spaces of human want and woe. The South was finding, through her blacks' perpetual defiance of torture and death for freedom, that there was perhaps something, even in a negro, which most vexatiously refused to be counted in with the figures of the auctioneer's bill of sale; and now the North's lesson was coming to her — that the soul of a century's civilization was still less purchasable than the soul of a slave. A growing feeling of humanity was stirring through the northern States. It was not the work, I think, of any man or body of men; it was rather itself a creative force, and made men and bodies of men the results of its awakening influence. To such a power, my father's nature was quickly responsive. Both his head and his heart recognized the terrible wrongs of the enslaved, and the urgency with which they pressed for remedy; but where was the means? From the first, he felt that the movement which brought Freedom and Slavery fairly into the field and squarely against each other, threw unnecessary obstacles in its own way by the violence with which it was begun and prosecuted. If he were to work at all in the cause, he determined to work within the limits of recognized law. The Colonization Society held out a good hope; at least, he could see no other as close to the true but closer to the feasible; and, after connecting himself with it, he seems to have been content for a while on the score of political matters, and to have devoted himself to what he had adopted as his chief purpose in life. This was, enlarging the sphere of female education, and giving it a more vigorous tone. To this he tasked all his abilities. His convictions on the subject were very earnest; his strength of character sufficient to bear them out; so that, in a short time, he was able to establish his school so firmly in the respect of this community, that, for twenty-five years, all the odium that his activity in the Anti-slavery cause drew upon him did not for a moment abate the public confidence accorded to his professional power.

It was in 1836, in one of his vacations, that his mind was violently turned inwards to re-examine his status upon the Anti-slavery question. He happened to be visiting his old college-friend, Salmon P. Chase, at Cincinnati, and, fortunately for the spiritual life of both men, it was at the time of the terrible riots that broke up the press of John G. Birney. Both being known as already favoring the cause of the slave, they stood in much peril for several days; but when the dark time was passed, the clearness that defined their sentiments was seen to be worth all the personal danger that had bought it. Self-delusion on the subject was no longer possible. The deductions from the facts were as plain as the facts themselves. The two friends took counsel together, and adopted the policy from which thenceforward neither ever swerved. A great cloud was rolled from their eyes. In

all this turmoil of riot, they saw on the one side, indeed, a love of man great
in its devotion; but on the other, a moral deadness in the North so profound
and determined that it threatened thus brutally any voice that would disturb
it Their duty, then, was evident: to fling all the forces of their lives, and
by all social and political means, right against this inertness, and shatter it
if they could. To Mr. Chase, the course of things gave the larger political
work; to my father, the larger social. His diary records how amazed he
was, when he returned to Philadelphia, at his former blindness, and how
thankful to the spirit of love that had touched and cleansed his eyes that he
might see God's image erect. He knew now that his lot had been cast in
the very stronghold of apathy, the home of a lukewarm spirit, which, not containing anything positive to keep it close to the right, let its sullen negative-
ness gravitate towards the wrong. It will be difficult to make coming
generations understand, not the flaming antagonism to humanity, but the
more brutal avoidance of it that ruled the political tone in this latitude, from
1836 to 1861. I have thought of the word *bitterness*, as expressing it; but
though that might convey somewhat of its recoil when disturbed, it pictures
nothing of its inhuman solicitude against all disturbance. Conservatism, it
was called; and certainly it did conserve the devil admirably. At the
South, one race of men were so basely wielding a greater physical power
over another race of men, as to crush from them the attributes of self-respon-
sible creatures; Philadelphia, the city of the North nearest the wrong, made
no plea for humanity's claims. It went on, this monstrous abrogation of
everything that lends sanctity to man's relations on earth, till slaves were
beasts, with instincts annihilated, and masters demons, with instincts re-
versed; Philadelphia made no plea for the violated rhythm of life on
either side. Even the Church betrayed its mission, and practically aided
in stamping out from millions the spirit that related them to the Divine;
still Philadelphia made no plea for God's love in his humanity. Utterly
insensible to the most piercing appeals that man can make to man, she loved
her hardness, clung to it; and if, now and then, a voice from the North blew
down, warningly as a trumpet, the great city turned sluggishly in her bed
of spiritual and political torpor, and cried: Let be, let be! a little more
slumber! a little more folding of the hands to my moral death-sleep!

The souring of faith, this half-paralysis of the heart's beating, this
blurring of the intuitions that make manhood possible, were what my
father found here in that year of our Lord's grace, 1836. It will be worth
while to watch him move into the fight and bear his part in its thickest, just
to learn how largely history lays her humanitarian advances on a few willing souls.

The means which lay readiest to his use for rousing the dormant spirit
of the city was his social position. And yet how hard, one would think,
it must have been to make this sacrifice. He came accredited by all

the claims of finished culture, a man consecrated to the scholar's life.* Then, with the sensitiveness that springs from intellectual breeding, one will look to see him shrink from conflict with the callous condition of feeling around him. The glamour of book-lore will spread over it, and hide it from his sight. He has a noble enough mission, at all events: to raise the standard of educational culture in a city that hardly knows the meaning of the term; and if any glimpse should come to him of the lethargic inhumanity around him, he can afford to let it pass as a glimpse—his look being fixed on the sacred heights which the scholar's feet must tread.

Ah, how his course, so different, proves to us that the true scholar is always a scholar of truth. No matter what element of the public sentiment he met—the listlessness of pampered wealth; the brutal prejudice of some voting savage; the refined sneer of lettered dilettanteism; the purposed aversion of trade or pulpit fearing disturbed markets or pews;—he beat lustily and incessantly at all the parts of the iron image of wrong sitting stolidly here with close-shut eyes. No matter when it was, on holiday or working-day or Sabbath; at home and abroad; in the parlor, the street, the counting-room; in his school and in the Church;—he bore down on this apathy and its brood of scorns like a west wind that sweeps through a city dying under weight of miasma. And the wind might as well cease blowing yet not cease to be wind, as my father's influence stop and himself live. It scattered the good seed everywhere. How often have I heard him say, "I know nothing of what the harvest will be; I am responsible only for the sowing." And bravely went the sowing on, with the broadcast largesse of love. There was no breeze of talk that did not carry the seeds;— to the wayside, for from those that even chance upon the truth the fowls of the air cannot take it all; to thin soil and among thorns, for no heart so feeble or choked that will not find in a single day's growth of truth germination for eternity; to stony places, for no cranny in the rocks that can hold a seed but can be a home for riving roots;—"And other fell on good ground and did bring forth fruit."

Thus it was primarily to rouse those of his own class that he labored, to gall them into seeing (though they should turn again and rend him) that moral supineness is moral decay, that the soul shrivels into nothingness when wrong is acquiesced in, as surely as it is torn and scattered by the furies let loose within it, when wrong is done. But just there lay the difficulty and pain of his mission: that, from his acknowledged standing in the literary world, and as a leader in the interests of higher education, his path brought him into contact mainly with the cultured, and it was among these

---

* All that I here write of my father, I write equally of his co-laborer in the same sphere of work—Rev. W. H. Furness; and if it is true of others whom I did not know, then to their memory also I bear this record of the two whose labors and characters it has been the deepest privilege of my life to know so well.

that the pro-slavery spirit ruled with its bitterest stringency. Not cultured: let us unsay the word; rather, with the gloss and hard polish which reading and wealth and the finer appointments of living can throw over spiritual arrest or decay. Culture is a holy word, and dare be used of intellectual advance only when the moral sympathies have kept equal step. It includes something beyond an amateur sentiment in favor of what we favor. If it does not open the ear to every cry of humanity, struggling up or slipping back, it is no culture properly so called, but a sham, a mask of wax, a varnish with cruel glitter; and what a double wrath will be poured on him who cracks the wax and the varnish, not only because of the rude awakening, but because the crack shows the sham.

It is impossible for us now to realize what revenge this class dealt to my father for twenty-five years. Consider their power of revenge. They could not force a loss of property or of life, it is true; they made no open assault in the street; their 'delicacy' held itself above common vituperation. But they wielded a greater power than all these over a man whose every accomplishment made him their equal, and they used it without stint. They doomed him to the slow martyrdom of social scorn. They shut their doors against him. They elbowed him from every position to which he had a wish or a right, except public respect, and they could not elbow him from that unless they pushed his character from its poise. They cut him off from every friendly regard which would else have been devotedly his, on that level of educated life, and limited him to 'solitary confinement' within himself. They compelled him to walk as if under a ban or an anathema. Had he been a leper in Syrian deserts, or a disciple of Jesus among Pharisees, he could not have been more utterly banished from the region of homes and self-constituted piety. They showered ineffable contempt upon him in every way consistent with their littleness and—refinement. Slight, sneer, insult, all the myriad indignities that only 'good society' can devise, these were what my father received in return for his love and his work in love.

How little personal relation all this obloquy bore to him, let this stand as evidence: that he not only continued his work, but daily gave it more caustic energy and wider scope. As I have hinted, he did not, in political matters, give in his adherence to that class of abolitionists who, as he thought, threw away their best chances of success in refusing to work within constitutional provisions. He was prouder that this single community should call him " abolitionist," though it spat the word at him, than if the whole earth should hail him with the kingliest title; but he loved the name too well not to make it stand for some practical fact, some feasible and organized effort. He believed that our National Constitution did, indeed, hold many compromises with Slavery, but was framed, in the majority of its provisions and certainly in the totality of its spirit, in the interests of freedom; and that it only needed enforcement by the choice of the ballot-box to bring the

South either to an amicable or a hostile settlement of the question. Which, he did not ask or care. The duty of the present could not be mis-read; it was written in *the vote.*

With these views, he gave much time and work to organizing in this State, " The National Liberty Party," in 1840, and to securing from Pennsylvania some of the seven thousand votes that were cast for John G. Birney in that year throughout the Union. By the time another election came, the party had swelled its numbers to seventy thousand. To contribute his share towards this success, tract after tract, address after address, were written and sent broadcast; meetings were convened, committees formed, resolutions framed, speeches made, petitions and remonstrances sent, public action fearlessly sifted and criticised ; in short, because he held a steady faith in men's humane promptings when ultimately reached, he 'cried aloud' to them by every access, and 'spared not' to call them from their timidity and time-serving to manly utterance through the ballot-box.

Of such appeals, his address of the " Liberty Party of Pennsylvania, to the people of the State," issued in 1844, may stand as a sample. It is a vivid portrayal of the slave power's insidious encroachments, and of its monopolized guidance of the Government. It gathers up the national statistics into groups, shows how new meaning is reflected from them thus related, that all unite to illustrate the single fact of the South's steady increase of power, her tightening grasp about the throat of government, and her buffets of threat to the North when a weedling palm failed to palsy fast enough. It warns northern voters of the undertow that is drawing them, and adjures them, by every consideration of political common sense, not to cast their ballots for either of the pro-slavery candidates presented. The conclusion of this address is as follows :

OUR OBJECT.

" And now, fellow-citizens, you may ask, what is our object in thus exhibiting to you the alarming influence of the slave power? Do we wish to excite in your bosoms feelings of hatred against citizens of a common country? Do we wish to array the Free states against the Slave states in hostile strife ? No, fellow-citizens. But we wish to show you that, while the slave states are inferior to us in free population, having not even one half of ours ; inferior in morals, being the region of bowie knives and duels, of assassinations and lynch law ; inferior in mental attainments, having not one-fourth of the number that can read and write ; inferior in intelligence, having not one-fifth of the number of literary and scientific periodicals ; inferior in the products of agriculture and manufactures, of mines, of fisheries, and of the forest ; inferior, in short, in everything that constitutes the wealth, the honor, the dignity, the stability, the happiness, the true greatness of a nation,—it is wrong, it is unjust, it is absurd, that they should have an influence in all the departments of government so entirely disproportionate to our own. We would arouse you to your own true interests. We would have you, like men, firmly resolved to maintain your own rights. We would have you say to the South,—if you choose to hug to your bosom that system which is continually injuring and impoverishing you ; that system which reduces two millions and a half of native Americans in your midst to the most abject condition of ignorance and vice, withholding from them the very key of knowledge ; that system which is at war with every principle of justice, every feeling of humanity ; that system which makes man the property of man, and perpetuates that relation from one generation to another ; that system which tramples, continually, upon a majority of the commandments of the Decalogue ; that system which could not live a day if it did not give one party supreme control over the persons, the health, the liberty, the happiness, the marriage relations, the parental authority and filial obligations of the other ;—if you choose to cling to such a system, cling to it ; but you shall not cross our line ; you shall not bring that foul thing here. We know, and we here repeat it for the thousandth time to meet, for the thousandth time, the calumnies of our enemies, that while we may present to you every consideration of duty, we have no right, as well as no power, to alter your State laws. But remember, that slavery is the mere creature of local or statute law, and cannot exist out of the region where such law has force. 'It is so odious,' says Lord Mansfield, ' that nothing can be suffered to support it but *positive* law.'

" We would, therefore, say to you again, in the strength of that Constitution under which we live, and which no where countenances slavery, you shall not bring that foul thing here. You shall not force the corrupted and corrupting blood of that system into every vein and artery of our body politic. You shall not have the controlling power in all the departments of our government at home and abroad. You shall not so negotiate with foreign powers, as to open markets for the products of slave labor alone. You shall not so manage things at home, as every few years to bring bankruptcy upon our country. You shall not, in the apportionment of public moneys, have what you call your ' property ' represented, and thus get that which, by no right, belongs to you. You shall not have the power to bring your slaves upon our free soil, and take them away at pleasure ; nor to reclaim them, when they, panting for liberty, have been able to escape your grasp ; for we would have it said of us, as the eloquent Curran said of Britain, the moment the slave touches our soil, 'The ground on which he stands is holy, and consecrated to the Genius of UNIVERSAL EMANCIPATION.'

" Thus, fellow-citizens, we come to *the great object of the Liberty Party:* ABSOLUTE AND UNQALIFIED DIVORCE OF THE GENERAL GOVERNMENT FROM ALL CONNECTION WITH SLAVERY. We would employ every *constitutional* means to eradicate it from our entire country, because it would be for the highest welfare of our entire country. We would have liberty established in the District, and in all the Territories.   *   *   We would have liberty of speech and of the press, which the Constitution guarantees to us. We would have the right of petition most sacredly regarded. We would secure to every man what the Constitution secures, ' The right of trial by jury.' We would do what we can for the encouragement and improvement of the colored race, and restore to them that inestimable right of which they have been so meanly, as well as unjustly, deprived, the RIGHT OF SUFFRAGE. We would look to the best interests of the country, and the *whole* country, and not legislate for the good of an Oligarchy, the most arrogant that ever lorded it over an insulted people. We would have our commercial treaties with foreign nations regard the interests of the Free states. We would provide safe, adequate, and permanent markets for the produce of free labor. And, when reproached with slavery, we would be able to say to the world, with an open front and a clear conscience, our General Government has nothing to do with it, either to promote, to sustain, to defend, to sanction, or to approve.

" Thus, fellow-citizens, you see our objects. You may now ask, by what means we hope to attain them. We answer, by POLITICAL ACTION. What is political action ? It is *acting in a manner appropriate to those objects which we wish to secure through the agency of the different departments of Government.*   *   *   The only way in which we can act *constitutionally*, is to go to the ballot box, and there, silently and unostentatiously, deposit a vote for such men as will do what they can to carry out those principles which we have so much at heart.   *   *   *   *   *   *

"Come, then, men of Pennsylvania, come and join us in this good work. Join us, to use such moral means as to co: ect public sentiment throughout the region where slavery exists, and to impress upon the people of the Free states a manly sense of their own rights. Join us, to place "just men" in all our public offices; men whose example a whole people may safely imitate. Join us to free our General Government from the ig- nomiuious reproach of slavery ; to restore to our country those principles which our fathers so labored to establish ; and to hand these principles down afresh to successive genera- tions. It is the cause of truth, of humanity, and of God, to which we invite your aid. It is a cause of which you never need be ashamed. Living, you may be thankful, and dying, you may be thankful, for having labored ·in it. We have, as co-laborers with us, the noblest allies that man can wish. Within, we have the deepest convictions of conscience, the clearest deductions of reason ; and, all over the world, wherever man is found, the first, the most ardent longings of the human soul. Without, we have the happiness of nearly three millions of the human race; the honor, as well as the best interests of our whole country ; and the universal consent of all good men whose moral vision is not obscured by the mist of a low, misguided selfishness : while we seem to hear, as it were, the voices of the great and the good, the patriot and the philanthropist, of a past generation, calling to us and cheering us on. But, above all these, and beyond all these, we have with us the highest attributes of God, Justice and Mercy. With such allies, and in such a cause, who can doubt on which side the victory will ultimately rest.

"May He who guides the destinies of nations, and without whose aid 'they labor in vain that build,' so incline your hearts to exert your whole influence to place in all our public offices just and good men, that our country may be preserved, her best interests advanced, and her institutions, free in reality as in name, handed down to the latest pos- terity."

Is not the love of God and man ingrained in every line of this writing? Yet let us see how it was received by the most Christian (?) body in this city.

I need hardly say that my father's mind had been largely impressed, from earliest manhood, with the highest subject human thought can touch. His library records his wide religious reading ; but he could not see an honest path towards the profession of any definite views till 1836. The change wrought in him then, can best be gathered from his own simple words (under date, 1842) written in a fly-leaf of "The Unitarian Miscellany :" "Though I humbly trust that God made my trials in 1836 the means of bringing me to true repentance, yet I have kept these books as monuments of what I once was, and to remind me how grateful I should be to Him for having snatched me as a 'brand from the burning.'" Such a faith as this, born of the spiritual travail of years, what a life it always has for the heart that forms it! It tells not of a persuasion, but of a conviction ; a disproof of skepticism through the gathered forces of the soul ; a struggle, through epochs of doubt and dismay, into an attitude of positive vital faith. Its process is the only one that gives real right to ultimate peace. In comparison with the method and measure of such a conviction, what matters its specific form ? Self-truth is the point,—the fact for starting, the line for guiding; and as for result, this lonely and solemn rally on the deepest within us, as it is continuously unfolded, must lead to a glad and solemn union with the Highest without us. Who can know unfailing inward energy except through this new birth? It proved an ever-fresh spring of vigor to my father, and because of it he was chosen, in 1839, president of "The Philadelphia Bible Society." What changes were wrought in the policy of the Society, what numerous plans were devised and executed for multiplying its operations, how it was made a cordial alliance of all denominations, will presently appear. This is now to be said: that, after filling his office for five years, he found that his Anti-slavery testimony had engendered in the managers a bitterness that would seize the address of 1844 for pretext, and make retaliation in his sacrifice. Thankful, for the thousandth time, to be a sacrifice for the cause he loved, he sent in his resignation in a letter full of Christian kindness and sorrow. A short extract will show its tone :

" One whose great heart wishes the best for humanity calls to us from the West: ' When your Society propose to put a Bible into every family, and yet omit all reference to the slaves ; and when, giving an account of the destitution of the land, they make no mention of two and a half millions of people perishing in our midst without the Scriptures, can we help feeling that something is dreadfully wrong?' This, brethren, is a most solemn question. It is a question which I verily believe the American Bible Society, so far as they may have yielded, directly or indirectly, openly or silently, to a corrupt public sentiment on this subject, will have to answer at the bar of Him who has declared, that, ' If ye have respect to persons, ye commit sin ;' and that ' Inasmuch as ye did it not to one of the least of these, ye did it not to me.' The spirit of Christianity is a spirit of universal love and philanthropy. She looks down with pity, and, if she could, she would look with scorn upon all the petty distinctions that exist among men. She casts her benignant eye abroad over the earth, and, wherever she sees man, she sees him *as man*, as a being made in the image of God, whether an Indian, an African, or a Caucasian sun may shine upon him. She stoops from heaven to raise the fallen, to bind up the broken-hearted, to release the oppressed, to give liberty to the captive, and to break the fetters of those that are bound. She is marching onward with accelerated step, and, wherever she leaves the true impress of her heavenly influence, the moral wilderness is changed into the garden of the Lord. May it never be ours to do what may seem to be even the slightest obstacle to her universal sway.   *   *

" But I have already written more than I intended. In bringing this communication to a close, allow me to express to you individually, and as a Board, my most sincere Christian attachment. Whatever course any members may have taken in relation to this matter, I must believe that they have acted from what has seemed to them a sense of duty. Far be it from me to impeach their motives. Time, the great test of truth, may show them their course in a very different light from that in which they now view it. I may, as a Christian, lament that their views of duty are not more in unison with my own. I may, as a man, feel heart-sickened at the diseased, the deplorably diseased state of the public mind, in relation to two and a half millions of my fellow-men in bondage. I may, as a citizen of a Free state, blush at the humiliating fact, that not only the tyranny, but the ubiquity of the slave power is everywhere so manifest ; that it has insinuated itself into our free domain to such a degree that there seems to be as much mental Slavery in the Free states, as there is personal in the Slave states. I may feel all this, but I must not impeach the motives by which others have been governed."

There were twenty-one managers present at the reading of this letter, and, at its conclusion, a noble friend of the slave moved that the resignation be not accepted; the motion was lost by a vote of fourteen against seven. It was then moved that it be accepted 'with regret:' this was carried by the same vote! But 'with regret' was not an empty form for easing this action to its recipient; how much it meant is seen in the resolution that was added by unanimous acceptance: "*Resolved*,—That this Board are mainly indebted to Professor C. D. Cleveland for the prominent and influential position it has attained in the regards of this Christian community, and that they bear an 'earnest testimony to the sound judgment and unwearied zeal which have ever characterized the discharge of his duties in his responsible office." Let this tribute, coming from the bitterest personal opposition that ever man encountered, measure the work that extorted it. Looking at it, it will be difficult for the reader to believe that a sacrifice was made of the man to whom it refers by a representative Christian body, and merely to sate for a time the inhuman slave-greed; yet it is only one fact out of many that might be adduced, and I have brought it forward because it is, in my father's words, "a fair exponent of the position of the Christian Church at that time upon the subject of Slavery." Henceforward, he ceased not to rain blows, not only at his own (the Presbyterian) denomination, but at all the organized expressions of Christian purpose,—the Sunday-School Union, the Tract Society, etc.

While working thus by voice and pen, he was incessantly busy in personal rescue of the slave. Especially was this the case when it became the duty of every lover of his kind to defy the Fugitive Slave Law. How eagerly he then sprang to aid the escape of those against whom a law of the land impotently tried to bar the law of our common humanity! During the years that followed the passage of this infamous bill, the position he had attained here was of particular service. Recognized as one, who, being a sort of standing sacrifice, might as well continue to battle in the front; trusted implicitly even by his bitterest foes; with such a broad philanthropy to back his appeals; pushing straight into every breach where work was needed; blind to everything but his one light of moral instinct;—he became an organ for the charities of those whose softer natures longingly whispered the cry, but could not do the cut and thrust work, of deliverance. Dr. Furness held the same position, and others who, like him, refused to be enrolled in the 'Underground Committee,' or in any definite Anti-Slavery organization. These men knew that they were of greater service to the cause by being its body-guard, by standing between it and the public, by making the appeals and taking the blows, and by affording access, pecuniary and other, of each to each.

Thus the times moved on—growing hotter, more difficult and dangerous, but always working these two results: redoubling the labors of this noble band, and shaking the city from lethargy into ferment. Men were compelled to take sides, and but one result could follow, (the result which always follows when human nature is stung and quickened to find its highest instincts,) the Party of Right steadily moved to triumph.

For a lesson to us in courage, it is worth while to ask, how these Apostles of Freedom stood the terrible strain put upon them for so many years. I can answer for the two of whom I write, and do not doubt that the answer is true of the rest : This self-forgetfulness was made easy by a love that filled and overfilled all their moral energies—the simple love of man, as God's highest creation, and of his natural rights, as God's best gift. Their work was not a mere result of will, not an outcome of faculty, not an unsupported impulse of heart. It was character living itself out, an utterance of its entire unity, something drawn from the solemn depths of those life-convictions which all the personal and impersonal powers of a man, aglow and welded, unite in producing. Hence, their work was not apart from them, even so far as to be called ahead of them ; nor parallel with them ; it was *one* with them by a necessary spiritual inclusion. Will and Duty ceased to be separate powers ; they were transfused through the whole breadth of their human sympathies, adding to their warmth a fixity of purpose that bore them without a falter, through thirty years of such bitter obloquy, as, in these latter days, only the early Anti-Slavery disciples have had to endure. These men never said, in reference to the Anti-slavery cause, *I ought* or *I will,* because they never needed to say them. The sun shines without them, and life expands without them ; and here were souls as unconsciously beneficent as the one, as spontaneous in growth and shaping as the other. Theirs was not a force that moved mechanically in right lines, with limited objects before it. It did, indeed, sweep with arrowy swiftness of assail on every point that offered ; but when I remember that it more often pleaded than stormed, that it penetrated into every secret recess that mercy casually opened, and gently stirred into fuller life those roots of human feeling that can be numbed by apathy but not killed even by hate, I know that it was persuasive, diffusive, inbreathing force, an influence vital in others because an effluence vitalized from themselves.

So they stood, self-consecrated, enveloped by the love of God, permeated by the love of man,—twin Perfect Loves that cast out all dream of fear. And so they walked, calm as if a thousand stabs of personal insult never brought them one of personal pain, passing through all as if nothing but the serenest skies were above them. And, as I have said, right there is one explanation of the anomaly ; there *were* the serenest skies above them— heaven's love perpetually shining. Why should it not shine ? all the powers of the men were dedicated to rescuing the image of God on this earth,—

not man as he suffered physically, but the moral instinct threatened with annihilation. It was sacred to them, this soul so sacred to redeeming love, but too brutalized to find its way to it. Nor merely the slave. Their love embraced, with yet more pitying fervor, the master compelling his spiritual nature into death, and the northern apologist letting his die; and this over-mastering love of saving spiritual integrity, was one power that made them and heart-ease hold unfailing friends through the obloquy of those days; the other must be found in the fact mentioned,—that neither resolve nor impulse was their spur, but personal character moving from its depths.

From such a motive-power as this can come no parade of results. The nature that works, proceeds from the necessary laws and forces of its being, and is as simple and unconscious as any other natural law or force. Hence there are no startling epochs to record in my father's history, no supreme efforts; in filling the measure of daily opportunity lay his chief work. I cannot measure it by our ten fingers' counting. I can only show a life unfolding, and, by the essential laws of its growth, embracing the noblest cause of its time. But if action means vivifying public sentiment decaying under insidious poison; if it includes the doing of this amid a storm of odium that would quickly have shattered any soul irresolute for an instant; if it means incessant toil quietly performed, vast sums collected and disbursed, time sacrificed, strength spent; if it means holding up a great iniquity to loathing by a powerful pen, and nailing moral cowardice wherever it showed; if it be risking livelihood by introducing the cause of the slave into every literary work, and by mingling the school-culture of fifty future mothers, year by year, with hatred of the sin; if it means one's life in one's hand, friendships yielded, society defied, and position in it cheerfully renounced; above all, if action means a wealth of goodness overliving all scorns, compelling respect from a community rebuked, fellowship from a Church charged with ungodliness, and acknowledgment of unstained repute from a public eager to blacken with scandal; if to do thus, and bear thus, and live thus, is action, then my father did act to the full purpose of life in the struggle that freed the slave.

S. M. C.

WILLIAM WHIPPER.

The locality of Columbia, where Mr. Whipper resided for many years, was, as is well-known, a place of much note as a station on the Underground Rail Road. The firm of Smith and Whipper (lumber merchants), was likewise well-known throughout a wide range of country. Who, indeed, amongst those familiar with the history of public matters connected with the colored people of this country, has not heard of William Whipper? For the last thirty years, as an able business man, it has been very generally admitted, that he hardly had a superior.

Although an unassuming man, deeply engrossed with business—Anti-slavery papers, conventions, and public movements having for their aim the elevation of the colored man, have always commanded Mr. Whipper's interest and patronage. In the more important conventions which have been held amongst the colored people for the last thirty years, perhaps no other colored man has been so often called on to draft resolutions and prepare addresses, as the modest and earnest William Whipper. He has worked effectively in a quiet way, although not as a public speaker. He is self-made, and well read on the subject of the reforms of the day. Having been highly successful in his business, he is now at the age of seventy, in possession of a handsome fortune ; the reward of long years of assiduous labor. He is also cashier of the Freedman's Bank, in Philadelphia. For the last few years he has resided at New Brunswick, New Jersey, although his property and business confine him mainly to his native State, Pennsylvania.

Owing to a late affliction in his family, compelling him to devote the most of his time thereto, it has been impossible to obtain from him the material for completing such a sketch as was desired. Prior to this affliction, in answer to our request, he furnished some reminiscences of his labors as conductor of the Underground Rail Road, and at the same time, promised other facts relative to his life, but for the reason assigned, they were not worked up, which is to be regretted.

NEW BRUNSWICK, N. J., December 4, 1871.

MR. WILLIAM STILL, DEAR SIR:—I sincerely regret the absence of statistics that would enable me to furnish you with many events, that would assist you in describing the operations of the Underground Rail Road. I never kept any record of those persons passing through my hands, nor did I ever anticipate that the history of that perilous period would ever be written. I can only refer to the part I took in it from memory, and if I could delineate the actual facts as they occurred they would savor so much of egotism that I should feel ashamed to make them public. I willingly refer to a few incidents which you may select and use as you may think proper.

You are perfectly cognizant of the fact, that after the decision in York, Pa., of the celebrated Prigg case, Pennsylvania was regarded as free territory, which Canada afterwards proved to be, and that the Susquehanna river was the recognized northern boundary of the slave-holding empire. The borough of Columbia, situated on its eastern bank, in the county of Lancaster, was the great depot where the fugitives from Virginia and Maryland first landed. The long bridge connecting Wrightsville with Columbia, was the only safe outlet by which they could successfully escape their pursuers. When they had crossed this bridge they could look back over its broad silvery stream on its western shore, and say to the slave power: "Thus far shalt thou come, and no farther." Previous to that period, the line of fugitive travel was from Baltimore, by the way of Havre de Grace to Philadelphia; but the difficulty of a safe passage across the river, at that place caused the route to be changed to York, Pa., a distance of fifty-eight miles, the fare being forty dollars, and thence to Columbia, in the dead hour of the night. My house was at the end of the bridge, and as I kept the station, I was frequently called up in the night to take charge of the passengers.

On their arrival they were generally hungry and penniless. I have received hundreds in this condition; fed and sheltered from one to seventeen at a time in a single night. At this point the road forked; some I sent west by boats, to Pittsburgh, and others to you in our cars to Philadelphia, and the incidents of their trials form a portion of the history you have compiled. In a period of three years from 1847 to 1850, I passed hundreds to the land of freedom, while others, induced by high wages, and the feeling that they were safe in Columbia, worked in the lumber and coal yards of that place. I always persuaded them to go to Canada, as I had no faith in their being able to elude the grasp of the slave-hunters. Indeed, the merchants had the confidence of their security and desired them to remain; several of my friends told me that I was injuring the trade of the place by persuading the laborers to leave. Indeed, many of the fugitives themselves looked upon me with jealousy, and expressed their indignation at my efforts to have them removed from peace and plenty to a land that was cold and barren, to starve to death.

It was a period of great prosperity in our borough, and everything passed on favorably and successfully until the passage of the fugitive slave bill in 1850. At first the law was derided and condemned by our liberty-loving citizens, and the fugitives did not fear its operations because they asserted that they could protect themselves. This fatal dream was of short duration. A prominent man, by the name of Baker, was arrested and taken to Philadelphia, and given up by the commissioner, and afterwards purchased by our citizens; another, by the name of Smith, was shot dead in one of our lumber yards, because he refused to surrender, and his pursuer permitted to escape without arrest or trial. This produced not only a shock, but a crisis in the affairs of our little borough. It made the stoutest hearts quail before the unjust sovereignty of the law. The white citizens fearing the danger of a successful resistance to the majesty of the law, began to talk of the insecurity of these exiles. The fugitives themselves, whose faith and hope had been buoyed up by the promises held up to them of protection, began to be apprehensive of danger, and talked of leaving, while others, more bold, were ready to set the dangers that surrounded them at defiance, and if necessary, die in the defence of their freedom and the homes they had acquired.

At this juncture private meetings were held by the colored people, and the discussions and resolves bore a peculiar resemblance in sentiment and expression to the patriotic outbursts of the American revolution.

Some were in favor, if again attacked, of killing and slaying all within their reach; of setting their own houses on fire, and then going and burning the town. It was the old spirit which animated the Russians at Moscow, and the blacks of Hayti. At this point my self-interest mingled with my sense of humanity, and I felt that I occupied a more responsible position than I shall ever attain to again. I, therefore, determined to make the most of it. I exhorted them to peace and patience under their present difficulties, and for their own sakes as well as the innocent sufferers, besought them to leave as early as they could. If I had advocated a different course I could have caused the burning of the town. The result of our meeting produced a calm that lasted only for a few days, when it was announced, one evening, that the claimants of a Methodist preacher, by the name of Dorsey, were in the borough, and that it was expected that they would attempt to take him that night.

It was about nine o'clock in the evening when I went to his house, but was refused admittance, until those inside ascertained who I was. There were several men in the house all armed with deadly weapons, awaiting the approach of the intruders. Had they come the whole party would have been massacred. I advised Dorsey to leave, but he very pointedly refused, saying he had been taken up once before alive, but never would be again. The men told him to stand his ground, and they would stand by him and defend him, they had lived together, and would die together. I told them that they knew the strength of the pro-slavery feeling that surrounded them, and that they would be overpowered, and perhaps many lives lost, which might be saved by his changing his place of residence. He said, he had no money, and would rather die with his family, than be killed on the road. I said, how much money do you want to start with, and we will send you more if you need it. Here is one hundred dollars in gold.

47

"That is not enough." "Will two hundred dollars do?" "Yes." I shall bring it to you to-morrow. I got the money the next morning, and when I came with it, he said, he could not leave unless his family was taken care of. I told him I would furnish his family with provisions for the next six months. Then he said he had two small houses, worth four hundred and seventy-five dollars. My reply was that I will sell them for you, and give the money to your family. He then gave me a power of attorney to do so, and attended to all his affairs. He left the next day, being the Sabbath, and has never returned since, although he has lived in the City of Boston ever since, except about six months in Canada.

I wish to notice this case a little further, as the only one out of many to which I will refer. About the year 1831 or 1832, Mr. Joseph Purvis, a younger brother of Robert Purvis, about nineteen or twenty years of age, was visiting Mr. Stephen Smith, of Columbia, and while there the claimants of Dorsey came and secured him, and had proceeded about two miles with him on the way to Lancaster. Young Purvis heard of it, and his natural and instinctive love of freedom fired up his warm southern blood at the very recital. He was one of nature's noblemen. Fierce, fiery, and impulsive, he was as quick to decide as to perform. He demanded an immediate rescue. Though he was advised of the danger of such an attempt, his spirit and determination made him invincible. He proceeded to a place where some colored men were working. With a firm and determined look, and a herculean shout, he called out to them, "To arms, to arms! boys, we must rescue this man; I shall lead if you will follow." "We will," was the immediate response. And they went and overtook them, and dispersed his claimants. They brought Dorsey back in triumph to Columbia.

He then gave Dorsey his pistol, with the injunction that he should use it and die in defence of his liberty rather than again be taken into bondage. He promised he would. I found him with this pistol on his table, the night I called on him, and I have every reason to believe that the promise gave to Mr. Purvis was one of the chief causes of his obstinacy. The lesson he had taught him had not only become incorporated in his nature, but had become a part of his religion.

The history of this brave and noble effort of young Purvis, in rescuing a fellow-being from the jaws of Slavery has been handed down, in Columbia, to a generation that was born since that event has transpired. He always exhibited the same devotion and manly daring in the cause of the flying bondman that inspired his youthful ardor in behalf of freedom. The youngest of a family distinguished for their devotion to freedom, he was without superiors in the trying hour of battle. Like John Brown, he often discarded theories, but was eminently practical. He has passed to another sphere. Peace to his ashes! I honor his name as a hero, and friend of man. I loved him for the noble characteristics of his nature, and above all for his noble daring in defense of the right. As a friend I admired him, and owe his memory this tribute to departed worth.

At this point a conscientious regard for truth dictates that I should state that my disposition to make a sacrifice for the removal of Dorsey and some other leading spirits was aided by my own desire for *self-preservation.*

I knew that it had been asserted, far down in the slave region, that Smith & Whipper, the negro lumber merchants, were engaged in secreting fugitive slaves. And on two occasions attempts had been made to set fire to their yard for the purpose of punishing them for such illegal acts. And I felt that if a collision took place, we should not only be made to suffer the penalty, but the most valuable property in the village be destroyed, besides a prodigal waste of human life be the consequence. In such an event I felt that I should not only lose all I had ever earned, but peril the hopes and property of others, so that I would have freely given one thousand dollars to have been insured against the consequences of such a riot. I then borrowed fourteen hundred dollars on my own individual account, and assisted many others to go to a land where the virgin soil was not polluted by the foot-prints of a slave.

The colored population of the Borough of Columbia, in 1850, was nine hundred and forty-three, about one-fifth the whole population, and in five years they were reduced to four hundred and eighty-seven by emigration to Canada.

In the summer of 1853, I visited Canada for the purpose of ascertaining the actual condition of many of those I had assisted in reaching a land of freedom ; and I was much gratified to find them contented, prosperous, and happy. I was induced by the prospects of the new emigrants to purchase lands on the Sydenham River, with the intention of making it my future home.

In the spring of 1861, when I was preparing to leave, the war broke out, and with its progress I began to realize the prospect of a new civilization, and, therefore, concluded to remain and share the fortunes of my hitherto ill-fated country.

I will say in conclusion that it would have been fortunate for us if Columbia, being a port of entry for flying fugitives, had been also the seat of great capitalists and freedom-loving inhabitants ; but such was not the case. There was but little Anti-slavery sentiment among the whites, yet there were many strong and valiant friends among them who contributed freely ; the colored population were too poor to render much aid, except in feeding and secreting strangers. I was doing a prosperous business at that time and felt it my duty to contribute liberally out of my earnings. Much as I loved Anti-slavery meetings I did not feel that I could afford to attend them, as my immediate duty was to the flying fugitive.

Now, my friend, I have extended this letter far beyond the limits intended, not with the expectation that it will be published, but for your own private use to select any matter that you might desire to use in your history. I have to regret that I am compelled to refer so often to my own exertions.

I know that I speak within bounds when I say that directly and indirectly from 1847 to 1860, I have contributed from my earnings one thousand dollars annually, and for the five years during the war a like amount to put down the rebellion.

Now the slaves are emancipated, and we are all enfranchised, after struggling for existence, freedom and manhood — I feel thankful for having had the glorious privilege of laboring with others for the redemption of my race from oppression and thraldom; and I would prefer to-day to be penniless in the streets, rather than to have withheld a single hour's labor or a dollar from the sacred cause of liberty, justice, and humanity.

I remain yours in the sacred cause of liberty and equality,

WM. WHIPPER.

ISAAC T. HOPPER.

The distinctive characteristics of this individual were so admirably portrayed in the newspapers and other periodicals published at the time of his death, that we shall make free use of them without hesitation. He was distinguished from his early life by his devotion to the relief of the oppressed colored race. He was an active member of the old Pennsylvania Abolition Society, and labored zealously with Dr. Benjamin Rush, Dr. Rogers, Dr. Wistar, and other distinguished philanthropists of the time. No man at that day, not even eminent judges and advocates, was better acquainted with the intricacies of law questions connected with slavery. His accurate legal knowledge, his natural acuteness, his ready tact in avoiding dangerous corners and slipping through unseen loop-holes, often gave him the victory in cases that seemed hopeless to other minds. In many of these cases, physical courage was needed as much as moral firmness; and he possessed these qualities in a very unusual degree.

Being for many years an inspector of the public prisons, his practical sagacity and benevolence were used with marked results. His enlarged sympathies had always embraced the criminal and the imprisoned, as well as the oppressed; and the last years of his life were especially devoted to the improvement of prisons and prisoners. In this department of benevolence he manifested the same zealous kindness and untiring diligence that had so long been exerted for the colored people, for whose welfare he labored to the end of his days.

He possessed a wonderful wisdom in furnishing relief to all who were in difficulty and embarrassment. This caused a very extensive demand upon his time and talents, which were rarely withheld when honestly sought, and seldom applied in vain.

Mrs. Kirkland prepared, under the title of "The Helping Hand," a small volume, for the benefit of "The Home" for discharged female convicts, containing a brief description of the institution, and a detail of facts illustrating the happy results of its operation. Its closing chapter is appropriately devoted to the following well-deserved tribute to the veteran philanthropist, to whose zeal and discretion that and so many other similar institutions owe their existence, or to a large degree their prosperity.

" Not to inform the public what it knows very well already, nor to forestall the volume now preparing by Mrs. Child, a kindred spirit, but to gratify my own feelings, and to give grace and sanctity to this little book, I wish to say a few words of Mr. Hopper, the devoted friend of the prisoner as of the slave; one whose long life, and whose last thoughts, were given to the care and succor of human weakness, error, and suffering. To make even the most unpretending book for the benefit of ' The Home,' without bringing forward the name of Isaac T. Hopper, and recognizing the part he took in its affairs, from the earliest moment of its existence until the close of his life, would be an unpardonable omission. A few words must be said where a volume would scarcely suffice.

" ' The rich and the poor meet together, and the Lord is the Father of them all,' might stand for the motto of Mr. Hopper's life. That the most remote of these two classes stood on the same level of benevolent interest in his mind, his whole career made obvious; he was the last man to represent as naturally opposite those whom God has always, even to the end of the world, made mutually dependent. He told the simple truth to each with equal frankness; helped both with equal readiness. The palace owed him no more than the hovel suggested thoughts of superiority. Nothing human, however grand, or however degraded, was a stranger to him. In the light that came to him from heaven, all stood alike children of the Great Father ; earthly distinction disappearing the moment the sinking soul or the suffering body was in question. No amount of depravity could extinguish his hope of reform ; no recurrence of ingratitude could paralyze his efforts. Early and late, supported or unsupported, praised or ridiculed, he went forward in the great work of relief, looking neither to the right hand, nor to the left; and when the object was accomplished, he shrank back into modest obscurity, only to wait till a new necessity called for his reappearance. Who can number the poor, aching, conscious, despairing hearts that have felt new life come to them from his kind words, his benignant smile, his helping hand. If the record of his long life could be fully written, which it can never be, since every day and all day, in company, in the family circle, with children, with prisoners, with the insane, ' virtue went out of him ' that no human observation could measure or describe, what touching interest would be added to the history of our poor and vicious population for more than half a century past; what new honor and blessing would surround the venerated name of our departed friend and leader!

"But he desired nothing of this. Without claiming for him a position above humanity, which alone would account for a willingness to be wholly unrecognized as a friend of the afflicted, it is not too much to say that no man was ever less desirous of public praise or outward honor. He was even unwilling that any care should be taken to preserve the remembrance of his features, sweet and beautiful as they were, though he was brought reluctantly to yield to the anxious wish of his children and friends that the countenance on which every eye loved to dwell, should not be wholly lost when the grave should close above it. He loved to talk of interesting cases of reform and recovery, both because those things occupied his mind, and because every one loved to hear him; but the hearer who made these disclosures the occasion for unmeaning compliment, as if he fancied a craving vanity to have prompted them, soon found himself rebuked by the straightforward and plain-spoken patriarch. Precious indeed were those seasons of outpouring, when one interesting recital suggested another, till the listener seemed to see the whole mystery of prison-life and obscure wretchedness laid open before him with the distinctness of a picture. For, strange as it may seem, our friend had under his plain garb—unchanged in form since the days of Franklin, to go no further back—a fine dramatic talent, and could not relate the humblest incident without giving it a picturesque or dramatic turn, speaking now for one character, now for another, with a variety and discrimination very remarkable. This made his company greatly sought, and as his strongly social nature readily responded, his acquaintance was very large. To every one that knew him personally, I can appeal for the truth and moderation of these views of his character and manners.

"A few biographical items will close what I venture to offer here.

"Isaac T. Hopper was born December 3, 1771, in the township of Deptford, Gloucester county, New Jersey, but spent a large portion of his life in Philadelphia, where he served his apprenticeship to the humble calling of a tailor. But neither the necessity for constant occupation nor the temptations of youthful gaiety, prevented his commencing, even then, the devotion of a portion of his time, to the care of the poor and needy. He had scarcely reached man's estate when we find him an active member of a benevolent association, and his volume of notes of cases, plans and efforts, date back to that early period. To that time also, we are to refer the beginning of his warm Anti-slavery sentiment, a feeling so prominent and effective throughout his life, and the source of some of his noblest efforts and sacrifices. For many years he served as inspector of prisons in Philadelphia, and thus, by long and constant practical observation, was accumulated that knowledge of the human heart in its darkest windings, that often astonished the objects of his care, when they thought they had been able cunningly to blind his eyes to their real character and intentions. After his removal to New York, and when the occasion for his personal labors in the cause of the slave had in some measure, ceased or slackened, he threw his whole heart into the Prison Association, whose aims and plans of action were entirely in accordance with his views, and indeed, in a great degree, based on his experience and advice. The intent of the Prison Association is threefold : first to protect and defend those who are arrested, and who, as is well known, often suffer greatly from want of honest and intelligent counsel ; secondly, to attend to the treatment and instruction of convicts while in prison ; and thirdly, on their discharge to render them such practical aid as shall enable the repentant to return to society by means of the pursuit of some honest calling. The latter branch occupied Mr. Hopper's time and attention, and he devoted himself to it with an affectionate and religious earnestness that ceased only with his life. No disposition was too perverse for his efforts at reform ; no heart was so black that he did not at least try the balm of healing upon it ; no relapses could tire out his patience, which, without weak waste of means still apostolically went on ' hoping all things,' while even a dying spark of good feeling remained.

Up to February last did this venerable saint continue his abundant labors ; when a severe cold, co-operating with the decay of nature, brought him his sentence of dismissal. He felt that it was on the way, and with the serious grace that marked everything he did, he began at once to gather his earthly robes about him and prepare for the great change which no one could dread less. It was hard for those who saw his ruddy cheek and sparkling eye, his soft brown hair, and sprightly movements to feel that the time of his departure was drawing nigh : but he knew and felt it, with more composure than his friends could summon. It might well be said of this our beloved patriarch, that his eye was not dim, nor his natural force abated. To the last of his daily journeyings through the city, for which he generally used the rail road, he would never allow the drivers to stop for him to get on or off the car, feeling, as he used smilingly to observe, ' very jealous on that point.' Few ever passed him in the street without asking who he was ; for not only did his primitive dress, his broad-brimmed hat, and his antique shoe buckles attract attention, but the beauty and benevolence of his face was sure to fix the eye of ordinary discernment. He was a living temperance lecture, and those who desire to preserve good looks could not ask a more infallible receipt, than that sweet temper and out-flowing benevolence which made his countenance please every eye. Gay and cheerful as a boy, he had ever some pleasant anecdote or amusing turn to relate, and in all perhaps not one without a moral bearing, not thrust forward, but left to be picked out by the hearer at his leisure. He seemed born to show how great strictness in essentials could exist without the least asceticism in trifles. Anything but a Simeon Stylites in his sainthood, he could go among 'publicans and sinners' without the least fear of being mistaken by them for one of themselves. An influence radiated from him that made itself felt in every company, though he would very likely be the most modest man present. More gentlemanly manners and address no court in Christendom need require; his resolute simplicity and candor, always under the guidance of a delicate taste, never for a moment degenerated into coarseness or disregard even of the prejudices of others. His life, even in these minute particulars, showed how the whole man is harmonized by the sense of being

'Ever in the Great Taskmaster's eye.'

"He died on the 7th of May, 1852, in his eighty-first year, and a public funeral in the Tabernacle brought together thousands desirous of showing respect to his memory."

Mrs. Child has written a full, and in many respects, an exceedingly interesting biography of the subject of this memoir, towards the close of which she says:

"From the numerous notices in papers of all parties and sects, I will merely quote the following. 'The New York Observer' thus announces his death:

"'The venerable Isaac T. Hopper, whose placid, benevolent face has so long irradiated almost every public meeting for doing good, and whose name, influence, and labors, have been devoted with an apostolic simplicity and constancy to humanity, died on Friday last, at an advanced age. He was a Quaker of that early sort illustrated by such philanthropists as Anthony Benezet, Thomas Clarkson, Mrs. Fry, and the like.

"'He was a most self-denying, patient, loving friend of the poor, and the suffering of every kind; and his life was an unbroken history of beneficence. Thousands of hearts will feel a touch of grief at the news of his death; for few men have so large a wealth in the blessings of the poor, and the grateful remembrance of kindness and benevolence, as he.'

"'The New York Times' contained the following:

"'Most of our readers will call to mind, in connection with the name of Isaac T. Hopper, the compact, well-knit figure of a Quaker gentleman, apparently about sixty years of age, dressed in drab or brown clothes of the plainest cut, and bearing on his handsome, manly face the impress of that benevolence with which his whole heart was filled.

"'He was twenty years older than he seemed. The fountain of benevolence within freshened his old age with its continuous flow. The step of the octogenarian was elastic as that of a boy, his form erect as a mountain pine.

"'His whole physique was a splendid sample of nature's handiwork. We see him now with our mind's eye, but with the eye of flesh we shall see him no more. Void of intentional offence to God or man, his spirit has joined its happy kindred in a world where there is neither sorrow nor perplexity.'

" I sent the following communication to 'The New York Tribune':

" In this world of shadows, few things strengthen the soul like seeing the calm and cheerful exit of a truly good man; and this has been my privilege by the bedside of Isaac T. Hopper.

" He was a man of remarkable endowments, both of head and heart. His clear discrimination, his unconquerable will, his total unconsciousness of fear, his extraordinary tact in circumventing plans he wished to frustrate, would have made him illustrious as the general of an army; and these qualities might have become faults, if they had not been balanced by an unusual degree of conscientiousness and benevolence. He battled courageously, not from ambition, but from an inborn love of truth. He circumvented as adroitly as the most practiced politician; but it was always to defeat the plans of those who oppressed God's poor; never to advance his own self-interest.

" ' Few men have been more strongly attached to any religious society than he was to the Society of Friends, which he joined in the days of its purity, impelled by his own religious convictions. But when the time came that he must either be faithless to duty in the cause of his enslaved brethren, or part company with the Society to which he was bound by the strong and sacred ties of early religious feeling, this sacrifice he also calmly laid on the altar of humanity.

" ' During nine years that I lived in his household, my respect and affection for him continually increased. Never have I seen a man who so completely fulfilled the Scripture injunction, to forgive an erring brother, 'not only seven times, but seventy times seven.' I have witnessed relapse after relapse into vice, under circumstances which seemed like the most heartless ingratitude to him; but he joyfully hailed the first symptom of repentance, and was always ready to grant a new probation.

" ' Farewell, thou brave and kind old Friend! The prayers of ransomed ones ascended to Heaven for thee, and a glorious company have welcomed thee to the Eternal City.' "

SAMUEL D. BURRIS,

Referred to by John Hunn, was also a brave conductor on the Underground Rail Road leading down into Maryland (via Hunn's place). Mr. Burris was a native of Delaware, but being a free man and possessing more than usual intelligence, and withal an ardent love of liberty, he left "slavedom" and moved with his family to Philadelphia. Here his abhorrence of Slavery was greatly increased, especially after becoming acquainted with the Anti-slavery Office and the Abolition doctrine. Under whose auspices or by what influence he was first induced to visit the South with a view of aiding slaves to escape, the writer does not recollect; nevertheless, from personal knowledge, prior to 1851, he well knew that Burris was an accredited agent on the road above alluded to, and that he had been considered a safe, wise, and useful man in his day and calling. Probably the simple conviction that he would not otherwise be doing as he would be done by actuated him in going down South occasionally to assist some of his suffering friends to get the yokes off their necks, and with him escape to freedom. A number were thus aided by Burris. But finally he found himself within the fatal snare; the slave-holders caught him at last, and Burris was made a prisoner in Dover jail. His wife and children were thereby left without their protector and head. The friends of the slave in Philadelphia and elsewhere deeply sympathized with him in this dreadful hour. Being able to use the pen, although he could not write without having his letters inspected, he kept up a constant correspondence with his friends both in Delaware and Philadelphia. John Hunn and Thomas Garrett were as faithful to him as brothers. After lying in prison for many months, his trial came on and Slavery gained the victory. The court decided that he must be sold in or out of the State to serve for seven years. No change, pardon or relief, could be expected from the spirit and power that held sway over Delaware at that time.

The case was one of great interest to Mr. McKim, as indeed to the entire Executive Committee of the Pennsylvania Anti-slavery Society, who felt constrained to do all they could to save the poor man from his threatened fate, although they had not advised or encouraged him in the act for which he was condemned and about to suffer. In viewing his condition, but a faint ray of hope was entertained from one single direction. It was this: to raise money privately and have a man at the auction on the day of sale to purchase him.

John Hunn and Thomas Garrett were too well known as Abolitionists to undertake this mission. A friend indeed, was desirable, but none other would do than such an one as would not be suspected. Mr. McKim thought that a man who might be taken for a negro trader would be the right kind of a man to send on this errand. Garrett and Hunn being consulted heartily acquiesced in this plan, and after much reflection and inquiry, Isaac S. Flint, an uncompromising abolitionist, living in Wilmington, Delaware, was elected to buy Burris at the sale, providing that he was not run up to a figure exceeding the amount in hand.

Flint's abhorrence of Slavery combined with his fearlessness, cool bearing, and perfect knowledge from what he had read of the usages of traders at slave sales, without question admirably fitted him to play the part of a trader for the time being.

When the hour arrived, the doomed man was placed on the auction-block. Two traders from Baltimore were known to be present; how many others the friends of Burris knew not. The usual opportunity was given to traders and speculators to thoroughly examine the property on the block, and most skillfully was Burris examined from the soles of his feet to the crown of his head; legs, arms and body, being handled as horse-jockies treat horses. Flint watched the ways of the traders and followed for effect their example. The auctioneer began and soon had a bid of five hundred dollars. A Baltimore trader was now in the lead, when Flint, if we mistake not, bought off the trader for one hundred dollars. The bids were thus suddenly checked, and Burris was knocked down to Isaac S. Flint (a strange trader). Of course he had left his abolition name at home and had adopted one suited to the occasion. When the crier's hammer indicated the last bid, although Burris had borne up heroically throughout the trying ordeal, he was not by any means aware of the fact that he had fallen into the hands of friends, but, on the contrary, evidently labored under the impression that his freedom was gone. But a few moments were allowed to pass ere Flint had the bill of sale for his property, and the joyful news was whispered in the ear of Burris that all was right; that he had been bought with abolition gold to save him from going south. Once more Burris found himself in Philadelphia with his wife and children and friends, a stronger opponent than ever of Slavery. Having thus escaped by the skin of his teeth, he never again ventured South.

After remaining a year or two in Philadelphia, about the year 1852 he went to California to seek more lucrative employment than he had hitherto found. Becoming somewhat satisfactorily situated he sent for his family, who joined him. In the meanwhile, his interest in the cause of freedom did not falter; he always kept posted on the subject of the Underground Rail Road and Anti-slavery questions; and after the war, when appeals were made on behalf of contrabands who flocked into Washington daily in a state of utter destitution, Burris was among the first to present the matter to the colored churches of San Francisco, with a view of raising means to aid in this good work, and as the result, a handsome collection was taken up and forwarded to the proper committee in Washington.

About three years ago, Samuel D. Burris died, in the city of San Francisco, at about the age of sixty years. To the slave he had been a true friend, and had labored faithfully for the improvement of his own mind as well as the general elevation of his race.

MARIANN, GRACE ANNA, AND ELIZABETH R. LEWIS.

Near Kimberton, in Chester county, Pa., was the birth-place, and, till within a few years, the home of three sisters, Mariann, Grace Anna and Elizabeth R. Lewis, who were among the most faithful, devoted, and quietly efficient workers in the Anti-slavery cause, including that department of it which is the subject of this volume.

Birth-right members of the Society of Friends, they were born into more than the traditional Anti-slavery faith and feeling of that Society. A deep abhorrence of slavery, and an earnest will to put that feeling into act, as opportunity should serve, were in the very life-blood which they drew from father and mother both.

Left fatherless at an early age, they were taught by their mother to remember that their father, on his visits to their maternal grandfather, living then in Maryland, was wont, as he expressed it, to feel the black shadow of slavery over his spirit, from the time he entered, till he left, the State; and that, on his death-bed, he had regretted having let ill-health prevent his meeting with, and joining one of the Anti-slavery Societies of that day. Of the mother's share in the transmission of their hereditary feeling, it is enough, to all acquainted with the history of Anti-slavery work in Pennsylvania, to say that she was sister, not by blood alone, but in heart and soul, to that early, active, untiring abolitionist, Dr. Bartholomew Fussell.

It is easy to see that the children of such parents, growing up under the influence of such a mother, needed no conversion, no sacrifices of prejudice or hostile opinions, to make them Anti-slavery; but were ready, simply as a matter of course, to work for the good cause whenever any way appeared in which their work could serve it. What was called " modern abolitionism," as distinguished from the less aggressive form of opposition to slavery, which preceded the movement pioneered by Garrison, they at once accepted, as soon as it was set before them, through the agents of the American Anti-Slavery·Society, in the campaign in Pennsylvania, begun in 1836. Regarding it but as the next step forward in the way they had already entered, they instinctively fell into line with the new movement, assisted in forming a society auxiliary to it, in their own neighborhood, and were constant to the end in working for its advancement.

Auxiliary to the influences already mentioned, was a very early recollection of seeing a colored man, Henry, bound with ropes and carried off to slavery. Grace Anna, not more than four or five years old at the time, declared that the man's face of agony is before her now; nor is it likely that her sisters were impressed less deeply. Of natures keenly sensitive, they hated slavery, from that hour, as only children of such natures can; and—as yet too young and immature for that charity to have been developed in them, which can

GRACE ANNE LEWIS.
See p. 748.

MRS. FRANCIS E. W. HARPER.
See p. 753.

JOHN NEEDLES.

EARNEST IN THE CAUSE.

see a brother even in the evil-doer, and pity while condemning him,—they even more intensely hated, while they feared, the actors in the outrage, and despised the girl who had betrayed the victim. Ever after, any one of them could be trusted to be faithful to the hunted fugitive, though an army of kidnappers might surround her.

Another of their early recollections was of a white handkerchief which was to be waved from a back window, as a signal of danger, to a colored man at work in a wood near by. And, all the while, the feelings aroused by such events were kept alive by little Anti-slavery poems, which they were wont to learn by heart and recite in the evenings. Grace Anna, on her first visit to Philadelphia, when nine years old, bought a copy of one of these, entitled "Zambo's Story," pleased to recognize in it a favorite of her still earlier childhood.

By means like these they were unconsciously preparing themselves for the predestined tasks of their after-life; and if there were danger that such a strain upon their sympathies, as they often underwent, might prove unhealthful, it was fully counteracted by ball-playing, and all kinds of active out-door amusements of childhood, so that it was never known to result in harm.

As time passed on, their home, always open to fugitives, became an important centre of Underground Rail Road operations for the region extending from Wilmington, Del., into Adams county, Pa.; and they, grown to womanhood, had glided into the management of its very considerable business. They received passengers from Thomas Garrett, and sometimes others, perhaps, of Wilmington, when it was thought unsafe to send them thence directly through Philadelphia; from Wm. and Phebe Wright, in Adams county, and from friends, more than we have room to name, in York, Columbia, and the southern parts of Lancaster and Chester counties; the several lines, from Adams county to Wilmington, converging upon the house of John Vickers, of Lionville, whose wagon, laden apparently with innocent-looking earthen ware from his pottery, sometimes conveyed, unseen beneath the visible load, a precious burden of Southern chattels, on their way to manhood.

[At a later period, the trains from Adams county generally took another course, going to Harrisburg, and on to Canada, by way of the Susquehanna Valley; though still, when pursuit that way was apprehended, the former course was taken.]

These passengers, the Lewises forwarded in diverse ways; usually, in the earlier times, by wagon or carriage, to Richard Moore, of Quakertown, in Bucks county, about thirty miles distant; but later, when abolitionists were more numerous, and easier stages could be safely made, either directly to the writer, or to one or other of ten or twelve stations which had become established at places less remote, in the counties of Chester and Montgomery. During portions of the time, their married sister Rebecca, and her husband,

Edwin Fussell, and their uncle, Dr. B. Fussell, and, after him, his brother William, lived on farms adjoining theirs, and were their active helpers in this work.

The receiving and passing on of fugitives, was not all they had to do. Often it was necessary to fit out whole families with clothing suitable for the journey. In cases of emergency they would sometimes gather a sewing-circle from such neighboring families as could be trusted; and, with its help, accomplish rapidly the needed work. One instance is remembered, of a woman, with her little boy, whom they put into girls' attire; and, changing also the woman's dress, sent both, by cars, to Canada, accompanied by a friend. In this kind of work, too, they had generous aid from friends at neighboring stations. From Lawrenceville and Limerick, and Pottstown and Pughtown, came contributions of clothing; at one time a supply which filled compactly three three-bushel bags, and of which a small remainder, still on hand when slavery was abolished, was sent South to the freedmen.

The prudence, skill, and watchful care with which the business was conducted, are well attested by the fact that, so far as can be remembered, during all the many years of their connection with the Underground Rail Road, not a plan miscarried, and not a slave that reached their station was retaken; although among their neighbors there were bitter adversaries of the Antislavery cause, eager to find occasion for hostile acts against any abolitionist; and, at times, especially vindictive against the noble sisters, because of their effective co-operation with other friends of Temperance, in preventing the licensing of a liquor-selling tavern in the neighborhood. On one occasion, when, within a week, they had passed on to freedom no less than forty fugitives, eleven of whom had been in the house at once, they were amused at hearing a remark by some of their pro-slavery neighbors, to the effect that "there used to be a pretty brisk trade of running off niggers, but there was not much of it done now."

Though parties of four, five or six sometimes arrived in open day, they seldom sent any away till about nightfall or later, and, whenever the danger was greater than usual, the coming was also at night. The fugitives, in attempting to capture whom, Gorsuch was killed, near Christiana, were brought to them at midnight, by Dr. Fussell; and in this case such caution was observed, that not even the hired girl knew of the presence of persons not of the family.

For one reason or another,—perhaps to let a hot pursuit go by; perhaps to allow opportunity for recovering from fatigue and recruiting exhausted strength, or for earning means to pursue the journey by the common railroads,—it was often thought advisable that passengers should remain with them for a considerable period; and numbers of these were, at different times, employed as laborers in some capacity. Grace Anna testifies that some of the best assistants they ever had in the house or on the farm, were these escaped slaves; that in general they were thrifty and economical, one man, for instance, who spent several years with them, having accumulated five hundred dollars before he went on to Canada; and another, enough to furnish an old coat with a full set of buttons, each of which was a golden half-eagle, covered with cloth, and firmly sewed on, besides an ample supply of good clothing for himself and his wife; and that, almost without exception, they were honest and loyal to their benefactors, and only too happy to find opportunities of showing their gratitude.   One man sent back to the sisters a letter of thanks, through a gentleman in England, whither he had gone.   And once, when Grace Anna was passing an elegant mansion in Philadelphia, a colored woman rushed out upon her with such an impetuous demonstration of affection, joy, and thankfulness—all thought of fitness of time and place swept away by the swell of strong emotion—as might well have amused, or slightly astonished, the passers in the street, who knew not that in her arms the woman's child had died.   But it is no marvel that to her the memory of that poor runaway slave-woman's true affection is more than could have been the warmest welcome from her educated and refined mistress.

One case, of which the sisters for a time had charge, seems worthy of a somewhat more extended mention.   In the fall of 1855 a slave named Johnson, who, in fleeing from bondage, had come as far as Wilmington, thinking he saw his master on the train by which he was journeying northward, sprang from the car and hurt his foot severely.   The Kennett abolitionists having taken him in hand, and fearing that suspicious eyes were on him in their region, felt it necessary to send him onward without waiting for his wound to heal.   He was therefore taken to the Lewises, suffering very much in his removal, and arriving in a condition which required the most assiduous care.   For more than four months he remained with them, patient and gentle in his helplessness and suffering, and very thankful for the ministrations of kindness he received.   He was nursed as tenderly as if his own sisters had attended him, instead of strangers, and was so carefully concealed that the nearest neighbors knew not of his being with them.   Their cousin, Morris Fussell, who lived near, being a physician, they had not to depend for even medical advice upon the outside world.

As the sufferer's wound, in natural course, became offensive, the care of it could not but have been disagreeable as well as toilsome; and the feeble health of one of the sisters at that time must have made heavier the burden to be borne.   But it was borne with a cheerful constancy.   In a letter which Grace Anna wrote after she had attended for some time in person to the patient, with the care and sympathy which his condition demanded, and begun to feel her strength unequal to the task, in addition to her household duties, she asked a friend in Philadelphia to procure for her a trusty colored woman fit to be a helper in the work, offering higher wages than were common in that region for the services required, and adding that, indeed, they could not stand upon the amount of pay, but must have help, if it could be obtained, though not in a condition to bear undue expenditure. But, she said, the man "is unable to be removed; and if he were not, I know of no place where the charge would not be equally severe." So, in perfect keeping with her character, she just quietly regarded it as a matter of course that it should still continue where it was. And there it did continue until spring, when the man, now able to bear removal, was conveyed to the writer, and, after a time, went thence to Boston. There his foot, pronounced incurable, was amputated, and the abolitionists supplied him with a wooden limb. He then returned and spent another winter with the Lewises, assisting in the household work, and rendering services invaluable at a time when it was almost impossible to obtain female help. The next spring, hoping vainly to recover in a warmer climate from the disease induced by the drain his wounded foot had made upon his system, he went to Hayti, and there died; happy, we may well believe, to have escaped from slavery, though only to have won scarely two years of freedom as an invalid and a cripple.

The sisters were so thoroughly united in their work, as well as in all the experiences of life, that this brief sketch has not attempted what indeed it could not have achieved—a separation of their spheres of beneficent activity. Yet they had each her individual traits and adaptations to their common task; "diversities of gifts, but the same spirit." Elizabeth, although for many years shut out by feeble health from any part requiring much bodily exertion, was ever a wise counsellor, as well as ready with such help as her state of health would warrant. Though weak in body, in spirit she was strong and calm and self-reliant, with a clear, discriminating intellect, a keen sense of right, and a certain solidity and balanced symmetry of the spiritual nature which made her an appreciable power wherever she was known. Of Mariann, Grace Anna says, that if a flash of inspiration was required, it usually came from her. Taught by her love for others, and by a sensitiveness almost preternaturally quick, "she always knew exactly the right thing to do," and put all the poetry of a nature exquisitely fine into her efforts to diffuse around her purity and peace and happiness. Her constant, utterly unselfish endeavors to this end contributed in ample measure to the blessedness of a delightful home, rich in the virtues, charities and graces which make home blessed. Veiled by her modest and retiring disposition, to few beyond the circle of her home were known the beauty and beneficence of her noiseless life; but those who did look in upon it testified her worth in terms so strong as showed how deeply it impressed them. "Just the best woman I ever knew," said a young man for whom she had long cared like a mother. "I cannot remember," said another, "ever hearing from her one ungentle word;" and it may be safely doubted whether she was ever heard to utter such. And one who "knew her every mood" cannot recall an instance of selfishness in her, even when a child. "The most womanly woman I ever knew," declared a friend long closely intimate with her, "and such as would have been adored, if found by any man worthy of her."

The ideal element in her was chastened by sound sense and blended with a quick sagacity; but her shrinking sensitiveness, too keen to be quite healthy, and an extreme of self-forgetfulness, amounting possibly to a defect in one sojourning amid this world's diverse dispositions and experiences, rendered her, on the whole, less balanced and complete than her younger sisters, and not well fitted for rough encounter with life's trials. So it became Grace Anna's province, especially after their mother's death, to stand a shelter between her and whatever would unpleasantly affect her by its contact; to be in some sort as a brother to her, seeing there was no brother in the house. But from this it must not be inferred that Grace Anna is less gifted with the distinctive qualities of her sex. For the native fineness of her spiritual texture, her gentle dignity and feminine delicacy and grace, mark her as "every inch" a true and noble woman. In her combine in happy union the calm strength of soul and self-reliance of her younger, with the poetic ideality and a just degree of the quick sensibility of her elder sister, with better health than either, making her foremost of the three in that executive efficiency which did so much to give their plans the uniform success already mentioned. Kindness and warm affection, clearness of moral vision, and purity of heart, with a lively relish for quiet intellectual pleasures, for society and books adapted to refine, improve and elevate, were among the characteristics common to them all.

Mariann and Elizabeth, having lived to see the triumph of the Right, in the Presidential Proclamation of Freedom to the slaves, have gone from their earthly labors to their heavenly rest; which, we may well believe, is that whereof the poet speaks:

"Rest in harmonious action like the stars,
Doing the deeds which make heaven musical,
The earth a heaven, and brothers of us all."

Grace Anna still continues here, working for human welfare in such fields as still demand the laborer's toil; and finding mental profit and delight in the pursuit of natural science.

CUNNINGHAM'S RACHE.

BY MISS GRACE A. LEWIS.

Among the many fugitives whose stories were full of interest, was that of a woman named Rachel. She was tall, muscular, slight, with an extremely sensitive nervous organization, a brain of large size, and an expression of remarkable sagacity and quickness. She was living in West Chester, Chester county, Pa., when attempts were made to retake her to Slavery.

48

With wonderful swiftness and adroitness she eluded pursuit, and was soon hurried away. Speedily reaching our house, she hid herself away during the day, and in the evening, as a place of greater safety, she was transferred to the house of our uncle, Dr. Fussell, then residing on an adjoining farm. As was his wont, this kind-hearted man soon entered into a conversation with her, and in a few minutes discovered that she had once been a pupil of his during his residence in Maryland many years before.

At the moment of recognition she sprang up, overwhelming him with her manifestations of delight, crying: "You Dr. Fussell? You Dr. Fussell? Don't you remember me? I'm Rache—Cunningham's Rache, down at Bush River Neck." Then receding to view him better, "Lord bless de child! how he is grown!"

Her tongue once loosened, she poured forth her whole history, expressing in every lineament her concentrated abhorrence of her libertine master, "Mort Cunningham." Over that story, it is needful to pass lightly, simply saying, she endured all outraged nature could endure and survive. For the sake of humanity we may trust there were few such fiends even among southern masters as this monster in human shape. Cunningham finally sold her to go further South, with a master whose name cannot now be recalled. This man was in ill health, and after a time he and his wife started northward, bringing Rache with them. On the voyage the master grew worse, and one night when he was about to die, a fearful storm arose, which Rache devoutly believed was sent from Heaven. In describing this scene, she impersonated her surroundings with wonderful vividness and marvellous power. At one moment she was the howling wind; at another the tumultuous sea—then the lurching ship—the bellowing cow frightened by the storm—the devil, who came to carry away her master's soul, and finally the weak, dying man, as he passed to eternity.

They proceeded on their voyage and landed at their place of destination. Rache sees the cow snuffing the land breeze and darting off through the crowd. The captain of the vessel points to the cow and motions her to follow its example. She needs nothing more. Again she is acting—she is now the cow; but human caution, shrewdness, purpose, are lent to animal instinct. She looks around her with wary eye—scents the air—a flash, and she is hidden from the crowd which you see around her—she is free! Making her way northward, she finally arrived at the house of Emmer Kimber, Kimberton, Chester county, Pa., and proving a remarkably capable woman, she remained a considerable time in his family, as a cook. She finally married, and settled in West Chester, where the pair prospered and were soon surrounded by the comforts of a neat home. After several years of peaceful life there, she was one day alarmed, not by the heirs of her dead master, but by the loathed "Mort Cunningham," who, without the shadow of legal right, had come to carry her back to Slavery. Fear lent her wings.

She darted into a hatter's shop and out through the back buildings, springing over a dye kettle in her way, and cleared a board fence at a bound. On her way to a place of safety she looked back to see, with keen enjoyment, " Mort Cunningham " falling backward from the fence she had leaped. Secure in a garret, she looked down into the streets below, to see his vacant, dazed look as he sought, unable to find her. Her rendering of the expression of his face at this time, was irresistibly ludicrous, as was that of his whole bearing while searching for her. "Mort Cunningham " did not get her, but whether or not she ever returned to the enjoyment of her happy home, in West Chester, we never knew, as this sudden flight was the last we ever heard of her. She was one of the most wide-awake of human beings, and the world certainly lost in the uneducated slave, an actor of great dramatic power.

FRANCES ELLEN WATKINS HARPER.

The narratives and labors of eminent colored men such as Banneker, Douglass, Brown, Garnet, and others, have been written and sketched very fully for the public, and doubtless with advantage to the cause of freedom. But there is not to be found in any written work portraying the Anti-Slavery struggle, (except in the form of narratives,) as we are aware of, a sketch of the labors of any eminent colored woman. We feel, therefore, not only glad of the opportunity to present a sketch not merely of the leading colored poet in the United States, but also of one of the most liberal contributors, as well as one of the ablest advocates of the Underground Rail Road and of the slave.

No extravagant praise of any kind,—only simple facts are needed to portray the noble deeds of this faithful worker.

The want of space forbids more than a brief reference to her early life.

Frances Ellen Watkins Harper (Watkins being her maiden name) was born in the City of Baltimore in 1825, not of slave parentage, but subjected of course to the oppressive influence which bond and free alike endured under slave laws. Since reaching her majority, in looking back, the following sentences from her own pen express the loneliness of her childhood days. " Have I yearned for a mother's love? The grave was my robber. Before three years had scattered their blight around my path, death had won my mother from me. Would the strong arm of a brother have been welcome? I was my mother's only child." Thus she fell into the hands of an aunt, who watched over her during these early helpless years. Rev. William Watkins, an uncle, taught a school in Baltimore for free colored children, to which she was sent until she was about thirteen years of age. After this period, she was put out to work to earn her own living.

She had many trials to endure which she would fain forget; but in the midst of them all she had an ardent thirst for knowledge and a remarkable talent for composition, as she evinced at the age of fourteen in an article which attracted the attention of the lady in whose family she was employed, and others. In this situation she was taught sewing, took care of the children, &c.; and at the same time, through the kindness of her employer, her greed for books was satisfied so far as was possible from occasional half-hours of leisure. She was noted for her industry, rarely trifling away time as most girls are wont to do in similar circumstances. Scarcely had she reached her majority ere she had written a number of prose and poetic pieces which were deemed of sufficient merit to publish in a small volume called "Forest Leaves." Some of her productions found their way into newspapers and attracted attention. The ability exhibited in some of her productions was so remarkable that some doubted and others denied their originality. Of this character we here copy an extract from one of her early prose productions:

CHRISTIANITY.

"Christianity is a system claiming God for its author, and the welfare of man for its object. It is a system so uniform, exalted and pure, that the loftiest intellects have acknowledged its influence, and acquiesced in the justness of its claims. Genius has bent from his erratic course to gather fire from her altars, and pathos from the agony of Gethsemane and the sufferings of Calvary. Philosophy and science have paused amid their speculative researches and wondrous revelations to gain wisdom from her teachings and knowledge from her precepts. Poetry has culled her fairest flowers and wreathed her softest to bind her Author's 'bleeding brow.' Music has strung her sweetest lyres and breathed her noblest strains to celebrate his fame; whilst Learning has bent from her lofty heights to bow at the lowly cross. The constant friend of man, she has stood by him in his hour of greatest need. She has cheered the prisoner in his cell, and strengthened the martyr at the stake. She has nerved the frail and shrinking heart of woman for high and holy deeds. The worn and weary have rested their fainting heads upon her bosom, and gathered strength from her words and courage from her counsels. She has been the staff of decrepit age and the joy of manhood in its strength. She has bent over the form of lovely childhood, and suffered it to have a place in the Redeemer's arms. She has stood by the bed of the dying, and unveiled the glories of eternal life, gilding the darkness of the tomb with the glory of the resurrection."

Her mind being of a strictly religious caste, the effusions from her pen all savor of a highly moral and elevating tone.

About the year 1851 she left Baltimore to seek a home in a Free State, and for a short time resided in Ohio, where she was engaged in teaching. Contrary to her expectations, her adopted home and calling not proving satisfactory, she left that State and came to Pennsylvania as a last resort, and again engaged in teaching at Little York. Here she not only had to encounter the trouble of dealing with unruly children, she was sorely oppressed with the thought of the condition of her people in Maryland. Not unfrequently she gave utterance to such expressions as the following:

"Not that we have not a right to breathe the air as freely as anybody else here (in Baltimore), but we are treated worse than aliens among a people whose language we speak, whose religion we profess, and whose blood flows and mingles in our veins.   *   *   *   Homeless in the land of our birth and worse off than strangers in the home of our nativity." During her stay in York she had frequent opportunities of seeing passengers on the Underground Rail Road. In one of her letters she thus alluded to a traveler: "I saw a passenger *per* the Underground Rail Road yesterday; did he arrive safely? Notwithstanding that abomination of the nineteenth century —the Fugitive Slave Law—men still determine to be free. Notwithstanding all the darkness in which they keep the slaves, it seems that somehow light is dawning upon their minds.   *   * These poor fugitives are a property that can walk. Just to think that from the rainbow-crowned Niagara to the swollen waters of the Mexican Gulf, from the restless murmur of the Atlantic to the ceaseless roar of the Pacific, the poor, half-starved, flying fugitive has no resting-place for the sole of his foot!"

Whilst hesitating whether or not it would be best to continue teaching, she wrote to a friend for advice as follows: "What would you do if you were in my place? Would you give up and go back and work at your trade (dress-making)? There are no people that need all the benefits resulting from a well-directed education more than we do. The condition of our people, the wants of our children, and the welfare of our race demand the aid of every helping hand, the God-speed of every Christian heart. It is a work of time, a labor of patience, to become an effective school teacher; and it should be a work of love in which they who engage should not abate heart or hope until it is done. And after all, it is one of woman's most sacred rights to have the privilege of forming the symmetry and rightly adjusting the mental balance of an immortal mind." "I have written a lecture on education, and I am also writing a small book."

Thus, whilst filling her vocation as a teacher in Little York, was she deeply engrossed in thought as to how she could best promote the welfare of her race. But as she was devoted to the work in hand, she soon found that fifty-three untrained little urchins overtaxed her naturally delicate physical powers; it also happened just about this time that she was further moved to enter the Anti-Slavery field as a lecturer substantially by the following circumstance: About the year 1853, Maryland, her native State, had enacted a law forbidding free people of color from the North from coming into the State on pain of being imprisoned and sold into slavery. A free man, who had unwittingly violated this infamous statute, had recently been sold to Georgia, and had escaped thence by secreting himself behind the wheel-house of a boat bound northward; but before he reached the desired haven, he was discovered and remanded to slavery. It was reported that he died soon after from the effects of exposure and suffering. In a letter to a friend referring to this outrage, Mrs. Harper thus wrote: "Upon that grave I pledged myself to the Anti-Slavery cause."

Having thus decided, she wrote in a subsequent letter, "It may be that God himself has written upon both my heart and brain a commission to use time, talent and energy in the cause of freedom." In this abiding faith she came to Philadelphia, hoping that the way would open for usefulness, and to publish her little book (above referred to). She visited the Anti-Slavery Office and read Anti-Slavery documents with great avidity; in the mean time making her home at the station of the Underground Rail Road, where she frequently saw passengers and heard their melting tales of suffering and wrong, which intensely increased her sympathy in their behalf. Although anxious to enter the Anti-Slavery field as a worker, her modesty prevented her from pressing her claims; consequently as she was but little known, being a young and homeless maiden (an exile by law), no especial encouragement was tendered her by Anti-Slavery friends in Philadelphia.

During her stay in Philadelphia she published some verses entitled, "Eliza Harris crossing the River on the Ice." It was deemed best to delay the issuing of the book.

After spending some weeks in Philadelphia, she concluded to visit Boston. Here she was treated with the kindness characteristic of the friends in the Anti-Slavery Office whom she visited, but only made a brief stay, after which she proceeded to New Bedford, the "hot-bed of the fugitives" in Massachusetts, where by invitation she addressed a public meeting on the subject of Education and the Elevation of the Colored Race.

The occasion and result of the commencement of her public career was thus given by her own pen in a letter dated August, 1854:

"Well, I am out lecturing. I have lectured every night this week; besides addressed a Sunday-school, and I shall speak, if nothing prevent, to-night. My lectures have met with success. Last night I lectured in a white church in Providence. Mr. Gardener was present, and made the estimate of about six hundred persons. Never, perhaps, was a speaker, old or young, favored with a more attentive audience. * * * My voice is not wanting in strength, as I am aware of, to reach pretty well over the house. The church was the Roger Williams; the pastor, a Mr. Furnell, who appeared to be a kind and Christian man. * * * My maiden lecture was Monday night in New Bedford on the Elevation and Education of our People. Perhaps as intellectual a place as any I was ever at of its size."

Having thus won her way to a favorable position as a lecturer, the following month she was engaged by the State Anti-Slavery Society of Maine, with what success appears from one of her letters bearing date — Buckstown Centre, Sept. 28, 1854:

"The agent of the State Anti-Slavery Society of Maine travels with me, and she is a pleasant, dear, sweet lady. I do like her so. We travel together, eat together, and sleep together. (She is a white woman.) In fact I have not been in one colored person's house since I left Massachusetts; but I have a pleasant time. My life reminds me of a beautiful dream. What a difference between this and York! * * I have met with some of the kindest treatment up here that I have ever received. * * I have lectured three times this week. After I went from Limerick, I went to Springvale; there I spoke on Sunday night at an Anti-Slavery meeting. Some of the people are Anti-Slavery, Anti-rum and Anti-Catholic; and if you could see our Maine ladies,—some of them among the noblest types of womanhood you have ever seen! They are for putting men of Anti-Slavery principles in office, * * to cleanse the corrupt fountains of our government by sending men to Congress who will plead for our down-trodden and oppressed brethren, our crushed and helpless sisters, whose tears and blood bedew our soil, whose chains are clanking 'neath our proudest banners, whose cries and groans amid our loudest pæans rise."

Everywhere in this latitude doors opened before her, and her gifts were universally recognized as a valuable acquisition to the cause. In the letter above referred to she said: "I spoke in Boston on Monday night. * * * Well, I am but one, but can do something, and, God helping me, I will try. Mr. Brister from Lowell addressed the meeting; also Rev. ——. Howe. We had a good demonstration."

Having read the narrative of Solomon Northrup (12 years a slave), she was led to embrace the Free Labor doctrine most thoroughly; and in a letter dated at Temple, Maine, Oct. 20, 1854, after expressing the interest she took in the annual meeting of the Anti-Slavery Society of that state, she remarked:

"I spoke on Free Produce, and now by the way I believe in that kind of Abolition. Oh, it does seem to strike at one of the principal roots of the matter. I have commenced since I read Solomon Northrup. Oh, if Mrs. Stowe has clothed American slavery in the graceful garb of fiction, Solomon Northrup comes up from the dark habitation of Southern cruelty where slavery fattens and feasts on human blood with such mournful revelations that one might almost wish for the sake of humanity that the tales of horror which he reveals were not so. Oh, how can we pamper our appetites upon luxuries drawn from reluctant fingers? Oh, could slavery exist long if it did not sit on a commercial throne? I have read somewhere, if I remember aright, of a Hindoo being loth to cut a tree because being a believer in the transmigration of souls, he thought the soul of his father had passed into it. * * * Oh, friend, beneath the most delicate preparations of the cane can you not see the stinging lash and clotted whip? I have reason to be thankful that I am able to give a little more for a Free Labor dress, if it is coarser. I can thank God that upon its warp and woof I see no stain of blood and tears; that to procure a little finer muslin for my limbs no crushed and broken heart went out in sighs, and that from the field where it was raised went up no wild and startling cry unto the throne of God to witness there in language deep and strong, that in demanding that cotton I was nerving oppression's hand for deeds of guilt and crime. If the liberation of the slave demanded it, I could consent to part with a portion of the blood from my own veins if that would do him any good."

After having thus alluded to free labor, she gave a short journal of the different places where she had recently lectured from the 5th of September to the 20th of October, which we mention here simply to show the perseverance which characterized her as an advocate of her enslaved race, and at the same time show how doors everywhere opened to her: Portland, Monmouth Centre, North Berwick, Limerick (two meetings), Springvale, Portsmouth, Elliott, Waterborough (spoke four times), Lyman, Saccarappo, Moderation, Steep Falls (twice), North Buxton, Goram, Gardner, Litchfield, twice, Monmouth Ridge twice, Monmouth Centre three times, Litchfield second time, West Waterville twice, Livermore Temple. Her ability and labors were everywhere appreciated, and her meetings largely attended. In a subsequent letter referring to the manner that she was received, she wrote, "A short while ago when I was down this way I took breakfast with the then Governor of Maine."

For a year and a half she continued in the Eastern States, speaking in most or all of them with marked success; the papers meting out to her full commendation for her efforts. The following extract clipped from the Portland Daily Press, respecting a lecture that she was invited to deliver after the war by the Mayor (Mr. Washburne) and others, is a fair sample of notices from this source:

"She spoke for nearly an hour and a half, her subject being 'The Mission of the War, and the Demands of the Colored Race in the Work of Reconstruction;' and we have seldom seen an audience more attentive, better pleased, or more enthusiastic. Mrs. Harper has a splendid articulation, uses chaste, pure language, has a pleasant voice, and allows no one to tire of hearing her. We shall attempt no abstract of her address; none that we could make would do her justice. It was one of which any lecturer might feel proud, and her reception by a Portland audience was all that could be desired. We have seen no praises of her that were overdrawn. We have heard Miss Dickinson, and do not hesitate to award the palm to her darker colored sister."

In 1856, desiring to see the fugitives in Canada, she visited the Upper Province, and in a letter dated at Niagara Falls, Sept. 12th, she unfolded her mind in the following language:

"Well, I have gazed for the first time upon Free Land, and, would you believe it, tears sprang to my eyes, and I wept. Oh, it was a glorious sight to gaze for the first time on a land where a poor slave flying from our glorious land of liberty would in a moment find his fetters broken, his shackles loosed, and whatever he was in the land of Washington, beneath the shadow of Bunker Hill Monument or even Plymouth Rock, here he becomes a man and a brother. I have gazed on Harper's Ferry, or rather the rock at the Ferry; I have seen it towering up in simple grandeur, with the gentle Potomac gliding peacefully at its feet, and felt that that was God's masonry, and my soul had expanded in gazing on its sublimity. I have seen the ocean singing its wild chorus of sounding waves, and ecstacy has thrilled upon the living chords of my heart. I have since then seen the rainbow-crowned Niagara chanting the choral hymn of Omnipotence, girdled with grandeur, and robed with glory; but none of these things have melted me as the first sight of Free Land. Towering mountains lifting their hoary summits to catch the first faint flush of day when the sunbeams kiss the shadows from morning's drowsy face may expand and exalt your soul. The first view of the ocean may fill you with strange delight. Niagara—the great, the glorious Niagara—may hush your spirit with its ceaseless thunder; it may charm you with its robe of crested spray and rainbow crown; but the land of Freedom was a lesson of deeper significance than foaming waves or towering mounts."

While in Toronto she lectured, and was listened to with great interest; but she made only a brief visit, thence returning to Philadelphia, her adopted home.

With her newly acquired reputation as a lecturer, from 1856 to 1859 she continued her labors in Pennsylvania, New Jersey, New York, Ohio, &c. In the meantime she often came in contact with Underground Rail Road passengers, especially in Philadelphia. None sympathized with them more sincerely or showed a greater willingness to render them material aid. She contributed apparently with the same liberality as though they were her own near kin. Even when at a distance, so deep was her interest in the success of the Road, she frequently made it her business to forward donations, and carefully inquire into the state of the treasury. The Chairman of the Committee might publish a volume of interesting letters from her pen relating to the Underground Rail Road and kindred topics; but a few extracts must suffice. We here copy from a letter dated at Rushsylvania, Ohio, Dec. 15th: "I send you to-day two dollars for the Underground Rail Road. It is only a part of what I subscribed at your meeting. May God speed the flight of the slave as he speeds through our Republic to gain his liberty in a monarchical land. I am still in the lecturing field, though not very strong physically. * * * Send me word what I can do for the fugitive."

From Tiffin, Ohio, March 31st, touching the news of a rescue in Philadelphia, she thus wrote:

" I see by the Cincinnati papers that you have had an attempted rescue and a failure. That is sad! Can you not give me the particulars? and if there is anything that I can do for them in money or words, call upon me. This is a common cause; and if there is any burden to be borne in the Anti-Slavery cause—anything to be done to weaken our hateful chains or assert our manhood and womanhood, I have a right to do my share of the work. The humblest and feeblest of us can do something; and though I may be deficient in many of the conventionalisms of city life, and be considered as a person of good impulses, but unfinished, yet if there is common rough work to be done, call on me."

Mrs. Harper was not content to make speeches and receive plaudits, but was ever willing to do the rough work and to give material aid wherever needed.

From another letter dated Lewis Centre, Ohio, we copy the following characteristic extract:

" Yesterday I sent you thirty dollars. Take five of it for the rescuers (who were in prison), and the rest pay away on the books. My offering is not large; but if you need more, send me word. Also how comes on the Underground Rail Road? Do you need anything for that? You have probably heard of the shameful outrage of a colored man or boy named Wagner, who was kidnapped in Ohio and carried across the river and sold for a slave. * * * Ohio has become a kind of a negro hunting ground, a new Cor go's coast and Guinea's shore. A man was kidnapped almost under the shadow of our capital. Oh, was it not dreadful? * * * Oh, may the living God prepare me for an earnest and faithful advocacy of the cause of justice and right!"

In those days the blows struck by the hero, John Brown, were agitating the nation. Scarcely was it possible for a living soul to be more deeply affected than this female advocate. Nor did her sympathies end in mere words. She tendered material aid as well as heartfelt commiseration.

To John Brown's wife * she sent through the writer the following letter:

LETTER TO JOHN BROWN'S WIFE.

FARMER CENTRE, OHIO, Nov. 14th.

MY DEAR MADAM:—In an hour like this the common words of sympathy may seem like idle words, and yet I want to say something to you, the noble wife of the hero of the nineteenth century. Belonging to the race your dear husband reached forth his hand to assist, I need not tell you that my sympathies are with you. I thank you for the brave words you have spoken. A republic that produces such a wife and mother may hope for better days. Our heart may grow more hopeful for humanity when it sees the sublime sacrifice it is about to receive from his hands. Not in vain has your dear husband periled all, if the martyrdom of one hero is worth more than the life of a million cowards. From the prison comes forth a shout of triumph over that power whose ethics are robbery of the feeble and oppression of the weak, the trophies of whose chivalry are a plundered cradle and a scourged and bleeding woman. Dear sister, I thank you for the brave and noble words that you have spoken. Enclosed I send you a few dollars as a token of my gratitude, reverence and love.

Yours respectfully,   FRANCES ELLEN WATKINS.

Post Office address: care of William Still, 107 Fifth St., Philadelphia, Penn.

May God, our own God, sustain you in the hour of trial. If there is one thing on earth I can do for you or yours, let me be apprized. I am at your service.

Not forgetting Brown's comrades, who were then lying in prison under sentence of death, true to the best impulses of her generous heart, she thus wrote relative to these ill-fated prisoners, from Montpelier, Dec. 12th:

"I thank you for complying with my request. (She had previously ordered a box of things to be forwarded to them.) And also that you wrote to them. You see Brown towered up so bravely that these doomed and fated men may have been almost overlooked, and just think that I am able to send one ray through the night around them. And as their letters came too late to answer in time, I am better satisfied that you wrote. I hope the things will reach them. Poor doomed and fated men! Why did you not send them more things? Please send me the bill of expense. * * Send me word what I can do for the fugitives. Do you need any money? Do I not owe you on the old bill (pledge)? Look carefully and see if I have paid all. Along with this letter I send you one for Mr. Stephens (one of Brown's men), and would ask you to send him a box of nice things every week till he dies or is acquitted. I understand the balls have not been extracted from him. Has not this suffering been overshadowed by the glory that gathered around the brave old

* Mrs. Harper passed two weeks with Mrs. Brown at the house of the writer while she was awaiting the execution of her husband, and sympathized with her most deeply.

man ? * * * Spare no expense to make the last hours of his (Stephens') life as bright as possible with sympathy. * * * Now, my friend, fulfil this to the letter. Oh, is it not a privilege, if you are sisterless and lonely, to be a sister to the human race, and to place your heart where it may throb close to down-trodden humanity ?"

On another occasion in writing from the lecturing field hundreds of miles away from Philadelphia, the sympathy she felt for the fugitives found expression in the following language:

"How fared the girl who came robed in male attire? Do write me every time you write how many come to your house; and, my dear friend, if you have that much in hand of mine from my books, will you please pay the Vigilance Committee two or three dollars for me to help carry on the glorious enterprise. Now, please do not write back that you are not going to do any such thing. Let me explain a few matters to you. In the first place, I am able to give something. In the second place, I am willing to do so. * * * Oh, life is fading away, and we have but an hour of time! Should we not, therefore, endeavor to let its history gladden the earth? The nearer we ally ourselves to the wants and woes of humanity in the spirit of Christ, the closer we get to the great heart of God; the nearer we stand by the beating of the pulse of universal love."

Doubtless it has not often been found necessary for persons desirous of contributing to benevolent causes to first have to remove anticipated objections. Nevertheless in some cases it would seem necessary to admonish her not to be quite so liberal; to husband with a little more care her hard-earned income for a "rainy day," as her health was not strong.

"My health," she wrote at that time, "is not very strong, and I may have to give up before long. I may have to yield on account of my voice, which I think, has become somewhat affected. I might be so glad if it was only so that I could go home among my own kindred and people, but slavery comes up like a dark shadow between me and the home of my childhood. Well, perhaps it is my lot to die from home and be buried among strangers; and yet I do not regret that I have espoused this cause; perhaps I have been of some service to the cause of human rights, and I hope the consciousness that I have not lived in vain, will be a halo of peace around my dying bed; a heavenly sunshine lighting up the dark valley and shadow of death."

Notwithstanding this yearning for home, she was far from desiring at her death, a burial in a Slave State, as the following clearly expressed views show:

"I have lived in the midst of oppression and wrong, and I am saddened by every captured fugitive in the North; a blow has been struck at my freedom, in every hunted and down-trodden slave in the South; North and South have both been guilty, and they that sin must suffer."

Also, in harmony with the above sentiments, came a number of verses appropriate to her desires in this respect, one of which we here give as a sample:

> "Make me a grave where'er you will,
> In a lowly plain, or a lofty hill,
> Make it among earth's humblest graves,
> But not in a land where men are slaves."

In the State of Maine the papers brought to her notice the capture of Margaret Garner, and the tragic and bloody deed connected therewith. And she writes:

"Rome had her altars where the trembling criminal, and the worn and weary slave might fly for an asylum—Judea her cities of refuge; but Ohio, with her Bibles and churches, her baptisms and prayers, had not one temple so dedicated to human rights, one altar so consecrated to human liberty, that trampled upon and down-trodden innocence knew that it could find protection for a night, or shelter for a day."

In the fall of 1860, in the city of Cincinnati, Mrs. Harper was married to Fenton Harper, a widower, and resident of Ohio. It seemed obvious that this change would necessarily take her from the sphere of her former usefulness. The means she had saved from the sale of her books and from her lectures, she invested in a small farm near Columbus, and in a short time after her marriage she entered upon house-keeping.

Notwithstanding her family cares, consequent upon married life, she only ceased from her literary and anti-slavery labors, when compelled to do so by other duties.

On the 23d of May, 1864, death deprived her of her husband.

Whilst she could not give so much attention to writing as she could have desired in her household days, she, nevertheless, did then produce some of her best productions. Take the following for a sample, on the return from Cleveland, Ohio, of a poor, ill-fated slave-girl, (under the Fugitive Slave Law):

TO THE UNION SAVERS OF CLEVELAND.

Men of Cleveland, had a vulture
    Sought a timid dove for prey,
Would you not, with human pity,
    Drive the gory bird away?

Had you seen a feeble lambkin,
    Shrinking from a wolf so bold, -
Would ye not to shield the trembler,
    In your arms have made its fold?

But when she, a hunted sister,
    Stretched her hands that ye might **save**,
Colder far than Zembla's regions
    Was the answer that ye gave.

On the Union's bloody altar,
    Was your hapless victim laid;
Mercy, truth and justice shuddered,
    But your hands would give no aid.

And ye sent her back to torture,
    Robbed of freedom and of right.
Thrust the wretched, captive stranger.
    Back to slavery's gloomy night.

Back where brutal men may trample,
 On her honor and her fame ;
And unto her lips so dusky,
 Press the cup of woe and shame.

There is blood upon your city,
 Dark and dismal is the stain ;
And your hands would fail to cleanse it,
 Though Lake Erie ye should drain.

There's a curse upon your Union,
 Fearful sounds are in the air;
As if thunderbolts were framing,
 Answers to the bondsman's prayer.

Ye may offer human victims,
 Like the heathen priests of old;
And may barter manly honor
 For the Union and for gold.

But ye can not stay the whirlwind,
 When the storm begins to break;
And our God doth rise in judgment,
 For the poor and needy's sake.

And, your sin-cursed, guilty Union,
 Shall be shaken to its base,
Till ye learn that simple justice,
 Is the right of every race.

Mrs. Harper took the deepest interest in the war, and looked with extreme anxiety for the results ; and she never lost an opportunity to write, speak, or serve the cause in any way that she thought would best promote the freedom of the slave. On the proclamation of General Fremont, the passages from her pen are worthy to be long remembered :

"Well, what think you of the war? To me one of the most interesting features is Fremont's Proclamation freeing the slaves of the rebels. Is there no ray of hope in that? I should not wonder if Edward M. Davis breathed that into his ear. His proclamation looks like real earnestness; no mincing the matter with the rebels. Death to the traitors and confiscation of their slaves is no child's play. I hope that the boldness of his stand will inspire others to look the real cause of the war in the face and inspire the government with uncompromising earnestness to remove the festering curse. And yet I am not uneasy about the result of this war. We may look upon it as God's controversy with the nation; His arising to plead by fire and blood the cause of His poor and needy people. Some time since Breckinridge, in writing to Sumner, asks, if I rightly remember, What is the fate of a few negroes to me or mine? Bound up in one great bundle of humanity our fates seem linked together, our destiny entwined with theirs, and our rights are interwoven together."

Finally when the long-looked-for Emancipation Proclamation came, although Mrs. Harper was not at that time very well, she accepted an invitation to address a public meeting in Columbus, Ohio, an allusion to which we find in a letter dated at Grove City, O., which we copy with the feeling that many who may read this volume will sympathize with every word uttered relative to the Proclamation:

"I spoke in Columbus on the President's Proclamation. * * But was not such an event worthy the awakening of every power—the congratulation of every faculty? What hath God wrought! We may well exclaim how event after event has paved the way for freedom. In the crucible of disaster and defeat God has stirred the nation, and permitted no permanent victory to crown her banners while she kept her hand upon the trembling slave and held him back from freedom. And even now the scale may still seem to oscillate between the contending parties, and some may say, Why does not God give us full and quick victory? My friend, do not despair if even deeper shadows gather around the fate of the nation, that truth will not ultimately triumph, and the right be established and vindicated; but the deadly gangrene has taken such deep and almost fatal hold upon the nation that the very centres of its life seem to be involved in its eradication. Just look, after all the trials deep and fiery through which the nation has waded, how mournfully suggestive was the response the proclamation received from the democratic triumphs which followed so close upon its footsteps. Well, thank God that the President did not fail us, that the fierce rumbling of democratic thunder did not shake from his hand the bolt he leveled against slavery. Oh, it would have been so sad if, after all the desolation and carnage that have dyed our plains with blood and crimsoned our borders with warfare, the pale young corpses trodden down by the hoofs of war, the dim eyes that have looked their last upon the loved and lost, had the arm of Executive power failed us in the nation's fearful crisis! For how mournful it is when the unrighted wrongs and fearful agonies of ages reach their culminating point, and events solemn, terrible and sublime marshal themselves in dread array to mould the destiny of nations, the hands appointed to hold the helm of affairs, instead of grasping the mighty occasions and stamping them with the great seals of duty and right, permit them to float along the current of circumstances without comprehending the hour of visitation or the momentous day of opportunity. Yes, we may thank God that in the hour when the nation's life was convulsed, and fearful gloom had shed its shadows over the land, the President reached out his hand through the darkness to break the chains on which the rust of centuries had gathered. Well, did you ever expect to see this day? I know that all is not accomplished; but we may rejoice in what has been already wrought,—the wondrous change in so short a time. Just a little while since the American flag to the flying bondman was an ensign of bondage; now it has become a symbol of protection and freedom. Once the slave was a despised and trampled on pariah; now he has become a useful ally to the American government. From the crimson sods of war springs the white flower of freedom, and songs of deliverance mingle with the crash and roar of war. The shadow of the American army becomes a covert for the slave, and beneath the American Eagle he grasps the key of knowledge and is lifted to a higher destiny."

This letter we had intended should complete the sketch of Mrs. Harper's Anti-Slavery labors; but in turning to another epistle dated Boston, April 19th, on the Assassination of the President, we feel that a part of it is too interesting to omit:

"Sorrow treads on the footsteps of the nation's joy. A few days since the telegraph thrilled and throbbed with a nation's joy. To-day a nation sits down beneath the shadow of its mournful grief. Oh, what a terrible lesson does this event read to us! A few years since slavery tortured, burned, hung and outraged us, and the nation passed by and said, they had nothing to do with slavery where it was, slavery would have something to do with them where they were. Oh, how fearfully the judgments of Ichabod have pressed upon the nation's life! Well, it may be in the providence of God this blow was needed to intensify the nation's hatred of slavery, to show the utter fallacy of basing national reconstruction upon the votes of returned rebels, and rejecting loyal black men; making (after all the blood poured out like water, and wealth scattered like chaff) a return to the old idea that a white rebel is better or of more account in the body politic than a loyal black man. * * Moses, the meekest man on earth, led the children of Israel over the Red Sea, but was not permitted to see them settled in Canaan. Mr. Lincoln has led up through another Red Sea to the table land of triumphant victory, and God has seen fit to summon for the new era another man. It is ours then to bow to the Chastener and let our honored and loved chieftain go. Surely the everlasting arms that have hushed him so strangely to sleep are able to guide the nation through its untrod future; but in vain should be this fearful baptism of blood if from the dark bosom of slavery springs such terrible crimes. Let the whole nation resolve that the whole virus shall be eliminated from its body; that in the future slavery shall only be remembered as a thing of the past that shall never have the faintest hope of a resurrection."

Up to this point, we have spoken of Mrs. Harper as a laborer, battling for freedom under slavery and the war. She is equally earnest in laboring for Equality before the law—education, and a higher manhood, especially in the South, among the Freedmen.

For the best part of several years, since the war, she has traveled very extensively through the Southern States, going on the plantations and amongst the lowly, as well as to the cities and towns, addressing schools, Churches, meetings in Court Houses, Legislative Halls, &c., and, sometimes, under the most trying and hazardous circumstances; influenced in her labor of love, wholly by the noble impulses of her own heart, working her way along unsustained by any Society. In this mission, she has come in contact with all classes—the original slaveholders and the Freedmen, before and since the Fifteenth Amendment bill was enacted. Excepting two of the Southern States (Texas and Arkansas), she has traveled largely over all the others, and in no instance has she permitted herself, through fear, to disappoint an audience, when engagements had been made for her to speak, although frequently admonished that it would be dangerous to venture in so doing.

We first quote from a letter dated Darlington, S. C., May 13, 1867:

" You will see by this that I am in the sunny South. * * * I here read and see human nature under new lights and phases. I meet with a people eager to hear, ready to listen, as if they felt that the slumber of the ages had been broken, and that they were to sleep no more. * * * I am glad that the colored man gets his freedom and suffrage together; that he is not forced to go through the same condition of things here, that has inclined him so much to apathy, isolation, and indifference, in the North. You, perhaps, wonder why I have been so slow in writing to you, but if you knew how busy I am, just working up to or past the limit of my strength. Traveling, conversing, addressing day and Sunday-schools (picking up scraps of information, takes up a large portion of my time), besides what I give to reading. For my audiences I have both white and colored. On the cars, some find out that I am a lecturer, and then, again, I am drawn into conversation. ' What are you lecturing about ?' the question comes up, and if I say, among other topics politics, then I may look for an onset. There is a sensitiveness on this subject, a dread, it may be, that some one will 'put the devil in the nigger's head,' or exert some influence inimical to them ; still, I get along somewhat pleasantly. Last week I had a small congregation of listeners in the cars, where I sat. I got in conversation with a former slave dealer, and we had rather an exciting time. I was traveling alone, but it is not worth while to show any signs of fear. * * * Last Saturday I spoke in Sumter ; a number of white persons were present, and I had been invited to speak there by the Mayor and editor of the paper. There had been some violence in the district, and some of my friends did not wish me to go, but I had promised, and, of course, I went. * * * * I am in Darlington, and spoke yesterday, but my congregation was so large, that I stood near the door of the church, so that I might be heard both inside and out, for a large portion, perhaps nearly half my congregation were on the outside ; and this, in Darlington, where, about two years ago, a girl was hung for making a childish and indiscreet speech. Victory was perched on our banners. Our army had been through, and this poor, ill-fated girl, almost a child in years, about seventeen years of age, rejoiced over the event, and said that she was going to marry a Yankee and set up housekeeping. She was reported as having made an incendiary speech and arrested, cruelly scourged, and then brutally hung. Poor child ! she had been a faithful servant—her master tried to save her, but the tide of fury swept away his efforts. * * * Oh, friend, perhaps, sometimes your heart would ache, if you were only here and heard of the wrongs and abuses to which these people have been subjected. * * * Things, I believe, are a little more hopeful ; at least, I believe, some of the colored people are getting better contracts, and, I understand, that there's less murdering. While I am writing, a colored man stands here, with a tale of wrong—he has worked a whole year, year before last, and now he has been put off with fifteen bushels of corn and his food ; yesterday he went to see about getting his money, and the person to whom he went, threatened to kick him off, and accused him of stealing. I don't know how the colored man will vote, but perhaps many of them will be intimidated at the polls."

From a letter dated Cheraw, June 17th, 1867, the following remarks are taken :

" Well, Carolina is an interesting place. There is not a state in the Union I prefer to Carolina. Kinder, more hospitable, warmer-hearted people perhaps you will not find anywhere. I have been to Georgia · but Carolina is my preference. * * The South is to be a great theatre for the colored man's development and progress. There is brain-power here. If any doubt it, let him come into our schools, or even converse with some of our Freedmen either in their homes or by the way-side."

A few days later she gave an account of a visit she had just made in Florence, where our poor soldiers had been prisoners ; saw some of the huts where they were exposed to rain and heat and cold with only the temporary shelter they made for themselves, which was a sad sight. Then she visited the grave-yards of some thousands of Union soldiers. Here in " eastern South Carolina " she was in " one of the worst parts of the State " in the days of Slavery ; but under the new order of things, instead of the lash, she saw school books, and over the ruins of slavery, education and free speech springing up, at which she was moved to exclaim, " Thank God for the wonderful change! I have lectured several nights this week, and the weather is quite warm; but I do like South Carolina. No state in the Union as far as colored people are concerned, do I like better—the land of warm welcomes and friendly hearts. God bless her and give her great peace!"

At a later period she visited Charleston and Columbia, and was well received in both places. She spoke a number of times in the different Freedmen schools and the colored churches in Charleston, once in the Legislative Hall, and also in one of the colored churches in Columbia. She received special encouragement and kindness from Hon. H. Cadoza, Secretary of State, and his family, and regarded him as a wise and upright leader of his race in that state.

The following are some stirring lines which she wrote upon the Fifteenth Amendment:

FIFTEENTH AMENDMENT.

Beneath the burden of our joy
    Tremble, O wires, from East to West!
Fashion with words your tongues of fire,
    To tell the nation's high behest.

Outstrip the winds, and leave behind
    The murmur of the restless waves;
Nor tarry with your glorious news,
    Amid the ocean's coral caves.

Ring out! ring out! your sweetest chimes,
    Ye bells, that call to praise;
Let every heart with gladness thrill,
    And songs of joyful triumph raise.

Shake off the dust, O rising race!
    Crowned as a brother and a man;
Justice to-day asserts her claim,
    And from thy brow fades out the ban.

With freedom's chrism upon thy head,
    Her precious ensign in thy hand,
Go place thy once despised name
    Amid the noblest of the land.

O ransomed race! give God the praise,
    Who led thee through a crimson sea,
And 'mid the storm of fire and blood,
    Turned out the war-cloud's light to thee.

Mrs. Harper, in writing from Kingstree, S. C., July 11th, 1867, in midsummer (laboring almost without any pecuniary reward), gave an account of a fearful catastrophe which had just occurred there in the burning of the jail with a number of colored prisoners in it. "It was a very sad affair. There was only one white prisoner and he got out. I believe

49

there was some effort made to release some of the prisoners : but the smoke was such that the effort proved ineffectual. Well, for the credit of our common human nature we may hope that it was so. * * * Last night I had some of the 'rebs' to hear me (part of the time some of the white folks come out). Our meetings are just as quiet'and as orderly on the whole in Carolina as one might desire. * * I like General Sickles as a Military Governor. 'Massa Daniel, he King of the Carolinas.' I like his Mastership. Under him we ride in the City Cars, and get first-class passage on the railroad." At this place a colored man was in prison under sentence of death for "participating in a riot;" and the next day (after the date of her letter) was fixed for his execution. With some others, Mrs. Harper called at General Sickles' Head Quarters, hoping to elicit his sympathies whereby the poor fellow's life might be saved ; but he was not in. Hence they were not able to do anything.

"Next week," continued Mrs. Harper, "I am to speak in a place where one of our teachers was struck and a colored man shot, who, I believe, gave offence by some words spoken at a public meeting. I do not feel any particular fear."

Her Philadelphia correspondent had jestingly suggested to her in one of his letters, that she should be careful not to allow herself to be "bought by the rebels." To which she replied :

" Now, in reference to being bought by rebels and becoming a Johnsonite I hold that between the white people and the colored there is a community of interests, and the sooner they find it out, the better it will be for both parties ; but that community of interests does not consist in increasing the privileges of one class and curtailing the rights of the other, but in getting every citizen interested in the welfare, progress and durability of the state. I do not in lecturing confine myself to the political side of the question. While I am in favor of Universal suffrage, yet I know that the colored man needs something more than a vote in his hand : he needs to know the value of a home life ; to rightly appreciate and value the marriage relation ; to know how and to be incited to leave behind him the old shards and shells of slavery and to rise in the scale of character, wealth and influence. Like the Nautilus outgrowing his home to build for himself more 'stately temples' of social condition. A man landless, ignorant and poor may use the vote against his interests ; but with intelligence and land he holds in his hand the basis of power and elements of strength."

While contemplating the great demand for laborers, in a letter from Athens, February 1st, 1870, after referring to some who had been "discouraged from the field," she wisely added that it was "no time to be discouraged."

　　　　　　　　　　　　 * * If those who can benefit our people will hang around places where they are not needed, they may expect to be discouraged. * * Here is ignorance to be instructed ; a race who needs to be helped up to higher planes of thought and action ; and whether we are hindered or helped, we should try to be true to the commission God has written upon our souls. As far as the colored people are concerned, they are beginning to get homes for themselves and depositing money in Bank. They have hundreds of homes in Kentucky. There is progress in Tennessee, and even in this State while a number have been leaving, some who stay seem to be getting along prosperously. In Augusta colored persons are in the Revenue Office and Post Office. I have just been having some good meetings there. Some of my meet-

ings pay me poorly; but I have a chance to instruct and visit among the people and talk to their Sunday-schools and day-schools also. Of course I do not pretend that all are saving money or getting homes. I rather think from what I hear that the interest of the grown-up people in getting education has somewhat subsided, owing, perhaps, in a measure, to the novelty having worn off and the absorption or rather direction of the mind to other matters. Still I don't think that I have visited scarcely a place since last August where there was no desire for a teacher; and Mr. Fidler, who is a Captain or Colonel, thought some time since that there were more colored than white who were learning or had learned to read. There has been quite an amount of violence and trouble in the State; but we have the military here, and if they can keep Georgia out of the Union about a year or two longer, and the colored people continue to live as they have been doing, from what I hear, perhaps these rebels will learn a little more sense. I have been in Atlanta for some time, but did not stay until the Legislature was organized; but I was there when colored members returned and took their seats. It was rather a stormy time in the House; but no blood was shed. Since then there has been some 'sticking;' but I don't think any of the colored ones were in it."

In the neighborhood of Eufaula, Ala., in December, 1870, Mrs. Harper did a good work, as may be seen from the following extract taken from a letter, dated December 9th:

Last evening I visited one of the plantations, and had an interesting time. Oh, how warm was the welcome! I went out near dark, and between that time and attending my lecture, I was out to supper in two homes. The people are living in the old cabins of slavery; some of them have no windows, at all, that I see; in fact, I don't remember of having seen a pane of window-glass in the settlement. But, humble as their homes were, I was kindly treated, and well received; and what a chance one has for observation among these people, if one takes with her a manner that unlocks other hearts. I had quite a little gathering, after less, perhaps, than a day's notice; the minister did not know that I was coming, till he met me in the afternoon. There was no fire in the church, and so they lit fires outside, and we gathered, or at least a number of us, around the fire. To-night I am going over to Georgia to lecture. In consequence of the low price of cotton, the people may not be able to pay much, and I am giving all my lectures free. You speak of things looking dark in the South; there is no trouble here that I know of—cotton is low, but the people do not seem to be particularly depressed about it; this emigration question has been on the carpet, and I do not wonder if some of them, with their limited knowledge, lose hope in seeing full justice done to them, among their life-long oppressors; Congress has been agitating the St. Domingo question; a legitimate theme for discussion, and one that comes nearer home, is how they can give more security and strength to the government which we have established in the South—for there has been a miserable weakness in the security to human life. The man with whom I stopped, had a son who married a white woman, or girl, and was shot down, and there was, as I understand, no investigation by the jury; and a number of cases have occurred of murders, for which the punishment has been very lax, or not at all, and, it may be, never will be; however, I rather think things are somewhat quieter. A few days ago a shameful outrage occurred at this place—some men had been out fox hunting, and came to the door of a colored woman and demanded entrance, making out they wanted fire; she replied that she had none, and refused to open the door; the miserable cowards broke open the door, and shamefully beat her. I am going to see her this afternoon. It is remarkable, however, in spite of circumstances, how some of these people are getting along. Here is a woman who, with her husband, at the surrender, had a single dollar; and now they have a home of their own, and several acres attached—five altogether; but, as that was rather small, her husband has contracted for two hundred and forty acres more, and has now gone out and commenced operations."

From Columbiana, February 20th, she wrote concerning her work, and presented the "lights and shades" of affairs as they came under her notice.

"I am almost constantly either traveling or speaking. I do not think that I have missed more than one Sunday that I have not addressed some Sunday-school, and I have not missed many day-schools either. And as I am giving all my lectures free the proceeds of the collections are not often very large; still as ignorant as part of the people are perhaps a number of them would not hear at all, and may be prejudice others if I charged even ten cents, and so perhaps in the long run, even if my work is wearing, I may be of some real benefit to my race. * * I don't know but that you would laugh if you were to hear some of the remarks which my lectures call forth: 'She is a man,' again 'She is not colored, she is painted.' Both white and colored come out to hear me, and I have very fine meetings; and then part of the time I am talking in between times, and how tired I am some of the time. Still I am standing with my race on the threshold of a new era, and though some be far past me in the learning of the schools, yet to-day, with my limited and fragmentary knowledge, I may help the race forward a little. Some of our people remind me of sheep without a shepherd."

PRIVATE LECTURES TO FREEDWOMEN.

Desiring to speak to women who have been the objects of so much wrong and abuse under Slavery, and even since Emancipation, in a state of ignorance, not accessible always to those who would or could urge the proper kind of education respecting their morals and general improvement, Mrs. Harper has made it her business not to overlook this all important duty to her poor sisters.

The following extract taken from a letter dated "Greenville, Georgia, March 29th," will show what she was doing in this direction:

"But really my hands are almost constantly full of work; sometimes I speak twice a day. Part of my lectures are given privately to women, and for them I never make any charge, or take up any collection. But this part of the country reminds me of heathen ground, and though my work may not be recognized as part of it used to be in the North, yet never perhaps were my services more needed; and according to their intelligence and means perhaps never better appreciated than here among these lowly people. I am now going to have a private meeting with the women of this place if they will come out. I am going to talk with them about their daughters, and about things connected with the welfare of the race. Now is the time for our women to begin to try to lift up their heads and plant the roots of progress under the hearthstone. Last night I spoke in a school-house, where there was not, to my knowledge, a single window glass; to-day I write to you in a lowly cabin, where the windows in the room are formed by two apertures in the wall. There is a wide-spread and almost universal appearance of poverty in this State where I have been, but thus far I have seen no, or scarcely any, pauperism. I am not sure that I have seen any. The climate is so fine, so little cold that poor people can live off of less than they can in the North. Last night my table was adorned with roses, although I did not get one cent for my lecture. * * * *

"The political heavens are getting somewhat overcast. Some of this old rebel element, I think, are in favor of taking away the colored man's vote, and if he loses it now it may be generations before he gets it again. Well, after all perhaps the colored man generally is not really developed enough to value his vote and equality with other races, so he gets enough to eat and drink, and be comfortable, perhaps the loss of his vote would not be a serious grievance to many ; but his children differently educated and trained by circumstances might feel political inferiority rather a bitter cup."

" After all whether they encourage or discourage me, I belong to this race, and when it is down I belong to a down race ; when it is up I belong to a risen race."

She writes thus from Montgomery, December 29th, 1870 :

" Did you ever read a little poem commencing, I think, with these words :

A mother cried, Oh, give me joy,
For I have born a darling boy !
A darling boy ! why the world is full
Of the men who play at push and pull.

Well, as full as the room was of beds and tenants, on the morning of the twenty-second, there arose a wail upon the air, and this mundane sphere had another inhabitant, and my room another occupant. I left after that, and when I came back the house was fuller than it was before, and my hostess gave me to understand that she would rather I should be somewhere else, and I left again. How did I fare ? Well, I had been stopping with one of our teachers and went back ; but the room in which I stopped was one of those southern shells through which both light and cold enter at the same time ; it had one window and perhaps more than half or one half the panes gone. I don't know that I was ever more conquered by the cold than I had been at that house, and I have lived parts of winter after winter amid the snows of New England ; but if it was cold out of doors, there was warmth and light within doors ; but here, if you opened the door for light, the cold would also enter, and so part of the time I sat by the fire, and that and the crevices in the house supplied me with light in one room, and we had the deficient window-sash, or perhaps it never had had any lights in it. You could put your finger through some of the apertures in the house ; at least I could mine, and the water froze down to the bottom of the tumbler. From another such domicile may kind fate save me. And then the man asked me four dollars and a half a week board.

One of the nights there was no fire in the stove, and the next time we had fires, one stove might have been a second-hand chamber stove. Now perhaps you think these people very poor, but the man with whom I stopped has no family that I saw, but himself and wife, and he would make two dollars and a half a day, and she worked out and kept a boarder. And yet, except the beds and bed clothing, I wouldn't have given fifteen dollars for all their house furniture. I should think that this has been one of the lowest down States in the South, as far as civilization has been concerned. In the future, until these people are educated, look out for Democratic victories, for here are two materials with which Democracy can work, ignorance and poverty. Men talk about missionary work among the heathen, but if any lover of Christ wants a field for civilizing work, here is a field. Part of the time I am preaching against men ill-treating their wives. I have heard though, that often during the war men hired out their wives and drew their pay.

*   *   *   *   *   *   *   *   *   *

" And then there is another trouble, some of our Northern men have been down this way and by some means they have not made the best impression on every mind here. One woman here has been expressing her mind very freely to me about some of our Northerners, and we are not all considered here as saints and angels, and of course in their minds I get associated with some or all the humbugs that have been before me. But I am not discouraged, my race needs me, if I will only be faithful, and in spite of suspicion and distrust, I will work on ; the deeper our degradation, the louder our call for redemption. If they have little or no faith in goodness and earnestness, that is only one reason why we should be more faithful and earnest, and so I shall probably stay here in the South all winter. I am not making much money, and perhaps will hardly clear expenses this winter ; but after all what matters it when I am in my grave whether I have been rich or poor, loved or hated, despised or respected, if Christ will only own me to His Father, and I be permitted a place in one of the mansions of rest."

Col. J. W. Forney, editor of " The Press," published July 12, 1871, with the brief editorial heading by his own hand, the document appended :

The following letter, written by Mrs. F. E. W. Harper, the well-known colored orator, to a friend, Mr. Wm. Still, of Philadelphia, will be read with surprise and pleasure by all classes ; especially supplemented as it is by an article from the Mobile (Alabama) *Register*, referring to one of her addresses in that city. The *Register* is the organ of the fire-eaters of the South, conducted by John Forsyth, heretofore one of the most intolerant of that school. Mrs. Harper describes the manner in which the old plantation of Jefferson Davis in Mississippi was cultivated by his brother's former slave, having been a guest in the Davis mansion, now occupied by Mr. Montgomery, the aforesaid slave. She also draws a graphic picture of her own marvellous advancement from utter obscurity to the platform of a public lecturer, honored by her own race and applauded by their oppressors. While we regret, as she says, that her experience and that of Mr. Montgomery is exceptional, it is easy to anticipate the harvest of such a sowing. The same culture—the same courage on the part of the men and women who undertake to advocate Republican doctrines in the South—the same perseverance and intelligence on the part of those who are earning their bread by the cultivation of the soil, will be crowned with the same success. Violence, bloodshed, and murder cannot rule long in communities where these resistless elements are allowed to work. No scene in the unparalleled tragedy of the rebellion, or in the drama which succeeded that tragedy, can be compared to the picture outlined by Mrs. Harper herself, and filled in by the ready pen of the rebel editor of the Mobile *Register* :

MOBILE, July 5, 1871.

MY DEAR FRIEND :—It is said that truth is stranger than fiction; and if ten years since some one had entered my humble log house and seen me kneading bread and making butter, and said that in less than ten years you will be in the lecture field, you will be a welcome guest under the roof of the President of the Confederacy, though not by special invitation from him, that you will see his brother's former slave a man of business and influence, that hundreds of colored men will congregate on the old baronial possessions, that a school will spring up there like a well in the desert dust, that this former slave will be a magistrate upon that plantation, that labor will be organized upon a new basis, and that under the sole auspices and moulding hands of this man and his sons will be developed a business whose transactions will be numbered in hundreds of thousands of dollars, would you not have smiled incredulously ? And I have lived to see the day when the plantation has passed into new hands, and these hands once wore the fetters of slavery. Mr. Montgomery, the present proprietor by contract of between five and six thousand acres of land, has one of the most interesting families that I have ever seen in the South. They are building up a future which if exceptional now I hope will become more general hereafter. Every hand of his family is adding its quota to the success of this experiment of a colored man both trading and farming on an extensive scale. Last year his wife took on her hands about 130 acres of land, and with her force she raised about 107 bales of cotton. She has a number of orphan children employed, and not only does she supervise their labor, but she works herself. One daughter, an intelligent young lady, is postmistress and I believe assistant book-keeper. One son attends to the planting interest, and another daughter attends to one of the stores. The business of this firm of Montgomery & Sons has amounted, I understand, to between three and four hundred thousand dollars in a year. I stayed on the place several days and was hospitably entertained and kindly treated. When I come, if nothing prevents, I will tell you more about them. Now for the next strange truth Enclosed I send you a notice from one of the leading and representative papers of rebeldom. The editor has been, or is considered, one of the representative men of the South. I have given a lecture since this notice, which brought out some of the most noted rebels, among whom was Admiral Semmes. In my speech I referred to the Alabama sweeping away our comm⌐ce, and his son sat near him and seemed to receive it with much good humor. I don't know what the papers will say to-day ; perhaps they will think that I dwelt upon the past too much. Oh, if you had seen the rebs I had out last night, perhaps you would have felt a little nervous for me. However, I lived through it, and gave them more gospel truth than perhaps some of them have heard for some time.

A LECTURE.

We received a polite invitation from the trustees of the State-street African Methodist Episcopal Zion Church to attend a lecture in that edifice on Thursday evening. Being told that the discourse would be delivered by a female colored lecturer from Maryland, curiosity, as well as an interest to see how the colored citizens were managing their own institutions, led us at once to accept the invitation. We found a very spacious church, gas-light, and the balustrades of the galleries copiously hung with wreaths and festoons of flowers, and a large audience of both sexes, which, both in appearance and behaviour, was respectable and decorously observant of the proprieties of the place. The services were opened, as usual, with prayer and a hymn, the latter inspired by powerful lungs, and in which the musical ear at once caught the negro talent for melody. The lecturer was then introduced as Mrs. F. E. W. Harper, from Maryland. Without a moment's hesitation she started off in the flow of her discourse, which rolled smoothly and uninterruptedly on for nearly two hours. It was very apparent that it was not a cut and dried speech, for she was as fluent and as felicitous in her allusions to circumstances immediately around her as she was when she rose to a more exalted pitch of laudation of the " Union," or of execration of the old slavery system. Her voice was remarkable—as sweet as any woman's voice we ever heard, and so clear and distinct as to pass every syllable to the most distant ear in the house.

Without any effort at attentive listening we followed the speaker to the end, not discerning a single grammatical inaccuracy of speech, or the slightest violation of good taste in manner or matter. At times the current of thoughts flowed in eloquent and poetic expression, and often her quaint humor would expose the ivory in half a thousand mouths. We confess that we began to wonder, and we asked a fine-looking man before us, " What is her color ? Is she dark or light ?" He answered, " She is mulatto ; what they call a red mulatto." The ' red ' was new to us. Our neighbor asked, " How do you like her ? " We replied, " She is giving your people the best kind and the very wisest of advice." He rejoined, " I wish I had her education." To which we added, " That's just what she tells you is your great duty and your need, and if you are too old to get it yourselves, you must give it to your children."

The speaker left the impression on our mind that she was not only intelligent and educated, but—the great end of education—she was enlightened. She comprehends perfectly the situation of her people, to whose interests she seems ardently devoted. The main theme of her discourse, the one string to the harmony of which all the others were attuned, was the grand opportunity that emancipation had afforded to the black race to lift itself to the level of the duties and responsibilities enjoined by it. " You have muscle power and brain power," she said ; " you must utilize them, or be content to remain forever the inferior race. Get land, every one that can, and as fast as you can. A landless people must be dependent upon the landed people. A few acres to till for food and a roof, however humble, over your head, are the castle of your independence, and when you have it you are fortified to act and vote independently whenever your interests are at stake." That part of her lecture (and there was much of it) that dwelt on the moral duties and domestic relations of the colored people was pitched on the highest key of sound morality. She urged the cultivation of the "home life," the sanctity of the marriage state (a happy contrast to her strong-minded, free-love, white sisters of the North), and the duties of mothers to their daughters. "Why," said she in a voice of much surprise, "I have actually heard since I have been South that sometimes colored husbands positively beat their wives! I do not mean to insinuate for a moment that such things can possibly happen in Mobile. The very appearance of this congregation forbids it; but I did hear of one terrible husband defending himself for the unmanly practice with "Well, I have got to whip her or leave her."

There were parts of the lecturer's discourse that grated a little on a white Southern ear, but it was lost and forgiven in the genuine earnestness and profound good sense with which the woman spoke to her kind in words of sound advice.

On the whole, we are very glad we accepted the Zion's invitation. It gave us much food for new thought. It reminded us, perhaps, of neglected duties to these people, and it impressed strongly on our minds that these people are getting along, getting onward, and progress was a star becoming familiar to their gaze and their desires. Whatever the negroes have done in the path of advancement, they have done largely without white aid. But politics and white pride have kept the white people aloof from offering that earnest and moral assistance which would be so useful to a people just starting from infancy into a life of self-dependence.

In writing from Columbiana and Demopolis, Alabama, about the first of March, 1871, Mrs. Harper painted the state of affairs in her usually graphic manner, and diligently was she endeavoring to inspire the people with hope and encouragement.

"Oh, what a field there is here in this region! Let me give you a short account of this week's work. Sunday I addressed a Sunday-school in Taladega; on Monday afternoon a day-school. On Monday I rode several miles to a meeting; addressed it, and came back the same night. Got back about or after twelve o'clock. The next day I had a meeting of women and addressed them, and then lectured in the evening in the Court-House to both colored and white. Last night I spoke again, about ten miles from where I am now stopping, and returned the same night, and to-morrow evening probably I shall speak again. I grow quite tired part of the time. * * * And now let me give you an anecdote or two of some of our new citizens. While in Taladega I was entertained and well entertained, at the house of one of our new citizens. He is living in the house of his former master. He is a brick-maker by trade, and I rather think mason also. He was worth to his owner, it was reckoned, fifteen hundred or about that a year. He worked with him seven years; and in that seven years he remembers receiving from him fifty cents. Now mark the contrast! That man is now free, owns the home of his former master, has I think more than sixty acres of land, and his master is in the poor-house. I heard of another such case not long since: A woman was cruelly treated once, or more than once. She escaped and ran naked into town. The villain in whose clutch she found herself was trying to drag her downward to his own low level of impurity, and at last she fell. She was poorly fed, so that she was tempted to sell her person. Even scraps thrown to the dog she was hunger-bitten enough to aim for. Poor thing, was there anything in the future for her? Had not hunger and cruelty and prostitution done their work, and left her an entire wreck for life? It seems not. Freedom came, and with it dawned a new era upon that poor, overshadowed, and sin-darkened life. Freedom brought opportunity for work and wages combined. She went to work, and got ten dollars a month. She has contrived to get some education, and has since been teaching school. While her former mistress has been to her for help.

"Do not the mills of God grind exceedingly fine? And she has helped that mistress, and so has the colored man given money, from what I heard, to his former master. After all, friend, do we not belong to one of the best branches of the human race? And yet, how have our people been murdered in the South, and their bones scattered at the grave's mouth! Oh, when will we have a government strong enough to make human life safe? Only yesterday I heard of a murder committed on a man for an old grudge of several years' standing. I had visited the place, but had just got away. Last summer a Mr. Luke was hung, and several other men also, I heard."

While surrounded with this state of affairs, an appeal reached her through the columns of the National Standard, setting forth a state of very great suffering and want, especially on the part of the old, blind and decrepit Freedmen of the District of Columbia. After expressing deep pity for these unfortunates, she added: " Please send ten dollars to Josephine Griffing for me for the suffering poor of the District of Columbia. Just send it by mail, and charge to my account."

Many more letters written by Mrs. Harper are before us, containing highly interesting information from Louisiana, Mississippi, Florida, North Carolina, Virginia, Kentucky, Tennessee, Missouri, Maryland, and even poor little Delaware. Through all these States she has traveled and labored extensively, as has been already stated; but our space in this volume will admit of only one more letter:

"I have been traveling the best part of the day. * * Can you spare a little time from your book to just take a peep at some of our Alabama people? If you would see some instances of apparent poverty and ignorance that I have seen perhaps you would not wonder very much at the conservative voting in the State. A few days since I was about to pay a woman a dollar and a quarter for some washing in ten cent (currency) notes, when she informed me that she could not count it; she must trust to my honesty—she could count forty cents. Since I left Eufaula I have seen something of plantation life. The first plantation I visited was about five or six miles from Eufaula, and I should think that the improvement in some of the cabins was not very much in advance of what it was in Slavery. The cabins are made with doors, but not, to my recollection, a single window pane or speck of plastering; and yet even in some of those lowly homes I met with hospitality. A room to myself is a luxury that I do not always enjoy. Still I live through it, and find life rather interesting. The people have much to learn. The condition of the women is not very enviable in some cases. They have had some of them a terribly hard time in Slavery, and their subjection has not ceased in freedom. * * One man said of some women, that a man must leave them or whip them. * * Let me introduce you to another scene: here is a gathering; a large fire is burning out of doors, and here are one or two boys with hats on. Here is a little girl with her bonnet on, and there a little boy moves off and commences to climb a tree. Do you know what the gathering means? It is a school, and the teacher, I believe, is paid from the school fund. He says he is from New Hampshire. That may be. But to look at him and to hear him teach, you would perhaps think him not very lately from the North; at least I do not think he is a model teacher. They have a church; but somehow they have burnt a hole, I understand, in the top, and so I lectured inside, and they gathered around the fire outside. Here is another—what shall I call it?—meeting-place. It is a brush arbor. And what pray is that? Shall I call it an edifice or an improvised meeting-house? Well, it is called a brush arbor. It is a kind of brush house with seats, and a kind of covering made partly, I rather think, of branches of trees, and an humble place for pulpit. I lectured in a place where they seemed to have no other church; but I spoke at a house. In Glenville, a little out-of-the-way place, I spent part of a week. There they have two unfinished churches. One has not a single pane of glass, and the same aperture that admits the light also gives ingress to the air; and the other one, I rather think, is less finished than that. I spoke in one, and then the white people gave me a hall, and quite a number attended. * * * I am now at Union Springs, where I shall probably room with three women. But amid all this roughing it in the bush, I find a field of work where kindness and hospitality have thrown their sunshine around my way. And Oh what a field of work is here! How much one needs the Spirit of our dear Master to make one's life a living, loving force to help men to higher planes of thought and action. I am giving all my lectures with free admission; but still I get along, and the way has been opening for me almost ever since I have been South. Oh, if some more of our young women would only consecrate their lives to the work of upbuilding the race! Oh, if I could only see our young men and women aiming to build up a future for themselves which would grandly contrast with the past —with its pain, ignorance and low social condition."

It may be well to add that Mrs. Harper's letters from which we have copied were simply private, never intended for publication; and while they bear obvious marks of truthfulness, discrimination and impartiality, it becomes us to say that a more strictly conscientious woman we have never known.

Returning to Philadelphia after many months of hard labor in the South, Mrs. Harper, instead of seeking needed rest and recreation, scarcely allows a day to pass without seeking to aid in the reformation of the outcast and degraded. The earnest advice which she gives on the subject of temperance and moral reforms generally causes some to reflect, even among adults, and induces a number of poor children to attend day and Sabbath-schools. The condition of this class, she feels, appeals loudly for a remedy to respectable and intelligent colored citizens; and whilst not discouraged, she is often quite saddened at the supineness of the better class. During the past summer when it was too warm to labor in the South she spent several months in this field without a farthing's reward. She assisted in organizing a Sabbath-school, and accepted the office of Assistant Superintendent under the auspices of the Young Men's Christian Association.

Mrs. Harper reads the best magazines and ablest weeklies, as well as more elaborate works, not excepting such authors as De Tocqueville, Mill, Ruskin, Buckle, Guizot, &c. In espousing the cause of the oppressed as a poet and lecturer, had she neglected to fortify her mind in the manner she did, she would have been weighed and found wanting long since. Before friends and foes, the learned and the unlearned, North and South, Mrs. Harper has pleaded the cause of her race in a manner that has commanded the greatest respect; indeed, it is hardly too much to say, that during seventeen years of public labor she has made thousands of speeches without doing herself or people discredit in a single instance, but has accomplished a great deal in the way of removing prejudice. May we not hope that the rising generation at least will take encouragement by her example and find an argument of rare force in favor of mental and moral equality, and above all be awakened to see how prejudices and difficulties may be surmounted by continual struggles, intelligence and a virtuous character?

Fifty thousand copies at least of her four small books have been sold to those who have listened to her eloquent lectures. One of those productions entitled " Moses " has been used to entertain audiences with evening readings in various parts of the country. With what effect may be seen from the two brief notices as follows :

" Mrs. F. E. W. Harper delivered a poem upon ' Moses' in Wilbraham to a large and delighted audience. She is a woman of high moral tone, with superior native powers highly cultivated, and a captivating eloquence that hold her audience in rapt attention from the beginning to the close. She will delight any intelligent audience, and those who wish first-class lecturers cannot do better than to secure her services."—*Zion's Herald, Boston.*

" Mrs. Frances E. W. Harper read her poem of ' Moses' last evening at Rev. Mr. Harrison's church to a good audience. It deals with the story of the Hebrew Moses from his finding in the wicker basket on the Nile to his death on Mount Nebo and his burial in an unknown grave; following closely the Scripture account. It contains about 700 lines, beginning with blank verse of the common measure, and changing to other measures, but always without rhyme ; and is a pathetic and well-sustained piece. Mrs. Harper recited it with good effect, and it was well received. She is a lady of much talent, and always speaks well, particularly when her subject relates to the condition of her own people, in whose welfare, before and since the war, she has taken the deepest interest. As a lecturer Mrs. Harper is more effective than most of those who come before our lyceums ; with a natural eloquence that is very moving."—*Galesburgh Register, Ill.*

Grace Greenwood, in the Independent in noticing a Course of Lectures in which Mrs. Harper spoke (in Philadelphia) pays this tribute to her :

" Next on the course was Mrs Harper, a colored woman ; about as colored as some of the Cuban belles I have met with at Saratoga. She has a noble head, this bronze muse ; a strong face, with a shadowed glow upon it, indicative of thoughtful fervor, and of a nature most femininely sensitive, but not in the least morbid. Her form is delicate, her hands daintily small. She stands quietly beside her desk, and speaks without notes, with gestures few and fitting. Her manner is marked by dignity and composure. She is never assuming, never theatrical. In the first part of her lecture she was most impressive in her pleading for the race with whom her lot is cast. There was something touching in her attitude as their representative. The woe of two hundred years sighed through her tones. Every glance of her sad eyes was a mournful remonstrance against injustice and wrong. Feeling on her soul, as she must have felt it, the chilling weight of caste, she seemed to say:

> ' I lift my heavy heart up solemnly,
> As once Electra her sepulchral urn.'

* * * As I listened to her, there swept over me, in a chill wave of horror, the realization that this noble woman had she not been rescued from her mother's condition, might have been sold on the auction-block, to the highest bidder—her intellect, fancy, eloquence, the flashing wit, that might make the delight of a Parisian saloon, and her pure, Christian character all thrown in—the recollection that women like her could be dragged out of public conveyances in our own city, or frowned out of fashionable churches by Anglo-Saxon saints."

THE END.